Java™

HOW TO PROGRAM

TENTH EDITION
LATE OBJECTS VERSION

Deitel® Series Page

How To Program Series

Android How to Program, 2/E
C++ How to Program, 9/E
C How to Program, 7/E
Java™ How to Program, 10/E
Java™ How to Program, Late Objects Version, 10/E
Internet & World Wide Web How to Program, 5/E
Visual C++® 2008 How to Program, 2/E
Visual Basic® 2012 How to Program, 6/E
Visual C#® 2012 How to Program, 5/E

Simply Series

Simply C++: An App-Driven Tutorial Approach
Simply Java™ Programming: An App-Driven
    Tutorial Approach
Simply C#: An App-Driven Tutorial Approach
Simply Visual Basic® 2010: An App-Driven
    Approach, 4/E

CourseSmart Web Books

www.deitel.com/books/CourseSmart/

C++ How to Program, 8/E and 9/E
Simply C++: An App-Driven Tutorial Approach
Java™ How to Program, 9/E and 10/E
Simply Visual Basic® 2010: An App-Driven
    Approach, 4/E

(continued from previous column)
Visual Basic® 2012 How to Program, 6/E
Visual Basic® 2010 How to Program, 5/E
Visual C#® 2012 How to Program, 5/E
Visual C#® 2010 How to Program, 4/E

Deitel® Developer Series

Android for Programmers: An App-Driven
    Approach, 2/E, Volume 1
C for Programmers with an Introduction to C11
C++11 for Programmers
C# 2012 for Programmers
Dive Into® iOS 6 for Programmers: An App-Driven
    Approach
Java™ for Programmers, 3/E
JavaScript for Programmers

LiveLessons Video Learning Products

www.deitel.com/books/LiveLessons/

Android App Development Fundamentals
C++ Fundamentals
Java™ Fundamentals
C# 2012 Fundamentals
C# 2010 Fundamentals
iOS® 6 App Development Fundamentals
JavaScript Fundamentals
Visual Basic® Fundamentals

To receive updates on Deitel publications, Resource Centers, training courses, partner offers and more, please join the Deitel communities on

- Facebook®—facebook.com/DeitelFan
- Twitter®—@deitel
- Google+™—google.com/+DeitelFan
- YouTube™—youtube.com/DeitelTV
- LinkedIn®—linkedin.com/company/deitel-&-associates

and register for the free *Deitel® Buzz Online* e-mail newsletter at:

www.deitel.com/newsletter/subscribe.html

To communicate with the authors, send e-mail to:

deitel@deitel.com

For information on *Dive-Into®* Series on-site seminars offered by Deitel & Associates, Inc. worldwide, write to us at deitel@deitel.com or visit:

www.deitel.com/training/

For continuing updates on Pearson/Deitel publications visit:

www.deitel.com
www.pearsonhighered.com/deitel/

Visit the Deitel Resource Centers that will help you master programming languages, software development, Android and iOS app development, and Internet- and web-related topics:

www.deitel.com/ResourceCenters.html

Java™

HOW TO PROGRAM

TENTH EDITION
LATE OBJECTS VERSION

Paul Deitel
Deitel & Associates, Inc.

Harvey Deitel
Deitel & Associates, Inc.

DEITEL®

PEARSON

Boston   Columbus   Indianapolis   New York   San Francisco   Upper Saddle River
Amsterdam   Cape Town   Dubai   London   Madrid   Milan   Munich   Paris   Montreal   Toronto
Delhi   Mexico City   Sao Paulo   Sydney   Hong Kong   Seoul   Singapore   Taipei   Tokyo

Editorial Director, ECS: *Marcia Horton*
Executive Editor: *Tracy Johnson (Dunkelberger)*
Director of Marketing: *Christy Lesko*
Marketing Manager: *Yez Alayan*
Marketing Assistant: *Jon Bryant*
Director of Program Management: *Erin Gregg*
Program Management—Team Lead: *Scott Disanno*
Program Manager: *Carole Snyder*
Project Management—Team Lead: *Laura Burgess*
Project Manager: *Robert Engelhardt*
Procurement Specialist: *Linda Sager*
Cover Design: *Paul Deitel, Harvey Deitel, Abbey Deitel, Barbara Deitel, Marta Samsel*
Permissions Supervisor: *Michael Joyce*
Permissions Administrator: *Jenell Forschler*
Director, Image Asset Services: *Annie Atherton*
Manager, Visual Research: *Karen Sanatar*
Cover Art: © *Elina Elisseeva/Shutterstock*
Media Project Manager: *Renata Butera*

Credits and acknowledgments borrowed from other sources and reproduced, with permission, in this textbook appear on page vi.

Library of Congress Cataloging-in-Publication Data
On file

10 9 8 7 6 5 4 3 2
ISBN-10: 0-13-257565-5
ISBN-13: 978-0-13-257565-2

To Brian Goetz,
   Oracle's Java Language Architect and
   Specification Lead for Java SE 8's Project Lambda:

   Your mentorship helped us make a better book.
   Thank you for insisting that we get it right.

   Paul and Harvey Deitel

Trademarks

DEITEL, the double-thumbs-up bug and DIVE INTO are registered trademarks of Deitel and Associates, Inc.

Oracle and Java are registered trademarks of Oracle and/or its affiliates. Other names may be trademarks of their respective owners.

Microsoft and/or its respective suppliers make no representations about the suitability of the information contained in the documents and related graphics published as part of the services for any purpose. All such documents and related graphics are provided "as is" without warranty of any kind. Microsoft and/or its respective suppliers hereby disclaim all warranties and conditions with regard to this information, including all warranties and conditions of merchantability, whether express, implied or statutory, fitness for a particular purpose, title and non-infringement. In no event shall Microsoft and/or its respective suppliers be liable for any special, indirect or consequential damages or any damages whatsoever resulting from loss of use, data or profits, whether in an action of contract, negligence or other tortious action, arising out of or in connection with the use or performance of information available from the services.

The documents and related graphics contained herein could include technical inaccuracies or typographical errors. Changes are periodically added to the information herein. Microsoft and/or its respective suppliers may make improvements and/or changes in the product(s) and/or the program(s) described herein at any time. Partial screen shots may be viewed in full within the software version specified.

Microsoft® and Windows® are registered trademarks of the Microsoft Corporation in the U.S.A. and other countries. Screen shots and icons reprinted with permission from the Microsoft Corporation. This book is not sponsored or endorsed by or affiliated with the Microsoft Corporation.UNIX is a registered trademark of The Open Group.

Apache is a trademark of The Apache Software Foundation.

CSS and XML are registered trademarks of the World Wide Web Consortium.

Firefox is a registered trademark of the Mozilla Foundation.

Google is a trademark of Google, Inc.

Mac and OS X are trademarks of Apple Inc., registered in the U.S. and other countries.

Linux is a registered trademark of Linus Torvalds. All trademarks are property of their respective owners.

Throughout this book, trademarks are used. Rather than put a trademark symbol in every occurrence of a trademarked name, we state that we are using the names in an editorial fashion only and to the benefit of the trademark owner, with no intention of infringement of the trademark.

Contents

Chapters 26–34 and Appendices F–N are PDF documents posted online at the book's Companion Website (located at www.pearsonhighered.com/deitel/). See the inside front cover for information on accessing the Companion Website.

7 Introduction to Classes and Objects 265

11 Exception Handling: A Deeper Look   433

17 Java SE 8 Lambdas and Streams

18   Recursion   768

19   Searching, Sorting and Big O   802

Online Chapters and Appendices

Chapters 26–34 and Appendices F–N are PDF documents posted online at the book's Companion Website (located at www.pearsonhighered.com/deitel/). See the inside front cover for information on accessing the Companion Website.

26   JavaFX GUI: Part 2

27   JavaFX Graphics and Multimedia

28   Networking

Foreword

I've been enamored with Java even prior to its 1.0 release in 1995, and have subsequently been a Java developer, author, speaker, teacher and Oracle Java Technology Ambassador. In this journey, it has been my privilege to call Paul Deitel a colleague, and to often leverage and recommend his *Java How To Program* book. In its many editions, this book has proven to be a great text for college and professional courses that I and others have developed to teach the Java programming language.

One of the qualities that makes this book a great resource is its thorough and insightful coverage of Java concepts, including those introduced recently in Java SE 8. Another useful quality is its treatment of concepts and practices essential to effective software development.

As a long-time fan of this book, I'd like to point out some of the features of this tenth edition about which I'm most excited:

- An ambitious new chapter on Java lambda expressions and streams. This chapter starts out with a primer on functional programming, introducing Java lambda expressions and how to use streams to perform functional programming tasks on collections.

- Although concurrency has been addressed since the first edition of the book, it is increasingly important because of multi-core architectures. There are timing examples—using the new Date/Time API classes introduced in Java SE 8—in the concurrency chapter that show the performance improvements with multi-core over single-core.

- JavaFX is Java's GUI/graphics/multimedia technology moving forward, so it is nice to see a three-chapter treatment of JavaFX in the Deitel live-code pedagogic style. One of these chapters is in the printed book and the other two are online.

Please join me in congratulating Paul and Harvey Deitel on their latest edition of a wonderful resource for computer science students and software developers alike!

James L. Weaver
Java Technology Ambassador
Oracle Corporation

Preface

"The chief merit of language is clearness…"
—Galen

Welcome to the Java programming language and *Java How to Program, Tenth Edition, Late Objects Version*! This book, which we call *"Java Love,"* presents leading-edge computing technologies for students, instructors and software developers. It's appropriate for introductory academic and professional course sequences based on the curriculum recommendations of the ACM and the IEEE, and for AP Computer Science exam preparation. If you haven't already done so, please read the back cover and inside back cover—these concisely capture the essence of the book. In this Preface we provide more detail.

We focus on software engineering best practices. At the heart of the book is the Deitel signature "live-code approach"—rather than using code snippets, we present concepts in the context of complete working programs that run on recent versions of Windows®, OS X® and Linux®. Each complete code example is accompanied by live sample executions.

Keeping in Touch with the Authors
As you read the book, if you have questions, send an e-mail to us at

> `deitel@deitel.com`

and we'll respond promptly. For updates on this book, visit

> `http://www.deitel.com/books/jhtp10LOV`

subscribe to the *Deitel® Buzz Online* newsletter at

> `http://www.deitel.com/newsletter/subscribe.html`

and join the Deitel social networking communities on

- Facebook® (`http://www.deitel.com/deitelfan`)
- Twitter® (`@deitel`)
- Google+™ (`http://google.com/+DeitelFan`)
- YouTube® (`http://youtube.com/DeitelTV`)
- LinkedIn® (`http://linkedin.com/company/deitel-&-associates`)

Source Code and VideoNotes
All the source code is available at:

> `http://www.deitel.com/books/jhtp10LOV`

and at the book's Companion Website (which also contains extensive VideoNotes):

> `http://www.pearsonhighered.com/deitel`

Motivation for *Java How to Program, 10/e, Late Objects Version*

There are several approaches to teaching first courses in Java programming. The two most popular are the *late objects approach* and the *early objects approach*. To meet these diverse needs, we have published two versions of this book:

- *Java How to Program, 10/e, Late Objects Version*, and
- *Java How to Program, 10/e, Early Objects*

The key difference between these two editions is the order in which topics are presented in Chapters 1–7. The books have identical content from Chapters 8 to 31.

Chapters 1–6 in *Java How to Program, 10/e, Late Objects Version*, form the core of a pure-procedural programming CS1 course that covers operators, data types, input/output, control statements, methods and arrays. Instructors who want to cover some key material on strings early can present Sections 14.1–14.3 immediately after Chapter 6. Instructors who want to cover some key material on files early can present Sections 15.1–15.4 immediately after Chapter 6. Instructors who want to introduce *some* object-oriented programming in a first course can include some or all of Chapters 7–11 (see below).

Modular Organization[1]

Java How to Program, 10/e, Late Objects Version, is appropriate for programming courses at various levels, most notably CS 1 and CS 2 courses and introductory course sequences in related disciplines. The book's modular organization helps instructors plan their syllabi:

Introduction
- Chapter 1, Introduction to Computers, the Internet and Java
- Chapter 2, Introduction to Java Applications; Input/Output and Operators

Additional Programming Fundamentals
- Chapter 3, Control Statements: Part 1; Assignment, ++ and −− Operators
- Chapter 4, Control Statements: Part 2; Logical Operators
- Chapter 5, Methods
- Chapter 6, Arrays and ArrayLists
- Chapter 14, Strings, Characters and Regular Expressions
- Chapter 15, Files, Streams and Object Serialization

Object-Oriented Programming and Object-Oriented Design
- Chapter 7, Introduction to Classes and Objects
- Chapter 8, Classes and Objects: A Deeper Look
- Chapter 9, Object-Oriented Programming: Inheritance
- Chapter 10, Object-Oriented Programming: Polymorphism and Interfaces
- Chapter 11, Exception Handling: A Deeper Look
- (**Online optional module**) Chapter 33, ATM Case Study, Part 1: Object-Oriented Design with the UML

1. The online chapters will be available on the book's Companion Website for Fall 2014 classes.

- (**Online optional module**) Chapter 34, ATM Case Study Part 2: Implementing an Object-Oriented Design

Swing Graphical User Interfaces and Java 2D Graphics
- Chapter 12, GUI Components: Part 1
- Chapter 13, Graphics and Java 2D
- Chapter 22, GUI Components: Part 2

Data Structures, Collections, Lambdas and Streams
- Chapter 16, Generic Collections
- Chapter 17, Java SE 8 Lambdas and Streams
- Chapter 18, Recursion
- Chapter 19, Searching, Sorting and Big O
- Chapter 20, Generic Classes and Methods
- Chapter 21, Custom Generic Data Structures

Concurrency; Networking
- Chapter 23, Concurrency
- (**Online**) Chapter 28, Networking

JavaFX Graphical User Interfaces, Graphics and Multimedia
- Chapter 25, JavaFX GUI: Part 1
- (**Online**) Chapter 26, JavaFX GUI: Part 2
- (**Online**) Chapter 27, JavaFX Graphics and Multimedia

Database-Driven Desktop and Web Development
- Chapter 24, Accessing Databases with JDBC
- (**Online**) Chapter 29, Java Persistence API (JPA)
- (**Online**) Chapter 30, JavaServer™ Faces Web Apps: Part 1
- (**Online**) Chapter 31, JavaServer™ Faces Web Apps: Part 2
- (**Online**) Chapter 32, REST-Based Web Services

New and Updated Features

Here are the updates we've made for *Java How to Program, 10/e, Late Objects Version*:

Java Standard Edition: Java SE 7 and the New Java SE 8

- *Easy to use with Java SE 7 or Java SE 8.* To meet the needs of our audiences, we designed the book for college and professional courses based on Java SE 7, Java SE 8 or a mixture of both. The Java SE 8 features are covered in optional, easy-to-include-or-omit sections. The new Java SE 8 capabilities can dramatically improve the programming process. Figure 1 lists some new Java SE 8 features that we cover.

Java SE 8 features
Lambda expressions
Type-inference improvements
@FunctionalInterface annotation
Parallel array sorting
Bulk data operations for Java Collections—filter, map and reduce
Library enhancements to support lambdas (e.g., java.util.stream, java.util.function)
Date & Time API (java.time)
Java concurrency API improvements
static and default methods in interfaces
Functional interfaces—interfaces that define only one abstract method and can include static and default methods
JavaFX enhancements

Fig. 1 | Some new Java SE 8 features.

- *Java SE 8 lambdas, streams, and interfaces with **default** and **static** methods.* The most significant new features in JavaSE 8 are lambdas and complementary technologies, which we cover in detail in the optional Chapter 17 and optional sections marked "Java SE 8" in later chapters. In Chapter 17, you'll see that functional programming with lambdas and streams can help you write programs faster, more concisely, more simply, with fewer bugs and that are easier to parallelize (to get performance improvements on multi-core systems) than programs written with previous techniques. You'll see that functional programming complements object-oriented programming. After you read Chapter 17, you'll be able to cleverly reimplement many of the Java SE 7 examples throughout the book (Fig. 2).

Pre-Java-SE-8 topics	Corresponding Java SE 8 discussions and examples
Chapter 6, Arrays and ArrayLists	Sections 17.3—17.4 introduce basic lambda and streams capabilities that process one-dimensional arrays.
Chapter 10, Object-Oriented Programming: Polymorphism and Interfaces	Section 10.10 introduces the new Java SE 8 interface features (default methods, static methods and the concept of functional interfaces) that support functional programming with lambdas and streams.
Chapters 12 and 22, GUI Components: Part 1 and 2, respectively	Section 17.9 shows how to use a lambda to implement a Swing event-listener functional interface.
Chapter 14, Strings, Characters and Regular Expressions	Section 17.5 shows how to use lambdas and streams to process collections of String objects.

Fig. 2 | Java SE 8 lambdas and streams discussions and examples. (Part 1 of 2.)

Pre-Java-SE-8 topics	Corresponding Java SE 8 discussions and examples
Chapter 15, Files, Streams and Object Serialization	Section 17.7 shows how to use lambdas and streams to process lines of text from a file.
Chapter 23, Concurrency	Shows that functional programs are easier to parallelize so that they can take advantage of multi-core architectures to enhance performance. Demonstrates parallel stream processing. Shows that Arrays method parallelSort improves performance on multi-core architectures when sorting large arrays.
Chapter 25, JavaFX GUI: Part 1	Section 25.5.5 shows how to use a lambda to implement a JavaFX event-listener functional interface.

Fig. 2 | Java SE 8 lambdas and streams discussions and examples. (Part 2 of 2.)

- *Java SE 7's **try-with-resources statement and the AutoClosable Interface.** Auto-Closable objects reduce the likelihood of resource leaks when you use them with the try-with-resources statement, which automatically closes the AutoClosable objects. In this edition, we use try-with-resources and AutoClosable objects as appropriate starting in Chapter 15, Files, Streams and Object Serialization.

- *Java security.* We audited our book against the CERT Oracle Secure Coding Standard for Java as appropriate for an introductory textbook.

  `http://bit.ly/CERTOracleSecureJava`

  See the Secure Java Programming section of this Preface for more information about CERT.

- *Java NIO API.* We updated the file-processing examples in Chapter 15 to use features from the Java NIO (new IO) API.

- *Java Documentation.* Throughout the book, we provide links to Java documentation where you can learn more about various topics that we present. For Java SE 7 documentation, the links begin with

  `http://docs.oracle.com/javase/7/`

  and for Java SE 8 documentation, the links begin with

  `http://download.java.net/jdk8/`

  These links could change when Oracle releases Java SE 8—*possibly* to links beginning with

  `http://docs.oracle.com/javase/8/`

  For any links that change after publication, we'll post updates at

  `http://www.deitel.com/books/jhtp10LOV`

Swing and JavaFX GUI, Graphics and Multimedia

- *Swing GUI and Java 2D graphics.* Java's Swing GUI is discussed in the optional GUI and graphics sections in Chapters 2–6 and 8–10, and in Chapters 12 and

22. Swing is now in maintenance mode—Oracle has stopped development and will provide only bug fixes going forward, however it will remain part of Java and is still widely used. Chapter 13 discusses Java 2D graphics.

- *JavaFX GUI, graphics and multimedia.* Java's GUI, graphics and multimedia API going forward is JavaFX. In Chapter 25, we use JavaFX 2.2 (released in 2012) with Java SE 7. Our online Chapters 26 and 27—located on the book's companion website (see the inside front cover of this book)—present additional JavaFX GUI features and introduce JavaFX graphics and multimedia in the context of Java FX 8 and Java SE 8. In Chapters 25–27 we use Scene Builder—a drag-and-drop tool for creating JavaFX GUIs quickly and conveniently. It's a standalone tool that you can use separately or with any of the Java IDEs.

- *Scalable GUI and graphics presentation.* Instructors teaching introductory courses have a broad choice of the amount of GUI, graphics and multimedia to cover—from none at all, to optional introductory sections in the early chapters, to a deep treatment of Swing GUI and Java 2D graphics in Chapters 12, 13 and 22, and a deep treatment of JavaFX GUI, graphics and multimedia in Chapter 25 and online Chapters 26–27.

Concurrency

- *Concurrency for optimal multi-core performance.* In this edition, we were privileged to have as a reviewer Brian Goetz, co-author of *Java Concurrency in Practice* (Addison-Wesley). We updated Chapter 23, with Java SE 8 technology and idiom. We added a parallelSort vs. sort example that uses the Java SE 8 Date/Time API to time each operation and demonstrate parallelSort's better performance on a multi-core system. We include a Java SE 8 parallel vs. sequential stream processing example, again using the Date/Time API to show performance improvements. Finally, we added a Java SE 8 CompletableFuture example that demonstrates sequential and parallel execution of long-running calculations.

- *SwingWorker class.* We use class SwingWorker to create multithreaded user interfaces. In online Chapter 26, we show how JavaFX handles concurrency.

- *Concurrency is challenging.* Programming concurrent applications is difficult and error-prone. There's a great variety of concurrency features. We point out the ones that most people should use and mention those that should be left to the experts.

Getting Monetary Amounts Right

- *Monetary amounts.* In the early chapters, for convenience, we use type double to represent monetary amounts. Due to the potential for incorrect monetary calculations with type double, class BigDecimal (which is a bit more complex) should be used to represent monetary amounts. We demonstrate BigDecimal in Chapters 8 and 25.

Object Technology

- *Object-oriented programming and design.* We use a *late objects* approach, covering programming fundamentals such as data types, variables, operators, control stattements, methods and arrays in the early chapters. Then students develop their first customized classes and objects in Chapter 7. [For courses that require an early-objects approach, consider *Java How to Program, 10/e, Early Objects.*]

- *Real-world case studies.* The object-oriented programing presentation features `Account`, `Time`, `Employee`, `GradeBook` and `Card` shuffling-and-dealing case studies.

- *Inheritance, Interfaces, Polymorphism and Composition.* We use a series of real-world case studies to illustrate these OO concepts and explain situations in which each is preferred in building industrial-strength applications.

- *Exception handling.* We integrate basic exception handling early in the book then present a deeper treatment in Chapter 11. Exception handling is important for building "mission-critical" and "business-critical" applications. Programmers need to be concerned with, "What happens when the component I call on to do a job experiences difficulty? How will that component signal that it had a problem?" To use a Java component, you need to know not only how that component behaves when "things go well," but also what exceptions that component "throws" when "things go poorly."

- *Class* `Arrays` *and* `ArrayList`. Chapter 6 covers class `Arrays`—which contains methods for performing common array manipulations—and class `ArrayList`— which implements a dynamically resizable array-like data structure. The chapter's rich selection of exercises includes a substantial project on building your own computer through the technique of software simulation. The Chapter 21 exercises include a follow-on project on building your own compiler that can compile high-level language programs into machine language code that will execute on your computer simulator.

- *Optional Online Case Study: Developing an Object-Oriented Design and Java Implementation of an ATM.* Online Chapters 33–34 include an *optional* case study on object-oriented design using the UML (Unified Modeling Language™)—the industry-standard graphical language for modeling object-oriented systems. We design and implement the software for a simple automated teller machine (ATM). We analyze a typical requirements document that specifies the system to be built. We determine the classes needed to implement that system, the attributes the classes need to have, the behaviors the classes need to exhibit and specify how the classes must interact with one another to meet the system requirements. From the design we produce a complete Java implementation. Students often report having a "light-bulb moment"—the case study helps them "tie it all together" and really understand object orientation.

Data Structures and Generic Collections

- *Data structures presentation.* We begin with generic class `ArrayList` in Chapter 6. Our later data structures discussions (Chapters 16–21) provide a deeper treatment of generic collections—showing how to use the built-in collections of the Java API. We discuss recursion, which is important for implementing tree-like, data-structure classes. We discuss popular searching and sorting algorithms for manipulating the contents of collections, and provide a friendly introduction to Big O—a means of describing how hard an algorithm might have to work to solve a problem. We then show how to implement generic methods and classes, and *custom* generic data structures (this is intended for computer-science majors—most programmers should use the pre-built generic collections). Lambdas and streams (introduced in Chapter 17) are especially useful for working with generic collections.

Database

- *JDBC.* Chapter 24 covers JDBC and uses the Java DB database management system. The chapter introduces Structured Query Language (SQL) and features an OO case study on developing a database-driven address book that demonstrates PreparedStatements.

- *Java Persistence API.* The new online Chapter 29 covers the Java Persistence API (JPA)—a standard for object relational mapping (ORM) that uses JDBC "under the hood." ORM tools can look at a database's schema and generate a set of classes that enabled you to interact with a database without having to use JDBC and SQL directly. This speeds database-application development, reduces errors and produces more portable code.

Web Application Development

- *Java Server Faces (JSF).* Online Chapters 30–31 have been updated to introduce the latest JavaServer Faces (JSF) technology for building web-based applications. Chapter 30 includes examples on building web application GUIs, validating forms and session tracking. Chapter 31 discusses data-driven, Ajax-enabled JSF applications—the chapter features a database-driven multitier web address book that allows users to add and search for contacts.

- *Web services.* Chapter 32 now concentrates on creating and consuming REST-based web services. The vast majority of today's web services now use REST.

Secure Java Programming

It's difficult to build industrial-strength systems that stand up to attacks from viruses, worms, and other forms of "malware." Today, via the Internet, such attacks can be instantaneous and global in scope. Building security into software from the beginning of the development cycle can greatly reduce vulnerabilities. We incorporate various secure Java coding practices (as appropriate for an introductory textbook) into our discussions and code examples.

The CERT® Coordination Center (www.cert.org) was created to analyze and respond promptly to attacks. CERT—the Computer Emergency Response Team—is a government-funded organization within the Carnegie Mellon University Software Engineering Institute™. CERT publishes and promotes secure coding standards for various popular programming languages to help software developers implement industrial-strength systems that avoid the programming practices which leave systems open to attack.

We'd like to thank Robert C. Seacord, Secure Coding Manager at CERT and an adjunct professor in the Carnegie Mellon University School of Computer Science. Mr. Seacord was a technical reviewer for our book, *C How to Program, 7/e*, where he scrutinized our C programs from a security standpoint, recommending that we adhere to the *CERT C Secure Coding Standard*. This experience influenced our coding practices in *C++ How to Program, 9/e* and *Java How to Program, 10/e, Late Objects Version* as well.

Optional GUI and Graphics Case Study

Students enjoy building GUI and graphics applications. For courses that introduce GUI and graphics early, we've integrated an optional 10-segment introduction to creating graphics and Swing-based graphical user interfaces (GUIs). The goal of this case study is to create a simple polymorphic drawing application in which the user can select a shape to draw, select the characteristics of the shape (such as its color) and use the mouse to draw the shape. The case study builds gradually toward that goal, with the reader implementing polymorphic drawing in Chapter 10, adding an event-driven GUI in Chapter 12 and enhancing the drawing capabilities in Chapter 13 with Java 2D.

- Section 2.9—Using Dialog Boxes
- Section 3.14—Creating Simple Drawings
- Section 4.10—Drawing Rectangles and Ovals
- Section 5.13—Colors and Filled Shapes
- Section 6.14—Drawing Arcs
- Section 8.16—Using Objects with Graphics
- Section 9.7—Displaying Text and Images Using Labels
- Section 10.11—Drawing with Polymorphism
- Exercise 12.17—Expanding the Interface
- Exercise 13.31—Adding Java2D

Teaching Approach

Java How to Program, 10/e, Late Objects Version contains hundreds of complete working examples. We stress program clarity and concentrate on building well-engineered software.

VideoNotes. The Companion Website includes extensive VideoNotes in which co-author Paul Deitel explains in detail most of the programs in the book's core chapters. Students like viewing the VideoNotes for reinforcement of core concepts and for additional insights.

Syntax Shading. For readability, we syntax shade all the Java code, similar to the way most Java integrated-development environments and code editors syntax color code. Our syntax-shading conventions are as follows:

```
comments appear in light gray like this
keywords appear bold black like this
constants and literal values appear in bold dark gray like this
all other code appears in black like this
```

Code Highlighting. We place gray rectangles around key code segments.

Using Fonts for Emphasis. We place the key terms and the index's page reference for each defining occurrence in **bold** text for easier reference. We emphasize on-screen components in the **bold Helvetica** font (e.g., the **File** menu) and emphasize Java program text in the Lucida font (for example, int x = 5;).

Web Access. All of the source-code examples can be downloaded from:

```
http://www.deitel.com/books/jhtp10LOV
http://www.pearsonhighered.com/deitel
```

Objectives. The opening quotes are followed by a list of chapter objectives.

Illustrations/Figures. Abundant tables, line drawings, UML diagrams, programs and program outputs are included.

Programming Tips. We include programming tips to help you focus on important aspects of program development. These tips and practices represent the best we've gleaned from a combined seven decades of programming and teaching experience.

Good Programming Practice

The Good Programming Practices *call attention to techniques that will help you produce programs that are clearer, more understandable and more maintainable.*

Common Programming Error

Pointing out these Common Programming Errors *reduces the likelihood that you'll make them.*

Error-Prevention Tip

These tips contain suggestions for exposing bugs and removing them from your programs; many describe aspects of Java that prevent bugs from getting into programs in the first place.

Performance Tip

These tips highlight opportunities for making your programs run faster or minimizing the amount of memory that they occupy.

Portability Tip

The Portability Tips *help you write code that will run on a variety of platforms.*

Software Engineering Observation

The Software Engineering Observations *highlight architectural and design issues that affect the construction of software systems, especially large-scale systems.*

Look-and-Feel Observation

The Look-and-Feel Observations *highlight graphical-user-interface conventions. These observations help you design attractive, user-friendly graphical user interfaces that conform to industry norms.*

Summary Bullets. We present a section-by-section bullet-list summary of the chapter. For ease of reference, we include the page number of each key term's defining occurrence in the text.

Self-Review Exercises and Answers. Extensive self-review exercises *and* answers are included for self study. All of the exercises in the optional ATM case study are fully solved.

Exercises. The chapter exercises include:

- simple recall of important terminology and concepts

- What's wrong with this code?

- What does this code do?

- writing individual statements and small portions of methods and classes

- writing complete methods, classes and programs

- major projects

- in many chapters, Making a Difference exercises that encourage you to use computers and the Internet to research and solve significant social problems.

Exercises that are purely SE 8 are marked as such. Check out our Programming Projects Resource Center for lots of additional exercise and project possibilities (www.deitel.com/ ProgrammingProjects/).

Index. We've included an extensive index. Defining occurrences of key terms are highlighted with a **bold** page number. The print book index mentions only those terms used in the print book. The online chapters index includes all the print book terms and the online chapter terms.

Software Used in *Java How to Program, 10/e, Late Objects* Version

All the software you'll need for this book is available free for download from the Internet. See the Before You Begin section that follows this Preface for links to each download.

We wrote most of the examples in *Java How to Program, 10/e, Late Objects Version*, using the free Java Standard Edition Development Kit (JDK) 7. For the optional Java SE 8 modules, we used the OpenJDK's early access version of JDK 8. In Chapter 25 and several online chapters, we also used the Netbeans IDE. See the Before You Begin section that follows this Preface for more information.

Instructor Supplements

The following supplements are available to qualified instructors only through Pearson Education's Instructor Resource Center (www.pearsonhighered.com/irc):

- *PowerPoint® slides* containing all the code and figures in the text, plus bulleted items that summarize key points.

- *Test Item File* of multiple-choice questions (approximately two per book section).

- *Solutions Manual* with solutions to the vast majority of the end-of-chapter exercises. **Check the IRC to determine the exercises for which we provide solutions.**

Please do not write to us requesting access to the Pearson Instructor's Resource Center which contains the book's instructor supplements, including the exercise solutions. Access is limited strictly to college instructors teaching from the book. Instructors may obtain access only through their Pearson representatives. Solutions are *not* provided for "project" exercises.

If you're not a registered faculty member, contact your Pearson representative or visit www.pearsonhighered.com/educator/replocator/.

Acknowledgments

We'd like to thank Abbey Deitel and Barbara Deitel for long hours devoted to this project. We're fortunate to have worked on this project with the dedicated team of publishing professionals at Pearson. We appreciate the guidance, wisdom and energy of Tracy Johnson, Executive Editor, Computer Science. Tracy and her team handle all of our academic textbooks. Carole Snyder recruited the book's academic reviewers and managed the review process. Bob Engelhardt managed the book's publication. We selected the cover art and Laura Gardner designed the cover.

Reviewers

We wish to acknowledge the efforts of our recent editions reviewers—a distinguished group of academics, Oracle Java team members, Oracle Java Champions and other industry professionals. They scrutinized the text and the programs and provided countless suggestions for improving the presentation.

Tenth Edition reviewers: Lance Andersen (Oracle Corporation), Dr. Danny Coward (Oracle Corporation), Brian Goetz (Oracle Corporation), Evan Golub (University of Maryland), Dr. Huiwei Guan (Professor, Department of Computer & Information Science, North Shore Community College), Manfred Riem (Java Champion), Simon Ritter (Oracle Corporation), Robert C. Seacord (CERT, Software Engineering Institute, Carnegie Mellon University), Khallai Taylor (Assistant Professor, Triton College and Adjunct Professor, Lonestar College—Kingwood), Jorge Vargas (Yumbling and a Java Champion), Johan Vos (LodgON, co-author of *Pro JavaFX 2* and Oracle Java Champion) and James L. Weaver (Oracle Corporation and co-author of *Pro JavaFX 2*).

Previous editions reviewers: Soundararajan Angusamy (Sun Microsystems), Joseph Bowbeer (Consultant), William E. Duncan (Louisiana State University), Diana Franklin (University of California, Santa Barbara), Edward F. Gehringer (North Carolina State University), Ric Heishman (George Mason University), Dr. Heinz Kabutz (JavaSpecialists.eu), Patty Kraft (San Diego State University), Lawrence Premkumar (Sun Microsystems), Tim Margush (University of Akron), Sue McFarland Metzger (Villanova University), Shyamal Mitra (The University of Texas at Austin), Peter Pilgrim (Consultant), Manjeet Rege, Ph.D. (Rochester Institute of Technology), Susan Rodger (Duke University), Amr Sabry (Indiana University), José Antonio González Seco (Parliament of Andalusia), Sang Shin (Sun Microsystems), S. Sivakumar (Astra Infotech Private Limited), Raghavan "Rags" Srinivas (Intuit), Monica Sweat (Georgia Tech), Vinod Varma (Astra Infotech Private Limited) and Alexander Zuev (Sun Microsystems).

A Special Thank You to Brian Goetz

We were privileged to have Brian Goetz, Oracle's Java Language Architect and Specification Lead for Java SE 8's Project Lambda, and co-author of *Java Concurrency in Practice*, do a detailed full-book review. He thoroughly scrutinized every chapter, providing extremely helpful insights and constructive comments. Any remaining faults in the book are our own.

Well, there you have it! As you read the book, we'd appreciate your comments, criticisms, corrections and suggestions for improvement. Please address all correspondence to:

`deitel@deitel.com`

We'll respond promptly. We hope you enjoy working with *Java How to Program, 10/e, Late Objects Version* as much as we enjoyed writing it!

Paul and Harvey Deitel

About the Authors

Paul Deitel, CEO and Chief Technical Officer of Deitel & Associates, Inc., is a graduate of MIT, where he studied Information Technology. He holds the Java Certified Programmer and Java Certified Developer designations, and is an Oracle Java Champion. Through Deitel & Associates, Inc., he has delivered hundreds of programming courses worldwide to clients, including Cisco, IBM, Siemens, Sun Microsystems, Dell, Fidelity, NASA at the Kennedy Space Center, the National Severe Storm Laboratory, White Sands Missile Range, Rogue Wave Software, Boeing, SunGard Higher Education, Nortel Networks, Puma, iRobot, Invensys and many more. He and his co-author, Dr. Harvey M. Deitel, are the world's best-selling programming-language textbook/professional book/video authors.

Dr. Harvey Deitel, Chairman and Chief Strategy Officer of Deitel & Associates, Inc., has over 50 years of experience in the computer field. Dr. Deitel earned B.S. and M.S. degrees in Electrical Engineering from MIT and a Ph.D. in Mathematics from Boston University. He has extensive college teaching experience, including earning tenure and serving as the Chairman of the Computer Science Department at Boston College before founding Deitel & Associates, Inc., in 1991 with his son, Paul. The Deitels' publications have earned international recognition, with translations published in Japanese, German, Russian, Spanish, French, Polish, Italian, Simplified Chinese, Traditional Chinese, Korean, Portuguese, Greek, Urdu and Turkish. Dr. Deitel has delivered hundreds of programming courses to corporate, academic, government and military clients.

About Deitel® & Associates, Inc.

Deitel & Associates, Inc., founded by Paul Deitel and Harvey Deitel, is an internationally recognized authoring and corporate training organization, specializing in computer programming languages, object technology, mobile app development and Internet and web software technology. The company's training clients include many of the world's largest companies, government agencies, branches of the military and academic institutions. The company offers instructor-led training courses delivered at client sites worldwide on major programming languages and platforms, including Java™, Android app development, Objective-C and iOS app development, C++, C, Visual C#®, Visual Basic®, Visual C++®, Python®, object technology, Internet and web programming and a growing list of additional programming and software development courses.

Through its 39-year publishing partnership with Pearson/Prentice Hall, Deitel & Associates, Inc., publishes leading-edge programming textbooks and professional books in print and a wide range of e-book formats, and *LiveLessons* video courses. Deitel & Associates, Inc. and the authors can be reached at:

```
deitel@deitel.com
```

To learn more about Deitel's *Dive-Into*® *Series* Corporate Training curriculum, visit:

```
http://www.deitel.com/training
```

To request a proposal for worldwide on-site, instructor-led training at your organization, e-mail deitel@deitel.com.

Individuals wishing to purchase Deitel books and *LiveLessons* video training can do so through www.deitel.com. Bulk orders by corporations, the government, the military and academic institutions should be placed directly with Pearson. For more information, visit

```
http://www.informit.com/store/sales.aspx
```

Before You Begin

This section contains information you should review before using this book. Any updates to the information presented here will be posted at:

```
http://www.deitel.com/books/jhtp10LOV
```

In addition, we provide Dive-Into® videos (which will be available in time for Fall 2014 classes) that demonstrate the instructions in this Before You Begin section.

Font and Naming Conventions

We use fonts to distinguish between on-screen components (such as menu names and menu items) and Java code or commands. Our convention is to emphasize on-screen components in a sans-serif bold **Helvetica** font (for example, **File** menu) and to emphasize Java code and commands in a sans-serif Lucida font (for example, System.out.println()).

Software Used in the Book

All the software you'll need for this book is available free for download from the web. With the exception of the examples that are specific to Java SE 8, all of the examples were tested with the Java SE 7 and Java SE 8 Java Standard Edition Development Kits (JDKs).

Java Standard Edition Development Kit 7 (JDK 7)
JDK 7 for Windows, OS X and Linux platforms is available from:

```
http://www.oracle.com/technetwork/java/javase/downloads/index.html
```

Java Standard Edition Development Kit (JDK) 8
At the time of this publication, the near-final version of JDK 8 for Windows, OS X and Linux platforms was available from:

```
https://jdk8.java.net/download.html
```

Once JDK 8 is released as final, it will be available from:

```
http://www.oracle.com/technetwork/java/javase/downloads/index.html
```

JDK Installation Instructions

After downloading the JDK installer, be sure to carefully follow the JDK installation instructions for your platform at:

```
http://docs.oracle.com/javase/7/docs/webnotes/install/index.html
```

Though these instructions are for JDK 7, they also apply to JDK 8—you'll need to update the JDK version number in any version-specific instructions.

Setting the PATH Environment Variable

The PATH environment variable on your computer designates which directories the computer searches when looking for applications, such as the applications that enable you to compile and run your Java applications (called javac and java, respectively). *Carefully follow the installation instructions for Java on your platform to ensure that you set the PATH environment variable correctly.* The steps for setting environment variables differ by operating system and sometimes by operating system version (e.g., Windows 7 vs. Windows 8). Instructions for various platforms are listed at:

```
http://www.java.com/en/download/help/path.xml
```

If you do not set the PATH variable correctly on Windows and some Linux installations, when you use the JDK's tools, you'll receive a message like:

```
'java' is not recognized as an internal or external command,
operable program or batch file.
```

In this case, go back to the installation instructions for setting the PATH and recheck your steps. If you've downloaded a newer version of the JDK, you may need to change the name of the JDK's installation directory in the PATH variable.

JDK Installation Directory and the **bin** Subdirectory

The JDK's installation directory varies by platform. The directories listed below are for Oracle's JDK 7 update 51:

- 32-bit JDK on Windows:
  `C:\Program Files (x86)\Java\jdk1.7.0_51`

- 64-bit JDK on Windows:
  `C:\Program Files\Java\jdk1.7.0_51`

- Mac OS X:
  `/Library/Java/JavaVirtualMachines/jdk1.7.0_51.jdk/Contents/Home`

- Ubuntu Linux:
  `/usr/lib/jvm/java-7-oracle`

Depending on your platform, the JDK installation folder's name might differ if you're using a different update of JDK 7 or using JDK 8. For Linux, the install location depends on the installer you use and possibly the version of Linux that you use. We used Ubuntu Linux. The PATH environment variable must point to the JDK installation directory's **bin** subdirectory.

When setting the PATH, be sure to use the proper JDK-installation-directory name for the specific version of the JDK you installed—as newer JDK releases become available, the JDK-installation-directory name changes to include an *update version number*. For example, at the time of this writing, the most recent JDK 7 release was update 51. For this version, the JDK-installation-directory name ends with "_51".

Setting the CLASSPATH Environment Variable

If you attempt to run a Java program and receive a message like

```
Exception in thread "main" java.lang.NoClassDefFoundError: YourClass
```

then your system has a `CLASSPATH` environment variable that must be modified. To fix the preceding error, follow the steps in setting the `PATH` environment variable, to locate the `CLASSPATH` variable, then edit the variable's value to include the local directory—typically represented as a dot (.). On Windows add

```
.;
```

at the beginning of the `CLASSPATH`'s value (with no spaces before or after these characters). On other platforms, replace the semicolon with the appropriate path separator characters—typically a colon (:).

Setting the `JAVA_HOME` Environment Variable

The Java DB database software that you'll use in Chapter 24 and several online chapters requires you to set the `JAVA_HOME` environment variable to your JDK's installation directory. The same steps you used to set the `PATH` may also be used to set other environment variables, such as `JAVA_HOME`.

Java Integrated Development Environments (IDEs)

There are many Java integrated development environments that you can use for Java programming. For this reason, we used only the JDK command-line tools for most of the book's examples. We provide Dive-Into® videos (which will be available in time for Fall 2014 classes) that show how to download, install and use three popular IDEs—NetBeans, Eclipse and IntelliJ IDEA. We use NetBeans in Chapter 25 and several of the book's online chapters.

NetBeans Downloads
You can download the JDK/NetBeans bundle from:

```
http://www.oracle.com/technetwork/java/javase/downloads/index.html
```

The NetBeans version that's bundled with the JDK is for Java SE development. The online JavaServer Faces (JSF) chapters and web services chapter use the Java Enterprise Edition (Java EE) version of NetBeans, which you can download from:

```
https://netbeans.org/downloads/
```

This version supports both Java SE and Java EE development.

Eclipse Downloads
You can download the Eclipse IDE from:

```
https://www.eclipse.org/downloads/
```

For Java SE development choose the Eclipse IDE for Java Developers. For Java Enterprise Edition (Java EE) development (such as JSF and web services), choose the Eclipse IDE for Java EE Developers—this version supports both Java SE and Java EE development.

IntelliJ IDEA Community Edition Downloads
You can download the free IntelliJ IDEA Community Edition from:

```
http://www.jetbrains.com/idea/download/index.html
```

The free version supports only Java SE development.

Obtaining the Code Examples

The examples for *Java How to Program, 10/e, Late Objects Version* are available for download at

```
http://www.deitel.com/books/jhtp10LOV/
```

under the heading **Download Code Examples and Other Premium Content**. The examples are also available from

```
http://www.pearsonhighered.com/deitel
```

When you download the ZIP archive file, write down the location where you choose to save it on your computer.

Extract the contents of examples.zip using a ZIP extraction tool such as 7-Zip (www.7-zip.org), WinZip (www.winzip.com) or the built-in capabilities of your operating system. Instructions throughout the book assume that the examples are located at:

- C:\examples on Windows
- your user account home folder's examples subfolder on Linux
- your Documents folders examples subfolder on Mac OS X

Java's Nimbus Look-and-Feel

Java comes bundled with a cross-platform look-and-feel known as Nimbus. For programs with Swing graphical user interfaces (e.g., Chapters 12 and 22), we configured our test computers to use Nimbus as the default look-and-feel.

To set Nimbus as the default for all Java applications, you must create a text file named swing.properties in the lib folder of both your JDK installation folder and your JRE installation folder. Place the following line of code in the file:

```
swing.defaultlaf=com.sun.java.swing.plaf.nimbus.NimbusLookAndFeel
```

For more information on locating these folders visit http://docs.oracle.com/javase/7/docs/webnotes/install/index.html. [*Note:* In addition to the standalone JRE, there's a JRE nested in your JDK's installation folder. If you're using an IDE that depends on the JDK (e.g., NetBeans), you may also need to place the swing.properties file in the nested jre folder's lib folder.]

You're now ready to begin your Java studies with *Java How to Program, 10/e, Late Objects Version*. We hope you enjoy the book!

Introduction to Computers, the Internet and Java

1

Man is still the most extraordinary computer of all.
—John F. Kennedy

Good design is good business.
—Thomas J. Watson, Founder of IBM

Objectives

In this chapter you'll:

- Learn about exciting recent developments in the computer field.
- Learn computer hardware, software and networking basics.
- Understand the data hierarchy.
- Understand the different types of programming languages.
- Understand the importance of Java and other leading programming languages.
- Understand object-oriented programming basics.
- Learn the importance of the Internet and the web.
- Learn a typical Java program-development environment.
- Test-drive a Java application.
- Learn some key recent software technologies.
- See how to keep up-to-date with information technologies.

1.1 Introduction

Welcome to Java—one of the world's most widely used computer programming languages. You're already familiar with the powerful tasks computers perform. Using this textbook, you'll write instructions commanding computers to perform those tasks. **Software** (i.e., the instructions you write) controls **hardware** (i.e., computers).

You'll learn *object-oriented programming*—today's key programming methodology. You'll create and work with many *software objects*.

For many organizations, the preferred language for meeting their enterprise programming needs is Java. Java is also widely used for implementing Internet-based applications and software for devices that communicate over a network.

Forrester Research predicts more than two billion PCs will be in use by 2015.[1] According to Oracle, 97% of enterprise desktops, 89% of PC desktops, three billion devices (Fig. 1.1) and 100% of all Blu-ray Disc™ players run Java, and there are over 9 million Java developers.[2]

According to a study by Gartner, mobile devices will continue to outpace PCs as users' primary computing devices; an estimated 1.96 billion smartphones and 388 million tablets will be shipped in 2015—8.7 times the number of PCs.[3] By 2018, the mobile applications

---

1.   http://www.worldometers.info/computers.
2.   http://www.oracle.com/technetwork/articles/java/javaone12review-1863742.html.
3.   http://www.gartner.com/newsroom/id/2645115.

Devices		
Airplane systems	ATMs	Automobile infotainment systems
Blu-ray Disc™ players	Cable boxes	Copiers
Credit cards	CT scanners	Desktop computers
e-Readers	Game consoles	GPS navigation systems
Home appliances	Home security systems	Light switches
Lottery terminals	Medical devices	Mobile phones
MRIs	Parking payment stations	Printers
Transportation passes	Robots	Routers
Smart cards	Smart meters	Smartpens
Smartphones	Tablets	Televisions
TV set-top boxes	Thermostats	Vehicle diagnostic systems

Fig. 1.1 | Some devices that use Java.

(apps) market is expected to reach $92 billion.[4] This is creating significant career opportunities for people who program mobile applications, many of which are programmed in Java (see Section 1.6.3).

Java Standard Edition

Java has evolved so rapidly that this tenth edition of *Java How to Program*—based on **Java Standard Edition 7 (Java SE 7)** and **Java Standard Edition 8 (Java SE 8)**—was published just 17 years after the first edition. Java Standard Edition contains the capabilities needed to develop desktop and server applications. The book can be used with *either* Java SE 7 *or* Java SE 8 (released just after this book was published). All of the Java SE 8 features are discussed in modular, easy-to-include-or-omit sections throughout the book.

Prior to Java SE 8, Java supported three programming paradigms—*procedural programming, object-oriented programming* and *generic programming.* Java SE 8 adds *functional programming*. In Chapter 17, we'll show how to use functional programming to write programs faster, more concisely, with fewer bugs and that are easier to *parallelize* (i.e., perform multiple calculations simultaneously) to take advantage of today's multi-core hardware architectures to enhance application performance.

Java Enterprise Edition

Java is used in such a broad spectrum of applications that it has two other editions. The **Java Enterprise Edition (Java EE)** is geared toward developing large-scale, distributed networking applications and web-based applications. In the past, most computer applications ran on "standalone" computers (computers that were not networked together). Today's applications can be written with the aim of communicating among the world's computers via the Internet and the web. Later in this book we discuss how to build such web-based applications with Java.

---

4. https://www.abiresearch.com/press/tablets-will-generate-35-of-this-years-25-billion-.

Java Micro Edition
The **Java Micro Edition** (**Java ME**)—a subset of Java SE—is geared toward developing applications for resource-constrained embedded devices, such as smartwatches, MP3 players, television set-top boxes, smart meters (for monitoring electric energy usage) and more.

1.2 Hardware and Software

Computers can perform calculations and make logical decisions phenomenally faster than human beings can. Many of today's personal computers can perform billions of calculations in one second—more than a human can perform in a lifetime. *Supercomputers* are already performing *thousands of trillions (quadrillions)* of instructions per second! China's National University of Defense Technology's Tianhe-2 supercomputer can perform over 33 quadrillion calculations per second (33.86 *petaflops*)![5] To put that in perspective, *the Tianhe-2 supercomputer can perform in one second about 3 million calculations for every person on the planet!* And—these supercomputing "upper limits" are growing quickly.

Computers process data under the control of sequences of instructions called **computer programs**. These software programs guide the computer through ordered actions specified by people called computer **programmers**. In this book, you'll learn a key programming methodology that's enhancing programmer productivity, thereby reducing software development costs—*object-oriented programming*.

A computer consists of various devices referred to as hardware (e.g., the keyboard, screen, mouse, hard disks, memory, DVD drives and processing units). Computing costs are *dropping dramatically*, owing to rapid developments in hardware and software technologies. Computers that might have filled large rooms and cost millions of dollars decades ago are now inscribed on silicon chips smaller than a fingernail, costing perhaps a few dollars each. Ironically, silicon is one of the most abundant materials on Earth—it's an ingredient in common sand. Silicon-chip technology has made computing so economical that computers have become a commodity.

1.2.1 Moore's Law

Every year, you probably expect to pay at least a little more for most products and services. The opposite has been the case in the computer and communications fields, especially with regard to the hardware supporting these technologies. For many decades, hardware costs have fallen rapidly.

Every year or two, the capacities of computers have approximately *doubled* inexpensively. This remarkable trend often is called **Moore's Law**, named for the person who identified it in the 1960s, Gordon Moore, co-founder of Intel—the leading manufacturer of the processors in today's computers and embedded systems. Moore's Law and related observations apply especially to the amount of memory that computers have for programs, the amount of secondary storage (such as disk storage) they have to hold programs and data over longer periods of time, and their processor speeds—the speeds at which they *execute* their programs (i.e., do their work).

---

5. http://www.top500.org/.

Similar growth has occurred in the communications field—costs have plummeted as enormous demand for communications *bandwidth* (i.e., information-carrying capacity) has attracted intense competition. We know of no other fields in which technology improves so quickly and costs fall so rapidly. Such phenomenal improvement is truly fostering the *Information Revolution*.

1.2.2 Computer Organization

Regardless of differences in *physical* appearance, computers can be envisioned as divided into various **logical units** or sections (Fig. 1.2).

Logical unit	Description
Input unit	This "receiving" section obtains information (data and computer programs) from **input devices** and places it at the disposal of the other units for processing. Most user input is entered into computers through keyboards, touch screens and mouse devices. Other forms of input include receiving voice commands, scanning images and barcodes, reading from secondary storage devices (such as hard drives, DVD drives, Blu-ray Disc™ drives and USB flash drives—also called "thumb drives" or "memory sticks"), receiving video from a webcam and having your computer receive information from the Internet (such as when you stream videos from YouTube® or download e-books from Amazon). Newer forms of input include position data from a GPS device, and motion and orientation information from an *accelerometer* (a device that responds to up/down, left/right and forward/backward acceleration) in a smartphone or game controller (such as Microsoft® Kinect® and Xbox®, Wii™ Remote and Sony® PlayStation® Move).
Output unit	This "shipping" section takes information the computer has processed and places it on various **output devices** to make it available for use outside the computer. Most information that's output from computers today is displayed on screens (including touch screens), printed on paper ("going green" discourages this), played as audio or video on PCs and media players (such as Apple's iPods) and giant screens in sports stadiums, transmitted over the Internet or used to control other devices, such as robots and "intelligent" appliances. Information is also commonly output to secondary storage devices, such as hard drives, DVD drives and USB flash drives. A popular recent form of output is smartphone vibration.
Memory unit	This rapid-access, relatively low-capacity "warehouse" section retains information that has been entered through the input unit, making it immediately available for processing when needed. The memory unit also retains processed information until it can be placed on output devices by the output unit. Information in the memory unit is *volatile*—it's typically lost when the computer's power is turned off. The memory unit is often called either **memory, primary memory** or **RAM** (Random Access Memory). Main memories on desktop and notebook computers contain as much as 128 GB of RAM. GB stands for gigabytes; a gigabyte is approximately one billion bytes. A **byte** is eight bits. A bit is either a 0 or a 1.

Fig. 1.2 | Logical units of a computer. (Part 1 of 2.)

Logical unit	Description
Arithmetic and logic unit (ALU)	This "manufacturing" section performs *calculations*, such as addition, subtraction, multiplication and division. It also contains the *decision* mechanisms that allow the computer, for example, to compare two items from the memory unit to determine whether they're equal. In today's systems, the ALU is implemented as part of the next logical unit, the CPU.
Central processing unit (CPU)	This "administrative" section coordinates and supervises the operation of the other sections. The CPU tells the input unit when information should be read into the memory unit, tells the ALU when information from the memory unit should be used in calculations and tells the output unit when to send information from the memory unit to certain output devices. Many of today's computers have multiple CPUs and, hence, can perform many operations simultaneously. A **multi-core processor** implements multiple processors on a single integrated-circuit chip—a *dual-core processor* has two CPUs and a *quad-core processor* has four CPUs. Today's desktop computers have processors that can execute billions of instructions per second.
Secondary storage unit	This is the long-term, high-capacity "warehousing" section. Programs or data not actively being used by the other units normally are placed on secondary storage devices (e.g., your *hard drive*) until they're again needed, possibly hours, days, months or even years later. Information on secondary storage devices is *persistent*—it's preserved even when the computer's power is turned off. Secondary storage information takes much longer to access than information in primary memory, but its cost per unit is much less. Examples of secondary storage devices include hard drives, DVD drives and USB flash drives, some of which can hold over 2 TB (TB stands for terabytes; a terabyte is approximately one trillion bytes). Typical hard drives on desktop and notebook computers hold up to 2 TB, and some desktop hard drives can hold up to 4 TB.

Fig. 1.2 | Logical units of a computer. (Part 2 of 2.)

1.3 Data Hierarchy

Data items processed by computers form a **data hierarchy** that becomes larger and more complex in structure as we progress from the simplest data items (called "bits") to richer ones, such as characters and fields. Figure 1.3 illustrates a portion of the data hierarchy.

Bits
The smallest data item in a computer can assume the value 0 or the value 1. It's called a **bit** (short for "binary digit"—a digit that can assume one of *two* values). Remarkably, the impressive functions performed by computers involve only the simplest manipulations of 0s and 1s—*examining a bit's value*, *setting a bit's value* and *reversing a bit's value* (from 1 to 0 or from 0 to 1).

Characters
It's tedious for people to work with data in the low-level form of bits. Instead, they prefer to work with *decimal digits* (0–9), *letters* (A–Z and a–z), and *special symbols* (e.g., $, @, %,

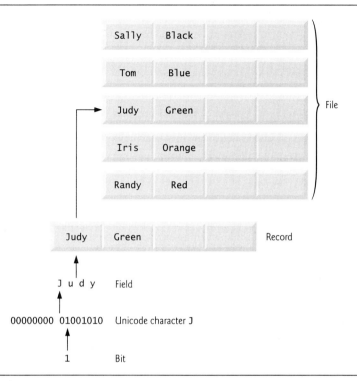

Fig. 1.3 | Data hierarchy.

&, *, (,), –, +, ", :, ? and /). Digits, letters and special symbols are known as **characters**. The computer's **character set** is the set of all the characters used to write programs and represent data items. Computers process only 1s and 0s, so a computer's character set represents every character as a pattern of 1s and 0s. Java uses **Unicode®** characters that are composed of one, two or four bytes (8, 16 or 32 bits). Unicode contains characters for many of the world's languages. See Appendix H for more information on Unicode. See Appendix B for more information on the **ASCII (American Standard Code for Information Interchange)** character set—the popular subset of Unicode that represents uppercase and lowercase letters, digits and some common special characters.

Fields
Just as characters are composed of bits, **fields** are composed of characters or bytes. A field is a group of characters or bytes that conveys meaning. For example, a field consisting of uppercase and lowercase letters can be used to represent a person's name, and a field consisting of decimal digits could represent a person's age.

Records
Several related fields can be used to compose a **record** (implemented as a class in Java). In a payroll system, for example, the record for an employee might consist of the following fields (possible types for these fields are shown in parentheses):

- Employee identification number (a whole number)
- Name (a string of characters)
- Address (a string of characters)
- Hourly pay rate (a number with a decimal point)
- Year-to-date earnings (a number with a decimal point)
- Amount of taxes withheld (a number with a decimal point)

Thus, a record is a group of related fields. In the preceding example, all the fields belong to the *same* employee. A company might have many employees and a payroll record for each.

Files

A **file** is a group of related records. [*Note:* More generally, a file contains arbitrary data in arbitrary formats. In some operating systems, a file is viewed simply as a *sequence of bytes*— any organization of the bytes in a file, such as organizing the data into records, is a view created by the application programmer. You'll see how to do that in Chapter 15.] It's not unusual for an organization to have many files, some containing billions, or even trillions, of characters of information.

Database

A **database** is a collection of data organized for easy access and manipulation. The most popular model is the *relational database*, in which data is stored in simple *tables*. A table includes *records* and *fields*. For example, a table of students might include first name, last name, major, year, student ID number and grade point average fields. The data for each student is a record, and the individual pieces of information in each record are the fields. You can *search*, *sort* and otherwise manipulate the data based on its relationship to multiple tables or databases. For example, a university might use data from the student database in combination with data from databases of courses, on-campus housing, meal plans, etc. We discuss databases in Chapter 24.

Big Data

The amount of data being produced worldwide is enormous and growing quickly. According to IBM, approximately 2.5 quintillion bytes (2.5 *exabytes*) of data are created daily and 90% of the world's data was created in just the past two years![6] According to a Digital Universe study, the global data supply reached 2.8 *zettabytes* (equal to 2.8 trillion gigabytes) in 2012.[7] Figure 1.4 shows some common byte measurements. **Big data** applications deal with such massive amounts of data and this field is growing quickly, creating lots of opportunity for software developers. According to a study by Gartner Group, over 4 million IT jobs globally will support big data by by 2015.[8]

---

6. `http://www-01.ibm.com/software/data/bigdata/`.
7. `http://www.guardian.co.uk/news/datablog/2012/dec/19/big-data-study-digital-universe-global-volume`.
8. `http://tech.fortune.cnn.com/2013/09/04/big-data-employment-boom/`.

Unit	Bytes	Which is approximately
1 kilobyte (KB)	1024 bytes	10^3 (1024 bytes exactly)
1 megabyte (MB)	1024 kilobytes	10^6 (1,000,000 bytes)
1 gigabyte (GB)	1024 megabytes	10^9 (1,000,000,000 bytes)
1 terabyte (TB)	1024 gigabytes	10^{12} (1,000,000,000,000 bytes)
1 petabyte (PB)	1024 terabytes	10^{15} (1,000,000,000,000,000 bytes)
1 exabyte (EB)	1024 petabytes	10^{18} (1,000,000,000,000,000,000 bytes)
1 zettabyte (ZB)	1024 exabytes	10^{21} (1,000,000,000,000,000,000,000 bytes)

Fig. 1.4 | Byte measurements.

1.4 Machine Languages, Assembly Languages and High-Level Languages

Programmers write instructions in various programming languages, some directly understandable by computers and others requiring intermediate *translation* steps. Hundreds of such languages are in use today. These may be divided into three general types:

1. Machine languages
2. Assembly languages
3. High-level languages

Machine Languages

Any computer can directly understand only its own **machine language**, defined by its hardware design. Machine languages generally consist of strings of numbers (ultimately reduced to 1s and 0s) that instruct computers to perform their most elementary operations one at a time. Machine languages are *machine dependent* (a particular machine language can be used on only one type of computer). Such languages are cumbersome for humans. For example, here's a section of an early machine-language payroll program that adds overtime pay to base pay and stores the result in gross pay:

```
+1300042774
+1400593419
+1200274027
```

Assembly Languages and Assemblers

Programming in machine language was simply too slow and tedious for most programmers. Instead of using the strings of numbers that computers could directly understand, programmers began using English-like abbreviations to represent elementary operations. These abbreviations formed the basis of **assembly languages**. *Translator programs* called **assemblers** were developed to convert early assembly-language programs to machine language at computer speeds. The following section of an assembly-language payroll program also adds overtime pay to base pay and stores the result in gross pay:

```
load    basepay
add     overpay
store   grosspay
```

Although such code is clearer to humans, it's incomprehensible to computers until translated to machine language.

High-Level Languages and Compilers
With the advent of assembly languages, computer usage increased rapidly, but programmers still had to use numerous instructions to accomplish even the simplest tasks. To speed the programming process, **high-level languages** were developed in which single statements could be written to accomplish substantial tasks. Translator programs called **compilers** convert high-level language programs into machine language. High-level languages allow you to write instructions that look almost like everyday English and contain commonly used mathematical notations. A payroll program written in a high-level language might contain a *single* statement such as

```
grossPay = basePay + overTimePay
```

From the programmer's standpoint, high-level languages are preferable to machine and assembly languages. Java is one of the most widely used high-level programming languages.

Interpreters
Compiling a large high-level language program into machine language can take considerable computer time. *Interpreter* programs, developed to execute high-level language programs directly, avoid the delay of compilation, although they run slower than compiled programs. We'll say more about interpreters in Section 1.9, where you'll learn that Java uses a clever performance-tuned mixture of compilation and interpretation to run programs.

1.5 Introduction to Object Technology

Today, as demands for new and more powerful software are soaring, building software quickly, correctly and economically remains an elusive goal. *Objects*, or more precisely, the *classes* objects come from, are essentially *reusable* software components. There are date objects, time objects, audio objects, video objects, automobile objects, people objects, etc. Almost any *noun* can be reasonably represented as a software object in terms of *attributes* (e.g., name, color and size) and *behaviors* (e.g., calculating, moving and communicating). Software-development groups can use a modular, object-oriented design-and-implementation approach to be much more productive than with earlier popular techniques like "structured programming"—object-oriented programs are often easier to understand, correct and modify.

1.5.1 The Automobile as an Object

To help you understand objects and their contents, let's begin with a simple analogy. Suppose you want to *drive a car and make it go faster by pressing its accelerator pedal.* What must happen before you can do this? Well, before you can drive a car, someone has to *design* it. A car typically begins as engineering drawings, similar to the *blueprints* that describe the design of a house. These drawings include the design for an accelerator pedal. The pedal *hides* from the driver the complex mechanisms that actually make the car go faster, just as the brake pedal "hides" the mechanisms that slow the car, and the steering wheel "hides" the mechanisms that turn the car. This enables people with little or no knowledge of how engines, braking and steering mechanisms work to drive a car easily.

Just as you cannot cook meals in the kitchen of a blueprint, you cannot drive a car's engineering drawings. Before you can drive a car, it must be *built* from the engineering drawings that describe it. A completed car has an *actual* accelerator pedal to make it go faster, but even that's not enough—the car won't accelerate on its own (hopefully!), so the driver must *press* the pedal to accelerate the car.

1.5.2 Methods and Classes

Let's use our car example to introduce some key object-oriented programming concepts. Performing a task in a program requires a **method**. The method houses the program statements that actually perform its tasks. The method hides these statements from its user, just as the accelerator pedal of a car hides from the driver the mechanisms of making the car go faster. In Java, we create a program unit called a **class** to house the set of methods that perform the class's tasks. For example, a class that represents a bank account might contain one method to *deposit* money to an account, another to *withdraw* money from an account and a third to *inquire* what the account's current balance is. A class is similar in concept to a car's engineering drawings, which house the design of an accelerator pedal, steering wheel, and so on.

1.5.3 Instantiation

Just as someone has to *build a car* from its engineering drawings before you can actually drive a car, you must *build an object* of a class before a program can perform the tasks that the class's methods define. The process of doing this is called *instantiation*. An object is then referred to as an **instance** of its class.

1.5.4 Reuse

Just as a car's engineering drawings can be *reused* many times to build many cars, you can *reuse* a class many times to build many objects. Reuse of existing classes when building new classes and programs saves time and effort. Reuse also helps you build more reliable and effective systems, because existing classes and components often have undergone extensive *testing*, *debugging* and *performance* tuning. Just as the notion of *interchangeable parts* was crucial to the Industrial Revolution, reusable classes are crucial to the software revolution that has been spurred by object technology.

Software Engineering Observation 1.1

Use a building-block approach to creating your programs. Avoid reinventing the wheel— use existing high-quality pieces wherever possible. This software reuse *is a key benefit of object-oriented programming.*

1.5.5 Messages and Method Calls

When you drive a car, pressing its gas pedal sends a *message* to the car to perform a task— that is, to go faster. Similarly, you *send messages to an object*. Each message is implemented as a **method call** that tells a method of the object to perform its task. For example, a program might call a bank-account object's *deposit* method to increase the account's balance.

1.5.6 Attributes and Instance Variables

A car, besides having capabilities to accomplish tasks, also has *attributes*, such as its color, its number of doors, the amount of gas in its tank, its current speed and its record of total miles driven (i.e., its odometer reading). Like its capabilities, the car's attributes are represented as part of its design in its engineering diagrams (which, for example, include an odometer and a fuel gauge). As you drive an actual car, these attributes are carried along with the car. Every car maintains its *own* attributes. For example, each car knows how much gas is in its own gas tank, but *not* how much is in the tanks of *other* cars.

An object, similarly, has attributes that it carries along as it's used in a program. These attributes are specified as part of the object's class. For example, a bank-account object has a *balance attribute* that represents the amount of money in the account. Each bank-account object knows the balance in the account it represents, but *not* the balances of the *other* accounts in the bank. Attributes are specified by the class's **instance variables**.

1.5.7 Encapsulation and Information Hiding

Classes (and their objects) **encapsulate**, i.e., encase, their attributes and methods. A class's (and its object's) attributes and methods are intimately related. Objects may communicate with one another, but they're normally not allowed to know how other objects are implemented—implementation details are *hidden* within the objects themselves. This **information hiding**, as we'll see, is crucial to good software engineering.

1.5.8 Inheritance

A new class of objects can be created conveniently by **inheritance**—the new class (called the **subclass**) starts with the characteristics of an existing class (called the **superclass**), possibly customizing them and adding unique characteristics of its own. In our car analogy, an object of class "convertible" certainly *is an* object of the more *general* class "automobile," but more *specifically*, the roof can be raised or lowered.

1.5.9 Interfaces

Java also supports **interfaces**—collections of related methods that typically enable you to tell objects *what* to do, but not *how* to do it (we'll see an exception to this in Java SE 8). In the car analogy, a "basic-driving-capabilities" interface consisting of a steering wheel, an accelerator pedal and a brake pedal would enable a driver to tell the car *what* to do. Once you know how to use this interface for turning, accelerating and braking, you can drive many types of cars, even though manufacturers may *implement* these systems *differently*.

A class **implements** zero or more interfaces, each of which can have one or more methods, just as a car implements separate interfaces for basic driving functions, controlling the radio, controlling the heating and air conditioning systems, and the like. Just as car manufacturers implement capabilities *differently*, classes may implement an interface's methods *differently*. For example a software system may include a "backup" interface that offers the methods *save* and *restore*. Classes may implement those methods differently, depending on the types of things being backed up, such as programs, text, audios, videos, etc., and the types of devices where these items will be stored.

1.5.10 Object-Oriented Analysis and Design (OOAD)

Soon you'll be writing programs in Java. How will you create the **code** (i.e., the program instructions) for your programs? Perhaps, like many programmers, you'll simply turn on your computer and start typing. This approach may work for small programs (like the ones we present in the early chapters of the book), but what if you were asked to create a software system to control thousands of automated teller machines for a major bank? Or suppose you were asked to work on a team of 1,000 software developers building the next generation of the U.S. air traffic control system? For projects so large and complex, you should not simply sit down and start writing programs.

To create the best solutions, you should follow a detailed **analysis** process for determining your project's **requirements** (i.e., defining *what* the system is supposed to do) and developing a **design** that satisfies them (i.e., specifying *how* the system should do it). Ideally, you'd go through this process and carefully review the design (and have your design reviewed by other software professionals) before writing any code. If this process involves analyzing and designing your system from an object-oriented point of view, it's called an **object-oriented analysis-and-design (OOAD) process**. Languages like Java are object oriented. Programming in such a language, called **object-oriented programming (OOP)**, allows you to implement an object-oriented design as a working system.

1.5.11 The UML (Unified Modeling Language)

Although many different OOAD processes exist, a single graphical language for communicating the results of *any* OOAD process has come into wide use. The Unified Modeling Language (UML) is now the most widely used graphical scheme for modeling object-oriented systems. We present our first UML diagrams in Chapters 3 and 4, then use them in our deeper treatment of object-oriented programming through Chapter 11. In our *optional* online ATM Software Engineering Case Study in Chapters 33–34 we present a simple subset of the UML's features as we guide you through an object-oriented design experience.

1.6 Operating Systems

Operating systems are software systems that make using computers more convenient for users, application developers and system administrators. They provide services that allow each application to execute safely, efficiently and *concurrently* (i.e., in parallel) with other applications. The software that contains the core components of the operating system is the **kernel**. Popular desktop operating systems include Linux, Windows and Mac OS X. Popular mobile operating systems used in smartphones and tablets include Google's Android, Apple's iOS (for its iPhone, iPad and iPod Touch devices), Windows Phone 8 and BlackBerry OS.

1.6.1 Windows—A Proprietary Operating System

In the mid-1980s, Microsoft developed the **Windows operating system**, consisting of a graphical user interface built on top of DOS—an enormously popular personal-computer operating system that users interacted with by typing commands. Windows borrowed many concepts (such as icons, menus and windows) popularized by early Apple Macintosh operating systems and originally developed by Xerox PARC. Windows 8 is Microsoft's latest operating system—its features include PC and tablet support, a tiles-based user interface, security enhancements, touch-screen and multi-touch support, and more. Windows is a *proprietary* operating system—it's controlled by Microsoft exclusively. It's by far the world's most widely used operating system.

1.6.2 Linux—An Open-Source Operating System

The **Linux** operating system—which is popular in servers, personal computers and embedded systems—is perhaps the greatest success of the *open-source* movement. The **open-source software** development style departs from the *proprietary* development style (used, for example, with Microsoft's Windows and Apple's Mac OS X). With open-source development, individuals and companies—often worldwide—contribute their efforts in developing, maintaining and evolving software. Anyone can use and customize it for their own purposes, typically at no charge. The Java Development Kit and many related Java technologies are now open source.

Some organizations in the open-source community are the *Eclipse Foundation* (the *Eclipse Integrated Development Environment* helps Java programmers conveniently develop software), the *Mozilla Foundation* (creators of the *Firefox web browser*), the *Apache Software Foundation* (creators of the *Apache web server* that *delivers web pages over the Internet* in response to web-browser requests) and *GitHub* and *SourceForge* (which provide the *tools for managing open-source projects*).

Rapid improvements to computing and communications, decreasing costs and open-source software have made it easier and more economical to create software-based businesses now than just a few decades ago. Facebook, which was launched from a college dorm room, was built with open-source software.[9]

A variety of issues—such as Microsoft's market power, the relatively small number of user-friendly Linux applications and the diversity of Linux distributions (Red Hat Linux, Ubuntu Linux and many others)—have prevented widespread Linux use on desktop computers. But Linux has become extremely popular on servers and in embedded systems, such as Google's Android-based smartphones.

1.6.3 Android

Android—the fastest-growing mobile and smartphone operating system—is based on the Linux kernel and uses Java. Experienced Java programmers can quickly dive into Android development. One benefit of developing Android apps is the openness of the platform. The operating system is open source and free.

The Android operating system was developed by Android, Inc., which was acquired by Google in 2005. In 2007, the Open Handset Alliance™—which now has 87 company members worldwide (`http://www.openhandsetalliance.com/oha_members.html`)—was formed to develop, maintain and evolve Android, driving innovation in mobile technology and improving the user experience while reducing costs. As of April 2013, more than 1.5 million Android devices (smartphones, tablets, etc.) were being activated *daily*.[10] By October 2013, a Strategy Analytics report showed that Android had 81.3% of the global *smartphone* market share, compared to 13.4% for Apple, 4.1% for Microsoft and 1% for Blackberry.[11] Android devices now include smartphones, tablets, e-readers, robots, jet engines, NASA satellites, game consoles, refrigerators, televisions, cameras, health-care

---

9. `http://developers.facebook.com/opensource`.
10. `http://www.technobuffalo.com/2013/04/16/google-daily-android-activations-1-5-million/`.
11. `http://blogs.strategyanalytics.com/WSS/post/2013/10/31/Android-Captures-Record-81-Percent-Share-of-Global-Smartphone-Shipments-in-Q3-2013.aspx`.

devices, smartwatches, automobile in-vehicle infotainment systems (for controlling the radio, GPS, phone calls, thermostat, etc.) and more.[12]

Android smartphones include the functionality of a mobile phone, Internet client (for web browsing and Internet communication), MP3 player, gaming console, digital camera and more. These handheld devices feature full-color *multitouch screens* which allow you to control the device with *gestures* involving one touch or multiple simultaneous touches. You can download apps directly onto your Android device through Google Play and other app marketplaces. At the time of this writing, there were over one million apps in **Google Play**, and the number is growing quickly.[13]

We present an introduction to Android app development in our textbook, *Android How to Program, Second Edition,* and in our professional book, *Android for Programmers: An App-Driven Approach, Second Edition*. After you learn Java, you'll find it straightforward to begin developing and running Android apps. You can place your apps on Google Play (play.google.com), and if they're successful, you may even be able to launch a business. Just remember—Facebook, Microsoft and Dell were all launched from college dorm rooms.

1.7 Programming Languages

In this section, we comment briefly on several popular programming languages (Fig. 1.5). In the next section, we introduce Java.

Programming language	Description
Fortran	Fortran (FORmula TRANslator) was developed by IBM Corporation in the mid-1950s for scientific and engineering applications that require complex mathematical computations. It's still widely used, and its latest versions support object-oriented programming.
COBOL	COBOL (COmmon Business Oriented Language) was developed in the late 1950s by computer manufacturers, the U.S. government and industrial computer users based on a language developed by Grace Hopper, a U.S. Navy Rear Admiral and computer scientist who also advocated for the international standardization of programming languages. COBOL is still widely used for commercial applications that require precise and efficient manipulation of large amounts of data. Its latest version supports object-oriented programming.
Pascal	Research in the 1960s resulted in *structured programming*—a disciplined approach to writing programs that are clearer, easier to test and debug and easier to modify than large programs produced with previous techniques. One result of this research was the development in 1971 of the Pascal programming language, which was designed for teaching structured programming and was popular in college courses for several decades.

Fig. 1.5 | Some other programming languages. (Part 1 of 3.)

12. http://www.businessweek.com/articles/2013-05-29/behind-the-internet-of-things-is-android-and-its-everywhere.
13. http://en.wikipedia.org/wiki/Google_Play.

Programming language	Description
Ada	Ada, based on Pascal, was developed under the sponsorship of the U.S. Department of Defense (DOD) during the 1970s and early 1980s. The DOD wanted a single language that would fill most of its needs. The Ada language was named after Lady Ada Lovelace, daughter of the poet Lord Byron. She's credited with writing the world's first computer program in the early 1800s (for the Analytical Engine mechanical computing device designed by Charles Babbage). Ada also supports object-oriented programming.
Basic	Basic was developed in the 1960s at Dartmouth College to familiarize novices with programming techniques. Many of its latest versions are object oriented.
C	C was developed in the early 1970s by Dennis Ritchie at Bell Laboratories. It initially became widely known as the UNIX operating system's development language. Today, most of the code for general-purpose operating systems is written in C or C++.
C++	C++, which is based on C, was developed by Bjarne Stroustrup in the early 1980s at Bell Laboratories. C++ provides several features that "spruce up" the C language, but more important, it provides capabilities for object-oriented programming.
Objective-C	Objective-C is another object-oriented language based on C. It was developed in the early 1980s and later acquired by NeXT, which in turn was acquired by Apple. It has become the key programming language for the OS X operating system and all iOS-powered devices (such as iPods, iPhones and iPads).
Visual Basic	Microsoft's Visual Basic language was introduced in the early 1990s to simplify the development of Microsoft Windows applications. Its latest versions support object-oriented programming.
Visual C#	Microsoft's three object-oriented primary programming languages are Visual Basic (based on the original Basic), Visual C++ (based on C++) and Visual C# (based on C++ and Java, and developed for integrating the Internet and the web into computer applications).
PHP	PHP, an object-oriented, open-source scripting language supported by a community of users and developers, is used by millions of websites. PHP is platform independent—implementations exist for all major UNIX, Linux, Mac and Windows operating systems. PHP also supports many databases, including the popular open-source MySQL.
Perl	Perl (Practical Extraction and Report Language), one of the most widely used object-oriented scripting languages for web programming, was developed in 1987 by Larry Wall. It features rich text-processing capabilities.
Python	Python, another object-oriented scripting language, was released publicly in 1991. Developed by Guido van Rossum of the National Research Institute for Mathematics and Computer Science in Amsterdam (CWI), Python draws heavily from Modula-3—a systems programming language. Python is "extensible"—it can be extended through classes and programming interfaces.
JavaScript	JavaScript is the most widely used scripting language. It's primarily used to add dynamic behavior to web pages—for example, animations and improved interactivity with the user. It's provided with all major web browsers.

Fig. 1.5 | Some other programming languages. (Part 2 of 3.)

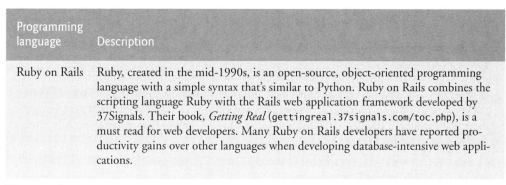

Programming language	Description
Ruby on Rails	Ruby, created in the mid-1990s, is an open-source, object-oriented programming language with a simple syntax that's similar to Python. Ruby on Rails combines the scripting language Ruby with the Rails web application framework developed by 37Signals. Their book, *Getting Real* (gettingreal.37signals.com/toc.php), is a must read for web developers. Many Ruby on Rails developers have reported productivity gains over other languages when developing database-intensive web applications.

Fig. 1.5 | Some other programming languages. (Part 3 of 3.)

1.8 Java

The microprocessor revolution's most important contribution to date is that it enabled the development of personal computers. Microprocessors have had a profound impact in intelligent consumer-electronic devices. Recognizing this, Sun Microsystems in 1991 funded an internal corporate research project led by James Gosling, which resulted in a C++-based object-oriented programming language that Sun called Java.

A key goal of Java is to be able to write programs that will run on a great variety of computer systems and computer-controlled devices. This is sometimes called "write once, run anywhere."

The web exploded in popularity in 1993, and Sun saw the potential of using Java to add *dynamic content*, such as interactivity and animations, to web pages. Java drew the attention of the business community because of the phenomenal interest in the web. Java is now used to develop large-scale enterprise applications, to enhance the functionality of web servers (the computers that provide the content we see in our web browsers), to provide applications for consumer devices (cell phones, smartphones, television set-top boxes and more) and for many other purposes. Java is also the key language for developing Android smartphone and tablet apps. Sun Microsystems was acquired by Oracle in 2010.

Java Class Libraries
You can create each class and method you need to form your Java programs. However, most Java programmers take advantage of the rich collections of existing classes and methods in the **Java class libraries**, also known as the **Java APIs** (**Application Programming Interfaces**).

Performance Tip 1.1
Using Java API classes and methods instead of writing your own versions can improve program performance, because they're carefully written to perform efficiently. This also shortens program development time.

1.9 A Typical Java Development Environment

We now explain the steps to create and execute a Java application. Normally there are five phases—edit, compile, load, verify and execute. We discuss them in the context of the Java

SE 8 Development Kit (JDK). See the *Before You Begin* section *for information on downloading and installing the JDK on Windows, Linux and OS X.*

Phase 1: Creating a Program

Phase 1 consists of editing a file with an *editor program*, normally known simply as an *editor* (Fig. 1.6). Using the editor, you type a Java program (typically referred to as **source code**), make any necessary corrections and save it on a secondary storage device, such as your hard drive. Java source code files are given a name ending with the **.java extension**, indicating that the file contains Java source code.

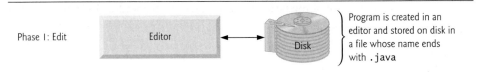

Fig. 1.6 | Typical Java development environment—editing phase.

Two editors widely used on Linux systems are vi and emacs. Windows provides **Notepad**. OS X provides **TextEdit**. Many freeware and shareware editors are also available online, including Notepad++ (notepad-plus-plus.org), EditPlus (www.editplus.com), TextPad (www.textpad.com) and jEdit (www.jedit.org).

Integrated development environments (IDEs) provide tools that support the software development process, such as editors, debuggers for locating **logic errors** (errors that cause programs to execute incorrectly) and more. There are many popular Java IDEs, including:

- Eclipse (www.eclipse.org)
- NetBeans (www.netbeans.org)
- IntelliJ IDEA (www.jetbrains.com)

On the book's website at

```
www.deitel.com/books/jhtp10lov
```

we provide Dive-Into® videos that show you how to executes this book's Java applications and how to develop new Java applications with Eclipse, NetBeans and IntelliJ IDEA.

Phase 2: Compiling a Java Program into Bytecodes

In Phase 2, you use the command **javac** (the **Java compiler**) to **compile** a program (Fig. 1.7). For example, to compile a program called Welcome.java, you'd type

```
javac Welcome.java
```

in your system's command window (i.e., the **Command Prompt** in Windows, the **Terminal** application in OS X) or a Linux shell (also called **Terminal** in some versions of Linux). If the program compiles, the compiler produces a **.class** file called Welcome.class that contains the compiled version. IDEs typically provide a menu item, such as **Build** or **Make**, that invokes the javac command for you. If the compiler detects errors, you'll need to go back to Phase 1 and correct them. In Chapter 2, we'll say more about the kinds of errors the compiler can detect.

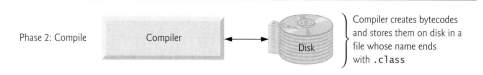

Fig. 1.7 | Typical Java development environment—compilation phase.

The Java compiler translates Java source code into **bytecodes** that represent the tasks to execute in the execution phase (Phase 5). The **Java Virtual Machine** (**JVM**)—a part of the JDK and the foundation of the Java platform—executes bytecodes. A **virtual machine** (**VM**) is a software application that simulates a computer but hides the underlying operating system and hardware from the programs that interact with it. If the same VM is implemented on many computer platforms, applications written for that type of VM can be used on all those platforms. The JVM is one of the most widely used virtual machines. Microsoft's .NET uses a similar virtual-machine architecture.

Unlike machine-language instructions, which are *platform dependent* (that is, dependent on specific computer hardware), bytecode instructions are *platform independent*. So, Java's bytecodes are **portable**—without recompiling the source code, the same bytecode instructions can execute on any platform containing a JVM that understands the version of Java in which the bytecodes were compiled. The JVM is invoked by the **java** command. For example, to execute a Java application called Welcome, you'd type the command

```
java Welcome
```

in a command window to invoke the JVM, which would then initiate the steps necessary to execute the application. This begins Phase 3. IDEs typically provide a menu item, such as **Run**, that invokes the java command for you.

Phase 3: Loading a Program into Memory

In Phase 3, the JVM places the program in memory to execute it—this is known as **loading** (Fig. 1.8). The JVM's **class loader** takes the .class files containing the program's byte-codes and transfers them to primary memory. It also loads any of the .class files provided by Java that your program uses. The .class files can be loaded from a disk on your system or over a network (e.g., your local college or company network, or the Internet).

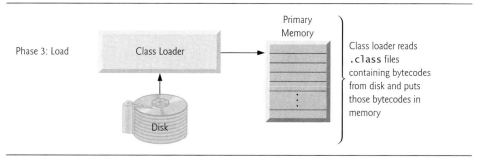

Fig. 1.8 | Typical Java development environment—loading phase.

Phase 4: Bytecode Verification

In Phase 4, as the classes are loaded, the **bytecode verifier** examines their bytecodes to ensure that they're valid and do not violate Java's security restrictions (Fig. 1.9). Java enforces strong security to make sure that Java programs arriving over the network do not damage your files or your system (as computer viruses and worms might).

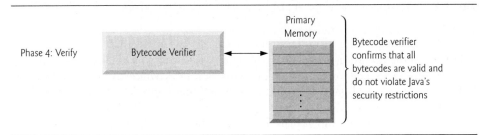

Fig. 1.9 | Typical Java development environment—verification phase.

Phase 5: Execution

In Phase 5, the JVM **executes** the program's bytecodes, thus performing the actions specified by the program (Fig. 1.10). In early Java versions, the JVM was simply an *interpreter* for Java bytecodes. Most Java programs would execute slowly, because the JVM would interpret and execute one bytecode at a time. Some modern computer architectures can execute several instructions in parallel. Today's JVMs typically execute bytecodes using a combination of interpretation and so-called **just-in-time (JIT) compilation**. In this process, the JVM analyzes the bytecodes as they're interpreted, searching for *hot spots*—parts of the bytecodes that execute frequently. For these parts, a **just-in-time (JIT) compiler**, such as Oracle's **Java HotSpot™ compiler**, translates the bytecodes into the underlying computer's machine language. When the JVM encounters these compiled parts again, the faster machine-language code executes. Thus Java programs actually go through *two* compilation phases—one in which source code is translated into bytecodes (for portability across JVMs on different computer platforms) and a second in which, during execution, the *bytecodes* are translated into *machine language* for the actual computer on which the program executes.

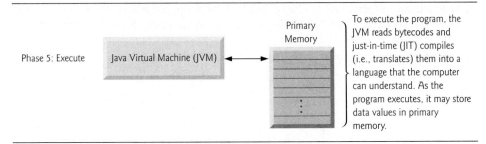

Fig. 1.10 | Typical Java development environment—execution phase.

Problems That May Occur at Execution Time

Programs might not work on the first try. Each of the preceding phases can fail because of various errors that we'll discuss throughout this book. For example, an executing program might try to divide by zero (an illegal operation for whole-number arithmetic in Java). This would cause the Java program to display an error message. If this occurred, you'd have to return to the edit phase, make the necessary corrections and proceed through the remaining phases again to determine that the corrections fixed the problem(s). [*Note:* Most programs in Java input or output data. When we say that a program displays a message, we normally mean that it displays that message on your computer's screen. Messages and other data may be output to other devices, such as disks and hardcopy printers, or even to a network for transmission to other computers.]

Common Programming Error 1.1

*Errors such as division by zero occur as a program runs, so they're called **runtime errors** or **execution-time errors**. Fatal runtime errors cause programs to terminate immediately without having successfully performed their jobs. **Nonfatal runtime errors** allow programs to run to completion, often producing incorrect results.*

1.10 Test-Driving a Java Application

In this section, you'll run and interact with your first Java application. The **Painter** application, which you'll build over the course of several exercises, allows you to drag the mouse to "paint." The elements and functionality you see here are typical of what you'll learn to program in this book. Using the **Painter**'s graphical user interface (GUI), you can control the drawing color, the shape to draw (line, rectangle or oval) and whether the shape is filled with the drawing color. You can also undo the last shape you added to the drawing or clear the entire drawing. [*Note:* We use fonts to distinguish between features. Our convention is to emphasize screen features like titles and menus (e.g., the **File** menu) in a semibold **sans-serif Helvetica** font and to emphasize nonscreen elements, such as file names, program code or input (e.g., `ProgramName.java`), in a `sans-serif Lucida` font.]

The steps in this section show you how to execute the **Painter** app from a **Command Prompt** (Windows), **Terminal** (OS X) or shell (Linux) window on your system. Throughout the book, we'll refer to these windows simply as *command windows*. Perform the following steps to use the **Painter** application to draw a smiley face:

1. *Checking your setup.* Read the Before You Begin section to confirm that you've set up Java properly on your computer, that you've copied the book's examples to your hard drive and that you know how to open a command window on your system.

2. *Changing to the completed application's directory.* Open a command window and use the `cd` command to change to the directory (also called a *folder*) for the **Painter** application. We assume that the book's examples are located in `C:\examples` on Windows or in your user account's `Documents/examples` folder on Linux/OS X. On Windows type `cd C:\examples\ch01\painter`, then press *Enter*. On Linux/OS X, type `cd ~/Documents/examples/ch01/painter`, then press *Enter*.

3. *Running the **Painter** application.* Recall that the `java` command, followed by the name of the application's `.class` file (in this case, `Painter`), executes the application. Type the command `java Painter` and press *Enter* to execute the app. Figure 1.11 shows the app running on Windows, Linux and OS X, respectively—we shortened the windows to save space.

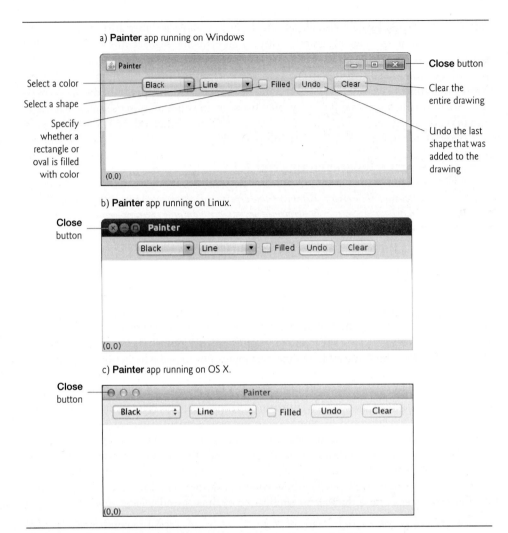

Fig. 1.11 | **Painter** app executing in Windows 7, Linux and OS X.

[*Note:* Java commands are *case sensitive*—that is, uppercase letters are different from lowercase letters. It's important to type the name of this application as Painter with a capital P. Otherwise, the application will *not* execute. Specifying the .class extension when using the java command results in an error. Also, if you receive the error message, "Exception in thread "main" java.lang.NoClassDefFoundError: Painter," your system has a CLASSPATH problem. Please refer to the Before You Begin section for instructions to help you fix this problem.]

4. *Drawing a filled yellow oval for the face.* Select **Yellow** as the drawing color, **Oval** as the shape and check the **Filled** checkbox, then drag the mouse to draw a large oval (Fig. 1.12).

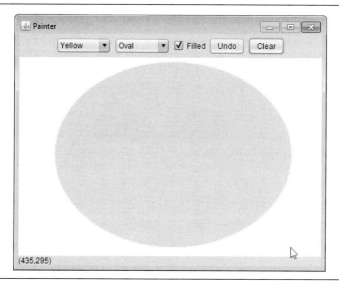

Fig. 1.12 | Drawing a filled yellow oval for the face.

   5. *Drawing blue eyes.* Select **Blue** as the drawing color, then draw two small ovals as the eyes (Fig. 1.13).

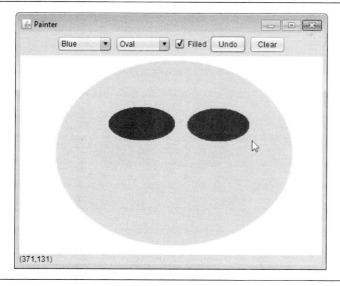

Fig. 1.13 | Drawing blue eyes.

   6. *Drawing black eyebrows and a nose.* Select **Black** as the drawing color and **Line** as the shape, then draw eyebrows and a nose (Fig. 1.14). Lines do not have fill, so leaving the **Filled** checkbox checked has no effect when drawing lines.

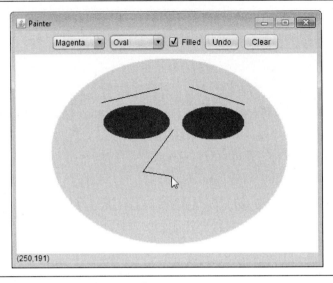

Fig. 1.14 | Drawing black eyebrows and a nose.

7. *Drawing a magenta mouth.* Select **Magenta** as the drawing color and **Oval** as the shape, then draw a mouth (Fig. 1.15).

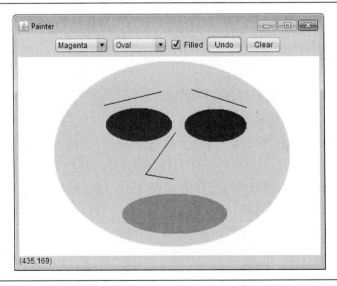

Fig. 1.15 | Drawing a magenta mouth.

8. *Drawing a yellow oval on the mouth to make a smile.* Select **Yellow** as the drawing color, then draw an oval to change the magenta oval into a smile (Fig. 1.16).

Fig. 1.16 | Drawing a yellow oval on the mouth to make a smile.

9. *Exiting the Painter application.* To exit the **Painter** application, click the **Close** button (in the window's upper-right corner on Windows and the upper-left corner on Linux and OS X). Closing the window causes the **Painter** application to terminate.

1.11 Internet and World Wide Web

In the late 1960s, ARPA—the Advanced Research Projects Agency of the United States Department of Defense—rolled out plans for networking the main computer systems of approximately a dozen ARPA-funded universities and research institutions. The computers were to be connected with communications lines operating at speeds on the order of 50,000 bits per second, a stunning rate at a time when most people (of the few who even had networking access) were connecting over telephone lines to computers at a rate of 110 bits per second. Academic research was about to take a giant leap forward. ARPA proceeded to implement what quickly became known as the ARPANET, the precursor to today's **Internet**. Today's fastest Internet speeds are on the order of billions of bits per second with trillion-bit-per-second speeds on the horizon!

Things worked out differently from the original plan. Although the ARPANET enabled researchers to network their computers, its main benefit proved to be the capability for quick and easy communication via what came to be known as electronic mail (e-mail). This is true even on today's Internet, with e-mail, instant messaging, file transfer and social media such as Facebook and Twitter enabling billions of people worldwide to communicate quickly and easily.

The protocol (set of rules) for communicating over the ARPANET became known as the **Transmission Control Protocol (TCP)**. TCP ensured that messages, consisting of sequentially numbered pieces called *packets*, were properly routed from sender to receiver, arrived intact and were assembled in the correct order.

1.11.1 The Internet: A Network of Networks

In parallel with the early evolution of the Internet, organizations worldwide were implementing their own networks for both intraorganization (that is, within an organization) and interorganization (that is, between organizations) communication. A huge variety of networking hardware and software appeared. One challenge was to enable these different networks to communicate with each other. ARPA accomplished this by developing the Internet Protocol (IP), which created a true "network of networks," the current architecture of the Internet. The combined set of protocols is now called **TCP/IP**.

Businesses rapidly realized that by using the Internet, they could improve their operations and offer new and better services to their clients. Companies started spending large amounts of money to develop and enhance their Internet presence. This generated fierce competition among communications carriers and hardware and software suppliers to meet the increased infrastructure demand. As a result, **bandwidth**—the information-carrying capacity of communications lines—on the Internet has increased tremendously, while hardware costs have plummeted.

1.11.2 The World Wide Web: Making the Internet User-Friendly

The **World Wide Web** (simply called "the web") is a collection of hardware and software associated with the Internet that allows computer users to locate and view multimedia-based documents (documents with various combinations of text, graphics, animations, audios and videos) on almost any subject. The introduction of the web was a relatively recent event. In 1989, Tim Berners-Lee of CERN (the European Organization for Nuclear Research) began to develop a technology for sharing information via "hyperlinked" text documents. Berners-Lee called his invention the **HyperText Markup Language** (HTML). He also wrote communication protocols such as **HyperText Transfer Protocol** (HTTP) to form the backbone of his new hypertext information system, which he referred to as the World Wide Web.

In 1994, Berners-Lee founded an organization, called the **World Wide Web Consortium** (W3C, www.w3.org), devoted to developing web technologies. One of the W3C's primary goals is to make the web universally accessible to everyone regardless of disabilities, language or culture. In this book, you'll use Java to build web-based applications.

1.11.3 Web Services and Mashups

In online Chapter 32, we include a substantial treatment of web services (Fig. 1.17). The applications-development methodology of *mashups* enables you to rapidly develop powerful software applications by combining (often free) complementary web services and other forms of information feeds. One of the first mashups combined the real-estate listings provided by www.craigslist.org with the mapping capabilities of *Google Maps* to offer maps that showed the locations of homes for sale or rent in a given area.

Web services source	How it's used
Google Maps	Mapping services
Twitter	Microblogging

Fig. 1.17 | Some popular web services (www.programmableweb.com/apis/directory/1?sort=mashups). (Part 1 of 2.)

Web services source	How it's used
YouTube	Video search
Facebook	Social networking
Instagram	Photo sharing
Foursquare	Mobile check-in
LinkedIn	Social networking for business
Groupon	Social commerce
Netflix	Movie rentals
eBay	Internet auctions
Wikipedia	Collaborative encyclopedia
PayPal	Payments
Last.fm	Internet radio
Amazon eCommerce	Shopping for books and many other products
Salesforce.com	Customer Relationship Management (CRM)
Skype	Internet telephony
Microsoft Bing	Search
Flickr	Photo sharing
Zillow	Real-estate pricing
Yahoo Search	Search
WeatherBug	Weather

Fig. 1.17 | Some popular web services (`www.programmableweb.com/apis/directory/1?sort=mashups`). (Part 2 of 2.)

1.11.4 Ajax

Ajax helps Internet-based applications perform like desktop applications—a difficult task, given that such applications suffer transmission delays as data is shuttled back and forth between your computer and server computers on the Internet. Using Ajax, applications like Google Maps have achieved excellent performance and approach the look-and-feel of desktop applications. Although we don't discuss "raw" Ajax programming (which is quite complex) in this text, we do show in online Chapter 31 how to build Ajax-enabled applications using JavaServer Faces (JSF) Ajax-enabled components.

1.11.5 The Internet of Things

The Internet is no longer just a network of computers—it's an **Internet of Things**. A *thing* is any object with an IP address and the ability to send data automatically over a network—e.g., a car with a transponder for paying tolls, a heart monitor implanted in a human, a smart meter that reports energy usage, mobile apps that can track your movement and location, and smart thermostats that adjust room temperatures based on weather forecasts and activity in the home. You'll use IP addresses to build networked applications in online Chapter 28.

1.12 Software Technologies

Figure 1.18 lists a number of buzzwords that you'll hear in the software development community. We've created Resource Centers on most of these topics, with more on the way.

Technology	Description
Agile software development	**Agile software development** is a set of methodologies that try to get software implemented faster and using fewer resources. Check out the Agile Alliance (www.agilealliance.org) and the Agile Manifesto (www.agilemanifesto.org).
Refactoring	**Refactoring** involves reworking programs to make them clearer and easier to maintain while preserving their correctness and functionality. It's widely employed with agile development methodologies. Many IDEs contain built-in *refactoring tools* to do major portions of the reworking automatically.
Design patterns	**Design patterns** are proven architectures for constructing flexible and maintainable object-oriented software. The field of design patterns tries to enumerate those recurring patterns, encouraging software designers to *reuse* them to develop better-quality software using less time, money and effort. We discuss Java design patterns in the online Appendix N.
LAMP	**LAMP** is an acronym for the open-source technologies that many developers use to build web applications—it stands for *Linux, Apache, MySQL* and *PHP* (or *Perl* or *Python*—two other scripting languages). MySQL is an open-source database management system. PHP is the most popular open-source server-side "scripting" language for developing web applications. Apache is the most popular web server software. The equivalent for Windows development is WAMP—*Windows*, Apache, MySQL and PHP.
Software as a Service (SaaS)	Software has generally been viewed as a product; most software still is offered this way. If you want to run an application, you buy a software package from a software vendor—often a CD, DVD or web download. You then install that software on your computer and run it as needed. As new versions appear, you upgrade your software, often at considerable cost in time and money. This process can become cumbersome for organizations that must maintain tens of thousands of systems on a diverse array of computer equipment. With **Software as a Service (SaaS)**, the software runs on servers elsewhere on the Internet. When that server is updated, all clients worldwide see the new capabilities—no local installation is needed. You access the service through a browser. Browsers are quite portable, so you can run the same applications on a wide variety of computers from anywhere in the world. Salesforce.com, Google, and Microsoft's Office Live and Windows Live all offer SaaS.
Platform as a Service (PaaS)	**Platform as a Service (PaaS)** provides a computing platform for developing and running applications as a service over the web, rather than installing the tools on your computer. Some PaaS providers are Google App Engine, Amazon EC2 and Windows Azure™.

Fig. 1.18 | Software technologies. (Part 1 of 2.)

Technology	Description
Cloud computing	SaaS and PaaS are examples of **cloud computing**. You can use software and data stored in the "cloud"—i.e., accessed on remote computers (or servers) via the Internet and available on demand—rather than having it stored on your desktop, notebook computer or mobile device. This allows you to increase or decrease computing resources to meet your needs at any given time, which is more cost effective than purchasing hardware to provide enough storage and processing power to meet occasional peak demands. Cloud computing also saves money by shifting the burden of managing these apps to the service provider.
Software Development Kit (SDK)	**Software Development Kits (SDKs)** include the tools and documentation developers use to program applications. For example, you'll use the Java Development Kit (JDK) to build and run Java applications.

Fig. 1.18 | Software technologies. (Part 2 of 2.)

Software is complex. Large, real-world software applications can take many months or even years to design and implement. When large software products are under development, they typically are made available to the user communities as a series of releases, each more complete and polished than the last (Fig. 1.19).

Version	Description
Alpha	*Alpha* software is the earliest release of a software product that's still under active development. Alpha versions are often buggy, incomplete and unstable and are released to a relatively small number of developers for testing new features, getting early feedback, etc.
Beta	*Beta* versions are released to a larger number of developers later in the development process after most major bugs have been fixed and new features are nearly complete. Beta software is more stable, but still subject to change.
Release candidates	*Release candidates* are generally *feature complete*, (mostly) bug free and ready for use by the community, which provides a diverse testing environment—the software is used on different systems, with varying constraints and for a variety of purposes.
Final release	Any bugs that appear in the release candidate are corrected, and eventually the final product is released to the general public. Software companies often distribute incremental updates over the Internet.
Continuous beta	Software that's developed using this approach (for example, Google search or Gmail) generally does not have version numbers. It's hosted in the *cloud* (not installed on your computer) and is constantly evolving so that users always have the latest version.

Fig. 1.19 | Software product-release terminology.

1.13 Keeping Up-to-Date with Information Technologies

Figure 1.20 lists key technical and business publications that will help you stay up-to-date with the latest news and trends and technology. You can also find a growing list of Internet- and web-related Resource Centers at www.deitel.com/ResourceCenters.html.

Publication	URL
AllThingsD	allthingsd.com
Bloomberg BusinessWeek	www.businessweek.com
CNET	news.cnet.com
Communications of the ACM	cacm.acm.org
Computerworld	www.computerworld.com
Engadget	www.engadget.com
eWeek	www.eweek.com
Fast Company	www.fastcompany.com/
Fortune	money.cnn.com/magazines/fortune
GigaOM	gigaom.com
Hacker News	news.ycombinator.com
IEEE Computer Magazine	www.computer.org/portal/web/computingnow/computer
InfoWorld	www.infoworld.com
Mashable	mashable.com
PCWorld	www.pcworld.com
SD Times	www.sdtimes.com
Slashdot	slashdot.org/
Technology Review	technologyreview.com
Techcrunch	techcrunch.com
The Next Web	thenextweb.com
The Verge	www.theverge.com
Wired	www.wired.com

Fig. 1.20 | Technical and business publications.

Self-Review Exercises

1.1 Fill in the blanks in each of the following statements:
  a) Computers process data under the control of sets of instructions called _____.
  b) The key logical units of the computer are the _____, _____, _____, _____, _____ and _____.
  c) The three types of languages discussed in the chapter are _____, _____ and _____.
  d) The programs that translate high-level language programs into machine language are called _____.

e) _____ is an operating system for mobile devices based on the Linux kernel and Java.
f) _____ software is generally feature complete, (supposedly) bug free and ready for use by the community.
g) The Wii Remote, as well as many smartphones, use a(n) _____ which allows the device to respond to motion.

1.2 Fill in the blanks in each of the following sentences about the Java environment:
a) The _____ command from the JDK executes a Java application.
b) The _____ command from the JDK compiles a Java program.
c) A Java source code file must end with the _____ file extension.
d) When a Java program is compiled, the file produced by the compiler ends with the _____ file extension.
e) The file produced by the Java compiler contains _____ that are executed by the Java Virtual Machine.

1.3 Fill in the blanks in each of the following statements (based on Section 1.5):
a) Objects enable the design practice of _____—although they may know how to communicate with one another across well-defined interfaces, they normally are not allowed to know how other objects are implemented.
b) Java programmers concentrate on creating _____, which contain fields and the set of methods that manipulate those fields and provide services to clients.
c) The process of analyzing and designing a system from an object-oriented point of view is called _____.
d) A new class of objects can be created conveniently by _____ —the new class (called the subclass) starts with the characteristics of an existing class (called the superclass), possibly customizing them and adding unique characteristics of its own.
e) _____ is a graphical language that allows people who design software systems to use an industry-standard notation to represent them.
f) The size, shape, color and weight of an object are considered _____ of the object's class.

Answers to Self-Review Exercises

1.1 a) programs. b) input unit, output unit, memory unit, central processing unit, arithmetic and logic unit, secondary storage unit. c) machine languages, assembly languages, high-level languages. d) compilers. e) Android. f) Release candidate. g) accelerometer.

1.2 a) `java`. b) `javac`. c) `.java`. d) `.class`. e) bytecodes.

1.3 a) information hiding. b) classes. c) object-oriented analysis and design (OOAD). d) inheritance. e) The Unified Modeling Language (UML). f) attributes.

Exercises

1.4 Fill in the blanks in each of the following statements:
a) The logical unit that receives information from outside the computer for use by the computer is the _____.
b) The process of instructing the computer to solve a problem is called _____.
c) _____ is a type of computer language that uses Englishlike abbreviations for machine-language instructions.
d) _____ is a logical unit that sends information which has already been processed by the computer to various devices so that it may be used outside the computer.
e) _____ and _____ are logical units of the computer that retain information.
f) _____ is a logical unit of the computer that performs calculations.
g) _____ is a logical unit of the computer that makes logical decisions.

  h) _____ languages are most convenient to the programmer for writing programs quickly and easily.

  i) The only language a computer can directly understand is that computer's _____.

  j) _____ is a logical unit of the computer that coordinates the activities of all the other logical units.

1.5 Fill in the blanks in each of the following statements:

  a) The _____ programming language is now used to develop large-scale enterprise applications, to enhance the functionality of web servers, to provide applications for consumer devices and for many other purposes.

  b) _____ initially became widely known as the development language of the UNIX operating system.

  c) The _____ ensures that messages, consisting of sequentially numbered pieces called bytes, were properly routed from sender to receiver, arrived intact and were assembled in the correct order.

  d) The _____ programming language was developed by Bjarne Stroustrup in the early 1980s at Bell Laboratories.

1.6 Fill in the blanks in each of the following statements:

  a) Java programs normally go through five phases—_____, _____, _____, _____ and _____.

  b) A(n) _____ provides many tools that support the software development process, such as editors for writing and editing programs, debuggers for locating logic errors in programs, and many other features.

  c) The command `java` invokes the _____, which executes Java programs.

  d) A(n) _____ is a software application that simulates a computer, but hides the underlying operating system and hardware from the programs that interact with it.

  e) The _____ takes the `.class` files containing the program's bytecodes and transfers them to primary memory.

  f) The _____ examines bytecodes to ensure that they're valid.

1.7 Explain the two compilation phases of Java programs.

1.8 One of the world's most common objects is a wrist watch. Discuss how each of the following terms and concepts applies to the notion of a watch: object, attributes, behaviors, class, inheritance (consider, for example, an alarm clock), modeling, messages, encapsulation, interface and information hiding.

Making a Difference

Throughout the book we've included Making a Difference exercises in which you'll be asked to work on problems that really matter to individuals, communities, countries and the world. For more information about worldwide organizations working to make a difference, and for related programming project ideas, visit our Making a Difference Resource Center at www.deitel.com/makingadifference.

1.9 *(Test-Drive: Carbon Footprint Calculator)* Some scientists believe that carbon emissions, especially from the burning of fossil fuels, contribute significantly to global warming and that this can be combatted if individuals take steps to limit their use of carbon-based fuels. Organizations and individuals are increasingly concerned about their "carbon footprints." Websites such as TerraPass

    http://www.terrapass.com/carbon-footprint-calculator/

and Carbon Footprint

    http://www.carbonfootprint.com/calculator.aspx

provide carbon-footprint calculators. Test-drive these calculators to determine your carbon footprint. Exercises in later chapters will ask you to program your own carbon-footprint calculator. To prepare for this, use the web to research the formulas for calculating carbon footprints.

1.10   *(Test-Drive: Body Mass Index Calculator)* Obesity causes significant increases in illnesses such as diabetes and heart disease. To determine whether a person is overweight or obese, you can use a measure called the body mass index (BMI). The United States Department of Health and Human Services provides a BMI calculator at `http://www.nhlbi.nih.gov/guidelines/obesity/BMI/bmicalc.htm`. Use it to calculate your own BMI. A forthcoming exercise will ask you to program your own BMI calculator. To prepare for this, use the web to research the formulas for calculating BMI.

1.11   *(Attributes of Hybrid Vehicles)* In this chapter you learned some basics of classes. Now you'll "flesh out" aspects of a class called "Hybrid Vehicle." Hybrid vehicles are becoming increasingly popular, because they often get much better mileage than purely gasoline-powered vehicles. Browse the web and study the features of four or five of today's popular hybrid cars, then list as many of their hybrid-related attributes as you can. Some common attributes include city-miles-per-gallon and highway-miles-per-gallon. Also list the attributes of the batteries (type, weight, etc.).

1.12   *(Gender Neutrality)* Many people want to eliminate sexism in all forms of communication. You've been asked to create a program that can process a paragraph of text and replace gender-specific words with gender-neutral ones. Assuming that you've been given a list of gender-specific words and their gender-neutral replacements (e.g., replace both "wife" and "husband" with "spouse," "man" and "woman" with "person," "daughter" and "son" with "child"), explain the procedure you'd use to read through a paragraph of text and manually perform these replacements. How might your procedure generate a strange term like "woperchild?" You'll soon learn that a more formal term for "procedure" is "algorithm," and that an algorithm specifies the steps to be performed and the order in which to perform them. We'll show how to develop algorithms then convert them to Java programs which can be run on computers.

2

Introduction to Java Applications; Input/Output and Operators

What's in a name?
That which we call a rose
By any other name would
smell as sweet.
—William Shakespeare

The chief merit of language
is clearness.
—Galen

One person can make a
difference and every person
should try.
—John F. Kennedy

Objectives

In this chapter you'll:

- Write simple Java applications.

- Use input and output statements.

- Learn about Java's primitive types.

- Understand basic memory concepts.

- Use arithmetic operators.

- Learn the precedence of arithmetic operators.

- Write decision-making statements.

- Use relational and equality operators.

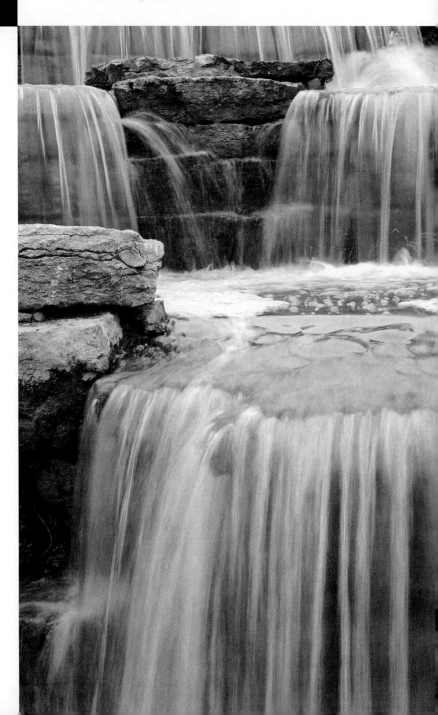

2.1 Introduction

This chapter introduces Java application programming. We begin with examples of programs that display (output) messages on the screen. We then present a program that obtains (inputs) two numbers from a user, calculates their sum and displays the result. You'll learn how to instruct the computer to perform arithmetic calculations and save their results for later use. The last example demonstrates how to make decisions. The application compares two numbers, then displays messages that show the comparison results. You'll use the JDK command-line tools to compile and run this chapter's programs. If you prefer to use an integrated development environment (IDE), we've also posted Dive Into® videos at http://www.deitel.com/books/jhtp10LOV/ for Eclipse, NetBeans and IntelliJ IDEA.

2.2 Your First Program in Java: Printing a Line of Text

A Java **application** is a computer program that executes when you use the **java command** to launch the Java Virtual Machine (JVM). Later in this section we'll discuss how to compile and run a Java application. First we consider a simple application that displays a line of text. Figure 2.1 shows the program followed by a box that displays its output.

```
1   // Fig. 2.1: Welcome1.java
2   // Text-printing program.
3
4   public class Welcome1
5   {
6      // main method begins execution of Java application
7      public static void main(String[] args)
8      {
9         System.out.println("Welcome to Java Programming!");
10     } // end method main
11  } // end class Welcome1
```

Fig. 2.1 | Text-printing program. (Part 1 of 2.)

```
Welcome to Java Programming!
```

Fig. 2.1 | Text-printing program. (Part 2 of 2.)

The program includes line numbers. We've added these for instructional purposes—they're *not* part of a Java program. This example illustrates several important Java features. We'll see that line 9 does the work—displaying the phrase Welcome to Java Programming! on the screen.

Commenting Your Programs

We insert **comments** to **document programs** and improve their readability. The Java compiler *ignores* comments, so they do *not* cause the computer to perform any action when the program is run.

By convention, we begin every program with a comment indicating the figure number and filename. The comment in line 1

```
// Fig. 2.1: Welcome1.java
```

begins with //, indicating that it's an **end-of-line comment**—it terminates at the end of the line on which the // appears. An end-of-line comment need not begin a line; it also can begin in the middle of a line and continue until the end (as in lines 6, 10 and 11). Line 2

```
// Text-printing program.
```

by our convention, is a comment that describes the purpose of the program.

Java also has **traditional comments**, which can be spread over several lines as in

```
/* This is a traditional comment. It
   can be split over multiple lines */
```

These begin and end with delimiters, /* and */. The compiler ignores all text between the delimiters. Java incorporated traditional comments and end-of-line comments from the C and C++ programming languages, respectively. We prefer using // comments.

Java provides comments of a third type—**Javadoc comments**. These are delimited by /** and */. The compiler ignores all text between the delimiters. Javadoc comments enable you to embed program documentation directly in your programs. Such comments are the preferred Java documenting format in industry. The **javadoc utility program** (part of the JDK) reads Javadoc comments and uses them to prepare program documentation in HTML format. We demonstrate Javadoc comments and the javadoc utility in online Appendix G, Creating Documentation with javadoc.

 Common Programming Error 2.1

Forgetting one of the delimiters of a traditional or Javadoc comment is a syntax error. A ***syntax error*** *occurs when the compiler encounters code that violates Java's language rules (i.e., its syntax). These rules are similar to a natural language's grammar rules specifying sentence structure. Syntax errors are also called* ***compiler errors***, ***compile-time errors*** *or* ***compilation errors***, *because the compiler detects them when compiling the program. When a syntax error is encountered, the compiler issues an error message. You must eliminate all compilation errors before your program will compile properly.*

Good Programming Practice 2.1

Some organizations require that every program begin with a comment that states the purpose of the program and the author, date and time when the program was last modified.

Using Blank Lines

Line 3 is a blank line. Blank lines, space characters and tabs make programs easier to read. Together, they're known as **white space** (or whitespace). The compiler ignores white space.

Good Programming Practice 2.2

Use blank lines and spaces to enhance program readability.

Declaring a Class

Line 4

    public class Welcome1

begins a **class declaration** for class Welcome1. Every Java program consists of at least one class that you (the programmer) define. The **class keyword** introduces a class declaration and is immediately followed by the **class name** (Welcome1). **Keywords** (sometimes called **reserved words**) are reserved for use by Java and are always spelled with all lowercase letters. The complete list of keywords is shown in Appendix C.

In Chapters 1–7, every class we define begins with the **public** keyword. For now, we simply require public. You'll learn more about public and non-public classes in Chapter 8.

Filename for a **public** Class

A public class *must* be placed in a file that has a filename of the form *ClassName*.java, so class Welcome1 is stored in the file Welcome1.java.

Common Programming Error 2.2

A compilation error occurs if a public class's filename is not exactly same name as the class (in terms of both spelling and capitalization) followed by the .java extension.

Class Names and Identifiers

By convention, class names begin with a capital letter and capitalize the first letter of each word they include (e.g., SampleClassName). A class name is an **identifier**—a series of characters consisting of letters, digits, underscores (_) and dollar signs ($) that does *not* begin with a digit and does *not* contain spaces. Some valid identifiers are Welcome1, $value, _value, m_inputField1 and button7. The name 7button is *not* a valid identifier because it begins with a digit, and the name input field is *not* a valid identifier because it contains a space. Normally, an identifier that does not begin with a capital letter is not a class name. Java is **case sensitive**—uppercase and lowercase letters are distinct—so value and Value are different (but both valid) identifiers.

Class Body

A **left brace** (as in line 5), {, begins the **body** of every class declaration. A corresponding **right brace** (at line 11), }, must end each class declaration. Lines 6–10 are indented.

Good Programming Practice 2.3

Indent the entire body of each class declaration one "level" between the left brace and the right brace that delimit the body of the class. This format emphasizes the class declaration's structure and makes it easier to read. We use three spaces to form a level of indent—many programmers prefer two or four spaces. Whatever you choose, use it consistently.

Error-Prevention Tip 2.1

When you type an opening left brace, {, immediately type the closing right brace, }, then reposition the cursor between the braces and indent to begin typing the body. This practice helps prevent errors due to missing braces. Many IDEs insert the closing right brace for you when you type the opening left brace.

Common Programming Error 2.3

It's a syntax error if braces do not occur in matching pairs.

Good Programming Practice 2.4

IDEs typically indent code for you. The Tab *key may also be used to indent code. You can configure each IDE to specify the number of spaces inserted when you press* Tab.

Declaring a Method
Line 6

```
    // main method begins execution of Java application
```

is an end-of-line comment indicating the purpose of lines 7–10 of the program. Line 7

```
    public static void main(String[] args)
```

is the starting point of every Java application. The **parentheses** after the identifier main indicate that it's a program building block called a **method**. Java class declarations normally contain one or more methods. For a Java application, one of the methods *must* be called main and must be defined as shown in line 7; otherwise, the Java Virtual Machine (JVM) will not execute the application. Methods perform tasks and can return information when they complete their tasks. We'll explain the purpose of keyword static in Chapter 5. Keyword **void** indicates that this method will *not* return any information. Later, we'll see how a method can return information. For now, simply mimic main's first line in your Java applications. In line 7, the String[] args in parentheses is a required part of the method main's declaration—we discuss this in Chapter 6.

The left brace in line 8 begins the **body of the method declaration**. A corresponding right brace must end it (line 10). Line 9 in the method body is indented between the braces.

Good Programming Practice 2.5

Indent the entire body of each method declaration one "level" between the braces that define the body of the method. This makes the structure of the method stand out and makes the method declaration easier to read.

Performing Output with **System.out.println**
Line 9

```
    System.out.println("Welcome to Java Programming!");
```

instructs the computer to perform an action—namely, to display the characters contained between the double quotation marks (the quotation marks themselves are *not* displayed). Together, the quotation marks and the characters between them are a **string**—also known as a **character string** or a **string literal**. White-space characters in strings are *not* ignored by the compiler. Strings *cannot* span multiple lines of code.

The `System.out` object—which is predefined for you—is known as the **standard output object**. It allows a Java application to display information in the **command window** from which it executes. In recent versions of Microsoft Windows, the command window is the **Command Prompt**. In UNIX/Linux/Mac OS X, the command window is called a **terminal window** or a **shell**. Many programmers call it simply the **command line**.

Method `System.out.println` displays (or prints) a line of text in the command window. The string in the parentheses in line 9 is the **argument** to the method. When `System.out.println` completes its task, it positions the output cursor (the location where the next character will be displayed) at the beginning of the next line in the command window. This is similar to what happens when you press the *Enter* key while typing in a text editor—the cursor appears at the beginning of the next line in the document.

The entire line 9, including `System.out.println`, the argument `"Welcome to Java Programming!"` in the parentheses and the **semicolon** (`;`), is called a **statement**. A method typically contains one or more statements that perform its task. Most statements end with a semicolon. When the statement in line 9 executes, it displays `Welcome to Java Programming!` in the command window.

When learning how to program, sometimes it's helpful to "break" a working program so you can familiarize yourself with the compiler's syntax-error messages. These messages do not always state the exact problem in the code. When you encounter an error message, it will give you an idea of what caused the error. [Try removing a semicolon or brace from the program of Fig. 2.1, then recompile the program to see the error messages generated by the omission.]

Error-Prevention Tip 2.2
When the compiler reports a syntax error, it may not be on the line that the error message indicates. First, check the line for which the error was reported. If you don't find an error on that line, check several preceding lines.

Using End-of-Line Comments on Right Braces for Readability
As an aid to programming novices, we include an end-of-line comment after a closing brace that ends a method declaration and after a closing brace that ends a class declaration. For example, line 10

```
      } // end method main
```

indicates the closing brace of method `main`, and line 11

```
   } // end class Welcome1
```

indicates the closing brace of class `Welcome1`. Each comment indicates the method or class that the right brace terminates. We'll omit such ending comments after this chapter.

Compiling Your First Java Application
We're now ready to compile and execute our program. We assume you're using the Java Development Kit's command-line tools, not an IDE. To help you compile and run your

programs in an IDE, we provide online Dive Into® videos for the popular IDEs Eclipse, NetBeans and IntelliJ IDEA. These are located on the book's website:

```
http://www.deitel.com/books/jhtp10LOV
```

To prepare to compile the program, open a command window and change to the directory where the program is stored. Many operating systems use the command cd to change directories. On Windows, for example,

```
cd c:\examples\ch02\fig02_01
```

changes to the fig02_01 directory. On UNIX/Linux/Max OS X, the command

```
cd ~/examples/ch02/fig02_01
```

changes to the fig02_01 directory. To compile the program, type

```
javac Welcome1.java
```

If the program contains no compilation errors, this command creates a new file called Welcome1.class (known as the **class file** for Welcome1) containing the platform-independent Java bytecodes that represent our application. When we use the java command to execute the application on a given platform, the JVM will translate these bytecodes into instructions that are understood by the underlying operating system and hardware.

Common Programming Error 2.4

When using javac, if you receive a message such as "bad command or filename," "javac: command not found" or "'javac' is not recognized as an internal or external command, operable program or batch file," then your Java software installation was not completed properly. This indicates that the system's PATH environment variable was not set properly. Carefully review the installation instructions in the Before You Begin section of this book. On some systems, after correcting the PATH, you may need to reboot your computer or open a new command window for these settings to take effect.

Each syntax-error message contains the filename and line number where the error occurred. For example, Welcome1.java:6 indicates that an error occurred at line 6 in Welcome1.java. The rest of the message provides information about the syntax error.

Common Programming Error 2.5

The compiler error message "class Welcome1 is public, should be declared in a file named Welcome1.java" indicates that the filename does not match the name of the public class in the file or that you typed the class name incorrectly when compiling the class.

*Executing the **Welcome1** Application*
The following instructions assume that the book's examples are located in C:\examples on Windows or in your user account's Documents/examples folder on Linux/OS X. To execute this program in a command window, change to the directory containing Welcome1.java—C:\examples\ch02\fig02_01 on Microsoft Windows or ~/Documents/examples/ch02/fig02_01 on Linux/OS X. Next, type

```
java Welcome1
```

and press *Enter*. This command launches the JVM, which loads the Welcome1.class file. The command *omits* the .class file-name extension; otherwise, the JVM will *not* execute the program. The JVM calls class `Welcome1`'s `main` method. Next, the statement at line 9 of `main` displays `"Welcome to Java Programming!"`. Figure 2.2 shows the program executing in a Microsoft Windows **Command Prompt** window. [*Note:* Many environments show command windows with black backgrounds and white text. We adjusted these settings to make our screen captures more readable.]

Error-Prevention Tip 2.3

When attempting to run a Java program, if you receive a message such as "Exception in thread "main" java.lang.NoClassDefFoundError: Welcome1," *your CLASSPATH environment variable has not been set properly. Please carefully review the installation instructions in the Before You Begin section of this book. On some systems, you may need to reboot your computer or open a new command window after configuring the CLASSPATH.*

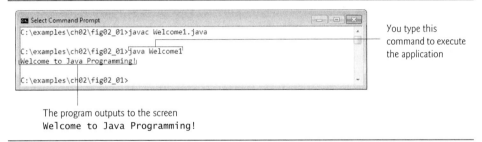

You type this command to execute the application

The program outputs to the screen
`Welcome to Java Programming!`

Fig. 2.2 | Executing `Welcome1` from the **Command Prompt**.

2.3 Modifying Your First Java Program

In this section, we modify the example in Fig. 2.1 to print text on one line by using multiple statements and to print text on several lines by using a single statement.

Displaying a Single Line of Text with Multiple Statements
`Welcome to Java Programming!` can be displayed several ways. Class `Welcome2`, shown in Fig. 2.3, uses two statements (lines 9–10) to produce the output shown in Fig. 2.1. [*Note:* From this point forward, we highlight with a yellow background the new and key features in each code listing, as we've done for lines 9–10.]

```
 1   // Fig. 2.3: Welcome2.java
 2   // Printing a line of text with multiple statements.
 3
 4   public class Welcome2
 5   {
 6      // main method begins execution of Java application
 7      public static void main(String[] args)
 8      {
 9         System.out.print("Welcome to ");
10         System.out.println("Java Programming!");
11      } // end method main
12   } // end class Welcome2
```

Fig. 2.3 | Printing a line of text with multiple statements. (Part 1 of 2.)

```
Welcome to Java Programming!
```

Fig. 2.3 | Printing a line of text with multiple statements. (Part 2 of 2.)

The program is similar to Fig. 2.1, so we discuss only the changes here. Line 2

```
// Printing a line of text with multiple statements.
```

is an end-of-line comment stating the purpose of the program. Line 4 begins the Welcome2 class declaration. Lines 9–10 of method main

```
System.out.print("Welcome to ");
System.out.println("Java Programming!");
```

display one line of text. The first statement uses System.out's method print to display a string. Each print or println statement resumes displaying characters from where the last print or println statement stopped displaying characters. Unlike println, after displaying its argument, print does *not* position the output cursor at the beginning of the next line in the command window—the next character the program displays will appear *immediately after* the last character that print displays. So, line 10 positions the first character in its argument (the letter "J") immediately after the last character that line 9 displays (the *space character* before the string's closing double-quote character).

Displaying Multiple Lines of Text with a Single Statement

A single statement can display multiple lines by using **newline characters**, which indicate to System.out's print and println methods when to position the output cursor at the beginning of the next line in the command window. Like blank lines, space characters and tab characters, newline characters are whitespace characters. The program in Fig. 2.4 outputs four lines of text, using newline characters to determine when to begin each new line. Most of the program is identical to those in Figs. 2.1 and 2.3.

```
 1    // Fig. 2.4: Welcome3.java
 2    // Printing multiple lines of text with a single statement.
 3
 4    public class Welcome3
 5    {
 6       // main method begins execution of Java application
 7       public static void main(String[] args)
 8       {
 9          System.out.println("Welcome\nto\nJava\nProgramming!");
10       } // end method main
11    } // end class Welcome3
```

```
Welcome
to
Java
Programming!
```

Fig. 2.4 | Printing multiple lines of text with a single statement.

Line 9

```
System.out.println("Welcome\nto\nJava\nProgramming!");
```

displays four separate lines of text in the command window. Normally, the characters in a string are displayed *exactly* as they appear in the double quotes. Note, however, that the paired characters \ and n (repeated three times in the statement) do *not* appear on the screen. The **backslash** (\) is an **escape character**, which has special meaning to System.out's print and println methods. When a backslash appears in a string, Java combines it with the next character to form an **escape sequence**. The escape sequence \n represents the newline character. When a newline character appears in a string being output with System.out, the newline character causes the screen's output cursor to move to the beginning of the next line in the command window.

Figure 2.5 lists several common escape sequences and describes how they affect the display of characters in the command window. For the complete list of escape sequences, visit

```
http://docs.oracle.com/javase/specs/jls/se7/html/
    jls-3.html#jls-3.10.6
```

Escape sequence	Description
\n	Newline. Position the screen cursor at the beginning of the *next* line.
\t	Horizontal tab. Move the screen cursor to the next tab stop.
\r	Carriage return. Position the screen cursor at the beginning of the *current* line—do *not* advance to the next line. Any characters output after the carriage return *overwrite* the characters previously output on that line.
\\	Backslash. Used to print a backslash character.
\"	Double quote. Used to print a double-quote character. For example, System.out.println("\"in quotes\""); displays "in quotes".

Fig. 2.5 | Some common escape sequences.

2.4 Displaying Text with `printf`

The **System.out.printf** method (f means "formatted") displays *formatted* data. Figure 2.6 uses this method to output on two lines the strings "Welcome to" and "Java Programming!". Lines 9–10

```
System.out.printf("%s%n%s%n",
    "Welcome to", "Java Programming!");
```

call method System.out.printf to display the program's output. The method call specifies three arguments. When a method requires multiple arguments, they're placed in a **comma-separated list**.

Good Programming Practice 2.6

Place a space after each comma (,) in an argument list to make programs more readable.

```
 1   // Fig. 2.6: Welcome4.java
 2   // Displaying multiple lines with method System.out.printf.
 3
 4   public class Welcome4
 5   {
 6      // main method begins execution of Java application
 7      public static void main(String[] args)
 8      {
 9         System.out.printf("%s%n%s%n",
10            "Welcome to", "Java Programming!");
11      } // end method main
12   } // end class Welcome4
```

```
Welcome to
Java Programming!
```

Fig. 2.6 | Displaying multiple lines with method System.out.printf.

Lines 9–10 represent only *one* statement. Java allows large statements to be split over many lines. We indent line 10 to indicate that it's a *continuation* of line 9.

Common Programming Error 2.6

Splitting a statement in the middle of an identifier or a string is a syntax error.

Method printf's first argument is a **format string** that may consist of **fixed text** and **format specifiers**. Fixed text is output by printf just as it would be by print or println. Each format specifier is a *placeholder* for a value and specifies the *type of data* to output. Format specifiers also may include optional formatting information.

Format specifiers begin with a percent sign (%) followed by a character that represents the *data type*. For example, the format specifier **%s** is a placeholder for a string. The format string in line 9 specifies that printf should output two strings, each followed by a newline character. At the first format specifier's position, printf substitutes the value of the first argument after the format string. At each subsequent format specifier's position, printf substitutes the value of the next argument. So this example substitutes "Welcome to" for the first %s and "Java Programming!" for the second %s. The output shows that two lines of text are displayed on two lines.

Notice that instead of using the escape sequence \n, we used the **%n** format specifier, which is a line separator that's *portable* across operating systems. You cannot use %n in the argument to System.out.print or System.out.println; however, the line separator output by System.out.println *after* it displays its argument *is* portable across operating systems. Online Appendix I presents more details of formatting output with printf.

2.5 Another Application: Adding Integers

Our next application reads (or inputs) two **integers** (whole numbers, such as –22, 7, 0 and 1024) typed by a user at the keyboard, computes their sum and displays it. This program must keep track of the numbers supplied by the user for the calculation later in the program. Programs remember numbers and other data in the computer's memory and access that data through program elements called **variables**. The program of Fig. 2.7 demonstrates these concepts. In the sample output, we use bold text to identify the user's input (i.e., **45** and **72**). As in prior programs, Lines 1–2 state the figure number, filename and purpose of the program.

```java
1   // Fig. 2.7: Addition.java
2   // Addition program that inputs two numbers then displays their sum.
3   import java.util.Scanner; // program uses class Scanner
4
5   public class Addition
6   {
7      // main method begins execution of Java application
8      public static void main(String[] args)
9      {
10        // create a Scanner to obtain input from the command window
11        Scanner input = new Scanner(System.in);
12
13        int number1; // first number to add
14        int number2; // second number to add
15        int sum; // sum of number1 and number2
16
17        System.out.print("Enter first integer: "); // prompt
18        number1 = input.nextInt(); // read first number from user
19
20        System.out.print("Enter second integer: "); // prompt
21        number2 = input.nextInt(); // read second number from user
22
23        sum = number1 + number2; // add numbers, then store total in sum
24
25        System.out.printf("Sum is %d%n", sum); // display sum
26     } // end method main
27  } // end class Addition
```

```
Enter first integer: 45
Enter second integer: 72
Sum is 117
```

Fig. 2.7 | Addition program that inputs two numbers then displays their sum.

2.5.1 import Declarations

A great strength of Java is its rich set of predefined classes that you can *reuse* rather than "reinventing the wheel." These classes are grouped into **packages**—*named groups of related classes*—and are collectively referred to as the **Java class library**, or the **Java Application Programming Interface (Java API)**. Line 3

```java
import java.util.Scanner; // program uses class Scanner
```

is an **import declaration** that helps the compiler locate a class that's used in this program. It indicates that this example uses Java's predefined Scanner class (discussed shortly) from the package that is named **java.util**. This enables the compiler to ensure that you use the class correctly.

Common Programming Error 2.7

All import declarations must appear before the first class declaration in the file. Placing an import declaration inside or after a class declaration is a syntax error.

Common Programming Error 2.8

Forgetting to include an import declaration for a class that must be imported results in a compilation error containing a message such as "cannot find symbol." When this occurs, check that you provided the proper import declarations and that the names in them are correct, including proper capitalization.

Software Engineering Observation 2.1

*In each new Java version, the APIs typically contain new capabilities that fix bugs, improve performance or offer better means for accomplishing tasks. The corresponding older versions are no longer needed and should not be used. Such APIs are said to be **deprecated** and might be removed from later Java versions.*

You'll often encounter deprecated APIs when browsing the online API documentation. The compiler will warn you when you compile code that uses deprecated APIs. If you compile your code with javac using the command-line argument -deprecation, the compiler will tell you which deprecated features you're using. For each one, the online documentation (http://docs.oracle.com/javase/7/docs/api/) indicates and typically links to the new feature that replaces the deprecated one.

2.5.2 Declaring Class Addition

Line 5

```
public class Addition
```

begins the declaration of class Addition. The filename for this public class must be Addition.java. Remember that the body of each class declaration starts with an opening left brace (line 6) and ends with a closing right brace (line 27).

The application begins execution with the main method (lines 8–26). The left brace (line 9) marks the beginning of method main's body, and the corresponding right brace (line 26) marks its end. Method main is indented one level in the body of class Addition, and the code in the body of main is indented another level for readability.

2.5.3 Declaring and Creating a Scanner to Obtain User Input from the Keyboard

A **variable** is a location in the computer's memory where a value can be stored for use later in a program. All Java variables *must* be declared with a **name** and a **type** *before* they can be used. A variable's *name* enables the program to access the *value* of the variable in memory. A variable's name can be any valid identifier—again, a series of characters consisting of letters, digits, underscores (_) and dollar signs ($) that does *not* begin with a digit and does *not* contain spaces. A variable's *type* specifies what kind of information is stored at that location in memory. Like other statements, declaration statements end with a semicolon (;).

Line 11

```
Scanner input = new Scanner(System.in);
```

is a **variable declaration statement** that specifies the *name* (input) and *type* (Scanner) of a variable that's used in this program. A **Scanner** enables a program to read data (e.g., numbers and strings) for use in a program. The data can come from many sources, such as the user at the keyboard or a file on disk. Before using a Scanner, you must create it and specify the *source* of the data.

The = in line 11 indicates that Scanner variable input should be **initialized** (i.e., prepared for use in the program) in its declaration with the result of the expression to the right of the equals sign—new Scanner(System.in). This expression uses the **new** keyword to create a Scanner object that reads characters typed by the user at the keyboard. The **standard input object**, **System.in**, enables applications to read *bytes* of data typed by the user. The Scanner translates these bytes into types (like ints) that can be used in a program.

2.5.4 Declaring Variables to Store Integers

The variable declaration statements in lines 13–15

```
int number1; // first number to add
int number2; // second number to add
int sum; // sum of number1 and number2
```

declare that variables number1, number2 and sum hold data of type **int**—they can hold *integer* values (whole numbers such as 72, –1127 and 0). These variables are *not* yet initialized. The range of values for an int is –2,147,483,648 to +2,147,483,647. [*Note:* The int values you use in a program may not contain commas.]

Some other types of data are **float** and **double**, for holding real numbers, and **char**, for holding character data. Real numbers contain decimal points, such as in 3.4, 0.0 and –11.19. Variables of type char represent individual characters, such as an uppercase letter (e.g., A), a digit (e.g., 7), a special character (e.g., * or %) or an escape sequence (e.g., the tab character, \t). The types int, float, double and char are called **primitive types**. Primitive-type names are keywords and must appear in all lowercase letters. Appendix D summarizes the characteristics of the eight primitive types (boolean, byte, char, short, int, long, float and double).

Several variables of the same type may be declared in a single declaration with the variable names separated by commas (i.e., a comma-separated list of variable names). For example, lines 13–15 can also be written as:

```
int number1, // first number to add
    number2, // second number to add
    sum; // sum of number1 and number2
```

Good Programming Practice 2.7
Declare each variable in its own declaration. This format allows a descriptive comment to be inserted next to each variable being declared.

Good Programming Practice 2.8
Choosing meaningful variable names helps a program to be self-documenting (i.e., one can understand the program simply by reading it rather than by reading associated documentation or creating and viewing an excessive number of comments).

Good Programming Practice 2.9

*By convention, variable-name identifiers begin with a lowercase letter, and every word in the name after the first word begins with a capital letter. For example, variable-name identifier firstNumber starts its second word, Number, with a capital N. This naming convention is known as **camel case**, because the uppercase letters stand out like a camel's humps.*

2.5.5 Prompting the User for Input

Line 17

```
System.out.print("Enter first integer: "); // prompt
```

uses System.out.print to display the message "Enter first integer: ". This message is called a **prompt** because it directs the user to take a specific action. We use method print here rather than println so that the user's input appears on the same line as the prompt. Recall from Section 2.2 that identifiers starting with capital letters typically represent class names. Class System is part of package **java.lang**. Notice that class System is *not* imported with an import declaration at the beginning of the program.

Software Engineering Observation 2.2

By default, package java.lang is imported in every Java program; thus, classes in java.lang are the only ones in the Java API that do not require an import declaration.

2.5.6 Obtaining an int as Input from the User

Line 18

```
number1 = input.nextInt(); // read first number from user
```

uses Scanner object input's nextInt method to obtain an integer from the user at the keyboard. At this point the program *waits* for the user to type the number and press the *Enter* key to submit the number to the program.

Our program assumes that the user enters a valid integer value. If not, a runtime logic error will occur and the program will terminate. Chapter 11, Exception Handling: A Deeper Look, discusses how to make your programs more robust by enabling them to handle such errors. This is also known as making your program *fault tolerant*.

In line 18, we place the result of the call to method nextInt (an int value) in variable number1 by using the **assignment operator**, =. The statement is read as "number1 *gets* the value of input.nextInt()." Operator = is called a **binary operator**, because it has *two* operands—number1 and the result of the method call input.nextInt(). This statement is called an *assignment statement*, because it *assigns* a value to a variable. Everything to the *right* of the assignment operator, =, is always evaluated *before* the assignment is performed.

Good Programming Practice 2.10

Place spaces on either side of a binary operator for readability.

2.5.7 Prompting for and Inputting a Second `int`

Line 20

```
System.out.print("Enter second integer: "); // prompt
```

prompts the user to enter the second integer. Line 21

```
number2 = input.nextInt(); // read second number from user
```

reads the second integer and assigns it to variable `number2`.

2.5.8 Using Variables in a Calculation

Line 23

```
sum = number1 + number2; // add numbers then store total in sum
```

is an assignment statement that calculates the sum of the variables `number1` and `number2` then assigns the result to variable `sum` by using the assignment operator, =. The statement is read as "sum *gets* the value of `number1` + `number2`." When the program encounters the addition operation, it performs the calculation using the values stored in the variables `number1` and `number2`. In the preceding statement, the addition operator is a *binary oper-ator*—its *two* operands are the variables `number1` and `number2`. Portions of statements that contain calculations are called **expressions**. In fact, an expression is any portion of a statement that has a *value* associated with it. For example, the value of the expression `number1 + number2` is the *sum* of the numbers. Similarly, the value of the expression `input.nextInt()` is the integer typed by the user.

2.5.9 Displaying the Result of the Calculation

After the calculation has been performed, line 25

```
System.out.printf("Sum is %d%n", sum); // display sum
```

uses method `System.out.printf` to display the sum. The format specifier **%d** is a *placeholder* for an `int` value (in this case the value of `sum`)—the letter d stands for "decimal integer." The remaining characters in the format string are all fixed text. So, method `printf` displays "Sum is ", followed by the value of sum (in the position of the %d format specifier) and a newline.

Calculations can also be performed *inside* `printf` statements. We could have combined the statements at lines 23 and 25 into the statement

```
System.out.printf("Sum is %d%n", (number1 + number2));
```

The parentheses around the expression `number1 + number2` are optional—they're included to emphasize that the value of the *entire* expression is output in the position of the %d format specifier. Such parentheses are said to be **redundant**.

2.5.10 Java API Documentation

For each new Java API class we use, we indicate the package in which it's located. This information helps you locate descriptions of each package and class in the Java API documentation. A web-based version of this documentation can be found at

```
http://docs.oracle.com/javase/7/docs/api/index.html
```

You can download it from the Additional Resources section at

```
http://www.oracle.com/technetwork/java/javase/downloads/index.html
```

Appendix F shows how to use this documentation.

2.6 Memory Concepts

Variable names such as `number1`, `number2` and `sum` actually correspond to *locations* in the computer's memory. Every variable has a **name**, a **type**, a **size** (in bytes) and a **value**.

In the addition program of Fig. 2.7, when the following statement (line 18) executes:

```
number1 = input.nextInt(); // read first number from user
```

the number typed by the user is placed into a memory location corresponding to the name `number1`. Suppose that the user enters 45. The computer places that integer value into location `number1` (Fig. 2.8), replacing the previous value (if any) in that location. The previous value is lost, so this process is said to be *destructive*.

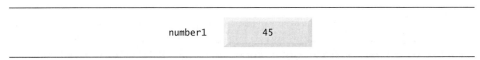

| number1 | 45 |

Fig. 2.8 | Memory location showing the name and value of variable `number1`.

When the statement (line 21)

```
number2 = input.nextInt(); // read second number from user
```

executes, suppose that the user enters 72. The computer places that integer value into location `number2`. The memory now appears as shown in Fig. 2.9.

| number1 | 45 |
| number2 | 72 |

Fig. 2.9 | Memory locations after storing values for `number1` and `number2`.

After the program of Fig. 2.7 obtains values for `number1` and `number2`, it adds the values and places the total into variable `sum`. The statement (line 23)

```
sum = number1 + number2; // add numbers, then store total in sum
```

performs the addition, then replaces any previous value in `sum`. After `sum` has been calculated, memory appears as shown in Fig. 2.10. The values of `number1` and `number2` appear exactly as they did before they were used in the calculation of `sum`. These values were used, but *not* destroyed, as the computer performed the calculation. When a value is read from a memory location, the process is *nondestructive*.

number1	45
number2	72
sum	117

Fig. 2.10 | Memory locations after storing the sum of number1 and number2.

2.7 Arithmetic

Most programs perform arithmetic calculations. The **arithmetic operators** are summarized in Fig. 2.11. Note the use of various special symbols not used in algebra. The **asterisk** (*****) indicates multiplication, and the percent sign (**%**) is the **remainder operator**, which we'll discuss shortly. The arithmetic operators in Fig. 2.11 are *binary* operators, because each operates on *two* operands. For example, the expression f + 7 contains the binary operator + and the two operands f and 7.

Java operation	Operator	Algebraic expression	Java expression
Addition	+	$f + 7$	f + 7
Subtraction	–	$p - c$	p - c
Multiplication	*	bm	b * m
Division	/	x / y or $\frac{x}{y}$ or $x \div y$	x / y
Remainder	%	$r \bmod s$	r % s

Fig. 2.11 | Arithmetic operators.

Integer division yields an integer quotient. For example, the expression 7 / 4 evaluates to 1, and the expression 17 / 5 evaluates to 3. Any fractional part in integer division is simply *truncated* (i.e., *discarded*)—no *rounding* occurs. Java provides the remainder operator, %, which yields the remainder after division. The expression x % y yields the remainder after x is divided by y. Thus, 7 % 4 yields 3, and 17 % 5 yields 2. This operator is most commonly used with integer operands but it can also be used with other arithmetic types. In this chapter's exercises and in later chapters, we consider several interesting applications of the remainder operator, such as determining whether one number is a multiple of another.

Arithmetic Expressions in Straight-Line Form

Arithmetic expressions in Java must be written in **straight-line form** to facilitate entering programs into the computer. Thus, expressions such as "a divided by b" must be written as a / b, so that all constants, variables and operators appear in a straight line. The following algebraic notation is generally not acceptable to compilers:

$$\frac{a}{b}$$

Parentheses for Grouping Subexpressions
Parentheses are used to group terms in Java expressions in the same manner as in algebraic expressions. For example, to multiply a times the quantity b + c, we write

```
    a * (b + c)
```

If an expression contains **nested parentheses**, such as

```
    ((a + b) * c)
```

the expression in the *innermost* set of parentheses (a + b in this case) is evaluated *first*.

Rules of Operator Precedence
Java applies the operators in arithmetic expressions in a precise sequence determined by the **rules of operator precedence**, which are generally the same as those followed in algebra:

1. Multiplication, division and remainder operations are applied first. If an expression contains several such operations, they're applied from left to right. Multiplication, division and remainder operators have the same level of precedence.

2. Addition and subtraction operations are applied next. If an expression contains several such operations, the operators are applied from left to right. Addition and subtraction operators have the same level of precedence.

These rules enable Java to apply operators in the correct *order*.[1] When we say that operators are applied from left to right, we're referring to their **associativity**. Some operators associate from right to left. Figure 2.12 summarizes these rules of operator precedence. A complete precedence chart is included in Appendix A.

Operator(s)	Operation(s)	Order of evaluation (precedence)
* / %	Multiplication Division Remainder	Evaluated first. If there are several operators of this type, they're evaluated from *left to right*.
+ -	Addition Subtraction	Evaluated next. If there are several operators of this type, they're evaluated from *left to right*.
=	Assignment	Evaluated last.

Fig. 2.12 | Precedence of arithmetic operators.

Sample Algebraic and Java Expressions
Now let's consider several expressions in light of the rules of operator precedence. Each example lists an algebraic expression and its Java equivalent. The following is an example of an arithmetic mean (average) of five terms:

1. We use simple examples to explain the *order of evaluation* of expressions. Subtle issues occur in the more complex expressions you'll encounter later in the book. For more information on order of evaluation, see Chapter 15 of *The Java™ Language Specification* (http://docs.oracle.com/javase/specs/jls/se7/html/index.html).

Algebra: $\quad m = \dfrac{a + b + c + d + e}{5}$

Java: $\quad$ m = (a + b + c + d + e) / 5;

The parentheses are required because division has higher precedence than addition. The entire quantity (a + b + c + d + e) is to be divided by 5. If the parentheses are erroneously omitted, we obtain a + b + c + d + e / 5, which evaluates as

$$a + b + c + d + \dfrac{e}{5}$$

Here's an example of the equation of a straight line:

Algebra: $\quad y = mx + b$
Java: $\quad$ y = m * x + b;

No parentheses are required. The multiplication operator is applied first because multiplication has a higher precedence than addition. The assignment occurs last because it has a lower precedence than multiplication or addition.

The following example contains remainder (%), multiplication, division, addition and subtraction operations:

Algebra: $\quad z = pr\,\%\,q + w/x - y$

Java: $\quad$ z = p * r % q + w / x - y;

             6   1   2   4   3   5

The circled numbers under the statement indicate the *order* in which Java applies the operators. The *, % and / operations are evaluated first in *left-to-right* order (i.e., they associate from left to right), because they have higher precedence than + and -. The + and - operations are evaluated next. These operations are also applied from *left to right*. The assignment (=) operation is evaluated last.

Evaluation of a Second-Degree Polynomial

To develop a better understanding of the rules of operator precedence, consider the evaluation of an assignment expression that includes a second-degree polynomial $ax^2 + bx + c$:

y = a * x * x + b * x + c;

    6   1   2   4   3   5

The multiplication operations are evaluated first in left-to-right order (i.e., they associate from left to right), because they have higher precedence than addition. (Java has no arithmetic operator for exponentiation, so x^2 is represented as x * x. Section 4.4 shows an alternative for performing exponentiation.) The addition operations are evaluated next from *left to right*. Suppose that a, b, c and x are initialized (given values) as follows: a = 2, b = 3, c = 7 and x = 5. Figure 2.13 illustrates the order in which the operators are applied.

You can use *redundant parentheses* (unnecessary parentheses) to make an expression clearer. For example, the preceding statement might be parenthesized as follows:

y = (a * x * x) + (b * x) + c;

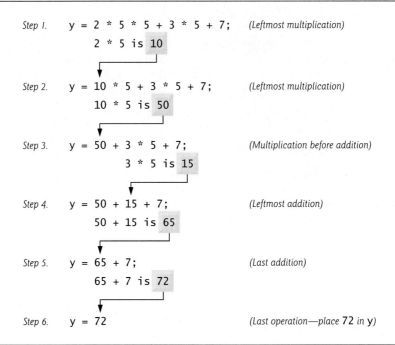

Step 1.   y = 2 * 5 * 5 + 3 * 5 + 7;   (Leftmost multiplication)

          2 * 5 is 10

Step 2.   y = 10 * 5 + 3 * 5 + 7;   (Leftmost multiplication)

          10 * 5 is 50

Step 3.   y = 50 + 3 * 5 + 7;   (Multiplication before addition)

                   3 * 5 is 15

Step 4.   y = 50 + 15 + 7;   (Leftmost addition)

          50 + 15 is 65

Step 5.   y = 65 + 7;   (Last addition)

          65 + 7 is 72

Step 6.   y = 72   (Last operation—place 72 in y)

Fig. 2.13 | Order in which a second-degree polynomial is evaluated.

2.8 Decision Making: Equality and Relational Operators

A **condition** is an expression that can be **true** or **false**. This section introduces Java's **if selection statement**, which allows a program to make a **decision** based on a condition's value. For example, the condition "grade is greater than or equal to 60" determines whether a student passed a test. If the condition in an if statement is *true*, the body of the if statement executes. If the condition is *false*, the body does not execute. We'll see an example shortly.

Conditions in if statements can be formed by using the **equality operators** (== and !=) and **relational operators** (>, <, >= and <=) summarized in Fig. 2.14. Both equality operators have the same level of precedence, which is *lower* than that of the relational operators. The equality operators associate from *left to right*. The relational operators all have the same level of precedence and also associate from *left to right*.

Algebraic operator	Java equality or relational operator	Sample Java condition	Meaning of Java condition
Equality operators			
=	==	x == y	x is equal to y
≠	!=	x != y	x is not equal to y

Fig. 2.14 | Equality and relational operators. (Part 1 of 2.)

Algebraic operator	Java equality or relational operator	Sample Java condition	Meaning of Java condition
Relational operators			
>	>	x > y	x is greater than y
<	<	x < y	x is less than y
≥	>=	x >= y	x is greater than or equal to y
≤	<=	x <= y	x is less than or equal to y

Fig. 2.14 | Equality and relational operators. (Part 2 of 2.)

Figure 2.15 uses six if statements to compare two integers input by the user. If the condition in any of these if statements is *true*, the statement associated with that if statement executes; otherwise, the statement is skipped. We use a Scanner to input the integers from the user and store them in variables number1 and number2. The program *compares* the numbers and displays the results of the comparisons that are true.

```
1   // Fig. 2.15: Comparison.java
2   // Compare integers using if statements, relational operators
3   // and equality operators.
4   import java.util.Scanner; // program uses class Scanner
5
6   public class Comparison
7   {
8      // main method begins execution of Java application
9      public static void main(String[] args)
10     {
11        // create Scanner to obtain input from command line
12        Scanner input = new Scanner(System.in);
13
14        int number1; // first number to compare
15        int number2; // second number to compare
16
17        System.out.print("Enter first integer: "); // prompt
18        number1 = input.nextInt(); // read first number from user
19
20        System.out.print("Enter second integer: "); // prompt
21        number2 = input.nextInt(); // read second number from user
22
23        if (number1 == number2)
24           System.out.printf("%d == %d%n", number1, number2);
25
26        if (number1 != number2)
27           System.out.printf("%d != %d%n", number1, number2);
28
29        if (number1 < number2)
30           System.out.printf("%d < %d%n", number1, number2);
```

Fig. 2.15 | Compare integers using if statements, relational operators and equality operators. (Part 1 of 2.)

```
31
32          if (number1 > number2)
33             System.out.printf("%d > %d%n", number1, number2);
34
35          if (number1 <= number2)
36             System.out.printf("%d <= %d%n", number1, number2);
37
38          if (number1 >= number2)
39             System.out.printf("%d >= %d%n", number1, number2);
40       } // end method main
41    } // end class Comparison
```

```
Enter first integer: 777
Enter second integer: 777
777 == 777
777 <= 777
777 >= 777
```

```
Enter first integer: 1000
Enter second integer: 2000
1000 != 2000
1000 < 2000
1000 <= 2000
```

```
Enter first integer: 2000
Enter second integer: 1000
2000 != 1000
2000 > 1000
2000 >= 1000
```

Fig. 2.15 | Compare integers using if statements, relational operators and equality operators. (Part 2 of 2.)

The declaration of class Comparison begins at line 6

```
public class Comparison
```

The class's main method (lines 9–40) begins the execution of the program. Line 12

```
Scanner input = new Scanner(System.in);
```

declares Scanner variable input and assigns it a Scanner that inputs data from the standard input (i.e., the keyboard).

Lines 14–15

```
int number1; // first number to compare
int number2; // second number to compare
```

declare the int variables used to store the values input from the user.

Lines 17–18

```
System.out.print("Enter first integer: "); // prompt
number1 = input.nextInt(); // read first number from user
```

prompt the user to enter the first integer and input the value, respectively. The value is stored in variable `number1`.

Lines 20–21

```
System.out.print("Enter second integer: "); // prompt
number2 = input.nextInt(); // read second number from user
```

prompt the user to enter the second integer and input the value, respectively. The value is stored in variable `number2`.

Lines 23–24

```
if (number1 == number2)
    System.out.printf("%d == %d%n", number1, number2);
```

compare the values of `number1` and `number2` to determine whether they're equal. An `if` statement always begins with keyword `if`, followed by a condition in parentheses. An `if` statement expects one statement in its body, but may contain multiple statements if they're enclosed in a set of braces ({}). The indentation of the body statement shown here is not required, but it improves the program's readability by emphasizing that the statement in line 24 *is part of* the `if` statement that begins at line 23. Line 24 executes only if the numbers stored in variables `number1` and `number2` are equal (i.e., the condition is *true*). The `if` statements in lines 26–27, 29–30, 32–33, 35–36 and 38–39 compare `number1` and `number2` using the operators `!=`, `<`, `>`, `<=` and `>=`, respectively. If the condition in one or more of the `if` statements is *true*, the corresponding body statement executes.

Common Programming Error 2.9

Confusing the equality operator, ==, with the assignment operator, =, can cause a logic error or a compilation error. The equality operator should be read as "is equal to" and the assignment operator as "gets" or "gets the value of." To avoid confusion, some people read the equality operator as "double equals" or "equals equals."

Good Programming Practice 2.11

Place only one statement per line in a program for readability.

There's no semicolon (;) at the end of the first line of each `if` statement. Such a semicolon would result in a logic error at execution time. For example,

```
if (number1 == number2); // logic error
    System.out.printf("%d == %d%n", number1, number2);
```

would actually be interpreted by Java as

```
if (number1 == number2)
    ; // empty statement
System.out.printf("%d == %d%n", number1, number2);
```

where the semicolon on the line by itself—called the **empty statement**—is the statement to execute if the condition in the `if` statement is *true*. When the empty statement executes, no task is performed. The program then continues with the output statement, which *always* executes, *regardless* of whether the condition is true or false, because the output statement is *not* part of the `if` statement.

White space

Note the use of white space in Fig. 2.15. Recall that the compiler normally ignores white space. So, statements may be split over several lines and may be spaced according to your preferences without affecting a program's meaning. It's incorrect to split identifiers and strings. Ideally, statements should be kept small, but this is not always possible.

Error-Prevention Tip 2.4

A lengthy statement can be spread over several lines. If a single statement must be split across lines, choose natural breaking points, such as after a comma in a comma-separated list, or after an operator in a lengthy expression. If a statement is split across two or more lines, indent all subsequent lines until the end of the statement.

Operators Discussed So Far

Figure 2.16 shows the operators discussed so far in decreasing order of precedence. All but the assignment operator, =, associate from *left to right*. The assignment operator, =, associates from *right to left*. An assignment expression's value is whatever was assigned to the variable on the = operator's left side—for example, the value of the expression x = 7 is 7. So an expression like x = y = 0 is evaluated as if it had been written as x = (y = 0), which first assigns the value 0 to variable y, then assigns the result of that assignment, 0, to x.

Good Programming Practice 2.12

When writing expressions containing many operators, refer to the operator precedence chart (Appendix A). Confirm that the operations in the expression are performed in the order you expect. If, in a complex expression, you're uncertain about the order of evaluation, use parentheses to force the order, exactly as you'd do in algebraic expressions.

Operators				Associativity	Type
*	/	%		left to right	multiplicative
+	-			left to right	additive
<	<=	>	>=	left to right	relational
==	!=			left to right	equality
=				right to left	assignment

Fig. 2.16 | Precedence and associativity of operators discussed.

2.9 (Optional) GUI and Graphics Case Study: Using Dialog Boxes

This optional case study is designed for those who want to begin learning Java's capabilities for creating graphical user interfaces (GUIs) and graphics early in the book, before the deeper discussions of these topics later in the book. This case study features Java's mature Swing technology, which as of this writing is still a bit more popular than the newer JavaFX technology presented in later chapters.

This GUI and Graphics Case Study appears in 10 brief sections (see Fig. 2.17). Each section introduces new concepts and provides examples with screen captures that show sample interactions and results. In the first few sections, you'll create your first graphical apps. In subsequent sections, you'll use object-oriented programming concepts to create an app that draws a variety of shapes. When we formally introduce GUIs in Chapter 12, we use the mouse to choose exactly which shapes to draw and where to draw them. In Chapter 13, we add capabilities of the Java 2D graphics API to draw the shapes with different line thicknesses and fills. We hope you find this case study informative and entertaining.

Location	Title—Exercise(s)
Section 2.4	Using Dialog Boxes—Basic input and output with dialog boxes
Section 3.14	Creating Simple Drawings—Displaying and drawing lines on the screen
Section 4.10	Drawing Rectangles and Ovals—Using shapes to represent data
Section 5.13	Colors and Filled Shapes—Drawing a bull's-eye and random graphics
Section 6.14	Drawing Arcs—Drawing spirals with arcs
Section 8.16	Using Objects with Graphics—Storing shapes as objects
Section 9.7	Displaying Text and Images Using Labels—Providing status information
Section 10.11	Drawing with Polymorphism—Identifying the similarities between shapes
Exercise 12.17	Expanding the Interface—Using GUI components and event handling
Exercise 13.31	Adding Java 2D—Using the Java 2D API to enhance drawings

Fig. 2.17 | Summary of the GUI and Graphics Case Study in each chapter.

Displaying Text in a Dialog Box

The programs presented thus far display output in the *command window*. Many apps use windows or **dialog boxes** (also called **dialogs**) to display output. Web browsers such as Chrome, Firefox, Internet Explorer, Safari and Opera display web pages in their own windows. E-mail programs allow you to type and read messages in a window. Typically, dialog boxes are windows in which programs display important messages to users. Class **JOption-Pane** provides prebuilt dialog boxes that enable programs to display windows containing messages—such windows are called **message dialogs**. Figure 2.18 displays the String "Welcome to Java" in a message dialog.

```java
1  // Fig. 2.18: Dialog1.java
2  // Using JOptionPane to display multiple lines in a dialog box.
3  import javax.swing.JOptionPane;
4
5  public class Dialog1
6  {
7     public static void main(String[] args)
8     {
9        // display a dialog with a message
10       JOptionPane.showMessageDialog(null, "Welcome to Java");
11    }
12 } // end class Dialog1
```

Fig. 2.18 | Using JOptionPane to display multiple lines in a dialog box. (Part 1 of 2.)

Fig. 2.18 | Using JOptionPane to display multiple lines in a dialog box. (Part 2 of 2.)

JOptionPane *Class* static *Method* showMessagDialog

Line 3 indicates that the program uses class JOptionPane from package **javax.swing**. This package contains many classes that help you create **graphical user interfaces (GUIs)**. **GUI components** facilitate data entry by a program's user and presentation of outputs to the user. Line 10 calls JOptionPane method **showMessageDialog** to display a dialog box containing a message. The method requires two arguments. The first helps the Java app determine where to position the dialog box. A dialog is typically displayed from a GUI app with its own window. The first argument refers to that window (known as the *parent window*) and causes the dialog to appear centered over the app's window. If the first argument is null, the dialog box is displayed at the center of your screen. The second argument is the String to display in the dialog box.

Introducing static *Methods*

JOptionPane method showMessageDialog is a so-called **static method**. Such methods often define frequently used tasks. For example, many programs display dialog boxes, and the code to do this is the same each time. Rather than requiring you to "reinvent the wheel" and create code to display a dialog, the designers of class JOptionPane declared a static method that performs this task for you. A static method is called by using its class name followed by a dot (.) and the method name, as in

> *ClassName*.*methodName*(*arguments*)

Notice that you do *not* create an object of class JOptionPane to use its static method showMessageDialog. We discuss static methods in more detail in Chapter 5.

Entering Text in a Dialog

Figure 2.19 uses another predefined JOptionPane dialog called an **input dialog** that allows the user to *enter data* into a program. The program asks for the user's name and responds with a message dialog containing a greeting and the name that the user entered.

```
1    // Fig. 2.19: NameDialog.java
2    // Obtaining user input from a dialog.
3    import javax.swing.JOptionPane;
4
5    public class NameDialog
6    {
7       public static void main(String[] args)
8       {
```

Fig. 2.19 | Obtaining user input from a dialog. (Part 1 of 2.)

```
9            // prompt user to enter name
10           String name = JOptionPane.showInputDialog("What is your name?");
11
12           // create the message
13           String message =
14              String.format("Welcome, %s, to Java Programming!", name);
15
16           // display the message to welcome the user by name
17           JOptionPane.showMessageDialog(null, message);
18        } // end main
19     } // end class NameDialog
```

Fig. 2.19 | Obtaining user input from a dialog. (Part 2 of 2.)

JOptionPane Class `static` Method `showInputDialog`

Line 10 uses JOptionPane method **showInputDialog** to display an input dialog containing a prompt and a *field* (known as a **text field**) in which you can enter text. Method showInputDialog's argument is the prompt that indicates what you should enter. You type characters in the text field, then click the **OK** button or press the *Enter* key to return the String to the program. Method showInputDialog returns a String containing the characters you typed. We store the String in variable name. If you press the dialog's **Cancel** button or press the *Esc* key, the method returns null and the program displays the word "null" as the name.

String Class `static` Method `format`

Lines 13–14 use static String method **format** to return a String containing a greeting with the user's name. Method format works like method System.out.printf, except that format returns the formatted String rather than displaying it in a command window. Line 17 displays the greeting in a message dialog, just as we did in Fig. 2.18.

GUI and Graphics Case Study Exercise

2.1   Modify the addition program in Fig. 2.7 to use dialog-based input and output with the methods of class JOptionPane. Since method showInputDialog returns a String, you must convert the String the user enters to an int for use in calculations. The static method parseInt of class Integer (package java.lang) takes a String argument representing an integer and returns the value as an int. If the String does not contain a valid integer, the program will terminate with an error.

2.10 Wrap-Up

In this chapter, you learned many important features of Java, including displaying data on the screen in a **Command Prompt**, inputting data from the keyboard, performing calculations and making decisions. The applications presented here introduced you to many basic programming concepts. In the next chapter we begin our introduction to control statements, which specify the order in which a program's actions are performed.

Summary

Section 2.2 Your First Program in Java: Printing a Line of Text

- A Java application (p. 35) executes when you use the java command to launch the JVM.

- Comments (p. 36) document programs and improve their readability. The compiler ignores them.

- A comment that begins with // is an end-of-line comment—it terminates at the end of the line on which it appears.

- Traditional comments (p. 36) can be spread over several lines and are delimited by /* and */.

- Javadoc comments (p. 36), delimited by /** and */, enable you to embed program documentation in your code. The javadoc utility program generates HTML pages based on these comments.

- A syntax error (p. 36; also called a compiler error, compile-time error or compilation error) occurs when the compiler encounters code that violates Java's language rules. It's similar to a grammar error in a natural language.

- Blank lines, space characters and tab characters are known as white space (p. 37). White space makes programs easier to read and is ignored by the compiler.

- Keywords (p. 37) are reserved for use by Java and are always spelled with all lowercase letters.

- Keyword class (p. 37) introduces a class declaration.

- By convention, all class names in Java begin with a capital letter and capitalize the first letter of each word they include (e.g., SampleClassName).

- A Java class name is an identifier—a series of characters consisting of letters, digits, underscores (_) and dollar signs ($) that does not begin with a digit and does not contain spaces.

- Java is case sensitive (p. 37)—that is, uppercase and lowercase letters are distinct.

- The body of every class declaration (p. 37) is delimited by braces, { and }.

- A public (p. 37) class declaration must be saved in a file with the same name as the class followed by the ".java" file-name extension.

- Method main (p. 38) is the starting point of every Java application and must begin with

```
public static void main(String[] args)
```

otherwise, the JVM will not execute the application.

- Methods perform tasks and return information when they complete them. Keyword void (p. 38) indicates that a method will perform a task but return no information.

- Statements instruct the computer to perform actions.

- A string (p. 39) in double quotes is sometimes called a character string or a string literal.

- The standard output object (System.out; p. 39) displays characters in the command window.

- Method System.out.println (p. 39) displays its argument (p. 39) in the command window followed by a newline character to position the output cursor to the beginning of the next line.

- You compile a program with the command javac. If the program contains no syntax errors, a class file (p. 40) containing the Java bytecodes that represent the application is created. These bytecodes are interpreted by the JVM when you execute the program.

- To run an application, type java followed by the name of the class that contains the main method.

Section 2.3 Modifying Your First Java Program

- System.out.print (p. 42) displays its argument and positions the output cursor immediately after the last character displayed.

- A backslash (\) in a string is an escape character (p. 43). Java combines it with the next character to form an escape sequence (p. 43). The escape sequence \n (p. 43) represents the newline character.

Section 2.4 Displaying Text with `printf`

- `System.out.printf` method (p. 43; f means "formatted") displays formatted data.
- Method `printf`'s first argument is a format string (p. 44) containing fixed text and/or format specifiers. Each format specifier (p. 44) indicates the type of data to output and is a placeholder for a corresponding argument that appears after the format string.
- Format specifiers begin with a percent sign (%) and are followed by a character that represents the data type. The format specifier `%s` (p. 44) is a placeholder for a string.
- The `%n` format specifier (p. 44) is a portable line separator. You cannot use `%n` in the argument to `System.out.print` or `System.out.println`; however, the line separator output by `System.out.println` after it displays its argument is portable across operating systems.

Section 2.5 Another Application: Adding Integers

- An `import` declaration (p. 45) helps the compiler locate a class that's used in a program.
- Java's rich set of predefined classes are grouped into packages (p. 45)—named groups of classes. These are referred to as the Java class library (p. 45), or the Java Application Programming Interface (Java API).
- A variable (p. 46) is a location in the computer's memory where a value can be stored for use later in a program. All variables must be declared with a name and a type before they can be used.
- A variable's name enables the program to access the variable's value in memory.
- A `Scanner` (package `java.util`; p. 47) enables a program to read data that the program will use. Before a `Scanner` can be used, the program must create it and specify the source of the data.
- Variables should be initialized (p. 47) to prepare them for use in a program.
- The expression `new Scanner(System.in)` creates a `Scanner` that reads from the standard input object (`System.in`; p. 47)—normally the keyboard.
- Data type `int` (p. 47) is used to declare variables that will hold integer values. The range of values for an `int` is –2,147,483,648 to +2,147,483,647.
- Types `float` and `double` (p. 47) specify real numbers with decimal points, such as `3.4` and `-11.19`.
- Variables of type `char` (p. 47) represent individual characters, such as an uppercase letter (e.g., A), a digit (e.g., 7), a special character (e.g., * or %) or an escape sequence (e.g., tab, \t).
- Types such as `int`, `float`, `double` and `char` are primitive types (p. 47). Primitive-type names are keywords; thus, they must appear in all lowercase letters.
- A prompt (p. 48) directs the user to take a specific action.
- `Scanner` method `nextInt` obtains an integer for use in a program.
- The assignment operator, `=` (p. 48), enables the program to give a value to a variable. It's called a binary operator (p. 48) because it has two operands.
- Portions of statements that have values are called expressions (p. 49).
- The format specifier `%d` (p. 49) is a placeholder for an `int` value.

Section 2.6 Memory Concepts

- Variable names (p. 50) correspond to locations in the computer's memory. Every variable has a name, a type, a size and a value.
- A value that's placed in a memory location replaces the location's previous value, which is lost.

Section 2.7 Arithmetic

- The arithmetic operators (p. 51) are + (addition), - (subtraction), * (multiplication), / (division) and % (remainder).

- Integer division (p. 51) yields an integer quotient.
- The remainder operator, % (p. 51), yields the remainder after division.
- Arithmetic expressions must be written in straight-line form (p. 51).
- If an expression contains nested parentheses (p. 52), the innermost set is evaluated first.
- Java applies the operators in arithmetic expressions in a precise sequence determined by the rules of operator precedence (p. 52).
- When we say that operators are applied from left to right, we're referring to their associativity (p. 52). Some operators associate from right to left.
- Redundant parentheses (p. 53) can make an expression clearer.

Section 2.8 Decision Making: Equality and Relational Operators
- The if statement (p. 54) makes a decision based on a condition's value (true or false).
- Conditions in if statements can be formed by using the equality (== and !=) and relational (>, <, >= and <=) operators (p. 54).
- An if statement begins with keyword if followed by a condition in parentheses and expects one statement in its body.
- The empty statement (p. 57) is a statement that does not perform a task.

Self-Review Exercises

2.1 Fill in the blanks in each of the following statements:
   a) A(n) _____ begins the body of every method, and a(n) _____ ends the body of every method.
   b) You can use the _____ statement to make decisions.
   c) _____ begins an end-of-line comment.
   d) _____, _____ and _____ are called white space.
   e) _____ are reserved for use by Java.
   f) Java applications begin execution at method _____.
   g) Methods _____, _____ and _____ display information in a command window.

2.2 State whether each of the following is *true* or *false*. If *false*, explain why.
   a) Comments cause the computer to print the text after the // on the screen when the program executes.
   b) All variables must be given a type when they're declared.
   c) Java considers the variables number and NuMbEr to be identical.
   d) The remainder operator (%) can be used only with integer operands.
   e) The arithmetic operators *, /, %, + and - all have the same level of precedence.

2.3 Write statements to accomplish each of the following tasks:
   a) Declare variables c, thisIsAVariable, q76354 and number to be of type int.
   b) Prompt the user to enter an integer.
   c) Input an integer and assign the result to int variable value. Assume Scanner variable input can be used to read a value from the keyboard.
   d) Print "This is a Java program" on one line in the command window. Use method System.out.println.
   e) Print "This is a Java program" on two lines in the command window. The first line should end with Java. Use method System.out.printf and two %s format specifiers.
   f) If the variable number is not equal to 7, display "The variable number is not equal to 7".

2.4   Identify and correct the errors in each of the following statements:

a) `if (c < 7);`
```
    System.out.println("c is less than 7");
```

b) `if (c => 7)`
```
    System.out.println("c is equal to or greater than 7");
```

2.5   Write declarations, statements or comments that accomplish each of the following tasks:

a) State that a program will calculate the product of three integers.

b) Create a `Scanner` called `input` that reads values from the standard input.

c) Declare the variables x, y, z and `result` to be of type `int`.

d) Prompt the user to enter the first integer.

e) Read the first integer from the user and store it in the variable x.

f) Prompt the user to enter the second integer.

g) Read the second integer from the user and store it in the variable y.

h) Prompt the user to enter the third integer.

i) Read the third integer from the user and store it in the variable z.

j) Compute the product of the three integers contained in variables x, y and z, and assign the result to the variable `result`.

k) Use `System.out.printf` to display the message `"Product is"` followed by the value of the variable `result`.

2.6   Using the statements you wrote in Exercise 2.5, write a complete program that calculates and prints the product of three integers.

Answers to Self-Review Exercises

2.1   a) left brace ({), right brace (}). b) `if`. c) `//`. d) Space characters, newlines and tabs. e) Keywords. f) `main`. g) `System.out.print`, `System.out.println` and `System.out.printf`.

2.2   a) False. Comments do not cause any action to be performed when the program executes. They're used to document programs and improve their readability.

b) True.

c) False. Java is case sensitive, so these variables are distinct.

d) False. The remainder operator can also be used with noninteger operands in Java.

e) False. The operators *, / and % are higher precedence than operators + and -.

2.3   a) `int c, thisIsAVariable, q76354, number;`

or
```
int c;
int thisIsAVariable;
int q76354;
int number;
```

b) `System.out.print("Enter an integer: ");`

c) `value = input.nextInt();`

d) `System.out.println("This is a Java program");`

e) `System.out.printf("%s%n%s%n", "This is a Java", "program");`

f) `if (number != 7)`
```
    System.out.println("The variable number is not equal to 7");
```

2.4   a) Error: Semicolon after the right parenthesis of the condition (c < 7) in the `if`. Correction: Remove the semicolon after the right parenthesis. [*Note:* As a result, the output statement will execute regardless of whether the condition in the `if` is true.]

b) Error: The relational operator => is incorrect. Correction: Change => to >=.

2.5   a) `// Calculate the product of three integers`
b) `Scanner input = new Scanner(System.in);`
c) `int x, y, z, result;`
    or
    `int x;`
    `int y;`
    `int z;`
    `int result;`
d) `System.out.print("Enter first integer: ");`
e) `x = input.nextInt();`
f) `System.out.print("Enter second integer: ");`
g) `y = input.nextInt();`
h) `System.out.print("Enter third integer: ");`
i) `z = input.nextInt();`
j) `result = x * y * z;`
k) `System.out.printf("Product is %d%n", result);`

2.6   The solution to Self-Review Exercise 2.6 is as follows:

```
1   // Ex. 2.6: Product.java
2   // Calculate the product of three integers.
3   import java.util.Scanner; // program uses Scanner
4
5   public class Product
6   {
7      public static void main(String[] args)
8      {
9         // create Scanner to obtain input from command window
10        Scanner input = new Scanner(System.in);
11
12        int x; // first number input by user
13        int y; // second number input by user
14        int z; // third number input by user
15        int result; // product of numbers
16
17        System.out.print("Enter first integer: "); // prompt for input
18        x = input.nextInt(); // read first integer
19
20        System.out.print("Enter second integer: "); // prompt for input
21        y = input.nextInt(); // read second integer
22
23        System.out.print("Enter third integer: "); // prompt for input
24        z = input.nextInt(); // read third integer
25
26        result = x * y * z; // calculate product of numbers
27
28        System.out.printf("Product is %d%n", result);
29     } // end method main
30  } // end class Product
```

```
Enter first integer: 10
Enter second integer: 20
Enter third integer: 30
Product is 6000
```

Exercises

2.7   Fill in the blanks in each of the following statements:

a) _____ are used to document a program and improve its readability.

b) A decision can be made in a Java program with a(n) _____.

c) Calculations are normally performed by _____ statements.

d) The arithmetic operators with the same precedence as multiplication are _____ and _____.

e) When parentheses in an arithmetic expression are nested, the _____ set of parentheses is evaluated first.

f) A location in the computer's memory that may contain different values at various times throughout the execution of a program is called a(n) _____.

2.8   Write Java statements that accomplish each of the following tasks:

a) Display the message `"Enter an integer: "`, leaving the cursor on the same line.

b) Assign the product of variables b and c to variable a.

c) Use a comment to state that a program performs a sample payroll calculation.

2.9   State whether each of the following is *true* or *false*. If *false*, explain why.

a) Java operators are evaluated from left to right.

b) The following are all valid variable names: `_under_bar_`, `m928134`, `t5`, `j7`, `her_sales$`, `his_$account_total`, `a`, `b$`, `c`, `z` and `z2`.

c) A valid Java arithmetic expression with no parentheses is evaluated from left to right.

d) The following are all invalid variable names: `3g`, `87`, `67h2`, `h22` and `2h`.

2.10   Assuming that x = 2 and y = 3, what does each of the following statements display?

a) `System.out.printf("x = %d%n", x);`

b) `System.out.printf("Value of %d + %d is %d%n", x, x, (x + x));`

c) `System.out.printf("x =");`

d) `System.out.printf("%d = %d%n", (x + y), (y + x));`

2.11   Which of the following Java statements contain variables whose values are modified?

a) `p = i + j + k + 7;`

b) `System.out.println("variables whose values are modified");`

c) `System.out.println("a = 5");`

d) `value = input.nextInt();`

2.12   Given that $y = ax^3 + 7$, which of the following are correct Java statements for this equation?

a) `y = a * x * x * x + 7;`

b) `y = a * x * x * (x + 7);`

c) `y = (a * x) * x * (x + 7);`

d) `y = (a * x) * x * x + 7;`

e) `y = a * (x * x * x) + 7;`

f) `y = a * x * (x * x + 7);`

2.13   State the order of evaluation of the operators in each of the following Java statements, and show the value of x after each statement is performed:

a) `x = 7 + 3 * 6 / 2 - 1;`

b) `x = 2 % 2 + 2 * 2 - 2 / 2;`

c) `x = (3 * 9 * (3 + (9 * 3 / (3))));`

2.14   Write an application that displays the numbers 1 to 4 on the same line, with each pair of adjacent numbers separated by one space. Use the following techniques:

a) Use one `System.out.println` statement.

b) Use four `System.out.print` statements.

c) Use one `System.out.printf` statement.

2.15   *(Arithmetic)* Write an application that asks the user to enter two integers, obtains them from the user and prints their sum, product, difference and quotient (division). Use the techniques shown in Fig. 2.7.

2.16   *(Comparing Integers)* Write an application that asks the user to enter two integers, obtains them from the user and displays the larger number followed by the words "is larger". If the numbers are equal, print the message "These numbers are equal". Use the techniques shown in Fig. 2.15.

2.17   *(Arithmetic, Smallest and Largest)* Write an application that inputs three integers from the user and displays the sum, average, product, smallest and largest of the numbers. Use the techniques shown in Fig. 2.15. [*Note:* The calculation of the average in this exercise should result in an integer representation of the average. So, if the sum of the values is 7, the average should be 2, not 2.3333….]

2.18   *(Displaying Shapes with Asterisks)* Write an application that displays a box, an oval, an arrow and a diamond using asterisks (*), as follows:

```
*********        ***        *            *
*       *      *     *     ***          * *
*       *     *       *   *****        *   *
*       *     *       *     *         *     *
*       *     *       *     *        *       *
*       *     *       *     *         *     *
*       *     *       *     *          *   *
*       *      *     *      *           * *
*********        ***        *            *
```

2.19   What does the following code print?

```java
System.out.printf("*%n***%n****%n****%n*****%n");
```

2.20   What does the following code print?

```java
System.out.println("*");
System.out.println("***");
System.out.println("*****");
System.out.println("****");
System.out.println("**");
```

2.21   What does the following code print?

```java
System.out.print("*");
System.out.print("***");
System.out.print("*****");
System.out.print("****");
System.out.println("**");
```

2.22   What does the following code print?

```java
System.out.print("*");
System.out.println("***");
System.out.println("*****");
System.out.print("****");
System.out.println("**");
```

2.23   What does the following code print?

```java
System.out.printf("%s%n%s%n%s%n", "*", "***", "*****");
```

2.24   *(Largest and Smallest Integers)* Write an application that reads five integers and determines and prints the largest and smallest integers in the group. Use only the programming techniques you learned in this chapter.

2.25   *(Odd or Even)* Write an application that reads an integer and determines and prints whether it's odd or even. [*Hint:* Use the remainder operator. An even number is a multiple of 2. Any multiple of 2 leaves a remainder of 0 when divided by 2.]

2.26   *(Multiples)* Write an application that reads two integers, determines whether the first is a multiple of the second and prints the result. [*Hint:* Use the remainder operator.]

2.27   *(Checkerboard Pattern of Asterisks)* Write an application that displays a checkerboard pattern, as follows:

```
* * * * * * * *
 * * * * * * * *
* * * * * * * *
 * * * * * * * *
* * * * * * * *
 * * * * * * * *
* * * * * * * *
 * * * * * * * *
```

2.28   *(Diameter, Circumference and Area of a Circle)* Here's a peek ahead. In this chapter, you learned about integers and the type `int`. Java can also represent floating-point numbers that contain decimal points, such as 3.14159. Write an application that inputs from the user the radius of a circle as an integer and prints the circle's diameter, circumference and area using the floating-point value 3.14159 for π. Use the techniques shown in Fig. 2.7. [*Note:* You may also use the predefined constant `Math.PI` for the value of π. This constant is more precise than the value 3.14159. Class `Math` is defined in package `java.lang`. Classes in that package are imported automatically, so you do not need to `import` class `Math` to use it.] Use the following formulas (*r* is the radius):

$$diameter = 2r$$
$$circumference = 2\pi r$$
$$area = \pi r^2$$

Do not store the results of each calculation in a variable. Rather, specify each calculation as the value that will be output in a `System.out.printf` statement. The values produced by the circumference and area calculations are floating-point numbers. Such values can be output with the format specifier `%f` in a `System.out.printf` statement. You'll learn more about floating-point numbers in Chapter 3.

2.29   *(Integer Value of a Character)* Here's another peek ahead. In this chapter, you learned about integers and the type `int`. Java can also represent uppercase letters, lowercase letters and a considerable variety of special symbols. Every character has a corresponding integer representation. The set of characters a computer uses together with the corresponding integer representations for those characters is called that computer's character set. You can indicate a character value in a program simply by enclosing that character in single quotes, as in `'A'`.

You can determine a character's integer equivalent by preceding that character with `(int)`, as in

```
(int) 'A'
```

An operator of this form is called a cast operator. (You'll learn about cast operators in Chapter 3.) The following statement outputs a character and its integer equivalent:

```
System.out.printf("The character %c has the value %d%n", 'A', ((int) 'A'));
```

When the preceding statement executes, it displays the character A and the value 65 (from the Unicode® character set) as part of the string. The format specifier `%c` is a placeholder for a character (in this case, the character `'A'`).

Using statements similar to the one shown earlier in this exercise, write an application that displays the integer equivalents of some uppercase letters, lowercase letters, digits and special symbols. Display the integer equivalents of the following: A B C a b c 0 1 2 $ * + / and the blank character.

2.30 *(Separating the Digits in an Integer)* Write an application that inputs one number consisting of five digits from the user, separates the number into its individual digits and prints the digits separated from one another by three spaces each. For example, if the user types in the number 42339, the program should print

```
4   2   3   3   9
```

Assume that the user enters the correct number of digits. What happens when you enter a number with more than five digits? What happens when you enter a number with fewer than five digits? [*Hint:* It's possible to do this exercise with the techniques you learned in this chapter. You'll need to use both division and remainder operations to "pick off" each digit.]

2.31 *(Table of Squares and Cubes)* Using only the programming techniques you learned in this chapter, write an application that calculates the squares and cubes of the numbers from 0 to 10 and prints the resulting values in table format, as shown below.

```
number  square  cube
0       0       0
1       1       1
2       4       8
3       9       27
4       16      64
5       25      125
6       36      216
7       49      343
8       64      512
9       81      729
10      100     1000
```

2.32 *(Negative, Positive and Zero Values)* Write a program that inputs five numbers and determines and prints the number of negative numbers input, the number of positive numbers input and the number of zeros input.

Making a Difference

2.33 *(Body Mass Index Calculator)* We introduced the body mass index (BMI) calculator in Exercise 1.10. The formulas for calculating BMI are

$$BMI = \frac{weightInPounds \times 703}{heightInInches \times heightInInches}$$

or

$$BMI = \frac{weightInKilograms}{heightInMeters \times heightInMeters}$$

Create a BMI calculator that reads the user's weight in pounds and height in inches (or, if you prefer, the user's weight in kilograms and height in meters), then calculates and displays the user's body mass index. Also, display the following information from the Department of Health and Human Services/National Institutes of Health so the user can evaluate his/her BMI:

```
BMI VALUES
Underweight: less than 18.5
Normal:      between 18.5 and 24.9
Overweight:  between 25 and 29.9
Obese:       30 or greater
```

[*Note:* In this chapter, you learned to use the int type to represent whole numbers. The BMI calculations when done with int values will both produce whole-number results. In Chapter 3, you'll learn to use the double type to represent numbers with decimal points. When the BMI calculations are performed with doubles, they'll both produce numbers with decimal points—these are called "floating-point" numbers.]

2.34   *(World Population Growth Calculator)* Use the web to determine the current world population and the annual world population growth rate. Write an application that inputs these values, then displays the estimated world population after one, two, three, four and five years.

2.35   *(Car-Pool Savings Calculator)* Research several car-pooling websites. Create an application that calculates your daily driving cost, so that you can estimate how much money could be saved by car pooling, which also has other advantages such as reducing carbon emissions and reducing traffic congestion. The application should input the following information and display the user's cost per day of driving to work:

a) Total miles driven per day.
b) Cost per gallon of gasoline.
c) Average miles per gallon.
d) Parking fees per day.
e) Tolls per day.

3

Control Statements: Part 1; Assignment, ++ and -- Operators

Let's all move one place on.
—Lewis Carroll

How many apples fell on Newton's head before he took the hint!
—Robert Frost

Objectives

In this chapter you'll:

- Learn basic problem-solving techniques.

- Develop algorithms through the process of top-down, stepwise refinement.

- Use the `if` and `if...else` selection statements to choose between alternative actions.

- Use the `while` repetition statement to execute statements in a program repeatedly.

- Use counter-controlled repetition and sentinel-controlled repetition.

- Use the compound assignment operator, and the increment and decrement operators.

- Learn about the portability of primitive data types.

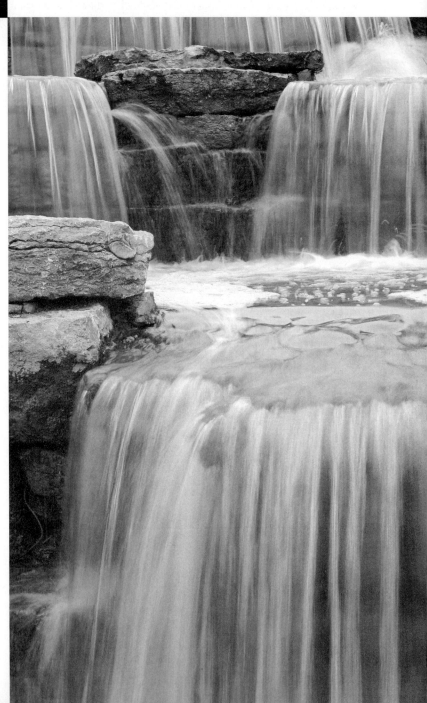

3.1 Introduction

Before writing a program to solve a problem, you should have a thorough understanding of the problem and a carefully planned approach to solving it. When writing a program, you also should understand the available building blocks and employ proven program-construction techniques. In this chapter and the next, we discuss these issues in presenting the theory and principles of structured programming. As you'll see when we get into object-oriented programming (starting in Chapter 7), the concepts presented here are crucial in constructing classes and manipulating objects. We discuss Java's `if` statement in additional detail, and introduce the `if...else` and `while` statements—all of these building blocks allow you to specify the logic required for methods to perform their tasks. We also introduce the compound assignment operator and the increment and decrement operators. Finally, we consider the portability of Java's primitive types.

3.2 Algorithms

Any computing problem can be solved by executing a series of actions in a specific order. A *procedure* for solving a problem in terms of

> **1.** the **actions** to execute and
>
> **2.** the **order** in which these actions execute

is called an **algorithm**. The following example demonstrates that correctly specifying the order in which the actions execute is important.

Consider the "rise-and-shine algorithm" followed by one executive for getting out of bed and going to work: (1) Get out of bed; (2) take off pajamas; (3) take a shower; (4) get dressed; (5) eat breakfast; (6) carpool to work. This routine gets the executive to work well prepared to make critical decisions. Suppose that the same steps are performed in a slightly different order: (1) Get out of bed; (2) take off pajamas; (3) get dressed; (4) take a shower; (5) eat breakfast; (6) carpool to work. In this case, our executive shows up for work soaking wet. Specifying the order in which statements (actions) execute in a program is called **program control**. This chapter investigates program control using Java's **control statements**.

3.3 Pseudocode

Pseudocode is an informal language that helps you develop algorithms without having to worry about the strict details of Java language syntax. The pseudocode we present is particularly useful for developing algorithms that will be converted to structured portions of Java programs. The pseudocode we use in this book is similar to everyday English—it's convenient and user friendly, but it's not an actual computer programming language. You'll see an algorithm written in pseudocode in Fig. 3.5. You may, of course, use your own native language(s) to develop your own pseudocode.

Pseudocode does not execute on computers. Rather, it helps you "think out" a program before attempting to write it in a programming language, such as Java. This chapter provides several examples of using pseudocode to develop Java programs.

The style of pseudocode we present consists purely of characters, so you can type pseudocode conveniently, using any text-editor program. A carefully prepared pseudocode program can easily be converted to a corresponding Java program.

Pseudocode normally describes only statements representing the *actions* that occur after you convert a program from pseudocode to Java and the program is run on a computer. Such actions might include *input, output* or *calculations*. In our pseudocode, we typically do *not* include variable declarations, but some programmers choose to list variables and mention their purposes.

3.4 Control Structures

Normally, statements in a program are executed one after the other in the order in which they're written. This process is called **sequential execution**. Various Java statements, which we'll soon discuss, enable you to specify that the next statement to execute is *not* necessarily the *next* one in sequence. This is called **transfer of control**.

During the 1960s, it became clear that the indiscriminate use of transfers of control was the root of much difficulty experienced by software development groups. The blame was pointed at the **goto statement** (used in most programming languages of the time), which allows you to specify a transfer of control to one of a wide range of destinations in a program. [*Note:* Java does *not* have a goto statement; however, the word goto is *reserved* by Java and should *not* be used as an identifier in programs.]

The research of Bohm and Jacopini[1] had demonstrated that programs could be written *without* any goto statements. The challenge of the era for programmers was to shift their styles to "goto-less programming." The term **structured programming** became almost synonymous with "goto elimination." Not until the 1970s did most programmers start taking structured programming seriously. The results were impressive. Software development groups reported shorter development times, more frequent on-time delivery of systems and more frequent within-budget completion of software projects. The key to these successes was that structured programs were clearer, easier to debug and modify, and more likely to be bug free in the first place.

Bohm and Jacopini's work demonstrated that all programs could be written in terms of only three control structures—the **sequence structure**, the **selection structure** and the

1.   C. Bohm, and G. Jacopini, "Flow Diagrams, Turing Machines, and Languages with Only Two Formation Rules," *Communications of the ACM*, Vol. 9, No. 5, May 1966, pp. 336–371.

repetition structure. When we introduce Java's control-structure implementations, we'll refer to them in the terminology of the *Java Language Specification* as "control statements."

Sequence Structure in Java

The sequence structure is built into Java. Unless directed otherwise, the computer executes Java statements one after the other in the order in which they're written—that is, in sequence. The **activity diagram** in Fig. 3.1 illustrates a typical sequence structure in which two calculations are performed in order. Java lets you have as many actions as you want in a sequence structure. As we'll soon see, anywhere a single action may be placed, we may place several actions in sequence.

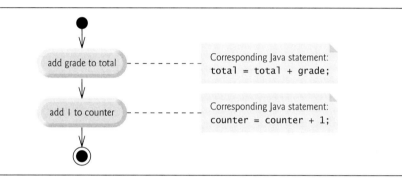

Fig. 3.1 | Sequence-structure activity diagram.

A UML activity diagram models the **workflow** (also called the **activity**) of a portion of a software system. Such workflows may include a portion of an algorithm, like the sequence structure in Fig. 3.1. Activity diagrams are composed of symbols, such as **action-state symbols** (rectangles with their left and right sides replaced with outward arcs), **diamonds** and **small circles**. These symbols are connected by **transition arrows**, which represent the *flow of the activity*—that is, the *order* in which the actions should occur.

Like pseudocode, activity diagrams help you develop and represent algorithms. Activity diagrams clearly show how control structures operate. We use the UML in this chapter and Chapter 4 to show control flow in control statements. Online Chapters 33–34 use the UML in a real-world automated-teller-machine case study.

Consider the sequence-structure activity diagram in Fig. 3.1. It contains two **action states**, each containing an **action expression**—for example, "add grade to total" or "add 1 to counter"—that specifies a particular action to perform. Other actions might include calculations or input/output operations. The arrows in the activity diagram represent **transitions**, which indicate the *order* in which the actions represented by the action states occur. The program that implements the activities illustrated by the diagram in Fig. 3.1 first adds grade to total, then adds 1 to counter.

The **solid circle** at the top of the activity diagram represents the **initial state**—the *beginning* of the workflow *before* the program performs the modeled actions. The **solid circle surrounded by a hollow circle** at the bottom of the diagram represents the **final state**—the *end* of the workflow *after* the program performs its actions.

Figure 3.1 also includes rectangles with the upper-right corners folded over. These are UML **notes** (like comments in Java)—explanatory remarks that describe the purpose of symbols in the diagram. Figure 3.1 uses UML notes to show the Java code associated with each action state. A **dotted line** connects each note with the element it describes. Activity diagrams normally do *not* show the Java code that implements the activity. We do this here to illustrate how the diagram relates to Java code. For more information on the UML, see our optional online object-oriented design case study (Chapters 33–34) or visit `www.uml.org`.

Selection Statements in Java

Java has three types of **selection statements** (discussed in this chapter and Chapter 4). The `if` *statement* either performs (selects) an action, if a condition is *true*, or skips it, if the condition is *false*. The `if...else` *statement* performs an action if a condition is *true* and performs a different action if the condition is *false*. The `switch` *statement* (Chapter 4) performs one of *many* different actions, depending on the value of an expression.

The `if` statement is a **single-selection statement** because it selects or ignores a *single* action (or, as we'll soon see, a *single group of actions*). The `if...else` statement is called a **double-selection statement** because it selects between *two different actions* (or *groups of actions*). The `switch` statement is called a **multiple-selection statement** because it selects among *many different actions* (or *groups of actions*).

Repetition Statements in Java

Java provides three **repetition statements** (also called **iteration statements** or **looping statements**) that enable programs to perform statements repeatedly as long as a condition (called the **loop-continuation condition**) remains *true*. The repetition statements are the `while`, `do...while`, `for` and enhanced `for` statements. (Chapter 4 presents the `do...while` and `for` statements and Chapter 6 presents the enhanced `for` statement.) The `while` and `for` statements perform the action (or group of actions) in their bodies zero or more times—if the loop-continuation condition is initially *false*, the action (or group of actions) will *not* execute. The `do...while` statement performs the action (or group of actions) in its body *one or more* times. The words `if`, `else`, `switch`, `while`, `do` and `for` are Java keywords. A complete list of Java keywords appears in Appendix C.

Summary of Control Statements in Java

Java has only three kinds of control structures, which from this point forward we refer to as *control statements*: the *sequence statement*, *selection statements* (three types) and *repetition statements* (three types). Every program is formed by combining as many of these statements as is appropriate for the algorithm the program implements. We can model each control statement as an activity diagram. Like Fig. 3.1, each diagram contains an initial state and a final state that represent a control statement's entry point and exit point, respectively. **Single-entry/single-exit control statements** make it easy to build programs—we simply connect the exit point of one to the entry point of the next. We call this **control-statement stacking**. We'll learn that there's only one other way in which control statements may be connected—**control-statement nesting**—in which one control statement appears *inside* another. Thus, algorithms in Java programs are constructed from only three kinds of control statements, combined in only two ways. This is the essence of simplicity.

3.5 `if` Single-Selection Statement

Programs use selection statements to choose among alternative courses of action. For example, suppose that the passing grade on an exam is 60. The *pseudocode* statement

> *If student's grade is greater than or equal to 60*
>   *Print "Passed"*

determines whether the *condition* "student's grade is greater than or equal to 60" is *true*. If so, "Passed" is printed, and the next pseudocode statement in order is "performed." (Remember, pseudocode is not a real programming language.) If the condition is *false*, the *Print* statement is ignored, and the next pseudocode statement in order is performed. The indentation of the second line of this selection statement is optional, but recommended, because it emphasizes the inherent structure of structured programs.

The preceding pseudocode *If* statement may be written in Java as

```java
if (studentGrade >= 60)
    System.out.println("Passed");
```

The Java code corresponds closely to the pseudocode. This is one of the properties of pseudocode that makes it such a useful program development tool.

UML Activity Diagram for an **if** Statement

Figure 3.2 illustrates the single-selection if statement. This figure contains the most important symbol in an activity diagram—the *diamond*, or **decision symbol**, which indicates that a *decision* is to be made. The workflow continues along a path determined by the symbol's associated **guard conditions**, which can be *true* or *false*. Each transition arrow emerging from a decision symbol has a guard condition (specified in *square brackets* next to the arrow). If a guard condition is *true*, the workflow enters the action state to which the transition arrow points. In Fig. 3.2, if the grade is greater than or equal to 60, the program prints "Passed," then transitions to the activity's final state. If the grade is less than 60, the program immediately transitions to the final state without displaying a message.

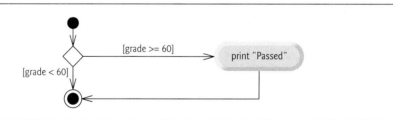

Fig. 3.2 | if single-selection statement UML activity diagram.

The if statement is a single-entry/single-exit control statement. We'll see that the activity diagrams for the remaining control statements also contain initial states, transition arrows, action states that indicate actions to perform, decision symbols (with associated guard conditions) that indicate decisions to be made, and final states.

3.6 if...else Double-Selection Statement

The if single-selection statement performs an indicated action only when the condition is true; otherwise, the action is skipped. The **if...else double-selection statement** allows you to specify an action to perform when the condition is *true* and another action when the condition is *false*. For example, the pseudocode statement

> *If student's grade is greater than or equal to 60*
>   *Print "Passed"*
> *Else*
>   *Print "Failed"*

prints "Passed" if the student's grade is greater than or equal to 60, but prints "Failed" if it's less than 60. In either case, after printing occurs, the next pseudocode statement in sequence is "performed."

The preceding *If…Else* pseudocode statement can be written in Java as

```java
if (grade >= 60)
    System.out.println("Passed");
else
    System.out.println("Failed");
```

The body of the `else` is also indented. Whatever indentation convention you choose should be applied consistently throughout your programs.

Good Programming Practice 3.1
Indent both body statements of an `if…else` statement. Many IDEs do this for you.

Good Programming Practice 3.2
If there are several levels of indentation, each level should be indented the same additional amount of space.

UML Activity Diagram for an `if…else` Statement
Figure 3.3 illustrates the flow of control in the `if…else` statement. Once again, the symbols in the UML activity diagram (besides the initial state, transition arrows and final state) represent action states and decisions.

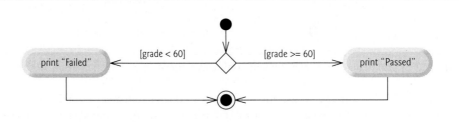

Fig. 3.3 | `if…else` double-selection statement UML activity diagram.

Nested `if…else` Statements
A program can test multiple cases by placing `if…else` statements inside other `if…else` statements to create nested **`if…else` statements**. For example, the following pseudocode represents a nested `if…else` that prints A for exam grades greater than or equal to 90, B for grades 80 to 89, C for grades 70 to 79, D for grades 60 to 69 and F for all other grades:

If student's grade is greater than or equal to 90
    Print "A"
else
        If student's grade is greater than or equal to 80
            Print "B"
        else
                If student's grade is greater than or equal to 70
                    Print "C"
                else
                        If student's grade is greater than or equal to 60
                            Print "D"
                        else
                            Print "F"

This pseudocode may be written in Java as

```java
if (studentGrade >= 90)
    System.out.println("A");
else
    if (studentGrade >= 80)
        System.out.println("B");
    else
        if (studentGrade >= 70)
            System.out.println("C");
        else
            if (studentGrade >= 60)
                System.out.println("D");
            else
                System.out.println("F");
```

Error-Prevention Tip 3.1

In a nested if...else *statement, ensure that you test for all possible cases.*

If variable studentGrade is greater than or equal to 90, the first four conditions in the nested if...else statement will be true, but only the statement in the if part of the first if...else statement will execute. After that statement executes, the else part of the "outermost" if...else statement is skipped. Many programmers prefer to write the preceding nested if...else statement as

```java
if (studentGrade >= 90)
    System.out.println("A");
else if (studentGrade >= 80)
    System.out.println("B");
else if (studentGrade >= 70)
    System.out.println("C");
else if (studentGrade >= 60)
    System.out.println("D");
else
    System.out.println("F");
```

The two forms are identical except for the spacing and indentation, which the compiler ignores. The latter form avoids deep indentation of the code to the right. Such indentation often leaves little room on a line of source code, forcing lines to be split.

*Dangling-**else** Problem*

The Java compiler always associates an else with the immediately preceding if unless told to do otherwise by the placement of braces ({ and }). This behavior can lead to what is referred to as the **dangling-else problem**. For example,

```
if (x > 5)
    if (y > 5)
        System.out.println("x and y are > 5");
else
    System.out.println("x is <= 5");
```

appears to indicate that if x is greater than 5, the nested if statement determines whether y is also greater than 5. If so, the string "x and y are > 5" is output. Otherwise, it appears that if x is not greater than 5, the else part of the if...else outputs the string "x is <= 5". Beware! This nested if...else statement does *not* execute as it appears. The compiler actually interprets the statement as

```
if (x > 5)
    if (y > 5)
        System.out.println("x and y are > 5");
    else
        System.out.println("x is <= 5");
```

in which the body of the first if is a *nested* if...else. The outer if statement tests whether x is greater than 5. If so, execution continues by testing whether y is also greater than 5. If the second condition is *true*, the proper string—"x and y are > 5"—is displayed. However, if the second condition is *false*, the string "x is <= 5" is displayed, even though we know that x is greater than 5. Equally bad, if the outer if statement's condition is false, the inner if...else is skipped and nothing is displayed.

To force the nested if...else statement to execute as it was originally intended, we must write it as follows:

```
if (x > 5)
{
    if (y > 5)
        System.out.println("x and y are > 5");
}
else
    System.out.println("x is <= 5");
```

The braces indicate that the second if is in the body of the first and that the else is associated with the *first* if. Exercises 3.27–3.28 investigate the dangling-else problem further.

Blocks

The if statement normally expects only *one* statement in its body. To include *several* statements in the body of an if (or the body of an else for an if...else statement), enclose the statements in braces. Statements contained in a pair of braces (such as the body of a method) form a **block**. A block can be placed anywhere in a method that a single statement can be placed.

The following example includes a block in the else part of an if...else statement:

```
if (grade >= 60)
   System.out.println("Passed");
else
{
   System.out.println("Failed");
   System.out.println("You must take this course again.");
}
```

In this case, if grade is less than 60, the program executes *both* statements in the body of the else and prints

```
Failed
You must take this course again.
```

Note the braces surrounding the two statements in the else clause. These braces are important. Without the braces, the statement

```
System.out.println("You must take this course again.");
```

would be outside the body of the else part of the if...else statement and would execute *regardless* of whether the grade was less than 60.

Syntax errors (e.g., when one brace in a block is left out of the program) are caught by the compiler. A **logic error** (e.g., when both braces in a block are left out of the program) has its effect at execution time. A **fatal logic error** causes a program to fail and terminate prematurely. A **nonfatal logic error** allows a program to continue executing but causes it to produce incorrect results.

Just as a block can be placed anywhere a single statement can be placed, it's also possible to have an empty statement. Recall from Section 2.8 that the empty statement is represented by placing a semicolon (;) where a statement would normally be.

Common Programming Error 3.1
Placing a semicolon after the condition in an if or if...else statement leads to a logic error in single-selection if statements and a syntax error in double-selection if...else statements (when the if-part contains an actual body statement).

Conditional Operator (?:)

Java provides the **conditional operator (?:)** that can be used in place of an if...else statement. This can make your code shorter and clearer. The conditional operator is Java's only **ternary operator** (i.e., an operator that takes *three* operands). Together, the operands and the ?: symbol form a **conditional expression**. The first operand (to the left of the ?) is a **boolean expression** (i.e., a *condition* that evaluates to a boolean value—**true** or **false**), the second operand (between the ? and :) is the value of the conditional expression if the boolean expression is true and the third operand (to the right of the :) is the value of the conditional expression if the boolean expression evaluates to false. For example, the statement

```
System.out.println(studentGrade >= 60 ? "Passed" : "Failed");
```

prints the value of println's conditional-expression argument. The conditional expression in this statement evaluates to the string "Passed" if the boolean expression student-Grade >= 60 is true and to the string "Failed" if it's false. Thus, this statement with the conditional operator performs essentially the same function as the if...else statement shown earlier in this section. The precedence of the conditional operator is low, so the entire conditional expression is normally placed in parentheses. We'll see that conditional expressions can be used in some situations where if...else statements cannot.

Error-Prevention Tip 3.2

Use expressions of the same type for the second and third operands of the ?: operator to avoid subtle errors.

3.7 while Repetition Statement

A repetition statement allows you to specify that a program should repeat an action while some condition remains *true*. The pseudocode statement

> *While there are more items on my shopping list*
> *Purchase next item and cross it off my list*

describes the repetition during a shopping trip. The condition "there are more items on my shopping list" may be true or false. If it's *true*, then the action "Purchase next item and cross it off my list" is performed. This action will be performed *repeatedly* while the condition remains *true*. The statement(s) contained in the *While* repetition statement constitute its body, which may be a single statement or a block. Eventually, the condition will become *false* (when the shopping list's last item has been purchased and crossed off). At this point, the repetition terminates, and the first statement after the repetition statement executes.

As an example of Java's **while repetition statement**, consider a program segment that finds the first power of 3 larger than 100. Suppose that the int variable product is initialized to 3. After the following while statement executes, product contains the result:

```
while (product <= 100)
   product = 3 * product;
```

Each iteration of the while statement multiplies product by 3, so product takes on the values 9, 27, 81 and 243 successively. When product becomes 243, product <= 100 becomes false. This terminates the repetition, so the final value of product is 243. At this point, program execution continues with the next statement after the while statement.

Common Programming Error 3.2

*Not providing in the body of a while statement an action that eventually causes the condition in the while to become false normally results in a logic error called an **infinite loop** (the loop never terminates).*

UML Activity Diagram for a while Statement
The UML activity diagram in Fig. 3.4 illustrates the flow of control in the preceding while statement. Once again, the symbols in the diagram (besides the initial state, transition arrows, a final state and three notes) represent an action state and a decision. This diagram introduces the UML's **merge symbol**. The UML represents both the merge symbol

and the decision symbol as diamonds. The merge symbol joins two flows of activity into one. In this diagram, the merge symbol joins the transitions from the initial state and from the action state, so they both flow into the decision that determines whether the loop should begin (or continue) executing.

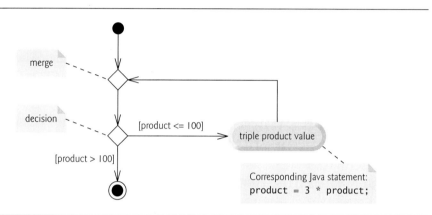

Fig. 3.4 | while repetition statement UML activity diagram.

The decision and merge symbols can be distinguished by the number of "incoming" and "outgoing" transition arrows. A decision symbol has one transition arrow pointing to the diamond and two or more pointing out from it to indicate possible transitions from that point. In addition, each transition arrow pointing out of a decision symbol has a guard condition next to it. A merge symbol has two or more transition arrows pointing to the diamond and only one pointing from the diamond, to indicate multiple activity flows merging to continue the activity. *None* of the transition arrows associated with a merge symbol has a guard condition.

Figure 3.4 clearly shows the repetition of the while statement discussed earlier in this section. The transition arrow emerging from the action state points back to the merge, from which program flow transitions back to the decision that's tested at the beginning of each iteration of the loop. The loop continues to execute until the guard condition product > 100 becomes true. Then the while statement exits (reaches its final state), and control passes to the next statement in sequence in the program.

3.8 Formulating Algorithms: Counter-Controlled Repetition

To illustrate how algorithms are developed, we solve two variations of a problem that averages student grades. Consider the following problem statement:

> *A class of ten students took a quiz. The grades (integers in the range 0–100) for this quiz are available to you. Determine the class average on the quiz.*

The class average is equal to the sum of the grades divided by the number of students. The algorithm for solving this problem on a computer must input each grade, keep track of the total of all grades input, perform the averaging calculation and print the result.

Pseudocode Algorithm with Counter-Controlled Repetition
Let's use pseudocode to list the actions to execute and specify the order in which they should execute. We use **counter-controlled repetition** to input the grades one at a time. This technique uses a variable called a **counter** (or **control variable**) to control the number of times a set of statements will execute. Counter-controlled repetition is often called **definite repetition**, because the number of repetitions is known *before* the loop begins executing. In this example, repetition terminates when the counter exceeds 10. This section presents a fully developed pseudocode algorithm (Fig. 3.5) and a corresponding Java program (Fig. 3.6) that implements the algorithm. In Section 3.9, we demonstrate how to use pseudocode to develop such an algorithm from scratch.

Note the references in the algorithm of Fig. 3.5 to a total and a counter. A **total** is a variable used to accumulate the sum of several values. A counter is a variable used to count—in this case, the grade counter indicates which of the 10 grades is about to be entered by the user. Variables used to store totals are normally initialized to zero before being used in a program.

Software Engineering Observation 3.1

Experience has shown that the most difficult part of solving a problem on a computer is developing the algorithm for the solution. Once a correct algorithm has been specified, producing a working Java program from it is usually straightforward.

1	*Set total to zero*
2	*Set grade counter to one*
3	
4	*While grade counter is less than or equal to ten*
5	*Prompt the user to enter the next grade*
6	*Input the next grade*
7	*Add the grade into the total*
8	*Add one to the grade counter*
9	
10	*Set the class average to the total divided by ten*
11	*Print the class average*

Fig. 3.5 | Pseudocode algorithm that uses counter-controlled repetition to solve the class-average problem.

Implementing Counter-Controlled Repetition
In Fig. 3.6, class ClassAverage's main method (lines 7–31) implements the class-averaging algorithm described by the pseudocode in Fig. 3.5—it allows the user to enter 10 grades, then calculates and displays the average.

```
1    // Fig. 3.6: ClassAverage.java
2    // Solving the class-average problem using counter-controlled repetition.
3    import java.util.Scanner; // program uses class Scanner
4
```

Fig. 3.6 | Solving the class-average problem using counter-controlled repetition. (Part 1 of 2.)

```
5   public class ClassAverage
6   {
7      public static void main(String[] args)
8      {
9         // create Scanner to obtain input from command window
10        Scanner input = new Scanner(System.in);
11
12        // initialization phase
13        int total = 0;   // initialize sum of grades entered by the user
14        int gradeCounter = 1; // initialize # of grade to be entered next
15
16        // processing phase uses counter-controlled repetition
17        while (gradeCounter <= 10) // loop 10 times
18        {
19           System.out.print("Enter grade: "); // prompt
20           int grade = input.nextInt(); // input next grade
21           total = total + grade; // add grade to total
22           gradeCounter = gradeCounter + 1; // increment counter by 1
23        }
24
25        // termination phase
26        int average = total / 10; // integer division yields integer result
27
28        // display total and average of grades
29        System.out.printf("%nTotal of all 10 grades is %d%n", total);
30        System.out.printf("Class average is %d%n", average);
31     }
32  } // end class ClassAverage
```

```
Enter grade: 67
Enter grade: 78
Enter grade: 89
Enter grade: 67
Enter grade: 87
Enter grade: 98
Enter grade: 93
Enter grade: 85
Enter grade: 82
Enter grade: 100

Total of all 10 grades is 846
Class average is 84
```

Fig. 3.6 | Solving the class-average problem using counter-controlled repetition. (Part 2 of 2.)

Local Variables in Method main

Line 10 declares and initializes Scanner object input, which is used to read values entered by the user. Lines 13, 14, 20 and 26 declare local variables total, gradeCounter, grade and average, respectively, to be of type int. Variable grade stores the user input.

These declarations appear in the body of method main. Recall that variables declared in a method body are local variables and can be used only from the line of their declaration to the closing right brace of the method declaration. A local variable's declaration must appear *before* the variable is used in that method. A local variable cannot be accessed outside the method in which it's declared. Variable grade, declared in the body of the while loop, can be used only in that block.

Initialization Phase: Initializing Variables total *and* gradeCounter

The assignments (in lines 13–14) initialize total to 0 and gradeCounter to 1. These initializations occur *before* the variables are used in calculations.

Common Programming Error 3.3

Using the value of a local variable before it's initialized results in a compilation error. All local variables must be initialized before their values are used in expressions.

Error-Prevention Tip 3.3

Initialize each total and counter, either in its declaration or in an assignment statement. Totals are normally initialized to 0. Counters are normally initialized to 0 or 1, depending on how they're used (we'll show examples of when to use 0 and when to use 1).

Processing Phase: Reading 10 Grades from the User

Line 17 indicates that the while statement should continue looping (also called **iterating**) as long as gradeCounter's value is less than or equal to 10. While this condition remains *true*, the while statement repeatedly executes the statements between the braces that delimit its body (lines 18–23).

Line 19 displays the prompt "Enter grade: ". Line 20 reads the grade entered by the user and assigns it to variable grade. Then line 21 adds the new grade entered by the user to the total and assigns the result to total, which replaces its previous value.

Line 22 adds 1 to gradeCounter to indicate that the program has processed a grade and is ready to input the next grade from the user. Incrementing gradeCounter eventually causes it to exceed 10. Then the loop terminates, because its condition (line 17) becomes *false*.

Termination Phase: Calculating and Displaying the Class Average

When the loop terminates, line 26 performs the averaging calculation and assigns its result to the variable average. Line 29 uses System.out's printf method to display the text "Total of all 10 grades is " followed by variable total's value. Line 30 then uses printf to display the text "Class average is " followed by variable average's value. When execution reaches line 31, the program terminates.

Notes on Integer Division and Truncation

The averaging calculation performed by method main produces an integer result. The program's output indicates that the sum of the grade values in the sample execution is 846, which, when divided by 10, should yield the floating-point number 84.6. However, the result of the calculation total / 10 (line 26 of Fig. 3.6) is the integer 84, because total and 10 are both integers. Dividing two integers results in **integer division**—any fractional part of the calculation is **truncated** (i.e., *lost*). In the next section we'll see how to obtain a floating-point result from the averaging calculation.

Common Programming Error 3.4

Assuming that integer division rounds (rather than truncates) can lead to incorrect results. For example, 7 ÷ 4, which yields 1.75 in conventional arithmetic, truncates to 1 in integer arithmetic, rather than rounding to 2.

A Note About Arithmetic Overflow
In Fig. 3.6, line 21

```
total = total + grade; // add grade to total
```

added each `grade` entered by the user to the `total`. Even this simple statement has a *potential* problem—adding the integers could result in a value that's *too large* to store in an `int` variable. This is known as **arithmetic overflow** and causes *undefined behavior*, which can lead to unintended results (`http://en.wikipedia.org/wiki/Integer_overflow#Security_ramifications`). Figure 2.7's `Addition` program had the same issue in line 23, which calculated the sum of two `int` values entered by the user:

```
sum = number1 + number2; // add numbers, then store total in sum
```

The maximum and minimum values that can be stored in an `int` variable are represented by the constants `MIN_VALUE` and `MAX_VALUE`, respectively, which are defined in class `Integer`. There are similar constants for the other integral types and for floating-point types. Each primitive type has a corresponding class type in package `java.lang`. You can see the values of these constants in each class's online documentation. The online documentation for class Integer is located at:

```
http://docs.oracle.com/javase/7/docs/api/java/lang/Integer.html
```

It's considered a good practice to ensure, *before* you perform arithmetic calculations like those in line 21 of Fig. 3.6 and line 23 of Fig. 2.7, that they will *not* overflow. The code for doing this is shown on the CERT website `www.securecoding.cert.org`—just search for guideline "NUM00-J." The code uses the `&&` (logical AND) and `||` (logical OR) operators, which are introduced in Chapter 4. In industrial-strength code, you should perform checks like these for *all* calculations.

A Deeper Look at Receiving User Input
Any time a program receives input from the user, various problems might occur. For example, in line 20 of Fig. 3.6

```
int grade = input.nextInt(); // input next grade
```

we assume that the user will enter an integer grade in the range 0 to 100. However, the person entering a grade could enter an integer less than 0, an integer greater than 100, an integer outside the range of values that can be stored in an `int` variable, a number containing a decimal point or a value containing letters or special symbols that's not even an integer.

To ensure that inputs are valid, industrial-strength programs must test for all possible erroneous cases. A program that inputs grades should **validate** the grades by using **range checking** to ensure that hey are values from 0 to 100. You can then ask the user to reenter any value that's out of range. If a program requires inputs from a specific set of values (e.g., nonsequential product codes), you can ensure that each input matches a value in the set.

3.9 Formulating Algorithms: Sentinel-Controlled Repetition

Let's generalize Section 3.8's class-average problem. Consider the following problem:

> *Develop a class-averaging program that processes grades for an arbitrary number of students each time it's run.*

In the previous class-average example, the problem statement specified the number of students, so the number of grades (10) was known in advance. In this example, no indication is given of how many grades the user will enter during the program's execution. The program must process an arbitrary number of grades. How can it determine when to stop the input of grades? How will it know when to calculate and print the class average?

One way to solve this problem is to use a special value called a **sentinel value** (also called a **signal value**, a **dummy value** or a **flag value**) to indicate "end of data entry." The user enters grades until all legitimate grades have been entered. The user then types the sentinel value to indicate that no more grades will be entered. **Sentinel-controlled repetition** is often called **indefinite repetition** because the number of repetitions is *not* known before the loop begins executing.

Clearly, a sentinel value must be chosen that cannot be confused with an acceptable input value. Grades on a quiz are nonnegative integers, so -1 is an acceptable sentinel value for this problem. Thus, a run of the class-average program might process a stream of inputs such as 95, 96, 75, 74, 89 and -1. The program would then compute and print the class average for the grades 95, 96, 75, 74 and 89; since -1 is the sentinel value, it should *not* enter into the averaging calculation.

Developing the Pseudocode Algorithm with Top-Down, Stepwise Refinement: The Top and First Refinement

We approach this class-average program with a technique called **top-down, stepwise refinement**, which is essential to the development of well-structured programs. We begin with a pseudocode representation of the **top**—a single statement that conveys the overall function of the program:

> *Determine the class average for the quiz*

The top is, in effect, a *complete* representation of a program. Unfortunately, the top rarely conveys sufficient detail from which to write a Java program. So we now begin the refinement process. We divide the top into a series of smaller tasks and list these in the order in which they'll be performed. This results in the following **first refinement**:

> *Initialize variables*
> *Input, sum and count the quiz grades*
> *Calculate and print the class average*

This refinement uses only the *sequence structure*—the steps listed should execute in order, one after the other.

Software Engineering Observation 3.2

Each refinement, as well as the top itself, is a complete specification of the algorithm—only the level of detail varies.

Software Engineering Observation 3.3

Many programs can be divided logically into three phases: an initialization phase *that initializes the variables; a* processing phase *that inputs data values and adjusts program variables accordingly; and a* termination phase *that calculates and outputs the final results.*

Proceeding to the Second Refinement

The preceding Software Engineering Observation is often all you need for the first refinement in the top-down process. To proceed to the next level of refinement—that is, the **second refinement**—we commit to specific variables. In this example, we need a running total of the numbers, a count of how many numbers have been processed, a variable to receive the value of each grade as it's input by the user and a variable to hold the calculated average. The pseudocode statement

> *Initialize variables*

can be refined as follows:

> *Initialize total to zero*
> *Initialize counter to zero*

Only the variables *total* and *counter* need to be initialized before they're used. The variables *average* and *grade* (for the calculated average and the user input, respectively) need not be initialized, because their values will be replaced as they're calculated or input.

The pseudocode statement

> *Input, sum and count the quiz grades*

requires *repetition* to successively input each grade. We do not know in advance how many grades will be entered, so we'll use sentinel-controlled repetition. The user enters grades one at a time. After entering the last grade, the user enters the sentinel value. The program tests for the sentinel value after each grade is input and terminates the loop when the user enters the sentinel value. The second refinement of the preceding pseudocode statement is then

> *Prompt the user to enter the first grade*
> *Input the first grade (possibly the sentinel)*
>
> *While the user has not yet entered the sentinel*
>   *Add this grade into the running total*
>   *Add one to the grade counter*
>   *Prompt the user to enter the next grade*
>   *Input the next grade (possibly the sentinel)*

In pseudocode, we do *not* use braces around the statements that form the body of the *While* structure. We simply indent the statements under the *While* to show that they belong to the *While*. Again, pseudocode is only an informal program development aid.

The pseudocode statement

> *Calculate and print the class average*

can be refined as follows:

> *If the counter is not equal to zero*
>   *Set the average to the total divided by the counter*
>   *Print the average*
> *else*
>   *Print "No grades were entered"*

We're careful here to test for the possibility of *division by zero*—a *logic error* that, if undetected, would cause the program to fail or produce invalid output. The complete second refinement of the pseudocode for the class-average problem is shown in Fig. 3.7.

Error-Prevention Tip 3.4

When performing division (/) or remainder (%) calculations in which the right operand could be zero, test for this and handle it (e.g., display an error message) rather than allowing the error to occur.

---

1   *Initialize total to zero*
2   *Initialize counter to zero*
3
4   *Prompt the user to enter the first grade*
5   *Input the first grade (possibly the sentinel)*
6
7   *While the user has not yet entered the sentinel*
8   *Add this grade into the running total*
9   *Add one to the grade counter*
10   *Prompt the user to enter the next grade*
11   *Input the next grade (possibly the sentinel)*
12
13   *If the counter is not equal to zero*
14   *Set the average to the total divided by the counter*
15   *Print the average*
16   *else*
17   *Print "No grades were entered"*

Fig. 3.7 | Class-average pseudocode algorithm with sentinel-controlled repetition.

In Figs. 3.5 and 3.7, we included blank lines and indentation in the pseudocode to make it more readable. The blank lines separate the algorithms into their phases and set off control statements; the indentation emphasizes the bodies of the control statements.

The pseudocode algorithm in Fig. 3.7 solves the more general class-average problem. This algorithm was developed after two refinements. Sometimes more are needed.

Software Engineering Observation 3.4

Terminate the top-down, stepwise refinement process when you've specified the pseudocode algorithm in sufficient detail for you to convert the pseudocode to Java. Normally, implementing the Java program is then straightforward.

Software Engineering Observation 3.5

Some programmers do not use program development tools like pseudocode. They feel that their ultimate goal is to solve the problem on a computer and that writing pseudocode merely delays the production of final outputs. Although this may work for simple and familiar problems, it can lead to serious errors and delays in large, complex projects.

Implementing Sentinel-Controlled Repetition

In Fig. 3.8, method `main` (lines 7–46) implements the pseudocode algorithm of Fig. 3.7. Although each grade is an `int`, the averaging calculation is likely to produce a number with a *decimal point*—in other words, a real (floating-point) number. The type `int` cannot represent such a number, so this class uses type `double` to do so. You'll also see that control statements may be *stacked* on top of one another (in sequence). The `while` statement (lines 22–30) is followed in sequence by an `if...else` statement (lines 34–45). Much of the code in this program is identical to that in Fig. 3.6, so we concentrate on the new concepts.

```java
1   // Fig. 3.8: ClassAverage.java
2   // Solving the class-average problem using sentinel-controlled repetition.
3   import java.util.Scanner; // program uses class Scanner
4
5   public class ClassAverage
6   {
7      public static void main(String[] args)
8      {
9         // create Scanner to obtain input from command window
10        Scanner input = new Scanner(System.in);
11
12        // initialization phase
13        int total = 0; // initialize sum of grades
14        int gradeCounter = 0; // initialize # of grades entered so far
15
16        // processing phase
17        // prompt for input and read grade from user
18        System.out.print("Enter grade or -1 to quit: ");
19        int grade = input.nextInt();
20
21        // loop until sentinel value read from user
22        while (grade != -1)
23        {
24           total = total + grade; // add grade to total
25           gradeCounter = gradeCounter + 1; // increment counter
26
27           // prompt for input and read next grade from user
28           System.out.print("Enter grade or -1 to quit: ");
29           grade = input.nextInt();
30        }
31
32        // termination phase
33        // if user entered at least one grade...
34        if (gradeCounter != 0)
35        {
36           // use number with decimal point to calculate average of grades
37           double average = (double) total / gradeCounter;
38
39           // display total and average (with two digits of precision)
40           System.out.printf("%nTotal of the %d grades entered is %d%n",
41              gradeCounter, total);
```

Fig. 3.8 | Solving the class-average problem using sentinel-controlled repetition. (Part 1 of 2.)

```
42                  System.out.printf("Class average is %.2f%n", average);
43          }
44          else // no grades were entered, so output appropriate message
45              System.out.println("No grades were entered");
46      }
47  } // end class ClassAverage
```

```
Enter grade or -1 to quit: 97
Enter grade or -1 to quit: 88
Enter grade or -1 to quit: 72
Enter grade or -1 to quit: -1

Total of the 3 grades entered is 257
Class average is 85.67
```

Fig. 3.8 | Solving the class-average problem using sentinel-controlled repetition. (Part 2 of 2.)

Floating-Point Number Precision and Memory Requirements

Most averages are not integers. So, this example calculates the class average as a **floating-point number**—a number with a *decimal point*, such as 43.95, 0.0, –129.8873. Java provides two primitive types for storing floating-point numbers in memory—float and double. Variables of type **float** represent **single-precision floating-point numbers** and can hold up to *seven significant digits*. Variables of type **double** represent **double-precision floating-point numbers**. These require *twice* as much memory as float variables and can hold up to *15 significant digits*—about *double* the precision of float variables.

Most programmers represent floating-point numbers with type double. In fact, Java treats all floating-point numbers you type in a program's source code (such as 7.33 and 0.0975) as double values by default. Such values in the source code are known as **floating-point literals**. See Appendix D, Primitive Types, for the precise ranges of values for floats and doubles.

Program Logic for Sentinel-Controlled Repetition vs. Counter-Controlled Repetition

Line 37 declares double variable average, which allows us to store the class average as a floating-point number. Line 14 initializes gradeCounter to 0, because no grades have been entered yet. Remember that this program uses *sentinel-controlled repetition* to input the grades. To keep an accurate record of the number of grades entered, the program increments gradeCounter only when the user enters a valid grade.

Compare the program logic for sentinel-controlled repetition in this application with that for counter-controlled repetition in Fig. 3.6. In counter-controlled repetition, each iteration of the while statement (lines 17–23 of Fig. 3.6) reads a value from the user, for the specified number of iterations. In sentinel-controlled repetition, the program reads the first value (lines 18–19 of Fig. 3.8) before reaching the while. This value determines whether the program's flow of control should enter the body of the while. If the condition of the while is false, the user entered the sentinel value, so the body of the while does not execute (i.e., no grades were entered). If, on the other hand, the condition is *true*, the body begins execution, and the loop adds the grade value to the total and increments the gradeCounter (lines 24–25). Then lines 28–29 in the loop body input the next value from the user. Next, program control reaches the closing right brace of the loop body at line 30, so execution continues with the test of the `while`'s condition (line 22). The condition uses the most recent `grade` input by the user to determine whether the loop body should execute again. The value of variable `grade` is always input from the user immediately before the program tests the `while` condition. This allows the program to determine whether the value just input is the sentinel value *before* the program processes that value (i.e., adds it to the `total`). If the sentinel value is input, the loop terminates, and the program does not add –1 to the `total`.

Good Programming Practice 3.3
In a sentinel-controlled loop, prompts should remind the user of the sentinel.

After the loop terminates, the `if...else` statement at lines 34–45 executes. The condition at line 34 determines whether any grades were input. If none were input, the `else` part (lines 44–45) of the `if...else` statement executes and displays the message "No grades were entered" and the method returns control to the calling method.

Braces in a `while` statement
Notice the `while` statement's *block* in Fig. 3.8 (lines 23–30). Without the braces, the loop would consider its body to be only the first statement, which adds the `grade` to the `total`. The last three statements in the block would fall outside the loop body, causing the computer to interpret the code incorrectly as follows:

```
while (grade != -1)
    total = total + grade; // add grade to total
gradeCounter = gradeCounter + 1; // increment counter

// prompt for input and read next grade from user
System.out.print("Enter grade or -1 to quit: ");
grade = input.nextInt();
```

The preceding code would cause an *infinite loop* in the program if the user did not input the sentinel -1 at line 19 (before the `while` statement).

Common Programming Error 3.5
Omitting the braces that delimit a block can lead to logic errors, such as infinite loops. To prevent this problem, some programmers enclose the body of every control statement in braces, even if the body contains only a single statement.

Explicitly and Implicitly Converting Between Primitive Types
If at least one grade was entered, line 37 of Fig. 3.8 calculates the average of the grades. Recall from Fig. 3.6 that integer division yields an integer result. Even though variable `average` is declared as a `double`, if we had written the averaging calculation as

```
double average = total / gradeCounter;
```

it would lose the fractional part of the quotient *before* the result of the division is assigned to `average`. This occurs because `total` and `gradeCounter` are *both* integers, and integer division yields an integer result.

Most averages are not whole numbers (e.g., 0, –22 and 1024). For this reason, we calculate the class average in this example as a floating-point number. To perform a floating-point calculation with integer values, we must *temporarily* treat these values as floating-point numbers for use in the calculation. Java provides the **unary cast operator** to accomplish this task. Line 37 of Fig. 3.8 uses the **(double)** cast operator—a unary operator—to create a *temporary* floating-point copy of its operand total (which appears to the right of the operator). Using a cast operator in this manner is called **explicit conversion** or **type casting**. The value stored in total is still an integer.

The calculation now consists of a floating-point value (the temporary double copy of total) divided by the integer gradeCounter. Java can evaluate only arithmetic expressions in which the operands' types are *identical*. To ensure this, Java performs an operation called **promotion** (or **implicit conversion**) on selected operands. For example, in an expression containing int and double values, the int values are promoted to double values for use in the expression. In this example, the value of gradeCounter is promoted to type double, then floating-point division is performed and the result of the calculation is assigned to average. As long as the (double) cast operator is applied to *any* variable in the calculation, the calculation will yield a double result. Later in this chapter, we discuss all the primitive types. You'll learn more about the promotion rules in Section 5.7.

 Common Programming Error 3.6

A cast operator can be used to convert between primitive numeric types, such as int and double. Casting to the wrong type may cause compilation errors.

A cast operator is formed by placing parentheses around any type's name. The operator is a **unary operator** (i.e., an operator that takes only one operand). Java also supports unary versions of the plus (+) and minus (−) operators, so you can write expressions like −7 or +5. Cast operators associate from *right to left* and have the same precedence as other unary operators, such as unary + and unary −. This precedence is one level higher than that of the **multiplicative operators** *, / and %. (See the operator precedence chart in Appendix A.) We indicate the cast operator with the notation (*type*) in our precedence charts, to indicate that any type name can be used to form a cast operator.

Line 42 displays the class average. In this example, we display the class average *rounded* to the nearest hundredth. The format specifier %.2f in printf's format control string indicates that variable average's value should be displayed with two digits of precision to the right of the decimal point—indicated by .2 in the format specifier. The three grades entered during the sample execution (Fig. 3.8) total 257, which yields the average 85.666666.... Method printf uses the precision in the format specifier to round the value to the specified number of digits. In this program, the average is rounded to the hundredths position and is displayed as 85.67.

Floating-Point Number Precision
Floating-point numbers are not always 100% precise, but they have numerous applications. For example, when we speak of a "normal" body temperature of 98.6, we do not need to be precise to a large number of digits. When we read the temperature on a thermometer as 98.6, it may actually be 98.5999473210643. Calling this number simply 98.6 is fine for most applications involving body temperatures.

Floating-point numbers often arise as a result of division, such as in this example's class-average calculation. In conventional arithmetic, when we divide 10 by 3, the result is 3.3333333..., with the sequence of 3s repeating infinitely. The computer allocates only a fixed amount of space to hold such a value, so clearly the stored floating-point value can be only an approximation.

Owing to the imprecise nature of floating-point numbers, type double is preferred over type float, because double variables can represent floating-point numbers more accurately. For this reason, we primarily use type double throughout the book. In some applications, the precision of float and double variables will be inadequate. For precise floating-point numbers (such as those required by monetary calculations), Java provides class BigDecimal (package java.math), which we'll discuss in Chapter 8.

Common Programming Error 3.7
Using floating-point numbers in a manner that assumes they're represented precisely can lead to incorrect results.

3.10 Formulating Algorithms: Nested Control Statements

For the next example, we once again formulate an algorithm by using pseudocode and top-down, stepwise refinement, and write a corresponding Java program. We've seen that control statements can be stacked on top of one another (in sequence). In this case study, we examine the only other structured way control statements can be connected—namely, by **nesting** one control statement within another.

Consider the following problem statement:

A college offers a course that prepares students for the state licensing exam for real-estate brokers. Last year, ten of the students who completed this course took the exam. The college wants to know how well its students did on the exam. You've been asked to write a program to summarize the results. You've been given a list of these 10 students. Next to each name is written a 1 if the student passed the exam or a 2 if the student failed.

Your program should analyze the results of the exam as follows:

1. *Input each test result (i.e., a 1 or a 2). Display the message "Enter result" on the screen each time the program requests another test result.*

2. *Count the number of test results of each type.*

3. *Display a summary of the test results, indicating the number of students who passed and the number who failed.*

4. *If more than eight students passed the exam, print "Bonus to instructor!"*

After reading the problem statement carefully, we make the following observations:

1. The program must process test results for 10 students. A counter-controlled loop can be used, because the number of test results is known in advance.

2. Each test result has a numeric value—either a 1 or a 2. Each time it reads a test result, the program must determine whether it's a 1 or a 2. We test for a 1 in our algorithm. If the number is not a 1, we assume that it's a 2. (Exercise 3.24 considers the consequences of this assumption.)

3. Two counters are used to keep track of the exam results—one to count the number of students who passed the exam and one to count the number who failed.

4. After the program has processed all the results, it must decide whether more than eight students passed the exam.

Let's proceed with top-down, stepwise refinement. We begin with a pseudocode representation of the top:

Analyze exam results and decide whether a bonus should be paid

Once again, the top is a *complete* representation of the program, but several refinements are likely to be needed before the pseudocode can evolve naturally into a Java program.

Our first refinement is

Initialize variables
Input the 10 exam results, and count passes and failures
Print a summary of the exam results and decide whether a bonus should be paid

Here, too, even though we have a *complete* representation of the entire program, further refinement is necessary. We now commit to specific variables. Counters are needed to record the passes and failures, a counter will be used to control the looping process and a variable is needed to store the user input. The variable in which the user input will be stored is *not* initialized at the start of the algorithm, because its value is read from the user during each iteration of the loop.

The pseudocode statement

Initialize variables

can be refined as follows:

Initialize passes to zero
Initialize failures to zero
Initialize student counter to one

Notice that only the counters are initialized at the start of the algorithm.

The pseudocode statement

Input the 10 exam results, and count passes and failures

requires a loop that successively inputs the result of each exam. We know in advance that there are precisely 10 exam results, so counter-controlled looping is appropriate. Inside the loop (i.e., *nested* within the loop), a double-selection structure will determine whether each exam result is a pass or a failure and will increment the appropriate counter. The refinement of the preceding pseudocode statement is then

While student counter is less than or equal to 10
*   Prompt the user to enter the next exam result*
*   Input the next exam result*

*   If the student passed*
*   Add one to passes*
*   Else*
*   Add one to failures*

*   Add one to student counter*

We use blank lines to isolate the *If…Else* control structure, which improves readability.

The pseudocode statement

Print a summary of the exam results and decide whether a bonus should be paid

can be refined as follows:

Print the number of passes
Print the number of failures

If more than eight students passed
    Print "Bonus to instructor!"

Complete Second Refinement of Pseudocode and Conversion to Class `Analysis`

The complete second refinement appears in Fig. 3.9. Notice that blank lines are also used to set off the *While* structure for program readability. This pseudocode is now sufficiently refined for conversion to Java.

1	*Initialize passes to zero*
2	*Initialize failures to zero*
3	*Initialize student counter to one*
4	
5	*While student counter is less than or equal to 10*
6	*Prompt the user to enter the next exam result*
7	*Input the next exam result*
8	
9	*If the student passed*
10	*Add one to passes*
11	*Else*
12	*Add one to failures*
13	
14	*Add one to student counter*
15	
16	*Print the number of passes*
17	*Print the number of failures*
18	
19	*If more than eight students passed*
20	*Print "Bonus to instructor!"*

Fig. 3.9 | Pseudocode for examination-results problem.

The Java class that implements the pseudocode algorithm and two sample executions are shown in Fig. 3.10. Lines 13, 14, 15 and 22 of `main` declare the variables that are used to process the examination results.

Error-Prevention Tip 3.5

Initializing local variables when they're declared helps you avoid compilation errors that might arise from attempts to use uninitialized variables. While Java does not require that local-variable initializations be incorporated into declarations, it does require that each local variable be given a value before its value is used in an expression.

The while statement (lines 18–32) loops 10 times. During each iteration, the loop inputs and processes one exam result. Notice that the if...else statement (lines 25–28) for processing each result is *nested* in the while statement. If the result is 1, the if...else statement increments passes; otherwise, it assumes the result is 2 and increments failures. Line 31 increments studentCounter before the loop condition is tested again at line 18. After 10 values have been input, the loop terminates and line 35 displays the number of passes and failures. The if statement at lines 38–39 determines whether more than eight students passed the exam and, if so, outputs the message "Bonus to instructor!".

```java
1   // Fig. 3.10: Analysis.java
2   // Analysis of examination results using nested control statements.
3   import java.util.Scanner; // class uses class Scanner
4
5   public class Analysis
6   {
7      public static void main(String[] args)
8      {
9         // create Scanner to obtain input from command window
10        Scanner input = new Scanner(System.in);
11
12        // initializing variables in declarations
13        int passes = 0;
14        int failures = 0;
15        int studentCounter = 1;
16
17        // process 10 students using counter-controlled loop
18        while (studentCounter <= 10)
19        {
20           // prompt user for input and obtain value from user
21           System.out.print("Enter result (1 = pass, 2 = fail): ");
22           int result = input.nextInt();
23
24           // if...else is nested in the while statement
25           if (result == 1)
26              passes = passes + 1;
27           else
28              failures = failures + 1;
29
30           // increment studentCounter so loop eventually terminates
31           studentCounter = studentCounter + 1;
32        }
33
34        // termination phase; prepare and display results
35        System.out.printf("Passed: %d%nFailed: %d%n", passes, failures);
36
37        // determine whether more than 8 students passed
38        if (passes > 8)
39           System.out.println("Bonus to instructor!");
40     }
41  } // end class Analysis
```

Fig. 3.10 | Analysis of examination results using nested control statements. (Part 1 of 2.)

```
Enter result (1 = pass, 2 = fail): 1
Enter result (1 = pass, 2 = fail): 2
Enter result (1 = pass, 2 = fail): 1
Enter result (1 = pass, 2 = fail): 1
Enter result (1 = pass, 2 = fail): 1
Enter result (1 = pass, 2 = fail): 1
Enter result (1 = pass, 2 = fail): 1
Enter result (1 = pass, 2 = fail): 1
Enter result (1 = pass, 2 = fail): 1
Enter result (1 = pass, 2 = fail): 1
Passed: 9
Failed: 1
Bonus to instructor!
```

```
Enter result (1 = pass, 2 = fail): 1
Enter result (1 = pass, 2 = fail): 2
Enter result (1 = pass, 2 = fail): 1
Enter result (1 = pass, 2 = fail): 2
Enter result (1 = pass, 2 = fail): 1
Enter result (1 = pass, 2 = fail): 2
Enter result (1 = pass, 2 = fail): 2
Enter result (1 = pass, 2 = fail): 1
Enter result (1 = pass, 2 = fail): 1
Enter result (1 = pass, 2 = fail): 1
Passed: 6
Failed: 4
```

Fig. 3.10 | Analysis of examination results using nested control statements. (Part 2 of 2.)

Figure 3.10 shows the input and output from two sample excutions of the program. During the first, the condition at line 38 of method main is true—more than eight students passed the exam, so the program outputs a message to bonus the instructor.

3.11 Compound Assignment Operators

The **compound assignment operators** abbreviate assignment expressions. Statements like

  variable = variable   operator   expression;

where *operator* is one of the binary operators +, -, *, / or % (or others we discuss later in the text) can be written in the form

  variable   operator= expression;

For example, you can abbreviate the statement

  c = c + 3;

with the **addition compound assignment operator, +=,** as

  c += 3;

The += operator adds the value of the expression on its right to the value of the variable on its left and stores the result in the variable on the left of the operator. Thus, the assignment expression c += 3 adds 3 to c. Figure 3.11 shows the arithmetic compound assignment operators, sample expressions using the operators and explanations of what the operators do.

Assignment operator	Sample expression	Explanation	Assigns
Assume: int c = 3, d = 5, e = 4, f = 6, g = 12;			
+=	c += 7	c = c + 7	10 to c
-=	d -= 4	d = d - 4	1 to d
*=	e *= 5	e = e * 5	20 to e
/=	f /= 3	f = f / 3	2 to f
%=	g %= 9	g = g % 9	3 to g

Fig. 3.11 | Arithmetic compound assignment operators.

3.12 Increment and Decrement Operators

Java provides two unary operators (summarized in Fig. 3.12) for adding 1 to or subtracting 1 from the value of a numeric variable. These are the unary **increment operator**, ++, and the unary **decrement operator**, --. A program can increment by 1 the value of a variable called c using the increment operator, ++, rather than the expression c = c + 1 or c += 1. An increment or decrement operator that's prefixed to (placed before) a variable is referred to as the **prefix increment** or **prefix decrement operator**, respectively. An increment or decrement operator that's postfixed to (placed after) a variable is referred to as the **postfix increment** or **postfix decrement operator**, respectively.

Operator	Operator name	Sample expression	Explanation
++	prefix increment	++a	Increment a by 1, then use the new value of a in the expression in which a resides.
++	postfix increment	a++	Use the current value of a in the expression in which a resides, then increment a by 1.
--	prefix decrement	--b	Decrement b by 1, then use the new value of b in the expression in which b resides.
--	postfix decrement	b--	Use the current value of b in the expression in which b resides, then decrement b by 1.

Fig. 3.12 | Increment and decrement operators.

Using the prefix increment (or decrement) operator to add 1 to (or subtract 1 from) a variable is known as **preincrementing** (or **predecrementing**). This causes the variable to be incremented (decremented) by 1; then the new value of the variable is used in the expression in which it appears. Using the postfix increment (or decrement) operator to add 1 to (or subtract 1 from) a variable is known as **postincrementing** (or **postdecrementing**).

This causes the current value of the variable to be used in the expression in which it appears; then the variable's value is incremented (decremented) by 1.

Good Programming Practice 3.4

Unlike binary operators, the unary increment and decrement operators should be placed next to their operands, with no intervening spaces.

Difference Between Prefix Increment and Postfix Increment Operators

Figure 3.13 demonstrates the difference between the prefix increment and postfix increment versions of the ++ increment operator. The decrement operator (--) works similarly.

Line 9 initializes the variable c to 5, and line 10 outputs c's initial value. Line 11 outputs the value of the expression c++. This expression postincrements the variable c, so c's *original* value (5) is output, then c's value is incremented (to 6). Thus, line 11 outputs c's initial value (5) again. Line 12 outputs c's new value (6) to prove that the variable's value was indeed incremented in line 11.

Line 17 resets c's value to 5, and line 18 outputs c's value. Line 19 outputs the value of the expression ++c. This expression preincrements c, so its value is incremented; then the *new* value (6) is output. Line 20 outputs c's value again to show that the value of c is still 6 after line 19 executes.

```java
1   // Fig. 3.13: Increment.java
2   // Prefix increment and postfix increment operators.
3
4   public class Increment
5   {
6      public static void main(String[] args)
7      {
8         // demonstrate postfix increment operator
9         int c = 5;
10        System.out.printf("c before postincrement: %d%n", c); // prints 5
11        System.out.printf("   postincrementing c: %d%n", c++); // prints 5
12        System.out.printf(" c after postincrement: %d%n", c); // prints 6
13
14        System.out.println(); // skip a line
15
16        // demonstrate prefix increment operator
17        c = 5;
18        System.out.printf(" c before preincrement: %d%n", c); // prints 5
19        System.out.printf("    preincrementing c: %d%n", ++c); // prints 6
20        System.out.printf("  c after preincrement: %d%n", c); // prints 6
21     }
22  } // end class Increment
```

```
c before postincrement: 5
   postincrementing c: 5
 c after postincrement: 6

 c before preincrement: 5
    preincrementing c: 6
  c after preincrement: 6
```

Fig. 3.13 | Prefix increment and postfix increment operators.

Simplifying Statements with the Arithmetic Compound Assignment, Increment and Decrement Operators

The arithmetic compound assignment operators and the increment and decrement operators can be used to simplify program statements. For example, the three assignment statements in Fig. 3.10 (lines 26, 28 and 31)

```
passes = passes + 1;
failures = failures + 1;
studentCounter = studentCounter + 1;
```

can be written more concisely with compound assignment operators as

```
passes += 1;
failures += 1;
studentCounter += 1;
```

with prefix increment operators as

```
++passes;
++failures;
++studentCounter;
```

or with postfix increment operators as

```
passes++;
failures++;
studentCounter++;
```

When incrementing or decrementing a variable in a statement by itself, the prefix increment and postfix increment forms have the *same* effect, and the prefix decrement and postfix decrement forms have the *same* effect. It's only when a variable appears in the context of a larger expression that preincrementing and postincrementing the variable have different effects (and similarly for predecrementing and postdecrementing).

Common Programming Error 3.8

Attempting to use the increment or decrement operator on an expression other than one to which a value can be assigned is a syntax error. For example, writing ++(x + 1) is a syntax error, because (x + 1) is not a variable.

Operator Precedence and Associativity

Figure 3.14 shows the precedence and associativity of the operators we've introduced. They're shown from top to bottom in decreasing order of precedence. The second column describes the associativity of the operators at each level of precedence. The conditional operator (?:); the unary operators increment (++), decrement (--), plus (+) and minus (-); the cast operators and the assignment operators =, +=, -=, *=, /= and %= associate from *right to left*. All the other operators in the operator precedence chart in Fig. 3.14 associate from left to right. The third column lists the type of each group of operators.

Good Programming Practice 3.5

Refer to Appendix A, Operator Precedence Chart, when writing expressions containing many operators. Confirm that the operators in the expression are performed in the order you expect. If you're uncertain about the evaluation order, break the expression into smaller statements or use parentheses to force the evaluation order, exactly as you'd do in an algebraic expression. Some operators such as assignment (=) associate right to left rather than left to right.

Operators					Associativity	Type
++	--				right to left	unary postfix
++	--	+	-	(*type*)	right to left	unary prefix
*	/	%			left to right	multiplicative
+	-				left to right	additive
<	<=	>	>=		left to right	relational
==	!=				left to right	equality
?:					right to left	conditional
=	+=	-=	*=	/= %=	right to left	assignment

Fig. 3.14 | Precedence and associativity of the operators discussed so far.

3.13 Primitive Types

The table in Appendix D lists the eight primitive types in Java. Like its predecessor languages C and C++, Java requires all variables to have a type. For this reason, Java is referred to as a **strongly typed language**.

In C and C++, programmers frequently have to write separate versions of programs to support different computer platforms, because the primitive types are not guaranteed to be identical from computer to computer. For example, an `int` on one machine might be represented by 16 bits (2 bytes) of memory, on a second machine by 32 bits (4 bytes), and on another machine by 64 bits (8 bytes). In Java, `int` values are always 32 bits (4 bytes).

Portability Tip 3.1

The primitive types in Java are portable across all computer platforms that support Java.

Each type in Appendix D is listed with its size in bits (there are eight bits to a byte) and its range of values. Because the designers of Java want to ensure portability, they use internationally recognized standards for character formats (Unicode; for more information, visit www.unicode.org) and floating-point numbers (IEEE 754; for more information, visit grouper.ieee.org/groups/754/).

3.14 (Optional) GUI and Graphics Case Study: Creating Simple Drawings

An appealing feature of Java is its graphics support, which enables you to visually enhance your applications. We now introduce one of Java's graphical capabilities—drawing lines. It also covers the basics of creating a window to display a drawing on the computer screen.

Java's Coordinate System

To draw in Java, you must understand Java's **coordinate system** (Fig. 3.15), a scheme for identifying points on the screen. By default, the upper-left corner of a GUI component has the coordinates (0, 0). A coordinate pair is composed of an *x*-coordinate (the **horizontal coordinate**) and a *y*-coordinate (the **vertical coordinate**). The *x*-coordinate is the horizontal location moving from *left to right*. The *y*-coordinate is the vertical location moving from *top to bottom*. The **x-axis** describes every horizontal coordinate, and the **y-axis** every vertical coordinate. Coordinates indicate where graphics should be displayed on a screen. Coordinate units are measured in **pixels**. The term pixel stands for "picture element." A pixel is a display monitor's smallest unit of resolution.

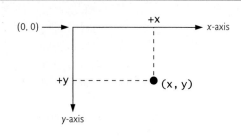

Fig. 3.15 | Java coordinate system. Units are measured in pixels.

First Drawing Application

Our first drawing application simply draws two lines. Class DrawPanel (Fig. 3.16) performs the actual drawing, while class DrawPanelTest (Fig. 3.17) creates a window to display the drawing. In class DrawPanel, the import statements in lines 3–4 allow us to use class **Graphics** (from package java.awt), which provides various methods for drawing text and shapes onto the screen, and class **JPanel** (from package javax.swing), which provides an area on which we can draw.

```
 1   // Fig. 3.16: DrawPanel.java
 2   // Using drawLine to connect the corners of a panel.
 3   import java.awt.Graphics;
 4   import javax.swing.JPanel;
 5
 6   public class DrawPanel extends JPanel
 7   {
 8      // draws an X from the corners of the panel
 9      public void paintComponent(Graphics g)
10      {
11         // call paintComponent to ensure the panel displays correctly
12         super.paintComponent(g);
13
14         int width = getWidth(); // total width
15         int height = getHeight(); // total height
16
17         // draw a line from the upper-left to the lower-right
18         g.drawLine(0, 0, width, height);
19
20         // draw a line from the lower-left to the upper-right
21         g.drawLine(0, height, width, 0);
22      }
23   } // end class DrawPanel
```

Fig. 3.16 | Using drawLine to connect the corners of a panel.

```
1   // Fig. 3.17: DrawPanelTest.java
2   // Creating JFrame to display DrawPanel.
3   import javax.swing.JFrame;
4
5   public class DrawPanelTest
6   {
7      public static void main(String[] args)
8      {
9         // create a panel that contains our drawing
10        DrawPanel panel = new DrawPanel();
11
12        // create a new frame to hold the panel
13        JFrame application = new JFrame();
14
15        // set the frame to exit when it is closed
16        application.setDefaultCloseOperation(JFrame.EXIT_ON_CLOSE);
17
18        application.add(panel); // add the panel to the frame
19        application.setSize(250, 250); // set the size of the frame
20        application.setVisible(true); // make the frame visible
21     }
22  } // end class DrawPanelTest
```

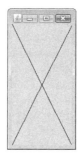

Fig. 3.17 | Creating JFrame to display DrawPanel.

Line 6 uses the keyword **extends** to indicate that class DrawPanel is an enhanced type of JPanel. The keyword extends represents a so-called *inheritance* relationship in which our new class DrawPanel begins with the existing members (data and methods) from class JPanel. The class from which DrawPanel **inherits**, JPanel, appears to the right of keyword extends. In this inheritance relationship, JPanel is called the **superclass** and DrawPanel is called the **subclass**. This results in a DrawPanel class that has the attributes (data) and behaviors (methods) of class JPanel as well as the new features we're adding in our Draw-Panel class declaration—specifically, the ability to draw two lines along the diagonals of the panel. Inheritance is explained in detail in Chapter 9. For now, you should mimic our DrawPanel class when creating your own graphics programs.

Method *paintComponent*
Every JPanel, including our DrawPanel, has a **paintComponent** method (lines 9–22), which the system automatically calls every time it needs to display the DrawPanel. Method paintComponent must be declared as shown in line 9—otherwise, the system will not call

it. This method is called when a JPanel is first displayed on the screen, when it's *covered* then *uncovered* by a window on the screen, and when the window in which it appears is *resized*. Method paintComponent requires one argument, a Graphics object, that's provided by the system when it calls paintComponent. This Graphics object is used to draw lines, rectangles, ovals and other graphics.

The first statement in every paintComponent method you create should always be

```
super.paintComponent(g);
```

which ensures that the panel is properly rendered before we begin drawing on it. Next, lines 14–15 call methods that class DrawPanel inherits from JPanel. Because DrawPanel extends JPanel, DrawPanel can use any public methods of JPanel. Methods **getWidth** and **getHeight** return the JPanel's width and height, respectively. Lines 14–15 store these values in the local variables width and height. Finally, lines 18 and 21 use the Graphics variable g to call method **drawLine** to draw the two lines. Method drawLine draws a line between two points represented by its four arguments. The first two arguments are the *x*- and *y*-coordinates for one endpoint, and the last two arguments are the coordinates for the other endpoint. If you *resize* the window, the lines will *scale* accordingly, because the arguments are based on the width and height of the panel. Resizing the window in this application causes the system to call paintComponent to *redraw* the DrawPanel's contents.

Class *DrawPanelTest*

To display the DrawPanel on the screen, you must place it in a window. You create a window with an object of class **JFrame**. In DrawPanelTest.java (Fig. 3.17), line 3 imports class JFrame from package javax.swing. Line 10 in main creates a DrawPanel object, which contains our drawing, and line 13 creates a new JFrame that can hold and display our panel. Line 16 calls JFrame method **setDefaultCloseOperation** with the argument **JFrame.EXIT_ON_CLOSE** to indicate that the application should terminate when the user closes the window. Line 18 uses class JFrame's **add method** to *attach* the DrawPanel to the JFrame. Line 19 sets the *size* of the JFrame. Method **setSize** takes two parameters that represent the width and height of the JFrame, respectively. Finally, line 20 *displays* the JFrame by calling its **setVisible method** with the argument true. When the JFrame is displayed, the DrawPanel's paintComponent method (lines 9–22 of Fig. 3.16) is implicitly called, and the two lines are drawn (see the sample outputs in Fig. 3.17). Try resizing the window to see that the lines always draw based on the window's current width and height.

GUI and Graphics Case Study Exercises

3.1 Using loops and control statements to draw lines can lead to many interesting designs.

    a) Create the design in the left screen capture of Fig. 3.18. This design draws lines from the top-left corner, fanning them out until they cover the upper-left half of the panel. One approach is to divide the width and height into an equal number of steps (we found 15 steps worked well). The first endpoint of a line will always be in the top-left corner (0, 0). The second endpoint can be found by starting at the bottom-left corner and moving up one vertical step and right one horizontal step. Draw a line between the two endpoints. Continue moving up and to the right one step to find each successive endpoint. The figure should scale accordingly as you resize the window.

    b) Modify part (a) to have lines fan out from all four corners, as shown in the right screen capture of Fig. 3.18. Lines from opposite corners should intersect along the middle.

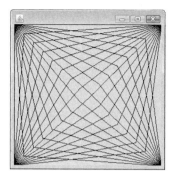

Fig. 3.18 | Lines fanning from a corner.

3.2   Figure 3.19 displays two additional designs created using `while` loops and `drawLine`.
   a) Create the design in the left screen capture of Fig. 3.19. Begin by dividing each edge into an equal number of increments (we chose 15 again). The first line starts in the top-left corner and ends one step right on the bottom edge. For each successive line, move down one increment on the left edge and right one increment on the bottom edge. Continue drawing lines until you reach the bottom-right corner. The figure should scale as you resize the window so that the endpoints always touch the edges.
   b) Modify your answer in part (a) to mirror the design in all four corners, as shown in the right screen capture of Fig. 3.19.

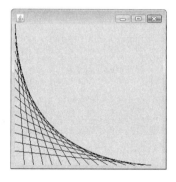
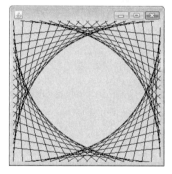

Fig. 3.19 | Line art with loops and `drawLine`.

3.15 Wrap-Up

This chapter presented basic problem solving for building classes and developing methods for these classes. We demonstrated how to construct an algorithm (i.e., an approach to solving a problem), then how to refine the algorithm through several phases of pseudocode development, resulting in Java code that can be executed as part of a method. The chapter showed how to use top-down, stepwise refinement to plan out the specific actions that a method must perform and the order in which the method must perform these actions.

Only three types of control structures—sequence, selection and repetition—are needed to develop any problem-solving algorithm. Specifically, this chapter demonstrated the if single-selection statement, the if...else double-selection statement and the while repetition statement. These are some of the building blocks used to construct solutions to many problems. We used control-statement stacking to total and compute the average of a set of student grades with counter- and sentinel-controlled repetition, and we used control-statement nesting to analyze and make decisions based on a set of exam results. We introduced Java's compound assignment operators and its increment and decrement operators. Finally, we discussed Java's primitive types. In Chapter 4, we continue our discussion of control statements, introducing the for, do...while and switch statements.

Summary

Section 3.1 Introduction
- Before writing a program to solve a problem, you must have a thorough understanding of the problem and a carefully planned approach to solving it. You must also understand the building blocks that are available and employ proven program-construction techniques.

Section 3.2 Algorithms
- Any computing problem can be solved by executing a series of actions (p. 73) in a specific order.
- A procedure for solving a problem in terms of the actions to execute and the order in which they execute is called an algorithm (p. 73).
- Specifying the order in which statements execute in a program is called program control (p. 73).

Section 3.3 Pseudocode
- Pseudocode (p. 74) is an informal language that helps you develop algorithms without having to worry about the strict details of Java language syntax.
- The pseudocode we use in this book is similar to everyday English—it's convenient and user friendly, but it's not an actual computer programming language. You may, of course, use your own native language(s) to develop your own pseudocode.
- Pseudocode helps you "think out" a program before attempting to write it in a programming language, such as Java.
- Carefully prepared pseudocode can easily be converted to a corresponding Java program.

Section 3.4 Control Structures
- Normally, statements in a program are executed one after the other in the order in which they're written. This process is called sequential execution (p. 74).
- Various Java statements enable you to specify that the next statement to execute is not necessarily the next one in sequence. This is called transfer of control (p. 74).
- Bohm and Jacopini demonstrated that all programs could be written in terms of only three control structures (p. 74)—the sequence structure, the selection structure and the repetition structure.
- The term "control structures" comes from the field of computer science. The *Java Language Specification* refers to "control structures" as "control statements" (p. 75).

- The sequence structure is built into Java. Unless directed otherwise, the computer executes Java statements one after the other in the order in which they're written—that is, in sequence.
- Anywhere a single action may be placed, several actions may be placed in sequence.
- Activity diagrams (p. 75) are part of the UML. An activity diagram models the workflow (p. 75; also called the activity) of a portion of a software system.
- Activity diagrams are composed of symbols (p. 75)—such as action-state symbols, diamonds and small circles—that are connected by transition arrows, which represent the flow of the activity.
- Action states (p. 75) contain action expressions that specify particular actions to perform.
- The arrows in an activity diagram represent transitions, which indicate the order in which the actions represented by the action states occur.
- The solid circle located at the top of an activity diagram represents the activity's initial state (p. 75)—the beginning of the workflow before the program performs the modeled actions.
- The solid circle surrounded by a hollow circle that appears at the bottom of the diagram represents the final state (p. 75)—the end of the workflow after the program performs its actions.
- Rectangles with their upper-right corners folded over are UML notes (p. 75)—explanatory remarks that describe the purpose of symbols in the diagram.
- Java has three types of selection statements (p. 76).
- The `if` single-selection statement (p. 76) selects or ignores one or more actions.
- The `if...else` double-selection statement selects between two actions or groups of actions.
- The `switch` statement is called a multiple-selection statement (p. 76) because it selects among many different actions or groups of actions.
- Java provides the `while`, `do...while` and `for` repetition (also called iteration or looping) statements that enable programs to perform statements repeatedly as long as a loop-continuation condition remains true.
- The `while` and `for` statements perform the action(s) in their bodies zero or more times—if the loop-continuation condition (p. 76) is initially false, the action(s) will not execute. The `do...while` statement performs the action(s) in its body one or more times.
- The words `if`, `else`, `switch`, `while`, `do` and `for` are Java keywords. Keywords cannot be used as identifiers, such as variable names.
- Every program is formed by combining as many sequence, selection and repetition statements (p. 76) as is appropriate for the algorithm the program implements.
- Single-entry/single-exit control statements (p. 76) are attached to one another by connecting the exit point of one to the entry point of the next. This is known as control-statement stacking.
- A control statement may also be nested (p. 76) inside another control statement.

Section 3.5 `if` Single-Selection Statement
- Programs use selection statements to choose among alternative courses of action.
- The single-selection `if` statement's activity diagram contains the diamond symbol, which indicates that a decision is to be made. The workflow follows a path determined by the symbol's associated guard conditions (p. 77). If a guard condition is true, the workflow enters the action state to which the corresponding transition arrow points.
- The `if` statement is a single-entry/single-exit control statement.

Section 3.6 `if...else` Double-Selection Statement
- The `if` single-selection statement performs an indicated action only when the condition is true.

- The `if...else` double-selection (p. 76) statement performs one action when the condition is true and another action when the condition is false.
- A program can test multiple cases with nested `if...else` statements (p. 78).
- The conditional operator (`?:`, p. 81) is Java's only ternary operator—it takes three operands. Together, the operands and the `?:` symbol form a conditional expression (p. 81).
- The Java compiler associates an `else` with the immediately preceding `if` unless told to do otherwise by the placement of braces.
- The `if` statement expects one statement in its body. To include several statements in the body of an `if` (or the body of an `else` for an `if...else` statement), enclose the statements in braces.
- A block (p. 81) of statements can be placed anywhere that a single statement can be placed.
- A logic error (p. 81) has its effect at execution time. A fatal logic error (p. 81) causes a program to fail and terminate prematurely. A nonfatal logic error (p. 81) allows a program to continue executing, but causes it to produce incorrect results.
- Just as a block can be placed anywhere a single statement can be placed, you can also use an empty statement, represented by placing a semicolon (`;`) where a statement would normally be.

Section 3.7 `while` Repetition Statement
- The `while` repetition statement (p. 82) allows you to specify that a program should repeat an action while some condition remains true.
- The UML's merge (p. 82) symbol joins two flows of activity into one.
- The decision and merge symbols can be distinguished by the number of incoming and outgoing transition arrows. A decision symbol has one transition arrow pointing to the diamond and two or more transition arrows pointing out from the diamond to indicate possible transitions from that point. Each transition arrow pointing out of a decision symbol has a guard condition. A merge symbol has two or more transition arrows pointing to the diamond and only one transition arrow pointing from the diamond, to indicate multiple activity flows merging to continue the activity. None of the transition arrows associated with a merge symbol has a guard condition.

Section 3.8 Formulating Algorithms: Counter-Controlled Repetition
- Counter-controlled repetition (p. 84) uses a variable called a counter (or control variable) to control the number of times a set of statements execute.
- Counter-controlled repetition is often called definite repetition (p. 84), because the number of repetitions is known before the loop begins executing.
- A total (p. 84) is a variable used to accumulate the sum of several values. Variables used to store totals are normally initialized to zero before being used in a program.
- A local variable's declaration must appear before the variable is used in that method. A local variable cannot be accessed outside the method in which it's declared.
- Dividing two integers results in integer division—the calculation's fractional part is truncated.

Section 3.9 Formulating Algorithms: Sentinel-Controlled Repetition
- In sentinel-controlled repetition (p. 88), a special value called a sentinel value (also called a signal value, a dummy value or a flag value) is used to indicate "end of data entry."
- A sentinel value must be chosen that cannot be confused with an acceptable input value.
- Top-down, stepwise refinement (p. 88) is essential to the development of well-structured programs.
- Division by zero is a logic error.
- To perform a floating-point calculation with integer values, cast one of the integers to type `double`.

- Java knows how to evaluate only arithmetic expressions in which the operands' types are identical. To ensure this, Java performs an operation called promotion on selected operands.
- The unary cast operator is formed by placing parentheses around the name of a type.

Section 3.11 Compound Assignment Operators
- The compound assignment operators (p. 99) abbreviate assignment expressions. Statements of the form

    variable = *variable*   *operator*   *expression*;

  where *operator* is one of the binary operators +, -, *, / or %, can be written in the form

    variable   *operator*=   *expression*;

- The += operator adds the value of the expression on the right of the operator to the value of the variable on the left of the operator and stores the result in the variable on the left of the operator.

Section 3.12 Increment and Decrement Operators
- The unary increment operator, ++, and the unary decrement operator, --, add 1 to or subtract 1 from the value of a numeric variable (p. 100).
- An increment or decrement operator that's prefixed (p. 100) to a variable is the prefix increment or prefix decrement operator, respectively. An increment or decrement operator that's postfixed (p. 100) to a variable is the postfix increment or postfix decrement operator, respectively.
- Using the prefix increment or decrement operator to add or subtract 1 is known as preincrementing or predecrementing, respectively.
- Preincrementing or predecrementing a variable causes the variable to be incremented or decremented by 1; then the new value of the variable is used in the expression in which it appears.
- Using the postfix increment or decrement operator to add or subtract 1 is known as postincrementing or postdecrementing, respectively.
- Postincrementing or postdecrementing the variable causes its value to be used in the expression in which it appears; then the variable's value is incremented or decremented by 1.
- When incrementing or decrementing a variable in a statement by itself, the prefix and postfix increment have the same effect, and the prefix and postfix decrement have the same effect.

Section 3.13 Primitive Types
- Java requires all variables to have a type. Thus, Java is referred to as a strongly typed language (p. 103).
- Java uses Unicode characters and IEEE 754 floating-point numbers.

Self-Review Exercises

3.1   Fill in the blanks in each of the following statements:
  a) All programs can be written in terms of three types of control structures: _____, _____ and _____.
  b) The _____ statement is used to execute one action when a condition is true and another when that condition is false.
  c) Repeating a set of instructions a specific number of times is called _____ repetition.
  d) When it's not known in advance how many times a set of statements will be repeated, a(n) _____ value can be used to terminate the repetition.
  e) The _____ structure is built into Java; by default, statements execute in the order they appear.

     f)   Instance variables of types char, byte, short, int, long, float and double are all given the value _____ by default.

     g)   Java is a(n) _____ language; it requires all variables to have a type.

     h)   If the increment operator is _____ to a variable, first the variable is incremented by 1, then its new value is used in the expression.

3.2   State whether each of the following is *true* or *false*. If *false*, explain why.

     a)   An algorithm is a procedure for solving a problem in terms of the actions to execute and the order in which they execute.

     b)   A set of statements contained within a pair of parentheses is called a block.

     c)   A selection statement specifies that an action is to be repeated while some condition remains true.

     d)   A nested control statement appears in the body of another control statement.

     e)   Java provides the arithmetic compound assignment operators +=, −=, *=, /= and %= for abbreviating assignment expressions.

     f)   The primitive types (boolean, char, byte, short, int, long, float and double) are portable across only Windows platforms.

     g)   Specifying the order in which statements execute in a program is called program control.

     h)   The unary cast operator (double) creates a temporary integer copy of its operand.

     i)   Instance variables of type boolean are given the value true by default.

     j)   Pseudocode helps you think out a program before attempting to write it in a programming language.

3.3   Write four different Java statements that each add 1 to integer variable x.

3.4   Write Java statements to accomplish each of the following tasks:

     a)   Use one statement to assign the sum of x and y to z, then increment x by 1.

     b)   Test whether variable count is greater than 10. If it is, print "Count is greater than 10".

     c)   Use one statement to decrement the variable x by 1, then subtract it from variable total and store the result in variable total.

     d)   Calculate the remainder after q is divided by divisor, and assign the result to q. Write this statement in two different ways.

3.5   Write a Java statement to accomplish each of the following tasks:

     a)   Declare variables sum of type int and initialize it to 0.

     b)   Declare variables x of type int and initialize it to 1.

     c)   Add variable x to variable sum, and assign the result to variable sum.

     d)   Print "The sum is: ", followed by the value of variable sum.

3.6   Combine the statements that you wrote in Exercise 3.5 into a Java application that calculates and prints the sum of the integers from 1 to 10. Use a while statement to loop through the calculation and increment statements. The loop should terminate when the value of x becomes 11.

3.7   Determine the value of the variables in the statement product *= x++; after the calculation is performed. Assume that all variables are type int and initially have the value 5.

3.8   Identify and correct the errors in each of the following sets of code:

     a)

```
while (c <= 5)
{
    product *= c;
    ++c;
```

     b)

```
if (gender == 1)
    System.out.println("Woman");
else;
    System.out.println("Man");
```

3.9   What is wrong with the following `while` statement?

```
while (z >= 0)
    sum += z;
```

Answers to Self-Review Exercises

3.1   a) sequence, selection, repetition. b) `if...else`. c) counter-controlled (or definite). d) sentinel, signal, flag or dummy. e) sequence. f) 0 (zero). g) strongly typed. h) prefixed.

3.2   a) True. b) False. A set of statements contained within a pair of braces ({ and }) is called a block. c) False. A repetition statement specifies that an action is to be repeated while some condition remains true. d) True. e) True. f) False. The primitive types (`boolean`, `char`, `byte`, `short`, `int`, `long`, `float` and `double`) are portable across all computer platforms that support Java. g) True. h) False. The unary cast operator (`double`) creates a temporary floating-point copy of its operand. i) False. Instance variables of type `boolean` are given the value `false` by default. j) True.

3.3
```
x = x + 1;
x += 1;
++x;
x++;
```

3.4   a) `z = x++ + y;`
      b) `if (count > 10)`
             `System.out.println("Count is greater than 10");`
      c) `total -= --x;`
      d) `q %= divisor;`
         `q = q % divisor;`

3.5   a) `int sum = 0;`
      b) `int x = 1;`
      c) `sum += x; or sum = sum + x;`
      d) `System.out.printf("The sum is: %d%n", sum);`

3.6   The program is as follows:

```
1   // Exercise 3.6: Calculate.java
2   // Calculate the sum of the integers from 1 to 10
3   public class Calculate
4   {
5      public static void main(String[] args)
6      {
7         int sum = 0;
8         int x = 1;
9
10        while (x <= 10) // while x is less than or equal to 10
11        {
12           sum += x; // add x to sum
13           ++x; // increment x
14        }
15
16        System.out.printf("The sum is: %d%n", sum);
17     }
18  } // end class Calculate
```

```
The sum is: 55
```

3.7   product = 25, x = 6

3.8   a) Error: The closing right brace of the `while` statement's body is missing.
        Correction: Add a closing right brace after the statement `++c;`.
    b) Error: The semicolon after `else` results in a logic error. The second output statement will always be executed.
        Correction: Remove the semicolon after `else`.

3.9   The value of the variable z is never changed in the `while` statement. Therefore, if the loop-continuation condition (z >= 0) is true, an infinite loop is created. To prevent an infinite loop from occurring, z must be decremented so that it eventually becomes less than 0.

Exercises

3.10   Compare and contrast the `if` single-selection statement and the `while` repetition statement. How are these two statements similar? How are they different?

3.11   Explain what happens when a Java program attempts to divide one integer by another. What happens to the fractional part of the calculation? How can you avoid that outcome?

3.12   Describe the two ways in which control statements can be combined.

3.13   What type of repetition would be appropriate for calculating the sum of the first 100 positive integers? What type would be appropriate for calculating the sum of an arbitrary number of positive integers? Briefly describe how each of these tasks could be performed.

3.14   What is the difference between preincrementing and postincrementing a variable?

3.15   Identify and correct the errors in each of the following pieces of code. [*Note:* There may be more than one error in each piece of code.]

```
a) if (age >= 65);
      System.out.println("Age is greater than or equal to 65");
   else
      System.out.println("Age is less than 65)";
b) int x = 1, total;
   while (x <= 10)
   {
      total += x;
      ++x;
   }
c) while (x <= 100)
      total += x;
      ++x;
d) while (y > 0)
   {
      System.out.println(y);
      ++y;
```

3.16   What does the following program print?

```
1   // Exercise 3.16: Mystery.java
2   public class Mystery
3   {
4      public static void main(String[] args)
5      {
6         int x = 1;
7         int total = 0;
```

```
 8
 9          while (x <= 10)
10          {
11              int y = x * x;
12              System.out.println(y);
13              total += y;
14              ++x;
15          }
16
17          System.out.printf("Total is %d%n", total);
18      }
19  } // end class Mystery
```

For Exercises 3.17 through 3.20, perform each of the following steps:
  a) Read the problem statement.
  b) Formulate the algorithm using pseudocode and top-down, stepwise refinement.
  c) Write a Java program.
  d) Test, debug and execute the Java program.
  e) Process three complete sets of data.

3.17   *(Gas Mileage)* Drivers are concerned with the mileage their automobiles get. One driver has kept track of several trips by recording the miles driven and gallons used for each tankful. Develop a Java application that will input the miles driven and gallons used (both as integers) for each trip. The program should calculate and display the miles per gallon obtained for each trip and print the combined miles per gallon obtained for all trips up to this point. All averaging calculations should produce floating-point results. Use class Scanner and sentinel-controlled repetition to obtain the data from the user.

3.18   *(Credit Limit Calculator)* Develop a Java application that determines whether any of several department-store customers has exceeded the credit limit on a charge account. For each customer, the following facts are available:
  a) account number
  b) balance at the beginning of the month
  c) total of all items charged by the customer this month
  d) total of all credits applied to the customer's account this month
  e) allowed credit limit.

The program should input all these facts as integers, calculate the new balance (= *beginning balance + charges − credits*), display the new balance and determine whether the new balance exceeds the customer's credit limit. For those customers whose credit limit is exceeded, the program should display the message "Credit limit exceeded".

3.19   *(Sales Commission Calculator)* A large company pays its salespeople on a commission basis. The salespeople receive $200 per week plus 9% of their gross sales for that week. For example, a salesperson who sells $5,000 worth of merchandise in a week receives $200 plus 9% of $5000, or a total of $650. You've been supplied with a list of the items sold by each salesperson. The values of these items are as follows:

Item	Value
1	239.99
2	129.75
3	99.95
4	350.89

Develop a Java application that inputs one salesperson's items sold for last week and calculates and displays that salesperson's earnings. There's no limit to the number of items that can be sold.

3.20   *(Salary Calculator)* Develop a Java application that determines the gross pay for each of three employees. The company pays straight time for the first 40 hours worked by each employee and time and a half for all hours worked in excess of 40. You're given a list of the employees, their number of hours worked last week and their hourly rates. Your program should input this information for each employee, then determine and display the employee's gross pay. Use class Scanner to input the data.

3.21   *(Find the Largest Number)* The process of finding the largest value is used frequently in computer applications. For example, a program that determines the winner of a sales contest would input the number of units sold by each salesperson. The salesperson who sells the most units wins the contest. Write a pseudocode program, then a Java application that inputs a series of 10 integers and determines and prints the largest integer. Your program should use at least the following three variables:

  a) counter: A counter to count to 10 (i.e., to keep track of how many numbers have been input and to determine when all 10 numbers have been processed).

  b) number: The integer most recently input by the user.

  c) largest: The largest number found so far.

3.22   *(Tabular Output)* Write a Java application that uses looping to print the following table of values:

N	10*N	100*N	1000*N
1	10	100	1000
2	20	200	2000
3	30	300	3000
4	40	400	4000
5	50	500	5000

3.23   *(Find the Two Largest Numbers)* Using an approach similar to that for Exercise 3.21, find the *two* largest values of the 10 values entered. [*Note:* You may input each number only once.]

3.24   *(Validating User Input)* Modify the program in Fig. 3.10 to validate its inputs. For any input, if the value entered is other than 1 or 2, keep looping until the user enters a correct value.

3.25   What does the following program print?

```java
// Exercise 3.25: Mystery2.java
public class Mystery2
{
   public static void main(String[] args)
   {
      int count = 1;

      while (count <= 10)
      {
         System.out.println(count % 2 == 1 ? "****" : "++++++++");
         ++count;
      }
   }
} // end class Mystery2
```

3.26   What does the following program print?

```java
// Exercise 3.26: Mystery3.java
public class Mystery3
{
   public static void main(String[] args)
   {
```

```
6          int row = 10;
7
8          while (row >= 1)
9          {
10            int column = 1;
11
12            while (column <= 10)
13            {
14               System.out.print(row % 2 == 1 ? "<" : ">");
15               ++column;
16            }
17
18            --row;
19            System.out.println();
20         }
21      }
22   } // end class Mystery3
```

3.27   *(Dangling-else Problem)* Determine the output for each of the given sets of code when x
is 9 and y is 11 and when x is 11 and y is 9. The compiler ignores the indentation in a Java program.
Also, the Java compiler always associates an else with the immediately preceding if unless told to
do otherwise by the placement of braces ({}). On first glance, you may not be sure which if a particular else matches—this situation is referred to as the "dangling-else problem." We've eliminated the indentation from the following code to make the problem more challenging. [*Hint:* Apply
the indentation conventions you've learned.]

a)
```
if (x < 10)
if (y > 10)
System.out.println("*****");
else
System.out.println("#####");
System.out.println("$$$$$");
```

b)
```
if (x < 10)
{
if (y > 10)
System.out.println("*****");
}
else
{
System.out.println("#####");
System.out.println("$$$$$");
}
```

3.28   *(Another Dangling-else Problem)* Modify the given code to produce the output shown in
each part of the problem. Use proper indentation techniques. Make no changes other than inserting
braces and changing the indentation of the code. The compiler ignores indentation in a Java program. We've eliminated the indentation from the given code to make the problem more challenging. [*Note:* It's possible that no modification is necessary for some of the parts.]

```
if (y == 8)
if (x == 5)
System.out.println("@@@@@");
else
System.out.println("#####");
System.out.println("$$$$$");
System.out.println("&&&&&");
```

a) Assuming that x = 5 and y = 8, the following output is produced:

```
@@@@@
$$$$$
&&&&&
```

b) Assuming that x = 5 and y = 8, the following output is produced:

```
@@@@@
```

c) Assuming that x = 5 and y = 8, the following output is produced:

```
@@@@@
```

d) Assuming that x = 5 and y = 7, the following output is produced. [*Note:* The last three output statements after the `else` are all part of a block.]

```
#####
$$$$$
&&&&&
```

3.29 *(Square of Asterisks)* Write an application that prompts the user to enter the size of the side of a square, then displays a hollow square of that size made of asterisks. Your program should work for squares of all side lengths between 1 and 20.

3.30 *(Palindromes)* A palindrome is a sequence of characters that reads the same backward as forward. For example, each of the following five-digit integers is a palindrome: 12321, 55555, 45554 and 11611. Write an application that reads in a five-digit integer and determines whether it's a palindrome. If the number is not five digits long, display an error message and allow the user to enter a new value.

3.31 *(Printing the Decimal Equivalent of a Binary Number)* Write an application that inputs an integer containing only 0s and 1s (i.e., a binary integer) and prints its decimal equivalent. [*Hint:* Use the remainder and division operators to pick off the binary number's digits one at a time, from right to left. In the decimal number system, the rightmost digit has a positional value of 1 and the next digit to the left a positional value of 10, then 100, then 1000, and so on. The decimal number 234 can be interpreted as 4 * 1 + 3 * 10 + 2 * 100. In the binary number system, the rightmost digit has a positional value of 1, the next digit to the left a positional value of 2, then 4, then 8, and so on. The decimal equivalent of binary 1101 is 1 * 1 + 0 * 2 + 1 * 4 + 1 * 8, or 1 + 0 + 4 + 8 or, 13.]

3.32 *(Checkerboard Pattern of Asterisks)* Write an application that uses only the output statements

```
System.out.print("* ");
System.out.print(" ");
System.out.println();
```

to display the checkerboard pattern that follows. A `System.out.println` method call with no arguments causes the program to output a single newline character. [*Hint:* Repetition statements are required.]

```
* * * * * * * *
 * * * * * * * *
* * * * * * * *
 * * * * * * * *
* * * * * * * *
 * * * * * * * *
* * * * * * * *
 * * * * * * * *
```

3.33 *(Multiples of 2 with an Infinite Loop)* Write an application that keeps displaying in the command window the multiples of the integer 2—namely, 2, 4, 8, 16, 32, 64, and so on. Your loop should not terminate (i.e., it should create an infinite loop). What happens when you run this program?

3.34   *(What's Wrong with This Code?)* What is wrong with the following statement? Provide the correct statement to add one to the sum of x and y.

```
System.out.println(++(x + y));
```

3.35   *(Sides of a Triangle)* Write an application that reads three nonzero values entered by the user and determines and prints whether they could represent the sides of a triangle.

3.36   *(Sides of a Right Triangle)* Write an application that reads three nonzero integers and determines and prints whether they could represent the sides of a right triangle.

3.37   *(Factorial)* The factorial of a nonnegative integer n is written as $n!$ (pronounced "n factorial") and is defined as follows:

$n! = n \cdot (n-1) \cdot (n-2) \cdot \ldots \cdot 1$ (for values of n greater than or equal to 1)

and

$n! = 1$ (for $n = 0$)

For example, $5! = 5 \cdot 4 \cdot 3 \cdot 2 \cdot 1$, which is 120.

    a) Write an application that reads a nonnegative integer and computes and prints its factorial.

    b) Write an application that estimates the value of the mathematical constant e by using the following formula. Allow the user to enter the number of terms to calculate.

$$e = 1 + \frac{1}{1!} + \frac{1}{2!} + \frac{1}{3!} + \ldots$$

    c) Write an application that computes the value of e^x by using the following formula. Allow the user to enter the number of terms to calculate.

$$e^x = 1 + \frac{x}{1!} + \frac{x^2}{2!} + \frac{x^3}{3!} + \ldots$$

Making a Difference

3.38   *(Enforcing Privacy with Cryptography)* The explosive growth of Internet communications and data storage on Internet-connected computers has greatly increased privacy concerns. The field of cryptography is concerned with coding data to make it difficult (and hopefully—with the most advanced schemes—impossible) for unauthorized users to read. In this exercise you'll investigate a simple scheme for encrypting and decrypting data. A company that wants to send data over the Internet has asked you to write a program that will encrypt it so that it may be transmitted more securely. All the data is transmitted as four-digit integers. Your application should read a four-digit integer entered by the user and encrypt it as follows: Replace each digit with the result of adding 7 to the digit and getting the remainder after dividing the new value by 10. Then swap the first digit with the third, and swap the second digit with the fourth. Then print the encrypted integer. Write a separate application that inputs an encrypted four-digit integer and decrypts it (by reversing the encryption scheme) to form the original number. [*Optional reading project:* Research "public key cryptography" in general and the PGP (Pretty Good Privacy) specific public key scheme. You may also want to investigate the RSA scheme, which is widely used in industrial-strength applications.]

3.39   *(World Population Growth)* World population has grown considerably over the centuries. Continued growth could eventually challenge the limits of breathable air, drinkable water, arable cropland and other limited resources. There's evidence that growth has been slowing in recent years and that world population could peak sometime this century, then start to decline.

    For this exercise, research world population growth issues online. *Be sure to investigate various viewpoints.* Get estimates for the current world population and its growth rate (the percentage by which it's likely to increase this year). Write a program that calculates world population growth each year for the next 75 years, *using the simplifying assumption that the current growth rate will stay constant.* Print the results in a table. The first column should display the year from year 1 to year 75. The second column should display the anticipated world population at the end of that year. The third column should display the numerical increase in the world population that would occur that year. Using your results, determine the year in which the population would be double what it is today, if this year's growth rate were to persist.

Control Statements: Part 2;
Logical Operators

4

The wheel is come full circle.
—William Shakespeare

All the evolution we know of proceeds from the vague to the definite.
—Charles Sanders Peirce

Objectives

In this chapter you'll:

- Learn the essentials of counter-controlled repetition.

- Use the **for** and **do...while** repetition statements to execute statements in a program repeatedly.

- Understand multiple selection using the **switch** selection statement.

- Use the **break** and **continue** program control statements to alter the flow of control.

- Use the logical operators to form complex conditional expressions in control statements.

4.1 Introduction

This chapter continues our presentation of structured programming theory and principles by introducing all but one of Java's remaining control statements. We demonstrate Java's for, do...while and switch statements. Through a series of short examples using while and for, we explore the essentials of counter-controlled repetition. We use a switch statement to count the number of A, B, C, D and F grade equivalents in a set of numeric grades entered by the user. We introduce the break and continue program-control statements. We discuss Java's logical operators, which enable you to use more complex conditional expressions in control statements. Finally, we summarize Java's control statements and the proven problem-solving techniques presented in this chapter and Chapter 3.

4.2 Essentials of Counter-Controlled Repetition

This section uses the while repetition statement introduced in Chapter 3 to formalize the elements required to perform counter-controlled repetition, which requires

1. a **control variable** (or loop counter)

2. the **initial value** of the control variable

3. the **increment** by which the control variable is modified each time through the loop (also known as **each iteration of the loop**)

4. the **loop-continuation condition** that determines if looping should continue.

To see these elements of counter-controlled repetition, consider the application of Fig. 4.1, which uses a loop to display the numbers from 1 through 10.

```
1   // Fig. 4.1: WhileCounter.java
2   // Counter-controlled repetition with the while repetition statement.
3
4   public class WhileCounter
5   {
6      public static void main(String[] args)
7      {
```

Fig. 4.1 | Counter-controlled repetition with the while repetition statement. (Part 1 of 2.)

```
 8          int counter = 1; // declare and initialize control variable
 9
10          while (counter <= 10) // loop-continuation condition
11          {
12             System.out.printf("%d  ", counter);
13             ++counter; // increment control variable
14          }
15
16          System.out.println();
17       }
18   } // end class WhileCounter
```

| 1 | 2 | 3 | 4 | 5 | 6 | 7 | 8 | 9 | 10 |

Fig. 4.1 | Counter-controlled repetition with the `while` repetition statement. (Part 2 of 2.)

In Fig. 4.1, the elements of counter-controlled repetition are defined in lines 8, 10 and 13. Line 8 *declares* the control variable (`counter`) as an `int`, *reserves space* for it in memory and sets its *initial value* to 1. Variable `counter` also could have been declared and initialized with the following local-variable declaration and assignment statements:

```
int counter; // declare counter
counter = 1; // initialize counter to 1
```

Line 12 displays control variable `counter`'s value during each iteration of the loop. Line 13 *increments* the control variable by 1 for each iteration of the loop. The loop-continuation condition in the `while` (line 10) tests whether the value of the control variable is less than or equal to 10 (the final value for which the condition is `true`). The program performs the body of this `while` even when the control variable is 10. The loop terminates when the control variable exceeds 10 (i.e., `counter` becomes 11).

Common Programming Error 4.1
Because floating-point values may be approximate, controlling loops with floating-point variables may result in imprecise counter values and inaccurate termination tests.

Error-Prevention Tip 4.1
Use integers to control counting loops.

The program in Fig. 4.1 can be made more concise by initializing `counter` to 0 in line 8 and *preincrementing* `counter` in the `while` condition as follows:

```
while (++counter <= 10) // loop-continuation condition
   System.out.printf("%d  ", counter);
```

This code saves a statement, because the `while` condition performs the increment before testing the condition. (Recall from Section 3.12 that the precedence of `++` is higher than that of `<=`.) Coding in such a condensed fashion takes practice, might make code more difficult to read, debug, modify and maintain, and typically should be avoided.

Software Engineering Observation 4.1
"Keep it simple" is good advice for most of the code you'll write.

4.3 for Repetition Statement

Section 4.2 presented the essentials of counter-controlled repetition. The while statement can be used to implement any counter-controlled loop. Java also provides the **for repetition statement**, which specifies the counter-controlled-repetition details in a single line of code. Figure 4.2 reimplements the application of Fig. 4.1 using for.

```
1   // Fig. 4.2: ForCounter.java
2   // Counter-controlled repetition with the for repetition statement.
3
4   public class ForCounter
5   {
6      public static void main(String[] args)
7      {
8         // for statement header includes initialization,
9         // loop-continuation condition and increment
10        for (int counter = 1; counter <= 10; counter++)
11           System.out.printf("%d  ", counter);
12
13        System.out.println();
14     }
15  } // end class ForCounter
```

```
1  2  3  4  5  6  7  8  9  10
```

Fig. 4.2 | Counter-controlled repetition with the for repetition statement.

When the for statement (lines 10–11) begins executing, the control variable counter is *declared* and *initialized* to 1. (Recall from Section 4.2 that the first two elements of counter-controlled repetition are the *control variable* and its *initial value*.) Next, the program checks the *loop-continuation condition*, counter <= 10, which is between the two required semicolons. Because the initial value of counter is 1, the condition initially is true. Therefore, the body statement (line 11) displays control variable counter's value, namely 1. After executing the loop's body, the program increments counter in the expression counter++, which appears to the right of the second semicolon. Then the loop-continuation test is performed again to determine whether the program should continue with the next iteration of the loop. At this point, the control variable's value is 2, so the condition is still true (the *final value* is not exceeded)—thus, the program performs the body statement again (i.e., the next iteration of the loop). This process continues until the numbers 1 through 10 have been displayed and the counter's value becomes 11, causing the loop-continuation test to fail and repetition to terminate (after 10 repetitions of the loop body). Then the program performs the first statement after the for—in this case, line 13.

Figure 4.2 uses (in line 10) the loop-continuation condition counter <= 10. If you incorrectly specified counter < 10 as the condition, the loop would iterate only nine times. This is a common *logic error* called an **off-by-one error**.

Common Programming Error 4.2

Using an incorrect relational operator or an incorrect final value of a loop counter in the loop-continuation condition of a repetition statement can cause an off-by-one error.

Error-Prevention Tip 4.2

Using the final value and operator <= in a loop's condition helps avoid off-by-one errors. For a loop that outputs 1 to 10, the loop-continuation condition should be counter <= 10 *rather than* counter < 10 *(which causes an off-by-one error) or* counter < 11 *(which is correct). Many programmers prefer so-called zero-based counting, in which to count 10 times,* counter *would be initialized to zero and the loop-continuation test would be* counter < 10.

Error-Prevention Tip 4.3

As Chapter 3 mentioned, integers can overflow, causing logic errors. A loop's control variable also could overflow. Write your loop conditions carefully to prevent this.

A Closer Look at the **for** *Statement's Header*

Figure 4.3 takes a closer look at the for statement in Fig. 4.2. The first line—including the keyword for and everything in parentheses after for (line 10 in Fig. 4.2)—is sometimes called the **for statement header**. The for header "does it all"—it specifies each item needed for counter-controlled repetition with a control variable. If there's more than one statement in the body of the for, braces are required to define the body of the loop.

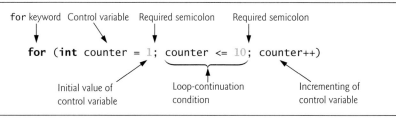

Fig. 4.3 | for statement header components.

General Format of a **for** *Statement*

The general format of the for statement is

```
for (initialization; loopContinuationCondition; increment)
    statement
```

where the *initialization* expression names the loop's control variable and *optionally* provides its initial value, *loopContinuationCondition* determines whether the loop should continue executing and *increment* modifies the control variable's value, so that the loop-continuation condition eventually becomes false. The two semicolons in the for header are required. If the loop-continuation condition is initially false, the program does *not* execute the for statement's body. Instead, execution proceeds with the statement following the for.

Representing a **for** *Statement with an Equivalent* **while** *Statement*

The for statement often can be represented with an equivalent while statement as follows:

```
initialization;
while (loopContinuationCondition)
{
    statement
    increment;
}
```

In Section 4.7, we show a case in which a for statement cannot be represented with an equivalent while statement. Typically, for statements are used for counter-controlled repetition and while statements for sentinel-controlled repetition. However, while and for can each be used for either repetition type.

Scope of a *for* Statement's Control Variable

If the *initialization* expression in the for header declares the control variable (i.e., the control variable's type is specified before the variable name, as in Fig. 4.2), the control variable can be used *only* in that for statement—it will not exist outside it. This restricted use is known as the variable's **scope**. The scope of a variable defines where it can be used in a program. For example, a *local variable* can be used *only* in the method that declares it and *only* from the point of declaration through the end of the method. Scope is discussed in detail in Chapter 5, Methods.

Common Programming Error 4.3

When a for statement's control variable is declared in the initialization section of the for's header, using the control variable after the for's body is a compilation error.

Expressions in a *for* Statement's Header Are Optional

All three expressions in a for header are optional. If the *loopContinuationCondition* is omitted, Java assumes that the loop-continuation condition is *always true*, thus creating an *infinite loop*. You might omit the *initialization* expression if the program initializes the control variable *before* the loop. You might omit the *increment* expression if the program calculates the increment with statements in the loop's body or if no increment is needed. The increment expression in a for acts as if it were a standalone statement at the end of the for's body. Therefore, the expressions

```
counter = counter + 1
counter += 1
++counter
counter++
```

are equivalent increment expressions in a for statement. Many programmers prefer counter++ because it's concise and because a for loop evaluates its increment expression *after* its body executes, so the postfix increment form seems more natural. In this case, the variable being incremented does not appear in a larger expression, so preincrementing and postincrementing actually have the *same* effect.

Common Programming Error 4.4

Placing a semicolon immediately to the right of the right parenthesis of a for header makes that for's body an empty statement. This is normally a logic error.

Error-Prevention Tip 4.4

Infinite loops occur when the loop-continuation condition in a repetition statement never becomes false. To prevent this situation in a counter-controlled loop, ensure that the control variable is modified during each iteration of the loop so that the loop-continuation condition will eventually become false. In a sentinel-controlled loop, ensure that the sentinel value is able to be input.

*Placing Arithmetic Expressions in a **for** Statement's Header*

The initialization, loop-continuation condition and increment portions of a for statement can contain arithmetic expressions. For example, assume that x = 2 and y = 10. If x and y are not modified in the body of the loop, the statement

```
for (int j = x; j <= 4 * x * y; j += y / x)
```

is equivalent to the statement

```
for (int j = 2; j <= 80; j += 5)
```

The increment of a for statement may also be *negative*, in which case it's a **decrement**, and the loop counts *downward*.

*Using a **for** Statement's Control Variable in the Statement's Body*

Programs frequently display the control-variable value or use it in calculations in the loop body, but this use is *not* required. The control variable is commonly used to control repetition *without* being mentioned in the body of the for.

Error-Prevention Tip 4.5

Although the value of the control variable can be changed in the body of a for loop, avoid doing so, because this practice can lead to subtle errors.

*UML Activity Diagram for the **for** Statement*

The for statement's UML activity diagram is similar to that of the while statement (Fig. 3.4). Figure 4.4 shows the activity diagram of the for statement in Fig. 4.2. The diagram makes it clear that initialization occurs *once before* the loop-continuation test is evaluated the first time, and that incrementing occurs *each* time through the loop *after* the body statement executes.

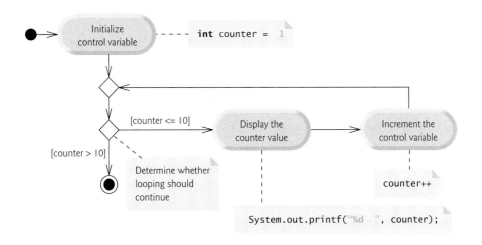

Fig. 4.4 | UML activity diagram for the for statement in Fig. 4.2.

4.4 Examples Using the for Statement

The following examples show techniques for varying the control variable in a for statement. In each case, we write *only* the appropriate for header. Note the change in the relational operator for the loops that *decrement* the control variable.

a) Vary the control variable from 1 to 100 in increments of 1.

```
for (int i = 1; i <= 100; i++)
```

b) Vary the control variable from 100 to 1 in *decrements* of 1.

```
for (int i = 100; i >= 1; i--)
```

c) Vary the control variable from 7 to 77 in increments of 7.

```
for (int i = 7; i <= 77; i += 7)
```

d) Vary the control variable from 20 to 2 in *decrements* of 2.

```
for (int i = 20; i >= 2; i -= 2)
```

e) Vary the control variable over the values 2, 5, 8, 11, 14, 17, 20.

```
for (int i = 2; i <= 20; i += 3)
```

f) Vary the control variable over the values 99, 88, 77, 66, 55, 44, 33, 22, 11, 0.

```
for (int i = 99; i >= 0; i -= 11)
```

Common Programming Error 4.5

Using an incorrect relational operator in the loop-continuation condition of a loop that counts downward (e.g., using i <= 1 instead of i >= 1 in a loop counting down to 1) is usually a logic error.

Common Programming Error 4.6

Do not use equality operators (!= or ==) in a loop-continuation condition if the loop's control variable increments or decrements by more than 1. For example, consider the for statement header for (int counter = 1; counter != 10; counter += 2). The loop-continuation test counter != 10 never becomes false (resulting in an infinite loop) because counter increments by 2 after each iteration.

Application: Summing the Even Integers from 2 to 20

We now consider two sample applications that demonstrate simple uses of for. The application in Fig. 4.5 uses a for statement to sum the even integers from 2 to 20 and store the result in an int variable called total.

```
1   // Fig. 4.5: Sum.java
2   // Summing integers with the for statement.
3
4   public class Sum
5   {
```

Fig. 4.5 | Summing integers with the for statement. (Part 1 of 2.)

```
6      public static void main(String[] args)
7      {
8         int total = 0;
9
10        // total even integers from 2 through 20
11        for (int number = 2; number <= 20; number += 2)
12           total += number;
13
14        System.out.printf("Sum is %d%n", total);
15     }
16  } // end class Sum
```

```
Sum is 110
```

Fig. 4.5 | Summing integers with the `for` statement. (Part 2 of 2.)

The *initialization* and *increment* expressions can be comma-separated lists that enable you to use multiple initialization expressions or multiple increment expressions. For example, *although this is discouraged*, you could merge the body of the `for` statement in lines 11–12 of Fig. 4.5 into the increment portion of the `for` header by using a comma as follows:

```
for (int number = 2; number <= 20; total += number, number += 2)
   ; // empty statement
```

Good Programming Practice 4.1
For readability limit the size of control-statement headers to a single line if possible.

Application: Compound-Interest Calculations

Let's use the `for` statement to compute compound interest. Consider the following problem:

> A person invests $1,000 in a savings account yielding 5% interest. Assuming that all the interest is left on deposit, calculate and print the amount of money in the account at the end of each year for 10 years. Use the following formula to determine the amounts:
>
> $$a = p (1 + r)^n$$
>
> where
>
> p is the original amount invested (i.e., the principal)
> r is the annual interest rate (e.g., use 0.05 for 5%)
> n is the number of years
> a is the amount on deposit at the end of the nth year.

The solution to this problem (Fig. 4.6) involves a loop that performs the indicated calculation for each of the 10 years the money remains on deposit. Lines 8–10 in method `main` declare `double` variables `amount`, `principal` and `rate`, and initialize `principal` to `1000.0` and `rate` to `0.05`. Java treats floating-point constants like `1000.0` and `0.05` as type `double`. Similarly, Java treats whole-number constants like `7` and `-22` as type `int`.

```java
1   // Fig. 4.6: Interest.java
2   // Compound-interest calculations with for.
3
4   public class Interest
5   {
6      public static void main(String[] args)
7      {
8         double amount; // amount on deposit at end of each year
9         double principal = 1000.0; // initial amount before interest
10        double rate = 0.05; // interest rate
11
12        // display headers
13        System.out.printf("%s%20s%n", "Year", "Amount on deposit");
14
15        // calculate amount on deposit for each of ten years
16        for (int year = 1; year <= 10; ++year)
17        {
18           // calculate new amount for specified year
19           amount = principal * Math.pow(1.0 + rate, year);
20
21           // display the year and the amount
22           System.out.printf("%4d%,20.2f%n", year, amount);
23        }
24     }
25  } // end class Interest
```

```
Year    Amount on deposit
   1             1,050.00
   2             1,102.50
   3             1,157.63
   4             1,215.51
   5             1,276.28
   6             1,340.10
   7             1,407.10
   8             1,477.46
   9             1,551.33
  10             1,628.89
```

Fig. 4.6 | Compound-interest calculations with for.

Formatting Strings with Field Widths and Justification

Line 13 outputs the headers for two columns of output. The first column displays the year and the second column the amount on deposit at the end of that year. We use the format specifier %20s to output the String "Amount on Deposit". The integer 20 between the % and the conversion character s indicates that the value should be displayed with a **field width** of 20—that is, printf displays the value with at least 20 character positions. If the value to be output is less than 20 character positions wide (17 characters in this example), the value is **right justified** in the field by default. If the year value to be output were more than four character positions wide, the field width would be extended to the right to accommodate the entire value—this would push the amount field to the right, upsetting the neat columns of our tabular output. To output values **left justified**, simply precede the field width with the **minus sign (–) formatting flag** (e.g., %-20s).

Performing the Interest Calculations with static Method pow of Class Math
The for statement (lines 16–23) executes its body 10 times, varying control variable year from 1 to 10 in increments of 1. This loop terminates when year becomes 11. (Variable year represents *n* in the problem statement.)

Classes provide methods that perform common tasks on objects. In fact, most methods must be called on a specific object. For example, to output text in Fig. 4.6, line 13 calls method printf on the System.out object, and to input int values from the user at the keyboard you called method nextInt on a Scanner object. Some classes also provide methods that perform common tasks and do *not* require objects. These are called static methods. For example, Java does *not* include an exponentiation operator, so the designers of Java's Math class defined static method pow for raising a value to a power. You can call a static method by specifying the *class name* followed by a dot (.) and the method name, as in

ClassName.*methodName*(*arguments*)

In Chapter 5, you'll learn how to implement static methods in your own classes.

We use static method **pow** of class **Math** to perform the compound-interest calculation in Fig. 4.6. Math.pow(*x*, *y*) calculates the value of *x* raised to the *y*th power. The method receives two double arguments and returns a double value. Line 19 performs the calculation $a = p(1 + r)^n$, where *a* is amount, *p* is principal, *r* is rate and *n* is year. Class Math is defined in package java.lang, so you do *not* need to import class Math to use it.

The body of the for statement contains the calculation 1.0 + rate, which appears as an argument to the Math.pow method. In fact, this calculation produces the *same* result each time through the loop, so repeating it in every iteration of the loop is wasteful.

Performance Tip 4.1
In loops, avoid calculations for which the result never changes—such calculations should typically be placed before the loop. Many of today's sophisticated optimizing compilers will place such calculations outside loops in the compiled code.

Formatting Floating-Point Numbers
After each calculation, line 22 outputs the year and the amount on deposit at the end of that year. The year is output in a field width of four characters (as specified by %4d). The amount is output as a floating-point number with the format specifier %,20.2f. The **comma (,) formatting flag** indicates that the floating-point value should be output with a **grouping separator**. The actual separator used is specific to the user's locale (i.e., country). For example, in the United States, the number will be output using commas to separate every three digits and a decimal point to separate the fractional part of the number, as in 1,234.45. The number 20 in the format specification indicates that the value should be output right justified in a *field width* of 20 characters. The .2 specifies the formatted number's *precision*—in this case, the number is *rounded* to the nearest hundredth and output with two digits to the right of the decimal point.

A Warning about Displaying Rounded Values
We declared variables amount, principal and rate to be of type double in this example. We're dealing with fractional parts of dollars and thus need a type that allows decimal points in its values. Unfortunately, floating-point numbers can cause trouble. Here's a simple explanation of what can go wrong when using double (or float) to represent dollar

amounts (assuming that dollar amounts are displayed with two digits to the right of the decimal point): Two `double` dollar amounts stored in the machine could be 14.234 (which would normally be rounded to 14.23 for display purposes) and 18.673 (which would normally be rounded to 18.67 for display purposes). When these amounts are added, they produce the internal sum 32.907, which would normally be rounded to 32.91 for display purposes. Thus, your output could appear as

```
    14.23
 +  18.67
 -------
    32.91
```

but a person adding the individual numbers as displayed would expect the sum to be 32.90. You've been warned!

Error-Prevention Tip 4.6

Do not use variables of type double (or float) to perform precise monetary calculations. The imprecision of floating-point numbers can lead to errors. In the exercises, you'll learn how to use integers to perform precise monetary calculations—Java also provides class java.math.BigDecimal for this purpose, which we demonstrate in Fig. 8.16.

4.5 do...while Repetition Statement

The **do...while repetition statement** is similar to the `while` statement. In the `while`, the program tests the loop-continuation condition at the *beginning* of the loop, *before* executing the loop's body; if the condition is *false*, the body *never* executes. The do...while statement tests the loop-continuation condition *after* executing the loop's body; therefore, *the body always executes at least once*. When a do...while statement terminates, execution continues with the next statement in sequence. Figure 4.7 uses a do...while to output the numbers 1–10.

```java
1  // Fig. 4.7: DoWhileTest.java
2  // do...while repetition statement.
3
4  public class DoWhileTest
5  {
6     public static void main(String[] args)
7     {
8        int counter = 1;
9
10       do
11       {
12          System.out.printf("%d  ", counter);
13          ++counter;
14       } while (counter <= 10); // end do...while
15
16       System.out.println();
17    }
18 } // end class DoWhileTest
```

Fig. 4.7 | do...while repetition statement. (Part 1 of 2.)

```
1  2  3  4  5  6  7  8  9  10
```

Fig. 4.7 | do...while repetition statement. (Part 2 of 2.)

Line 8 declares and initializes control variable `counter`. Upon entering the do...while statement, line 12 outputs `counter`'s value and line 13 increments `counter`. Then the program evaluates the loop-continuation test at the *bottom* of the loop (line 14). If the condition is *true*, the loop continues at the first body statement (line 12). If the condition is *false*, the loop terminates and the program continues at the next statement after the loop.

*UML Activity Diagram for the **do...while** Repetition Statement*
Figure 4.8 contains the UML activity diagram for the do...while statement. This diagram makes it clear that the loop-continuation condition is not evaluated until *after* the loop performs the action state *at least once*. Compare this activity diagram with that of the while statement (Fig. 3.4).

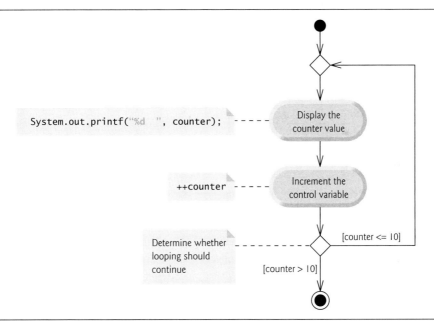

Fig. 4.8 | do...while repetition statement UML activity diagram.

*Braces in a **do...while** Repetition Statement*
It isn't necessary to use braces in the do...while repetition statement if there's only one statement in the body. However, many programmers include the braces, to avoid confusion between the while and do...while statements. For example,

while (*condition*)

is normally the first line of a while statement. A do...while statement with no braces around a single-statement body appears as:

```
do
    statement
while (condition);
```

which can be confusing. A reader may misinterpret the last line—while(*condition*);—as a while statement containing an empty statement (the semicolon by itself). Thus, the do...while statement with one body statement is usually written with braces as follows:

```
do
{
    statement
} while (condition);
```

Good Programming Practice 4.2

Always include braces in a do...while statement. This helps eliminate ambiguity between the while statement and a do...while statement containing only one statement.

4.6 switch Multiple-Selection Statement

Chapter 3 discussed the if single-selection statement and the if...else double-selection statement. The **switch multiple-selection statement** performs different actions based on the possible values of a **constant integral expression** of type byte, short, int or char. As of Java SE 7, the expression may also be a String.

Using a switch Statement to Count A, B, C, D and F Grades

Figure 4.9 calculates the class average of a set of numeric grades entered by the user, and uses a switch statement to determine whether each grade is the equivalent of an A, B, C, D or F and to increment the appropriate grade counter. The program also displays a summary of the number of students who received each grade.

Like earlier versions of the class-average program, the main method of class Letter-Grades (Fig. 4.9) declares local variables total (line 9) and gradeCounter (line 10) to keep track of the sum of the grades entered by the user and the number of grades entered, respectively. Lines 11–15 declare counter variables for each grade category. Note that the variables in lines 9–15 are explicitly initialized to 0.

Method main has two key parts. Lines 26–56 read an arbitrary number of integer grades from the user using sentinel-controlled repetition, update instance variables total and gradeCounter, and increment an appropriate letter-grade counter for each grade entered. Lines 59–80 output a report containing the total of all grades entered, the average of the grades and the number of students who received each letter grade. Let's examine these parts in more detail.

```
1   // Fig. 4.9: LetterGrades.java
2   // LetterGrades class uses the switch statement to count letter grades.
3   import java.util.Scanner;
4
5   public class LetterGrades
6   {
7       public static void main(String[] args)
8       {
```

Fig. 4.9 | LetterGrades class uses the switch statement to count letter grades. (Part 1 of 3.)

```
 9          int total = 0; // sum of grades
10          int gradeCounter = 0; // number of grades entered
11          int aCount = 0; // count of A grades
12          int bCount = 0; // count of B grades
13          int cCount = 0; // count of C grades
14          int dCount = 0; // count of D grades
15          int fCount = 0; // count of F grades
16
17          Scanner input = new Scanner(System.in);
18
19          System.out.printf("%s%n%s%n   %s%n   %s%n",
20             "Enter the integer grades in the range 0-100.",
21             "Type the end-of-file indicator to terminate input:",
22             "On UNIX/Linux/Mac OS X type <Ctrl> d then press Enter",
23             "On Windows type <Ctrl> z then press Enter");
24
25          // loop until user enters the end-of-file indicator
26          while (input.hasNext())
27          {
28             int grade = input.nextInt(); // read grade
29             total += grade; // add grade to total
30             ++gradeCounter; // increment number of grades
31
32             // increment appropriate letter-grade counter
33             switch (grade / 10)
34             {
35                case 9:  // grade was between 90
36                case 10: // and 100, inclusive
37                   ++aCount;
38                   break; // exits switch
39
40                case 8: // grade was between 80 and 89
41                   ++bCount;
42                   break; // exits switch
43
44                case 7: // grade was between 70 and 79
45                   ++cCount;
46                   break; // exits switch
47
48                case 6: // grade was between 60 and 69
49                   ++dCount;
50                   break; // exits switch
51
52                default: // grade was less than 60
53                   ++fCount;
54                   break; // optional; exits switch anyway
55             } // end switch
56          } // end while
57
58          // display grade report
59          System.out.printf("%nGrade Report:%n");
60
```

Fig. 4.9 | LetterGrades class uses the switch statement to count letter grades. (Part 2 of 3.)

```
61          // if user entered at least one grade...
62          if (gradeCounter != 0)
63          {
64             // calculate average of all grades entered
65             double average = (double) total / gradeCounter;
66
67             // output summary of results
68             System.out.printf("Total of the %d grades entered is %d%n",
69                gradeCounter, total);
70             System.out.printf("Class average is %.2f%n", average);
71             System.out.printf("%n%s%n%s%d%n%s%d%n%s%d%n%s%d%n%s%d%n",
72                "Number of students who received each grade:",
73                "A: ", aCount,   // display number of A grades
74                "B: ", bCount,   // display number of B grades
75                "C: ", cCount,   // display number of C grades
76                "D: ", dCount,   // display number of D grades
77                "F: ", fCount); // display number of F grades
78          } // end if
79          else // no grades were entered, so output appropriate message
80             System.out.println("No grades were entered");
81       } // end main
82    } // end class LetterGrades
```

```
Enter the integer grades in the range 0-100.
Type the end-of-file indicator to terminate input:
   On UNIX/Linux/Mac OS X type <Ctrl> d then press Enter
   On Windows type <Ctrl> z then press Enter
99
92
45
57
63
71
76
85
90
100
^Z

Grade Report:
Total of the 10 grades entered is 778
Class average is 77.80

Number of students who received each grade:
A: 4
B: 1
C: 2
D: 1
F: 2
```

Fig. 4.9 | LetterGrades class uses the switch statement to count letter grades. (Part 3 of 3.)

Reading Grades from the User

Lines 19–23 prompt the user to enter integer grades and to type the end-of-file indicator
to terminate the input. The **end-of-file indicator** is a system-dependent keystroke combi-

nation which the user enters to indicate that there's *no more data to input.* In Chapter 15, Files, Streams and Object Serialization, you'll see how the end-of-file indicator is used when a program reads its input from a file.

On UNIX/Linux/Mac OS X systems, end-of-file is entered by typing the sequence

> *<Ctrl> d*

on a line by itself. This notation means to simultaneously press both the *Ctrl* key and the *d* key. On Windows systems, end-of-file can be entered by typing

> *<Ctrl> z*

[*Note:* On some systems, you must press *Enter* after typing the end-of-file key sequence. Also, Windows typically displays the characters ^Z on the screen when the end-of-file indicator is typed, as shown in the output of Fig. 4.9.]

Portability Tip 4.1
The keystroke combinations for entering end-of-file are system dependent.

The while statement (lines 26–56) obtains the user input. The condition at line 26 calls Scanner method **hasNext** to determine whether there's more data to input. This method returns the boolean value true if there's more data; otherwise, it returns false. The returned value is then used as the value of the condition in the while statement. Method hasNext returns false once the user types the end-of-file indicator.

Line 28 inputs a grade value from the user. Line 29 adds grade to total. Line 30 increments gradeCounter. These variables are used to compute the average of the grades. Lines 33–55 use a switch statement to increment the appropriate letter-grade counter based on the numeric grade entered.

Processing the Grades

The switch statement (lines 33–55) determines which counter to increment. We assume that the user enters a valid grade in the range 0–100. A grade in the range 90–100 represents A, 80–89 represents B, 70–79 represents C, 60–69 represents D and 0–59 represents F. The switch statement consists of a block that contains a sequence of **case labels** and an optional **default case**. These are used in this example to determine which counter to increment based on the grade.

When the flow of control reaches the switch, the program evaluates the expression in the parentheses (grade / 10) following keyword switch. This is the switch's **controlling expression**. The program compares this expression's value (which must evaluate to an integral value of type byte, char, short or int, or to a String) with each case label. The controlling expression in line 33 performs integer division, which *truncates the fractional part* of the result. Thus, when we divide a value from 0 to 100 by 10, the result is always a value from 0 to 10. We use several of these values in our case labels. For example, if the user enters the integer 85, the controlling expression evaluates to 8. The switch compares 8 with each case label. If a match occurs (case 8: at line 40), the program executes that case's statements. For the integer 8, line 41 increments bCount, because a grade in the 80s is a B. The **break statement** (line 42) causes program control to proceed with the first statement after the switch—in this program, we reach the end of the while loop, so control returns to the loop-continuation condition in line 26 to determine whether the loop should continue executing.

The cases in our switch explicitly test for the values 10, 9, 8, 7 and 6. Note the cases at lines 35–36 that test for the values 9 and 10 (both of which represent the grade A). Listing cases consecutively in this manner with no statements between them enables the cases to perform the same set of statements—when the controlling expression evaluates to 9 or 10, the statements in lines 37–38 will execute. The switch statement does *not* provide a mechanism for testing *ranges* of values, so *every* value you need to test must be listed in a separate case label. Each case can have multiple statements. The switch statement differs from other control statements in that it does *not* require braces around multiple statements in a case.

case *without a* break *Statement*
Without break statements, each time a match occurs in the switch, the statements for that case and subsequent cases execute until a break statement or the end of the switch is encountered. This is often referred to as "falling through" to the statements in subsequent cases. (This feature is perfect for writing a concise program that displays the iterative song "The Twelve Days of Christmas" in Exercise 4.29.)

Common Programming Error 4.7
Forgetting a break statement when one is needed in a switch is a logic error.

The default *Case*
If no match occurs between the controlling expression's value and a case label, the default case (lines 52–54) executes. We use the default case in this example to process all controlling-expression values that are less than 6—that is, all failing grades. If no match occurs and the switch does not contain a default case, program control simply continues with the first statement after the switch.

Error-Prevention Tip 4.7
In a switch statement, ensure that you test for all possible values of the controlling expression.

Displaying the Grade Report
Lines 59–80 output a report based on the grades entered (as shown in the input/output window in Fig. 4.9). Line 62 determines whether the user entered at least one grade—this helps us avoid dividing by zero. If so, line 65 calculates the average of the grades. Lines 68–77 then output the total of all the grades, the class average and the number of students who received each letter grade. If no grades were entered, line 80 outputs an appropriate message. The output in Fig. 4.9 shows a sample grade report based on 10 grades.

switch *Statement UML Activity Diagram*
Figure 4.10 shows the UML activity diagram for the general switch statement. Most switch statements use a break in each case to terminate the switch statement after processing the case. Figure 4.10 emphasizes this by including break statements in the activity diagram. The diagram makes it clear that the break statement at the end of a case causes control to exit the switch statement immediately.

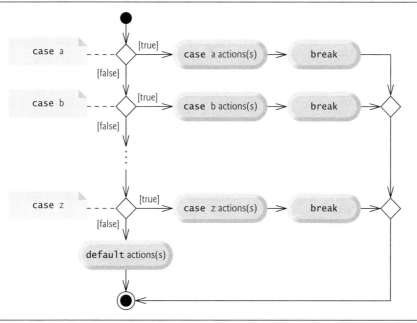

Fig. 4.10 | switch multiple-selection statement UML activity diagram with break statements.

The break statement is *not* required for the switch's last case (or the optional default case, when it appears last), because execution continues with the next statement after the switch.

Error-Prevention Tip 4.8
Provide a default case in switch statements. This focuses you on the need to process exceptional conditions.

Good Programming Practice 4.3
Although each case and the default case in a switch can occur in any order, place the default case last. When the default case is listed last, the break for that case is not required.

Notes on the Expression in Each case of a switch

When using the switch statement, remember that each case must contain a String ot a constant integral expression—that is, any combination of integer constants that evaluates to a constant integer value (e.g., –7, 0 or 221). An integer constant is simply an integer value. In addition, you can use **character constants**—specific characters in single quotes, such as 'A', '7' or '$'—which represent the integer values of characters and enum constants (introduced in Section 5.10). (Appendix B shows the integer values of the characters in the ASCII character set, which is a subset of the Unicode® character set used by Java.)

The expression in each case can also be a **constant variable**—a variable containing a value which does not change for the entire program. Such a variable is declared with keyword final (discussed in Chapter 5). Java has a feature called enum types, which we also present in Chapter 5—enum type constants can also be used in case labels.

In Chapter 10, Object-Oriented Programming: Polymorphism and Interfaces, we present a more elegant way to implement `switch` logic—we use a technique called *polymorphism* to create programs that are often clearer, easier to maintain and easier to extend than programs using `switch` logic.

4.7 break and continue Statements

In addition to selection and repetition statements, Java provides statements `break` (which we discussed in the context of the `switch` statement)and **continue** (presented in this section and online Appendix L) to alter the flow of control. The preceding section showed how `break` can be used to terminate a `switch` statement's execution. This section discusses how to use `break` in repetition statements.

break *Statement*
The `break` statement, when executed in a `while`, `for`, `do...while` or `switch`, causes *immediate* exit from that statement. Execution continues with the first statement after the control statement. Common uses of the `break` statement are to escape early from a loop or to skip the remainder of a `switch` (as in Fig. 4.9). Figure 4.11 demonstrates a `break` statement exiting a `for`.

```java
1   // Fig. 4.11: BreakTest.java
2   // break statement exiting a for statement.
3   public class BreakTest
4   {
5      public static void main(String[] args)
6      {
7         int count; // control variable also used after loop terminates
8
9         for (count = 1; count <= 10; count++) // loop 10 times
10        {
11           if (count == 5)
12              break; // terminates loop if count is 5
13
14           System.out.printf("%d ", count);
15        }
16
17        System.out.printf("%nBroke out of loop at count = %d%n", count);
18     }
19  } // end class BreakTest
```

```
1 2 3 4
Broke out of loop at count = 5
```

Fig. 4.11 | break statement exiting a for statement.

When the `if` statement nested at lines 11–12 in the `for` statement (lines 9–15) detects that count is 5, the `break` statement at line 12 executes. This terminates the `for` statement, and the program proceeds to line 17 (immediately after the `for` statement), which displays a message indicating the value of the control variable when the loop terminated. The loop fully executes its body only four times instead of 10.

continue *Statement*

The continue statement, when executed in a while, for or do...while, skips the remaining statements in the loop body and proceeds with the *next iteration* of the loop. In while and do...while statements, the program evaluates the loop-continuation test immediately after the continue statement executes. In a for statement, the increment expression executes, then the program evaluates the loop-continuation test.

```java
1   // Fig. 4.12: ContinueTest.java
2   // continue statement terminating an iteration of a for statement.
3   public class ContinueTest
4   {
5      public static void main(String[] args)
6      {
7         for (int count = 1; count <= 10; count++) // loop 10 times
8         {
9            if (count == 5)
10               continue; // skip remaining code in loop body if count is 5
11
12            System.out.printf("%d ", count);
13         }
14
15         System.out.printf("%nUsed continue to skip printing 5%n");
16      }
17   } // end class ContinueTest
```

```
1 2 3 4 6 7 8 9 10
Used continue to skip printing 5
```

Fig. 4.12 | continue statement terminating an iteration of a for statement.

Figure 4.12 uses continue (line 10) to skip the statement at line 12 when the nested if determines that count's value is 5. When the continue statement executes, program control continues with the increment of the control variable in the for statement (line 7).

In Section 4.3, we stated that while could be used in most cases in place of for. This is *not* true when the increment expression in the while follows a continue statement. In this case, the increment does *not* execute before the program evaluates the repetition-continuation condition, so the while does not execute in the same manner as the for.

Software Engineering Observation 4.2
Some programmers feel that break and continue violate structured programming. Since the same effects are achievable with structured programming techniques, these programmers do not use break or continue.

Software Engineering Observation 4.3
There's a tension between achieving quality software engineering and achieving the best-performing software. Sometimes one of these goals is achieved at the expense of the other. For all but the most performance-intensive situations, apply the following rule of thumb: First, make your code simple and correct; then make it fast and small, but only if necessary.

4.8 Logical Operators

The if, if...else, while, do...while and for statements each require a *condition* to determine how to continue a program's flow of control. So far, we've studied only simple conditions, such as count <= 10, number != sentinelValue and total > 1000. Simple conditions are expressed in terms of the relational operators >, <, >= and <= and the equality operators == and !=, and each expression tests only one condition. To test *multiple* conditions in the process of making a decision, we performed these tests in separate statements or in nested if or if...else statements. Sometimes control statements require more complex conditions to determine a program's flow of control.

Java's **logical operators** enable you to form more complex conditions by *combining* simple conditions. The logical operators are && (conditional AND), || (conditional OR), & (boolean logical AND), | (boolean logical inclusive OR), ∧ (boolean logical exclusive OR) and ! (logical NOT). [*Note:* The &, | and ∧ operators are also bitwise operators when they're applied to integral operands. We discuss the bitwise operators in online Appendix K.]

Conditional AND (&&) Operator

Suppose we wish to ensure at some point in a program that two conditions are *both* true before we choose a certain path of execution. In this case, we can use the **&& (conditional AND)** operator, as follows:

```
if (gender == FEMALE && age >= 65)
    ++seniorFemales;
```

This if statement contains two simple conditions. The condition gender == FEMALE compares variable gender to the constant FEMALE to determine whether a person is female. The condition age >= 65 might be evaluated to determine whether a person is a senior citizen. The if statement considers the combined condition

```
gender == FEMALE && age >= 65
```

which is true if and only if *both* simple conditions are true. In this case, the if statement's body increments seniorFemales by 1. If either or both of the simple conditions are false, the program skips the increment. Some programmers find that the preceding combined condition is more readable when *redundant* parentheses are added, as in:

```
(gender == FEMALE) && (age >= 65)
```

The table in Fig. 4.13 summarizes the && operator. The table shows all four possible combinations of false and true values for *expression1* and *expression2*. Such tables are called **truth tables**. Java evaluates to false or true all expressions that include relational operators, equality operators or logical operators.

expression1	expression2	expression1 && expression2
false	false	false
false	true	false
true	false	false
true	true	true

Fig. 4.13 | && (conditional AND) operator truth table.

Conditional OR (||) Operator

Now suppose we wish to ensure that *either or both* of two conditions are true before we choose a certain path of execution. In this case, we use the || (**conditional OR**) operator, as in the following program segment:

```
if ((semesterAverage >= 90) || (finalExam >= 90))
    System.out.println ("Student grade is A");
```

The preceding statement also contains two simple conditions. The condition `semester-Average >= 90` evaluates to determine whether the student deserves an A in the course because of a solid performance throughout the semester. The condition `finalExam >= 90` evaluates to determine whether the student deserves an A in the course because of an outstanding performance on the final exam. The `if` statement then considers the combined condition

```
(semesterAverage >= 90) || (finalExam >= 90)
```

and awards the student an A if *either or both* of the simple conditions are true. The only time the message "Student grade is A" is *not* printed is when *both* of the simple conditions are *false*. Figure 4.14 shows the truth table for operator conditional OR (||). Operator && has a higher precedence than operator ||. Both operators associate from left to right.

expression I	expression2	expression I || expression2
false	false	false
false	true	true
true	false	true
true	true	true

Fig. 4.14 | || (conditional OR) operator truth table.

Short-Circuit Evaluation of Complex Conditions

The parts of an expression containing && or || operators are evaluated *only* until it's known whether the condition is true or false. Thus, evaluation of the expression

```
(gender == FEMALE) && (age >= 65)
```

stops immediately if gender *is not* equal to FEMALE (i.e., the entire expression is false) and continues if gender *is* equal to FEMALE (i.e., the entire expression could still be true if the condition age >= 65 is true). This feature of conditional AND and conditional OR expressions is called **short-circuit evaluation**.

Common Programming Error 4.8

In expressions using operator &&, a condition—we'll call this the dependent condition—*may require another condition to be true for the evaluation of the dependent condition to be meaningful. In this case, the dependent condition should be placed after the && operator to prevent errors. Consider the expression (i != 0) && (10 / i == 2). The dependent condition (10 / i == 2)* must *appear after the && operator to prevent the possibility of division by zero.*

Boolean Logical AND (&) and Boolean Logical Inclusive OR (|) Operators
The **boolean logical AND (&)** and **boolean logical inclusive OR (|)** operators are identical
to the && and || operators, except that the & and | operators *always* evaluate *both* of their
operands (i.e., they do *not* perform short-circuit evaluation). So, the expression

```
(gender == 1) & (age >= 65)
```

evaluates age >= 65 *regardless* of whether gender is equal to 1. This is useful if the right
operand has a required **side effect**—a modification of a variable's value. For example, the
expression

```
(birthday == true) | (++age >= 65)
```

guarantees that the condition ++age >= 65 will be evaluated. Thus, the variable age is incremented, regardless of whether the overall expression is true or false.

Error-Prevention Tip 4.9

*For clarity, avoid expressions with side effects (such as assignments) in conditions. They
can make code harder to understand and can lead to subtle logic errors.*

Error-Prevention Tip 4.10

Assignment (=) expressions generally should not *be used in conditions. Every condition
must* result in a boolean value; otherwise, a compilation error occurs. In a condition, an
assignment will compile only *if a* boolean expression *is assigned to a* boolean *variable.*

Boolean Logical Exclusive OR (^)
A simple condition containing the **boolean logical exclusive OR (^)** operator is true *if and
only if one of its operands is* true *and the other is* false. If both are true or both are false,
the entire condition is false. Figure 4.15 is a truth table for the boolean logical exclusive
OR operator (^). This operator is guaranteed to evaluate *both* of its operands.

expression1	expression2	expression1 ^ expression2
false	false	false
false	true	true
true	false	true
true	true	false

Fig. 4.15 | ^ (boolean logical exclusive OR) operator truth table.

Logical Negation (!) Operator
The **!** (**logical NOT**, also called **logical negation** or **logical complement**) operator "revers-
es" the meaning of a condition. Unlike the logical operators &&, ||, &, | and ^, which are
binary operators that combine two conditions, the logical negation operator is a *unary* operator that has only one condition as an operand. The operator is placed *before* a condition
to choose a path of execution if the original condition (without the logical negation operator) is false, as in the program segment

```
if (! (grade == sentinelValue))
    System.out.printf("The next grade is %d%n", grade);
```

which executes the `printf` call only if `grade` is *not* equal to `sentinelValue`. The parentheses around the condition `grade == sentinelValue` are needed because the logical negation operator has a *higher* precedence than the equality operator.

In most cases, you can avoid using logical negation by expressing the condition differently with an appropriate relational or equality operator. For example, the previous statement may also be written as follows:

```
if (grade != sentinelValue)
    System.out.printf("The next grade is %d%n", grade);
```

This flexibility can help you express a condition in a more convenient manner. Figure 4.16 is a truth table for the logical negation operator.

expression	!expression
false	true
true	false

Fig. 4.16 | ! (logical NOT) operator truth table.

Logical Operators Example

Figure 4.17 uses logical operators to produce the truth tables discussed in this section. The output shows the `boolean` expression that was evaluated and its result. We used the **%b format specifier** to display the word "true" or the word "false" based on a `boolean` expression's value. Lines 9–13 produce the truth table for &&. Lines 16–20 produce the truth table for ||. Lines 23–27 produce the truth table for &. Lines 30–35 produce the truth table for |. Lines 38–43 produce the truth table for ^. Lines 46–47 produce the truth table for !.

```java
1   // Fig. 4.17: LogicalOperators.java
2   // Logical operators.
3
4   public class LogicalOperators
5   {
6      public static void main(String[] args)
7      {
8         // create truth table for && (conditional AND) operator
9         System.out.printf("%s%n%s: %b%n%s: %b%n%s: %b%n%s: %b%n%n",
10           "Conditional AND (&&)", "false && false", (false && false) ,
11           "false && true", (false && true) ,
12           "true && false", (true && false) ,
13           "true && true", (true && true) );
14
15        // create truth table for || (conditional OR) operator
16        System.out.printf("%s%n%s: %b%n%s: %b%n%s: %b%n%s: %b%n%n",
17           "Conditional OR (||)", "false || false", (false || false) ,
18           "false || true", (false || true) ,
19           "true || false", (true || false) ,
20           "true || true", (true || true) );
```

Fig. 4.17 | Logical operators. (Part 1 of 3.)

```
21
22          // create truth table for & (boolean logical AND) operator
23          System.out.printf("%s%n%s: %b%n%s: %b%n%s: %b%n%s: %b%n%n",
24             "Boolean logical AND (&)", "false & false", (false & false)  ,
25             "false & true", (false & true)  ,
26             "true & false", (true & false)  ,
27             "true & true", (true & true)  );
28
29          // create truth table for | (boolean logical inclusive OR) operator
30          System.out.printf("%s%n%s: %b%n%s: %b%n%s: %b%n%s: %b%n%n",
31             "Boolean logical inclusive OR (|)",
32             "false | false", (false | false)  ,
33             "false | true", (false | true)  ,
34             "true | false", (true | false)  ,
35             "true | true", (true | true)  );
36
37          // create truth table for ^ (boolean logical exclusive OR) operator
38          System.out.printf("%s%n%s: %b%n%s: %b%n%s: %b%n%s: %b%n%n",
39             "Boolean logical exclusive OR (^)",
40             "false ^ false", (false ^ false)  ,
41             "false ^ true", (false ^ true)  ,
42             "true ^ false", (true ^ false)  ,
43             "true ^ true", (true ^ true)  );
44
45          // create truth table for ! (logical negation) operator
46          System.out.printf("%s%n%s: %b%n%s: %b%n", "Logical NOT (!)",
47             "!false", (!false)  , "!true", (!true)  );
48       }
49   } // end class LogicalOperators
```

```
Conditional AND (&&)
false && false: false
false && true: false
true && false: false
true && true: true

Conditional OR (||)
false || false: false
false || true: true
true || false: true
true || true: true

Boolean logical AND (&)
false & false: false
false & true: false
true & false: false
true & true: true

Boolean logical inclusive OR (|)
false | false: false
false | true: true
true | false: true
true | true: true
```

Fig. 4.17 | Logical operators. (Part 2 of 3.)

```
Boolean logical exclusive OR (^)
false ^ false: false
false ^ true: true
true ^ false: true
true ^ true: false

Logical NOT (!)
!false: true
!true: false
```

Fig. 4.17 | Logical operators. (Part 3 of 3.)

Precedence and Associativity of the Operators Presented So Far
Figure 4.18 shows the precedence and associativity of the Java operators introduced so far. The operators are shown from top to bottom in decreasing order of precedence.

Operators	Associativity	Type
++ --	right to left	unary postfix
++ -- + - ! (*type*)	right to left	unary prefix
* / %	left to right	multiplicative
+ -	left to right	additive
< <= > >=	left to right	relational
== !=	left to right	equality
&	left to right	boolean logical AND
^	left to right	boolean logical exclusive OR
|	left to right	boolean logical inclusive OR
&&	left to right	conditional AND
||	left to right	conditional OR
?:	right to left	conditional
= += -= *= /= %=	right to left	assignment

Fig. 4.18 | Precedence/associativity of the operators discussed so far.

4.9 Structured Programming Summary

Just as architects design buildings by employing the collective wisdom of their profession, so should programmers design programs. Our field is much younger than architecture, and our collective wisdom is considerably sparser. We've learned that structured programming produces programs that are easier than unstructured programs to understand, test, debug, modify and even prove correct in a mathematical sense.

Java Control Statements Are Single-Entry/Single-Exit
Figure 4.19 uses UML activity diagrams to summarize Java's control statements. The initial and final states indicate the *single entry point* and the *single exit point* of each control

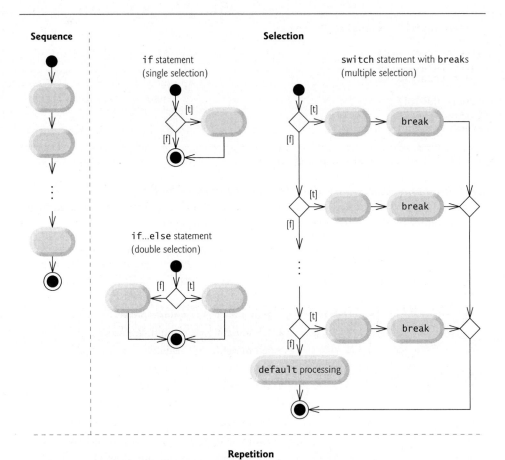

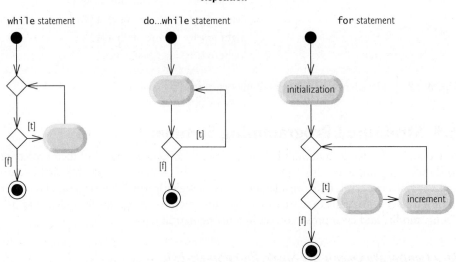

Fig. 4.19 | Java's single-entry/single-exit sequence, selection and repetition statements.

statement. Arbitrarily connecting individual symbols in an activity diagram can lead to unstructured programs. Therefore, the programming profession has chosen a limited set of control statements that can be combined in only two simple ways to build structured programs.

For simplicity, Java includes only *single-entry/single-exit* control statements—there's only one way to enter and only one way to exit each control statement. Connecting control statements in sequence to form structured programs is simple. The final state of one control statement is connected to the initial state of the next—that is, the control statements are placed one after another in a program in sequence. We call this *control-statement stacking*. The rules for forming structured programs also allow for control statements to be *nested*.

Rules for Forming Structured Programs

Figure 4.20 shows the rules for forming structured programs. The rules assume that action states may be used to indicate *any* action. The rules also assume that we begin with the simplest activity diagram (Fig. 4.21) consisting of only an initial state, an action state, a final state and transition arrows.

Rules for forming structured programs

1. Begin with the simplest activity diagram (Fig. 4.21).
2. Any action state can be replaced by two action states in sequence.
3. Any action state can be replaced by any control statement (sequence of action states, `if`, `if...else`, `switch`, `while`, `do...while` or `for`).
4. Rules 2 and 3 can be applied as often as you like and in any order.

Fig. 4.20 | Rules for forming structured programs.

Fig. 4.21 | Simplest activity diagram.

Applying the rules in Fig. 4.20 always results in a properly structured activity diagram with a neat, building-block appearance. For example, repeatedly applying rule 2 to the simplest activity diagram results in an activity diagram containing many action states in sequence (Fig. 4.22). Rule 2 generates a *stack* of control statements, so let's call rule 2 the **stacking rule**. The vertical dashed lines in Fig. 4.22 are not part of the UML—we use them to separate the four activity diagrams that demonstrate rule 2 of Fig. 4.20 being applied.

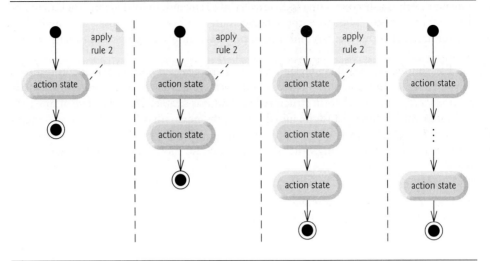

Fig. 4.22 | Repeatedly applying rule 2 of Fig. 4.20 to the simplest activity diagram.

Rule 3 is called the **nesting rule**. Repeatedly applying rule 3 to the simplest activity diagram results in one with neatly *nested* control statements. For example, in Fig. 4.23, the action state in the simplest activity diagram is replaced with a double-selection (if...else) statement. Then rule 3 is applied again to the action states in the double-selection statement, replacing each with a double-selection statement. The dashed action-state symbol around each double-selection statement represents the action state that was replaced. [*Note:* The dashed arrows and dashed action-state symbols shown in Fig. 4.23 are not part of the UML. They're used here to illustrate that *any* action state can be replaced with a control statement.]

Rule 4 generates larger, more involved and more deeply nested statements. The diagrams that emerge from applying the rules in Fig. 4.20 constitute the set of all possible structured activity diagrams and hence the set of all possible structured programs. The beauty of the structured approach is that we use *only seven* simple single-entry/single-exit control statements and assemble them in *only two* simple ways.

If the rules in Fig. 4.20 are followed, an "unstructured" activity diagram (like the one in Fig. 4.24) cannot be created. If you're uncertain about whether a particular diagram is structured, apply the rules of Fig. 4.20 in reverse to reduce it to the simplest activity diagram. If you can reduce it, the original diagram is structured; otherwise, it's not.

Three Forms of Control

Structured programming promotes simplicity. Only three forms of control are needed to implement an algorithm:

- sequence
- selection
- repetition

The sequence structure is trivial. Simply list the statements to execute in the order in which they should execute. Selection is implemented in one of three ways:

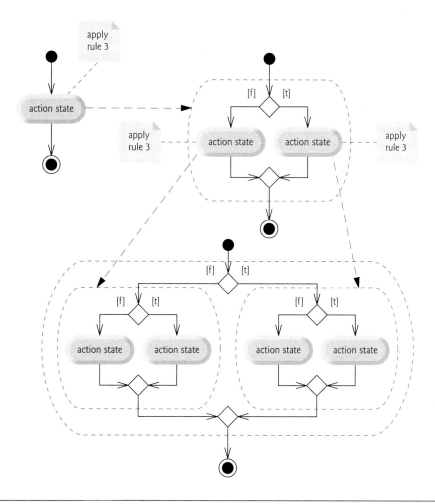

Fig. 4.23 | Repeatedly applying rule 3 of Fig. 4.20 to the simplest activity diagram.

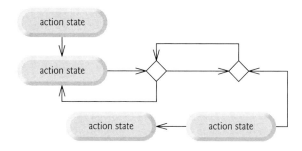

Fig. 4.24 | "Unstructured" activity diagram.

- if statement (single selection)
- if...else statement (double selection)
- switch statement (multiple selection)

In fact, it's straightforward to prove that the simple if statement is sufficient to provide *any* form of selection—everything that can be done with the if...else statement and the switch statement can be implemented by combining if statements (although perhaps not as clearly and efficiently).

Repetition is implemented in one of three ways:

- while statement
- do...while statement
- for statement

[*Note:* There's a fourth repetition statement—the *enhanced for statement*—that we discuss in Section 6.6.] It's straightforward to prove that the while statement is sufficient to provide *any* form of repetition. Everything that can be done with do...while and for can be done with the while statement (although perhaps not as conveniently).

Combining these results illustrates that *any* form of control ever needed in a Java program can be expressed in terms of

- sequence
- if statement (selection)
- while statement (repetition)

and that these can be combined in only two ways—*stacking* and *nesting*. Indeed, structured programming is the essence of simplicity.

4.10 (Optional) GUI and Graphics Case Study: Drawing Rectangles and Ovals

Our next program (Fig. 4.25) demonstrates drawing rectangles and ovals, using the Graphics methods **drawRect** and **drawOval**, respectively. Method paintComponent (lines 10–21) performs the actual drawing. Remember, the first statement in every paintComponent method must be a call to super.paintComponent, as in line 12. Lines 14–20 loop 10 times to draw 10 rectangles and 10 ovals.

```
1   // Fig. 4.25: Shapes.java
2   // Drawing a cascade of shapes based on the user's choice.
3   import java.awt.Graphics;
4   import javax.swing.JPanel;
5   import javax.swing.JFrame;
6
7   public class Shapes extends JPanel
8   {
```

Fig. 4.25 | Drawing a cascade of shapes based on the user's choice. (Part 1 of 2.)

```
 9        // draws a cascade of shapes starting from the top-left corner
10        public void paintComponent(Graphics g)
11        {
12           super.paintComponent(g);
13
14           for (int i = 0; i < 10; i++)
15           {
16              g.drawRect(10 + i * 10, 10 + i * 10,
17                 50 + i * 10, 50 + i * 10);
18              g.drawOval(240 + i * 10, 10 + i * 10,
19                 50 + i * 10, 50 + i * 10);
20           }
21        }
22
23        public static void main( String[] args )
24        {
25           Shapes panel = new Shapes(); // create the panel
26           JFrame application = new JFrame(); // creates a new JFrame
27
28           application.setDefaultCloseOperation(JFrame.EXIT_ON_CLOSE);
29           application.add(panel);
30           application.setSize(500, 290);
31           application.setVisible(true);
32        }
33     } // end class Shapes
```

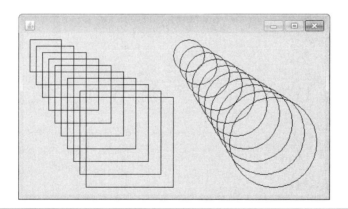

Fig. 4.25 | Drawing a cascade of shapes based on the user's choice. (Part 2 of 2.)

Lines 16–17 call Graphics method drawRect, which requires four arguments. The first two represent the *x*- and *y*-coordinates of the upper-left corner of the rectangle; the next two represent the rectangle's width and height. In this example, we start at a position 10 pixels down and 10 pixels right of the top-left corner, and every iteration of the loop moves the upper-left corner another 10 pixels down and to the right. The width and the height of the rectangle start at 50 pixels and increase by 10 pixels in each iteration.

Lines 18–19 in the loop draw ovals. Method drawOval creates an imaginary rectangle called a **bounding rectangle** and places inside it an oval that touches the midpoints of all four sides. The method's four arguments represent the *x*- and *y*-coordinates of the upper-left corner of the bounding rectangle and the bounding rectangle's width and height. The values passed to drawOval in this example are exactly the same as those passed to drawRect in lines 16–17, except that the first oval's bounding box has an *x*-coordinate that starts 240 pixels from the left side of the panel. Since the width and height of the bounding rectangle are identical in this example, lines 18–19 draw a circle. As an exercise, modify the program to draw both rectangles and ovals with the same arguments. This will allow you to see how each oval touches all four sides of the corresponding rectangle.

Line 25 in main creates a Shapes object. Lines 26–31 perform the standard operations that create and set up a window in this case study—create a frame, set it to exit the application when closed, add the drawing to the frame, set the frame size and make it visible.

GUI and Graphics Case Study Exercise

4.1 Draw 12 concentric circles in the center of a JPanel (Fig. 4.26). The innermost circle should have a radius of 10 pixels, and each successive circle should have a radius 10 pixels larger than the previous one. Begin by finding the center of the JPanel. To get the upper-left corner of a circle, move up one radius and to the left one radius from the center. The width and height of the bounding rectangle are both the same as the circle's diameter (i.e., twice the radius).

Fig. 4.26 | Drawing concentric circles.

4.11 Wrap-Up

In this chapter, we completed our introduction to control statements, which enable you to control the flow of execution in methods. Chapter 3 discussed if, if...else and while. This chapter demonstrated for, do...while and switch. We showed that any algorithm can be developed using combinations of the sequence structure, the three types of selection statements—if, if...else and switch—and the three types of repetition statements—while, do...while and for. In this chapter and Chapter 3, we discussed how you can combine these building blocks to utilize proven program-construction and problem-solving techniques. You used the break statement to exit a switch statement and to immediately terminate a loop, and used a continue statement to terminate a loop's current iteration and proceed with the loop's next iteration. This chapter also introduced Java's logical operators, which enable you to use more complex conditional expressions in control statements. In Chapter 5, we examine methods.

Summary

Section 4.2 Essentials of Counter-Controlled Repetition

- Counter-controlled repetition (p. 122) requires a control variable, the initial value of the control variable, the increment by which the control variable is modified each time through the loop (also known as each iteration of the loop) and the loop-continuation condition that determines whether looping should continue.
- You can declare a variable and initialize it in the same statement.

Section 4.3 for Repetition Statement

- The `while` statement can be used to implement any counter-controlled loop.
- The `for` statement (p. 124) specifies all the details of counter-controlled repetition in its header
- When the `for` statement begins executing, its control variable is declared and initialized. If the loop-continuation condition is initially true, the body executes. After executing the loop's body, the increment expression executes. Then the loop-continuation test is performed again to determine whether the program should continue with the next iteration of the loop.
- The general format of the `for` statement is

  for (*initialization*; *loopContinuationCondition*; *increment*)
     statement

  where the *initialization* expression names the loop's control variable and provides its initial value, *loopContinuationCondition* determines whether the loop should continue executing and *increment* modifies the control variable's value, so that the loop-continuation condition eventually becomes false. The two semicolons in the `for` header are required.
- Most `for` statements can be represented with equivalent `while` statements as follows:

  initialization;

  while (*loopContinuationCondition*)
  {
     statement
     increment;
  }
- Typically, `for` statements are used for counter-controlled repetition and `while` statements for sentinel-controlled repetition.
- If the *initialization* expression in the `for` header declares the control variable, the control variable can be used only in that `for` statement—it will not exist outside the `for` statement.
- The expressions in a `for` header are optional. If the *loopContinuationCondition* is omitted, Java assumes that it's always true, thus creating an infinite loop. You might omit the *initialization* expression if the control variable is initialized before the loop. You might omit the *increment* expression if the increment is calculated with statements in the loop's body or if no increment is needed.
- The increment expression in a `for` acts as if it's a standalone statement at the end of the `for`'s body.
- A `for` statement can count downward by using a negative increment—i.e., a decrement (p. 127).
- If the loop-continuation condition is initially `false`, the `for` statement's body does not execute.

Section 4.4 Examples Using the for Statement

- Java treats floating-point constants like `1000.0` and `0.05` as type `double`. Similarly, Java treats whole-number constants like `7` and `-22` as type `int`.
- The format specifier `%4s` outputs a `String` in a field width (p. 130) of 4—that is, `printf` displays the value with at least 4 character positions. If the value to be output is less than 4 character po-

sitions wide, the value is right justified (p. 130) in the field by default. If the value is greater than 4 character positions wide, the field width expands to accommodate the appropriate number of characters. To left justify (p. 130) the value, use a negative integer to specify the field width.

- Math.pow(*x*, *y*) (p. 131) calculates the value of *x* raised to the *y*th power. The method receives two double arguments and returns a double value.

- The comma (,) formatting flag (p. 131) in a format specifier indicates that a floating-point value should be output with a grouping separator (p. 131). The actual separator used is specific to the user's locale (i.e., country). In the United States, the number will have commas separating every three digits and a decimal point separating the fractional part of the number, as in 1,234.45.

- The . in a format specifier indicates that the integer to its right is the number's precision.

Section 4.5 *do...while Repetition Statement*
- The do...while statement (p. 132) is similar to the while statement. In the while, the program tests the loop-continuation condition at the beginning of the loop, before executing its body; if the condition is false, the body never executes. The do...while statement tests the loop-continuation condition *after* executing the loop's body; therefore, the body always executes at least once.

Section 4.6 *switch Multiple-Selection Statement*
- The switch statement (p. 134) performs different actions based on the possible values of a constant integral expression (a constant value of type byte, short, int or char, but not long), or a String.

- The end-of-file indicator is a system-dependent keystroke combination that terminates user input. On UNIX/Linux/Mac OS X systems, end-of-file is entered by typing the sequence *<Ctrl> d* on a line by itself. This notation means to simultaneously press both the *Ctrl* key and the *d* key. On Windows systems, enter end-of-file by typing *<Ctrl> z*.

- Scanner method hasNext (p. 137) determines whether there's more data to input. This method returns the boolean value true if there's more data; otherwise, it returns false. As long as the end-of-file indicator has not been typed, method hasNext will return true.

- The switch statement consists of a block that contains a sequence of case labels (p. 137) and an optional default case (p. 137).

- In a switch, the program evaluates the controlling expression and compares its value with each case label. If a match occurs, the program executes the statements for that case.

- Listing cases consecutively with no statements between them enables the cases to perform the same set of statements.

- Every value you wish to test in a switch must be listed in a separate case label.

- Each case can have multiple statements, and these need not be placed in braces.

- A case's statements typically end with a break statement (p. 137) that terminates the switch's execution.

- Without break statements, each time a match occurs in the switch, the statements for that case and subsequent cases execute until a break statement or the end of the switch is encountered.

- If no match occurs between the controlling expression's value and a case label, the optional default case executes. If no match occurs and the switch does not contain a default case, program control simply continues with the first statement after the switch.

Section 4.7 *break and continue Statements*
- The break statement, when executed in a while, for, do...while or switch, causes immediate exit from that statement.

- The `continue` statement (p. 140), when executed in a `while`, `for` or `do...while`, skips the loop's remaining body statements and proceeds with its next iteration. In `while` and `do...while` statements, the program evaluates the loop-continuation test immediately. In a `for` statement, the increment expression executes, then the program evaluates the loop-continuation test.

Section 4.8 Logical Operators

- Simple conditions are expressed in terms of the relational operators >, <, >= and <= and the equality operators == and !=, and each expression tests only one condition.

- Logical operators (p. 142) enable you to form more complex conditions by combining simple conditions. The logical operators are && (conditional AND), || (conditional OR), & (boolean logical AND), | (boolean logical inclusive OR), ^ (boolean logical exclusive OR) and ! (logical NOT).

- To ensure that two conditions are *both* true, use the && (conditional AND) operator. If either or both of the simple conditions are false, the entire expression is false.

- To ensure that either *or* both of two conditions are true, use the || (conditional OR) operator, which evaluates to true if either or both of its simple conditions are true.

- A condition using && or || operators (p. 142) uses short-circuit evaluation (p. 143)—they're evaluated only until it's known whether the condition is true or false.

- The & and | operators (p. 144) work identically to the && and || operators but always evaluate both operands.

- A simple condition containing the boolean logical exclusive OR (^; p. 144) operator is `true` *if and only if one of its operands is* `true` *and the other is* `false`. If both operands are `true` or both are `false`, the entire condition is `false`. This operator is also guaranteed to evaluate both of its operands.

- The unary ! (logical NOT; p. 144) operator "reverses" the value of a condition.

Self-Review Exercises

4.1   Fill in the blanks in each of the following statements:
a) Typically, _____ statements are used for counter-controlled repetition and _____ statements for sentinel-controlled repetition.
b) The `do...while` statement tests the loop-continuation condition _____ executing the loop's body; therefore, the body always executes at least once.
c) The _____ statement selects among multiple actions based on the possible values of an integer variable or expression, or a `String`.
d) The _____ statement, when executed in a repetition statement, skips the remaining statements in the loop body and proceeds with the next iteration of the loop.
e) The _____ operator can be used to ensure that two conditions are *both* true before choosing a certain path of execution.
f) If the loop-continuation condition in a `for` header is initially _____, the program does not execute the `for` statement's body.
g) Methods that perform common tasks and do not require objects are called _____ methods.

4.2   State whether each of the following is *true* or *false*. If *false*, explain why.
a) The `default` case is required in the `switch` selection statement.
b) The `break` statement is required in the last case of a `switch` selection statement.
c) The expression `((x > y) && (a < b))` is true if either `x > y` is true or `a < b` is true.
d) An expression containing the || operator is true if either or both of its operands are true.
e) The comma (,) formatting flag in a format specifier (e.g., `%,20.2f`) indicates that a value should be output with a thousands separator.

    f) To test for a range of values in a `switch` statement, use a hyphen (–) between the start and end values of the range in a `case` label.

    g) Listing cases consecutively with no statements between them enables the cases to perform the same set of statements.

4.3 Write a Java statement or a set of Java statements to accomplish each of the following tasks:

    a) Sum the odd integers between 1 and 99, using a `for` statement. Assume that the integer variables `sum` and `count` have been declared.

    b) Calculate the value of `2.5` raised to the power of `3`, using the `pow` method.

    c) Print the integers from 1 to 20, using a `while` loop and the counter variable `i`. Assume that the variable `i` has been declared, but not initialized. Print only five integers per line. [*Hint:* Use the calculation `i % 5`. When the value of this expression is 0, print a newline character; otherwise, print a tab character. Assume that this code is an application. Use the `System.out.println()` method to output the newline character, and use the `System.out.print('\t')` method to output the tab character.]

    d) Repeat part (c), using a `for` statement.

4.4 Find the error in each of the following code segments, and explain how to correct it:

    a)
```
i = 1;
while (i <= 10);
   ++i;
}
```

    b)
```
for (k = 0.1; k != 1.0; k += 0.1)
   System.out.println(k);
```

    c)
```
switch (n)
{
   case 1:
      System.out.println("The number is 1");
   case 2:
      System.out.println("The number is 2");
      break;
   default:
      System.out.println("The number is not 1 or 2");
      break;
}
```

    d) The following code should print the values 1 to 10:
```
n = 1;
while (n < 10)
   System.out.println(n++);
```

Answers to Self-Review Exercises

4.1 a) `for`, `while`. b) after. c) `switch`. d) `continue`. e) `&&` (conditional AND). f) `false`. g) `static`.

4.2 a) False. The `default` case is optional. If no default action is needed, then there's no need for a `default` case. b) False. The `break` statement is used to exit the `switch` statement. The `break` statement is not required for the last case in a `switch` statement. c) False. *Both* of the relational expressions must be true for the entire expression to be true when using the `&&` operator. d) True. e) True. f) False. The `switch` statement does not provide a mechanism for testing ranges of values, so every value that must be tested should be listed in a separate case label. g) True.

4.3 a)
```
sum = 0;
for (count = 1; count <= 99; count += 2)
   sum += count;
```

b) **double** result = Math.pow(2.5, 3);
c) i = 1;

```
while (i <= 20)
{
    System.out.print(i);

    if (i % 5 == 0)
        System.out.println();
    else
        System.out.print('\t');

    ++i;
}
```
d) **for** (i = 1; i <= 20; i++)
```
{
    System.out.print(i);

    if (i % 5 == 0)
        System.out.println();
    else
        System.out.print('\t');
}
```

4.4   a) Error: The semicolon after the `while` header causes an infinite loop, and there's a missing left brace.
Correction: Replace the semicolon by a {, or remove both the ; and the }.
   b) Error: Using a floating-point number to control a `for` statement may not work, because floating-point numbers are represented only approximately by most computers.
Correction: Use an integer, and perform the proper calculation in order to get the values you desire:

```
for (k = 1; k != 10; k++)
    System.out.println((double) k / 10);
```

   c) Error: The missing code is the `break` statement in the statements for the first case.
Correction: Add a `break` statement at the end of the statements for the first case. This omission is not necessarily an error if you want the statement of `case 2:` to execute every time the `case 1:` statement executes.
   d) Error: An improper relational operator is used in the `while`'s continuation condition.
Correction: Use `<=` rather than `<`, or change 10 to 11.

Exercises

4.5   Describe the four basic elements of counter-controlled repetition.

4.6   Compare and contrast the `while` and `for` repetition statements.

4.7   Discuss a situation in which it would be more appropriate to use a do...while statement than a `while` statement. Explain why.

4.8   Compare and contrast the `break` and `continue` statements.

4.9   Find and correct the error(s) in each of the following segments of code:
   a) **For** (i = 100, i >= 1, i++)
```
        System.out.println(i);
```

b) The following code should print whether integer `value` is odd or even:

```
switch (value % 2)
{
   case 0:
      System.out.println("Even integer");

   case 1:
      System.out.println("Odd integer");
}
```

c) The following code should output the odd integers from 19 to 1:

```
for (i = 19; i >= 1; i += 2)
   System.out.println(i);
```

d) The following code should output the even integers from 2 to 100:

```
counter = 2;

do
{
   System.out.println(counter);
   counter += 2;
} While (counter < 100);
```

4.10   What does the following program do?

```
 1   // Exercise 4.10: Printing.java
 2   public class Printing
 3   {
 4      public static void main(String[] args)
 5      {
 6         for (int i = 1; i <= 10; i++)
 7         {
 8            for (int j = 1; j <= 5; j++)
 9               System.out.print('@');
10
11            System.out.println();
12         }
13      }
14   } // end class Printing
```

4.11   *(Find the Smallest Value)* Write an application that finds the smallest of several integers. Assume that the first value read specifies the number of values to input from the user.

4.12   *(Calculating the Product of Odd Integers)* Write an application that calculates the product of the odd integers from 1 to 15.

4.13   *(Factorials) Factorials* are used frequently in probability problems. The factorial of a positive integer *n* (written *n*! and pronounced "*n* factorial") is equal to the product of the positive integers from 1 to *n*. Write an application that calculates the factorials of 1 through 20. Use type `long`. Display the results in tabular format. What difficulty might prevent you from calculating the factorial of 100?

4.14   *(Modified Compound-Interest Program)* Modify the compound-interest application of Fig. 4.6 to repeat its steps for interest rates of 5%, 6%, 7%, 8%, 9% and 10%. Use a `for` loop to vary the interest rate.

4.15   *(Triangle Printing Program)* Write an application that displays the following patterns separately, one below the other. Use for loops to generate the patterns. All asterisks (*) should be printed by a single statement of the form `System.out.print('*');` which causes the asterisks to print side by side. A statement of the form `System.out.println();` can be used to move to the next line. A statement of the form `System.out.print(' ');` can be used to display a space for the last two patterns. There should be no other output statements in the program. [*Hint:* The last two patterns require that each line begin with an appropriate number of blank spaces.]

```
(a)              (b)              (c)              (d)
*                **********       **********                *
**               *********        *********                **
***              ********         ********                 ***
****             *******          *******                  ****
*****            ******           ******                   *****
******           *****            *****                    ******
*******          ****             ****                     *******
********         ***              ***                      ********
*********        **               **                       *********
**********       *                *                        **********
```

4.16 *(Bar Chart Printing Program)* One interesting application of computers is to display graphs and bar charts. Write an application that reads five numbers between 1 and 30. For each number that's read, your program should display the same number of adjacent asterisks. For example, if your program reads the number 7, it should display *******. Display the bars of asterisks *after* you read all five numbers.

4.17 *(Calculating Sales)* An online retailer sells five products whose retail prices are as follows: Product 1, $2.98; product 2, $4.50; product 3, $9.98; product 4, $4.49 and product 5, $6.87. Write an application that reads a series of pairs of numbers as follows:
   a) product number
   b) quantity sold

Your program should use a `switch` statement to determine the retail price for each product. It should calculate and display the total retail value of all products sold. Use a sentinel-controlled loop to determine when the program should stop looping and display the final results.

4.18 *(Modified Compound-Interest Program)* Modify the application in Fig. 4.6 to use only integers to calculate the compound interest. [*Hint:* Treat all monetary amounts as integral numbers of pennies. Then break the result into its dollars and cents portions by using the division and remainder operations, respectively. Insert a period between the dollars and the cents portions.]

4.19 Assume that i = 1, j = 2, k = 3 and m = 2. What does each of the following statements print?
   a) `System.out.println(i == 1);`
   b) `System.out.println(j == 3);`
   c) `System.out.println((i >= 1) && (j < 4));`
   d) `System.out.println((m <= 99) & (k < m));`
   e) `System.out.println((j >= i) || (k == m));`
   f) `System.out.println((k + m < j) | (3 - j >= k));`
   g) `System.out.println(!(k > m));`

4.20 *(Calculating the Value of π)* Calculate the value of π from the infinite series

$$\pi = 4 - \frac{4}{3} + \frac{4}{5} - \frac{4}{7} + \frac{4}{9} - \frac{4}{11} + \cdots$$

Print a table that shows the value of π approximated by computing the first 200,000 terms of this series. How many terms do you have to use before you first get a value that begins with 3.14159?

4.21   *(Pythagorean Triples)* A right triangle can have sides whose lengths are all integers. The set of three integer values for the lengths of the sides of a right triangle is called a Pythagorean triple. The lengths of the three sides must satisfy the relationship that the sum of the squares of two of the sides is equal to the square of the hypotenuse. Write an application that displays a table of the Pythagorean triples for side1, side2 and the hypotenuse, all no larger than 500. Use a triple-nested for loop that tries all possibilities. This method is an example of "brute-force" computing. You'll learn in more advanced computer science courses that for many interesting problems there's no known algorithmic approach other than using sheer brute force.

4.22   *(Modified Triangle Printing Program)* Modify Exercise 4.15 to combine your code from the four separate triangles of asterisks such that all four patterns print side by side. [*Hint:* Make clever use of nested for loops.]

4.23   *(De Morgan's Laws)* In this chapter, we discussed the logical operators &&, &, ||, |, ∧ and !. De Morgan's laws can sometimes make it more convenient for us to express a logical expression. These laws state that the expression !(*condition1* && *condition2*) is logically equivalent to the expression (!*condition1* || !*condition2*). Also, the expression !(*condition1* || *condition2*) is logically equivalent to the expression (!*condition1* && !*condition2*). Use De Morgan's laws to write equivalent expressions for each of the following, then write an application to that both the original expression and the new expression in each case produce the same value:

a) `!(x < 5) && !(y >= 7)`
b) `!(a == b) || !(g != 5)`
c) `!((x <= 8) && (y > 4))`
d) `!((i > 4) || (j <= 6))`

4.24   *(Diamond Printing Program)* Write an application that prints the following diamond shape. You may use output statements that print a single asterisk (*), a single space or a single new-line character. Maximize your use of repetition (with nested for statements), and minimize the number of output statements.

```
    *
   ***
  *****
 *******
*********
 *******
  *****
   ***
    *
```

4.25   *(Modified Diamond Printing Program)* Modify the application you wrote in Exercise 4.24 to read an odd number in the range 1–19 to specify the number of rows in the diamond. Your program should then display a diamond of the appropriate size.

4.26   A criticism of the break statement and the continue statement is that each is unstructured. Actually, these statements can always be replaced by structured statements, although doing so can be awkward. Describe in general how you'd remove any break statement from a loop in a program and replace it with some structured equivalent. [*Hint:* The break statement exits a loop from the body of the loop. The other way to exit is by failing the loop-continuation test. Consider using in the loop-continuation test a second test that indicates "early exit because of a 'break' condition."] Use the technique you develop here to remove the break statement from the application in Fig. 4.11.

4.27   What does the following program segment do?

```
for (i = 1; i <= 5; i++)
{
   for (j = 1; j <= 3; j++)
   {
      for (k = 1; k <= 4; k++)
         System.out.print('*');

      System.out.println();
   } // end inner for

   System.out.println();
} // end outer for
```

4.28   Describe in general how you'd remove any `continue` statement from a loop in a program and replace it with some structured equivalent. Use the technique you develop here to remove the `continue` statement from the program in Fig. 4.12.

4.29   *("The Twelve Days of Christmas" Song)* Write an application that uses repetition and `switch` statements to print the song "The Twelve Days of Christmas." One `switch` statement should be used to print the day ("first," "second," and so on). A separate `switch` statement should be used to print the remainder of each verse. Visit the website en.wikipedia.org/wiki/The_Twelve_Days_of_Christmas_(song) for the lyrics of the song.

Making a Difference

4.30   *(Global Warming Facts Quiz)* The controversial issue of global warming has been widely publicized by the film "An Inconvenient Truth," featuring former Vice President Al Gore. Mr. Gore and a U.N. network of scientists, the Intergovernmental Panel on Climate Change, shared the 2007 Nobel Peace Prize in recognition of "their efforts to build up and disseminate greater knowledge about man-made climate change." Research *both* sides of the global warming issue online (you might want to search for phrases like "global warming skeptics"). Create a five-question multiple-choice quiz on global warming, each question having four possible answers (numbered 1–4). Be objective and try to fairly represent both sides of the issue. Next, write an application that administers the quiz, calculates the number of correct answers (zero through five) and returns a message to the user. If the user correctly answers five questions, print "Excellent"; if four, print "Very good"; if three or fewer, print "Time to brush up on your knowledge of global warming," and include a list of some of the websites where you found your facts.

4.31   *(Tax Plan Alternatives; The "FairTax")* There are many proposals to make taxation fairer. Check out the FairTax initiative in the United States at www.fairtax.org. Research how the proposed FairTax works. One suggestion is to eliminate income taxes and most other taxes in favor of a 23% consumption tax on all products and services that you buy. Some FairTax opponents question the 23% figure and say that because of the way the tax is calculated, it would be more accurate to say the rate is 30%—check this carefully. Write a program that prompts the user to enter expenses in various expense categories they have (e.g., housing, food, clothing, transportation, education, health care, vacations), then prints the estimated FairTax that person would pay.

4.32   *(Facebook User Base Growth)* According to CNNMoney.com, Facebook hit one billion users in October 2012. Using the compound-growth technique you learned in Fig. 4.6 and assuming its user base grows at a rate of 4% per month, how many months will it take for Facebook to grow its user base to 1.5 billion users? How many months will it take for Facebook to grow its user base to two billion users?

5

Methods

Form ever follows function.
—Louis Henri Sullivan

E pluribus unum.
(One composed of many.)
—Virgil

O! call back yesterday,
bid time return.
—William Shakespeare

Answer me in one word.
—William Shakespeare

Objectives

In this chapter you'll:

- Declare your own methods and call them.

- Use common `Math` methods from the Java API.

- Understand how the method-call/return mechanism is supported by the method-call stack.

- Learn about argument promotion and casting.

- Use secure random-number generation to implement game-playing applications.

- Understand how the visibility of declarations is limited to specific regions of programs.

- Understand what method overloading is and how to create overloaded methods.

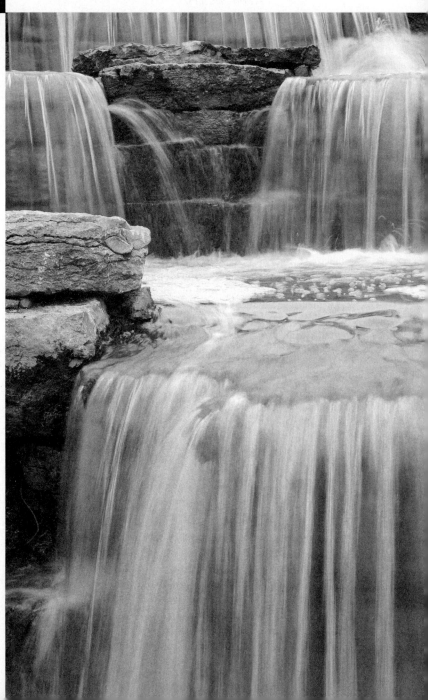

5.1 Introduction

Experience has shown that the best way to develop and maintain a large program is to construct it from small, simple pieces, or **modules**. This technique is called **divide and conquer**. In this chapter, you'll learn how to declare and use methods to facilitate the design, implementation, operation and maintenance of large programs.

Previously, you've called methods on specific objects—for example, method nextInt on Scanner objects and methods printf and println on the System.out object. You'll see that it's possible for certain methods, called static methods, to be called on a class rather than an object. You'll learn how to declare static methods, then call them from other methods (such as main). You'll also learn how Java is able to keep track of which method is currently executing, how local variables of methods are maintained in memory and how a method knows where to return after it completes execution.

We'll take a brief diversion into simulation techniques with random-number generation and develop a version of the dice game called craps that uses most of the programming techniques you've used to this point in the book. In addition, you'll learn how to declare constants in your programs.

Many of the classes you'll use or create while developing applications will have more than one method of the same name. This technique, called *overloading*, is used to implement methods that perform similar tasks for arguments of different types or for different numbers of arguments.

We continue discussing methods in Chapter 7, Introduction to Classes and Objects, where you'll declare your own classes, create objects of those classes and invoke their methods. We discuss methods further in Chapter 18, Recursion. Recursion provides an intriguing way of thinking about methods and algorithms.

5.2 Program Modules in Java

You write Java programs by combining new methods and classes with predefined ones available in the **Java Application Programming Interface** (also referred to as the **Java API** or **Java class library**) and in various other class libraries. Related classes are typically grouped into *packages* so that they can be *imported* into programs and *reused*. You'll learn how to group your own classes into *packages* in Section 21.4.10. The Java API provides a rich collection of predefined classes that contain methods for performing common mathematical calculations, string manipulations, character manipulations, input/output operations, database operations, networking operations, file processing, error checking and more.

Software Engineering Observation 5.1

Familiarize yourself with the rich collection of classes and methods provided by the Java API (http://docs.oracle.com/javase/7/docs/api/). Section 5.8 overviews several common packages. Online Appendix F explains how to navigate the API documentation. Don't reinvent the wheel. When possible, reuse Java API classes and methods. This reduces program development time and avoids introducing programming errors.

Divide and Conquer with Methods

Methods help you modularize a program by separating its tasks into self-contained units. You've declared a main method in every program you've written. The main method is special in that it is called once to begin a program's execution. When you create other methods, the statements in the method bodies are written only once, are hidden from other methods and can be reused from several locations in a program.

One motivation for modularizing a program into methods is the *divide-and-conquer* approach, which makes program development more manageable by constructing programs from small, simple pieces. Another is **software reusability**—using existing methods as building blocks to create new programs. Often, you can create programs mostly from existing classes and methods rather than by building customized code. For example, in earlier programs, we did not define how to read data from the keyboard—Java provides these capabilities in the Scanner class's methods. A third motivation is to *avoid repeating code*. Dividing a program into meaningful methods—and as you'll see starting in Chapter 7, classes—makes the program easier to debug and maintain.

Software Engineering Observation 5.2

To promote software reusability, every method should be limited to performing a single, well-defined task, and the name of the method should express that task effectively.

Error-Prevention Tip 5.1

A method that performs one task is easier to test and debug than one that performs many tasks.

Software Engineering Observation 5.3

If you cannot choose a concise name that expresses a method's task, your method might be attempting to perform too many tasks. Break such a method into several smaller ones.

Hierarchical Relationship Between Method Calls

A method is invoked by a method call, and when the called method completes its task, it returns control—and possibly a result—to the caller. An analogy to this program structure is the hierarchical form of management (Fig. 5.1). A boss (the caller) asks a worker (the called method) to perform a task and report back (return) the results after completing the task. The boss method does not know how the worker method performs its designated tasks. The worker may also call other worker methods, unbeknown to the boss. This "hiding" of implementation details promotes good software engineering. Figure 5.1 shows the boss method communicating with several worker methods in a hierarchical manner. The boss method divides its responsibilities among the various worker methods. Here, worker1 acts as a "boss method" to worker4 and worker5.

> **Error-Prevention Tip 5.2**
> *When you call a method that returns a value indicating whether the method performed its task successfully, be sure to check the return value of that method and, if that method was unsuccessful, deal with the issue appropriately.*

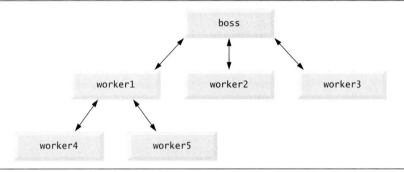

Fig. 5.1 | Hierarchical boss-method/worker-method relationship.

5.3 static Methods, static Variables and Class Math

Most methods execute in response to method calls *on specific objects* (but this is not always the case. Sometimes a method performs a task that does not depend on an object. Such a method applies to the class in which it's declared as a whole and is known as a static method or a **class method**.

It's common for classes to contain convenient static methods to perform common tasks. For example, recall that we used static method pow of class Math to raise a value to a power in Fig. 4.6. For any class imported into your program, you can call the class's static methods by specifying the name of the class in which the method is declared, followed by a dot (.) and the method name, as in

ClassName.methodName(arguments)

Math Class Methods

We use Math class methods here to present the concept of static methods. Class Math provides a collection of methods that enable you to perform common mathematical calculations. For example, you can calculate the square root of 900.0 with the static method call

```
Math.sqrt(900.0)
```

This expression evaluates to 30.0. Method sqrt takes an argument of type double and returns a result of type double. To output the value of the preceding method call in the command window, you might write the statement

```
System.out.println(Math.sqrt(900.0));
```

In this statement, the value that `sqrt` returns becomes the argument to method `println`. There was no need to create a `Math` object before calling method `sqrt`. Also *all* `Math` class methods are `static`—therefore, each is called by preceding its name with the class name `Math` and the dot (.) separator.

Software Engineering Observation 5.4

Class `Math` is part of the `java.lang` package, which is implicitly imported by the compiler, so it's not necessary to import class `Math` to use its methods.

Method arguments may be constants, variables or expressions. If c = 13.0, d = 3.0 and f = 4.0, then the statement

```
System.out.println(Math.sqrt(c + d * f));
```

calculates and prints the square root of 13.0 + 3.0 * 4.0 = 25.0—namely, 5.0. Figure 5.2 summarizes several `Math` class methods. In the figure, *x* and *y* are of type `double`.

Method	Description	Example
abs(*x*)	absolute value of *x*	abs(23.7) is 23.7 abs(0.0) is 0.0 abs(-23.7) is 23.7
ceil(*x*)	rounds *x* to the smallest integer not less than *x*	ceil(9.2) is 10.0 ceil(-9.8) is -9.0
cos(*x*)	trigonometric cosine of *x* (*x* in radians)	cos(0.0) is 1.0
exp(*x*)	exponential method e^x	exp(1.0) is 2.71828 exp(2.0) is 7.38906
floor(*x*)	rounds *x* to the largest integer not greater than *x*	floor(9.2) is 9.0 floor(-9.8) is -10.0
log(*x*)	natural logarithm of *x* (base *e*)	log(Math.E) is 1.0 log(Math.E * Math.E) is 2.0
max(*x*, *y*)	larger value of *x* and *y*	max(2.3, 12.7) is 12.7 max(-2.3, -12.7) is -2.3
min(*x*, *y*)	smaller value of *x* and *y*	min(2.3, 12.7) is 2.3 min(-2.3, -12.7) is -12.7
pow(*x*, *y*)	*x* raised to the power *y* (i.e., x^y)	pow(2.0, 7.0) is 128.0 pow(9.0, 0.5) is 3.0
sin(*x*)	trigonometric sine of *x* (*x* in radians)	sin(0.0) is 0.0
sqrt(*x*)	square root of *x*	sqrt(900.0) is 30.0
tan(*x*)	trigonometric tangent of *x* (*x* in radians)	tan(0.0) is 0.0

Fig. 5.2 | Math class methods.

Class Variables and `Math` Class `static` Constants `PI` and `E`

Just as a class may contain `static` methods, a class also may contain `static` variables. Such variables are known as **class variables**. Class `Math` declares two constants, **Math.PI** and **Math.E**, that represent *high-precision approximations* to commonly used mathematical constants. Math.PI (3.141592653589793) is the ratio of a circle's circumference to its diameter. Math.E (2.718281828459045) is the base value for natural logarithms (calculated with static Math method log). These constants are declared in class Math with the modifiers public, static and final:

- Making them public allows you to use them in your own classes.

- Making them static allows them to be accessed via the class name Math and a dot (.) separator, just as class Math's methods are.

- Making them **final** indicates that they are *constants*—their values cannot change after they are initialized. As you'll see in Fig. 5.8, static variables are not required to be constants.

A class's variables are sometimes called **fields**. You'll learn in Chapter 7 that a class's fields consist of its static variables and instance variables. You'll learn more about static fields in Section 8.11.

Why Is Method main Declared static?

When you execute the Java Virtual Machine (JVM) with the java command, the JVM attempts to invoke the main method of the class you specify. Declaring main as static allows the JVM to invoke main without creating an object of the class. When you execute your application, you specify its class name as an argument to the java command, as in

> java *ClassName argument1 argument2 ...*

The JVM loads the class specified by *ClassName* and uses that class name to invoke method main. In the preceding command, *ClassName* is a **command-line argument** to the JVM that tells it which class to execute. Following the *ClassName*, you can also specify a list of Strings (separated by spaces) as command-line arguments that the JVM will pass to your application. Such arguments might be used to specify options (e.g., a filename) to run the application. As you'll learn in Chapter 6, Arrays and ArrayLists, your application can access those command-line arguments and use them to customize the application.

5.4 Declaring Methods

So far, each class we declared contained one method named main. Class MaximumFinder (Fig. 5.3) has two methods—main (lines 8–25) and maximum (lines 28–41). The maximum method determines and returns the largest of three double values. Recall that main is a special method that is always called automatically by the Java Virtual Machine (JVM) when you execute an application. Most methods do not get called automatically. As you'll soon see, you must call method maximum explicitly to tell it to perform its task. We begin our discussion with method maximum's declaration.

```
1   // Fig. 5.3: MaximumFinder.java
2   // Programmer-declared method maximum with three double parameters.
3   import java.util.Scanner;
```

Fig. 5.3 | Programmer-declared method maximum with three double parameters. (Part I of 2.)

```
 4
 5   public class MaximumFinder
 6   {
 7      // obtain three floating-point values and locate the maximum value
 8      public static void main(String[] args)
 9      {
10         // create Scanner for input from command window
11         Scanner input = new Scanner(System.in);
12
13         // prompt for and input three floating-point values
14         System.out.print(
15            "Enter three floating-point values separated by spaces: ");
16         double number1 = input.nextDouble(); // read first double
17         double number2 = input.nextDouble(); // read second double
18         double number3 = input.nextDouble(); // read third double
19
20         // determine the maximum value
21         double result = maximum(number1, number2, number3);
22
23         // display maximum value
24         System.out.println("Maximum is: " + result);
25      }
26
27      // returns the maximum of its three double parameters
28      public static double maximum(double x, double y, double z)
29      {
30         double maximumValue = x; // assume x is the largest to start
31
32         // determine whether y is greater than maximumValue
33         if (y > maximumValue)
34            maximumValue = y;
35
36         // determine whether z is greater than maximumValue
37         if (z > maximumValue)
38            maximumValue = z;
39
40         return maximumValue;
41      }
42   } // end class MaximumFinder
```

```
Enter three floating-point values separated by spaces: 9.35 2.74 5.1
Maximum is: 9.35
```

```
Enter three floating-point values separated by spaces: 5.8 12.45 8.32
Maximum is: 12.45
```

```
Enter three floating-point values separated by spaces: 6.46 4.12 10.54
Maximum is: 10.54
```

Fig. 5.3 | Programmer-declared method `maximum` with three `double` parameters. (Part 2 of 2.)

The **public** and **static** Keywords

Method maximum's declaration begins with keyword public to indicate that the method is "available to the public"—it can be called from methods of other classes. The keyword static enables the main method (another static method) to call maximum as shown in line 21 without qualifying the method name with the class name MaximumFinder—static methods in the same class can call each other directly. Any other class that uses maximum must fully qualify the method name with the class name. The examples in this chapter and the next begin every method declaration with the keywords public and static. (You'll learn about non-public and non-static methods in Chapter 7.)

The Return Type

After keywords public and static is the method's **return type**, which specifies the type of data the method returns (that is, gives back to its *caller*) after performing its task. For example, when you go to an automated teller machine (ATM) and request your account balance, you expect the ATM to give you back a value that represents your balance. Similarly, when a statement calls method maximum in this example, the statement expects to receive back the largest of the three values. The return type double indicates that this method will perform a task then return a double value to the **calling method** (that is, main in this example). You've already used methods that return information—for example, Scanner method nextInt inputs an integer typed by the user at the keyboard, then returns that value for use in the program. In some cases, you'll define methods that perform a task but will *not* return any information. Such methods use the return type void (as in main).

The Method Name and Parameters

The method name, maximum, follows the return type. Class names, method names and variable names are all *identifiers* and by convention all use the same *camel case* naming scheme we discussed in Chapter 2. Also by convention, class names begin with an initial *uppercase* letter, and method names and variable names begin with an initial *lowercase* letter.

The parentheses after the method name indicate that this is a method. For a method that requires additional information to perform its task, the method can specify one or more **parameters** that represent that additional information. If the parentheses are empty, the method does not require additional information to perform its task.

Parameters are defined in a comma-separated **parameter list**, which is located in the parentheses that follow the method name. Each parameter must specify a type and an identifier. Method maximum requires three double parameters, which we named x, y and z. A method's parameters are considered to be local variables of that method and can be used only in that method's body. Collectively, the elements in line 28 are often referred to as the **method header**.

Common Programming Error 5.1
Declaring method parameters of the same type as float x, y *instead of* float x, float y *is a syntax error—a type is required for each parameter in the parameter list.*

The Method Body

The method header is always followed by the method's body, which is delimited by left and right braces, as in lines 29 and 41. A method's body contains one or more statements that perform the method's task. To determine the maximum value, we begin with the assumption that parameter x contains the largest value, so line 30 declares local variable max-imumValue and initializes it with the value of parameter x. Of course, it's possible that parameter y or z contains the actual largest value, so we must compare each of these values with maximumValue. The if statement at lines 33–34 determines whether y is greater than maximumValue. If so, line 34 assigns y to maximumValue. The if statement at lines 37–38 determines whether z is greater than maximumValue. If so, line 38 assigns z to maximum-Value. At this point the largest of the three values resides in maximumValue, so line 40 uses the **return** statement to return that value to the point in the program from which maximum was called (line 21). When program control returns to that point, maximum's parameters x, y and z no longer exist in memory.

Method main and Calling Method maximum

Lines 14–18 in main prompt the user to enter three double values, then read them from the user via Scanner method **nextDouble**, which returns the user input as a double value.

A method call supplies values—called arguments—for each of the method's parameters. For example, the argument to method System.out.println specifies the data to display in a command window. When maximum is called from line 21 in main, its parameters x, y and z (line 28) are initialized with the values of *arguments* number1, number2 and number3, respectively. There must be one argument in the method call for each parameter in the method declaration. Also, each argument must be *consistent* with the type of the corresponding parameter. For example, a parameter of type double can receive values like 7.35, 22 or –0.03456, but not Strings like "hello" nor the boolean values true or false. Section 5.7 discusses the argument types that can be provided in a method call for each parameter of a primitive type.

When method maximum returns the result to line 21, the program assigns maximum's return value to main's local variable result. Then line 24 outputs the maximum value.

Common Programming Error 5.2

A compilation error occurs if the number of arguments in a method call does not match the number of parameters in the method declaration.

Assembling Strings with String Concatenation

Java allows you to assemble String objects into larger strings by using operators + or +=. This is known as **string concatenation**. When both operands of operator + are String objects, operator + creates a new String object in which the characters of the right operand are placed at the end of those in the left operand—e.g., the expression "hello " + "there" creates the String "hello there".

In line 24 of Fig. 5.3, the expression "Maximum is: " + result uses operator + with operands of types String and double. *Every primitive value and object in Java can be represented as a String.* When one of the + operator's operands is a String, the other is converted to a String, then the two are *concatenated*. In line 24, the double value is converted to its String representation and placed at the end of the String "Maximum is: ". If there are any *trailing zeros* in a double value, these will be *discarded* when the number is converted to a String—for example 9.3500 would be represented as 9.35.

Primitive values used in String concatenation are converted to Strings. A boolean concatenated with a String is converted to the String "true" or "false". In Chapter 7, you'll learn that *all objects have a toString method that returns a String representation of the object.* When an object is concatenated with a `String`, the object's `toString` method is implicitly called to obtain the `String` representation of the object.

You can break large `String` literals into several smaller `Strings` and place them on multiple lines of code for readability. In this case, the `Strings` can be reassembled using concatenation. We discuss the details of `Strings` in Chapter 14.

Common Programming Error 5.3

It's a syntax error to break a `String` literal across lines. If necessary, you can split a `String` into several smaller `Strings` and use concatenation to form the desired `String`.

Common Programming Error 5.4

Confusing the + operator used for string concatenation with the + operator used for addition can lead to strange results. Java evaluates the operands of an operator from left to right. For example, if integer variable y has the value 5, the expression "y + 2 = " + y + 2 results in the string "y + 2 = 52", not "y + 2 = 7", because first the value of y (5) is concatenated to the string "y + 2 = ", then the value 2 is concatenated to the new larger string "y + 2 = 5". The expression "y + 2 = " + (y + 2) produces the desired result "y + 2 = 7".

Implementing Method `maximum` by Reusing Method `Math.max`

The entire body of our `maximum` method could also be implemented with two calls to `Math.max`, as follows:

```
return Math.max(x, Math.max(y, z));
```

The outer call to `Math.max` specifies arguments x and `Math.max(y, z)`. *Before* any method can be called, its arguments must be evaluated to determine their values. If an argument is a method call, the method call must be performed to determine its return value. So, in the preceding statement, `Math.max(y, z)` is evaluated to determine the maximum of y and z. Then the result is passed as the second argument to the other call to `Math.max`, which returns the larger of its two arguments. This is a good example of *software reuse*—we find the largest of three values by reusing `Math.max`, which finds the larger of two values. Notice how concise this code is compared to lines 30–38 of Fig. 5.3.

5.5 Notes on Declaring and Using Methods

There are three ways to call a method:

1. Using a method name by itself to call another method of the *same* class—such as `maximum(number1, number2, number3)` in line 21 of Fig. 5.3.

2. Using an object's variable name followed by a dot (.) and the method name to call a non-`static` method of the object—such as the method call in line 16 of Fig. 5.3, `input.nextDouble()`, which calls a method of class `Scanner`. Non-`static` methods are typically called **instance methods**.

3. Using the class name and a dot (.) to call a `static` method of a class—such as `Math.sqrt(900.0)` in Section 5.3.

There are three ways to return control to the statement that calls a method. If the method does not return a result, control returns when the program flow reaches the method-ending right brace or when the statement

```
      return;
```

is executed. If the method returns a result, the statement

```
      return expression;
```

evaluates the *expression*, then returns the result to the caller.

Common Programming Error 5.5

Declaring a method outside the body of a class declaration or inside the body of another method is a syntax error.

Common Programming Error 5.6

Redeclaring a parameter as a local variable in the method's body is a compilation error.

Common Programming Error 5.7

Forgetting to return a value from a method that should return a value is a compilation error. If a return type other than void *is specified, the method* must *contain a* return *statement that returns a value consistent with the method's return type. Returning a value from a method whose return type is* void *is a compilation error.*

5.6 Method-Call Stack and Stack Frames

To understand how Java performs method calls, we first need to consider a data structure (i.e., collection of related data items) known as a **stack**. You can think of a stack as analogous to a pile of dishes. When a dish is placed on the pile, it's normally placed at the top (referred to as **pushing** the dish onto the stack). Similarly, when a dish is removed from the pile, it's normally removed from the top (referred to as **popping** the dish off the stack). Stacks are known as **last-in, first-out (LIFO) data structures**—the *last* item pushed onto the stack is the *first* item popped from the stack.

When a program *calls* a method, the called method must know how to *return* to its caller, so the *return address* of the calling method is *pushed* onto the **method-call stack**. If a series of method calls occurs, the successive return addresses are pushed onto the stack in last-in, first-out order so that each method can return to its caller.

The method-call stack also contains the memory for the *local variables* (including the method parameters) used in each invocation of a method during a program's execution. This data, stored as a portion of the method-call stack, is known as the **stack frame** (or **activation record**) of the method call. When a method call is made, the stack frame for that method call is *pushed* onto the method-call stack. When the method returns to its caller, the stack frame for this method call is *popped* off the stack and those local variables are no longer known to the program.

Of course, a computer's memory is finite, so only a certain amount can be used to store stack frames on the method-call stack. If more method calls occur than can have their stack frames stored, an error known as a **stack overflow** occurs—we'll talk more about this in Chapter 11, Exception Handling: A Deeper Look.

5.7 Argument Promotion and Casting

Another important feature of method calls is **argument promotion**—converting an *argument's value*, if possible, to the type that the method expects to receive in its corresponding *parameter*. For example, a program can call Math method sqrt with an int argument even though a double argument is expected. The statement

```
System.out.println(Math.sqrt(4));
```

correctly evaluates Math.sqrt(4) and prints the value 2.0. The method declaration's parameter list causes Java to convert the int value 4 to the double value 4.0 *before* passing the value to method sqrt. Such conversions may lead to compilation errors if Java's **promotion rules** are not satisfied. These rules specify which conversions are allowed—that is, which ones can be performed *without losing data*. In the sqrt example above, an int is converted to a double without changing its value. However, converting a double to an int *truncates* the fractional part of the double value—thus, part of the value is lost. Converting large integer types to small integer types (e.g., long to int, or int to short) may also result in changed values.

The promotion rules apply to expressions containing values of two or more primitive types and to primitive-type values passed as arguments to methods. Each value is promoted to the "highest" type in the expression. Actually, the expression uses a *temporary copy* of each value—the types of the original values remain unchanged. Figure 5.4 lists the primitive types and the types to which each can be promoted. The valid promotions for a given type are always to a type higher in the table. For example, an int can be promoted to the higher types long, float and double.

Converting values to types lower in the table of Fig. 5.4 will result in different values if the lower type cannot represent the value of the higher type (e.g., the int value 2000000 cannot be represented as a short, and any floating-point number with digits after its decimal point cannot be represented in an integer type such as long, int or short). Therefore, in cases where information may be lost due to conversion, the Java compiler requires you to use a *cast operator* (introduced in Section 3.9) to explicitly force the conversion to occur—otherwise a compilation error occurs. This enables you to "take control" from the compiler. You essentially say, "I know this conversion might cause loss of information, but

Type	Valid promotions
double	None
float	double
long	float or double
int	long, float or double
char	int, long, float or double
short	int, long, float or double (but not char)
byte	short, int, long, float or double (but not char)
boolean	None (boolean values are not considered to be numbers in Java)

Fig. 5.4 | Promotions allowed for primitive types.

for my purposes here, that's fine." Suppose method `square` calculates the square of an integer and thus requires an `int` argument. To call `square` with a `double` argument named `doubleValue`, we would be required to write the method call as

```
square((int) doubleValue)
```

This method call explicitly casts (converts) `doubleValue`'s value to a a temporary integer for use in method `square`. Thus, if `doubleValue`'s value is 4.5, the method receives the value 4 and returns 16, not 20.25.

Common Programming Error 5.8

Casting a primitive-type value to another primitive type may change the value if the new type is not a valid promotion. For example, casting a floating-point value to an integer value may introduce truncation errors (loss of the fractional part) into the result.

5.8 Java API Packages

As you've seen, Java contains many *predefined* classes that are grouped into categories of related classes called *packages*. Together, these are known as the Java Application Programming Interface (Java API), or the Java class library. A great strength of Java is the Java API's thousands of classes. Some key Java API packages that we use in this book are described in Fig. 5.5, which represents only a small portion of the *reusable components* in the Java API.

Package	Description
java.awt.event	The **Java Abstract Window Toolkit Event Package** contains classes and interfaces that enable event handling for GUI components in both the java.awt and javax.swing packages. (See Chapter 12, GUI Components: Part 1, and Chapter 22, GUI Components: Part 2.)
java.awt.geom	The **Java 2D Shapes Package** contains classes and interfaces for working with Java's advanced two-dimensional graphics capabilities. (See Chapter 13, Graphics and Java 2D.)
java.io	The **Java Input/Output Package** contains classes and interfaces that enable programs to input and output data. (See Chapter 15, Files, Streams and Object Serialization.)
java.lang	The **Java Language Package** contains classes and interfaces (discussed throughout the book) that are required by many Java programs. This package is imported by the compiler into all programs.
java.net	The **Java Networking Package** contains classes and interfaces that enable programs to communicate via computer networks like the Internet. (See online Chapter 28, Networking.)
java.security	The **Java Security Package** contains classes and interfaces for enhancing application security.
java.sql	The **JDBC Package** contains classes and interfaces for working with databases. (See Chapter 24, Accessing Databases with JDBC.)

Fig. 5.5 | Java API packages (a subset). (Part 1 of 2.)

Package	Description
java.util	The **Java Utilities Package** contains utility classes and interfaces that enable storing and processing of large amounts of data. Many of these classes and interfaces have been updated to support Java SE 8's new lambda capabilities. (See Chapter 16, Generic Collections.)
java.util.concurrent	The **Java Concurrency Package** contains utility classes and interfaces for implementing programs that can perform multiple tasks in parallel. (See Chapter 23, Concurrency.)
javax.swing	The **Java Swing GUI Components Package** contains classes and interfaces for Java's Swing GUI components that provide support for portable GUIs. This package still uses some elements of the older java.awt package. (See Chapter 12, GUI Components: Part 1, and Chapter 22, GUI Components: Part 2.)
javax.swing.event	The **Java Swing Event Package** contains classes and interfaces that enable event handling (e.g., responding to button clicks) for GUI components in package javax.swing. (See Chapter 12, GUI Components: Part 1, and Chapter 22, GUI Components: Part 2.)
javax.xml.ws	The **JAX-WS Package** contains classes and interfaces for working with web services in Java. (See online Chapter 32, REST-Based Web Services.)
javafx packages	JavaFX is the preferred GUI technology for the future. We discuss these packages in Chapter 25, JavaFX GUI: Part 1 and in the online JavaFX GUI and multimedia chapters.
Some Java SE 8 Packages Used in This Book	
java.time	The new Java SE 8 **Date/Time API Package** contains classes and interfaces for working with dates and times. These features are designed to replace the older date and time capabilities of package java.util. (See Chapter 23, Concurrency.)
java.util.function and java.util.stream	These packages contain classes and interfaces for working with Java SE 8's functional programming capabilities. (See Chapter 17, Java SE 8 Lambdas and Streams.)

Fig. 5.5 | Java API packages (a subset). (Part 2 of 2.)

The set of packages available in Java is quite large. In addition to those summarized in Fig. 5.5, Java includes packages for complex graphics, advanced graphical user interfaces, printing, advanced networking, security, database processing, multimedia, accessibility (for people with disabilities), concurrent programming, cryptography, XML processing and many other capabilities. For an overview of the packages in Java, visit

```
http://docs.oracle.com/javase/7/docs/api/overview-summary.html
http://download.java.net/jdk8/docs/api/overview-summary.html
```

You can locate additional information about a predefined Java class's methods in the Java API documentation at

```
http://docs.oracle.com/javase/7/docs/api/
```

When you visit this site, click the **Index** link to see an alphabetical listing of all the classes and methods in the Java API. Locate the class name and click its link to see the online description of the class. Click the **METHOD** link to see a table of the class's methods. Each `static` method will be listed with the word "`static`" preceding its return type.

5.9 Case Study: Secure Random-Number Generation

We now take a brief diversion into a popular type of programming application—simulation and game playing. In this and the next section, we develop a game-playing program with multiple methods. The program uses most of the control statements presented thus far in the book and introduces several new programming concepts.

The **element of chance** can be introduced in a program via an object of class **Secure-Random** (package `java.security`). Such objects can produce random `boolean`, `byte`, `float`, `double`, `int`, `long` and Gaussian values. In the next several examples, we use objects of class `SecureRandom` to produce random values.

Moving to Secure Random Numbers

Recent editions of this book used Java's `Random` class to obtain "random" values. This class produced *deterministic* values that could be *predicted* by malicious programmers. Secure-Random objects produce **nondeterministic random numbers** that *cannot* be predicted.

Deterministic random numbers have been the source of many software security breaches. Most programming languages now have library features similar to Java's Secure-Random class for producing nondeterministic random numbers to help prevent such problems. From this point forward in the text, when we refer to "random numbers" we mean "secure random numbers."

Creating a SecureRandom Object

A new secure random-number generator object can be created as follows:

```
SecureRandom randomNumbers = new SecureRandom();
```

It can then be used to generate random values—we discuss only random `int` values here. For more information on the `SecureRandom` class, see `docs.oracle.com/javase/7/docs/api/java/security/SecureRandom.html`.

Obtaining a Random `int` Value

Consider the following statement:

```
int randomValue = randomNumbers.nextInt();
```

`SecureRandom` method **nextInt** generates a random `int` value. If it truly produces values *at random*, then every value in the range should have an *equal chance* (or probability) of being chosen each time `nextInt` is called.

Changing the Range of Values Produced By `nextInt`

The range of values produced by method `nextInt` generally differs from the range of values required in a particular Java application. For example, a program that simulates coin tossing might require only 0 for "heads" and 1 for "tails." A program that simulates the rolling of a six-sided die might require random integers in the range 1–6. A program that randomly predicts the next type of spaceship (out of four possibilities) that will fly across the horizon in a video game might require random integers in the range 1–4. For cases like these, class SecureRandom provides another version of method nextInt that receives an int argument and returns a value from 0 up to, but not including, the argument's value. For example, for coin tossing, the following statement returns 0 or 1.

```
int randomValue = randomNumbers.nextInt(2);
```

Rolling a Six-Sided Die

To demonstrate random numbers, let's develop a program that simulates 20 rolls of a six-sided die and displays the value of each roll. We begin by using nextInt to produce random values in the range 0–5, as follows:

```
int face = randomNumbers.nextInt(6);
```

The argument 6—called the **scaling factor**—represents the number of unique values that nextInt should produce (in this case six—0, 1, 2, 3, 4 and 5). This manipulation is called **scaling** the range of values produced by SecureRandom method nextInt.

A six-sided die has the numbers 1–6 on its faces, not 0–5. So we **shift** the range of numbers produced by adding a **shifting value**—in this case 1—to our previous result, as in

```
int face = 1 + randomNumbers.nextInt(6);
```

The shifting value (1) specifies the *first* value in the desired range of random integers. The preceding statement assigns face a random integer in the range 1–6.

Rolling a Six-Sided Die 20 Times

Figure 5.6 shows two sample outputs which confirm that the results of the preceding calculation are integers in the range 1–6, and that each run of the program can produce a *different* sequence of random numbers. Line 3 imports class SecureRandom from the java.security package. Line 10 creates the SecureRandom object randomNumbers to produce random values. Line 16 executes 20 times in a loop to roll the die. The if statement (lines 21–22) in the loop starts a new line of output after every five numbers to create a neat, five-column format.

```
 1    // Fig. 5.6: RandomIntegers.java
 2    // Shifted and scaled random integers.
 3    import java.security.SecureRandom; // program uses class SecureRandom
 4
 5    public class RandomIntegers
 6    {
 7       public static void main(String[] args)
 8       {
 9          // randomNumbers object will produce secure random numbers
10          SecureRandom randomNumbers = new SecureRandom();
11
12          // loop 20 times
13          for (int counter = 1; counter <= 20; counter++)
14          {
15             // pick random integer from 1 to 6
16             int face = 1 + randomNumbers.nextInt(6);
```

Fig. 5.6 | Shifted and scaled random integers. (Part 1 of 2.)

```
17
18              System.out.printf("%d  ", face); // display generated value
19
20              // if counter is divisible by 5, start a new line of output
21              if (counter % 5 == 0)
22                  System.out.println();
23          }
24      }
25  } // end class RandomIntegers
```

```
1  5  3  6  2
5  2  6  5  2
4  4  4  2  6
3  1  6  2  2
```

```
6  5  4  2  6
1  2  5  1  3
6  3  2  2  1
6  4  2  6  4
```

Fig. 5.6 | Shifted and scaled random integers. (Part 2 of 2.)

Rolling a Six-Sided Die 6,000,000 Times

To show that the numbers produced by nextInt occur with approximately equal likelihood, let's simulate 6,000,000 rolls of a die with the application in Fig. 5.7. Each integer from 1 to 6 should appear approximately 1,000,000 times.

```java
1   // Fig. 5.7: RollDie.java
2   // Roll a six-sided die 6,000,000 times.
3   import java.security.SecureRandom;
4
5   public class RollDie
6   {
7      public static void main(String[] args)
8      {
9         // randomNumbers object will produce secure random numbers
10        SecureRandom randomNumbers = new SecureRandom();
11
12        int frequency1 = 0; // count of 1s rolled
13        int frequency2 = 0; // count of 2s rolled
14        int frequency3 = 0; // count of 3s rolled
15        int frequency4 = 0; // count of 4s rolled
16        int frequency5 = 0; // count of 5s rolled
17        int frequency6 = 0; // count of 6s rolled
18
19        // tally counts for 6,000,000 rolls of a die
20        for (int roll = 1; roll <= 6000000; roll++)
21        {
22           int face = 1 + randomNumbers.nextInt(6); // number from 1 to 6
```

Fig. 5.7 | Roll a six-sided die 6,000,000 times. (Part 1 of 2.)

```
23
24              // use face value 1-6 to determine which counter to increment
25              switch (face)
26              {
27                  case 1:
28                      ++frequency1; // increment the 1s counter
29                      break;
30                  case 2:
31                      ++frequency2; // increment the 2s counter
32                      break;
33                  case 3:
34                      ++frequency3; // increment the 3s counter
35                      break;
36                  case 4:
37                      ++frequency4; // increment the 4s counter
38                      break;
39                  case 5:
40                      ++frequency5; // increment the 5s counter
41                      break;
42                  case 6:
43                      ++frequency6; // increment the 6s counter
44                      break;
45              }
46          }
47
48          System.out.println("Face\tFrequency"); // output headers
49          System.out.printf("1\t%d%n2\t%d%n3\t%d%n4\t%d%n5\t%d%n6\t%d%n",
50              frequency1, frequency2, frequency3, frequency4,
51              frequency5, frequency6);
52      }
53  } // end class RollDie
```

```
Face    Frequency
1       999501
2       1000412
3       998262
4       1000820
5       1002245
6       998760
```

```
Face    Frequency
1       999647
2       999557
3       999571
4       1000376
5       1000701
6       1000148
```

Fig. 5.7 | Roll a six-sided die 6,000,000 times. (Part 2 of 2.)

As the sample outputs show, scaling and shifting the values produced by nextInt enables the program to simulate rolling a six-sided die. The application uses nested control statements (the switch is nested inside the for) to determine the number of times each side of the die appears. The for statement (lines 20–46) iterates 6,000,000 times. During each iteration, line 22 produces a random value from 1 to 6. That value is then used as the controlling expression (line 25) of the switch statement (lines 25–45). Based on the face value, the switch statement increments one of the six counter variables during each iteration of the loop. This switch statement has no default case, because we have a case for every possible die value that the expression in line 22 could produce. Run the program, and observe the results. As you'll see, every time you run this program, it produces *different* results.

When we study arrays in Chapter 6, we'll show an elegant way to replace the entire switch statement in this program with a *single* statement. Then, when we study Java SE 8's new functional programming capabilities in Chapter 17, we'll show how to replace the loop that rolls the dice, the switch statement *and* the statement that displays the results with a *single* statement!

Generalized Scaling and Shifting of Random Numbers

Previously, we simulated the rolling of a six-sided die with the statement

```java
int face = 1 + randomNumbers.nextInt(6);
```

This statement always assigns to variable face an integer in the range $1 \leq face \leq 6$. The *width* of this range (i.e., the number of consecutive integers in the range) is 6, and the *starting number* in the range is 1. In the preceding statement, the width of the range is determined by the number 6 that's passed as an argument to SecureRandom method nextInt, and the starting number of the range is the number 1 that's added to randomNumbers.nextInt(6). We can generalize this result as

```java
int number = shiftingValue + randomNumbers.nextInt(scalingFactor);
```

where *shiftingValue* specifies the *first number* in the desired range of consecutive integers and *scalingFactor* specifies *how many numbers* are in the range.

It's also possible to choose integers at random from sets of values other than ranges of consecutive integers. For example, to obtain a random value from the sequence 2, 5, 8, 11 and 14, you could use the statement

```java
int number = 2 + 3 * randomNumbers.nextInt(5);
```

In this case, randomNumbers.nextInt(5) produces values in the range 0–4. Each value produced is multiplied by 3 to produce a number in the sequence 0, 3, 6, 9 and 12. We add 2 to that value to *shift* the range of values and obtain a value from the sequence 2, 5, 8, 11 and 14. We can generalize this result as

```java
int number = shiftingValue +
    differenceBetweenValues * randomNumbers.nextInt(scalingFactor);
```

where *shiftingValue* specifies the first number in the desired range of values, *differenceBetweenValues* represents the *constant difference* between consecutive numbers in the sequence and *scalingFactor* specifies how many numbers are in the range.

A Note About Performance

Using SecureRandom instead of Random to achieve higher levels of security incurs a significant performance penalty. For "casual" applications, you might want to use class Random from package java.util—simply replace SecureRandom with Random.

5.10 Case Study: A Game of Chance; Introducing enum Types

A popular game of chance is a dice game known as craps, which is played in casinos and back alleys throughout the world. The rules of the game are straightforward:

> *You roll two dice. Each die has six faces, which contain one, two, three, four, five and six spots, respectively. After the dice have come to rest, the sum of the spots on the two upward faces is calculated. If the sum is 7 or 11 on the first throw, you win. If the sum is 2, 3 or 12 on the first throw (called "craps"), you lose (i.e., the "house" wins). If the sum is 4, 5, 6, 8, 9 or 10 on the first throw, that sum becomes your "point." To win, you must continue rolling the dice until you "make your point" (i.e., roll that same point value). You lose by rolling a 7 before making your point.*

Figure 5.8 simulates the game of craps, using methods to implement the game's logic. The main method (lines 21–65) calls the rollDice method (lines 68–81) as necessary to roll the dice and compute their sum. The sample outputs show winning and losing on the first roll, and winning and losing on a subsequent roll.

```
1   // Fig. 5.8: Craps.java
2   // Craps class simulates the dice game craps.
3   import java.security.SecureRandom;
4
5   public class Craps
6   {
7      // create secure random number generator for use in method rollDice
8      private static final SecureRandom randomNumbers = new SecureRandom();
9
10     // enum type with constants that represent the game status
11     private enum Status { CONTINUE, WON, LOST };
12
13     // constants that represent common rolls of the dice
14     private static final int SNAKE_EYES = 2;
15     private static final int TREY = 3;
16     private static final int SEVEN = 7;
17     private static final int YO_LEVEN = 11;
18     private static final int BOX_CARS = 12;
19
20     // plays one game of craps
21     public static void main(String[] args)
22     {
23        int myPoint = 0; // point if no win or loss on first roll
24        Status gameStatus; // can contain CONTINUE, WON or LOST
25
26        int sumOfDice = rollDice(); // first roll of the dice
27
28        // determine game status and point based on first roll
29        switch (sumOfDice)
30        {
```

Fig. 5.8 | Craps class simulates the dice game craps. (Part 1 of 3.)

```
31              case SEVEN: // win with 7 on first roll
32              case YO_LEVEN: // win with 11 on first roll
33                 gameStatus = Status.WON;
34                 break;
35              case SNAKE_EYES: // lose with 2 on first roll
36              case TREY: // lose with 3 on first roll
37              case BOX_CARS: // lose with 12 on first roll
38                 gameStatus = Status.LOST;
39                 break;
40              default: // did not win or lose, so remember point
41                 gameStatus = Status.CONTINUE; // game is not over
42                 myPoint = sumOfDice; // remember the point
43                 System.out.printf("Point is %d%n", myPoint);
44                 break;
45           }
46
47        // while game is not complete
48        while (gameStatus == Status.CONTINUE) // not WON or LOST
49        {
50           sumOfDice = rollDice(); // roll dice again
51
52           // determine game status
53           if (sumOfDice == myPoint) // win by making point
54              gameStatus = Status.WON;
55           else
56              if (sumOfDice == SEVEN) // lose by rolling 7 before point
57                 gameStatus = Status.LOST;
58        }
59
60        // display won or lost message
61        if (gameStatus == Status.WON)
62           System.out.println("Player wins");
63        else
64           System.out.println("Player loses");
65     }
66
67     // roll dice, calculate sum and display results
68     public static int rollDice()
69     {
70        // pick random die values
71        int die1 = 1 + randomNumbers.nextInt(6); // first die roll
72        int die2 = 1 + randomNumbers.nextInt(6); // second die roll
73
74        int sum = die1 + die2; // sum of die values
75
76        // display results of this roll
77        System.out.printf("Player rolled %d + %d = %d%n",
78           die1, die2, sum);
79
80        return sum;
81     }
82 } // end class Craps
```

Fig. 5.8 | Craps class simulates the dice game craps. (Part 2 of 3.)

```
Player rolled 5 + 6 = 11
Player wins
```

```
Player rolled 5 + 4 = 9
Point is 9
Player rolled 4 + 2 = 6
Player rolled 3 + 6 = 9
Player wins
```

```
Player rolled 1 + 2 = 3
Player loses
```

```
Player rolled 2 + 6 = 8
Point is 8
Player rolled 5 + 1 = 6
Player rolled 2 + 1 = 3
Player rolled 1 + 6 = 7
Player loses
```

Fig. 5.8 | Craps class simulates the dice game craps. (Part 3 of 3.)

Method rollDice

In the rules of the game, the player must roll *two* dice on the first and all subsequent rolls. We declare method rollDice (lines 68–81) to roll the dice and compute and print their sum. Method rollDice is declared once, but it's called from two places (lines 26 and 50) in main, which contains the logic for one complete game of craps. Method rollDice takes no arguments, so it has an empty parameter list. Each time it's called, rollDice returns the sum of the dice, so the return type int is indicated in the method header (line 68). Although lines 71 and 72 look the same (except for the die names), they do not necessarily produce the same result. Each of these statements produces a *random* value in the range 1– 6. Variable randomNumbers (used in lines 71–72) is *not* declared in the method. Instead it's declared as a private static final variable of the class and initialized in line 8. This enables us to create one SecureRandom object that's reused in each call to rollDice.

Method main's Local Variables

The game is reasonably involved. The player may win or lose on the first roll, or may win or lose on any subsequent roll. Method main (lines 21–65) uses local variable myPoint (line 23) to store the "point" if the player doesn't win or lose on the first roll, local variable gameStatus (line 24) to keep track of the overall game status and local variable sumOfDice (line 26) to hold the sum of the dice for the most recent roll. Variable myPoint is initialized to 0 to ensure that the application will compile. If you do not initialize myPoint, the compiler issues an error, because myPoint is not assigned a value in *every* case of the switch statement, and thus the program could try to use myPoint before it's assigned a value. By contrast, gameStatus *is* assigned a value in *every* case of the switch statement (including the `default` case)—thus, it's guaranteed to be initialized before it's used, so we do not need to initialize it in line 24.

enum *Type* Status

Local variable `gameStatus` (line 24) is declared to be of a new type called `Status` (declared at line 11). Type `Status` is a `private` member of class `Craps`, because `Status` will be used only in that class. `Status` is a type called an **enum type**, which, in its simplest form, declares a set of constants represented by identifiers. An enum type is a special kind of class that's introduced by the keyword enum and a type name (in this case, `Status`). As with classes, braces delimit an enum declaration's body. Inside the braces is a comma-separated list of **enum constants**, each representing a unique value. The identifiers in an enum must be *unique*. You'll learn more about enum types in Chapter 8.

Good Programming Practice 5.1

Use only uppercase letters in the names of enum constants to make them stand out and remind you that they're not variables.

Variables of type `Status` can be assigned only the three constants declared in the enum (line 11) or a compilation error will occur. When the game is won, the program sets local variable `gameStatus` to `Status.WON` (lines 33 and 54). When the game is lost, the program sets local variable `gameStatus` to `Status.LOST` (lines 38 and 57). Otherwise, the program sets local variable `gameStatus` to `Status.CONTINUE` (line 41) to indicate that the game is not over and the dice must be rolled again.

Good Programming Practice 5.2

Using enum constants (like Status.WON, Status.LOST and Status.CONTINUE) rather than literal values (such as 0, 1 and 2) makes programs easier to read and maintain.

Logic of the main *Method*

Line 26 in `main` calls `rollDice`, which picks two random values from 1 to 6, displays the values of the first die, the second die and their sum, and returns the sum. Method `main` next enters the `switch` statement (lines 29–45), which uses the `sumOfDice` value from line 26 to determine whether the game has been won or lost, or should continue with another roll. The values that result in a win or loss on the first roll are declared as `private static final int` constants in lines 14–18. The identifier names use casino parlance for these sums. These constants, like enum constants, are declared by convention with all capital letters, to make them stand out in the program. Lines 31–34 determine whether the player won on the first roll with `SEVEN` (7) or `YO_LEVEN` (11). Lines 35–39 determine whether the player lost on the first roll with `SNAKE_EYES` (2), `TREY` (3), or `BOX_CARS` (12). After the first roll, if the game is not over, the `default` case (lines 40–44) sets `gameStatus` to `Status.CONTINUE`, saves `sumOfDice` in `myPoint` and displays the point.

If we're still trying to "make our point" (i.e., the game is continuing from a prior roll), lines 48–58 execute. Line 50 rolls the dice again. If `sumOfDice` matches `myPoint` (line 53), line 54 sets `gameStatus` to `Status.WON`, then the loop terminates because the game is complete. If `sumOfDice` is `SEVEN` (line 56), line 57 sets `gameStatus` to `Status.LOST`, and the loop terminates because the game is complete. When the game completes, lines 61–64 display a message indicating whether the player won or lost, and the program terminates.

The program uses the various program-control mechanisms we've discussed. The Craps class uses two methods—main and rollDice (called twice from main)—and the switch, while, if...else and nested if control statements. Note also the use of multiple case labels in the switch statement to execute the same statements for sums of SEVEN and YO_LEVEN (lines 31–32) and for sums of SNAKE_EYES, TREY and BOX_CARS (lines 35–37).

Why Some Constants Are Not Defined as enum Constants

You might be wondering why we declared the sums of the dice as private static final int constants rather than as enum constants. The reason is that the program must compare the int variable sumOfDice (line 26) to these constants to determine the outcome of each roll. Suppose we declared enum Sum containing constants (e.g., Sum.SNAKE_EYES) representing the five sums used in the game, then used these constants in the switch statement (lines 29–45). Doing so would prevent us from using sumOfDice as the switch statement's controlling expression, because Java does *not* allow an int to be compared to an enum constant. To achieve the same functionality as the current program, we would have to use a variable currentSum of type Sum as the switch's controlling expression. Unfortunately, Java does not provide an easy way to convert an int value to a particular enum constant. This could be done with a separate switch statement. This would be cumbersome and would not improve the program's readability (thus defeating the purpose of using an enum).

5.11 Scope of Declarations

You've seen declarations of various Java entities, such as classes, methods, variables and parameters. Declarations introduce names that can be used to refer to such Java entities. The **scope** of a declaration is the portion of the program that can refer to the declared entity by its name. Such an entity is said to be "in scope" for that portion of the program. This section introduces several important scope issues.

The basic scope rules are as follows:

1. The scope of a parameter declaration is the body of the method in which the declaration appears.

2. The scope of a local-variable declaration is from the point at which the declaration appears to the end of that block.

3. The scope of a local-variable declaration that appears in the initialization section of a for statement's header is the body of the for statement and the other expressions in the header.

4. A method or field's scope is the entire body of the class.

Any block may contain variable declarations. If a local variable or parameter in a method has the same name as a field of the class, the field is *hidden* until the block terminates execution—this is called **shadowing**. You can access a shadowed static variable of a class by preceding its name with the class's name and a dot (.), as in *ClassName*.x. (Section 7.2.1 discusses shadowing of so-called instance variables.)

Figure 5.9 demonstrates scoping issues with static and local variables. Line 7 declares and initializes the static variable x to 1. This variable is *shadowed* in any block (or method) that declares a local variable named x. Method main (lines 11–23) declares a local variable x (line 13) and initializes it to 5. This local variable's value is output to show that the static variable x (whose value is 1) is *shadowed* in main. The program declares two other methods—useLocalVariable (lines 26–35) and useField (lines 38–45)—that each take no arguments and return no results. Method main calls each method twice (lines 17–20). Method useLocalVariable declares local variable x (line 28). When useLocalVariable is first called (line 17), it creates local variable x and initializes it to 25 (line 28), outputs the value of x (lines 30–31), increments x (line 32) and outputs the value of x again (lines 33–34). When useLocalVariable is called a second time (line 19), it *recreates* local variable x and *reinitializes* it to 25, so the output of each useLocalVariable call is identical.

```java
1   // Fig. 5.9: Scope.java
2   // Scope class demonstrates field and local variable scopes.
3
4   public class Scope
5   {
6      // field that is accessible to all methods of this class
7      private static int x = 1;
8
9      // method main creates and initializes local variable x
10     // and calls methods useLocalVariable and useField
11     public static void main(String[] args)
12     {
13        int x = 5; // method's local variable x shadows field x
14
15        System.out.printf("local x in main is %d%n", x);
16
17        useLocalVariable(); // useLocalVariable has local x
18        useField(); // useField uses class Scope's field x
19        useLocalVariable(); // useLocalVariable reinitializes local x
20        useField(); // class Scope's field x retains its value
21
22        System.out.printf("%nlocal x in main is %d%n", x);
23     }
24
25     // create and initialize local variable x during each call
26     public static void useLocalVariable()
27     {
28        int x = 25; // initialized each time useLocalVariable is called
29
30        System.out.printf(
31           "%nlocal x on entering method useLocalVariable is %d%n", x);
32        ++x; // modifies this method's local variable x
33        System.out.printf(
34           "local x before exiting method useLocalVariable is %d%n", x);
35     }
36
37     // modify class Scope's field x during each call
38     public static void useField()
39     {
40        System.out.printf(
41           "%nfield x on entering method useField is %d%n", x);
```

Fig. 5.9 | Scope class demonstrates field and local-variable scopes. (Part 1 of 2.)

```
42            x *= 10; // modifies class Scope's field x
43            System.out.printf(
44               "field x before exiting method useField is %d%n", x);
45         }
46      } // end class Scope
```

```
local x in main is 5

local x on entering method useLocalVariable is 25
local x before exiting method useLocalVariable is 26

field x on entering method useField is 1
field x before exiting method useField is 10

local x on entering method useLocalVariable is 25
local x before exiting method useLocalVariable is 26

field x on entering method useField is 10
field x before exiting method useField is 100

local x in main is 5
```

Fig. 5.9 | Scope class demonstrates field and local-variable scopes. (Part 2 of 2.)

Method useField does not declare any local variables. Therefore, when it refers to x, the static variable x (line 7) of the class is used. When method useField is first called (line 18), it outputs the value (1) of static variable x (lines 40–41), multiplies it by 10 (line 42) and outputs its value (10) again (lines 43–44) before returning. The next time method useField is called (line 20), the static variable has its modified value (10), so the method outputs 10, then 100. Finally, in method main, the program outputs the value of local variable x again (line 22) to show that none of the method calls modified main's local variable x, because the methods all referred to variables named x in other scopes.

Principle of Least Privilege

In a general sense, "things" should have the capabilities they need to get their job done, but no more. An example is the scope of a variable. A variable should not be visible when it's not needed.

Good Programming Practice 5.3

Declare local variables as close to where they're first used as possible.

5.12 Method Overloading

Methods of the *same* name can be declared in the same class, as long as they have *different* sets of parameters (determined by the number, types and order of the parameters)—this is called **method overloading**. When an overloaded method is called, the compiler selects the appropriate method by examining the number, types and order of the arguments in the call. Method overloading is commonly used to create several methods with the *same* name that perform the *same* or *similar* tasks, but on *different* types or *different* numbers of arguments. For example, Math methods abs, min and max (summarized in Section 5.3) are overloaded with four versions each:

1. One with two double parameters.

2. One with two float parameters.

3. One with two int parameters.

4. One with two long parameters.

Our next example demonstrates declaring and invoking overloaded methods. We demonstrate overloaded constructors in Chapter 8.

Declaring Overloaded Methods

Class MethodOverload (Fig. 5.10) includes two overloaded versions of method square—one that calculates the square of an int (and returns an int) and one that calculates the square of a double (and returns a double). Although these methods have the same name and similar parameter lists and bodies, think of them simply as *different* methods. It may help to think of the method names as "square of int" and "square of double," respectively.

Line 9 invokes method square with the argument 7. Literal integer values are treated as type int, so the method call in line 9 invokes the version of square at lines 14–19 that specifies an int parameter. Similarly, line 10 invokes method square with the argument

```java
 1   // Fig. 5.10: MethodOverload.java
 2   // Overloaded method declarations.
 3
 4   public class MethodOverload
 5   {
 6      // test overloaded square methods
 7      public static void main(String[] args)
 8      {
 9         System.out.printf("Square of integer 7 is %d%n", square(7));
10         System.out.printf("Square of double 7.5 is %f%n", square(7.5));
11      }
12
13      // square method with int argument
14      public static int square(int intValue)
15      {
16         System.out.printf("%nCalled square with int argument: %d%n",
17            intValue);
18         return intValue * intValue;
19      }
20
21      // square method with double argument
22      public static double square(double doubleValue)
23      {
24         System.out.printf("%nCalled square with double argument: %f%n",
25            doubleValue);
26         return doubleValue * doubleValue;
27      }
28   } // end class MethodOverload
```

Fig. 5.10 | Overloaded method declarations. (Part 1 of 2.)

```
Called square with int argument: 7
Square of integer 7 is 49

Called square with double argument: 7.500000
Square of double 7.5 is 56.250000
```

Fig. 5.10 | Overloaded method declarations. (Part 2 of 2.)

7.5. Literal floating-point values are treated as type double, so the method call in line 10 invokes the version of square at lines 22–27 that specifies a double parameter. Each method first outputs a line of text to prove that the proper method was called in each case. The values in lines 10 and 24 are displayed with the format specifier %f. We did not specify a precision in either case. By default, floating-point values are displayed with six digits of precision if the precision is *not* specified in the format specifier.

Distinguishing Between Overloaded Methods
The compiler distinguishes overloaded methods by their **signatures**—a combination of the method's *name* and the *number*, *types* and *order* of its parameters, but *not* its return type. If the compiler looked only at method names during compilation, the code in Fig. 5.10 would be ambiguous—the compiler would not know how to distinguish between the two square methods (lines 14–19 and 22–27). Internally, the compiler uses longer method names that include the original method name, the types of each parameter and the exact order of the parameters to determine whether the methods in a class are *unique* in that class.

For example, in Fig. 5.10, the compiler might (internally) use the logical name "square of int" for the square method that specifies an int parameter and "square of double" for the square method that specifies a double parameter (the actual names the compiler uses are messier). If method1's declaration begins as

        void method1(int a, float b)

then the compiler might use the logical name "method1 of int and float." If the parameters are specified as

        void method1(float a, int b)

then the compiler might use the logical name "method1 of float and int." The *order* of the parameter types is important—the compiler considers the preceding two method1 headers to be *distinct*.

Return Types of Overloaded Methods
In discussing the logical names of methods used by the compiler, we did not mention the return types of the methods. *Method calls cannot be distinguished only by return type.* If you had overloaded methods that differed *only* by their return types and you called one of the methods in a standalone statement as in:

        square(2);

the compiler would *not* be able to determine the version of the method to call, because the return value is *ignored*. When two methods have the *same* signature and *different* return types, the compiler issues an error message indicating that the method is already defined in the class. Overloaded methods *can* have *different* return types if the methods have *different* parameter lists. Also, overloaded methods need *not* have the same number of parameters.

Common Programming Error 5.9

Declaring overloaded methods with identical parameter lists is a compilation error regardless of whether the return types are different.

5.13 (Optional) GUI and Graphics Case Study: Colors and Filled Shapes

Although you can create many interesting designs with just lines and basic shapes, class Graphics provides many more capabilities. The next two features we introduce are colors and filled shapes. Adding color enriches the drawings a user sees on the computer screen. Shapes can be filled with solid colors.

Colors displayed on computer screens are defined by their *red*, *green*, and *blue* components (called **RGB values**) that have integer values from 0 to 255. The higher the value of a component color, the richer that color's shade will be. Java uses class **Color** (package java.awt) to represent colors using their RGB values. For convenience, class Color contains various predefined static Color objects—BLACK, BLUE, CYAN, DARK_GRAY, GRAY, GREEN, LIGHT_GRAY, MAGENTA, ORANGE, PINK, RED, WHITE and YELLOW. Each can be accessed via the class name and a dot (.) as in Color.RED. You can create custom colors by passing the red-, green- and blue-component values to class Color's constructor:

```
public Color(int r, int g, int b)
```

Graphics methods **fillRect** and **fillOval** draw filled rectangles and ovals, respectively. These have the same parameters as drawRect and drawOval; the first two are the coordinates for the *upper-left corner* of the shape, while the next two determine the *width* and *height*. The example in Fig. 5.11 demonstrates colors and filled shapes by drawing and displaying a yellow smiley face on the screen.

```
1   // Fig. 5.11: DrawSmiley.java
2   // Drawing a smiley face using colors and filled shapes.
3   import java.awt.Color;
4   import java.awt.Graphics;
5   import javax.swing.JPanel;
6
7   public class DrawSmiley extends JPanel
8   {
9      public void paintComponent(Graphics g)
10     {
11        super.paintComponent(g);
12
13        // draw the face
14        g.setColor(Color.YELLOW);
15        g.fillOval(10, 10, 200, 200);
16
```

Fig. 5.11 | Drawing a smiley face using colors and filled shapes. (Part 1 of 2.)

```
17          // draw the eyes
18          g.setColor(Color.BLACK);
19          g.fillOval(55, 65, 30, 30);
20          g.fillOval(135, 65, 30, 30);
21
22          // draw the mouth
23          g.fillOval(50, 110, 120, 60);
24
25          // "touch up" the mouth into a smile
26          g.setColor(Color.YELLOW);
27          g.fillRect(50, 110, 120, 30);
28          g.fillOval(50, 120, 120, 40);
29      }
30
31      public static void main(String[] args)
32      {
33          DrawSmiley panel = new DrawSmiley();
34          JFrame application = new JFrame();
35
36          application.setDefaultCloseOperation(JFrame.EXIT_ON_CLOSE);
37          application.add(panel);
38          application.setSize(230, 250);
39          application.setVisible(true);
40      }
41  } // end class DrawSmiley
```

Fig. 5.11 | Drawing a smiley face using colors and filled shapes. (Part 2 of 2.)

The import statements in lines 3–5 import classes Color, Graphics and JPanel. Class DrawSmiley uses class Color to specify drawing colors, and uses class Graphics to draw.

Class JPanel again provides the area in which we draw. Line 14 in method paintComponent uses Graphics method **setColor** to set the current drawing color to Color.YELLOW. Method setColor requires one argument, the Color to set as the drawing color. In this case, we use the predefined object Color.YELLOW.

Line 15 draws a circle with diameter 200 to represent the face—when the width and height arguments are identical, method fillOval draws a circle. Next, line 18 sets the color to Color.Black, and lines 19–20 draw the eyes. Line 23 draws the mouth as an oval, but this is not quite what we want.

To create a happy face, we'll touch up the mouth. Line 26 sets the color to Color.YELLOW, so any shapes we draw will blend in with the face. Line 27 draws a rectangle that's half the mouth's height. This erases the top half of the mouth, leaving just the bottom half. To create a better smile, line 28 draws another oval to slightly cover the upper portion of the mouth. Method main (lines 31–40) creates and displays a JFrame containing the drawing. When the JFrame is displayed, the system calls method paintComponent to draw the smiley face.

GUI and Graphics Case Study Exercises

5.1   Using method fillOval, draw a bull's-eye that alternates between two random colors, as in Fig. 5.12. Use the constructor Color(int r, int g, int b) with random arguments to generate random colors.

5.2   Create a program that draws 10 random filled shapes in random colors, positions and sizes (Fig. 5.13). Method paintComponent should contain a loop that iterates 10 times. In each iteration, the loop should determine whether to draw a filled rectangle or an oval, create a random color and choose coordinates and dimensions at random. The coordinates should be chosen based on the panel's width and height. Lengths of sides should be limited to half the width or height of the window.

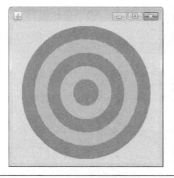

Fig. 5.12 | A bulls-eye with two alternating, random colors.

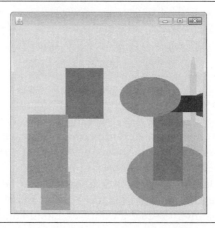

Fig. 5.13 | Randomly generated shapes.

5.14 Wrap-Up

In this chapter, you learned about method declarations and how to call call static methods. You learned how to use operators + and += to perform string concatenations. We discussed how the method-call stack and stack frames keep track of the methods that have been called and where each method must return to when it completes its task. We also discussed Java's promotion rules for converting implicitly between primitive types and how to perform explicit conversions with cast operators. Next, you learned about some of the commonly used packages in the Java API.

You saw how to declare named constants using both enum types and private static final variables. You used class SecureRandom to generate random numbers for simulations. You also learned about the scope of fields and local variables in a class. Finally, you learned that multiple methods in one class can be overloaded by providing methods with the same name and different signatures. Such methods can be used to perform the same or similar tasks using different types or different numbers of parameters.

In Chapter 6, you'll learn how to maintain lists and tables of data in arrays. You'll see a more elegant implementation of the application that rolls a die 6,000,000 times. You'll also learn how to access an application's command-line arguments that are passed to method main when an application begins execution.

Summary

Section 5.1 Introduction
- Experience has shown that the best way to develop and maintain a large program is to construct it from small, simple pieces, or modules. This technique is called divide and conquer (p. 165).

Section 5.2 Program Modules in Java
- Methods are declared within classes. Classes are typically grouped into packages so they can be imported and reused.
- Methods allow you to modularize a program by separating its tasks into self-contained units. The statements in a method are written only once and hidden from other methods.
- Using existing methods as building blocks to create new programs is a form of software reusability (p. 166) that allows you to avoid repeating code within a program.

Section 5.3 static Methods, static Fields and Class Math
- A method call specifies the name of the method to call and provides the arguments that the called method requires to perform its task. When the method call completes, the method returns either a result, or simply control, to its caller.
- A class may contain static methods to perform common tasks that do not require an object of the class. Any data a static method might require to perform its tasks can be sent to the method as arguments in a method call. A static method is called by specifying the name of the class in which the method is declared followed by a dot (.) and the method name, as in

    ClassName.methodName(arguments)

- Class Math provides static methods for performing common mathematical calculations.
- Math.PI (3.141592653589793; p. 169) is the ratio of a circle's circumference to its diameter. Math.E (2.718281828459045; p. 169) is the base value for natural logarithms.

- `Math.PI` and `Math.E` are declared `public`, `static` and `final`. Making them `public` allows you to use these fields in your own classes. Making them `static` allows them to be accessed via the class name `Math` and a dot (.) separator, just like class `Math`'s methods. Making them `final` (p. 169) indicates that they are constants—their values cannot be changed after they're initialized.

- When you execute the Java Virtual Machine (JVM) with the `java` command, the JVM loads the class you specify and uses that class name to invoke method `main`. You can specify additional command-line arguments (p. 169) that the JVM will pass to your application.

- You can place a `main` method in every class you declare—only the `main` method in the class you use to execute the application will be called by the `java` command.

Section 5.4 Declaring Methods

- Class, method and variable names are identifiers. By convention all use camel case names. Class names begin with an uppercase letter, and method and variable names begin with a lowercase letter.

- Parameters are declared in a comma-separated parameter list (p. 171), which is located inside the parentheses that follow the method name in the method declaration. Multiple parameters are separated by commas. Each parameter must specify a type followed by a variable name.

- Every method's body is delimited by left and right braces ({ and }).

- Each method's body contains one or more statements that perform the method's task(s).

- The method's return type specifies the type of data returned to a method's caller. Keyword `void` indicates that a method will perform a task but will not return any information.

- Empty parentheses following a method name indicate that the method does not require any parameters to perform its task.

- When a method that specifies a return type (p. 171) other than `void` is called and completes its task, the method must return a result to its calling method.

- The `return` statement (p. 172) passes a value from a called method back to its caller.

- When a method is called, the program makes a copy of the method's argument values and assigns them to the method's corresponding parameters. When program control returns to the point in the program where the method was called, the method's parameters are removed from memory.

- `String`s can be concatenated (p. 172) using operator +, which places the characters of the right operand at the end of those in the left operand.

- Every primitive value and object in Java can be represented as a `String`.

- If a `boolean` is concatenated with a `String`, the word `"true"` or the word `"false"` is used to represent the `boolean` value.

- All objects in Java have a special method named `toString` that returns a `String` representation of the object's contents. When an object is concatenated with a `String`, the JVM implicitly calls the object's `toString` method to obtain the string representation of the object.

- You can break large `String` literals into several smaller `String`s and place them on multiple lines of code for readability, then reassemble the `String`s using concatenation.

Section 5.5 Notes on Declaring and Using Methods

- There are three ways to call a method—using a method name by itself to call another method of the same class; using an object's variable name followed by a dot (.) and the method name to call a method of the object; and using the class name and a dot (.) to call a `static` method of a class.

- There are three ways to return control to a statement that calls a method. If the method does not return a result, control returns when the program flow reaches the method-ending right brace or when the statement

```
return;
```

is executed. If the method returns a result, the statement

> **return** *expression*;

evaluates the *expression*, then immediately returns the resulting value to the caller.

Section 5.6 Method-Call Stack and Stack Frames
- Stacks (p. 174) are known as last-in, first-out (LIFO) data structures—the last item pushed (inserted) onto the stack is the first item popped (removed) from the stack.
- A called method must know how to return to its caller, so the return address of the calling method is pushed onto the method-call stack when the method is called. If a series of method calls occurs, the successive return addresses are pushed onto the stack in last-in, first-out order so that the last method to execute will be the first to return to its caller.
- The method-call stack (p. 174) contains the memory for the local variables used in each invocation of a method during a program's execution. This data is known as the method call's stack frame or activation record. When a method call is made, the stack frame for that method call is pushed onto the method-call stack. When the method returns to its caller, its stack frame call is popped off the stack and the local variables are no longer known to the program.
- If there are more method calls than can have their stack frames stored on the method-call stack, an error known as a stack overflow (p. 174) occurs. The application will compile correctly, but its execution causes a stack overflow.

Section 5.7 Argument Promotion and Casting
- Argument promotion (p. 175) converts an argument's value to the type that the method expects to receive in its corresponding parameter.
- Promotion rules (p. 175) apply to expressions containing values of two or more primitive types and to primitive-type values passed as arguments to methods. Each value is promoted to the "highest" type in the expression. In cases where information may be lost due to conversion, the Java compiler requires you to use a cast operator to explicitly force the conversion to occur.

Section 5.9 Case Study: Secure Random-Number Generation
- `SecureRandom` objects can produce nondeterministic random values.
- `SecureRandom` method `nextInt` (p. 178) generates a random `int` value.
- Class `SecureRandom` provides another version of method `nextInt` that receives an `int` argument and returns a value from 0 up to, but not including, the argument's value.
- Random numbers in a range (p. 179) can be generated with

> **int** number = *shiftingValue* + randomNumbers.nextInt(*scalingFactor*);

where *shiftingValue* specifies the first number in the desired range of consecutive integers, and *scalingFactor* specifies how many numbers are in the range.
- Random numbers can be chosen from nonconsecutive integer ranges, as in

> **int** number = *shiftingValue* +
>   *differenceBetweenValues* * randomNumbers.nextInt(*scalingFactor*);

where *shiftingValue* specifies the first number in the range of values, *differenceBetweenValues* represents the difference between consecutive numbers in the sequence and *scalingFactor* specifies how many numbers are in the range.

Section 5.10 Case Study: A Game of Chance; Introducing **enum** Types
- An `enum` type (p. 186) is introduced by the keyword enum and a type name. As with any class, braces ({ and }) delimit the body of an enum declaration. Inside the braces is a comma-separated

list of `enum` constants, each representing a unique value. The identifiers in an `enum` must be unique. Variables of an `enum` type can be assigned only constants of that `enum` type.

- Constants can also be declared as `private static final` variables. Such constants are declared by convention with all capital letters to make them stand out in the program.

Section 5.11 Scope of Declarations

- Scope (p. 187) is the portion of the program in which an entity, such as a variable or a method, can be referred to by its name. Such an entity is said to be "in scope" for that portion of the program.
- The scope of a parameter declaration is the body of the method in which the declaration appears.
- The scope of a local-variable declaration is from the point at which the declaration appears to the end of that block.
- The scope of a local-variable declaration that appears in the initialization section of a `for` statement's header is the body of the `for` statement and the other expressions in the header.
- The scope of a method or field of a class is the entire body of the class. This enables a class's methods to use simple names to call the class's other methods and to access the class's fields.
- Any block may contain variable declarations. If a local variable or parameter in a method has the same name as a variable of the class, the class's variable is shadowed (p. 187) until the block terminates execution.

Section 5.12 Method Overloading

- Java allows overloaded methods (p. 189) in a class, as long as the methods have different sets of parameters (determined by the number, order and types of the parameters).
- Overloaded methods are distinguished by their signatures (p. 191)—combinations of the methods' names and the number, types and order of their parameters, but not their return types.

Self-Review Exercises

5.1 Fill in the blanks in each of the following statements:
a) A method is invoked with a(n) _____.
b) A variable known only within the method in which it's declared is called a(n) _____.
c) The _____ statement in a called method can be used to pass the value of an expression back to the calling method.
d) The keyword _____ indicates that a method does not return a value.
e) Data can be added or removed only from the _____ of a stack.
f) Stacks are known as _____ data structures; the last item pushed (inserted) onto the stack is the first item popped (removed) from the stack.
g) The three ways to return control from a called method to a caller are _____, _____ and _____.
h) An object of class _____ produces truly random numbers.
i) The method-call stack contains the memory for local variables on each invocation of a method during a program's execution. This data, stored as a portion of the method-call stack, is known as the _____ or _____ of the method call.
j) If there are more method calls than can be stored on the method-call stack, an error known as a(n) _____ occurs.
k) The _____ of a declaration is the portion of a program that can refer to the entity in the declaration by name.
l) It's possible to have several methods with the same name that each operate on different types or numbers of arguments. This feature is called method _____.

5.2   For the class `Craps` in Fig. 5.8, state the scope of each of the following entities:

a) the variable `randomNumbers`.

b) the variable `die1`.

c) the method `rollDice`.

d) the method `main`.

e) the variable `sumOfDice`.

5.3   Write an application that tests whether the examples of the `Math` class method calls shown in Fig. 5.2 actually produce the indicated results.

5.4   Give the method header for each of the following methods:

a) Method `hypotenuse`, which takes two double-precision, floating-point arguments `side1` and `side2` and returns a double-precision, floating-point result.

b) Method `smallest`, which takes three integers `x`, `y` and `z` and returns an integer.

c) Method `instructions`, which does not take any arguments and does not return a value. [*Note:* Such methods are commonly used to display instructions to a user.]

d) Method `intToFloat`, which takes integer argument `number` and returns a `float`.

5.5   Find the error in each of the following program segments. Explain how to correct the error.

a) ```
void g()
{
    System.out.println("Inside method g");

    void h()
    {
        System.out.println("Inside method h");
    }
}
```

b)  ```
int sum(int x, int y)
{
    int result;
    result = x + y;
}
```

c) ```
void f(float a);
{
    float a;
    System.out.println(a);
}
```

d)  ```
void product()
{
    int a = 6, b = 5, c = 4, result;
    result = a * b * c;
    System.out.printf("Result is %d%n", result);
    return result;
}
```

5.6   Declare method `sphereVolume` to calculate and return the volume of the sphere. Use the following statement to calculate the volume:

```
double volume = (4.0 / 3.0) * Math.PI * Math.pow(radius, 3)
```

Write a Java application that prompts the user for the `double` radius of a sphere, calls `sphereVolume` to calculate the volume and displays the result.

Answers to Self-Review Exercises

5.1 a) method call. b) local variable. c) return. d) void. e) top. f) last-in, first-out (LIFO). g) return; or return *expression*; or encountering the closing right brace of a method. h) SecureRandom. i) stack frame, activation record. j) stack overflow. k) scope. l) method overloading.

5.2 a) class body. b) block that defines method rollDice's body. c) class body. d) class body. e) block that defines method main's body.

5.3 The following solution demonstrates the Math class methods in Fig. 5.2:

```
1   // Exercise 5.3: MathTest.java
2   // Testing the Math class methods.
3   public class MathTest
4   {
5      public static void main(String[] args)
6      {
7         System.out.printf("Math.abs(23.7) = %f%n", Math.abs(23.7));
8         System.out.printf("Math.abs(0.0) = %f%n", Math.abs(0.0));
9         System.out.printf("Math.abs(-23.7) = %f%n", Math.abs(-23.7));
10        System.out.printf("Math.ceil(9.2) = %f%n", Math.ceil(9.2));
11        System.out.printf("Math.ceil(-9.8) = %f%n", Math.ceil(-9.8));
12        System.out.printf("Math.cos(0.0) = %f%n", Math.cos(0.0));
13        System.out.printf("Math.exp(1.0) = %f%n", Math.exp(1.0));
14        System.out.printf("Math.exp(2.0) = %f%n", Math.exp(2.0));
15        System.out.printf("Math.floor(9.2) = %f%n", Math.floor(9.2));
16        System.out.printf("Math.floor(-9.8) = %f%n", Math.floor(-9.8));
17        System.out.printf("Math.log(Math.E) = %f%n", Math.log(Math.E));
18        System.out.printf("Math.log(Math.E * Math.E) = %f%n",
19           Math.log(Math.E * Math.E));
20        System.out.printf("Math.max(2.3, 12.7) = %f%n", Math.max(2.3, 12.7));
21        System.out.printf("Math.max(-2.3, -12.7) = %f%n",
22           Math.max(-2.3, -12.7));
23        System.out.printf("Math.min(2.3, 12.7) = %f%n", Math.min(2.3, 12.7));
24        System.out.printf("Math.min(-2.3, -12.7) = %f%n",
25           Math.min(-2.3, -12.7));
26        System.out.printf("Math.pow(2.0, 7.0) = %f%n", Math.pow(2.0, 7.0));
27        System.out.printf("Math.pow(9.0, 0.5) = %f%n", Math.pow(9.0, 0.5));
28        System.out.printf("Math.sin(0.0) = %f%n", Math.sin(0.0));
29        System.out.printf("Math.sqrt(900.0) = %f%n", Math.sqrt(900.0));
30        System.out.printf("Math.tan(0.0) = %f%n", Math.tan(0.0));
31     } // end main
32  } // end class MathTest
```

```
Math.abs(23.7) = 23.700000
Math.abs(0.0) = 0.000000
Math.abs(-23.7) = 23.700000
Math.ceil(9.2) = 10.000000
Math.ceil(-9.8) = -9.000000
Math.cos(0.0) = 1.000000
Math.exp(1.0) = 2.718282
Math.exp(2.0) = 7.389056
Math.floor(9.2) = 9.000000
Math.floor(-9.8) = -10.000000
Math.log(Math.E) = 1.000000
Math.log(Math.E * Math.E) = 2.000000
Math.max(2.3, 12.7) = 12.700000
Math.max(-2.3, -12.7) = -2.300000
Math.min(2.3, 12.7) = 2.300000
Math.min(-2.3, -12.7) = -12.700000
```

```
Math.pow(2.0, 7.0) = 128.000000
Math.pow(9.0, 0.5) = 3.000000
Math.sin(0.0) = 0.000000
Math.sqrt(900.0) = 30.000000
Math.tan(0.0) = 0.000000
```

5.4   a) **double** hypotenuse(**double** side1, **double** side2)
   b) **int** smallest(**int** x, **int** y, **int** z)
   c) **void** instructions()
   d) **float** intToFloat(**int** number)

5.5   a) Error: Method h is declared within method g.
      Correction: Move the declaration of h outside the declaration of g.
   b) Error: The method is supposed to return an integer, but does not.
      Correction: Delete the variable result, and place the statement

         return x + y;

      in the method, or add the following statement at the end of the method body:

         return result;

   c) Error: The semicolon after the right parenthesis of the parameter list is incorrect, and
      the parameter a should not be redeclared in the method.
      Correction: Delete the semicolon after the right parenthesis of the parameter list, and
      delete the declaration float a;.
   d) Error: The method returns a value when it's not supposed to.
      Correction: Change the return type from void to int.

5.6   The following solution calculates the volume of a sphere, using the radius entered by the user:

```
 1  // Exercise 5.6: Sphere.java
 2  // Calculate the volume of a sphere.
 3  import java.util.Scanner;
 4
 5  public class Sphere
 6  {
 7     // obtain radius from user and display volume of sphere
 8     public static void main(String[] args)
 9     {
10        Scanner input = new Scanner(System.in);
11
12        System.out.print("Enter radius of sphere: ");
13        double radius = input.nextDouble();
14
15        System.out.printf("Volume is %f%n", sphereVolume(radius));
16     } // end method determineSphereVolume
17
18     // calculate and return sphere volume
19     public static double sphereVolume(double radius)
20     {
21        double volume = (4.0 / 3.0) * Math.PI * Math.pow(radius, 3);
22        return volume;
23     } // end method sphereVolume
24  } // end class Sphere
```

```
Enter radius of sphere: 4
Volume is 268.082573
```

Exercises

5.7 What is the value of x after each of the following statements is executed?

a) x = Math.abs(7.5);
b) x = Math.floor(7.5);
c) x = Math.abs(0.0);
d) x = Math.ceil(0.0);
e) x = Math.abs(-6.4);
f) x = Math.ceil(-6.4);
g) x = Math.ceil(-Math.abs(-8 + Math.floor(-5.5)));

5.8 *(Parking Charges)* A parking garage charges a $2.00 minimum fee to park for up to three hours. The garage charges an additional $0.50 per hour for each hour *or part thereof* in excess of three hours. The maximum charge for any given 24-hour period is $10.00. Assume that no car parks for longer than 24 hours at a time. Write an application that calculates and displays the parking charges for each customer who parked in the garage yesterday. You should enter the hours parked for each customer. The program should display the charge for the current customer and should calculate and display the running total of yesterday's receipts. It should use the method calculateCharges to determine the charge for each customer.

5.9 *(Rounding Numbers)* Math.floor can be used to round values to the nearest integer—e.g.,

    y = Math.floor(x + 0.5);

will round the number x to the nearest integer and assign the result to y. Write an application that reads double values and uses the preceding statement to round each of the numbers to the nearest integer. For each number processed, display both the original number and the rounded number.

5.10 *(Rounding Numbers)* To round numbers to specific decimal places, use a statement like

    y = Math.floor(x * 10 + 0.5) / 10;

which rounds x to the tenths position (i.e., the first position to the right of the decimal point), or

    y = Math.floor(x * 100 + 0.5) / 100;

which rounds x to the hundredths position (i.e., the second position to the right of the decimal point). Write an application that defines four methods for rounding a number x in various ways:

a) roundToInteger(number)
b) roundToTenths(number)
c) roundToHundredths(number)
d) roundToThousandths(number)

For each value read, your program should display the original value, the number rounded to the nearest integer, the number rounded to the nearest tenth, the number rounded to the nearest hundredth and the number rounded to the nearest thousandth.

5.11 Answer each of the following questions:

a) What does it mean to choose numbers "at random"?
b) Why is the nextInt method of class SecureRandom useful for simulating games of chance?
c) Why is it often necessary to scale or shift the values produced by a SecureRandom object?
d) Why is computerized simulation of real-world situations a useful technique?

5.12 Write statements that assign random integers to the variable *n* in the following ranges:

a) $1 \leq n \leq 2$.
b) $1 \leq n \leq 100$.
c) $0 \leq n \leq 9$.
d) $1000 \leq n \leq 1112$.

e) $-1 \leq n \leq 1$.
f) $-3 \leq n \leq 11$.

5.13   Write statements that will display a random number from each of the following sets:
a) 2, 4, 6, 8, 10.
b) 3, 5, 7, 9, 11.
c) 6, 10, 14, 18, 22.

5.14   *(Exponentiation)* Write a method `integerPower(base, exponent)` that returns the value of

$$base^{\,exponent}$$

For example, `integerPower(3, 4)` calculates 3^4 (or 3 * 3 * 3 * 3). Assume that `exponent` is a positive, nonzero integer and that `base` is an integer. Use a `for` or `while` statement to control the calculation. Do not use any `Math` class methods. Incorporate this method into an application that reads integer values for `base` and `exponent` and performs the calculation with the `integerPower` method.

5.15   *(Hypotenuse Calculations)* Define a method `hypotenuse` that calculates the hypotenuse of a right triangle when the lengths of the other two sides are given. The method should take two arguments of type `double` and return the hypotenuse as a `double`. Incorporate this method into an application that reads values for `side1` and `side2` and performs the calculation with the `hypotenuse` method. Use `Math` methods `pow` and `sqrt` to determine the length of the hypotenuse for each of the triangles in Fig. 5.14. [*Note:* Class `Math` also provides method `hypot` to perform this calculation.]

Triangle	Side 1	Side 2
1	3.0	4.0
2	5.0	12.0
3	8.0	15.0

Fig. 5.14 | Values for the sides of triangles in Exercise 5.15.

5.16   *(Multiples)* Write a method `isMultiple` that determines, for a pair of integers, whether the second integer is a multiple of the first. The method should take two integer arguments and return `true` if the second is a multiple of the first and `false` otherwise. [*Hint:* Use the remainder operator.] Incorporate this method into an application that inputs a series of pairs of integers (one pair at a time) and determines whether the second value in each pair is a multiple of the first.

5.17   *(Even or Odd)* Write a method `isEven` that uses the remainder operator (%) to determine whether an integer is even. The method should take an integer argument and return `true` if the integer is even and `false` otherwise. Incorporate this method into an application that inputs a sequence of integers (one at a time) and determines whether each is even or odd.

5.18   *(Displaying a Square of Asterisks)* Write a method `squareOfAsterisks` that displays a solid square (the same number of rows and columns) of asterisks whose side is specified in integer parameter `side`. For example, if `side` is 4, the method should display

```
****
****
****
****
```

Incorporate this method into an application that reads an integer value for `side` from the user and outputs the asterisks with the `squareOfAsterisks` method.

5.19 *(Displaying a Square of Any Character)* Modify the method created in Exercise 5.18 to receive a second parameter of type char called fillCharacter. Form the square using the char provided as an argument. Thus, if side is 5 and fillCharacter is #, the method should display

```
#####
#####
#####
#####
#####
```

Use the following statement (in which input is a Scanner object) to read a character from the user at the keyboard:

```
char fill = input.next().charAt(0);
```

5.20 *(Circle Area)* Write an application that prompts the user for the radius of a circle and uses a method called circleArea to calculate the area of the circle.

5.21 *(Separating Digits)* Write methods that accomplish each of the following tasks:
a) Calculate the integer part of the quotient when integer a is divided by integer b.
b) Calculate the integer remainder when integer a is divided by integer b.
c) Use the methods developed in parts (a) and (b) to write a method displayDigits that receives an integer between 1 and 99999 and displays it as a sequence of digits, separating each pair of digits by two spaces. For example, the integer 4562 should appear as

```
    4  5  6  2
```

Incorporate the methods into an application that inputs an integer and calls displayDigits by passing the method the integer entered. Display the results.

5.22 *(Temperature Conversions)* Implement the following integer methods:
a) Method celsius returns the Celsius equivalent of a Fahrenheit temperature, using the calculation

```
celsius = 5.0 / 9.0 * (fahrenheit - 32);
```

b) Method fahrenheit returns the Fahrenheit equivalent of a Celsius temperature, using the calculation

```
fahrenheit = 9.0 / 5.0 * celsius + 32;
```

c) Use the methods from parts (a) and (b) to write an application that enables the user either to enter a Fahrenheit temperature and display the Celsius equivalent or to enter a Celsius temperature and display the Fahrenheit equivalent.

5.23 *(Find the Minimum)* Write a method minimum3 that returns the smallest of three floating-point numbers. Use the Math.min method to implement minimum3. Incorporate the method into an application that reads three values from the user, determines the smallest value and displays the result.

5.24 *(Perfect Numbers)* An integer number is said to be a *perfect number* if its factors, including 1 (but not the number itself), sum to the number. For example, 6 is a perfect number, because 6 = 1 + 2 + 3. Write a method isPerfect that determines whether parameter number is a perfect number. Use this method in an application that displays all the perfect numbers between 1 and 1000. Display the factors of each perfect number to confirm that the number is indeed perfect. Challenge the computing power of your computer by testing numbers much larger than 1000. Display the results.

5.25 *(Prime Numbers)* A positive integer is *prime* if it's divisible by only 1 and itself. For example, 2, 3, 5 and 7 are prime, but 4, 6, 8 and 9 are not. The number 1, by definition, is not prime.
a) Write a method that determines whether a number is prime.

b) Use this method in an application that determines and displays all the prime numbers less than 10,000. How many numbers up to 10,000 do you have to test to ensure that you've found all the primes?

c) Initially, you might think that $n/2$ is the upper limit for which you must test to see whether a number n is prime, but you need only go as high as the square root of n. Rewrite the program, and run it both ways.

5.26 *(Reversing Digits)* Write a method that takes an integer value and returns the number with its digits reversed. For example, given the number 7631, the method should return 1367. Incorporate the method into an application that reads a value from the user and displays the result.

5.27 *(Greatest Common Divisor)* The *greatest common divisor* (*GCD*) of two integers is the largest integer that evenly divides each of the two numbers. Write a method gcd that returns the greatest common divisor of two integers. [*Hint:* You might want to use Euclid's algorithm. You can find information about it at en.wikipedia.org/wiki/Euclidean_algorithm.] Incorporate the method into an application that reads two values from the user and displays the result.

5.28 Write a method qualityPoints that inputs a student's average and returns 4 if it's 90–100, 3 if 80–89, 2 if 70–79, 1 if 60–69 and 0 if lower than 60. Incorporate the method into an application that reads a value from the user and displays the result.

5.29 *(Coin Tossing)* Write an application that simulates coin tossing. Let the program toss a coin each time the user chooses the "Toss Coin" menu option. Count the number of times each side of the coin appears. Display the results. The program should call a separate method flip that takes no arguments and returns a value from a Coin enum (HEADS and TAILS). [*Note:* If the program realistically simulates coin tossing, each side of the coin should appear approximately half the time.]

5.30 *(Guess the Number)* Write an application that plays "guess the number" as follows: Your program chooses the number to be guessed by selecting a random integer in the range 1 to 1000. The application displays the prompt Guess a number between 1 and 1000. The player inputs a first guess. If the player's guess is incorrect, your program should display Too high. Try again. or Too low. Try again. to help the player "zero in" on the correct answer. The program should prompt the user for the next guess. When the user enters the correct answer, display Congratulations. You guessed the number!, and allow the user to choose whether to play again. [*Note:* The guessing technique employed in this problem is similar to a binary search, which is discussed in Chapter 19, Searching, Sorting and Big O.]

5.31 *(Guess the Number Modification)* Modify the program of Exercise 5.30 to count the number of guesses the player makes. If the number is 10 or fewer, display Either you know the secret or you got lucky! If the player guesses the number in 10 tries, display Aha! You know the secret! If the player makes more than 10 guesses, display You should be able to do better! Why should it take no more than 10 guesses? Well, with each "good guess," the player should be able to eliminate half of the numbers, then half of the remaining numbers, and so on.

5.32 *(Distance Between Points)* Write method distance to calculate the distance between two points $(x1, y1)$ and $(x2, y2)$. All numbers and return values should be of type double. Incorporate this method into an application that enables the user to enter the coordinates of the points.

5.33 *(Craps Game Modification)* Modify the craps program of Fig. 5.8 to allow wagering. Initialize variable bankBalance to 1000 dollars. Prompt the player to enter a wager. Check that wager is less than or equal to bankBalance, and if it's not, have the user reenter wager until a valid wager is entered. Then, run one game of craps. If the player wins, increase bankBalance by wager and display the new bankBalance. If the player loses, decrease bankBalance by wager, display the new bankBalance, check whether bankBalance has become zero and, if so, display the message "Sorry. You busted!" As the game progresses, display various messages to create some "chatter," such as "Oh, you're going for broke, huh?" or "Aw c'mon, take a chance!" or "You're up big. Now's the time to cash in your chips!". Implement the "chatter" as a separate method that randomly chooses the string to display.

5.34 *(Table of Binary, Octal and Hexadecimal Numbers)* Write an application that displays a table of the binary, octal and hexadecimal equivalents of the decimal numbers in the range 1 through 256. If you aren't familiar with these number systems, read online Appendix J first.

Making a Difference

As computer costs decline, it becomes feasible for every student, regardless of economic circumstance, to have a computer and use it in school. This creates exciting possibilities for improving the educational experience of all students worldwide, as suggested by the next five exercises. [*Note:* Check out initiatives such as the One Laptop Per Child Project (www.laptop.org). Also, research "green" laptops—what are some key "going green" characteristics of these devices? Look into the Electronic Product Environmental Assessment Tool (www.epeat.net), which can help you assess the "greenness" of desktops, notebooks and monitors to help you decide which products to purchase.]

5.35 *(Computer-Assisted Instruction)* The use of computers in education is referred to as *computer-assisted instruction* (*CAI*). Write a program that will help an elementary school student learn multiplication. Use a SecureRandom object to produce two positive one-digit integers. The program should then prompt the user with a question, such as

```
How much is 6 times 7?
```

The student then inputs the answer. Next, the program checks the student's answer. If it's correct, display the message "Very good!" and ask another multiplication question. If the answer is wrong, display the message "No. Please try again." and let the student try the same question repeatedly until the student finally gets it right. A separate method should be used to generate each new question. This method should be called once when the application begins execution and each time the user answers the question correctly.

5.36 *(Computer-Assisted Instruction: Reducing Student Fatigue)* One problem in CAI environments is student fatigue. This can be reduced by varying the computer's responses to hold the student's attention. Modify the program of Exercise 5.35 so that various comments are displayed for each answer as follows:

Possible responses to a correct answer:

```
Very good!
Excellent!
Nice work!
Keep up the good work!
```

Possible responses to an incorrect answer:

```
No. Please try again.
Wrong. Try once more.
Don't give up!
No. Keep trying.
```

Use random-number generation to choose a number from 1 to 4 that will be used to select one of the four appropriate responses to each correct or incorrect answer. Use a switch statement to issue the responses.

5.37 *(Computer-Assisted Instruction: Monitoring Student Performance)* More sophisticated computer-assisted instruction systems monitor the student's performance over a period of time. The decision to begin a new topic is often based on the student's success with previous topics. Modify the program of Exercise 5.36 to count the number of correct and incorrect responses typed by the student. After the student types 10 answers, your program should calculate the percentage that are correct. If the percentage is lower than 75%, display `"Please ask your teacher for extra help."`, then reset the program so another student can try it. If the percentage is 75% or higher, display `"Congratulations, you are ready to go to the next level!"`, then reset the program so another student can try it.

5.38   *(Computer-Assisted Instruction: Difficulty Levels)* Exercises 5.35–5.37 developed a computer-assisted instruction program to help teach an elementary school student multiplication. Modify the program to allow the user to enter a difficulty level. At a difficulty level of 1, the program should use only single-digit numbers in the problems; at a difficulty level of 2, numbers as large as two digits, and so on.

5.39   *(Computer-Assisted Instruction: Varying the Types of Problems)* Modify the program of Exercise 5.38 to allow the user to pick a type of arithmetic problem to study. An option of 1 means addition problems only, 2 means subtraction problems only, 3 means multiplication problems only, 4 means division problems only and 5 means a random mixture of all these types.

6

Arrays and ArrayLists

Begin at the beginning, ... and go on till you come to the end: then stop.
—Lewis Carroll

To go beyond is as wrong as to fall short.
—Confucius

Objectives

In this chapter you'll:

- Learn what primitive types and reference types are.

- Learn what arrays are.

- Use arrays to store data in and retrieve data from lists and tables of values.

- Declare arrays, initialize arrays and refer to individual elements of arrays.

- Iterate through arrays with the enhanced **for** statement.

- Pass arrays to methods.

- Declare and manipulate multidimensional arrays.

- Use variable-length argument lists.

- Read command-line arguments into a program.

- Search, sort and fill arrays with the methods of class **Arrays**, which contains methods for common array manipulations.

- Use class **ArrayList** to manipulate a dynamically resizable arraylike data structure.

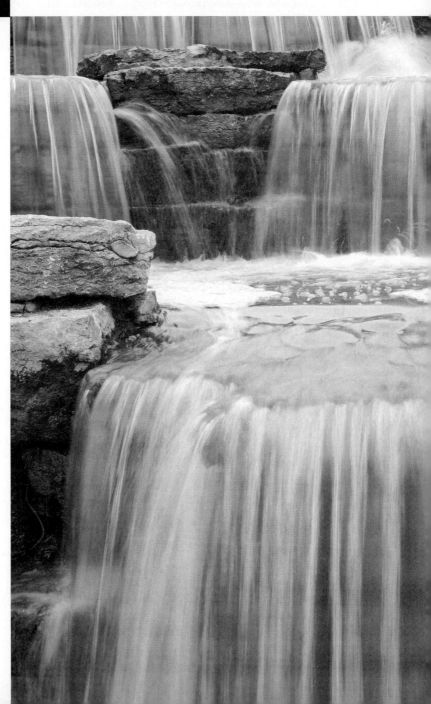

6.1 Introduction

This chapter introduces **data structures**—collections of related data items. **Array** objects are data structures consisting of related data items of the same type. Arrays make it convenient to process related groups of values. Arrays remain the same length once they're created. We study data structures in depth in Chapters 16–21.

After discussing how arrays are declared, created and initialized, we present practical examples that demonstrate common array manipulations. We introduce Java's *exception-handling* mechanism and use it to allow a program to continue executing when it attempts to access an array element that does not exist. We introduce Java's *enhanced* `for` *statement*, which allows a program to access the data in an array more easily than does the counter-controlled `for` statement presented in Section 4.3. We show how to use *variable-length argument lists* to create methods that can be called with varying numbers of arguments, and we demonstrate how to process *command-line arguments* in method `main`. Next, we present some common array manipulations with `static` methods of class `Arrays` from the `java.util` package.

Although commonly used, arrays have limited capabilities. For instance, you must specify an array's size, and if at execution time you wish to modify the size, you must do so by creating a new array. At the end of this chapter, we introduce one of Java's prebuilt data structures from the Java API's *collection classes*. These offer greater capabilities than traditional arrays. They're reusable, reliable, powerful and efficient. We focus on the `ArrayList` collection. `ArrayList`s are similar to arrays but provide additional functionality, such as **dynamic resizing** as necessary to accommodate more or fewer elements.

Java SE 8
After reading Chapter 17, Java SE 8 Lambdas and Streams, you'll be able to reimplement many of Chapter 6's examples in a more concise and elegant manner, and in a way that makes them easier to parallelize to improve performance on today's multi-core systems.

6.2 Primitive Types vs. Reference Types

Java's types are divided into primitive types and **reference types**. In Chapters 2–5, you worked primarily with variables of types int and double—two of the primitive types. The other six primitive types are boolean, byte, char, short, long and float—these are summarized in Appendix D. All nonprimitive types are *reference types*, so classes, which specify the types of objects, are reference types. In earlier chapters, you used variables of the *reference types* Scanner (Chapters 2–4) and SecureRandom (Chapter 5).

Software Engineering Observation 6.1

A variable's declared type (e.g., int, double or Scanner) indicates whether the variable is of a primitive or a reference type. If a variable's type is not one of the eight primitive types, then it's a reference type.

A primitive-type variable can hold exactly *one* value of its declared type at a time. For example, an int variable can store one integer at a time. When another value is assigned to that variable, the new value replaces the previous one—which is *lost*.

Programs use variables of reference types (normally called **references**) to store the *addresses* of objects in the computer's memory. Such a variable is said to **refer to an object** in the program. For example, the statement:

```
Scanner input = new Scanner(System.in);
```

which you've used in many programs, creates a Scanner object, then assigns to the variable input a *reference* to that Scanner object.

To call an object's methods, you need a reference to the object. For example, the statement

```
int number = input.nextInt();
```

uses the variable input, which refers to a Scanner object, to call the Scanner object's method nextInt.

If an object's method requires additional data to perform its task, then you'd pass arguments in the method call. For example, the statement

```
int face = 1 + randomNumbers.nextInt(6);
```

from line 16 of Fig. 5.6 uses the variable randomNumbers, which refers to a SecureRandom object, to call a the object's nextInt method and pass it the argument 6. Note that primitive-type variables do *not* refer to objects, so such variables cannot be used to invoke methods.

6.3 Arrays

An array is a group of variables (called **elements** or **components**) containing values that all have the *same* type. Arrays are *objects*, so they're considered *reference types*. As you'll soon see, what we typically think of as an array is actually a *reference* to an array object in memory. The *elements* of an array can be either *primitive types* or *reference types* (including arrays, as we'll see in Section 6.10). To refer to a particular element in an array, we specify the *name* of the reference to the array and the *position number* of the element in the array. The position number of the element is called the element's **index** or **subscript**.

Logical Array Representation

Figure 6.1 shows a logical representation of an integer array called c. This array contains 12 *elements*. A program refers to any one of these elements with an **array-access expression** that includes the *name* of the array followed by the *index* of the particular element in **square brackets** (**[]**). The first element in every array has **index zero** and is sometimes called the **zeroth element**. Thus, the elements of array c are c[0], c[1], c[2] and so on. The highest index in array c is 11, which is 1 less than 12—the number of elements in the array. Array names follow the same conventions as other variable names.

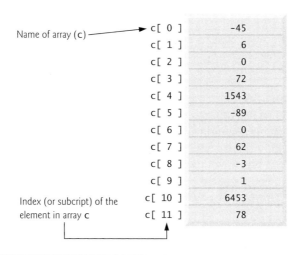

Fig. 6.1 | A 12-element array.

An index must be a *nonnegative integer*. A program can use an expression as an index. For example, if we assume that variable a is 5 and variable b is 6, then the statement

```
c[a + b] += 2;
```

adds 2 to array element c[11]. An indexed array name is an *array-access expression*, which can be used on the left side of an assignment to place a new value into an array element.

Common Programming Error 6.1

An index must be an int value or a value of a type that can be promoted to int—namely, byte, short or char, but not long; otherwise, a compilation error occurs.

Let's examine array c in Fig. 6.1 more closely. The **name** of the array is c. Every array object knows its own length and stores it in a **length instance variable**. The expression c.length returns array c's length. Even though the length instance variable of an array is public, it cannot be changed because it's a final variable. This array's 12 elements are referred to as c[0], c[1], c[2], ..., c[11]. The value of c[0] is -45, the value of c[1] is 6, the value of c[2] is 0, the value of c[7] is 62 and the value of c[11] is 78. To calculate the sum of the values contained in the first three elements of array c and store the result in variable sum, we would write

```
sum = c[0] + c[1] + c[2];
```

To divide the value of c[6] by 2 and assign the result to the variable x, we would write

```
x = c[6] / 2;
```

6.4 Declaring and Creating Arrays

Array objects occupy space in memory. Like other objects, arrays are created with keyword new. To create an array object, you specify the type of the array elements and the number of elements as part of an **array-creation expression** that uses keyword new. Such an expression returns a *reference* that can be stored in an array variable. The following declaration and array-creation expression create an array object containing 12 int elements and store the array's reference in the array variable named c:

```
int[] c = new int[12];
```

This expression can be used to create the array in Fig. 6.1. When an array is created, each of its elements receives a default value—zero for the numeric primitive-type elements, false for boolean elements and null for references. As you'll soon see, you can provide nondefault element values when you create an array.

Creating the array in Fig. 6.1 can also be performed in two steps as follows:

```
int[] c; // declare the array variable
c = new int[12]; // create the array; assign to array variable
```

In the declaration, the *square brackets* following the type indicate that c is a variable that will refer to an array (i.e., the variable will store an array *reference*). In the assignment statement, the array variable c receives the reference to a new array of 12 int elements.

Common Programming Error 6.2

In an array declaration, specifying the number of elements in the square brackets of the declaration (e.g., int[12] c;) is a syntax error.

A program can create several arrays in a single declaration. The following declaration reserves 100 elements for b and 27 elements for x:

```
String[] b = new String[100], x = new String[27];
```

When the type of the array and the square brackets are combined at the beginning of the declaration, all the identifiers in the declaration are array variables. In this case, variables b and x refer to String arrays. For readability, we prefer to declare only *one* variable per declaration. The preceding declaration is equivalent to:

```
String[] b = new String[100]; // create array b
String[] x = new String[27]; // create array x
```

Good Programming Practice 6.1

For readability, declare only one variable per declaration. Keep each declaration on a separate line, and include a comment describing the variable being declared.

When only one variable is declared in each declaration, the square brackets can be placed either after the type or after the array variable name, as in:

```
String b[] = new String[100]; // create array b
String x[] = new String[27]; // create array x
```

but placing the square brackets after the type is preferred.

Common Programming Error 6.3

Declaring multiple array variables in a single declaration can lead to subtle errors. Consider the declaration int[] a, b, c;. If a, b and c should be declared as array variables, then this declaration is correct—placing square brackets directly following the type indicates that all the identifiers in the declaration are array variables. However, if only a is intended to be an array variable, and b and c are intended to be individual int variables, then this declaration is incorrect—the declaration int a[], b, c; would achieve the desired result.

A program can declare arrays of any type. Every element of a primitive-type array contains a value of the array's declared element type. Similarly, in an array of a reference type, every element is a reference to an object of the array's declared element type. For example, every element of an int array is an int value, and every element of a String array is a reference to a String object.

6.5 Examples Using Arrays

This section presents several examples that demonstrate declaring arrays, creating arrays, initializing arrays and manipulating array elements.

6.5.1 Creating and Initializing an Array

The application of Fig. 6.2 uses keyword new to create an array of 10 int elements, which are initially zero (the default initial value for int variables). Line 9 declares array—a reference capable of referring to an array of int elements—then initializes the variable with a reference to an array object containing 10 int elements. Line 11 outputs the column headings. The first column contains the index (0–9) of each array element, and the second column contains the default initial value (0) of each array element.

```
1   // Fig. 6.2: InitArray.java
2   // Initializing the elements of an array to default values of zero.
3
4   public class InitArray
5   {
6      public static void main(String[] args)
7      {
```

Fig. 6.2 | Initializing the elements of an array to default values of zero. (Part 1 of 2.)

```
 8              // declare variable array and initialize it with an array object
 9              int[] array = new int[10]; // create the array object
10
11              System.out.printf("%s%8s%n", "Index", "Value"); // column headings
12
13              // output each array element's value
14              for (int counter = 0; counter < array.length; counter++)
15                 System.out.printf("%5d%8d%n", counter, array[counter]);
16         }
17     } // end class InitArray
```

```
Index   Value
    0       0
    1       0
    2       0
    3       0
    4       0
    5       0
    6       0
    7       0
    8       0
    9       0
```

Fig. 6.2 | Initializing the elements of an array to default values of zero. (Part 2 of 2.)

The for statement (lines 14–15) outputs the index (represented by counter) and value of each array element (represented by array[counter]). Control variable counter is initially 0—index values start at 0, so using **zero-based counting** allows the loop to access every element of the array. The for's loop-continuation condition uses the expression array.length (line 14) to determine the length of the array. In this example, the length of the array is 10, so the loop continues executing as long as the value of control variable counter is less than 10. The highest index value of a 10-element array is 9, so using the less-than operator in the loop-continuation condition guarantees that the loop does not attempt to access an element *beyond* the end of the array (i.e., during the final iteration of the loop, counter is 9). We'll soon see what Java does when it encounters such an *out-of-range index* at execution time.

6.5.2 Using an Array Initializer

You can create an array and initialize its elements with an **array initializer**—a comma-separated list of expressions (called an **initializer list**) enclosed in braces. In this case, the array length is determined by the number of elements in the initializer list. For example,

```
int[] n = { 10, 20, 30, 40, 50 };
```

creates a *five*-element array with index values 0–4. Element n[0] is initialized to 10, n[1] is initialized to 20, and so on. When the compiler encounters an array declaration that includes an initializer list, it *counts* the number of initializers in the list to determine the size of the array, then sets up the appropriate new operation "behind the scenes."

The application in Fig. 6.3 initializes an integer array with 10 values (line 9) and displays the array in tabular format. The code for displaying the array elements (lines 14–15) is identical to that in Fig. 6.2 (lines 15–16).

```
 1   // Fig. 6.3: InitArray.java
 2   // Initializing the elements of an array with an array initializer.
 3
 4   public class InitArray
 5   {
 6      public static void main(String[] args)
 7      {
 8         // initializer list specifies the initial value for each element
 9         int[] array = { 32, 27, 64, 18, 95, 14, 90, 70, 60, 37 };
10
11         System.out.printf("%s%8s%n", "Index", "Value"); // column headings
12
13         // output each array element's value
14         for (int counter = 0; counter < array.length; counter++)
15            System.out.printf("%5d%8d%n", counter, array[counter]);
16
17   } // end class InitArray
```

```
Index   Value
    0      32
    1      27
    2      64
    3      18
    4      95
    5      14
    6      90
    7      70
    8      60
    9      37
```

Fig. 6.3 | Initializing the elements of an array with an array initializer.

6.5.3 Calculating the Values to Store in an Array

The application in Fig. 6.4 creates a 10-element array and assigns to each element one of the even integers from 2 to 20 (2, 4, 6, ..., 20). Then the application displays the array in tabular format. The for statement at lines 12–13 calculates an array element's value by multiplying the current value of the control variable counter by 2, then adding 2.

```
 1   // Fig. 6.4: InitArray.java
 2   // Calculating the values to be placed into the elements of an array.
 3
 4   public class InitArray
 5   {
 6      public static void main(String[] args)
 7      {
 8         final int ARRAY_LENGTH = 10; // declare constant
 9         int[] array = new int[ARRAY_LENGTH]; // create array
10
```

Fig. 6.4 | Calculating the values to be placed into the elements of an array. (Part 1 of 2.)

```
11        // calculate value for each array element
12        for (int counter = 0; counter < array.length; counter++)
13           array[counter] = 2 + 2 * counter;
14
15        System.out.printf("%s%8s%n", "Index", "Value"); // column headings
16
17        // output each array element's value
18        for (int counter = 0; counter < array.length; counter++)
19           System.out.printf("%5d%8d%n", counter, array[counter]);
20     }
21  } // end class InitArray
```

```
Index  Value
    0      2
    1      4
    2      6
    3      8
    4     10
    5     12
    6     14
    7     16
    8     18
    9     20
```

Fig. 6.4 | Calculating the values to be placed into the elements of an array. (Part 2 of 2.)

Line 8 uses the modifier `final` to declare the constant variable `ARRAY_LENGTH` with the value 10. Constant variables must be initialized *before* they're used and *cannot* be modified thereafter. If you attempt to *modify* a `final` variable after it's initialized in its declaration, the compiler issues an error message like

```
cannot assign a value to final variable variableName
```

Good Programming Practice 6.2
*Constant variables also are called **named constants**. They often make programs more readable than programs that use literal values (e.g., 10)—a named constant such as `ARRAY_LENGTH` clearly indicates its purpose, whereas a literal value could have different meanings based on its context.*

Good Programming Practice 6.3
Multiword named constants should have each word separated from the next with an underscore (_) as in `ARRAY_LENGTH`.

Common Programming Error 6.4
Assigning a value to a `final` variable after it has been initialized is a compilation error. Similarly, attempting to access the value of a `final` variable before it's initialized results in a compilation error like, "`variable variableName might not have been initialized.`"

6.5.4 Summing the Elements of an Array

Often, the elements of an array represent a series of values to be used in a calculation. If, for example, they represent exam grades, a professor may wish to total the elements of the array and use that sum to calculate the class average for the exam.

Figure 6.5 sums the values contained in a 10-element integer array. The program declares, creates and initializes the array at line 8. The for statement performs the calculations. [*Note:* The values supplied as array initializers are often read into a program rather than specified in an initializer list. For example, an application could input the values from a user or from a file on disk (as discussed in Chapter 15, Files, Streams and Object Serialization). Reading the data into a program (rather than "hand coding" it into the program) makes the program more reusable, because it can be used with *different* sets of data.]

```java
1   // Fig. 6.5: SumArray.java
2   // Computing the sum of the elements of an array.
3
4   public class SumArray
5   {
6      public static void main(String[] args)
7      {
8         int[] array = { 87, 68, 94, 100, 83, 78, 85, 91, 76, 87 };
9         int total = 0;
10
11         // add each element's value to total
12         for (int counter = 0; counter < array.length; counter++)
13            total += array[counter];
14
15         System.out.printf("Total of array elements: %d%n", total);
16      }
17   } // end class SumArray
```

```
Total of array elements: 849
```

Fig. 6.5 | Computing the sum of the elements of an array.

6.5.5 Using Bar Charts to Display Array Data Graphically

Many programs present data to users in a graphical manner. For example, numeric values are often displayed as bars in a bar chart. In such a chart, longer bars represent proportionally larger numeric values. One simple way to display numeric data graphically is with a bar chart that shows each numeric value as a bar of asterisks (*).

Professors often like to examine the distribution of grades on an exam. A professor might graph the number of grades in each of several categories to visualize the grade distribution. Suppose the grades on an exam were 87, 68, 94, 100, 83, 78, 85, 91, 76 and 87. They include one grade of 100, two grades in the 90s, four grades in the 80s, two grades in the 70s, one grade in the 60s and no grades below 60. Our next application (Fig. 6.6) stores this grade distribution data in an array of 11 elements, each corresponding to a category of grades. For example, array[0] indicates the number of grades in the range 0–9, array[7] the number of grades in the range 70–79 and array[10] the number of 100 grades. The GradeBook case studies in Chapter 7 contain code that calculates these grade frequencies based on a set of grades. For now, we manually create the array with the given grade frequencies.

```java
1   // Fig. 6.6: BarChart.java
2   // Bar chart printing program.
3
4   public class BarChart
5   {
6      public static void main(String[] args)
7      {
8         int[] array = {0, 0, 0, 0, 0, 0, 1, 2, 4, 2, 1};
9
10        System.out.println("Grade distribution:");
11
12        // for each array element, output a bar of the chart
13        for (int counter = 0; counter < array.length; counter++)
14        {
15           // output bar label ("00-09: ", ..., "90-99: ", "100: ")
16           if (counter == 10)
17              System.out.printf("%5d: ", 100);
18           else
19              System.out.printf("%02d-%02d: ",
20                 counter * 10, counter * 10 + 9);
21
22           // print bar of asterisks
23           for (int stars = 0; stars < array[counter]; stars++)
24              System.out.print("*");
25
26           System.out.println();
27        }
28     }
29  } // end class BarChart
```

```
Grade distribution:
00-09:
10-19:
20-29:
30-39:
40-49:
50-59:
60-69: *
70-79: **
80-89: ****
90-99: **
  100: *
```

Fig. 6.6 | Bar chart printing program.

The application reads the numbers from the array and graphs the information as a bar chart. It displays each grade range followed by a bar of asterisks indicating the number of grades in that range. To label each bar, lines 16–20 output a grade range (e.g., "70-79: ") based on the current value of counter. When counter is 10, line 17 outputs 100 with a field width of 5, followed by a colon and a space, to align the label "100: " with the other bar labels. The nested for statement (lines 23–24) outputs the bars. Note the loop-continuation condition at line 23 (stars < array[counter]). Each time the program reaches the inner for, the loop counts from 0 up to array[counter], thus using a value in array to determine the number of asterisks to display. In this example, *no* students received a grade below 60, so array[0]–array[5] contain zeroes, and *no* asterisks are displayed next to the first six grade ranges. In line 19, the format specifier %02d indicates that an int value should be formatted as a field of two digits. The **0 flag** in the format specifier displays a leading 0 for values with fewer digits than the field width (2).

6.5.6 Using the Elements of an Array as Counters

Sometimes, programs use counter variables to summarize data, such as the results of a survey. In Fig. 5.7, we used separate counters in our die-rolling program to track the number of occurrences of each side of a six-sided die as the program rolled the die 6,000,000 times. An array version of this application is shown in Fig. 6.7.

```
 1   // Fig. 6.7: RollDie.java
 2   // Die-rolling program using arrays instead of switch.
 3   import java.security.SecureRandom;
 4
 5   public class RollDie
 6   {
 7      public static void main(String[] args)
 8      {
 9         SecureRandom randomNumbers = new SecureRandom();
10         int[] frequency = new int[7]; // array of frequency counters
11
12         // roll die 6,000,000 times; use die value as frequency index
13         for (int roll = 1; roll <= 6000000; roll++)
14            ++frequency[1 + randomNumbers.nextInt(6)];
15
16         System.out.printf("%s%10s%n", "Face", "Frequency");
17
18         // output each array element's value
19         for (int face = 1; face < frequency.length; face++)
20            System.out.printf("%4d%10d%n", face, frequency[face]);
21      }
22   } // end class RollDie
```

```
Face Frequency
   1    999690
   2    999512
   3   1000575
   4    999815
   5    999781
   6   1000627
```

Fig. 6.7 | Die-rolling program using arrays instead of switch.

Figure 6.7 uses the array frequency (line 10) to count the occurrences of each side of the die. *The single statement in line 14 of this program replaces lines 22–45 of Fig. 5.7.* Line

14 uses the random value to determine which frequency element to increment during each iteration of the loop. The calculation in line 14 produces random numbers from 1 to 6, so the array frequency must be large enough to store six counters. However, we use a seven-element array in which we ignore frequency[0]—it's more logical to have the face value 1 increment frequency[1] than frequency[0]. Thus, each face value is used as an index for array frequency. In line 14, the calculation inside the square brackets evaluates first to determine which element of the array to increment, then the ++ operator adds one to that element. We also replaced lines 49–51 from Fig. 5.7 by looping through array frequency to output the results (lines 19–20). When we study Java SE 8's new functional programming capabilities in Chapter 17, we'll show how to replace lines 13–14 and 19–20 with a *single* statement!

6.5.7 Using Arrays to Analyze Survey Results

Our next example uses arrays to summarize data collected in a survey. Consider the following problem statement:

> *Twenty students were asked to rate on a scale of 1 to 5 the quality of the food in the student cafeteria, with 1 being "awful" and 5 being "excellent." Place the 20 responses in an integer array and determine the frequency of each rating.*

This is a typical array-processing application (Fig. 6.8). We wish to summarize the number of responses of each type (that is, 1–5). Array responses (lines 9–10) is a 20-element integer array containing the students' survey responses. The last value in the array *is intentionally* an incorrect response (14). When a Java program executes, array element indices are checked for validity—all indices must be greater than or equal to 0 and less than the length of the array. Any attempt to access an element outside that range of indices results in a runtime error that's known as an ArrayIndexOutOfBoundsException. At the end of this section, we'll discuss the invalid response value, demonstrate array **bounds checking** and introduce Java's *exception-handling* mechanism, which can be used to detect and handle an ArrayIndexOutOfBoundsException.

```
1   // Fig. 6.8: StudentPoll.java
2   // Poll analysis program.
3
4   public class StudentPoll
5   {
6      public static void main(String[] args)
7      {
8         // student response array (more typically, input at runtime)
9         int[] responses = { 1, 2, 5, 4, 3, 5, 2, 1, 3, 3, 1, 4, 3, 3, 3,
10           2, 3, 3, 2, 14 };
11        int[] frequency = new int[6]; // array of frequency counters
12
13        // for each answer, select responses element and use that value
14        // as frequency index to determine element to increment
15        for (int answer = 0; answer < responses.length; answer++)
16        {
```

Fig. 6.8 | Poll analysis program. (Part 1 of 2.)

```
17                    try
18                    {
19                        ++frequency[responses[answer]];
20                    }
21                    catch (ArrayIndexOutOfBoundsException e)
22                    {
23                        System.out.println(e); // invokes toString method
24                        System.out.printf("    responses[%d] = %d%n%n",
25                            answer, responses[answer]);
26                    }
27                }
28
29                System.out.printf("%s%10s%n", "Rating", "Frequency");
30
31                // output each array element's value
32                for (int rating = 1; rating < frequency.length; rating++)
33                    System.out.printf("%6d%10d%n", rating, frequency[rating]);
34            }
35    } // end class StudentPoll
```

```
java.lang.ArrayIndexOutOfBoundsException: 14
    responses[19] = 14

Rating Frequency
    1        3
    2        4
    3        8
    4        2
    5        2
```

Fig. 6.8 | Poll analysis program. (Part 2 of 2.)

The *frequency* Array

We use the *six-element* array frequency (line 11) to count the number of occurrences of each response. Each element is used as a *counter* for one of the possible types of survey responses—frequency[1] counts the number of students who rated the food as 1, frequency[2] counts the number of students who rated the food as 2, and so on.

Summarizing the Results

The for statement (lines 15–27) reads the responses from the array responses one at a time and increments one of the counters frequency[1] to frequency[5]; we ignore frequency[0] because the survey responses are limited to the range 1–5. The key statement in the loop appears in line 19. This statement increments the appropriate frequency counter as determined by the value of responses[answer].

Let's step through the first few iterations of the for statement:

- When the counter answer is 0, responses[answer] is the value of responses[0] (that is, 1—see line 9). In this case, frequency[responses[answer]] is interpreted as frequency[1], and the counter frequency[1] is incremented by one. To evaluate the expression, we begin with the value in the *innermost* set of brackets (answer, currently 0). The value of answer is plugged into the expression, and the next set of brackets (responses[answer]) is evaluated. That value is used as the index for the frequency array to determine which counter to increment (in this case, frequency[1]).

- The next time through the loop answer is 1, responses[answer] is the value of responses[1] (that is, 2—see line 9), so frequency[responses[answer]] is interpreted as frequency[2], causing frequency[2] to be incremented.

- When answer is 2, responses[answer] is the value of responses[2] (that is, 5—see line 9), so frequency[responses[answer]] is interpreted as frequency[5], causing frequency[5] to be incremented, and so on.

Regardless of the number of responses processed, only a six-element array (in which we ignore element zero) is required to summarize the results, because all the correct response values are values from 1 to 5, and the index values for a six-element array are 0–5. In the program's output, the Frequency column summarizes only 19 of the 20 values in the responses array—the last element of the array responses contains an (intentionally) incorrect response that was not counted. Section 6.6 discusses what happens when the program in Fig. 6.8 encounters the invalid response (14) in the last element of array responses.

6.6 Exception Handling: Processing the Incorrect Response

An **exception** indicates a problem that occurs while a program executes. The name "exception" suggests that the problem occurs infrequently—if the "rule" is that a statement normally executes correctly, then the problem represents the "exception to the rule." **Exception handling** helps you create **fault-tolerant programs** that can resolve (or handle) exceptions. In many cases, this allows a program to continue executing as if no problems were encountered. For example, the StudentPoll application still displays results (Fig. 6.8), even though one of the responses was out of range. More severe problems might prevent a program from continuing normal execution, instead requiring the program to notify the user of the problem, then terminate. When the JVM or a method detects a problem, such as an invalid array index or an invalid method argument, it **throws** an exception—that is, an exception occurs. Methods in your own classes can also throw exceptions, as you'll learn in Chapter 8.

6.6.1 The try Statement

To handle an exception, place any code that might throw an exception in a **try statement** (lines 17–26). The **try block** (lines 17–20) contains the code that might *throw* an exception, and the **catch block** (lines 21–26) contains the code that *handles* the exception if one occurs. You can have *many* catch blocks to handle different *types* of exceptions that might be thrown in the corresponding try block. When line 19 correctly increments an element of the frequency array, lines 21–26 are ignored. The braces that delimit the bodies of the try and catch blocks are required.

6.6.2 Executing the catch Block

When the program encounters the invalid value 14 in the responses array, it attempts to add 1 to frequency[14], which is *outside* the bounds of the array—the frequency array has only six elements (with indexes 0–5). Because array bounds checking is performed at execution time, the JVM generates an *exception*—specifically line 19 throws an **ArrayIndexOutOf-BoundsException** to notify the program of this problem. At this point the try block terminates and the catch block begins executing—any local variables declared in the try block are now *out of scope* (and no longer exist), so they're not accessible in the catch block.

The catch block declares an exception parameter (e) of type (IndexOutOfRangeException). The catch block can handle exceptions of the specified type. Inside the catch block, you can use the parameter's identifier to interact with a caught exception object.

Error-Prevention Tip 6.1

When writing code to access an array element, ensure that the array index remains greater than or equal to 0 and less than the length of the array. This would prevent ArrayIndexOutOfBoundsExceptions if your program is correct.

6.6.3 toString Method of the Exception Parameter

When lines 21–26 *catch* the exception, the program displays a message indicating the problem that occurred. Line 23 *implicitly* calls the exception object's toString method to get the error message that's implicitly stored in the exception object and display it. Once the message is displayed in this example, the exception is considered *handled* and the program continues with the next statement after the catch block's closing brace. In this example, the end of the for statement is reached (line 27), so the program continues with the increment of the control variable in line 15. We discuss exception handling again in Chapter 8, and more deeply in Chapter 11.

6.7 Enhanced for Statement

The **enhanced for statement** iterates through the elements of an array *without* using a counter, thus avoiding the possibility of "stepping outside" the array. We show how to use the enhanced for statement with the Java API's prebuilt data structures (called collections) in Section 6.14. The syntax of an enhanced for statement is:

```
for (parameter : arrayName)
   statement
```

where *parameter* has a *type* and an *identifier* (e.g., int number), and *arrayName* is the array through which to iterate. The type of the parameter must be *consistent* with the type of the elements in the array. As the next example illustrates, the identifier represents successive element values in the array on successive iterations of the loop.

Figure 6.9 uses the enhanced for statement (lines 12–13) to sum the integers in an array of student grades. The enhanced for's parameter is of type int, because array contains int values—the loop selects one int value from the array during each iteration. The enhanced for statement iterates through successive values in the array one by one. The statement's header can be read as "for each iteration, assign the next element of array to int variable number, then execute the following statement." Thus, for each iteration, identifier number represents an int value in array. Lines 12–13 are equivalent to the following counter-controlled repetition used in lines 12–13 of Fig. 6.5 to total the integers in array, except that counter *cannot be accessed* in the enhanced for statement:

```
for (int counter = 0; counter < array.length; counter++)
   total += array[counter];
```

```
 1   // Fig. 6.9: EnhancedForTest.java
 2   // Using the enhanced for statement to total integers in an array.
 3
 4   public class EnhancedForTest
 5   {
 6      public static void main(String[] args)
 7      {
 8         int[] array = { 87, 68, 94, 100, 83, 78, 85, 91, 76, 87 };
 9         int total = 0;
10
11         // add each element's value to total
12         for (int number : array)
13            total += number;
14
15         System.out.printf("Total of array elements: %d%n", total);
16      }
17   } // end class EnhancedForTest
```

```
Total of array elements: 849
```

Fig. 6.9 | Using the enhanced for statement to total integers in an array.

The enhanced for statement can be used *only* to obtain array elements—it *cannot* be used to *modify* elements. If your program needs to modify elements, use the traditional counter-controlled for statement.

The enhanced for statement can be used in place of the counter-controlled for statement whenever code looping through an array does *not* require access to the counter indicating the index of the current array element. For example, totaling the integers in an array requires access only to the element values—the index of each element is irrelevant. However, if a program must use a counter for some reason other than simply to loop through an array (e.g., to print an index number next to each array element value, as in the examples earlier in this chapter), use the counter-controlled for statement.

Error-Prevention Tip 6.2

The enhanced for statement simplifies the code for iterating through an array making the code more readable and eliminating several error possibilities, such as improperly specifying the control variable's initial value, the loop-continuation test and the increment expression.

Java SE 8

The for statement and the enhanced for statement each iterate sequentially from a starting value to an ending value. In Chapter 17, Java SE 8 Lambdas and Streams, you'll learn about class Stream and its forEach method. Working together, these provide an elegant, more concise and less error prone means for iterating through collections so that some of the iterations may occur in parallel with others to achieve better multi-core system performance.

6.8 Passing Arrays to Methods

This section demonstrates how to pass arrays and individual array elements as arguments to methods. To pass an array argument to a method, specify the name of the array *without any brackets*. For example, if array hourlyTemperatures is declared as

```
        double[] hourlyTemperatures = new double[24];
```
then the method call

```
        modifyArray(hourlyTemperatures);
```

passes the reference of array `hourlyTemperatures` to method `modifyArray`. Every array object "knows" its own length. Thus, when we pass an array object's reference into a method, we need not pass the array length as an additional argument.

For a method to receive an array reference through a method call, the method's parameter list must specify an *array parameter*. For example, the method header for method `modifyArray` might be written as

```
        void modifyArray(double[] b)
```

indicating that `modifyArray` receives the reference of a `double` array in parameter b. The method call passes array `hourlyTemperature`'s reference, so when the called method uses the array variable b, it *refers to* the same array object as `hourlyTemperatures` in the caller.

When an argument to a method is an entire array or an individual array element of a reference type, the called method receives a *copy* of the reference. However, when an argument to a method is an individual array element of a primitive type, the called method receives a copy of the element's *value*. Such primitive values are called **scalars** or **scalar quantities**. To pass an individual array element to a method, use the indexed name of the array element as an argument in the method call.

Figure 6.10 demonstrates the difference between passing an entire array and passing a primitive-type array element to a method. Notice that `main` invokes `static` methods `modifyArray` (line 19) and `modifyElement` (line 30) directly. Recall from Section 5.4 that a `static` method of a class can invoke other `static` methods of the same class directly.

```
 I   // Fig. 6.10: PassArray.java
 2   // Passing arrays and individual array elements to methods.
 3
 4   public class PassArray
 5   {
 6      // main creates array and calls modifyArray and modifyElement
 7      public static void main(String[] args)
 8      {
 9         int[] array = { 1, 2, 3, 4, 5 };
10
11         System.out.printf(
12            "Effects of passing reference to entire array:%n" +
13            "The values of the original array are:%n");
14
15         // output original array elements
16         for (int value : array)
17            System.out.printf("   %d", value);
18
19         modifyArray(array); // pass array reference
20         System.out.printf("%n%nThe values of the modified array are:%n");
21
```

Fig. 6.10 | Passing arrays and individual array elements to methods. (Part I of 2.)

```
22          // output modified array elements
23          for (int value : array)
24             System.out.printf("   %d", value);
25
26          System.out.printf(
27             "%n%nEffects of passing array element value:%n" +
28             "array[3] before modifyElement: %d%n", array[3]);
29
30          modifyElement(array[3]); // attempt to modify array[3]
31          System.out.printf(
32             "array[3] after modifyElement: %d%n", array[3]);
33       }
34
35       // multiply each element of an array by 2
36       public static void modifyArray(int[] array2)
37       {
38          for (int counter = 0; counter < array2.length; counter++)
39             array2[counter] *= 2;
40       }
41
42       // multiply argument by 2
43       public static void modifyElement(int element)
44       {
45          element *= 2;
46          System.out.printf(
47             "Value of element in modifyElement: %d%n", element);
48       }
49    } // end class PassArray
```

```
Effects of passing reference to entire array:
The values of the original array are:
   1   2   3   4   5

The values of the modified array are:
   2   4   6   8   10

Effects of passing array element value:
array[3] before modifyElement: 8
Value of element in modifyElement: 16
array[3] after modifyElement: 8
```

Fig. 6.10 | Passing arrays and individual array elements to methods. (Part 2 of 2.)

The enhanced for statement at lines 16–17 outputs the elements of array. Line 19 invokes method modifyArray, passing array as an argument. The method (lines 36–40) receives a copy of array's reference and uses it to multiply each of array's elements by 2. To prove that array's elements were modified, lines 23–24 output array's elements again. As the output shows, method modifyArray doubled the value of each element. We could *not* use the enhanced for statement in lines 38–39 because we're modifying the array's elements.

Figure 6.10 next demonstrates that when a copy of an individual primitive-type array element is passed to a method, modifying the *copy* in the called method does *not* affect the original value of that element in the calling method's array. Lines 26–28 output the value of array[3] *before* invoking method modifyElement. Remember that the value of this element is now 8 after it was modified in the call to modifyArray. Line 30 calls method modifyElement and passes array[3] as an argument. Remember that array[3] is actually one int value (8) in array. Therefore, the program passes a copy of the value of array[3]. Method modifyElement (lines 43–48) multiplies the value received as an argument by 2, stores the result in its parameter element, then outputs the value of element (16). Since method parameters, like local variables, cease to exist when the method in which they're declared completes execution, the method parameter element is destroyed when method modifyElement terminates. When the program returns control to main, lines 31–32 output the *unmodified* value of array[3] (i.e., 8).

6.9 Pass-By-Value vs. Pass-By-Reference

The preceding example demonstrated how arrays and primitive-type array elements are passed as arguments to methods. We now take a closer look at how arguments in general are passed to methods. Two ways to pass arguments in method calls in many programming languages are **pass-by-value** and **pass-by-reference** (sometimes called **call-by-value** and **call-by-reference**). When an argument is passed by value, a *copy* of the argument's *value* is passed to the called method. The called method works exclusively with the copy. Changes to the called method's copy do *not* affect the original variable's value in the caller.

When an argument is passed by reference, the called method can access the argument's value in the caller directly and modify that data, if necessary. Pass-by-reference improves performance by eliminating the need to copy possibly large amounts of data.

Unlike some other languages, Java does *not* allow you to choose pass-by-value or pass-by-reference—*all arguments are passed by value*. A method call can pass two types of values to a method—copies of primitive values (e.g., values of type int and double) and copies of references to objects. Objects themselves cannot be passed to methods. When a method modifies a primitive-type parameter, changes to the parameter have no effect on the original argument value in the calling method. For example, when line 30 in main of Fig. 6.10 passes array[3] to method modifyElement, the statement in line 45 that doubles the value of parameter element has *no* effect on the value of array[3] in main. This is also true for reference-type parameters. If you modify a reference-type parameter so that it refers to another object, only the parameter refers to the new object—the reference stored in the caller's variable still refers to the original object.

Although an object's reference is passed by value, a method can still interact with the referenced object by calling its public methods using the copy of the object's reference. Since the reference stored in the parameter is a copy of the reference that was passed as an argument, the parameter in the called method and the argument in the calling method refer to the *same* object in memory. For example, in Fig. 6.10, both parameter array2 in method modifyArray and variable array in main refer to the *same* array object in memory. Any changes made using the parameter array2 are carried out on the object that array references in the calling method. In Fig. 6.10, the changes made in modifyArray using array2 affect the contents of the array object referenced by array in main. Thus, with a reference to an object, the called method *can* manipulate the caller's object directly.

> **Performance Tip 6.1**
> *Passing references to arrays, instead of the array objects themselves, makes sense for performance reasons. Because everything in Java is passed by value, if array objects were passed, a copy of each element would be passed. For large arrays, this would waste time and consume considerable storage for the copies of the elements.*

6.10 Multidimensional Arrays

Multidimensional arrays with two dimensions are often used to represent *tables* of values with data arranged in *rows* and *columns*. To identify a particular table element, you specify *two* indices. *By convention*, the first identifies the element's row and the second its column. Arrays that require two indices to identify each element are called **two-dimensional arrays**. (Multidimensional arrays can have more than two dimensions.) Java does not support multidimensional arrays directly, but it allows you to specify one-dimensional arrays whose elements are also one-dimensional arrays, thus achieving the same effect. Figure 6.11 illustrates a two-dimensional array named a with three rows and four columns (i.e., a three-by-four array). In general, an array with *m* rows and *n* columns is called an ***m*-by-*n* array**.

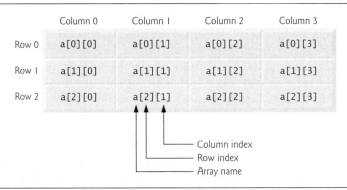

Fig. 6.11 | Two-dimensional array with three rows and four columns.

Every element in array a is identified in Fig. 6.11 by an *array-access expression* of the form a[*row*][*column*]; a is the name of the array, and *row* and *column* are the indices that uniquely identify each element by row and column index. The names of the elements in *row* 0 all have a *first* index of 0, and the names of the elements in *column* 3 all have a *second* index of 3.

Arrays of One-Dimensional Arrays
Like one-dimensional arrays, multidimensional arrays can be initialized with array initializers in declarations. A two-dimensional array b with two rows and two columns could be declared and initialized with **nested array initializers** as follows:

```
int[][] b = {{1, 2}, {3, 4}};
```

The initial values are *grouped by row* in braces. So 1 and 2 initialize b[0][0] and b[0][1], respectively, and 3 and 4 initialize b[1][0] and b[1][1], respectively. The compiler counts the number of nested array initializers (represented by sets of braces within the outer braces) to determine the number of *rows* in array b. The compiler counts the initializer values in the nested array initializer for a row to determine the number of *columns* in that row. As we'll see momentarily, this means that *rows can have different lengths*.

Multidimensional arrays are maintained as *arrays of one-dimensional arrays*. Therefore array b in the preceding declaration is actually composed of two separate one-dimensional arrays—one containing the values in the first nested initializer list {1, 2} and one containing the values in the second nested initializer list {3, 4}. Thus, array b itself is an array of two elements, each a one-dimensional array of int values.

Two-Dimensional Arrays with Rows of Different Lengths

The manner in which multidimensional arrays are represented makes them quite flexible. In fact, the lengths of the rows in array b are *not* required to be the same. For example,

```
int[][] b = {{1, 2}, {3, 4, 5}};
```

creates integer array b with two elements (determined by the number of nested array initializers) that represent the rows of the two-dimensional array. Each element of b is a *reference* to a one-dimensional array of int variables. The int array for row 0 is a one-dimensional array with *two* elements (1 and 2), and the int array for row 1 is a one-dimensional array with *three* elements (3, 4 and 5).

Creating Two-Dimensional Arrays with Array-Creation Expressions

A multidimensional array with the *same* number of columns in every row can be created with an array-creation expression. For example, the following line declares array b and assign it a reference to a three-by-four array:

```
int[][] b = new int[3][4];
```

In this case, we use the literal values 3 and 4 to specify the number of rows and number of columns, respectively, but this is *not* required. Programs can also use variables to specify array dimensions, because *new creates arrays at execution time—not at compile time*. The elements of a multidimensional array are initialized when the array object is created.

A multidimensional array in which each row has a *different* number of columns can be created as follows:

```
int[][] b = new int[2][];   // create 2 rows
b[0] = new int[5]; // create 5 columns for row 0
b[1] = new int[3]; // create 3 columns for row 1
```

The preceding statements create a two-dimensional array with two rows. Row 0 has *five* columns, and row 1 has *three* columns.

Two-Dimensional Array Example: Displaying Element Values

Figure 6.12 demonstrates initializing two-dimensional arrays with array initializers, and using nested for loops to **traverse** the arrays—that is, manipulate *every* element of each array. (In Chapter 7, we'll show a GradeBook case study in which we use a two-dimensional array to store student grades on multiple exams.) Class InitArray's main declares two arrays. The declaration of array1 (line 9) uses nested array initializers of the *same* length to initialize the first row to the values 1, 2 and 3, and the second row to the values 4, 5 and 6. The declaration of array2 (line 10) uses nested initializers of *different* lengths. In this case, the first row is initialized to two elements with the values 1 and 2, respectively. The second row is initialized to one element with the value 3. The third row is initialized to three elements with the values 4, 5 and 6, respectively.

```java
1    // Fig. 6.12: InitArray.java
2    // Initializing two-dimensional arrays.
3
4    public class InitArray
5    {
6       // create and output two-dimensional arrays
7       public static void main(String[] args)
8       {
9          int[][] array1 = {{1, 2, 3}, {4, 5, 6}};
10         int[][] array2 = {{1, 2}, {3}, {4, 5, 6}};
11
12         System.out.println("Values in array1 by row are");
13         outputArray(array1); // displays array1 by row
14
15         System.out.printf("%nValues in array2 by row are%n");
16         outputArray(array2); // displays array2 by row
17      }
18
19      // output rows and columns of a two-dimensional array
20      public static void outputArray(int[][] array)
21      {
22         // loop through array's rows
23         for (int row = 0; row < array.length; row++)
24         {
25            // loop through columns of current row
26            for (int column = 0; column < array[row].length; column++)
27               System.out.printf("%d  ", array[row][column]);
28
29            System.out.println();
30         }
31      }
32   } // end class InitArray
```

```
Values in array1 by row are
1  2  3
4  5  6

Values in array2 by row are
1  2
3
4  5  6
```

Fig. 6.12 | Initializing two-dimensional arrays.

Lines 13 and 16 call method outputArray (lines 20–31) to output the elements of array1 and array2, respectively. Method outputArray's parameter—int[][] array— indicates that the method receives a two-dimensional array. The nested for statement (lines 23–30) outputs the rows of a two-dimensional array. In the loop-continuation condition of the outer for statement, the expression array.length determines the number of rows in the array. In the inner for statement, the expression array[row].length determines the number of columns in the current row of the array. The inner `for` statement's condition enables the loop to determine the exact number of columns in each row.

Nested Enhanced-for Statements
The nested loop in method `outputArray` may also be implemented with nested enhanced-for statements as follows:

```
// loop through array's rows
for (int[] row : array)
{
   // loop through columns of current row
   for (int column : row)
      System.out.printf("%d  ", column);

   System.out.println();
}
```

Common Multidimensional-Array Manipulations Performed with for Statements
Many common array manipulations use `for` statements. As an example, the following `for` statement sets all the elements in row 2 of array a in Fig. 6.11 to zero:

```
for (int column = 0; column < a[2].length; column++)
   a[2][column] = 0;
```

We specified row 2; therefore, we know that the *first* index is always 2 (0 is the first row, and 1 is the second row). This `for` loop varies only the *second* index (i.e., the column index). If row 2 of array a contains four elements, then the preceding `for` statement is equivalent to the assignment statements

```
a[2][0] = 0;
a[2][1] = 0;
a[2][2] = 0;
a[2][3] = 0;
```

The following nested `for` statement totals the values of all the elements in array a:

```
int total = 0;
for (int row = 0; row < a.length; row++)
{
   for (int column = 0; column < a[row].length; column++)
      total += a[row][column];
}
```

These nested `for` statements total the array elements *one row at a time*. The outer `for` statement begins by setting the row index to 0 so that the first row's elements can be totaled by the inner `for` statement. The outer `for` then increments row to 1 so that the second row can be totaled. Then, the outer `for` increments row to 2 so that the third row can be totaled.

6.11 Variable-Length Argument Lists

With **variable-length argument lists**, you can create methods that receive an unspecified number of arguments. A type followed by an **ellipsis (. . .)** in a method's parameter list indicates that the method receives a variable number of arguments of that particular type. This use of the ellipsis can occur only *once* in a parameter list, and the ellipsis, together with its type and the parameter name, must be placed at the *end* of the parameter list. While you can use method overloading and array passing to accomplish much of what is accomplished with variable-length argument lists, using an ellipsis in a method's parameter list is more concise.

Figure 6.13 demonstrates method average (lines 7–16), which receives a variable-length sequence of doubles. Java treats the variable-length argument list as an array whose elements are all of the same type. So, the method body can manipulate the parameter numbers as an array of doubles. Lines 12–13 use the enhanced for loop to walk through the array and calculate the total of the doubles in the array. Line 15 accesses numbers.length to obtain the size of the numbers array for use in the averaging calculation. Lines 29, 31 and 33 in main call method average with two, three and four arguments, respectively. Method average has a variable-length argument list (line 7), so it can average as many double arguments as the caller passes. The output shows that each call to method average returns the correct value.

 Common Programming Error 6.5
Placing an ellipsis indicating a variable-length argument list in the middle of a parameter list is a syntax error. An ellipsis may be placed only at the end of the parameter list.

```
1   // Fig. 6.13: VarargsTest.java
2   // Using variable-length argument lists.
3
4   public class VarargsTest
5   {
6      // calculate average
7      public static double average(double... numbers)
8      {
9         double total = 0.0;
10
11        // calculate total using the enhanced for statement
12        for (double d : numbers)
13           total += d;
14
15        return total / numbers.length;
16     }
17
18     public static void main(String[] args)
19     {
20        double d1 = 10.0;
21        double d2 = 20.0;
22        double d3 = 30.0;
23        double d4 = 40.0;
24
25        System.out.printf("d1 = %.1f%nd2 = %.1f%nd3 = %.1f%nd4 = %.1f%n%n",
26           d1, d2, d3, d4);
27
28        System.out.printf("Average of d1 and d2 is %.1f%n",
29           average(d1, d2)  );
30        System.out.printf("Average of d1, d2 and d3 is %.1f%n",
31           average(d1, d2, d3)  );
```

Fig. 6.13 | Using variable-length argument lists. (Part 1 of 2.)

```
32              System.out.printf("Average of d1, d2, d3 and d4 is %.1f%n",
33                 average(d1, d2, d3, d4) );
34        }
35  } // end class VarargsTest
```

```
d1 = 10.0
d2 = 20.0
d3 = 30.0
d4 = 40.0

Average of d1 and d2 is 15.0
Average of d1, d2 and d3 is 20.0
Average of d1, d2, d3 and d4 is 25.0
```

Fig. 6.13 | Using variable-length argument lists. (Part 2 of 2.)

6.12 Using Command-Line Arguments

It's possible to pass arguments from the command line to an application via method main's String[] parameter, which receives an array of Strings. By convention, this parameter is named args. When an application is executed using the java command, Java passes the **command-line arguments** that appear after the class name in the java command to the application's main method as Strings in the array args. The number of command-line arguments is obtained by accessing the array's length attribute. Common uses of command-line arguments include passing options and filenames to applications.

Our next example uses command-line arguments to determine the size of an array, the value of its first element and the increment used to calculate the values of the array's remaining elements. The command

        java InitArray 5 0 4

passes three arguments, 5, 0 and 4, to the application InitArray. Command-line arguments are separated by white space, *not* commas. When this command executes, InitArray's main method receives the three-element array args (i.e., args.length is 3) in which args[0] contains the String "5", args[1] contains the String "0" and args[2] contains the String "4". The program determines how to use these arguments—in Fig. 6.14 we convert the three command-line arguments to int values and use them to initialize an array. When the program executes, if args.length is not 3, the program prints an error message and terminates (lines 9–12). Otherwise, lines 14–32 initialize and display the array based on the values of the command-line arguments.

```
1   // Fig. 6.14: InitArray.java
2   // Initializing an array using command-line arguments.
3
4   public class InitArray
5   {
6      public static void main(String[] args)
7      {
```

Fig. 6.14 | Initializing an array using command-line arguments. (Part 1 of 2.)

```
 8          // check number of command-line arguments
 9          if (args.length != 3)
10             System.out.printf(
11                "Error: Please re-enter the entire command, including%n" +
12                "an array size, initial value and increment.%n");
13          else
14          {
15             // get array size from first command-line argument
16             int arrayLength = Integer.parseInt(args[0]);
17             int[] array = new int[arrayLength];
18
19             // get initial value and increment from command-line arguments
20             int initialValue = Integer.parseInt(args[1]);
21             int increment = Integer.parseInt(args[2]);
22
23             // calculate value for each array element
24             for (int counter = 0; counter < array.length; counter++)
25                array[counter] = initialValue + increment * counter;
26
27             System.out.printf("%s%8s%n", "Index", "Value");
28
29             // display array index and value
30             for (int counter = 0; counter < array.length; counter++)
31                System.out.printf("%5d%8d%n", counter, array[counter]);
32          }
33       }
34    } // end class InitArray
```

```
java InitArray
Error: Please re-enter the entire command, including
an array size, initial value and increment.
```

```
java InitArray 5 0 4
Index    Value
    0        0
    1        4
    2        8
    3       12
    4       16
```

```
java InitArray 8 1 2
Index    Value
    0        1
    1        3
    2        5
    3        7
    4        9
    5       11
    6       13
    7       15
```

Fig. 6.14 | Initializing an array using command-line arguments. (Part 2 of 2.)

Line 16 gets `args[0]`—a `String` that specifies the array size—and converts it to an `int` value that the program uses to create the array in line 17. The `static` method `parseInt` of class `Integer` converts its `String` argument to an `int`.

Lines 20–21 convert the `args[1]` and `args[2]` command-line arguments to `int` values and store them in `initialValue` and `increment`, respectively. Lines 24–25 calculate the value for each array element.

The output of the first execution shows that the application received an insufficient number of command-line arguments. The second execution uses command-line arguments 5, 0 and 4 to specify the size of the array (5), the value of the first element (0) and the increment of each value in the array (4), respectively. The corresponding output shows that these values create an array containing the integers 0, 4, 8, 12 and 16. The output from the third execution shows that the command-line arguments 8, 1 and 2 produce an array whose 8 elements are the nonnegative odd integers from 1 to 15.

6.13 Class Arrays

Class **Arrays** helps you avoid reinventing the wheel by providing `static` methods for common array manipulations. These methods include **sort** for *sorting* an array (i.e., arranging elements into ascending order), **binarySearch** for *searching* a *sorted* array (i.e., determining whether an array contains a specific value and, if so, where the value is located), **equals** for *comparing* arrays and **fill** for *placing values into an array*. These methods are overloaded for primitive-type arrays and for arrays of objects. Our focus in this section is on using the built-in capabilities provided by the Java API. Chapter 19, Searching, Sorting and Big O, shows how to implement your own sorting and searching algorithms, a subject of great interest to computer-science researchers and students.

Figure 6.15 uses `Arrays` methods `sort`, `binarySearch`, `equals` and `fill`, and shows how to *copy* arrays with class `System`'s `static` **arraycopy** method. In `main`, line 11 sorts the elements of array `doubleArray`. The `static` method `sort` of class `Arrays` orders the array's elements in *ascending* order by default. We discuss how to sort in *descending* order later in the chapter. Overloaded versions of `sort` allow you to sort a specific range of elements within the array. Lines 12–15 output the sorted array.

```
1   // Fig. 6.15: ArrayManipulations.java
2   // Arrays class methods and System.arraycopy.
3   import java.util.Arrays;
4
5   public class ArrayManipulations
6   {
7      public static void main(String[] args)
8      {
9         // sort doubleArray into ascending order
10        double[] doubleArray = { 8.4, 9.3, 0.2, 7.9, 3.4 };
11        Arrays.sort(doubleArray);
12        System.out.printf("%ndoubleArray: ");
13
14        for (double value : doubleArray)
15           System.out.printf("%.1f ", value);
```

Fig. 6.15 | Arrays class methods and `System.arraycopy`. (Part 1 of 3.)

```
16
17          // fill 10-element array with 7s
18          int[] filledIntArray = new int[10];
19          Arrays.fill(filledIntArray, 7);
20          displayArray(filledIntArray, "filledIntArray");
21
22          // copy array intArray into array intArrayCopy
23          int[] intArray = { 1, 2, 3, 4, 5, 6 };
24          int[] intArrayCopy = new int[intArray.length];
25          System.arraycopy(intArray, 0, intArrayCopy, 0, intArray.length);
26          displayArray(intArray, "intArray");
27          displayArray(intArrayCopy, "intArrayCopy");
28
29          // compare intArray and intArrayCopy for equality
30          boolean b = Arrays.equals(intArray, intArrayCopy);
31          System.out.printf("%n%nintArray %s intArrayCopy%n",
32             (b ? "==" : "!="));
33
34          // compare intArray and filledIntArray for equality
35          b = Arrays.equals(intArray, filledIntArray);
36          System.out.printf("intArray %s filledIntArray%n",
37             (b ? "==" : "!="));
38
39          // search intArray for the value 5
40          int location = Arrays.binarySearch(intArray, 5);
41
42          if (location >= 0)
43             System.out.printf(
44                "Found 5 at element %d in intArray%n", location);
45          else
46             System.out.println("5 not found in intArray");
47
48          // search intArray for the value 8763
49          location = Arrays.binarySearch(intArray, 8763);
50
51          if (location >= 0)
52             System.out.printf(
53                "Found 8763 at element %d in intArray%n", location);
54          else
55             System.out.println("8763 not found in intArray");
56       }
57
58       // output values in each array
59       public static void displayArray(int[] array, String description)
60       {
61          System.out.printf("%n%s: ", description);
62
63          for (int value : array)
64             System.out.printf("%d ", value);
65       }
66    } // end class ArrayManipulations
```

Fig. 6.15 | Arrays class methods and System.arraycopy. (Part 2 of 3.)

```
doubleArray: 0.2 3.4 7.9 8.4 9.3
filledIntArray: 7 7 7 7 7 7 7 7 7 7
intArray: 1 2 3 4 5 6
intArrayCopy: 1 2 3 4 5 6

intArray == intArrayCopy
intArray != filledIntArray
Found 5 at element 4 in intArray
8763 not found in intArray
```

Fig. 6.15 | Arrays class methods and `System.arraycopy`. (Part 3 of 3.)

Line 19 calls `static` method `fill` of class `Arrays` to populate all 10 elements of `filledIntArray` with 7s. Overloaded versions of `fill` allow you to populate a specific range of elements with the same value. Line 20 calls our class's `displayArray` method (declared at lines 59–65) to output the contents of `filledIntArray`.

Line 25 copies the elements of `intArray` into `intArrayCopy`. The first argument (`intArray`) passed to `System` method `arraycopy` is the array from which elements are to be copied. The second argument (0) is the index that specifies the *starting point* in the range of elements to copy from the array. This value can be any valid array index. The third argument (`intArrayCopy`) specifies the *destination array* that will store the copy. The fourth argument (0) specifies the index in the destination array *where the first copied element should be stored*. The last argument specifies the *number of elements to copy* from the array in the first argument. In this case, we copy all the elements in the array.

Lines 30 and 35 call `static` method `equals` of class `Arrays` to determine whether all the elements of two arrays are equivalent. If the arrays contain the same elements in the same order, the method returns `true`; otherwise, it returns `false`.

Error-Prevention Tip 6.3

When comparing array contents, always use `Arrays.equals(array1, array2)`, which compares the two arrays' contents, rather than `array1.equals(array2)`, which compares whether `array1` and `array2` refer to the same array object.

Lines 40 and 49 call `static` method `binarySearch` of class `Arrays` to perform a binary search on `intArray`, using the second argument (5 and 8763, respectively) as the key. If `value` is found, `binarySearch` returns the index of the element; otherwise, `binarySearch` returns a negative value. The negative value returned is based on the search key's *insertion point*—the index where the key would be inserted in the array if we were performing an insert operation. After `binarySearch` determines the insertion point, it changes its sign to negative and subtracts 1 to obtain the return value. For example, in Fig. 6.15, the insertion point for the value 8763 is the element with index 6 in the array. Method `binarySearch` changes the insertion point to –6, subtracts 1 from it and returns the value –7. Subtracting 1 from the insertion point guarantees that method `binarySearch` returns positive values (>= 0) if and only if the key is found. This return value is useful for inserting elements in a sorted array. Chapter 19 discusses binary searching in detail.

Common Programming Error 6.6

Passing an unsorted array to `binarySearch` is a logic error—the value returned is undefined.

Java SE 8—Class **Arrays** *Method* **parallelSort**

The Arrays class now has several new "parallel" methods that take advantage of multi-core hardware. Arrays method parallelSort can sort large arrays more efficiently on multi-core systems. In Section 23.12, we create a very large array and use features of the Java SE 8 Date/Time API to compare how long it takes to sort the array with methods sort and parallelSort.

6.14 Introduction to Collections and Class **ArrayList**

The Java API provides several predefined data structures, called **collections**, used to store groups of related objects in memory. These classes provide efficient methods that organize, store and retrieve your data *without* requiring knowledge of how the data is being *stored*. This reduces application-development time.

You've used arrays to store sequences of objects. Arrays do not automatically change their size at execution time to accommodate additional elements. The collection class **ArrayList<T>** (package java.util) provides a convenient solution to this problem—it can *dynamically* change its size to accommodate more elements. The T (by convention) is a *placeholder*—when declaring a new ArrayList, replace it with the type of elements that you want the ArrayList to hold. For example,

```
ArrayList<String> list;
```

declares list as an ArrayList collection that can store only Strings. Classes with this kind of placeholder that can be used with any type are called **generic classes**. *Only nonprimitive types can be used to declare variables and create objects of generic classes.* However, Java provides a mechanism—known as *boxing*—that allows primitive values to be wrapped as objects for use with generic classes. So, for example,

```
ArrayList<Integer> integers;
```

declares integers as an ArrayList that can store only Integers. When you place an int value into an ArrayList<Integer>, the int value is *boxed* (wrapped) as an Integer object, and when you get an Integer object from an ArrayList<Integer>, then assign the object to an int variable, the int value inside the object is *unboxed* (unwrapped).

Additional generic collection classes and generics are discussed in Chapters 16 and 20, respectively. Figure 6.16 shows some common methods of class ArrayList<T>.

Method	Description
add	Adds an element to the *end* of the ArrayList.
clear	Removes all the elements from the ArrayList.
contains	Returns true if the ArrayList contains the specified element; otherwise, returns false.
get	Returns the element at the specified index.
indexOf	Returns the index of the first occurrence of the specified element in the ArrayList.

Fig. 6.16 | Some methods and properties of class ArrayList<T>. (Part 1 of 2.)

Method	Description
remove	Overloaded. Removes the first occurrence of the specified value or the element at the specified index.
size	Returns the number of elements stored in the `ArrayList`.
trimToSize	Trims the capacity of the `ArrayList` to the current number of elements.

Fig. 6.16 | Some methods and properties of class `ArrayList<T>`. (Part 2 of 2.)

Demonstrating an *ArrayList<String>*

Figure 6.17 demonstrates some common `ArrayList` capabilities. Line 10 creates a new empty `ArrayList` of `String`s with a default initial capacity of 10 elements. The capacity indicates how many items the `ArrayList` can hold *without growing*. `ArrayList` is implemented using a conventional array behind the scenes. When the `ArrayList` grows, it must create a larger internal array and *copy* each element to the new array. This is a time-consuming operation. It would be inefficient for the `ArrayList` to grow each time an element is added. Instead, it grows only when an element is added *and* the number of elements is equal to the capacity—i.e., there's no space for the new element.

```
1   // Fig. 6.17: ArrayListCollection.java
2   // Generic ArrayList<T> collection demonstration.
3   import java.util.ArrayList;
4
5   public class ArrayListCollection
6   {
7      public static void main(String[] args)
8      {
9         // create a new ArrayList of Strings with an initial capacity of 10
10        ArrayList<String> items = new ArrayList<String>();
11
12        items.add("red"); // append an item to the list
13        items.add(0, "yellow"); // insert "yellow" at index 0
14
15        // header
16        System.out.print(
17           "Display list contents with counter-controlled loop:");
18
19        // display the colors in the list
20        for (int i = 0; i < items.size(); i++)
21           System.out.printf(" %s", items.get(i));
22
23        // display colors using enhanced for in the display method
24        display(items,
25           "%nDisplay list contents with enhanced for statement:");
26
27        items.add("green"); // add "green" to the end of the list
28        items.add("yellow"); // add "yellow" to the end of the list
```

Fig. 6.17 | Generic `ArrayList<T>` collection demonstration. (Part 1 of 2.)

```
29          display(items, "List with two new elements:");
30
31          items.remove("yellow"); // remove the first "yellow"
32          display(items, "Remove first instance of yellow:");
33
34          items.remove(1); // remove item at index 1
35          display(items, "Remove second list element (green):");
36
37          // check if a value is in the List
38          System.out.printf("\"red\" is %sin the list%n",
39              items.contains("red") ? "" : "not ");
40
41          // display number of elements in the List
42          System.out.printf("Size: %s%n", items.size());
43      }
44
45      // display the ArrayList's elements on the console
46      public static void display(ArrayList<String> items, String header)
47      {
48          System.out.printf(header); // display header
49
50          // display each element in items
51          for (String item : items)
52              System.out.printf(" %s", item);
53
54          System.out.println();
55      }
56  } // end class ArrayListCollection
```

```
Display list contents with counter-controlled loop: yellow red
Display list contents with enhanced for statement: yellow red
List with two new elements: yellow red green yellow
Remove first instance of yellow: red green yellow
Remove second list element (green): red yellow
"red" is in the list
Size: 2
```

Fig. 6.17 | Generic ArrayList<T> collection demonstration. (Part 2 of 2.)

The **add** method adds elements to the ArrayList (lines 12–13). The add method with *one* argument *appends* its argument to the *end* of the ArrayList. The add method with *two* arguments *inserts* a new element at the specified *position*. The first argument is an index. As with arrays, collection indices start at zero. The second argument is the *value* to insert at that *index*. The indices of all subsequent elements are incremented by one. Inserting an element is usually slower than adding an element to the end of the ArrayList

Lines 20–21 display the items in the ArrayList. Method **size** returns the number of elements currently in the ArrayList. Method **get** (line 21) obtains the element at a specified index. Lines 24–25 display the elements again by invoking method display (defined at lines 46–55). Lines 27–28 add two more elements to the ArrayList, then line 29 displays the elements again to confirm that the two elements were added to the *end* of the collection.

The **remove** method is used to remove an element with a specific value (line 31). It removes only the first such element. If no such element is in the ArrayList, remove does nothing. An overloaded version of the method removes the element at the specified index (line 34). When an element is removed, the indices of any elements after the removed element decrease by one.

Line 39 uses the **contains** method to check if an item is in the ArrayList. The contains method returns true if the element is found in the ArrayList, and false otherwise. The method compares its argument to each element of the ArrayList in order, so using contains on a large ArrayList can be *inefficient*. Line 42 displays the ArrayList's size.

Java SE 7—Diamond (<>) Notation for Creating an Object of a Generic Class
Consider line 10 of Fig. 6.17:

```
ArrayList<String> items = new ArrayList<String>();
```

Notice that ArrayList<String> appears in the variable declaration *and* in the class instance creation expression. Java SE 7 introduced the **diamond (<>) notation** to simplify statements like this. Using <> in a class instance creation expression for an object of a *generic* class tells the compiler to determine what belongs in the angle brackets. In Java SE 7 and higher, the preceding statement can be written as:

```
ArrayList<String> items = new ArrayList<>();
```

When the compiler encounters the diamond (<>) in the class instance creation expression, it uses the declaration of variable items to determine the ArrayList's element type (String)—this is known as *inferring the element type*.

6.15 (Optional) GUI and Graphics Case Study: Drawing Arcs

Using Java's graphics features, we can create complex drawings that would be more tedious to code line by line. In Figs. 6.18–6.19, we use arrays and repetition statements to draw a rainbow by using Graphics method fillArc. Drawing arcs in Java is similar to drawing ovals—an arc is simply a section of an oval.

In Fig. 6.18, lines 10–11 declare and create two new color constants—VIOLET and INDIGO. As you may know, the colors of a rainbow are red, orange, yellow, green, blue, indigo and violet. Java has predefined constants only for the first five colors. Lines 15–17 initialize an array with the colors of the rainbow, starting with the innermost arcs first. The array begins with two Color.WHITE elements, which, as you'll soon see, are for drawing the empty arcs at the center of the rainbow. The instance variables can be initialized when they're declared, as shown in lines 10–17. The constructor (lines 20–23) contains a single statement that calls method **setBackground** (which is inherited from class JPanel) with the parameter Color.WHITE. Method setBackground takes a single Color argument and sets the background of the component to that color.

Line 30 in paintComponent declares local variable radius, which determines the radius of each arc. Local variables centerX and centerY (lines 33–34) determine the location of the midpoint on the base of the rainbow. The loop at lines 37–46 uses control variable counter to count backward from the end of the array, drawing the largest arcs first and placing each successive smaller arc on top of the previous one. Line 40 sets the color to draw the current arc from the array. The reason we have Color.WHITE entries at the beginning of the array is to create the empty arc in the center. Otherwise, the center of the rainbow would just be a solid violet semicircle. You can change the individual colors and the number of entries in the array to create new designs.

```java
1   // Fig. 6.18: DrawRainbow.java
2   // Drawing a rainbow using arcs and an array of colors.
3   import java.awt.Color;
4   import java.awt.Graphics;
5   import javax.swing.JPanel;
6
7   public class DrawRainbow extends JPanel
8   {
9      // define indigo and violet
10     private final static Color VIOLET = new Color(128, 0, 128);
11     private final static Color INDIGO = new Color(75, 0, 130);
12
13     // colors to use in the rainbow, starting from the innermost
14     // The two white entries result in an empty arc in the center
15     private Color[] colors =
16        { Color.WHITE, Color.WHITE, VIOLET, INDIGO, Color.BLUE,
17          Color.GREEN, Color.YELLOW, Color.ORANGE, Color.RED };
18
19     // constructor
20     public DrawRainbow()
21     {
22        setBackground(Color.WHITE); // set the background to white
23     }
24
25     // draws a rainbow using concentric arcs
26     public void paintComponent(Graphics g)
27     {
28        super.paintComponent(g);
29
30        int radius = 20; // radius of an arc
31
32        // draw the rainbow near the bottom-center
33        int centerX = getWidth() / 2;
34        int centerY = getHeight() - 10;
35
36        // draws filled arcs starting with the outermost
37        for (int counter = colors.length; counter > 0; counter--)
38        {
39           // set the color for the current arc
40           g.setColor(colors[counter - 1]);
41
42           // fill the arc from 0 to 180 degrees
43           g.fillArc(centerX - counter * radius,
44              centerY - counter * radius,
45              counter * radius * 2, counter * radius * 2, 0, 180);
46        }
47     }
48  } // end class DrawRainbow
```

Fig. 6.18 | Drawing a rainbow using arcs and an array of colors.

The **fillArc** method call at lines 43–45 draws a filled semicircle. Method fillArc requires six parameters. The first four represent the bounding rectangle in which the arc will be drawn. The first two of these specify the coordinates for the *upper-left* corner of the bounding rectangle, and the next two specify its width and height. The fifth parameter is the starting angle on the oval, and the sixth specifies the **sweep**, or the amount of arc to cover. The starting angle and sweep are measured in degrees, with zero degrees pointing right. A *positive* sweep draws the arc *counterclockwise*, while a *negative* sweep draws the arc *clockwise*. A method similar to fillArc is **drawArc**—it requires the same parameters as fillArc, but draws the edge of the arc rather than filling it.

Class DrawRainbowTest (Fig. 6.19) creates and sets up a JFrame to display the rainbow. Once the program makes the JFrame visible, the system calls the paintComponent method in class DrawRainbow to draw the rainbow on the screen.

```java
1   // Fig. 6.19: DrawRainbowTest.java
2   // Test application to display a rainbow.
3   import javax.swing.JFrame;
4
5   public class DrawRainbowTest
6   {
7      public static void main(String[] args)
8      {
9         DrawRainbow panel = new DrawRainbow();
10        JFrame application = new JFrame();
11
12        application.setDefaultCloseOperation(JFrame.EXIT_ON_CLOSE);
13        application.add(panel);
14        application.setSize(400, 250);
15        application.setVisible(true);
16     }
17  } // end class DrawRainbowTest
```

Fig. 6.19 | Test application to display a rainbow.

GUI and Graphics Case Study Exercise

6.1   *(Drawing Spirals)* In this exercise, you'll draw spirals with methods drawLine and drawArc.

a) Draw a square-shaped spiral (as in the left screen capture of Fig. 6.20), centered on the panel, using method drawLine. One technique is to use a loop that increases the line length after drawing every second line. The direction in which to draw the next line should follow a distinct pattern, such as down, left, up, right.

b) Draw a circular spiral (as in the right screen capture of Fig. 6.20), using method `drawArc` to draw one semicircle at a time. Each successive semicircle should have a larger radius (as specified by the bounding rectangle's width) and should continue drawing where the previous semicircle finished.

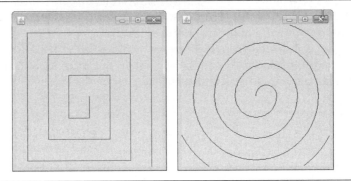

Fig. 6.20 | Drawing a spiral using `drawLine` (left) and `drawArc` (right).

6.16 Wrap-Up

This chapter began our introduction to data structures, exploring the use of arrays to store data in and retrieve data from lists and tables of values. The chapter examples demonstrated how to declare an array, initialize an array and refer to individual elements of an array. The chapter introduced the enhanced `for` statement to iterate through arrays. We used exception handling to test for `ArrayIndexOutOfBoundsExceptions` that occur when a program attempts to access an array element outside the bounds of an array. We also illustrated how to pass arrays to methods and how to declare and manipulate multidimensional arrays. Finally, the chapter showed how to write methods that use variable-length argument lists and how to read arguments passed to a program from the command line.

We introduced the `ArrayList<T>` generic collection, which provides all the functionality and performance of arrays, along with other useful capabilities such as dynamic resizing. We used the `add` methods to add new items to the end of an `ArrayList` and to insert items in an `ArrayList`. The `remove` method was used to remove the first occurrence of a specified item, and an overloaded version of `remove` was used to remove an item at a specified index. We used the `size` method to obtain the number of items in the `ArrayList`.

We continue our coverage of data structures in Chapter 16, Generic Collections, which introduces the Java Collections Framework and Java's other predefined data structures. Like `ArrayList`, the other predefined data structures use generics to allow you to specify the exact types of objects that a particular data structure will store. Chapter 16 also covers additional methods of class `Arrays`—you'll be able to use some of these after reading the Chapter 6, but others require knowledge of concepts presented later in the book. Chapter 20 discusses generics, which enable you to create general models of methods and classes that can be declared once, but used with many different data types. Chapter 21, Custom Generic Data Structures, shows how to build dynamic data structures, such as lists, queues, stacks and trees, that can grow and shrink as programs execute.

We've now introduced the basic concepts of control statements, methods, arrays and collections. As you'll see in Chapter 7, Java applications typically contain just a few lines of code in method `main`—these statements normally create the objects that perform the work of the application. In Chapter 7, you'll learn how to implement your own classes and use objects of those classes in applications.

Summary

Section 6.1 Introduction
- Arrays (p. 209) are fixed-length data structures consisting of related data items of the same type.

Section 6.2 Primitive Types vs. Reference Types
- Types in Java are divided into two categories—primitive types and reference types. The primitive types are `boolean`, `byte`, `char`, `short`, `int`, `long`, `float` and `double`. All other types are reference types, so classes, which specify the types of objects, are reference types.
- A primitive-type variable can store exactly one value of its declared type at a time.
- Reference-type variables (called references; p. 210) store the location of an object in the computer's memory. Such variables refer to objects in the program.
- A reference to an object (p. 210) is required to invoke an object's methods. A primitive-type variable does not refer to an object and therefore cannot be used to invoke a method.

Section 6.3 Arrays
- An array is a group of variables (called elements or components; p. 210) containing values that all have the same type. Arrays are objects, so they're considered reference types.
- A program refers to any one of an array's elements with an array-access expression (p. 211) that includes the name of the array followed by the index of the particular element in square brackets (`[]`; p. 211).
- The first element in every array has index zero (p. 211) and is sometimes called the zeroth element.
- An index must be a nonnegative integer. A program can use an expression as an index.
- An array object's `length` instance variable (p. 211) stores the array's length.

Section 6.4 Declaring and Creating Arrays
- To create an array object, specify the array's element type and the number of elements as part of an array-creation expression (p. 212) that uses keyword `new`.
- When an array is created, each element receives a default value—zero for numeric primitive-type elements, `false` for boolean elements and `null` for references.
- In an array declaration, the type and the square brackets can be combined at the beginning of the declaration to indicate that all the identifiers in the declaration are array variables.
- Every element of a primitive-type array contains a variable of the array's declared type. Every element of a reference-type array is a reference to an object of the array's declared type.

Section 6.5 Examples Using Arrays
- A program can create an array and initialize its elements with an array initializer (p. 214).
- Constant variables (p. 216) are declared with keyword `final`, must be initialized before they're used and cannot be modified thereafter.

Section 6.6 Exception Handling: Processing the Incorrect Response

- An exception indicates a problem that occurs while a program executes. The name "exception" suggests that the problem occurs infrequently—if the "rule" is that a statement normally executes correctly, then the problem represents the "exception to the rule."

- Exception handling (p. 222) enables you to create fault-tolerant programs.

- When a Java program executes, the JVM checks array indices to ensure that they're greater than or equal to 0 and less than the array's length. If a program uses an invalid index, Java generates an exception (p. 222) to indicate that an error occurred in the program at execution time.

- To handle an exception, place any code that might throw an exception (p. 222) in a try statement.

- The try block (p. 222) contains the code that might throw an exception, and the catch block (p. 222) contains the code that handles the exception if one occurs.

- You can have many catch blocks to handle different types of exceptions that might be thrown in the corresponding try block.

- When a try block terminates, any variables declared in the try block go out of scope.

- A catch block declares a type and an exception parameter. Inside the catch block, you can use the parameter's identifier to interact with a caught exception object.

- When a program is executed, array element indices are checked for validity—all indices must be greater than or equal to 0 and less than the length of the array. If an attempt is made to use an invalid index to access an element, an ArrayIndexOutOfRangeException (p. 223) exception occurs.

- An exception object's toString method returns the exception's error message.

Section 6.7 Enhanced **for** Statement

- The enhanced for statement (p. 223) allows you to iterate through the elements of an array or a collection without using a counter. The syntax of an enhanced for statement is:

    for (*parameter* : *arrayName*)
        statement

  where *parameter* has a type and an identifier, and *arrayName* is the array through which to iterate.

- The enhanced for statement cannot be used to modify elements in an array. If a program needs to modify elements, use the traditional counter-controlled for statement.

Section 6.8 Passing Arrays to Methods

- When an argument is passed by value, a copy of the argument's value is made and passed to the called method. The called method works exclusively with the copy.

Section 6.9 Pass-By-Value vs. Pass-By-Reference

- When an argument is passed by reference (p. 227), the called method can access the argument's value in the caller directly and possibly modify it.

- All arguments in Java are passed by value. A method call can pass two types of values to a method—copies of primitive values and copies of references to objects. Although an object's reference is passed by value (p. 227), a method can still interact with the referenced object by calling its public methods using the copy of the object's reference.

- To pass an object reference to a method, simply specify in the method call the name of the variable that refers to the object.

- When you pass an array or an individual array element of a reference type to a method, the called method receives a copy of the array or element's reference. When you pass an individual element of a primitive type, the called method receives a copy of the element's value.

- To pass an individual array element to a method, use the indexed name of the array.

Section 6.10 Multidimensional Arrays

- Multidimensional arrays with two dimensions are often used to represent tables of values consisting of information arranged in rows and columns.
- A two-dimensional array (p. 228) with *m* rows and *n* columns is called an *m*-by-*n* array. Such an array can be initialized with an array initializer of the form

    arrayType[][] *arrayName* = {{*row1 initializer*}, {*row2 initializer*}, ...};

- Multidimensional arrays are maintained as arrays of separate one-dimensional arrays. As a result, the lengths of the rows in a two-dimensional array are not required to be the same.
- A multidimensional array with the same number of columns in every row can be created with an array-creation expression of the form

    arrayType[][] *arrayName* = **new** *arrayType*[*numRows*][*numColumns*];

Section 6.11 Variable-Length Argument Lists

- An argument type followed by an ellipsis (...; p. 231) in a method's parameter list indicates that the method receives a variable number of arguments of that particular type. The ellipsis can occur only once in a method's parameter list. It must be at the end of the parameter list.
- A variable-length argument list (p. 231) is treated as an array within the method body. The number of arguments in the array can be obtained using the array's length field.

Section 6.12 Using Command-Line Arguments

- Passing arguments to main (p. 233) from the command line is achieved by including a parameter of type String[] in the parameter list of main. By convention, main's parameter is named args.
- Java passes command-line arguments that appear after the class name in the java command to the application's main method as Strings in the array args.

Section 6.13 Class **Arrays**

- Class Arrays' (p. 235) static methods peform common array manipulations, including sort, binarySearch, equals and fill.
- Class System's arraycopy method (p. 235) enables you to copy the elements of one array into another.

Section 6.14 Introduction to Collections and Class **ArrayList**

- The Java API's collection classes provide efficient methods that organize, store and retrieve data without requiring knowledge of how the data is being stored.
- An ArrayList<T> (p. 238) is similar to an array but can be dynamically resized.
- The add method (p. 240) with one argument appends an element to the end of an ArrayList.
- The add method with two arguments inserts a new element at a specified position in an ArrayList.
- The size method (p. 240) returns the number of elements currently in an ArrayList.
- The remove method with a reference to an object as an argument removes the first element that matches the argument's value.
- The remove method with an integer argument removes the element at the specified index, and all elements above that index are shifted down by one.
- The contains method returns true if the element is found in the ArrayList, and false otherwise.

Self-Review Exercises

6.1 Fill in the blank(s) in each of the following statements:
a) Lists and tables of values can be stored in _____ and _____.
b) An array is a group of _____ (called elements or components) containing values that all have the same _____.
c) The _____ allows you to iterate through an array's elements without using a counter.
d) The number used to refer to a particular array element is called the element's _____.
e) An array that uses two indices is referred to as a(n) _____ array.
f) Use the enhanced `for` statement _____ to walk through `double` array `numbers`.
g) Command-line arguments are stored in _____.
h) Use the expression _____ to receive the total number of arguments in a command line. Assume that command-line arguments are stored in `String[] args`.
i) Given the command `java MyClass test`, the first command-line argument is _____.
j) A(n) _____ in the parameter list of a method indicates that the method can receive a variable number of arguments.

6.2 Determine whether each of the following is *true* or *false*. If *false*, explain why.
a) An array can store many different types of values.
b) An array index should normally be of type `float`.
c) An individual array element that's passed to a method and modified in that method will contain the modified value when the called method completes execution.
d) Command-line arguments are separated by commas.

6.3 Perform the following tasks for an array called `fractions`:
a) Declare a constant `ARRAY_SIZE` that's initialized to 10.
b) Declare an array with `ARRAY_SIZE` elements of type `double`, and initialize the elements to 0.
c) Refer to array element 4.
d) Assign the value `1.667` to array element 9.
e) Assign the value `3.333` to array element 6.
f) Sum all the elements of the array, using a `for` statement. Declare the integer variable x as a control variable for the loop.

6.4 Perform the following tasks for an array called `table`:
a) Declare and create the array as an integer array that has three rows and three columns. Assume that the constant `ARRAY_SIZE` has been declared to be 3.
b) How many elements does the array contain?
c) Use a `for` statement to initialize each element of the array to the sum of its indices. Assume that the integer variables x and y are declared as control variables.

6.5 Find and correct the error in each of the following program segments:
a) `final int ARRAY_SIZE = 5;`
   `ARRAY_SIZE = 10;`
b) Assume `int[] b = new int[10];`
   `for (int i = 0; i <= b.length; i++)`
   `    b[i] = 1;`
c) Assume `int[][] a = {{1, 2}, {3, 4}};`
   `    a[1, 1] = 5;`

Answers to Self-Review Exercises

6.1 a) arrays, collections. b) variables, type. c) enhanced `for` statement. d) index (or subscript or position number). e) two-dimensional. f) `for (double d : numbers)`. g) an array of `Strings`, called args by convention. h) `args.length`. i) `test`. j) ellipsis (`...`).

6.2   a) False. An array can store only values of the same type.
   b) False. An array index must be an integer or an integer expression.
   c) For individual primitive-type elements of an array: False. A called method receives and manipulates a copy of the element value, so modifications do not affect the original. If the reference of an array is passed to a method, however, modifications to the array elements made in the called method *are* reflected in the original. For individual elements of a reference type: True. A called method receives a copy of the element's reference, and changes to the referenced object will be reflected in the original array element.
   d) False. Command-line arguments are separated by white space.

6.3   a) `final int ARRAY_SIZE = 10;`
   b) `double[] fractions = new double[ARRAY_SIZE];`
   c) `fractions[4]`
   d) `fractions[9] = 1.667;`
   e) `fractions[6] = 3.333;`
   f) `double total = 0.0;`
   `for (int x = 0; x < fractions.length; x++)`
   `    total += fractions[x];`

6.4   a) `int[][] table = new int[ARRAY_SIZE][ARRAY_SIZE];`
   b) Nine.
   c) `for (int x = 0; x < table.length; x++)`
   `    for (int y = 0; y < table[x].length; y++)`
   `        table[x][y] = x + y;`

6.5   a) Error: Assigning a value to a constant after it has been initialized.
   Correction: Assign the correct value to the constant in a `final int ARRAY_SIZE` declaration or declare another variable.
   b) Error: Referencing an array element outside the bounds of the array (`b[10]`).
   Correction: Change the `<=` operator to `<`.
   c) Error: Array indexing is performed incorrectly.
   Correction: Change the statement to `a[1][1] = 5;`.

Exercises

6.6   Fill in the blanks in each of the following statements:
   a) One-dimensional array p contains four elements. The names of those elements are _____, _____, _____ and _____.
   b) Naming an array, stating its type and specifying the number of dimensions in the array is called _____ the array.
   c) In a two-dimensional array, the first index identifies the _____ of an element and the second index identifies the _____ of an element.
   d) An *m*-by-*n* array contains _____ rows, _____ columns and _____ elements.
   e) The name of the element in row 3 and column 5 of array d is _____.

6.7   Determine whether each of the following is *true* or *false*. If *false*, explain why.
   a) To refer to a particular location or element within an array, we specify the name of the array and the value of the particular element.
   b) An array declaration reserves space for the array.
   c) To indicate that 100 locations should be reserved for integer array p, you write the declaration
   `p[100];`

d) An application that initializes the elements of a 15-element array to zero must contain at least one for statement.

e) An application that totals the elements of a two-dimensional array must contain nested for statements.

6.8   Write Java statements to accomplish each of the following tasks:

a) Display the value of element 6 of array f.

b) Initialize each of the five elements of one-dimensional integer array g to 8.

c) Total the 100 elements of floating-point array c.

d) Copy 11-element array a into the first portion of array b, which contains 34 elements.

e) Determine and display the smallest and largest values contained in 99-element floating-point array w.

6.9   Consider a two-by-three integer array t.

a) Write a statement that declares and creates t.

b) How many rows does t have?

c) How many columns does t have?

d) How many elements does t have?

e) Write access expressions for all the elements in row 1 of t.

f) Write access expressions for all the elements in column 2 of t.

g) Write a single statement that sets the element of t in row 0 and column 1 to zero.

h) Write individual statements to initialize each element of t to zero.

i) Write a nested for statement that initializes each element of t to zero.

j) Write a nested for statement that inputs the values for the elements of t from the user.

k) Write a series of statements that determines and displays the smallest value in t.

l) Write a single printf statement that displays the elements of the first row of t.

m) Write a statement that totals the elements of the third column of t. Do not use repetition.

n) Write a series of statements that displays the contents of t in tabular format. List the column indices as headings across the top, and list the row indices at the left of each row.

6.10   *(Sales Commissions)* Use a one-dimensional array to solve the following problem: A company pays its salespeople on a commission basis. The salespeople receive $200 per week plus 9% of their gross sales for that week. For example, a salesperson who grosses $5,000 in sales in a week receives $200 plus 9% of $5,000, or a total of $650. Write an application (using an array of counters) that determines how many of the salespeople earned salaries in each of the following ranges (assume that each salesperson's salary is truncated to an integer amount):

a) $200–299

b) $300–399

c) $400–499

d) $500–599

e) $600–699

f) $700–799

g) $800–899

h) $900–999

i) $1,000 and over

Summarize the results in tabular format.

6.11   Write statements that perform the following one-dimensional-array operations:

a) Set the 10 elements of integer array counts to zero.

b) Add one to each of the 15 elements of integer array bonus.

c) Display the five values of integer array bestScores in column format.

6.12   *(Duplicate Elimination)* Use a one-dimensional array to solve the following problem: Write an application that inputs five numbers, each between 10 and 100, inclusive. As each number is read, display it only if it's not a duplicate of a number already read. Provide for the "worst case," in which all five numbers are different. Use the smallest possible array to solve this problem. Display the complete set of unique values input after the user enters each new value.

6.13   Label the elements of three-by-five two-dimensional array sales to indicate the order in which they're set to zero by the following program segment:

```
for (int row = 0; row < sales.length; row++)
{
    for (int col = 0; col < sales[row].length; col++)
    {
        sales[row][col] = 0;
    }
}
```

6.14   *(Variable-Length Argument List)* Write an application that calculates the product of a series of integers that are passed to method product using a variable-length argument list. Test your method with several calls, each with a different number of arguments.

6.15   *(Command-Line Arguments)* Rewrite Fig. 6.2 so that the size of the array is specified by the first command-line argument. If no command-line argument is supplied, use 10 as the default size of the array.

6.16   *(Using the Enhanced for Statement)* Write an application that uses an enhanced for statement to sum the double values passed by the command-line arguments. [*Hint:* Use the static method parseDouble of class Double to convert a String to a double value.]

6.17   *(Dice Rolling)* Write an application to simulate the rolling of two dice. The application should use an object of class Random once to roll the first die and again to roll the second die. The sum of the two values should then be calculated. Each die can show an integer value from 1 to 6, so the sum of the values will vary from 2 to 12, with 7 being the most frequent sum, and 2 and 12 the least frequent. Figure 6.21 shows the 36 possible combinations of the two dice. Your application should roll the dice 36,000,000 times. Use a one-dimensional array to tally the number of times each possible sum appears. Display the results in tabular format.

	1	2	3	4	5	6
1	2	3	4	5	6	7
2	3	4	5	6	7	8
3	4	5	6	7	8	9
4	5	6	7	8	9	10
5	6	7	8	9	10	11
6	7	8	9	10	11	12

Fig. 6.21 | The 36 possible sums of two dice.

6.18   *(Game of Craps)* Write an application that runs 1,000,000 games of craps (Fig. 5.8) and answers the following questions:

a) How many games are won on the first roll, second roll, ..., twentieth roll and after the twentieth roll?

b) How many games are lost on the first roll, second roll, ..., twentieth roll and after the twentieth roll?

c) What are the chances of winning at craps? [*Note:* You should discover that craps is one of the fairest casino games. What do you suppose this means?]

d) What is the average length of a game of craps?

e) Do the chances of winning improve with the length of the game?

6.19 *(Airline Reservations System)* A small airline has just purchased a computer for its new automated reservations system. You've been asked to develop the new system. You're to write an application to assign seats on each flight of the airline's only plane (capacity: 10 seats).

Your application should display the following alternatives: Please type 1 for First Class and Please type 2 for Economy. If the user types 1, your application should assign a seat in the first-class section (seats 1–5). If the user types 2, your application should assign a seat in the economy section (seats 6–10). Your application should then display a boarding pass indicating the person's seat number and whether it's in the first-class or economy section of the plane.

Use a one-dimensional array of primitive type boolean to represent the seating chart of the plane. Initialize all the elements of the array to false to indicate that all the seats are empty. As each seat is assigned, set the corresponding element of the array to true to indicate that the seat is no longer available.

Your application should never assign a seat that has already been assigned. When the economy section is full, your application should ask the person if it's acceptable to be placed in the first-class section (and vice versa). If yes, make the appropriate seat assignment. If no, display the message "Next flight leaves in 3 hours."

6.20 *(Total Sales)* Use a two-dimensional array to solve the following problem: A company has four salespeople (1 to 4) who sell five different products (1 to 5). Once a day, each salesperson passes in a slip for each type of product sold. Each slip contains the following:

a) The salesperson number

b) The product number

c) The total dollar value of that product sold that day

Thus, each salesperson passes in between 0 and 5 sales slips per day. Assume that the information from all the slips for last month is available. Write an application that will read all this information for last month's sales and summarize the total sales by salesperson and by product. All totals should be stored in the two-dimensional array sales. After processing all the information for last month, display the results in tabular format, with each column representing a salesperson and each row representing a particular product. Cross-total each row to get the total sales of each product for last month. Cross-total each column to get the total sales by salesperson for last month. Your output should include these cross-totals to the right of the totaled rows and to the bottom of the totaled columns.

6.21 *(Turtle Graphics)* The Logo language made the concept of *turtle graphics* famous. Imagine a mechanical turtle that walks around the room under the control of a Java application. The turtle holds a pen in one of two positions, up or down. While the pen is down, the turtle traces out shapes as it moves, and while the pen is up, the turtle moves about freely without writing anything. In this problem, you'll simulate the operation of the turtle and create a computerized sketchpad.

Use a 20-by-20 array floor that's initialized to zeros. Read commands from an array that contains them. Keep track of the current position of the turtle at all times and whether the pen is currently up or down. Assume that the turtle always starts at position (0, 0) of the floor with its pen up. The set of turtle commands your application must process are shown in Fig. 6.22.

Command	Meaning
1	Pen up
2	Pen down

Fig. 6.22 | Turtle graphics commands. (Part 1 of 2.)

Command	Meaning
3	Turn right
4	Turn left
5,10	Move forward 10 spaces (replace 10 for a different number of spaces)
6	Display the 20-by-20 array
9	End of data (sentinel)

Fig. 6.22 | Turtle graphics commands. (Part 2 of 2.)

Suppose that the turtle is somewhere near the center of the floor. The following "program" would draw and display a 12-by-12 square, leaving the pen in the up position:

```
2
5,12
3
5,12
3
5,12
3
5,12
1
6
9
```

As the turtle moves with the pen down, set the appropriate elements of array floor to 1s. When the 6 command (display the array) is given, wherever there's a 1 in the array, display an asterisk or any character you choose. Wherever there's a 0, display a blank.

Write an application to implement the turtle graphics capabilities discussed here. Write several turtle graphics programs to draw interesting shapes. Add other commands to increase the power of your turtle graphics language.

6.22 *(Knight's Tour)* An interesting puzzler for chess buffs is the Knight's Tour problem, originally proposed by the mathematician Euler. Can the knight piece move around an empty chessboard and touch each of the 64 squares once and only once? We study this intriguing problem in depth here.

The knight makes only L-shaped moves (two spaces in one direction and one space in a perpendicular direction). Thus, as shown in Fig. 6.23, from a square near the middle of an empty chessboard, the knight (labeled K) can make eight different moves (numbered 0 through 7).

a) Draw an eight-by-eight chessboard on a sheet of paper, and attempt a Knight's Tour by hand. Put a 1 in the starting square, a 2 in the second square, a 3 in the third, and so on. Before starting the tour, estimate how far you think you'll get, remembering that a full tour consists of 64 moves. How far did you get? Was this close to your estimate?

b) Now let's develop an application that will move the knight around a chessboard. The board is represented by an eight-by-eight two-dimensional array board. Each square is initialized to zero. We describe each of the eight possible moves in terms of its horizontal and vertical components. For example, a move of type 0, as shown in Fig. 6.23, consists of moving two squares horizontally to the right and one square vertically upward. A move of type 2 consists of moving one square horizontally to the left and two squares vertically upward. Horizontal moves to the left and vertical moves upward are indicated with negative numbers. The eight moves may be described by two one-dimensional arrays, horizontal and vertical, as follows:

Fig. 6.23 | The eight possible moves of the knight.

```
horizontal[0] = 2       vertical[0] = -1
horizontal[1] = 1       vertical[1] = -2
horizontal[2] = -1      vertical[2] = -2
horizontal[3] = -2      vertical[3] = -1
horizontal[4] = -2      vertical[4] = 1
horizontal[5] = -1      vertical[5] = 2
horizontal[6] = 1       vertical[6] = 2
horizontal[7] = 2       vertical[7] = 1
```

Let the variables `currentRow` and `currentColumn` indicate the row and column, respectively, of the knight's current position. To make a move of type `moveNumber`, where `moveNumber` is between 0 and 7, your application should use the statements

```
currentRow += vertical[moveNumber];
currentColumn += horizontal[moveNumber];
```

Write an application to move the knight around the chessboard. Keep a counter that varies from 1 to 64. Record the latest count in each square the knight moves to. Test each potential move to see if the knight has already visited that square. Test every potential move to ensure that the knight does not land off the chessboard. Run the application. How many moves did the knight make?

c) After attempting to write and run a Knight's Tour application, you've probably developed some valuable insights. We'll use these insights to develop a *heuristic* (i.e., a common-sense rule) for moving the knight. Heuristics do not guarantee success, but a carefully developed heuristic greatly improves the chance of success. You may have observed that the outer squares are more troublesome than the squares nearer the center of the board. In fact, the most troublesome or inaccessible squares are the four corners.

Intuition may suggest that you should attempt to move the knight to the most troublesome squares first and leave open those that are easiest to get to, so that when the board gets congested near the end of the tour, there will be a greater chance of success.

We could develop an "accessibility heuristic" by classifying each of the squares according to how accessible it is and always moving the knight (using the knight's L-shaped moves) to the most inaccessible square. We label a two-dimensional array `accessibility` with numbers indicating from how many squares each particular square is accessible. On a blank chessboard, each of the 16 squares nearest the center is rated as 8, each corner square is rated as 2, and the other squares have accessibility numbers of 3, 4 or 6 as follows:

```
2   3   4   4   4   4   3   2
3   4   6   6   6   6   4   3
4   6   8   8   8   8   6   4
4   6   8   8   8   8   6   4
4   6   8   8   8   8   6   4
4   6   8   8   8   8   6   4
3   4   6   6   6   6   4   3
2   3   4   4   4   4   3   2
```

Write a new version of the Knight's Tour, using the accessibility heuristic. The knight should always move to the square with the lowest accessibility number. In case of a tie, the knight may move to any of the tied squares. Therefore, the tour may begin in any of the four corners. [*Note:* As the knight moves around the chessboard, your application should reduce the accessibility numbers as more squares become occupied. In this way, at any given time during the tour, each available square's accessibility number will remain equal to precisely the number of squares from which that square may be reached.] Run this version of your application. Did you get a full tour? Modify the application to run 64 tours, one starting from each square of the chessboard. How many full tours did you get?

d) Write a version of the Knight's Tour application that, when encountering a tie between two or more squares, decides what square to choose by looking ahead to those squares reachable from the "tied" squares. Your application should move to the tied square for which the next move would arrive at a square with the lowest accessibility number.

6.23 *(Knight's Tour: Brute-Force Approaches)* In part (c) of Exercise 6.22, we developed a solution to the Knight's Tour problem. The approach used, called the "accessibility heuristic," generates many solutions and executes efficiently.

As computers continue to increase in power, we'll be able to solve more problems with sheer computer power and relatively unsophisticated algorithms. Let's call this approach "brute-force" problem solving.

a) Use random-number generation to enable the knight to walk around the chessboard (in its legitimate L-shaped moves) at random. Your application should run one tour and display the final chessboard. How far did the knight get?

b) Most likely, the application in part (a) produced a relatively short tour. Now modify your application to attempt 1,000 tours. Use a one-dimensional array to keep track of the number of tours of each length. When your application finishes attempting the 1,000 tours, it should display this information in neat tabular format. What was the best result?

c) Most likely, the application in part (b) gave you some "respectable" tours, but no full tours. Now let your application run until it produces a full tour. [*Caution:* This version of the application could run for hours on a powerful computer.] Once again, keep a table of the number of tours of each length, and display this table when the first full tour is found. How many tours did your application attempt before producing a full tour? How much time did it take?

d) Compare the brute-force version of the Knight's Tour with the accessibility-heuristic version. Which required a more careful study of the problem? Which algorithm was more difficult to develop? Which required more computer power? Could we be certain (in advance) of obtaining a full tour with the accessibility-heuristic approach? Could we be certain (in advance) of obtaining a full tour with the brute-force approach? Argue the pros and cons of brute-force problem solving in general.

6.24 *(Eight Queens)* Another puzzler for chess buffs is the Eight Queens problem, which asks the following: Is it possible to place eight queens on an empty chessboard so that no queen is "attacking" any other (i.e., no two queens are in the same row, in the same column or along the same diagonal)?

Use the thinking developed in Exercise 6.22 to formulate a heuristic for solving the Eight Queens problem. Run your application. [*Hint:* It's possible to assign a value to each square of the chessboard to indicate how many squares of an empty chessboard are "eliminated" if a queen is placed in that square. Each of the corners would be assigned the value 22, as demonstrated by Fig. 6.24. Once these "elimination numbers" are placed in all 64 squares, an appropriate heuristic might be as follows: Place the next queen in the square with the smallest elimination number. Why is this strategy intuitively appealing?]

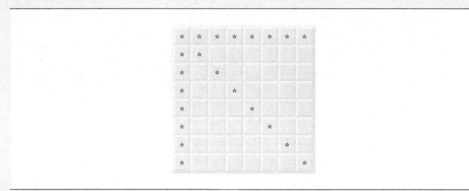

Fig. 6.24 | The 22 squares eliminated by placing a queen in the upper left corner.

6.25 *(Eight Queens: Brute-Force Approaches)* In this exercise, you'll develop several brute-force approaches to solving the Eight Queens problem introduced in Exercise 6.24.

    a) Use the random brute-force technique developed in Exercise 6.23 to solve the Eight Queens problem.

    b) Use an exhaustive technique (i.e., try all possible combinations of eight queens on the chessboard) to solve the Eight Queens problem.

    c) Why might the exhaustive brute-force approach not be appropriate for solving the Knight's Tour problem?

    d) Compare and contrast the random brute-force and exhaustive brute-force approaches.

6.26 *(Knight's Tour: Closed-Tour Test)* In the Knight's Tour (Exercise 6.22), a full tour occurs when the knight makes 64 moves, touching each square of the chessboard once and only once. A closed tour occurs when the 64th move is one move away from the square in which the knight started the tour. Modify the application you wrote in Exercise 6.22 to test for a closed tour if a full tour has occurred.

6.27 *(Sieve of Eratosthenes)* A prime number is any integer greater than 1 that's evenly divisible only by itself and 1. The Sieve of Eratosthenes is a method of finding prime numbers. It operates as follows:

    a) Create a primitive-type boolean array with all elements initialized to true. Array elements with prime indices will remain true. All other array elements will eventually be set to false.

    b) Starting with array index 2, determine whether a given element is true. If so, loop through the remainder of the array and set to false every element whose index is a multiple of the index for the element with value true. Then continue the process with the next element with value true. For array index 2, all elements beyond element 2 in the array that have indices which are multiples of 2 (indices 4, 6, 8, 10, etc.) will be set to false; for array index 3, all elements beyond element 3 in the array that have indices which are multiples of 3 (indices 6, 9, 12, 15, etc.) will be set to false; and so on.

When this process completes, the array elements that are still true indicate that the index is a prime number. These indices can be displayed. Write an application that uses an array of 1,000 elements to determine and display the prime numbers between 2 and 999. Ignore array elements 0 and 1.

6.28   *(Simulation: The Tortoise and the Hare)* In this problem, you'll re-create the classic race of the tortoise and the hare. You'll use random-number generation to develop a simulation of this memorable event.

Our contenders begin the race at square 1 of 70 squares. Each square represents a possible position along the race course. The finish line is at square 70. The first contender to reach or pass square 70 is rewarded with a pail of fresh carrots and lettuce. The course weaves its way up the side of a slippery mountain, so occasionally the contenders lose ground.

A clock ticks once per second. With each tick of the clock, your application should adjust the position of the animals according to the rules in Fig. 6.25. Use variables to keep track of the positions of the animals (i.e., position numbers are 1–70). Start each animal at position 1 (the "starting gate"). If an animal slips left before square 1, move it back to square 1.

Animal	Move type	Percentage of the time	Actual move
Tortoise	Fast plod	50%	3 squares to the right
	Slip	20%	6 squares to the left
	Slow plod	30%	1 square to the right
Hare	Sleep	20%	No move at all
	Big hop	20%	9 squares to the right
	Big slip	10%	12 squares to the left
	Small hop	30%	1 square to the right
	Small slip	20%	2 squares to the left

Fig. 6.25 | Rules for adjusting the positions of the tortoise and the hare.

Generate the percentages in Fig. 6.25 by producing a random integer i in the range $1 \leq i \leq 10$. For the tortoise, perform a "fast plod" when $1 \leq i \leq 5$, a "slip" when $6 \leq i \leq 7$ or a "slow plod" when $8 \leq i \leq 10$. Use a similar technique to move the hare.

Begin the race by displaying

```
BANG !!!!!
AND THEY'RE OFF !!!!!
```

Then, for each tick of the clock (i.e., each repetition of a loop), display a 70-position line showing the letter T in the position of the tortoise and the letter H in the position of the hare. Occasionally, the contenders will land on the same square. In this case, the tortoise bites the hare, and your application should display OUCH!!! beginning at that position. All output positions other than the T, the H or the OUCH!!! (in case of a tie) should be blank.

After each line is displayed, test for whether either animal has reached or passed square 70. If so, display the winner and terminate the simulation. If the tortoise wins, display TORTOISE WINS!!! YAY!!! If the hare wins, display Hare wins. Yuch. If both animals win on the same tick of the clock, you may want to favor the tortoise (the "underdog"), or you may want to display It's a tie. If neither animal wins, perform the loop again to simulate the next tick of the clock. When you're ready to run your application, assemble a group of fans to watch the race. You'll be amazed at how involved your audience gets!

Later in the book, we introduce a number of Java capabilities, such as graphics, images, animation, sound and multithreading. As you study those features, you might enjoy enhancing your tortoise-and-hare contest simulation.

6.29 *(Fibonacci Series)* The Fibonacci series

0, 1, 1, 2, 3, 5, 8, 13, 21, …

begins with the terms 0 and 1 and has the property that each succeeding term is the sum of the two preceding terms.

a) Write a method fibonacci(n) that calculates the nth Fibonacci number. Incorporate this method into an application that enables the user to enter the value of n.

b) Determine the largest Fibonacci number that can be displayed on your system.

c) Modify the application you wrote in part (a) to use double instead of int to calculate and return Fibonacci numbers, and use this modified application to repeat part (b).

Special Section: Building Your Own Computer

In the next several problems, we take a temporary diversion from the world of high-level language programming to "peel open" a computer and look at its internal structure. We introduce machine-language programming and write several machine-language programs. To make this an especially valuable experience, we then build a computer (through the technique of software-based *simulation*) on which you can execute your machine-language programs.

6.30 *(Machine-Language Programming)* Let's create a computer called the Simpletron. As its name implies, it's a simple machine, but powerful. The Simpletron runs programs written in the only language it directly understands: Simpletron Machine Language (SML).

The Simpletron contains an *accumulator*—a special register in which information is put before the Simpletron uses that information in calculations or examines it in various ways. All the information in the Simpletron is handled in terms of *words*. A word is a signed four-digit decimal number, such as +3364, -1293, +0007 and -0001. The Simpletron is equipped with a 100-word memory, and these words are referenced by their location numbers 00, 01, …, 99.

Before running an SML program, we must *load*, or place, the program into memory. The first instruction (or statement) of every SML program is always placed in location 00. The simulator will start executing at this location.

Each instruction written in SML occupies one word of the Simpletron's memory (so instructions are signed four-digit decimal numbers). We shall assume that the sign of an SML instruction is always plus, but the sign of a data word may be either plus or minus. Each location in the Simpletron's memory may contain an instruction, a data value used by a program or an unused (and so undefined) area of memory. The first two digits of each SML instruction are the *operation code* specifying the operation to be performed. SML operation codes are summarized in Fig. 6.26.

The last two digits of an SML instruction are the *operand*—the address of the memory location containing the word to which the operation applies. Let's consider several simple SML programs.

Operation code	Meaning
Input/output operations:	
final int READ = 10;	Read a word from the keyboard into a specific location in memory.

Fig. 6.26 | Simpletron Machine Language (SML) operation codes. (Part 1 of 2.)

Operation code	Meaning
`final int WRITE = 11;`	Write a word from a specific location in memory to the screen.
Load/store operations:	
`final int LOAD = 20;`	Load a word from a specific location in memory into the accumulator.
`final int STORE = 21;`	Store a word from the accumulator into a specific location in memory.
Arithmetic operations:	
`final int ADD = 30;`	Add a word from a specific location in memory to the word in the accumulator (leave the result in the accumulator).
`final int SUBTRACT = 31;`	Subtract a word from a specific location in memory from the word in the accumulator (leave the result in the accumulator).
`final int DIVIDE = 32;`	Divide a word from a specific location in memory into the word in the accumulator (leave result in the accumulator).
`final int MULTIPLY = 33;`	Multiply a word from a specific location in memory by the word in the accumulator (leave the result in the accumulator).
Transfer-of-control operations:	
`final int BRANCH = 40;`	Branch to a specific location in memory.
`final int BRANCHNEG = 41;`	Branch to a specific location in memory if the accumulator is negative.
`final int BRANCHZERO = 42;`	Branch to a specific location in memory if the accumulator is zero.
`final int HALT = 43;`	Halt. The program has completed its task.

Fig. 6.26 | Simpletron Machine Language (SML) operation codes. (Part 2 of 2.)

The first SML program (Fig. 6.27) reads two numbers from the keyboard and computes and displays their sum. The instruction +1007 reads the first number from the keyboard and places it into location 07 (which has been initialized to 0). Then instruction +1008 reads the next number into location 08. The *load* instruction, +2007, puts the first number into the accumulator, and the *add* instruction, +3008, adds the second number to the number in the accumulator. *All SML arithmetic instructions leave their results in the accumulator.* The *store* instruction, +2109, places the result back into memory location 09, from which the *write* instruction, +1109, takes the number and displays it (as a signed four-digit decimal number). The *halt* instruction, +4300, terminates execution.

Location	Number	Instruction
00	+1007	(Read A)
01	+1008	(Read B)
02	+2007	(Load A)
03	+3008	(Add B)

Fig. 6.27 | SML program that reads two integers and computes their sum. (Part 1 of 2.)

Location	Number	Instruction
04	+2109	(Store C)
05	+1109	(Write C)
06	+4300	(Halt)
07	+0000	(Variable A)
08	+0000	(Variable B)
09	+0000	(Result C)

Fig. 6.27 | SML program that reads two integers and computes their sum. (Part 2 of 2.)

The second SML program (Fig. 6.28) reads two numbers from the keyboard and determines and displays the larger value. Note the use of the instruction +4107 as a conditional transfer of control, much the same as Java's if statement.

Location	Number	Instruction
00	+1009	(Read A)
01	+1010	(Read B)
02	+2009	(Load A)
03	+3110	(Subtract B)
04	+4107	(Branch negative to 07)
05	+1109	(Write A)
06	+4300	(Halt)
07	+1110	(Write B)
08	+4300	(Halt)
09	+0000	(Variable A)
10	+0000	(Variable B)

Fig. 6.28 | SML program that reads two integers and determines the larger.

Now write SML programs to accomplish each of the following tasks:

a) Use a sentinel-controlled loop to read 10 positive numbers. Compute and display their sum.

b) Use a counter-controlled loop to read seven numbers, some positive and some negative, and compute and display their average.

c) Read a series of numbers, and determine and display the largest number. The first number read indicates how many numbers should be processed.

6.31 *(Computer Simulator)* In this problem, you're going to build your own computer. No, you'll not be soldering components together. Rather, you'll use the powerful technique of *software-based simulation* to create an object-oriented *software model* of the Simpletron of Exercise 6.30. Your Simpletron simulator will turn the computer you're using into a Simpletron, and you'll actually be able to run, test and debug the SML programs you wrote in Exercise 6.30.

When you run your Simpletron simulator, it should begin by displaying:

```
*** Welcome to Simpletron! ***
*** Please enter your program one instruction    ***
*** (or data word) at a time. I will display     ***
*** the location number and a question mark (?). ***
*** You then type the word for that location.    ***
*** Type -99999 to stop entering your program.   ***
```

Your application should simulate the memory of the Simpletron with a one-dimensional array `memory` that has 100 elements. Now assume that the simulator is running, and let's examine the dialog as we enter the program of Fig. 6.28 (Exercise 6.30):

```
00 ? +1009
01 ? +1010
02 ? +2009
03 ? +3110
04 ? +4107
05 ? +1109
06 ? +4300
07 ? +1110
08 ? +4300
09 ? +0000
10 ? +0000
11 ? -99999
```

Your program should display the memory location followed by a question mark. Each value to the right of a question mark is input by the user. When the sentinel value -99999 is input, the program should display the following:

```
*** Program loading completed ***
*** Program execution begins   ***
```

The SML program has now been placed (or loaded) in array `memory`. Now the Simpletron executes the SML program. Execution begins with the instruction in location 00 and, as in Java, continues sequentially, unless directed to some other part of the program by a transfer of control.

Use the variable `accumulator` to represent the accumulator register. Use the variable `instructionCounter` to keep track of the location in memory that contains the instruction being performed. Use the variable `operationCode` to indicate the operation currently being performed (i.e., the left two digits of the instruction word). Use the variable `operand` to indicate the memory location on which the current instruction operates. Thus, `operand` is the rightmost two digits of the instruction currently being performed. Do not execute instructions directly from memory. Rather, transfer the next instruction to be performed from memory to a variable called `instructionRegister`. Then pick off the left two digits and place them in `operationCode`, and pick off the right two digits and place them in `operand`. When the Simpletron begins execution, the special registers are all initialized to zero.

Now, let's walk through execution of the first SML instruction, +1009 in memory location 00. This procedure is called an *instruction-execution cycle*.

The `instructionCounter` tells us the location of the next instruction to be performed. We *fetch* the contents of that location from `memory` by using the Java statement

```
instructionRegister = memory[instructionCounter];
```

The operation code and the operand are extracted from the instruction register by the statements

```
operationCode = instructionRegister / 100;
operand = instructionRegister % 100;
```

Now the Simpletron must determine that the operation code is actually a *read* (versus a *write*, a *load*, and so on). A `switch` differentiates among the 12 operations of SML. In the `switch` statement, the behavior of various SML instructions is simulated as shown in Fig. 6.29. We discuss branch instructions shortly and leave the others to you.

When the SML program completes execution, the name and contents of each register as well as the complete contents of memory should be displayed. Such a printout is often called a computer dump (no, a computer dump is not a place where old computers go). To help you program your dump method, a sample dump format is shown in Fig. 6.30. A dump after executing a Simpletron program would show the actual values of instructions and data values at the moment execution terminated.

Instruction	Description
read:	Display the prompt "Enter an integer", then input the integer and store it in location memory[operand].
load:	accumulator = memory[operand];
add:	accumulator += memory[operand];
halt:	This instruction displays the message *** Simpletron execution terminated ***

Fig. 6.29 | Behavior of several SML instructions in the Simpletron.

```
REGISTERS:
accumulator          +0000
instructionCounter      00
instructionRegister  +0000
operationCode           00
operand                 00

MEMORY:
        0     1     2     3     4     5     6     7     8     9
 0  +0000 +0000 +0000 +0000 +0000 +0000 +0000 +0000 +0000 +0000
10  +0000 +0000 +0000 +0000 +0000 +0000 +0000 +0000 +0000 +0000
20  +0000 +0000 +0000 +0000 +0000 +0000 +0000 +0000 +0000 +0000
30  +0000 +0000 +0000 +0000 +0000 +0000 +0000 +0000 +0000 +0000
40  +0000 +0000 +0000 +0000 +0000 +0000 +0000 +0000 +0000 +0000
50  +0000 +0000 +0000 +0000 +0000 +0000 +0000 +0000 +0000 +0000
60  +0000 +0000 +0000 +0000 +0000 +0000 +0000 +0000 +0000 +0000
70  +0000 +0000 +0000 +0000 +0000 +0000 +0000 +0000 +0000 +0000
80  +0000 +0000 +0000 +0000 +0000 +0000 +0000 +0000 +0000 +0000
90  +0000 +0000 +0000 +0000 +0000 +0000 +0000 +0000 +0000 +0000
```

Fig. 6.30 | A sample dump.

Let's proceed with the execution of our program's first instruction—namely, the +1009 in location 00. As we've indicated, the switch statement simulates this task by prompting the user to enter a value, reading the value and storing it in memory location memory[operand]. The value is then read into location 09.

At this point, simulation of the first instruction is completed. All that remains is to prepare the Simpletron to execute the next instruction. Since the instruction just performed was not a transfer of control, we need merely increment the instruction-counter register as follows:

```
instructionCounter++;
```

This action completes the simulated execution of the first instruction. The entire process (i.e., the instruction-execution cycle) begins anew with the fetch of the next instruction to execute.

Now let's consider how the branching instructions—the transfers of control—are simulated. All we need to do is adjust the value in the instruction counter appropriately. Therefore, the unconditional branch instruction (40) is simulated within the `switch` as

```
instructionCounter = operand;
```

The conditional "branch if accumulator is zero" instruction is simulated as

```
if (accumulator == 0)
    instructionCounter = operand;
```

At this point, you should implement your Simpletron simulator and run each of the SML programs you wrote in Exercise 6.30. If you desire, you may embellish SML with additional features and provide for these features in your simulator.

Your simulator should check for various types of errors. During the program-loading phase, for example, each number the user types into the Simpletron's `memory` must be in the range -9999 to +9999. Your simulator should test that each number entered is in this range and, if not, keep prompting the user to re-enter the number until the user enters a correct number.

During the execution phase, your simulator should check for various serious errors, such as attempts to divide by zero, attempts to execute invalid operation codes, and accumulator overflows (i.e., arithmetic operations resulting in values larger than +9999 or smaller than -9999). Such serious errors are called *fatal errors*. When a fatal error is detected, your simulator should display an error message, such as

```
*** Attempt to divide by zero ***
*** Simpletron execution abnormally terminated ***
```

and should display a full computer dump in the format we discussed previously. This treatment will help the user locate the error in the program.

6.32 *(Simpletron Simulator Modifications)* In Exercise 6.31, you wrote a software simulation of a computer that executes programs written in Simpletron Machine Language (SML). In this exercise, we propose several modifications and enhancements to the Simpletron Simulator. In the exercises of Chapter 21, we propose building a compiler that converts programs written in a high-level programming language (a variation of Basic) to Simpletron Machine Language. Some of the following modifications and enhancements may be required to execute the programs produced by the compiler:

a) Extend the Simpletron Simulator's memory to contain 1,000 memory locations to enable the Simpletron to handle larger programs.

b) Allow the simulator to perform remainder calculations. This modification requires an additional SML instruction.

c) Allow the simulator to perform exponentiation calculations. This modification requires an additional SML instruction.

d) Modify the simulator to use hexadecimal rather than integer values to represent SML instructions.

e) Modify the simulator to allow output of a newline. This modification requires an additional SML instruction.

f) Modify the simulator to process floating-point values in addition to integer values.

g) Modify the simulator to handle string input. [*Hint:* Each Simpletron word can be divided into two groups, each holding a two-digit integer. Each two-digit integer represents the ASCII (see Appendix B) decimal equivalent of a character. Add a machine-language instruction that will input a string and store the string, beginning at a specific Simpletron memory location. The first half of the word at that location will be a count of the number of characters in the string (i.e., the length of the string). Each succeeding half-word contains one ASCII character expressed as two decimal digits. The machine-language instruction converts each character into its ASCII equivalent and assigns it to a half-word.]

h) Modify the simulator to handle output of strings stored in the format of part (g). [*Hint:* Add a machine-language instruction that will display a string, beginning at a certain Simpletron memory location. The first half of the word at that location is a count of the number of characters in the string (i.e., the length of the string). Each succeeding half-word contains one ASCII character expressed as two decimal digits. The machine-language instruction checks the length and displays the string by translating each two-digit number into its equivalent character.]

Making a Difference

6.33   *(Polling)* The Internet and the web are enabling more people to network, join a cause, voice opinions, and so on. Recent presidential candidates have used the Internet intensively to get out their messages and raise money for their campaigns. In this exercise, you'll write a simple polling program that allows users to rate five social-consciousness issues from 1 (least important) to 10 (most important). Pick five causes that are important to you (e.g., political issues, global environmental issues). Use a one-dimensional array `topics` (of type `String`) to store the five causes. To summarize the survey responses, use a 5-row, 10-column two-dimensional array `responses` (of type `int`), each row corresponding to an element in the `topics` array. When the program runs, it should ask the user to rate each issue. Have your friends and family respond to the survey. Then have the program display a summary of the results, including:

a) A tabular report with the five topics down the left side and the 10 ratings across the top, listing in each column the number of ratings received for each topic.

b) To the right of each row, show the average of the ratings for that issue.

c) Which issue received the highest point total? Display both the issue and the point total.

d) Which issue received the lowest point total? Display both the issue and the point total.

Introduction to Classes
and Objects

Your public servants serve you right.
—Adlai E. Stevenson

Nothing can have value without being an object of utility.
—Karl Marx

Objectives

In this chapter you'll learn:

- How to declare a class and use it to create an object.

- How to implement a class's behaviors as methods.

- How to implement a class's attributes as instance variables.

- How to call an object's methods to make them perform their tasks.

- What local variables of a method are and how they differ from instance variables.

- How to use a constructor to initialize an object's data.

- How to represent and use numbers containing decimal points.

7.1 Introduction

[*Note:* This chapter depends on the terminology and concepts of object-oriented programming introduced in Section 1.5, Introduction to Object Technology.]

In the preceding chapters, you worked with *existing* classes, objects and methods. For example, you used the predefined standard output object System.out, invoking its methods print, println and printf to display information on the screen, and you used the existing Scanner class to create an object that reads into memory integer data typed by the user at the keyboard. Throughout the book, you'll use many more preexisting classes and objects—this is one of the great strengths of Java as an object-oriented programming language.

In this chapter, you'll learn how to create your own classes. Each new *class* you create becomes a new *type* that can be used to declare variables and create objects. You can declare new classes as needed; this is one reason why Java is known as an *extensible* language.

In this chapter, Sections 7.2–7.5 present a case study on creating and using a simple, real-world bank account class—Account. Such a class should maintain as *instance variables* attributes such as its name and balance, and provide *methods* for tasks such as querying the balance (getBalance), making deposits that increase the balance (deposit) and making withdrawals that decrease the balance (withdraw). We'll build the getBalance and deposit methods into the class in the chapter's examples and you'll add the withdraw method in the exercises.

Next, we present additional case studies, including a card shuffling and dealing simulation and two GradeBook case studies that use arrays to store and manipulate student grades. The first GradeBook case study uses a one-dimensional array to represent grades for ten students on a single exam. The second uses a two-dimensional array to represent the grades for ten students on each of three exams.

Typically, the apps you develop in this chapter and later will consist of two or more classes. If you become part of a development team in industry, you might work on apps that contain hundreds, or even thousands, of classes.

7.2 Instance Variables, *set* Methods and *get* Methods

In this section, you'll create two classes—Account (Fig. 7.1) and AccountTest (Fig. 7.2). Class AccountTest is an *application class* in which the main method will create and use an Account object to demonstrate class Account's capabilities.

7.2.1 Account Class with an Instance Variable, a *set* Method and a *get* Method

Different accounts typically have different names. For this reason, class Account (Fig. 7.1) contains a name *instance variable*. A class's instance variables maintain data for each object (that is, each instance) of the class. Later in the chapter we'll add an instance variable named balance so we can keep track of how much money is in the account. Class Account contains two methods—method setName stores a name in an Account object and method getName obtains a name from an Account object.

```java
1   // Fig. 7.1: Account.java
2   // Account class that contains a name instance variable
3   // and methods to set and get its value.
4
5   public class Account
6   {
7      private String name; // instance variable
8
9      // method to set the name in the object
10     public void setName(String name)
11     {
12        this.name = name; // store the name
13     }
14
15     // method to retrieve the name from the object
16     public String getName()
17     {
18        return name; // return value of name to caller
19     }
20  } // end class Account
```

Fig. 7.1 | Account class that contains a name instance variable and methods to *set* and *get* its value.

Class Declaration
The *class declaration* begins in line 5:

```java
public class Account
```

The keyword public (which Chapter 8 explains in detail) is an **access modifier**. For now, we'll simply declare every class public. Each public class declaration must be stored in a file having the *same* name as the class and ending with the .java filename extension; otherwise, a compilation error will occur. Thus, public classes Account and AccountTest (Fig. 7.2) *must* be declared in the *separate* files Account.java and AccountTest.java, respectively.

Every class declaration contains the keyword class followed immediately by the class's name—in this case, Account. Every class's body is enclosed in a pair of left and right braces as in lines 6 and 20 of Fig. 7.1.

Identifiers and Camel Case Naming
Class names, method names and variable names are all *identifiers* and by convention all use the same *camel case* naming scheme we discussed in Chapter 2. Also by convention, class names begin with an initial *uppercase* letter, and method names and variable names begin with an initial *lowercase* letter.

Instance Variable name
Recall from Section 1.5 that an object has attributes, implemented as instance variables and carried with it throughout its lifetime. Instance variables exist before methods are called on an object, while the methods are executing and after the methods complete execution. Each object (instance) of the class has its *own* copy of the class's instance variables. A class normally contains one or more methods that manipulate the instance variables belonging to particular objects of the class.

Instance variables are declared *inside* a class declaration but *outside* the bodies of the class's methods. Line 7

```
    private String name; // instance variable
```

declares instance variable name of type String *outside* the bodies of methods setName (lines 10–13) and getName (lines 16–19). String variables can hold character string values such as "Jane Green". If there are many Account objects, each has its own name. Because name is an instance variable, it can be manipulated by each of the class's methods.

Good Programming Practice 7.1
We prefer to list a class's instance variables first in the class's body, so that you see the names and types of the variables before they're used in the class's methods. You can list the class's instance variables anywhere in the class outside its method declarations, but scattering the instance variables can lead to hard-to-read code.

Access Modifiers public and private
Most instance-variable declarations are preceded with the keyword private (as in line 7). Like public, **private** is an *access modifier*. Variables or methods declared with access modifier private are accessible only to methods of the class in which they're declared. So, the variable name can be used only in each Account object's methods (setName and getName in this case). You'll soon see that this presents powerful software engineering opportunities.

Instance Method setName of Class Account
In the preceding chapters, you've declared only static methods in each class. A class's non-static methods are known as **instance methods**. Method setName's declaration

(lines 10–13) indicates that setName receives parameter name of type String—which represents the name that will be passed to the method as an argument.

Recall that variables declared in a particular method's body (such as main) are local variables which can be used only in that method and that a method's parameters also are local variables of the method.

Method setName's body contains a single statement (line 12) that assigns the value of the name *parameter* (a String) to the class's name *instance variable*, thus storing the account name in the object. If a method contains a local variable with the *same* name as an instance variable (as in lines 10 and 7, respectively), that method's body will refer to the local variable rather than the instance variable. In this case, the local variable is said to *shadow* the instance variable in the method's body. The method's body can use the keyword **this** to refer to the shadowed instance variable explicitly, as shown on the left side of the assignment in line 12.

> **Good Programming Practice 7.2**
> *We could have avoided the need for keyword* this *here by choosing a different name for the parameter in line 10, but using the* this *keyword as shown in line 12 is a widely accepted practice to minimize the proliferation of identifier names.*

After line 12 executes, the method has completed its task, so it returns to its *caller*. As you'll soon see, the statement in line 21 of main (Fig. 7.2) calls method setName.

getName *Method of Class* Account

Method getName (lines 16–19 of Fig. 7.1) returns a particular Account object's name to the caller. The method has an empty parameter list, so it does *not* require additional information to perform its task.

7.2.2 AccountTest Class That Creates and Uses an Object of Class Account

Next, we'd like to use class Account in an app and *call* each of its methods. A class that contains a main method begins the execution of a Java app. Class Account *cannot* execute by itself because it does *not* contain a main method—if you type java Account in the command window, you'll get an error indicating "Main method not found in class Account." To fix this problem, you must either declare a *separate* class that contains a main method or place a main method in class Account.

Driver Class AccountTest

To help you prepare for the larger programs you'll encounter later in this book and in industry, we use a separate class AccountTest (Fig. 7.2) containing method main to test class Account. Once main begins executing, it may call other methods in this and other classes; those may, in turn, call other methods, and so on. Class AccountTest's main method creates one Account object and calls its getName and setName methods. Such a class is sometimes called a *driver class*—just as a Person object drives a Car object by telling it what to do (go faster, go slower, turn left, turn right, etc.), class AccountTest drives an Account object, telling it what to do by calling its methods.

```
 1   // Fig. 7.2: AccountTest.java
 2   // Creating and manipulating an Account object.
 3   import java.util.Scanner;
 4
 5   public class AccountTest
 6   {
 7      public static void main(String[] args)
 8      {
 9         // create a Scanner object to obtain input from the command window
10         Scanner input = new Scanner(System.in);
11
12         // create an Account object and assign it to myAccount
13         Account myAccount = new Account();
14
15         // display initial value of name (null)
16         System.out.printf("Initial name is: %s%n%n", myAccount.getName());
17
18         // prompt for and read name
19         System.out.println("Please enter the name:");
20         String theName = input.nextLine(); // read a line of text
21         myAccount.setName(theName); // put theName in myAccount
22         System.out.println(); // outputs a blank line
23
24         // display the name stored in object myAccount
25         System.out.printf("Name in object myAccount is:%n%s%n",
26            myAccount.getName());
27      }
28   } // end class AccountTest
```

```
Initial name is: null

Please enter the name:
Jane Green

Name in object myAccount is:
Jane Green
```

Fig. 7.2 | Creating and manipulating an Account object.

Scanner *Object for Receiving Input from the User*

Line 10 creates a Scanner object named input for inputting the name from the user. Line 19 prompts the user to enter a name. Line 20 uses the Scanner object's **nextLine** method to read the name from the user and assign it to the local variable theName. You type the name and press *Enter* to submit it to the program. Pressing *Enter* inserts a newline character after the characters you typed. Method nextLine reads characters (including white-space characters, such as the blank in "Jane Green") until it encounters the newline, then returns a String containing the characters up to, but *not* including, the newline, which is *discarded*.

As you've seen, class Scanner provides various other input methods. A Scanner method similar to nextLine—named **next**—reads the *next word*. When you press *Enter* after typing some text, method next reads characters until it encounters a *white-space character* (such as a space, tab or newline), then returns a String containing the characters up to, but *not* including, the white-space character, which is *discarded*. All information after the first white-space character is *not lost*—it can be read by subsequent statements that call the Scanner's methods later in the program.

Instantiating an Object—Keyword **new** *and Constructors*

Line 13 creates an Account object and assigns it to variable myAccount of type Account. Variable myAccount is initialized with the result of the **class instance creation expression** new Account(). Keyword **new** creates a new object of the specified class—in this case, Account. The parentheses to the right of Account are *required*. As you'll learn in Section 7.4, those parentheses in combination with a class name represent a call to a **constructor**, which is *similar* to a method but is called implicitly by the new operator to *initialize* an object's instance variables when the object is *created*. In Section 7.4, you'll see how to place an *argument* in the parentheses to specify an *initial value* for an Account object's name instance variable—you'll enhance class Account to enable this. For now, we simply leave the parentheses *empty*. Line 10 contains a class instance creation expression for a Scanner object—the expression initializes the Scanner with System.in, which tells the Scanner where to read the input from (i.e., the keyboard).

Calling Class **Account***'s* **getName** *Method*

Line 16 displays the *initial* name, which is obtained by calling the object's getName method. Just as we can use object System.out to call its methods print, printf and println, we can use object myAccount to call its methods getName and setName. Line 16 calls getName using the myAccount object created in line 13, followed by a dot separator (.), then the method name getName and an *empty* set of parentheses because no arguments are being passed. When getName is called:

1. The app transfers program execution from the call (line 16 in main) to method get-Name's declaration (lines 16–19 of Fig. 7.1). Because getName was called via the my-Account object, getName "knows" which object's instance variable to manipulate.

2. Next, method getName performs its task—that is, it *returns* the name (line 18 of Fig. 7.1). When the return statement executes, program execution continues where getName was called (line 16 in Fig. 7.2).

3. System.out.printf displays the String returned by method getName, then the program continues executing at line 19 in main.

Error-Prevention Tip 7.1

Never use as a format-control a string that was input from the user. When method System.out.printf evaluates the format-control string in its first argument, the method performs tasks based on the conversion specifier(s) in that string. If the format-control string were obtained from the user, a malicious user could supply conversion specifiers that would be executed by System.out.printf, possibly causing a security breach.

null*—the Default Initial Value for* **String** *Variables*

The first line of the output shows the name "null." Unlike local variables, which are *not* automatically initialized, *every instance variable has a* **default initial value**—a value provided by Java when you do *not* specify the instance variable's initial value. Thus, *instance variables are not* required to be explicitly initialized before they're used in a program—unless they must be initialized to values *other than* their default values. The default value for an instance variable of type String (like name in this example) is null, which we discuss further in Section 7.3.

Calling Class Account's setName Method

Line 21 calls myAccounts's setName method. Recall that a method call can supply arguments whose values are assigned to the corresponding method parameters. In this case, the value of main's local variable theName in parentheses is the argument that's passed to setName so that the method can perform its task. When setName is called:

1. The app transfers program execution from line 21 in main to setName method's declaration (lines 10–13 of Fig. 7.1), and the argument value in the call's parentheses (theName) is assigned to the corresponding parameter (name) in the method header (line 10 of Fig. 7.1). Because setName was called via the myAccount object, setName "knows" which object's instance variable to manipulate.

2. Next, method setName performs its task—that is, it assigns the name parameter's value to instance variable name (line 12 of Fig. 7.1).

3. When program execution reaches setName's closing right brace, it returns to where setName was called in line 21 of Fig. 7.2, then continues at line 22.

Displaying the Name That Was Entered by the User

When the second call to method getName (line 26) executes, the name entered by the user in line 20 is displayed. When the statement at lines 25–26 completes execution, the end of method main is reached, so the program terminates.

7.2.3 Compiling and Executing an App with Multiple Classes

You must compile the classes in Figs. 7.1 and 7.2 before you can *execute* the app. This is the first time you've created an app with *multiple* classes. Class AccountTest has a main method; class Account does not. To compile this app, first change to the directory that contains the app's source-code files. Next, type the command

```
javac Account.java AccountTest.java
```

to compile *both* classes at once. If the directory containing the app includes *only* this app's files, you can compile both classes with the command

```
javac *.java
```

The asterisk (*) in *.java indicates that *all* files in the *current* directory ending with the filename extension ".java" should be compiled. If both classes compile correctly—that is, no compilation errors are displayed—you can then run the app with the command

```
java AccountTest
```

7.2.4 Account UML Class Diagram with an Instance Variable and *set* and *get* Methods

We'll often use UML class diagrams to summarize a class's *attributes* and *operations*. In industry, UML diagrams help systems designers specify a system in a concise, graphical, programming-language-independent manner, before programmers implement the system in a specific programming language. Figure 7.3 presents a **UML class diagram** for class Account of Fig. 7.1.

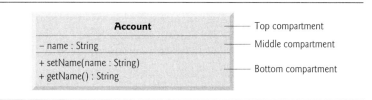

Fig. 7.3 | UML class diagram for class Account of Fig. 7.1.

Top Compartment
In the UML, each class is modeled in a class diagram as a rectangle with three compartments. In this diagram the *top* compartment contains the *class name* Account centered horizontally in boldface type.

Middle Compartment
The *middle* compartment contains the *class's attribute* name, which corresponds to the instance variable of the same name in Java. Instance variable name is private in Java, so the UML class diagram lists a *minus sign (–) access modifier* before the attribute name. Following the attribute name are a *colon* and the *attribute type*, in this case String.

Bottom Compartment
The *bottom* compartment contains the class's **operations**, setName and getName, which correspond to the methods of the same names in Java. The UML models operations by listing the operation name preceded by an *access modifier*, in this case + getName. This plus sign (+) indicates that getName is a *public* operation in the UML (because it's a public method in Java). Operation getName does *not* have any parameters, so the parentheses following the operation name in the class diagram are *empty*, just as they are in the method's declaration in line 16 of Fig. 7.1. Operation setName, also a public operation, has a String parameter called name.

Return Types
The UML indicates the *return type* of an operation by placing a colon and the return type *after* the parentheses following the operation name. Account method getName (Fig. 7.1) has a String return type. Method setName *does not* return a value (because it returns void in Java), so the UML class diagram *does not* specify a return type after the parentheses of this operation.

Parameters
The UML models a parameter a bit differently from Java by listing the parameter name, followed by a colon and the parameter type in the parentheses after the operation name. The UML has its own data types similar to those of Java, but for simplicity, we'll use the Java data types. Account method setName (Fig. 7.1) has a String parameter named name, so Fig. 7.3 lists name : String between the parentheses following the method name.

7.2.5 Additional Notes on This Example

Notes on **static** *Methods*

A static method can call other static methods of the same class directly (i.e., using the method name by itself) and can manipulate static variables in the same class directly. To access the class's instance variables and instance methods, a static method must use a reference to an object of the class. Instance methods can access all fields (static variables and instance variables) and methods of the class.

Recall that static methods relate to a class as a whole, whereas instance methods are associated with a specific instance (object) of the class and may manipulate the instance variables of that object. Many objects of a class, each with its *own* copies of the instance variables, may exist at the same time. Suppose a static method were to invoke an instance method directly. How would the static method know which object's instance variables to manipulate? What would happen if *no* objects of the class existed at the time the instance method was invoked? Thus, Java does *not* allow a static method to directly access instance variables and instance methods of the same class.

Notes on **import** *Declarations*

Notice the import declaration in Fig. 7.2 (line 3), which indicates to the compiler that the program uses class Scanner. As you learned in Chapter 2, classes System and String are in package java.lang, which is *implicitly* imported into *every* Java program, so all programs can use that package's classes *without* explicitly importing them. *Most* other classes you'll use in Java programs *must* be imported *explicitly*.

There's a special relationship between classes that are compiled in the *same* directory, like classes Account and AccountTest. By default, such classes are considered to be in the *same* package—known as the **default package**. Classes in the *same* package are *implicitly imported* into the source-code files of other classes in that package. Thus, an import declaration is *not* required when one class in a package uses another in the *same* package—such as when class AccountTest uses class Account.

The import declaration in line 3 is *not* required if we refer to class Scanner throughout this file as java.util.Scanner, which includes the *full package name and class name*. This is known as the class's **fully qualified class name**. For example, line 10 of Fig. 7.2 also could be written as

```
java.util.Scanner input = new java.util.Scanner(System.in);
```

Software Engineering Observation 7.1

The Java compiler does not require import *declarations in a Java source-code file if the fully qualified class name is specified every time a class name is used. Most Java programmers prefer the more concise programming style enabled by* import *declarations.*

7.2.6 Software Engineering with **private** Instance Variables and **public** *set* and *get* Methods

As you'll see, through the use of *set* and *get* methods, you can *validate* attempted modifications to private data and control how that data is presented to the caller—these are compelling software engineering benefits. We'll discuss this in more detail in Section 7.5.

If the instance variable were `public`, any **client** of the class—that is, any other class that calls the class's methods—could see the data and do whatever it wanted with it, including setting it to an *invalid* value.

You might think that even though a client of the class cannot directly access a `private` instance variable, the client can do whatever it wants with the variable through `public` *set* and *get* methods. You would think that you could peek at the `private` data any time with the `public` *get* method and that you could modify the `private` data at will through the `public` *set* method. But *set* methods can be programmed to *validate* their arguments and reject any attempts to *set* the data to bad values, such as a negative body temperature, a day in March out of the range 1 through 31, a product code not in the company's product catalog, etc. And a *get* method can present the data in a different form. For example, a `Grade` class might store a grade as an `int` between 0 and 100, but a `getGrade` method might return a letter grade as a `String`, such as `"A"` for grades between 90 and 100, `"B"` for grades between 80 and 89, etc. Tightly controlling the access to and presentation of `private` data can greatly reduce errors, while increasing the robustness and security of your programs.

Declaring instance variables with access modifier `private` is known as *data hiding* or *information hiding*. When a program creates (instantiates) an object of class `Account`, variable `name` is *encapsulated* (hidden) in the object and can be accessed only by methods of the object's class.

Software Engineering Observation 7.2

Precede each instance variable and method declaration with an access modifier. Generally, instance variables should be declared `private` and methods `public`. Later in the book, we'll discuss why you might want to declare a method `private`.

Conceptual View of an *Account* Object with Encapsulated Data

You can think of an `Account` object as shown in Fig. 7.4. The `private` instance variable `name` is *hidden inside* the object (represented by the inner circle containing `name`) and *protected by an outer layer* of `public` methods (represented by the outer circle containing `getName` and `setName`). Any client code that needs to interact with the `Account` object can do so *only* by calling the `public` methods of the protective outer layer.

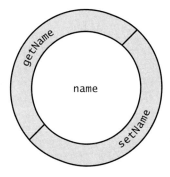

Fig. 7.4 | Conceptual view of an `Account` object with its encapsulated `private` instance variable `name` and protective layer of `public` methods.

7.3 Default and Explicit Initialization for Instance Variables

Recall that local variables are *not* initialized by default. Primitive-type instance variables *are* initialized by default—instance variables of types byte, char, short, int, long, float and double are initialized to 0, and variables of type boolean are initialized to false.

You can specify your own initial value for a primitive-type instance variable by assigning the variable a value in its declaration, as in

```
private int numberOfStudents = 10;
```

Reference-type instance variables (such as those of type String), if not explicitly initialized, are initialized by default to the value null—which represents a "reference to nothing." That's why the first call to getName in line 16 of Fig. 7.2 returns null—the value of name has *not* yet been set, so the *default initial value* null is returned.

7.4 Account Class: Initializing Objects with Constructors

As mentioned in Section 7.2, when an object of class Account (Fig. 7.1) is created, its String instance variable name is initialized to null by *default*. But what if you want to provide a name when you *create* an Account object?

Each class you declare can optionally provide a *constructor* with parameters that can be used to initialize an object of a class when the object is created. Java *requires* a constructor call for *every* object that's created, so this is the ideal point to initialize an object's instance variables. The next example enhances class Account (Fig. 7.5) with a constructor that can receive a name and use it to initialize instance variable name when an Account object is created (Fig. 7.6).

7.4.1 Declaring an Account Constructor for Custom Object Initialization

When you declare a class, you can provide your own constructor to specify *custom initialization* for objects of your class. For example, you might want to specify a name for an Account object when the object is created, as in line 10 of Fig. 7.6:

```
Account account1 = new Account("Jane Green");
```

In this case, the String argument "Jane Green" is passed to the Account object's constructor and used to initialize the name instance variable. The preceding statement requires that the class provide a constructor that takes only a String parameter. Figure 7.5 contains a modified Account class with such a constructor.

```
1   // Fig. 7.5: Account.java
2   // Account class with a constructor that initializes the name.
3
4   public class Account
5   {
6      private String name; // instance variable
7
8      // constructor initializes name with parameter name
9      public Account(String name) // constructor name is class name
10     {
```

Fig. 7.5 | Account class with a constructor that initializes the name. (Part 1 of 2.)

```
11            this.name = name;
12        }
13
14        // method to set the name
15        public void setName(String name)
16        {
17            this.name = name;
18        }
19
20        // method to retrieve the name
21        public String getName()
22        {
23            return name;
24        }
25    } // end class Account
```

Fig. 7.5 | Account class with a constructor that initializes the name. (Part 2 of 2.)

Account Constructor Declaration

Lines 9–12 of Fig. 7.5 declare Account's constructor. A constructor *must* have the *same name* as the class. A constructor's *parameter list* specifies that the constructor requires one or more pieces of data to perform its task. Line 9 indicates that the constructor has a String parameter called name. When you create a new Account object (as you'll see in Fig. 7.6), you'll pass a person's name to the constructor, which will receive that name in the parameter name. The constructor will then assign name to *instance variable* name in line 11.

Error-Prevention Tip 7.2

Even though it's possible to do so, do not call methods from constructors. We'll explain this in Chapter 10, Object-Oriented Programming: Polymorphism and Interfaces.

Parameter **name** of Class **Account**'s Constructor and Method **setName**

Recall from Section 7.2.1 that method parameters are local variables. In Fig. 7.5, the constructor and method setName both have a parameter called name. Although these parameters have the same identifier (name), the parameter in line 9 is a local variable of the constructor that's *not* visible to method setName, and the one in line 15 is a local variable of setName that's *not* visible to the constructor.

7.4.2 Class AccountTest: Initializing Account Objects When They're Created

The AccountTest program (Fig. 7.6) initializes two Account objects using the constructor. Line 10 creates and initializes the Account object account1. Keyword new requests memory from the system to store the Account object, then implicitly calls the class's constructor to *initialize* the object. The call is indicated by the parentheses after the class name, which contain the *argument* "Jane Green" that's used to initialize the new object's name. The class instance creation expression in line 10 returns a *reference* to the new object, which is assigned to the variable account1. Line 11 repeats this process, passing the argument "John Blue" to initialize the name for account2. Lines 14–15 use each object's getName method to obtain the names and show that they were indeed initialized when the objects were *created*. The output shows *different* names, confirming that each Account maintains its *own copy* of instance variable name.

```
1   // Fig. 7.6: AccountTest.java
2   // Using the Account constructor to initialize the name instance
3   // variable at the time each Account object is created.
4
5   public class AccountTest
6   {
7      public static void main(String[] args)
8      {
9         // create two Account objects
10        Account account1 = new Account("Jane Green");
11        Account account2 = new Account("John Blue");
12
13        // display initial value of name for each Account
14        System.out.printf("account1 name is: %s%n", account1.getName());
15        System.out.printf("account2 name is: %s%n", account2.getName());
16     }
17  } // end class AccountTest
```

```
account1 name is: Jane Green
account2 name is: John Blue
```

Fig. 7.6 | Using the Account constructor to initialize the name instance variable at the time each Account object is created.

Constructors Cannot Return Values

An important difference between constructors and methods is that *constructors cannot return values*, so they *cannot* specify a return type (not even void). Normally, constructors are declared public—later in the book we'll explain when to use private constructors.

Default Constructor

Recall that line 13 of Fig. 7.2

```
Account myAccount = new Account();
```

used new to create an Account object. The *empty* parentheses after "new Account" indicate a call to the class's **default constructor**—in any class that does *not* explicitly declare a constructor, the compiler provides a default constructor (which always has no parameters). When a class has only the default constructor, the class's instance variables are initialized to their *default values*. In Section 8.5, you'll learn that classes can have multiple constructors.

There's No Default Constructor in a Class That Declares a Constructor

If you declare a constructor for a class, the compiler will *not* create a *default constructor* for that class. In that case, you will not be able to create an Account object with the class instance creation expression new Account() as we did in Fig. 7.2—unless the custom constructor you declare takes *no* parameters.

Software Engineering Observation 7.3
Unless default initialization of your class's instance variables is acceptable, provide a custom constructor to ensure that your instance variables are properly initialized with meaningful values when each new object of your class is created.

Adding the Constructor to Class *Account's* UML Class Diagram

The UML class diagram of Fig. 7.7 models class Account of Fig. 7.5, which has a constructor with a String name parameter. Like operations, the UML models constructors in the *third* compartment of a class diagram. To distinguish a constructor from the class's operations, the UML requires that the word "constructor" be enclosed in **guillemets (« and »)** and placed before the constructor's name. It's customary to list constructors *before* other operations in the third compartment.

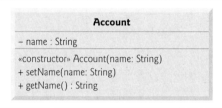

Fig. 7.7 | UML class diagram for Account class of Fig. 7.5.

7.5 Account Class with a Balance; Floating-Point Numbers

We now declare an Account class that maintains the *balance* of a bank account in addition to the name. Most account balances are not integers. So, class Account represents the account balance as a double. [In Section 8.15, as we study object-oriented programming in more depth, we'll begin representing monetary amounts precisely with class BigDecimal as you should do when writing industrial-strength monetary applications.]

7.5.1 Account Class with a balance Instance Variable of Type double

Our next app contains a version of class Account (Fig. 7.8) that maintains as instance variables the name *and* the balance of a bank account. A typical bank services *many* accounts, each with its *own* balance, so line 8 declares an instance variable balance of type double. Every instance (i.e., object) of class Account contains its *own* copies of *both* the name and the balance.

```
1   // Fig. 7.8: Account.java
2   // Account class with a double instance variable balance and a constructor
3   // and deposit method that perform validation.
4
```

Fig. 7.8 | Account class with a double instance variable balance and a constructor and deposit method that perform validation. (Part I of 2.)

```
5   public class Account
6   {
7      private String name; // instance variable
8      private double balance; // instance variable
9
10     // Account constructor that receives two parameters
11     public Account(String name, double balance)
12     {
13        this.name = name; // assign name to instance variable name
14
15        // validate that the balance is greater than 0.0; if it's not,
16        // instance variable balance keeps its default initial value of 0.0
17        if (balance > 0.0) // if the balance is valid
18           this.balance = balance; // assign it to instance variable balance
19     }
20
21     // method that deposits (adds) only a valid amount to the balance
22     public void deposit(double depositAmount)
23     {
24        if (depositAmount > 0.0) // if the depositAmount is valid
25           balance += depositAmount; // add it to the balance
26     }
27
28     // method returns the account balance
29     public double getBalance()
30     {
31        return balance;
32     }
33
34     // method that sets the name
35     public void setName(String name)
36     {
37        this.name = name;
38     }
39
40     // method that returns the name
41     public String getName()
42     {
43        return name; // give value of name back to caller
44     } // end method getName
45  } // end class Account
```

Fig. 7.8 | Account class with a double instance variable balance and a constructor and deposit method that perform validation. (Part 2 of 2.)

Account Class Two-Parameter Constructor

The class has a *constructor* and four *methods*. It's common for someone opening an account to deposit money immediately, so the constructor (lines 11–19) now receives a second parameter—initialBalance of type double that represents the *starting balance*. Lines 17–18 ensure that initialBalance is greater than 0.0. If so, initialBalance's value is assigned to instance variable balance. Otherwise, balance remains at 0.0—its *default initial value*.

Account *Class* deposit *Method*

Method deposit (lines 22–26) does *not* return any data when it completes its task, so its return type is void. The method receives one parameter named depositAmount—a double value that's added to the balance *only* if the parameter value is *valid* (i.e., greater than zero). Line 25 adds the depositAmount to the current balance.

Account *Class* getBalance *Method*

Method getBalance (lines 29–32) allows *clients* of the class (i.e., other classes whose methods call the methods of this class) to obtain the value of a particular Account object's balance. The method specifies return type double and an *empty* parameter list.

Account's *Methods Can All Use* balance

Once again, the statements in lines 18, 25 and 31 use the variable balance even though it was *not* declared in *any* of the methods. We can use balance in these methods because it's an *instance variable* of the class.

7.5.2 AccountTest Class to Use Class Account

Class AccountTest (Fig. 7.9) creates two Account objects (lines 9–10) and initializes them with a *valid* balance of 50.00 and an *invalid* balance of -7.53, respectively—for the purpose of our examples, we assume that balances must be greater than or equal to zero. The calls to method System.out.printf in lines 13–16 output the account names and balances, which are obtained by calling each Account's getName and getBalance methods.

```java
1   // Fig. 7.9: AccountTest.java
2   // Inputting and outputting floating-point numbers with Account objects.
3   import java.util.Scanner;
4
5   public class AccountTest
6   {
7      public static void main(String[] args)
8      {
9         Account account1 = new Account("Jane Green", 50.00);
10        Account account2 = new Account("John Blue", -7.53);
11
12        // display initial balance of each object
13        System.out.printf("%s balance: $%.2f%n",
14           account1.getName(), account1.getBalance());
15        System.out.printf("%s balance: $%.2f%n%n",
16           account2.getName(), account2.getBalance());
17
18        // create a Scanner to obtain input from the command window
19        Scanner input = new Scanner(System.in);
20
21        System.out.print("Enter deposit amount for account1: "); // prompt
22        double depositAmount = input.nextDouble(); // obtain user input
23        System.out.printf("%nadding %.2f to account1 balance%n%n",
24           depositAmount);
25        account1.deposit(depositAmount); // add to account1's balance
```

Fig. 7.9 | Inputting and outputting floating-point numbers with Account objects. (Part 1 of 2.)

```
26
27          // display balances
28          System.out.printf("%s balance: $%.2f%n",
29              account1.getName(), account1.getBalance());
30          System.out.printf("%s balance: $%.2f%n%n",
31              account2.getName(), account2.getBalance());
32
33          System.out.print("Enter deposit amount for account2: "); // prompt
34          depositAmount = input.nextDouble(); // obtain user input
35          System.out.printf("%nadding %.2f to account2 balance%n%n",
36              depositAmount);
37          account2.deposit(depositAmount); // add to account2 balance
38
39          // display balances
40          System.out.printf("%s balance: $%.2f%n",
41              account1.getName(), account1.getBalance());
42          System.out.printf("%s balance: $%.2f%n%n",
43              account2.getName(), account2.getBalance());
44      } // end main
45  } // end class AccountTest
```

```
Jane Green balance: $50.00
John Blue balance: $0.00

Enter deposit amount for account1: 25.53

adding 25.53 to account1 balance

Jane Green balance: $75.53
John Blue balance: $0.00
```

```
Enter deposit amount for account2: 123.45

adding 123.45 to account2 balance

Jane Green balance: $75.53
John Blue balance: $123.45
```

Fig. 7.9 | Inputting and outputting floating-point numbers with Account objects. (Part 2 of 2.)

Displaying the Account Objects' Initial Balances

When method getBalance is called for account1 from line 14, the value of account1's balance is returned from line 31 of Fig. 7.8 and displayed by the System.out.printf statement (Fig. 7.9, lines 13–14). Similarly, when method getBalance is called for account2 from line 16, the value of the account2's balance is returned from line 31 of Fig. 7.8 and displayed by the System.out.printf statement (Fig. 7.9, lines 15–16). The balance of account2 is initially 0.00, because the constructor rejected the attempt to start account2 with a *negative* balance, so the balance retains its default initial value.

Formatting Floating-Point Numbers for Display

Each of the balances is output by printf with the format specifier %.2f. The **%f format specifier** is used to output values of type float or double. The .2 between % and f represents the number of *decimal places* (2) that should be output to the *right* of the decimal point in the floating-point number—also known as the number's **precision**. Any floating-point value output with %.2f will be *rounded* to the *hundredths position*—for example, 123.457 would be rounded to 123.46 and 27.33379 would be rounded to 27.33.

Reading a Floating-Point Value from the User and Making a Deposit

Line 21 (Fig. 7.9) prompts the user to enter a deposit amount for account1. Line 22 declares *local* variable depositAmount to store each deposit amount entered by the user. Unlike *instance* variables (such as name and balance in class Account), *local* variables (like depositAmount in main) are *not* initialized by default, so they normally must be initialized explicitly. As you'll learn momentarily, variable depositAmount's initial value will be determined by the user's input.

Common Programming Error 7.1

The Java compiler will issue a compilation error if you attempt to use the value of an uninitialized local variable. This helps you avoid dangerous execution-time logic errors. It's always better to get the errors out of your programs at compilation time rather than execution time.

Line 22 obtains the input from the user by calling Scanner object input's nextDouble method. Lines 23–24 display the depositAmount. Line 25 calls object account1's deposit method with the depositAmount as the method's argument. When the method is called, the argument's value is assigned to the parameter depositAmount of method deposit (line 22 of Fig. 7.8); then method deposit adds that value to the balance. Lines 28–31 (Fig. 7.9) output the names and balances of both Accounts *again* to show that *only* account1's balance has changed.

Line 33 prompts the user to enter a deposit amount for account2. Line 34 obtains the input from the user by calling Scanner object input's nextDouble method. Lines 35–36 display the depositAmount. Line 37 calls object account2's deposit method with depositAmount as the method's *argument*; then method deposit adds that value to the balance. Finally, lines 40–43 output the names and balances of both Accounts *again* to show that *only* account2's balance has changed.

Duplicated Code in Method main

The six statements at lines 13–14, 15–16, 28–29, 30–31, 40–41 and 42–43 are almost *identical*—they each output an Account's name and balance. They differ only in the name of the Account object—account1 or account2. Duplicate code like this can create *code maintenance problems* when that code needs to be updated—if *six* copies of the same code all have the same error or update to be made, you must make that change *six* times, *without making errors*. Exercise 7.14 asks you to modify Fig. 7.9 to include a displayAccount method that takes as a parameter an Account object and outputs the object's name and balance. You'll then replace main's duplicated statements with six calls to displayAccount, thus reducing the size of your program and improving its maintainability by having *one* copy of the code that displays an Account's name and balance.

Software Engineering Observation 7.4

Replacing duplicated code with calls to a method that contains one copy of that code can reduce the size of your program and improve its maintainability.

*UML Class Diagram for Class **Account***

The UML class diagram in Fig. 7.10 concisely models class Account of Fig. 7.8. The diagram models in its *second* compartment the private attributes name of type String and balance of type double.

Account
– name : String
– balance : double
«constructor» Account(name : String, balance: double)
+ deposit(depositAmount : double)
+ getBalance() : double
+ setName(name : String)
+ getName() : String

Fig. 7.10 | UML class diagram for Account class of Fig. 7.8.

Class Account's *constructor* is modeled in the *third* compartment with parameters name of type String and initialBalance of type double. The class's four public methods also are modeled in the *third* compartment—operation deposit with a depositAmount parameter of type double, operation getBalance with a return type of double, operation setName with a name parameter of type String and operation getName with a return type of String.

7.6 Case Study: Card Shuffling and Dealing Simulation

The examples in Chapter 6 demonstrated arrays containing only elements of primitive types. The elements of an array can be either primitive types or reference types. This section uses random-number generation and an array of reference-type elements—namely objects representing playing cards—to develop a class that simulates card shuffling and dealing. This class can then be used to implement applications that play specific card games. The exercises at the end of the chapter use the classes developed here to build a simple poker application.

We first develop class Card (Fig. 7.11), which represents a playing card that has a face (e.g., "Ace", "Deuce", "Three", ..., "Jack", "Queen", "King") and a suit (e.g., "Hearts", "Diamonds", "Clubs", "Spades"). Next, we develop the DeckOfCards class (Fig. 7.12), which creates a deck of 52 playing cards in which each element is a Card object. We then build a test application (Fig. 7.13) that demonstrates class DeckOfCards's card shuffling and dealing capabilities.

*Class **Card***

Class Card (Fig. 7.11) contains two String instance variables—face and suit—that are used to store references to the face name and suit name for a specific Card. The constructor for the class (lines 10–14) receives two Strings that it uses to initialize face and suit. Method toString (lines 17–20) creates a String consisting of the face of the card, the String " of " and the suit of the card. Card's toString method can be invoked *explicitly* to obtain a string representation of a Card object (e.g., "Ace of Spades"). The toString method of an object is called *implicitly* when the object is used where a String is expected (e.g., when printf outputs the object as a String using the %s format specifier or when the object is concatenated to a String using the + operator). For this behavior to occur, toString must be declared with the header shown in Fig. 7.11.

```java
1   // Fig. 7.11: Card.java
2   // Card class represents a playing card.
3
4   public class Card
5   {
6      private final String face; // face of card ("Ace", "Deuce", ...)
7      private final String suit; // suit of card ("Hearts", "Diamonds", ...)
8
9      // two-argument constructor initializes card's face and suit
10     public Card(String cardFace, String cardSuit)
11     {
12        this.face = cardFace; // initialize face of card
13        this.suit = cardSuit; // initialize suit of card
14     }
15
16     // return String representation of Card
17     public String toString()
18     {
19        return face + " of " + suit;
20     }
21  } // end class Card
```

Fig. 7.11 | Card class represents a playing card.

Class DeckOfCards

Class DeckOfCards (Fig. 7.12) declares as an instance variable a Card array named deck (line 7). An array of a *reference* type is declared like any other array. Class DeckOfCards also declares an integer instance variable currentCard (line 8) representing the sequence number (0–51) of the next Card to be dealt from the deck array, and a named constant NUMBER_OF_CARDS (line 9) indicating the number of Cards in the deck (52).

```java
1   // Fig. 7.12: DeckOfCards.java
2   // DeckOfCards class represents a deck of playing cards.
3   import java.security.SecureRandom;
4
5   public class DeckOfCards
6   {
7      private Card[] deck; // array of Card objects
8      private int currentCard; // index of next Card to be dealt (0-51)
9      private static final int NUMBER_OF_CARDS = 52; // constant # of Cards
10     // random number generator
11     private static final SecureRandom randomNumbers = new SecureRandom();
12
```

Fig. 7.12 | DeckOfCards class represents a deck of playing cards. (Part 1 of 2.)

```
13      // constructor fills deck of Cards
14      public DeckOfCards()
15      {
16          String[] faces = { "Ace", "Deuce", "Three", "Four", "Five", "Six",
17              "Seven", "Eight", "Nine", "Ten", "Jack", "Queen", "King" };
18          String[] suits = { "Hearts", "Diamonds", "Clubs", "Spades" };
19
20          deck = new Card[NUMBER_OF_CARDS]; // create array of Card objects
21          currentCard = 0; // first Card dealt will be deck[0]
22
23          // populate deck with Card objects
24          for (int count = 0; count < deck.length; count++)
25              deck[count] =
26                  new Card(faces[count % 13], suits[count / 13]);
27      }
28
29      // shuffle deck of Cards with one-pass algorithm
30      public void shuffle()
31      {
32          // next call to method dealCard should start at deck[0] again
33          currentCard = 0;
34
35          // for each Card, pick another random Card (0-51) and swap them
36          for (int first = 0; first < deck.length; first++)
37          {
38              // select a random number between 0 and 51
39              int second = randomNumbers.nextInt(NUMBER_OF_CARDS);
40
41              // swap current Card with randomly selected Card
42              Card temp = deck[first];
43              deck[first] = deck[second];
44              deck[second] = temp;
45          }
46      }
47
48      // deal one Card
49      public Card dealCard()
50      {
51          // determine whether Cards remain to be dealt
52          if (currentCard < deck.length)
53              return deck[currentCard++]; // return current Card in array
54          else
55              return null; // return null to indicate that all Cards were dealt
56      }
57  } // end class DeckOfCards
```

Fig. 7.12 | DeckOfCards class represents a deck of playing cards. (Part 2 of 2.)

DeckOfCards *Constructor*

The class's constructor instantiates the deck array (line 20) with NUMBER_OF_CARDS (52) elements. The elements of deck are null by default, so the constructor uses a for statement (lines 24–26) to fill the deck with Cards. The loop initializes control variable count to 0 and loops while count is less than deck.length, causing count to take on each integer value from 0 to 51 (the indices of the deck array). Each Card is instantiated and initialized with two Strings—one from the faces array (which contains the Strings "Ace" through "King") and one from the suits array (which contains the Strings "Hearts", "Diamonds", "Clubs" and "Spades"). The calculation count % 13 always results in a value from 0 to 12 (the 13 indices of the faces array in lines 16–17), and the calculation count / 13 always results in a value from 0 to 3 (the four indices of the suits array in line 18). When the deck array is initialized, it contains the Cards with faces "Ace" through "King" in order for each suit (all 13 "Hearts", then all the "Diamonds", then the "Clubs", then the "Spades"). We use arrays of Strings to represent the faces and suits in this example. In Exercise 7.20, we ask you to modify this example to use arrays of enum constants to represent the faces and suits.

DeckOfCards *Method* shuffle

Method shuffle (lines 30–46) shuffles the Cards in the deck. The method loops through all 52 Cards (array indices 0 to 51). For each Card, a number between 0 and 51 is picked randomly to select another Card. Next, the current Card object and the randomly selected Card object are swapped in the array. This exchange is performed by the three assignments in lines 42–44. The extra variable temp temporarily stores one of the two Card objects being swapped. The swap cannot be performed with only the two statements

```
deck[first] = deck[second];
deck[second] = deck[first];
```

If deck[first] is the "Ace" of "Spades" and deck[second] is the "Queen" of "Hearts", after the first assignment, both array elements contain the "Queen" of "Hearts" and the "Ace" of "Spades" is lost—so, the extra variable temp is needed. After the for loop terminates, the Card objects are randomly ordered. A total of only 52 swaps are made in a single pass of the entire array, and the array of Card objects is shuffled!

[*Note:* It's recommended that you use a so-called *unbiased* shuffling algorithm for real card games. Such an algorithm ensures that all possible shuffled card sequences are equally likely to occur. Exercise 7.21 asks you to research the popular unbiased Fisher-Yates shuffling algorithm and use it to reimplement the DeckOfCards method shuffle.]

DeckOfCards *Method* dealCard

Method dealCard (lines 49–56) deals one Card in the array. Recall that currentCard indicates the index of the next Card to be dealt (i.e., the Card at the *top* of the deck). Thus, line 52 compares currentCard to the length of the deck array. If the deck is not empty (i.e., currentCard is less than 52), line 53 returns the "top" Card and postincrements currentCard to prepare for the next call to dealCard—otherwise, null is returned. Recall that null represents a "reference to nothing."

Shuffling and Dealing Cards

Figure 7.13 demonstrates class DeckOfCards. Line 9 creates a DeckOfCards object named myDeckOfCards. The DeckOfCards constructor creates the deck with the 52 Card objects in order by suit and face. Line 10 invokes myDeckOfCards's shuffle method to rearrange the Card objects. Lines 13–20 deal all 52 Cards and print them in four columns of 13 Cards each. Line 16 deals one Card object by invoking myDeckOfCards's dealCard method, then displays the Card left justified in a field of 19 characters. When a Card is output as a String, the Card's toString method (lines 17–20 of Fig. 7.11) is implicitly invoked. Lines 18–19 start a new line after every four Cards.

```
1   // Fig. 7.13: DeckOfCardsTest.java
2   // Card shuffling and dealing.
3
4   public class DeckOfCardsTest
5   {
6      // execute application
7      public static void main(String[] args)
8      {
9         DeckOfCards myDeckOfCards = new DeckOfCards();
10        myDeckOfCards.shuffle(); // place Cards in random order
11
12        // print all 52 Cards in the order in which they are dealt
13        for (int i = 1; i <= 52; i++)
14        {
15           // deal and display a Card
16           System.out.printf("%-19s", myDeckOfCards.dealCard());
17
18           if (i % 4 == 0) // output a newline after every fourth card
19              System.out.println();
20        }
21     }
22  } // end class DeckOfCardsTest
```

Six of Spades	Eight of Spades	Six of Clubs	Nine of Hearts
Queen of Hearts	Seven of Clubs	Nine of Spades	King of Hearts
Three of Diamonds	Deuce of Clubs	Ace of Hearts	Ten of Spades
Four of Spades	Ace of Clubs	Seven of Diamonds	Four of Hearts
Three of Clubs	Deuce of Hearts	Five of Spades	Jack of Diamonds
King of Clubs	Ten of Hearts	Three of Hearts	Six of Diamonds
Queen of Clubs	Eight of Diamonds	Deuce of Diamonds	Ten of Diamonds
Three of Spades	King of Diamonds	Nine of Clubs	Six of Hearts
Ace of Spades	Four of Diamonds	Seven of Hearts	Eight of Clubs
Deuce of Spades	Eight of Hearts	Five of Hearts	Queen of Spades
Jack of Hearts	Seven of Spades	Four of Clubs	Nine of Diamonds
Ace of Diamonds	Queen of Diamonds	Five of Clubs	King of Spades
Five of Diamonds	Ten of Clubs	Jack of Spades	Jack of Clubs

Fig. 7.13 | Card shuffling and dealing.

Preventing *NullPointerExceptions*

In Fig. 7.12, we created a deck array of 52 Card references—each element of every reference-type array created with new is default initialized to null. Reference-type variables which are fields of a class are also initialized to null by default. A NullPointerException occurs when you try to call a method on a null reference. In industrial-strength code, ensuring that references are not null before you use them to call methods prevents Null-PointerExceptions.

7.7 Case Study: Class GradeBook Using an Array to Store Grades

We now present the first part of our case study on developing a GradeBook class that instructors can use to maintain students' grades on an exam and display a grade report that includes the grades, class average, lowest grade, highest grade and a grade distribution bar chart. The version of class GradeBook presented in this section stores the grades for one exam in a one-dimensional array. In Section 7.8, we present a version of class GradeBook that uses a two-dimensional array to store students' grades for *several* exams.

Storing Student Grades in an Array in Class *GradeBook*

Class GradeBook (Fig. 7.14) uses an array of ints to store several students' grades on a single exam. Array grades is declared as an instance variable (line 7), so each GradeBook object maintains its *own* set of grades. The constructor (lines 10–14) has two parameters—the name of the course and an array of grades. When an application (e.g., class GradeBookTest in Fig. 7.15) creates a GradeBook object, the application passes an existing int array to the constructor, which assigns the array's reference to instance variable grades (line 13). The grades array's *size* is determined by the length instance variable of the constructor's array parameter. Thus, a GradeBook object can process a *variable* number of grades. The grade values in the argument could have been input from a user, read from a file on disk (as discussed in Chapter 15) or come from a variety of other sources. In class GradeBookTest, we initialize an array with grade values (Fig. 7.15, line 10). Once the grades are stored in *instance variable* grades of class GradeBook, all the class's methods can access the elements of grades.

```
 1   // Fig. 7.14: GradeBook.java
 2   // GradeBook class using an array to store test grades.
 3
 4   public class GradeBook
 5   {
 6      private String courseName; // name of course this GradeBook represents
 7      private int[] grades; // array of student grades
 8
 9      // constructor
10      public GradeBook(String courseName, int[] grades)
11      {
12         this.courseName = courseName;
13         this.grades = grades;
14      }
15
16      // method to set the course name
17      public void setCourseName(String courseName)
18      {
19         this.courseName = courseName;
20      }
```

Fig. 7.14 | GradeBook class using an array to store test grades. (Part 1 of 4.)

```
21
22      // method to retrieve the course name
23      public String getCourseName()
24      {
25         return courseName;
26      }
27
28      // perform various operations on the data
29      public void processGrades()
30      {
31         // output grades array
32         outputGrades();
33
34         // call method getAverage to calculate the average grade
35         System.out.printf("%nClass average is %.2f%n", getAverage());
36
37         // call methods getMinimum and getMaximum
38         System.out.printf("Lowest grade is %d%nHighest grade is %d%n%n",
39            getMinimum(), getMaximum());
40
41         // call outputBarChart to print grade distribution chart
42         outputBarChart();
43      }
44
45      // find minimum grade
46      public int getMinimum()
47      {
48         int lowGrade = grades[0]; // assume grades[0] is smallest
49
50         // loop through grades array
51         for (int grade : grades)
52         {
53            // if grade lower than lowGrade, assign it to lowGrade
54            if (grade < lowGrade)
55               lowGrade = grade; // new lowest grade
56         }
57
58         return lowGrade;
59      }
60
61      // find maximum grade
62      public int getMaximum()
63      {
64         int highGrade = grades[0]; // assume grades[0] is largest
65
66         // loop through grades array
67         for (int grade : grades)
68         {
69            // if grade greater than highGrade, assign it to highGrade
70            if (grade > highGrade)
71               highGrade = grade; // new highest grade
72         }
```

Fig. 7.14 | GradeBook class using an array to store test grades. (Part 2 of 4.)

```
 73
 74        return highGrade;
 75     }
 76
 77     // determine average grade for test
 78     public double getAverage()
 79     {
 80        int total = 0;
 81
 82        // sum grades for one student
 83        for (int grade : grades)
 84           total += grade;
 85
 86        // return average of grades
 87        return (double) total / grades.length;
 88     }
 89
 90     // output bar chart displaying grade distribution
 91     public void outputBarChart()
 92     {
 93        System.out.println("Grade distribution:");
 94
 95        // stores frequency of grades in each range of 10 grades
 96        int[] frequency = new int[11];
 97
 98        // for each grade, increment the appropriate frequency
 99        for (int grade : grades)
100           ++frequency[grade / 10];
101
102        // for each grade frequency, print bar in chart
103        for (int count = 0; count < frequency.length; count++)
104        {
105           // output bar label ("00-09: ", ..., "90-99: ", "100: ")
106           if (count == 10)
107              System.out.printf("%5d: ", 100);
108           else
109              System.out.printf("%02d-%02d: ",
110                 count * 10, count * 10 + 9);
111
112           // print bar of asterisks
113           for (int stars = 0; stars < frequency[count]; stars++)
114              System.out.print("*");
115
116           System.out.println();
117        }
118     }
119
120     // output the contents of the grades array
121     public void outputGrades()
122     {
123        System.out.printf("The grades are:%n%n");
124
```

Fig. 7.14 | GradeBook class using an array to store test grades. (Part 3 of 4.)

```
125          // output each student's grade
126          for (int student = 0; student < grades.length; student++)
127             System.out.printf("Student %2d: %3d%n",
128                student + 1, grades[student]);
129      }
130   } // end class GradeBook
```

Fig. 7.14 | GradeBook class using an array to store test grades. (Part 4 of 4.)

Method processGrades (lines 29–43) contains a series of method calls that output a report summarizing the grades. Line 32 calls method outputGrades to print the contents of the array grades. Lines 126–128 in method outputGrades output the students' grades. A counter-controlled for statement *must* be used in this case, because lines 127–128 use counter variable student's value to output each grade next to a particular student number (see the output in Fig. 7.15). Although array indices start at 0, a professor might typically number students starting at 1. Thus, lines 127–128 output student + 1 as the student number to produce grade labels "Student 1: ", "Student 2: ", and so on.

Method processGrades next calls method getAverage (line 35) to obtain the average of the grades in the array. Method getAverage (lines 78–88) uses an enhanced for statement to total the values in array grades before calculating the average. The parameter in the enhanced for's header (e.g., int grade) indicates that for each iteration, the int variable grade takes on a value in the array grades. The averaging calculation in line 87 uses grades.length to determine the number of grades being averaged.

Lines 38–39 in method processGrades call methods getMinimum and getMaximum to determine the lowest and highest grades of any student on the exam, respectively. Each of these methods uses an enhanced for statement to loop through array grades. Lines 51–56 in method getMinimum loop through the array. Lines 54–55 compare each grade to lowGrade; if a grade is less than lowGrade, lowGrade is set to that grade. When line 58 executes, lowGrade contains the lowest grade in the array. Method getMaximum (lines 62–75) works similarly to method getMinimum.

Finally, line 42 in method processGrades calls outputBarChart to print a grade distribution chart using a technique similar to that in Fig. 6.6. In that example, we manually calculated the number of grades in each category (i.e., 0–9, 10–19, …, 90–99 and 100) by simply looking at a set of grades. Here, lines 99–100 use a technique similar to that in Fig. 6.8 to calculate the frequency of grades in each category. Line 96 declares and creates array frequency of 11 ints to store the frequency of grades in each category. For each grade in array grades, lines 99–100 increment the appropriate frequency array element. To determine which one to increment, line 100 divides the current grade by 10 using *integer division*—e.g., if grade is 85, line 100 increments frequency[8] to update the count of grades in the range 80–89. Lines 103–117 print the bar chart (as shown in Fig. 7.15) based on the values in array frequency. Like lines 23–24 of Fig. 6.6, lines 113–116 of Fig. 7.14 use a value in array frequency to determine the number of asterisks to display in each bar.

Class *GradeBookTest* That Demonstrates Class *GradeBook*

The application of Fig. 7.15 creates an object of class GradeBook (Fig. 7.14) using the int array gradesArray (declared and initialized in line 10). Lines 12–13 pass a course name and gradesArray to the GradeBook constructor. Lines 14–15 display a welcome message that includes the course name stored in the GradeBook object. Line 16 invokes the GradeBook object's processGrades method. The output summarizes the 10 grades in myGradeBook.

Software Engineering Observation 7.5

A test harness (or test application) is responsible for creating an object of the class being tested and providing it with data. This data could come from any of several sources. Test data can be placed directly into an array with an array initializer, it can come from the user at the keyboard, from a file (as you'll see in Chapter 15), from a database (as you'll see in Chapter 24) or from a network (as you'll see in online Chapter 28). After passing this data to the class's constructor to instantiate the object, the test harness should call upon the object to test its methods and manipulate its data. Gathering data in the test harness like this allows the class to be more reusable, able to manipulate data from several sources.

```java
1   // Fig. 7.15: GradeBookTest.java
2   // GradeBookTest creates a GradeBook object using an array of grades,
3   // then invokes method processGrades to analyze them.
4   public class GradeBookTest
5   {
6      // main method begins program execution
7      public static void main(String[] args)
8      {
9         // array of student grades
10        int[] gradesArray = { 87, 68, 94, 100, 83, 78, 85, 91, 76, 87 };
11
12        GradeBook myGradeBook = new GradeBook(
13           "CS101 Introduction to Java Programming", gradesArray);
14        System.out.printf("Welcome to the grade book for%n%s%n%n",
15           myGradeBook.getCourseName());
16        myGradeBook.processGrades();
17     }
18  } // end class GradeBookTest
```

```
Welcome to the grade book for
CS101 Introduction to Java Programming

The grades are:

Student  1:  87
Student  2:  68
Student  3:  94
Student  4: 100
Student  5:  83
Student  6:  78
Student  7:  85
Student  8:  91
Student  9:  76
Student 10:  87

Class average is 84.90
Lowest grade is 68
Highest grade is 100
```

Fig. 7.15 │ GradeBookTest creates a GradeBook object using an array of grades, then invokes method processGrades to analyze them. (Part 1 of 2.)

```
Grade distribution:
00-09:
10-19:
20-29:
30-39:
40-49:
50-59:
60-69: *
70-79: **
80-89: ****
90-99: **
  100: *
```

Fig. 7.15 | GradeBookTest creates a GradeBook object using an array of grades, then invokes method processGrades to analyze them. (Part 2 of 2.)

Java SE 8

In Chapter 17, Java SE 8 Lambdas and Streams, the example of Fig. 17.5 uses stream methods min, max, count and average to process the elements of an int array elegantly and concisely without having to write repetition statements. In Chapter 23, Concurrency, the example of Fig. 23.29 uses stream method summaryStatistics to perform all of these operations in one method call.

7.8 Case Study: Class GradeBook Using a Two-Dimensional Array

In Section 7.7, we presented class GradeBook (Fig. 7.14), which used a one-dimensional array to store student grades on a single exam. In most semesters, students take several exams. Professors are likely to want to analyze grades across the entire semester, both for a single student and for the class as a whole.

Storing Student Grades in a Two-Dimensional Array in Class GradeBook

Figure 7.16 contains a GradeBook class that uses a two-dimensional array grades to store the grades of *several* students on *multiple* exams. Each *row* of the array represents a *single* student's grades for the entire course, and each *column* represents the grades of *all* the students who took a particular exam. Class GradeBookTest (Fig. 7.17) passes the array as an argument to the GradeBook constructor. In this example, we use a ten-by-three array for ten students' grades on three exams. Five methods perform array manipulations to process the grades. Each method is similar to its counterpart in the earlier one-dimensional array version of GradeBook (Fig. 7.14). Method getMinimum (lines 46–62) determines the lowest grade of any student for the semester. Method getMaximum (lines 65–83) determines the highest grade of any student for the semester. Method getAverage (lines 86–96) determines a particular student's semester average. Method outputBarChart (lines 99–129) outputs a grade bar chart for the entire semester's student grades. Method outputGrades (lines 132–156) outputs the array in a tabular format, along with each student's semester average.

```
 1   // Fig. 7.16: GradeBook.java
 2   // GradeBook class using a two-dimensional array to store grades.
 3
 4   public class GradeBook
 5   {
 6      private String courseName; // name of course this grade book represents
 7      private int[][] grades; // two-dimensional array of student grades
 8
 9      // two-argument constructor initializes courseName and grades array
10      public GradeBook(String courseName, int[][] grades)
11      {
12         this.courseName = courseName;
13         this.grades = grades;
14      }
15
16      // method to set the course name
17      public void setCourseName(String courseName)
18      {
19         this.courseName = courseName;
20      }
21
22      // method to retrieve the course name
23      public String getCourseName()
24      {
25         return courseName;
26      }
27
28      // perform various operations on the data
29      public void processGrades()
30      {
31         // output grades array
32         outputGrades();
33
34         // call methods getMinimum and getMaximum
35         System.out.printf("%n%s %d%n%s %d%n%n",
36            "Lowest grade in the grade book is", getMinimum(),
37            "Highest grade in the grade book is", getMaximum());
38
39         // output grade distribution chart of all grades on all tests
40         outputBarChart();
41      }
42
43      // find minimum grade
44      public int getMinimum()
45      {
46         // assume first element of grades array is smallest
47         int lowGrade = grades[0][0];
48
49         // loop through rows of grades array
50         for (int[] studentGrades : grades)
51         {
```

Fig. 7.16 | GradeBook class using a two-dimensional array to store grades. (Part 1 of 4.)

```
52          // loop through columns of current row
53          for (int grade : studentGrades)
54          {
55              // if grade less than lowGrade, assign it to lowGrade
56              if (grade < lowGrade)
57                  lowGrade = grade;
58          }
59      }
60
61      return lowGrade;
62  }
63
64  // find maximum grade
65  public int getMaximum()
66  {
67      // assume first element of grades array is largest
68      int highGrade = grades[0][0];
69
70      // loop through rows of grades array
71      for (int[] studentGrades : grades)
72      {
73          // loop through columns of current row
74          for (int grade : studentGrades)
75          {
76              // if grade greater than highGrade, assign it to highGrade
77              if (grade > highGrade)
78                  highGrade = grade;
79          }
80      }
81
82      return highGrade;
83  }
84
85  // determine average grade for particular set of grades
86  public double getAverage(int[] setOfGrades)
87  {
88      int total = 0;
89
90      // sum grades for one student
91      for (int grade : setOfGrades)
92          total += grade;
93
94      // return average of grades
95      return (double) total / setOfGrades.length;
96  }
97
98  // output bar chart displaying overall grade distribution
99  public void outputBarChart()
100 {
101     System.out.println("Overall grade distribution:");
102
```

Fig. 7.16 | GradeBook class using a two-dimensional array to store grades. (Part 2 of 4.)

```
103        // stores frequency of grades in each range of 10 grades
104        int[] frequency = new int[11];
105
106        // for each grade in GradeBook, increment the appropriate frequency
107        for (int[] studentGrades : grades)
108        {
109           for (int grade : studentGrades)
110              ++frequency[grade / 10];
111        }
112
113        // for each grade frequency, print bar in chart
114        for (int count = 0; count < frequency.length; count++)
115        {
116           // output bar label ("00-09: ", ..., "90-99: ", "100: ")
117           if (count == 10)
118              System.out.printf("%5d: ", 100);
119           else
120              System.out.printf("%02d-%02d: ",
121                 count * 10, count * 10 + 9);
122
123           // print bar of asterisks
124           for (int stars = 0; stars < frequency[count]; stars++)
125              System.out.print("*");
126
127           System.out.println();
128        }
129     }
130
131     // output the contents of the grades array
132     public void outputGrades()
133     {
134        System.out.printf("The grades are:%n%n");
135        System.out.print("                ");  // align column heads
136
137        // create a column heading for each of the tests
138        for (int test = 0; test < grades[0].length; test++)
139           System.out.printf("Test %d  ", test + 1);
140
141        System.out.println("Average"); // student average column heading
142
143        // create rows/columns of text representing array grades
144        for (int student = 0; student < grades.length; student++)
145        {
146           System.out.printf("Student %2d", student + 1);
147
148           for (int test : grades[student]) // output student's grades
149              System.out.printf("%8d", test);
150
151           // call method getAverage to calculate student's average grade;
152           // pass row of grades as the argument to getAverage
153           double average = getAverage(grades[student]);
```

Fig. 7.16 │ GradeBook class using a two-dimensional array to store grades. (Part 3 of 4.)

```
154            System.out.printf("%9.2f%n", average);
155        }
156    }
157 } // end class GradeBook
```

Fig. 7.16 | GradeBook class using a two-dimensional array to store grades. (Part 4 of 4.)

*Methods **getMinimum** and **getMaximum***
Methods getMinimum, getMaximum, outputBarChart and outputGrades each loop through array grades by using nested for statements—for example, the nested enhanced for statement (lines 50–59) from the declaration of method getMinimum. The outer enhanced for statement iterates through the two-dimensional array grades, assigning successive rows to parameter studentGrades on successive iterations. The square brackets following the parameter name indicate that studentGrades refers to a one-dimensional int array—namely, a row in array grades containing one student's grades. To find the lowest overall grade, the inner for statement compares the elements of the current one-dimensional array studentGrades to variable lowGrade. For example, on the first iteration of the outer for, row 0 of grades is assigned to parameter studentGrades. The inner enhanced for statement then loops through studentGrades and compares each grade value with lowGrade. If a grade is less than lowGrade, lowGrade is set to that grade. On the second iteration of the outer enhanced for statement, row 1 of grades is assigned to studentGrades, and the elements of this row are compared with variable lowGrade. This repeats until all rows of grades have been traversed. When execution of the nested statement is complete, lowGrade contains the lowest grade in the two-dimensional array. Method getMaximum works similarly to method getMinimum.

*Method **outputBarChart***
Method outputBarChart in Fig. 7.16 is nearly identical to the one in Fig. 7.14. However, to output the overall grade distribution for a whole semester, the method here uses nested enhanced for statements (lines 107–111) to create the one-dimensional array frequency based on all the grades in the two-dimensional array. The rest of the code in each of the two outputBarChart methods that displays the chart is identical.

*Method **outputGrades***
Method outputGrades (lines 132–156) uses nested for statements to output values of the array grades and each student's semester average. The output (Fig. 7.17) shows the result, which resembles the tabular format of a professor's physical grade book. Lines 138–139 print the column headings for each test. We use a counter-controlled for statement here so that we can identify each test with a number. Similarly, the for statement in lines 144–155 first outputs a row label using a counter variable to identify each student (line 146). Although array indices start at 0, lines 139 and 146 output test + 1 and student + 1, respectively, to produce test and student numbers starting at 1 (see the output in Fig. 7.17). The inner for statement (lines 148–149) uses the outer for statement's counter variable student to loop through a specific row of array grades and output each student's test grade. An enhanced for statement can be nested in a counter-controlled for statement, and vice versa. Finally, line 153 obtains each student's semester average by passing the current row of grades (i.e., grades[student]) to method getAverage.

Method getAverage

Method getAverage (lines 86–96) takes one argument—a one-dimensional array of test results for a particular student. When line 153 calls getAverage, the argument is grades[student], which specifies that a particular row of the two-dimensional array grades should be passed to getAverage. For example, based on the array created in Fig. 7.17, the argument grades[1] represents the three values (a one-dimensional array of grades) stored in row 1 of the two-dimensional array grades. Recall that a two-dimensional array is one whose elements are one-dimensional arrays. Method getAverage calculates the sum of the array elements, divides the total by the number of test results and returns the floating-point result as a double value (line 95).

Class GradeBookTest That Demonstrates Class GradeBook

Figure 7.17 creates an object of class GradeBook (Fig. 7.16) using the two-dimensional array of ints named gradesArray (declared and initialized in lines 10–19). Lines 21–22 pass a course name and gradesArray to the GradeBook constructor. Lines 23–24 display a welcome message containing the course name, then line 25 invokes myGradeBook's processGrades method to display a report summarizing the students' grades for the semester.

```
1   // Fig. 7.17: GradeBookTest.java
2   // GradeBookTest creates GradeBook object using a two-dimensional array
3   // of grades, then invokes method processGrades to analyze them.
4   public class GradeBookTest
5   {
6      // main method begins program execution
7      public static void main(String[] args)
8      {
9         // two-dimensional array of student grades
10        int[][] gradesArray = {{87, 96, 70},
11                               {68, 87, 90},
12                               {94, 100, 90},
13                               {100, 81, 82},
14                               {83, 65, 85},
15                               {78, 87, 65},
16                               {85, 75, 83},
17                               {91, 94, 100},
18                               {76, 72, 84},
19                               {87, 93, 73}};
20
21        GradeBook myGradeBook = new GradeBook(
22           "CS101 Introduction to Java Programming", gradesArray);
23        System.out.printf("Welcome to the grade book for%n%s%n%n",
24           myGradeBook.getCourseName());
25        myGradeBook.processGrades();
26     }
27  } // end class GradeBookTest
```

Fig. 7.17 | GradeBookTest creates GradeBook object using a two-dimensional array of grades, then invokes method processGrades to analyze them. (Part 1 of 2.)

```
Welcome to the grade book for
CS101 Introduction to Java Programming

The grades are:
            Test 1  Test 2  Test 3  Average
Student  1     87      96      70    84.33
Student  2     68      87      90    81.67
Student  3     94     100      90    94.67
Student  4    100      81      82    87.67
Student  5     83      65      85    77.67
Student  6     78      87      65    76.67
Student  7     85      75      83    81.00
Student  8     91      94     100    95.00
Student  9     76      72      84    77.33
Student 10     87      93      73    84.33

Lowest grade in the grade book is 65
Highest grade in the grade book is 100

Overall grade distribution:
00-09:
10-19:
20-29:
30-39:
40-49:
50-59:
60-69: ***
70-79: ******
80-89: ***********
90-99: *******
  100: ***
```

Fig. 7.17 | GradeBookTest creates GradeBook object using a two-dimensional array of grades, then invokes method processGrades to analyze them. (Part 2 of 2.)

7.9 Wrap-Up

In this chapter, you learned how to create your own classes, create objects of those classes and call methods of those objects to perform useful actions. You declared instance variables maintain data for each object of the class, and you declared your own methods to operate on that data. You learned the difference between a local variable of a method and an instance variable of a class, and that only instance variables are initialized automatically. You used a class's constructor to specify the initial values for an object's instance variables. You studied an Account class, then three substantial object-oriented case studies—one card shuffling and dealing and two variations of a GradeBook class. The first used a one-dimensional array of grades for 10 students on a single exam. The second used a two-dimensional array of grades for 10 students on three exams. In Chapter 8, we take a deeper look at classes and objects.

Summary

Section 7.2 Instance Variables, set Methods and get Methods
- Each class you create becomes a new type that can be used to declare variables and create objects.
- You can declare new classes as needed; this is one reason Java is known as an extensible language.

Section 7.2.1 Account *Class with an Instance Variable, a* set *Method and a* get *Method*

- Each class declaration that begins with the access modifier (p. 268) `public` must be stored in a file that has the same name as the class and ends with the `.java` filename extension.
- Every class declaration contains keyword `class` followed immediately by the class's name.
- Class, method and variable names are identifiers. By convention all use camel case names. Class names begin with an uppercase letter, and method and variable names begin with a lowercase letter.
- An object has attributes that are implemented as instance variables (p. 268) and carried with it throughout its lifetime.
- Instance variables exist before methods are called on an object, while the methods are executing and after the methods complete execution.
- A class normally contains one or more methods that manipulate the instance variables that belong to particular objects of the class.
- Instance variables are declared inside a class declaration but outside the bodies of the class's method declarations.
- Each object (instance) of the class has its own copy of each of the class's instance variables.
- Most instance-variable declarations are preceded with the keyword `private` (p. 268), which is an access modifier. Variables or methods declared with access modifier `private` are accessible only to methods of the class in which they're declared.
- Classes often provide `public` methods to allow the class's clients to *set* or *get* `private` instance variables. The names of these methods need not begin with *set* or *get*, but this naming convention is recommended.

Section 7.2.2 AccountTest *Class That Creates and Uses an Object of Class* Account

- A class that creates an object of another class, then calls the object's methods, is a driver class.
- `Scanner` method `nextLine` (p. 270) reads characters until a newline character is encountered, then returns the characters as a `String`.
- `Scanner` method `next` (p. 270) reads characters until any white-space character is encountered, then returns the characters as a `String`.
- A class instance creation expression (p. 271) begins with keyword `new` and creates a new object.
- A constructor is similar to a method but is called implicitly by the `new` operator to initialize an object's instance variables at the time the object is created.
- To call a method of an object, follow the object name with a dot separator (p. 271), the method name and a set of parentheses containing the method's arguments.
- Local variables are not automatically initialized. Every instance variable has a default initial value—a value provided by Java when you do not specify the instance variable's initial value.
- The default value for an instance variable of type `String` is `null`.
- A method call supplies values—known as arguments—for each of the method's parameters. Each argument's value is assigned to the corresponding parameter in the method header.
- The number of arguments in a method call must match the number of parameters in the method declaration's parameter list.
- The argument types in the method call must be consistent with the types of the corresponding parameters in the method's declaration.

Section 7.2.3 Compiling and Executing an App with Multiple Classes

- The `javac` command can compile multiple classes at once. Simply list the source-code filenames after the command with each filename separated by a space from the next. If the directory containing the app includes only one app's files, you can compile all of its classes with the command javac *.java. The asterisk (*) in *.java indicates that all files in the current directory ending with the filename extension ".java" should be compiled.

Section 7.2.4 **Account** *UML Class Diagram with an Instance Variable and* set *and* get *Methods*
- In the UML, each class is modeled in a class diagram (p. 273) as a rectangle with three compartments. The top one contains the class's name centered horizontally in boldface. The middle one contains the class's attributes, which correspond to instance variables in Java. The bottom one contains the class's operations (p. 273), which correspond to methods and constructors in Java.
- The UML represents instance variables as an attribute name, followed by a colon and the type.
- Private attributes are preceded by a minus sign (–) in the UML.
- The UML models operations by listing the operation name followed by a set of parentheses. A plus sign (+) in front of the operation name indicates that the operation is a public one in the UML (i.e., a public method in Java).
- The UML models a parameter of an operation by listing the parameter name, followed by a colon and the parameter type between the parentheses after the operation name.
- The UML indicates an operation's return type by placing a colon and the return type after the parentheses following the operation name.
- UML class diagrams do not specify return types for operations that do not return values.
- Declaring instance variables private is known as data hiding or information hiding.

Section 7.2.5 *Additional Notes on This Example*
- Most classes you'll use in Java programs must be imported explicitly. There's a special relationship between classes that are compiled in the same directory. By default, such classes are considered to be in the same package—known as the default package. Classes in the same package are implicitly imported into the source-code files of other classes in that package. An import declaration is not required when one class in a package uses another in the same package.
- An import declaration is not required if you always refer to a class with its fully qualified class name, which includes its package name and class name.

Section 7.2.6 *Software Engineering with* **private** *Instance Variables and* **public** set *and* get *Methods*
- Declaring instance variables private is known as data hiding or information hiding.

Section 7.3 *Default and Explicit Initialization for Instance Variables*
- Primitive-type instance variables are initialized by default. Variables of types byte, char, short, int, long, float and double are initialized to 0. Variables of type boolean are initialized to false.
- Reference-type instance variables are initialized by default to the value null.

Section 7.4 **Account** *Class: Initializing Objects with Constructors*
- Each class you declare can optionally provide a constructor with parameters that can be used to initialize an object of a class when the object is created.
- Java requires a constructor call for every object that's created.
- Constructors can specify parameters but not return types.
- If a class does not define constructors, the compiler provides a default constructor (p. 278) with no parameters, and the class's instance variables are initialized to their default values.
- If you declare a constructor for a class, the compiler will *not* create a *default constructor* for that class.

- The UML models constructors in the third compartment of a class diagram. To distinguish a constructor from a class's operations, the UML places the word "constructor" between guillemets (« and »; p. 279) before the constructor's name.

Section 7.5 *Account Class with a Balance; Floating-Point Numbers*
- Scanner method nextDouble returns a double value.
- The format specifier %f (p. 282) is used to output values of type float or double. The format specifier %.2f specifies that two digits of precision (p. 283) should be output to the right of the decimal point in the floating-point number.
- The default value for an instance variable of type double is 0.0, and the default value for an instance variable of type int is 0.

Section 7.6 *Case Study: Card Shuffling and Dealing Simulation*
- The toString method of an object is called implicitly when the object is used where a String is expected (e.g., when printf outputs the object as a String using the %s format specifier or when the object is concatenated to a String using the + operator).

Self-Review Exercises

7.1 Fill in the blanks in each of the following:
a) Each class declaration that begins with keyword _____ must be stored in a file that has exactly the same name as the class and ends with the .java filename extension.
b) Keyword _____ in a class declaration is followed immediately by the class's name.
c) Keyword _____ requests memory from the system to store an object, then calls the corresponding class's constructor to initialize the object.
d) Each parameter must specify both a(n) _____ and a(n) _____.
e) By default, classes that are compiled in the same directory are considered to be in the same package, known as the _____.
f) Variables of type double represent _____ floating-point numbers.
g) Scanner method _____ returns a double value.
h) Keyword public is an access _____.
i) Scanner method _____ reads characters until it encounters a newline character, then returns those characters as a String.
j) Class String is in package _____.
k) A(n) _____ is not required if you always refer to a class with its fully qualified class name.

7.2 State whether each of the following is *true* or *false*. If *false*, explain why.
a) An import declaration is not required when one class in a package uses another in the same package.
b) Variables declared in the body of a particular method are known as instance variables and can be used in all methods of the class.
c) Primitive-type local variables are initialized by default.
d) Reference-type instance variables are initialized by default to the value null.

7.3 What is the difference between a local variable and an instance variable?

Answers to Self-Review Exercises

7.1 a) public. b) class. c) new. d) type, name. e) default package. f) double-precision. g) next-Double. h) modifier. i) nextLine. j) java.lang. k) import declaration.

7.2　a)　True. b) False. Such variables are called local variables and can be used only in the method in which they're declared. c) False. Primitive-type instance variables are initialized by default. Each local variable must explicitly be assigned a value. d) True.

7.3　A local variable is declared in the body of a method and can be used only from the point at which it's declared through the end of the method declaration. An instance variable is declared in a class, but not in the body of any of the class's methods. Also, instance variables are accessible to all methods of the class. (We'll see an exception to this in Chapter 8.)

Exercises

7.4　*(Keyword new)* What's the purpose of keyword new? Explain what happens when you use it.

7.5　*(Default Constructors)* What is a default constructor? How are an object's instance variables initialized if a class has only a default constructor?

7.6　*(Instance Variables)* Explain the purpose of an instance variable.

7.7　*(Using Classes without Importing Them)* Most classes need to be imported before they can be used in an app. Why is every app allowed to use classes System and String without first importing them?

7.8　*(Using a Class without Importing It)* Explain how a program could use class Scanner without importing it.

7.9　*(set and get Methods)* Explain why a class might provide a *set* method and a *get* method for an instance variable.

7.10　*(Modified Account Class)* Modify class Account (Fig. 7.8) to provide a method called withdraw that withdraws money from an Account. Ensure that the withdrawal amount does not exceed the Account's balance. If it does, the balance should be left unchanged and the method should print a message indicating "Withdrawal amount exceeded account balance." Modify class AccountTest (Fig. 7.9) to test method withdraw.

7.11　*(Invoice Class)* Create a class called Invoice that a hardware store might use to represent an invoice for an item sold at the store. An Invoice should include four pieces of information as instance variables—a part number (type String), a part description (type String), a quantity of the item being purchased (type int) and a price per item (double). Your class should have a constructor that initializes the four instance variables. Provide a *set* and a *get* method for each instance variable. In addition, provide a method named getInvoiceAmount that calculates the invoice amount (i.e., multiplies the quantity by the price per item), then returns the amount as a double value. If the quantity is not positive, it should be set to 0. If the price per item is not positive, it should be set to 0.0. Write a test app named InvoiceTest that demonstrates class Invoice's capabilities.

7.12　*(Employee Class)* Create a class called Employee that includes three instance variables—a first name (type String), a last name (type String) and a monthly salary (double). Provide a constructor that initializes the three instance variables. Provide a *set* and a *get* method for each instance variable. If the monthly salary is not positive, do not set its value. Write a test app named EmployeeTest that demonstrates class Employee's capabilities. Create two Employee objects and display each object's *yearly* salary. Then give each Employee a 10% raise and display each Employee's yearly salary again.

7.13　*(Date Class)* Create a class called Date that includes three instance variables—a month (type int), a day (type int) and a year (type int). Provide a constructor that initializes the three instance variables and assumes that the values provided are correct. Provide a *set* and a *get* method for each instance variable. Provide a method displayDate that displays the month, day and year separated by forward slashes (/). Write a test app named DateTest that demonstrates class Date's capabilities.

7.14 *(Removing Duplicated Code in Method* `main`*)* In the `AccountTest` class of Fig. 7.9, method `main` contains six statements (lines 13–14, 15–16, 28–29, 30–31, 40–41 and 42–43) that each display an `Account` object's `name` and `balance`. Study these statements and you'll notice that they differ only in the `Account` object being manipulated—`account1` or `account2`. In this exercise, you'll define a new `displayAccount` method that contains *one* copy of that output statement. The method's parameter will be an `Account` object and the method will output the object's `name` and `balance`. You'll then replace the six duplicated statements in `main` with calls to `displayAccount`, passing as an argument the specific `Account` object to output.

Modify class `AccountTest` class of Fig. 7.9 to declare the following `displayAccount` method *after* the closing right brace of `main` and *before* the closing right brace of class `AccountTest`:

```
public static void displayAccount(Account accountToDisplay)
{
   // place the statement that displays
   // accountToDisplay's name and balance here
}
```

Replace the comment in the method's body with a statement that displays `accountToDisplay`'s `name` and `balance`.

Recall that `main` is a `static` method, so it can be called without first creating an object of the class in which `main` is declared. We also declared method `displayAccount` as a `static` method. When `main` needs to call another method in the same class without first creating an object of that class, the other method *also* must be declared `static`.

Once you've completed `displayAccount`'s declaration, modify `main` to replace the statements that display each `Account`'s `name` and `balance` with calls to `displayAccount`—each receiving as its argument the `account1` or `account2` object, as appropriate. Then, test the updated `AccountTest` class to ensure that it produces the same output as shown in Fig. 7.9.

7.15 *(Enhanced GradeBook)* Modify the `GradeBook` class of Fig. 7.16 so that the constructor accepts as parameters the number of students and the number of exams, then builds an appropriately sized two-dimensional array, rather than receiving a preinitialized two-dimensional array as it does now. Set each element of the new two-dimensional array to -1 to indicate that no grade has been entered for that element. Add a `setGrade` method that sets one grade for a particular student on a particular exam. Modify class `GradeBookTest` of Fig. 7.17 to input the number of students and number of exams for the `GradeBook` and to allow the instructor to enter one grade at a time.

Exercises 7.16–7.20 are reasonably challenging. Once you've done them, you ought to be able to implement most popular card games easily.

7.16 *(Card Shuffling and Dealing)* Modify the application of Fig. 7.13 to deal a five-card poker hand. Then modify class `DeckOfCards` of Fig. 7.12 to include methods that determine whether a hand contains

a) a pair
b) two pairs
c) three of a kind (e.g., three jacks)
d) four of a kind (e.g., four aces)
e) a flush (i.e., all five cards of the same suit)
f) a straight (i.e., five cards of consecutive face values)
g) a full house (i.e., two cards of one face value and three cards of another face value)

[*Hint:* Add methods `getFace` and `getSuit` to class `Card` of Fig. 7.11.]

7.17 *(Card Shuffling and Dealing)* Use the methods developed in Exercise 7.16 to write an application that deals two five-card poker hands, evaluates each hand and determines which is better.

7.18 *(Project: Card Shuffling and Dealing)* Modify the application developed in Exercise 7.17 so that it can simulate the dealer. The dealer's five-card hand is dealt "face down," so the player cannot see it. The application should then evaluate the dealer's hand, and, based on the quality of the hand, the dealer should draw one, two or three more cards to replace the corresponding number of unneeded cards in the original hand. The application should then reevaluate the dealer's hand. [*Caution:* This is a difficult problem!]

7.19 *(Project: Card Shuffling and Dealing)* Modify the application developed in Exercise 7.18 so that it can handle the dealer's hand automatically, but the player is allowed to decide which cards of the player's hand to replace. The application should then evaluate both hands and determine who wins. Now use this new application to play 20 games against the computer. Who wins more games, you or the computer? Have a friend play 20 games against the computer. Who wins more games? Based on the results of these games, refine your poker-playing application. (This, too, is a difficult problem.) Play 20 more games. Does your modified application play a better game?

7.20 *(Project: Card Shuffling and Dealing)* Modify the application of Figs. 7.11–7.13 to use Face and Suit enum types to represent the faces and suits of the cards. Declare each of these enum types as a public type in its own source-code file. Each Card should have a Face and a Suit instance variable. These should be initialized by the Card constructor. In class DeckOfCards, create an array of Faces that's initialized with the names of the constants in the Face enum type and an array of Suits that's initialized with the names of the constants in the Suit enum type. [*Note:* When you output an enum constant as a String, the name of the constant is displayed.]

7.21 *(Fisher-Yates Shuffling Algorithm)* Research the Fisher-Yates shuffling algorithm online, then use it to reimplement the shuffle method in Fig. 7.12.

Making a Difference

7.22 *(Target-Heart-Rate Calculator)* While exercising, you can use a heart-rate monitor to see that your heart rate stays within a safe range suggested by your trainers and doctors. According to the American Heart Association (AHA) (www.americanheart.org/presenter.jhtml?identifier =4736), the formula for calculating your *maximum heart rate* in beats per minute is 220 minus your age in years. Your *target heart rate* is a range that's 50–85% of your maximum heart rate. [*Note:* These formulas are estimates provided by the AHA. Maximum and target heart rates may vary based on the health, fitness and gender of the individual. **Always consult a physician or qualified health-care professional before beginning or modifying an exercise program.**] Create a class called Heart-Rates. The class attributes should include the person's first name, last name and date of birth (consisting of separate attributes for the month, day and year of birth). Your class should have a constructor that receives this data as parameters. For each attribute provide *set* and *get* methods. The class also should include a method that calculates and returns the person's age (in years), a method that calculates and returns the person's maximum heart rate and a method that calculates and returns the person's target heart rate. Write a Java app that prompts for the person's information, instantiates an object of class HeartRates and prints the information from that object—including the person's first name, last name and date of birth—then calculates and prints the person's age in (years), maximum heart rate and target-heart-rate range.

Classes and Objects: A Deeper Look

Is it a world to hide virtues in?
—William Shakespeare

*But what, to serve
our private ends,
Forbids the cheating
of our friends?*
—Charles Churchill

*This above all: to thine own self
be true.*
—William Shakespeare.

Objectives

In this chapter you'll:

- Use the **throw** statement to indicate that a problem has occurred.

- Use keyword **this** in a constructor to call another constructor in the same class.

- Use **static** variables and methods.

- Import **static** members of a class.

- Use the **enum** type to create sets of constants with unique identifiers.

- Declare **enum** constants with parameters.

- Use **BigDecimal** for precise monetary calculations.

8.1 Introduction

We now take a deeper look at building classes, controlling access to members of a class and creating constructors. We show how to throw an exception to indicate that a problem has occurred (Section 6.5 discussed catching exceptions). We use the this keyword to enable one constructor to conveniently call another constructor of the same class. We discuss *composition*—a capability that allows a class to have references to objects of other classes as members. We reexamine the use of *set* and *get* methods. Recall that Section 5.10 introduced the basic enum type to declare a set of constants. In this chapter, we discuss the relationship between enum types and classes, demonstrating that an enum type, like a class, can be declared in its own file with constructors, methods and fields. The chapter also discusses static class members and final instance variables in detail. We show a special relationship between classes in the same package. Finally, we demonstrate how to use class BigDecimal to perform precise monetary calculations. Two additional types of classes—nested classes and anonymous inner classes—are discussed in Chapter 12.

8.2 Time Class Case Study

Our first example consists of two classes—Time1 (Fig. 8.1) and Time1Test (Fig. 8.2). Class Time1 represents the time of day. Class Time1Test's main method creates one object of class Time1 and invokes its methods. The output of this program appears in Fig. 8.2.

Time1 Class Declaration
Class Time1's private int instance variables hour, minute and second (lines 6–8) represent the time in universal-time format (24-hour clock format in which hours are in the range 0–23, and minutes and seconds are each in the range 0–59). Time1 contains public methods setTime (lines 12–25), toUniversalString (lines 28–31) and toString (lines 34–39). These methods are also called the **public services** or the **public interface** that the class provides to its clients.

```
 1   // Fig. 8.1: Time1.java
 2   // Time1 class declaration maintains the time in 24-hour format.
 3
 4   public class Time1
 5   {
 6      private int hour;   // 0 - 23
 7      private int minute; // 0 - 59
 8      private int second; // 0 - 59
 9
10      // set a new time value using universal time; throw an
11      // exception if the hour, minute or second is invalid
12      public void setTime(int hour, int minute, int second)
13      {
14         // validate hour, minute and second
15         if (hour < 0 || hour >= 24 || minute < 0 || minute >= 60 ||
16            second < 0 || second >= 60)
17         {
18            throw new IllegalArgumentException(
19               "hour, minute and/or second was out of range");
20         }
21
22         this.hour = hour;
23         this.minute = minute;
24         this.second = second;
25      }
26
27      // convert to String in universal-time format (HH:MM:SS)
28      public String toUniversalString()
29      {
30         return String.format("%02d:%02d:%02d", hour, minute, second);
31      }
32
33      // convert to String in standard-time format (H:MM:SS AM or PM)
34      public String toString()
35      {
36         return String.format("%d:%02d:%02d %s",
37            ((hour == 0 || hour == 12) ? 12 : hour % 12),
38            minute, second, (hour < 12 ? "AM" : "PM"));
39      }
40   } // end class Time1
```

Fig. 8.1 | Time1 class declaration maintains the time in 24-hour format.

Default Constructor

In this example, class Time1 does *not* declare a constructor, so the compiler supplies a default constructor. Each instance variable implicitly receives the default int value. Instance variables also can be initialized when they're declared in the class body, using the same initialization syntax as with a local variable.

Method setTime and Throwing Exceptions

Method setTime (lines 12–25) is a public method that declares three int parameters and uses them to set the time. Lines 15–16 test each argument to determine whether the value is outside the proper range. The hour value must be greater than or equal to 0 and less than

24, because universal-time format represents hours as integers from 0 to 23 (e.g., 1 PM is hour 13 and 11 PM is hour 23; midnight is hour 0 and noon is hour 12). Similarly, both minute and second values must be greater than or equal to 0 and less than 60. For values outside these ranges, setTime **throws an exception** of type **IllegalArgumentException** (lines 18–19), which notifies the client code that an invalid argument was passed to the method. As you learned in Section 6.5, you can use try...catch to catch exceptions and attempt to recover from them, which we'll do in Fig. 8.2. The class instance creation expression in the **throw statement** (Fig. 8.1; line 18) creates a new object of type Illegal-ArgumentException. The parentheses following the class name indicate a call to the IllegalArgumentException constructor. In this case, we call the constructor that allows us to specify a custom error message. After the exception object is created, the throw statement immediately terminates method setTime and the exception is returned to the calling method that attempted to set the time. If the argument values are all valid, lines 22–24 assign them to the hour, minute and second instance variables.

 Software Engineering Observation 8.1

For a method like setTime in Fig. 8.1, validate all of the method's arguments before using them to set instance variable values to ensure that the object's data is modified only if all the arguments are valid.

Method *toUniversalString*

Method toUniversalString (lines 28–31) takes no arguments and returns a String in *universal-time format*, consisting of two digits each for the hour, minute and second—recall that you can use the 0 flag in a printf format specification (e.g., "%02d") to display leading zeros for a value that doesn't use all the character positions in the specified field width. For example, if the time were 1:30:07 PM, the method would return 13:30:07. Line 30 uses static method **format** of class String to return a String containing the formatted hour, minute and second values, each with two digits and possibly a leading 0 (specified with the 0 flag). Method format is similar to method System.out.printf except that format *returns* a formatted String rather than displaying it in a command window. The formatted String is returned by method toUniversalString.

Method *toString*

Method toString (lines 34–39) takes no arguments and returns a String in *standard-time format*, consisting of the hour, minute and second values separated by colons and followed by AM or PM (e.g., 11:30:17 AM or 1:27:06 PM). Like method toUniversalString, method toString uses static String method format to format the minute and second as two-digit values, with leading zeros if necessary. Line 37 uses a conditional operator (?:) to determine the value for hour in the String—if the hour is 0 or 12 (AM or PM), it appears as 12; otherwise, it appears as a value from 1 to 11. The conditional operator in line 30 determines whether AM or PM will be returned as part of the String.

Recall all objects in Java have a toString method that returns a String representation of the object. We chose to return a String containing the time in standard-time format. Method toString is called *implicitly* whenever a Time1 object appears in the code where a String is needed, such as the value to output with a %s format specifier in a call to System.out.printf. You may also call toString *explicitly* to obtain a String representation of a Time object.

Using Class *Time1*

Class Time1Test (Fig. 8.2) uses class Time1. Line 9 declares and creates a Time1 object time. Operator new implicitly invokes class Time1's default constructor, because Time1 does not declare any constructors. To confirm that the Time1 object was initialized properly, line 12 calls the private method displayTime (lines 35–39), which, in turn, calls the Time1 object's toUniversalString and toString methods to output the time in universal-time format and standard-time format, respectively. Note that toString could have been called implicitly here rather than explicitly. Next, line 16 invokes method setTime of the time object to change the time. Then line 17 calls displayTime again to output the time in both formats to confirm that it was set correctly.

Software Engineering Observation 8.2

*Recall from Chapter 7 that methods declared with access modifier private can be called only by other methods of the class in which the private methods are declared. Such methods are commonly referred to as **utility methods** or **helper methods** because they're typically used to support the operation of the class's other methods.*

```java
1   // Fig. 8.2: Time1Test.java
2   // Time1 object used in an app.
3
4   public class Time1Test
5   {
6      public static void main(String[] args)
7      {
8         // create and initialize a Time1 object
9         Time1 time = new Time1(); // invokes Time1 constructor
10
11        // output string representations of the time
12        displayTime("After time object is created", time);
13        System.out.println();
14
15        // change time and output updated time
16        time.setTime(13, 27, 6);
17        displayTime("After calling setTime", time);
18        System.out.println();
19
20        // attempt to set time with invalid values
21        try
22        {
23           time.setTime(99, 99, 99); // all values out of range
24        }
25        catch (IllegalArgumentException e)
26        {
27           System.out.printf("Exception: %s%n%n", e.getMessage());
28        }
29
30        // display time after attempt to set invalid values
31        displayTime("After calling setTime with invalid values", time);
32     }
```

Fig. 8.2 | Time1 object used in an app. (Part 1 of 2.)

```
33
34      // displays a Time1 object in 24-hour and 12-hour formats
35      private static void displayTime(String header, Time1 t)
36      {
37         System.out.printf("%s%nUniversal time: %s%nStandard time: %s%n",
38            header, t.toUniversalString(), t.toString());
39      }
40   } // end class Time1Test
```

```
After time object is created
Universal time: 00:00:00
Standard time: 12:00:00 AM

After calling setTime
Universal time: 13:27:06
Standard time: 1:27:06 PM

Exception: hour, minute and/or second was out of range

After calling setTime with invalid values
Universal time: 13:27:06
Standard time: 1:27:06 PM
```

Fig. 8.2 | Time1 object used in an app. (Part 2 of 2.)

Calling *Time1 Method* `setTime` *with Invalid Values*

To illustrate that method `setTime` *validates* its arguments, line 23 calls method `setTime` with *invalid* arguments of 99 for the `hour`, `minute` and `second`. This statement is placed in a `try` block (lines 21–24) in case `setTime` throws an `IllegalArgumentException`, which it will do since the arguments are all invalid. When this occurs, the exception is caught at lines 25–28, and line 27 displays the exception's error message by calling its `getMessage` method. Line 31 outputs the time again in both formats to confirm that `setTime` did *not* change the time when invalid arguments were supplied.

Software Engineering of the *Time1 Class Declaration*

Consider several issues of class design with respect to class `Time1`. The instance variables `hour`, `minute` and `second` are each declared `private`. The actual data representation used within the class is of no concern to the class's clients. For example, it would be perfectly reasonable for `Time1` to represent the time internally as the number of seconds since midnight or the number of minutes and seconds since midnight. Clients could use the same `public` methods and get the same results without being aware of this. (Exercise 8.5 asks you to represent the time in class `Time2` of Fig. 8.5 as the number of seconds since midnight and show that indeed no change is visible to the clients of the class.)

Software Engineering Observation 8.3

Classes simplify programming, because the client can use only a class's `public` *methods. Such methods are usually client oriented rather than implementation oriented. Clients are neither aware of, nor involved in, a class's implementation. Clients generally care about what the class does but not how the class does it.*

Software Engineering Observation 8.4

Interfaces change less frequently than implementations. When an implementation changes, implementation-dependent code must change accordingly. Hiding the implementation reduces the possibility that other program parts will become dependent on class implementation details.

Java SE 8—Date/Time API

This section's example and several of this chapter's later examples demonstrate various class-implementation concepts in classes that represent dates and times. In professional Java development, rather than building your own date and time classes, you'll typically re-use the ones provided by the Java API. Though Java has always had classes for manipulating dates and times, Java SE 8 introduces a new **Date/Time API**—defined by the classes in the package **java.time**—applications built with Java SE 8 should use the Date/Time API's capabilities, rather than those in earlier Java versions. The new API fixes various issues with the older classes and provides more robust, easier-to-use capabilities for manipulating dates, times, time zones, calendars and more. We use some Date/Time API features in Chapter 23. You can learn more about the Date/Time API's classes at:

```
download.java.net/jdk8/docs/api/java/time/package-summary.html
```

8.3 Controlling Access to Members

The access modifiers public and private control access to a class's variables and methods. In Chapter 9, we'll introduce the additional access modifier protected. The primary purpose of public methods is to present to the class's clients a view of the services the class provides (i.e., the class's public interface). Clients need not be concerned with how the class accomplishes its tasks. For this reason, the class's private variables and private methods (i.e., its *implementation details*) are *not* accessible to its clients.

Figure 8.3 demonstrates that private class members are *not* accessible outside the class. Lines 9–11 attempt to access the private instance variables hour, minute and second of the Time1 object time. When this program is compiled, the compiler generates error messages that these private members are not accessible. This program assumes that the Time1 class from Fig. 8.1 is used.

```java
 1   // Fig. 8.3: MemberAccessTest.java
 2   // Private members of class Time1 are not accessible.
 3   public class MemberAccessTest
 4   {
 5      public static void main(String[] args)
 6      {
 7         Time1 time = new Time1(); // create and initialize Time1 object
 8
 9         time.hour = 7; // error: hour has private access in Time1
10         time.minute = 15; // error: minute has private access in Time1
11         time.second = 30; // error: second has private access in Time1
12      }
13   } // end class MemberAccessTest
```

Fig. 8.3 | Private members of class Time1 are not accessible. (Part 1 of 2.)

```
MemberAccessTest.java:9: hour has private access in Time1
      time.hour = 7; // error: hour has private access in Time1
          ^
MemberAccessTest.java:10: minute has private access in Time1
      time.minute = 15; // error: minute has private access in Time1
          ^
MemberAccessTest.java:11: second has private access in Time1
      time.second = 30; // error: second has private access in Time1
          ^
3 errors
```

Fig. 8.3 | Private members of class `Time1` are not accessible. (Part 2 of 2.)

Common Programming Error 8.1

An attempt by a method that's not a member of a class to access a private member of that class generates a compilation error.

8.4 Referring to the Current Object's Members with the this Reference

Every object can access a *reference to itself* with keyword **this** (sometimes called the **this reference**). When an instance method is called for a particular object, the method's body *implicitly* uses keyword this to refer to the object's instance variables and other methods. This enables the class's code to know which object should be manipulated. As you'll see in Fig. 8.4, you can also use keyword this *explicitly* in an instance method's body. Section 8.5 shows another interesting use of keyword this. Section 8.11 explains why keyword this cannot be used in a static method.

We now demonstrate implicit and explicit use of the this reference (Fig. 8.4). This example is the first in which we declare *two* classes in one file—class ThisTest is declared in lines 4–11, and class SimpleTime in lines 14–47. We do this to demonstrate that when you compile a .java file containing more than one class, the compiler produces a separate class file with the .class extension for every compiled class. In this case, two separate files are produced—SimpleTime.class and ThisTest.class. When one source-code (.java) file contains multiple class declarations, the compiler places both class files for those classes in the *same* directory. Note also in Fig. 8.4 that only class ThisTest is declared public. A source-code file can contain only *one* public class—otherwise, a compilation error occurs. *Non-public classes* can be used only by other classes in the *same package*. So, in this example, class SimpleTime can be used only by class ThisTest.

```
1    // Fig. 8.4: ThisTest.java
2    // this used implicitly and explicitly to refer to members of an object.
3
4    public class ThisTest
5    {
6       public static void main(String[] args)
7       {
```

Fig. 8.4 | this used implicitly and explicitly to refer to members of an object. (Part 1 of 2.)

```
8              SimpleTime time = new SimpleTime(15, 30, 19);
9              System.out.println(time.buildString());
10         }
11    } // end class ThisTest
12
13    // class SimpleTime demonstrates the "this" reference
14    class SimpleTime
15    {
16        private int hour;   // 0-23
17        private int minute; // 0-59
18        private int second; // 0-59
19
20        // if the constructor uses parameter names identical to
21        // instance variable names the "this" reference is
22        // required to distinguish between the names
23        public SimpleTime(int hour, int minute, int second)
24        {
25            this.hour = hour;     // set "this" object's hour
26            this.minute = minute; // set "this" object's minute
27            this.second = second; // set "this" object's second
28        }
29
30        // use explicit and implicit "this" to call toUniversalString
31        public String buildString()
32        {
33            return String.format("%24s: %s%n%24s: %s",
34                "this.toUniversalString()", this.toUniversalString(),
35                "toUniversalString()", toUniversalString());
36        }
37
38        // convert to String in universal-time format (HH:MM:SS)
39        public String toUniversalString()
40        {
41            // "this" is not required here to access instance variables,
42            // because method does not have local variables with same
43            // names as instance variables
44            return String.format("%02d:%02d:%02d",
45                this.hour, this.minute, this.second);
46        }
47    } // end class SimpleTime
```

```
this.toUniversalString(): 15:30:19
    toUniversalString(): 15:30:19
```

Fig. 8.4 | `this` used implicitly and explicitly to refer to members of an object. (Part 2 of 2.)

Class SimpleTime (lines 14–47) declares three private instance variables—hour, minute and second (lines 16–18). The class's constructor (lines 23–28) receives three int arguments to initialize a SimpleTime object. Once again, we used parameter names for the constructor (line 23) that are *identical* to the class's instance-variable names (lines 16–18), so we use the this reference to refer to the instance variables in lines 25–27.

Error-Prevention Tip 8.1

Most IDEs will issue a warning if you say x = x; *instead of* this.x = x;. *The statement* x = x; *is often called a no-op (no operation).*

Method buildString (lines 31–36) returns a String created by a statement that uses the this reference explicitly and implicitly. Line 34 uses it *explicitly* to call method toUniversalString. Line 35 uses it *implicitly* to call the same method. Both lines perform the same task. You typically will not use this explicitly to reference other methods within the current object. Also, line 45 in method toUniversalString explicitly uses the this reference to access each instance variable. This is *not* necessary here, because the method does *not* have any local variables that shadow the instance variables of the class.

Performance Tip 8.1

Java conserves storage by maintaining only one copy of each method per class—this method is invoked by every object of the class. Each object, on the other hand, has its own copy of the class's instance variables. Each method of the class implicitly uses this *to determine the specific object of the class to manipulate.*

Class ThisTest's main method (lines 6–10) demonstrates class SimpleTime. Line 8 creates an instance of class SimpleTime and invokes its constructor. Line 9 invokes the object's buildString method, then displays the results.

8.5 Time Class Case Study: Overloaded Constructors

As you know, you can declare your own constructor to specify how objects of a class should be initialized. Next, we demonstrate a class with several **overloaded constructors** that enable objects of that class to be initialized in different ways. To overload constructors, simply provide multiple constructor declarations with different signatures.

Class *Time2 with Overloaded Constructors*

The Time1 class's default constructor in Fig. 8.1 initialized hour, minute and second to their default 0 values (i.e., midnight in universal time). The default constructor does not enable the class's clients to initialize the time with nonzero values. Class Time2 (Fig. 8.5) contains five overloaded constructors that provide convenient ways to initialize objects. In this program, four of the constructors invoke a fifth, which in turn ensures that the value supplied for hour is in the range 0 to 23, and the values for minute and second are each in the range 0 to 59. The compiler invokes the appropriate constructor by matching the number, types and order of the types of the arguments specified in the constructor call with the number, types and order of the types of the parameters specified in each constructor declaration. Class Time2 also provides *set* and *get* methods for each instance variable.

```
1   // Fig. 8.5: Time2.java
2   // Time2 class declaration with overloaded constructors.
3
4   public class Time2
5   {
```

Fig. 8.5 | Time2 class with overloaded constructors. (Part 1 of 4.)

```
 6      private int hour; // 0 - 23
 7      private int minute; // 0 - 59
 8      private int second; // 0 - 59
 9
10      // Time2 no-argument constructor:
11      // initializes each instance variable to zero
12      public Time2()
13      {
14         this(0, 0, 0); // invoke constructor with three arguments
15      }
16
17      // Time2 constructor: hour supplied, minute and second defaulted to 0
18      public Time2(int hour)
19      {
20         this(hour, 0, 0); // invoke constructor with three arguments
21      }
22
23      // Time2 constructor: hour and minute supplied, second defaulted to 0
24      public Time2(int hour, int minute)
25      {
26         this(hour, minute, 0); // invoke constructor with three arguments
27      }
28
29      // Time2 constructor: hour, minute and second supplied
30      public Time2(int hour, int minute, int second)
31      {
32         if (hour < 0 || hour >= 24)
33            throw new IllegalArgumentException("hour must be 0-23");
34
35         if (minute < 0 || minute >= 60)
36            throw new IllegalArgumentException("minute must be 0-59");
37
38         if (second < 0 || second >= 60)
39            throw new IllegalArgumentException("second must be 0-59");
40
41         this.hour = hour;
42         this.minute = minute;
43         this.second = second;
44      }
45
46      // Time2 constructor: another Time2 object supplied
47      public Time2(Time2 time)
48      {
49         // invoke constructor with three arguments
50         this(time.getHour(), time.getMinute(), time.getSecond());
51      }
52
53      // Set Methods
54      // set a new time value using universal time;
55      // validate the data
56      public void setTime(int hour, int minute, int second)
57      {
```

Fig. 8.5 | Time2 class with overloaded constructors. (Part 2 of 4.)

```
58          if (hour < 0 || hour >= 24)
59             throw new IllegalArgumentException("hour must be 0-23");
60
61          if (minute < 0 || minute >= 60)
62             throw new IllegalArgumentException("minute must be 0-59");
63
64          if (second < 0 || second >= 60)
65             throw new IllegalArgumentException("second must be 0-59");
66
67          this.hour = hour;
68          this.minute = minute;
69          this.second = second;
70       }
71
72       // validate and set hour
73       public void setHour(int hour)
74       {
75          if (hour < 0 || hour >= 24)
76             throw new IllegalArgumentException("hour must be 0-23");
77
78          this.hour = hour;
79       }
80
81       // validate and set minute
82       public void setMinute(int minute)
83       {
84          if (minute < 0 && minute >= 60)
85             throw new IllegalArgumentException("minute must be 0-59");
86
87          this.minute = minute;
88       }
89
90       // validate and set second
91       public void setSecond(int second)
92       {
93          if (second >= 0 && second < 60)
94             throw new IllegalArgumentException("second must be 0-59");
95
96          this.second = second;
97       }
98
99       // Get Methods
100      // get hour value
101      public int getHour()
102      {
103         return hour;
104      }
105
106      // get minute value
107      public int getMinute()
108      {
109         return minute;
110      }
```

Fig. 8.5 | Time2 class with overloaded constructors. (Part 3 of 4.)

```
111
112    // get second value
113    public int getSecond()
114    {
115       return second;
116    }
117
118    // convert to String in universal-time format (HH:MM:SS)
119    public String toUniversalString()
120    {
121       return String.format(
122          "%02d:%02d:%02d", getHour(), getMinute(), getSecond());
123    }
124
125    // convert to String in standard-time format (H:MM:SS AM or PM)
126    public String toString()
127    {
128       return String.format("%d:%02d:%02d %s",
129          ((getHour() == 0 || getHour() == 12) ? 12 : getHour() % 12),
130          getMinute(), getSecond(), (getHour() < 12 ? "AM" : "PM"));
131    }
132 } // end class Time2
```

Fig. 8.5 | Time2 class with overloaded constructors. (Part 4 of 4.)

Class **Time2***'s Constructors—Calling One Constructor from Another via* **this**

Lines 12–15 declare a so-called **no-argument constructor** that's invoked without arguments. Once you declare any constructors in a class, the compiler will *not* provide a *default constructor*. This no-argument constructor ensures that class Time2's clients can create Time2 objects with default values. Such a constructor simply initializes the object as specified in the constructor's body. In the body, we introduce a use of this that's allowed only as the *first* statement in a constructor's body. Line 14 uses this in method-call syntax to invoke the Time2 constructor that takes three parameters (lines 30–44) with values of 0 for the hour, minute and second. Using this as shown here is a popular way to *reuse* initialization code provided by another of the class's constructors rather than defining similar code in the no-argument constructor's body. We use this syntax in four of the five Time2 constructors to make the class easier to maintain and modify. If we need to change how objects of class Time2 are initialized, only the constructor that the class's other constructors call will need to be modified.

Common Programming Error 8.2

It's a compilation error when this is used in a constructor's body to call another of the class's constructors if that call is not the first statement in the constructor. It's also a compilation error when a method attempts to invoke a constructor directly via this.

Lines 18–21 declare a Time2 constructor with a single int parameter representing the hour, which is passed with 0 for the minute and second to the constructor at lines 30–44. Lines 24–27 declare a Time2 constructor that receives two int parameters representing the hour and minute, which are passed with 0 for the second to the constructor at lines 30–44. Like the no-argument constructor, each of these constructors invokes the constructor at lines 30–44 to minimize code duplication. Lines 30–44 declare the Time2 constructor that receives three `int` parameters representing the `hour`, `minute` and `second`. This constructor validates and initializes the instance variables.

Lines 47–51 declare a `Time2` constructor that receives a reference to another `Time2` object. The values from the `Time2` argument are passed to the three-argument constructor at lines 30–44 to initialize the `hour`, `minute` and `second`. Line 50 could have directly accessed the `hour`, `minute` and `second` values of the argument `time` with the expressions `time.hour`, `time.minute` and `time.second`—even though `hour`, `minute` and `second` are declared as `private` variables of class `Time2`. This is due to a special relationship between objects of the same class. We'll see in a moment why it's preferable to use the *get* methods.

Software Engineering Observation 8.5

When one object of a class has a reference to another object of the same class, the first object can access all *the second object's data and methods (including those that are* `private`*).*

Class *Time2's* `setTime` *Method*

Method `setTime` (lines 56–70) throws an `IllegalArgumentException` (lines 59, 62 and 65) if any the method's arguments is out of range. Otherwise, it sets `Time2`'s instance variables to the argument values (lines 67–69).

Notes Regarding Class *Time2's* set *and* get *Methods and Constructors*

`Time2`'s *get* methods are called throughout the class. In particular, methods `toUniversalString` and `toString` call methods `getHour`, `getMinute` and `getSecond` in line 122 and lines 129–130, respectively. In each case, these methods could have accessed the class's private data directly without calling the *get* methods. However, consider changing the representation of the time from three `int` values (requiring 12 bytes of memory) to a single `int` value representing the total number of seconds that have elapsed since midnight (requiring only four bytes of memory). If we made such a change, only the bodies of the methods that access the `private` data directly would need to change—in particular, the three-argument constructor, the `setTime` method and the individual *set* and *get* methods for the hour, `minute` and `second`. There would be no need to modify the bodies of methods `toUniversalString` or `toString` because they do *not* access the data directly. Designing the class in this manner reduces the likelihood of programming errors when altering the class's implementation.

Similarly, each `Time2` constructor could include a copy of the appropriate statements from the three-argument constructor. Doing so may be slightly more efficient, because the extra constructor calls are eliminated. But, *duplicating* statements makes changing the class's internal data representation more difficult. Having the `Time2` constructors call the constructor with three arguments requires that any changes to the implementation of the three-argument constructor be made only once. Also, the compiler can optimize programs by removing calls to simple methods and replacing them with the expanded code of their declarations—a technique known as **inlining the code**, which improves program performance.

Using Class *Time2's* Overloaded Constructors

Class `Time2Test` (Fig. 8.6) invokes the overloaded `Time2` constructors (lines 8–12 and 24). Line 8 invokes the `Time2` no-argument constructor. Lines 9–12 demonstrate passing arguments to the other `Time2` constructors. Line 9 invokes the single-argument constructor that receives an `int` at lines 18–21 of Fig. 8.5. Line 10 invokes the two-argument constructor at lines 24–27 of Fig. 8.5. Line 11 invokes the three-argument constructor at lines 30–44 of

Fig. 8.5. Line 12 invokes the single-argument constructor that takes a Time2 at lines 47–51 of Fig. 8.5. Next, the app displays the String representations of each Time2 object to confirm that it was initialized properly (lines 15–19). Line 24 attempts to initialize t6 by creating a new Time2 object and passing three *invalid* values to the constructor. When the constructor attempts to use the invalid hour value to initialize the object's hour, an IllegalArgumentException occurs. We catch this exception at line 26 and display its error message, which results in the last line of the output.

```
1   // Fig. 8.6: Time2Test.java
2   // Overloaded constructors used to initialize Time2 objects.
3
4   public class Time2Test
5   {
6      public static void main(String[] args)
7      {
8         Time2 t1 = new Time2(); // 00:00:00
9         Time2 t2 = new Time2(2); // 02:00:00
10        Time2 t3 = new Time2(21, 34); // 21:34:00
11        Time2 t4 = new Time2(12, 25, 42); // 12:25:42
12        Time2 t5 = new Time2(t4); // 12:25:42
13
14        System.out.println("Constructed with:");
15        displayTime("t1: all default arguments", t1);
16        displayTime("t2: hour specified; default minute and second", t2);
17        displayTime("t3: hour and minute specified; default second", t3);
18        displayTime("t4: hour, minute and second specified", t4);
19        displayTime("t5: Time2 object t4 specified", t5);
20
21        // attempt to initialize t6 with invalid values
22        try
23        {
24           Time2 t6 = new Time2(27, 74, 99); // invalid values
25        }
26        catch (IllegalArgumentException e)
27        {
28           System.out.printf("%nException while initializing t6: %s%n",
29              e.getMessage());
30        }
31     }
32
33     // displays a Time2 object in 24-hour and 12-hour formats
34     private static void displayTime(String header, Time2 t)
35     {
36        System.out.printf("%s%n   %s%n   %s%n",
37           header, t.toUniversalString(), t.toString());
38     }
39  } // end class Time2Test
```

```
Constructed with:
t1: all default arguments
   00:00:00
   12:00:00 AM
```

Fig. 8.6 | Overloaded constructors used to initialize Time2 objects. (Part 1 of 2.)

```
t2: hour specified; default minute and second
   02:00:00
   2:00:00 AM
t3: hour and minute specified; default second
   21:34:00
   9:34:00 PM
t4: hour, minute and second specified
   12:25:42
   12:25:42 PM
t5: Time2 object t4 specified
   12:25:42
   12:25:42 PM

Exception while initializing t6: hour must be 0-23
```

Fig. 8.6 | Overloaded constructors used to initialize `Time2` objects. (Part 2 of 2.)

8.6 Default and No-Argument Constructors

Every class *must* have at least *one* constructor. If you do not provide any in a class's declaration, the compiler creates a *default constructor* that takes *no* arguments when it's invoked. The default constructor initializes the instance variables to the initial values specified in their declarations or to their default values (zero for primitive numeric types, `false` for `boolean` values and `null` for references). In Section 9.4.1, you'll learn that the default constructor also performs another task.

Recall that if your class declares constructors, the compiler will *not* create a default constructor. In this case, you must declare a no-argument constructor if default initialization is required. Like a default constructor, a no-argument constructor is invoked with empty parentheses. The `Time2` no-argument constructor (lines 12–15 of Fig. 8.5) explicitly initializes a `Time2` object by passing to the three-argument constructor 0 for each parameter. Since 0 is the default value for `int` instance variables, the no-argument constructor in this example could actually be declared with an empty body. In this case, each instance variable would receive its default value when the no-argument constructor is called. If we omit the no-argument constructor, clients of this class would not be able to create a `Time2` object with the expression `new Time2()`.

Error-Prevention Tip 8.2

Ensure that you do not *include a return type in a constructor definition. Java allows other methods of the class besides its constructors to have the same name as the class and to specify return types. Such methods are* not *constructors and will* not *be called when an object of the class is instantiated.*

Common Programming Error 8.3

A compilation error occurs if a program attempts to initialize an object of a class by passing the wrong number or types of arguments to the class's constructor.

8.7 Notes on *Set* and *Get* Methods

As you know, a class's `private` fields can be manipulated *only* by its methods. A typical manipulation might be the adjustment of a customer's bank balance (e.g., a `private` instance variable of a class `BankAccount`) by a method `computeInterest`. *Set* methods are also commonly called **mutator methods**, because they typically *change* an object's state—i.e., *modify* the values of instance variables. *Get* methods are also commonly called **accessor methods** or **query methods**.

Set *and* Get *Methods vs.* `public` *Data*

It would seem that providing *set* and *get* capabilities is essentially the same as making a class's instance variables `public`. This is one of the subtleties that makes Java so desirable for software engineering. A `public` instance variable can be read or written by any method that has a reference to an object containing that variable. If an instance variable is declared `private`, a `public` *get* method certainly allows other methods to access it, but the *get* method can *control* how the client can access it. For example, a *get* method might control the format of the data it returns, shielding the client code from the actual data representation. A `public` *set* method can—and should—carefully scrutinize attempts to modify the variable's value and throw an exception if necessary. For example, attempts to *set* the day of the month to 37 or a person's weight to a negative value should be rejected. Thus, although *set* and *get* methods provide access to `private` data, the access is restricted by the implementation of the methods. This helps promote good software engineering.

Software Engineering Observation 8.6

Classes should never have `public` *nonconstant data, but declaring data* `public static final` *enables you to make constants available to clients of your class. For example, class* Math *offers* `public static final` *constants* Math.E *and* Math.PI.

Error-Prevention Tip 8.3

Do not provide `public static final` *constants if the constants' values are likely to change in future versions of your software.*

Validity Checking in Set *Methods*

The benefits of data integrity do not follow automatically simply because instance variables are declared `private`—you must provide validity checking. A class's *set* methods could determine that attempts were made to assign invalid data to objects of the class. Typically *set* methods have `void` return type and use exception handling to indicate attempts to assign invalid data. We discuss exception handling in detail in Chapter 11.

Software Engineering Observation 8.7

When appropriate, provide `public` *methods to change and retrieve the values of* `private` *instance variables. This architecture helps hide the implementation of a class from its clients, which improves program modifiability.*

Error-Prevention Tip 8.4

Using set *and* get *methods helps you create classes that are easier to debug and maintain. If only one method performs a particular task, such as setting an instance variable in an object, it's easier to debug and maintain the class. If the instance variable is not being set properly, the code that actually modifies instance variable is localized to one* set *method. Your debugging efforts can be focused on that one method.*

Predicate Methods

Another common use for accessor methods is to test whether a condition is *true* or *false*—such methods are often called **predicate methods.** An example would be class ArrayList's isEmpty method, which returns true if the ArrayList is empty and false otherwise. A program might test isEmpty before attempting to read another item from an ArrayList.

8.8 Composition

A class can have references to objects of other classes as members. This is called **composition** and is sometimes referred to as a *has-a* relationship. For example, an AlarmClock object needs to know the current time *and* the time when it's supposed to sound its alarm, so it's reasonable to include *two* references to Time objects in an AlarmClock object. A car *has-a* steering wheel, a break pedal and an accelerator pedal.

Class **Date**

This composition example contains classes Date (Fig. 8.7), Employee (Fig. 8.8) and EmployeeTest (Fig. 8.9). Class Date (Fig. 8.7) declares instance variables month, day and year (lines 6–8) to represent a date. The constructor receives three int parameters. Lines 17–19 validate the month—if it's out-of-range, lines 18–19 throw an exception. Lines 22–25 validate the day. If the day is incorrect based on the number of days in the particular month (except February 29th which requires special testing for leap years), lines 24–25 throw an exception. Lines 28–31 perform the leap year testing for February. If the month is February and the day is 29 and the year is not a leap year, lines 30–31 throw an exception. If no exceptions are thrown, then lines 33–35 initialize the Date's instance variables and lines 38–38 output the this reference as a String. Since this is a reference to the current Date object, the object's toString method (lines 42–45) is called *implicitly* to obtain the object's String representation. In this example, we assume that the value for year is correct—an industrial-strength Date class should also validate the year.

```
1   // Fig. 8.7: Date.java
2   // Date class declaration.
3
4   public class Date
5   {
6      private int month; // 1-12
7      private int day; // 1-31 based on month
8      private int year; // any year
9
10     private static final int[] daysPerMonth =
11        { 0, 31, 28, 31, 30, 31, 30, 31, 31, 30, 31, 30, 31 };
12
13     // constructor: confirm proper value for month and day given the year
14     public Date(int month, int day, int year)
15     {
16        // check if month in range
17        if (month <= 0 || month > 12)
18           throw new IllegalArgumentException(
19              "month (" + month + ") must be 1-12");
```

Fig. 8.7 | Date class declaration. (Part 1 of 2.)

```
20
21          // check if day in range for month
22          if (day <= 0 ||
23              (day > daysPerMonth[month] && !(month == 2 && day == 29)))
24              throw new IllegalArgumentException("day (" + day +
25                  ") out-of-range for the specified month and year");
26
27          // check for leap year if month is 2 and day is 29
28          if (month == 2 && day == 29 && !(year % 400 == 0 ||
29              (year % 4 == 0 && year % 100 != 0)))
30              throw new IllegalArgumentException("day (" + day +
31                  ") out-of-range for the specified month and year");
32
33          this.month = month;
34          this.day = day;
35          this.year = year;
36
37          System.out.printf(
38              "Date object constructor for date %s%n", this);
39      }
40
41      // return a String of the form month/day/year
42      public String toString()
43      {
44          return String.format("%d/%d/%d", month, day, year);
45      }
46  } // end class Date
```

Fig. 8.7 | Date class declaration. (Part 2 of 2.)

Class Employee

Class Employee (Fig. 8.8) has instance variables firstName, lastName, birthDate and hireDate. Members firstName and lastName are references to String objects. Members birthDate and hireDate are references to Date objects. This demonstrates that a class can have as instance variables references to objects of other classes. The Employee constructor (lines 12–19) takes four parameters representing the first name, last name, birth date and hire date. The objects referenced by the parameters are assigned to the Employee object's instance variables. When class Employee's toString method is called, it returns a String containing the employee's name and the String representations of the two Date objects. Each of these Strings is obtained with an *implicit* call to the Date class's toString method.

```
1   // Fig. 8.8: Employee.java
2   // Employee class with references to other objects.
3
4   public class Employee
5   {
6       private String firstName;
7       private String lastName;
8       private Date birthDate;
9       private Date hireDate;
```

Fig. 8.8 | Employee class with references to other objects. (Part 1 of 2.)

```
10
11      // constructor to initialize name, birth date and hire date
12      public Employee(String firstName, String lastName, Date birthDate,
13         Date hireDate)
14      {
15         this.firstName = firstName;
16         this.lastName = lastName;
17         this.birthDate = birthDate;
18         this.hireDate = hireDate;
19      }
20
21      // convert Employee to String format
22      public String toString()
23      {
24         return String.format("%s, %s  Hired: %s  Birthday: %s",
25            lastName, firstName, hireDate, birthDate);
26      }
27   } // end class Employee
```

Fig. 8.8 | Employee class with references to other objects. (Part 2 of 2.)

Class *EmployeeTest*

Class EmployeeTest (Fig. 8.9) creates two Date objects to represent an Employee's birthday and hire date, respectively. Line 10 creates an Employee and initializes its instance variables by passing to the constructor two Strings (representing the Employee's first and last names) and two Date objects (representing the birthday and hire date). Line 12 *implicitly* invokes the Employee's toString method to display the values of its instance variables and demonstrate that the object was initialized properly.

```
1   // Fig. 8.9: EmployeeTest.java
2   // Composition demonstration.
3
4   public class EmployeeTest
5   {
6      public static void main(String[] args)
7      {
8         Date birth = new Date(7, 24, 1949);
9         Date hire = new Date(3, 12, 1988);
10         Employee employee = new Employee("Bob", "Blue", birth, hire);
11
12         System.out.println(employee);
13      }
14   } // end class EmployeeTest
```

```
Date object constructor for date 7/24/1949
Date object constructor for date 3/12/1988
Blue, Bob  Hired: 3/12/1988  Birthday: 7/24/1949
```

Fig. 8.9 | Composition demonstration.

8.9 enum Types

In Fig. 5.8, we introduced the basic enum type, which defines a set of constants represented as unique identifiers. In that program the enum constants represented the game's status. In this section we discuss the relationship between enum types and classes. Like classes, all enum types are *reference* types. An enum type is declared with an **enum declaration**, which is a comma-separated list of *enum constants*—the declaration may optionally include other components of traditional classes, such as constructors, fields and methods (as you'll see momentarily). Each enum declaration declares an enum class with the following restrictions:

1. enum constants are *implicitly* final.

2. enum constants are *implicitly* static.

3. Any attempt to create an object of an enum type with operator new results in a compilation error.

The enum constants can be used anywhere constants can be used, such as in the case labels of switch statements and to control enhanced for statements.

Declaring Instance Variables, a Constructor and Methods in an enum Type

Figure 8.10 demonstrates instance variables, a constructor and methods in an enum type. The enum declaration (lines 5–37) contains two parts—the enum constants and the other members of the enum type. The first part (lines 8–13) declares six constants. Each is optionally followed by arguments that are passed to the **enum constructor** (lines 20–24). Like the constructors you've seen in classes, an enum constructor can specify any number of parameters and can be overloaded. In this example, the enum constructor requires two String parameters. To properly initialize each enum constant, we follow it with parentheses containing two String arguments. The second part (lines 16–36) declares the other members of the enum type—two instance variables (lines 16–17), a constructor (lines 20–24) and two methods (lines 27–30 and 33–36).

Lines 16–17 declare the instance variables title and copyrightYear. Each enum constant in enum type Book is actually an object of enum type Book that has its own copy of instance variables title and copyrightYear. The constructor (lines 20–24) takes two String parameters, one that specifies the book's title and one that specifies its copyright year. Lines 22–23 assign these parameters to the instance variables. Lines 27–36 declare methods, which return the book title and copyright year, respectively.

```
1   // Fig. 8.10: Book.java
2   // Declaring an enum type with a constructor and explicit instance fields
3   // and accessors for these fields
4
5   public enum Book
6   {
7      // declare constants of enum type
8      JHTP("Java How to Program", "2015"),
9      CHTP("C How to Program", "2013"),
10     IW3HTP("Internet & World Wide Web How to Program", "2012"),
```

Fig. 8.10 | Declaring an enum type with a constructor and explicit instance fields and accessors for these fields. (Part 1 of 2.)

```
11          CPPHTP("C++ How to Program", "2014"),
12          VBHTP("Visual Basic How to Program", "2014"),
13          CSHARPHTP("Visual C# How to Program", "2014");
14
15          // instance fields
16          private final String title; // book title
17          private final String copyrightYear; // copyright year
18
19          // enum constructor
20          Book(String title, String copyrightYear)
21          {
22             this.title = title;
23             this.copyrightYear = copyrightYear;
24          }
25
26          // accessor for field title
27          public String getTitle()
28          {
29             return title;
30          }
31
32          // accessor for field copyrightYear
33          public String getCopyrightYear()
34          {
35             return copyrightYear;
36          }
37       } // end enum Book
```

Fig. 8.10 | Declaring an enum type with a constructor and explicit instance fields and accessors for these fields. (Part 2 of 2.)

Using enum type Book

Figure 8.11 tests the enum type Book and illustrates how to iterate through a range of enum constants. For every enum, the compiler generates the static method **values** (called in line 12) that returns an array of the enum's constants in the order they were declared. Lines 12–14 use the enhanced for statement to display all the constants declared in the enum Book. Line 14 invokes the enum Book's getTitle and getCopyrightYear methods to get the title and copyright year associated with the constant. When an enum constant is converted to a String (e.g., book in line 13), the constant's identifier is used as the String representation (e.g., JHTP for the first enum constant).

```
1    // Fig. 8.11: EnumTest.java
2    // Testing enum type Book.
3    import java.util.EnumSet;
4
5    public class EnumTest
6    {
7       public static void main(String[] args)
8       {
```

Fig. 8.11 | Testing enum type Book. (Part 1 of 2.)

```
9            System.out.println("All books:");
10
11           // print all books in enum Book
12           for (Book book : Book.values())
13              System.out.printf("%-10s%-45s%s%n", book,
14                 book.getTitle(), book.getCopyrightYear());
15
16           System.out.printf("%nDisplay a range of enum constants:%n");
17
18           // print first four books
19           for (Book book : EnumSet.range(Book.JHTP, Book.CPPHTP))
20              System.out.printf("%-10s%-45s%s%n", book,
21                 book.getTitle(), book.getCopyrightYear());
22       }
23    } // end class EnumTest
```

```
All books:
JHTP       Java How to Program                          2015
CHTP       C How to Program                             2013
IW3HTP     Internet & World Wide Web How to Program     2012
CPPHTP     C++ How to Program                           2014
VBHTP      Visual Basic How to Program                  2014
CSHARPHTP  Visual C# How to Program                     2014

Display a range of enum constants:
JHTP       Java How to Program                          2015
CHTP       C How to Program                             2013
IW3HTP     Internet & World Wide Web How to Program     2012
CPPHTP     C++ How to Program                           2014
```

Fig. 8.11 | Testing enum type Book. (Part 2 of 2.)

Lines 19–21 use the `static` method **range** of class **EnumSet** (declared in package `java.util`) to display a range of the enum Book's constants. Method `range` takes two parameters—the first and the last enum constants in the range—and returns an `EnumSet` that contains all the constants between these two constants, inclusive. For example, the expression `EnumSet.range(Book.JHTP, Book.CPPHTP)` returns an `EnumSet` containing `Book.JHTP`, `Book.CHTP`, `Book.IW3HTP` and `Book.CPPHTP`. The enhanced `for` statement can be used with an `EnumSet` just as it can with an array, so lines 12–14 use it to display the title and copyright year of every book in the `EnumSet`. Class `EnumSet` provides several other `static` methods for creating sets of enum constants from the same enum type.

Common Programming Error 8.4
In an enum declaration, it's a syntax error to declare enum constants after the enum type's constructors, fields and methods.

8.10 Garbage Collection

Every object uses system resources, such as memory. We need a disciplined way to give resources back to the system when they're no longer needed; otherwise, "resource leaks" might occur that would prevent resources from being reused by your program or possibly by other programs. The JVM performs automatic **garbage collection** to reclaim the *memory* occupied by objects that are no longer used. When there are *no more references* to an object, the object is *eligible* to be collected. Collection typically occurs when the JVM executes its **garbage collector**, which may not happen for a while, or even at all before a program terminates. So, memory leaks that are common in other languages like C and C++ (because memory is *not* automatically reclaimed in those languages) are *less* likely in Java, but some can still happen in subtle ways. Resource leaks other than memory leaks can also occur. For example, an app may open a file on disk to modify its contents—if the app does not close the file, it must terminate before any other app can use the file.

A Note about Class `Object`'s `finalize` Method
Every class in Java has the methods of class `Object` (package `java.lang`), one of which is method **`finalize`**. (You'll learn more about class `Object` in Chapter 9.) You should *never* use method `finalize`, because it can cause many problems and there's uncertainty as to whether it will *ever* get called before a program terminates.

The original intent of `finalize` was to allow the garbage collector to perform **termination housekeeping** on an object just before reclaiming the object's memory. Now, it's considered better practice for any class that uses system resources—such as files on disk—to provide a method that programmers can call to release resources when they're no longer needed in a program. `AutoClosable` objects reduce the likelihood of resource leaks when you use them with the try-with-resources statement. As its name implies, an `AutoClosable` object is closed automatically, once a try-with-resources statement finishes using the object. We discuss this in more detail in Section 11.12.

> **Software Engineering Observation 8.8**
> *Many Java API classes (e.g., class Scanner and classes that read files from or write files to disk) provide close or dispose methods that programmers can call to release resources when they're no longer needed in a program.*

8.11 `static` Class Members
Every object has its own copy of all the instance variables of the class. In certain cases, only one copy of a particular variable should be *shared* by all objects of a class. A **static field**—called a **class variable**—is used in such cases. A `static` variable represents **classwide information**—all objects of the class share the *same* piece of data. The declaration of a `static` variable begins with the keyword `static`.

Motivating `static`
Let's motivate `static` data with an example. Suppose that we have a video game with Martians and other space creatures. Each `Martian` tends to be brave and willing to attack other space creatures when the `Martian` is aware that at least four other `Martian`s are present. If fewer than five `Martian`s are present, each of them becomes cowardly. Thus, each `Martian` needs to know the `martianCount`. We could endow class `Martian` with `martianCount` as an *instance variable*. If we do this, then every `Martian` will have *a separate copy* of the instance variable, and every time we create a new `Martian`, we'll have to update the instance variable `martianCount` in every `Martian` object. This wastes space with the redundant copies, wastes time in updating the separate copies and is error prone. Instead, we declare mar-

tianCount to be static, making martianCount classwide data. Every Martian can see the martianCount as if it were an instance variable of class Martian, but only *one* copy of the static martianCount is maintained. This saves space. We save time by having the Martian constructor increment the static martianCount—there's only one copy, so we do not have to increment separate copies for each Martian object.

Software Engineering Observation 8.9
Use a static variable when all objects of a class must use the same copy of the variable.

Class Scope

Static variables have *class scope*—they can be used in all of the class's methods. We can access a class's public static members through a reference to any object of the class, or by qualifying the member name with the class name and a dot (.), as in Math.random(). A class's private static class members can be accessed by client code only through methods of the class. Actually, *static class members exist even when no objects of the class exist*— they're available as soon as the class is loaded into memory at execution time. To access a public static member when no objects of the class exist (and even when they do), prefix the class name and a dot (.) to the static member, as in Math.PI. To access a private static member when no objects of the class exist, provide a public static method and call it by qualifying its name with the class name and a dot.

Software Engineering Observation 8.10
Static class variables and methods exist, and can be used, even if no objects of that class have been instantiated.

static *Methods Cannot Directly Access Instance Variables and Instance Methods*

A static method *cannot* access a class's instance variables and instance methods, because a static method can be called even when no objects of the class have been instantiated. For the same reason, the this reference *cannot* be used in a static method. The this reference must refer to a specific object of the class, and when a static method is called, there might not be any objects of its class in memory.

Common Programming Error 8.5
A compilation error occurs if a static method calls an instance method in the same class by using only the method name. Similarly, a compilation error occurs if a static method attempts to access an instance variable in the same class by using only the variable name.

Common Programming Error 8.6
Referring to this in a static method is a compilation error.

Tracking the Number of Employee Objects That Have Been Created

Our next program declares two classes—Employee (Fig. 8.12) and EmployeeTest (Fig. 8.13). Class Employee declares private static variable count (Fig. 8.12, line 7) and public static method getCount (lines 36–39). The static variable count maintains a count of the number of objects of class Employee that have been created so far. This class variable is initialized to zero in line 7. If a static variable is *not* initialized, the compiler assigns it a default value—in this case 0, the default value for type int.

```java
1    // Fig. 8.12: Employee.java
2    // static variable used to maintain a count of the number of
3    // Employee objects in memory.
4
5    public class Employee
6    {
7       private static int count = 0; // number of Employees created
8       private String firstName;
9       private String lastName;
10
11      // initialize Employee, add 1 to static count and
12      // output String indicating that constructor was called
13      public Employee(String firstName, String lastName)
14      {
15         this.firstName = firstName;
16         this.lastName = lastName;
17
18         ++count;  // increment static count of employees
19         System.out.printf("Employee constructor: %s %s; count = %d%n",
20            firstName, lastName, count);
21      }
22
23      // get first name
24      public String getFirstName()
25      {
26         return firstName;
27      }
28
29      // get last name
30      public String getLastName()
31      {
32         return lastName;
33      }
34
35      // static method to get static count value
36      public static int getCount()
37      {
38         return count;
39      }
40   } // end class Employee
```

Fig. 8.12 | static variable used to maintain a count of the number of Employee objects in memory.

When Employee objects exist, variable count can be used in any method of an Employee object—this example increments count in the constructor (line 18). The public static method getCount (lines 36–39) returns the number of Employee objects that have been created so far. When no objects of class Employee exist, client code can access variable count by calling method getCount via the class name, as in Employee.getCount(). When objects exist, method getCount can also be called via any reference to an Employee object.

Good Programming Practice 8.1

Invoke every static method by using the class name and a dot (.) to emphasize that the method being called is a static method.

Class EmployeeTest

EmployeeTest method main (Fig. 8.13) instantiates two Employee objects (lines 13–14). When each Employee object's constructor is invoked, lines 15–16 of Fig. 8.12 assign the Employee's first name and last name to instance variables firstName and lastName. These two statements do *not* make copies of the original String arguments. Actually, String objects in Java are **immutable**—they cannot be modified after they're created. Therefore, it's safe to have *many* references to one String object. This is not normally the case for objects of most other classes in Java. If String objects are immutable, you might wonder why we're able to use operators + and += to concatenate String objects. String-concatenation actually results in a *new* String object containing the concatenated values. The original String objects are *not* modified.

```java
1  // Fig. 8.13: EmployeeTest.java
2  // static member demonstration.
3
4  public class EmployeeTest
5  {
6     public static void main(String[] args)
7     {
8        // show that count is 0 before creating Employees
9        System.out.printf("Employees before instantiation: %d%n",
10          Employee.getCount());
11
12       // create two Employees; count should be 2
13       Employee e1 = new Employee("Susan", "Baker");
14       Employee e2 = new Employee("Bob", "Blue");
15
16       // show that count is 2 after creating two Employees
17       System.out.printf("%nEmployees after instantiation:%n");
18       System.out.printf("via e1.getCount(): %d%n", e1.getCount());
19       System.out.printf("via e2.getCount(): %d%n", e2.getCount());
20       System.out.printf("via Employee.getCount(): %d%n",
21          Employee.getCount());
22
23       // get names of Employees
24       System.out.printf("%nEmployee 1: %s %s%nEmployee 2: %s %s%n",
25          e1.getFirstName(), e1.getLastName(),
26          e2.getFirstName(), e2.getLastName());
27    }
28 } // end class EmployeeTest
```

```
Employees before instantiation: 0
Employee constructor: Susan Baker; count = 1
Employee constructor: Bob Blue; count = 2
```

Fig. 8.13 | static member demonstration. (Part 1 of 2.)

```
Employees after instantiation:
via e1.getCount(): 2
via e2.getCount(): 2
via Employee.getCount(): 2

Employee 1: Susan Baker
Employee 2: Bob Blue
```

Fig. 8.13 | `static` member demonstration. (Part 2 of 2.)

When `main` terminates, local variables `e1` and `e2` are discarded—remember that a local variable exists *only* until the block in which it's declared completes execution. Because `e1` and `e2` were the only references to the `Employee` objects created in lines 13–14 (Fig. 8.13), these objects become "eligible for garbage collection" as `main` terminates.

In a typical app, the garbage collector *might* eventually reclaim the memory for any objects that are eligible for collection. If any objects are not reclaimed before the program terminates, the operating system will reclaim the memory used by the program. The JVM does *not* guarantee when, or even whether, the garbage collector will execute. When it does, it's possible that no objects or only a subset of the eligible objects will be collected.

8.12 static Import

In Section 5.3, you learned about the `static` fields and methods of class `Math`. We access class `Math`'s `static` fields and *methods* by preceding each with the class name `Math` and a dot (`.`). A **static import** declaration enables you to import the `static` members of a class or interface so you can access them via their *unqualified names* in your class—that is, the class name and a dot (`.`) are *not* required when using an imported `static` member.

static *Import Forms*
A static import declaration has two forms—one that imports a particular `static` member (which is known as **single static import**) and one that imports *all* `static` members of a class (known as **static import on demand**). The following syntax imports a particular static member:

> **import static** *packageName*.*ClassName*.*staticMemberName*;

where *packageName* is the package of the class (e.g., `java.lang`), *ClassName* is the name of the class (e.g., `Math`) and *staticMemberName* is the name of the `static` field or method (e.g., `PI` or `abs`). The following syntax imports *all* `static` members of a class:

> **import static** *packageName*.*ClassName*.*;

The asterisk (`*`) indicates that *all* `static` members of the specified class should be available for use in the file. `static` import declarations import *only* `static` class members. Regular `import` statements should be used to specify the classes used in a program.

Demonstrating static *Import*
Figure 8.14 demonstrates a `static` import. Line 3 is a `static` import declaration, which imports *all* `static` fields and methods of class `Math` from package `java.lang`. Lines 9–12 access the `Math` class's `static` fields `E` (line 11) and `PI` (line 12) and the `static` methods

sqrt (line 9) and ceil (line 10) *without* preceding the field names or method names with class name Math and a dot.

Common Programming Error 8.7

A compilation error occurs if a program attempts to import two or more classes' static methods that have the same signature or static fields that have the same name.

```java
1   // Fig. 8.14: StaticImportTest.java
2   // Static import of Math class methods.
3   import static java.lang.Math.*;
4
5   public class StaticImportTest
6   {
7      public static void main(String[] args)
8      {
9         System.out.printf("sqrt(900.0) = %.1f%n", sqrt(900.0));
10        System.out.printf("ceil(-9.8) = %.1f%n", ceil(-9.8));
11        System.out.printf("E = %f%n", E);
12        System.out.printf("PI = %f%n", PI);
13     }
14  } // end class StaticImportTest
```

```
sqrt(900.0) = 30.0
ceil(-9.8) = -9.0
E = 2.718282
PI = 3.141593
```

Fig. 8.14 | static import of Math class methods.

8.13 final Instance Variables

The **principle of least privilege** is fundamental to good software engineering. In the context of an app's code, it states that code should be granted only the amount of privilege and access that it needs to accomplish its designated task, but no more. This makes your programs more robust by preventing code from accidentally (or maliciously) modifying variable values and calling methods that should *not* be accessible.

Let's see how this principle applies to instance variables. Some of them need to be *modifiable* and some do not. You can use the keyword final to specify that a variable is *not* modifiable (i.e., it's a *constant*) and that any attempt to modify it is an error. For example,

        private final int INCREMENT;

declares a final (constant) instance variable INCREMENT of type int. Such variables can be initialized when they're declared. If they're not, they *must* be initialized in every constructor of the class. Initializing constants in constructors enables each object of the class to have a different value for the constant. If a final variable is *not* initialized in its declaration or in every constructor, a compilation error occurs.

Software Engineering Observation 8.11

Declaring an instance variable as final helps enforce the principle of least privilege. If an instance variable should not be modified, declare it to be final to prevent modification. For example, in Fig. 8.8, the instance variables firstName, lastName, birthDate and hireDate are never modified after they're initialized, so they should be declared final. We'll enforce this practice in all programs going forward. You'll see additional benefits of final in Chapter 23, Concurrency.

Common Programming Error 8.8

Attempting to modify a final instance variable after it's initialized is a compilation error.

Error-Prevention Tip 8.5

Attempts to modify a final instance variable are caught at compilation time rather than causing execution-time errors. It's always preferable to get bugs out at compilation time, if possible, rather than allow them to slip through to execution time (where experience has found that repair is often many times more expensive).

Software Engineering Observation 8.12

A final field should also be declared static if it's initialized in its declaration to a value that's the same for all objects of the class. After this initialization, its value can never change. Therefore, we don't need a separate copy of the field for every object of the class. Making the field static enables all objects of the class to share the final field.

8.14 Package Access

If no access modifier (public, protected or private—we discuss protected in Chapter 9) is specified for a method or variable when it's declared in a class, the method or variable is considered to have **package access**. In a program that consists of one class declaration, this has no specific effect. However, if a program uses *multiple* classes from the *same* package (i.e., a group of related classes), these classes can access each other's package-access members directly through references to objects of the appropriate classes, or in the case of static members through the class name. Package access is rarely used.

Figure 8.15 demonstrates package access. The app contains two classes in one source-code file—the PackageDataTest class containing main (lines 5–21) and the PackageData class (lines 24–41). Classes in the same source file are part of the same package. Consequently, class PackageDataTest is allowed to modify the package-access data of Package-Data objects. When you compile this program, the compiler produces two separate .class files—PackageDataTest.class and PackageData.class. The compiler places the two .class files in the same directory. You can also place class PackageData (lines 24–41) in a separate source-code file.

In the PackageData class declaration, lines 26–27 declare the instance variables number and string with no access modifiers—therefore, these are package-access instance variables. Class PackageDataTest's main method creates an instance of the PackageData class (line 9) to demonstrate the ability to modify the PackageData instance variables directly (as shown in lines 15–16). The results of the modification can be seen in the output window.

```
 1   // Fig. 8.15: PackageDataTest.java
 2   // Package-access members of a class are accessible by other classes
 3   // in the same package.
 4
 5   public class PackageDataTest
 6   {
 7      public static void main(String[] args)
 8      {
 9         PackageData packageData = new PackageData();
10
11         // output String representation of packageData
12         System.out.printf("After instantiation:%n%s%n", packageData);
13
14         // change package access data in packageData object
15         packageData.number = 77;
16         packageData.string = "Goodbye";
17
18         // output String representation of packageData
19         System.out.printf("%nAfter changing values:%n%s%n", packageData);
20      }
21   } // end class PackageDataTest
22
23   // class with package access instance variables
24   class PackageData
25   {
26      int number; // package-access instance variable
27      String string; // package-access instance variable
28
29      // constructor
30      public PackageData()
31      {
32         number = 0;
33         string = "Hello";
34      }
35
36      // return PackageData object String representation
37      public String toString()
38      {
39         return String.format("number: %d; string: %s", number, string);
40      }
41   } // end class PackageData
```

```
After instantiation:
number: 0; string: Hello

After changing values:
number: 77; string: Goodbye
```

Fig. 8.15 | Package-access members of a class are accessible by other classes in the same package.

8.15 Using BigDecimal for Precise Monetary Calculations

In earlier chapters, we demonstrated monetary calculations using values of type double. In Chapter 4, we discussed the fact that some double values are represented *approximately*.

Any application that requires precise floating-point calculations—such as those in financial applications—should instead use class **BigDecimal** (from package **java.math**).

Interest Calculations Using *BigDecimal*

Figure 8.16 reimplements the interest calculation example of Fig. 4.6 using objects of class BigDecimal to perform the calculations. We also introduce class **NumberFormat** (package **java.text**) for formatting numeric values as *locale-specific* Strings—for example, in the U.S. locale, the value 1234.56, would be formatted as "1,234.56", whereas in many European locales it would be formatted as "1.234,56".

```java
1  // Interest.java
2  // Compound-interest calculations with BigDecimal.
3  import java.math.BigDecimal;
4  import java.text.NumberFormat;
5
6  public class Interest
7  {
8     public static void main(String args[])
9     {
10        // initial principal amount before interest
11        BigDecimal principal = BigDecimal.valueOf(1000.0);
12        BigDecimal rate = BigDecimal.valueOf(0.05); // interest rate
13
14        // display headers
15        System.out.printf("%s%20s%n", "Year", "Amount on deposit");
16
17        // calculate amount on deposit for each of ten years
18        for (int year = 1; year <= 10; year++)
19        {
20           // calculate new amount for specified year
21           BigDecimal amount =
22              principal.multiply(rate.add(BigDecimal.ONE).pow(year));
23
24           // display the year and the amount
25           System.out.printf("%4d%20s%n", year,
26              NumberFormat.getCurrencyInstance().format(amount));
27        }
28     }
29  } // end class Interest
```

```
Year    Amount on deposit
   1           $1,050.00
   2           $1,102.50
   3           $1,157.62
   4           $1,215.51
   5           $1,276.28
   6           $1,340.10
   7           $1,407.10
   8           $1,477.46
   9           $1,551.33
  10           $1,628.89
```

Fig. 8.16 | Compound-interest calculations with BigDecimal.

Creating BigDecimal Objects

Lines 11–12 declare and initialize `BigDecimal` variables `principal` and `rate` using the `BigDecimal` static method **valueOf** that receives a `double` argument and returns a `Big-Decimal` object that represents the *exact* value specified.

Performing the Interest Calculations with BigDecimal

Lines 21–22 perform the interest calculation using `BigDecimal` methods **multiply**, **add** and **pow**. The expression in line 22 evaluates as follows:

1. First, the expression `rate.add(BigDecimal.ONE)` adds 1 to the `rate` to produce a `BigDecimal` containing 1.05—this is equivalent to 1.0 + rate in line 19 of Fig. 4.6. The `BigDecimal` constant **ONE** represents the value 1. Class `BigDecimal` also provides the commonly used constants **ZERO** (0) and **TEN** (10).

2. Next, `BigDecimal` method pow is called on the preceding result to raise 1.05 to the power year—this is equivalent to passing 1.0 + rate and year to method `Math.pow` in line 19 of Fig. 4.6.

3. Finally, we call `BigDecimal` method `multiply` on the `principal` object, passing the preceding result as the argument. This returns a `BigDecimal` representing the amount on deposit at the end of the specified year.

Since the expression `rate.add(BigDecimal.ONE)` produces the same value in each iteration of the loop, we could have simply initialized rate to 1.05 in line 12; however, we chose to mimic the precise calculations we used in line 19 of Fig. 4.6.

Formatting Currency Values with NumberFormat

During each iteration of the loop, line 26

```
NumberFormat.getCurrencyInstance().format(amount)
```

evaluates as follows:

1. First, the expression uses `NumberFormat`'s static method **getCurrencyInstance** to get a `NumberFormat` that's pre-configured to format numeric values as locale-specific currency `Strings`—for example, in the U.S. locale, the numeric value 1628.89 is formatted as $1,628.89. Locale-specific formatting is an important part of **internationalization**—the process of customizing your applications for users' various locales and spoken languages.

2. Next, the expression invokes method `NumberFormat` method **format** (on the object returned by `getCurrencyInstance`) to perform the formatting of the amount value. Method `format` then returns the locale-specific `String` representation, rounded to two-digits to the right of the decimal point.

Rounding BigDecimal Values

In addition to precise calculations, `BigDecimal` also gives you control over how values are rounded—by default all calculations are exact and *no* rounding occurs. If you do not specify how to round `BigDecimal` values and a given value cannot be represented exactly—such as the result of 1 divided by 3, which is 0.3333333...—an `ArithmeticException` occurs.

Though we do not do so in this example, you can specify the *rounding mode* for `Big-Decimal` by supplying a `MathContext` object (package `java.math`) to class `BigDecimal`'s constructor when you create a `BigDecimal`. You may also provide a `MathContext` to various `BigDecimal` methods that perform calculations. Class `MathContext` contains several pre-configured `MathContext` objects that you can learn about at

> http://docs.oracle.com/javase/7/docs/api/java/math/MathContext.html

By default, each pre-configured `MathContext` uses so called "bankers rounding" as explained for the `RoundingMode` constant `HALF_EVEN` at:

> http://docs.oracle.com/javase/7/docs/api/java/math/
> RoundingMode.html#HALF_EVEN

Scaling *BigDecimal* Values

A `BigDecimal`'s scale is the number of digits to the right of its decimal point. If you need a `BigDecimal` rounded to a specific digit, you can call `BigDecimal` method `setScale`. For example, the following expression returns a `BigDecimal` with two digits to the right of the decimal point and using bankers rounding:

> amount.setScale(2, RoundingMode.HALF_EVEN)

8.16 (Optional) GUI and Graphics Case Study: Using Objects with Graphics

Most of the graphics you've seen to this point did not vary with each program execution. Exercise 5.2 in Section 5.13 asked you to create a program that generated shapes and colors at random. In that exercise, the drawing changed every time the system called paint-Component. To create a more consistent drawing that remains the same each time it's drawn, we must store information about the displayed shapes so that we can reproduce them each time the system calls paintComponent. To do this, we'll create a set of shape classes that store information about each shape. We'll make these classes "smart" by allowing objects of these classes to draw themselves by using a Graphics object.

Class *MyLine*

Figure 8.17 declares class `MyLine`, which has all these capabilities. Class `MyLine` imports classes `Color` and `Graphics` (lines 3–4). Lines 8–11 declare instance variables for the coordinates of the endpoints needed to draw a line, and line 12 declares the instance variable that stores the color of the line. The constructor at lines 15–22 takes five parameters, one for each instance variable that it initializes. Method draw at lines 25–29 requires a Graphics object and uses it to draw the line in the proper color and between the endpoints.

```
1   // Fig. 8.17: MyLine.java
2   // MyLine class represents a line.
3   import java.awt.Color;
4   import java.awt.Graphics;
5
6   public class MyLine
7   {
```

Fig. 8.17 | MyLine class represents a line. (Part 1 of 2.)

```
 8        private int x1; // x-coordinate of first endpoint
 9        private int y1; // y-coordinate of first endpoint
10        private int x2; // x-coordinate of second endpoint
11        private int y2; // y-coordinate of second endpoint
12        private Color color; // color of this line
13
14        // constructor with input values
15        public MyLine(int x1, int y1, int x2, int y2, Color color)
16        {
17           this.x1 = x1;
18           this.y1 = y1;
19           this.x2 = x2;
20           this.y2 = y2;
21           this.color = color;
22        }
23
24        // Draw the line in the specified color
25        public void draw(Graphics g)
26        {
27           g.setColor(color);
28           g.drawLine(x1, y1, x2, y2);
29        }
30     } // end class MyLine
```

Fig. 8.17 | MyLine class represents a line. (Part 2 of 2.)

Class *DrawPanel*

In Fig. 8.18, we declare class DrawPanel, which will generate random objects of class MyLine. Line 12 declares the MyLine array lines to store the lines to draw. Inside the constructor (lines 15–37), line 17 sets the background color to Color.WHITE. Line 19 creates the array with a random length between 5 and 9. The loop at lines 22–36 creates a new MyLine for every element in the array. Lines 25–28 generate random coordinates for each line's endpoints, and lines 31–32 generate a random color for the line. Line 35 creates a new MyLine object with the randomly generated values and stores it in the array. Method paintComponent iterates through the MyLine objects in array lines using an enhanced for statement (lines 45–46). Each iteration calls the draw method of the current MyLine object and passes it the Graphics object for drawing on the panel.

```
 1     // Fig. 8.18: DrawPanel.java
 2     // Program that uses class MyLine
 3     // to draw random lines.
 4     import java.awt.Color;
 5     import java.awt.Graphics;
 6     import java.security.SecureRandom;
 7     import javax.swing.JPanel;
 8
 9     public class DrawPanel extends JPanel
10     {
11        private SecureRandom randomNumbers = new SecureRandom();
12        private MyLine[] lines; // array of lines
```

Fig. 8.18 | Program that uses class MyLine to draw random lines. (Part 1 of 2.)

```
13
14      // constructor, creates a panel with random shapes
15      public DrawPanel()
16      {
17         setBackground(Color.WHITE);
18
19         lines = new MyLine[5 + randomNumbers.nextInt(5)];
20
21         // create lines
22         for (int count = 0; count < lines.length; count++)
23         {
24            // generate random coordinates
25            int x1 = randomNumbers.nextInt(300);
26            int y1 = randomNumbers.nextInt(300);
27            int x2 = randomNumbers.nextInt(300);
28            int y2 = randomNumbers.nextInt(300);
29
30            // generate a random color
31            Color color = new Color(randomNumbers.nextInt(256),
32               randomNumbers.nextInt(256), randomNumbers.nextInt(256));
33
34            // add the line to the list of lines to be displayed
35            lines[count] = new MyLine(x1, y1, x2, y2, color);
36         }
37      }
38
39      // for each shape array, draw the individual shapes
40      public void paintComponent(Graphics g)
41      {
42         super.paintComponent(g);
43
44         // draw the lines
45         for (MyLine line : lines)
46            line.draw(g);
47      }
48   } // end class DrawPanel
```

Fig. 8.18 | Program that uses class MyLine to draw random lines. (Part 2 of 2.)

Class TestDraw

Class TestDraw in Fig. 8.19 sets up a new window to display our drawing. Since we're setting the coordinates for the lines only once in the constructor, the drawing does not change if paintComponent is called to refresh the drawing on the screen.

```
1   // Fig. 8.19: TestDraw.java
2   // Creating a JFrame to display a DrawPanel.
3   import javax.swing.JFrame;
4
5   public class TestDraw
6   {
```

Fig. 8.19 | Creating a JFrame to display a DrawPanel. (Part 1 of 2.)

```
 7      public static void main(String[] args)
 8      {
 9         DrawPanel panel = new DrawPanel();
10         JFrame app = new JFrame();
11
12         app.setDefaultCloseOperation(JFrame.EXIT_ON_CLOSE);
13         app.add(panel);
14         app.setSize(300, 300);
15         app.setVisible(true);
16      }
17   } // end class TestDraw
```

Fig. 8.19 | Creating a JFrame to display a DrawPanel. (Part 2 of 2.)

GUI and Graphics Case Study Exercise

8.1   Extend the program in Figs. 8.17–8.19 to randomly draw rectangles and ovals. Create classes MyRectangle and MyOval. Both of these classes should include *x1*, *y1*, *x2*, *y2* coordinates, a color and a boolean flag to determine whether the shape is filled. Declare a constructor in each class with arguments for initializing all the instance variables. To help draw rectangles and ovals, each class should provide methods getUpperLeftX, getUpperLeftY, getWidth and getHeight that calculate the upper-left *x*-coordinate, upper-left *y*-coordinate, width and height, respectively. The upper-left *x*-coordinate is the smaller of the two *x*-coordinate values, the upper-left *y*-coordinate is the smaller of the two *y*-coordinate values, the width is the absolute value of the difference between the two *x*-coordinate values, and the height is the absolute value of the difference between the two *y*-coordinate values.

   Class DrawPanel, which extends JPanel and handles the creation of the shapes, should declare three arrays, one for each shape type. The length of each array should be a random number between 1 and 5. The constructor of class DrawPanel will fill each array with shapes of random position, size, color and fill.

   In addition, modify all three shape classes to include the following:
   a) A constructor with no arguments that sets the shape's coordinates to 0, the color of the shape to Color.BLACK, and the filled property to false (MyRectangle and MyOval only).
   b) *Set* methods for the instance variables in each class. The methods that set a coordinate value should verify that the argument is greater than or equal to zero before setting the coordinate—if it's not, they should set the coordinate to zero. The constructor should call the *set* methods rather than initialize the local variables directly.
   c) *Get* methods for the instance variables in each class. Method draw should reference the coordinates by the *get* methods rather than access them directly.

8.17 Wrap-Up

In this chapter, we presented additional class concepts. The Time class case study showed a complete class declaration consisting of private data, overloaded public constructors for initialization flexibility, *set* and *get* methods for manipulating the class's data, and methods that returned String representations of a Time object in two different formats. You also learned that every class can declare a toString method that returns a String representation of an object of the class and that method toString can be called implicitly whenever an object of a class appears in the code where a String is expected. We showed how to throw an exception to indicate that a problem has occurred.

You learned that the this reference is used implicitly in a class's instance methods to access the class's instance variables and other instance methods. You also saw explicit uses of the this reference to access the class's members (including shadowed fields) and how to use keyword this in a constructor to call another constructor of the class.

We discussed the differences between default constructors provided by the compiler and no-argument constructors provided by the programmer. You learned that a class can have references to objects of other classes as members—a concept known as composition. You learned more about enum types and how they can be used to create a set of constants for use in a program. You learned about Java's garbage-collection capability and how it (unpredictably) reclaims the memory of objects that are no longer used. The chapter explained the motivation for static fields in a class and demonstrated how to declare and use static fields and methods in your own classes. You also learned how to declare and initialize final variables.

You learned that fields declared without an access modifier are given package access by default. You saw the relationship between classes in the same package that allows each class in a package to access the package-access members of other classes in the package. Finally, we demonstrated how to use class BigDecimal to perform precise monetary calculations.

In the next chapter, you'll learn about an important aspect of object-oriented programming in Java—inheritance. You'll see that all classes in Java are related by inheritance, directly or indirectly, to the class called Object. You'll also begin to understand how the relationships between classes enable you to build more powerful apps.

Summary

Section 8.2 Time Class Case Study
- The public methods of a class are also known as the class's public services or public interface (p. 308). They present to the class's clients a view of the services the class provides.
- A class's private members are not accessible to its clients.
- String class static method format (p. 310) is similar to method System.out.printf except that format returns a formatted String rather than displaying it in a command window.
- All objects in Java have a toString method that returns a String representation of the object. Method toString is called implicitly when an object appears in code where a String is needed.

Section 8.3 Controlling Access to Members
- The access modifiers public and private control access to a class's variables and methods.

- The primary purpose of public methods is to present to the class's clients a view of the services the class provides. Clients need not be concerned with how the class accomplishes its tasks.

- A class's private variables and private methods (i.e., its implementation details) are not accessible to its clients.

Section 8.4 Referring to the Current Object's Members with the this Reference
- An instance method of an object implicitly uses keyword this (p. 314) to refer to the object's instance variables and other methods. Keyword this can also be used explicitly.

- The compiler produces a separate file with the .class extension for every compiled class.

- If a local variable has the same name as a class's field, the local variable shadows the field. You can use the this reference in a method to refer to the shadowed field explicitly.

Section 8.5 Time Class Case Study: Overloaded Constructors
- Overloaded constructors enable objects of a class to be initialized in different ways. The compiler differentiates overloaded constructors (p. 316) by their signatures.

- To call one constructor of a class from another of the same class, you can use the this keyword followed by parentheses containing the constructor arguments. If used, such a constructor call must appear as the first statement in the constructor's body.

Section 8.6 Default and No-Argument Constructors
- If no constructors are provided in a class, the compiler creates a default constructor.

- If a class declares constructors, the compiler will not create a default constructor. In this case, you must declare a no-argument constructor (p. 319) if default initialization is required.

Section 8.7 Notes on Set and Get Methods
- *Set* methods are commonly called mutator methods (p. 323) because they typically change a value. *Get* methods are commonly called accessor methods (p. 323) or query methods. A predicate method (p. 324) tests whether a condition is true or false.

Section 8.8 Composition
- A class can have references to objects of other classes as members. This is called composition (p. 324) and is sometimes referred to as a *has-a* relationship.

Section 8.9 enum Types
- All enum types (p. 327) are reference types. An enum type is declared with an enum declaration, which is a comma-separated list of enum constants. The declaration may optionally include other components of traditional classes, such as constructors, fields and methods.

- enum constants are implicitly final, because they declare constants that should not be modified.

- enum constants are implicitly static.

- Any attempt to create an object of an enum type with operator new results in a compilation error.

- enum constants can be used anywhere constants can be used, such as in the case labels of switch statements and to control enhanced for statements.

- Each enum constant in an enum declaration is optionally followed by arguments which are passed to the enum constructor.

- For every enum, the compiler generates a static method called values (p. 328) that returns an array of the enum's constants in the order in which they were declared.

- EnumSet static method range (p. 329) receives the first and last enum constants in a range and returns an EnumSet that contains all the constants between these two constants, inclusive.

Section 8.10 Garbage Collection

- The Java Virtual Machine (JVM) performs automatic garbage collection (p. 330) to reclaim the memory occupied by objects that are no longer in use. When there are no more references to an object, the object is eligible for garbage collection. The memory for such an object can be reclaimed when the JVM executes its garbage collector.

Section 8.11 `static` Class Members

- A `static` variable (p. 330) represents classwide information that's shared among the class's objects.
- `static` variables have class scope. A class's `public static` members can be accessed through a reference to any object of the class, or they can be accessed by qualifying the member name with the class name and a dot (`.`). Client code can access a class's `private static` class members only through methods of the class.
- `static` class members exist as soon as the class is loaded into memory.
- A method declared `static` cannot access a class's instance variables and instance methods, because a `static` method can be called even when no objects of the class have been instantiated.
- The `this` reference cannot be used in a `static` method.

Section 8.12 `static` Import

- A `static` import declaration (p. 334) enables you to refer to imported `static` members without the class name and a dot (`.`). A single `static` import declaration imports one `static` member, and a `static` import on demand imports all `static` members of a class.

Section 8.13 `final` Instance Variables

- In the context of an app's code, the principle of least privilege (p. 335) states that code should be granted only the amount of privilege and access that it needs to accomplish its designated task.
- Keyword `final` specifies that a variable is not modifiable. Such variables must be initialized when they're declared or by each of a class's constructors.

Section 8.14 Package Access

- If no access modifier is specified for a method or variable when it's declared in a class, the method or variable is considered to have package access (p. 336).

Section 8.15 Using `BigDecimal` for Precise Monetary Calculations

- Any application that requires precise floating-point calculations without rounding errors—such as those in financial applications—should instead use class `BigDecimal` (package `java.math`; p. 338).
- `BigDecimal static` method `valueOf` (p. 339) with a `double` argument returns a `BigDecimal` that represents the exact value specified.
- `BigDecimal` method `add` (p. 339) adds its argument `BigDecimal` to the `BigDecimal` on which the method is called and returns the result.
- `BigDecimal` provides the constants `ONE` (1), `ZERO` (0) and `TEN` (10).
- `BigDecimal` method `pow` (p. 339) raises its first argument to the power specified in its second argument.
- `BigDecimal` method `multiply` (p. 339) multiplies its argument `BigDecimal` with the `BigDecimal` on which the method is called and returns the result.
- Class `NumberFormat` (package `java.text`; p. 339) provides capabilities for formatting numeric values as locale-specific `String`s. The class's `static` method `getCurrencyInstance` returns a preconfigured `NumberFormat` for local-specific currency values. `NumberFormat` method `format` performs the formatting.

- Locale-specific formatting is an important part of internationalization—the process of customizing your applications for users' various locales and spoken languages.

- BigDecimal gives you control over how values are rounded—by default all calculations are exact and no rounding occurs. If you do not specify how to round BigDecimal values and a given value cannot be represented exactly an ArithmeticException occurs.

- You can specify the rounding mode for BigDecimal by supplying a MathContext object (package java.math) to class BigDecimal's constructor when you create a BigDecimal. You may also provide a MathContext to various BigDecimal methods that perform calculations. By default, each pre-configured MathContext uses so called "bankers rounding."

- A BigDecimal's scale is the number of digits to the right of its decimal point. If you need a BigDecimal rounded to a specific digit, you can call BigDecimal method setScale.

Self-Review Exercise

8.1 Fill in the blanks in each of the following statements:
  a) A(n) _____ imports all static members of a class.
  b) String class static method _____ is similar to method System.out.printf, but returns a formatted String rather than displaying a String in a command window.
  c) If a method contains a local variable with the same name as one of its class's fields, the local variable _____ the field in that method's scope.
  d) The public methods of a class are also known as the class's _____ or _____.
  e) A(n) _____ declaration specifies one class to import.
  f) If a class declares constructors, the compiler will not create a(n) _____.
  g) An object's _____ method is called implicitly when an object appears in code where a String is needed.
  h) *Get* methods are commonly called _____ or _____.
  i) A(n) _____ method tests whether a condition is true or false.
  j) For every enum, the compiler generates a static method called _____ that returns an array of the enum's constants in the order in which they were declared.
  k) Composition is sometimes referred to as a(n) _____ relationship.
  l) A(n) _____ declaration contains a comma-separated list of constants.
  m) A(n) _____ variable represents classwide information that's shared by all the objects of the class.
  n) A(n) _____ declaration imports one static member.
  o) The _____ states that code should be granted only the amount of privilege and access that it needs to accomplish its designated task.
  p) Keyword _____ specifies that a variable is not modifiable after initialiation in a declaration or constructor.
  q) A(n) _____ declaration imports only the classes that the program uses from a particular package.
  r) *Set* methods are commonly called _____ because they typically change a value.
  s) Use class _____ to perform precise monetary calculations.
  t) Use the _____ statement to indicate that a problem has occurred.

Answers to Self-Review Exercise

8.1 a) static import on demand. b) format. c) shadows. d) public services, public interface. e) single-type-import. f) default constructor. g) toString. h) accessor methods, query methods. i) predicate. j) values. k) *has-a*. l) enum. m) static. n) single static import. o) principle of least privilege. p) final. q) type-import-on-demand. r) mutator methods. s) BigDecimal. t) throw.

Exercises

8.2   *(Based on Section 8.14)* Explain the notion of package access in Java. Explain the negative aspects of package access.

8.3   What happens when a return type, even void, is specified for a constructor?

8.4   *(Rectangle Class)* Create a class Rectangle with attributes length and width, each of which defaults to 1. Provide methods that calculate the rectangle's perimeter and area. It has *set* and *get* methods for both length and width. The *set* methods should verify that length and width are each floating-point numbers larger than 0.0 and less than 20.0. Write a program to test class Rectangle.

8.5   *(Modifying the Internal Data Representation of a Class)* It would be perfectly reasonable for the Time2 class of Fig. 8.5 to represent the time internally as the number of seconds since midnight rather than the three integer values hour, minute and second. Clients could use the same public methods and get the same results. Modify the Time2 class of Fig. 8.5 to implement the time as the number of seconds since midnight and show that no change is visible to the clients of the class.

8.6   *(Savings Account Class)* Create class SavingsAccount. Use a static variable annualInterestRate to store the annual interest rate for all account holders. Each object of the class contains a private instance variable savingsBalance indicating the amount the saver currently has on deposit. Provide method calculateMonthlyInterest to calculate the monthly interest by multiplying the savingsBalance by annualInterestRate divided by 12—this interest should be added to savingsBalance. Provide a static method modifyInterestRate that sets the annualInterestRate to a new value. Write a program to test class SavingsAccount. Instantiate two savingsAccount objects, saver1 and saver2, with balances of $2000.00 and $3000.00, respectively. Set annualInterestRate to 4%, then calculate the monthly interest for each of 12 months and print the new balances for both savers. Next, set the annualInterestRate to 5%, calculate the next month's interest and print the new balances for both savers.

8.7   *(Enhancing Class Time2)* Modify class Time2 of Fig. 8.5 to include a tick method that increments the time stored in a Time2 object by one second. Provide method incrementMinute to increment the minute by one and method incrementHour to increment the hour by one. Write a program that tests the tick method, the incrementMinute method and the incrementHour method to ensure that they work correctly. Be sure to test the following cases:

a) incrementing into the next minute,

b) incrementing into the next hour and

c) incrementing into the next day (i.e., 11:59:59 PM to 12:00:00 AM).

8.8   *(Enhancing Class Date)* Modify class Date of Fig. 8.7 to perform error checking on the initializer values for instance variables month, day and year (currently it validates only the month and day). Provide a method nextDay to increment the day by one. Write a program that tests method nextDay in a loop that prints the date during each iteration to illustrate that the method works correctly. Test the following cases:

a) incrementing into the next month and

b) incrementing into the next year.

8.9   Rewrite the code in Fig. 8.14 to use a separate import declaration for each static member of class Math that's used in the example.

8.10   Write an enum type TrafficLight, whose constants (RED, GREEN, YELLOW) take one parameter—the duration of the light. Write a program to test the TrafficLight enum so that it displays the enum constants and their durations.

8.11   *(Complex Numbers)* Create a class called Complex for performing arithmetic with complex numbers. Complex numbers have the form

realPart + *imaginaryPart* * *i*

where i is

$$\sqrt{-1}$$

Write a program to test your class. Use floating-point variables to represent the private data of the class. Provide a constructor that enables an object of this class to be initialized when it's declared. Provide a no-argument constructor with default values in case no initializers are provided. Provide public methods that perform the following operations:

   a) Add two Complex numbers: The real parts are added together and the imaginary parts are added together.

   b) Subtract two Complex numbers: The real part of the right operand is subtracted from the real part of the left operand, and the imaginary part of the right operand is subtracted from the imaginary part of the left operand.

   c) Print Complex numbers in the form (*realPart*, *imaginaryPart*).

8.12   *(Date and Time Class)* Create class DateAndTime that combines the modified Time2 class of Exercise 8.7 and the modified Date class of Exercise 8.8. Modify method incrementHour to call method nextDay if the time is incremented into the next day. Modify methods toString and toUniversalString to output the date in addition to the time. Write a program to test the new class DateAndTime. Specifically, test incrementing the time to the next day.

8.13   *(Set of Integers)* Create class IntegerSet. Each IntegerSet object can hold integers in the range 0–100. The set is represented by an array of booleans. Array element a[i] is true if integer i is in the set. Array element a[j] is false if integer j is not in the set. The no-argument constructor initializes the array to the "empty set" (i.e., all false values).

   Provide the following methods: The static method union creates a set that's the set-theoretic union of two existing sets (i.e., an element of the new set's array is set to true if that element is true in either or both of the existing sets—otherwise, the new set's element is set to false). The static method intersection creates a set which is the set-theoretic intersection of two existing sets (i.e., an element of the new set's array is set to false if that element is false in either or both of the existing sets—otherwise, the new set's element is set to true). Method insertElement inserts a new integer k into a set (by setting a[k] to true). Method deleteElement deletes integer m (by setting a[m] to false). Method toString returns a String containing a set as a list of numbers separated by spaces. Include only those elements that are present in the set. Use --- to represent an empty set. Method isEqualTo determines whether two sets are equal. Write a program to test class IntegerSet. Instantiate several IntegerSet objects. Test that all your methods work properly.

8.14   *(Date Class)* Create class Date with the following capabilities:

   a) Output the date in multiple formats, such as

```
MM/DD/YYYY
June 14, 1992
DDD YYYY
```

   b) Use overloaded constructors to create Date objects initialized with dates of the formats in part (a). In the first case the constructor should receive three integer values. In the second case it should receive a String and two integer values. In the third case it should receive two integer values, the first of which represents the day number in the year. [*Hint:* To convert the String representation of the month to a numeric value, compare Strings using the equals method. For example, if s1 and s2 are Strings, the method call s1.equals(s2) returns true if the Strings are identical and otherwise returns false.]

8.15   *(Rational Numbers)* Create a class called Rational for performing arithmetic with fractions. Write a program to test your class. Use integer variables to represent the private instance variables of the class—the numerator and the denominator. Provide a constructor that enables an object of this class to be initialized when it's declared. The constructor should store the fraction in reduced form. The fraction

2/4

is equivalent to 1/2 and would be stored in the object as 1 in the numerator and 2 in the denominator. Provide a no-argument constructor with default values in case no initializers are provided. Provide public methods that perform each of the following operations:

a) Add two Rational numbers: The result of the addition should be stored in reduced form. Implement this as a static method.

b) Subtract two Rational numbers: The result of the subtraction should be stored in reduced form. Implement this as a static method.

c) Multiply two Rational numbers: The result of the multiplication should be stored in reduced form. Implement this as a static method.

d) Divide two Rational numbers: The result of the division should be stored in reduced form. Implement this as a static method.

e) Return a String representation of a Rational number in the form a/b, where a is the numerator and b is the denominator.

f) Return a String representation of a Rational number in floating-point format. (Consider providing formatting capabilities that enable the user of the class to specify the number of digits of precision to the right of the decimal point.)

8.16 *(Huge Integer Class)* Create a class HugeInteger which uses a 40-element array of digits to store integers as large as 40 digits each. Provide methods parse, toString, add and subtract. Method parse should receive a String, extract each digit using method charAt and place the integer equivalent of each digit into the integer array. For comparing HugeInteger objects, provide the following methods: isEqualTo, isNotEqualTo, isGreaterThan, isLessThan, isGreaterThanOrEqualTo and isLessThanOrEqualTo. Each of these is a predicate method that returns true if the relationship holds between the two HugeInteger objects and returns false if the relationship does not hold. Provide a predicate method isZero. If you feel ambitious, also provide methods multiply, divide and remainder. [*Note:* Primitive boolean values can be output as the word "true" or the word "false" with format specifier %b.]

8.17 *(Tic-Tac-Toe)* Create a class TicTacToe that will enable you to write a program to play Tic-Tac-Toe. The class contains a private 3-by-3 two-dimensional array. Use an enum type to represent the value in each cell of the array. The enum's constants should be named X, O and EMPTY (for a position that does not contain an X or an O). The constructor should initialize the board elements to EMPTY. Allow two human players. Wherever the first player moves, place an X in the specified square, and place an O wherever the second player moves. Each move must be to an empty square. After each move, determine whether the game has been won and whether it's a draw. If you feel ambitious, modify your program so that the computer makes the moves for one of the players. Also, allow the player to specify whether he or she wants to go first or second. If you feel exceptionally ambitious, develop a program that will play three-dimensional Tic-Tac-Toe on a 4-by-4-by-4 board [*Note:* This is an extremely challenging project!].

8.18 *(Account Class with BigDecimal balance)* Rewrite the Account class of Section 7.5 to store the balance as a BigDecimal object and to perform all calculations using BigDecimals.

Making a Difference

8.19 *(Project: Emergency Response Class)* The North American emergency response service, *9-1-1*, connects callers to a *local* Public Service Answering Point (PSAP). Traditionally, the PSAP would ask the caller for identification information—including the caller's address, phone number and the nature of the emergency, then dispatch the appropriate emergency responders (such as the police, an ambulance or the fire department). *Enhanced 9-1-1 (or E9-1-1)* uses computers and databases to determine the caller's physical address, directs the call to the nearest PSAP, and displays the caller's phone number and address to the call taker. *Wireless Enhanced 9-1-1* provides call takers with identification information for wireless calls. Rolled out in two phases, the first phase required carriers to provide the wireless phone number and the location of the cell site or base station transmitting the call. The second phase required carriers to provide the location of the caller (using technologies such as GPS). To learn more about 9-1-1, visit http://www.fcc.gov/pshs/services/911-services/Welcome.html and http://people.howstuffworks.com/9-1-1.htm.

An important part of creating a class is determining the class's attributes (instance variables). For this class design exercise, research 9-1-1 services on the Internet. Then, design a class called Emergency that might be used in an object-oriented 9-1-1 emergency response system. List the attributes that an object of this class might use to represent the emergency. For example, the class might include information on who reported the emergency (including their phone number), the location of the emergency, the time of the report, the nature of the emergency, the type of response and the status of the response. The class attributes should completely describe the nature of the problem and what's happening to resolve that problem.

9

Object-Oriented Programming: Inheritance

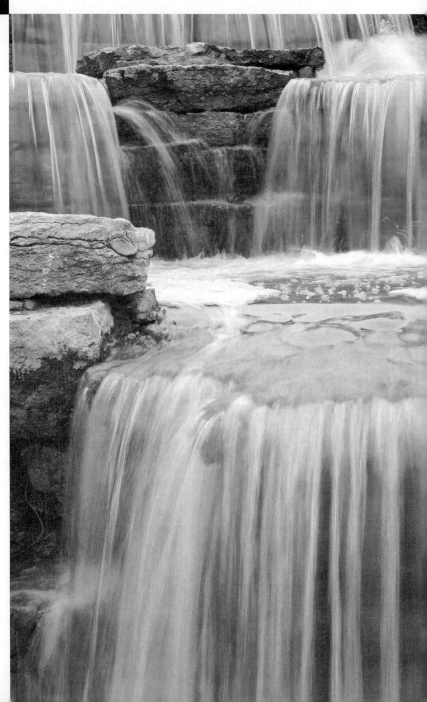

Say not you know another entirely,
till you have divided an
inheritance with him.
—Johann Kasper Lavater

This method is to define as the
number of a class the class of all
classes similar to the given class.
—Bertrand Russell

Objectives

In this chapter you'll:

- Understand inheritance and how to use it to develop new classes based on existing classes.

- Learn the notions of superclasses and subclasses and the relationship between them.

- Use keyword **extends** to create a class that inherits attributes and behaviors from another class.

- Use access modifier **protected** in a superclass to give subclass methods access to these superclass members.

- Access superclass members with **super** from a subclass.

- Learn how constructors are used in inheritance hierarchies.

- Learn about the methods of class **Object**, the direct or indirect superclass of all classes.

9.1 Introduction

This chapter continues our discussion of object-oriented programming (OOP) by introducing **inheritance**, in which a new class is created by acquiring an existing class's members and possibly embellishing them with new or modified capabilities. With inheritance, you can save time during program development by basing new classes on existing proven and debugged high-quality software. This also increases the likelihood that a system will be implemented and maintained effectively.

When creating a class, rather than declaring completely new members, you can designate that the new class should *inherit* the members of an existing class. The existing class is called the **superclass**, and the new class is the **subclass.** (The C++ programming language refers to the superclass as the **base class** and the subclass as the **derived class.**) A subclass can become a superclass for future subclasses.

A subclass can add its own fields and methods. Therefore, a subclass is *more specific* than its superclass and represents a more specialized group of objects. The subclass exhibits the behaviors of its superclass and can modify those behaviors so that they operate appropriately for the subclass. This is why inheritance is sometimes referred to as **specialization**.

The **direct superclass** is the superclass from which the subclass explicitly inherits. An **indirect superclass** is any class above the direct superclass in the **class hierarchy**, which defines the inheritance relationships among classes—as you'll see in Section 9.2, diagrams help you understand these relationships. In Java, the class hierarchy begins with class Object (in package java.lang), which *every* class in Java directly or indirectly **extends** (or "inherits from"). Section 9.6 lists the methods of class Object that are inherited by all other Java classes. Java supports only **single inheritance**, in which each class is derived from exactly *one* direct superclass. Unlike C++, Java does *not* support multiple inheritance (which occurs when a class is derived from more than one direct superclass). Chapter 10, Object-Oriented Programming: Polymorphism and Interfaces, explains how to use Java *interfaces* to realize many of the benefits of multiple inheritance while avoiding the associated problems.

We distinguish between the *is-a* **relationship** and the *has-a* **relationship**. *Is-a* represents inheritance. In an *is-a* relationship, *an object of a subclass can also be treated as an object of its superclass*—e.g., a car *is a* vehicle. By contrast, *has-a* represents composition (see Chapter 8). In a *has-a* relationship, *an object contains as members references to other objects*—e.g., a car *has a* steering wheel (and a car object has a reference to a steering-wheel object).

New classes can inherit from classes in **class libraries**. Organizations develop their own class libraries and can take advantage of others available worldwide. Some day, most new software likely will be constructed from **standardized reusable components**, just as automobiles and most computer hardware are constructed today. This will facilitate the rapid development of more powerful, abundant and economical software.

9.2 Superclasses and Subclasses

Often, an object of one class *is an* object of another class as well. For example, a CarLoan *is a* Loan as are HomeImprovementLoans and MortgageLoans. Thus, in Java, class CarLoan can be said to inherit from class Loan. In this context, class Loan is a superclass and class CarLoan is a subclass. A CarLoan *is a* specific type of Loan, but it's incorrect to claim that every Loan *is a* CarLoan—the Loan could be any type of loan. Figure 9.1 lists several simple examples of superclasses and subclasses—superclasses tend to be "more general" and subclasses "more specific."

Superclass	Subclasses
Student	GraduateStudent, UndergraduateStudent
Shape	Circle, Triangle, Rectangle, Sphere, Cube
Loan	CarLoan, HomeImprovementLoan, MortgageLoan
Employee	Faculty, Staff
BankAccount	CheckingAccount, SavingsAccount

Fig. 9.1 | Inheritance examples.

Because every subclass object *is an* object of its superclass, and one superclass can have many subclasses, the set of objects represented by a superclass is often larger than the set of objects represented by any of its subclasses. For example, the superclass Vehicle represents *all* vehicles, including cars, trucks, boats, bicycles and so on. By contrast, subclass Car represents a smaller, more specific subset of vehicles.

University Community Member Hierarchy
Inheritance relationships form treelike *hierarchical* structures. A superclass exists in a hierarchical relationship with its subclasses. Let's develop a sample class hierarchy (Fig. 9.2), also called an **inheritance hierarchy**. A university community has thousands of members, including employees, students and alumni. Employees are either faculty or staff members. Faculty members are either administrators (e.g., deans and department chairpersons) or teachers. The hierarchy could contain many other classes. For example, students can be graduate or undergraduate students. Undergraduate students can be freshmen, sophomores, juniors or seniors.

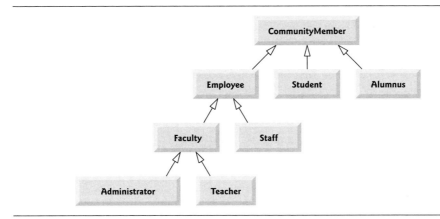

Fig. 9.2 | Inheritance hierarchy UML class diagram for university CommunityMembers.

Each arrow in the hierarchy represents an *is-a* relationship. As we follow the arrows upward in this class hierarchy, we can state, for example, that "an Employee *is a* CommunityMember" and "a Teacher *is a* Faculty member." CommunityMember is the direct superclass of Employee, Student and Alumnus and is an indirect superclass of all the other classes in the diagram. Starting from the bottom, you can follow the arrows and apply the *is-a* relationship up to the topmost superclass. For example, an Administrator *is a* Faculty member, *is an* Employee, *is a* CommunityMember and, of course, *is an* Object.

Shape Hierarchy
Now consider the Shape inheritance hierarchy in Fig. 9.3. This hierarchy begins with superclass Shape, which is extended by subclasses TwoDimensionalShape and ThreeDimensionalShape—Shapes are either TwoDimensionalShapes or ThreeDimensionalShapes. The third level of this hierarchy contains *specific* types of TwoDimensionalShapes and ThreeDimensionalShapes. As in Fig. 9.2, we can follow the arrows from the bottom of the diagram to the topmost superclass in this class hierarchy to identify several *is-a* relationships. For example, a Triangle *is a* TwoDimensionalShape and *is a* Shape, while a Sphere *is a* ThreeDimensionalShape and *is a* Shape. This hierarchy could contain many other classes. For example, ellipses and trapezoids also are TwoDimensionalShapes.

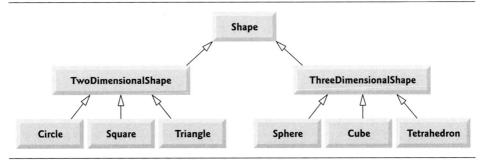

Fig. 9.3 | Inheritance hierarchy UML class diagram for Shapes.

Not every class relationship is an inheritance relationship. In Chapter 8, we discussed the *has-a* relationship, in which classes have members that are references to objects of other classes. Such relationships create classes by *composition* of existing classes. For example, given the classes Employee, BirthDate and TelephoneNumber, it's improper to say that an Employee *is a* BirthDate or that an Employee *is a* TelephoneNumber. However, an Employee *has a* BirthDate, and an Employee *has a* TelephoneNumber.

It's possible to treat superclass objects and subclass objects similarly—their commonalities are expressed in the superclass's members. Objects of all classes that extend a common superclass can be treated as objects of that superclass—such objects have an *is-a* relationship with the superclass. Later in this chapter and in Chapter 10, we consider many examples that take advantage of the *is-a* relationship.

A subclass can customize methods that it inherits from its superclass. To do this, the subclass **overrides** (*redefines*) the superclass method with an appropriate implementation, as we'll see in the chapter's code examples.

9.3 protected Members

Chapter 8 discussed access modifiers public and private. A class's public members are accessible wherever the program has a *reference* to an *object* of that class or one of its *subclasses*. A class's private members are accessible only within the class itself. In this section, we introduce the access modifier **protected**. Using protected access offers an intermediate level of access between public and private. A superclass's protected members can be accessed by members of that superclass, by members of its subclasses and by members of other classes in the *same package*—protected members also have *package access*.

All public and protected superclass members retain their original access modifier when they become members of the subclass—public members of the superclass become public members of the subclass, and protected members of the superclass become protected members of the subclass. A superclass's private members are *not* accessible outside the class itself. Rather, they're *hidden* from its subclasses and can be accessed only through the public or protected methods inherited from the superclass.

Subclass methods can refer to public and protected members inherited from the superclass simply by using the member names. When a subclass method *overrides* an inherited superclass method, the *superclass* version of the method can be accessed from the *subclass* by preceding the superclass method name with keyword **super** and a dot (.) separator. We discuss accessing overridden members of the superclass in Section 9.4.

Software Engineering Observation 9.1

Methods of a subclass cannot directly access private members of their superclass. A subclass can change the state of private superclass instance variables only through non-private methods provided in the superclass and inherited by the subclass.

Software Engineering Observation 9.2

Declaring private instance variables helps you test, debug and correctly modify systems. If a subclass could access its superclass's private instance variables, classes that inherit from that subclass could access the instance variables as well. This would propagate access to what should be private instance variables, and the benefits of information hiding would be lost.

9.4 Relationship Between Superclasses and Subclasses

We now use an inheritance hierarchy containing types of *employees* in a company's payroll application to discuss the relationship between a superclass and its subclass. In this company, *commission employees* (who will be represented as objects of a superclass) are paid a percentage of their sales, while *base-salaried commission employees* (who will be represented as objects of a subclass) receive a base salary *plus* a percentage of their sales.

We divide our discussion of the relationship between these classes into five examples. The first declares class CommissionEmployee, which directly inherits from class Object and declares as private instance variables a first name, last name, social security number, commission rate and gross (i.e., total) sales amount.

The second example declares class BasePlusCommissionEmployee, which also directly inherits from class Object and declares as private instance variables a first name, last name, social security number, commission rate, gross sales amount *and* base salary. We create this class by *writing every line of code* the class requires—we'll soon see that it's much more efficient to create it by inheriting from class CommissionEmployee.

The third example declares a new BasePlusCommissionEmployee class that *extends* class CommissionEmployee (i.e., a BasePlusCommissionEmployee *is a* CommissionEmployee who also has a base salary). This *software reuse lets us write much less code* when developing the new subclass. In this example, class BasePlusCommissionEmployee attempts to access class CommissionEmployee's private members—this results in compilation errors, because the subclass *cannot* access the superclass's private instance variables.

The fourth example shows that if CommissionEmployee's instance variables are declared as protected, the BasePlusCommissionEmployee subclass *can* access that data directly. Both BasePlusCommissionEmployee classes contain identical functionality, but we show how the inherited version is easier to create and manage.

After we discuss the convenience of using protected instance variables, we create the fifth example, which sets the CommissionEmployee instance variables back to private to enforce good software engineering. Then we show how the BasePlusCommissionEmployee subclass can use CommissionEmployee's public methods to manipulate (in a controlled manner) the private instance variables inherited from CommissionEmployee.

9.4.1 Creating and Using a CommissionEmployee Class

We begin by declaring class CommissionEmployee (Fig. 9.4). Line 4 begins the class declaration and indicates that class CommissionEmployee **extends** (i.e., *inherits from*) class **Object** (from package java.lang). This causes class CommissionEmployee to inherit the class Object's methods—class Object does not have any fields. If you don't explicitly specify which class a new class extends, the class extends Object implicitly. For this reason, you typically will not include "extends Object" in your code—we do so in this one example only for demonstration purposes.

Overview of Class CommissionEmployee's Methods and Instance Variables
Class CommissionEmployee's public services include a constructor (lines 13–34) and methods earnings (lines 87–90) and toString (lines 93–101). Lines 37–52 declare public *get* methods for the class's final instance variables (declared in lines 6–8) firstName, lastName and socialSecurityNumber. These three instance variables are declared final because they do not need to be modified after they're initialized—this is also why we do

not provide corresponding *set* methods. Lines 55–84 declare public *set* and *get* methods for the class's grossSales and commissionRate instance variables (declared in lines 9–10). The class declares its instance variables as private, so objects of other classes cannot directly access these variables.

```java
1   // Fig. 9.4: CommissionEmployee.java
2   // CommissionEmployee class represents an employee paid a
3   // percentage of gross sales.
4   public class CommissionEmployee extends Object
5   {
6      private final String firstName;
7      private final String lastName;
8      private final String socialSecurityNumber;
9      private double grossSales; // gross weekly sales
10     private double commissionRate; // commission percentage
11
12     // five-argument constructor
13     public CommissionEmployee(String firstName, String lastName,
14        String socialSecurityNumber, double grossSales,
15        double commissionRate)
16     {
17        // implicit call to Object's default constructor occurs here
18
19        // if grossSales is invalid throw exception
20        if (grossSales < 0.0)
21           throw new IllegalArgumentException(
22              "Gross sales must be >= 0.0");
23
24        // if commissionRate is invalid throw exception
25        if (commissionRate <= 0.0 || commissionRate >= 1.0)
26           throw new IllegalArgumentException(
27              "Commission rate must be > 0.0 and < 1.0");
28
29        this.firstName = firstName;
30        this.lastName = lastName;
31        this.socialSecurityNumber = socialSecurityNumber;
32        this.grossSales = grossSales;
33        this.commissionRate = commissionRate;
34     } // end constructor
35
36     // return first name
37     public String getFirstName()
38     {
39        return firstName;
40     }
41
42     // return last name
43     public String getLastName()
44     {
45        return lastName;
46     }
```

Fig. 9.4 | CommissionEmployee class represents an employee paid a percentage of gross sales. (Part 1 of 3.)

```
47
48        // return social security number
49        public String getSocialSecurityNumber()
50        {
51           return socialSecurityNumber;
52        }
53
54        // set gross sales amount
55        public void setGrossSales(double grossSales)
56        {
57           if (grossSales < 0.0)
58              throw new IllegalArgumentException(
59                 "Gross sales must be >= 0.0");
60
61           this.grossSales = grossSales;
62        }
63
64        // return gross sales amount
65        public double getGrossSales()
66        {
67           return grossSales;
68        }
69
70        // set commission rate
71        public void setCommissionRate(double commissionRate)
72        {
73           if (commissionRate <= 0.0 || commissionRate >= 1.0)
74              throw new IllegalArgumentException(
75                 "Commission rate must be > 0.0 and < 1.0");
76
77           this.commissionRate = commissionRate;
78        }
79
80        // return commission rate
81        public double getCommissionRate()
82        {
83           return commissionRate;
84        }
85
86        // calculate earnings
87        public double earnings()
88        {
89           return commissionRate * grossSales;
90        }
91
92        // return String representation of CommissionEmployee object
93        @Override // indicates that this method overrides a superclass method
94        public String toString()
95        {
96           return String.format("%s: %s %s%n%s: %s%n%s: %.2f%n%s: %.2f",
97              "commission employee", firstName, lastName,
98              "social security number", socialSecurityNumber,
```

Fig. 9.4 | CommissionEmployee class represents an employee paid a percentage of gross sales. (Part 2 of 3.)

```
 99            "gross sales", grossSales,
100            "commission rate", commissionRate);
101    }
102 } // end class CommissionEmployee
```

Fig. 9.4 | CommissionEmployee class represents an employee paid a percentage of gross sales. (Part 3 of 3.)

Class CommissionEmployee's Constructor

Constructors are *not* inherited, so class CommissionEmployee does not inherit class Object's constructor. However, a superclass's constructors are still available to be called by subclasses. In fact, Java requires that *the first task of any subclass constructor is to call its direct superclass's constructor*, either explicitly or implicitly (if no constructor call is specified), to ensure that the instance variables inherited from the superclass are initialized properly. The syntax for calling a superclass constructor explicitly is discussed in Section 9.4.3. In this example, class CommissionEmployee's constructor calls class Object's constructor implicitly. If the code does not include an explicit call to the superclass constructor, Java *implicitly* calls the superclass's default or *no-argument* constructor. The comment in line 17 of Fig. 9.4 indicates where the implicit call to the superclass Object's default constructor is made (you do *not* write the code for this call). Object's default constructor does nothing. Even if a class does not have constructors, the default constructor that the compiler implicitly declares for the class will call the superclass's default or no-argument constructor.

After the implicit call to Object's constructor, lines 20–22 and 25–27 validate the grossSales and commissionRate arguments. If these are valid (that is, the constructor does not throw an IllegalArgumentException), lines 29–33 assign the constructor's arguments to the class's instance variables.

We did not validate the values of arguments firstName, lastName and socialSecurityNumber before assigning them to the corresponding instance variables. We could validate the first and last names—perhaps to ensure that they're of a reasonable length. Similarly, a social security number could be validated using regular expressions (Section 14.7) to ensure that it contains nine digits, with or without dashes (e.g., 123-45-6789 or 123456789).

Class CommissionEmployee's earnings Method

Method earnings (lines 87–90) calculates a CommissionEmployee's earnings. Line 89 multiplies the commissionRate by the grossSales and returns the result.

Class CommissionEmployee's toString Method and the @Override Annotation

Method toString (lines 93–101) is special—it's one of the methods that *every* class inherits directly or indirectly from class Object (summarized in Section 9.6). Method toString returns a String representing an object. It's called implicitly whenever an object must be converted to a String representation, such as when an object is output by printf or output by String method format via the %s format specifier. Class Object's toString method returns a String that includes the name of the object's class. It's primarily a placeholder that can be *overridden* by a subclass to specify an appropriate String representation of the data in a subclass object. Method toString of class CommissionEmployee overrides (redefines) class Object's toString method. When invoked, CommissionEmployee's toString method uses `String` method `format` to return a `String` containing information about the `CommissionEmployee`. To override a superclass method, a subclass must declare a method with the *same signature* (method name, number of parameters, parameter types and order of parameter types) as the superclass method—`Object`'s `toString` method takes no parameters, so `CommissionEmployee` declares `toString` with no parameters.

Line 93 uses the optional **@Override annotation** to indicate that the following method declaration (i.e., `toString`) should *override* an *existing* superclass method. This annotation helps the compiler catch a few common errors. For example, in this case, you intend to override superclass method `toString`, which is spelled with a lowercase "t" and an uppercase "S." If you inadvertently use a lowercase "s," the compiler will flag this as an error because the superclass does not contain a method named `toString`. If you didn't use the @Override annotation, `toString` would be an entirely different method that would *not* be called if a `CommissionEmployee` were used where a `String` was needed.

Another common overriding error is declaring the wrong number or types of parameters in the parameter list. This creates an *unintentional overload* of the superclass method, rather than overriding the existing method. If you then attempt to call the method (with the correct number and types of parameters) on a subclass object, the superclass's version is invoked—potentially leading to subtle logic errors. When the compiler encounters a method declared with @Override, it compares the method's signature with the superclass's method signatures. If there isn't an exact match, the compiler issues an error message, such as "method does not override or implement a method from a supertype." You would then correct your method's signature so that it matches one in the superclass.

Error-Prevention Tip 9.1

Though the @Override annotation is optional, declare overridden methods with it to ensure at compilation time that you defined their signatures correctly. It's always better to find errors at compile time rather than at runtime. For this reason, the toString *methods in Fig. 7.11 and in Chapter 8's examples should have been declared with* @Override.

Common Programming Error 9.1

It's a compilation error to override a method with a more restricted access modifier—a public *superclass method cannot become a* protected *or* private *subclass method; a* protected *superclass method cannot become a* private *subclass method. Doing so would break the* is-a *relationship, which requires that all subclass objects be able to respond to method calls made to* public *methods declared in the superclass. If a* public *method, could be overridden as a* protected *or* private *method, the subclass objects would not be able to respond to the same method calls as superclass objects. Once a method is declared* public *in a superclass, the method remains* public *for all that class's direct and indirect subclasses.*

Class CommissionEmployeeTest

Figure 9.5 tests class `CommissionEmployee`. Lines 9–10 instantiate a `CommissionEmployee` object and invoke `CommissionEmployee`'s constructor (lines 13–34 of Fig. 9.4) to initialize it with `"Sue"` as the first name, `"Jones"` as the last name, `"222-22-2222"` as the social security number, 10000 as the gross sales amount ($10,000) and `.06` as the commission rate (i.e., 6%). Lines 15–24 use `CommissionEmployee`'s *get* methods to retrieve the object's instance-variable values for output. Lines 26–27 invoke the object's `setGrossSales` and `setCommissionRate` methods to change the values of instance variables grossSales and commission-

Rate. Lines 29–30 output the String representation of the updated CommissionEmployee. When an object is output using the %s format specifier, the object's toString method is invoked *implicitly* to obtain the object's String representation. [*Note:* In this chapter, we do not use the earnings method in each class, but it's used extensively in Chapter 10.]

```java
1   // Fig. 9.5: CommissionEmployeeTest.java
2   // CommissionEmployee class test program.
3
4   public class CommissionEmployeeTest
5   {
6      public static void main(String[] args)
7      {
8         // instantiate CommissionEmployee object
9         CommissionEmployee employee = new CommissionEmployee(
10           "Sue", "Jones", "222-22-2222", 10000, .06);
11
12        // get commission employee data
13        System.out.println(
14           "Employee information obtained by get methods:");
15        System.out.printf("%n%s %s%n", "First name is",
16           employee.getFirstName());
17        System.out.printf("%s %s%n", "Last name is",
18           employee.getLastName());
19        System.out.printf("%s %s%n", "Social security number is",
20           employee.getSocialSecurityNumber());
21        System.out.printf("%s %.2f%n", "Gross sales is",
22           employee.getGrossSales());
23        System.out.printf("%s %.2f%n", "Commission rate is",
24           employee.getCommissionRate());
25
26        employee.setGrossSales(5000);
27        employee.setCommissionRate(.1);
28
29        System.out.printf("%n%s:%n%n%s%n",
30           "Updated employee information obtained by toString", employee);
31     } // end main
32  } // end class CommissionEmployeeTest
```

```
Employee information obtained by get methods:

First name is Sue
Last name is Jones
Social security number is 222-22-2222
Gross sales is 10000.00
Commission rate is 0.06

Updated employee information obtained by toString:

commission employee: Sue Jones
social security number: 222-22-2222
gross sales: 5000.00
commission rate: 0.10
```

Fig. 9.5 | CommissionEmployee class test program.

9.4.2 Creating and Using a BasePlusCommissionEmployee Class

We now discuss the second part of our introduction to inheritance by declaring and testing (a completely new and independent) class BasePlusCommissionEmployee (Fig. 9.6), which contains a first name, last name, social security number, gross sales amount, commission rate *and* base salary. Class BasePlusCommissionEmployee's public services include a BasePlusCommissionEmployee constructor (lines 15–42) and methods earnings (lines 111–114) and toString (lines 117–126). Lines 45–108 declare public *get* and *set* methods for the class's private instance variables (declared in lines 7–12) firstName, lastName, socialSecurityNumber, grossSales, commissionRate and baseSalary. These variables and methods encapsulate all the necessary features of a base-salaried commission employee. Note the *similarity* between this class and class CommissionEmployee (Fig. 9.4)—in this example, we'll not yet exploit that similarity.

```java
1   // Fig. 9.6: BasePlusCommissionEmployee.java
2   // BasePlusCommissionEmployee class represents an employee who receives
3   // a base salary in addition to commission.
4
5   public class BasePlusCommissionEmployee
6   {
7      private final String firstName;
8      private final String lastName;
9      private final String socialSecurityNumber;
10     private double grossSales; // gross weekly sales
11     private double commissionRate; // commission percentage
12     private double baseSalary; // base salary per week
13
14     // six-argument constructor
15     public BasePlusCommissionEmployee(String firstName, String lastName,
16        String socialSecurityNumber, double grossSales,
17        double commissionRate, double baseSalary)
18     {
19        // implicit call to Object's default constructor occurs here
20
21        // if grossSales is invalid throw exception
22        if (grossSales < 0.0)
23           throw new IllegalArgumentException(
24              "Gross sales must be >= 0.0");
25
26        // if commissionRate is invalid throw exception
27        if (commissionRate <= 0.0 || commissionRate >= 1.0)
28           throw new IllegalArgumentException(
29              "Commission rate must be > 0.0 and < 1.0");
30
31        // if baseSalary is invalid throw exception
32        if (baseSalary < 0.0)
33           throw new IllegalArgumentException(
34              "Base salary must be >= 0.0");
35
```

Fig. 9.6 | BasePlusCommissionEmployee class represents an employee who receives a base salary in addition to a commission. (Part 1 of 3.)

```
36              this.firstName = firstName;
37              this.lastName = lastName;
38              this.socialSecurityNumber = socialSecurityNumber;
39              this.grossSales = grossSales;
40              this.commissionRate = commissionRate;
41              this.baseSalary = baseSalary;
42          } // end constructor
43
44          // return first name
45          public String getFirstName()
46          {
47              return firstName;
48          }
49
50          // return last name
51          public String getLastName()
52          {
53              return lastName;
54          }
55
56          // return social security number
57          public String getSocialSecurityNumber()
58          {
59              return socialSecurityNumber;
60          }
61
62          // set gross sales amount
63          public void setGrossSales(double grossSales)
64          {
65              if (grossSales < 0.0)
66                  throw new IllegalArgumentException(
67                      "Gross sales must be >= 0.0");
68
69              this.grossSales = grossSales;
70          }
71
72          // return gross sales amount
73          public double getGrossSales()
74          {
75              return grossSales;
76          }
77
78          // set commission rate
79          public void setCommissionRate(double commissionRate)
80          {
81              if (commissionRate <= 0.0 || commissionRate >= 1.0)
82                  throw new IllegalArgumentException(
83                      "Commission rate must be > 0.0 and < 1.0");
84
85              this.commissionRate = commissionRate;
86          }
87
```

Fig. 9.6 | BasePlusCommissionEmployee class represents an employee who receives a base salary in addition to a commission. (Part 2 of 3.)

```
88        // return commission rate
89        public double getCommissionRate()
90        {
91           return commissionRate;
92        }
93
94        // set base salary
95        public void setBaseSalary(double baseSalary)
96        {
97           if (baseSalary < 0.0)
98              throw new IllegalArgumentException(
99                 "Base salary must be >= 0.0");
100
101          this.baseSalary = baseSalary;
102       }
103
104       // return base salary
105       public double getBaseSalary()
106       {
107          return baseSalary;
108       }
109
110       // calculate earnings
111       public double earnings()
112       {
113          return baseSalary + (commissionRate * grossSales);
114       }
115
116       // return String representation of BasePlusCommissionEmployee
117       @Override
118       public String toString()
119       {
120          return String.format(
121             "%s: %s %s%n%s: %s%n%s: %.2f%n%s: %.2f%n%s: %.2f",
122             "base-salaried commission employee", firstName, lastName,
123             "social security number", socialSecurityNumber,
124             "gross sales", grossSales, "commission rate", commissionRate,
125             "base salary", baseSalary);
126       }
127 } // end class BasePlusCommissionEmployee
```

Fig. 9.6 | BasePlusCommissionEmployee class represents an employee who receives a base salary in addition to a commission. (Part 3 of 3.)

Class BasePlusCommissionEmployee does *not* specify "extends Object" in line 5, so the class *implicitly* extends Object. Also, like class CommissionEmployee's constructor (lines 13–34 of Fig. 9.4), class BasePlusCommissionEmployee's constructor invokes class Object's default constructor *implicitly*, as noted in the comment in line 19.

Class BasePlusCommissionEmployee's earnings method (lines 111–114) returns the result of adding the BasePlusCommissionEmployee's base salary to the product of the commission rate and the employee's gross sales.

Class BasePlusCommissionEmployee overrides Object method toString to return a String containing the BasePlusCommissionEmployee's information. Once again, we use format specifier %.2f to format the gross sales, commission rate and base salary with two digits of precision to the right of the decimal point (line 121).

Testing Class *BasePlusCommissionEmployee*

Figure 9.7 tests class BasePlusCommissionEmployee. Lines 9–11 create a BasePlusCommissionEmployee object and pass "Bob", "Lewis", "333-33-3333", 5000, .04 and 300 to the constructor as the first name, last name, social security number, gross sales, commission rate and base salary, respectively. Lines 16–27 use BasePlusCommissionEmployee's *get* methods to retrieve the values of the object's instance variables for output. Line 29 invokes the object's setBaseSalary method to change the base salary. Method setBaseSalary (Fig. 9.6, lines 95–102) ensures that instance variable baseSalary is not assigned a negative value. Line 33 of Fig. 9.7 invokes method toString *explicitly* to get the object's String representation.

```java
 1   // Fig. 9.7: BasePlusCommissionEmployeeTest.java
 2   // BasePlusCommissionEmployee test program.
 3
 4   public class BasePlusCommissionEmployeeTest
 5   {
 6      public static void main(String[] args)
 7      {
 8         // instantiate BasePlusCommissionEmployee object
 9         BasePlusCommissionEmployee employee =
10            new BasePlusCommissionEmployee(
11            "Bob", "Lewis", "333-33-3333", 5000, .04, 300);
12
13         // get base-salaried commission employee data
14         System.out.println(
15            "Employee information obtained by get methods:%n");
16         System.out.printf("%s %s%n", "First name is",
17            employee.getFirstName());
18         System.out.printf("%s %s%n", "Last name is",
19            employee.getLastName());
20         System.out.printf("%s %s%n", "Social security number is",
21            employee.getSocialSecurityNumber());
22         System.out.printf("%s %.2f%n", "Gross sales is",
23            employee.getGrossSales());
24         System.out.printf("%s %.2f%n", "Commission rate is",
25            employee.getCommissionRate());
26         System.out.printf("%s %.2f%n", "Base salary is",
27            employee.getBaseSalary());
28
29         employee.setBaseSalary(1000);
30
31         System.out.printf("%n%s:%n%n%s%n",
32            "Updated employee information obtained by toString",
33            employee.toString());
34      } // end main
35   } // end class BasePlusCommissionEmployeeTest
```

Fig. 9.7 | BasePlusCommissionEmployee test program. (Part 1 of 2.)

```
Employee information obtained by get methods:

First name is Bob
Last name is Lewis
Social security number is 333-33-3333
Gross sales is 5000.00
Commission rate is 0.04
Base salary is 300.00

Updated employee information obtained by toString:

base-salaried commission employee: Bob Lewis
social security number: 333-33-3333
gross sales: 5000.00
commission rate: 0.04
base salary: 1000.00
```

Fig. 9.7 | BasePlusCommissionEmployee test program. (Part 2 of 2.)

Notes on Class *BasePlusCommissionEmployee*

Much of class BasePlusCommissionEmployee's code (Fig. 9.6) is *similar*, or *identical*, to that of class CommissionEmployee (Fig. 9.4). For example, private instance variables firstName and lastName and methods setFirstName, getFirstName, setLastName and getLastName are identical to those of class CommissionEmployee. The classes also both contain private instance variables socialSecurityNumber, commissionRate and gross-Sales, and corresponding *get* and *set* methods. In addition, the BasePlusCommissionEmployee constructor is *almost* identical to that of class CommissionEmployee, except that BasePlusCommissionEmployee's constructor also sets the baseSalary. The other additions to class BasePlusCommissionEmployee are private instance variable baseSalary and methods setBaseSalary and getBaseSalary. Class BasePlusCommissionEmployee's toString method is *almost* identical to that of class CommissionEmployee except that it also outputs instance variable baseSalary with two digits of precision to the right of the decimal point.

We literally *copied* code from class CommissionEmployee and *pasted* it into class Base-PlusCommissionEmployee, then modified class BasePlusCommissionEmployee to include a base salary and methods that manipulate the base salary. This *"copy-and-paste" approach* is often error prone and time consuming. Worse yet, it spreads copies of the same code throughout a system, creating code-maintenance problems—changes to the code would need to be made in multiple classes. Is there a way to "acquire" the instance variables and methods of one class in a way that makes them part of other classes *without duplicating code*? Next we answer this question, using a more elegant approach to building classes that emphasizes the benefits of inheritance.

Software Engineering Observation 9.3

With inheritance, the instance variables and methods that are the same for all the classes in the hierarchy are declared in a superclass. Changes made to these common features in the superclass are inherited by the subclass. Without inheritance, changes would need to be made to all *the source-code files that contain a copy of the code in question.*

9.4.3 Creating a CommissionEmployee–BasePlusCommissionEmployee Inheritance Hierarchy

Now we declare class BasePlusCommissionEmployee (Fig. 9.8) to *extend* class CommissionEmployee (Fig. 9.4). A BasePlusCommissionEmployee object *is a* CommissionEmployee, because inheritance passes on class CommissionEmployee's capabilities. Class BasePlusCommissionEmployee also has instance variable baseSalary (Fig. 9.8, line 6). Keyword extends (line 4) indicates inheritance. BasePlusCommissionEmployee *inherits* CommissionEmployee's instance variables and methods.

Software Engineering Observation 9.4

At the design stage in an object-oriented system, you'll often find that certain classes are closely related. You should "factor out" common instance variables and methods and place them in a superclass. Then use inheritance to develop subclasses, specializing them with capabilities beyond those inherited from the superclass.

Software Engineering Observation 9.5

Declaring a subclass does not affect its superclass's source code. Inheritance preserves the integrity of the superclass.

Only CommissionEmployee's public and protected members are directly accessible in the subclass. The CommissionEmployee constructor is *not* inherited. So, the public BasePlusCommissionEmployee services include its constructor (lines 9–23), public methods inherited from CommissionEmployee, and methods setBaseSalary (lines 26–33), getBaseSalary (lines 36–39), earnings (lines 42–47) and toString (lines 50–60). Methods earnings and toString *override* the corresponding methods in class CommissionEmployee because their superclass versions do not properly calculate a BasePlusCommissionEmployee's earnings or return an appropriate String representation, respectively.

```java
1   // Fig. 9.8: BasePlusCommissionEmployee.java
2   // private superclass members cannot be accessed in a subclass.
3
4   public class BasePlusCommissionEmployee extends CommissionEmployee
5   {
6      private double baseSalary; // base salary per week
7
8      // six-argument constructor
9      public BasePlusCommissionEmployee(String firstName, String lastName,
10         String socialSecurityNumber, double grossSales,
11         double commissionRate, double baseSalary)
12      {
13         // explicit call to superclass CommissionEmployee constructor
14         super(firstName, lastName, socialSecurityNumber,
15            grossSales, commissionRate);
16
17         // if baseSalary is invalid throw exception
18         if (baseSalary < 0.0)
19            throw new IllegalArgumentException(
20               "Base salary must be >= 0.0");
21
```

Fig. 9.8 | private superclass members cannot be accessed in a subclass. (Part I of 3.)

```
22          this.baseSalary = baseSalary;
23      }
24
25      // set base salary
26      public void setBaseSalary(double baseSalary)
27      {
28          if (baseSalary < 0.0)
29              throw new IllegalArgumentException(
30                  "Base salary must be >= 0.0");
31
32          this.baseSalary = baseSalary;
33      }
34
35      // return base salary
36      public double getBaseSalary()
37      {
38          return baseSalary;
39      }
40
41      // calculate earnings
42      @Override
43      public double earnings()
44      {
45          // not allowed: commissionRate and grossSales private in superclass
46          return baseSalary + (commissionRate * grossSales);
47      }
48
49      // return String representation of BasePlusCommissionEmployee
50      @Override
51      public String toString()
52      {
53          // not allowed: attempts to access private superclass members
54          return String.format(
55              "%s: %s %s%n%s: %s%n%s: %.2f%n%s: %.2f%n%s: %.2f",
56              "base-salaried commission employee", firstName, lastName,
57              "social security number", socialSecurityNumber,
58              "gross sales", grossSales, "commission rate", commissionRate,
59              "base salary", baseSalary);
60      }
61  } // end class BasePlusCommissionEmployee
```

```
BasePlusCommissionEmployee.java:46: error: commissionRate has private access
in CommissionEmployee
      return baseSalary + (commissionRate * grossSales);
                           ^
BasePlusCommissionEmployee.java:46: error: grossSales has private access in
CommissionEmployee
      return baseSalary + (commissionRate * grossSales);
                                            ^
BasePlusCommissionEmployee.java:56: error: firstName has private access in
CommissionEmployee
          "base-salaried commission employee", firstName, lastName,
                                                ^
```

Fig. 9.8 | private superclass members cannot be accessed in a subclass. (Part 2 of 3.)

```
BasePlusCommissionEmployee.java:56: error: lastName has private access in Com-
missionEmployee
        "base-salaried commission employee", firstName, lastName,
                                                         ^
BasePlusCommissionEmployee.java:57: error: socialSecurityNumber has private
access in CommissionEmployee
        "social security number", socialSecurityNumber,
                                  ^
BasePlusCommissionEmployee.java:58: error: grossSales has private access in
CommissionEmployee
        "gross sales", grossSales, "commission rate", commissionRate,
                       ^
BasePlusCommissionEmployee.java:58: error: commissionRate has private access
inCommissionEmployee
        "gross sales", grossSales, "commission rate", commissionRate,
                                                      ^
```

Fig. 9.8 | `private` superclass members cannot be accessed in a subclass. (Part 3 of 3.)

A Subclass's Constructor Must Call Its Superclass's Constructor

Each subclass constructor must implicitly or explicitly call one of its superclass's constructors to initialize the instance variables inherited from the superclass. Lines 14–15 in Base-
PlusCommissionEmployee's six-argument constructor (lines 9–23) explicitly call class
CommissionEmployee's five-argument constructor (declared at lines 13–34 of Fig. 9.4) to
initialize the superclass portion of a BasePlusCommissionEmployee object (i.e., variables
firstName, lastName, socialSecurityNumber, grossSales and commissionRate). We
do this by using the **superclass constructor call syntax**—keyword super, followed by a set
of parentheses containing the superclass constructor arguments, which are used to initialize the superclass instance variables firstName, lastName, socialSecurityNumber,
grossSales and commissionRate, respectively. If BasePlusCommissionEmployee's constructor did not invoke the superclass's constructor explicitly, the compiler would attempt
to insert a call to the superclass's default or no-argument constructor. Class Commission-
Employee does not have such a constructor, so the compiler would issue an error. The explicit superclass constructor call in lines 14–15 of Fig. 9.8 must be the *first* statement in
the constructor's body. When a superclass contains a no-argument constructor, you can
use super() to call that constructor explicitly, but this is rarely done.

> ### Software Engineering Observation 9.6
> *You learned previously that you should not call a class's instance methods from its*
> *constructors and that we'll say why in Chapter 10. Calling a superclass constructor from*
> *a subclass constructor does not contradict this advice.*

BasePlusCommissionEmployee Methods Earnings and toString

The compiler generates errors for line 46 (Fig. 9.8) because CommissionEmployee's instance variables commissionRate and grossSales are private—subclass BasePlusCommissionEmployee's methods are *not* allowed to access superclass CommissionEmployee's
private instance variables. The compiler issues additional errors at lines 56–58 of
BasePlusCommissionEmployee's toString method for the same reason. The errors in
BasePlusCommissionEmployee could have been prevented by using the *get* methods inherited from class CommissionEmployee. For example, line 46 could have called getCommis-

sionRate and getGrossSales to access CommissionEmployee's private instance variables commissionRate and grossSales, respectively. Lines 56–58 also could have used appropriate *get* methods to retrieve the values of the superclass's instance variables.

9.4.4 CommissionEmployee–BasePlusCommissionEmployee Inheritance Hierarchy Using protected Instance Variables

To enable class BasePlusCommissionEmployee to directly access superclass instance variables firstName, lastName, socialSecurityNumber, grossSales and commissionRate, we can declare those members as protected in the superclass. As we discussed in Section 9.3, a superclass's protected members are accessible by all subclasses of that superclass. In the new CommissionEmployee class, we modified only lines 6–10 of Fig. 9.4 to declare the instance variables with the protected access modifier as follows:

```
protected final String firstName;
protected final String lastName;
protected final String socialSecurityNumber;
protected double grossSales; // gross weekly sales
protected double commissionRate; // commission percentage
```

The rest of the class declaration (which is not shown here) is identical to that of Fig. 9.4.

We could have declared CommissionEmployee's instance variables public to enable subclass BasePlusCommissionEmployee to access them. However, declaring public instance variables is poor software engineering because it allows unrestricted access to the these variables from any class, greatly increasing the chance of errors. With protected instance variables, the subclass gets access to the instance variables, but classes that are not subclasses and classes that are not in the same package cannot access these variables directly—recall that protected class members are also visible to other classes in the same package.

Class BasePlusCommissionEmployee

Class BasePlusCommissionEmployee (Fig. 9.9) extends the new version of class CommissionEmployee with protected instance variables. BasePlusCommissionEmployee objects inherit CommissionEmployee's protected instance variables firstName, lastName, socialSecurityNumber, grossSales and commissionRate—all these variables are now protected members of BasePlusCommissionEmployee. As a result, the compiler does not generate errors when compiling line 45 of method earnings and lines 54–56 of method toString. If another class extends this version of class BasePlusCommissionEmployee, the new subclass also can access the protected members.

```
1    // Fig. 9.9: BasePlusCommissionEmployee.java
2    // BasePlusCommissionEmployee inherits protected instance
3    // variables from CommissionEmployee.
4
5    public class BasePlusCommissionEmployee extends CommissionEmployee
6    {
7       private double baseSalary; // base salary per week
```

Fig. 9.9 | BasePlusCommissionEmployee inherits protected instance variables from CommissionEmployee. (Part 1 of 2.)

```java
 8
 9      // six-argument constructor
10      public BasePlusCommissionEmployee(String firstName, String lastName,
11          String socialSecurityNumber, double grossSales,
12          double commissionRate, double baseSalary)
13      {
14          super(firstName, lastName, socialSecurityNumber,
15             grossSales, commissionRate);
16
17          // if baseSalary is invalid throw exception
18          if (baseSalary < 0.0)
19             throw new IllegalArgumentException(
20                "Base salary must be >= 0.0");
21
22          this.baseSalary = baseSalary;
23      }
24
25      // set base salary
26      public void setBaseSalary(double baseSalary)
27      {
28          if (baseSalary < 0.0)
29             throw new IllegalArgumentException(
30                "Base salary must be >= 0.0");
31
32          this.baseSalary = baseSalary;
33      }
34
35      // return base salary
36      public double getBaseSalary()
37      {
38          return baseSalary;
39      }
40
41      // calculate earnings
42      @Override // indicates that this method overrides a superclass method
43      public double earnings()
44      {
45          return baseSalary + (commissionRate * grossSales);
46      }
47
48      // return String representation of BasePlusCommissionEmployee
49      @Override
50      public String toString()
51      {
52          return String.format(
53             "%s: %s %s%n%s: %s%n%s: %.2f%n%s: %.2f%n%s: %.2f",
54             "base-salaried commission employee", firstName, lastName,
55             "social security number", socialSecurityNumber,
56             "gross sales", grossSales, "commission rate", commissionRate,
57             "base salary", baseSalary);
58      }
59  } // end class BasePlusCommissionEmployee
```

Fig. 9.9 | BasePlusCommissionEmployee inherits protected instance variables from CommissionEmployee. (Part 2 of 2.)

A Subclass Object Contains the Instance Variables of All of Its Superclasses

When you create a BasePlusCommissionEmployee object, it contains all instance variables declared in the class hierarchy to that point—that is, those from classes Object (which does not have instance variables), CommissionEmployee and BasePlusCommissionEmployee. Class BasePlusCommissionEmployee does *not* inherit CommissionEmployee's five-argument constructor, but *explicitly invokes* it (lines 14–15) to initialize the instance variables that BasePlusCommissionEmployee inherited from CommissionEmployee. Similarly, CommissionEmployee's constructor *implicitly* calls class Object's constructor. BasePlusCommissionEmployee's constructor must *explicitly* call CommissionEmployee's constructor because CommissionEmployee does *not* have a no-argument constructor that could be invoked implicitly.

Testing Class BasePlusCommissionEmployee

The BasePlusCommissionEmployeeTest class for this example is identical to that of Fig. 9.7 and produces the same output, so we do not show it here. Although the version of class BasePlusCommissionEmployee in Fig. 9.6 does not use inheritance and the version in Fig. 9.9 does, both classes provide the *same* functionality. The source code in Fig. 9.9 (59 lines) is considerably shorter than that in Fig. 9.6 (127 lines), because most of the class's functionality is now inherited from CommissionEmployee—there's now only one copy of the CommissionEmployee functionality. This makes the code easier to maintain, modify and debug, because the code related to a CommissionEmployee exists only in that class.

Notes on Using protected Instance Variables

In this example, we declared superclass instance variables as protected so that subclasses could access them. Inheriting protected instance variables enables direct access to the variables by subclasses. In most cases, however, it's better to use private instance variables to encourage proper software engineering. Your code will be easier to maintain, modify and debug.

Using protected instance variables creates several potential problems. First, the subclass object can set an inherited variable's value directly without using a *set* method. Therefore, a subclass object can assign an invalid value to the variable, possibly leaving the object in an inconsistent state. For example, if we were to declare CommissionEmployee's instance variable grossSales as protected, a subclass object (e.g., BasePlusCommissionEmployee) could then assign a negative value to grossSales. Another problem with using protected instance variables is that subclass methods are more likely to be written so that they depend on the superclass's data implementation. In practice, subclasses should depend only on the superclass services (i.e., non-private methods) and not on the superclass data implementation. With protected instance variables in the superclass, we may need to modify all the subclasses of the superclass if the superclass implementation changes. For example, if for some reason we were to change the names of instance variables firstName and lastName to first and last, then we would have to do so for all occurrences in which a subclass directly references superclass instance variables firstName and lastName. Such a class is said to be **fragile** or **brittle**, because a small change in the superclass can "break" subclass implementation. You should be able to change the superclass implementation while still providing the same services to the subclasses. Of course, if the superclass services change, we must reimplement our subclasses. A third problem is that a class's protected members are visible to all classes in the same package as the class containing the protected members—this is not always desirable.

Software Engineering Observation 9.7

Use the protected access modifier when a superclass should provide a method only to its subclasses and other classes in the same package, but not to other clients.

Software Engineering Observation 9.8

Declaring superclass instance variables private (as opposed to protected) enables the superclass implementation of these instance variables to change without affecting subclass implementations.

Error-Prevention Tip 9.2

When possible, do not include protected instance variables in a superclass. Instead, include non-private methods that access private instance variables. This will help ensure that objects of the class maintain consistent states.

9.4.5 CommissionEmployee–BasePlusCommissionEmployee Inheritance Hierarchy Using private Instance Variables

Let's reexamine our hierarchy once more, this time using good software engineering practices.

Class CommissionEmployee

Class CommissionEmployee (Fig. 9.10) declares instance variables firstName, lastName, socialSecurityNumber, grossSales and commissionRate as *private* (lines 6–10) and provides public methods getFirstName, getLastName, getSocialSecurityNumber, set-GrossSales, getGrossSales, setCommissionRate, getCommissionRate, earnings and toString for manipulating these values. Methods earnings (lines 87–90) and toString (lines 93–101) use the class's *get* methods to obtain the values of its instance variables. If we decide to change the names of the instance variables, the earnings and toString declarations will *not* require modification—only the bodies of the *get* and *set* methods that directly manipulate the instance variables will need to change. These changes occur solely within the superclass—no changes to the subclass are needed. *Localizing the effects of changes* like this is a good software engineering practice.

```
1   // Fig. 9.10: CommissionEmployee.java
2   // CommissionEmployee class uses methods to manipulate its
3   // private instance variables.
4   public class CommissionEmployee
5   {
6      private final String firstName;
7      private final String lastName;
8      private final String socialSecurityNumber;
9      private double grossSales; // gross weekly sales
10     private double commissionRate; // commission percentage
```

Fig. 9.10 | CommissionEmployee class uses methods to manipulate its private instance variables. (Part 1 of 3.)

```
11
12      // five-argument constructor
13      public CommissionEmployee(String firstName, String lastName,
14         String socialSecurityNumber, double grossSales,
15         double commissionRate)
16      {
17         // implicit call to Object constructor occurs here
18
19         // if grossSales is invalid throw exception
20         if (grossSales < 0.0)
21            throw new IllegalArgumentException(
22               "Gross sales must be >= 0.0");
23
24         // if commissionRate is invalid throw exception
25         if (commissionRate <= 0.0 || commissionRate >= 1.0)
26            throw new IllegalArgumentException(
27               "Commission rate must be > 0.0 and < 1.0");
28
29         this.firstName = firstName;
30         this.lastName = lastName;
31         this.socialSecurityNumber = socialSecurityNumber;
32         this.grossSales = grossSales;
33         this.commissionRate = commissionRate;
34      } // end constructor
35
36      // return first name
37      public String getFirstName()
38      {
39         return firstName;
40      }
41
42      // return last name
43      public String getLastName()
44      {
45         return lastName;
46      }
47
48      // return social security number
49      public String getSocialSecurityNumber()
50      {
51         return socialSecurityNumber;
52      }
53
54      // set gross sales amount
55      public void setGrossSales(double grossSales)
56      {
57         if (grossSales < 0.0)
58            throw new IllegalArgumentException(
59               "Gross sales must be >= 0.0");
60
61         this.grossSales = grossSales;
62      }
```

Fig. 9.10 | CommissionEmployee class uses methods to manipulate its private instance variables. (Part 2 of 3.)

```
63
64      // return gross sales amount
65      public double getGrossSales()
66      {
67         return grossSales;
68      }
69
70      // set commission rate
71      public void setCommissionRate(double commissionRate)
72      {
73         if (commissionRate <= 0.0 || commissionRate >= 1.0)
74            throw new IllegalArgumentException(
75               "Commission rate must be > 0.0 and < 1.0");
76
77         this.commissionRate = commissionRate;
78      }
79
80      // return commission rate
81      public double getCommissionRate()
82      {
83         return commissionRate;
84      }
85
86      // calculate earnings
87      public double earnings()
88      {
89         return getCommissionRate() * getGrossSales();
90      }
91
92      // return String representation of CommissionEmployee object
93      @Override
94      public String toString()
95      {
96         return String.format("%s: %s %s%n%s: %s%n%s: %.2f%n%s: %.2f",
97            "commission employee", getFirstName(), getLastName(),
98            "social security number", getSocialSecurityNumber(),
99            "gross sales", getGrossSales(),
100           "commission rate", getCommissionRate());
101      }
102 } // end class CommissionEmployee
```

Fig. 9.10 | CommissionEmployee class uses methods to manipulate its private instance variables. (Part 3 of 3.)

Class *BasePlusCommissionEmployee*

Subclass BasePlusCommissionEmployee (Fig. 9.11) inherits CommissionEmployee's non-private methods and can access (in a controlled way) the private superclass members via those methods. Class BasePlusCommissionEmployee has several changes that distinguish it from Fig. 9.9. Methods earnings (lines 43–47) and toString (lines 50–55) each invoke method getBaseSalary to obtain the base salary value, rather than accessing baseSalary directly. If we decide to rename instance variable baseSalary, only the bodies of method setBaseSalary and getBaseSalary will need to change.

```
1   // Fig. 9.11: BasePlusCommissionEmployee.java
2   // BasePlusCommissionEmployee class inherits from CommissionEmployee
3   // and accesses the superclass's private data via inherited
4   // public methods.
5
6   public class BasePlusCommissionEmployee extends CommissionEmployee
7   {
8      private double baseSalary; // base salary per week
9
10     // six-argument constructor
11     public BasePlusCommissionEmployee(String firstName, String lastName,
12        String socialSecurityNumber, double grossSales,
13        double commissionRate, double baseSalary)
14     {
15        super(firstName, lastName, socialSecurityNumber,
16           grossSales, commissionRate);
17
18        // if baseSalary is invalid throw exception
19        if (baseSalary < 0.0)
20           throw new IllegalArgumentException(
21              "Base salary must be >= 0.0");
22
23        this.baseSalary = baseSalary;
24     }
25
26     // set base salary
27     public void setBaseSalary(double baseSalary)
28     {
29        if (baseSalary < 0.0)
30           throw new IllegalArgumentException(
31              "Base salary must be >= 0.0");
32
33        this.baseSalary = baseSalary;
34     }
35
36     // return base salary
37     public double getBaseSalary()
38     {
39        return baseSalary;
40     }
41
42     // calculate earnings
43     @Override
44     public double earnings()
45     {
46        return getBaseSalary() + super.earnings();
47     }
48
49     // return String representation of BasePlusCommissionEmployee
50     @Override
51     public String toString()
52     {
```

Fig. 9.11 | BasePlusCommissionEmployee class inherits from CommissionEmployee and accesses the superclass's private data via inherited public methods. (Part 1 of 2.)

```
53          return String.format("%s %s%n%s: %.2f", "base-salaried",
54              super.toString(), "base salary", getBaseSalary());
55      }
56  } // end class BasePlusCommissionEmployee
```

Fig. 9.11 | BasePlusCommissionEmployee class inherits from CommissionEmployee and accesses the superclass's private data via inherited public methods. (Part 2 of 2.)

Class *BasePlusCommissionEmployee's* **earnings** *Method*

Method earnings (lines 43–47) overrides class CommissionEmployee's earnings method (Fig. 9.10, lines 87–90) to calculate a base-salaried commission employee's earnings. The new version obtains the portion of the earnings based on commission alone by calling CommissionEmployee's earnings method with super.earnings() (line 46), then adds the base salary to this value to calculate the total earnings. Note the syntax used to invoke an *overridden* superclass method from a subclass—place the keyword super and a dot (.) separator before the superclass method name. This method invocation is a good software engineering practice—if a method performs all or some of the actions needed by another method, call that method rather than duplicate its code. By having BasePlusCommission-Employee's earnings method invoke CommissionEmployee's earnings method to calculate part of a BasePlusCommissionEmployee object's earnings, we *avoid duplicating the code* and *reduce code-maintenance problems.*

Common Programming Error 9.2

When a superclass method is overridden in a subclass, the subclass version often calls the superclass version to do a portion of the work. Failure to prefix the superclass method name with the keyword super and the dot (.) separator when calling the superclass's method causes the subclass method to call itself, potentially creating an error called infinite recursion, which would eventually cause the method-call stack to overflow—a fatal runtime error. Recursion, used correctly, is a powerful capability discussed in Chapter 18.

Class *BasePlusCommissionEmployee's* **toString** *Method*

Similarly, BasePlusCommissionEmployee's toString method (Fig. 9.11, lines 50–55) overrides CommissionEmployee's toString method (Fig. 9.10, lines 93–101) to return a String representation that's appropriate for a base-salaried commission employee. The new version creates part of a BasePlusCommissionEmployee object's String representation (i.e., the String "commission employee" and the values of class CommissionEmployee's private instance variables) by calling CommissionEmployee's toString method with the expression super.toString() (Fig. 9.11, line 54). BasePlusCommissionEmployee's toString method then completes the remainder of a BasePlusCommissionEmployee object's String representation (i.e., the value of class BasePlusCommissionEmployee's base salary).

Testing Class *BasePlusCommissionEmployee*

Class BasePlusCommissionEmployeeTest performs the same manipulations on a BasePlusCommissionEmployee object as in Fig. 9.7 and produces the same output, so we do not show it here. Although each BasePlusCommissionEmployee class you've seen behaves identically, the version in Fig. 9.11 is the best engineered. By using inheritance and by calling methods that hide the data and ensure consistency, we've efficiently and effectively constructed a well-engineered class.

9.5 Constructors in Subclasses

As we explained, instantiating a subclass object begins a chain of constructor calls in which the subclass constructor, before performing its own tasks, explicitly uses super to call one of the constructors in its direct superclass or implicitly calls the superclass's default or no-argument constructor. Similarly, if the superclass is derived from another class—true of every class except Object—the superclass constructor invokes the constructor of the next class up the hierarchy, and so on. The last constructor called in the chain is *always* Object's constructor. The original subclass constructor's body finishes executing *last*. Each superclass's constructor manipulates the superclass instance variables that the subclass object inherits. For example, consider again the CommissionEmployee–BasePlusCommissionEmployee hierarchy from Figs. 9.10–9.11. When an app creates a BasePlusCommissionEmployee object, its constructor is called. That constructor calls CommissionEmployee's constructor, which in turn calls Object's constructor. Class Object's constructor has an *empty body*, so it immediately returns control to CommissionEmployee's constructor, which then initializes the CommissionEmployee instance variables that are part of the BasePlusCommissionEmployee object. When CommissionEmployee's constructor completes execution, it returns control to BasePlusCommissionEmployee's constructor, which initializes the baseSalary.

Software Engineering Observation 9.9

Java ensures that even if a constructor does not assign a value to an instance variable, the variable is still initialized to its default value (e.g., 0 for primitive numeric types, false for booleans, null for references).

9.6 Class Object

As we discussed earlier in this chapter, all classes in Java inherit directly or indirectly from class Object (package java.lang), so its 11 methods (some are overloaded) are inherited by all other classes. Figure 9.12 summarizes Object's methods. We discuss several Object methods throughout this book (as indicated in Fig. 9.12).

Method	Description
equals	This method compares two objects for equality and returns true if they're equal and false otherwise. The method takes any Object as an argument. When objects of a particular class must be compared for equality, the class should override method equals to compare the *contents* of the two objects. For the requirements of implementing this method (which include also overriding method hashCode), refer to the method's documentation at docs.oracle.com/javase/7/docs/api/java/lang/Object.html#equals(java.lang.Object). The default equals implementation uses operator == to determine whether two references *refer to the same object* in memory. Section 14.3.3 demonstrates class String's equals method and differentiates between comparing String objects with == and with equals.
hashCode	Hashcodes are int values used for high-speed storage and retrieval of information stored in a data structure that's known as a hashtable (see Section 16.11). This method is also called as part of Object's default toString method implementation.

Fig. 9.12 | Object methods. (Part 1 of 2.)

Method	Description
toString	This method (introduced in Section 9.4.1) returns a String representation of an object. The default implementation of this method returns the package name and class name of the object's class typically followed by a hexadecimal representation of the value returned by the object's hashCode method.
wait, notify, notifyAll	Methods notify, notifyAll and the three overloaded versions of wait are related to multithreading, which is discussed in Chapter 23.
getClass	Every object in Java knows its own type at execution time. Method getClass (used in Sections 10.5– and 12.5) returns an object of class Class (package java.lang) that contains information about the object's type, such as its class name (returned by Class method getName).
finalize	This protected method is called by the garbage collector to perform termination housekeeping on an object just before the garbage collector reclaims the object's memory. Recall from Section 8.10 that it's unclear whether, or when, finalize will be called. For this reason, most programmers should avoid method finalize.
clone	This protected method, which takes no arguments and returns an Object reference, makes a copy of the object on which it's called. The default implementation performs a so-called **shallow copy**—instance-variable values in one object are copied into another object of the same type. For reference types, only the references are copied. A typical overridden clone method's implementation would perform a **deep copy** that creates a new object for each reference-type instance variable. *Implementing clone correctly is difficult. For this reason, its use is discouraged.* Some industry experts suggest that object serialization should be used instead. We discuss object serialization in Chapter 15. Recall from Chapter 7 that arrays are objects. As a result, like all other objects, arrays inherit the members of class Object. Every array has an overridden clone method that copies the array. However, if the array stores references to objects, the objects are not copied—a shallow copy is performed.

Fig. 9.12 | Object methods. (Part 2 of 2.)

9.7 (Optional) GUI and Graphics Case Study: Displaying Text and Images Using Labels

Programs often use labels when they need to display information or instructions to the user in a graphical user interface. **Labels** are a convenient way of identifying GUI components on the screen and keeping the user informed about the current state of the program. In Java, an object of class **JLabel** (from package javax.swing) can display text, an image or both. The example in Fig. 9.13 demonstrates several JLabel features, including a plain text label, an image label and a label with both text and an image.

```
1   // Fig 9.13: LabelDemo.java
2   // Demonstrates the use of labels.
3   import java.awt.BorderLayout;
4   import javax.swing.ImageIcon;
```

Fig. 9.13 | JLabel with text and with images. (Part 1 of 2.)

```
5   import javax.swing.JLabel;
6   import javax.swing.JFrame;
7
8   public class LabelDemo
9   {
10     public static void main(String[] args)
11     {
12        // Create a label with plain text
13        JLabel northLabel = new JLabel("North");
14
15        // create an icon from an image so we can put it on a JLabel
16        ImageIcon labelIcon = new ImageIcon("GUItip.gif");
17
18        // create a label with an Icon instead of text
19        JLabel centerLabel = new JLabel(labelIcon);
20
21        // create another label with an Icon
22        JLabel southLabel = new JLabel(labelIcon);
23
24        // set the label to display text (as well as an icon)
25        southLabel.setText("South");
26
27        // create a frame to hold the labels
28        JFrame application = new JFrame();
29
30        application.setDefaultCloseOperation(JFrame.EXIT_ON_CLOSE);
31
32        // add the labels to the frame; the second argument specifies
33        // where on the frame to add the label
34        application.add(northLabel, BorderLayout.NORTH);
35        application.add(centerLabel, BorderLayout.CENTER);
36        application.add(southLabel, BorderLayout.SOUTH);
37
38        application.setSize(300, 300);
39        application.setVisible(true);
40     } // end main
41  } // end class LabelDemo
```

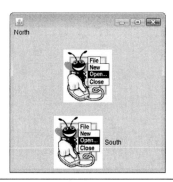

Fig. 9.13 | JLabel with text and with images. (Part 2 of 2.)

Lines 3–6 import the classes we need to display JLabels. BorderLayout from package java.awt contains constants that specify where we can place GUI components in the

JFrame. Class **ImageIcon** represents an image that can be displayed on a JLabel, and class JFrame represents the window that will contain all the labels.

Line 13 creates a JLabel that displays its constructor argument—the string "North". Line 16 declares local variable labelIcon and assigns it a new ImageIcon. The constructor for ImageIcon receives a String that specifies the path to the image. Since we specify only a filename, Java assumes that it's in the same directory as class LabelDemo. ImageIcon can load images in GIF, JPEG and PNG image formats. Line 19 declares and initializes local variable centerLabel with a JLabel that displays the labelIcon. Line 22 declares and initializes local variable southLabel with a JLabel similar to the one in line 19. However, line 25 calls method **setText** to change the text the label displays. Method setText can be called on any JLabel to change its text. This JLabel displays both the icon and the text.

Line 28 creates the JFrame that displays the JLabels, and line 30 indicates that the program should terminate when the JFrame is closed. We attach the labels to the JFrame in lines 34–36 by calling an overloaded version of method add that takes two parameters. The first parameter is the component we want to attach, and the second is the region in which it should be placed. Each JFrame has an associated **layout** that helps the JFrame position the GUI components that are attached to it. The default layout for a JFrame is known as a **BorderLayout** and has five regions—NORTH (top), SOUTH (bottom), EAST (right side), WEST (left side) and CENTER. Each of these is declared as a constant in class BorderLayout. When calling method add with one argument, the JFrame places the component in the CENTER automatically. If a position already contains a component, then the new component takes its place. Lines 38 and 39 set the size of the JFrame and make it visible on screen.

GUI and Graphics Case Study Exercise

9.1 Modify GUI and Graphics Case Study Exercise 8.1 to include a JLabel as a status bar that displays counts representing the number of each shape displayed. Class DrawPanel should declare a method that returns a String containing the status text. In main, first create the DrawPanel, then create the JLabel with the status text as an argument to the JLabel's constructor. Attach the JLabel to the SOUTH region of the JFrame, as shown in Fig. 9.14.

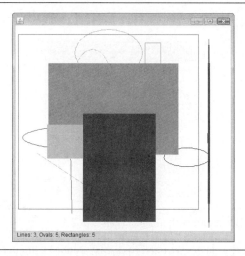

Fig. 9.14 | JLabel displaying shape statistics.

9.8 Wrap-Up

This chapter introduced inheritance—the ability to create classes by acquiring an existing class's members (without copying and pasting the code) and having the ability to embellish them with new capabilities. You learned the notions of superclasses and subclasses and used keyword extends to create a subclass that inherits members from a superclass. We showed how to use the @Override annotation to prevent unintended overloading by indicating that a method overrides a superclass method. We introduced the access modifier protected; subclass methods can directly access protected superclass members. You learned how to use super to access overridden superclass members. You also saw how constructors are used in inheritance hierarchies. Finally, you learned about the methods of class Object, the direct or indirect superclass of all Java classes.

In Chapter 10, Object-Oriented Programming: Polymorphism and Interfaces, we build on our discussion of inheritance by introducing *polymorphism*—an object-oriented concept that enables us to write programs that conveniently handle, in a more general and convenient manner, objects of a wide variety of classes related by inheritance. After studying Chapter 10, you'll be familiar with classes, objects, encapsulation, inheritance and polymorphism—the key technologies of object-oriented programming.

Summary

Section 9.1 Introduction
- Inheritance (p. 353) reduces program-development time.
- The direct superclass (p. 353) of a subclass is the one from which the subclass inherits. An indirect superclass (p. 353) of a subclass is two or more levels up the class hierarchy from that subclass.
- In single inheritance (p. 353), a class is derived from one superclass. In multiple inheritance, a class is derived from more than one direct superclass. Java does not support multiple inheritance.
- A subclass is more specific than its superclass and represents a smaller group of objects (p. 353).
- Every object of a subclass is also an object of that class's superclass. However, a superclass object is not an object of its class's subclasses.
- An *is-a* relationship (p. 354) represents inheritance. In an *is-a* relationship, an object of a subclass also can be treated as an object of its superclass.
- A *has-a* relationship (p. 354) represents composition. In a *has-a* relationship, a class object contains references to objects of other classes.

Section 9.2 Superclasses and Subclasses
- Single-inheritance relationships form treelike hierarchical structures—a superclass exists in a hierarchical relationship with its subclasses.

Section 9.3 protected Members
- A superclass's public members are accessible wherever the program has a reference to an object of that superclass or one of its subclasses.
- A superclass's private members can be accessed directly only within the superclass's declaration.
- A superclass's protected members (p. 356) have an intermediate level of protection between public and private access. They can be accessed by members of the superclass, by members of its subclasses and by members of other classes in the same package.

- A superclass's private members are hidden in its subclasses and can be accessed only through the public or protected methods inherited from the superclass.

- An overridden superclass method can be accessed from a subclass if the superclass method name is preceded by super (p. 356) and a dot (.) separator.

Section 9.4 Relationship Between Superclasses and Subclasses

- A subclass cannot access the private members of its superclass, but it can access the non-private members.

- A subclass can invoke a constructor of its superclass by using the keyword super, followed by a set of parentheses containing the superclass constructor arguments. This must appear as the first statement in the subclass constructor's body.

- A superclass method can be overridden in a subclass to declare an appropriate implementation for the subclass.

- The @Override annotation (p. 361) indicates that a method should override a superclass method. When the compiler encounters a method declared with @Override, it compares the method's signature with the superclass's method signatures. If there isn't an exact match, the compiler issues an error message, such as "method does not override or implement a method from a supertype."

- Method toString takes no arguments and returns a String. The Object class's toString method is normally overridden by a subclass.

- When an object is output using the %s format specifier, the object's toString method is called implicitly to obtain its String representation.

Section 9.5 Constructors in Subclasses

- The first task of a subclass constructor is to call its direct superclass's constructor (p. 370) to ensure that the instance variables inherited from the superclass are initialized.

Section 9.6 Class Object

- See the table of class Object's methods in Fig. 9.12.

Self-Review Exercises

9.1 Fill in the blanks in each of the following statements:
  a) _____ is a form of software reusability in which new classes acquire the members of existing classes and embellish those classes with new capabilities.
  b) A superclass's _____ members can be accessed in the superclass declaration *and in* subclass declarations.
  c) In a(n) _____ relationship, an object of a subclass can also be treated as an object of its superclass.
  d) In a(n) _____ relationship, a class object has references to objects of other classes as members.
  e) In single inheritance, a class exists in a(n) _____ relationship with its subclasses.
  f) A superclass's _____ members are accessible anywhere that the program has a reference to an object of that superclass or to an object of one of its subclasses.
  g) When an object of a subclass is instantiated, a superclass _____ is called implicitly or explicitly.
  h) Subclass constructors can call superclass constructors via the _____ keyword.

9.2 State whether each of the following is *true* or *false*. If a statement is *false*, explain why.
  a) Superclass constructors are not inherited by subclasses.
  b) A *has-a* relationship is implemented via inheritance.

c) A Car class has an *is-a* relationship with the SteeringWheel and Brakes classes.
d) When a subclass redefines a superclass method by using the same signature, the subclass is said to overload that superclass method.

Answers to Self-Review Exercises

9.1 a) Inheritance. b) public and protected. c) *is-a* or inheritance. d) *has-a* or composition. e) hierarchical. f) public. g) constructor. h) super.

9.2 a) True. b) False. A *has-a* relationship is implemented via composition. An *is-a* relationship is implemented via inheritance. c) False. This is an example of a *has-a* relationship. Class Car has an *is-a* relationship with class Vehicle. d) False. This is known as overriding, not overloading—an overloaded method has the same name, but a different signature.

Exercises

9.3 *(Using Composition Rather Than Inheritance)* Many programs written with inheritance could be written with composition instead, and vice versa. Rewrite class BasePlusCommissionEmployee (Fig. 9.11) of the CommissionEmployee–BasePlusCommissionEmployee hierarchy to use composition rather than inheritance.

9.4 *(Software Reuse)* Discuss the ways in which inheritance promotes software reuse, saves time during program development and helps prevent errors.

9.5 *(Student Inheritance Hierarchy)* Draw an inheritance hierarchy for students at a university similar to the hierarchy shown in Fig. 9.2. Use Student as the superclass of the hierarchy, then extend Student with classes UndergraduateStudent and GraduateStudent. Continue to extend the hierarchy as deep (i.e., as many levels) as possible. For example, Freshman, Sophomore, Junior and Senior might extend UndergraduateStudent, and DoctoralStudent and MastersStudent might be subclasses of GraduateStudent. After drawing the hierarchy, discuss the relationships that exist between the classes. [*Note:* You do not need to write any code for this exercise.]

9.6 *(Shape Inheritance Hierarchy)* The world of shapes is much richer than the shapes included in the inheritance hierarchy of Fig. 9.3. Write down all the shapes you can think of—both two-dimensional and three-dimensional—and form them into a more complete Shape hierarchy with as many levels as possible. Your hierarchy should have class Shape at the top. Classes TwoDimensionalShape and ThreeDimensionalShape should extend Shape. Add additional subclasses, such as Quadrilateral and Sphere, at their correct locations in the hierarchy as necessary.

9.7 *(protected vs. private)* Some programmers prefer not to use protected access, because they believe it breaks the encapsulation of the superclass. Discuss the relative merits of using protected access vs. using private access in superclasses.

9.8 *(Quadrilateral Inheritance Hierarchy)* Write an inheritance hierarchy for classes Quadrilateral, Trapezoid, Parallelogram, Rectangle and Square. Use Quadrilateral as the superclass of the hierarchy. Create and use a Point class to represent the points in each shape. Make the hierarchy as deep (i.e., as many levels) as possible. Specify the instance variables and methods for each class. The private instance variables of Quadrilateral should be the *x-y* coordinate pairs for the four endpoints of the Quadrilateral. Write a program that instantiates objects of your classes and outputs each object's area (except Quadrilateral).

9.9 *(What Does Each Code Snippet Do?)*
a) Assume that the following method call is located in an overridden earnings method in a subclass:

```
super.earnings()
```

b) Assume that the following line of code appears before a method declaration:

```
@Override
```

c) Assume that the following line of code appears as the first statement in a constructor's body:

```
super(firstArgument, secondArgument);
```

9.10   *(Write a Line of Code)* Write a line of code that performs each of the following tasks:
   a) Specify that class PieceWorker inherits from class Employee.
   b) Call superclass Employee's toString method from subclass PieceWorker's toString method.
   c) Call superclass Employee's constructor from subclass PieceWorker's constructor—assume that the superclass constructor receives three Strings representing the first name, last name and social security number.

9.11   *(Using super in a Constructor's Body)* Explain why you would use super in the first statement of a subclass constructor's body.

9.12   *(Using super in an Instance Method's Body)* Explain why you would use super in the body of a subclass's instance method.

9.13   *(Calling get Methods in a Class's Body)* In Figs. 9.10–9.11 methods earnings and toString each call various *get* methods within the same class. Explain the benefits of calling these *get* methods within the classes.

9.14   *(Employee Hierarchy)* In this chapter, you studied an inheritance hierarchy in which class BasePlusCommissionEmployee inherited from class CommissionEmployee. However, not all types of employees are CommissionEmployees. In this exercise, you'll create a more general Employee superclass that *factors out* the attributes and behaviors in class CommissionEmployee that are common to all Employees. The common attributes and behaviors for all Employees are firstName, lastName, socialSecurityNumber, getFirstName, getLastName, getSocialSecurityNumber and a portion of method toString. Create a new superclass Employee that contains these instance variables and methods and a constructor. Next, rewrite class CommissionEmployee from Section 9.4.5 as a subclass of Employee. Class CommissionEmployee should contain only the instance variables and methods that are not declared in superclass Employee. Class CommissionEmployee's constructor should invoke class Employee's constructor and CommissionEmployee's toString method should invoke Employee's toString method. Once you've completed these modifications, run the CommissionEmployeeTest and BasePlusCommissionEmployeeTest apps using these new classes to ensure that the apps still display the same results for a CommissionEmployee object and BasePlusCommissionEmployee object, respectively.

9.15   *(Creating a New Subclass of Employee)* Other types of Employees might include SalariedEmployees who get paid a fixed weekly salary, PieceWorkers who get paid by the number of pieces they produce or HourlyEmployees who get paid an hourly wage with time-and-a-half—1.5 times the hourly wage—for hours worked over 40 hours.
   Create class HourlyEmployee that inherits from class Employee (Exercise 9.14) and has instance variable hours (a double) that represents the hours worked, instance variable wage (a double) that represents the wages per hour, a constructor that takes as arguments a first name, a last name, a social security number, an hourly wage and the number of hours worked, *set* and *get* methods for manipulating the hours and wage, an earnings method to calculate an HourlyEmployee's earnings based on the hours worked and a toString method that returns the HourlyEmployee's String representation. Method setWage should ensure that wage is nonnegative, and setHours should ensure that the value of hours is between 0 and 168 (the total number of hours in a week). Use class HourlyEmployee in a test program that's similar to the one in Fig. 9.5.

Object-Oriented Programming: Polymorphism and Interfaces

General propositions do not decide concrete cases.
—Oliver Wendell Holmes

A philosopher of imposing stature doesn't think in a vacuum. Even his most abstract ideas are, to some extent, conditioned by what is or is not known in the time when he lives.
—Alfred North Whitehead

Objectives

In this chapter you'll:

- Learn the concept of polymorphism.

- Use overridden methods to effect polymorphism.

- Distinguish between abstract and concrete classes.

- Declare abstract methods to create abstract classes.

- Learn how polymorphism makes systems extensible and maintainable.

- Determine an object's type at execution time.

- Declare and implement interfaces, and become familiar with the Java SE 8 interface enhancements.

10.1 Introduction

We continue our study of object-oriented programming by explaining and demonstrating **polymorphism** with inheritance hierarchies. Polymorphism enables you to "program in the *general*" rather than "program in the *specific*." In particular, polymorphism enables you to write programs that process objects that share the same superclass, either directly or indirectly, as if they were all objects of the superclass; this can simplify programming.

Consider the following example of polymorphism. Suppose we create a program that simulates the movement of several types of animals for a biological study. Classes Fish, Frog and Bird represent the types of animals under investigation. Imagine that each class extends superclass Animal, which contains a method move and maintains an animal's current location as *x-y* coordinates. Each subclass implements method move. Our program maintains an Animal array containing references to objects of the various Animal subclasses. To simulate the animals' movements, the program sends each object the *same* message once per second—namely, move. Each specific type of Animal responds to a move message in its own way—a Fish might swim three feet, a Frog might jump five feet and a Bird might fly ten feet. Each object knows how to modify its *x-y* coordinates appropriately for its *specific* type of movement. Relying on each object to know how to "do the right thing" (i.e., do what's appropriate for that type of object) in response to the *same* method call is the key concept of polymorphism. The *same* message (in this case, move) sent to a *variety* of objects has *many forms* of results—hence the term polymorphism.

Implementing for Extensibility

With polymorphism, we can design and implement systems that are easily *extensible*—new classes can be added with little or no modification to the general portions of the program, as long as the new classes are part of the inheritance hierarchy that the program processes generically. The new classes simply "plug right in." The only parts of a program that must be altered are those that require direct knowledge of the new classes that we add to the hierarchy. For example, if we extend class Animal to create class Tortoise (which might respond to a move message by crawling one inch), we need to write only the Tortoise class and the part of the simulation that instantiates a Tortoise object. The portions of the simulation that tell each Animal to move generically can remain the same.

Chapter Overview

First, we discuss common examples of polymorphism. We then provide a simple example demonstrating polymorphic behavior. We use superclass references to manipulate *both* superclass objects and subclass objects polymorphically.

We then present a case study that revisits the employee hierarchy of Section 9.4.5. We develop a simple payroll application that polymorphically calculates the weekly pay of several different types of employees using each employee's earnings method. Though the earnings of each type of employee are calculated in a *specific* way, polymorphism allows us to process the employees "in the *general*." In the case study, we enlarge the hierarchy to include two new classes—SalariedEmployee (for people paid a fixed weekly salary) and HourlyEmployee (for people paid an hourly salary and "time-and-a-half" for overtime). We declare a common set of functionality for all the classes in the updated hierarchy in an "abstract" class, Employee, from which "concrete" classes SalariedEmployee, HourlyEmployee and CommissionEmployee inherit directly and "concrete" class BasePlusCommissionEmployee inherits indirectly. As you'll soon see, *when we invoke each employee's* earnings *method off a superclass* Employee *reference (regardless of the employee's type), the correct earnings subclass calculation is performed,* due to Java's polymorphic capabilities.

Programming in the Specific

Occasionally, when performing polymorphic processing, we need to program "in the *specific*." Our Employee case study demonstrates that a program can determine the *type* of an object at *execution time* and act on that object accordingly. In the case study, we've decided that BasePlusCommissionEmployees should receive 10% raises on their base salaries. So, we use these capabilities to determine whether a particular employee object *is a* BasePlusCommissionEmployee. If so, we increase that employee's base salary by 10%.

Interfaces

The chapter continues with an introduction to Java *interfaces*, which are particularly useful for assigning *common* functionality to possibly *unrelated* classes. This allows objects of these classes to be processed polymorphically—objects of classes that **implement** the *same* interface can respond to all of the interface method calls. To demonstrate creating and using interfaces, we modify our payroll application to create a generalized accounts payable application that can calculate payments due for company employees *and* invoice amounts to be billed for purchased goods.

10.2 Polymorphism Examples

Let's consider several additional examples of polymorphism.

Quadrilaterals

If class `Rectangle` is derived from class `Quadrilateral`, then a `Rectangle` object *is a* more *specific* version of a `Quadrilateral`. Any operation (e.g., calculating the perimeter or the area) that can be performed on a `Quadrilateral` can also be performed on a `Rectangle`. These operations can also be performed on other `Quadrilateral`s, such as `Square`s, `Parallelogram`s and `Trapezoid`s. The polymorphism occurs when a program invokes a method through a superclass `Quadrilateral` variable—at execution time, the correct subclass version of the method is called, based on the type of the reference stored in the superclass variable. You'll see a simple code example that illustrates this process in Section 10.3.

Space Objects in a Video Game

Suppose we design a video game that manipulates objects of classes `Martian`, `Venusian`, `Plutonian`, `SpaceShip` and `LaserBeam`. Imagine that each class inherits from the superclass `SpaceObject`, which contains method `draw`. Each subclass implements this method. A screen manager maintains a collection (e.g., a `SpaceObject` array) of references to objects of the various classes. To refresh the screen, the screen manager periodically sends each object the *same* message—namely, `draw`. However, each object responds its *own* way, based on its class. For example, a `Martian` object might draw itself in red with green eyes and the appropriate number of antennae. A `SpaceShip` object might draw itself as a bright silver flying saucer. A `LaserBeam` object might draw itself as a bright red beam across the screen. Again, the *same* message (in this case, `draw`) sent to a *variety* of objects has "many forms" of results.

A screen manager might use polymorphism to facilitate adding new classes to a system with minimal modifications to the system's code. Suppose that we want to add `Mercurian` objects to our video game. To do so, we'd build a class `Mercurian` that extends `SpaceObject` and provides its own `draw` method implementation. When `Mercurian` objects appear in the `SpaceObject` collection, the screen-manager code *invokes method draw, exactly as it does for every other object in the collection, regardless of its type.* So the new `Mercurian` objects simply "plug right in" without any modification of the screen manager code by the programmer. Thus, without modifying the system (other than to build new classes and modify the code that creates new objects), you can use polymorphism to conveniently include additional types that were not even considered when the system was created.

Software Engineering Observation 10.1

Polymorphism enables you to deal in generalities and let the execution-time environment handle the specifics. You can tell objects to behave in manners appropriate to those objects, without knowing their specific types, as long as they belong to the same inheritance hierarchy.

Software Engineering Observation 10.2

Polymorphism promotes extensibility: Software that invokes polymorphic behavior is independent of the object types to which messages are sent. New object types that can respond to existing method calls can be incorporated into a system without modifying the base system. Only client code that instantiates new objects must be modified to accommodate new types.

10.3 Demonstrating Polymorphic Behavior

Section 9.4 created a class hierarchy, in which class `BasePlusCommissionEmployee` inherited from `CommissionEmployee`. The examples in that section manipulated `CommissionEmployee` and `BasePlusCommissionEmployee` objects by using references to them to invoke their methods—we aimed superclass variables at superclass objects and subclass variables at subclass objects. These assignments are natural and straightforward—superclass variables are *intended* to refer to superclass objects, and subclass variables are *intended* to refer to subclass objects. However, as you'll soon see, other assignments are possible.

In the next example, we aim a *superclass* reference at a *subclass* object. We then show how invoking a method on a subclass object via a superclass reference invokes the *subclass* functionality—the type of the *referenced object*, not the type of the *variable*, determines which method is called. This example demonstrates that *an object of a subclass can be treated as an object of its superclass,* enabling various interesting manipulations. A program can create an array of superclass variables that refer to objects of many subclass types. This is allowed because each subclass object *is an* object of its superclass. For instance, we can assign the reference of a `BasePlusCommissionEmployee` object to a superclass `CommissionEmployee` variable, because a `BasePlusCommissionEmployee` *is a* `CommissionEmployee`—so we can treat a `BasePlusCommissionEmployee` as a `CommissionEmployee`.

As you'll learn later in the chapter, you *cannot treat a superclass object as a subclass object,* because a superclass object is *not* an object of any of its subclasses. For example, we cannot assign the reference of a `CommissionEmployee` object to a subclass `BasePlusCommissionEmployee` variable, because a `CommissionEmployee` is *not* a `BasePlusCommissionEmployee`—a `CommissionEmployee` does *not* have a `baseSalary` instance variable and does *not* have methods `setBaseSalary` and `getBaseSalary`. The *is-a* relationship applies only *up the hierarchy* from a subclass to its direct (and indirect) superclasses, and *not* vice versa (i.e., not down the hierarchy from a superclass to its subclasses or indirect subclasses).

The Java compiler *does* allow the assignment of a superclass reference to a subclass variable if we explicitly *cast* the superclass reference to the subclass type. Why would we ever want to perform such an assignment? A superclass reference can be used to invoke *only* the methods declared in the superclass—attempting to invoke *subclass-only* methods through a superclass reference results in compilation errors. If a program needs to perform a subclass-specific operation on a subclass object referenced by a superclass variable, the program must first cast the superclass reference to a subclass reference through a technique known as **downcasting**. This enables the program to invoke subclass methods that are *not* in the superclass. We demonstrate the mechanics of downcasting in Section 10.5.

> ### Software Engineering Observation 10.3
> *Although it's allowed, you should generally avoid downcasting.*

The example in Fig. 10.1 demonstrates three ways to use superclass and subclass variables to store references to superclass and subclass objects. The first two are straightforward—as in Section 9.4, we assign a superclass reference to a superclass variable, and a subclass reference to a subclass variable. Then we demonstrate the relationship between subclasses and superclasses (i.e., the *is-a* relationship) by assigning a subclass reference to a superclass variable. This program uses classes `CommissionEmployee` and `BasePlusCommissionEmployee` from Fig. 9.10 and Fig. 9.11, respectively.

```
1   // Fig. 10.1: PolymorphismTest.java
2   // Assigning superclass and subclass references to superclass and
3   // subclass variables.
4
5   public class PolymorphismTest
6   {
7      public static void main(String[] args)
8      {
9         // assign superclass reference to superclass variable
10        CommissionEmployee commissionEmployee = new CommissionEmployee(
11           "Sue", "Jones", "222-22-2222", 10000, .06);
12
13        // assign subclass reference to subclass variable
14        BasePlusCommissionEmployee basePlusCommissionEmployee =
15           new BasePlusCommissionEmployee(
16           "Bob", "Lewis", "333-33-3333", 5000, .04, 300);
17
18        // invoke toString on superclass object using superclass variable
19        System.out.printf("%s %s:%n%n%s%n%n",
20           "Call CommissionEmployee's toString with superclass reference ",
21           "to superclass object", commissionEmployee.toString());
22
23        // invoke toString on subclass object using subclass variable
24        System.out.printf("%s %s:%n%n%s%n%n",
25           "Call BasePlusCommissionEmployee's toString with subclass",
26           "reference to subclass object",
27           basePlusCommissionEmployee.toString());
28
29        // invoke toString on subclass object using superclass variable
30        CommissionEmployee commissionEmployee2 =
31           basePlusCommissionEmployee;
32        System.out.printf("%s %s:%n%n%s%n",
33           "Call BasePlusCommissionEmployee's toString with superclass",
34           "reference to subclass object", commissionEmployee2.toString());
35     } // end main
36  } // end class PolymorphismTest
```

```
Call CommissionEmployee's toString with superclass reference to superclass
object:

commission employee: Sue Jones
social security number: 222-22-2222
gross sales: 10000.00
commission rate: 0.06

Call BasePlusCommissionEmployee's toString with subclass reference to
subclass object:

base-salaried commission employee: Bob Lewis
social security number: 333-33-3333
gross sales: 5000.00
commission rate: 0.04
base salary: 300.00
```

Fig. 10.1 | Assigning superclass and subclass references to superclass and subclass variables. (Part 1 of 2.)

```
Call BasePlusCommissionEmployee's toString with superclass reference to
subclass object:

base-salaried commission employee: Bob Lewis
social security number: 333-33-3333
gross sales: 5000.00
commission rate: 0.04
base salary: 300.00
```

Fig. 10.1 | Assigning superclass and subclass references to superclass and subclass variables. (Part 2 of 2.)

In Fig. 10.1, lines 10–11 create a CommissionEmployee object and assign its reference to a CommissionEmployee variable. Lines 14–16 create a BasePlusCommissionEmployee object and assign its reference to a BasePlusCommissionEmployee variable. These assignments are natural—for example, a CommissionEmployee variable's primary purpose is to hold a reference to a CommissionEmployee object. Lines 19–21 use commissionEmployee to invoke toString *explicitly*. Because commissionEmployee refers to a CommissionEmployee object, superclass CommissionEmployee's version of toString is called. Similarly, lines 24–27 use basePlusCommissionEmployee to invoke toString *explicitly* on the BasePlusCommissionEmployee object. This invokes subclass BasePlusCommissionEmployee's version of toString.

Lines 30–31 then assign the reference of subclass object basePlusCommissionEmployee to a superclass CommissionEmployee variable, which lines 32–34 use to invoke method toString. *When a superclass variable contains a reference to a subclass object, and that reference is used to call a method, the subclass version of the method is called.* Hence, commissionEmployee2.toString() in line 34 actually calls class BasePlusCommissionEmployee's toString method. The Java compiler allows this "crossover" because an object of a subclass *is an* object of its superclass (but *not* vice versa). When the compiler encounters a method call made through a variable, the compiler determines if the method can be called by checking the variable's class type. If that class contains the proper method declaration (or inherits one), the call is compiled. At execution time, the type of the object to which the variable refers determines the actual method to use. This process, called *dynamic binding*, is discussed in detail in Section 10.5.

10.4 Abstract Classes and Methods

When we think of a class, we assume that programs will create objects of that type. Sometimes it's useful to declare classes—called **abstract classes**—for which you *never* intend to create objects. Because they're used only as superclasses in inheritance hierarchies, we refer to them as **abstract superclasses**. These classes cannot be used to instantiate objects, because, as we'll soon see, abstract classes are *incomplete*. Subclasses must declare the "missing pieces" to become "concrete" classes, from which you can instantiate objects. Otherwise, these subclasses, too, will be abstract. We demonstrate abstract classes in Section 10.5.

Purpose of Abstract Classes
An abstract class's purpose is to provide an appropriate superclass from which other classes can inherit and thus share a common design. In the Shape hierarchy of Fig. 9.3, for exam-

ple, subclasses inherit the notion of what it means to be a Shape—perhaps common attributes such as location, color and borderThickness, and behaviors such as draw, move, resize and changeColor. Classes that can be used to instantiate objects are called **concrete classes**. Such classes provide implementations of *every* method they declare (some of the implementations can be inherited). For example, we could derive concrete classes Circle, Square and Triangle from abstract superclass TwoDimensionalShape. Similarly, we could derive concrete classes Sphere, Cube and Tetrahedron from abstract superclass ThreeDimensionalShape. Abstract superclasses are *too general* to create real objects—they specify only what is common among subclasses. We need to be more *specific* before we can create objects. For example, if you send the draw message to abstract class TwoDimensionalShape, the class knows that two-dimensional shapes should be *drawable*, but it does not know what *specific* shape to draw, so it cannot implement a real draw method. Concrete classes provide the specifics that make it reasonable to instantiate objects.

Not all hierarchies contain abstract classes. However, you'll often write client code that uses only abstract superclass types to reduce the client code's dependencies on a range of subclass types. For example, you can write a method with a parameter of an abstract superclass type. When called, such a method can receive an object of *any* concrete class that directly or indirectly extends the superclass specified as the parameter's type.

Abstract classes sometimes constitute several levels of a hierarchy. For example, the Shape hierarchy of Fig. 9.3 begins with abstract class Shape. On the next level of the hierarchy are *abstract* classes TwoDimensionalShape and ThreeDimensionalShape. The next level of the hierarchy declares *concrete* classes for TwoDimensionalShapes (Circle, Square and Triangle) and for ThreeDimensionalShapes (Sphere, Cube and Tetrahedron).

Declaring an Abstract Class and Abstract Methods

You make a class abstract by declaring it with keyword **abstract**. An abstract class normally contains one or more **abstract methods**. An abstract method is an *instance method* with keyword abstract in its declaration, as in

```
public abstract void draw(); // abstract method
```

Abstract methods do *not* provide implementations. A class that contains *any* abstract methods must be explicitly declared abstract even if that class contains some concrete (nonabstract) methods. Each concrete subclass of an abstract superclass also must provide concrete implementations of each of the superclass's abstract methods. Constructors and static methods cannot be declared abstract. Constructors are *not* inherited, so an abstract constructor could never be implemented. Though non-private static methods are inherited, they cannot be overridden. Since abstract methods are meant to be overridden so that they can process objects based on their types, it would not make sense to declare a static method as abstract.

Software Engineering Observation 10.4

An abstract class declares common attributes and behaviors (both abstract and concrete) of the various classes in a class hierarchy. An abstract class typically contains one or more abstract methods that subclasses must override if they are to be concrete. The instance variables and concrete methods of an abstract class are subject to the normal rules of inheritance.

Common Programming Error 10.1

Attempting to instantiate an object of an abstract class is a compilation error.

Common Programming Error 10.2

Failure to implement a superclass's abstract methods in a subclass is a compilation error unless the subclass is also declared abstract.

Using Abstract Classes to Declare Variables

Although we cannot instantiate objects of abstract superclasses, you'll soon see that we *can* use abstract superclasses to declare variables that can hold references to objects of *any* concrete class *derived from* those abstract superclasses. We'll use such variables to manipulate subclass objects *polymorphically*. You also can use abstract superclass names to invoke static methods declared in those abstract superclasses.

Consider another application of polymorphism. A drawing program needs to display many shapes, including types of new shapes that you'll *add* to the system *after* writing the drawing program. The drawing program might need to display shapes, such as Circles, Triangles, Rectangles or others, that derive from abstract class Shape. The drawing program uses Shape variables to manage the objects that are displayed. To draw any object in this inheritance hierarchy, the drawing program uses a superclass Shape variable containing a reference to the subclass object to invoke the object's draw method. This method is declared abstract in superclass Shape, so each concrete subclass *must* implement method draw in a manner specific to that shape—each object in the Shape inheritance hierarchy *knows how to draw itself.* The drawing program does not have to worry about the type of each object or whether the program has ever encountered objects of that type.

Layered Software Systems

Polymorphism is particularly effective for implementing so-called *layered software systems*. In operating systems, for example, each type of physical device could operate quite differently from the others. Even so, commands to read or write data from and to devices may have a certain uniformity. For each device, the operating system uses a piece of software called a *device driver* to control all communication between the system and the device. The write message sent to a device-driver object needs to be interpreted specifically in the context of that driver and how it manipulates devices of a specific type. However, the write call itself really is no different from the write to any other device in the system—place some number of bytes from memory onto that device. An object-oriented operating system might use an abstract superclass to provide an "interface" appropriate for all device drivers. Then, through inheritance from that abstract superclass, subclasses are formed that all behave similarly. The device-driver methods are declared as abstract methods in the abstract superclass. The implementations of these abstract methods are provided in the concrete subclasses that correspond to the specific types of device drivers. New devices are always being developed, often long after the operating system has been released. When you buy a new device, it comes with a device driver provided by the device vendor. The device is immediately operational after you connect it to your computer and install the driver. This is another elegant example of how polymorphism makes systems *extensible.*

10.5 Case Study: Payroll System Using Polymorphism

This section reexamines the CommissionEmployee-BasePlusCommissionEmployee hierarchy that we explored throughout Section 9.4. Now we use an abstract method and polymorphism to perform payroll calculations based on an enhanced employee inheritance hierarchy that meets the following requirements:

> *A company pays its employees on a weekly basis. The employees are of four types: Salaried employees are paid a fixed weekly salary regardless of the number of hours worked, hourly employees are paid by the hour and receive overtime pay (i.e., 1.5 times their hourly salary rate) for all hours worked in excess of 40 hours, commission employees are paid a percentage of their sales and base-salaried commission employees receive a base salary plus a percentage of their sales. For the current pay period, the company has decided to reward salaried-commission employees by adding 10% to their base salaries. The company wants you to write an application that performs its payroll calculations polymorphically.*

We use abstract class Employee to represent the general concept of an employee. The classes that extend Employee are SalariedEmployee, CommissionEmployee and HourlyEmployee. Class BasePlusCommissionEmployee—which extends CommissionEmployee—represents the last employee type. The UML class diagram in Fig. 10.2 shows the inheritance hierarchy for our polymorphic employee-payroll application. Abstract class name Employee is italicized—a convention of the UML.

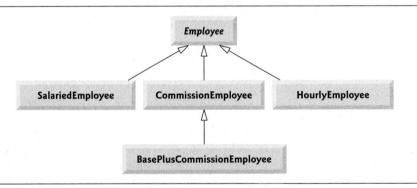

Fig. 10.2 | Employee hierarchy UML class diagram.

Abstract superclass Employee declares the "interface" to the hierarchy—that is, the set of methods that a program can invoke on all Employee objects. We use the term "interface" here in a *general* sense to refer to the various ways programs can communicate with objects of *any* Employee subclass. Be careful not to confuse the general notion of an "interface" with the formal notion of a Java interface, the subject of Section 10.9. Each employee, regardless of the way his or her earnings are calculated, has a first name, a last name and a social security number, so private instance variables firstName, lastName and socialSecurityNumber appear in abstract superclass Employee.

The diagram in Fig. 10.3 shows each of the five classes in the hierarchy down the left side and methods earnings and toString across the top. For each class, the diagram shows the desired results of each method. We do not list superclass Employee's *get* methods because they're *not* overridden in any of the subclasses—each of these methods is inherited and used "as is" by each subclass.

	earnings	toString
Employee	`abstract`	*firstName lastName* `social security number:` *SSN*
Salaried-Employee	`weeklySalary`	`salaried employee:` *firstName lastName* `social security number:` *SSN* `weekly salary:` *weeklySalary*

Hourly-Employee	`if (hours <= 40)`
	`    wage * hours`
	`else if (hours > 40)`
	`{`
	`    40 * wage +`
	`    ( hours - 40 ) *`
	`    wage * 1.5`
	`}`
		`hourly employee:` *firstName lastName*
		`social security number:` *SSN*
		`hourly wage:` *wage*`; hours worked:` *hours*

Commission-Employee	`commissionRate *` `grossSales`	`commission employee:` *firstName lastName* `social security number:` *SSN* `gross sales:` *grossSales*`;` `commission rate:` *commissionRate*

BasePlus-Commission-Employee	`(commissionRate *`
	`grossSales) +`
	`baseSalary`
		`base salaried commission employee:`
		    firstName lastName
		`social security number:` *SSN*
		`gross sales:` *grossSales*`;`
		`commission rate:` *commissionRate*`;`
		`base salary:` *baseSalary*

Fig. 10.3 | Polymorphic interface for the `Employee` hierarchy classes.

The following sections implement the `Employee` class hierarchy of Fig. 10.2. The first section implements *abstract superclass* `Employee`. The next four sections each implement one of the *concrete* classes. The last section implements a test program that builds objects of all these classes and processes those objects polymorphically.

10.5.1 Abstract Superclass Employee

Class `Employee` (Fig. 10.4) provides methods `earnings` and `toString`, in addition to the *get* methods that return the values of `Employee`'s instance variables. An `earnings` method certainly applies *generically* to all employees. But each earnings calculation depends on the employee's particular class. So we declare `earnings` as `abstract` in superclass `Employee` because a *specific* default implementation does not make sense for that method—there isn't enough information to determine what amount `earnings` should return.

Each subclass overrides `earnings` with an appropriate implementation. To calculate an employee's earnings, the program assigns to a superclass `Employee` variable a reference to the employee's object, then invokes the `earnings` method on that variable. We maintain an array of `Employee` variables, each holding a reference to an `Employee` object. You *cannot* use class `Employee` directly to create `Employee` *objects*, because `Employee` is an *abstract* class. Due to inheritance, however, all objects of all `Employee` subclasses may be thought of as `Employee` objects. The program will iterate through the array and call method earnings for each Employee object. Java processes these method calls *polymorphically*. Declaring earnings as an abstract method in Employee enables the calls to earnings through Employee variables to compile and forces every direct *concrete* subclass of Employee to *override* earnings.

Method toString in class Employee returns a String containing the first name, last name and social security number of the employee. As we'll see, each subclass of Employee *overrides* method toString to create a String representation of an object of that class that contains the employee's type (e.g., "salaried employee:") followed by the rest of the employee's information.

Let's consider class Employee's declaration (Fig. 10.4). The class includes a constructor that receives the first name, last name and social security number (lines 11–17); *get* methods that return the first name, last name and social security number (lines 20–23, 26–29 and 32–35, respectively); method toString (lines 38–43), which returns the String representation of an Employee; and abstract method earnings (line 46), which will be implemented by each of the *concrete* subclasses. The Employee constructor does *not* validate its parameters in this example; normally, such validation should be provided.

```java
1   // Fig. 10.4: Employee.java
2   // Employee abstract superclass.
3
4   public abstract class Employee
5   {
6      private final String firstName;
7      private final String lastName;
8      private final String socialSecurityNumber;
9
10     // constructor
11     public Employee(String firstName, String lastName,
12        String socialSecurityNumber)
13     {
14        this.firstName = firstName;
15        this.lastName = lastName;
16        this.socialSecurityNumber = socialSecurityNumber;
17     }
18
19     // return first name
20     public String getFirstName()
21     {
22        return firstName;
23     }
24
25     // return last name
26     public String getLastName()
27     {
28        return lastName;
29     }
30
31     // return social security number
32     public String getSocialSecurityNumber()
33     {
```

Fig. 10.4 | Employee abstract superclass. (Part 1 of 2.)

```
34        return socialSecurityNumber;
35     }
36
37     // return String representation of Employee object
38     @Override
39     public String toString()
40     {
41        return String.format("%s %s%nsocial security number: %s",
42            getFirstName(), getLastName(), getSocialSecurityNumber());
43     }
44
45     // abstract method must be overridden by concrete subclasses
46     public abstract double earnings(); // no implementation here
47  } // end abstract class Employee
```

Fig. 10.4 | Employee abstract superclass. (Part 2 of 2.)

Why did we decide to declare earnings as an abstract method? It simply does not make sense to provide a *specific* implementation of this method in class Employee. We cannot calculate the earnings for a *general* Employee—we first must know the *specific* type of Employee to determine the appropriate earnings calculation. By declaring this method abstract, we indicate that each concrete subclass *must* provide an appropriate earnings implementation and that a program will be able to use superclass Employee variables to invoke method earnings *polymorphically* for any type of Employee.

10.5.2 Concrete Subclass SalariedEmployee

Class SalariedEmployee (Fig. 10.5) extends class Employee (line 4) and overrides *abstract* method earnings (lines 38–42), which makes SalariedEmployee a *concrete* class. The class includes a constructor (lines 9–19) that receives a first name, a last name, a social security number and a weekly salary; a *set* method to assign a new *nonnegative* value to instance variable weeklySalary (lines 22–29); a *get* method to return weeklySalary's value (lines 32–35); a method earnings (lines 38–42) to calculate a SalariedEmployee's earnings; and a method toString (lines 45–50), which returns a String including "salaried employee: " followed by employee-specific information produced by superclass Employee's toString method and Salaried-Employee's getWeeklySalary method. Class SalariedEmployee's constructor passes the first name, last name and social security number to the Employee constructor (line 12) to initialize the private instance variables of the superclass. Once again, we've duplicated the weeklySalary validation code in the constructor and the setWeekly-Salary method. Recall that more complex validation could be placed in a static class method that's called from the constructor and the *set* method.

> **Error-Prevention Tip 10.1**
>
> *We've said that you should not call a class's instance methods from its constructors—you can call static class methods and make the required call to one of the superclass's constructors. If you follow this advice, you'll avoid the problem of calling the class's overridable methods either directly or indirectly, which can lead to runtime errors.*

Method earnings overrides Employee's *abstract* method earnings to provide a *concrete* implementation that returns the SalariedEmployee's weekly salary. If we do not

```java
1    // Fig. 10.5: SalariedEmployee.java
2    // SalariedEmployee concrete class extends abstract class Employee.
3
4    public class SalariedEmployee extends Employee
5    {
6       private double weeklySalary;
7
8       // constructor
9       public SalariedEmployee(String firstName, String lastName,
10          String socialSecurityNumber, double weeklySalary)
11       {
12          super(firstName, lastName, socialSecurityNumber);
13
14          if (weeklySalary < 0.0)
15             throw new IllegalArgumentException(
16                "Weekly salary must be >= 0.0");
17
18          this.weeklySalary = weeklySalary;
19       }
20
21       // set salary
22       public void setWeeklySalary(double weeklySalary)
23       {
24          if (weeklySalary < 0.0)
25             throw new IllegalArgumentException(
26                "Weekly salary must be >= 0.0");
27
28          this.weeklySalary = weeklySalary;
29       }
30
31       // return salary
32       public double getWeeklySalary()
33       {
34          return weeklySalary;
35       }
36
37       // calculate earnings; override abstract method earnings in Employee
38       @Override
39       public double earnings()
40       {
41          return getWeeklySalary();
42       }
43
44       // return String representation of SalariedEmployee object
45       @Override
46       public String toString()
47       {
48          return String.format("salaried employee: %s%n%s: $%,.2f",
49             super.toString(), "weekly salary", getWeeklySalary());
50       }
51    } // end class SalariedEmployee
```

Fig. 10.5 | SalariedEmployee concrete class extends abstract class Employee.

implement earnings, class SalariedEmployee must be declared abstract—otherwise, class SalariedEmployee will not compile. Of course, we want SalariedEmployee to be a *concrete* class in this example.

Method toString (lines 45–50) overrides Employee method toString. If class SalariedEmployee did *not* override toString, SalariedEmployee would have inherited the Employee version of toString. In that case, SalariedEmployee's toString method would simply return the employee's full name and social security number, which does *not* adequately represent a SalariedEmployee. To produce a complete String representation of a SalariedEmployee, the subclass's toString method returns "salaried employee: " followed by the superclass Employee-specific information (i.e., first name, last name and social security number) obtained by invoking the *superclass's* toString method (line 49)—this is a nice example of *code reuse*. The String representation of a SalariedEmployee also contains the employee's weekly salary obtained by invoking the class's getWeeklySalary method.

10.5.3 Concrete Subclass HourlyEmployee

Class HourlyEmployee (Fig. 10.6) also extends Employee (line 4). The class includes a constructor (lines 10–25) that receives a first name, a last name, a social security number, an hourly wage and the number of hours worked. Lines 28–35 and 44–51 declare *set* methods that assign new values to instance variables wage and hours, respectively. Method setWage (lines 28–35) ensures that wage is *nonnegative*, and method setHours (lines 44–51) ensures that the value of hours is between 0 and 168 (the total number of hours in a week) inclusive. Class HourlyEmployee also includes *get* methods (lines 38–41 and 54–57) to return the values of wage and hours, respectively; a method earnings (lines 60–67) to calculate an HourlyEmployee's earnings; and a method toString (lines 70–76), which returns a String containing the employee's type ("hourly employee: ") and the employee-specific information. The HourlyEmployee constructor, like the SalariedEmployee constructor, passes the first name, last name and social security number to the superclass Employee constructor (line 13) to initialize the private instance variables. In addition, method toString calls *superclass* method toString (line 74) to obtain the Employee-specific information (i.e., first name, last name and social security number)—this is another nice example of *code reuse*.

```
1   // Fig. 10.6: HourlyEmployee.java
2   // HourlyEmployee class extends Employee.
3
4   public class HourlyEmployee extends Employee
5   {
6      private double wage; // wage per hour
7      private double hours; // hours worked for week
8
9      // constructor
10     public HourlyEmployee(String firstName, String lastName,
11        String socialSecurityNumber, double wage, double hours)
12     {
13        super(firstName, lastName, socialSecurityNumber);
14
```

Fig. 10.6 | HourlyEmployee class extends Employee. (Part 1 of 3.)

```
15          if (wage < 0.0) // validate wage
16             throw new IllegalArgumentException(
17                "Hourly wage must be >= 0.0");
18
19          if ((hours < 0.0) || (hours > 168.0)) // validate hours
20             throw new IllegalArgumentException(
21                "Hours worked must be >= 0.0 and <= 168.0");
22
23          this.wage = wage;
24          this.hours = hours;
25       }
26
27       // set wage
28       public void setWage(double wage)
29       {
30          if (wage < 0.0) // validate wage
31             throw new IllegalArgumentException(
32                "Hourly wage must be >= 0.0");
33
34          this.wage = wage;
35       }
36
37       // return wage
38       public double getWage()
39       {
40          return wage;
41       }
42
43       // set hours worked
44       public void setHours(double hours)
45       {
46          if ((hours < 0.0) || (hours > 168.0)) // validate hours
47             throw new IllegalArgumentException(
48                "Hours worked must be >= 0.0 and <= 168.0");
49
50          this.hours = hours;
51       }
52
53       // return hours worked
54       public double getHours()
55       {
56          return hours;
57       }
58
59       // calculate earnings; override abstract method earnings in Employee
60       @Override
61       public double earnings()
62       {
63          if (getHours() <= 40) // no overtime
64             return getWage() * getHours();
65          else
66             return 40 * getWage() + (getHours() - 40) * getWage() * 1.5;
67       }
```

Fig. 10.6 | HourlyEmployee class extends Employee. (Part 2 of 3.)

```
68
69      // return String representation of HourlyEmployee object
70      @Override
71      public String toString()
72      {
73         return String.format("hourly employee: %s%n%s: $%,.2f; %s: %,.2f",
74            super.toString(), "hourly wage", getWage(),
75            "hours worked", getHours());
76      }
77   } // end class HourlyEmployee
```

Fig. 10.6 | HourlyEmployee class extends Employee. (Part 3 of 3.)

10.5.4 Concrete Subclass CommissionEmployee

Class CommissionEmployee (Fig. 10.7) extends class Employee (line 4). The class includes a constructor (lines 10–25) that takes a first name, a last name, a social security number, a sales amount and a commission rate; *set* methods (lines 28–34 and 43–50) to assign valid new values to instance variables commissionRate and grossSales, respectively; *get* methods (lines 37–40 and 53–56) that retrieve the values of these instance variables; method earnings (lines 59–63) to calculate a CommissionEmployee's earnings; and method toString (lines 66–73), which returns the employee's type, namely, "commission employee: " and employee-specific information. The constructor also passes the first name, last name and social security number to *superclass* Employee's constructor (line 14) to initialize Employee's private instance variables. Method toString calls *superclass* method toString (line 70) to obtain the Employee-specific information (i.e., first name, last name and social security number).

```
1    // Fig. 10.7: CommissionEmployee.java
2    // CommissionEmployee class extends Employee.
3
4    public class CommissionEmployee extends Employee
5    {
6       private double grossSales; // gross weekly sales
7       private double commissionRate; // commission percentage
8
9       // constructor
10      public CommissionEmployee(String firstName, String lastName,
11         String socialSecurityNumber, double grossSales,
12         double commissionRate)
13      {
14         super(firstName, lastName, socialSecurityNumber);
15
16         if (commissionRate <= 0.0 || commissionRate >= 1.0) // validate
17            throw new IllegalArgumentException(
18               "Commission rate must be > 0.0 and < 1.0");
19
20         if (grossSales < 0.0) // validate
21            throw new IllegalArgumentException("Gross sales must be >= 0.0");
22
```

Fig. 10.7 | CommissionEmployee class extends Employee. (Part 1 of 2.)

```
23          this.grossSales = grossSales;
24          this.commissionRate = commissionRate;
25      }
26
27      // set gross sales amount
28      public void setGrossSales(double grossSales)
29      {
30          if (grossSales < 0.0) // validate
31              throw new IllegalArgumentException("Gross sales must be >= 0.0");
32
33          this.grossSales = grossSales;
34      }
35
36      // return gross sales amount
37      public double getGrossSales()
38      {
39          return grossSales;
40      }
41
42      // set commission rate
43      public void setCommissionRate(double commissionRate)
44      {
45          if (commissionRate <= 0.0 || commissionRate >= 1.0) // validate
46              throw new IllegalArgumentException(
47                  "Commission rate must be > 0.0 and < 1.0");
48
49          this.commissionRate = commissionRate;
50      }
51
52      // return commission rate
53      public double getCommissionRate()
54      {
55          return commissionRate;
56      }
57
58      // calculate earnings; override abstract method earnings in Employee
59      @Override
60      public double earnings()
61      {
62          return getCommissionRate() * getGrossSales();
63      }
64
65      // return String representation of CommissionEmployee object
66      @Override
67      public String toString()
68      {
69          return String.format("%s: %s%n%s: $%,.2f; %s: %.2f",
70              "commission employee", super.toString(),
71              "gross sales", getGrossSales(),
72              "commission rate", getCommissionRate());
73      }
74  } // end class CommissionEmployee
```

Fig. 10.7 | CommissionEmployee class extends Employee. (Part 2 of 2.)

10.5.5 Indirect Concrete Subclass BasePlusCommissionEmployee

Class BasePlusCommissionEmployee (Fig. 10.8) extends class CommissionEmployee (line 4) and therefore is an *indirect* subclass of class Employee. Class BasePlusCommission-Employee has a constructor (lines 9–20) that receives a first name, a last name, a social security number, a sales amount, a commission rate and a base salary. It then passes all of these except the base salary to the CommissionEmployee constructor (lines 13–14) to initialize the superclass instance variables. BasePlusCommissionEmployee also contains a *set* method (lines 23–29) to assign a new value to instance variable baseSalary and a *get* method (lines 32–35) to return baseSalary's value. Method earnings (lines 38–42) calculates a BasePlusCommissionEmployee's earnings. Line 41 in method earnings calls *superclass* CommissionEmployee's earnings method to calculate the commission-based portion of the employee's earnings—this is another nice example of *code reuse*. Base-PlusCommissionEmployee's toString method (lines 45–51) creates a String representation of a BasePlusCommissionEmployee that contains "base-salaried", followed by the String obtained by invoking *superclass* CommissionEmployee's toString method (line 49), then the base salary. The result is a String beginning with "base-salaried commission employee" followed by the rest of the BasePlusCommissionEmployee's information. Recall that CommissionEmployee's toString obtains the employee's first name, last name and social security number by invoking the toString method of its *superclass* (i.e., Employee)—yet another example of *code reuse*. BasePlusCommissionEmployee's toString initiates a *chain of method calls* that span all three levels of the Employee hierarchy.

```java
 1   // Fig. 10.8: BasePlusCommissionEmployee.java
 2   // BasePlusCommissionEmployee class extends CommissionEmployee.
 3
 4   public class BasePlusCommissionEmployee extends CommissionEmployee
 5   {
 6      private double baseSalary; // base salary per week
 7
 8      // constructor
 9      public BasePlusCommissionEmployee(String firstName, String lastName,
10         String socialSecurityNumber, double grossSales,
11         double commissionRate, double baseSalary)
12      {
13         super(firstName, lastName, socialSecurityNumber,
14            grossSales, commissionRate);
15
16         if (baseSalary < 0.0) // validate baseSalary
17            throw new IllegalArgumentException("Base salary must be >= 0.0");
18
19         this.baseSalary = baseSalary;
20      }
21
22      // set base salary
23      public void setBaseSalary(double baseSalary)
24      {
25         if (baseSalary < 0.0) // validate baseSalary
26            throw new IllegalArgumentException("Base salary must be >= 0.0");
```

Fig. 10.8 | BasePlusCommissionEmployee class extends CommissionEmployee. (Part 1 of 2.)

```
27
28          this.baseSalary = baseSalary;
29      }
30
31      // return base salary
32      public double getBaseSalary()
33      {
34          return baseSalary;
35      }
36
37      // calculate earnings; override method earnings in CommissionEmployee
38      @Override
39      public double earnings()
40      {
41          return getBaseSalary() + super.earnings();
42      }
43
44      // return String representation of BasePlusCommissionEmployee object
45      @Override
46      public String toString()
47      {
48          return String.format("%s %s; %s: $%,.2f",
49              "base-salaried", super.toString(),
50              "base salary", getBaseSalary());
51      }
52  } // end class BasePlusCommissionEmployee
```

Fig. 10.8 | BasePlusCommissionEmployee class extends CommissionEmployee. (Part 2 of 2.)

10.5.6 Polymorphic Processing, Operator instanceof and Downcasting

To test our Employee hierarchy, the application in Fig. 10.9 creates an object of each of the four *concrete* classes SalariedEmployee, HourlyEmployee, CommissionEmployee and BasePlusCommissionEmployee. The program manipulates these objects *nonpolymorphically*, via variables of each object's own type, then *polymorphically*, using an array of Employee variables. While processing the objects polymorphically, the program increases the base salary of each BasePlusCommissionEmployee by 10%—this requires *determining the object's type at execution time*. Finally, the program polymorphically determines and outputs the *type* of each object in the Employee array. Lines 9–18 create objects of each of the four concrete Employee subclasses. Lines 22–30 output the String representation and earnings of each of these objects *nonpolymorphically*. Each object's toString method is called *implicitly* by printf when the object is output as a String with the %s format specifier.

```
1   // Fig. 10.9: PayrollSystemTest.java
2   // Employee hierarchy test program.
3
4   public class PayrollSystemTest
5   {
```

Fig. 10.9 | Employee hierarchy test program. (Part 1 of 4.)

```
 6        public static void main(String[] args)
 7        {
 8           // create subclass objects
 9           SalariedEmployee salariedEmployee =
10              new SalariedEmployee("John", "Smith", "111-11-1111", 800.00);
11           HourlyEmployee hourlyEmployee =
12              new HourlyEmployee("Karen", "Price", "222-22-2222", 16.75, 40);
13           CommissionEmployee commissionEmployee =
14              new CommissionEmployee(
15              "Sue", "Jones", "333-33-3333", 10000, .06);
16           BasePlusCommissionEmployee basePlusCommissionEmployee =
17              new BasePlusCommissionEmployee(
18              "Bob", "Lewis", "444-44-4444", 5000, .04, 300);
19
20           System.out.println("Employees processed individually:");
21
22           System.out.printf("%n%s%n%s: $%,.2f%n%n",
23              salariedEmployee, "earned", salariedEmployee.earnings());
24           System.out.printf("%s%n%s: $%,.2f%n%n",
25              hourlyEmployee, "earned", hourlyEmployee.earnings());
26           System.out.printf("%s%n%s: $%,.2f%n%n",
27              commissionEmployee, "earned", commissionEmployee.earnings());
28           System.out.printf("%s%n%s: $%,.2f%n%n",
29              basePlusCommissionEmployee,
30              "earned", basePlusCommissionEmployee.earnings());
31
32           // create four-element Employee array
33           Employee[] employees = new Employee[4];
34
35           // initialize array with Employees
36           employees[0] = salariedEmployee;
37           employees[1] = hourlyEmployee;
38           employees[2] = commissionEmployee;
39           employees[3] = basePlusCommissionEmployee;
40
41           System.out.printf("Employees processed polymorphically:%n%n");
42
43           // generically process each element in array employees
44           for (Employee currentEmployee : employees)
45           {
46              System.out.println(currentEmployee); // invokes toString
47
48              // determine whether element is a BasePlusCommissionEmployee
49              if (currentEmployee instanceof BasePlusCommissionEmployee)
50              {
51                 // downcast Employee reference to
52                 // BasePlusCommissionEmployee reference
53                 BasePlusCommissionEmployee employee =
54                    (BasePlusCommissionEmployee) currentEmployee ;
55
56                 employee.setBaseSalary(1.10 * employee.getBaseSalary());
57
```

Fig. 10.9 | Employee hierarchy test program. (Part 2 of 4.)

```
58                    System.out.printf(
59                        "new base salary with 10%% increase is: $%,.2f%n",
60                        employee.getBaseSalary());
61                } // end if
62
63                System.out.printf(
64                    "earned $%,.2f%n%n", currentEmployee.earnings());
65            } // end for
66
67            // get type name of each object in employees array
68            for (int j = 0; j < employees.length; j++)
69                System.out.printf("Employee %d is a %s%n", j,
70                    employees[j].getClass().getName());
71        } // end main
72    } // end class PayrollSystemTest
```

```
Employees processed individually:

salaried employee: John Smith
social security number: 111-11-1111
weekly salary: $800.00
earned: $800.00

hourly employee: Karen Price
social security number: 222-22-2222
hourly wage: $16.75; hours worked: 40.00
earned: $670.00

commission employee: Sue Jones
social security number: 333-33-3333
gross sales: $10,000.00; commission rate: 0.06
earned: $600.00

base-salaried commission employee: Bob Lewis
social security number: 444-44-4444
gross sales: $5,000.00; commission rate: 0.04; base salary: $300.00
earned: $500.00

Employees processed polymorphically:

salaried employee: John Smith
social security number: 111-11-1111
weekly salary: $800.00
earned $800.00

hourly employee: Karen Price
social security number: 222-22-2222
hourly wage: $16.75; hours worked: 40.00
earned $670.00

commission employee: Sue Jones
social security number: 333-33-3333
gross sales: $10,000.00; commission rate: 0.06
earned $600.00
```

Fig. 10.9 | Employee hierarchy test program. (Part 3 of 4.)

```
base-salaried commission employee: Bob Lewis
social security number: 444-44-4444
gross sales: $5,000.00; commission rate: 0.04; base salary: $300.00
new base salary with 10% increase is: $330.00
earned $530.00

Employee 0 is a SalariedEmployee
Employee 1 is a HourlyEmployee
Employee 2 is a CommissionEmployee
Employee 3 is a BasePlusCommissionEmployee
```

Fig. 10.9 | Employee hierarchy test program. (Part 4 of 4.)

Creating the Array of Employees

Line 33 declares employees and assigns it an array of four Employee variables. Line 36 assigns to employees[0] a reference to a SalariedEmployee object. Line 37 assigns to employees[1] a reference to an HourlyEmployee object. Line 38 assigns to employees[2] a reference to a CommissionEmployee object. Line 39 assigns to employee[3] a reference to a BasePlusCommissionEmployee object. These assignments are allowed, because a SalariedEmployee *is an* Employee, an HourlyEmployee *is an* Employee, a CommissionEmployee *is an* Employee and a BasePlusCommissionEmployee *is an* Employee. Therefore, we can assign the references of SalariedEmployee, HourlyEmployee, CommissionEmployee and BasePlusCommissionEmployee objects to *superclass* Employee variables, *even though Employee is an abstract class.*

Polymorphically Processing Employees

Lines 44–65 iterate through array employees and invoke methods toString and earnings with Employee variable currentEmployee, which is assigned the reference to a different Employee in the array on each iteration. The output illustrates that the specific methods for each class are indeed invoked. All calls to method toString and earnings are resolved at *execution* time, based on the *type* of the object to which currentEmployee refers. This process is known as **dynamic binding** or **late binding**. For example, line 46 *implicitly* invokes method toString of the object to which currentEmployee refers. As a result of *dynamic binding*, Java decides which class's toString method to call *at execution time rather than at compile time.* Only the methods of class Employee can be called via an Employee variable (and Employee, of course, includes the methods of class Object). A superclass reference can be used to invoke only methods of the *superclass*—the *subclass* method implementations are invoked *polymorphically.*

Performing Type-Specific Operations on BasePlusCommissionEmployees

We perform special processing on BasePlusCommissionEmployee objects—as we encounter these objects at execution time, we increase their base salary by 10%. When processing objects *polymorphically*, we typically do not need to worry about the *specifics*, but to adjust the base salary, we *do* have to determine the *specific* type of Employee object at *execution time.* Line 49 uses the **instanceof** operator to determine whether a particular Employee object's type is BasePlusCommissionEmployee. The condition in line 49 is *true* if the object referenced by currentEmployee *is a* BasePlusCommissionEmployee. This would also be *true* for any object of a BasePlusCommissionEmployee subclass because of the *is-a* relationship a subclass has with its superclass. Lines 53–54 *downcast* currentEmployee from type Employee to type BasePlusCommissionEmployee—this cast is allowed only if the object has an *is-a* relationship with BasePlusCommissionEmployee. The condition at line 49 ensures that this is the case. This cast is required if we're to invoke subclass BasePlusCommissionEmployee methods getBaseSalary and setBaseSalary on the current Employee object—as you'll see momentarily, *attempting to invoke a subclass-only method directly on a superclass reference is a compilation error.*

Common Programming Error 10.3

Assigning a superclass variable to a subclass variable is a compilation error.

Common Programming Error 10.4

When downcasting a reference, a ClassCastException *occurs if the referenced object at execution time does not have an* is-a *relationship with the type specified in the cast operator.*

If the instanceof expression in line 49 is true, lines 53–60 perform the special processing required for the BasePlusCommissionEmployee object. Using BasePlusCommissionEmployee variable employee, line 56 invokes subclass-only methods getBaseSalary and setBaseSalary to retrieve and update the employee's base salary with the 10% raise.

Calling earnings *Polymorphically*
Lines 63–64 invoke method earnings on currentEmployee, which polymorphically calls the appropriate subclass object's earnings method. Obtaining the earnings of the SalariedEmployee, HourlyEmployee and CommissionEmployee polymorphically in lines 63–64 produces the same results as obtaining these employees' earnings individually in lines 22–27. The earnings amount obtained for the BasePlusCommissionEmployee in lines 63–64 is higher than that obtained in lines 28–30, due to the 10% increase in its base salary.

Getting Each Employee's *Class Name*
Lines 68–70 display each employee's type as a String. Every object *knows its own class* and can access this information through the **getClass** method, which all classes inherit from class Object. Method getClass returns an object of type **Class** (from package java.lang), which contains information about the object's type, including its class name. Line 70 invokes getClass on the current object to get its class. The result of the getClass call is used to invoke **getName** to get the object's class name.

Avoiding Compilation Errors with Downcasting
In the previous example, we avoided several compilation errors by *downcasting* an Employee variable to a BasePlusCommissionEmployee variable in lines 53–54. If you remove the cast operator (BasePlusCommissionEmployee) from line 54 and attempt to assign Employee variable currentEmployee directly to BasePlusCommissionEmployee variable employee, you'll receive an "incompatible types" compilation error. This error indicates that the attempt to assign the reference of superclass object currentEmployee to subclass variable employee is *not* allowed. The compiler prevents this assignment because a CommissionEmployee is *not* a BasePlusCommissionEmployee—*the* is-a *relationship applies only between the subclass and its superclasses, not vice versa.*

Similarly, if lines 56 and 60 used superclass variable `currentEmployee` to invoke sub-class-only methods `getBaseSalary` and `setBaseSalary`, we'd receive "`cannot find symbol`" compilation errors at these lines. Attempting to invoke subclass-only methods via a superclass variable is *not* allowed—even though lines 56 and 60 execute only if `instanceof` in line 49 returns `true` to indicate that `currentEmployee` holds a reference to a `BasePlusCommissionEmployee` object. Using a superclass `Employee` variable, we can invoke only methods found in class `Employee`—`earnings`, `toString` and `Employee`'s *get* and *set* methods.

Software Engineering Observation 10.5

Although the actual method that's called depends on the runtime type of the object to which a variable refers, a variable can be used to invoke only those methods that are members of that variable's type, which the compiler verifies.

10.6 Allowed Assignments Between Superclass and Subclass Variables

Now that you've seen a complete application that processes diverse subclass objects *polymorphically*, we summarize what you can and cannot do with superclass and subclass objects and variables. Although a subclass object also *is a* superclass object, the two classes are nevertheless different. As discussed previously, subclass objects can be treated as objects of their superclass. But because the subclass can have additional subclass-only members, assigning a superclass reference to a subclass variable is not allowed without an *explicit cast*—such an assignment would leave the subclass members undefined for the superclass object.

We've discussed three proper ways to assign superclass and subclass references to variables of superclass and subclass types:

1. Assigning a superclass reference to a superclass variable is straightforward.

2. Assigning a subclass reference to a subclass variable is straightforward.

3. Assigning a subclass reference to a superclass variable is safe, because the subclass object *is an* object of its superclass. However, the superclass variable can be used to refer *only* to superclass members. If this code refers to subclass-only members through the superclass variable, the compiler reports errors.

10.7 `final` Methods and Classes

We saw in Sections 5.3– and 5.10 that variables can be declared `final` to indicate that they cannot be modified *after* they're initialized—such variables represent constant values. It's also possible to declare methods, method parameters and classes with the `final` modifier.

Final Methods Cannot Be Overridden
A **`final` method** in a superclass *cannot* be overridden in a subclass—this guarantees that the `final` method implementation will be used by all direct and indirect subclasses in the hierarchy. Methods that are declared `private` are implicitly `final`, because it's not possible to override them in a subclass. Methods that are declared `static` are also implicitly `final`. A `final` method's declaration can never change, so all subclasses use the same method

implementation, and calls to final methods are resolved at compile time—this is known as **static binding**.

Final Classes Cannot Be Superclasses
A **final class** cannot extended to create a subclass. All methods in a final class are implicitly final. Class String is an example of a final class. If you were allowed to create a subclass of String, objects of that subclass could be used wherever Strings are expected. Since class String cannot be extended, programs that use Strings can rely on the functionality of String objects as specified in the Java API. Making the class final also prevents programmers from creating subclasses that might bypass security restrictions.

We've now discussed declaring variables, methods and classes final, and we've emphasized that if something *can* be final it *should* be final. Compilers can perform various optimizations when they know something is final. When we study concurrency in Chapter 23, you'll see that final variables make it much easier to parallelize your programs for use on today's multi-core processors. For more insights on the use of final, visit

> http://docs.oracle.com/javase/tutorial/java/IandI/final.html

Common Programming Error 10.5
Attempting to declare a subclass of a final class is a compilation error.

Software Engineering Observation 10.6
In the Java API, the vast majority of classes are not declared final. This enables inheritance and polymorphism. However, in some cases, it's important to declare classes final—typically for security reasons. Also, unless you carefully design a class for extension, you should declare the class as final to avoid (often subtle) errors.

10.8 A Deeper Explanation of Issues with Calling Methods from Constructors

Do not call overridable methods from constructors. When creating a *subclass* object, this could lead to an overridden method being called before the *subclass* object is fully initialized.

Recall that when you construct a *subclass* object, its constructor first calls one of the direct *superclass's* constructors. If the *superclass* constructor calls an overridable method, the *subclass's* version of that method will be called by the *superclass* constructor—before the *subclass* constructor's body has a chance to execute. This could lead to subtle, difficult-to-detect errors if the *subclass* method that was called depends on initialization that has not yet been performed in the *subclass* constructor's body.

It's acceptable to call a static method from a constructor. For example, a constructor and a *set* method often perform the same validation for a particular instance variable. If the validation code is brief, it's acceptable to duplicate it in the constructor and the *set* method. If lengthier validation is required, define a static validation method (typically a private helper method) then call it from the constructor and the *set* method. It's also acceptable for a constructor to call a final instance method, provided that the method does not directly or indirectly call an overridable instance method.

10.9 Creating and Using Interfaces

[Note: As written, this section and its code example apply through Java SE 7. Java SE 8's interface enhancements are introduced in Section 10.10 and discussed in more detail in Chapter 17.]

Our next example (Figs. 10.11–10.15) reexamines the payroll system of Section 10.5. Suppose that the company involved wishes to perform several accounting operations in a single accounts payable application—in addition to calculating the earnings that must be paid to each employee, the company must also calculate the payment due on each of several invoices (i.e., bills for goods purchased). Though applied to *unrelated* things (i.e., employees and invoices), both operations have to do with obtaining some kind of payment amount. For an employee, the payment refers to the employee's earnings. For an invoice, the payment refers to the total cost of the goods listed on the invoice. Can we calculate such *different* things as the payments due for employees and invoices in *a single* application *polymorphically*? Does Java offer a capability requiring that *unrelated* classes implement a set of *common* methods (e.g., a method that calculates a payment amount)? Java **interfaces** offer exactly this capability.

Standardizing Interactions

Interfaces define and standardize the ways in which things such as people and systems can interact with one another. For example, the controls on a radio serve as an interface between radio users and a radio's internal components. The controls allow users to perform only a limited set of operations (e.g., change the station, adjust the volume, choose between AM and FM), and different radios may implement the controls in different ways (e.g., using push buttons, dials, voice commands). The interface specifies *what* operations a radio must permit users to perform but does not specify *how* the operations are performed.

Software Objects Communicate Via Interfaces

Software objects also communicate via interfaces. A Java interface describes a set of methods that can be called on an object to tell it, for example, to perform some task or return some piece of information. The next example introduces an interface named `Payable` to describe the functionality of any object that must be "capable of being paid" and thus must offer a method to determine the proper payment amount due. An **interface declaration** begins with the keyword **interface** and contains *only* constants and `abstract` methods. Unlike classes, all interface members *must* be `public`, and *interfaces may not specify any implementation details*, such as concrete method declarations and instance variables. All methods declared in an interface are implicitly `public abstract` methods, and all fields are implicitly `public`, `static` and `final`.

> **Good Programming Practice 10.1**
>
> *According to the* Java Language Specification, *it's proper style to declare an interface's* `abstract` *methods without keywords* `public` *and* `abstract`, *because they're redundant in interface-method declarations. Similarly, an interface's constants should be declared without keywords* `public`, `static` *and* `final`, *because they, too, are redundant.*

Using an Interface

To use an interface, a concrete class must specify that it **implements** the interface and must declare each method in the interface with the signature specified in the interface declaration. To specify that a class implements an interface, add the `implements` keyword and the name of the interface to the end of your class declaration's first line. A class that does not implement *all* the methods of the interface is an *abstract* class and must be declared abstract. Implementing an interface is like signing a *contract* with the compiler that states, "I will declare all the methods specified by the interface or I will declare my class abstract."

Common Programming Error 10.6

Failing to implement any method of an interface in a concrete class that implements the interface results in a compilation error indicating that the class must be declared abstract.

Relating Disparate Types

An interface is often used when *disparate* classes—i.e., classes that are not related by a class hierarchy—need to share common methods and constants. This allows objects of *unrelated* classes to be processed *polymorphically*—objects of classes that implement the *same* interface can respond to the *same* method calls. You can create an interface that describes the desired functionality, then implement this interface in any classes that require that functionality. For example, in the accounts payable application developed in this section, we implement interface Payable in any class that must be able to calculate a payment amount (e.g., Employee, Invoice).

Interfaces vs. Abstract Classes

An interface is often used in place of an abstract class when there's no default implementation to inherit—that is, no fields and no default method implementations. Like public abstract classes, interfaces are typically public types. Like a public class, a public interface must be declared in a file with the same name as the interface and the .java filename extension.

Software Engineering Observation 10.7

Many developers feel that interfaces are an even more important modeling technology than classes, especially with the new interface enhancements in Java SE 8 (see Section 10.10).

Tagging Interfaces

We'll see in Chapter 15, Files, Streams and Object Serialization, the notion of *tagging interfaces* (also called *marker interfaces*)—empty interfaces that have *no* methods or constant values. They're used to add *is-a* relationships to classes. For example, in Chapter 15 we'll discuss a mechanism called *object serialization*, which can convert objects to byte representations and can convert those byte representations back to objects. To enable this mechanism to work with your objects, you simply have to mark them as Serializable by adding implements Serializable to the end of your class declaration's first line. Then, all the objects of your class have the *is-a* relationship with Serializable.

10.9.1 Developing a Payable Hierarchy

To build an application that can determine payments for employees and invoices alike, we first create interface Payable, which contains method getPaymentAmount that returns a double amount that must be paid for an object of any class that implements the interface. Method getPaymentAmount is a general-purpose version of method earnings of the Employee hierarchy—method earnings calculates a payment amount specifically for an Employee, while getPaymentAmount can be applied to a broad range of possibly unrelated objects. After declaring interface Payable, we introduce class Invoice, which implements interface `Payable`. We then modify class `Employee` such that it also implements interface `Payable`. Finally, we update `Employee` subclass `SalariedEmployee` to "fit" into the Payable hierarchy by renaming `SalariedEmployee` method `earnings` as `getPaymentAmount`.

> ### Good Programming Practice 10.2
> *When declaring a method in an interface, choose a method name that describes the method's purpose in a* general *manner, because the method may be implemented by many* unrelated *classes.*

Classes `Invoice` and `Employee` both represent things for which the company must be able to calculate a payment amount. Both classes implement the `Payable` interface, so a program can invoke method `getPaymentAmount` on `Invoice` objects and `Employee` objects alike. As we'll soon see, this enables the *polymorphic* processing of `Invoice`s and `Employee`s required for the company's accounts payable application.

The UML class diagram in Fig. 10.10 shows the interface and class hierarchy used in our accounts payable application. The hierarchy begins with interface `Payable`. The UML distinguishes an interface from other classes by placing the word "interface" in guillemets (« and ») above the interface name. The UML expresses the relationship between a class and an interface through a relationship known as **realization**. A class is said to *realize*, or *implement*, the methods of an interface. A class diagram models a realization as a dashed arrow with a hollow arrowhead pointing from the implementing class to the interface. The diagram in Fig. 10.10 indicates that classes `Invoice` and `Employee` each realize interface `Payable`. As in the class diagram of Fig. 10.2, class `Employee` appears in *italics*, indicating that it's an *abstract class*. *Concrete* class `SalariedEmployee` extends `Employee`, *inheriting its superclass's realization relationship* with interface `Payable`.

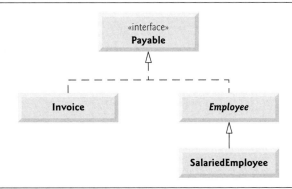

Fig. 10.10 | `Payable` hierarchy UML class diagram.

10.9.2 Interface `Payable`

The declaration of interface `Payable` begins in Fig. 10.11 at line 4. Interface `Payable` contains `public` `abstract` method `getPaymentAmount`. Interface methods are always `public` and `abstract`, so they do not need to be declared as such. Interface `Payable` has only one method, but interfaces can have *any* number of methods. In addition, method `getPaymentAmount` has no parameters, but interface methods *can* have parameters. Interfaces may also contain `final` `static` constants.

```
1  // Fig. 10.11: Payable.java
2  // Payable interface declaration.
3
4  public interface Payable
5  {
6     double getPaymentAmount(); // calculate payment; no implementation
7  }
```

Fig. 10.11 | Payable interface declaration.

10.9.3 Class Invoice

We now create class Invoice (Fig. 10.12) to represent a simple invoice that contains billing information for only one kind of part. The class declares private instance variables partNumber, partDescription, quantity and pricePerItem (in lines 6–9) that indicate the part number, a description of the part, the quantity of the part ordered and the price per item. Class Invoice also contains a constructor (lines 12–26), *get* and *set* methods (lines 29–69) that manipulate the class's instance variables and a toString method (lines 72–78) that returns a String representation of an Invoice object. Methods setQuantity (lines 41–47) and setPricePerItem (lines 56–63) ensure that quantity and pricePerItem obtain only nonnegative values.

```
1  // Fig. 10.12: Invoice.java
2  // Invoice class that implements Payable.
3
4  public class Invoice implements Payable
5  {
6     private final String partNumber;
7     private final String partDescription;
8     private int quantity;
9     private double pricePerItem;
10
11    // constructor
12    public Invoice(String partNumber, String partDescription, int quantity,
13       double pricePerItem)
14    {
15       if (quantity < 0) // validate quantity
16          throw new IllegalArgumentException("Quantity must be >= 0");
17
18       if (pricePerItem < 0.0) // validate pricePerItem
19          throw new IllegalArgumentException(
20             "Price per item must be >= 0");
21
22       this.quantity = quantity;
23       this.partNumber = partNumber;
24       this.partDescription = partDescription;
25       this.pricePerItem = pricePerItem;
26    } // end constructor
27
```

Fig. 10.12 | Invoice class that implements Payable. (Part 1 of 3.)

```
28        // get part number
29        public String getPartNumber()
30        {
31           return partNumber; // should validate
32        }
33
34        // get description
35        public String getPartDescription()
36        {
37           return partDescription;
38        }
39
40        // set quantity
41        public void setQuantity(int quantity)
42        {
43           if (quantity < 0) // validate quantity
44              throw new IllegalArgumentException("Quantity must be >= 0");
45
46           this.quantity = quantity;
47        }
48
49        // get quantity
50        public int getQuantity()
51        {
52           return quantity;
53        }
54
55        // set price per item
56        public void setPricePerItem(double pricePerItem)
57        {
58           if (pricePerItem < 0.0) // validate pricePerItem
59              throw new IllegalArgumentException(
60                 "Price per item must be >= 0");
61
62           this.pricePerItem = pricePerItem;
63        }
64
65        // get price per item
66        public double getPricePerItem()
67        {
68           return pricePerItem;
69        }
70
71        // return String representation of Invoice object
72        @Override
73        public String toString()
74        {
75           return String.format("%s: %n%s: %s (%s) %n%s: %d %n%s: $%,.2f",
76              "invoice", "part number", getPartNumber(), getPartDescription(),
77              "quantity", getQuantity(), "price per item", getPricePerItem());
78        }
79
```

Fig. 10.12 | Invoice class that implements Payable. (Part 2 of 3.)

```
80      // method required to carry out contract with interface Payable
81      @Override
82      public double getPaymentAmount()
83      {
84          return getQuantity() * getPricePerItem(); // calculate total cost
85      }
86  } // end class Invoice
```

Fig. 10.12 | Invoice class that implements Payable. (Part 3 of 3.)

A Class Can Extend Only One Other Class But Can Implement Many Interfaces

Line 4 indicates that class Invoice implements interface Payable. Like all classes, class Invoice also *implicitly* extends Object. Java does not allow subclasses to inherit from more than one superclass, but it allows a class to *inherit* from one *superclass* and *implement* as many *interfaces* as it needs. To implement more than one interface, use a comma-separated list of interface names after keyword implements in the class declaration, as in:

> public class *ClassName* extends *SuperclassName* implements *FirstInterface*, *SecondInterface*, ...

Software Engineering Observation 10.8

All objects of a class that implements multiple interfaces have the is-a *relationship with each implemented interface type.*

Class Invoice implements the one abstract method in interface Payable—method getPaymentAmount is declared in lines 81–85. The method calculates the total payment required to pay the invoice. The method multiplies the values of quantity and pricePerItem (obtained through the appropriate *get* methods) and returns the result. This method satisfies the implementation requirement for this method in interface Payable—we've *fulfilled* the *interface contract* with the compiler.

10.9.4 Modifying Class Employee to Implement Interface Payable

We now modify class Employee such that it implements interface Payable. Figure 10.13 contains the modified class, which is identical to that of Fig. 10.4 with two exceptions. First, line 4 of Fig. 10.13 indicates that class Employee now implements interface Payable. For this example, we renamed method earnings to getPaymentAmount throughout the Employee hierarchy. As with method earnings in the version of class Employee in Fig. 10.4, however, it does not make sense to *implement* method getPaymentAmount in class Employee because we cannot calculate the earnings payment owed to a *general* Employee—we must first know the *specific* type of Employee. In Fig. 10.4, we declared method earnings as abstract for this reason, so class Employee had to be declared abstract. This forced each Employee *concrete* subclass to *override* earnings with an implementation.

```
1  // Fig. 10.13: Employee.java
2  // Employee abstract superclass that implements Payable.
3
```

Fig. 10.13 | Employee abstract superclass that implements Payable. (Part 1 of 2.)

```
4   public abstract class Employee implements Payable
5   {
6      private final String firstName;
7      private final String lastName;
8      private final String socialSecurityNumber;
9
10     // constructor
11     public Employee(String firstName, String lastName,
12        String socialSecurityNumber)
13     {
14        this.firstName = firstName;
15        this.lastName = lastName;
16        this.socialSecurityNumber = socialSecurityNumber;
17     }
18
19     // return first name
20     public String getFirstName()
21     {
22        return firstName;
23     }
24
25     // return last name
26     public String getLastName()
27     {
28        return lastName;
29     }
30
31     // return social security number
32     public String getSocialSecurityNumber()
33     {
34        return socialSecurityNumber;
35     }
36
37     // return String representation of Employee object
38     @Override
39     public String toString()
40     {
41        return String.format("%s %s%nsocial security number: %s",
42           getFirstName(), getLastName(), getSocialSecurityNumber());
43     }
44
45     // Note: We do not implement Payable method getPaymentAmount here so
46     // this class must be declared abstract to avoid a compilation error.
47   } // end abstract class Employee
```

Fig. 10.13 | Employee abstract superclass that implements Payable. (Part 2 of 2.)

In Fig. 10.13, we handle this situation differently. Recall that when a class implements an interface, it makes a *contract* with the compiler stating either that the class will implement *each* method in the interface or the class will be declared abstract. Because class Employee does not provide a getPaymentAmount method, the class must be declared abstract. Any concrete subclass of the abstract class *must* implement the interface methods to fulfill the superclass's contract with the compiler. If the subclass does *not* do so, it too *must* be declared abstract. As indicated by the comments in lines 45–46, class Employee of Fig. 10.13 does *not* implement method getPaymentAmount, so the class is declared abstract. Each direct Employee subclass *inherits the superclass's contract* to implement method getPaymentAmount and thus must implement this method to become a concrete class for which objects can be instantiated. A class that extends one of Employee's concrete subclasses will inherit an implementation of getPaymentAmount and thus will also be a concrete class.

10.9.5 Modifying Class SalariedEmployee for Use in the Payable Hierarchy

Figure 10.14 contains a modified SalariedEmployee class that extends Employee and fulfills superclass Employee's contract to implement Payable method getPaymentAmount. This version of SalariedEmployee is identical to that of Fig. 10.5, but it replaces method earnings with method getPaymentAmount (lines 39–43). Recall that the Payable version of the method has a more *general* name to be applicable to possibly *disparate* classes. (If we included the remaining Employee subclasses from Section 10.5—HourlyEmployee, CommissionEmployee and BasePlusCommissionEmployee—in this example, their earnings methods should also be renamed getPaymentAmount. We leave these modifications to Exercise 10.15 and use only SalariedEmployee in our test program here. Exercise 10.16 asks you to implement interface Payable in the entire Employee class hierarchy of Figs. 10.4–10.9 *without* modifying the Employee subclasses.)

```java
1    // Fig. 10.14: SalariedEmployee.java
2    // SalariedEmployee class that implements interface Payable.
3    // method getPaymentAmount.
4    public class SalariedEmployee extends Employee
5    {
6       private double weeklySalary;
7
8       // constructor
9       public SalariedEmployee(String firstName, String lastName,
10          String socialSecurityNumber, double weeklySalary)
11       {
12          super(firstName, lastName, socialSecurityNumber);
13
14          if (weeklySalary < 0.0)
15             throw new IllegalArgumentException(
16                "Weekly salary must be >= 0.0");
17
18          this.weeklySalary = weeklySalary;
19       }
20
21       // set salary
22       public void setWeeklySalary(double weeklySalary)
23       {
24          if (weeklySalary < 0.0)
25             throw new IllegalArgumentException(
26                "Weekly salary must be >= 0.0");
```

Fig. 10.14 | SalariedEmployee class that implements interface Payable method getPaymentAmount. (Part 1 of 2.)

```
27
28          this.weeklySalary = weeklySalary;
29      }
30
31      // return salary
32      public double getWeeklySalary()
33      {
34          return weeklySalary;
35      }
36
37      // calculate earnings; implement interface Payable method that was
38      // abstract in superclass Employee
39      @Override
40      public double getPaymentAmount()
41      {
42          return getWeeklySalary();
43      }
44
45      // return String representation of SalariedEmployee object
46      @Override
47      public String toString()
48      {
49          return String.format("salaried employee: %s%n%s: $%,.2f",
50              super.toString(), "weekly salary", getWeeklySalary());
51      }
52  } // end class SalariedEmployee
```

Fig. 10.14 | `SalariedEmployee` class that implements interface `Payable` method getPaymentAmount. (Part 2 of 2.)

When a class implements an interface, the same *is-a* relationship provided by inheritance applies. Class `Employee` implements `Payable`, so we can say that an `Employee` *is a* `Payable`. In fact, objects of any classes that extend `Employee` are also `Payable` objects. SalariedEmployee objects, for instance, are `Payable` objects. Objects of any subclasses of the class that `implements` the interface can also be thought of as objects of the interface type. Thus, just as we can assign the reference of a `SalariedEmployee` object to a superclass `Employee` variable, we can assign the reference of a `SalariedEmployee` object to an interface `Payable` variable. `Invoice` implements `Payable`, so an `Invoice` object also *is a* `Payable` object, and we can assign the reference of an `Invoice` object to a `Payable` variable.

Software Engineering Observation 10.9

When a method parameter is declared with a superclass or interface type, the method processes the object passed as an argument polymorphically.

Software Engineering Observation 10.10

Using a superclass reference, we can polymorphically invoke any method declared in the superclass and its superclasses (e.g., class `Object`). Using an interface reference, we can polymorphically invoke any method declared in the interface, its superinterfaces (one interface can extend another) and in class `Object`—a variable of an interface type must refer to an object to call methods, and all objects have the methods of class `Object`.

10.9.6 Using Interface Payable to Process Invoices and Employees Polymorphically

PayableInterfaceTest (Fig. 10.15) illustrates that interface Payable can be used to process a set of Invoices and Employees *polymorphically* in a single application. Line 9 declares payableObjects and assigns it an array of four Payable variables. Lines 12–13 assign the references of Invoice objects to the first two elements of payableObjects. Lines 14–17 then assign the references of SalariedEmployee objects to the remaining two elements of payableObjects. These assignments are allowed because an Invoice *is a* Payable, a SalariedEmployee *is an* Employee and an Employee *is a* Payable. Lines 23–29 use the enhanced for statement to *polymorphically* process each Payable object in payableObjects, printing the object as a String, along with the payment amount due. Line 27 invokes method toString via a Payable interface reference, even though toString is not declared in interface Payable—*all references (including those of interface types) refer to objects that extend Object and therefore have a toString method.* (Method toString also can be invoked *implicitly* here.) Line 28 invokes Payable method getPaymentAmount to obtain the payment amount for each object in payableObjects, *regardless* of the actual type of the object. The output reveals that each of the method calls in lines 27–28 invokes the appropriate class's implementation of methods toString and getPaymentAmount. For instance, when currentPayable refers to an Invoice during the first iteration of the for loop, class Invoice's toString and getPaymentAmount execute.

```
1   // Fig. 10.15: PayableInterfaceTest.java
2   // Payable interface test program processing Invoices and
3   // Employees polymorphically.
4   public class PayableInterfaceTest
5   {
6      public static void main(String[] args)
7      {
8         // create four-element Payable array
9         Payable[] payableObjects = new Payable[4];
10
11        // populate array with objects that implement Payable
12        payableObjects[0] = new Invoice("01234", "seat", 2, 375.00);
13        payableObjects[1] = new Invoice("56789", "tire", 4, 79.95);
14        payableObjects[2] =
15           new SalariedEmployee("John", "Smith", "111-11-1111", 800.00);
16        payableObjects[3] =
17           new SalariedEmployee("Lisa", "Barnes", "888-88-8888", 1200.00);
18
19        System.out.println(
20           "Invoices and Employees processed polymorphically:");
21
22        // generically process each element in array payableObjects
23        for (Payable currentPayable : payableObjects)
24        {
```

Fig. 10.15 | Payable interface test program processing Invoices and Employees polymorphically. (Part 1 of 2.)

```
25              // output currentPayable and its appropriate payment amount
26              System.out.printf("%n%s %n%s: $%,.2f%n",
27                  currentPayable.toString(), // could invoke implicitly
28                  "payment due", currentPayable.getPaymentAmount());
29          }
30      } // end main
31  } // end class PayableInterfaceTest
```

```
Invoices and Employees processed polymorphically:

invoice:
part number: 01234 (seat)
quantity: 2
price per item: $375.00
payment due: $750.00

invoice:
part number: 56789 (tire)
quantity: 4
price per item: $79.95
payment due: $319.80

salaried employee: John Smith
social security number: 111-11-1111
weekly salary: $800.00
payment due: $800.00

salaried employee: Lisa Barnes
social security number: 888-88-8888
weekly salary: $1,200.00
payment due: $1,200.00
```

Fig. 10.15 | `Payable` interface test program processing `Invoices` and `Employees` polymorphically. (Part 2 of 2.)

10.9.7 Some Common Interfaces of the Java API

You'll use interfaces extensively when developing Java applications. The Java API contains numerous interfaces, and many of the Java API methods take interface arguments and return interface values. Figure 10.16 overviews a few of the more popular interfaces of the Java API that we use in later chapters.

Interface	Description
Comparable	Java contains several comparison operators (e.g., <, <=, >, >=, ==, !=) that allow you to compare primitive values. However, these operators *cannot* be used to compare objects. Interface Comparable is used to allow objects of a class that `implements` the interface to be compared to one another. Interface Comparable is commonly used for ordering objects in a collection such as an array. We use Comparable in Chapter 16, Generic Collections, and Chapter 20, Generic Classes and Methods.

Fig. 10.16 | Common interfaces of the Java API. (Part 1 of 2.)

Interface	Description
Serializable	An interface used to identify classes whose objects can be written to (i.e., serialized) or read from (i.e., deserialized) some type of storage (e.g., file on disk, database field) or transmitted across a network. We use Serializable in Chapter 15, Files, Streams and Object Serialization, and Chapter 28, Networking.
Runnable	Implemented by any class that represents a task to perform. Objects of such as class are often executed in parallel using a technique called *multithreading* (discussed in Chapter 23, Concurrency). The interface contains one method, run, which specifies the behavior of an object when executed.
GUI event-listener interfaces	You work with graphical user interfaces (GUIs) every day. In your web browser, you might type the address of a website to visit, or you might click a button to return to a previous site. The browser responds to your interaction and performs the desired task. Your interaction is known as an *event*, and the code that the browser uses to respond to an event is known as an *event handler*. In Chapter 12, GUI Components: Part 1, and Chapter 22, GUI Components: Part 2, you'll learn how to build GUIs and event handlers that respond to user interactions. Event handlers are declared in classes that implement an appropriate *event-listener interface*. Each event-listener interface specifies one or more methods that must be implemented to respond to user interactions.
AutoCloseable	Implemented by classes that can be used with the try-with-resources statement (Chapter 11, Exception Handling: A Deeper Look) to help prevent resource leaks.

Fig. 10.16 | Common interfaces of the Java API. (Part 2 of 2.)

10.10 Java SE 8 Interface Enhancements

This section introduces Java SE 8's new interface features. We discuss these in more detail in later chapters.

10.10.1 default Interface Methods

Prior to Java SE 8, interface methods could be *only* public abstract methods. This meant that an interface specified *what* operations an implementing class must perform but not *how* the class should perform them.

In Java SE 8, interfaces also may contain public **default methods** with *concrete* default implementations that specify *how* operations are performed when an implementing class does not override the methods. If a class implements such an interface, the class also receives the interface's default implementations (if any). To declare a default method, place the keyword default before the method's return type and provide a concrete method implementation.

Adding Methods to Existing Interfaces

Prior to Java SE 8, adding methods to an interface would break any implementing classes that did not implement the new methods. Recall that if you didn't implement each of an interface's methods, you had to declare your class abstract.

Any class that implements the original interface will *not* break when a default method is added—the class simply receives the new default method. When a class implements a Java SE 8 interface, the class "signs a contract" with the compiler that says, "I will declare all the *abstract* methods specified by the interface or I will declare my class abstract"—the implementing class is not required to override the interface's default methods, but it can if necessary.

> **Software Engineering Observation 10.11**
> *Java SE 8* default *methods enable you to evolve existing interfaces by adding new methods to those interfaces without breaking code that uses them.*

Interfaces vs. *abstract* Classes

Prior to Java SE 8, an interface was typically used (rather than an abstract class) when there were no implementation details to inherit—no fields and no method implementations. With default methods, you can instead declare common method implementations in interfaces, which gives you more flexibility in designing your classes.

10.10.2 static Interface Methods

Prior to Java SE 8, it was common to associate with an interface a class containing static helper methods for working with objects that implemented the interface. In Chapter 16, you'll learn about class Collections which contains many static helper methods for working with objects that implement interfaces Collection, List, Set and more. For example, Collections method sort can sort objects of *any* class that implements interface List. With static interface methods, such helper methods can now be declared directly in interfaces rather than in separate classes.

10.10.3 Functional Interfaces

As of Java SE 8, any interface containing only one abstract method is known as a **functional interface**. There are many such interfaces throughout the Java SE 7 APIs, and many new ones in Java SE 8. Some functional interfaces that you'll use in this book include:

- ActionListener (Chapter 12)—You'll implement this interface to define a method that's called when the user clicks a button.

- Comparator (Chapter 16)—You'll implement this interface to define a method that can compare two objects of a given type to determine whether the first object is less than, equal to or greater than the second.

- Runnable (Chapter 23)—You'll implement this interface to define a task that may be run in parallel with other parts of your program.

Functional interfaces are used extensively with Java SE 8's new lambda capabilities that we introduce in Chapter 17. In Chapter 12, you'll often implement an interface by creating a so-called anonymous inner class that implements the interface's method(s). In Java SE 8, lambdas provide a shorthand notation for creating *anonymous methods* that the compiler automatically translates into anonymous inner classes for you.

10.11 (Optional) GUI and Graphics Case Study: Drawing with Polymorphism

You may have noticed in the drawing program created in GUI and Graphics Case Study Exercise 8.1 (and modified in GUI and Graphics Case Study Exercise 9.1) that shape classes have many similarities. Using inheritance, we can "factor out" the common features from all three classes and place them in a single shape *superclass*. Then, using variables of the superclass type, we can manipulate shape objects *polymorphically*. Removing the redundant code will result in a smaller, more flexible program that's easier to maintain.

GUI and Graphics Case Study Exercises

10.1   Modify the MyLine, MyOval and MyRectangle classes of GUI and Graphics Case Study Exercise 8.1 and Exercise 9.1 to create the class hierarchy in Fig. 10.17. Classes of the MyShape hierarchy should be "smart" shape classes that know how to draw themselves (if provided with a Graphics object that tells them where to draw). Once the program creates an object from this hierarchy, it can manipulate it *polymorphically* for the rest of its lifetime as a MyShape.

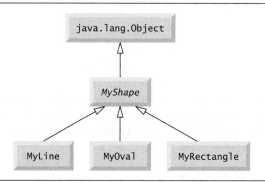

Fig. 10.17 | MyShape hierarchy.

In your solution, class MyShape in Fig. 10.17 *must* be abstract. Since MyShape represents any shape in general, you cannot implement a draw method without knowing *specifically* what shape it is. The data representing the coordinates and color of the shapes in the hierarchy should be declared as private members of class MyShape. In addition to the common data, class MyShape should declare the following methods:

a)   A *no-argument constructor* that sets all the coordinates of the shape to 0 and the color to Color.BLACK.

b)   A constructor that initializes the coordinates and color to the values of the arguments supplied.

c)   *Set* methods for the individual coordinates and color that allow the programmer to set any piece of data independently for a shape in the hierarchy.

d)   *Get* methods for the individual coordinates and color that allow the programmer to retrieve any piece of data independently for a shape in the hierarchy.

e)   The abstract method

```
public abstract void draw(Graphics g);
```

which the program's paintComponent method will call to draw a shape on the screen.

To ensure proper encapsulation, all data in class MyShape must be private. This requires declaring proper *set* and *get* methods to manipulate the data. Class MyLine should provide a no-argument constructor and a constructor with arguments for the coordinates and color. Classes MyOval and MyRectangle should provide a no-argument constructor and a constructor with arguments for the coordinates, color and determining whether the shape is filled. The no-argument constructor should, in addition to setting the default values, set the shape to be an unfilled shape.

You can draw lines, rectangles and ovals if you know two points in space. Lines require *x1*, *y1*, *x2* and *y2* coordinates. The drawLine method of the Graphics class will connect the two points supplied with a line. If you have the same four coordinate values (*x1*, *y1*, *x2* and *y2*) for ovals and rectangles, you can calculate the four arguments needed to draw them. Each requires an upper-left *x*-coordinate value (the smaller of the two *x*-coordinate values), an upper-left *y*-coordinate value (the smaller of the two *y*-coordinate values), a *width* (the absolute value of the difference between the two *x*-coordinate values) and a *height* (the absolute value of the difference between the two *y*-coordinate values). Rectangles and ovals should also have a filled flag that determines whether to draw the shape as a filled shape.

There should be no MyLine, MyOval or MyRectangle variables in the program—only MyShape variables that contain references to MyLine, MyOval and MyRectangle objects. The program should generate random shapes and store them in an array of type MyShape. Method paintComponent should walk through the MyShape array and draw every shape, by polymorphically calling every shape's draw method.

Allow the user to specify (via an input dialog) the number of shapes to generate. The program will then generate and display the shapes along with a status bar that informs the user how many of each shape were created.

10.2   *(Drawing Application Modification)* In the preceding exercise, you created a MyShape hierarchy in which classes MyLine, MyOval and MyRectangle extend MyShape directly. If your hierarchy was properly designed, you should be able to see the similarities between the MyOval and MyRectangle classes. Redesign and reimplement the code for the MyOval and MyRectangle classes to "factor out" the common features into the abstract class MyBoundedShape to produce the hierarchy in Fig. 10.18.

Class MyBoundedShape should declare two constructors that mimic those of class MyShape, only with an added parameter to specify whether the shape is filled. Class MyBoundedShape should also declare *get* and *set* methods for manipulating the filled flag and methods that calculate the upper-left *x*-coordinate, upper-left *y*-coordinate, width and height. Remember, the values needed to draw an oval or a rectangle can be calculated from two *(x, y)* coordinates. If designed properly, the new MyOval and MyRectangle classes should each have two constructors and a draw method.

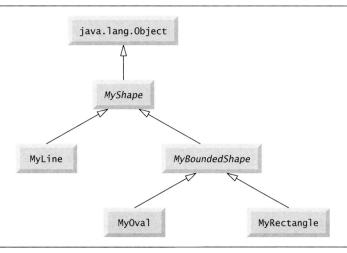

Fig. 10.18 | MyShape hierarchy with MyBoundedShape.

10.12 Wrap-Up

This chapter introduced polymorphism—the ability to process objects that share the same superclass in a class hierarchy as if they were all objects of the superclass. We discussed how polymorphism makes systems extensible and maintainable, then demonstrated how to use overridden methods to effect polymorphic behavior. We introduced abstract classes, which allow you to provide an appropriate superclass from which other classes can inherit. You learned that an abstract class can declare abstract methods that each subclass must implement to become a concrete class and that a program can use variables of an abstract class to invoke the subclasses' implementations of abstract methods polymorphically. You also learned how to determine an object's type at execution time. We explained the notions of final methods and classes. Finally, the chapter discussed declaring and implementing an interface as a way for possibly disparate classes to implement common functionality, enabling objects of those classes to be processed polymorphically.

You should now be familiar with classes, objects, encapsulation, inheritance, interfaces and polymorphism—the most essential aspects of object-oriented programming.

In the next chapter, you'll learn about exceptions, useful for handling errors during a program's execution. Exception handling provides for more robust programs.

Summary

Section 10.1 Introduction
- Polymorphism (p. 388) enables us to write programs that process objects that share the same superclass as if they were all objects of the superclass; this can simplify programming.
- With polymorphism, we can design and implement systems that are easily extensible. The only parts of a program that must be altered to accommodate new classes are those that require direct knowledge of the new classes that you add to the hierarchy.

Section 10.3 Demonstrating Polymorphic Behavior
- When the compiler encounters a method call made through a variable, it determines if the method can be called by checking the variable's class type. If that class contains the proper method declaration (or inherits one), the call is compiled. At execution time, the type of the object to which the variable refers determines the actual method to use.

Section 10.4 Abstract Classes and Methods
- Abstract classes (p. 393) cannot be used to instantiate objects, because they're incomplete.
- The primary purpose of an abstract class is to provide an appropriate superclass from which other classes can inherit and thus share a common design.
- Classes that can be used to instantiate objects are called concrete classes (p. 394). They provide implementations of every method they declare (some of the implementations can be inherited).
- Programmers often write client code that uses only abstract superclasses (p. 394) to reduce client code's dependencies on specific subclass types.
- Abstract classes sometimes constitute several levels of a hierarchy.
- An abstract class normally contains one or more abstract methods (p. 394).
- Abstract methods do not provide implementations.
- A class that contains any abstract methods must be declared as an abstract class (p. 394). Each concrete subclass must provide implementations of each of the superclass's abstract methods.

- Constructors and `static` methods cannot be declared `abstract`.
- Abstract superclass variables can hold references to objects of any concrete class derived from the superclass. Programs typically use such variables to manipulate subclass objects polymorphically.
- Polymorphism is particularly effective for implementing layered software systems.

Section 10.5 Case Study: Payroll System Using Polymorphism
- A hierarchy designer can demand that each concrete subclass provide an appropriate method implementation by including an `abstract` method in a superclass.
- Most method calls are resolved at execution time, based on the type of the object being manipulated. This process is known as dynamic binding (p. 409) or late binding.
- A superclass variable can be used to invoke only methods declared in the superclass.
- Operator `instanceof` (p. 409) determines if an object has the *is-a* relationship with a specific type.
- Every object in Java knows its own class and can access it through `Object` method `getClass` (p. 410), which returns an object of type `Class` (package `java.lang`).
- The *is-a* relationship applies only between the subclass and its superclasses, not vice versa.

Section 10.7 `final` Methods and Classes
- A method that's declared `final` (p. 411) in a superclass cannot be overridden in a subclass.
- Methods declared `private` are implicitly `final`, because you can't override them in a subclass.
- Methods that are declared `static` are implicitly `final`.
- A `final` method's declaration can never change, so all subclasses use the same implementation, and calls to `final` methods are resolved at compile time—this is known as static binding (p. 412).
- The compiler can optimize programs by removing calls to `final` methods and inlining their expanded code at each method-call location.
- A class that's declared `final` cannot be extended (p. 412).
- All methods in a `final` class are implicitly `final`.

Section 10.9 Creating and Using Interfaces
- An interface (p. 413) specifies *what* operations are allowed but not *how* they're performed.
- A Java interface describes a set of methods that can be called on an object.
- An interface declaration begins with the keyword `interface` (p. 413).
- All interface members must be `public`, and interfaces may not specify any implementation details, such as concrete method declarations and instance variables.
- All methods declared in an interface are implicitly `public abstract` methods and all fields are implicitly `public`, `static` and `final`.
- To use an interface, a concrete class must specify that it `implements` (p. 413) the interface and must declare each interface method with the signature specified in the interface declaration. A class that does not implement all the interface's methods must be declared `abstract`.
- Implementing an interface is like signing a contract with the compiler that states, "I will declare all the methods specified by the interface or I will declare my class `abstract`."
- An interface is typically used when disparate (i.e., unrelated) classes need to share common methods and constants. This allows objects of unrelated classes to be processed polymorphically—objects of classes that implement the same interface can respond to the same method calls.
- You can create an interface that describes the desired functionality, then implement the interface in any classes that require that functionality.

- An interface is often used in place of an abstract class when there's no default implementation to inherit—that is, no instance variables and no default method implementations.
- Like public abstract classes, interfaces are typically public types, so they're normally declared in files by themselves with the same name as the interface and the .java filename extension.
- Java does not allow subclasses to inherit from more than one superclass, but it does allow a class to inherit from a superclass and implement more than one interface.
- All objects of a class that implement multiple interfaces have the *is-a* relationship with each implemented interface type.
- An interface can declare constants. The constants are implicitly public, static and final.

Section 10.10 Java SE 8 Interface Enhancements
- In Java SE 8, an interface may declare default methods—that is, public methods with concrete implementations that specify how an operation should be performed.
- When a class implements an interface, the class receives the interface's default concrete implementations if it does not override them.
- To declare a default method in an interface, you simply place the keyword default before the method's return type and provide a complete method body.
- When you enhance an existing an interface with default methods—any classes that implemented the original interface will not break—it'll simply receive the default method implementations.
- With default methods, you can declare common method implementations in interfaces (rather than abstract classes), which gives you more flexibility in designing your classes.
- As of Java SE 8, interfaces may now include public static methods.
- As of Java SE 8, any interface containing only one method is known as a functional interface. There are many such interfaces throughout the Java APIs.
- Functional interfaces are used extensively with Java SE 8's new lambda capabilities. As you'll see, lambdas provide a shorthand notation for creating anonymous methods.

Self-Review Exercises

10.1 Fill in the blanks in each of the following statements:
   a) If a class contains at least one abstract method, it's a(n) _____ class.
   b) Classes from which objects can be instantiated are called _____ classes.
   c) _____ involves using a superclass variable to invoke methods on superclass and subclass objects, enabling you to "program in the general."
   d) Methods that are not interface methods and that do not provide implementations must be declared using keyword _____.
   e) Casting a reference stored in a superclass variable to a subclass type is called _____.

10.2 State whether each of the statements that follows is *true* or *false*. If *false*, explain why.
   a) All methods in an abstract class must be declared as abstract methods.
   b) Invoking a subclass-only method through a subclass variable is not allowed.
   c) If a superclass declares an abstract method, a subclass must implement that method.
   d) An object of a class that implements an interface may be thought of as an object of that interface type.

10.3 *(Java SE 8 interfaces)* Fill in the blanks in each of the following statements:
   a) In Java SE 8, an interface may declare _____—that is, public methods with concrete implementations that specify how an operation should be performed.
   b) As of Java SE 8, interfaces can now include _____ helper methods.
   c) As of Java SE 8, any interface containing only one method is known as a(n) _____.

Answers to Self-Review Exercises

10.1   a) abstract. b) concrete. c) Polymorphism. d) `abstract`. e) downcasting.

10.2   a)   False. An abstract class can include methods with implementations and `abstract` methods. b) False. Trying to invoke a subclass-only method with a superclass variable is not allowed. c) False. Only a concrete subclass must implement the method. d) True.

10.3   a) `default` methods. b) `static`. c) functional interface.

Exercises

10.4   How does polymorphism enable you to program "in the general" rather than "in the specific"? Discuss the key advantages of programming "in the general."

10.5   What are abstract methods? Describe the circumstances in which an abstract method would be appropriate.

10.6   How does polymorphism promote extensibility?

10.7   Discuss three proper ways in which you can assign superclass and subclass references to variables of superclass and subclass types.

10.8   Compare and contrast abstract classes and interfaces. Why would you use an abstract class? Why would you use an interface?

10.9   *(Java SE 8 Interfaces)* Explain how `default` methods enable you to add new methods to an existing interface without breaking the classes that implemented the original interface.

10.10   *(Java SE 8 Interfaces)* What is a functional interface?

10.11   *(Java SE 8 Interfaces)* Why is it useful to be able to add `static` methods to interfaces?

10.12   *(Payroll System Modification)* Modify the payroll system of Figs. 10.4–10.9 to include private instance variable `birthDate` in class `Employee`. Use class `Date` of Fig. 8.7 to represent an employee's birthday. Add *get* methods to class `Date`. Assume that payroll is processed once per month. Create an array of `Employee` variables to store references to the various employee objects. In a loop, calculate the payroll for each `Employee` (polymorphically), and add a $100.00 bonus to the person's payroll amount if the current month is the one in which the `Employee`'s birthday occurs.

10.13   *(Project: Shape Hierarchy)* Implement the `Shape` hierarchy shown in Fig. 9.3. Each `TwoDimensionalShape` should contain method `getArea` to calculate the area of the two-dimensional shape. Each `ThreeDimensionalShape` should have methods `getArea` and `getVolume` to calculate the surface area and volume, respectively, of the three-dimensional shape. Create a program that uses an array of `Shape` references to objects of each concrete class in the hierarchy. The program should print a text description of the object to which each array element refers. Also, in the loop that processes all the shapes in the array, determine whether each shape is a `TwoDimensionalShape` or a `ThreeDimensionalShape`. If it's a `TwoDimensionalShape`, display its area. If it's a `ThreeDimensionalShape`, display its area and volume.

10.14   *(Payroll System Modification)* Modify the payroll system of Figs. 10.4–10.9 to include an additional `Employee` subclass `PieceWorker` that represents an employee whose pay is based on the number of pieces of merchandise produced. Class `PieceWorker` should contain private instance variables `wage` (to store the employee's wage per piece) and `pieces` (to store the number of pieces produced). Provide a concrete implementation of method `earnings` in class `PieceWorker` that calculates the employee's earnings by multiplying the number of pieces produced by the wage per piece. Create an array of `Employee` variables to store references to objects of each concrete class in the new `Employee` hierarchy. For each `Employee`, display its `String` representation and earnings.

10.15 *(Accounts Payable System Modification)* In this exercise, we modify the accounts payable application of Figs. 10.11–10.15 to include the complete functionality of the payroll application of Figs. 10.4–10.9. The application should still process two `Invoice` objects, but now should process one object of each of the four `Employee` subclasses. If the object currently being processed is a `BasePlusCommissionEmployee`, the application should increase the `BasePlusCommissionEmployee`'s base salary by 10%. Finally, the application should output the payment amount for each object. Complete the following steps to create the new application:

    a) Modify classes `HourlyEmployee` (Fig. 10.6) and `CommissionEmployee` (Fig. 10.7) to place them in the `Payable` hierarchy as subclasses of the version of `Employee` (Fig. 10.13) that implements `Payable`. [*Hint:* Change the name of method `earnings` to `getPaymentAmount` in each subclass so that the class satisfies its inherited contract with interface `Payable`.]

    b) Modify class `BasePlusCommissionEmployee` (Fig. 10.8) such that it extends the version of class `CommissionEmployee` created in part (a).

    c) Modify `PayableInterfaceTest` (Fig. 10.15) to polymorphically process two `Invoices`, one `SalariedEmployee`, one `HourlyEmployee`, one `CommissionEmployee` and one `BasePlusCommissionEmployee`. First output a `String` representation of each `Payable` object. Next, if an object is a `BasePlusCommissionEmployee`, increase its base salary by 10%. Finally, output the payment amount for each `Payable` object.

10.16 *(Accounts Payable System Modification)* It's possible to include the functionality of the payroll application (Figs. 10.4–10.9) in the accounts payable application without modifying `Employee` subclasses `SalariedEmployee`, `HourlyEmployee`, `CommissionEmployee` or `BasePlusCommissionEmployee`. To do so, you can modify class `Employee` (Fig. 10.4) to implement interface `Payable` and declare method `getPaymentAmount` to invoke method `earnings`. Method `getPaymentAmount` would then be inherited by the subclasses in the `Employee` hierarchy. When `getPaymentAmount` is called for a particular subclass object, it polymorphically invokes the appropriate `earnings` method for that subclass. Reimplement Exercise 10.15 using the original `Employee` hierarchy from the payroll application of Figs. 10.4–10.9. Modify class `Employee` as described in this exercise, and *do not* modify any of class `Employee`'s subclasses.

Making a Difference

10.17 *(CarbonFootprint Interface: Polymorphism)* Using interfaces, as you learned in this chapter, you can specify similar behaviors for possibly disparate classes. Governments and companies worldwide are becoming increasingly concerned with carbon footprints (annual releases of carbon dioxide into the atmosphere) from buildings burning various types of fuels for heat, vehicles burning fuels for power, and the like. Many scientists blame these greenhouse gases for the phenomenon called global warming. Create three small classes unrelated by inheritance—classes `Building`, `Car` and `Bicycle`. Give each class some unique appropriate attributes and behaviors that it does not have in common with other classes. Write an interface `CarbonFootprint` with a `getCarbonFootprint` method. Have each of your classes implement that interface, so that its `getCarbonFootprint` method calculates an appropriate carbon footprint for that class (check out a few websites that explain how to calculate carbon footprints). Write an application that creates objects of each of the three classes, places references to those objects in `ArrayList<CarbonFootprint>`, then iterates through the `ArrayList`, polymorphically invoking each object's `getCarbonFootprint` method. For each object, print some identifying information and the object's carbon footprint.

Exception Handling: A Deeper Look

It is common sense to take a method and try it. If it fails, admit it frankly and try another. But above all, try something.
—Franklin Delano Roosevelt

O! throw away the worser part of it, And live the purer with the other half.
—William Shakespeare

If they're running and they don't look where they're going I have to come out from somewhere and catch them.
—Jerome David Salinger

Objectives

In this chapter you'll:

- Learn what exceptions are and how they're handled.
- Learn when to use exception handling.
- Use **try** blocks to delimit code in which exceptions might occur.
- Use **throw** to indicate a problem.
- Use **catch** blocks to specify exception handlers.
- Use the **finally** block to release resources.
- Understand the exception class hierarchy.
- Create user-defined exceptions.

11.1 Introduction

As you know from Chapter 6, an exception is an indication of a problem that occurs during a program's execution. Exception handling enables you to create applications that can resolve (or handle) exceptions. In many cases, handling an exception allows a program to continute executing as if no problem had been encountered. The features presented in this chapter help you write *robust* and *fault-tolerant* programs that can deal with problems and continue executing or *terminate gracefully.* Java exception handling is based in part on the work of Andrew Koenig and Bjarne Stroustrup.[1]

First, we demonstrate basic exception-handling techniques by handling an exception that occurs when a method attempts to divide an integer by zero. Next, we introduce several classes at the top of Java's exception-handling class hierarchy. As you'll see, only classes that extend Throwable (package java.lang) directly or indirectly can be used with exception handling. We then show how to use *chained exceptions*—when you invoke a method that indicates an exception, you can throw another exception and chain the original one to the new one. This enables you to add application-specific information to the orginal exception. Next, we introduce *preconditions* and *postconditions*, which must be true when your methods are called and when they return, respectively. We then present *assertions*, which you can use at development time to help debug your code. We also discuss two exception-handling features that were introduced in Java SE 7—catching multiple exceptions with one catch handler and the new try-with-resources statement that automatically releases a resource after it's used in the try block.

This chapter focuses on the exception-handling concepts and presents several mechanical examples that demonstrate various features. As you'll see in later chapters, many Java APIs methods throw exceptions that we handle in our code. Figure 11.1 shows some of the exception types you've already seen and others you'll learn about.

Chapter	Sample of exceptions used
Chapter 6	`ArrayIndexOutOfBoundsException`
Chapters 8–10	`IllegalArgumentException`
Chapter 11	`ArithmeticException, InputMismatchException`

Chapter 15	`SecurityException, FileNotFoundException, IOException,`
	`ClassNotFoundException, IllegalStateException,`
	`FormatterClosedException, NoSuchElementException`

Chapter 16	`ClassCastException, UnsupportedOperationException,` `NullPointerException,` custom exception types
Chapter 20	`ClassCastException,` custom exception types
Chapter 21	`IllegalArgumentException,` custom exception types
Chapter 23	`InterruptedException, IllegalMonitorStateException,` `ExecutionException, CancellationException`
Chapter 28	`MalformedURLException, EOFException, SocketException,` `InterruptedException, UnknownHostException`
Chapter 24	`SQLException, IllegalStateException, PatternSyntaxException`
Chapter 31	`SQLException`

Fig. 11.1 | Various exception types that you'll see throughout this book

11.2 Example: Divide by Zero without Exception Handling

First we demonstrate what happens when errors arise in an application that does not use exception handling. Figure 11.2 prompts the user for two integers and passes them to method `quotient`, which calculates the integer quotient and returns an `int` result. In this example, you'll see that exceptions are **thrown** (i.e., the exception occurs) by a method when it detects a problem and is unable to handle it.

```java
1  // Fig. 11.2: DivideByZeroNoExceptionHandling.java
2  // Integer division without exception handling.
3  import java.util.Scanner;
4
5  public class DivideByZeroNoExceptionHandling
6  {
7     // demonstrates throwing an exception when a divide-by-zero occurs
8     public static int quotient(int numerator, int denominator)
9     {
10        return numerator / denominator; // possible division by zero
11     }
12
13     public static void main(String[] args)
14     {
15        Scanner scanner = new Scanner(System.in);
```

Fig. 11.2 | Integer division without exception handling. (Part 1 of 2.)

```
16
17        System.out.print("Please enter an integer numerator: ");
18        int numerator = scanner.nextInt();
19        System.out.print("Please enter an integer denominator: ");
20        int denominator = scanner.nextInt();
21
22        int result = quotient(numerator, denominator);
23        System.out.printf(
24           "%nResult: %d / %d = %d%n", numerator, denominator, result);
25     }
26  } // end class DivideByZeroNoExceptionHandling
```

```
Please enter an integer numerator: 100
Please enter an integer denominator: 7

Result: 100 / 7 = 14
```

```
Please enter an integer numerator: 100
Please enter an integer denominator: 0
Exception in thread "main" java.lang.ArithmeticException: / by zero
        at DivideByZeroNoExceptionHandling.quotient(
            DivideByZeroNoExceptionHandling.java:10)
        at DivideByZeroNoExceptionHandling.main(
            DivideByZeroNoExceptionHandling.java:22)
```

```
Please enter an integer numerator: 100
Please enter an integer denominator: hello
Exception in thread "main" java.util.InputMismatchException
        at java.util.Scanner.throwFor(Unknown Source)
        at java.util.Scanner.next(Unknown Source)
        at java.util.Scanner.nextInt(Unknown Source)
        at java.util.Scanner.nextInt(Unknown Source)
        at DivideByZeroNoExceptionHandling.main(
            DivideByZeroNoExceptionHandling.java:20)
```

Fig. 11.2 | Integer division without exception handling. (Part 2 of 2.)

Stack Trace

The first sample execution in Fig. 11.2 shows a successful division. In the second execution, the user enters the value 0 as the denominator. Several lines of information are displayed in response to this invalid input. This information is known as a **stack trace**, which includes the name of the exception (java.lang.ArithmeticException) in a descriptive message that indicates the problem that occurred and the method-call stack (i.e., the call chain) at the time it occurred. The stack trace includes the path of execution that led to the exception method by method. This helps you debug the program.

*Stack Trace for an **ArithmeticException***

The first line specifies that an ArithmeticException has occurred. The text after the name of the exception ("/ by zero") indicates that this exception occurred as a result of an attempt to divide by zero. Java does not allow division by zero in integer arithmetic. When this occurs, Java throws an **ArithmeticException**. ArithmeticExceptions can arise from a number of different problems, so the extra data ("/ by zero") provides more specific information. Java *does* allow division by zero with floating-point values. Such a calculation results in the value positive or negative infinity, which is represented in Java as a floating-point value (but displays as the string Infinity or -Infinity). If 0.0 is divided by 0.0, the result is NaN (not a number), which is also represented in Java as a floating-point value (but displays as NaN). If you need to compare a floating-point value to NaN, use the method isNaN of class Float (for float values) or of class Double (for double values). Classes Float and Double are in package java.lang.

Starting from the last line of the stack trace, we see that the exception was detected in line 22 of method main. Each line of the stack trace contains the class name and method (e.g., DivideByZeroNoExceptionHandling.main) followed by the filename and line number (e.g., DivideByZeroNoExceptionHandling.java:22). Moving up the stack trace, we see that the exception occurs in line 10, in method quotient. The top row of the call chain indicates the **throw point**—the initial point at which the exception occurred. The throw point of this exception is in line 10 of method quotient.

Stack Trace for an **InputMismatchException**

In the third execution, the user enters the string "hello" as the denominator. Notice again that a stack trace is displayed. This informs us that an InputMismatchException has occurred (package java.util). Our prior examples that input numeric values assumed that the user would input a proper integer value. However, users sometimes make mistakes and input noninteger values. An **InputMismatchException** occurs when Scanner method nextInt receives a string that does not represent a valid integer. Starting from the end of the stack trace, we see that the exception was detected in line 20 of method main. Moving up the stack trace, we see that the exception occurred in method nextInt. Notice that in place of the filename and line number, we're provided with the text Unknown Source. This means that the so-called *debugging symbols* that provide the filename and line number information for that method's class were not available to the JVM—this is typically the case for the classes of the Java API. Many IDEs have access to the Java API source code and will display filenames and line numbers in stack traces.

Program Termination

In the sample executions of Fig. 11.2 when exceptions occur and stack traces are displayed, the program also *exits*. This does not always occur in Java. Sometimes a program may continue even though an exception has occurred and a stack trace has been printed. In such cases, the application may produce unexpected results. For example, a graphical user interface (GUI) application will often continue executing. In Fig. 11.2 both types of exceptions were detected in method main. In the next example, we'll see how to *handle* these exceptions so that you can enable the program to run to normal completion.

11.3 Example: Handling ArithmeticExceptions and InputMismatchExceptions

The application in Fig. 11.3, which is based on Fig. 11.2, uses *exception handling* to process any ArithmeticExceptions and InputMistmatchExceptions that arise. The application still prompts the user for two integers and passes them to method quotient, which calculates the quotient and returns an int result. This version of the application uses exception handling so that if the user makes a mistake, the program catches and handles (i.e., deals with) the exception—in this case, allowing the user to re-enter the input.

```java
1   // Fig. 11.3: DivideByZeroWithExceptionHandling.java
2   // Handling ArithmeticExceptions and InputMismatchExceptions.
3   import java.util.InputMismatchException;
4   import java.util.Scanner;
5
6   public class DivideByZeroWithExceptionHandling
7   {
8      // demonstrates throwing an exception when a divide-by-zero occurs
9      public static int quotient(int numerator, int denominator)
10        throws ArithmeticException
11     {
12        return numerator / denominator; // possible division by zero
13     }
14
15     public static void main(String[] args)
16     {
17        Scanner scanner = new Scanner(System.in);
18        boolean continueLoop = true; // determines if more input is needed
19
20        do
21        {
22           try // read two numbers and calculate quotient
23           {
24              System.out.print("Please enter an integer numerator: ");
25              int numerator = scanner.nextInt();
26              System.out.print("Please enter an integer denominator: ");
27              int denominator = scanner.nextInt();
28
29              int result = quotient(numerator, denominator);
30              System.out.printf("%nResult: %d / %d = %d%n", numerator,
31                 denominator, result);
32              continueLoop = false; // input successful; end looping
33           }
34           catch (InputMismatchException inputMismatchException)
35           {
36              System.err.printf("%nException: %s%n",
37                 inputMismatchException);
38              scanner.nextLine(); // discard input so user can try again
39              System.out.printf(
40                 "You must enter integers. Please try again.%n%n");
41           }
42           catch (ArithmeticException arithmeticException)
43           {
44              System.err.printf("%nException: %s%n", arithmeticException);
45              System.out.printf(
46                 "Zero is an invalid denominator. Please try again.%n%n");
47           }
48        } while (continueLoop);
49     }
50  } // end class DivideByZeroWithExceptionHandling
```

Fig. 11.3 | Handling ArithmeticExceptions and InputMismatchExceptions. (Part 1 of 2.)

```
Please enter an integer numerator: 100
Please enter an integer denominator: 7

Result: 100 / 7 = 14
```

```
Please enter an integer numerator: 100
Please enter an integer denominator: 0

Exception: java.lang.ArithmeticException: / by zero
Zero is an invalid denominator. Please try again.

Please enter an integer numerator: 100
Please enter an integer denominator: 7

Result: 100 / 7 = 14
```

```
Please enter an integer numerator: 100
Please enter an integer denominator: hello

Exception: java.util.InputMismatchException
You must enter integers. Please try again.

Please enter an integer numerator: 100
Please enter an integer denominator: 7

Result: 100 / 7 = 14
```

Fig. 11.3 | Handling ArithmeticExceptions and InputMismatchExceptions. (Part 2 of 2.)

The first sample execution in Fig. 11.3 does *not* encounter any problems. In the second execution the user enters a *zero denominator*, and an ArithmeticException exception occurs. In the third execution the user enters the string "hello" as the denominator, and an InputMismatchException occurs. For each exception, the user is informed of the mistake and asked to try again, then is prompted for two new integers. In each sample execution, the program runs to completion successfully.

Class InputMismatchException is imported in line 3. Class ArithmeticException does not need to be imported because it's in package java.lang. Line 18 creates the boolean variable continueLoop, which is true if the user has *not* yet entered valid input. Lines 20–48 repeatedly ask users for input until a *valid* input is received.

*Enclosing Code in a **try** Block*
Lines 22–33 contain a **try block**, which encloses the code that *might* throw an exception and the code that should *not* execute if an exception occurs (i.e., if an exception occurs, the remaining code in the try block will be skipped). A try block consists of the keyword try followed by a block of code enclosed in curly braces. [*Note:* The term "try block" sometimes refers only to the block of code that follows the try keyword (not including the try keyword itself). For simplicity, we use the term "try block" to refer to the block of

code that follows the try keyword, as well as the try keyword.] The statements that read the integers from the keyboard (lines 25 and 27) each use method nextInt to read an int value. Method nextInt throws an InputMismatchException if the value read in is *not* an integer.

The division that can cause an ArithmeticException is not performed in the try block. Rather, the call to method quotient (line 29) invokes the code that attempts the division (line 12); the JVM *throws* an ArithmeticException object when the denominator is zero.

Software Engineering Observation 11.1

Exceptions may surface through explicitly mentioned code in a try block, through deeply nested method calls initiated by code in a try block or from the Java Virtual Machine as it executes Java bytecodes.

Catching Exceptions

The try block in this example is followed by two catch blocks—one that handles an InputMismatchException (lines 34–41) and one that handles an ArithmeticException (lines 42–47). A **catch block** (also called a **catch clause** or **exception handler**) *catches* (i.e., receives) and *handles* an exception. A catch block begins with the keyword catch followed by a parameter in parentheses (called the *exception parameter*, discussed shortly) and a block of code enclosed in curly braces. [*Note:* The term "catch clause" is sometimes used to refer to the keyword catch followed by a block of code, whereas the term "catch block" refers to only the block of code following the catch keyword, but not including it. For simplicity, we use the term "catch block" to refer to the block of code following the catch keyword, as well as the keyword itself.]

At least one catch block or a **finally block** (discussed in Section 11.6) *must* immediately follow the try block. Each catch block specifies in parentheses an **exception parameter** that identifies the exception type the handler can process. When an exception occurs in a try block, the catch block that executes is the *first* one whose type matches the type of the exception that occurred (i.e., the type in the catch block matches the thrown exception type exactly or is a direct or indirect superclass of it). The exception parameter's name enables the catch block to interact with a caught exception object—e.g., to implicitly invoke the caught exception's toString method (as in lines 37 and 44), which displays basic information about the exception. Notice that we use the **System.err (standard error stream) object** to output error messages. By default, System.err's print methods, like those of System.out, display data to the *command prompt*.

Line 38 of the first catch block calls Scanner method nextLine. Because an InputMismatchException occurred, the call to method nextInt never successfully read in the user's data—so we read that input with a call to method nextLine. We do not do anything with the input at this point, because we know that it's *invalid*. Each catch block displays an error message and asks the user to try again. After either catch block terminates, the user is prompted for input. We'll soon take a deeper look at how this flow of control works in exception handling.

Common Programming Error 11.1

It's a syntax error to place code between a try block and its corresponding catch blocks.

Multi-catch

It's relatively common for a try block to be followed by several catch blocks to handle various types of exceptions. If the bodies of several catch blocks are identical, you can use the **multi-catch** feature (introduced in Java SE 7) to catch those exception types in a *single* catch handler and perform the same task. The syntax for a *multi-catch* is:

catch (*Type1* | *Type2* | *Type3* e)

Each exception type is separated from the next with a vertical bar (|). The preceding line of code indicates that *any* of the types (or their subclasses) can be caught in the exception handler. Any number of Throwable types can be specified in a multi-catch.

Uncaught Exceptions

An **uncaught exception** is one for which there are no matching catch blocks. You saw uncaught exceptions in the second and third outputs of Fig. 11.2. Recall that when exceptions occurred in that example, the application terminated early (after displaying the exception's *stack trace*). This does not always occur as a result of uncaught exceptions. Java uses a "multithreaded" model of program execution—each **thread** is a *concurrent activity*. One program can have many threads. If a program has only *one* thread, an uncaught exception will cause the program to terminate. If a program has *multiple* threads, an uncaught exception will terminate *only* the thread in which the exception occurred. In such programs, however, certain threads may rely on others, and if one thread terminates due to an uncaught exception, there may be adverse effects on the rest of the program. Chapter 23, Concurrency, discusses these issues in depth.

Termination Model of Exception Handling

If an exception occurs in a try block (such as an InputMismatchException being thrown as a result of the code at line 25 of Fig. 11.3), the try block *terminates* immediately and program control transfers to the *first* of the following catch blocks in which the exception parameter's type matches the thrown exception's type. In Fig. 11.3, the first catch block catches InputMismatchExceptions (which occur if invalid input is entered) and the second catch block catches ArithmeticExceptions (which occur if an attempt is made to divide by zero). After the exception is handled, program control does *not* return to the throw point, because the try block has *expired* (and its *local variables* have been *lost*). Rather, control resumes after the last catch block. This is known as the **termination model of exception handling**. Some languages use the **resumption model of exception handling**, in which, after an exception is handled, control resumes just after the *throw point*.

Notice that we name our exception parameters (inputMismatchException and arithmeticException) based on their type. Java programmers often simply use the letter e as the name of their exception parameters.

After executing a catch block, this program's flow of control proceeds to the first statement after the last catch block (line 48 in this case). The condition in the do...while statement is true (variable continueLoop contains its initial value of true), so control returns to the beginning of the loop and the user is again prompted for input. This control statement will loop until *valid* input is entered. At that point, program control reaches line 32, which assigns false to variable continueLoop. The try block then *terminates*. If no exceptions are thrown in the try block, the catch blocks are *skipped* and control continues with the first statement after the catch blocks (we'll learn about another possibility when we discuss the finally block in Section 11.6). Now the condition for the do...while loop is false, and method main ends.

The try block and its corresponding catch and/or finally blocks form a **try statement**. Do not confuse the terms "try block" and "try statement"—the latter includes the try block as well as the following catch blocks and/or finally block.

As with any other block of code, when a try block terminates, *local variables* declared in the block *go out of scope* and are no longer accessible; thus, the local variables of a try block are not accessible in the corresponding catch blocks. When a catch block *terminates*, *local variables* declared within the catch block (including the exception parameter of that catch block) also *go out of scope* and are *destroyed*. Any remaining catch blocks in the try statement are *ignored*, and execution resumes at the first line of code after the try...catch sequence—this will be a finally block, if one is present.

Using the throws Clause

In method quotient (Fig. 11.3, lines 9–13), line 10 is known as a **throws clause**. It specifies the exceptions the method *might* throw if problems occur. This clause, which must appear after the method's parameter list and before the body, contains a comma-separated list of the exception types. Such exceptions may be thrown by statements in the method's body or by methods called from there. We've added the throws clause to this application to indicate that this method might throw an ArithmeticException. Method quotient's callers are thus informed that the method might throw an ArithmeticException. Some exception types, such as ArithmeticException, are not required to be listed in the throws clause. For those that are, the method can throw exceptions that have the *is-a* relationship with the classes listed in the throws clause. You'll learn more about this in Section 11.5.

Error-Prevention Tip 11.1

Read the online API documentation for a method before using it in a program. The documentation specifies the exceptions thrown by the method (if any) and indicates reasons why such exceptions may occur. Next, read the online API documentation for the specified exception classes. The documentation for an exception class typically contains potential reasons that such exceptions occur. Finally, provide for handling those exceptions in your program.

When line 12 executes, if the denominator is zero, the JVM throws an ArithmeticException object. This object will be caught by the catch block at lines 42–47, which displays basic information about the exception by *implicitly* invoking the exception's toString method, then asks the user to try again.

If the denominator is not zero, method quotient performs the division and returns the result to the point of invocation of method quotient in the try block (line 29). Lines 30–31 display the result of the calculation and line 32 sets continueLoop to false. In this case, the try block completes successfully, so the program skips the catch blocks and fails the condition at line 48, and method main completes execution normally.

When quotient throws an ArithmeticException, quotient *terminates* and does *not* return a value, and quotient's *local variables go out of scope* (and are destroyed). If quotient contained local variables that were references to objects and there were no other references to those objects, the objects would be marked for *garbage collection*. Also, when an exception occurs, the try block from which quotient was called *terminates* before lines 30–32 can execute. Here, too, if local variables were created in the try block prior to the exception's being thrown, these variables would go out of scope.

If an `InputMismatchException` is generated by lines 25 or 27, the `try` block *termi-nates* and execution *continues* with the `catch` block at lines 34–41. In this case, method `quotient` is not called. Then method `main` continues after the last `catch` block (line 48).

11.4 When to Use Exception Handling

Exception handling is designed to process **synchronous errors**, which occur when a state-ment executes. Common examples we'll see throughout the book are *out-of-range array in-dices*, *arithmetic overflow* (i.e., a value outside the representable range of values), *division by zero*, *invalid method parameters* and *thread interruption* (as we'll see in Chapter 23). Excep-tion handling is not designed to process problems associated with **asynchronous events** (e.g., disk I/O completions, network message arrivals, mouse clicks and keystrokes), which occur in parallel with, and *independent of,* the program's flow of control.

Software Engineering Observation 11.2

Incorporate your exception-handling and error-recovery strategy into your system from the inception of the design process—including these after a system has been implemented can be difficult.

Software Engineering Observation 11.3

Exception handling provides a single, uniform technique for documenting, detecting and recovering from errors. This helps programmers working on large projects understand each other's error-processing code.

Software Engineering Observation 11.4

There's a great variety of situations that generate exceptions—some exceptions are easier to recover from than others.

11.5 Java Exception Hierarchy

All Java exception classes inherit directly or indirectly from class **Exception**, forming an *inheritance hierarchy*. You can extend this hierarchy with your own exception classes.

Figure 11.4 shows a small portion of the inheritance hierarchy for class **Throwable** (a subclass of `Object`), which is the superclass of class `Exception`. Only `Throwable` objects can be used with the exception-handling mechanism. Class `Throwable` has two direct sub-classes: `Exception` and `Error`. Class `Exception` and its subclasses—for instance, `Runtime-Exception` (package `java.lang`) and `IOException` (package `java.io`)—represent exceptional situations that can occur in a Java program and that can be caught by the application. Class **Error** and its subclasses represent *abnormal situations* that happen in the JVM. Most *Errors happen infrequently and should not be caught by applications—it's usually not possible for applications to recover from Errors.*

The Java exception hierarchy contains hundreds of classes. Information about Java's exception classes can be found throughout the Java API. You can view `Throwable`'s docu-mentation at `docs.oracle.com/javase/7/docs/api/java/lang/Throwable.html`. From there, you can look at this class's subclasses to get more information about Java's Excep-tions and Errors.

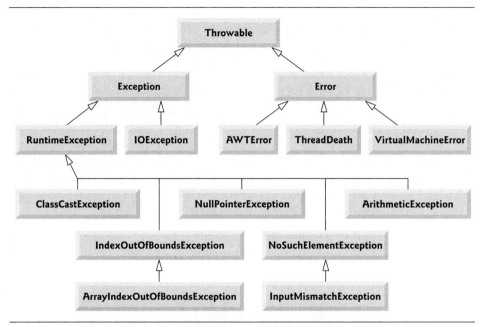

Fig. 11.4 | Portion of class Throwable's inheritance hierarchy.

Checked vs. Unchecked Exceptions

Java distinguishes between **checked exceptions** and **unchecked exceptions**. This distinction is important, because the Java compiler enforces special requirements for *checked* exceptions (discussed momentarily). An exception's type determines whether it's checked or unchecked.

RuntimeExceptions Are Unchecked Exceptions

All exception types that are direct or indirect subclasses of **RuntimeException** (package java.lang) are *unchecked* exceptions. These are typically caused by defects in your program's code. Examples of unchecked exceptions include:

- ArrayIndexOutOfBoundsExceptions (discussed in Chapter 6)—You can avoid these by ensuring that your array indices are always greater than or equal to 0 and less than the array's length.

- ArithmeticExceptions (shown in Fig. 11.3)—You can avoid the Arithmetic-Exception that occurs when you divide by zero by checking the denominator to determine whether it's 0 *before* performing the calculation.

Classes that inherit directly or indirectly from class Error (Fig. 11.4) are *unchecked*, because Errors are such serious problems that your program should not even attempt to deal with them.

Checked Exceptions

All classes that inherit from class Exception but *not* directly or indirectly from class RuntimeException are considered to be *checked* exceptions. Such exceptions are typically caused by conditions that are not under the control of the program—for example, in file processing, the program can't open a file if it does not exist.

The Compiler and Checked Exceptions

The compiler checks each method call and method declaration to determine whether the method throws a checked exception. If so, the compiler verifies that the checked exception is *caught* or is *declared* in a throws clause—this is known as the **catch-or-declare requirement**. We show how to catch or declare checked exceptions in the next several examples. Recall from Section 11.3 that the throws clause specifies the exceptions a method throws. Such exceptions are not caught in the method's body. To satisfy the *catch* part of the *catch-or-declare requirement*, the code that generates the exception must be wrapped in a try block and must provide a catch handler for the checked-exception type (or one of its superclasses). To satisfy the *declare* part of the catch-or-declare requirement, the method containing the code that generates the exception must provide a throws clause containing the checked-exception type after its parameter list and before its method body. If the catch-or-declare requirement is not satisfied, the compiler will issue an error message. This forces you to think about the problems that may occur when a method that throws checked exceptions is called.

Error-Prevention Tip 11.2

You must deal with checked exceptions. This results in more robust code than would be created if you were able to simply ignore them.

Common Programming Error 11.2

If a subclass method overrides a superclass method, it's an error for the subclass method to list more exceptions in its throws clause than the superclass method does. However, a subclass's throws clause can contain a subset of a superclass's throws clause.

Software Engineering Observation 11.5

If your method calls other methods that throw checked exceptions, those exceptions must be caught or declared. If an exception can be handled meaningfully in a method, the method should catch the exception rather than declare it.

The Compiler and Unchecked Exceptions

Unlike checked exceptions, the Java compiler does *not* examine the code to determine whether an unchecked exception is caught or declared. Unchecked exceptions typically can be *prevented* by proper coding. For example, the unchecked ArithmeticException thrown by method quotient (lines 9–13) in Fig. 11.3 can be avoided if the method ensures that the denominator is not zero *before* performing the division. Unchecked exceptions are *not* required to be listed in a method's throws clause—even if they are, it's *not* required that such exceptions be caught by an application.

Software Engineering Observation 11.6

Although the compiler does not enforce the catch-or-declare requirement for unchecked exceptions, provide appropriate exception-handling code when it's known that such exceptions might occur. For example, a program should process the NumberFormatException from Integer method parseInt, even though NumberFormatException is an indirect subclass of RuntimeException (and thus an unchecked exception). This makes your programs more robust.

Catching Subclass Exceptions

If a catch handler is written to catch *superclass* exception objects, it can also catch all objects of that class's *subclasses*. This enables catch to handle related exceptions *polymorphically*. You can catch each subclass individually if those exceptions require different processing.

Only the First Matching **catch** *Executes*

If *multiple* catch blocks match a particular exception type, only the *first* matching catch block executes when an exception of that type occurs. It's a compilation error to catch the *exact same type* in two different catch blocks associated with a particular try block. However, there can be several catch blocks that match an exception—i.e., several catch blocks whose types are the same as the exception type or a superclass of that type. For instance, we could follow a catch block for type ArithmeticException with a catch block for type Exception—both would match ArithmeticExceptions, but only the first matching catch block would execute.

Common Programming Error 11.3

Placing a catch block for a superclass exception type before other catch blocks that catch subclass exception types would prevent those catch blocks from executing, so a compilation error occurs.

Error-Prevention Tip 11.3

Catching subclass types individually is subject to error if you forget to test for one or more of the subclass types explicitly; catching the superclass guarantees that objects of all subclasses will be caught. Positioning a catch block for the superclass type after all other subclass catch blocks ensures that all subclass exceptions are eventually caught.

Software Engineering Observation 11.7

In industry, throwing or catching type Exception is discouraged—we use it here simply to demonstrate exception-handling mechanics. In subsequent chapters, we generally throw and catch more specific exception types.

11.6 finally Block

Programs that obtain certain resources must return them to the system to avoid so-called **resource leaks.** In programming languages such as C and C++, the most common resource leak is a *memory leak.* Java performs automatic *garbage collection* of memory no longer used by programs, thus avoiding most memory leaks. However, other types of resource leaks can occur. For example, files, database connections and network connections that are not closed properly after they're no longer needed might not be available for use in other programs.

Error-Prevention Tip 11.4

A subtle issue is that Java does not entirely eliminate memory leaks. Java will not garbage-collect an object until there are no remaining references to it. Thus, if you erroneously keep references to unwanted objects, memory leaks can occur.

The finally block (which consists of the finally keyword, followed by code enclosed in curly braces), sometimes referred to as the **finally clause,** is optional. If it's present, it's placed after the last catch block. If there are no catch blocks, the finally block, if present, immediately follows the try block.

When the *finally Block Executes*

The finally block will execute *whether or not* an exception is thrown in the corresponding try block. The finally block also will execute if a try block exits by using a return, break or continue statement or simply by reaching its closing right brace. The one case in which the finally block will *not* execute is if the application *exits early* from a try block by calling method **System.exit**. This method, which we demonstrate in Chapter 15, *immediately* terminates an application.

If an exception that occurs in a try block cannot be caught by one of that try block's catch handlers, the program skips the rest of the try block and control proceeds to the finally block. Then the program passes the exception to the next outer try block—normally in the calling method—where an associated catch block might catch it. This process can occur through many levels of try blocks. Also, the exception could go *uncaught* (as we discussed in Section 11.3).

If a catch block throws an exception, the finally block still executes. Then the exception is passed to the next outer try block—again, normally in the calling method.

Releasing Resources in a *finally Block*

Because a finally block always executes, it typically contains *resource-release code*. Suppose a resource is allocated in a try block. If no exception occurs, the catch blocks are *skipped* and control proceeds to the finally block, which frees the resource. Control then proceeds to the first statement after the finally block. If an exception occurs in the try block, the try block *terminates*. If the program catches the exception in one of the corresponding catch blocks, it processes the exception, then the finally block *releases the resource* and control proceeds to the first statement after the finally block. If the program doesn't catch the exception, the finally block *still* releases the resource and an attempt is made to catch the exception in a calling method.

Error-Prevention Tip 11.5

The finally block is an ideal place to release resources acquired in a try block (such as opened files), which helps eliminate resource leaks.

Performance Tip 11.1

Always release a resource explicitly and at the earliest possible moment at which it's no longer needed. This makes resources available for reuse as early as possible, thus improving resource utilization and program performance.

Demonstrating the *finally Block*

Figure 11.5 demonstrates that the finally block executes even if an exception is *not* thrown in the corresponding try block. The program contains static methods main (lines 6–18), throwException (lines 21–44) and doesNotThrowException (lines 47–64). Methods throwException and doesNotThrowException are declared static, so main can call them directly without instantiating a UsingExceptions object.

```
1   // Fig. 11.5: UsingExceptions.java
2   // try...catch...finally exception handling mechanism.
3
4   public class UsingExceptions
5   {
6      public static void main(String[] args)
7      {
8         try
9         {
10            throwException();
11         }
12         catch (Exception exception) // exception thrown by throwException
13         {
14            System.err.println("Exception handled in main");
15         }
16
17         doesNotThrowException();
18      }
19
20      // demonstrate try...catch...finally
21      public static void throwException() throws Exception
22      {
23         try // throw an exception and immediately catch it
24         {
25            System.out.println("Method throwException");
26            throw new Exception(); // generate exception
27         }
28         catch (Exception exception) // catch exception thrown in try
29         {
30            System.err.println(
31               "Exception handled in method throwException");
32            throw exception; // rethrow for further processing
33
34            // code here would not be reached; would cause compilation errors
35
36         }
37         finally // executes regardless of what occurs in try...catch
38         {
39            System.err.println("Finally executed in throwException");
40         }
41
42         // code here would not be reached; would cause compilation errors
43
44      }
45
46      // demonstrate finally when no exception occurs
47      public static void doesNotThrowException()
48      {
49         try // try block does not throw an exception
50         {
51            System.out.println("Method doesNotThrowException");
52         }
```

Fig. 11.5 | try...catch...finally exception-handling mechanism. (Part 1 of 2.)

```
53        catch (Exception exception) // does not execute
54        {
55            System.err.println(exception);
56        }
57        finally // executes regardless of what occurs in try...catch
58        {
59            System.err.println(
60                "Finally executed in doesNotThrowException");
61        }
62
63        System.out.println("End of method doesNotThrowException");
64    }
65 } // end class UsingExceptions
```

```
Method throwException
Exception handled in method throwException
Finally executed in throwException
Exception handled in main
Method doesNotThrowException
Finally executed in doesNotThrowException
End of method doesNotThrowException
```

Fig. 11.5 | try...catch...finally exception-handling mechanism. (Part 2 of 2.)

System.out and System.err are **streams**—sequences of bytes. While System.out (known as the **standard output stream**) displays a program's output, System.err (known as the **standard error stream**) displays a program's errors. Output from these streams can be *redirected* (i.e., sent to somewhere other than the *command prompt*, such as to a *file*). Using two different streams enables you to easily *separate* error messages from other output. For instance, data output from System.err could be sent to a log file, while data output from System.out can be displayed on the screen. For simplicity, this chapter will *not* redirect output from System.err, but will display such messages to the *command prompt*. You'll learn more about streams in Chapter 15.

*Throwing Exceptions Using the **throw** Statement*
Method main (Fig. 11.5) begins executing, enters its try block and immediately calls method throwException (line 10). Method throwException throws an Exception. The statement at line 26 is known as a **throw statement**—it's executed to indicate that an exception has occurred. So far, you've caught only exceptions thrown by called methods. You can throw exceptions yourself by using the throw statement. Just as with exceptions thrown by the Java API's methods, this indicates to client applications that an error has occurred. A throw statement specifies an object to be thrown. The operand of a throw can be of any class derived from class Throwable.

Software Engineering Observation 11.8
When toString is invoked on any Throwable object, its resulting String includes the descriptive string that was supplied to the constructor, or simply the class name if no string was supplied.

Software Engineering Observation 11.9

An exception can be thrown without containing information about the problem that occurred. In this case, simply knowing that an exception of a particular type occurred may provide sufficient information for the handler to process the problem correctly.

Software Engineering Observation 11.10

Throw exceptions from constructors to indicate that the constructor parameters are not valid—this prevents an object from being created in an invalid state.

Rethrowing Exceptions

Line 32 of Fig. 11.5 **rethrows the exception**. Exceptions are rethrown when a catch block, upon receiving an exception, decides either that it cannot process that exception or that it can only partially process it. Rethrowing an exception defers the exception handling (or perhaps a portion of it) to another catch block associated with an outer try statement. An exception is rethrown by using the **throw keyword**, followed by a reference to the exception object that was just caught. Exceptions cannot be rethrown from a finally block, as the exception parameter (a local variable) from the catch block no longer exists.

When a rethrow occurs, the *next enclosing try block* detects the rethrown exception, and that try block's catch blocks attempt to handle it. In this case, the next enclosing try block is found at lines 8–11 in method main. Before the rethrown exception is handled, however, the finally block (lines 37–40) executes. Then method main detects the rethrown exception in the try block and handles it in the catch block (lines 12–15).

Next, main calls method doesNotThrowException (line 17). No exception is thrown in doesNotThrowException's try block (lines 49–52), so the program skips the catch block (lines 53–56), but the finally block (lines 57–61) nevertheless executes. Control proceeds to the statement after the finally block (line 63). Then control returns to main and the program terminates.

Common Programming Error 11.4

If an exception has not been caught when control enters a finally block and the finally block throws an exception that's not caught in the finally block, the first exception will be lost and the exception from the finally block will be returned to the calling method.

Error-Prevention Tip 11.6

Avoid placing in a finally block code that can throw an exception. If such code is required, enclose the code in a try...catch within the finally block.

Common Programming Error 11.5

Assuming that an exception thrown from a catch block will be processed by that catch block or any other catch block associated with the same try statement can lead to logic errors.

Good Programming Practice 11.1

Exception handling removes error-processing code from the main line of a program's code to improve program clarity. Do not place try...catch... finally around every statement that may throw an exception. This decreases readability. Rather, place one try block around a significant portion of your code, follow the try with catch blocks that handle each possible exception and follow the catch blocks with a single finally block (if one is required).

11.7 Stack Unwinding and Obtaining Information from an Exception Object

When an exception is thrown but *not caught* in a particular scope, the method-call stack is "unwound," and an attempt is made to catch the exception in the next outer try block. This process is called **stack unwinding**. Unwinding the method-call stack means that the method in which the exception was not caught *terminates*, all local variables in that method *go out of scope* and control returns to the statement that originally invoked that method. If a try block encloses that statement, an attempt is made to catch the exception. If a try block does not enclose that statement or if the exception is not caught, stack unwinding occurs again. Figure 11.6 demonstrates stack unwinding, and the exception handler in main shows how to access the data in an exception object.

Stack Unwinding

In main, the try block (lines 8–11) calls method1 (declared at lines 35–38), which in turn calls method2 (declared at lines 41–44), which in turn calls method3 (declared at lines 47–50). Line 49 of method3 throws an Exception object—this is the *throw point*. Because the throw statement at line 49 is *not* enclosed in a try block, *stack unwinding* occurs—method3 terminates at line 49, then returns control to the statement in method2 that invoked method3 (i.e., line 43). Because *no* try block encloses line 43, *stack unwinding* occurs again—method2 terminates at line 43 and returns control to the statement in method1 that invoked method2 (i.e., line 37). Because *no* try block encloses line 37, *stack unwinding* occurs one more time—method1 terminates at line 37 and returns control to the statement in main that invoked method1 (i.e., line 10). The try block at lines 8–11 encloses this statement. The exception has not been handled, so the try block terminates and the first matching catch block (lines 12–31) catches and processes the exception. If there were no matching catch blocks, and the exception is *not declared* in each method that throws it, a compilation error would occur. Remember that this is not always the case—for *unchecked* exceptions, the application will compile, but it will run with unexpected results.

```
1   // Fig. 11.6: UsingExceptions.java
2   // Stack unwinding and obtaining data from an exception object.
3
4   public class UsingExceptions
5   {
6      public static void main(String[] args)
7      {
8         try
9         {
10            method1();
11         }
12         catch (Exception exception) // catch exception thrown in method1
13         {
14            System.err.printf("%s%n%n", exception.getMessage());
15            exception.printStackTrace();
16
```

Fig. 11.6 | Stack unwinding and obtaining data from an exception object. (Part 1 of 2.)

```
17            // obtain the stack-trace information
18            StackTraceElement[] traceElements = exception.getStackTrace();
19
20            System.out.printf("%nStack trace from getStackTrace:%n");
21            System.out.println("Class\t\tFile\t\t\tLine\tMethod");
22
23            // loop through traceElements to get exception description
24            for (StackTraceElement element : traceElements)
25            {
26               System.out.printf("%s\t", element.getClassName());
27               System.out.printf("%s\t", element.getFileName());
28               System.out.printf("%s\t", element.getLineNumber());
29               System.out.printf("%s%n", element.getMethodName());
30            }
31         }
32      } // end main
33
34      // call method2; throw exceptions back to main
35      public static void method1() throws Exception
36      {
37         method2();
38      }
39
40      // call method3; throw exceptions back to method1
41      public static void method2() throws Exception
42      {
43         method3();
44      }
45
46      // throw Exception back to method2
47      public static void method3() throws Exception
48      {
49         throw new Exception("Exception thrown in method3");
50      }
51   } // end class UsingExceptions
```

```
Exception thrown in method3

java.lang.Exception: Exception thrown in method3
        at UsingExceptions.method3(UsingExceptions.java:49)
        at UsingExceptions.method2(UsingExceptions.java:43)
        at UsingExceptions.method1(UsingExceptions.java:37)
        at UsingExceptions.main(UsingExceptions.java:10)

Stack trace from getStackTrace:
Class           File                    Line    Method
UsingExceptions UsingExceptions.java    49      method3
UsingExceptions UsingExceptions.java    43      method2
UsingExceptions UsingExceptions.java    37      method1
UsingExceptions UsingExceptions.java    10      main
```

Fig. 11.6 | Stack unwinding and obtaining data from an exception object. (Part 2 of 2.)

Obtaining Data from an Exception Object

All exceptions derive from class Throwable, which has a **printStackTrace** method that outputs to the standard error stream the *stack trace* (discussed in Section 11.2). Often this is helpful in testing and debugging. Class Throwable also provides a **getStackTrace** method that retrieves the stack-trace information that might be printed by printStackTrace. Class Throwable's **getMessage** method returns the descriptive string stored in an exception.

Error-Prevention Tip 11.7
An exception that's not caught in an application causes Java's default exception handler to run. This displays the name of the exception, a descriptive message that indicates the problem that occurred and a complete execution stack trace. In an application with a single thread of execution, the application terminates. In an application with multiple threads, the thread that caused the exception terminates. We discuss multithreading in Chapter 23.

Error-Prevention Tip 11.8
Throwable method toString *(inherited by all* Throwable *subclasses) returns a* String *containing the name of the exception's class and a descriptive message.*

The catch handler in Fig. 11.6 (lines 12–31) demonstrates getMessage, print-StackTrace and getStackTrace. If we wanted to output the stack-trace information to streams other than the standard error stream, we could use the information returned from getStackTrace and output it to another stream or use one of the overloaded versions of method printStackTrace. Sending data to other streams is discussed in Chapter 15.

Line 14 invokes the exception's getMessage method to get the *exception description*. Line 15 invokes the exception's printStackTrace method to output the *stack trace* that indicates where the exception occurred. Line 18 invokes the exception's getStackTrace method to obtain the stack-trace information as an array of **StackTraceElement** objects. Lines 24–30 get each StackTraceElement in the array and invoke its methods **getClassName**, **getFileName**, **getLineNumber** and **getMethodName** to get the class name, filename, line number and method name, respectively, for that StackTraceElement. Each StackTraceElement represents *one* method call on the *method-call stack*.

The program's output shows that output of printStackTrace follows the pattern: *className.methodName(fileName:lineNumber)*, where *className*, *methodName* and *fileName* indicate the names of the class, method and file in which the exception occurred, respectively, and the *lineNumber* indicates where in the file the exception occurred. You saw this in the output for Fig. 11.2. Method getStackTrace enables custom processing of the exception information. Compare the output of printStackTrace with the output created from the StackTraceElements to see that both contain the same stack-trace information.

Software Engineering Observation 11.11
Occasionally, you might want to ignore an exception by writing a catch *handler with an empty body. Before doing so, ensure that the exception doesn't indicate a condition that code higher up the stack might want to know about or recover from.*

11.8 Chained Exceptions

Sometimes a method responds to an exception by throwing a different exception type that's specific to the current application. If a catch block throws a new exception, the original exception's information and stack trace are *lost*. Earlier Java versions provided no mechanism to wrap the original exception information with the new exception's information to provide a complete stack trace showing where the original problem occurred. This made debugging such problems particularly difficult. **Chained exceptions** enable an exception object to maintain the complete stack-trace information from the original exception. Figure 11.7 demonstrates chained exceptions.

```java
1   // Fig. 11.7: UsingChainedExceptions.java
2   // Chained exceptions.
3
4   public class UsingChainedExceptions
5   {
6      public static void main(String[] args)
7      {
8         try
9         {
10            method1();
11         }
12         catch (Exception exception) // exceptions thrown from method1
13         {
14            exception.printStackTrace();
15         }
16      }
17
18      // call method2; throw exceptions back to main
19      public static void method1() throws Exception
20      {
21         try
22         {
23            method2();
24         } // end try
25         catch (Exception exception) // exception thrown from method2
26         {
27            throw new Exception("Exception thrown in method1", exception);
28         }
29      }
30
31      // call method3; throw exceptions back to method1
32      public static void method2() throws Exception
33      {
34         try
35         {
36            method3();
37         }
38         catch (Exception exception) // exception thrown from method3
39         {
40            throw new Exception("Exception thrown in method2", exception);
41         }
42      }
43
```

Fig. 11.7 | Chained exceptions. (Part 1 of 2.)

```
44        // throw Exception back to method2
45        public static void method3() throws Exception
46        {
47            throw new Exception("Exception thrown in method3");
48        }
49    } // end class UsingChainedExceptions
```

```
java.lang.Exception: Exception thrown in method1
        at UsingChainedExceptions.method1(UsingChainedExceptions.java:27)
        at UsingChainedExceptions.main(UsingChainedExceptions.java:10)
Caused by: java.lang.Exception: Exception thrown in method2
        at UsingChainedExceptions.method2(UsingChainedExceptions.java:40)
        at UsingChainedExceptions.method1(UsingChainedExceptions.java:23)
        ... 1 more
Caused by: java.lang.Exception: Exception thrown in method3
        at UsingChainedExceptions.method3(UsingChainedExceptions.java:47)
        at UsingChainedExceptions.method2(UsingChainedExceptions.java:36)
        ... 2 more
```

Fig. 11.7 | Chained exceptions. (Part 2 of 2.)

Program Flow of Control

The program consists of four methods—main (lines 6–16), method1 (lines 19–29), method2 (lines 32–42) and method3 (lines 45–48). Line 10 in method main's try block calls method1. Line 23 in method1's try block calls method2. Line 36 in method2's try block calls method3. In method3, line 47 throws a new Exception. Because this statement is not in a try block, method3 terminates, and the exception is returned to the calling method (method2) at line 36. This statement *is* in a try block; therefore, the try block terminates and the exception is caught at lines 38–41. Line 40 in the catch block throws a new exception. In this case, the Exception constructor with *two* arguments is called. The second argument represents the exception that was the original cause of the problem. In this program, that exception occurred at line 47. Because an exception is thrown from the catch block, method2 terminates and returns the new exception to the calling method (method1) at line 23. Once again, this statement is in a try block, so the try block terminates and the exception is caught at lines 25–28. Line 27 in the catch block throws a new exception and uses the exception that was caught as the second argument to the Exception constructor. Because an exception is thrown from the catch block, method1 terminates and returns the new exception to the calling method (main) at line 10. The try block in main terminates, and the exception is caught at lines 12–15. Line 14 prints a stack trace.

Program Output

Notice in the program output that the first three lines show the most recent exception that was thrown (i.e., the one from method1 at line 27). The next four lines indicate the exception that was thrown from method2 at line 40. Finally, the last four lines represent the exception that was thrown from method3 at line 47. Also notice that, as you read the output in reverse, it shows how many more chained exceptions remain.

11.9 Declaring New Exception Types

Most Java programmers use *existing* classes from the Java API, third-party vendors and freely available class libraries (usually downloadable from the Internet) to build Java applications. The methods of those classes typically are declared to throw appropriate exceptions when problems occur. You write code that processes these existing exceptions to make your programs more robust.

If you build classes that other programmers will use, it's often appropriate to declare your own exception classes that are specific to the problems that can occur when another programmer uses your reusable classes.

A New Exception Type Must Extend an Existing One

A new exception class must extend an existing exception class to ensure that the class can be used with the exception-handling mechanism. An exception class is like any other class; however, a typical new exception class contains only four constructors:

- one that takes no arguments and passes a default error message String to the superclass constructor

- one that receives a customized error message as a String and passes it to the superclass constructor

- one that receives a customized error message as a String and a Throwable (for chaining exceptions) and passes both to the superclass constructor

- one that receives a Throwable (for chaining exceptions) and passes it to the superclass constructor.

Good Programming Practice 11.2

Associating each type of serious execution-time malfunction with an appropriately named Exception class improves program clarity.

Software Engineering Observation 11.12

When defining your own exception type, study the existing exception classes in the Java API and try to extend a related exception class. For example, if you're creating a new class to represent when a method attempts a division by zero, you might extend class ArithmeticException because division by zero occurs during arithmetic. If the existing classes are not appropriate superclasses for your new exception class, decide whether your new class should be a checked or an unchecked exception class. If clients should be required to handle the exception, the new exception class should be a checked exception (i.e., extend Exception but not RuntimeException). The client application should be able to reasonably recover from such an exception. If the client code should be able to ignore the exception (i.e., the exception is an unchecked one), the new exception class should extend RuntimeException.

Example of a Custom Exception Class

In Chapter 21, Custom Generic Data Structures, we provide an example of a *custom* exception class. We declare a reusable class called List that's capable of storing a list of references to objects. Some operations typically performed on a List are not allowed if the List is empty, such as removing an item from the front or back of the list. For this reason, some List methods throw exceptions of exception class EmptyListException.

Good Programming Practice 11.3
By convention, all exception-class names should end with the word `Exception`.

11.10 Preconditions and Postconditions

Programmers spend significant amounts of time maintaining and debugging code. To facilitate these tasks and to improve the overall design, you can specify the expected states before and after a method's execution. These states are called preconditions and postconditions, respectively.

Preconditions

A **precondition** must be true when a method is *invoked*. Preconditions describe constraints on method parameters and any other expectations the method has about the current state of a program *just before it begins executing*. If the preconditions are *not* met, then the method's behavior is *undefined*—it may *throw an exception, proceed with an illegal value* or *attempt to recover* from the error. You should not expect consistent behavior if the preconditions are not satisfied.

Postconditions

A **postcondition** is true *after the method successfully returns*. Postconditions describe *constraints on the return value* and any other *side effects* the method may have. When defining a method, you should document all postconditions so that others know what to expect when they call your method, and you should make certain that your method honors all its postconditions if its preconditions are indeed met.

Throwing Exceptions When Preconditions or Postconditions Are Not Met

When their preconditions or postconditions are not met, methods typically throw exceptions. As an example, examine `String` method `charAt`, which has one `int` parameter—an index in the `String`. For a precondition, method `charAt` assumes that `index` is greater than or equal to zero and less than the length of the `String`. If the precondition is met, the postcondition states that the method will return the character at the position in the `String` specified by the parameter `index`. Otherwise, the method throws an `IndexOutOfBounds-Exception`. We trust that method `charAt` satisfies its postcondition, provided that we meet the precondition. We need not be concerned with the details of how the method actually retrieves the character at the index.

Typically, a method's preconditions and postconditions are described as part of its specification. When designing your own methods, you should state the preconditions and postconditions in a comment before the method declaration.

11.11 Assertions

When implementing and debugging a class, it's sometimes useful to state conditions that should be true at a particular point in a method. These conditions, called **assertions**, help ensure a program's validity by catching potential bugs and identifying possible logic errors during development. Preconditions and postconditions are two types of assertions. Preconditions are assertions about a program's state when a method is invoked, and postconditions are assertions about its state after a method finishes.

While assertions can be stated as comments to guide you during program development, Java includes two versions of the **assert** statement for validating assertions programatically. The assert statement evaluates a boolean expression and, if false, throws an **AssertionError** (a subclass of Error). The first form of the assert statement is

> **assert** *expression*;

which throws an AssertionError if *expression* is false. The second form is

> **assert** *expression1* : *expression2*;

which evaluates *expression1* and throws an AssertionError with *expression2* as the error message if *expression1* is false.

You can use assertions to implement *preconditions* and *postconditions* programmatically or to verify any other *intermediate* states that help you ensure that your code is working correctly. Figure 11.8 demonstrates the assert statement. Line 11 prompts the user to enter a number between 0 and 10, then line 12 reads the number. Line 15 determines whether the user entered a number within the valid range. If the number is out of range, the assert statement reports an error; otherwise, the program proceeds normally.

```java
1   // Fig. 11.8: AssertTest.java
2   // Checking with assert that a value is within range
3   import java.util.Scanner;
4
5   public class AssertTest
6   {
7      public static void main(String[] args)
8      {
9         Scanner input = new Scanner(System.in);
10
11         System.out.print("Enter a number between 0 and 10: ");
12         int number = input.nextInt();
13
14         // assert that the value is >= 0 and <= 10
15         assert (number >= 0 && number <= 10) : "bad number: " + number;
16
17         System.out.printf("You entered %d%n", number);
18      }
19   } // end class AssertTest
```

```
Enter a number between 0 and 10: 5
You entered 5
```

```
Enter a number between 0 and 10: 50
Exception in thread "main" java.lang.AssertionError: bad number: 50
        at AssertTest.main(AssertTest.java:15)
```

Fig. 11.8 | Checking with assert that a value is within range.

You use assertions primarily for debugging and identifying logic errors in an application. You must explicitly enable assertions when executing a program, because they reduce performance and are unnecessary for the program's user. To do so, use the java command's -ea command-line option, as in

```
java -ea AssertTest
```

Software Engineering Observation 11.13
Users shouldn't encounter AssertionErrors—these should be used only during program development. For this reason, you shouldn't catch AssertionErrors. Instead, allow the program to terminate, so you can see the error message, then locate and fix the source of the problem. You should not use assert to indicate runtime problems in production code (as we did in Fig. 11.8 for demonstration purposes)—use the exception mechanism for this purpose.

11.12 try-with-Resources: Automatic Resource Deallocation

Typically *resource-release code* should be placed in a finally block to ensure that a resource is released, regardless of whether there were exceptions when the resource was used in the corresponding try block. An alternative notation—the **try-with-resources** statement (introduced in Java SE 7)—simplifies writing code in which you obtain one or more resources, use them in a try block and release them in a corresponding finally block. For example, a file-processing application could process a file with a try-with-resources statement to ensure that the file is closed properly when it's no longer needed—we demonstrate this in Chapter 15. Each resource must be an object of a class that implements the **Auto-Closeable** interface, and thus provides a close method. The general form of a try-with-resources statement is

```
try (ClassName theObject = new ClassName())
{
    // use theObject here
}
catch (Exception e)
{
    // catch exceptions that occur while using the resource
}
```

where *ClassName* is a class that implements the AutoCloseable interface. This code creates an object of type *ClassName* and uses it in the try block, then calls its close method to release any resources used by the object. The try-with-resources statement *implicitly* calls the theObject's close method *at the end of the try block*. You can allocate multiple resources in the parentheses following try by separating them with a semicolon (;). You'll see examples of the try-with-resources statement in Chapters 15 and 24.

11.13 Wrap-Up

In this chapter, you learned how to use exception handling to deal with errors. You learned that exception handling enables you to remove error-handling code from the "main line" of the program's execution. We showed how to use try blocks to enclose code that may throw an exception, and how to use catch blocks to deal with exceptions that may arise.

You learned about the termination model of exception handling, which dictates that after an exception is handled, program control does not return to the throw point. We discussed checked vs. unchecked exceptions, and how to specify with the throws clause the exceptions that a method might throw.

You learned how to use the finally block to release resources whether or not an exception occurs. You also learned how to throw and rethrow exceptions. We showed how to obtain information about an exception using methods printStackTrace, getStackTrace and getMessage. Next, we presented chained exceptions, which allow you to wrap original exception information with new exception information. Then, we showed how to create your own exception classes.

We introduced preconditions and postconditions to help programmers using your methods understand conditions that must be true when the method is called and when it returns, respectively. When preconditions and postconditions are not met, methods typically throw exceptions. We discussed the assert statement and how it can be used to help you debug your programs. In particular, assert can be used to ensure that preconditions and postconditions are met.

We also introduced multi-catch for processing several types of exceptions in the same catch handler and the try-with-resources statement for automatically deallocating a resource after it's used in the try block. In the next chapter, we take a deeper look at graphical user interfaces (GUIs).

Summary

Section 11.1 Introduction
- An exception is an indication of a problem that occurs during a program's execution.
- Exception handling enables programmers to create applications that can resolve exceptions.

Section 11.2 Example: Divide by Zero without Exception Handling
- Exceptions are thrown (p. 435) when a method detects a problem and is unable to handle it.
- An exception's stack trace (p. 436) includes the name of the exception in a message that indicates the problem that occurred and the complete method-call stack at the time the exception occurred.
- The point in the program at which an exception occurs is called the throw point (p. 437).

Section 11.3 Example: Handling *ArithmeticExceptions* and *InputMismatchExceptions*
- A try block (p. 439) encloses code that might throw an exception and code that should not execute if that exception occurs.
- Exceptions may surface through explicitly mentioned code in a try block, through calls to other methods or even through deeply nested method calls initiated by code in the try block.
- A catch block (p. 440) begins with keyword catch and an exception parameter followed by a block of code that handles the exception. This code executes when the try block detects the exception.
- At least one catch block or a finally block (p. 440) must immediately follow the try block.
- A catch block specifies in parentheses an exception parameter identifying the exception type to handle. The parameter's name enables the catch block to interact with a caught exception object.
- An uncaught exception (p. 441) is an exception that occurs for which there are no matching catch blocks. An uncaught exception will cause a program to terminate early if that program contains only one thread. Otherwise, only the thread in which the exception occurred will terminate. The rest of the program will run but possibly with adverse results.

- Multi-catch (p. 441) enables you to catch multiple exception types in a single catch handler and perform the same task for each type of exception. The syntax for a multi-catch is:

  catch (*Type1* | *Type2* | *Type3* e)

- Each exception type is separated from the next with a vertical bar (|).

- If an exception occurs in a try block, the try block terminates immediately and program control transfers to the first catch block with a parameter type that matches the thrown exception's type.

- After an exception is handled, program control does not return to the throw point, because the try block has expired. This is known as the termination model of exception handling (p. 441).

- If there are multiple matching catch blocks when an exception occurs, only the first is executed.

- A throws clause (p. 442) specifies a comma-separated list of exceptions that the method might throw, and appears after the method's parameter list and before the method body.

Section 11.4 When to Use Exception Handling
- Exception handling processes synchronous errors (p. 443), which occur when a statement executes.

- Exception handling is not designed to process problems associated with asynchronous events (p. 443), which occur in parallel with, and independent of, the program's flow of control.

Section 11.5 Java Exception Hierarchy
- All Java exception classes inherit directly or indirectly from class Exception.

- Programmers can extend the Java exception hierarchy with their own exception classes.

- Class Throwable is the superclass of class Exception and is therefore also the superclass of all exceptions. Only Throwable objects can be used with the exception-handling mechanism.

- Class Throwable (p. 443) has two subclasses: Exception and Error.

- Class Exception and its subclasses represent problems that could occur in a Java program and be caught by the application.

- Class Error and its subclasses represent problems that could happen in the Java runtime system. Errors happen infrequently and typically should not be caught by an application.

- Java distinguishes between two categories of exceptions (p. 444): checked and unchecked.

- The Java compiler does not check to determine if an unchecked exception is caught or declared. Unchecked exceptions typically can be prevented by proper coding.

- Subclasses of RuntimeException represent unchecked exceptions. All exception types that inherit from class Exception but not from RuntimeException (p. 444) are checked.

- If a catch block is written to catch exception objects of a superclass type, it can also catch all objects of that class's subclasses. This allows for polymorphic processing of related exceptions.

Section 11.6 **finally** Block
- Programs that obtain certain types of resources must return them to the system to avoid so-called resource leaks (p. 446). Resource-release code typically is placed in a finally block (p. 446).

- The finally block is optional. If it's present, it's placed after the last catch block.

- The finally block will execute whether or not an exception is thrown in the corresponding try block or any of its corresponding catch blocks.

- If an exception cannot be caught by one of that try block's associated catch handlers, control proceeds to the finally block. Then the exception is passed to the next outer try block.

- If a catch block throws an exception, the finally block still executes. Then the exception is passed to the next outer try block.

- A throw statement (p. 449) can throw any Throwable object.
- Exceptions are rethrown (p. 450) when a catch block, upon receiving an exception, decides either that it cannot process that exception or that it can only partially process it. Rethrowing an exception defers the exception handling (or perhaps a portion of it) to another catch block.
- When a rethrow occurs, the next enclosing try block detects the rethrown exception, and that try block's catch blocks attempt to handle it.

Section 11.7 Stack Unwinding and Obtaining Information from an Exception Object
- When an exception is thrown but not caught in a particular scope, the method-call stack is unwound, and an attempt is made to catch the exception in the next outer try statement.
- Class Throwable offers a printStackTrace method that prints the method-call stack. Often, this is helpful in testing and debugging.
- Class Throwable also provides a getStackTrace method that obtains the same stack-trace information that's printed by printStackTrace (p. 453).
- Class Throwable's getMessage method (p. 453) returns the descriptive string stored in an exception.
- Method getStackTrace (p. 453) obtains the stack-trace information as an array of StackTrace-Element objects. Each StackTraceElement represents one method call on the method-call stack.
- StackTraceElement methods (p. 453) getClassName, getFileName, getLineNumber and get-MethodName get the class name, filename, line number and method name, respectively.

Section 11.8 Chained Exceptions
- Chained exceptions (p. 454) enable an exception object to maintain the complete stack-trace information, including information about previous exceptions that caused the current exception.

Section 11.9 Declaring New Exception Types
- A new exception class must extend an existing exception class to ensure that the class can be used with the exception-handling mechanism.

Section 11.10 Preconditions and Postconditions
- A method's precondition (p. 457) must be true when the method is invoked.
- A method's postcondition (p. 457) is true after the method successfully returns.
- When designing your own methods, you should state the preconditions and postconditions in a comment before the method declaration.

Section 11.11 Assertions
- Assertions (p. 457) help catch potential bugs and identify possible logic errors.
- The assert statement (p. 458) allows for validating assertions programmatically.
- To enable assertions at runtime, use the -ea switch when running the java command.

Section 11.12 **try-with-Resources: Automatic Resource Deallocation**
- The try-with-resources statement (p. 459) simplifies writing code in which you obtain a resource, use it in a try block and release the resource in a corresponding finally block. Instead, you allocate the resource in the parentheses following the try keyword and use the resource in the try block; then the statement implicitly calls the resource's close method at the end of the try block.
- Each resource must be an object of a class that implements the AutoCloseable interface (p. 459)—such a class has a close method.

- You can allocate multiple resources in the parentheses following `try` by separating them with a semicolon (`;`).

Self-Review Exercises

11.1   List five common examples of exceptions.

11.2   Why are exceptions particularly appropriate for dealing with errors produced by methods of classes in the Java API?

11.3   What is a "resource leak"?

11.4   If no exceptions are thrown in a `try` block, where does control proceed to when the `try` block completes execution?

11.5   Give a key advantage of using `catch(Exception `*exceptionName*`)`.

11.6   Should a conventional application catch `Error` objects? Explain.

11.7   What happens if no `catch` handler matches the type of a thrown object?

11.8   What happens if several `catch` blocks match the type of the thrown object?

11.9   Why would a programmer specify a superclass type as the type in a `catch` block?

11.10   What is the key reason for using `finally` blocks?

11.11   What happens when a `catch` block throws an `Exception`?

11.12   What does the statement `throw `*exceptionReference* do in a `catch` block?

11.13   What happens to a local reference in a `try` block when that block throws an `Exception`?

Answers to Self-Review Exercises

11.1   Memory exhaustion, array index out of bounds, arithmetic overflow, division by zero, invalid method parameters.

11.2   It's unlikely that methods of classes in the Java API could perform error processing that would meet the unique needs of all users.

11.3   A "resource leak" occurs when an executing program does not properly release a resource when it's no longer needed.

11.4   The `catch` blocks for that `try` statement are skipped, and the program resumes execution after the last `catch` block. If there's a `finally` block, it's executed first; then the program resumes execution after the `finally` block.

11.5   The form `catch(Exception `*exceptionName*`)` catches any type of exception thrown in a `try` block. An advantage is that no thrown `Exception` can slip by without being caught. You can handle the exception or rethrow it.

11.6   `Error`s are usually serious problems with the underlying Java system; most programs will not want to catch `Error`s because they will not be able to recover from them.

11.7   This causes the search for a match to continue in the next enclosing `try` statement. If there's a `finally` block, it will be executed before the exception goes to the next enclosing `try` statement. If there are no enclosing `try` statements for which there are matching `catch` blocks and the exceptions are declared (or unchecked), a stack trace is printed and the current thread terminates early. If the exceptions are checked, but not caught or declared, compilation errors occur.

11.8   The first matching `catch` block after the `try` block is executed.

11.9   This enables a program to catch related types of exceptions and process them in a uniform manner. However, it's often useful to process the subclass types individually for more precise exception handling.

11.10   The `finally` block is the preferred means for releasing resources to prevent resource leaks.

11.11   First, control passes to the `finally` block if there is one. Then the exception will be processed by a `catch` block (if one exists) associated with an enclosing `try` block (if one exists).

11.12   It rethrows the exception for processing by an exception handler of an enclosing `try` statement, after the `finally` block of the current `try` statement executes.

11.13   The reference goes out of scope. If the referenced object becomes unreachable, the object can be garbage collected.

Exercises

11.14   *(Exceptional Conditions)* List the various exceptional conditions that have occurred in programs throughout this text so far. List as many additional exceptional conditions as you can. For each of these, describe briefly how a program typically would handle the exception by using the exception-handling techniques discussed in this chapter. Typical exceptions include division by zero and array index out of bounds.

11.15   *(Exceptions and Constructor Failure)* Until this chapter, we've found dealing with errors detected by constructors to be a bit awkward. Explain why exception handling is an effective means for dealing with constructor failure.

11.16   *(Catching Exceptions with Superclasses)* Use inheritance to create an exception superclass (called `ExceptionA`) and exception subclasses `ExceptionB` and `ExceptionC`, where `ExceptionB` inherits from `ExceptionA` and `ExceptionC` inherits from `ExceptionB`. Write a program to demonstrate that the `catch` block for type `ExceptionA` catches exceptions of types `ExceptionB` and `ExceptionC`.

11.17   *(Catching Exceptions Using Class `Exception`)* Write a program that demonstrates how various exceptions are caught with

        `catch` (Exception exception)

This time, define classes `ExceptionA` (which inherits from class `Exception`) and `ExceptionB` (which inherits from class `ExceptionA`). In your program, create `try` blocks that throw exceptions of types `ExceptionA`, `ExceptionB`, `NullPointerException` and `IOException`. All exceptions should be caught with `catch` blocks specifying type `Exception`.

11.18   *(Order of `catch` Blocks)* Write a program demonstrating that the order of `catch` blocks is important. If you try to catch a superclass exception type before a subclass type, the compiler should generate errors.

11.19   *(Constructor Failure)* Write a program that shows a constructor passing information about constructor failure to an exception handler. Define class `SomeClass`, which throws an `Exception` in the constructor. Your program should try to create an object of type `SomeClass` and catch the exception that's thrown from the constructor.

11.20   *(Rethrowing Exceptions)* Write a program that illustrates rethrowing an exception. Define methods `someMethod` and `someMethod2`. Method `someMethod2` should initially throw an exception. Method `someMethod` should call `someMethod2`, catch the exception and rethrow it. Call `someMethod` from method `main`, and catch the rethrown exception. Print the stack trace of this exception.

11.21   *(Catching Exceptions Using Outer Scopes)* Write a program showing that a method with its own `try` block does not have to catch every possible error generated within the `try`. Some exceptions can slip through to, and be handled in, other scopes.

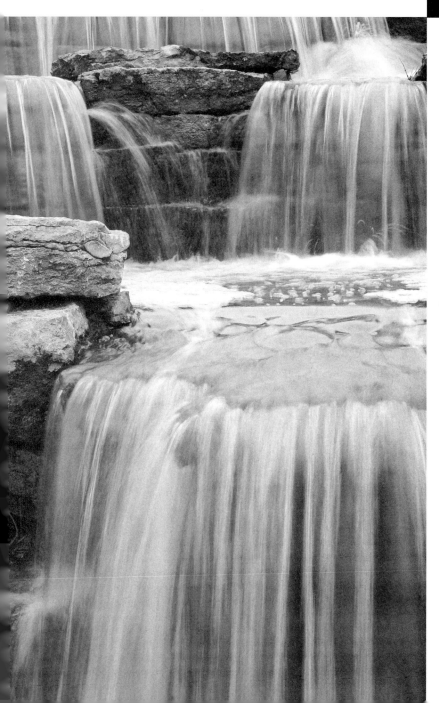

GUI Components: Part 1

*Do you think I can listen all day
to such stuff?*
—Lewis Carroll

*Even a minor event in the life of
a child is an event of that child's
world and thus a world event.*
—Gaston Bachelard

*You pays your money and you
takes your choice.*
—Punch

Objectives

In this chapter you'll:

- Learn how to use the Nimbus look-and-feel.

- Build GUIs and handle events generated by user interactions with GUIs.

- Understand the packages containing GUI components, event-handling classes and interfaces.

- Create and manipulate buttons, labels, lists, text fields and panels.

- Handle mouse events and keyboard events.

- Use layout managers to arrange GUI components.

12.1 Introduction

A **graphical user interface (GUI)** presents a user-friendly mechanism for interacting with an application. A GUI (pronounced "GOO-ee") gives an application a distinctive "look-and-feel." GUIs are built from **GUI components**. These are sometimes called *controls* or *widgets*—short for window gadgets. A GUI component is an object with which the user *interacts* via the mouse, the keyboard or another form of input, such as voice recognition. In this chapter and Chapter 22, GUI Components: Part 2, you'll learn about many of Java's so-called **Swing GUI components** from the **javax.swing** package. We cover other GUI components as they're needed throughout the book. In Chapter 25 and two online chapters, you'll learn about JavaFX—Java's latest APIs for GUI, graphics and multimedia.

Look-and-Feel Observation 12.1

Providing different applications with consistent, intuitive user-interface components gives users a sense of familiarity with a new application, so that they can learn it more quickly and use it more productively.

IDE Support for GUI Design
Many IDEs provide GUI design tools with which you can specify a component's *size*, *location* and other attributes in a visual manner by using the mouse, the keyboard and drag-and-drop. The IDEs generate the GUI code for you. This greatly simplifies creating GUIs, but each IDE generates this code differently. For this reason, we wrote the GUI code by hand, as you'll see in the source-code files for this chapter's examples. We encourage you to build each GUI visually using your preferred IDE(s).

Sample GUI: The SwingSet3 Demo Application

As an example of a GUI, consider Fig. 12.1, which shows the **SwingSet3** demo application from the JDK demos and samples download at `http://www.oracle.com/technetwork/java/javase/downloads/index.html`. This application is a nice way for you to browse through the various GUI components provided by Java's Swing GUI APIs. Simply click a component name (e.g., `JFrame`, `JTabbedPane`, etc.) in the **GUI Components** area at the left of the window to see a demonstration of the GUI component in the right side of the window. The source code for each demo is shown in the text area at the bottom of the window. We've labeled a few of the GUI components in the application. At the top of the window is a **title bar** that contains the window's title. Below that is a **menu bar** containing **menus** (**File** and **View**). In the top-right region of the window is a set of **buttons**—typically, users click buttons to perform tasks. In the **GUI Components** area of the window is a **combo box**; the user can click the down arrow at the right side of the box to select from a list of items. The menus, buttons and combo box are part of the application's GUI. They enable you to interact with the application.

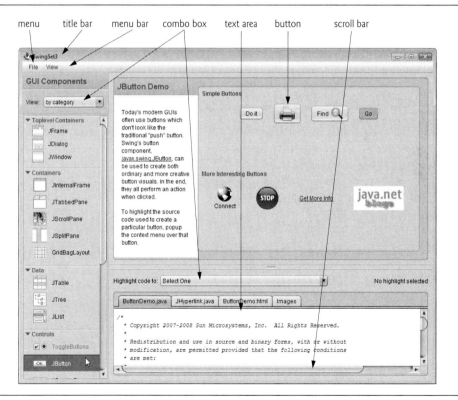

Fig. 12.1 | **SwingSet3** application demonstrates many of Java's Swing GUI components.

12.2 Java's Nimbus Look-and-Feel

A GUI's look consists of its visual aspects, such as its colors and fonts, and its feel consists of the components you use to interact with the GUI, such as buttons and menus. Together these are known as the GUI's look-and-feel. Swing has a cross-platform look-and-feel known as **Nimbus**. For GUI screen captures like Fig. 12.1, we've configured our systems to use Nimbus as the default look-and-feel. There are three ways that you can use Nimbus:

1. Set it as the default for all Java applications that run on your computer.

2. Set it as the look-and-feel at the time that you launch an application by passing a command-line argument to the java command.

3. Set it as the look-and-feel programatically in your application (see Section 22.6).

To set Nimbus as the default for all Java applications, you must create a text file named `swing.properties` in the `lib` folder of both your JDK installation folder and your JRE installation folder. Place the following line of code in the file:

```
swing.defaultlaf=com.sun.java.swing.plaf.nimbus.NimbusLookAndFeel
```

In addition to the standalone JRE, there is a JRE nested in your JDK's installation folder. If you're using an IDE that depends on the JDK, you may also need to place the `swing.properties` file in the nested `jre` folder's `lib` folder.

If you prefer to select Nimbus on an application-by-application basis, place the following command-line argument after the java command and before the application's name when you run the application:

```
-Dswing.defaultlaf=com.sun.java.swing.plaf.nimbus.NimbusLookAndFeel
```

12.3 Simple GUI-Based Input/Output with JOptionPane

The applications in Chapters 2–10 display text in the command window and obtain input from the command window. Most applications you use on a daily basis use windows or **dialog boxes** (also called **dialogs**) to interact with the user. For example, an e-mail program allows you to type and read messages in a window the program provides. Dialog boxes are windows in which programs display important messages to the user or obtain information from the user. Java's **JOptionPane** class (package `javax.swing`) provides prebuilt dialog boxes for both input and output. These are displayed by invoking static JOptionPane methods. Figure 12.2 presents a simple addition application that uses two **input dialogs** to obtain integers from the user and a **message dialog** to display the sum of the integers the user enters.

```
 1   // Fig. 12.2: Addition.java
 2   // Addition program that uses JOptionPane for input and output.
 3   import javax.swing.JOptionPane;
 4
 5   public class Addition
 6   {
 7      public static void main(String[] args)
 8      {
 9         // obtain user input from JOptionPane input dialogs
10         String firstNumber =
11            JOptionPane.showInputDialog("Enter first integer");
```

Fig. 12.2 | Addition program that uses JOptionPane for input and output. (Part 1 of 2.)

```
12          String secondNumber =
13             JOptionPane.showInputDialog("Enter second integer");
14
15          // convert String inputs to int values for use in a calculation
16          int number1 = Integer.parseInt(firstNumber);
17          int number2 = Integer.parseInt(secondNumber);
18
19          int sum = number1 + number2;
20
21          // display result in a JOptionPane message dialog
22          JOptionPane.showMessageDialog(null, "The sum is " + sum,
23             "Sum of Two Integers", JOptionPane.PLAIN_MESSAGE);
24       }
25    } // end class Addition
```

(a) Input dialog displayed by lines 10–11

Prompt to the user

When the user clicks **OK**,
showInputDialog returns
to the program the **100** typed
by the user as a **String**; the
program must convert the
String to an int

Text field in which the
user types a value

(b) Input dialog displayed by lines 12–13

(c) Message dialog displayed by lines 22–23—When the user clicks **OK**, the message dialog is dismissed (removed from the screen)

Fig. 12.2 | Addition program that uses JOptionPane for input and output. (Part 2 of 2.)

Input Dialogs

Line 3 imports class JOptionPane. Lines 10–11 declare the local String variable first-
Number and assign it the result of the call to JOptionPane static method **showInputDialog**. This method displays an input dialog (see the screen capture in Fig. 12.2(a)), using
the method's String argument ("Enter first integer") as a prompt.

Look-and-Feel Observation 12.2

*The prompt in an input dialog typically uses **sentence-style capitalization**—a style that
capitalizes only the first letter of the first word in the text unless the word is a proper noun
(for example, Jones).*

The user types characters in the text field, then clicks **OK** or presses the *Enter* key to
submit the String to the program. Clicking **OK** also **dismisses (hides) the dialog**. [*Note:*
If you type in the text field and nothing appears, activate the text field by clicking it with
the mouse.] Unlike Scanner, which can be used to input values of *several* types from the
user at the keyboard, *an input dialog can input only Strings*. This is typical of most GUI

components. The user can type *any* characters in the input dialog's text field. Our program assumes that the user enters a *valid* integer. If the user clicks **Cancel**, showInputDialog returns null. If the user either types a noninteger value or clicks the **Cancel** button in the input dialog, an exception will occur and the program will not operate correctly. Lines 12–13 display another input dialog that prompts the user to enter the second integer. Each JOptionPane dialog that you display is a so called **modal dialog**—while the dialog is on the screen, the user *cannot* interact with the rest of the application.

Look-and-Feel Observation 12.3

Do not overuse modal dialogs, as they can reduce the usability of your applications. Use a modal dialog only when it's necessary to prevent users from interacting with the rest of an application until they dismiss the dialog.

Converting *Strings* to *int* Values

To perform the calculation, we convert the Strings that the user entered to int values. Recall that the Integer class's static method parseInt converts its String argument to an int value and might throw a NumberFormatException. Lines 16–17 assign the converted values to local variables number1 and number2, and line 19 sums these values.

Message Dialogs

Lines 22–23 use JOptionPane static method **showMessageDialog** to display a message dialog (the last screen of Fig. 12.2) containing the sum. The first argument helps the Java application determine where to *position* the dialog box. A dialog is typically displayed from a GUI application with its own window. The first argument refers to that window (known as the *parent window*) and causes the dialog to appear centered over the parent (as we'll do in Section 12.9). If the first argument is null, the dialog box is displayed at the *center* of your screen. The second argument is the *message* to display—in this case, the result of concatenating the String "The sum is " and the value of sum. The third argument—"Sum of Two Integers"—is the String that should appear in the *title bar* at the top of the dialog. The fourth argument—**JOptionPane.PLAIN_MESSAGE**—is the *type of message dialog to display*. A PLAIN_MESSAGE dialog does *not* display an *icon* to the left of the message. Class JOptionPane provides several overloaded versions of methods showInputDialog and showMessageDialog, as well as methods that display other dialog types. For complete information, visit http://docs.oracle.com/javase/7/docs/api/javax/swing/JOptionPane.html.

Look-and-Feel Observation 12.4

*The title bar of a window typically uses **book-title capitalization**—a style that capitalizes the first letter of each significant word in the text and does not end with any punctuation (for example, Capitalization in a Book Title).*

JOptionPane Message Dialog Constants

The constants that represent the message dialog types are shown in Fig. 12.3. All message dialog types except PLAIN_MESSAGE display an icon to the *left* of the message. These icons provide a visual indication of the message's importance to the user. A QUESTION_MESSAGE icon is the *default icon* for an input dialog box (see Fig. 12.2).

Message dialog type	Icon	Description
ERROR_MESSAGE		Indicates an error.
INFORMATION_MESSAGE		Indicates an informational message.
WARNING_MESSAGE		Warns of a potential problem.
QUESTION_MESSAGE		Poses a question. This dialog normally requires a response, such as clicking a **Yes** or a **No** button.
PLAIN_MESSAGE	no icon	A dialog that contains a message, but no icon.

Fig. 12.3 | JOptionPane static constants for message dialogs.

12.4 Overview of Swing Components

Though it's possible to perform input and output using the JOptionPane dialogs, most GUI applications require more elaborate user interfaces. The remainder of this chapter discusses many GUI components that enable application developers to create robust GUIs. Figure 12.4 lists several basic Swing GUI components that we discuss.

Component	Description
JLabel	Displays *uneditable text* and/or icons.
JTextField	Typically *receives input* from the user.
JButton	Triggers an event when clicked with the mouse.
JCheckBox	Specifies an option that can be *selected* or *not selected*.
JComboBox	A *drop-down list of items* from which the *user* can make a *selection*.
JList	A *list of items* from which the user can make a *selection* by *clicking* on *any one* of them. *Multiple* elements *can* be selected.
JPanel	An area in which *components* can be *placed* and *organized*.

Fig. 12.4 | Some basic Swing GUI components.

Swing vs. AWT

There are actually *two* sets of Java GUI components. In Java's early days, GUIs were built with components from the **Abstract Window Toolkit (AWT)** in package **java.awt**. These look like the native GUI components of the platform on which a Java program executes. For example, a Button object displayed in a Java program running on Microsoft Windows looks like those in other *Windows* applications. On Apple Mac OS X, the Button looks like those in other *Mac* applications. Sometimes, even the manner in which a user can interact with an AWT component *differs between platforms*. The component's appearance and the way in which the user interacts with it are known as its **look-and-feel**.

Look-and-Feel Observation 12.5

Swing GUI components allow you to specify a uniform look-and-feel for your application across all platforms or to use each platform's custom look-and-feel. An application can even change the look-and-feel during execution to enable users to choose their own preferred look-and-feel.

Lightweight vs. Heavyweight GUI Components

Most Swing components are **lightweight components**—they're written, manipulated and displayed completely in Java. AWT components are **heavyweight components**, because they rely on the local platform's **windowing system** to determine their functionality and their look-and-feel. Several Swing components are *heavyweight* components.

Superclasses of Swing's Lightweight GUI Components

The UML class diagram of Fig. 12.5 shows an *inheritance hierarchy* of classes from which lightweight Swing components inherit their common attributes and behaviors.

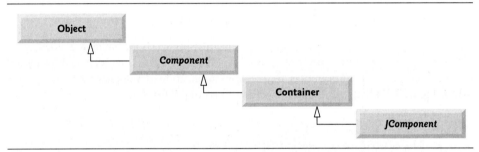

Fig. 12.5 | Common superclasses of the lightweight Swing components.

Class **Component** (package java.awt) is a superclass that declares the common features of GUI components in packages java.awt and javax.swing. Any object that *is a* **Container** (package java.awt) can be used to organize Components by *attaching* the Components to the Container. Containers can be placed in other Containers to organize a GUI.

Class **JComponent** (package javax.swing) is a subclass of Container. JComponent is the superclass of all *lightweight* Swing components and declares their common attributes and behaviors. Because JComponent is a subclass of Container, all lightweight Swing components are also Containers. Some common features supported by JComponent include:

1. A **pluggable look-and-feel** for *customizing* the appearance of components (e.g., for use on particular platforms). You'll see an example of this in Section 22.6.

2. Shortcut keys (called **mnemonics**) for direct access to GUI components through the keyboard. You'll see an example of this in Section 22.4.

3. Brief descriptions of a GUI component's purpose (called **tool tips**) that are displayed when the *mouse cursor is positioned over the component* for a short time. You'll see an example of this in the next section.

4. Support for *accessibility*, such as braille screen readers for the visually impaired.

5. Support for user-interface **localization**—that is, customizing the user interface to display in different languages and use local cultural conventions.

12.5 Displaying Text and Images in a Window

Our next example introduces a framework for building GUI applications. Several concepts in this framework will appear in many of our GUI applications. This is our first example in which the application appears in its own window. Most windows you'll create that can contain Swing GUI components are instances of class JFrame or a subclass of JFrame. JFrame is an *indirect* subclass of class java.awt.Window that provides the basic attributes and behaviors of a window—a *title bar* at the top, and *buttons* to *minimize, maximize* and *close* the window. Since an application's GUI is typically specific to the application, most of our examples will consist of *two* classes—a subclass of JFrame that helps us demonstrate new GUI concepts and an application class in which main creates and displays the application's primary window.

Labeling GUI Components

A typical GUI consists of many components. GUI designers often provide text stating the purpose of each. Such text is known as a **label** and is created with a **JLabel**—a subclass of JComponent. A JLabel displays read-only text, an image, or both text and an image. Applications rarely change a label's contents after creating it.

Look-and-Feel Observation 12.6

Text in a JLabel *normally uses sentence-style capitalization.*

The application of Figs. 12.6–12.7 demonstrates several JLabel features and presents the framework we use in most of our GUI examples. We did *not* highlight the code in this example, since most of it is new. [*Note:* There are many more features for each GUI component than we can cover in our examples. To learn the complete details of each GUI component, visit its page in the online documentation. For class JLabel, visit docs.oracle.com/javase/7/docs/api/javax/swing/JLabel.html.]

```
1   // Fig. 12.6: LabelFrame.java
2   // JLabels with text and icons.
3   import java.awt.FlowLayout; // specifies how components are arranged
4   import javax.swing.JFrame; // provides basic window features
5   import javax.swing.JLabel; // displays text and images
6   import javax.swing.SwingConstants; // common constants used with Swing
7   import javax.swing.Icon; // interface used to manipulate images
8   import javax.swing.ImageIcon; // loads images
9
10  public class LabelFrame extends JFrame
11  {
12     private final JLabel label1; // JLabel with just text
13     private final JLabel label2; // JLabel constructed with text and icon
14     private final JLabel label3; // JLabel with added text and icon
15
16     // LabelFrame constructor adds JLabels to JFrame
17     public LabelFrame()
18     {
```

Fig. 12.6 | JLabels with text and icons. (Part 1 of 2.)

```
19          super("Testing JLabel");
20          setLayout(new FlowLayout()); // set frame layout
21
22          // JLabel constructor with a string argument
23          label1 = new JLabel("Label with text");
24          label1.setToolTipText("This is label1");
25          add(label1); // add label1 to JFrame
26
27          // JLabel constructor with string, Icon and alignment arguments
28          Icon bug = new ImageIcon(getClass().getResource( "bug1.png"));
29          label2 = new JLabel("Label with text and icon", bug,
30             SwingConstants.LEFT);
31          label2.setToolTipText("This is label2");
32          add(label2); // add label2 to JFrame
33
34          label3 = new JLabel(); // JLabel constructor no arguments
35          label3.setText("Label with icon and text at bottom");
36          label3.setIcon(bug); // add icon to JLabel
37          label3.setHorizontalTextPosition(SwingConstants.CENTER);
38          label3.setVerticalTextPosition(SwingConstants.BOTTOM);
39          label3.setToolTipText("This is label3");
40          add(label3); // add label3 to JFrame
41       }
42    } // end class LabelFrame
```

Fig. 12.6 | JLabels with text and icons. (Part 2 of 2.)

```
1    // Fig. 12.7: LabelTest.java
2    // Testing LabelFrame.
3    import javax.swing.JFrame;
4
5    public class LabelTest
6    {
7       public static void main(String[] args)
8       {
9          LabelFrame labelFrame = new LabelFrame();
10         labelFrame.setDefaultCloseOperation(JFrame.EXIT_ON_CLOSE);
11         labelFrame.setSize(260, 180);
12         labelFrame.setVisible(true);
13      }
14   } // end class LabelTest
```

Fig. 12.7 | Testing LabelFrame.

Class `LabelFrame` (Fig. 12.6) extends `JFrame` to inherit the features of a window. We'll use an instance of class `LabelFrame` to display a window containing three `JLabel`s. Lines 12–14 declare the three `JLabel` instance variables that are instantiated in the `Label-Frame` constructor (lines 17–41). Typically, the `JFrame` subclass's constructor builds the GUI that's displayed in the window when the application executes. Line 19 invokes superclass `JFrame`'s constructor with the argument `"Testing JLabel"`. `JFrame`'s constructor uses this `String` as the text in the window's title bar.

Specifying the Layout

When building a GUI, you must attach each GUI component to a container, such as a window created with a `JFrame`. Also, you typically must decide where to *position* each GUI component—known as *specifying the layout*. Java provides several **layout managers** that can help you position components, as you'll learn later in this chapter and in Chapter 22.

Many IDEs provide GUI design tools in which you can specify components' exact *sizes* and *locations* in a visual manner by using the mouse; then the IDE will generate the GUI code for you. Such IDEs can greatly simplify GUI creation.

To ensure that our GUIs can be used with *any* IDE, we did *not* use an IDE to create the GUI code. We use Java's layout managers to *size* and *position* components. With the **FlowLayout** layout manager, components are placed in a *container* from left to right in the order in which they're added. When no more components can fit on the current line, they continue to display left to right on the next line. If the container is *resized*, a `FlowLayout` *reflows* the components, possibly with fewer or more rows based on the new container width. Every container has a *default layout*, which we're changing for `LabelFrame` to a `FlowLayout` (line 20). Method **setLayout** is inherited into class `LabelFrame` indirectly from class `Container`. The argument to the method must be an object of a class that implements the `LayoutManager` interface (e.g., `FlowLayout`). Line 20 creates a new `FlowLayout` object and passes its reference as the argument to `setLayout`.

Creating and Attaching *label1*

Now that we've specified the window's layout, we can begin creating and attaching GUI components to the window. Line 23 creates a `JLabel` object and passes `"Label with text"` to the constructor. The `JLabel` displays this text on the screen. Line 24 uses method **set-ToolTipText** (inherited by `JLabel` from `JComponent`) to specify the tool tip that's displayed when the user positions the mouse cursor over the `JLabel` in the GUI. You can see a sample tool tip in the second screen capture of Fig. 12.7. When you execute this application, hover the mouse pointer over each `JLabel` to see its tool tip. Line 25 (Fig. 12.6) attaches `label1` to the `LabelFrame` by passing `label1` to the **add** method, which is inherited indirectly from class `Container`.

Common Programming Error 12.1

If you do not explicitly add a GUI component to a container, the GUI component will not be displayed when the container appears on the screen.

Look-and-Feel Observation 12.7

Use tool tips to add descriptive text to your GUI components. This text helps the user determine the GUI component's purpose in the user interface.

The Icon Interface and Class ImageIcon

Icons are a popular way to enhance the look-and-feel of an application and are also commonly used to indicate functionality. For example, the same icon is used to play most of today's media on devices like DVD players and MP3 players. Several Swing components can display images. An icon is normally specified with an **Icon** (package javax.swing) argument to a constructor or to the component's **setIcon** method. Class **ImageIcon** supports several image formats, including Graphics Interchange Format (GIF), Portable Network Graphics (PNG) and Joint Photographic Experts Group (JPEG).

Line 28 declares an ImageIcon. The file bug1.png contains the image to load and store in the ImageIcon object. This image is included in the directory for this example. The ImageIcon object is assigned to Icon reference bug.

Loading an Image Resource

In line 28, the expression getClass().getResource("bug1.png") invokes method **get-Class** (inherited indirectly from class Object) to retrieve a reference to the Class object that represents the LabelFrame class declaration. That reference is then used to invoke Class method **getResource**, which returns the location of the image as a URL. The ImageIcon constructor uses the URL to locate the image, then loads it into memory. As we discussed in Chapter 1, the JVM loads class declarations into memory, using a class loader. The class loader knows where each class it loads is located on disk. Method getResource uses the Class object's class loader to determine the *location* of a resource, such as an image file. In this example, the image file is stored in the same location as the LabelFrame.class file. The techniques described here enable an application to load image files from locations that are relative to the class file's location.

Creating and Attaching label2

Lines 29–30 use another JLabel constructor to create a JLabel that displays the text "Label with text and icon" and the Icon bug created in line 28. The last constructor argument indicates that the label's contents are left justified, or left aligned (i.e., the icon and text are at the left side of the label's area on the screen). Interface **SwingConstants** (package javax.swing) declares a set of common integer constants (such as SwingConstants.LEFT, SwingConstants.CENTER and SwingConstants.RIGHT) that are used with many Swing components. By default, the text appears to the right of the image when a label contains both text and an image. The horizontal and vertical alignments of a JLabel can be set with methods **setHorizontalAlignment** and **setVerticalAlignment**, respectively. Line 31 specifies the tool-tip text for label2, and line 32 adds label2 to the JFrame.

Creating and Attaching label3

Class JLabel provides methods to change a JLabel's appearance after it's been instantiated. Line 34 creates an empty JLabel with the no-argument constructor. Line 35 uses JLabel method **setText** to set the text displayed on the label. Method **getText** can be used to retrieve the JLabel's current text. Line 36 uses JLabel method setIcon to specify the Icon to display. Method **getIcon** can be used to retrieve the current Icon displayed on a label. Lines 37–38 use JLabel methods **setHorizontalTextPosition** and **setVerticalTextPosition** to specify the text position in the label. In this case, the text will be centered *horizontally* and will appear at the *bottom* of the label. Thus, the Icon will appear *above* the text. The horizontal-position constants in SwingConstants are LEFT, CENTER and RIGHT (Fig. 12.8).

The vertical-position constants in SwingConstants are TOP, CENTER and BOTTOM (Fig. 12.8). Line 39 (Fig. 12.6) sets the tool-tip text for label3. Line 40 adds label3 to the JFrame.

Constant	Description	Constant	Description
Horizontal-position constants		*Vertical-position constants*	
LEFT	Place text on the left	TOP	Place text at the top
CENTER	Place text in the center	CENTER	Place text in the center
RIGHT	Place text on the right	BOTTOM	Place text at the bottom

Fig. 12.8 | Positioning constants (static members of interface SwingConstants).

Creating and Displaying a LabelFrame Window

Class LabelTest (Fig. 12.7) creates an object of class LabelFrame (line 9), then specifies the default close operation for the window. By default, closing a window simply *hides* the window. However, when the user closes the LabelFrame window, we would like the application to *terminate*. Line 10 invokes LabelFrame's **setDefaultCloseOperation** method (inherited from class JFrame) with constant **JFrame.EXIT_ON_CLOSE** as the argument to indicate that the program should *terminate* when the window is closed by the user. This line is important. Without it the application will *not* terminate when the user closes the window. Next, line 11 invokes LabelFrame's **setSize** method to specify the *width* and *height* of the window in *pixels*. Finally, line 12 invokes LabelFrame's **setVisible** method with the argument true to display the window on the screen. Try resizing the window to see how the FlowLayout changes the JLabel positions as the window width changes.

12.6 Text Fields and an Introduction to Event Handling with Nested Classes

Normally, a user interacts with an application's GUI to indicate the tasks that the application should perform. For example, when you write an e-mail in an e-mail application, clicking the **Send** button tells the application to send the e-mail to the specified e-mail addresses. GUIs are **event driven**. When the user interacts with a GUI component, the interaction—known as an **event**—drives the program to perform a task. Some common user interactions that cause an application to perform a task include *clicking* a button, *typing* in a text field, *selecting* an item from a menu, *closing* a window and *moving* the mouse. The code that performs a task in response to an event is called an **event handler**, and the process of responding to events is known as **event handling**.

Let's consider two other GUI components that can generate events—**JTextFields** and **JPasswordFields** (package javax.swing). Class JTextField extends class **JTextComponent** (package javax.swing.text), which provides many features common to Swing's text-based components. Class JPasswordField extends JTextField and adds methods that are specific to processing passwords. Each of these components is a single-line area in which the user can enter text via the keyboard. Applications can also display text in a JTextField (see the output of Fig. 12.10). A JPasswordField shows that characters are being typed as the user enters them, but hides the actual characters with an **echo character**, assuming that they represent a password that should remain known only to the user.

When the user types in a `JTextField` or a `JPasswordField`, then presses *Enter*, an *event* occurs. Our next example demonstrates how a program can perform a task *in response* to that event. The techniques shown here are applicable to all GUI components that generate events.

The application of Figs. 12.9–12.10 uses classes `JTextField` and `JPasswordField` to create and manipulate four text fields. When the user types in one of the text fields, then presses *Enter*, the application displays a message dialog box containing the text the user typed. You can type only in the text field that's "in **focus**." When you *click* a component, it *receives the focus*. This is important, because the text field with the focus is the one that generates an event when you press *Enter*. In this example, when you press *Enter* in the `JPasswordField`, the password is revealed. We begin by discussing the setup of the GUI, then discuss the event-handling code.

```java
1   // Fig. 12.9: TextFieldFrame.java
2   // JTextFields and JPasswordFields.
3   import java.awt.FlowLayout;
4   import java.awt.event.ActionListener;
5   import java.awt.event.ActionEvent;
6   import javax.swing.JFrame;
7   import javax.swing.JTextField;
8   import javax.swing.JPasswordField;
9   import javax.swing.JOptionPane;
10
11  public class TextFieldFrame extends JFrame
12  {
13     private final JTextField textField1; // text field with set size
14     private final JTextField textField2; // text field with text
15     private final JTextField textField3; // text field with text and size
16     private final JPasswordField passwordField; // password field with text
17
18     // TextFieldFrame constructor adds JTextFields to JFrame
19     public TextFieldFrame()
20     {
21        super("Testing JTextField and JPasswordField");
22        setLayout(new FlowLayout());
23
24        // construct text field with 10 columns
25        textField1 = new JTextField(10);
26        add(textField1); // add textField1 to JFrame
27
28        // construct text field with default text
29        textField2 = new JTextField("Enter text here");
30        add(textField2); // add textField2 to JFrame
31
32        // construct text field with default text and 21 columns
33        textField3 = new JTextField("Uneditable text field", 21);
34        textField3.setEditable(false); // disable editing
35        add(textField3); // add textField3 to JFrame
```

Fig. 12.9 | JTextFields and JPasswordFields. (Part 1 of 2.)

```
36
37          // construct password field with default text
38          passwordField = new JPasswordField("Hidden text");
39          add(passwordField); // add passwordField to JFrame
40
41          // register event handlers
42          TextFieldHandler handler = new TextFieldHandler();
43          textField1.addActionListener(handler);
44          textField2.addActionListener(handler);
45          textField3.addActionListener(handler);
46          passwordField.addActionListener(handler);
47      }
48
49      // private inner class for event handling
50      private class TextFieldHandler implements ActionListener
51      {
52          // process text field events
53          @Override
54          public void actionPerformed(ActionEvent event)
55          {
56              String string = "";
57
58              // user pressed Enter in JTextField textField1
59              if (event.getSource() == textField1)
60                  string = String.format("textField1: %s",
61                      event.getActionCommand());
62
63              // user pressed Enter in JTextField textField2
64              else if (event.getSource() == textField2)
65                  string = String.format("textField2: %s",
66                      event.getActionCommand());
67
68              // user pressed Enter in JTextField textField3
69              else if (event.getSource() == textField3)
70                  string = String.format("textField3: %s",
71                      event.getActionCommand());
72
73              // user pressed Enter in JTextField passwordField
74              else if (event.getSource() == passwordField)
75                  string = String.format("passwordField: %s",
76                      event.getActionCommand());
77
78              // display JTextField content
79              JOptionPane.showMessageDialog(null, string);
80          }
81      } // end private inner class TextFieldHandler
82  } // end class TextFieldFrame
```

Fig. 12.9 | JTextFields and JPasswordFields. (Part 2 of 2.)

Class TextFieldFrame extends JFrame and declares three JTextField variables and a JPasswordField variable (lines 13–16). Each of the corresponding text fields is instantiated and attached to the TextFieldFrame in the constructor (lines 19–47).

Creating the GUI
Line 22 sets the TextFieldFrame's layout to FlowLayout. Line 25 creates textField1 with 10 columns of text. A text column's width in *pixels* is determined by the average width of a character in the text field's current font. When text is displayed in a text field and the text is wider than the field itself, a portion of the text at the right side is not visible. If you're typing in a text field and the cursor reaches the right edge, the text at the left edge is pushed off the left side of the field and is no longer visible. Users can use the left and right arrow keys to move through the complete text. Line 26 adds textField1 to the JFrame.

Line 29 creates textField2 with the initial text "Enter text here" to display in the text field. The width of the field is determined by the width of the default text specified in the constructor. Line 30 adds textField2 to the JFrame.

Line 33 creates textField3 and calls the JTextField constructor with two arguments—the default text "Uneditable text field" to display and the text field's width in columns (21). Line 34 uses method **setEditable** (inherited by JTextField from class JTextComponent) to make the text field *uneditable*—i.e., the user cannot modify the text in the field. Line 35 adds textField3 to the JFrame.

Line 38 creates passwordField with the text "Hidden text" to display in the text field. The width of the field is determined by the width of the default text. When you execute the application, notice that the text is displayed as a string of asterisks. Line 39 adds passwordField to the JFrame.

Steps Required to Set Up Event Handling for a GUI Component
This example should display a message dialog containing the text from a text field when the user presses *Enter* in that text field. Before an application can respond to an event for a particular GUI component, you must:

1. Create a class that represents the event handler and implements an appropriate interface—known as an **event-listener interface**.

2. Indicate that an object of the class from *Step 1* should be notified when the event occurs—known as **registering the event handler**.

Using a Nested Class to Implement an Event Handler
All the classes discussed so far were so-called **top-level classes**—that is, they *were* not declared *inside* another class. Java allows you to declare classes *inside* other classes—these are called **nested classes**. Nested classes can be static or non-static. Non-static nested classes are called **inner classes** and are frequently used to implement *event handlers*.

An inner-class object must be created by an object of the top-level class that contains the inner class. Each inner-class object *implicitly* has a reference to an object of its top-level class. The inner-class object is allowed to use this implicit reference to directly access all the variables and methods of the top-level class. A nested class that's static does not require an object of its top-level class and does not implicitly have a reference to an object of the top-level class. As you'll see in Chapter 13, Graphics and Java 2D, the Java 2D graphics API uses static nested classes extensively.

Inner Class TextFieldHandler
The event handling in this example is performed by an object of the private *inner class* TextFieldHandler (lines 50–81). This class is private because it will be used only to create event handlers for the text fields in top-level class TextFieldFrame. As with other class

members, *inner classes* can be declared `public`, `protected` or `private`. Since event handlers tend to be specific to the application in which they're defined, they're often implemented as `private` inner classes or as *anonymous inner classes* (Section 12.11).

GUI components can generate many events in response to user interactions. Each event is represented by a class and can be processed only by the appropriate type of event handler. Normally, a component's supported events are described in the Java API documentation for that component's class and its superclasses. When the user presses *Enter* in a JTextField or JPasswordField, an **ActionEvent** (package java.awt.event) occurs. Such an event is processed by an object that implements the interface **ActionListener** (package java.awt.event). The information discussed here is available in the Java API documentation for classes JTextField and ActionEvent. Since JPasswordField is a subclass of JTextField, JPasswordField supports the same events.

To prepare to handle the events in this example, inner class TextFieldHandler implements interface ActionListener and declares the only method in that interface—actionPerformed (lines 53–80). This method specifies the tasks to perform when an ActionEvent occurs. So, inner class TextFieldHandler satisfies *Step 1* listed earlier in this section. We'll discuss the details of method actionPerformed shortly.

Registering the Event Handler for Each Text Field

In the TextFieldFrame constructor, line 42 creates a TextFieldHandler object and assigns it to variable handler. This object's actionPerformed method will be called automatically when the user presses *Enter* in any of the GUI's text fields. However, before this can occur, the program must register this object as the event handler for each text field. Lines 43–46 are the *event-registration* statements that specify handler as the event handler for the three JTextFields and the JPasswordField. The application calls JTextField method **addActionListener** to register the event handler for each component. This method receives as its argument an ActionListener object, which can be an object of any class that implements ActionListener. The object handler *is an* ActionListener, because class TextFieldHandler implements ActionListener. After lines 43–46 execute, the object handler **listens for events**. Now, when the user presses *Enter* in any of these four text fields, method actionPerformed (line 53–80) in class TextFieldHandler is called to handle the event. If an event handler is *not* registered for a particular text field, the event that occurs when the user presses *Enter* in that text field is **consumed**—i.e., it's simply *ignored* by the application.

Software Engineering Observation 12.1
The event listener for an event must implement the appropriate event-listener interface.

Common Programming Error 12.2
If you forget to register an event-handler object for a particular GUI component's event type, events of that type will be ignored.

Details of Class TextFieldHandler's actionPerformed Method

In this example, we use one event-handling object's actionPerformed method (lines 53–80) to handle the events generated by four text fields. Since we'd like to output the name of each text field's instance variable for demonstration purposes, we must determine *which* text field generated the event each time actionPerformed is called. The **event source** is the component with which the user interacted. When the user presses *Enter* while a text field or the password field *has the focus*, the system creates a unique ActionEvent object that contains information about the event that just occurred, such as the event source and the text in the text field. The system passes this ActionEvent object to the event listener's actionPerformed method. Line 56 declares the String that will be displayed. The variable is initialized with the **empty string**—a String containing no characters. The compiler requires the variable to be initialized in case none of the branches of the nested if in lines 59–76 executes.

ActionEvent method getSource (called in lines 59, 64, 69 and 74) returns a reference to the event source. The condition in line 59 asks, "Is the event source textField1?" This condition compares references with the == operator to determine if they refer to the same object. If they *both* refer to textField1, the user pressed *Enter* in textField1. Then, lines 60–61 create a String containing the message that line 79 displays in a message dialog. Line 61 uses ActionEvent method **getActionCommand** to obtain the text the user typed in the text field that generated the event.

In this example, we display the text of the password in the JPasswordField when the user presses *Enter* in that field. Sometimes it's necessary to programatically process the characters in a password. Class JPasswordField method **getPassword** returns the password's characters as an array of type char.

Class *TextFieldTest*

Class TextFieldTest (Fig. 12.10) contains the main method that executes this application and displays an object of class TextFieldFrame. When you execute the application, even the uneditable JTextField (textField3) can generate an ActionEvent. To test this, click the text field to give it the focus, then press *Enter*. Also, the actual text of the password is displayed when you press *Enter* in the JPasswordField. Of course, you would normally not display the password!

```
1   // Fig. 12.10: TextFieldTest.java
2   // Testing TextFieldFrame.
3   import javax.swing.JFrame;
4
5   public class TextFieldTest
6   {
7      public static void main(String[] args)
8      {
9         TextFieldFrame textFieldFrame = new TextFieldFrame();
10        textFieldFrame.setDefaultCloseOperation(JFrame.EXIT_ON_CLOSE);
11        textFieldFrame.setSize(350, 100);
12        textFieldFrame.setVisible(true);
13     }
14  } // end class TextFieldTest
```

Fig. 12.10 | Testing TextFieldFrame. (Part 1 of 2.)

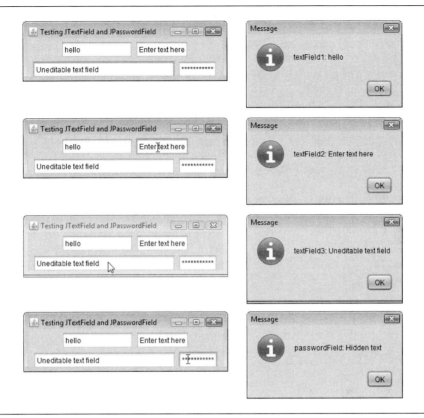

Fig. 12.10 | Testing `TextFieldFrame`. (Part 2 of 2.)

This application used a single object of class `TextFieldHandler` as the event listener for four text fields. Starting in Section 12.10, you'll see that it's possible to declare several event-listener objects of the same type and register each object for a separate GUI component's event. This technique enables us to eliminate the `if...else` logic used in this example's event handler by providing separate event handlers for each component's events.

Java SE 8: Implementing Event Listeners with Lambdas
Recall that interfaces like `ActionListener` that have only one `abstract` method are functional interfaces in Java SE 8. In Section 17.9, we show a more concise way to implement such event-listener interfaces with Java SE 8 lambdas.

12.7 Common GUI Event Types and Listener Interfaces

In Section 12.6, you learned that information about the event that occurs when the user presses *Enter* in a text field is stored in an `ActionEvent` object. Many different types of events can occur when the user interacts with a GUI. The event information is stored in an object of a class that extends `AWTEvent` (from package `java.awt`). Figure 12.11 illustrates a hierarchy containing many event classes from the package **java.awt.event**. Some of these are discussed in this chapter and Chapter 22. These event types are used with both

AWT and Swing components. Additional event types that are specific to Swing GUI components are declared in package `javax.swing.event`.

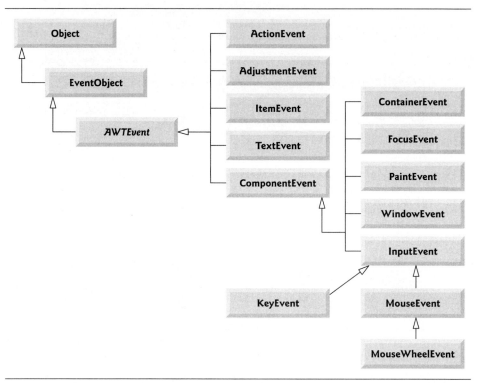

Fig. 12.11 | Some event classes of package `java.awt.event`.

Let's summarize the three parts to the event-handling mechanism that you saw in Section 12.6—the *event source*, the *event object* and the *event listener*. The event source is the GUI component with which the user interacts. The event object encapsulates information about the event that occurred, such as a reference to the event source and any event-specific information that may be required by the event listener for it to handle the event. The event listener is an object that's notified by the event source when an event occurs; in effect, it "listens" for an event, and one of its methods executes in response to the event. A method of the event listener receives an event object when the event listener is notified of the event. The event listener then uses the event object to respond to the event. This event-handling model is known as the **delegation event model**—an event's processing is delegated to an object (the event listener) in the application.

For each event-object type, there's typically a corresponding event-listener interface. An event listener for a GUI event is an object of a class that implements one or more of the event-listener interfaces from packages `java.awt.event` and `javax.swing.event`. Many of the event-listener types are common to both Swing and AWT components. Such types are declared in package `java.awt.event`, and some of them are shown in Fig. 12.12. Additional event-listener types that are specific to Swing components are declared in package `javax.swing.event`.

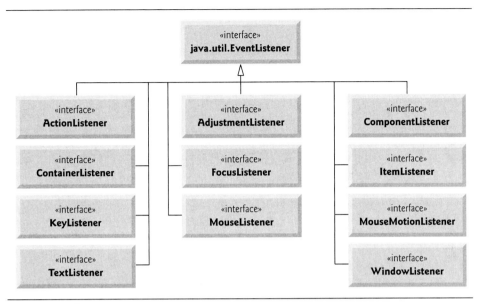

Fig. 12.12 | Some common event-listener interfaces of package `java.awt.event`.

Each event-listener interface specifies one or more event-handling methods that *must* be declared in the class that implements the interface. Recall from Section 10.9 that any class which implements an interface must declare *all* the abstract methods of that interface; otherwise, the class is an abstract class and cannot be used to create objects.

When an event occurs, the GUI component with which the user interacted notifies its *registered listeners* by calling each listener's appropriate *event-handling method*. For example, when the user presses the *Enter* key in a JTextField, the registered listener's actionPerformed method is called. In the next section, we complete our discussion of how the event handling works in the preceding example.

12.8 How Event Handling Works

Let's illustrate how the event-handling mechanism works, using textField1 from the example of Fig. 12.9. We have two remaining open questions from Section 12.7:

> **1.** How did the *event handler* get *registered*?
>
> **2.** How does the GUI component know to call actionPerformed rather than some other event-handling method?

The first question is answered by the event registration performed in lines 43–46 of Fig. 12.9. Figure 12.13 diagrams JTextField variable textField1, TextFieldHandler variable handler and the objects to which they refer.

Registering Events
Every JComponent has an instance variable called listenerList that refers to an object of class **EventListenerList** (package javax.swing.event). Each object of a JComponent

subclass maintains references to its *registered listeners* in the `listenerList`. For simplicity, we've diagramed `listenerList` as an array below the `JTextField` object in Fig. 12.13.

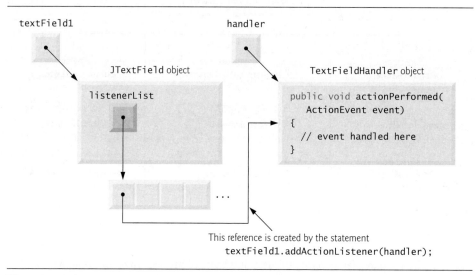

Fig. 12.13 | Event registration for `JTextField` `textField1`.

When the following statement (line 43 of Fig. 12.9) executes

```
textField1.addActionListener(handler);
```

a new entry containing a reference to the `TextFieldHandler` object is placed in `textField1`'s `listenerList`. Although not shown in the diagram, this new entry also includes the listener's type (`ActionListener`). Using this mechanism, each lightweight Swing component maintains its own list of *listeners* that were *registered* to *handle* the component's *events*.

Event-Handler Invocation

The event-listener type is important in answering the second question: How does the GUI component know to call `actionPerformed` rather than another method? Every GUI component supports several *event types*, including **mouse events**, **key events** and others. When an event occurs, the event is **dispatched** only to the *event listeners* of the appropriate type. Dispatching is simply the process by which the GUI component calls an event-handling method on each of its listeners that are registered for the event type that occurred.

Each *event type* has one or more corresponding *event-listener interfaces*. For example, `ActionEvent`s are handled by `ActionListener`s, **MouseEvents** by **MouseListeners** and **MouseMotionListeners**, and **KeyEvents** by **KeyListeners**. When an event occurs, the GUI component receives (from the JVM) a unique *event ID* specifying the event type. The GUI component uses the event ID to decide the listener type to which the event should be dispatched and to decide which method to call on each listener object. For an `ActionEvent`, the event is dispatched to *every* registered `ActionListener`'s `actionPerformed` method (the only method in interface `ActionListener`). For a `MouseEvent`, the event is dispatched to *every* registered `MouseListener` or `MouseMotionListener`, depending on the mouse event that occurs. The MouseEvent's event ID determines which of the several mouse event-handling methods are called. All these decisions are handled for you by the GUI components. All you need to do is register an event handler for the particular event type that your application requires, and the GUI component will ensure that the event handler's appropriate method gets called when the event occurs. We discuss other event types and event-listener interfaces as they're needed with each new component we introduce.

Performance Tip 12.1

GUIs should always remain responsive to the user. Performing a long-running task in an event handler prevents the user from interacting with the GUI until that task completes. Section 23.11 demonstrates techniques prevent such problems.

12.9 JButton

A **button** is a component the user clicks to trigger a specific action. A Java application can use several types of buttons, including **command buttons**, **checkboxes**, **toggle buttons** and **radio buttons**. Figure 12.14 shows the inheritance hierarchy of the Swing buttons we cover in this chapter. As you can see, all the button types are subclasses of **AbstractButton** (package javax.swing), which declares the common features of Swing buttons. In this section, we concentrate on buttons that are typically used to initiate a command.

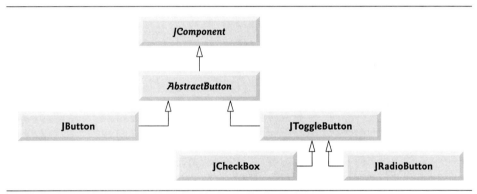

Fig. 12.14 | Swing button hierarchy.

A *command button* (see Fig. 12.16's output) generates an ActionEvent when the user clicks it. Command buttons are created with class **JButton**. The text on the face of a JButton is called a **button label**.

Look-and-Feel Observation 12.8

The text on buttons typically uses book-title capitalization.

Look-and-Feel Observation 12.9

A GUI can have many JButtons, but each button label should be unique in the portion of the GUI that's currently displayed. Having more than one JButton with the same label makes the JButtons ambiguous to the user.

The application of Figs. 12.15 and 12.16 creates two JButtons and demonstrates that JButtons can display Icons. Event handling for the buttons is performed by a single instance of *inner class* ButtonHandler (Fig. 12.15, lines 39–48).

```java
1   // Fig. 12.15: ButtonFrame.java
2   // Command buttons and action events.
3   import java.awt.FlowLayout;
4   import java.awt.event.ActionListener;
5   import java.awt.event.ActionEvent;
6   import javax.swing.JFrame;
7   import javax.swing.JButton;
8   import javax.swing.Icon;
9   import javax.swing.ImageIcon;
10  import javax.swing.JOptionPane;
11
12  public class ButtonFrame extends JFrame
13  {
14     private final JButton plainJButton; // button with just text
15     private final JButton fancyJButton; // button with icons
16
17     // ButtonFrame adds JButtons to JFrame
18     public ButtonFrame()
19     {
20        super("Testing Buttons");
21        setLayout(new FlowLayout());
22
23        plainJButton = new JButton("Plain Button"); // button with text
24        add(plainJButton); // add plainJButton to JFrame
25
26        Icon bug1 = new ImageIcon(getClass().getResource("bug1.gif"));
27        Icon bug2 = new ImageIcon(getClass().getResource("bug2.gif"));
28        fancyJButton = new JButton("Fancy Button", bug1); // set image
29        fancyJButton.setRolloverIcon(bug2); // set rollover image
30        add(fancyJButton); // add fancyJButton to JFrame
31
32        // create new ButtonHandler for button event handling
33        ButtonHandler handler = new ButtonHandler();
34        fancyJButton.addActionListener(handler);
35        plainJButton.addActionListener(handler);
36     }
37
38     // inner class for button event handling
39     private class ButtonHandler implements ActionListener
40     {
41        // handle button event
42        @Override
43        public void actionPerformed(ActionEvent event)
44        {
45           JOptionPane.showMessageDialog(ButtonFrame.this, String.format(
46              "You pressed: %s", event.getActionCommand()));
47        }
48     }
49  } // end class ButtonFrame
```

Fig. 12.15 | Command buttons and action events.

```
 1   // Fig. 12.16: ButtonTest.java
 2   // Testing ButtonFrame.
 3   import javax.swing.JFrame;
 4
 5   public class ButtonTest
 6   {
 7      public static void main(String[] args)
 8      {
 9         ButtonFrame buttonFrame = new ButtonFrame();
10         buttonFrame.setDefaultCloseOperation(JFrame.EXIT_ON_CLOSE);
11         buttonFrame.setSize(275, 110);
12         buttonFrame.setVisible(true);
13      }
14   } // end class ButtonTest
```

Fig. 12.16 | Testing ButtonFrame.

Lines 14–15 declare JButton variables plainJButton and fancyJButton. The corresponding objects are instantiated in the constructor. Line 23 creates plainJButton with the button label "Plain Button". Line 24 adds the JButton to the JFrame.

A JButton can display an Icon. To provide the user with an extra level of visual interaction with the GUI, a JButton can also have a **rollover Icon**—an Icon that's displayed when the user positions the mouse over the JButton. The icon on the JButton changes as the mouse moves in and out of the JButton's area on the screen. Lines 26–27 create two

ImageIcon objects that represent the default Icon and rollover Icon for the JButton created at line 28. Both statements assume that the image files are stored in the *same* directory as the application. Images are commonly placed in the *same* directory as the application or a subdirectory like images). These image files have been provided for you with the example.

Line 28 creates fancyButton with the text "Fancy Button" and the icon bug1. By default, the text is displayed to the *right* of the icon. Line 29 uses **setRolloverIcon** (inherited from class AbstractButton) to specify the image displayed on the JButton when the user positions the mouse over it. Line 30 adds the JButton to the JFrame.

Look-and-Feel Observation 12.10
Because class AbstractButton supports displaying text and images on a button, all subclasses of AbstractButton also support displaying text and images.

Look-and-Feel Observation 12.11
Rollover icons provide visual feedback indicating that an action will occur when when a JButton is clicked.

JButtons, like JTextFields, generate ActionEvents that can be processed by any ActionListener object. Lines 33–35 create an object of private *inner class* ButtonHandler and use addActionListener to *register* it as the *event handler* for each JButton. Class ButtonHandler (lines 39–48) declares actionPerformed to display a message dialog box containing the label for the button the user pressed. For a JButton event, ActionEvent method getActionCommand returns the label on the JButton.

*Accessing the **this** Reference in an Object of a Top-Level Class from an Inner Class*
When you execute this application and click one of its buttons, notice that the message dialog that appears is centered over the application's window. This occurs because the call to JOptionPane method showMessageDialog (lines 45–46) uses ButtonFrame.this rather than null as the first argument. When this argument is not null, it represents the so-called *parent GUI component* of the message dialog (in this case the application window is the parent component) and enables the dialog to be centered over that component when the dialog is displayed. ButtonFrame.this represents the this reference of the object of top-level class ButtonFrame.

Software Engineering Observation 12.2
When used in an inner class, keyword this refers to the current inner-class object being manipulated. An inner-class method can use its outer-class object's this by preceding this with the outer-class name and a dot (.) separator, as in ButtonFrame.this.

12.10 Buttons That Maintain State

The Swing GUI components contain three types of **state buttons**—**JToggleButton**, **JCheckBox** and **JRadioButton**—that have on/off or true/false values. Classes JCheckBox and JRadioButton are subclasses of JToggleButton (Fig. 12.14). A JRadioButton is different from a JCheckBox in that normally several JRadioButtons are grouped together and are *mutually exclusive*—only *one* in the group can be selected at any time, just like the buttons on a car radio. We first discuss class JCheckBox.

12.10.1 JCheckBox

The application of Figs. 12.17–12.18 uses two JCheckBoxes to select the desired font style of the text displayed in a JTextField. When selected, one applies a bold style and the other an italic style. If *both* are selected, the style is bold *and* italic. When the application initially executes, neither JCheckBox is checked (i.e., they're both false), so the font is plain. Class CheckBoxTest (Fig. 12.18) contains the main method that executes this application.

```java
1   // Fig. 12.17: CheckBoxFrame.java
2   // JCheckBoxes and item events.
3   import java.awt.FlowLayout;
4   import java.awt.Font;
5   import java.awt.event.ItemListener;
6   import java.awt.event.ItemEvent;
7   import javax.swing.JFrame;
8   import javax.swing.JTextField;
9   import javax.swing.JCheckBox;
10
11  public class CheckBoxFrame extends JFrame
12  {
13     private final JTextField textField; // displays text in changing fonts
14     private final JCheckBox boldJCheckBox; // to select/deselect bold
15     private final JCheckBox italicJCheckBox; // to select/deselect italic
16
17     // CheckBoxFrame constructor adds JCheckBoxes to JFrame
18     public CheckBoxFrame()
19     {
20        super("JCheckBox Test");
21        setLayout(new FlowLayout());
22
23        // set up JTextField and set its font
24        textField = new JTextField("Watch the font style change", 20);
25        textField.setFont(new Font("Serif", Font.PLAIN, 14));
26        add(textField); // add textField to JFrame
27
28        boldJCheckBox = new JCheckBox("Bold");
29        italicJCheckBox = new JCheckBox("Italic");
30        add(boldJCheckBox); // add bold checkbox to JFrame
31        add(italicJCheckBox); // add italic checkbox to JFrame
32
33        // register listeners for JCheckBoxes
34        CheckBoxHandler handler = new CheckBoxHandler();
35        boldJCheckBox.addItemListener(handler);
36        italicJCheckBox.addItemListener(handler);
37     }
38
39     // private inner class for ItemListener event handling
40     private class CheckBoxHandler implements ItemListener
41     {
```

Fig. 12.17 | JCheckBoxes and item events. (Part 1 of 2.)

```
42          // respond to checkbox events
43          @Override
44          public void itemStateChanged(ItemEvent event)
45          {
46              Font font = null; // stores the new Font
47
48              // determine which CheckBoxes are checked and create Font
49              if (boldJCheckBox.isSelected() && italicJCheckBox.isSelected())
50                  font = new Font("Serif", Font.BOLD + Font.ITALIC, 14);
51              else if (boldJCheckBox.isSelected())
52                  font = new Font("Serif", Font.BOLD, 14);
53              else if (italicJCheckBox.isSelected())
54                  font = new Font("Serif", Font.ITALIC, 14);
55              else
56                  font = new Font("Serif", Font.PLAIN, 14);
57
58              textField.setFont(font);
59          }
60      }
61  } // end class CheckBoxFrame
```

Fig. 12.17 | JCheckBoxes and item events. (Part 2 of 2.)

```
1   // Fig. 12.18: CheckBoxTest.java
2   // Testing CheckBoxFrame.
3   import javax.swing.JFrame;
4
5   public class CheckBoxTest
6   {
7       public static void main(String[] args)
8       {
9           CheckBoxFrame checkBoxFrame = new CheckBoxFrame();
10          checkBoxFrame.setDefaultCloseOperation(JFrame.EXIT_ON_CLOSE);
11          checkBoxFrame.setSize(275, 100);
12          checkBoxFrame.setVisible(true);
13      }
14  } // end class CheckBoxTest
```

Fig. 12.18 | Testing CheckBoxFrame.

After the JTextField is created and initialized (Fig. 12.17, line 24), line 25 uses method **setFont** (inherited by JTextField indirectly from class Component) to set the font of the JTextField to a new object of class **Font** (package java.awt). The new Font is initialized with "Serif" (a generic font name that represents a font such as Times and is supported on all Java platforms), Font.PLAIN style and 14-point size. Next, lines 28–29 create two JCheckBox objects. The String passed to the JCheckBox constructor is the **checkbox label** that appears to the right of the JCheckBox by default.

When the user clicks a JCheckBox, an **ItemEvent** occurs. This event can be handled by an **ItemListener** object, which *must* implement method **itemStateChanged**. In this example, the event handling is performed by an instance of private *inner class* CheckBox-Handler (lines 40–60). Lines 34–36 create an instance of class CheckBoxHandler and register it with method **addItemListener** as the listener for both the JCheckBox objects.

CheckBoxHandler method itemStateChanged (lines 43–59) is called when the user clicks the either boldJCheckBox or italicJCheckBox. In this example, we do not determine which JCheckBox was clicked—we use both of their states to determine the font to display. Line 49 uses JCheckBox method **isSelected** to determine if both JCheckBoxes are selected. If so, line 50 creates a bold italic font by adding the Font constants Font.BOLD and Font.ITALIC for the font-style argument of the Font constructor. Line 51 determines whether the boldJCheckBox is selected, and if so line 52 creates a bold font. Line 53 determines whether the italicJCheckBox is selected, and if so line 54 creates an italic font. If none of the preceding conditions are true, line 56 creates a plain font using the Font constant Font.PLAIN. Finally, line 58 sets textField's new font, which changes the font in the JTextField on the screen.

Relationship Between an Inner Class and Its Top-Level Class

Class CheckBoxHandler used variables boldJCheckBox (lines 49 and 51), italicJCheck-Box (lines 49 and 53) and textField (line 58) even though they are *not* declared in the inner class. Recall that an *inner class* has a special relationship with its *top-level class*—it's allowed to access *all* the variables and methods of the top-level class. CheckBoxHandler method itemStateChanged (line 43–59) uses this relationship to determine which JCheckBoxes are checked and to set the font on the JTextField. Notice that none of the code in inner class CheckBoxHandler requires an explicit reference to the top-level class object.

12.10.2 JRadioButton

Radio buttons (declared with class JRadioButton) are similar to checkboxes in that they have two states—*selected* and *not selected* (also called *deselected*). However, radio buttons normally appear as a **group** in which only *one* button can be selected at a time (see the output of Fig. 12.20). Radio buttons are used to represent **mutually exclusive options** (i.e., multiple options in the group *cannot* be selected at the same time). The logical relationship between radio buttons is maintained by a **ButtonGroup** object (package javax.swing), which itself is *not* a GUI component. A ButtonGroup object organizes a group of buttons and is *not* itself displayed in a user interface. Rather, the individual JRadioButton objects from the group are displayed in the GUI.

The application of Figs. 12.19–12.20 is similar to that of Figs. 12.17–12.18. The user can alter the font style of a JTextField's text. The application uses radio buttons that permit only a single font style in the group to be selected at a time. Class RadioButtonTest (Fig. 12.20) contains the main method that executes this application.

```
 1   // Fig. 12.19: RadioButtonFrame.java
 2   // Creating radio buttons using ButtonGroup and JRadioButton.
 3   import java.awt.FlowLayout;
 4   import java.awt.Font;
 5   import java.awt.event.ItemListener;
 6   import java.awt.event.ItemEvent;
 7   import javax.swing.JFrame;
 8   import javax.swing.JTextField;
 9   import javax.swing.JRadioButton;
10   import javax.swing.ButtonGroup;
11
12   public class RadioButtonFrame extends JFrame
13   {
14      private final JTextField textField; // used to display font changes
15      private final Font plainFont; // font for plain text
16      private final Font boldFont; // font for bold text
17      private final Font italicFont; // font for italic text
18      private final Font boldItalicFont; // font for bold and italic text
19      private final JRadioButton plainJRadioButton; // selects plain text
20      private final JRadioButton boldJRadioButton; // selects bold text
21      private final JRadioButton italicJRadioButton; // selects italic text
22      private final JRadioButton boldItalicJRadioButton; // bold and italic
23      private final ButtonGroup radioGroup; // holds radio buttons
24
25      // RadioButtonFrame constructor adds JRadioButtons to JFrame
26      public RadioButtonFrame()
27      {
28         super("RadioButton Test");
29         setLayout(new FlowLayout());
30
31         textField = new JTextField("Watch the font style change", 25);
32         add(textField); // add textField to JFrame
33
34         // create radio buttons
35         plainJRadioButton = new JRadioButton("Plain", true);
36         boldJRadioButton = new JRadioButton("Bold", false);
37         italicJRadioButton = new JRadioButton("Italic", false);
38         boldItalicJRadioButton = new JRadioButton("Bold/Italic", false);
39         add(plainJRadioButton); // add plain button to JFrame
40         add(boldJRadioButton); // add bold button to JFrame
41         add(italicJRadioButton); // add italic button to JFrame
42         add(boldItalicJRadioButton); // add bold and italic button
43
44         // create logical relationship between JRadioButtons
45         radioGroup = new ButtonGroup(); // create ButtonGroup
46         radioGroup.add(plainJRadioButton); // add plain to group
47         radioGroup.add(boldJRadioButton); // add bold to group
48         radioGroup.add(italicJRadioButton); // add italic to group
49         radioGroup.add(boldItalicJRadioButton); // add bold and italic
50
51         // create font objects
52         plainFont = new Font("Serif", Font.PLAIN, 14);
53         boldFont = new Font("Serif", Font.BOLD, 14);
```

Fig. 12.19 | Creating radio buttons using ButtonGroup and JRadioButton. (Part 1 of 2.)

```
54          italicFont = new Font("Serif", Font.ITALIC, 14);
55          boldItalicFont = new Font("Serif", Font.BOLD + Font.ITALIC, 14);
56          textField.setFont(plainFont);
57
58          // register events for JRadioButtons
59          plainJRadioButton.addItemListener(
60             new RadioButtonHandler(plainFont));
61          boldJRadioButton.addItemListener(
62             new RadioButtonHandler(boldFont));
63          italicJRadioButton.addItemListener(
64             new RadioButtonHandler(italicFont));
65          boldItalicJRadioButton.addItemListener(
66             new RadioButtonHandler(boldItalicFont));
67       }
68
69       // private inner class to handle radio button events
70       private class RadioButtonHandler implements ItemListener
71       {
72          private Font font; // font associated with this listener
73
74          public RadioButtonHandler(Font f)
75          {
76             font = f;
77          }
78
79          // handle radio button events
80          @Override
81          public void itemStateChanged(ItemEvent event)
82          {
83             textField.setFont(font);
84          }
85       }
86    } // end class RadioButtonFrame
```

Fig. 12.19 | Creating radio buttons using `ButtonGroup` and `JRadioButton`. (Part 2 of 2.)

```
1   // Fig. 12.20: RadioButtonTest.java
2   // Testing RadioButtonFrame.
3   import javax.swing.JFrame;
4
5   public class RadioButtonTest
6   {
7      public static void main(String[] args)
8      {
9         RadioButtonFrame radioButtonFrame = new RadioButtonFrame();
10        radioButtonFrame.setDefaultCloseOperation(JFrame.EXIT_ON_CLOSE);
11        radioButtonFrame.setSize(300, 100);
12        radioButtonFrame.setVisible(true);
13     }
14  } // end class RadioButtonTest
```

Fig. 12.20 | Testing `RadioButtonFrame`. (Part 1 of 2.)

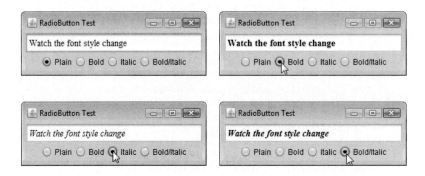

Fig. 12.20 | Testing `RadioButtonFrame`. (Part 2 of 2.)

Lines 35–42 (Fig. 12.19) in the constructor create four `JRadioButton` objects and add them to the `JFrame`. Each `JRadioButton` is created with a constructor call like that in line 35. This constructor specifies the label that appears to the right of the `JRadioButton` by default and the initial state of the `JRadioButton`. A `true` second argument indicates that the `JRadioButton` should appear *selected* when it's displayed.

Line 45 instantiates `ButtonGroup` object `radioGroup`. This object is the "glue" that forms the logical relationship between the four `JRadioButton` objects and allows only one of the four to be selected at a time. It's possible that no `JRadioButton`s in a `ButtonGroup` are selected, but this can occur *only* if *no* preselected `JRadioButton`s are added to the `ButtonGroup` and the user has *not* selected a `JRadioButton` yet. Lines 46–49 use `ButtonGroup` method **add** to associate each of the `JRadioButton`s with `radioGroup`. If more than one selected `JRadioButton` object is added to the group, the selected one that was added *first* will be selected when the GUI is displayed.

`JRadioButton`s, like `JCheckBox`es, generate `ItemEvent`s when they're *clicked*. Lines 59–66 create four instances of inner class `RadioButtonHandler` (declared at lines 70–85). In this example, each event-listener object is registered to handle the `ItemEvent` generated when the user clicks a particular `JRadioButton`. Notice that each `RadioButtonHandler` object is initialized with a particular `Font` object (created in lines 52–55).

Class `RadioButtonHandler` (line 70–85) implements interface `ItemListener` so it can handle `ItemEvent`s generated by the `JRadioButton`s. The constructor stores the `Font` object it receives as an argument in the event-listener object's instance variable `font` (declared at line 72). When the user clicks a `JRadioButton`, `radioGroup` turns off the previously selected `JRadioButton`, and method `itemStateChanged` (lines 80–84) sets the font in the `JTextField` to the `Font` stored in the `JRadioButton`'s corresponding event-listener object. Notice that line 83 of inner class `RadioButtonHandler` uses the top-level class's `textField` instance variable to set the font.

12.11 JComboBox; Using an Anonymous Inner Class for Event Handling

A combo box (sometimes called a **drop-down list**) enables the user to select *one* item from a list (Fig. 12.22). Combo boxes are implemented with class **JComboBox**, which extends class JComponent. JComboBox is a generic class, like the class ArrayList (Chapter 6). When you create a JComboBox, you specify the type of the objects that it manages—the JComboBox then displays a String representation of each object.

```java
1   // Fig. 12.21: ComboBoxFrame.java
2   // JComboBox that displays a list of image names.
3   import java.awt.FlowLayout;
4   import java.awt.event.ItemListener;
5   import java.awt.event.ItemEvent;
6   import javax.swing.JFrame;
7   import javax.swing.JLabel;
8   import javax.swing.JComboBox;
9   import javax.swing.Icon;
10  import javax.swing.ImageIcon;
11
12  public class ComboBoxFrame extends JFrame
13  {
14     private final JComboBox<String> imagesJComboBox; // holds icon names
15     private final JLabel label; // displays selected icon
16
17     private static final String[] names =
18        {"bug1.gif", "bug2.gif",  "travelbug.gif", "buganim.gif"};
19     private final Icon[] icons = {
20        new ImageIcon(getClass().getResource(names[0])),
21        new ImageIcon(getClass().getResource(names[1])),
22        new ImageIcon(getClass().getResource(names[2])),
23        new ImageIcon(getClass().getResource(names[3]))};
24
25     // ComboBoxFrame constructor adds JComboBox to JFrame
26     public ComboBoxFrame()
27     {
28        super("Testing JComboBox");
29        setLayout(new FlowLayout()); // set frame layout
30
31        imagesJComboBox = new JComboBox<String>(names); // set up JComboBox
32        imagesJComboBox.setMaximumRowCount(3); // display three rows
33
34        imagesJComboBox.addItemListener(
35           new ItemListener() // anonymous inner class
36           {
37              // handle JComboBox event
38              @Override
39              public void itemStateChanged(ItemEvent event)
40              {
41                 // determine whether item selected
42                 if (event.getStateChange() == ItemEvent.SELECTED)
43                    label.setIcon(icons[
44                       imagesJComboBox.getSelectedIndex()]);
45              }
46           } // end anonymous inner class
47        ); // end call to addItemListener
48
```

Fig. 12.21 | JComboBox that displays a list of image names. (Part 1 of 2.)

```
49          add(imagesJComboBox); // add combo box to JFrame
50          label = new JLabel(icons[0]); // display first icon
51          add(label); // add label to JFrame
52       }
53    } // end class ComboBoxFrame
```

Fig. 12.21 | JComboBox that displays a list of image names. (Part 2 of 2.)

```
 1    // Fig. 12.22: ComboBoxTest.java
 2    // Testing ComboBoxFrame.
 3    import javax.swing.JFrame;
 4
 5    public class ComboBoxTest
 6    {
 7       public static void main(String[] args)
 8       {
 9          ComboBoxFrame comboBoxFrame = new ComboBoxFrame();
10          comboBoxFrame.setDefaultCloseOperation(JFrame.EXIT_ON_CLOSE);
11          comboBoxFrame.setSize(350, 150);
12          comboBoxFrame.setVisible(true);
13       }
14    } // end class ComboBoxTest
```

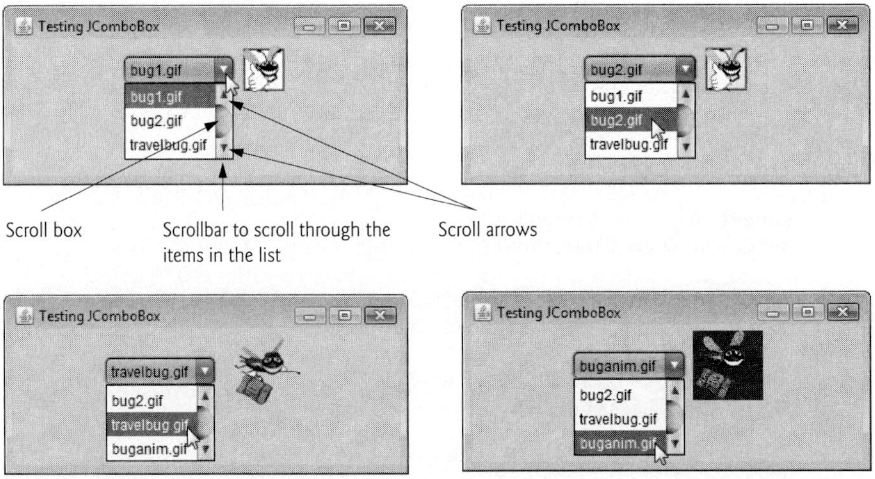

Scroll box   Scrollbar to scroll through the   Scroll arrows
                items in the list

Fig. 12.22 | Testing ComboBoxFrame.

JComboBoxes generate ItemEvents just as JCheckBoxes and JRadioButtons do. This example also demonstrates a special form of inner class that's used frequently in event handling. The application (Figs. 12.21–12.22) uses a JComboBox to provide a list of four image filenames from which the user can select one image to display. When the user selects a name, the application displays the corresponding image as an Icon on a JLabel. Class ComboBoxTest (Fig. 12.22) contains the main method that executes this application. The screen captures for this application show the JComboBox list after the selection was made to illustrate which image filename was selected.

Lines 19–23 (Fig. 12.21) declare and initialize array icons with four new ImageIcon objects. String array names (lines 17–18) contains the names of the four image files that are stored in the same directory as the application.

At line 31, the constructor initializes a JComboBox object with the Strings in array names as the elements in the list. Each item in the list has an **index**. The first item is added at index 0, the next at index 1 and so forth. The first item added to a JComboBox appears as the currently selected item when the JComboBox is displayed. Other items are selected by clicking the JComboBox, then selecting an item from the list that appears.

Line 32 uses JComboBox method **setMaximumRowCount** to set the maximum number of elements that are displayed when the user clicks the JComboBox. If there are additional items, the JComboBox provides a **scrollbar** (see the first screen) that allows the user to scroll through all the elements in the list. The user can click the **scroll arrows** at the top and bottom of the scrollbar to move up and down through the list one element at a time, or else drag the **scroll box** in the middle of the scrollbar up and down. To drag the scroll box, position the mouse cursor on it, hold the mouse button down and move the mouse. In this example, the drop-down list is too short to drag the scroll box, so you can click the up and down arrows or use your mouse's wheel to scroll through the four items in the list. Line 49 attaches the JComboBox to the ComboBoxFrame's FlowLayout (set in line 29). Line 50 creates the JLabel that displays ImageIcons and initializes it with the first ImageIcon in array icons. Line 51 attaches the JLabel to the ComboBoxFrame's FlowLayout.

Look-and-Feel Observation 12.12
Set the maximum row count for a JComboBox to a number of rows that prevents the list from expanding outside the bounds of the window in which it's used.

Using an Anonymous Inner Class for Event Handling

Lines 34–46 are one statement that declares the event listener's class, creates an object of that class and registers it as imagesJComboBox's ItemEvent listener. This event-listener object is an instance of an **anonymous inner class**—a class that's declared without a name and typically appears inside a method declaration. *As with other inner classes, an anonymous inner class can access its top-level class's members.* However, an anonymous inner class has limited access to the local variables of the method in which it's declared. Since an anonymous inner class has no name, one object of the class must be created at the point where the class is declared (starting at line 35).

Software Engineering Observation 12.3
An anonymous inner class declared in a method can access the instance variables and methods of the top-level class object that declared it, as well as the method's final local variables, but cannot access the method's non-final local variables. As of Java SE 8, anonymous inner classes may also access a methods "effectively final" local variables—see Chapter 17 for more information.

Lines 34–47 are a call to imagesJComboBox's addItemListener method. The argument to this method must be an object that *is an* ItemListener (i.e., any object of a class that implements ItemListener). Lines 35–46 are a class-instance creation expression that declares an anonymous inner class and creates one object of that class. A reference to that object is then passed as the argument to addItemListener. The syntax ItemListener()

after new begins the declaration of an anonymous inner class that implements interface ItemListener. This is similar to beginning a class declaration with

        public class MyHandler **implements** ItemListener

The opening left brace at line 36 and the closing right brace at line 46 delimit the body of the anonymous inner class. Lines 38–45 declare the ItemListener's itemStateChanged method. When the user makes a selection from imagesJComboBox, this method sets label's Icon. The Icon is selected from array icons by determining the index of the selected item in the JComboBox with method **getSelectedIndex** in line 44. For each item selected from a JComboBox, another item is first deselected—so two ItemEvents occur when an item is selected. We wish to display only the icon for the item the user just selected. For this reason, line 42 determines whether ItemEvent method **getStateChange** returns ItemEvent.SELECTED. If so, lines 43–44 set label's icon.

Software Engineering Observation 12.4
Like any other class, when an anonymous inner class implements an interface, the class must implement every abstract *method in the interface.*

The syntax shown in lines 35–46 for creating an event handler with an anonymous inner class is similar to the code that would be generated by a Java integrated development environment (IDE). Typically, an IDE enables you to design a GUI visually, then it generates code that implements the GUI. You simply insert statements in the event-handling methods that declare how to handle each event.

Java SE 8: Implementing Anonymous Inner Classes with Lambdas
In Section 17.9, we show how to use Java SE 8 lambdas to create event handlers. As you'll learn, the compiler translates a lambda into an object of an anonymous inner class.

12.12 JList

A list displays a series of items from which the user may *select one or more items* (see the output of Fig. 12.24). Lists are created with class JList, which directly extends class JComponent. Class JList—which like JComboBox is a generic class—supports **single-selection lists** (which allow only one item to be selected at a time) and **multiple-selection lists** (which allow any number of items to be selected). In this section, we discuss single-selection lists.

The application of Figs. 12.23–12.24 creates a JList containing 13 color names. When a color name is clicked in the JList, a **ListSelectionEvent** occurs and the application changes the background color of the application window to the selected color. Class ListTest (Fig. 12.24) contains the main method that executes this application.

```
1   // Fig. 12.23: ListFrame.java
2   // JList that displays a list of colors.
3   import java.awt.FlowLayout;
4   import java.awt.Color;
5   import javax.swing.JFrame;
6   import javax.swing.JList;
```

Fig. 12.23 | JList that displays a list of colors. (Part 1 of 2.)

```
 7    import javax.swing.JScrollPane;
 8    import javax.swing.event.ListSelectionListener;
 9    import javax.swing.event.ListSelectionEvent;
10    import javax.swing.ListSelectionModel;
11
12    public class ListFrame extends JFrame
13    {
14       private final JList<String> colorJList; // list to display colors
15       private static final String[] colorNames = {"Black", "Blue", "Cyan",
16          "Dark Gray", "Gray", "Green", "Light Gray", "Magenta",
17          "Orange", "Pink", "Red", "White", "Yellow"};
18       private static final Color[] colors = {Color.BLACK, Color.BLUE,
19          Color.CYAN, Color.DARK_GRAY, Color.GRAY, Color.GREEN,
20          Color.LIGHT_GRAY, Color.MAGENTA, Color.ORANGE, Color.PINK,
21          Color.RED, Color.WHITE, Color.YELLOW};
22
23       // ListFrame constructor add JScrollPane containing JList to JFrame
24       public ListFrame()
25       {
26          super("List Test");
27          setLayout(new FlowLayout());
28
29          colorJList = new JList<String>(colorNames); // list of colorNames
30          colorJList.setVisibleRowCount(5); // display five rows at once
31
32          // do not allow multiple selections
33          colorJList.setSelectionMode(ListSelectionModel.SINGLE_SELECTION);
34
35          // add a JScrollPane containing JList to frame
36          add(new JScrollPane(colorJList));
37
38          colorJList.addListSelectionListener(
39             new ListSelectionListener() // anonymous inner class
40             {
41                // handle list selection events
42                @Override
43                public void valueChanged(ListSelectionEvent event)
44                {
45                   getContentPane().setBackground(
46                      colors[colorJList.getSelectedIndex()]);
47                }
48             }
49          );
50       }
51    } // end class ListFrame
```

Fig. 12.23 | JList that displays a list of colors. (Part 2 of 2.)

```
1    // Fig. 12.24: ListTest.java
2    // Selecting colors from a JList.
3    import javax.swing.JFrame;
4
```

Fig. 12.24 | Selecting colors from a JList. (Part 1 of 2.)

```
5   public class ListTest
6   {
7      public static void main(String[] args)
8      {
9         ListFrame listFrame = new ListFrame(); // create ListFrame
10        listFrame.setDefaultCloseOperation(JFrame.EXIT_ON_CLOSE);
11        listFrame.setSize(350, 150);
12        listFrame.setVisible(true);
13     }
14  } // end class ListTest
```

Fig. 12.24 | Selecting colors from a JList. (Part 2 of 2.)

Line 29 (Fig. 12.23) creates JList object colorJList. The argument to the JList constructor is the array of Objects (in this case Strings) to display in the list. Line 30 uses JList method **setVisibleRowCount** to determine the number of items *visible* in the list.

Line 33 uses JList method **setSelectionMode** to specify the list's **selection mode**. Class **ListSelectionModel** (of package javax.swing) declares three constants that specify a JList's selection mode—**SINGLE_SELECTION** (which allows only one item to be selected at a time), **SINGLE_INTERVAL_SELECTION** (for a multiple-selection list that allows selection of several contiguous items) and **MULTIPLE_INTERVAL_SELECTION** (for a multiple-selection list that does not restrict the items that can be selected).

Unlike a JComboBox, a JList *does not provide a scrollbar* if there are more items in the list than the number of visible rows. In this case, a **JScrollPane** object is used to provide the scrolling capability. Line 36 adds a new instance of class JScrollPane to the JFrame. The JScrollPane constructor receives as its argument the JComponent that needs scrolling functionality (in this case, colorJList). Notice in the screen captures that a scrollbar created by the JScrollPane appears at the right side of the JList. By default, the scrollbar appears only when the number of items in the JList exceeds the number of visible items.

Lines 38–49 use JList method **addListSelectionListener** to register an object that implements **ListSelectionListener** (package javax.swing.event) as the listener for the JList's selection events. Once again, we use an instance of an anonymous inner class (lines 39–48) as the listener. In this example, when the user makes a selection from colorJList, method **valueChanged** (line 42–47) should change the background color of the List-Frame to the selected color. This is accomplished in lines 45–46. Note the use of JFrame method **getContentPane** in line 45. Each JFrame actually consists of *three layers*—the *background*, the *content pane* and the *glass pane*. The content pane appears in front of the background and is where the GUI components in the JFrame are displayed. The glass pane is used to display tool tips and other items that should appear in front of the GUI components on the screen. The content pane completely hides the background of the JFrame; thus, to change the background color behind the GUI components, you must change the content pane's background color. Method getContentPane returns a reference to the

JFrame's content pane (an object of class Container). In line 45, we then use that reference to call method **setBackground**, which sets the content pane's background color to an element in the colors array. The color is selected from the array by using the selected item's index. JList method **getSelectedIndex** returns the selected item's index. As with arrays and JComboBoxes, JList indexing is zero based.

12.13 Multiple-Selection Lists

A **multiple-selection list** enables the user to select many items from a JList (see the output of Fig. 12.26). A SINGLE_INTERVAL_SELECTION list allows selecting a contiguous range of items. To do so, click the first item, then press and hold the *Shift* key while clicking the last item in the range. A MULTIPLE_INTERVAL_SELECTION list (the default) allows continuous range selection as described for a SINGLE_INTERVAL_SELECTION list. Such a list also allows miscellaneous items to be selected by pressing and holding the *Ctrl* key while clicking each item to select. To *deselect* an item, press and hold the *Ctrl* key while clicking the item a second time.

The application of Figs. 12.25–12.26 uses multiple-selection lists to copy items from one JList to another. One list is a MULTIPLE_INTERVAL_SELECTION list and the other is a SINGLE_INTERVAL_SELECTION list. When you execute the application, try using the selection techniques described previously to select items in both lists.

```java
1   // Fig. 12.25: MultipleSelectionFrame.java
2   // JList that allows multiple selections.
3   import java.awt.FlowLayout;
4   import java.awt.event.ActionListener;
5   import java.awt.event.ActionEvent;
6   import javax.swing.JFrame;
7   import javax.swing.JList;
8   import javax.swing.JButton;
9   import javax.swing.JScrollPane;
10  import javax.swing.ListSelectionModel;
11
12  public class MultipleSelectionFrame extends JFrame
13  {
14     private final JList<String> colorJList; // list to hold color names
15     private final JList<String> copyJList; // list to hold copied names
16     private JButton copyJButton; // button to copy selected names
17     private static final String[] colorNames = {"Black", "Blue", "Cyan",
18        "Dark Gray", "Gray", "Green", "Light Gray", "Magenta", "Orange",
19        "Pink", "Red", "White", "Yellow"};
20
21     // MultipleSelectionFrame constructor
22     public MultipleSelectionFrame()
23     {
24        super("Multiple Selection Lists");
25        setLayout(new FlowLayout());
26
27        colorJList = new JList<String>(colorNames); // list of color names
28        colorJList.setVisibleRowCount(5); // show five rows
```

Fig. 12.25 | JList that allows multiple selections. (Part 1 of 2.)

```
29        colorJList.setSelectionMode(
30           ListSelectionModel.MULTIPLE_INTERVAL_SELECTION);
31        add(new JScrollPane(colorJList)); // add list with scrollpane
32
33        copyJButton = new JButton("Copy >>>");
34        copyJButton.addActionListener(
35           new ActionListener() // anonymous inner class
36           {
37              // handle button event
38              @Override
39              public void actionPerformed(ActionEvent event)
40              {
41                 // place selected values in copyJList
42                 copyJList.setListData(
43                    colorJList.getSelectedValuesList().toArray(
44                       new String[0]));
45              }
46           }
47        );
48
49        add(copyJButton); // add copy button to JFrame
50
51        copyJList = new JList<String>(); // list to hold copied color names
52        copyJList.setVisibleRowCount(5); // show 5 rows
53        copyJList.setFixedCellWidth(100); // set width
54        copyJList.setFixedCellHeight(15); // set height
55        copyJList.setSelectionMode(
56           ListSelectionModel.SINGLE_INTERVAL_SELECTION);
57        add(new JScrollPane(copyJList)); // add list with scrollpane
58     }
59  } // end class MultipleSelectionFrame
```

Fig. 12.25 | JList that allows multiple selections. (Part 2 of 2.)

```
1   // Fig. 12.26: MultipleSelectionTest.java
2   // Testing MultipleSelectionFrame.
3   import javax.swing.JFrame;
4
5   public class MultipleSelectionTest
6   {
7      public static void main(String[] args)
8      {
9         MultipleSelectionFrame multipleSelectionFrame =
10           new MultipleSelectionFrame();
11        multipleSelectionFrame.setDefaultCloseOperation(
12           JFrame.EXIT_ON_CLOSE);
13        multipleSelectionFrame.setSize(350, 150);
14        multipleSelectionFrame.setVisible(true);
15     }
16  } // end class MultipleSelectionTest
```

Fig. 12.26 | Testing MultipleSelectionFrame. (Part 1 of 2.)

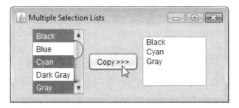

Fig. 12.26 | Testing `MultipleSelectionFrame`. (Part 2 of 2.)

Line 27 of Fig. 12.25 creates `JList` `colorJList` and initializes it with the `String`s in the array `colorNames`. Line 28 sets the number of visible rows in `colorJList` to 5. Lines 29–30 specify that `colorJList` is a `MULTIPLE_INTERVAL_SELECTION` list. Line 31 adds a new `JScrollPane` containing `colorJList` to the `JFrame`. Lines 51–57 perform similar tasks for `copyJList`, which is declared as a `SINGLE_INTERVAL_SELECTION` list. If a `JList` does not contain items, it will not diplay in a `FlowLayout`. For this reason, lines 53–54 use `JList` methods **`setFixedCellWidth`** and **`setFixedCellHeight`** to set `copyJList`'s width to 100 pixels and the height of each item in the `JList` to 15 pixels, respectively.

Normally, an event generated by another GUI component (known as an **external event**) specifies when the multiple selections in a `JList` should be processed. In this example, the user clicks the `JButton` called `copyJButton` to trigger the event that copies the selected items in `colorJList` to `copyJList`.

Lines 34–47 declare, create and register an `ActionListener` for the `copyJButton`. When the user clicks `copyJButton`, method `actionPerformed` (lines 38–45) uses `JList` method **`setListData`** to set the items displayed in `copyJList`. Lines 43–44 call `colorJList`'s method **`getSelectedValuesList`**, which returns a `List<String>` (because the `JList` was created as a `JList<String>`) representing the selected items in `colorJList`. We call the `List<String>`'s `toArray` method to convert this into an array of `String`s that can be passed as the argument to `copyJList`'s `setListData` method. `List` method `toArray` receives as its argument an array representing the type of array that the method will return. You'll learn more about `List` and `toArray` in Chapter 16.

You might be wondering why `copyJList` can be used in line 42 even though the application does not create the object to which it refers until line 49. Remember that method `actionPerformed` (lines 38–45) does not execute until the user presses the copyJButton, which cannot occur until after the constructor completes execution and the application displays the GUI. At that point in the application's execution, `copyJList` is already initialized with a new `JList` object.

12.14 Mouse Event Handling

This section presents the **`MouseListener`** and **`MouseMotionListener`** event-listener interfaces for handling **mouse events**. Mouse events can be processed for any GUI component that derives from `java.awt.Component`. The methods of interfaces `MouseListener` and `MouseMotionListener` are summarized in Figure 12.27. Package `javax.swing.event` contains interface **`MouseInputListener`**, which extends interfaces `MouseListener` and `MouseMotionListener` to create a single interface containing all the `MouseListener` and `MouseMotionListener` methods. The `MouseListener` and `MouseMotionListener` methods are called when the mouse interacts with a Component if appropriate event-listener objects are registered for that Component.

Each of the mouse event-handling methods receives as an argument a **MouseEvent** object that contains information about the mouse event that occurred, including the *x*- and *y*-coordinates of its location. These coordinates are measured from the *upper-left corner* of the GUI component on which the event occurred. The *x*-coordinates start at 0 and *increase from left to right*. The *y*-coordinates start at 0 and *increase from top to bottom*. The methods and constants of class **InputEvent** (MouseEvent's superclass) enable you to determine which mouse button the user clicked.

MouseListener and MouseMotionListener interface methods

Methods of interface MouseListener

`public void mousePressed(MouseEvent event)`

  Called when a mouse button is *pressed* while the mouse cursor is on a component.

`public void mouseClicked(MouseEvent event)`

  Called when a mouse button is *pressed and released* while the mouse cursor remains stationary on a component. Always preceded by a call to mousePressed and mouseReleased.

`public void mouseReleased(MouseEvent event)`

  Called when a mouse button is *released after being pressed*. Always preceded by a call to mousePressed and one or more calls to mouseDragged.

`public void mouseEntered(MouseEvent event)`

  Called when the mouse cursor *enters* the bounds of a component.

`public void mouseExited(MouseEvent event)`

  Called when the mouse cursor *leaves* the bounds of a component.

Methods of interface MouseMotionListener

`public void mouseDragged(MouseEvent event)`

  Called when the mouse button is *pressed* while the mouse cursor is on a component and the mouse is *moved* while the mouse button *remains pressed*. Always preceded by a call to mousePressed. All drag events are sent to the component on which the user began to drag the mouse.

`public void mouseMoved(MouseEvent event)`

  Called when the mouse is *moved* (with no mouse buttons pressed) when the mouse cursor is on a component. All move events are sent to the component over which the mouse is currently positioned.

Fig. 12.27 | MouseListener and MouseMotionListener interface methods.

Software Engineering Observation 12.5

Calls to mouseDragged are sent to the MouseMotionListener for the Component on which the drag started. Similarly, the mouseReleased call at the end of a drag operation is sent to the MouseListener for the Component on which the drag operation started.

Java also provides interface **MouseWheelListener** to enable applications to respond to the *rotation of a mouse wheel*. This interface declares method **mouseWheelMoved**, which receives a **MouseWheelEvent** as its argument. Class MouseWheelEvent (a subclass of Mouse-Event) contains methods that enable the event handler to obtain information about the amount of wheel rotation.

Tracking Mouse Events on a *JPanel*

The MouseTracker application (Figs. 12.28–12.29) demonstrates the MouseListener and MouseMotionListener interface methods. The event-handler class (lines 36–97 of Fig. 12.28) implements both interfaces. You *must* declare all seven methods from these two interfaces when your class implements them both. Each mouse event in this example displays a String in the JLabel called statusBar that is attached to the bottom of the window.

```
 1    // Fig. 12.28: MouseTrackerFrame.java
 2    // Mouse event handling.
 3    import java.awt.Color;
 4    import java.awt.BorderLayout;
 5    import java.awt.event.MouseListener;
 6    import java.awt.event.MouseMotionListener;
 7    import java.awt.event.MouseEvent;
 8    import javax.swing.JFrame;
 9    import javax.swing.JLabel;
10    import javax.swing.JPanel;
11
12    public class MouseTrackerFrame extends JFrame
13    {
14       private final JPanel mousePanel; // panel in which mouse events occur
15       private final JLabel statusBar; // displays event information
16
17       // MouseTrackerFrame constructor sets up GUI and
18       // registers mouse event handlers
19       public MouseTrackerFrame()
20       {
21          super("Demonstrating Mouse Events");
22
23          mousePanel = new JPanel();
24          mousePanel.setBackground(Color.WHITE);
25          add(mousePanel, BorderLayout.CENTER); // add panel to JFrame
26
27          statusBar = new JLabel("Mouse outside JPanel");
28          add(statusBar, BorderLayout.SOUTH); // add label to JFrame
29
30          // create and register listener for mouse and mouse motion events
31          MouseHandler handler = new MouseHandler();
32          mousePanel.addMouseListener(handler);
33          mousePanel.addMouseMotionListener(handler);
34       }
35
```

Fig. 12.28 | Mouse event handling. (Part 1 of 3.)

```
36    private class MouseHandler implements MouseListener,
37       MouseMotionListener
38    {
39       // MouseListener event handlers
40       // handle event when mouse released immediately after press
41       @Override
42       public void mouseClicked(MouseEvent event)'
43       {
44          statusBar.setText(String.format("Clicked at [%d, %d]",
45             event.getX(), event.getY()));
46       }
47
48       // handle event when mouse pressed
49       @Override
50       public void mousePressed(MouseEvent event)
51       {
52          statusBar.setText(String.format("Pressed at [%d, %d]",
53             event.getX(), event.getY()));
54       }
55
56       // handle event when mouse released
57       @Override
58       public void mouseReleased(MouseEvent event)
59       {
60          statusBar.setText(String.format("Released at [%d, %d]",
61             event.getX(), event.getY()));
62       }
63
64       // handle event when mouse enters area
65       @Override
66       public void mouseEntered(MouseEvent event)
67       {
68          statusBar.setText(String.format("Mouse entered at [%d, %d]",
69             event.getX(), event.getY()));
70          mousePanel.setBackground(Color.GREEN);
71       }
72
73       // handle event when mouse exits area
74       @Override
75       public void mouseExited(MouseEvent event)
76       {
77          statusBar.setText("Mouse outside JPanel");
78          mousePanel.setBackground(Color.WHITE);
79       }
80
81       // MouseMotionListener event handlers
82       // handle event when user drags mouse with button pressed
83       @Override
84       public void mouseDragged(MouseEvent event)
85       {
86          statusBar.setText(String.format("Dragged at [%d, %d]",
87             event.getX(), event.getY()));
88       }
```

Fig. 12.28 | Mouse event handling. (Part 2 of 3.)

```
89
90          // handle event when user moves mouse
91          @Override
92          public void mouseMoved(MouseEvent event)
93          {
94             statusBar.setText(String.format("Moved at [%d, %d]",
95                event.getX(), event.getY()));
96          }
97       } // end inner class MouseHandler
98    } // end class MouseTrackerFrame
```

Fig. 12.28 | Mouse event handling. (Part 3 of 3.)

```
 1    // Fig. 12.29: MouseTrackerFrame.java
 2    // Testing MouseTrackerFrame.
 3    import javax.swing.JFrame;
 4
 5    public class MouseTracker
 6    {
 7       public static void main(String[] args)
 8       {
 9          MouseTrackerFrame mouseTrackerFrame = new MouseTrackerFrame();
10          mouseTrackerFrame.setDefaultCloseOperation(JFrame.EXIT_ON_CLOSE);
11          mouseTrackerFrame.setSize(300, 100);
12          mouseTrackerFrame.setVisible(true);
13       }
14    } // end class MouseTracker
```

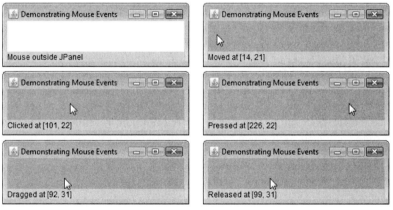

Fig. 12.29 | Testing MouseTrackerFrame.

Line 23 creates JPanel mousePanel. This JPanel's mouse events are tracked by the app. Line 24 sets mousePanel's background color to white. When the user moves the mouse into the mousePanel, the application will change mousePanel's background color to green. When the user moves the mouse out of the mousePanel, the application will change the background color back to white. Line 25 attaches mousePanel to the JFrame. As you've learned, you typically must specify the layout of the GUI components in a JFrame. In that section, we introduced the layout manager FlowLayout. Here we use the default layout of a JFrame's content pane—**BorderLayout**, which arranges component **NORTH**, **SOUTH**, **EAST**, **WEST** and **CENTER** regions. NORTH corresponds to the container's top. This example uses the CENTER and SOUTH regions. Line 25 uses a two-argument version of method add to place mousePanel in the CENTER region. The BorderLayout automatically sizes the component in the CENTER to use all the space in the JFrame that is not occupied by components in the other regions. Section 12.18.2 discusses BorderLayout in more detail.

Lines 27–28 in the constructor declare JLabel statusBar and attach it to the JFrame's SOUTH region. This JLabel occupies the width of the JFrame. The region's height is determined by the JLabel.

Line 31 creates an instance of inner class MouseHandler (lines 36–97) called handler that responds to mouse events. Lines 32–33 register handler as the listener for mouse-Panel's mouse events. Methods **addMouseListener** and **addMouseMotionListener** are inherited indirectly from class Component and can be used to register MouseListeners and MouseMotionListeners, respectively. A MouseHandler object *is a* MouseListener and *is a* MouseMotionListener because the class implements *both* interfaces. We chose to implement both interfaces here to demonstrate a class that implements more than one interface, but we could have implemented interface MouseInputListener instead.

When the mouse enters and exits mousePanel's area, methods mouseEntered (lines 65–71) and mouseExited (lines 74–79) are called, respectively. Method mouseEntered displays a message in the statusBar indicating that the mouse entered the JPanel and changes the background color to green. Method mouseExited displays a message in the statusBar indicating that the mouse is outside the JPanel (see the first sample output window) and changes the background color to white.

The other five events display a string in the statusBar that includes the event and the coordinates at which it occurred. MouseEvent methods **getX** and **getY** return the *x*- and *y*-coordinates, respectively, of the mouse at the time the event occurred.

12.15 Adapter Classes

Many event-listener interfaces, such as MouseListener and MouseMotionListener, contain multiple methods. It's not always desirable to declare every method in an event-listener interface. For instance, an application may need only the mouseClicked handler from MouseListener or the mouseDragged handler from MouseMotionListener. Interface WindowListener specifies seven window event-handling methods. For many of the listener interfaces that have multiple methods, packages java.awt.event and javax.swing.event provide event-listener adapter classes. An **adapter class** implements an interface and provides a default implementation (with an empty method body) of each method in the interface. Figure 12.30 shows several java.awt.event adapter classes and the interfaces they implement. You can extend an adapter class to inherit the default implementation of every method and subsequently override only the method(s) you need for event handling.

Software Engineering Observation 12.6

When a class implements an interface, the class has an is-a *relationship with that interface. All direct and indirect subclasses of that class inherit this interface. Thus, an object of a class that extends an event-adapter class is an object of the corresponding event-listener type (e.g., an object of a subclass of MouseAdapter is a MouseListener).*

Event-adapter class in `java.awt.event`	Implements interface
ComponentAdapter	ComponentListener
ContainerAdapter	ContainerListener
FocusAdapter	FocusListener
KeyAdapter	KeyListener
MouseAdapter	MouseListener
MouseMotionAdapter	MouseMotionListener
WindowAdapter	WindowListener

Fig. 12.30 | Event-adapter classes and the interfaces they implement.

Extending MouseAdapter

The application of Figs. 12.31–12.32 demonstrates how to determine the number of mouse clicks (i.e., the click count) and how to distinguish between the different mouse buttons. The event listener in this application is an object of inner class MouseClickHandler (Fig. 12.31, lines 25–46) that extends MouseAdapter, so we can declare just the mouseClicked method we need in this example.

```
 1   // Fig. 12.31: MouseDetailsFrame.java
 2   // Demonstrating mouse clicks and distinguishing between mouse buttons.
 3   import java.awt.BorderLayout;
 4   import java.awt.event.MouseAdapter;
 5   import java.awt.event.MouseEvent;
 6   import javax.swing.JFrame;
 7   import javax.swing.JLabel;
 8
 9   public class MouseDetailsFrame extends JFrame
10   {
11      private String details; // String displayed in the statusBar
12      private final JLabel statusBar; // JLabel at bottom of window
13
14      // constructor sets title bar String and register mouse listener
15      public MouseDetailsFrame()
16      {
17         super("Mouse clicks and buttons");
18
19         statusBar = new JLabel("Click the mouse");
20         add(statusBar, BorderLayout.SOUTH);
21         addMouseListener(new MouseClickHandler()); // add handler
22      }
23
24      // inner class to handle mouse events
25      private class MouseClickHandler extends MouseAdapter
26      {
27         // handle mouse-click event and determine which button was pressed
28         @Override
29         public void mouseClicked(MouseEvent event)
30         {
```

Fig. 12.31 | Demonstrating mouse clicks and distinguishing between mouse buttons. (Part 1 of 2.)

```
31              int xPos = event.getX(); // get x-position of mouse
32              int yPos = event.getY(); // get y-position of mouse
33
34              details = String.format("Clicked %d time(s)",
35                 event.getClickCount());
36
37              if (event.isMetaDown()) // right mouse button
38                 details += " with right mouse button";
39              else if (event.isAltDown()) // middle mouse button
40                 details += " with center mouse button";
41              else // left mouse button
42                 details += " with left mouse button";
43
44              statusBar.setText(details); // display message in statusBar
45           }
46        }
47     } // end class MouseDetailsFrame
```

Fig. 12.31 | Demonstrating mouse clicks and distinguishing between mouse buttons. (Part 2 of 2.)

```
 1    // Fig. 12.32: MouseDetails.java
 2    // Testing MouseDetailsFrame.
 3    import javax.swing.JFrame;
 4
 5    public class MouseDetails
 6    {
 7       public static void main(String[] args)
 8       {
 9          MouseDetailsFrame mouseDetailsFrame = new MouseDetailsFrame();
10          mouseDetailsFrame.setDefaultCloseOperation(JFrame.EXIT_ON_CLOSE);
11          mouseDetailsFrame.setSize(400, 150);
12          mouseDetailsFrame.setVisible(true);
13       }
14    } // end class MouseDetails
```

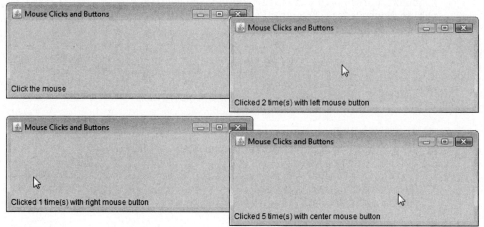

Fig. 12.32 | Testing MouseDetailsFrame.

Common Programming Error 12.3

If you extend an adapter class and misspell the name of the method you're overriding, and you do not declare the method with @Override, your method simply becomes another method in the class. This is a logic error that is difficult to detect, since the program will call the empty version of the method inherited from the adapter class.

A user of a Java application may be on a system with a one-, two- or three-button mouse. Class MouseEvent inherits several methods from class InputEvent that can distinguish among mouse buttons on a multibutton mouse or can mimic a multibutton mouse with a combined keystroke and mouse-button click. Figure 12.33 shows the InputEvent methods used to distinguish among mouse-button clicks. Java assumes that every mouse contains a left mouse button. Thus, it's simple to test for a left-mouse-button click. However, users with a one- or two-button mouse must use a combination of keystrokes and mouse-button clicks at the same time to simulate the missing buttons on the mouse. In the case of a one- or two-button mouse, a Java application assumes that the center mouse button is clicked if the user holds down the *Alt* key and clicks the left mouse button on a two-button mouse or the only mouse button on a one-button mouse. In the case of a one-button mouse, a Java application assumes that the right mouse button is clicked if the user holds down the *Meta* key (sometimes called the *Command* key or the "Apple" key on a Mac) and clicks the mouse button.

InputEvent method	Description
isMetaDown()	Returns true when the user clicks the *right mouse button* on a mouse with two or three buttons. To simulate a right-mouse-button click on a one-button mouse, the user can hold down the *Meta* key on the keyboard and click the mouse button.
isAltDown()	Returns true when the user clicks the *middle mouse button* on a mouse with three buttons. To simulate a middle-mouse-button click on a one- or two-button mouse, the user can press the *Alt* key and click the only or left mouse button, respectively.

Fig. 12.33 | InputEvent methods that help determine whether the right or center mouse button was clicked.

Line 21 of Fig. 12.31 registers a MouseListener for the MouseDetailsFrame. The event listener is an object of class MouseClickHandler, which extends MouseAdapter. This enables us to declare only method mouseClicked (lines 28–45). This method first captures the coordinates where the event occurred and stores them in local variables xPos and yPos (lines 31–32). Lines 34–35 create a String called details containing the number of consecutive mouse clicks, which is returned by MouseEvent method **getClickCount** at line 35. Lines 37–42 use methods **isMetaDown** and **isAltDown** to determine which mouse button the user clicked and append an appropriate String to details in each case. The resulting String is displayed in the statusBar. Class MouseDetails (Fig. 12.32) contains the main method that executes the application. Try clicking with each of your mouse's buttons repeatedly to see the click count increment.

12.16 JPanel Subclass for Drawing with the Mouse

Section 12.14 showed how to track mouse events in a JPanel. In this section, we use a JPanel as a **dedicated drawing area** in which the user can draw by dragging the mouse. In addition, this section demonstrates an event listener that extends an adapter class.

Method paintComponent

Lightweight Swing components that extend class JComponent (such as JPanel) contain method **paintComponent**, which is called when a lightweight Swing component is displayed. By overriding this method, you can specify how to draw shapes using Java's graphics capabilities. When customizing a JPanel for use as a dedicated drawing area, the subclass should override method paintComponent and call the superclass version of paint-Component as the first statement in the body of the overridden method to ensure that the component displays correctly. The reason is that subclasses of JComponent support **transparency**. To display a component correctly, the program must determine whether the component is transparent. The code that determines this is in superclass JComponent's paintComponent implementation. When a component is transparent, paintComponent will not clear its background when the program displays the component. When a component is **opaque**, paintComponent clears the component's background before the component is displayed. The transparency of a Swing lightweight component can be set with method **setOpaque** (a false argument indicates that the component is transparent).

Error-Prevention Tip 12.1

In a JComponent subclass's paintComponent method, the first statement should always call the superclass's paintComponent method to ensure that an object of the subclass displays correctly.

Common Programming Error 12.4

If an overridden paintComponent method does not call the superclass's version, the subclass component may not display properly. If an overridden paintComponent method calls the superclass's version after other drawing is performed, the drawing will be erased.

Defining the Custom Drawing Area

The Painter application of Figs. 12.34–12.35 demonstrates a customized subclass of JPanel that's used to create a dedicated drawing area. The application uses the mouseDragged event handler to create a simple drawing application. The user can draw pictures by dragging the mouse on the JPanel. This example does not use method mouseMoved, so our *event-listener class* (the *anonymous inner class* at lines 20–29 of Fig. 12.34) extends Mouse-MotionAdapter. Since this class already declares both mouseMoved and mouseDragged, we can simply override mouseDragged to provide the event handling this application requires.

```
1   // Fig. 12.34: PaintPanel.java
2   // Adapter class used to implement event handlers.
3   import java.awt.Point;
4   import java.awt.Graphics;
5   import java.awt.event.MouseEvent;
```

Fig. 12.34 | Adapter class used to implement event handlers. (Part 1 of 2.)

```
 6    import java.awt.event.MouseMotionAdapter;
 7    import java.util.ArrayList;
 8    import javax.swing.JPanel;
 9
10    public class PaintPanel extends JPanel
11    {
12       // list of Point references
13       private final ArrayList<Point> points = new ArrayList<>();
14
15       // set up GUI and register mouse event handler
16       public PaintPanel()
17       {
18          // handle frame mouse motion event
19          addMouseMotionListener(
20             new MouseMotionAdapter() // anonymous inner class
21             {
22                // store drag coordinates and repaint
23                @Override
24                public void mouseDragged(MouseEvent event)
25                {
26                   points.add(event.getPoint());
27                   repaint(); // repaint JFrame
28                }
29             }
30          );
31       }
32
33       // draw ovals in a 4-by-4 bounding box at specified locations on window
34       @Override
35       public void paintComponent(Graphics g)
36       {
37          super.paintComponent(g); // clears drawing area
38
39          // draw all points
40          for (Point point : points)
41             g.fillOval(point.x, point.y, 4, 4);
42       }
43    } // end class PaintPanel
```

Fig. 12.34 | Adapter class used to implement event handlers. (Part 2 of 2.)

Class PaintPanel (Fig. 12.34) extends JPanel to create the dedicated drawing area. Class **Point** (package java.awt) represents an *x-y* coordinate. We use objects of this class to store the coordinates of each mouse drag event. Class **Graphics** is used to draw. In this example, we use an ArrayList of Points (line 13) to store the location at which each mouse drag event occurs. As you'll see, method paintComponent uses these Points to draw.

Lines 19–30 register a MouseMotionListener to listen for the PaintPanel's mouse motion events. Lines 20–29 create an object of an anonymous inner class that extends the adapter class MouseMotionAdapter. Recall that MouseMotionAdapter implements Mouse-MotionListener, so the *anonymous inner class* object is a MouseMotionListener. The anonymous inner class inherits default mouseMoved and mouseDragged implementations, so it already implements all the interface's methods. However, the default implementations do nothing when they're called. So, we override method `mouseDragged` at lines 23–28 to capture the coordinates of a mouse drag event and store them as a `Point` object. Line 26 invokes the `MouseEvent`'s **getPoint** method to obtain the `Point` where the event occurred and stores it in the `ArrayList`. Line 27 calls method **repaint** (inherited indirectly from class `Component`) to indicate that the `PaintPanel` should be refreshed on the screen as soon as possible with a call to the `PaintPanel`'s `paintComponent` method.

Method `paintComponent` (lines 34–42), which receives a `Graphics` parameter, is called automatically any time the `PaintPanel` needs to be displayed on the screen—such as when the GUI is first displayed—or refreshed on the screen—such as when method `repaint` is called or when the GUI component has been *hidden* by another window on the screen and subsequently becomes visible again.

Look-and-Feel Observation 12.13

Calling repaint *for a Swing GUI component indicates that the component should be refreshed on the screen as soon as possible. The component's background is cleared only if the component is opaque.* JComponent *method* setOpaque *can be passed a* boolean *argument indicating whether the component is opaque (*true*) or transparent (*false*).*

Line 37 invokes the superclass version of `paintComponent` to clear the `PaintPanel`'s background (`JPanel`s are opaque by default). Lines 40–41 draw an oval at the location specified by each `Point` in the `ArrayList`. `Graphics` method **fillOval** draws a solid oval. The method's four parameters represent a rectangular area (called the *bounding box*) in which the oval is displayed. The first two parameters are the upper-left *x*-coordinate and the upper-left *y*-coordinate of the rectangular area. The last two coordinates represent the rectangular area's width and height. Method `fillOval` draws the oval so it touches the middle of each side of the rectangular area. In line 41, the first two arguments are specified by using class `Point`'s two `public` instance variables—`x` and `y`. You'll learn more `Graphics` features in Chapter 13.

Look-and-Feel Observation 12.14

Drawing on any GUI component is performed with coordinates that are measured from the upper-left corner (0, 0) of that GUI component, not the upper-left corner of the screen.

Using the Custom *JPanel* in an Application

Class `Painter` (Fig. 12.35) contains the `main` method that executes this application. Line 14 creates a `PaintPanel` object on which the user can drag the mouse to draw. Line 15 attaches the `PaintPanel` to the `JFrame`.

```
1   // Fig. 12.35: Painter.java
2   // Testing PaintPanel.
3   import java.awt.BorderLayout;
4   import javax.swing.JFrame;
5   import javax.swing.JLabel;
6
7   public class Painter
8   {
```

Fig. 12.35 | Testing `PaintPanel`. (Part 1 of 2.)

```
9      public static void main(String[] args)
10     {
11        // create JFrame
12        JFrame application = new JFrame("A simple paint program");
13
14        PaintPanel paintPanel = new PaintPanel();
15        application.add(paintPanel, BorderLayout.CENTER);
16
17        // create a label and place it in SOUTH of BorderLayout
18        application.add(new JLabel("Drag the mouse to draw"),
19           BorderLayout.SOUTH);
20
21        application.setDefaultCloseOperation(JFrame.EXIT_ON_CLOSE);
22        application.setSize(400, 200);
23        application.setVisible(true);
24     }
25  } // end class Painter
```

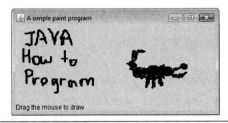

Fig. 12.35 | Testing `PaintPanel`. (Part 2 of 2.)

12.17 Key Event Handling

This section presents the `KeyListener` interface for handling **key events**. Key events are generated when keys on the keyboard are pressed and released. A class that implements `KeyListener` must provide declarations for methods **keyPressed**, **keyReleased** and **keyTyped**, each of which receives a `KeyEvent` as its argument. Class `KeyEvent` is a subclass of `InputEvent`. Method `keyPressed` is called in response to pressing any key. Method `keyTyped` is called in response to pressing any key that is not an **action key**. (The action keys are any arrow key, *Home*, *End*, *Page Up*, *Page Down*, any function key, etc.) Method `keyReleased` is called when the key is released after any `keyPressed` or `keyTyped` event.

The application of Figs. 12.36–12.37 demonstrates the `KeyListener` methods. Class `KeyDemoFrame` implements the `KeyListener` interface, so all three methods are declared in the application. The constructor (Fig. 12.36, lines 17–28) registers the application to handle its own key events by using method **addKeyListener** at line 27. Method addKey-Listener is declared in class `Component`, so every subclass of `Component` can notify Key-Listener objects of key events for that `Component`.

```
1  // Fig. 12.36: KeyDemoFrame.java
2  // Key event handling.
3  import java.awt.Color;
```

Fig. 12.36 | Key event handling. (Part 1 of 3.)

```java
 4    import java.awt.event.KeyListener;
 5    import java.awt.event.KeyEvent;
 6    import javax.swing.JFrame;
 7    import javax.swing.JTextArea;
 8
 9    public class KeyDemoFrame extends JFrame implements KeyListener
10    {
11       private final String line1 = ""; // first line of text area
12       private final String line2 = ""; // second line of text area
13       private final String line3 = ""; // third line of text area
14       private final JTextArea textArea; // text area to display output
15
16       // KeyDemoFrame constructor
17       public KeyDemoFrame()
18       {
19          super("Demonstrating Keystroke Events");
20
21          textArea = new JTextArea(10, 15); // set up JTextArea
22          textArea.setText("Press any key on the keyboard...");
23          textArea.setEnabled(false);
24          textArea.setDisabledTextColor(Color.BLACK);
25          add(textArea); // add text area to JFrame
26
27          addKeyListener(this); // allow frame to process key events
28       }
29
30       // handle press of any key
31       @Override
32       public void keyPressed(KeyEvent event)
33       {
34          line1 = String.format("Key pressed: %s",
35             KeyEvent.getKeyText(event.getKeyCode())); // show pressed key
36          setLines2and3(event); // set output lines two and three
37       }
38
39       // handle release of any key
40       @Override
41       public void keyReleased(KeyEvent event)
42       {
43          line1 = String.format("Key released: %s",
44             KeyEvent.getKeyText(event.getKeyCode())); // show released key
45          setLines2and3(event); // set output lines two and three
46       }
47
48       // handle press of an action key
49       @Override
50       public void keyTyped(KeyEvent event)
51       {
52          line1 = String.format("Key typed: %s", event.getKeyChar());
53          setLines2and3(event); // set output lines two and three
54       }
55
```

Fig. 12.36 | Key event handling. (Part 2 of 3.)

```
56      // set second and third lines of output
57      private void setLines2and3(KeyEvent event)
58      {
59         line2 = String.format("This key is %san action key",
60            (event.isActionKey() ? "" : "not "));
61
62         String temp = KeyEvent.getKeyModifiersText(event.getModifiers());
63
64         line3 = String.format("Modifier keys pressed: %s",
65            (temp.equals("") ? "none" : temp)); // output modifiers
66
67         textArea.setText(String.format("%s\n%s\n%s\n",
68            line1, line2, line3)); // output three lines of text
69      }
70   } // end class KeyDemoFrame
```

Fig. 12.36 | Key event handling. (Part 3 of 3.)

```
1    // Fig. 12.37: KeyDemo.java
2    // Testing KeyDemoFrame.
3    import javax.swing.JFrame;
4
5    public class KeyDemo
6    {
7       public static void main(String[] args)
8       {
9          KeyDemoFrame keyDemoFrame = new KeyDemoFrame();
10         keyDemoFrame.setDefaultCloseOperation(JFrame.EXIT_ON_CLOSE);
11         keyDemoFrame.setSize(350, 100);
12         keyDemoFrame.setVisible(true);
13      }
14   } // end class KeyDemo
```

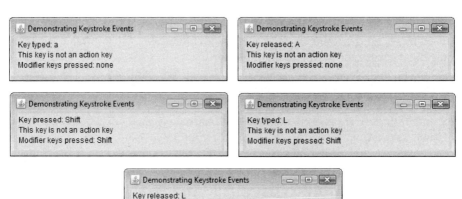

Fig. 12.37 | Testing KeyDemoFrame. (Part 1 of 2.)

Fig. 12.37 | Testing `KeyDemoFrame`. (Part 2 of 2.)

At line 25, the constructor adds the `JTextArea` `textArea` (where the application's output is displayed) to the `JFrame`. A `JTextArea` is a *multiline area* in which you can display text. (We discuss `JTextArea`s in more detail in Section 12.20.) Notice in the screen captures that `textArea` occupies the *entire window*. This is due to the `JFrame`'s default `BorderLayout` (discussed in Section 12.18.2 and demonstrated in Fig. 12.41). When a single `Component` is added to a `BorderLayout`, the `Component` occupies the *entire* Container. Line 23 disables the `JTextArea` so the user cannot type in it. This causes the text in the `JTextArea` to become gray. Line 24 uses method **`setDisabledTextColor`** to change the text color in the `JTextArea` to black for readability.

Methods `keyPressed` (lines 31–37) and `keyReleased` (lines 40–46) use `KeyEvent` method **`getKeyCode`** to get the **virtual key code** of the pressed key. Class `KeyEvent` contains virtual key-code constants that represent every key on the keyboard. These constants can be compared with `getKeyCode`'s return value to test for individual keys on the keyboard. The value returned by `getKeyCode` is passed to `static` `KeyEvent` method **`getKeyText`**, which returns a string containing the name of the key that was pressed. For a complete list of virtual key constants, see the online documentation for class `KeyEvent` (package `java.awt.event`). Method `keyTyped` (lines 49–54) uses `KeyEvent` method **`getKeyChar`** (which returns a char) to get the Unicode value of the character typed.

All three event-handling methods finish by calling method `setLines2and3` (lines 57–69) and passing it the `KeyEvent` object. This method uses `KeyEvent` method **`isActionKey`** (line 60) to determine whether the key in the event was an action key. Also, `InputEvent` method **`getModifiers`** is called (line 62) to determine whether any modifier keys (such as *Shift*, *Alt* and *Ctrl*) were pressed when the key event occurred. The result of this method is passed to `static` `KeyEvent` method **`getKeyModifiersText`**, which produces a `String` containing the names of the pressed modifier keys.

[*Note:* If you need to test for a specific key on the keyboard, class `KeyEvent` provides a **key constant** for each one. These constants can be used from the key event handlers to determine whether a particular key was pressed. Also, to determine whether the *Alt*, *Ctrl*, *Meta* and *Shift* keys are pressed individually, `InputEvent` methods **`isAltDown`**, **`isControlDown`**, **`isMetaDown`** and **`isShiftDown`** each return a `boolean` indicating whether the particular key was pressed during the key event.]

12.18 Introduction to Layout Managers

Layout managers *arrange* GUI components in a container for presentation purposes. You can use the layout managers for basic layout capabilities instead of determining every GUI component's exact position and size. This functionality enables you to concentrate on the basic look-and-feel and lets the layout managers process most of the layout details. All layout managers implement the interface **`LayoutManager`** (in package `java.awt`). Class Con-

`tainer`'s `setLayout` method takes an object that implements the `LayoutManager` interface as an argument. There are basically three ways for you to arrange components in a GUI:

1. *Absolute positioning:* This provides the greatest level of control over a GUI's appearance. By setting a `Container`'s layout to `null`, you can specify the *absolute position of each GUI component* with respect to the upper-left corner of the `Container` by using `Component` methods `setSize` and `setLocation` or `setBounds`. If you do this, you also must specify each GUI component's size. Programming a GUI with absolute positioning can be tedious, unless you have an integrated development environment (IDE) that can generate the code for you.

2. *Layout managers:* Using layout managers to position elements can be simpler and faster than creating a GUI with absolute positioning, and makes your GUIs more resizable, but you lose some control over the size and the precise positioning of each component.

3. *Visual programming in an IDE:* IDEs provide tools that make it easy to create GUIs. Each IDE typically provides a **GUI design tool** that allows you to drag and drop GUI components from a tool box onto a design area. You can then position, size and align GUI components as you like. The IDE generates the Java code that creates the GUI. In addition, you can typically add event-handling code for a particular component by double-clicking the component. Some design tools also allow you to use the layout managers described in this chapter and in Chapter 22.

Look-and-Feel Observation 12.15

Most Java IDEs provide GUI design tools for visually designing a GUI; the tools then write Java code that creates the GUI. Such tools often provide greater control over the size, position and alignment of GUI components than do the built-in layout managers.

Look-and-Feel Observation 12.16

It's possible to set a `Container`'s layout to `null`, which indicates that no layout manager should be used. In a `Container` without a layout manager, you must position and size the components and take care that, on resize events, all components are repositioned as necessary. A component's resize events can be processed by a `ComponentListener`.

Figure 12.38 summarizes the layout managers presented in this chapter. A couple of additional layout managers are discussed in Chapter 22.

Layout manager	Description
FlowLayout	Default for `javax.swing.JPanel`. Places components *sequentially, left to right*, in the order they were added. It's also possible to specify the order of the components by using the `Container` method `add`, which takes a `Component` and an integer index position as arguments.
BorderLayout	Default for `JFrame`s (and other windows). Arranges the components into five areas: NORTH, SOUTH, EAST, WEST and CENTER.
GridLayout	Arranges the components into rows and columns.

Fig. 12.38 | Layout managers.

12.18.1 FlowLayout

FlowLayout is the *simplest* layout manager. GUI components are placed in a container from left to right in the order in which they're added to the container. When the edge of the container is reached, components continue to display on the next line. Class FlowLayout allows GUI components to be *left aligned*, *centered* (the default) and *right aligned*.

The application of Figs. 12.39–12.40 creates three JButton objects and adds them to the application, using a FlowLayout. The components are center aligned by default. When the user clicks **Left**, the FlowLayout's alignment is changed to left aligned. When the user clicks **Right**, the FlowLayout's alignment is changed to right aligned. When the user clicks **Center**, the FlowLayout's alignment is changed to center aligned. The sample output windows show each alignment. The last sample output shows the centered alignment after the window has been resized to a smaller width so that the button **Right** flows onto a new line.

As seen previously, a container's layout is set with method setLayout of class Container. Line 25 (Fig. 12.39) sets the layout manager to the FlowLayout declared at line 23. Normally, the layout is set before any GUI components are added to a container.

Look-and-Feel Observation 12.17

Each individual container can have only one layout manager, but multiple containers in the same application can each use different layout managers.

```
1   // Fig. 12.39: FlowLayoutFrame.java
2   // FlowLayout allows components to flow over multiple lines.
3   import java.awt.FlowLayout;
4   import java.awt.Container;
5   import java.awt.event.ActionListener;
6   import java.awt.event.ActionEvent;
7   import javax.swing.JFrame;
8   import javax.swing.JButton;
9
10  public class FlowLayoutFrame extends JFrame
11  {
12     private final JButton leftJButton; // button to set alignment left
13     private final JButton centerJButton; // button to set alignment center
14     private final JButton rightJButton; // button to set alignment right
15     private final FlowLayout layout; // layout object
16     private final Container container; // container to set layout
17
18     // set up GUI and register button listeners
19     public FlowLayoutFrame()
20     {
21        super("FlowLayout Demo");
22
23        layout = new FlowLayout();
24        container = getContentPane(); // get container to layout
25        setLayout(layout);
26
27        // set up leftJButton and register listener
28        leftJButton = new JButton("Left");
29        add(leftJButton); // add Left button to frame
```

Fig. 12.39 | FlowLayout allows components to flow over multiple lines. (Part 1 of 2.)

```
30          leftJButton.addActionListener(
31             new ActionListener() // anonymous inner class
32             {
33                // process leftJButton event
34                @Override
35                public void actionPerformed(ActionEvent event)
36                {
37                   layout.setAlignment(FlowLayout.LEFT);
38
39                   // realign attached components
40                   layout.layoutContainer(container);
41                }
42             }
43          );
44
45          // set up centerJButton and register listener
46          centerJButton = new JButton("Center");
47          add(centerJButton); // add Center button to frame
48          centerJButton.addActionListener(
49             new ActionListener() // anonymous inner class
50             {
51                // process centerJButton event
52                @Override
53                public void actionPerformed(ActionEvent event)
54                {
55                   layout.setAlignment(FlowLayout.CENTER);
56
57                   // realign attached components
58                   layout.layoutContainer(container);
59                }
60             }
61          );
62
63          // set up rightJButton and register listener
64          rightJButton = new JButton("Right");
65          add(rightJButton); // add Right button to frame
66          rightJButton.addActionListener(
67             new ActionListener() // anonymous inner class
68             {
69                // process rightJButton event
70                @Override
71                public void actionPerformed(ActionEvent event)
72                {
73                   layout.setAlignment(FlowLayout.RIGHT);
74
75                   // realign attached components
76                   layout.layoutContainer(container);
77                }
78             }
79          );
80       } // end FlowLayoutFrame constructor
81    } // end class FlowLayoutFrame
```

Fig. 12.39 | FlowLayout allows components to flow over multiple lines. (Part 2 of 2.)

```
1   // Fig. 12.40: FlowLayoutDemo.java
2   // Testing FlowLayoutFrame.
3   import javax.swing.JFrame;
4
5   public class FlowLayoutDemo
6   {
7      public static void main(String[] args)
8      {
9         FlowLayoutFrame flowLayoutFrame = new FlowLayoutFrame();
10        flowLayoutFrame.setDefaultCloseOperation(JFrame.EXIT_ON_CLOSE);
11        flowLayoutFrame.setSize(300, 75);
12        flowLayoutFrame.setVisible(true);
13     }
14  } // end class FlowLayoutDemo
```

Fig. 12.40 | Testing `FlowLayoutFrame`.

Each button's event handler is specified with a separate anonymous inner-class object (lines 30–43, 48–61 and 66–79, respectively), and method `actionPerformed` in each case executes two statements. For example, line 37 in the event handler for `leftJButton` uses `FlowLayout` method **setAlignment** to change the alignment for the `FlowLayout` to a left-aligned (**FlowLayout.LEFT**) `FlowLayout`. Line 40 uses `LayoutManager` interface method **layoutContainer** (which is inherited by all layout managers) to specify that the `JFrame` should be rearranged based on the adjusted layout. According to which button was clicked, the `actionPerformed` method for each button sets the `FlowLayout`'s alignment to `Flow-Layout.LEFT` (line 37), **FlowLayout.CENTER** (line 55) or **FlowLayout.RIGHT** (line 73).

12.18.2 BorderLayout

The `BorderLayout` layout manager (the default layout manager for a `JFrame`) arranges components into five regions: NORTH, SOUTH, EAST, WEST and CENTER. NORTH corresponds to the top of the container. Class `BorderLayout` extends `Object` and implements interface **LayoutManager2** (a subinterface of `LayoutManager` that adds several methods for enhanced layout processing).

A `BorderLayout` limits a `Container` to containing *at most five components*—one in each region. The component placed in each region can be a container to which other components are attached. The components placed in the NORTH and SOUTH regions extend horizontally to the sides of the container and are as tall as the components placed in those regions. The EAST and WEST regions expand vertically between the NORTH and SOUTH regions and are as wide as the components placed in those regions. The component placed in the CENTER region *expands to fill all remaining space in the layout* (which is the reason the JTextArea in Fig. 12.37 occupies the entire window). If all five regions are occupied, the entire container's space is covered by GUI components. If the NORTH or SOUTH region is not occupied, the GUI components in the EAST, CENTER and WEST regions expand vertically to fill the remaining space. If the EAST or WEST region is not occupied, the GUI component in the CENTER region *expands horizontally to fill the remaining space*. If the CENTER region is *not* occupied, the area is left *empty*—the other GUI components do *not* expand to fill the remaining space. The application of Figs. 12.41–12.42 demonstrates the BorderLayout layout manager by using five JButtons.

```java
 1   // Fig. 12.41: BorderLayoutFrame.java
 2   // BorderLayout containing five buttons.
 3   import java.awt.BorderLayout;
 4   import java.awt.event.ActionListener;
 5   import java.awt.event.ActionEvent;
 6   import javax.swing.JFrame;
 7   import javax.swing.JButton;
 8
 9   public class BorderLayoutFrame extends JFrame implements ActionListener
10   {
11      private final JButton[] buttons; // array of buttons to hide portions
12      private static final String[] names = {"Hide North", "Hide South",
13         "Hide East", "Hide West", "Hide Center"};
14      private final BorderLayout layout;
15
16      // set up GUI and event handling
17      public BorderLayoutFrame()
18      {
19         super("BorderLayout Demo");
20
21         layout = new BorderLayout(5, 5); // 5 pixel gaps
22         setLayout(layout);
23         buttons = new JButton[names.length];
24
25         // create JButtons and register listeners for them
26         for (int count = 0; count < names.length; count++)
27         {
28            buttons[count] = new JButton(names[count]);
29            buttons[count].addActionListener(this);
30         }
31
32         add(buttons[0], BorderLayout.NORTH);
33         add(buttons[1], BorderLayout.SOUTH);
34         add(buttons[2], BorderLayout.EAST);
35         add(buttons[3], BorderLayout.WEST);
36         add(buttons[4], BorderLayout.CENTER);
37      }
```

Fig. 12.41 | BorderLayout containing five buttons. (Part 1 of 2.)

```
38
39      // handle button events
40      @Override
41      public void actionPerformed(ActionEvent event)
42      {
43         // check event source and lay out content pane correspondingly
44         for (JButton button : buttons)
45         {
46            if (event.getSource() == button)
47               button.setVisible(false); // hide the button that was clicked
48            else
49               button.setVisible(true); // show other buttons
50         }
51
52         layout.layoutContainer(getContentPane()); // lay out content pane
53      }
54   } // end class BorderLayoutFrame
```

Fig. 12.41 | BorderLayout containing five buttons. (Part 2 of 2.)

Line 21 of Fig. 12.41 creates a BorderLayout. The constructor arguments specify the number of pixels between components that are arranged horizontally (**horizontal gap space**) and between components that are arranged vertically (**vertical gap space**), respectively. The default is one pixel of gap space horizontally and vertically. Line 22 uses method setLayout to set the content pane's layout to layout.

We add Components to a BorderLayout with another version of Container method add that takes two arguments—the Component to add and the region in which the Component should appear. For example, line 32 specifies that buttons[0] should appear in the NORTH region. The components can be added in *any* order, but only *one* component should be added to each region.

Look-and-Feel Observation 12.18
If no region is specified when adding a Component to a BorderLayout, the layout manager assumes that the Component should be added to region BorderLayout.CENTER.

Common Programming Error 12.5
When more than one component is added to a region in a BorderLayout, only the last component added to that region will be displayed. There's no error that indicates this problem.

Class BorderLayoutFrame implements ActionListener directly in this example, so the BorderLayoutFrame will handle the events of the JButtons. For this reason, line 29 passes the this reference to the addActionListener method of each JButton. When the user clicks a particular JButton in the layout, method actionPerformed (lines 40–53) executes. The enhanced for statement at lines 44–50 uses an if...else to hide the particular JButton that generated the event. Method **setVisible** (inherited into JButton from class Component) is called with a false argument (line 47) to hide the JButton. If the current JButton in the array is not the one that generated the event, method setVisible is called with a true argument (line 49) to ensure that the JButton is displayed on the screen. Line 52 uses Layout-

Manager method layoutContainer to recalculate the layout of the content pane. Notice in the screen captures of Fig. 12.42 that certain regions in the BorderLayout change shape as JButtons are *hidden* and displayed in other regions. Try resizing the application window to see how the various regions resize based on the window's width and height. *For more complex layouts, group components in JPanels, each with a separate layout manager.* Place the JPanels on the JFrame using either the default BorderLayout or some other layout.

```java
1   // Fig. 12.42: BorderLayoutDemo.java
2   // Testing BorderLayoutFrame.
3   import javax.swing.JFrame;
4
5   public class BorderLayoutDemo
6   {
7      public static void main(String[] args)
8      {
9         BorderLayoutFrame borderLayoutFrame = new BorderLayoutFrame();
10        borderLayoutFrame.setDefaultCloseOperation(JFrame.EXIT_ON_CLOSE);
11        borderLayoutFrame.setSize(300, 200);
12        borderLayoutFrame.setVisible(true);
13     }
14  } // end class BorderLayoutDemo
```

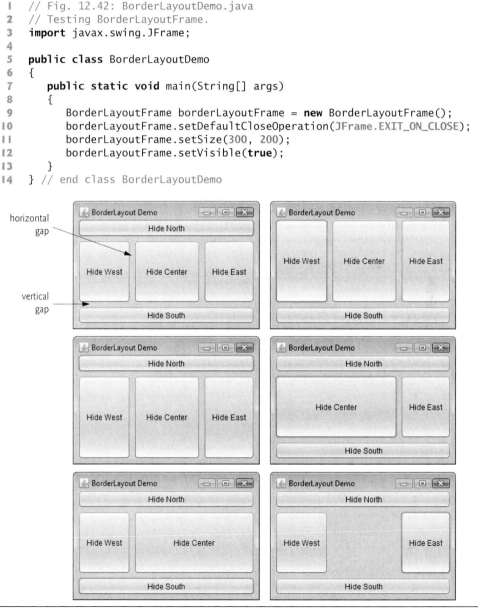

Fig. 12.42 | Testing BorderLayoutFrame.

12.18.3 GridLayout

The **GridLayout** layout manager divides the container into a *grid* so that components can be placed in *rows* and *columns*. Class GridLayout inherits directly from class Object and implements interface LayoutManager. Every Component in a GridLayout has the *same* width and height. Components are added to a GridLayout starting at the top-left cell of the grid and proceeding left to right until the row is full. Then the process continues left to right on the next row of the grid, and so on. The application of Figs. 12.43–12.44 demonstrates the GridLayout layout manager by using six JButtons.

```
 1   // Fig. 12.43: GridLayoutFrame.java
 2   // GridLayout containing six buttons.
 3   import java.awt.GridLayout;
 4   import java.awt.Container;
 5   import java.awt.event.ActionListener;
 6   import java.awt.event.ActionEvent;
 7   import javax.swing.JFrame;
 8   import javax.swing.JButton;
 9
10   public class GridLayoutFrame extends JFrame implements ActionListener
11   {
12      private final JButton[] buttons; // array of buttons
13      private static final String[] names =
14         { "one", "two", "three", "four", "five", "six" };
15      private boolean toggle = true; // toggle between two layouts
16      private final Container container; // frame container
17      private final GridLayout gridLayout1; // first gridlayout
18      private final GridLayout gridLayout2; // second gridlayout
19
20      // no-argument constructor
21      public GridLayoutFrame()
22      {
23         super("GridLayout Demo");
24         gridLayout1 = new GridLayout(2, 3, 5, 5); // 2 by 3; gaps of 5
25         gridLayout2 = new GridLayout(3, 2); // 3 by 2; no gaps
26         container = getContentPane();
27         setLayout(gridLayout1);
28         buttons = new JButton[names.length];
29
30         for (int count = 0; count < names.length; count++)
31         {
32            buttons[count] = new JButton(names[count]);
33            buttons[count].addActionListener(this); // register listener
34            add(buttons[count]); // add button to JFrame
35         }
36      }
37
38      // handle button events by toggling between layouts
39      @Override
40      public void actionPerformed(ActionEvent event)
41      {
```

Fig. 12.43 | GridLayout containing six buttons. (Part 1 of 2.)

```
42              if (toggle) // set layout based on toggle
43                  container.setLayout(gridLayout2);
44              else
45                  container.setLayout(gridLayout1);
46
47              toggle = !toggle;
48              container.validate(); // re-lay out container
49          }
50  } // end class GridLayoutFrame
```

Fig. 12.43 | GridLayout containing six buttons. (Part 2 of 2.)

```
 1  // Fig. 12.44: GridLayoutDemo.java
 2  // Testing GridLayoutFrame.
 3  import javax.swing.JFrame;
 4
 5  public class GridLayoutDemo
 6  {
 7     public static void main(String[] args)
 8     {
 9        GridLayoutFrame gridLayoutFrame = new GridLayoutFrame();
10        gridLayoutFrame.setDefaultCloseOperation(JFrame.EXIT_ON_CLOSE);
11        gridLayoutFrame.setSize(300, 200);
12        gridLayoutFrame.setVisible(true);
13     }
14  } // end class GridLayoutDemo
```

Fig. 12.44 | Testing GridLayoutFrame.

Lines 24–25 (Fig. 12.43) create two GridLayout objects. The GridLayout constructor used at line 24 specifies a GridLayout with 2 rows, 3 columns, 5 pixels of horizontal-gap space between Components in the grid and 5 pixels of vertical-gap space between Components in the grid. The GridLayout constructor used at line 25 specifies a GridLayout with 3 rows and 2 columns that uses the default gap space (1 pixel).

The JButton objects in this example initially are arranged using gridLayout1 (set for the content pane at line 27 with method setLayout). The first component is added to the first column of the first row. The next component is added to the second column of the first row, and so on. When a JButton is pressed, method actionPerformed (lines 39–49) is called. Every call to actionPerformed toggles the layout between gridLayout2 and gridLayout1, using boolean variable toggle to determine the next layout to set.

Line 48 shows another way to reformat a container for which the layout has changed. Container method **validate** recomputes the container's layout based on the current layout manager for the Container and the current set of displayed GUI components.

12.19 Using Panels to Manage More Complex Layouts

Complex GUIs (like Fig. 12.1) often require that each component be placed in an exact location. They often consist of multiple panels, with each panel's components arranged in a specific layout. Class JPanel extends JComponent and JComponent extends class Container, so every JPanel is a Container. Thus, every JPanel may have components, including other panels, attached to it with Container method add. The application of Figs. 12.45–12.46 demonstrates how a JPanel can be used to create a more complex layout in which several JButtons are placed in the SOUTH region of a BorderLayout.

```java
1  // Fig. 12.45: PanelFrame.java
2  // Using a JPanel to help lay out components.
3  import java.awt.GridLayout;
4  import java.awt.BorderLayout;
5  import javax.swing.JFrame;
6  import javax.swing.JPanel;
7  import javax.swing.JButton;
8
9  public class PanelFrame extends JFrame
10 {
11    private final JPanel buttonJPanel; // panel to hold buttons
12    private final JButton[] buttons;
13
14    // no-argument constructor
15    public PanelFrame()
16    {
17       super("Panel Demo");
18       buttons = new JButton[5];
19       buttonJPanel = new JPanel();
20       buttonJPanel.setLayout(new GridLayout(1, buttons.length));
21
22       // create and add buttons
23       for (int count = 0; count < buttons.length; count++)
24       {
25          buttons[count] = new JButton("Button " + (count + 1));
26          buttonJPanel.add(buttons[count]); // add button to panel
27       }
28
29       add(buttonJPanel, BorderLayout.SOUTH); // add panel to JFrame
30    }
31 } // end class PanelFrame
```

Fig. 12.45 | JPanel with five JButtons in a GridLayout attached to the SOUTH region of a BorderLayout.

```java
1  // Fig. 12.46: PanelDemo.java
2  // Testing PanelFrame.
3  import javax.swing.JFrame;
4
```

Fig. 12.46 | Testing PanelFrame. (Part 1 of 2.)

```
5   public class PanelDemo extends JFrame
6   {
7      public static void main(String[] args)
8      {
9         PanelFrame panelFrame = new PanelFrame();
10        panelFrame.setDefaultCloseOperation(JFrame.EXIT_ON_CLOSE);
11        panelFrame.setSize(450, 200);
12        panelFrame.setVisible(true);
13     }
14  } // end class PanelDemo
```

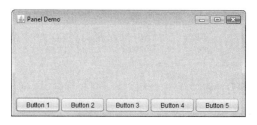

Fig. 12.46 | Testing PanelFrame. (Part 2 of 2.)

After JPanel buttonJPanel is declared (line 11 of Fig. 12.45) and created (line 19), line 20 sets buttonJPanel's layout to a GridLayout of one row and five columns (there are five JButtons in array buttons). Lines 23–27 add the JButtons in the array to the JPanel. Line 26 adds the buttons directly to the JPanel—class JPanel does not have a content pane, unlike a JFrame. Line 29 uses the JFrame's default BorderLayout to add buttonJPanel to the SOUTH region. The SOUTH region is as tall as the buttons on button-JPanel. A JPanel is sized to the components it contains. As more components are added, the JPanel *grows* (according to the restrictions of its layout manager) to accommodate the components. Resize the window to see how the layout manager affects the size of the JButtons.

12.20 JTextArea

A **JTextArea** provides an area for *manipulating multiple lines of text*. Like class JTextField, JTextArea is a subclass of JTextComponent, which declares common methods for JText-Fields, JTextAreas and several other text-based GUI components.

The application in Figs. 12.47–12.48 demonstrates JTextAreas. One JTextArea displays text that the user can select. The other is uneditable by the user and is used to display the text the user selected in the first JTextArea. Unlike JTextFields, JTextAreas do not have action events—when you press *Enter* while typing in a JTextArea, the cursor simply moves to the next line. As with multiple-selection JLists (Section 12.13), an external event from another GUI component indicates when to process the text in a JTextArea. For example, when typing an e-mail message, you normally click a **Send** button to send the text of the message to the recipient. Similarly, when editing a document in a word processor, you normally save the file by selecting a **Save** or **Save As...** menu item. In this program, the button **Copy >>>** generates the external event that copies the selected text in the left JTextArea and displays it in the right JTextArea.

```
1   // Fig. 12.47: TextAreaFrame.java
2   // Copying selected text from one JText area to another.
3   import java.awt.event.ActionListener;
4   import java.awt.event.ActionEvent;
5   import javax.swing.Box;
6   import javax.swing.JFrame;
7   import javax.swing.JTextArea;
8   import javax.swing.JButton;
9   import javax.swing.JScrollPane;
10
11  public class TextAreaFrame extends JFrame
12  {
13     private final JTextArea textArea1; // displays demo string
14     private final JTextArea textArea2; // highlighted text is copied here
15     private final JButton copyJButton; // initiates copying of text
16
17     // no-argument constructor
18     public TextAreaFrame()
19     {
20        super("TextArea Demo");
21        Box box = Box.createHorizontalBox(); // create box
22        String demo = "This is a demo string to\n" +
23           "illustrate copying text\nfrom one textarea to \n" +
24           "another textarea using an\nexternal event\n";
25
26        textArea1 = new JTextArea(demo, 10, 15);
27        box.add(new JScrollPane(textArea1)); // add scrollpane
28
29        copyJButton = new JButton("Copy >>>"); // create copy button
30        box.add(copyJButton); // add copy button to box
31        copyJButton.addActionListener(
32           new ActionListener() // anonymous inner class
33           {
34              // set text in textArea2 to selected text from textArea1
35              @Override
36              public void actionPerformed(ActionEvent event)
37              {
38                 textArea2.setText(textArea1.getSelectedText());
39              }
40           }
41        );
42
43        textArea2 = new JTextArea(10, 15);
44        textArea2.setEditable(false);
45        box.add(new JScrollPane(textArea2)); // add scrollpane
46
47        add(box); // add box to frame
48     }
49  } // end class TextAreaFrame
```

Fig. 12.47 | Copying selected text from one JTextArea to another.

In the constructor (lines 18–48), line 21 creates a **Box** container (package javax.swing) to organize the GUI components. Box is a subclass of Container that uses

```
 1  // Fig. 12.48: TextAreaDemo.java
 2  // Testing TextAreaFrame.
 3  import javax.swing.JFrame;
 4
 5  public class TextAreaDemo
 6  {
 7     public static void main(String[] args)
 8     {
 9        TextAreaFrame textAreaFrame = new TextAreaFrame();
10        textAreaFrame.setDefaultCloseOperation(JFrame.EXIT_ON_CLOSE);
11        textAreaFrame.setSize(425, 200);
12        textAreaFrame.setVisible(true);
13     }
14  } // end class TextAreaDemo
```

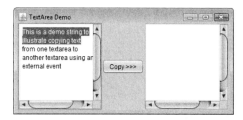 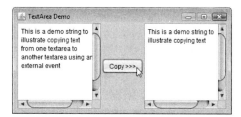

Fig. 12.48 | Testing TextAreaFrame.

a **BoxLayout** layout manager (discussed in detail in Section 22.9) to arrange the GUI components either horizontally or vertically. Box's static method **createHorizontalBox** creates a Box that arranges components from left to right in the order that they're attached.

Lines 26 and 43 create JTextAreas textArea1 and textArea2. Line 26 uses JText-Area's three-argument constructor, which takes a String representing the initial text and two ints specifying that the JTextArea has 10 rows and 15 columns. Line 43 uses JText-Area's two-argument constructor, specifying that the JTextArea has 10 rows and 15 columns. Line 26 specifies that demo should be displayed as the default JTextArea content. A JTextArea does not provide scrollbars if it cannot display its complete contents. So, line 27 creates a JScrollPane object, initializes it with textArea1 and attaches it to container box. By default, horizontal and vertical scrollbars appear as necessary in a JScrollPane.

Lines 29–41 create JButton object copyJButton with the label "Copy >>>", add copy-JButton to container box and register the event handler for copyJButton's ActionEvent. This button provides the external event that determines when the program should copy the selected text in textArea1 to textArea2. When the user clicks copyJButton, line 38 in actionPerformed indicates that method **getSelectedText** (inherited into JTextArea from JTextComponent) should return the selected text from textArea1. The user selects text by dragging the mouse over the desired text to highlight it. Method setText changes the text in textArea2 to the string returned by getSelectedText.

Lines 43–45 create textArea2, set its editable property to false and add it to container box. Line 47 adds box to the JFrame. Recall from Section 12.18.2 that the default layout of a JFrame is a BorderLayout and that the add method by default attaches its argument to the CENTER of the BorderLayout.

When text reaches the right edge of a JTextArea the text can wrap to the next line. This is referred to as **line wrapping**. By default, JTextArea does *not* wrap lines.

Look-and-Feel Observation 12.19

To provide line wrapping functionality for a JTextArea, invoke JTextArea method **set-LineWrap** *with a true argument.*

JScrollPane Scrollbar Policies

This example uses a JScrollPane to provide scrolling for a JTextArea. By default, JScrollPane displays scrollbars *only* if they're required. You can set the horizontal and vertical **scrollbar policies** of a JScrollPane when it's constructed. If a program has a reference to a JScrollPane, the program can use JScrollPane methods **setHorizontalScrollBarPolicy** and **setVerticalScrollBarPolicy** to change the scrollbar policies at any time. Class JScrollPane declares the constants

```
JScrollPane.VERTICAL_SCROLLBAR_ALWAYS
JScrollPane.HORIZONTAL_SCROLLBAR_ALWAYS
```

to indicate that *a scrollbar should always appear*, constants

```
JScrollPane.VERTICAL_SCROLLBAR_AS_NEEDED
JScrollPane.HORIZONTAL_SCROLLBAR_AS_NEEDED
```

to indicate that *a scrollbar should appear only if necessary* (the defaults) and constants

```
JScrollPane.VERTICAL_SCROLLBAR_NEVER
JScrollPane.HORIZONTAL_SCROLLBAR_NEVER
```

to indicate that *a scrollbar should never appear*. If the horizontal scrollbar policy is set to JScrollPane.HORIZONTAL_SCROLLBAR_NEVER, a JTextArea attached to the JScrollPane will automatically wrap lines.

12.21 Wrap-Up

In this chapter, you learned many GUI components and how to handle their events. You also learned about nested classes, inner classes and anonymous inner classes. You saw the special relationship between an inner-class object and an object of its top-level class. You learned how to use JOptionPane dialogs to obtain text input from the user and how to display messages to the user. You also learned how to create applications that execute in their own windows. We discussed class JFrame and components that enable a user to interact with an application. We also showed you how to display text and images to the user. You learned how to customize JPanels to create custom drawing areas, which you'll use extensively in the next chapter. You saw how to organize components on a window using layout managers and how to creating more complex GUIs by using JPanels to organize components. Finally, you learned about the JTextArea component in which a user can enter text and an application can display text. In Chapter 22, you'll learn about more advanced GUI components, such as sliders, menus and more complex layout managers. In the next chapter, you'll learn how to add graphics to your GUI application. Graphics allow you to draw shapes and text with colors and styles.

Summary

Section 12.1 Introduction

- A graphical user interface (GUI; p. 466) presents a user-friendly mechanism for interacting with an application. A GUI gives an application a distinctive look-and-feel (p. 466).
- Providing different applications with consistent, intuitive user-interface components gives users a sense of familarity with a new application, so that they can learn it more quickly.
- GUIs are built from GUI components (p. 466)—sometimes called controls or widgets.

Section 12.2 Java's Nimbus Look-and-Feel

- As of Java SE 6 update 10, Java comes bundled with a new, elegant, cross-platform look-and-feel known as Nimbus (p. 468).
- To set Nimbus as the default for all Java applications, create a `swing.properties` text file in the `lib` folder of your JDK and JRE installation folders. Place the following line of code in the file:

  ```
  swing.defaultlaf=com.sun.java.swing.plaf.nimbus.NimbusLookAndFeel
  ```

- To select Nimbus on an application-by-application basis, place the following command-line argument after the java command and before the application's name when you run the application:

  ```
  -Dswing.defaultlaf=com.sun.java.swing.plaf.nimbus.NimbusLookAndFeel
  ```

Section 12.3 Simple GUI-Based Input/Output with `JOptionPane`

- Most applications use windows or dialog boxes (p. 468) to interact with the user.
- Class `JOptionPane` (p. 468) of package `javax.swing` (p. 466) provides prebuilt dialog boxes for both input and output. `JOptionPane` static method `showInputDialog` (p. 469) displays an input dialog (p. 468).
- A prompt typically uses sentence-style capitalization—capitalizing only the first letter of the first word in the text unless the word is a proper noun.
- An input dialog can input only input `Strings`. This is typical of most GUI components.
- `JOptionPane` static method `showMessageDialog` (p. 470) displays a message dialog (p. 468).

Section 12.4 Overview of Swing Components

- Most Swing GUI components (p. 466) are located in package `javax.swing`.
- Together, the appearance and the way in which the user interacts with the application are known as that application's look-and-feel. Swing GUI components allow you to specify a uniform look-and-feel for your application across all platforms or to use each platform's custom look-and-feel.
- Lightweight Swing components are not tied to actual GUI components supported by the underlying platform on which an application executes.
- Several Swing components are heavyweight components (p. 472) that require direct interaction with the local windowing system (p. 472), which may restrict their appearance and functionality.
- Class `Component` (p. 472) of package `java.awt` declares many of the attributes and behaviors common to the GUI components in packages `java.awt` (p. 471) and `javax.swing`.
- Class `Container` (p. 472) of package `java.awt` is a subclass of `Component`. `Components` are attached to `Containers` so the `Components` can be organized and displayed on the screen.
- Class `JComponent` (p. 472) of package `javax.swing` is a subclass of `Container`. `JComponent` is the superclass of all lightweight Swing components and declares their common attributes and behaviors.
- Some common `JComponent` features include a pluggable look-and-feel (p. 472), shortcut keys called mnemonics (p. 472), tool tips (p. 472), support for assistive technologies and support for user-interface localization (p. 472).

Section 12.5 Displaying Text and Images in a Window

- Class JFrame provides the basic attributes and behaviors of a window.

- A JLabel (p. 473) displays read-only text, an image, or both text and an image. Text in a JLabel normally uses sentence-style capitalization.

- Each GUI component must be attached to a container, such as a window created with a JFrame (p. 475).

- Many IDEs provide GUI design tools (p. 521) in which you can specify the exact size and location of a component by using the mouse; then the IDE will generate the GUI code for you.

- JComponent method setToolTipText (p. 475) specifies the tool tip that's displayed when the user positions the mouse cursor over a lightweight component (p. 472).

- Container method add attaches a GUI component to a Container.

- Class ImageIcon (p. 476) supports several image formats, including GIF, PNG and JPEG.

- Method getClass of class Object (p. 476) retrieves a reference to the Class object that represents the the class declaration for the object on which the method is called.

- Class method getResource (p. 476) returns the location of its argument as a URL. The method getResource uses the Class object's class loader to determine the location of the resource.

- The horizontal and vertical alignments of a JLabel can be set with methods setHorizontalAlignment (p. 476) and setVerticalAlignment (p. 476), respectively.

- JLabel methods setText (p. 476) and getText (p. 476) set and get the text displayed on a label.

- JLabel methods setIcon (p. 476) and getIcon (p. 476) set and get the Icon (p. 476) on a label.

- JLabel methods setHorizontalTextPosition (p. 476) and setVerticalTextPosition (p. 476) specify the text position in the label.

- JFrame method setDefaultCloseOperation (p. 477) with constant JFrame.EXIT_ON_CLOSE as the argument indicates that the program should terminate when the window is closed by the user.

- Component method setSize (p. 477) specifies the width and height of a component.

- Component method setVisible (p. 477) with the argument true displays a JFrame on the screen.

Section 12.6 Text Fields and an Introduction to Event Handling with Nested Classes

- GUIs are event driven—when the user interacts with a GUI component, events (p. 477) drive the program to perform tasks.

- An event handler (p. 477) performs a task in response to an event.

- Class JTextField (p. 477) extends JTextComponent (p. 477) of package javax.swing.text, which provides common text-based component features. Class JPasswordField (p. 477) extends JTextField and adds several methods that are specific to processing passwords.

- A JPasswordField (p. 477) shows that characters are being typed as the user enters them, but hides the actual characters with echo characters (p. 477).

- A component receives the focus (p. 478) when the user clicks the component.

- JTextComponent method setEditable (p. 480) can be used to make a text field uneditable.

- To respond to an event for a particular GUI component, you must create a class that represents the event handler and implements an appropriate event-listener interface (p. 480), then register an object of the event-handling class as the event handler (p. 480).

- Non-static nested classes (p. 480) are called inner classes and are frequently used for event handling.

- An object of a non-static inner class (p. 480) must be created by an object of the top-level class (p. 480) that contains the inner class.

- An inner-class object can directly access the instance variables and methods of its top-level class.
- A nested class that's static does not require an object of its top-level class and does not implicitly have a reference to an object of the top-level class.
- Pressing *Enter* in a JTextField or JPasswordField generates an ActionEvent (p. 481) that can be handled by an ActionListener (p. 481) of package java.awt.event.
- JTextField method addActionListener (p. 481) registers an event handler for a text field's ActionEvent.
- The GUI component with which the user interacts is the event source (p. 482).
- An ActionEvent object contains information about the event that just occurred, such as the event source and the text in the text field.
- ActionEvent method getSource returns a reference to the event source. ActionEvent method getActionCommand (p. 482) returns the text the user typed in a text field or the label on a JButton.
- JPasswordField method getPassword (p. 482) returns the password the user typed.

Section 12.7 Common GUI Event Types and Listener Interfaces
- Each event-object type typically has a corresponding event-listener interface that specifies one or more event-handling methods, which must be declared in the class that implements the interface.

Section 12.8 How Event Handling Works
- When an event occurs, the GUI component with which the user interacted notifies its registered listeners by calling each listener's appropriate event-handling method.
- Every GUI component supports several event types. When an event occurs, the event is dispatched (p. 486) only to the event listeners of the appropriate type.

Section 12.9 JButton
- A button is a component the user clicks to trigger an action. All the button types are subclasses of AbstractButton (p. 487; package javax.swing). Button labels (p. 487) typically use book-title capitalization (p. 487).
- Command buttons (p. 487) are created with class JButton.
- A JButton can display an Icon. A JButton can also have a rollover Icon (p. 489)—an Icon that's displayed when the user positions the mouse over the button.
- Method setRolloverIcon (p. 490) of class AbstractButton specifies the image displayed on a button when the user positions the mouse over it.

Section 12.10 Buttons That Maintain State
- There are three Swing state button types—JToggleButton (p. 490), JCheckBox (p. 490) and JRadioButton (p. 490).
- Classes JCheckBox and JRadioButton are subclasses of JToggleButton.
- Component method setFont (p. 492) sets the component's font to a new Font object (p. 492) of package java.awt.
- Clicking a JCheckBox causes an ItemEvent (p. 493) that can be handled by an ItemListener (p. 493) which defines method itemStateChanged (p. 493). Method addItemListener registers the listener for the ItemEvent of a JCheckBox or JRadioButton object.
- JCheckBox method isSelected determines whether a JCheckBox is selected.
- JRadioButtons have two states—selected and not selected. Radio buttons (p. 487) normally appear as a group (p. 493) in which only one button can be selected at a time.

- JRadioButtons are used to represent mutually exclusive options (p. 493).
- The logical relationship between JRadioButtons is maintained by a ButtonGroup object (p. 493).
- ButtonGroup method add (p. 496) associates each JRadioButton with a ButtonGroup. If more than one selected JRadioButton object is added to a group, the selected one that was added first will be selected when the GUI is displayed.
- JRadioButtons generate ItemEvents when they're clicked.

Section 12.11 JComboBox; Using an Anonymous Inner Class for Event Handling

- A JComboBox (p. 496) provides a list of items from which the user can make a single selection. JComboBoxes generate ItemEvents.
- Each item in a JComboBox has an index (p. 499). The first item added to a JComboBox appears as the currently selected item when the JComboBox is displayed.
- JComboBox method setMaximumRowCount (p. 499) sets the maximum number of elements that are displayed when the user clicks the JComboBox.
- An anonymous inner class (p. 499) is a class without a name and typically appears inside a method declaration. One object of the anonymous inner class must be created when the class is declared.
- JComboBox method getSelectedIndex (p. 500) returns the index of the selected item.

Section 12.12 JList

- A JList displays a series of items from which the user may select one or more items. Class JList supports single-selection lists (p. 500) and multiple-selection lists (p. 500).
- When the user clicks an item in a JList, a ListSelectionEvent (p. 500) occurs. JList method addListSelectionListener (p. 502) registers a ListSelectionListener (p. 502) for a JList's selection events. A ListSelectionListener of package javax.swing.event(p. 484) must implement method valueChanged.
- JList method setVisibleRowCount (p. 502) specifies the number of visible items in the list.
- JList method setSelectionMode (p. 502) specifies a list's selection mode.
- A JList can be attached to a JScrollPane (p. 502) to provide a scrollbar for the JList.
- JFrame method getContentPane (p. 502) returns a reference to the JFrame's content pane where GUI components are displayed.
- JList method getSelectedIndex (p. 503) returns the selected item's index.

Section 12.13 Multiple-Selection Lists

- A multiple-selection list (p. 503) enables the user to select many items from a JList.
- JList method setFixedCellWidth (p. 505) sets a JList's width. Method setFixedCellHeight (p. 505) sets the height of each item in a JList.
- Normally, an external event (p. 505) generated by another GUI component (such as a JButton) specifies when the multiple selections in a JList should be processed.
- JList method setListData (p. 505) sets the items displayed in a JList. JList method getSelectedValues (p. 505) returns an array of Objects representing the selected items in a JList.

Section 12.14 Mouse Event Handling

- The MouseListener (p. 505) and MouseMotionListener (p. 505) event-listener interfaces are used to handle mouse events (p. 505). Mouse events can be trapped for any GUI component that extends Component.

- Interface MouseInputListener (p. 505) of package javax.swing.event extends interfaces MouseListener and MouseMotionListener to create a single interface containing all their methods.
- Each mouse event-handling method receives a MouseEvent object (p. 486) that contains information about the event, including the *x*- and *y*-coordinates where the event occurred. Coordinates are measured from the upper-left corner of the GUI component on which the event occurred.
- The methods and constants of class InputEvent (p. 506; MouseEvent's superclass) enable an application to determine which mouse button the user clicked.
- Interface MouseWheelListener (p. 507) enables applications to respond to mouse-wheel events.

Section 12.15 Adapter Classes
- An adapter class (p. 510) implements an interface and provides default implementations of its methods. When you extend an adapter class, you can override just the method(s) you need.
- MouseEvent method getClickCount (p. 513) returns the number of consecutive mouse-button clicks. Methods isMetaDown (p. 520) and isAltDown (p. 513) determine which button was clicked.

Section 12.16 JPanel Subclass for Drawing with the Mouse
- JComponents method paintComponent (p. 514) is called when a lightweight Swing component is displayed. Override this method to specify how to draw shapes using Java's graphics capabilities.
- When overriding paintComponent, call the superclass version as the first statement in the body.
- Subclasses of JComponent support transparency. When a component is opaque (p. 514), paintComponent clears its background before the component is displayed.
- The transparency of a Swing lightweight component can be set with method setOpaque (p. 514; a false argument indicates that the component is transparent).
- Class Point (p. 515) package java.awt represents an *x-y* coordinate.
- Class Graphics (p. 515) is used to draw.
- MouseEvent method getPoint (p. 516) obtains the Point where a mouse event occurred.
- Method repaint (p. 516), inherited indirectly from class Component, indicates that a component should be refreshed on the screen as soon as possible.
- Method paintComponent receives a Graphics parameter and is called automatically whenever a lightweight component needs to be displayed on the screen.
- Graphics method fillOval (p. 516) draws a solid oval. The first two arguments are the upper-left *x-y* coordinate of the bounding box, and the last two are the bounding box's width and height.

Section 12.17 Key Event Handling
- Interface KeyListener (p. 486) is used to handle key events (p. 486) that are generated when keys on the keyboard are pressed and released. Method addKeyListener of class Component (p. 517) registers a KeyListener.
- KeyEvent (p. 486) method getKeyCode (p. 520) gets the virtual key code (p. 520) of the pressed key. Class KeyEvent contains virtual key-code constants that represent every key on the keyboard.
- KeyEvent method getKeyText (p. 520) returns a string containing the name of the pressed key.
- KeyEvent method getKeyChar (p. 520) gets the Unicode value of the character typed.
- KeyEvent method isActionKey (p. 520) determines whether the key in an event was an action key (p. 517).
- InputEvent method getModifiers (p. 520) determines whether any modifier keys (such as *Shift*, *Alt* and *Ctrl*) were pressed when the key event occurred.

- `KeyEvent` method `getKeyModifiersText` (p. 520) returns a string containing the pressed modifier keys.

Section 12.18 Introduction to Layout Managers
- Layout managers (p. 520) arrange GUI components in a container for presentation purposes.
- All layout managers implement the interface `LayoutManager` (p. 520) of package `java.awt`.
- `Container` method `setLayout` specifies the layout of a container.
- `FlowLayout` places components left to right in the order in which they're added to the container. When the container's edge is reached, components continue to display on the next line. `FlowLayout` allows GUI components to be left aligned, centered (the default) and right aligned.
- `FlowLayout` method `setAlignment` (p. 524) changes the alignment for a `FlowLayout`.
- `BorderLayout` (p. 524) the default for a `JFrame`) arranges components into five regions: NORTH, SOUTH, EAST, WEST and CENTER. NORTH corresponds to the top of the container.
- A `BorderLayout` limits a `Container` to containing at most five components—one in each region.
- `GridLayout` (p. 528) divides a container into a grid of rows and columns.
- `Container` method `validate` (p. 529) recomputes a container's layout based on the current layout manager for the `Container` and the current set of displayed GUI components.

Section 12.19 Using Panels to Manage More Complex Layouts
- Complex GUIs often consist of multiple panels with different layouts. Every `JPanel` may have components, including other panels, attached to it with `Container` method `add`.

Section 12.20 JTextArea
- A `JTextArea` (p. 531)—a subclass of `JTextComponent`—may contain multiple lines of text.
- Class `Box` (p. 532) is a subclass of `Container` that uses a `BoxLayout` layout manager (p. 533) to arrange the GUI components either horizontally or vertically.
- `Box` static method `createHorizontalBox` (p. 533) creates a `Box` that arranges components from left to right in the order that they're attached.
- Method `getSelectedText` (p. 533) returns the selected text from a `JTextArea`.
- You can set the horizontal and vertical scrollbar policies (p. 534) of a `JScrollPane` when it's constructed. `JScrollPane` methods `setHorizontalScrollBarPolicy` (p. 534) and `setVertical-ScrollBarPolicy` (p. 534) can be used to change the scrollbar policies at any time.

Self-Review Exercises
12.1   Fill in the blanks in each of the following statements:
   a) Method _____ is called when the mouse is moved with no buttons pressed and an event listener is registered to handle the event.
   b) Text that cannot be modified by the user is called _____ text.
   c) A(n) _____ arranges GUI components in a `Container`.
   d) The add method for attaching GUI components is a method of class _____.
   e) GUI is an acronym for _____.
   f) Method _____ is used to specify the layout manager for a container.
   g) A `mouseDragged` method call is preceded by a(n) _____ method call and followed by a(n) _____ method call.
   h) Class _____ contains methods that display message dialogs and input dialogs.
   i) An input dialog capable of receiving input from the user is displayed with method _____ of class _____.

    j) A dialog capable of displaying a message to the user is displayed with method of class _____.

    k) Both JTextFields and JTextAreas directly extend class _____.

12.2   Determine whether each statement is *true* or *false*. If *false*, explain why.

    a) BorderLayout is the default layout manager for a JFrame's content pane.

    b) When the mouse cursor is moved into the bounds of a GUI component, method mouseOver is called.

    c) A JPanel cannot be added to another JPanel.

    d) In a BorderLayout, two buttons added to the NORTH region will be placed side by side.

    e) A maximum of five components can be added to a BorderLayout.

    f) Inner classes are not allowed to access the members of the enclosing class.

    g) A JTextArea's text is always read-only.

    h) Class JTextArea is a direct subclass of class Component.

12.3   Find the error(s) in each of the following statements, and explain how to correct it (them):

    a) buttonName = JButton("Caption");

    b) JLabel aLabel, JLabel;

    c) txtField = **new** JTextField(50, "Default Text");

    d) setLayout(**new** BorderLayout());
```
        button1 = new JButton("North Star");
        button2 = new JButton("South Pole");
        add(button1);
        add(button2);
```

Answers to Self-Review Exercises

12.1   a) mouseMoved. b) uneditable (read-only). c) layout manager. d) Container. e) graphical user interface. f) setLayout. g) mousePressed, mouseReleased. h) JOptionPane. i) showInputDialog, JOptionPane. j) showMessageDialog, JOptionPane. k) JTextComponent.

12.2   a) True.

    b) False. Method mouseEntered is called.

    c) False. A JPanel can be added to another JPanel, because JPanel is an indirect subclass of Component. So, a JPanel is a Component. Any Component can be added to a Container.

    d) False. Only the last button added will be displayed. Remember that only one component should be added to each region in a BorderLayout.

    e) True. [*Note:* Panels containing multiple components can be added to each region.]

    f) False. Inner classes have access to all members of the enclosing class declaration.

    g) False. JTextAreas are editable by default.

    h) False. JTextArea derives from class JTextComponent.

12.3   a) new is needed to create an object.

    b) JLabel is a class name and cannot be used as a variable name.

    c) The arguments passed to the constructor are reversed. The String must be passed first.

    d) BorderLayout has been set, and components are being added without specifying the region, so both are added to the center region. Proper add statements might be
```
        add(button1, BorderLayout.NORTH);
        add(button2, BorderLayout.SOUTH);
```

Exercises

12.4   Fill in the blanks in each of the following statements:

    a) The JTextField class directly extends class _____.

    b) Container method _____ attaches a GUI component to a container.

    c) Method _____ is called when a mouse button is released (without moving the mouse).

    d) The _____ class is used to create a group of JRadioButtons.

12.5 Determine whether each statement is *true* or *false*. If *false*, explain why.

    a) Only one layout manager can be used per Container.

    b) GUI components can be added to a Container in any order in a BorderLayout.

    c) JRadioButtons provide a series of mutually exclusive options (i.e., only one can be true at a time).

    d) Graphics method setFont is used to set the font for text fields.

    e) A JList displays a scrollbar if there are more items in the list than can be displayed.

    f) A Mouse object has a method called mouseDragged.

12.6 Determine whether each statement is *true* or *false*. If *false*, explain why.

    a) A JPanel is a JComponent.

    b) A JPanel is a Component.

    c) A JLabel is a Container.

    d) A JList is a JPanel.

    e) An AbstractButton is a JButton.

    f) A JTextField is an Object.

    g) ButtonGroup is a subclass of JComponent.

12.7 Find any errors in each of the following lines of code, and explain how to correct them.

    a) `import javax.swing.JFrame`

    b) `panelObject.GridLayout(8, 8);`

    c) `container.setLayout(new FlowLayout(FlowLayout.DEFAULT));`

    d) `container.add(eastButton, EAST); face`

12.8 Create the following GUI. You do not have to provide any functionality.

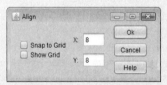

12.9 Create the following GUI. You do not have to provide any functionality.

12.10 Create the following GUI. You do not have to provide any functionality.

12.11 Create the following GUI. You do not have to provide any functionality.

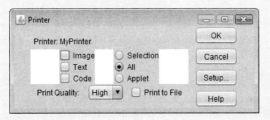

12.12 *(Temperature Conversion)* Write a temperature-conversion application that converts from Fahrenheit to Celsius. The Fahrenheit temperature should be entered from the keyboard (via a JTextField). A JLabel should be used to display the converted temperature. Use the following formula for the conversion:

$$Celsius = \frac{5}{9} \times (Fahrenheit - 32)$$

12.13 *(Temperature-Conversion Modification)* Enhance the temperature-conversion application of Exercise 12.12 by adding the Kelvin temperature scale. The application should also allow the user to make conversions between any two scales. Use the following formula for the conversion between Kelvin and Celsius (in addition to the formula in Exercise 12.12):

$$Kelvin = Celsius + 273.15$$

12.14 *(Guess-the-Number Game)* Write an application that plays "guess the number" as follows: Your application chooses the number to be guessed by selecting an integer at random in the range 1–1000. The application then displays the following in a label:

```
I have a number between 1 and 1000. Can you guess my number?
Please enter your first guess.
```

A JTextField should be used to input the guess. As each guess is input, the background color should change to either red or blue. Red indicates that the user is getting "warmer," and blue, "colder." A JLabel should display either "Too High" or "Too Low" to help the user zero in. When the user gets the correct answer, "Correct!" should be displayed, and the JTextField used for input should be changed to be uneditable. A JButton should be provided to allow the user to play the game again. When the JButton is clicked, a new random number should be generated and the input JTextField changed to be editable.

12.15 *(Displaying Events)* It's often useful to display the events that occur during the execution of an application. This can help you understand when the events occur and how they're generated. Write an application that enables the user to generate and process every event discussed in this chapter. The application should provide methods from the ActionListener, ItemListener, ListSelectionListener, MouseListener, MouseMotionListener and KeyListener interfaces to display messages when the events occur. Use method toString to convert the event objects received in each event handler into Strings that can be displayed. Method toString creates a String containing all the information in the event object.

12.16 *(GUI-Based Craps Game)* Modify the application of Section 5.10 to provide a GUI that enables the user to click a JButton to roll the dice. The application should also display four JLabels and four JTextFields, with one JLabel for each JTextField. The JTextFields should be used to display the values of each die and the sum of the dice after each roll. The point should be displayed in the fourth JTextField when the user does not win or lose on the first roll and should continue to be displayed until the game is lost.

(Optional) GUI and Graphics Case Study Exercise: Expanding the Interface

12.17 *(Interactive Drawing Application)* In this exercise, you'll implement a GUI application that uses the MyShape hierarchy from GUI and Graphics Case Study Exercise 10.2 to create an interactive drawing application. You'll create two classes for the GUI and provide a test class that launches the application. The classes of the MyShape hierarchy require no additional changes.

The first class to create is a subclass of JPanel called DrawPanel, which represents the area on which the user draws the shapes. Class DrawPanel should have the following instance variables:

 a) An array shapes of type MyShape that will store all the shapes the user draws.
 b) An integer shapeCount that counts the number of shapes in the array.
 c) An integer shapeType that determines the type of shape to draw.
 d) A MyShape currentShape that represents the current shape the user is drawing.
 e) A Color currentColor that represents the current drawing color.
 f) A boolean filledShape that determines whether to draw a filled shape.
 g) A JLabel statusLabel that represents the status bar. The status bar will display the coordinates of the current mouse position.

Class DrawPanel should also declare the following methods:

 a) Overridden method paintComponent that draws the shapes in the array. Use instance variable shapeCount to determine how many shapes to draw. Method paintComponent should also call currentShape's draw method, provided that currentShape is not null.
 b) Set methods for the shapeType, currentColor and filledShape.
 c) Method clearLastShape should clear the last shape drawn by decrementing instance variable shapeCount. Ensure that shapeCount is never less than zero.
 d) Method clearDrawing should remove all the shapes in the current drawing by setting shapeCount to zero.

Methods clearLastShape and clearDrawing should call repaint (inherited from JPanel) to refresh the drawing on the DrawPanel by indicating that the system should call method paintComponent.

Class DrawPanel should also provide event handling to enable the user to draw with the mouse. Create a single inner class that both extends MouseAdapter and implements MouseMotionListener to handle all mouse events in one class.

In the inner class, override method mousePressed so that it assigns currentShape a new shape of the type specified by shapeType and initializes both points to the mouse position. Next, override method mouseReleased to finish drawing the current shape and place it in the array. Set the second point of currentShape to the current mouse position and add currentShape to the array. Instance variable shapeCount determines the insertion index. Set currentShape to null and call method repaint to update the drawing with the new shape.

Override method mouseMoved to set the text of the statusLabel so that it displays the mouse coordinates—this will update the label with the coordinates every time the user moves (but does not drag) the mouse within the DrawPanel. Next, override method mouseDragged so that it sets the second point of the currentShape to the current mouse position and calls method repaint. This will allow the user to see the shape while dragging the mouse. Also, update the JLabel in mouseDragged with the current position of the mouse.

Create a constructor for DrawPanel that has a single JLabel parameter. In the constructor, initialize statusLabel with the value passed to the parameter. Also initialize array shapes with 100 entries, shapeCount to 0, shapeType to the value that represents a line, currentShape to null and currentColor to Color.BLACK. The constructor should then set the background color of the DrawPanel to Color.WHITE and register the MouseListener and MouseMotionListener so the JPanel properly handles mouse events.

Next, create a JFrame subclass called DrawFrame that provides a GUI that enables the user to control various aspects of drawing. For the layout of the DrawFrame, we recommend a BorderLayout, with the components in the NORTH region, the main drawing panel in the CENTER region, and a status bar in the SOUTH region, as in Fig. 12.49. In the top panel, create the components listed below. Each component's event handler should call the appropriate method in class DrawPanel.

    a) A button to undo the last shape drawn.

    b) A button to clear all shapes from the drawing.

    c) A combo box for selecting the color from the 13 predefined colors.

    d) A combo box for selecting the shape to draw.

    e) A checkbox that specifies whether a shape should be filled or unfilled.

Declare and create the interface components in DrawFrame's constructor. You'll need to create the status bar JLabel before you create the DrawPanel, so you can pass the JLabel as an argument to DrawPanel's constructor. Finally, create a test class that initializes and displays the DrawFrame to execute the application.

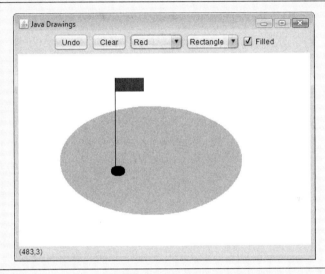

Fig. 12.49 | Interface for drawing shapes.

12.18 *(GUI-Based Version of the ATM Case Study)* Reimplement the Optional ATM Case Study of Chapters 33–34 as a GUI-based application. Use GUI components to approximate the ATM user interface shown in Fig. 33.1. For the cash dispenser and the deposit slot use JButtons labeled **Remove Cash** and **Insert Envelope**. This will enable the application to receive events indicating when the user takes the cash and inserts a deposit envelope, respectively.

Making a Difference

12.19 *(Ecofont)* Ecofont (www.ecofont.eu/ecofont_en.html)—developed by SPRANQ (a Netherlands-based company)—is a free, open-source computer font designed to reduce by as much as 20% the amount of ink used for printing, thus reducing also the number of ink cartridges used and the environmental impact of the manufacturing and shipping processes (using less energy, less fuel for shipping, and so on). The font, based on sans-serif Verdana, has small circular "holes" in the letters that are not visible in smaller sizes—such as the 9- or 10-point type frequently used. Download Ecofont, then install the font file Spranq_eco_sans_regular.ttf using the instructions from the Ecofont website. Next, develop a GUI-based program that allows you to type in a text string to be displayed in the Ecofont. Create **Increase Font Size** and **Decrease Font Size** buttons that allow you to scale up or down by one point at a time. Start with a default font size of 9 points. As you scale up, you'll be able to see the holes in the letters more clearly. As you scale down, the holes will be less apparent. What is the smallest font size at which you begin to notice the holes?

12.20 *(Typing Tutor: Tuning a Crucial Skill in the Computer Age)* Typing quickly and correctly is an essential skill for working effectively with computers and the Internet. In this exercise, you'll build a GUI application that can help users learn to "touch type" (i.e., type correctly without looking at the keyboard). The application should display a *virtual keyboard* (Fig. 12.50) and should allow the user to watch what he or she is typing on the screen without looking at the *actual keyboard*. Use JButtons to represent the keys. As the user presses each key, the application highlights the corresponding JButton on the GUI and adds the character to a JTextArea that shows what the user has typed so far. [*Hint:* To highlight a JButton, use its setBackground method to change its background color. When the key is released, reset its original background color. You can obtain the JButton's original background color with the getBackground method before you change its color.]

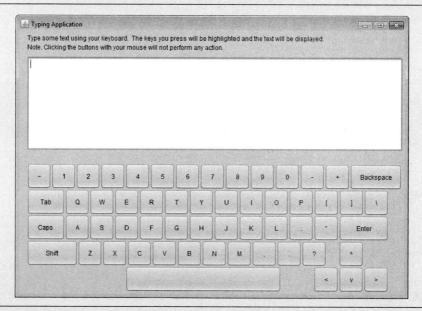

Fig. 12.50 | Typing tutor.

You can test your program by typing a pangram—a phrase that contains every letter of the alphabet at least once—such as "The quick brown fox jumped over a lazy dog." You can find other pangrams on the web.

To make the program more interesting you could monitor the user's accuracy. You could have the user type specific phrases that you've prestored in your program and that you display on the screen above the virtual keyboard. You could keep track of how many keystrokes the user types correctly and how many are typed incorrectly. You could also keep track of which keys the user is having difficulty with and display a report showing those keys.

Graphics and Java 2D

13

Treat nature in terms of the cylinder, the sphere, the cone, all in perspective.
—Paul Cézanne

Colors, like features, follow the changes of the emotions.
—Pablo Picasso

Nothing ever becomes real till it is experienced—even a proverb is no proverb to you till your life has illustrated it.
—John Keats

Objectives

In this chapter you'll:

- Understand graphics contexts and graphics objects.

- Manipulate colors and fonts.

- Use methods of class `Graphics` to draw various shapes.

- Use methods of class `Graphics2D` from the `Java 2D` API to draw various shapes.

- Specify `Paint` and `Stroke` characteristics of shapes displayed with `Graphics2D`.

13.1 Introduction

In this chapter, we overview several of Java's capabilities for drawing two-dimensional shapes, controlling colors and controlling fonts. Part of Java's initial appeal was its support for graphics that enabled programmers to visually enhance their applications. Java contains more sophisticated drawing capabilities as part of the Java 2D API (presented in this chapter) and its successor technology JavaFX (presented in Chapter 25 and two online chapters). This chapter begins by introducing many of Java's original drawing capabilities. Next we present several of the more powerful Java 2D capabilities, such as controlling the *style* of lines used to draw shapes and the way shapes are *filled* with *colors* and *patterns*. The classes that were part of Java's original graphics capabilities are now considered to be part of the Java 2D API.

Figure 13.1 shows a portion of the class hierarchy that includes various graphics classes and Java 2D API classes and interfaces covered in this chapter. Class **Color** contains methods and constants for manipulating colors. Class JComponent contains method paintComponent, which is used to draw graphics on a component. Class **Font** contains methods and constants for manipulating fonts. Class **FontMetrics** contains methods for obtaining *font* information. Class **Graphics** contains methods for drawing strings, lines, rectangles and other shapes. Class **Graphics2D**, which extends class Graphics, is used for drawing with the Java 2D API. Class **Polygon** contains methods for creating *polygons*. The bottom half of the figure lists several classes and interfaces from the Java 2D API. Class **BasicStroke** helps specify the drawing characteristics of *lines*. Classes **GradientPaint** and **TexturePaint** help specify the characteristics for filling *shapes* with *colors* or *patterns*. Classes GeneralPath, Line2D, Arc2D, Ellipse2D, Rectangle2D and RoundRectangle2D represent several Java 2D shapes.

To begin drawing in Java, we must first understand Java's **coordinate system** (Fig. 13.2), which is a scheme for identifying every *point* on the screen. By default, the *upper-left corner* of a GUI component (e.g., a window) has the coordinates (0, 0). A coordinate pair is composed of an *x*-coordinate (the **horizontal coordinate**) and a *y*-coordinate (the **vertical coordinate**). The *x*-coordinate is the horizontal distance moving *right* from the left edge of the screen. The *y*-coordinate is the vertical distance moving *down* from the *top* of the screen. The *x*-**axis** describes every horizontal coordinate, and the *y*-**axis** every vertical coordinate. The coordinates are used to indicate where graphics should be displayed on a screen. Coordinate units are measured in **pixels** (which stands for "picture elements"). A pixel is a display monitor's *smallest unit of resolution*.

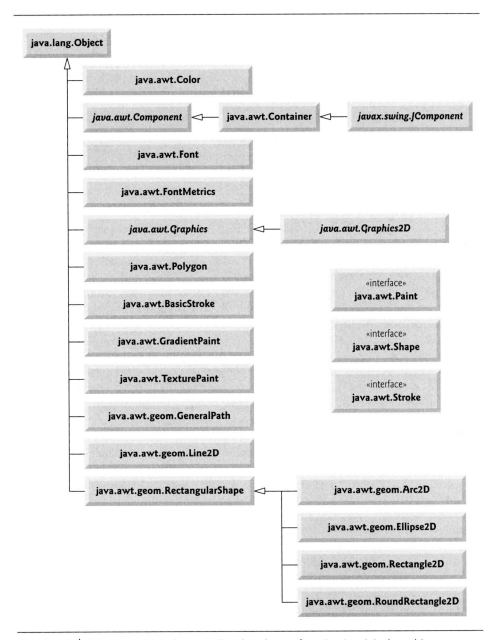

Fig. 13.1 | Classes and interfaces used in this chapter from Java's original graphics capabilities and from the Java 2D API.

Portability Tip 13.1

Different display monitors have different resolutions (i.e., the density of the pixels varies). This can cause graphics to appear in different sizes on different monitors or on the same monitor with different settings.

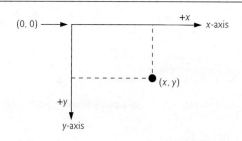

Fig. 13.2 | Java coordinate system. Units are measured in pixels.

13.2 Graphics Contexts and Graphics Objects

A **graphics context** enables drawing on the screen. A Graphics object manages a graphics context and draws pixels on the screen that represent *text* and other graphical objects (e.g., *lines, ellipses, rectangles* and other *polygons*). Graphics objects contain methods for *drawing, font manipulation, color manipulation* and the like.

Class Graphics is an abstract class (i.e., you cannot instantiate Graphics objects). This contributes to Java's portability. Because drawing is performed *differently* on every platform that supports Java, there cannot be only one implementation of the drawing capabilities across all systems. When Java is implemented on a particular platform, a subclass of Graphics is created that implements the drawing capabilities. This implementation is hidden by class Graphics, which supplies the interface that enables us to use graphics in a *platform-independent* manner.

Recall from Chapter 12 that class Component is the *superclass* for many of the classes in package java.awt. Class JComponent (package javax.swing), which inherits indirectly from class Component, contains a paintComponent method that can be used to draw graphics. Method paintComponent takes a Graphics object as an argument. This object is passed to the paintComponent method by the system when a lightweight Swing component needs to be repainted. The header for the paintComponent method is

```
public void paintComponent(Graphics g)
```

Parameter g receives a reference to an instance of the system-specific subclass of Graphics. The preceding method header should look familiar to you—it's the same one we used in some of the applications in Chapter 12. Actually, class JComponent is a *superclass* of JPanel. Many capabilities of class JPanel are inherited from class JComponent.

You seldom call method paintComponent directly, because drawing graphics is an *event-driven* process. As we mentioned in Chapter 11, Java uses a *multithreaded* model of program execution. Each thread is a *parallel* activity. Each program can have many threads. When you create a GUI-based application, one of those threads is known as the **event-dispatch thread** (**EDT**)—it's used to process all GUI events. All manipulation of the on-screen GUI components must be performed in that thread. When a GUI application executes, the application container calls method paintComponent (in the event-dispatch thread) for each lightweight component as the GUI is displayed. For paintComponent to be called again, an event must occur (such as *covering* and *uncovering* the component with another window).

If you need paintComponent to execute (i.e., if you want to update the graphics drawn on a Swing component), you can call method **repaint**, which returns void, takes no arguments and is inherited by all JComponents indirectly from class Component (package java.awt).

13.3 Color Control

Class Color declares methods and constants for manipulating colors in a Java program. The predeclared color constants are summarized in Fig. 13.3, and several color methods and constructors are summarized in Fig. 13.4. Two of the methods in Fig. 13.4 are Graphics methods that are specific to colors.

Color constant	RGB value
public static final Color RED	255, 0, 0
public static final Color GREEN	0, 255, 0
public static final Color BLUE	0, 0, 255
public static final Color ORANGE	255, 200, 0
public static final Color PINK	255, 175, 175
public static final Color CYAN	0, 255, 255
public static final Color MAGENTA	255, 0, 255
public static final Color YELLOW	255, 255, 0
public static final Color BLACK	0, 0, 0
public static final Color WHITE	255, 255, 255
public static final Color GRAY	128, 128, 128
public static final Color LIGHT_GRAY	192, 192, 192
public static final Color DARK_GRAY	64, 64, 64

Fig. 13.3 | Color constants and their RGB values.

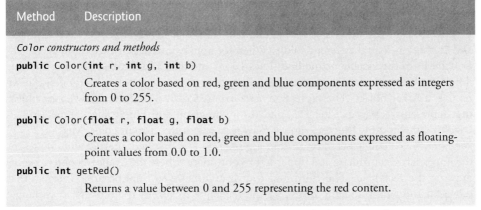

Method	Description

Color constructors and methods

public Color(**int** r, **int** g, **int** b)

Creates a color based on red, green and blue components expressed as integers from 0 to 255.

public Color(**float** r, **float** g, **float** b)

Creates a color based on red, green and blue components expressed as floating-point values from 0.0 to 1.0.

public int getRed()

Returns a value between 0 and 255 representing the red content.

Fig. 13.4 | Color methods and color-related Graphics methods. (Part 1 of 2.)

Method	Description

`public int getGreen()`

> Returns a value between 0 and 255 representing the green content.

`public int getBlue()`

> Returns a value between 0 and 255 representing the blue content.

Graphics methods for manipulating Colors

`public Color getColor()`

> Returns Color object representing current color for the graphics context.

`public void setColor(Color c)`

> Sets the current color for drawing with the graphics context.

Fig. 13.4 | Color methods and color-related Graphics methods. (Part 2 of 2.)

Every color is created from a red, a green and a blue value. Together these are called **RGB values**. All three RGB components can be integers in the range from 0 to 255, or all three can be floating-point values in the range 0.0 to 1.0. The first RGB component specifies the amount of red, the second the amount of green and the third the amount of blue. The larger the value, the greater the amount of that particular color. Java enables you to choose from $256 \times 256 \times 256$ (approximately 16.7 million) colors. Not all computers are capable of displaying all these colors. The screen will display the closest color it can.

Two of class Color's constructors are shown in Fig. 13.4—one that takes three int arguments and one that takes three float arguments, with each argument specifying the amount of red, green and blue. The int values must be in the range 0–255 and the float values in the range 0.0–1.0. The new Color object will have the specified amounts of red, green and blue. Color methods **getRed**, **getGreen** and **getBlue** return integer values from 0 to 255 representing the amounts of red, green and blue, respectively. Graphics method **getColor** returns a Color object representing the Graphics object's current drawing color. Graphics method **setColor** sets the current drawing color.

Drawing in Different Colors

Figures 13.5–13.6 demonstrate several methods from Fig. 13.4 by drawing *filled rectangles* and Strings in several different colors. When the application begins execution, class ColorJPanel's paintComponent method (lines 10–37 of Fig. 13.5) is called to paint the window. Line 17 uses Graphics method setColor to set the drawing color. Method setColor receives a Color object. The expression new Color(255, 0, 0) creates a new Color object that represents red (red value 255, and 0 for the green and blue values). Line 18 uses Graphics method **fillRect** to draw a *filled rectangle* in the current color. Method fillRect draws a rectangle based on its four arguments. The first two integer values represent the upper-left *x*-coordinate and upper-left *y*-coordinate, where the Graphics object begins drawing the rectangle. The third and fourth arguments are nonnegative integers that represent the width and the height of the rectangle in pixels, respectively. A rectangle drawn using method fillRect is filled by the current color of the Graphics object.

```
 1   // Fig. 13.5: ColorJPanel.java
 2   // Changing drawing colors.
 3   import java.awt.Graphics;
 4   import java.awt.Color;
 5   import javax.swing.JPanel;
 6
 7   public class ColorJPanel extends JPanel
 8   {
 9      // draw rectangles and Strings in different colors
10      @Override
11      public void paintComponent(Graphics g)
12      {
13         super.paintComponent(g);
14         this.setBackground(Color.WHITE);
15
16         // set new drawing color using integers
17         g.setColor(new Color(255, 0, 0));
18         g.fillRect(15, 25, 100, 20);
19         g.drawString("Current RGB: " + g.getColor(), 130, 40);
20
21         // set new drawing color using floats
22         g.setColor(new Color(0.50f, 0.75f, 0.0f));
23         g.fillRect(15, 50, 100, 20);
24         g.drawString("Current RGB: " + g.getColor(), 130, 65);
25
26         // set new drawing color using static Color objects
27         g.setColor(Color.BLUE);
28         g.fillRect(15, 75, 100, 20);
29         g.drawString("Current RGB: " + g.getColor(), 130, 90);
30
31         // display individual RGB values
32         Color color = Color.MAGENTA;
33         g.setColor(color);
34         g.fillRect(15, 100, 100, 20);
35         g.drawString("RGB values: " + color.getRed() + ", " +
36            color.getGreen() + ", " + color.getBlue(), 130, 115);
37      }
38   } // end class ColorJPanel
```

Fig. 13.5 | Changing drawing colors.

```
 1   // Fig. 13.6: ShowColors.java
 2   // Demonstrating Colors.
 3   import javax.swing.JFrame;
 4
 5   public class ShowColors
 6   {
 7      // execute application
 8      public static void main(String[] args)
 9      {
```

Fig. 13.6 | Demonstrating Colors. (Part 1 of 2.)

```
10          // create frame for ColorJPanel
11          JFrame frame = new JFrame("Using colors");
12          frame.setDefaultCloseOperation(JFrame.EXIT_ON_CLOSE);
13
14          ColorJPanel colorJPanel = new ColorJPanel();
15          frame.add(colorJPanel);
16          frame.setSize(400, 180);
17          frame.setVisible(true);
18      }
19  } // end class ShowColors
```

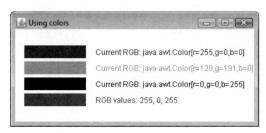

Fig. 13.6 | Demonstrating Colors. (Part 2 of 2.)

Line 19 uses Graphics method **drawString** to draw a String in the current color. The expression g.getColor() retrieves the current color from the Graphics object. We then concatenate the Color with string "Current RGB: ", resulting in an *implicit* call to class Color's toString method. The String representation of a Color contains the class name and package (java.awt.Color) and the red, green and blue values.

Look-and-Feel Observation 13.1

People perceive colors differently. Choose your colors carefully to ensure that your application is readable, both for people who can perceive color and for those who are color blind. Try to avoid using many different colors in close proximity.

Lines 22–24 and 27–29 perform the same tasks again. Line 22 uses the Color constructor with three float arguments to create a dark green color (0.50f for red, 0.75f for green and 0.0f for blue). Note the syntax of the values. The letter f appended to a floating-point literal indicates that the literal should be treated as type float. Recall that by default, floating-point literals are treated as type double.

Line 27 sets the current drawing color to one of the predeclared Color constants (Color.BLUE). The Color constants are static, so they're created when class Color is loaded into memory at execution time.

The statement in lines 35–36 makes calls to Color methods getRed, getGreen and getBlue on the predeclared Color.MAGENTA constant. Method main of class ShowColors (lines 8–18 of Fig. 13.6) creates the JFrame that will contain a ColorJPanel object where the colors will be displayed.

Software Engineering Observation 13.1

To change the color, you must create a new Color object (or use one of the predeclared Color constants). Like String objects, Color objects are immutable (not modifiable).

The **JColorChooser** component (package javax.swing) enables application users to select colors. Figures 13.7–13.8 demonstrate a JColorChooser dialog. When you click the **Change Color** button, a JColorChooser dialog appears. When you select a color and press the dialog's **OK** button, the background color of the application window changes.

```java
1  // Fig. 13.7: ShowColors2JFrame.java
2  // Choosing colors with JColorChooser.
3  import java.awt.BorderLayout;
4  import java.awt.Color;
5  import java.awt.event.ActionEvent;
6  import java.awt.event.ActionListener;
7  import javax.swing.JButton;
8  import javax.swing.JFrame;
9  import javax.swing.JColorChooser;
10 import javax.swing.JPanel;
11
12 public class ShowColors2JFrame extends JFrame
13 {
14    private final JButton changeColorJButton;
15    private Color color = Color.LIGHT_GRAY;
16    private final JPanel colorJPanel;
17
18    // set up GUI
19    public ShowColors2JFrame()
20    {
21       super("Using JColorChooser");
22
23       // create JPanel for display color
24       colorJPanel = new JPanel();
25       colorJPanel.setBackground(color);
26
27       // set up changeColorJButton and register its event handler
28       changeColorJButton = new JButton("Change Color");
29       changeColorJButton.addActionListener(
30          new ActionListener() // anonymous inner class
31          {
32             // display JColorChooser when user clicks button
33             @Override
34             public void actionPerformed(ActionEvent event)
35             {
36                color = JColorChooser.showDialog(
37                   ShowColors2JFrame.this, "Choose a color", color);
38
39                // set default color, if no color is returned
40                if (color == null)
41                   color = Color.LIGHT_GRAY;
42
43                // change content pane's background color
44                colorJPanel.setBackground(color);
45             } // end method actionPerformed
46          } // end anonymous inner class
47       ); // end call to addActionListener
```

Fig. 13.7 | Choosing colors with JColorChooser. (Part 1 of 2.)

```
48
49        add(colorJPanel, BorderLayout.CENTER);
50        add(changeColorJButton, BorderLayout.SOUTH);
51
52        setSize(400, 130);
53        setVisible(true);
54     } // end ShowColor2JFrame constructor
55  } // end class ShowColors2JFrame
```

Fig. 13.7 | Choosing colors with JColorChooser. (Part 2 of 2.)

```
1   // Fig. 13.8: ShowColors2.java
2   // Choosing colors with JColorChooser.
3   import javax.swing.JFrame;
4
5   public class ShowColors2
6   {
7      // execute application
8      public static void main(String[] args)
9      {
10        ShowColors2JFrame application = new ShowColors2JFrame();
11        application.setDefaultCloseOperation(JFrame.EXIT_ON_CLOSE);
12     }
13  } // end class ShowColors2
```

(a) Initial application window

(b) JColorChooser window

Select a color from one of the color swatches

(c) Application window after changing JPanel's background color

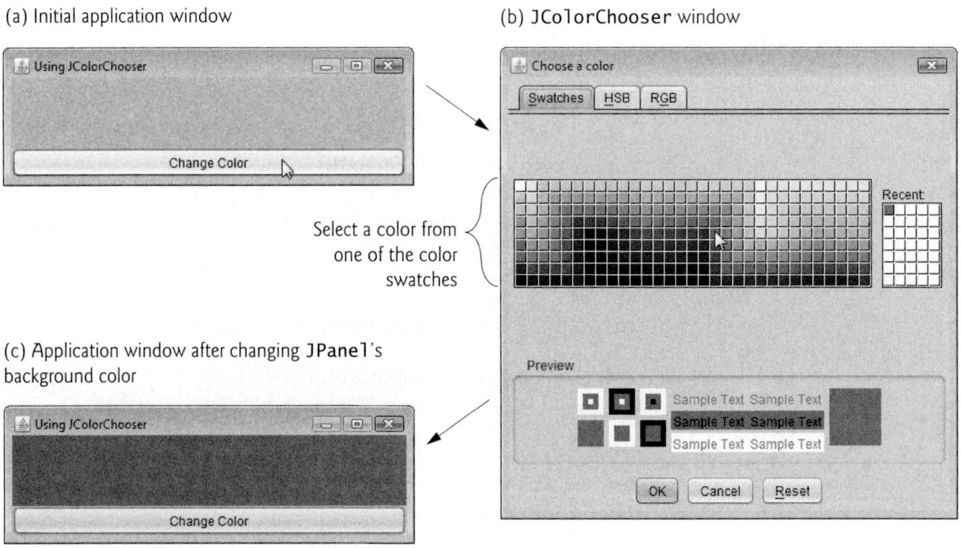

Fig. 13.8 | Choosing colors with JColorChooser.

Class JColorChooser provides static method **showDialog**, which creates a JColor-Chooser object, attaches it to a dialog box and displays the dialog. Lines 36–37 of Fig. 13.7

invoke this method to display the color-chooser dialog. Method `showDialog` returns the selected `Color` object, or `null` if the user presses **Cancel** or closes the dialog without pressing **OK**. The method takes three arguments—a reference to its parent `Component`, a `String` to display in the title bar of the dialog and the initial selected `Color` for the dialog. The parent component is a reference to the window from which the dialog is displayed (in this case the `JFrame`, with the reference name `frame`). The dialog will be centered on the parent. If the parent is `null`, the dialog is centered on the screen. While the color-chooser dialog is on the screen, the user cannot interact with the parent component until the dialog is dismissed. This type of dialog is called a modal dialog.

After the user selects a color, lines 40–41 determine whether `color` is `null`, and, if so, set `color` to `Color.LIGHT_GRAY`. Line 44 invokes method `setBackground` to change the background color of the `JPanel`. Method `setBackground` is one of the many `Component` methods that can be used on most GUI components. The user can continue to use the **Change Color** button to change the background color of the application. Figure 13.8 contains method `main`, which executes the program.

Figure 13.8(b) shows the default `JColorChooser` dialog that allows the user to select a color from a variety of **color swatches**. There are three tabs across the top of the dialog—**Swatches**, **HSB** and **RGB**. These represent three different ways to select a color. The **HSB** tab allows you to select a color based on **hue**, **saturation** and **brightness**—values that are used to define the amount of light in a color. Visit `http://en.wikipedia.org/wiki/HSL_and_HSV` for more information on HSB. The **RGB** tab allows you to select a color by using sliders to select the red, green and blue components. The **HSB** and **RGB** tabs are shown in Fig. 13.9.

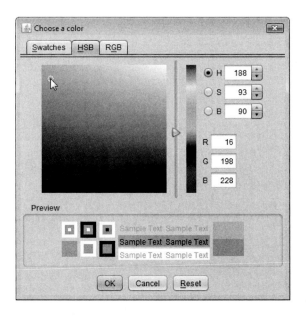

Fig. 13.9 | **HSB** and **RGB** tabs of the `JColorChooser` dialog. (Part 1 of 2.)

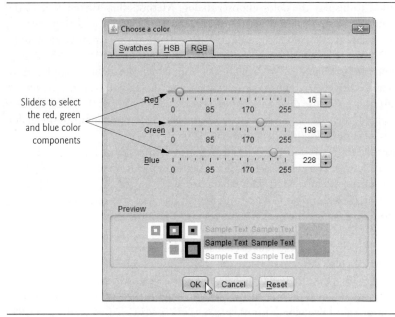

Sliders to select the red, green and blue color components

Fig. 13.9 | HSB and RGB tabs of the JColorChooser dialog. (Part 2 of 2.)

13.4 Manipulating Fonts

This section introduces methods and constants for manipulating fonts. Most font methods and font constants are part of class Font. Some constructors, methods and constants of class Font and class Graphics are summarized in Fig. 13.10.

Method or constant	Description
Font constants, constructors and methods	
`public static final int` PLAIN	A constant representing a plain font style.
`public static final int` BOLD	A constant representing a bold font style.
`public static final int` ITALIC	A constant representing an italic font style.
`public Font(String name,` `    int style, int size)`	Creates a Font object with the specified font name, style and size.
`public int getStyle()`	Returns an int indicating the current font style.
`public int getSize()`	Returns an int indicating the current font size.
`public String getName()`	Returns the current font name as a string.
`public String getFamily()`	Returns the font's family name as a string.
`public boolean isPlain()`	Returns true if the font is plain, else false.
`public boolean isBold()`	Returns true if the font is bold, else false.
`public boolean isItalic()`	Returns true if the font is italic, else false.

Fig. 13.10 | Font-related methods and constants. (Part 1 of 2.)

Method or constant	Description
Graphics methods for manipulating Fonts	
public Font getFont()	Returns a Font object reference representing the current font.
public void setFont(Font f)	Sets the current font to the font, style and size specified by the Font object reference f.

Fig. 13.10 | Font-related methods and constants. (Part 2 of 2.)

Class Font's constructor takes three arguments—the **font name**, **font style** and **font size**. The font name is any font currently supported by the system on which the program is running, such as standard Java fonts Monospaced, SansSerif and Serif. The font style is **Font.PLAIN**, **Font.ITALIC** or **Font.BOLD** (each is a static field of class Font). Font styles can be used in combination (e.g., Font.ITALIC + Font.BOLD). The font size is measured in points. A **point** is 1/72 of an inch. Graphics method **setFont** sets the current drawing font—the font in which text will be displayed—to its Font argument.

Portability Tip 13.2

The number of fonts varies across systems. Java provides five font names—Serif, Monospaced, SansSerif, Dialog and DialogInput—that can be used on all Java platforms. The Java runtime environment (JRE) on each platform maps these logical font names to actual fonts installed on the platform. The actual fonts used may vary by platform.

The application of Figs. 13.11–13.12 displays text in four different fonts, with each font in a different size. Figure 13.11 uses the Font constructor to initialize Font objects (in lines 17, 21, 25 and 30) that are each passed to Graphics method setFont to change the drawing font. Each call to the Font constructor passes a font name (Serif, Monospaced or SansSerif) as a string, a font style (Font.PLAIN, Font.ITALIC or Font.BOLD) and a font size. Once Graphics method setFont is invoked, all text displayed following the call will appear in the new font until the font is changed. Each font's information is displayed in lines 18, 22, 26 and 31–32 using method drawString. The coordinates passed to drawString correspond to the lower-left corner of the baseline of the font. Line 29 changes the drawing color to red, so the next string displayed appears in red. Lines 31–32 display information about the final Font object. Method **getFont** of class Graphics returns a Font object representing the current font. Method **getName** returns the current font name as a string. Method **getSize** returns the font size in points.

Software Engineering Observation 13.2

To change the font, you must create a new Font object. Font objects are immutable—class Font has no set methods to change the characteristics of the current font.

Figure 13.12 contains the main method, which creates a JFrame to display a FontJPanel. We add a FontJPanel object to this JFrame (line 15), which displays the graphics created in Fig. 13.11.

```java
 1   // Fig. 13.11: FontJPanel.java
 2   // Display strings in different fonts and colors.
 3   import java.awt.Font;
 4   import java.awt.Color;
 5   import java.awt.Graphics;
 6   import javax.swing.JPanel;
 7
 8   public class FontJPanel extends JPanel
 9   {
10      // display Strings in different fonts and colors
11      @Override
12      public void paintComponent(Graphics g)
13      {
14         super.paintComponent(g);
15
16         // set font to Serif (Times), bold, 12pt and draw a string
17         g.setFont(new Font("Serif", Font.BOLD, 12));
18         g.drawString("Serif 12 point bold.", 20, 30);
19
20         // set font to Monospaced (Courier), italic, 24pt and draw a string
21         g.setFont(new Font("Monospaced", Font.ITALIC, 24));
22         g.drawString("Monospaced 24 point italic.", 20, 50);
23
24         // set font to SansSerif (Helvetica), plain, 14pt and draw a string
25         g.setFont(new Font("SansSerif", Font.PLAIN, 14));
26         g.drawString("SansSerif 14 point plain.", 20, 70);
27
28         // set font to Serif (Times), bold/italic, 18pt and draw a string
29         g.setColor(Color.RED);
30         g.setFont(new Font("Serif", Font.BOLD + Font.ITALIC, 18));
31         g.drawString(g.getFont().getName() + " " + g.getFont().getSize() +
32            " point bold italic.", 20, 90);
33      }
34   } // end class FontJPanel
```

Fig. 13.11 | Display strings in different fonts and colors.

```java
 1   // Fig. 13.12: Fonts.java
 2   // Using fonts.
 3   import javax.swing.JFrame;
 4
 5   public class Fonts
 6   {
 7      // execute application
 8      public static void main(String[] args)
 9      {
10         // create frame for FontJPanel
11         JFrame frame = new JFrame("Using fonts");
12         frame.setDefaultCloseOperation(JFrame.EXIT_ON_CLOSE);
13
14         FontJPanel fontJPanel = new FontJPanel();
15         frame.add(fontJPanel);
```

Fig. 13.12 | Using fonts. (Part 1 of 2.)

```
16          frame.setSize(420, 150);
17          frame.setVisible(true);
18       }
19  } // end class Fonts
```

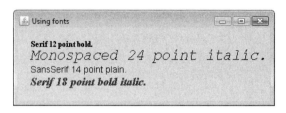

Fig. 13.12 | Using fonts. (Part 2 of 2.)

Font Metrics

Sometimes it's necessary to get information about the current drawing font, such as its name, style and size. Several Font methods used to get font information are summarized in Fig. 13.10. Method **getStyle** returns an integer value representing the current style. The integer value returned is either Font.PLAIN, Font.ITALIC, Font.BOLD or the combination of Font.ITALIC and Font.BOLD. Method **getFamily** returns the name of the font family to which the current font belongs. The name of the font family is platform specific. Font methods are also available to test the style of the current font, and these too are summarized in Fig. 13.10. Methods **isPlain**, **isBold** and **isItalic** return true if the current font style is plain, bold or italic, respectively.

Figure 13.13 illustrates some of the common **font metrics**, which provide precise information about a font, such as **height**, **descent** (the amount a character dips below the baseline), **ascent** (the amount a character rises above the baseline) and **leading** (the difference between the descent of one line of text and the ascent of the line of text below it—that is, the interline spacing).

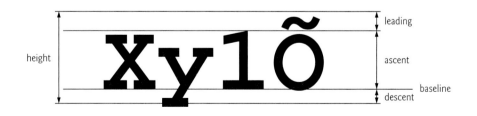

Fig. 13.13 | Font metrics.

Class **FontMetrics** declares several methods for obtaining font metrics. These methods and Graphics method **getFontMetrics** are summarized in Fig. 13.14. The application of Figs. 13.15–13.16 uses the methods of Fig. 13.14 to obtain font metric information for two fonts.

Method	Description
FontMetrics methods	
`public int getAscent()`	Returns the ascent of a font in points.
`public int getDescent()`	Returns the descent of a font in points.
`public int getLeading()`	Returns the leading of a font in points.
`public int getHeight()`	Returns the height of a font in points.
Graphics methods for getting a Font's FontMetrics	
`public FontMetrics getFontMetrics()`	
	Returns the `FontMetrics` object for the current drawing `Font`.
`public FontMetrics getFontMetrics(Font f)`	
	Returns the `FontMetrics` object for the specified `Font` argument.

Fig. 13.14 | FontMetrics and Graphics methods for obtaining font metrics.

```
1   // Fig. 13.15: MetricsJPanel.java
2   // FontMetrics and Graphics methods useful for obtaining font metrics.
3   import java.awt.Font;
4   import java.awt.FontMetrics;
5   import java.awt.Graphics;
6   import javax.swing.JPanel;
7
8   public class MetricsJPanel extends JPanel
9   {
10     // display font metrics
11     @Override
12     public void paintComponent(Graphics g)
13     {
14        super.paintComponent(g);
15
16        g.setFont(new Font("SansSerif", Font.BOLD, 12));
17        FontMetrics metrics = g.getFontMetrics();
18        g.drawString("Current font: " + g.getFont(), 10, 30);
19        g.drawString("Ascent: " + metrics.getAscent(), 10, 45);
20        g.drawString("Descent: " + metrics.getDescent(), 10, 60);
21        g.drawString("Height: " + metrics.getHeight(), 10, 75);
22        g.drawString("Leading: " + metrics.getLeading(), 10, 90);
23
24        Font font = new Font("Serif", Font.ITALIC, 14);
25        metrics = g.getFontMetrics(font);
26        g.setFont(font);
27        g.drawString("Current font: " + font, 10, 120);
28        g.drawString("Ascent: " + metrics.getAscent(), 10, 135);
29        g.drawString("Descent: " + metrics.getDescent(), 10, 150);
30        g.drawString("Height: " + metrics.getHeight(), 10, 165);
31        g.drawString("Leading: " + metrics.getLeading(), 10, 180);
32     }
33  } // end class MetricsJPanel
```

Fig. 13.15 | FontMetrics and Graphics methods useful for obtaining font metrics.

```
 I    // Fig. 13.16: Metrics.java
 2    // Displaying font metrics.
 3    import javax.swing.JFrame;
 4
 5    public class Metrics
 6    {
 7       // execute application
 8       public static void main(String[] args)
 9       {
10          // create frame for MetricsJPanel
11          JFrame frame = new JFrame("Demonstrating FontMetrics");
12          frame.setDefaultCloseOperation(JFrame.EXIT_ON_CLOSE);
13
14          MetricsJPanel metricsJPanel = new MetricsJPanel();
15          frame.add(metricsJPanel);
16          frame.setSize(510, 240);
17          frame.setVisible(true);
18       }
19    } // end class Metrics
```

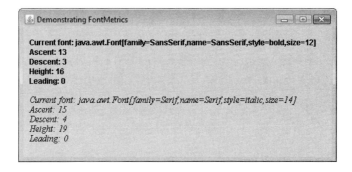

Fig. 13.16 | Displaying font metrics.

Line 16 of Fig. 13.15 creates and sets the current drawing font to a SansSerif, bold, 12-point font. Line 17 uses Graphics method getFontMetrics to obtain the FontMetrics object for the current font. Line 18 outputs the String representation of the Font returned by g.getFont(). Lines 19–22 use FontMetric methods to obtain the ascent, descent, height and leading for the font.

Line 24 creates a new Serif, italic, 14-point font. Line 25 uses a second version of Graphics method getFontMetrics, which accepts a Font argument and returns a corresponding FontMetrics object. Lines 28–31 obtain the ascent, descent, height and leading for the font. The font metrics are slightly different for the two fonts.

13.5 Drawing Lines, Rectangles and Ovals

This section presents Graphics methods for drawing lines, rectangles and ovals. The methods and their parameters are summarized in Fig. 13.17. For each drawing method that requires a width and height parameter, the width and height must be nonnegative values. Otherwise, the shape will not display.

Method	Description

`public void drawLine(int x1, int y1, int x2, int y2)`

Draws a line between the point (x1, y1) and the point (x2, y2).

`public void drawRect(int x, int y, int width, int height)`

Draws a rectangle of the specified width and height. The rectangle's top-left corner is located at (x, y). Only the outline of the rectangle is drawn using the Graphics object's color—the body of the rectangle is not filled with this color.

`public void fillRect(int x, int y, int width, int height)`

Draws a filled rectangle in the current color with the specified width and height. The rectangle's top-left corner is located at (x, y).

`public void clearRect(int x, int y, int width, int height)`

Draws a filled rectangle with the specified width and height in the current background color. The rectangle's *top-left* corner is located at (x, y). This method is useful if you want to remove a portion of an image.

`public void drawRoundRect(int x, int y, int width, int height, int arcWidth, int arcHeight)`

Draws a rectangle with rounded corners in the current color with the specified width and height. The arcWidth and arcHeight determine the rounding of the corners (see Fig. 13.20). Only the outline of the shape is drawn.

`public void fillRoundRect(int x, int y, int width, int height, int arcWidth, int arcHeight)`

Draws a filled rectangle in the current color with rounded corners with the specified width and height. The arcWidth and arcHeight determine the rounding of the corners (see Fig. 13.20).

`public void draw3DRect(int x, int y, int width, int height, boolean b)`

Draws a three-dimensional rectangle in the current color with the specified width and height. The rectangle's *top-left* corner is located at (x, y). The rectangle appears raised when b is true and lowered when b is false. Only the outline of the shape is drawn.

`public void fill3DRect(int x, int y, int width, int height, boolean b)`

Draws a filled three-dimensional rectangle in the current color with the specified width and height. The rectangle's *top-left* corner is located at (x, y). The rectangle appears raised when b is true and lowered when b is false.

`public void drawOval(int x, int y, int width, int height)`

Draws an oval in the current color with the specified width and height. The bounding rectangle's *top-left* corner is located at (x, y). The oval touches all four sides of the bounding rectangle at the center of each side (see Fig. 13.21). Only the outline of the shape is drawn.

`public void fillOval(int x, int y, int width, int height)`

Draws a filled oval in the current color with the specified width and height. The bounding rectangle's *top-left* corner is located at (x, y). The oval touches the center of all four sides of the bounding rectangle (see Fig. 13.21).

Fig. 13.17 | Graphics methods that draw lines, rectangles and ovals.

The application of Figs. 13.18–13.19 demonstrates drawing a variety of lines, rectangles, three-dimensional rectangles, rounded rectangles and ovals. In Fig. 13.18, line 17 draws a red line, line 20 draws an empty blue rectangle and line 21 draws a filled blue rectangle. Methods **fillRoundRect** (line 24) and **drawRoundRect** (line 25) draw rectangles with rounded corners. Their first two arguments specify the coordinates of the upper-left corner of the **bounding rectangle**—the area in which the rounded rectangle will be drawn. The upper-left corner coordinates are *not* the edge of the rounded rectangle, but the coordinates where the edge would be if the rectangle had square corners. The third and fourth arguments specify the width and height of the rectangle. The last two arguments determine the horizontal and vertical diameters of the arc (i.e., the arc width and arc height) used to represent the corners.

Figure 13.20 labels the arc width, arc height, width and height of a rounded rectangle. Using the same value for the arc width and arc height produces a quarter-circle at each

```java
1   // Fig. 13.18: LinesRectsOvalsJPanel.java
2   // Drawing lines, rectangles and ovals.
3   import java.awt.Color;
4   import java.awt.Graphics;
5   import javax.swing.JPanel;
6
7   public class LinesRectsOvalsJPanel extends JPanel
8   {
9      // display various lines, rectangles and ovals
10     @Override
11     public void paintComponent(Graphics g)
12     {
13        super.paintComponent(g);
14        this.setBackground(Color.WHITE);
15
16        g.setColor(Color.RED);
17        g.drawLine(5, 30, 380, 30);
18
19        g.setColor(Color.BLUE);
20        g.drawRect(5, 40, 90, 55);
21        g.fillRect(100, 40, 90, 55);
22
23        g.setColor(Color.CYAN);
24        g.fillRoundRect(195, 40, 90, 55, 50, 50);
25        g.drawRoundRect(290, 40, 90, 55, 20, 20);
26
27        g.setColor(Color.GREEN);
28        g.draw3DRect(5, 100, 90, 55, true);
29        g.fill3DRect(100, 100, 90, 55, false);
30
31        g.setColor(Color.MAGENTA);
32        g.drawOval(195, 100, 90, 55);
33        g.fillOval(290, 100, 90, 55);
34     }
35  } // end class LinesRectsOvalsJPanel
```

Fig. 13.18 | Drawing lines, rectangles and ovals.

```
1   // Fig. 13.19: LinesRectsOvals.java
2   // Testing LinesRectsOvalsJPanel.
3   import java.awt.Color;
4   import javax.swing.JFrame;
5
6   public class LinesRectsOvals
7   {
8      // execute application
9      public static void main(String[] args)
10     {
11        // create frame for LinesRectsOvalsJPanel
12        JFrame frame =
13           new JFrame("Drawing lines, rectangles and ovals");
14        frame.setDefaultCloseOperation(JFrame.EXIT_ON_CLOSE);
15
16        LinesRectsOvalsJPanel linesRectsOvalsJPanel =
17           new LinesRectsOvalsJPanel();
18        linesRectsOvalsJPanel.setBackground(Color.WHITE);
19        frame.add(linesRectsOvalsJPanel);
20        frame.setSize(400, 210);
21        frame.setVisible(true);
22     }
23  } // end class LinesRectsOvals
```

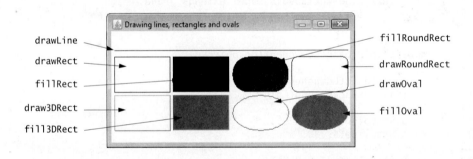

Fig. 13.19 | Testing LinesRectsOvalsJPanel.

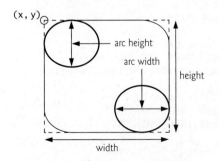

Fig. 13.20 | Arc width and arc height for rounded rectangles.

corner. When the arc width, arc height, width and height have the same values, the result is a circle. If the values for width and height are the same and the values of arcWidth and arcHeight are 0, the result is a square.

Methods **draw3DRect** (Fig. 13.18, line 28) and **fill3DRect** (line 29) take the same arguments. The first two specify the *top-left* corner of the rectangle. The next two arguments specify the width and height of the rectangle, respectively. The last argument determines whether the rectangle is **raised** (true) or **lowered** (false). The three-dimensional effect of draw3DRect appears as two edges of the rectangle in the original color and two edges in a slightly darker color. The three-dimensional effect of fill3DRect appears as two edges of the rectangle in the original drawing color and the fill and other two edges in a slightly darker color. Raised rectangles have the original drawing color edges at the top and left of the rectangle. Lowered rectangles have the original drawing color edges at the bottom and right of the rectangle. The three-dimensional effect is difficult to see in some colors.

Methods **drawOval** and **fillOval** (lines 32–33) take the same four arguments. The first two specify the top-left coordinate of the bounding rectangle that contains the oval. The last two specify the width and height of the bounding rectangle, respectively. Figure 13.21 shows an oval bounded by a rectangle. The oval touches the *center* of all four sides of the bounding rectangle. (The bounding rectangle is *not* displayed on the screen.)

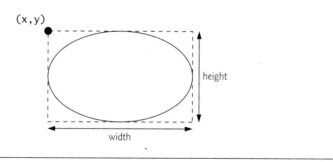

Fig. 13.21 | Oval bounded by a rectangle.

13.6 Drawing Arcs

An **arc** is drawn as a portion of an oval. Arc angles are measured in degrees. Arcs **sweep** (i.e., move along a curve) from a **starting angle** through the number of degrees specified by their **arc angle**. The starting angle indicates in degrees where the arc begins. The arc angle specifies the total number of degrees through which the arc sweeps. Figure 13.22 illustrates two arcs. The left set of axes shows an arc sweeping from zero degrees to approximately 110 degrees. Arcs that sweep in a *counterclockwise* direction are measured in **positive degrees**. The set of axes on the right shows an arc sweeping from zero degrees to approximately –110 degrees. Arcs that sweep in a *clockwise* direction are measured in **negative degrees**. Note the dashed boxes around the arcs in Fig. 13.22. When drawing an arc, we specify a bounding rectangle for an oval. The arc will sweep along part of the oval. Graphics methods **drawArc** and **fillArc** for drawing arcs are summarized in Fig. 13.23.

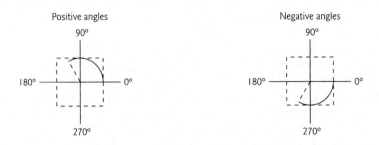

Fig. 13.22 | Positive and negative arc angles.

Method	Description
`public void drawArc(int x, int y, int width, int height, int startAngle, int arcAngle)`	
	Draws an arc relative to the bounding rectangle's top-left x- and y-coordinates with the specified `width` and `height`. The arc segment is drawn starting at `startAngle` and sweeps `arcAngle` degrees.
`public void fillArc(int x, int y, int width, int height, int startAngle, int arcAngle)`	
	Draws a filled arc (i.e., a sector) relative to the bounding rectangle's top-left x- and y-coordinates with the specified `width` and `height`. The arc segment is drawn starting at `startAngle` and sweeps `arcAngle` degrees.

Fig. 13.23 | Graphics methods for drawing arcs.

Figures 13.24–13.25 demonstrate the arc methods of Fig. 13.23. The application draws six arcs (three unfilled and three filled). To illustrate the bounding rectangle that helps determine where the arc appears, the first three arcs are displayed inside a red rectangle that has the same x, y, width and height arguments as the arcs.

```
1   // Fig. 13.24: ArcsJPanel.java
2   // Arcs displayed with drawArc and fillArc.
3   import java.awt.Color;
4   import java.awt.Graphics;
5   import javax.swing.JPanel;
6
7   public class ArcsJPanel extends JPanel
8   {
9      // draw rectangles and arcs
10     @Override
11     public void paintComponent(Graphics g)
12     {
13        super.paintComponent(g);
14
```

Fig. 13.24 | Arcs displayed with `drawArc` and `fillArc`. (Part 1 of 2.)

```
15            // start at 0 and sweep 360 degrees
16            g.setColor(Color.RED);
17            g.drawRect(15, 35, 80, 80);
18            g.setColor(Color.BLACK);
19            g.drawArc(15, 35, 80, 80, 0, 360);
20
21            // start at 0 and sweep 110 degrees
22            g.setColor(Color.RED);
23            g.drawRect(100, 35, 80, 80);
24            g.setColor(Color.BLACK);
25            g.drawArc(100, 35, 80, 80, 0, 110);
26
27            // start at 0 and sweep -270 degrees
28            g.setColor(Color.RED);
29            g.drawRect(185, 35, 80, 80);
30            g.setColor(Color.BLACK);
31            g.drawArc(185, 35, 80, 80, 0, -270);
32
33            // start at 0 and sweep 360 degrees
34            g.fillArc(15, 120, 80, 40, 0, 360);
35
36            // start at 270 and sweep -90 degrees
37            g.fillArc(100, 120, 80, 40, 270, -90);
38
39            // start at 0 and sweep -270 degrees
40            g.fillArc(185, 120, 80, 40, 0, -270);
41       }
42  } // end class ArcsJPanel
```

Fig. 13.24 | Arcs displayed with drawArc and fillArc. (Part 2 of 2.)

```
1   // Fig. 13.25: DrawArcs.java
2   // Drawing arcs.
3   import javax.swing.JFrame;
4
5   public class DrawArcs
6   {
7      // execute application
8      public static void main(String[] args)
9      {
10         // create frame for ArcsJPanel
11         JFrame frame = new JFrame("Drawing Arcs");
12         frame.setDefaultCloseOperation(JFrame.EXIT_ON_CLOSE);
13
14         ArcsJPanel arcsJPanel = new ArcsJPanel();
15         frame.add(arcsJPanel);
16         frame.setSize(300, 210);
17         frame.setVisible(true);
18      }
19  } // end class DrawArcs
```

Fig. 13.25 | Drawing arcs. (Part 1 of 2.)

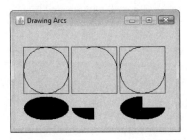

Fig. 13.25 | Drawing arcs. (Part 2 of 2.)

13.7 Drawing Polygons and Polylines

Polygons are *closed multisided shapes* composed of straight-line segments. **Polylines** are *sequences of connected points*. Figure 13.26 discusses methods for drawing polygons and polylines. Some methods require a **Polygon** object (package java.awt). Class Polygon's constructors are also described in Fig. 13.26. The application of Figs. 13.27–13.28 draws polygons and polylines.

Method	Description
Graphics methods for drawing polygons	
public void drawPolygon(**int**[] xPoints, **int**[] yPoints, **int** points)	Draws a polygon. The *x*-coordinate of each point is specified in the xPoints array and the *y*-coordinate of each point in the yPoints array. The last argument specifies the number of points. This method draws a *closed polygon*. If the last point is different from the first, the polygon is *closed* by a line that connects the last point to the first.
public void drawPolyline(**int**[] xPoints, **int**[] yPoints, **int** points)	Draws a sequence of connected lines. The *x*-coordinate of each point is specified in the xPoints array and the *y*-coordinate of each point in the yPoints array. The last argument specifies the number of points. If the last point is different from the first, the polyline is *not* closed.
public void drawPolygon(Polygon p)	Draws the specified polygon.
public void fillPolygon(**int**[] xPoints, **int**[] yPoints, **int** points)	Draws a *filled* polygon. The *x*-coordinate of each point is specified in the xPoints array and the *y*-coordinate of each point in the yPoints array. The last argument specifies the number of points. This method draws a *closed polygon*. If the last point is different from the first, the polygon is *closed* by a line that connects the last point to the first.
public void fillPolygon(Polygon p)	Draws the specified *filled* polygon. The polygon is *closed*.

Fig. 13.26 | Graphics methods for polygons and class Polygon methods. (Part 1 of 2.)

Method	Description

Polygon constructors and methods

public Polygon()

Constructs a new polygon object. The polygon does not contain any points.

public Polygon(**int**[] xValues, **int**[] yValues, **int** numberOfPoints)

Constructs a new polygon object. The polygon has numberOfPoints sides, with each point consisting of an *x*-coordinate from xValues and a *y*-coordinate from yValues.

public void addPoint(**int** x, **int** y)

Adds pairs of *x*- and *y*-coordinates to the Polygon.

Fig. 13.26 | Graphics methods for polygons and class Polygon methods. (Part 2 of 2.)

```
 1   // Fig. 13.27: PolygonsJPanel.java
 2   // Drawing polygons.
 3   import java.awt.Graphics;
 4   import java.awt.Polygon;
 5   import javax.swing.JPanel;
 6
 7   public class PolygonsJPanel extends JPanel
 8   {
 9      // draw polygons and polylines
10      @Override
11      public void paintComponent(Graphics g)
12      {
13         super.paintComponent(g);
14
15         // draw polygon with Polygon object
16         int[] xValues = {20, 40, 50, 30, 20, 15};
17         int[] yValues = {50, 50, 60, 80, 80, 60};
18         Polygon polygon1 = new Polygon(xValues, yValues, 6);
19         g.drawPolygon(polygon1);
20
21         // draw polylines with two arrays
22         int[] xValues2 = {70, 90, 100, 80, 70, 65, 60};
23         int[] yValues2 = {100, 100, 110, 110, 130, 110, 90};
24         g.drawPolyline(xValues2, yValues2, 7);
25
26         // fill polygon with two arrays
27         int[] xValues3 = {120, 140, 150, 190};
28         int[] yValues3 = {40, 70, 80, 60};
29         g.fillPolygon(xValues3, yValues3, 4);
30
31         // draw filled polygon with Polygon object
32         Polygon polygon2 = new Polygon();
33         polygon2.addPoint(165, 135);
34         polygon2.addPoint(175, 150);
35         polygon2.addPoint(270, 200);
```

Fig. 13.27 | Polygons displayed with drawPolygon and fillPolygon. (Part 1 of 2.)

```
36          polygon2.addPoint(200, 220);
37          polygon2.addPoint(130, 180);
38          g.fillPolygon(polygon2);
39       }
40    } // end class PolygonsJPanel
```

Fig. 13.27 | Polygons displayed with `drawPolygon` and `fillPolygon`. (Part 2 of 2.)

```
1    // Fig. 13.28: DrawPolygons.java
2    // Drawing polygons.
3    import javax.swing.JFrame;
4
5    public class DrawPolygons
6    {
7       // execute application
8       public static void main(String[] args)
9       {
10         // create frame for PolygonsJPanel
11         JFrame frame = new JFrame("Drawing Polygons");
12         frame.setDefaultCloseOperation(JFrame.EXIT_ON_CLOSE);
13
14         PolygonsJPanel polygonsJPanel = new PolygonsJPanel();
15         frame.add(polygonsJPanel);
16         frame.setSize(280, 270);
17         frame.setVisible(true);
18      }
19   } // end class DrawPolygons
```

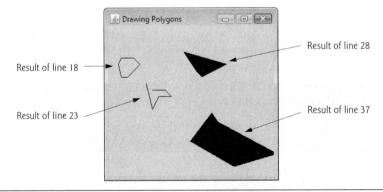

Fig. 13.28 | Drawing polygons.

Lines 16–17 of Fig. 13.27 create two int arrays and use them to specify the points for Polygon polygon1. The Polygon constructor call in line 18 receives array xValues, which contains the *x*-coordinate of each point; array yValues, which contains the *y*-coordinate of each point; and 6 (the number of points in the polygon). Line 19 displays polygon1 by passing it as an argument to Graphics method **drawPolygon**.

Lines 22–23 create two int arrays and use them to specify the points for a series of connected lines. Array xValues2 contains the *x*-coordinate of each point and array yValues2 the *y*-coordinate of each point. Line 24 uses Graphics method **drawPolyline** to display the series of connected lines specified with the arguments xValues2, yValues2 and 7 (the number of points).

Lines 27–28 create two int arrays and use them to specify the points of a polygon. Array xValues3 contains the *x*-coordinate of each point and array yValues3 the *y*-coordinate of each point. Line 29 displays a polygon by passing to Graphics method **fill-Polygon** the two arrays (xValues3 and yValues3) and the number of points to draw (4).

Common Programming Error 13.1

An ArrayIndexOutOfBoundsException is thrown if the number of points specified in the third argument to method drawPolygon or method fillPolygon is greater than the number of elements in the arrays of coordinates that specify the polygon to display.

Line 32 creates Polygon polygon2 with no points. Lines 33–37 use Polygon method **addPoint** to add pairs of *x*- and *y*-coordinates to the Polygon. Line 38 displays Polygon polygon2 by passing it to Graphics method fillPolygon.

13.8 Java 2D API

The **Java 2D API** provides advanced two-dimensional graphics capabilities for programmers who require detailed and complex graphical manipulations. The API includes features for processing line art, text and images in packages java.awt, java.awt.image, java.awt.color, java.awt.font, java.awt.geom, java.awt.print and java.awt.image.renderable. The capabilities of the API are far too broad to cover in this textbook. For an overview, visit http://docs.oracle.com/javase/7/docs/technotes/guides/2d/. In this section, we overview several Java 2D capabilities.

Drawing with the Java 2D API is accomplished with a **Graphics2D** reference (package java.awt). Graphics2D is an *abstract subclass* of class Graphics, so it has all the graphics capabilities demonstrated earlier in this chapter. In fact, the actual object used to draw in every paintComponent method is an instance of a *subclass* of Graphics2D that is passed to method paintComponent and accessed via the *superclass* Graphics. To access Graphics2D capabilities, we must cast the Graphics reference (g) passed to paintComponent into a Graphics2D reference with a statement such as

```
Graphics2D g2d = (Graphics2D) g;
```

The next two examples use this technique.

Lines, Rectangles, Round Rectangles, Arcs and Ellipses

This example demonstrates several Java 2D shapes from package java.awt.geom, including **Line2D.Double**, **Rectangle2D.Double**, **RoundRectangle2D.Double**, **Arc2D.Double** and **Ellipse2D.Double**. Note the syntax of each class name. Each class represents a shape with dimensions specified as double values. There's a *separate* version of each represented with float values (e.g., **Ellipse2D.Float**). In each case, Double is a public static nested class of the class specified to the left of the dot (e.g., Ellipse2D). To use the static nested class, we simply qualify its name with the outer-class name.

In Figs. 13.29–13.30, we draw Java 2D shapes and modify their drawing characteristics, such as changing line thickness, filling shapes with patterns and drawing dashed lines. These are just a few of the many capabilities provided by Java 2D.

Line 25 of Fig. 13.29 casts the `Graphics` reference received by `paintComponent` to a `Graphics2D` reference and assigns it to g2d to allow access to the Java 2D features.

```
 1   // Fig. 13.29: ShapesJPanel.java
 2   // Demonstrating some Java 2D shapes.
 3   import java.awt.Color;
 4   import java.awt.Graphics;
 5   import java.awt.BasicStroke;
 6   import java.awt.GradientPaint;
 7   import java.awt.TexturePaint;
 8   import java.awt.Rectangle;
 9   import java.awt.Graphics2D;
10   import java.awt.geom.Ellipse2D;
11   import java.awt.geom.Rectangle2D;
12   import java.awt.geom.RoundRectangle2D;
13   import java.awt.geom.Arc2D;
14   import java.awt.geom.Line2D;
15   import java.awt.image.BufferedImage;
16   import javax.swing.JPanel;
17
18   public class ShapesJPanel extends JPanel
19   {
20      // draw shapes with Java 2D API
21      @Override
22      public void paintComponent(Graphics g)
23      {
24         super.paintComponent(g);
25         Graphics2D g2d = (Graphics2D) g; // cast g to Graphics2D
26
27         // draw 2D ellipse filled with a blue-yellow gradient
28         g2d.setPaint(new GradientPaint(5, 30, Color.BLUE, 35, 100,
29            Color.YELLOW, true));
30         g2d.fill(new Ellipse2D.Double(5, 30, 65, 100));
31
32         // draw 2D rectangle in red
33         g2d.setPaint(Color.RED);
34         g2d.setStroke(new BasicStroke(10.0f));
35         g2d.draw(new Rectangle2D.Double(80, 30, 65, 100));
36
37         // draw 2D rounded rectangle with a buffered background
38         BufferedImage buffImage = new BufferedImage(10, 10,
39            BufferedImage.TYPE_INT_RGB);
40
41         // obtain Graphics2D from buffImage and draw on it
42         Graphics2D gg = buffImage.createGraphics();
43         gg.setColor(Color.YELLOW);
44         gg.fillRect(0, 0, 10, 10);
45         gg.setColor(Color.BLACK);
46         gg.drawRect(1, 1, 6, 6);
47         gg.setColor(Color.BLUE);
48         gg.fillRect(1, 1, 3, 3);
49         gg.setColor(Color.RED);
```

Fig. 13.29 | Demonstrating some Java 2D shapes. (Part 1 of 2.)

```
50          gg.fillRect(4, 4, 3, 3); // draw a filled rectangle
51
52          // paint buffImage onto the JFrame
53          g2d.setPaint(new TexturePaint(buffImage,
54             new Rectangle(10, 10)));
55          g2d.fill(
56             new RoundRectangle2D.Double(155, 30, 75, 100, 50, 50));
57
58          // draw 2D pie-shaped arc in white
59          g2d.setPaint(Color.WHITE);
60          g2d.setStroke(new BasicStroke(6.0f));
61          g2d.draw(
62             new Arc2D.Double(240, 30, 75, 100, 0, 270, Arc2D.PIE));
63
64          // draw 2D lines in green and yellow
65          g2d.setPaint(Color.GREEN);
66          g2d.draw(new Line2D.Double(395, 30, 320, 150));
67
68          // draw 2D line using stroke
69          float[] dashes = {10}; // specify dash pattern
70          g2d.setPaint(Color.YELLOW);
71          g2d.setStroke(new BasicStroke(4, BasicStroke.CAP_ROUND,
72             BasicStroke.JOIN_ROUND, 10, dashes, 0));
73          g2d.draw(new Line2D.Double(320, 30, 395, 150));
74       }
75   } // end class ShapesJPanel
```

Fig. 13.29 | Demonstrating some Java 2D shapes. (Part 2 of 2.)

```
1    // Fig. 13.30: Shapes.java
2    // Testing ShapesJPanel.
3    import javax.swing.JFrame;
4
5    public class Shapes
6    {
7       // execute application
8       public static void main(String[] args)
9       {
10          // create frame for ShapesJPanel
11          JFrame frame = new JFrame("Drawing 2D shapes");
12          frame.setDefaultCloseOperation(JFrame.EXIT_ON_CLOSE);
13
14          // create ShapesJPanel
15          ShapesJPanel shapesJPanel = new ShapesJPanel();
16
17          frame.add(shapesJPanel);
18          frame.setSize(425, 200);
19          frame.setVisible(true);
20       }
21   } // end class Shapes
```

Fig. 13.30 | Testing ShapesJPanel. (Part 1 of 2.)

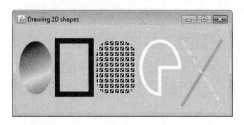

Fig. 13.30 | Testing ShapesJPanel. (Part 2 of 2.)

Ovals, Gradient Fills and Paint Objects

The first shape we draw is an *oval filled with gradually changing colors*. Lines 28–29 invoke Graphics2D method **setPaint** to set the **Paint** object that determines the color for the shape to display. A Paint object implements interface java.awt.Paint. It can be something as simple as one of the predeclared Color objects introduced in Section 13.3 (class Color implements Paint), or it can be an instance of the Java 2D API's GradientPaint, **SystemColor**, TexturePaint, LinearGradientPaint or RadialGradientPaint classes. In this case, we use a GradientPaint object.

Class GradientPaint helps draw a shape in *gradually changing colors*—called a **gradient**. The GradientPaint constructor used here requires seven arguments. The first two specify the starting coordinates for the gradient. The third specifies the starting Color for the gradient. The fourth and fifth specify the ending coordinates for the gradient. The sixth specifies the ending Color for the gradient. The last argument specifies whether the gradient is **cyclic** (true) or **acyclic** (false). The two sets of coordinates determine the direction of the gradient. Because the second coordinate (35, 100) is down and to the right of the first coordinate (5, 30), the gradient goes down and to the right at an angle. Because this gradient is cyclic (true), the color starts with blue, gradually becomes yellow, then gradually returns to blue. If the gradient is acyclic, the color transitions from the first color specified (e.g., blue) to the second color (e.g., yellow).

Line 30 uses Graphics2D method **fill** to draw a filled **Shape** object—an object that implements interface Shape (package java.awt). In this case, we display an Ellipse2D.Double object. The Ellipse2D.Double constructor receives four arguments specifying the *bounding rectangle* for the ellipse to display.

Rectangles, Strokes

Next we draw a red rectangle with a thick border. Line 33 invokes setPaint to set the Paint object to Color.RED. Line 34 uses Graphics2D method **setStroke** to set the characteristics of the rectangle's border (or the lines for any other shape). Method setStroke requires as its argument an object that implements interface **Stroke** (package java.awt). In this case, we use an instance of class BasicStroke. Class BasicStroke provides several constructors to specify the width of the line, how the line ends (called the **end caps**), how lines join together (called **line joins**) and the dash attributes of the line (if it's a dashed line). The constructor here specifies that the line should be 10 pixels wide.

Line 35 uses Graphics2D method **draw** to draw a Shape object—in this case, a Rectangle2D.Double. The Rectangle2D.Double constructor receives arguments specifying the rectangle's *upper-left x*-coordinate, upper-left *y*-coordinate, width and height.

Rounded Rectangles, **BufferedImage**s *and* **TexturePaint** *Objects*

Next we draw a rounded rectangle filled with a pattern created in a **BufferedImage** (package java.awt.image) object. Lines 38–39 create the BufferedImage object. Class BufferedImage can be used to produce images in color and grayscale. This particular BufferedImage is 10 pixels wide and 10 pixels tall (as specified by the first two arguments of the constructor). The third argument **BufferedImage.TYPE_INT_RGB** indicates that the image is stored in color using the RGB color scheme.

To create the rounded rectangle's fill pattern, we must first draw into the Buffered-Image. Line 42 creates a Graphics2D object (by calling BufferedImage method **create-Graphics**) that can be used to draw into the BufferedImage. Lines 43–50 use methods setColor, fillRect and drawRect to create the pattern.

Lines 53–54 set the Paint object to a new TexturePaint (package java.awt) object. A TexturePaint object uses the image stored in its associated BufferedImage (the first constructor argument) as the fill texture for a filled-in shape. The second argument specifies the Rectangle area from the BufferedImage that will be replicated through the texture. In this case, the Rectangle is the same size as the BufferedImage. However, a smaller portion of the BufferedImage can be used.

Lines 55–56 use Graphics2D method fill to draw a filled Shape object—in this case, a RoundRectangle2D.Double. The constructor for class RoundRectangle2D.Double receives six arguments specifying the rectangle dimensions and the arc width and arc height used to determine the rounding of the corners.

Arcs

Next we draw a pie-shaped arc with a thick white line. Line 59 sets the Paint object to Color.WHITE. Line 60 sets the Stroke object to a new BasicStroke for a line 6 pixels wide. Lines 61–62 use Graphics2D method draw to draw a Shape object—in this case, an Arc2D.Double. The Arc2D.Double constructor's first four arguments specify the upper-left *x*-coordinate, upper-left *y*-coordinate, width and height of the bounding rectangle for the arc. The fifth argument specifies the start angle. The sixth argument specifies the arc angle. The last argument specifies how the arc is *closed*. Constant **Arc2D.PIE** indicates that the arc is *closed* by drawing two lines—one line from the arc's starting point to the center of the bounding rectangle and one line from the center of the bounding rectangle to the ending point. Class Arc2D provides two other static constants for specifying how the arc is *closed*. Constant **Arc2D.CHORD** draws a line from the starting point to the ending point. Constant **Arc2D.OPEN** specifies that the arc should *not* be *closed*.

Lines

Finally, we draw two lines using **Line2D** objects—one solid and one dashed. Line 65 sets the Paint object to Color.GREEN. Line 66 uses Graphics2D method draw to draw a Shape object—in this case, an instance of class Line2D.Double. The Line2D.Double constructor's arguments specify the starting coordinates and ending coordinates of the line.

Line 69 declares a one-element float array containing the value 10. This array describes the dashes in the dashed line. In this case, each dash will be 10 pixels long. To create dashes of different lengths in a pattern, simply provide the length of each dash as an element in the array. Line 70 sets the Paint object to Color.YELLOW. Lines 71–72 set the Stroke object to a new BasicStroke. The line will be 4 pixels wide and will have rounded ends (**BasicStroke.CAP_ROUND**). If lines join together (as in a rectangle at the corners), their joining will be rounded (**BasicStroke.JOIN_ROUND**). The dashes argument specifies the dash lengths for the line. The last argument indicates the starting index in the dashes array for the first dash in the pattern. Line 73 then draws a line with the current Stroke.

Creating Your Own Shapes with General Paths

Next we present a **general path**—a shape constructed from straight lines and complex curves. A general path is represented with an object of class **GeneralPath** (package java.awt.geom). The application of Figs. 13.31 and 13.32 demonstrates drawing a general path in the shape of a five-pointed star.

```java
1   // Fig. 13.31: Shapes2JPanel.java
2   // Demonstrating a general path.
3   import java.awt.Color;
4   import java.awt.Graphics;
5   import java.awt.Graphics2D;
6   import java.awt.geom.GeneralPath;
7   import java.security.SecureRandom;
8   import javax.swing.JPanel;
9
10  public class Shapes2JPanel extends JPanel
11  {
12     // draw general paths
13     @Override
14     public void paintComponent(Graphics g)
15     {
16        super.paintComponent(g);
17        SecureRandom random = new SecureRandom();
18
19        int[] xPoints = {55, 67, 109, 73, 83, 55, 27, 37, 1, 43};
20        int[] yPoints = {0, 36, 36, 54, 96, 72, 96, 54, 36, 36};
21
22        Graphics2D g2d = (Graphics2D) g;
23        GeneralPath star = new GeneralPath();
24
25        // set the initial coordinate of the General Path
26        star.moveTo(xPoints[0], yPoints[0]);
27
28        // create the star--this does not draw the star
29        for (int count = 1; count < xPoints.length; count++)
30           star.lineTo(xPoints[count], yPoints[count]);
31
32        star.closePath(); // close the shape
33
34        g2d.translate(150, 150); // translate the origin to (150, 150)
35
36        // rotate around origin and draw stars in random colors
37        for (int count = 1; count <= 20; count++)
38        {
39           g2d.rotate(Math.PI / 10.0); // rotate coordinate system
40
```

Fig. 13.31 | Java 2D general paths. (Part 1 of 2.)

```
41              // set random drawing color
42              g2d.setColor(new Color(random.nextInt(256),
43                 random.nextInt(256), random.nextInt(256)));
44
45              g2d.fill(star); // draw filled star
46          }
47       }
48    } // end class Shapes2JPanel
```

Fig. 13.31 | Java 2D general paths. (Part 2 of 2.)

```
1   // Fig. 13.32: Shapes2.java
2   // Demonstrating a general path.
3   import java.awt.Color;
4   import javax.swing.JFrame;
5
6   public class Shapes2
7   {
8      // execute application
9      public static void main(String[] args)
10     {
11        // create frame for Shapes2JPanel
12        JFrame frame = new JFrame("Drawing 2D Shapes");
13        frame.setDefaultCloseOperation(JFrame.EXIT_ON_CLOSE);
14
15        Shapes2JPanel shapes2JPanel = new Shapes2JPanel();
16        frame.add(shapes2JPanel);
17        frame.setBackground(Color.WHITE);
18        frame.setSize(315, 330);
19        frame.setVisible(true);
20     }
21  } // end class Shapes2
```

Fig. 13.32 | Demonstrating a general path.

Lines 19–20 (Fig. 13.31) declare two int arrays representing the *x*- and *y*-coordinates of the points in the star. Line 23 creates GeneralPath object star. Line 26 uses General-Path method **moveTo** to specify the first point in the star. The for statement in lines 29–

30 uses GeneralPath method **lineTo** to draw a line to the next point in the star. Each new call to lineTo draws a line from the previous point to the current point. Line 32 uses GeneralPath method **closePath** to draw a line from the last point to the point specified in the last call to moveTo. This completes the general path.

Line 34 uses Graphics2D method **translate** to move the drawing origin to location (150, 150). All drawing operations now use location (150, 150) as (0, 0).

The for statement in lines 37–46 draws the star 20 times by rotating it around the new origin point. Line 39 uses Graphics2D method **rotate** to rotate the next displayed shape. The argument specifies the rotation angle in radians (with 360° = 2π radians). Line 45 uses Graphics2D method **fill** to draw a filled version of the star.

13.9 Wrap-Up

In this chapter, you learned how to use Java's graphics capabilities to produce colorful drawings. You learned how to specify the location of an object using Java's coordinate system, and how to draw on a window using the paintComponent method. You were introduced to class Color, and you learned how to use this class to specify different colors using their RGB components. You used the JColorChooser dialog to allow users to select colors in a program. You then learned how to work with fonts when drawing text on a window. You learned how to create a Font object from a font name, style and size, as well as how to access the metrics of a font. From there, you learned how to draw various shapes on a window, such as rectangles (regular, rounded and 3D), ovals and polygons, as well as lines and arcs. You then used the Java 2D API to create more complex shapes and to fill them with gradients or patterns. The chapter concluded with a discussion of general paths, used to construct shapes from straight lines and complex curves. In the next chapter, we discuss class String and its methods. We introduce regular expressions for pattern matching in strings and demonstrate how to validate user input with regular expressions.

Summary

Section 13.1 Introduction
- Java's coordinate system (p. 548) is a scheme for identifying every point (p. 559) on the screen.
- A coordinate pair (p. 548) has an *x*-coordinate (horizontal) and a *y*-coordinate (vertical).
- Coordinates are used to indicate where graphics should be displayed on a screen.
- Coordinate units are measured in pixels (p. 548). A pixel is a display monitor's smallest unit of resolution.

Section 13.2 Graphics Contexts and Graphics Objects
- A Java graphics context (p. 550) enables drawing on the screen.
- Class Graphics (p. 550) contains methods for drawing strings, lines, rectangles and other shapes. Methods are also included for font manipulation and color manipulation.
- A Graphics object manages a graphics context and draws pixels on the screen that represent text and other graphical objects, e.g., lines, ellipses, rectangles and other polygons (p. 550).
- Class Graphics is an abstract class. Each Java implementation has a Graphics subclass that provides drawing capabilities. This implementation is hidden from us by class Graphics, which supplies the interface that enables us to use graphics in a platform-independent manner.

- Method paintComponent can be used to draw graphics in any JComponent component.
- Method paintComponent receives a Graphics object that is passed to the method by the system when a lightweight Swing component needs to be repainted.
- When an application executes, the application container calls method paintComponent. For paintComponent to be called again, an event must occur.
- When a JComponent is displayed, its paintComponent method is called.
- Calling method repaint (p. 551) on a component updates the graphics drawn on that component.

Section 13.3 Color Control
- Class Color (p. 551) declares methods and constants for manipulating colors in a Java program.
- Every color is created from a red, a green and a blue component. Together these components are called RGB values (p. 552). The RGB components specify the amount of red, green and blue in a color, respectively. The larger the value, the greater the amount of that particular color.
- Color methods getRed, getGreen and getBlue (p. 552) return int values from 0 to 255 representing the amount of red, green and blue, respectively.
- Graphics method getColor (p. 552) returns a Color object with the current drawing color.
- Graphics method setColor (p. 552) sets the current drawing color.
- Graphics method fillRect (p. 552) draws a rectangle filled by the Graphics object's current color.
- Graphics method drawString (p. 554) draws a String in the current color.
- The JColorChooser GUI component (p. 555) enables application users to select colors.
- JColorChooser static method showDialog (p. 556) displays a modal JColorChooser dialog.

Section 13.4 Manipulating Fonts
- Class Font (p. 558) contains methods and constants for manipulating fonts.
- Class Font's constructor takes three arguments—the font name (p. 559), font style and font size.
- A Font's font style can be Font.PLAIN, Font.ITALIC or Font.BOLD (each is a static field of class Font). Font styles can be used in combination (e.g., Font.ITALIC + Font.BOLD).
- The font size is measured in points. A point is 1/72 of an inch.
- Graphics method setFont (p. 559) sets the drawing font in which text will be displayed.
- Font method getSize (p. 559) returns the font size in points.
- Font method getName (p. 559) returns the current font name as a string.
- Font method getStyle (p. 561) returns an integer value representing the current Font's style.
- Font method getFamily (p. 561) returns the name of the font family to which the current font belongs. The name of the font family is platform specific.
- Class FontMetrics (p. 561) contains methods for obtaining font information.
- Font metrics (p. 561) include height, descent and leading.

Section 13.5 Drawing Lines, Rectangles and Ovals
- Graphics methods fillRoundRect (p. 565) and drawRoundRect (p. 565) draw rectangles with rounded corners.
- Graphics methods draw3DRect (p. 567) and fill3DRect (p. 567) draw three-dimensional rectangles.
- Graphics methods drawOval (p. 567) and fillOval (p. 567) draw ovals.

Section 13.6 Drawing Arcs

- An arc (p. 567) is drawn as a portion of an oval.
- Arcs sweep from a starting angle by the number of degrees specified by their arc angle (p. 567).
- Graphics methods drawArc (p. 567) and fillArc (p. 567) are used for drawing arcs.

Section 13.7 Drawing Polygons and Polylines

- Class Polygon contains methods for creating polygons.
- Polygons are closed multisided shapes composed of straight-line segments.
- Polylines (p. 570) are sequences of connected points.
- Graphics method drawPolyline (p. 572) displays a series of connected lines.
- Graphics methods drawPolygon (p. 572) and fillPolygon (p. 573) are used to draw polygons.
- Polygon method addPoint (p. 573) adds pairs of x- and y-coordinates to the Polygon.

Section 13.8 Java 2D API

- The Java 2D API (p. 573) provides advanced two-dimensional graphics capabilities.
- Class Graphics2D (p. 573)—a subclass of Graphics—is used for drawing with the Java 2D API.
- The Java 2D API's classes for drawing shapes include Line2D.Double, Rectangle2D.Double, RoundRectangle2D.Double, Arc2D.Double and Ellipse2D.Double (p. 573).
- Class GradientPaint (p. 576) helps draw a shape in gradually changing colors—called a gradient (p. 576).
- Graphics2D method fill (p. 576) draws a filled object of any type that implements interface Shape (p. 576).
- Class BasicStroke (p. 576) helps specify the drawing characteristics of lines.
- Graphics2D method draw (p. 576) is used to draw a Shape object.
- Classes GradientPaint (p. 576) and TexturePaint (p. 577) help specify the characteristics for filling shapes with colors or patterns.
- A general path (p. 578) is a shape constructed from straight lines and complex curves and is represented with an object of class GeneralPath (p. 578).
- GeneralPath method moveTo (p. 579) specifies the first point in a general path.
- GeneralPath method lineTo (p. 580) draws a line to the next point in the path. Each new call to lineTo draws a line from the previous point to the current point.
- GeneralPath method closePath (p. 580) draws a line from the last point to the point specified in the last call to moveTo. This completes the general path.
- Graphics2D method translate (p. 580) is used to move the drawing origin to a new location.
- Graphics2D method rotate (p. 580) is used to rotate the next displayed shape.

Self-Review Exercises

13.1   Fill in the blanks in each of the following statements:

a) In Java 2D, method _____ of class _____ sets the characteristics of a stroke used to draw a shape.

b) Class _____ helps specify the fill for a shape such that the fill gradually changes from one color to another.

c) The _____ method of class Graphics draws a line between two points.

d) RGB is short for _____, _____ and _____.

    e) Font sizes are measured in units called _____.

    f) Class _____ helps specify the fill for a shape using a pattern drawn in a `BufferedImage`.

13.2   State whether each of the following is *true* or *false*. If *false*, explain why.

    a) The first two arguments of `Graphics` method `drawOval` specify the center coordinate of the oval.

    b) In the Java coordinate system, *x*-coordinates increase from left to right and *y*-coordinates from top to bottom.

    c) `Graphics` method `fillPolygon` draws a filled polygon in the current color.

    d) `Graphics` method `drawArc` allows negative angles.

    e) `Graphics` method `getSize` returns the size of the current font in centimeters.

    f) Pixel coordinate (0, 0) is located at the exact center of the monitor.

13.3   Find the error(s) in each of the following and explain how to correct them. Assume that `g` is a `Graphics` object.

    a) `g.setFont("SansSerif");`

    b) `g.erase(x, y, w, h);     // clear rectangle at (x, y)`

    c) `Font f = new Font("Serif", Font.BOLDITALIC, 12);`

    d) `g.setColor(255, 255, 0);  // change color to yellow`

Answers to Self-Review Exercises

13.1   a) `setStroke`, `Graphics2D`. b) `GradientPaint`. c) `drawLine`. d) red, green, blue. e) points. f) `TexturePaint`.

13.2   a) False. The first two arguments specify the upper-left corner of the bounding rectangle.

    b) True.

    c) True.

    d) True.

    e) False. Font sizes are measured in points.

    f) False. The coordinate (0,0) corresponds to the upper-left corner of a GUI component on which drawing occurs.

13.3   a) The `setFont` method takes a `Font` object as an argument—not a `String`.

    b) The `Graphics` class does not have an `erase` method. The `clearRect` method should be used.

    c) `Font.BOLDITALIC` is not a valid font style. To get a bold italic font, use `Font.BOLD + Font.ITALIC`.

    d) Method `setColor` takes a `Color` object as an argument, not three integers.

Exercises

13.4   Fill in the blanks in each of the following statements:

    a) Class _____ of the Java 2D API is used to draw ovals.

    b) Methods `draw` and `fill` of class `Graphics2D` require an object of type _____ as their argument.

    c) The three constants that specify font style are _____, _____ and _____.

    d) `Graphics2D` method _____ sets the painting color for Java 2D shapes.

13.5   State whether each of the following is *true* or *false*. If *false*, explain why.

    a) `Graphics` method `drawPolygon` automatically connects the endpoints of the polygon.

    b) `Graphics` method `drawLine` draws a line between two points.

    c) `Graphics` method `fillArc` uses degrees to specify the angle.

    d) In the Java coordinate system, values on the *y*-axis increase from left to right.

    e) `Graphics` inherits directly from class `Object`.

f) Graphics is an abstract class.

g) The Font class inherits directly from class Graphics.

13.6 *(Concentric Circles Using Method drawArc)* Write an application that draws a series of eight concentric circles. The circles should be separated by 10 pixels. Use Graphics method drawArc.

13.7 *(Concentric Circles Using Class Ellipse2D.Double)* Modify your solution to Exercise 13.6 to draw the ovals by using class Ellipse2D.Double and method draw of class Graphics2D.

13.8 *(Random Lines Using Class Line2D.Double)* Modify your solution to Exercise 13.7 to draw random lines in random colors and random thicknesses. Use class Line2D.Double and method draw of class Graphics2D to draw the lines.

13.9 *(Random Triangles)* Write an application that displays randomly generated triangles in different colors. Each triangle should be filled with a different color. Use class GeneralPath and method fill of class Graphics2D to draw the triangles.

13.10 *(Random Characters)* Write an application that randomly draws characters in different fonts, sizes and colors.

13.11 *(Grid Using Method drawLine)* Write an application that draws an 8-by-8 grid. Use Graphics method drawLine.

13.12 *(Grid Using Class Line2D.Double)* Modify your solution to Exercise 13.11 to draw the grid using instances of class Line2D.Double and method draw of class Graphics2D.

13.13 *(Grid Using Method drawRect)* Write an application that draws a 10-by-10 grid. Use the Graphics method drawRect.

13.14 *(Grid Using Class Rectangle2D.Double)* Modify your solution to Exercise 13.13 to draw the grid by using class Rectangle2D.Double and method draw of class Graphics2D.

13.15 *(Drawing Tetrahedrons)* Write an application that draws a tetrahedron (a three-dimensional shape with four triangular faces). Use class GeneralPath and method draw of class Graphics2D.

13.16 *(Drawing Cubes)* Write an application that draws a cube. Use class GeneralPath and method draw of class Graphics2D.

13.17 *(Circles Using Class Ellipse2D.Double)* Write an application that asks the user to input the radius of a circle as a floating-point number and draws the circle, as well as the values of the circle's diameter, circumference and area. Use the value 3.14159 for π. [*Note:* You may also use the predefined constant Math.PI for the value of π. This constant is more precise than the value 3.14159. Class Math is declared in the java.lang package, so you need not import it.] Use the following formulas (*r* is the radius):

$$diameter = 2r$$
$$circumference = 2\pi r$$
$$area = \pi r^2$$

The user should also be prompted for a set of coordinates in addition to the radius. Then draw the circle and display its diameter, circumference and area, using an Ellipse2D.Double object to represent the circle and method draw of class Graphics2D to display it.

13.18 *(Screen Saver)* Write an application that simulates a screen saver. The application should randomly draw lines using method drawLine of class Graphics. After drawing 100 lines, the application should clear itself and start drawing lines again. To allow the program to draw continuously, place a call to repaint as the last line in method paintComponent. Do you notice any problems with this on your system?

13.19 *(Screen Saver Using Timer)* Package javax.swing contains a class called Timer that is capable of calling method actionPerformed of interface ActionListener at a fixed time interval (specified in milliseconds). Modify your solution to Exercise 13.18 to remove the call to `repaint` from method `paintComponent`. Declare your class to implement `ActionListener`. (The `actionPerformed` method should simply call `repaint`.) Declare an instance variable of type `Timer` called `timer` in your class. In the constructor for your class, write the following statements:

```
timer = new Timer(1000, this);
timer.start();
```

This creates an instance of class `Timer` that will call `this` object's `actionPerformed` method every 1000 milliseconds (i.e., every second).

13.20 *(Screen Saver for a Random Number of Lines)* Modify your solution to Exercise 13.19 to enable the user to enter the number of random lines that should be drawn before the application clears itself and starts drawing lines again. Use a `JTextField` to obtain the value. The user should be able to type a new number into the `JTextField` at any time during the program's execution. Use an inner class to perform event handling for the `JTextField`.

13.21 *(Screen Saver with Shapes)* Modify your solution to Exercise 13.20 such that it uses random-number generation to choose different shapes to display. Use methods of class `Graphics`.

13.22 *(Screen Saver Using the Java 2D API)* Modify your solution to Exercise 13.21 to use classes and drawing capabilities of the Java 2D API. Draw shapes like rectangles and ellipses, with randomly generated gradients. Use class `GradientPaint` to generate the gradient.

13.23 *(Turtle Graphics)* Modify your solution to Exercise 6.21—*Turtle Graphics*—to add a graphical user interface using `JTextField`s and `JButton`s. Draw lines rather than asterisks (*). When the turtle graphics program specifies a move, translate the number of positions into a number of pixels on the screen by multiplying the number of positions by 10 (or any value you choose). Implement the drawing with Java 2D API features.

13.24 *(Knight's Tour)* Produce a graphical version of the Knight's Tour problem (Exercise 6.22, Exercise 6.23 and Exercise 6.26). As each move is made, the appropriate cell of the chessboard should be updated with the proper move number. If the result of the program is a *full tour* or a *closed tour*, the program should display an appropriate message. If you like, use class `Timer` (see Exercise 13.19) to help animate the Knight's Tour.

13.25 *(Tortoise and Hare)* Produce a graphical version of the *Tortoise and Hare* simulation (Exercise 6.28). Simulate the mountain by drawing an arc that extends from the bottom-left corner of the window to the top-right corner. The tortoise and the hare should race up the mountain. Implement the graphical output to actually print the tortoise and the hare on the arc for every move. [*Hint:* Extend the length of the race from 70 to 300 to allow yourself a larger graphics area.]

13.26 *(Drawing Spirals)* Write an application that uses `Graphics` method `drawPolyline` to draw a spiral similar to the one shown in Fig. 13.33.

13.27 *(Pie Chart)* Write a program that inputs four numbers and graphs them as a pie chart. Use class `Arc2D.Double` and method `fill` of class `Graphics2D` to perform the drawing. Draw each piece of the pie in a separate color.

13.28 *(Selecting Shapes)* Write an application that allows the user to select a shape from a `JCombo-Box` and draws it 20 times with random locations and dimensions in method `paintComponent`. The first item in the `JComboBox` should be the default shape that is displayed the first time `paintComponent` is called.

13.29 *(Random Colors)* Modify Exercise 13.28 to draw each of the 20 randomly sized shapes in a randomly selected color. Use all 13 predefined `Color` objects in an array of `Color`s.

13.30 *(JColorChooser Dialog)* Modify Exercise 13.28 to allow the user to select the color in which shapes should be drawn from a `JColorChooser` dialog.

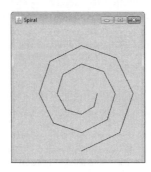

Fig. 13.33 | Spiral drawn using method `drawPolyline`.

(Optional) GUI and Graphics Case Study Exercise: Adding Java 2D

13.31 Java 2D introduces many new capabilities for creating unique and impressive graphics. We'll add a small subset of these features to the drawing application you created in Exercise 12.17. In this version, you'll enable the user to specify gradients for filling shapes and to change stroke characteristics for drawing lines and outlines of shapes. The user will be able to choose which colors compose the gradient and set the width and dash length of the stroke.

First, you must update the `MyShape` hierarchy to support Java 2D functionality. Make the following changes in class `MyShape`:

a) Change abstract method `draw`'s parameter type from `Graphics` to `Graphics2D`.

b) Change all variables of type `Color` to type `Paint` to enable support for gradients. [*Note:* Recall that class `Color` implements interface `Paint`.]

c) Add an instance variable of type `Stroke` in class `MyShape` and a `Stroke` parameter in the constructor to initialize the new instance variable. The default stroke should be an instance of class `BasicStroke`.

Classes `MyLine`, `MyBoundedShape`, `MyOval` and `MyRectangle` should each add a `Stroke` parameter to their constructors. In the `draw` methods, each shape should set the `Paint` and the `Stroke` before drawing or filling a shape. Since `Graphics2D` is a subclass of `Graphics`, we can continue to use `Graphics` methods `drawLine`, `drawOval`, `fillOval`, and so on to draw the shapes. When these methods are called, they'll draw the appropriate shape using the specified `Paint` and `Stroke` settings.

Next, you'll update the `DrawPanel` to handle the Java 2D features. Change all `Color` variables to `Paint` variables. Declare an instance variable `currentStroke` of type `Stroke` and provide a *set* method for it. Update the calls to the individual shape constructors to include the `Paint` and `Stroke` arguments. In method `paintComponent`, cast the `Graphics` reference to type `Graphics2D` and use the `Graphics2D` reference in each call to `MyShape` method `draw`.

Next, make the new Java 2D features accessible from the GUI. Create a `JPanel` of GUI components for setting the Java 2D options. Add these components at the top of the `DrawFrame` below the panel that currently contains the standard shape controls (see Fig. 13.34). These GUI components should include:

a) A checkbox to specify whether to paint using a gradient.

b) Two `JButtons` that each show a `JColorChooser` dialog to allow the user to choose the first and second color in the gradient. (These will replace the `JComboBox` used for choosing the color in Exercise 12.17.)

c) A text field for entering the `Stroke` width.

d) A text field for entering the `Stroke` dash length.

e) A checkbox for selecting whether to draw a dashed or solid line.

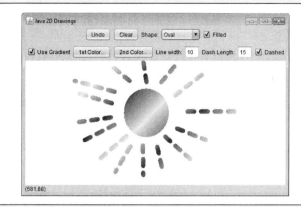

Fig. 13.34 | Drawing with Java 2D.

If the user selects to draw with a gradient, set the `Paint` on the `DrawPanel` to be a gradient of the two colors chosen by the user. The expression

new GradientPaint(0, 0, color1, 50, 50, color2, **true**))

creates a `GradientPaint` that cycles diagonally from the upper-left to the bottom-right every 50 pixels. Variables `color1` and `color2` represent the colors chosen by the user. If the user does not select to use a gradient, then simply set the `Paint` on the `DrawPanel` to be the first `Color` chosen by the user.

For strokes, if the user chooses a solid line, then create the `Stroke` with the expression

new BasicStroke(width, BasicStroke.CAP_ROUND, BasicStroke.JOIN_ROUND)

where variable `width` is the width specified by the user in the line-width text field. If the user chooses a dashed line, then create the `Stroke` with the expression

new BasicStroke(width, BasicStroke.CAP_ROUND, BasicStroke.JOIN_ROUND,
    10, dashes, 0)

where `width` again is the width in the line-width field, and `dashes` is an array with one element whose value is the length specified in the dash-length field. The `Panel` and `Stroke` objects should be passed to the shape object's constructor when the shape is created in `DrawPanel`.

Making a Difference

13.32 *(Large-Type Displays for People with Low Vision)* The accessibility of computers and the Internet to all people, regardless of disabilities, is becoming more important as these tools play increasing roles in our personal and business lives. According to a recent estimate by the World Health Organization (www.who.int/mediacentre/factsheets/fs282/en/), 246 million people worldwide have low vision. To learn more about low vision, check out the GUI-based low-vision simulation at www.webaim.org/simulations/lowvision.php. People with low vision might prefer to choose a font and/or a larger font size when reading electronic documents and web pages. Java has five built-in "logical" fonts that are guaranteed to be available in any Java implementation, including Serif, Sans-serif and Monospaced. Write a GUI application that provides a JTextArea in which the user can type text. Allow the user to select Serif, Sans-serif or Monospaced from a JComboBox. Provide a **Bold** JCheckBox, which, if checked, makes the text bold. Include **Increase Font Size** and **Decrease Font Size** JButtons that allow the user to scale the size of the font up or down, respectively, by one point at a time. Start with a font size of 18 points. For the purposes of this exercise, set the font size on the JComboBox, JButtons and JCheckBox to 20 points so that a person with low vision will be able to read the text on them.

14

Strings, Characters and Regular Expressions

The chief defect of Henry King
Was chewing little bits of string.
—Hilaire Belloc

Vigorous writing is concise. A
sentence should contain no
unnecessary words, a paragraph
no unnecessary sentences.
—William Strunk, Jr.

I have made this letter longer
than usual, because I lack the
time to make it short.
—Blaise Pascal

Objectives

In this chapter you'll:

■ Create and manipulate immutable character-string objects of class `String`.

■ Create and manipulate mutable character-string objects of class `StringBuilder`.

■ Create and manipulate objects of class `Character`.

■ Break a `String` object into tokens using `String` method `split`.

■ Use regular expressions to validate `String` data entered into an application.

14.1 Introduction

This chapter introduces Java's string- and character-processing capabilities. The techniques discussed here are appropriate for validating program input, displaying information to users and other text-based manipulations. They're also appropriate for developing text editors, word processors, page-layout software, computerized typesetting systems and other kinds of text-processing software. We've presented several string-processing capabilities in earlier chapters. This chapter discusses in detail the capabilities of classes `String`, `StringBuilder` and `Character` from the `java.lang` package—these classes provide the foundation for string and character manipulation in Java.

The chapter also discusses regular expressions that provide applications with the capability to validate input. The functionality is located in the `String` class along with classes `Matcher` and `Pattern` located in the `java.util.regex` package.

14.2 Fundamentals of Characters and Strings

Characters are the fundamental building blocks of Java source programs. Every program is composed of a sequence of characters that—when grouped together meaningfully—are interpreted by the Java compiler as a series of instructions used to accomplish a task. A program may contain **character literals**. A character literal is an integer value represented as a character in single quotes. For example, `'z'` represents the integer value of z, and `'\t'` represents the integer value of a tab character. The value of a character literal is the integer value of the character in the **Unicode character set**. Appendix B presents the integer equivalents of the characters in the ASCII character set, which is a subset of Unicode (discussed in online Appendix H).

Recall from Section 2.2 that a string is a sequence of characters treated as a single unit. A string may include letters, digits and various **special characters**, such as +, -, *, / and $. A string is an object of class `String`. **String literals** (stored in memory as `String` objects) are written as a sequence of characters in double quotation marks, as in:

```
"John Q. Doe"              (a name)
"9999 Main Street"         (a street address)
"Waltham, Massachusetts"   (a city and state)
"(201) 555-1212"           (a telephone number)
```

A string may be assigned to a `String` reference. The declaration

```
String color = "blue";
```

initializes `String` variable `color` to refer to a `String` object that contains the string "blue".

Performance Tip 14.1

To conserve memory, Java treats all string literals with the same contents as a single String object that has many references to it.

14.3 Class String

Class `String` is used to represent strings in Java. The next several subsections cover many of class `String`'s capabilities.

14.3.1 String Constructors

Class `String` provides constructors for initializing `String` objects in a variety of ways. Four of the constructors are demonstrated in the `main` method of Fig. 14.1.

```
 1   // Fig. 14.1: StringConstructors.java
 2   // String class constructors.
 3
 4   public class StringConstructors
 5   {
 6      public static void main(String[] args)
 7      {
 8         char[] charArray = {'b', 'i', 'r', 't', 'h', ' ', 'd', 'a', 'y'};
 9         String s = new String("hello");
10
11         // use String constructors
12         String s1 = new String();
13         String s2 = new String(s);
14         String s3 = new String(charArray);
15         String s4 = new String(charArray, 6, 3);
16
17         System.out.printf(
18            "s1 = %s%ns2 = %s%ns3 = %s%ns4 = %s%n", s1, s2, s3, s4);
19      }
20   } // end class StringConstructors
```

```
s1 =
s2 = hello
s3 = birth day
s4 = day
```

Fig. 14.1 | String class constructors.

Line 12 instantiates a new String using class String's no-argument constructor and assigns its reference to s1. The new String object contains no characters (i.e., the **empty string**, which can also be represented as "") and has a length of 0. Line 13 instantiates a new String object using class String's constructor that takes a String object as an argument and assigns its reference to s2. The new String object contains the same sequence of characters as the String object s that's passed as an argument to the constructor.

Performance Tip 14.2
It's not necessary to copy an existing String object. String objects are immutable, because class String does not provide methods that allow the contents of a String object to be modified after it is created.

Line 14 instantiates a new String object and assigns its reference to s3 using class String's constructor that takes a char array as an argument. The new String object contains a copy of the characters in the array.

Line 15 instantiates a new String object and assigns its reference to s4 using class String's constructor that takes a char array and two integers as arguments. The second argument specifies the starting position (the *offset*) from which characters in the array are accessed. Remember that the first character is at position 0. The third argument specifies the number of characters (the count) to access in the array. The new String object is formed from the accessed characters. If the offset or the count specified as an argument results in accessing an element outside the bounds of the character array, a StringIndex-OutOfBoundsException is thrown.

14.3.2 String Methods length, charAt and getChars

String methods **length**, **charAt** and **getChars** return the length of a String, obtain the character at a specific location in a String and retrieve a set of characters from a String as a char array, respectively. Figure 14.2 demonstrates each of these methods.

```
1   // Fig. 14.2: StringMiscellaneous.java
2   // This application demonstrates the length, charAt and getChars
3   // methods of the String class.
4
5   public class StringMiscellaneous
6   {
7      public static void main(String[] args)
8      {
9         String s1 = "hello there";
10        char[] charArray = new char[5];
11
12        System.out.printf("s1: %s", s1);
13
14        // test length method
15        System.out.printf("%nLength of s1: %d", s1.length());
16
17        // loop through characters in s1 with charAt and display reversed
18        System.out.printf("%nThe string reversed is: ");
```

Fig. 14.2 | String methods length, charAt and getChars. (Part 1 of 2.)

```
19
20          for (int count = s1.length() - 1; count >= 0; count--)
21             System.out.printf("%c ", s1.charAt(count));
22
23          // copy characters from string into charArray
24          s1.getChars(0, 5, charArray, 0);
25          System.out.printf("%nThe character array is: ");
26
27          for (char character : charArray)
28             System.out.print(character);
29
30          System.out.println();
31       }
32    } // end class StringMiscellaneous
```

```
s1: hello there
Length of s1: 11
The string reversed is: e r e h t   o l l e h
The character array is: hello
```

Fig. 14.2 | String methods length, charAt and getChars. (Part 2 of 2.)

Line 15 uses String method length to determine the number of characters in String s1. Like arrays, strings know their own length. However, unlike arrays, you access a String's length via class String's length method.

Lines 20–21 print the characters of the String s1 in reverse order (and separated by spaces). String method charAt (line 21) returns the character at a specific position in the String. Method charAt receives an integer argument that's used as the index and returns the character at that position. Like arrays, the first element of a String is at position 0.

Line 24 uses String method getChars to copy the characters of a String into a character array. The first argument is the starting index from which characters are to be copied. The second argument is the index that's one past the last character to be copied from the String. The third argument is the character array into which the characters are to be copied. The last argument is the starting index where the copied characters are placed in the target character array. Next, lines 27–28 print the char array contents one character at a time.

14.3.3 Comparing Strings

Chapter 19 discusses sorting and searching arrays. Frequently, the information being sorted or searched consists of Strings that must be compared to place them into order or to determine whether a string appears in an array (or other collection). Class String provides methods for *comparing* strings, as demonstrated in the next two examples.

To understand what it means for one string to be greater than or less than another, consider the process of alphabetizing a series of last names. No doubt, you'd place "Jones" before "Smith" because the first letter of "Jones" comes before the first letter of "Smith" in the alphabet. But the alphabet is more than just a list of 26 letters—it's an *ordered* list of characters. Each letter occurs in a specific position within the list. Z is more than just a letter of the alphabet—it's specifically the twenty-sixth letter of the alphabet.

How does the computer know that one letter "comes before" another? All characters are represented in the computer as numeric codes (see Appendix B). When the computer compares Strings, it actually compares the numeric codes of the characters in the Strings.

Figure 14.3 demonstrates String methods equals, equalsIgnoreCase, compareTo and **regionMatches** and using the equality operator == to compare String objects.

```java
1   // Fig. 14.3: StringCompare.java
2   // String methods equals, equalsIgnoreCase, compareTo and regionMatches.
3
4   public class StringCompare
5   {
6      public static void main(String[] args)
7      {
8         String s1 = new String("hello"); // s1 is a copy of "hello"
9         String s2 = "goodbye";
10        String s3 = "Happy Birthday";
11        String s4 = "happy birthday";
12
13        System.out.printf(
14           "s1 = %s%ns2 = %s%ns3 = %s%ns4 = %s%n%n", s1, s2, s3, s4);
15
16        // test for equality
17        if (s1.equals("hello"))  // true
18           System.out.println("s1 equals \"hello\"");
19        else
20           System.out.println("s1 does not equal \"hello\"");
21
22        // test for equality with ==
23        if (s1 == "hello")  // false; they are not the same object
24           System.out.println("s1 is the same object as \"hello\"");
25        else
26           System.out.println("s1 is not the same object as \"hello\"");
27
28        // test for equality (ignore case)
29        if (s3.equalsIgnoreCase(s4))  // true
30           System.out.printf("%s equals %s with case ignored%n", s3, s4);
31        else
32           System.out.println("s3 does not equal s4");
33
34        // test compareTo
35        System.out.printf(
36           "%ns1.compareTo(s2) is %d", s1.compareTo(s2));
37        System.out.printf(
38           "%ns2.compareTo(s1) is %d", s2.compareTo(s1));
39        System.out.printf(
40           "%ns1.compareTo(s1) is %d", s1.compareTo(s1));
41        System.out.printf(
42           "%ns3.compareTo(s4) is %d", s3.compareTo(s4));
43        System.out.printf(
44           "%ns4.compareTo(s3) is %d%n%n", s4.compareTo(s3));
```

Fig. 14.3 | String methods equals, equalsIgnoreCase, compareTo and regionMatches. (Part 1 of 2.)

```
45
46            // test regionMatches (case sensitive)
47            if (s3.regionMatches(0, s4, 0, 5))
48                System.out.println("First 5 characters of s3 and s4 match");
49            else
50                System.out.println(
51                    "First 5 characters of s3 and s4 do not match");
52
53            // test regionMatches (ignore case)
54            if (s3.regionMatches(true, 0, s4, 0, 5))
55                System.out.println(
56                    "First 5 characters of s3 and s4 match with case ignored");
57            else
58                System.out.println(
59                    "First 5 characters of s3 and s4 do not match");
60        }
61    } // end class StringCompare
```

```
s1 = hello
s2 = goodbye
s3 = Happy Birthday
s4 = happy birthday

s1 equals "hello"
s1 is not the same object as "hello"
Happy Birthday equals happy birthday with case ignored

s1.compareTo(s2) is 1
s2.compareTo(s1) is -1
s1.compareTo(s1) is 0
s3.compareTo(s4) is -32
s4.compareTo(s3) is 32

First 5 characters of s3 and s4 do not match
First 5 characters of s3 and s4 match with case ignored
```

Fig. 14.3 | String methods `equals`, `equalsIgnoreCase`, `compareTo` and `regionMatches`. (Part 2 of 2.)

String Method `equals`

The condition at line 17 uses method `equals` to compare `String` s1 and the `String` literal "hello" for equality. Method `equals` (a method of class `Object` overridden in `String`) tests any two objects for equality—the strings contained in the two objects are *identical*. The method returns `true` if the contents of the objects are equal, and `false` otherwise. The preceding condition is `true` because `String` s1 was initialized with the string literal "hello". Method `equals` uses a **lexicographical comparison**—it compares the integer Unicode values (see online Appendix H for more information) that represent each character in each `String`. Thus, if the `String` "hello" is compared to the string "HELLO", the result is `false`, because the integer representation of a lowercase letter is *different* from that of the corresponding uppercase letter.

*Comparing **String**s with the == Operator*
The condition at line 23 uses the equality operator == to compare String s1 for equality with the String literal "hello". When primitive-type values are compared with ==, the result is true if *both values are identical.* When references are compared with ==, the result is true if *both references refer to the same object in memory.* To compare the actual contents (or state information) of objects for equality, a method must be invoked. In the case of Strings, that method is equals. The preceding condition evaluates to false at line 23 because the reference s1 was initialized with the statement

```
s1 = new String("hello");
```

which creates a new String object with a copy of string literal "hello" and assigns the new object to variable s1. If s1 had been initialized with the statement

```
s1 = "hello";
```

which directly assigns the string literal "hello" to variable s1, the condition would be true. Remember that Java treats all string literal objects with the same contents as one String object to which there can be many references. Thus, lines 8, 17 and 23 all refer to the same String object "hello" in memory.

Common Programming Error 14.1

Comparing references with == can lead to logic errors, because == compares the references to determine whether they refer to the same object, not whether two objects have the same contents. *When two separate objects that contain the same values are compared with ==, the result will be* false. *When comparing objects to determine whether they have the same contents, use method* equals.

*String Method **equalsIgnoreCase***
If you're sorting Strings, you may compare them for equality with method equalsIgnoreCase, which ignores whether the letters in each String are uppercase or lowercase when performing the comparison. Thus, "hello" and "HELLO" compare as equal. Line 29 uses String method equalsIgnoreCase to compare String s3—Happy Birthday—for equality with String s4—happy birthday. The result of this comparison is true because the comparison ignores case.

*String Method **compareTo***
Lines 35–44 use method compareTo to compare Strings. Method compareTo is declared in the Comparable interface and implemented in the String class. Line 36 compares String s1 to String s2. Method compareTo returns 0 if the Strings are equal, a negative number if the String that invokes compareTo is less than the String that's passed as an argument and a positive number if the String that invokes compareTo is greater than the String that's passed as an argument. Method compareTo uses a *lexicographical* comparison—it compares the numeric values of corresponding characters in each String.

*String Method **regionMatches***
The condition at line 47 uses a version of String method regionMatches to compare portions of two Strings for equality. The first argument to this version of the method is the starting index in the String that invokes the method. The second argument is a compar-

ison String. The third argument is the starting index in the comparison String. The last argument is the number of characters to compare between the two Strings. The method returns true only if the specified number of characters are lexicographically equal.

Finally, the condition at line 54 uses a five-argument version of String method regionMatches to compare portions of two Strings for equality. When the first argument is true, the method ignores the case of the characters being compared. The remaining arguments are identical to those described for the four-argument regionMatches method.

String Methods startsWith and endsWith

The next example (Fig. 14.4) demonstrates String methods **startsWith** and **endsWith**. Method main creates array strings containing "started", "starting", "ended" and "ending". The remainder of method main consists of three for statements that test the elements of the array to determine whether they start with or end with a particular set of characters.

```java
1   // Fig. 14.4: StringStartEnd.java
2   // String methods startsWith and endsWith.
3
4   public class StringStartEnd
5   {
6      public static void main(String[] args)
7      {
8         String[] strings = {"started", "starting", "ended", "ending"};
9
10        // test method startsWith
11        for (String string : strings)
12        {
13           if (string.startsWith("st"))
14              System.out.printf("\"%s\" starts with \"st\"%n", string);
15        }
16
17        System.out.println();
18
19        // test method startsWith starting from position 2 of string
20        for (String string : strings)
21        {
22           if (string.startsWith("art", 2))
23              System.out.printf(
24                 "\"%s\" starts with \"art\" at position 2%n", string);
25        }
26
27        System.out.println();
28
29        // test method endsWith
30        for (String string : strings)
31        {
32           if (string.endsWith("ed"))
33              System.out.printf("\"%s\" ends with \"ed\"%n", string);
34        }
35     }
36  } // end class StringStartEnd
```

Fig. 14.4 | String methods startsWith and endsWith. (Part 1 of 2.)

```
"started" starts with "st"
"starting" starts with "st"

"started" starts with "art" at position 2
"starting" starts with "art" at position 2

"started" ends with "ed"
"ended" ends with "ed"
```

Fig. 14.4 | String methods startsWith and endsWith. (Part 2 of 2.)

Lines 11–15 use the version of method startsWith that takes a String argument. The condition in the if statement (line 13) determines whether each String in the array starts with the characters "st". If so, the method returns true and the application prints that String. Otherwise, the method returns false and nothing happens.

Lines 20–25 use the startsWith method that takes a String and an integer as arguments. The integer specifies the index at which the comparison should begin in the String. The condition in the if statement (line 22) determines whether each String in the array has the characters "art" beginning with the third character in each String. If so, the method returns true and the application prints the String.

The third for statement (lines 30–34) uses method endsWith, which takes a String argument. The condition at line 32 determines whether each String in the array ends with the characters "ed". If so, the method returns true and the application prints the String.

14.3.4 Locating Characters and Substrings in Strings

Often it's useful to search a string for a character or set of characters. For example, if you're creating your own word processor, you might want to provide a capability for searching through documents. Figure 14.5 demonstrates the many versions of String methods **indexOf** and **lastIndexOf** that search for a specified character or substring in a String.

```
 1   // Fig. 14.5: StringIndexMethods.java
 2   // String searching methods indexOf and lastIndexOf.
 3
 4   public class StringIndexMethods
 5   {
 6      public static void main(String[] args)
 7      {
 8         String letters = "abcdefghijklmabcdefghijklm";
 9
10         // test indexOf to locate a character in a string
11         System.out.printf(
12            "'c' is located at index %d%n", letters.indexOf('c'));
13         System.out.printf(
14            "'a' is located at index %d%n", letters.indexOf('a', 1));
15         System.out.printf(
16            "'$' is located at index %d%n%n", letters.indexOf('$'));
17
```

Fig. 14.5 | String-searching methods indexOf and lastIndexOf. (Part 1 of 2.)

```
18          // test lastIndexOf to find a character in a string
19          System.out.printf("Last 'c' is located at index %d%n",
20              letters.lastIndexOf('c'));
21          System.out.printf("Last 'a' is located at index %d%n",
22              letters.lastIndexOf('a', 25));
23          System.out.printf("Last '$' is located at index %d%n%n",
24              letters.lastIndexOf('$'));
25
26          // test indexOf to locate a substring in a string
27          System.out.printf("\"def\" is located at index %d%n",
28              letters.indexOf("def"));
29          System.out.printf("\"def\" is located at index %d%n",
30              letters.indexOf("def", 7));
31          System.out.printf("\"hello\" is located at index %d%n%n",
32              letters.indexOf("hello"));
33
34          // test lastIndexOf to find a substring in a string
35          System.out.printf("Last \"def\" is located at index %d%n",
36              letters.lastIndexOf("def"));
37          System.out.printf("Last \"def\" is located at index %d%n",
38              letters.lastIndexOf("def", 25));
39          System.out.printf("Last \"hello\" is located at index %d%n",
40              letters.lastIndexOf("hello"));
41      }
42   } // end class StringIndexMethods
```

```
'c' is located at index 2
'a' is located at index 13
'$' is located at index -1

Last 'c' is located at index 15
Last 'a' is located at index 13
Last '$' is located at index -1

"def" is located at index 3
"def" is located at index 16
"hello" is located at index -1

Last "def" is located at index 16
Last "def" is located at index 16
Last "hello" is located at index -1
```

Fig. 14.5 | String-searching methods indexOf and lastIndexOf. (Part 2 of 2.)

All the searches in this example are performed on the String letters (initialized with "abcdefghijklmabcdefghijklm"). Lines 11–16 use method indexOf to locate the first occurrence of a character in a String. If the method finds the character, it returns the character's index in the String—otherwise, it returns –1. There are two versions of indexOf that search for characters in a String. The expression in line 12 uses the version of method indexOf that takes an integer representation of the character to find. The expression at line 14 uses another version of method indexOf, which takes two integer arguments—the character and the starting index at which the search of the String should begin.

Lines 19–24 use method lastIndexOf to locate the last occurrence of a character in a String. The method searches from the end of the String toward the beginning. If it finds the character, it returns the character's index in the String—otherwise, it returns –1. There are two versions of lastIndexOf that search for characters in a String. The expression at line 20 uses the version that takes the integer representation of the character. The expression at line 22 uses the version that takes two integer arguments—the integer representation of the character and the index from which to begin searching *backward*.

Lines 27–40 demonstrate versions of methods indexOf and lastIndexOf that each take a String as the first argument. These versions perform identically to those described earlier except that they search for sequences of characters (or substrings) that are specified by their String arguments. If the substring is found, these methods return the index in the String of the first character in the substring.

14.3.5 Extracting Substrings from Strings

Class String provides two substring methods to enable a new String object to be created by copying part of an existing String object. Each method returns a new String object. Both methods are demonstrated in Fig. 14.6.

```java
1   // Fig. 14.6: SubString.java
2   // String class substring methods.
3
4   public class SubString
5   {
6      public static void main(String[] args)
7      {
8         String letters = "abcdefghijklmabcdefghijklm";
9
10        // test substring methods
11        System.out.printf("Substring from index 20 to end is \"%s\"%n",
12           letters.substring(20));
13        System.out.printf("%s \"%s\"%n",
14           "Substring from index 3 up to, but not including 6 is",
15           letters.substring(3, 6));
16     }
17  } // end class SubString
```

```
Substring from index 20 to end is "hijklm"
Substring from index 3 up to, but not including 6 is "def"
```

Fig. 14.6 | String class substring methods.

The expression letters.substring(20) at line 12 uses the substring method that takes one integer argument. The argument specifies the starting index in the original String letters from which characters are to be copied. The substring returned contains a copy of the characters from the starting index to the end of the String. Specifying an index outside the bounds of the String causes a **StringIndexOutOfBoundsException**.

Line 15 uses the substring method that takes two integer arguments—the starting index from which to copy characters in the original String and the index one beyond the last character to copy (i.e., copy up to, but *not including*, that index in the String). The substring returned contains a copy of the specified characters from the original String. An index outside the bounds of the String causes a StringIndexOutOfBoundsException.

14.3.6 Concatenating Strings

String method **concat** (Fig. 14.7) concatenates two String objects (similar to using the + operator) and returns a new String object containing the characters from both original Strings. The expression s1.concat(s2) at line 13 forms a String by appending the characters in s2 to the those in s1. The original Strings to which s1 and s2 refer are *not modified*.

```
 1   // Fig. 14.7: StringConcatenation.java
 2   // String method concat.
 3
 4   public class StringConcatenation
 5   {
 6      public static void main(String[] args)
 7      {
 8         String s1 = "Happy ";
 9         String s2 = "Birthday";
10
11         System.out.printf("s1 = %s%ns2 = %s%n%n",s1, s2);
12         System.out.printf(
13            "Result of s1.concat(s2) = %s%n", s1.concat(s2));
14         System.out.printf("s1 after concatenation = %s%n", s1);
15      }
16   } // end class StringConcatenation
```

```
s1 = Happy
s2 = Birthday

Result of s1.concat(s2) = Happy Birthday
s1 after concatenation = Happy
```

Fig. 14.7 | String method concat.

14.3.7 Miscellaneous String Methods

Class String provides several methods that return Strings or character arrays containing copies of an original String's contents which are then modified. These methods—none of which modify the String on which they're called—are demonstrated in Fig. 14.8.

```
 1   // Fig. 14.8: StringMiscellaneous2.java
 2   // String methods replace, toLowerCase, toUpperCase, trim and toCharArray.
 3
 4   public class StringMiscellaneous2
 5   {
 6      public static void main(String[] args)
 7      {
```

Fig. 14.8 | String methods replace, toLowerCase, toUpperCase, trim and toCharArray. (Part 1 of 2.)

```
8              String s1 = "hello";
9              String s2 = "GOODBYE";
10             String s3 = "   spaces   ";
11
12             System.out.printf("s1 = %s%ns2 = %s%ns3 = %s%n%n", s1, s2, s3);
13
14             // test method replace
15             System.out.printf(
16                "Replace 'l' with 'L' in s1: %s%n%n", s1.replace('l', 'L'));
17
18             // test toLowerCase and toUpperCase
19             System.out.printf("s1.toUpperCase() = %s%n", s1.toUpperCase());
20             System.out.printf("s2.toLowerCase() = %s%n%n", s2.toLowerCase());
21
22             // test trim method
23             System.out.printf("s3 after trim = \"%s\"%n%n", s3.trim());
24
25             // test toCharArray method
26             char[] charArray = s1.toCharArray();
27             System.out.print("s1 as a character array = ");
28
29             for (char character : charArray)
30                System.out.print(character);
31
32             System.out.println();
33          }
34    } // end class StringMiscellaneous2
```

```
s1 = hello
s2 = GOODBYE
s3 =    spaces

Replace 'l' with 'L' in s1: heLLo

s1.toUpperCase() = HELLO
s2.toLowerCase() = goodbye

s3 after trim = "spaces"

s1 as a character array = hello
```

Fig. 14.8 | String methods replace, toLowerCase, toUpperCase, trim and toCharArray. (Part 2 of 2.)

Line 16 uses String method replace to return a new String object in which every occurrence in s1 of character 'l' (lowercase el) is replaced with character 'L'. Method replace leaves the original String unchanged. If there are no occurrences of the first argument in the String, method replace returns the original String. An overloaded version of method replace enables you to replace substrings rather than individual characters.

Line 19 uses String method **toUpperCase** to generate a new String with uppercase letters where corresponding lowercase letters exist in s1. The method returns a new String object containing the converted String and leaves the original String unchanged. If there are no characters to convert, method toUpperCase returns the original String.

Line 20 uses String method **toLowerCase** to return a new String object with lower-case letters where corresponding uppercase letters exist in s2. The original String remains unchanged. If there are no characters in the original String to convert, toLowerCase returns the original String.

Line 23 uses String method **trim** to generate a new String object that removes all white-space characters that appear at the beginning and/or end of the String on which trim operates. The method returns a new String object containing the String without leading or trailing white space. The original String remains unchanged. If there are no white-space characters at the beginning and/or end, trim returns the original String.

Line 26 uses String method **toCharArray** to create a new character array containing a copy of the characters in s1. Lines 29–30 output each char in the array.

14.3.8 String Method `valueOf`

As we've seen, every object in Java has a toString method that enables a program to obtain the object's *string representation*. Unfortunately, this technique cannot be used with primitive types because they do not have methods. Class String provides static methods that take an argument of any type and convert it to a String object. Figure 14.9 demonstrates the String class **valueOf** methods.

The expression String.valueOf(charArray) at line 18 uses the character array charArray to create a new String object. The expression String.valueOf(charArray, 3, 3) at line 20 uses a portion of the character array charArray to create a new String object. The second argument specifies the starting index from which the characters are used. The third argument specifies the number of characters to be used.

```
1   // Fig. 14.9: StringValueOf.java
2   // String valueOf methods.
3
4   public class StringValueOf
5   {
6      public static void main(String[] args)
7      {
8         char[] charArray = {'a', 'b', 'c', 'd', 'e', 'f'};
9         boolean booleanValue = true;
10        char characterValue = 'Z';
11        int integerValue = 7;
12        long longValue = 10000000000L; // L suffix indicates long
13        float floatValue = 2.5f; // f indicates that 2.5 is a float
14        double doubleValue = 33.333; // no suffix, double is default
15        Object objectRef = "hello"; // assign string to an Object reference
16
17        System.out.printf(
18           "char array = %s%n", String.valueOf(charArray));
19        System.out.printf("part of char array = %s%n",
20           String.valueOf(charArray, 3, 3));
21        System.out.printf(
22           "boolean = %s%n", String.valueOf(booleanValue));
23        System.out.printf(
24           "char = %s%n", String.valueOf(characterValue));
```

Fig. 14.9 | String valueOf methods. (Part 1 of 2.)

```
25          System.out.printf("int = %s%n", String.valueOf(integerValue));
26          System.out.printf("long = %s%n", String.valueOf(longValue));
27          System.out.printf("float = %s%n", String.valueOf(floatValue));
28          System.out.printf(
29             "double = %s%n", String.valueOf(doubleValue));
30          System.out.printf("Object = %s", String.valueOf(objectRef));
31       }
32    } // end class StringValueOf
```

```
char array = abcdef
part of char array = def
boolean = true
char = Z
int = 7
long = 10000000000
float = 2.5
double = 33.333
Object = hello
```

Fig. 14.9 | String valueOf methods. (Part 2 of 2.)

There are seven other versions of method valueOf, which take arguments of type boolean, char, int, long, float, double and Object, respectively. These are demonstrated in lines 21–30. The version of valueOf that takes an Object as an argument can do so because all Objects can be converted to Strings with method toString.

[*Note:* Lines 12–13 use literal values 10000000000L and 2.5f as the initial values of long variable longValue and float variable floatValue, respectively. By default, Java treats integer literals as type int and floating-point literals as type double. Appending the letter L to the literal 10000000000 and appending letter f to the literal 2.5 indicates to the compiler that 10000000000 should be treated as a long and 2.5 as a float. An uppercase L or lowercase l can be used to denote a variable of type long and an uppercase F or lowercase f can be used to denote a variable of type float.]

14.4 Class StringBuilder

We now discuss the features of class **StringBuilder** for creating and manipulating *dynamic* string information—that is, *modifiable* strings. Every StringBuilder is capable of storing a number of characters specified by its *capacity*. If a StringBuilder's capacity is exceeded, the capacity expands to accommodate the additional characters.

Performance Tip 14.3

Java can perform certain optimizations involving String objects (such as referring to one String object from multiple variables) because it knows these objects will not change. Strings (not StringBuilders) should be used if the data will not change.

Performance Tip 14.4

In programs that frequently perform string concatenation, or other string modifications, it's often more efficient to implement the modifications with class StringBuilder.

Software Engineering Observation 14.1

*StringBuilders are not thread safe. If multiple threads require access to the same dynamic string information, use class **StringBuffer** in your code. Classes StringBuilder and StringBuffer provide identical capabilities, but class StringBuffer is thread safe. For more details on threading, see Chapter 23.*

14.4.1 StringBuilder Constructors

Class StringBuilder provides four constructors. We demonstrate three of these in Fig. 14.10. Line 8 uses the no-argument StringBuilder constructor to create a String-Builder with no characters in it and an initial capacity of 16 characters (the default for a StringBuilder). Line 9 uses the StringBuilder constructor that takes an integer argument to create a StringBuilder with no characters in it and the initial capacity specified by the integer argument (i.e., 10). Line 10 uses the StringBuilder constructor that takes a String argument to create a StringBuilder containing the characters in the String argument. The initial capacity is the number of characters in the String argument plus 16.

Lines 12–14 implicitly use the method toString of class StringBuilder to output the StringBuilders with the printf method. In Section 14.4.4, we discuss how Java uses StringBuilder objects to implement the + and += operators for string concatenation.

```java
1   // Fig. 14.10: StringBuilderConstructors.java
2   // StringBuilder constructors.
3
4   public class StringBuilderConstructors
5   {
6      public static void main(String[] args)
7      {
8         StringBuilder buffer1 = new StringBuilder();
9         StringBuilder buffer2 = new StringBuilder(10);
10        StringBuilder buffer3 = new StringBuilder("hello");
11
12        System.out.printf("buffer1 = \"%s\"%n", buffer1);
13        System.out.printf("buffer2 = \"%s\"%n", buffer2);
14        System.out.printf("buffer3 = \"%s\"%n", buffer3);
15     }
16   } // end class StringBuilderConstructors
```

```
buffer1 = ""
buffer2 = ""
buffer3 = "hello"
```

Fig. 14.10 | StringBuilder constructors.

14.4.2 StringBuilder Methods length, capacity, setLength and ensureCapacity

Class StringBuilder provides methods **length** and **capacity** to return the number of characters currently in a StringBuilder and the number of characters that can be stored in a StringBuilder without allocating more memory, respectively. Method **ensure-Capacity** guarantees that a StringBuilder has at least the specified capacity. Method **setLength** increases or decreases the length of a StringBuilder. Figure 14.11 demonstrates these methods.

```java
1   // Fig. 14.11: StringBuilderCapLen.java
2   // StringBuilder length, setLength, capacity and ensureCapacity methods.
3
4   public class StringBuilderCapLen
5   {
6      public static void main(String[] args)
7      {
8         StringBuilder buffer = new StringBuilder("Hello, how are you?");
9
10        System.out.printf("buffer = %s%nlength = %d%ncapacity = %d%n%n",
11           buffer.toString(), buffer.length(), buffer.capacity());
12
13        buffer.ensureCapacity(75);
14        System.out.printf("New capacity = %d%n%n", buffer.capacity());
15
16        buffer.setLength(10));
17        System.out.printf("New length = %d%nbuffer = %s%n",
18           buffer.length(), buffer.toString());
19     }
20  } // end class StringBuilderCapLen
```

```
buffer = Hello, how are you?
length = 19
capacity = 35

New capacity = 75

New length = 10
buffer = Hello, how
```

Fig. 14.11 | StringBuilder length, setLength, capacity and ensureCapacity methods.

The application contains one StringBuilder called buffer. Line 8 uses the StringBuilder constructor that takes a String argument to initialize the StringBuilder with "Hello, how are you?". Lines 10–11 print the contents, length and capacity of the StringBuilder. Note in the output window that the capacity of the StringBuilder is initially 35. Recall that the StringBuilder constructor that takes a String argument initializes the capacity to the length of the string passed as an argument plus 16.

Line 13 uses method ensureCapacity to expand the capacity of the StringBuilder to a minimum of 75 characters. Actually, if the original capacity is less than the argument, the method ensures a capacity that's the greater of the number specified as an argument and twice the original capacity plus 2. The StringBuilder's current capacity remains unchanged if it's more than the specified capacity.

> **Performance Tip 14.5**
> *Dynamically increasing the capacity of a StringBuilder can take a relatively long time. Executing a large number of these operations can degrade the performance of an application. If a StringBuilder is going to increase greatly in size, possibly multiple times, setting its capacity high at the beginning will increase performance.*

Line 16 uses method setLength to set the length of the StringBuilder to 10. If the specified length is less than the current number of characters in the StringBuilder, its contents are truncated to the specified length (i.e., the characters in the StringBuilder after the specified length are discarded). If the specified length is greater than the number of characters currently in the StringBuilder, null characters (characters with the numeric representation 0) are appended until the total number of characters in the StringBuilder is equal to the specified length.

14.4.3 StringBuilder Methods charAt, setCharAt, getChars and reverse

Class StringBuilder provides methods **charAt**, **setCharAt**, **getChars** and **reverse** to manipulate the characters in a StringBuilder (Fig. 14.12). Method charAt (line 12) takes an integer argument and returns the character in the StringBuilder at that index. Method getChars (line 15) copies characters from a StringBuilder into the character array passed as an argument. This method takes four arguments—the starting index from which characters should be copied in the StringBuilder, the index one past the last character to be copied from the StringBuilder, the character array into which the characters are to be copied and the starting location in the character array where the first character should be placed. Method setCharAt (lines 21 and 22) takes an integer and a character argument and sets the character at the specified position in the StringBuilder to the character argument. Method reverse (line 25) reverses the contents of the StringBuilder. Attempting to access a character that's outside the bounds of a StringBuilder results in a StringIndexOutOfBoundsException.

```
1   // Fig. 14.12: StringBuilderChars.java
2   // StringBuilder methods charAt, setCharAt, getChars and reverse.
3
4   public class StringBuilderChars
5   {
6      public static void main(String[] args)
7      {
8         StringBuilder buffer = new StringBuilder("hello there");
9
10        System.out.printf("buffer = %s%n", buffer.toString());
11        System.out.printf("Character at 0: %s%nCharacter at 4: %s%n%n",
12           buffer.charAt(0), buffer.charAt(4));
13
14        char[] charArray = new char[buffer.length()];
15        buffer.getChars(0, buffer.length(), charArray, 0);
16        System.out.print("The characters are: ");
```

Fig. 14.12 │ StringBuilder methods charAt, setCharAt, getChars and reverse. (Part 1 of 2.)

```
17
18          for (char character : charArray)
19             System.out.print(character);
20
21          buffer.setCharAt(0, 'H');
22          buffer.setCharAt(6, 'T');
23          System.out.printf("%n%nbuffer = %s", buffer.toString());
24
25          buffer.reverse();
26          System.out.printf("%n%nbuffer = %s%n", buffer.toString());
27       }
28    } // end class StringBuilderChars
```

```
buffer = hello there
Character at 0: h
Character at 4: o

The characters are: hello there

buffer = Hello There

buffer = erehT olleH
```

Fig. 14.12 | StringBuilder methods charAt, setCharAt, getChars and reverse. (Part 2 of 2.)

14.4.4 StringBuilder append Methods

Class StringBuilder provides *overloaded* **append** methods (Fig. 14.13) to allow values of various types to be appended to the end of a StringBuilder. Versions are provided for each of the primitive types and for character arrays, Strings, Objects, and more. (Remember that method toString produces a string representation of any Object.) Each method takes its argument, converts it to a string and appends it to the StringBuilder.

```
1   // Fig. 14.13: StringBuilderAppend.java
2   // StringBuilder append methods.
3
4   public class StringBuilderAppend
5   {
6      public static void main(String[] args)
7      {
8         Object objectRef = "hello";
9         String string = "goodbye";
10        char[] charArray = {'a', 'b', 'c', 'd', 'e', 'f'};
11        boolean booleanValue = true;
12        char characterValue = 'Z';
13        int integerValue = 7;
14        long longValue = 10000000000L;
15        float floatValue = 2.5f;
16        double doubleValue = 33.333;
```

Fig. 14.13 | StringBuilder append methods. (Part 1 of 2.)

```
17
18        StringBuilder lastBuffer = new StringBuilder("last buffer");
19        StringBuilder buffer = new StringBuilder();
20
21        buffer.append(objectRef)
22              .append("%n")
23              .append(string)
24              .append("%n")
25              .append(charArray)
26              .append("%n")
27              .append(charArray, 0, 3)
28              .append("%n")
29              .append(booleanValue)
30              .append("%n")
31              .append(characterValue);
32              .append("%n")
33              .append(integerValue)
34              .append("%n")
35              .append(longValue)
36              .append("%n")
37              .append(floatValue)
38              .append("%n")
39              .append(doubleValue)
40              .append("%n")
41              .append(lastBuffer);
42
43        System.out.printf("buffer contains%n%s%n", buffer.toString());
44     }
45  } // end StringBuilderAppend
```

```
buffer contains
hello
goodbye
abcdef
abc
true
Z
7
10000000000
2.5
33.333
last buffer
```

Fig. 14.13 | StringBuilder append methods. (Part 2 of 2.)

The compiler can use StringBuilder and the append methods to implement the + and += String concatenation operators. For example, assuming the declarations

```
String string1 = "hello";
String string2 = "BC";
int value = 22;
```

the statement

```
String s = string1 + string2 + value;
```

concatenates "hello", "BC" and 22. The concatenation can be performed as follows:

```
String s = new StringBuilder().append("hello").append("BC").
    append(22).toString();
```

First, the preceding statement creates an *empty* StringBuilder, then appends to it the strings "hello" and "BC" and the integer 22. Next, StringBuilder's toString method converts the StringBuilder to a String object to be assigned to String s. The statement

```
s += "!";
```

can be performed as follows (this may differ by compiler):

```
s = new StringBuilder().append(s).append("!").toString();
```

This creates an empty StringBuilder, then appends to it the current contents of s followed by "!". Next, StringBuilder's method toString (which must be called *explicitly* here) returns the StringBuilder's contents as a String, and the result is assigned to s.

14.4.5 StringBuilder Insertion and Deletion Methods

StringBuilder provides overloaded **insert** methods to insert values of various types at any position in a StringBuilder. Versions are provided for the primitive types and for character arrays, Strings, Objects and CharSequences. Each method takes its second argument and inserts it at the index specified by the first argument. If the first argument is less than 0 or greater than the StringBuilder's length, a StringIndexOutOfBoundsException occurs. Class StringBuilder also provides methods **delete** and **deleteCharAt** to delete characters at any position in a StringBuilder. Method delete takes two arguments—the starting index and the index one past the end of the characters to delete. All characters beginning at the starting index up to but *not* including the ending index are deleted. Method deleteCharAt takes one argument—the index of the character to delete. Invalid indices cause both methods to throw a StringIndexOutOfBoundsException. Figure 14.14 demonstrates methods insert, delete and deleteCharAt.

```
 1   // Fig. 14.14: StringBuilderInsertDelete.java
 2   // StringBuilder methods insert, delete and deleteCharAt.
 3
 4   public class StringBuilderInsertDelete
 5   {
 6      public static void main(String[] args)
 7      {
 8         Object objectRef = "hello";
 9         String string = "goodbye";
10         char[] charArray = {'a', 'b', 'c', 'd', 'e', 'f'};
11         boolean booleanValue = true;
12         char characterValue = 'K';
13         int integerValue = 7;
14         long longValue = 10000000;
15         float floatValue = 2.5f; // f suffix indicates that 2.5 is a float
16         double doubleValue = 33.333;
17
```

Fig. 14.14 | StringBuilder methods insert, delete and deleteCharAt. (Part 1 of 2.)

```
18          StringBuilder buffer = new StringBuilder();
19
20          buffer.insert(0, objectRef);
21          buffer.insert(0, "  "); // each of these contains two spaces
22          buffer.insert(0, string);
23          buffer.insert(0, "  ");
24          buffer.insert(0, charArray);
25          buffer.insert(0, "  ");
26          buffer.insert(0, charArray, 3, 3);
27          buffer.insert(0, "  ");
28          buffer.insert(0, booleanValue);
29          buffer.insert(0, "  ");
30          buffer.insert(0, characterValue);
31          buffer.insert(0, "  ");
32          buffer.insert(0, integerValue);
33          buffer.insert(0, "  ");
34          buffer.insert(0, longValue);
35          buffer.insert(0, "  ");
36          buffer.insert(0, floatValue);
37          buffer.insert(0, "  ");
38          buffer.insert(0, doubleValue);
39
40          System.out.printf(
41             "buffer after inserts:%n%s%n%n", buffer.toString());
42
43          buffer.deleteCharAt(10); // delete 5 in 2.5
44          buffer.delete(2, 6); // delete .333 in 33.333
45
46          System.out.printf(
47             "buffer after deletes:%n%s%n", buffer.toString());
48       }
49    } // end class StringBuilderInsertDelete
```

```
buffer after inserts:
33.333  2.5  10000000  7  K  true  def  abcdef  goodbye  hello

buffer after deletes:
33  2.  10000000  7  K  true  def  abcdef  goodbye  hello
```

Fig. 14.14 | StringBuilder methods insert, delete and deleteCharAt. (Part 2 of 2.)

14.5 Class Character

Java provides eight **type-wrapper classes**—Boolean, Character, Double, Float, Byte, Short, Integer and Long—that enable primitive-type values to be treated as objects. In this section, we present class Character—the type-wrapper class for primitive type char.

Most Character methods are static methods designed for convenience in processing individual char values. These methods take at least a character argument and perform either a test or a manipulation of the character. Class Character also contains a constructor that receives a char argument to initialize a Character object. Most of the methods of class Character are presented in the next three examples. For more information on class Character (and all the type-wrapper classes), see the java.lang package in the Java API documentation.

Figure 14.15 demonstrates static methods that test characters to determine whether they're a specific character type and the static methods that perform case conversions on characters. You can enter any character and apply the methods to the character.

```
1   // Fig. 14.15: StaticCharMethods.java
2   // Character static methods for testing characters and converting case.
3   import java.util.Scanner;
4
5   public class StaticCharMethods
6   {
7      public static void main(String[] args)
8      {
9         Scanner scanner = new Scanner(System.in); // create scanner
10        System.out.println("Enter a character and press Enter");
11        String input = scanner.next();
12        char c = input.charAt(0); // get input character
13
14        // display character info
15        System.out.printf("is defined: %b%n", Character.isDefined(c));
16        System.out.printf("is digit: %b%n", Character.isDigit(c));
17        System.out.printf("is first character in a Java identifier: %b%n",
18           Character.isJavaIdentifierStart(c));
19        System.out.printf("is part of a Java identifier: %b%n",
20           Character.isJavaIdentifierPart(c));
21        System.out.printf("is letter: %b%n", Character.isLetter(c));
22        System.out.printf(
23           "is letter or digit: %b%n", Character.isLetterOrDigit(c));
24        System.out.printf(
25           "is lower case: %b%n", Character.isLowerCase(c));
26        System.out.printf(
27           "is upper case: %b%n", Character.isUpperCase(c));
28        System.out.printf(
29           "to upper case: %s%n", Character.toUpperCase(c));
30        System.out.printf(
31           "to lower case: %s%n", Character.toLowerCase(c));
32     }
33  } // end class StaticCharMethods
```

```
Enter a character and press Enter
A
is defined: true
is digit: false
is first character in a Java identifier: true
is part of a Java identifier: true
is letter: true
is letter or digit: true
is lower case: false
is upper case: true
to upper case: A
to lower case: a
```

Fig. 14.15 | Character static methods for testing characters and converting case. (Part 1 of 2.)

```
Enter a character and press Enter
8
is defined: true
is digit: true
is first character in a Java identifier: false
is part of a Java identifier: true
is letter: false
is letter or digit: true
is lower case: false
is upper case: false
to upper case: 8
to lower case: 8
```

```
Enter a character and press Enter
$
is defined: true
is digit: false
is first character in a Java identifier: true
is part of a Java identifier: true
is letter: false
is letter or digit: false
is lower case: false
is upper case: false
to upper case: $
to lower case: $
```

Fig. 14.15 | Character static methods for testing characters and converting case. (Part 2 of 2.)

Line 15 uses Character method **isDefined** to determine whether character c is defined in the Unicode character set. If so, the method returns true; otherwise, it returns false. Line 16 uses Character method **isDigit** to determine whether character c is a defined Unicode digit. If so, the method returns true, and otherwise, false.

Line 18 uses Character method **isJavaIdentifierStart** to determine whether c is a character that can be the first character of an identifier in Java—that is, a letter, an underscore (_) or a dollar sign ($). If so, the method returns true, and otherwise, false. Line 20 uses Character method **isJavaIdentifierPart** to determine whether character c is a character that can be used in an identifier in Java—that is, a digit, a letter, an underscore (_) or a dollar sign ($). If so, the method returns true, and otherwise, false.

Line 21 uses Character method **isLetter** to determine whether character c is a letter. If so, the method returns true, and otherwise, false. Line 23 uses Character method **isLetterOrDigit** to determine whether character c is a letter or a digit. If so, the method returns true, and otherwise, false.

Line 25 uses Character method **isLowerCase** to determine whether character c is a lowercase letter. If so, the method returns true, and otherwise, false. Line 27 uses Character method **isUpperCase** to determine whether character c is an uppercase letter. If so, the method returns true, and otherwise, false.

Line 29 uses Character method **toUpperCase** to convert the character c to its uppercase equivalent. The method returns the converted character if the character has an uppercase equivalent, and otherwise, the method returns its original argument. Line 31 uses Character method **toLowerCase** to convert the character c to its lowercase equivalent. The method returns the converted character if the character has a lowercase equivalent, and otherwise, the method returns its original argument.

Figure 14.16 demonstrates static Character methods **digit** and **forDigit**, which convert characters to digits and digits to characters, respectively, in different number systems. Common number systems include decimal (base 10), octal (base 8), hexadecimal (base 16) and binary (base 2). The base of a number is also known as its **radix**. For more information on conversions between number systems, see online Appendix J.

```java
1   // Fig. 14.16: StaticCharMethods2.java
2   // Character class static conversion methods.
3   import java.util.Scanner;
4
5   public class StaticCharMethods2
6   {
7      // executes application
8      public static void main(String[] args)
9      {
10         Scanner scanner = new Scanner(System.in);
11
12         // get radix
13         System.out.println("Please enter a radix:");
14         int radix = scanner.nextInt();
15
16         // get user choice
17         System.out.printf("Please choose one:%n1 -- %s%n2 -- %s%n",
18            "Convert digit to character", "Convert character to digit");
19         int choice = scanner.nextInt();
20
21         // process request
22         switch (choice)
23         {
24            case 1: // convert digit to character
25               System.out.println("Enter a digit:");
26               int digit = scanner.nextInt();
27               System.out.printf("Convert digit to character: %s%n",
28                  Character.forDigit(digit, radix));
29               break;
30
31            case 2: // convert character to digit
32               System.out.println("Enter a character:");
33               char character = scanner.next().charAt(0);
34               System.out.printf("Convert character to digit: %s%n",
35                  Character.digit(character, radix));
36               break;
37         }
38      }
39   } // end class StaticCharMethods2
```

Fig. 14.16 | Character class static conversion methods. (Part 1 of 2.)

```
Please enter a radix:
16
Please choose one:
1 -- Convert digit to character
2 -- Convert character to digit
2
Enter a character:
A
Convert character to digit: 10
```

```
Please enter a radix:
16
Please choose one:
1 -- Convert digit to character
2 -- Convert character to digit
1
Enter a digit:
13
Convert digit to character: d
```

Fig. 14.16 | Character class static conversion methods. (Part 2 of 2.)

Line 28 uses method forDigit to convert the integer digit into a character in the number system specified by the integer radix (the base of the number). For example, the decimal integer 13 in base 16 (the radix) has the character value 'd'. Lowercase and uppercase letters represent the *same* value in number systems. Line 35 uses method digit to convert variable character into an integer in the number system specified by the integer radix (the base of the number). For example, the character 'A' is the base 16 (the radix) representation of the base 10 value 10. The radix must be between 2 and 36, inclusive.

Figure 14.17 demonstrates the constructor and several instance methods of class Character—**charValue**, toString and equals. Lines 7–8 instantiate two Character objects by assigning the character constants 'A' and 'a', respectively, to the Character variables. Java automatically converts these char literals into Character objects—a process known as *autoboxing* that we discuss in more detail in Section 16.4. Line 11 uses Character method charValue to return the char value stored in Character object c1. Line 11 returns a string representation of Character object c2 using method toString. The condition in line 13 uses method equals to determine whether the object c1 has the same contents as the object c2 (i.e., the characters inside each object are equal).

```
1   // Fig. 14.17: OtherCharMethods.java
2   // Character class instance methods.
3   public class OtherCharMethods
4   {
5      public static void main(String[] args)
6      {
7         Character c1 = 'A';
8         Character c2 = 'a';
```

Fig. 14.17 | Character class instance methods. (Part 1 of 2.)

```
 9
10            System.out.printf(
11               "c1 = %s%nc2 = %s%n%n", c1.charValue(), c2.toString());
12
13            if (c1.equals(c2))
14               System.out.println("c1 and c2 are equal%n");
15            else
16               System.out.println("c1 and c2 are not equal%n");
17         }
18    } // end class OtherCharMethods
```

```
c1 = A
c2 = a

c1 and c2 are not equal
```

Fig. 14.17 | Character class instance methods. (Part 2 of 2.)

14.6 Tokenizing Strings

When you read a sentence, your mind breaks it into **tokens**—individual words and punctuation marks that convey meaning to you. Compilers also perform tokenization. They break up statements into individual pieces like keywords, identifiers, operators and other programming-language elements. We now study class String's **split** method, which breaks a String into its component tokens. Tokens are separated from one another by **delimiters**, typically white-space characters such as space, tab, newline and carriage return. Other characters can also be used as delimiters to separate tokens. The application in Fig. 14.18 demonstrates String's split method.

When the user presses the *Enter* key, the input sentence is stored in variable sentence. Line 17 invokes String method split with the String argument " ", which returns an array of Strings. The space character in the argument String is the delimiter that method split uses to locate the tokens in the String. As you'll learn in the next section, the argument to method split can be a regular expression for more complex tokenizing. Line 19 displays the length of the array tokens—i.e., the number of tokens in sentence. Lines 21–22 output each token on a separate line.

```
 1    // Fig. 14.18: TokenTest.java
 2    // StringTokenizer object used to tokenize strings.
 3    import java.util.Scanner;
 4    import java.util.StringTokenizer;
 5
 6    public class TokenTest
 7    {
 8       // execute application
 9       public static void main(String[] args)
10       {
11          // get sentence
12          Scanner scanner = new Scanner(System.in);
```

Fig. 14.18 | StringTokenizer object used to tokenize strings. (Part 1 of 2.)

```
13          System.out.println("Enter a sentence and press Enter");
14          String sentence = scanner.nextLine();
15
16          // process user sentence
17          String[] tokens = sentence.split(" ");
18          System.out.printf("Number of elements: %d%nThe tokens are:%n",
19             tokens.length);
20
21          for (String token : tokens)
22             System.out.println(token);
23       }
24    } // end class TokenTest
```

```
Enter a sentence and press Enter
This is a sentence with seven tokens
Number of elements: 7
The tokens are:
This
is
a
sentence
with
seven
tokens
```

Fig. 14.18 | StringTokenizer object used to tokenize strings. (Part 2 of 2.)

14.7 Regular Expressions, Class Pattern and Class Matcher

A **regular expression** is a String that describes a *search pattern* for *matching* characters in other Strings. Such expressions are useful for *validating input* and ensuring that data is in a particular format. For example, a ZIP code must consist of five digits, and a last name must contain only letters, spaces, apostrophes and hyphens. One application of regular expressions is to facilitate the construction of a compiler. Often, a large and complex regular expression is used to *validate the syntax of a program*. If the program code does *not* match the regular expression, the compiler knows that there's a syntax error in the code.

Class String provides several methods for performing regular-expression operations, the simplest of which is the matching operation. String method **matches** receives a String that specifies the regular expression and matches the contents of the String object on which it's called to the regular expression. The method returns a boolean indicating whether the match succeeded.

A regular expression consists of literal characters and special symbols. Figure 14.19 specifies some **predefined character classes** that can be used with regular expressions. A character class is an *escape sequence* that represents a group of characters. A digit is any numeric character. A **word character** is any letter (uppercase or lowercase), any digit or the underscore character. A white-space character is a space, a tab, a carriage return, a newline or a form feed. Each character class matches a single character in the String we're attempting to match with the regular expression.

Character	Matches	Character	Matches
\d	any digit	\D	any nondigit
\w	any word character	\W	any nonword character
\s	any white-space character	\S	any non-whitespace character

Fig. 14.19 | Predefined character classes.

Regular expressions are not limited to these predefined character classes. The expressions employ various operators and other forms of notation to match complex patterns. We examine several of these techniques in the application in Figs. 14.20 and 14.21, which *validates user input* via regular expressions. [*Note:* This application is not designed to match all possible valid user input.]

```java
1   // Fig. 14.20: ValidateInput.java
2   // Validating user information using regular expressions.
3
4   public class ValidateInput
5   {
6      // validate first name
7      public static boolean validateFirstName(String firstName)
8      {
9         return firstName.matches("[A-Z][a-zA-Z]*");
10     }
11
12     // validate last name
13     public static boolean validateLastName(String lastName)
14     {
15        return lastName.matches("[a-zA-z]+(['-][a-zA-Z]+)*");
16     }
17
18     // validate address
19     public static boolean validateAddress(String address)
20     {
21        return address.matches(
22           "\\d+\\s+([a-zA-Z]+|[a-zA-Z]+\\s[a-zA-Z]+)");
23     }
24
25     // validate city
26     public static boolean validateCity(String city)
27     {
28        return city.matches("([a-zA-Z]+|[a-zA-Z]+\\s[a-zA-Z]+)");
29     }
30
31     // validate state
32     public static boolean validateState(String state)
33     {
```

Fig. 14.20 | Validating user information using regular expressions. (Part 1 of 2.)

```
34          return state.matches("([a-zA-Z]+|[a-zA-Z]+\\s[a-zA-Z]+)");
35      }
36
37      // validate zip
38      public static boolean validateZip(String zip)
39      {
40          return zip.matches("\\d{5}");
41      }
42
43      // validate phone
44      public static boolean validatePhone(String phone)
45      {
46          return phone.matches("[1-9]\\d{2}-[1-9]\\d{2}-\\d{4}");
47      }
48  } // end class ValidateInput
```

Fig. 14.20 | Validating user information using regular expressions. (Part 2 of 2.)

```
1   // Fig. 14.21: Validate.java
2   // Input and validate data from user using the ValidateInput class.
3   import java.util.Scanner;
4
5   public class Validate
6   {
7       public static void main(String[] args)
8       {
9           // get user input
10          Scanner scanner = new Scanner(System.in);
11          System.out.println("Please enter first name:");
12          String firstName = scanner.nextLine();
13          System.out.println("Please enter last name:");
14          String lastName = scanner.nextLine();
15          System.out.println("Please enter address:");
16          String address = scanner.nextLine();
17          System.out.println("Please enter city:");
18          String city = scanner.nextLine();
19          System.out.println("Please enter state:");
20          String state = scanner.nextLine();
21          System.out.println("Please enter zip:");
22          String zip = scanner.nextLine();
23          System.out.println("Please enter phone:");
24          String phone = scanner.nextLine();
25
26          // validate user input and display error message
27          System.out.println("%nValidate Result:");
28
29          if (!ValidateInput.validateFirstName(firstName))
30              System.out.println("Invalid first name");
31          else if (!ValidateInput.validateLastName(lastName))
32              System.out.println("Invalid last name");
33          else if (!ValidateInput.validateAddress(address))
34              System.out.println("Invalid address");
```

Fig. 14.21 | Input and validate data from user using the ValidateInput class. (Part 1 of 2.)

```
35              else if (!ValidateInput.validateCity(city))
36                  System.out.println("Invalid city");
37              else if (!ValidateInput.validateState(state))
38                  System.out.println("Invalid state");
39              else if (!ValidateInput.validateZip(zip))
40                  System.out.println("Invalid zip code");
41              else if (!ValidateInput.validatePhone(phone))
42                  System.out.println("Invalid phone number");
43              else
44                  System.out.println("Valid input.  Thank you.");
45         }
46    } // end class Validate
```

```
Please enter first name:
Jane
Please enter last name:
Doe
Please enter address:
123 Some Street
Please enter city:
Some City
Please enter state:
SS
Please enter zip:
123
Please enter phone:
123-456-7890

Validate Result:
Invalid zip code
```

```
Please enter first name:
Jane
Please enter last name:
Doe
Please enter address:
123 Some Street
Please enter city:
Some City
Please enter state:
SS
Please enter zip:
12345
Please enter phone:
123-456-7890

Validate Result:
Valid input.  Thank you.
```

Fig. 14.21 | Input and validate data from user using the ValidateInput class. (Part 2 of 2.)

Figure 14.20 validates user input. Line 9 validates the first name. To match a set of characters that does not have a predefined character class, use square brackets, []. For example, the pattern "[aeiou]" matches a single character that's a vowel. Character ranges are represented by placing a dash (-) between two characters. In the example, `"[A-Z]"` matches a single uppercase letter. If the first character in the brackets is `"^"`, the expression accepts any character other than those indicated. However, `"[^Z]"` is not the same as `"[A-Y]"`, which matches uppercase letters A–Y—`"[^Z]"` matches *any character other than* capital Z, including lowercase letters and nonletters such as the newline character. Ranges in character classes are determined by the letters' integer values. In this example, `"[A-Za-z]"` matches all uppercase and lowercase letters. The range `"[A-z]"` matches all letters and also matches those characters (such as [and \) with an integer value between uppercase Z and lowercase a (for more information on integer values of characters see Appendix B). Like predefined character classes, character classes delimited by square brackets match a single character in the search object.

In line 9, the asterisk after the second character class indicates that any number of letters can be matched. In general, when the regular-expression operator `"*"` appears in a regular expression, the application attempts to match zero or more occurrences of the subexpression immediately preceding the `"*"`. Operator `"+"` attempts to match one or more occurrences of the subexpression immediately preceding `"+"`. So both `"A*"` and `"A+"` will match `"AAA"` or `"A"`, but only `"A*"` will match an empty string.

If method `validateFirstName` returns `true` (line 29 of Fig. 14.21), the application attempts to validate the last name (line 31) by calling `validateLastName` (lines 13–16 of Fig. 14.20). The regular expression to validate the last name matches any number of letters split by spaces, apostrophes or hyphens.

Line 33 of Fig. 14.21 calls method `validateAddress` (lines 19–23 of Fig. 14.20) to validate the address. The first character class matches any digit one or more times (\\d+). Two \ characters are used, because \ normally starts an escape sequence in a string. So \\d in a `String` represents the regular-expression pattern \d. Then we match one or more white-space characters (\\s+). The character `"|"` matches the expression to its left or to its right. For example, `"Hi (John|Jane)"` matches both `"Hi John"` and `"Hi Jane"`. The parentheses are used to group parts of the regular expression. In this example, the left side of | matches a single word, and the right side matches two words separated by any amount of white space. So the address must contain a number followed by one or two words. Therefore, `"10 Broadway"` and `"10 Main Street"` are both valid addresses in this example. The city (lines 26–29 of Fig. 14.20) and state (lines 32–35 of Fig. 14.20) methods also match any word of at least one character or, alternatively, any two words of at least one character if the words are separated by a single space, so both `Waltham` and `West Newton` would match.

Quantifiers

The asterisk (*) and plus (+) are formally called **quantifiers**. Figure 14.22 lists all the quantifiers. We've already discussed how the asterisk (*) and plus (+) quantifiers work. All quantifiers affect only the subexpression immediately preceding the quantifier. Quantifier question mark (?) matches zero or one occurrences of the expression that it quantifies. A set of braces containing one number ({n}) matches exactly n occurrences of the expression it quantifies. We demonstrate this quantifier to validate the zip code in Fig. 14.20 at line 40. Including a comma after the number enclosed in braces matches at least n occurrences of the quantified expression. The set of braces containing two numbers ({n, m}), matches between n and m occurrences of the expression that it qualifies. Quantifiers may be applied to patterns enclosed in parentheses to create more complex regular expressions.

Quantifier	Matches
*	Matches zero or more occurrences of the pattern.
+	Matches one or more occurrences of the pattern.
?	Matches zero or one occurrences of the pattern.
$\{n\}$	Matches exactly n occurrences.
$\{n,\}$	Matches at least n occurrences.
$\{n,m\}$	Matches between n and m (inclusive) occurrences.

Fig. 14.22 | Quantifiers used in regular expressions.

All of the quantifiers are **greedy**. This means that they'll match as many occurrences as they can as long as the match is still successful. However, if any of these quantifiers is followed by a question mark (?), the quantifier becomes **reluctant** (sometimes called **lazy**). It then will match as few occurrences as possible as long as the match is still successful.

The zip code (line 40 in Fig. 14.20) matches a digit five times. This regular expression uses the digit character class and a quantifier with the digit 5 between braces. The phone number (line 46 in Fig. 14.20) matches three digits (the first one cannot be zero) followed by a dash followed by three more digits (again the first one cannot be zero) followed by four more digits.

String method matches checks whether an entire String conforms to a regular expression. For example, we want to accept "Smith" as a last name, but not "9@Smith#". If only a substring matches the regular expression, method matches returns false.

Replacing Substrings and Splitting Strings
Sometimes it's useful to replace parts of a string or to split a string into pieces. For this purpose, class String provides methods **replaceAll**, **replaceFirst** and **split**. These methods are demonstrated in Fig. 14.23.

```
1   // Fig. 14.23: RegexSubstitution.java
2   // String methods replaceFirst, replaceAll and split.
3   import java.util.Arrays;
4
5   public class RegexSubstitution
6   {
7      public static void main(String[] args)
8      {
9         String firstString = "This sentence ends in 5 stars *****";
10        String secondString = "1, 2, 3, 4, 5, 6, 7, 8";
11
12        System.out.printf("Original String 1: %s%n", firstString);
13
14        // replace '*' with '^'
15        firstString = firstString.replaceAll("\\*", "^");
16
17        System.out.printf("^ substituted for *: %s%n", firstString);
```

Fig. 14.23 | String methods replaceFirst, replaceAll and split. (Part 1 of 2.)

```
18
19          // replace 'stars' with 'carets'
20          firstString = firstString.replaceAll("stars", "carets");
21
22          System.out.printf(
23             "\"carets\" substituted for \"stars\": %s%n", firstString);
24
25          // replace words with 'word'
26          System.out.printf("Every word replaced by \"word\": %s%n%n",
27             firstString.replaceAll("\\w+", "word"));
28
29          System.out.printf("Original String 2: %s%n", secondString);
30
31          // replace first three digits with 'digit'
32          for (int i = 0; i < 3; i++)
33             secondString = secondString.replaceFirst("\\d", "digit");
34
35          System.out.printf(
36             "First 3 digits replaced by \"digit\" : %s%n", secondString);
37
38          System.out.print("String split at commas: ");
39          String[] results = secondString.split(",\\s*"); // split on commas
40          System.out.println(Arrays.toString(results));
41       }
42    } // end class RegexSubstitution
```

```
Original String 1: This sentence ends in 5 stars *****
^ substituted for *: This sentence ends in 5 stars ^^^^^
"carets" substituted for "stars": This sentence ends in 5 carets ^^^^^
Every word replaced by "word": word word word word word word ^^^^^

Original String 2: 1, 2, 3, 4, 5, 6, 7, 8
First 3 digits replaced by "digit" : digit, digit, digit, 4, 5, 6, 7, 8
String split at commas: ["digit", "digit", "digit", "4", "5", "6", "7", "8"]
```

Fig. 14.23 | String methods replaceFirst, replaceAll and split. (Part 2 of 2.)

Method replaceAll replaces text in a String with new text (the second argument) wherever the original String matches a regular expression (the first argument). Line 15 replaces every instance of "*" in firstString with "^". The regular expression ("*") precedes character * with two backslashes. Normally, * is a quantifier indicating that a regular expression should match *any number of occurrences* of a preceding pattern. However, in line 15, we want to find all occurrences of the literal character *—to do this, we must escape character * with character \. Escaping a special regular-expression character with \ instructs the matching engine to find the actual character. Since the expression is stored in a Java String and \ is a special character in Java Strings, we must include an additional \. So the Java String "*" represents the regular-expression pattern * which matches a single * character in the search string. In line 20, every match for the regular expression "stars" in firstString is replaced with "carets". Line 27 uses replaceAll to replace all words in the string with "word".

Method `replaceFirst` (line 33) replaces the first occurrence of a pattern match. Java `String`s are immutable; therefore, method `replaceFirst` returns a new `String` in which the appropriate characters have been replaced. This line takes the original `String` and replaces it with the `String` returned by `replaceFirst`. By iterating three times we replace the first three instances of a digit (`\d`) in `secondString` with the text `"digit"`.

Method `split` divides a `String` into several substrings. The original is broken in any location that matches a specified regular expression. Method `split` returns an array of `String`s containing the substrings between matches for the regular expression. In line 39, we use method `split` to tokenize a `String` of comma-separated integers. The argument is the regular expression that locates the delimiter. In this case, we use the regular expression `",\\s*"` to separate the substrings wherever a comma occurs. By matching any white-space characters, we eliminate extra spaces from the resulting substrings. The commas and white-space characters are not returned as part of the substrings. Again, the Java `String` `",\\s*"` represents the regular expression `,\s*`. Line 40 uses `Arrays` method `toString` to display the contents of array `results` in square brackets and separated by commas.

Classes *Pattern* and *Matcher*

In addition to the regular-expression capabilities of class `String`, Java provides other classes in package `java.util.regex` that help developers manipulate regular expressions. Class **Pattern** represents a regular expression. Class **Matcher** contains both a regular-expression pattern and a `CharSequence` in which to search for the pattern.

CharSequence (package `java.lang`) is an *interface* that allows read access to a sequence of characters. The interface requires that the methods `charAt`, `length`, `subSequence` and `toString` be declared. Both `String` and `StringBuilder` implement interface `CharSequence`, so an instance of either of these classes can be used with class `Matcher`.

Common Programming Error 14.2

A regular expression can be tested against an object of any class that implements interface CharSequence, but the regular expression must be a String. Attempting to create a regular expression as a StringBuilder is an error.

If a regular expression will be used only once, `static Pattern` method **matches** can be used. This method takes a `String` that specifies the regular expression and a `CharSequence` on which to perform the match. This method returns a `boolean` indicating whether the search object (the second argument) *matches* the regular expression.

If a regular expression will be used more than once (in a loop, for example), it's more efficient to use `static Pattern` method **compile** to create a specific `Pattern` object for that regular expression. This method receives a `String` representing the pattern and returns a new `Pattern` object, which can then be used to call method **matcher**. This method receives a `CharSequence` to search and returns a `Matcher` object.

`Matcher` provides method **matches**, which performs the same task as `Pattern` method `matches`, but receives no arguments—the search pattern and search object are encapsulated in the `Matcher` object. Class `Matcher` provides other methods, including **find**, **lookingAt**, **replaceFirst** and **replaceAll**.

Figure 14.24 presents a simple example that employs regular expressions. This program matches birthdays against a regular expression. The expression matches only birthdays that do not occur in April and that belong to people whose names begin with "J".

```
1   // Fig. 14.24: RegexMatches.java
2   // Classes Pattern and Matcher.
3   import java.util.regex.Matcher;
4   import java.util.regex.Pattern;
5
6   public class RegexMatches
7   {
8      public static void main(String[] args)
9      {
10        // create regular expression
11        Pattern expression =
12           Pattern.compile("J.*\\d[0-35-9]-\\d\\d-\\d\\d");
13
14        String string1 = "Jane's Birthday is 05-12-75\n" +
15           "Dave's Birthday is 11-04-68\n" +
16           "John's Birthday is 04-28-73\n" +
17           "Joe's Birthday is 12-17-77";
18
19        // match regular expression to string and print matches
20        Matcher matcher = expression.matcher(string1);
21
22        while (matcher.find())
23           System.out.println(matcher.group());
24     }
25  } // end class RegexMatches
```

```
Jane's Birthday is 05-12-75
Joe's Birthday is 12-17-77
```

Fig. 14.24 | Classes Pattern and Matcher.

Lines 11–12 create a Pattern by invoking static Pattern method compile. The *dot character "."* in the regular expression (line 12) matches any single character except a new-line character. Line 20 creates the Matcher object for the compiled regular expression and the matching sequence (string1). Lines 22–23 use a while loop to *iterate* through the String. Line 22 uses Matcher method find to attempt to match a piece of the search object to the search pattern. Each call to this method starts at the point where the last call ended, so multiple matches can be found. Matcher method lookingAt performs the same way, except that it always starts from the beginning of the search object and will always find the *first* match if there is one.

Common Programming Error 14.3

Method matches (from class String, Pattern or Matcher) will return true only if the entire search object matches the regular expression. Methods find and lookingAt (from class Matcher) will return true if a portion of the search object matches the regular expression.

Line 23 uses Matcher method **group**, which returns the String from the search object that matches the search pattern. The String that's returned is the one that was last matched by a call to find or lookingAt. The output in Fig. 14.24 shows the two matches that were found in string1.

Java SE 8

As you'll see in Section 17.7, you can combine regular-expression processing with Java SE 8 lambdas and streams to implement powerful String-and-file processing applications.

14.8 Wrap-Up

In this chapter, you learned about more String methods for selecting portions of Strings and manipulating Strings. You learned about the Character class and some of the methods it declares to handle chars. The chapter also discussed the capabilities of the String-Builder class for creating Strings. The end of the chapter discussed regular expressions, which provide a powerful capability to search and match portions of Strings that fit a particular pattern. In the next chapter, you'll learn about file processing, including how persistent data is stored and and retrieved.

Summary

Section 14.2 Fundamentals of Characters and Strings

- A character literal's value (p. 589) is its integer value in Unicode (p. 589). Strings can include letters, digits and special characters such as +, -, *, / and $. A string in Java is an object of class String. String literals (p. 589) are often referred to as String objects and are written in a program in double quotes.

Section 14.3 Class **String**

- String objects are immutable (p. 591)—after they're created, their character contents cannot be changed.
- String method length (p. 591) returns the number of characters in a String.
- String method charAt (p. 591) returns the character at a specific position.
- String method regionMatches (p. 593) compares portions of two strings for equality.
- String method equals tests for equality. The method returns true if the contents of the Strings are equal, false otherwise. Method equals uses a lexicographical comparison (p. 594) for Strings.
- When primitive-type values are compared with ==, the result is true if both values are identical. When references are compared with ==, the result is true if both refer to the same object.
- Java treats all string literals with the same contents as a single String object.
- String method equalsIgnoreCase performs a case-insensitive string comparison.
- String method compareTo uses a lexicographical comparison and returns 0 if the Strings are equal, a negative number if the string that calls compareTo is less than the argument String and a positive number if the string that calls compareTo is greater than than the argument String.
- String methods startsWith and endsWith (p. 596) determine whether a string starts with or ends with the specified characters, respectively.
- String method indexOf (p. 597) locates the first occurrence of a character or a substring in a string. String method lastIndexOf (p. 597) locates the last occurrence of a character or a substring in a string.
- String method substring copies and returns part of an existing string object.
- String method concat (p. 600) concatenates two string objects and returns a new string object.

- String method `replace` returns a new string object that replaces every occurrence in a `String` of its first character argument with its second character argument.
- String method `toUpperCase` (p. 601) returns a new string with uppercase letters in the positions where the original string had lowercase letters. `String` method `toLowerCase` (p. 602) returns a new string with lowercase letters in the positions where the original string had uppercase letters.
- String method `trim` (p. 602) returns a new string object in which all white-space characters (e.g., spaces, newlines and tabs) have been removed from the beginning and end of a string.
- String method `toCharArray` (p. 602) returns a `char` array containing a copy of the string's characters.
- String class `static` method `valueOf` returns its argument converted to a string.

Section 14.4 Class *StringBuilder*
- Class `StringBuilder` provides constructors that enable `StringBuilders` to be initialized with no characters and an initial capacity of 16 characters, with no characters and an initial capacity specified in the integer argument, or with a copy of the characters of the `String` argument and an initial capacity that's the number of characters in the `String` argument plus 16.
- `StringBuilder` method `length` (p. 604) returns the number of characters currently stored in a `StringBuilder`. `StringBuilder` method `capacity` (p. 604) returns the number of characters that can be stored in a `StringBuilder` without allocating more memory.
- `StringBuilder` method `ensureCapacity` (p. 605) ensures that a `StringBuilder` has at least the specified capacity. Method `setLength` increases or decreases the length of a `StringBuilder`.
- `StringBuilder` method `charAt` (p. 606) returns the character at the specified index. Method `setCharAt` (p. 606) sets the character at the specified position. `StringBuilder` method `getChars` (p. 606) copies characters in the `StringBuilder` into the character array passed as an argument.
- `StringBuilder`'s overloaded `append` methods (p. 607) add primitive-type, character-array, `String`, `Object` or `CharSequence` (p. 607) values to the end of a `StringBuilder`.
- `StringBuilder`'s overloaded `insert` (p. 609) methods insert primitive-type, character-array, `String`, `Object` or `CharSequence` values at any position in a `StringBuilder`.

Section 14.5 Class *Character*
- Character method `isDefined` (p. 612) determines whether a character is in the Unicode character set.
- Character method `isDigit` (p. 612) determines whether a character is a defined Unicode digit.
- Character method `isJavaIdentifierStart` (p. 612) determines whether a character can be used as the first character of a Java identifier. Character method `isJavaIdentifierPart` (p. 612) determines if a character can be used in an identifier.
- Character method `isLetter` (p. 612) determines whether a character is a letter. Character method `isLetterOrDigit` (p. 612) determines if a character is a letter or a digit.
- Character method `isLowerCase` (p. 612) determines whether a character is a lowercase letter. Character method `isUpperCase` (p. 612) determines whether a character is an uppercase letter.
- Character method `toUpperCase` (p. 612) converts a character to its uppercase equivalent. Character method `toLowerCase` (p. 613) converts a character to its lowercase equivalent.
- Character method `digit` (p. 613) converts its character argument into an integer in the number system specified by its integer argument `radix` (p. 613). Character method `forDigit` (p. 613) converts its integer argument `digit` into a character in the number system specified by its integer argument `radix`.

- Character method charValue (p. 614) returns the char stored in a Character object. Character method toString returns a String representation of a Character.

Section 14.6 Tokenizing *Strings*
- Class String's split method (p. 615) tokenizes a String based on the delimiter (p. 615) specified as an argument and returns an array of Strings containing the tokens (p. 615).

Section 14.7 Regular Expressions, Class *Pattern* and Class *Matcher*
- Regular expressions (p. 616) are sequences of characters and symbols that define a set of strings. They're useful for validating input and ensuring that data is in a particular format.
- String method matches (p. 616) receives a string that specifies the regular expression and matches the contents of the String object on which it's called to the regular expression. The method returns a boolean indicating whether the match succeeded.
- A character class is an escape sequence that represents a group of characters. Each character class matches a single character in the string we're attempting to match with the regular expression.
- A word character (\w; p. 616) is any letter (uppercase or lowercase), any digit or the underscore character.
- A white-space character (\s) is a space, a tab, a carriage return, a newline or a form feed.
- A digit (\d) is any numeric character.
- To match a set of characters that does not have a predefined character class (p. 616), use square brackets, []. Ranges can be represented by placing a dash (-) between two characters. If the first character in the brackets is "^", the expression accepts any character other than those indicated.
- When the regular expression operator "*" appears in a regular expression, the program attempts to match zero or more occurrences of the subexpression immediately preceding the "*".
- Operator "+" attempts to match one or more occurrences of the subexpression preceding it.
- The character "|" allows a match of the expression to its left or to its right.
- Parentheses () are used to group parts of the regular expression.
- The asterisk (*) and plus (+) are formally called quantifiers (p. 620).
- A quantifier affects only the subexpression immediately preceding it.
- Quantifier question mark (?) matches zero or one occurrences of the expression that it quantifies.
- A set of braces containing one number ({n}) matches exactly *n* occurrences of the expression it quantifies. Including a comma after the number enclosed in braces matches at least *n* occurrences.
- A set of braces containing two numbers ({n,m}) matches between *n* and *m* occurrences of the expression that it qualifies.
- Quantifiers are greedy (p. 621)—they'll match as many occurrences as they can as long as the match is successful. If a quantifier is followed by a question mark (?), the quantifier becomes reluctant (p. 621), matching as few occurrences as possible as long as the match is successful.
- String method replaceAll (p. 621) replaces text in a string with new text (the second argument) wherever the original string matches a regular expression (the first argument).
- Escaping a special regular-expression character with a \ instructs the regular-expression matching engine to find the actual character, as opposed to what it represents in a regular expression.
- String method replaceFirst (p. 621) replaces the first occurrence of a pattern match and returns a new string in which the appropriate characters have been replaced.
- String method split (p. 621) divides a string into substrings at any location that matches a specified regular expression and returns an array of the substrings.

- Class `Pattern` (p. 623) represents a regular expression.
- Class `Matcher` (p. 623) contains a regular-expression pattern and a `CharSequence` in which to search.
- `CharSequence` is an interface (p. 623) that allows read access to a sequence of characters. Both `String` and `StringBuilder` implement this interface, so they can be used with class `Matcher`.
- If a regular expression will be used only once, static `Pattern` method `matches` (p. 623) takes a string that specifies the regular expression and a `CharSequence` on which to perform the match. This method returns a `boolean` indicating whether the search object matches the regular expression.
- If a regular expression will be used more than once, it's more efficient to use static `Pattern` method `compile` (p. 623) to create a specific `Pattern` object for that regular expression. This method receives a string representing the pattern and returns a new `Pattern` object.
- `Pattern` method `matcher` (p. 623) receives a `CharSequence` to search and returns a `Matcher` object. `Matcher` method `matches` (p. 623) performs the same task as `Pattern` method `matches` but without arguments.
- `Matcher` method `find` (p. 623) attempts to match a piece of the search object to the search pattern. Each call to this method starts at the point where the last call ended, so multiple matches can be found.
- `Matcher` method `lookingAt` (p. 623) performs the same as `find`, except that it always starts from the beginning of the search object and will always find the first match if there is one.
- `Matcher` method `group` (p. 624) returns the string from the search object that matches the search pattern. The string returned is the one that was last matched by a call to `find` or `lookingAt`.

Self-Review Exercises

14.1 State whether each of the following is *true* or *false*. If *false*, explain why.
  a) When `String` objects are compared using `==`, the result is `true` if the `Strings` contain the same values.
  b) A `String` can be modified after it's created.

14.2 For each of the following, write a single statement that performs the indicated task:
  a) Compare the string in `s1` to the string in `s2` for equality of contents.
  b) Append the string `s2` to the string `s1`, using `+=`.
  c) Determine the length of the string in `s1`.

Answers to Self-Review Exercises

14.1 a) False. String objects are compared using operator `==` to determine whether they're the same object in memory.
  b) False. `String` objects are immutable and cannot be modified after they're created. `StringBuilder` objects can be modified after they're created.

14.2 a) `s1.equals(s2)`
  b) `s1 += s2;`
  c) `s1.length()`

Exercises

14.3 *(Comparing Strings)* Write an application that uses `String` method `compareTo` to compare two strings input by the user. Output whether the first string is less than, equal to or greater than the second.

14.4   *(Comparing Portions of Strings)* Write an application that uses String method region-Matches to compare two strings input by the user. The application should input the number of characters to be compared and the starting index of the comparison. The application should state whether the strings are equal. Ignore the case of the characters when performing the comparison.

14.5   *(Random Sentences)* Write an application that uses random-number generation to create sentences. Use four arrays of strings called article, noun, verb and preposition. Create a sentence by selecting a word at random from each array in the following order: article, noun, verb, preposition, article and noun. As each word is picked, concatenate it to the previous words in the sentence. The words should be separated by spaces. When the final sentence is output, it should start with a capital letter and end with a period. The application should generate and display 20 sentences.

The article array should contain the articles "the", "a", "one", "some" and "any"; the noun array should contain the nouns "boy", "girl", "dog", "town" and "car"; the verb array should contain the verbs "drove", "jumped", "ran", "walked" and "skipped"; the preposition array should contain the prepositions "to", "from", "over", "under" and "on".

14.6   *(Project: Limericks)* A limerick is a humorous five-line verse in which the first and second lines rhyme with the fifth, and the third line rhymes with the fourth. Using techniques similar to those developed in Exercise 14.5, write a Java application that produces random limericks. Polishing this application to produce good limericks is a challenging problem, but the result will be worth the effort!

14.7   *(Pig Latin)* Write an application that encodes English-language phrases into pig Latin. Pig Latin is a form of coded language. There are many different ways to form pig Latin phrases. For simplicity, use the following algorithm:

To form a pig Latin phrase from an English-language phrase, tokenize the phrase into words with String method split. To translate each English word into a pig Latin word, place the first letter of the English word at the end of the word and add the letters "ay." Thus, the word "jump" becomes "umpjay," the word "the" becomes "hetay," and the word "computer" becomes "omputercay." Blanks between words remain as blanks. Assume the following: The English phrase consists of words separated by blanks, there are no punctuation marks and all words have two or more letters. Method printLatinWord should display each word. Each token is passed to method printLatinWord to print the pig Latin word. Enable the user to input the sentence. Keep a running display of all the converted sentences in a text area.

14.8   *(Tokenizing Telephone Numbers)* Write an application that inputs a telephone number as a string in the form (555) 555-5555. The application should use String method split to extract the area code as a token, the first three digits of the phone number as a token and the last four digits of the phone number as a token. The seven digits of the phone number should be concatenated into one string. Both the area code and the phone number should be printed. Remember that you'll have to change delimiter characters during the tokenization process.

14.9   *(Displaying a Sentence with Its Words Reversed)* Write an application that inputs a line of text, tokenizes the line with String method split and outputs the tokens in reverse order. Use space characters as delimiters.

14.10   *(Displaying Strings in Uppercase and Lowercase)* Write an application that inputs a line of text and outputs the text twice—once in all uppercase letters and once in all lowercase letters.

14.11   *(Searching Strings)* Write an application that inputs a line of text and a search character and uses String method indexOf to determine the number of occurrences of the character in the text.

14.12   *(Searching Strings)* Write an application based on the application in Exercise 14.11 that inputs a line of text and uses String method indexOf to determine the total number of occurrences of each letter of the alphabet in the text. Uppercase and lowercase letters should be counted together. Store the totals for each letter in an array, and print the values in tabular format after the totals have been determined.

14.13 *(Tokenizing and Comparing Strings)* Write an application that reads a line of text, tokenizes the line using space characters as delimiters and outputs only those words beginning with the letter "b".

14.14 *(Tokenizing and Comparing Strings)* Write an application that reads a line of text, tokenizes it using space characters as delimiters and outputs only those words ending with the letters "ED".

14.15 *(Converting int Values to Characters)* Write an application that inputs an integer code for a character and displays the corresponding character. Modify this application so that it generates all possible three-digit codes in the range from 000 to 255 and attempts to print the corresponding characters.

14.16 *(Defining Your Own String Methods)* Write your own versions of String search methods indexOf and lastIndexOf.

14.17 *(Creating Three-Letter Strings from a Five-Letter Word)* Write an application that reads a five-letter word from the user and produces every possible three-letter string that can be derived from the letters of that word. For example, the three-letter words produced from the word "bathe" include "ate," "bat," "bet," "tab," "hat," "the" and "tea."

Special Section: Advanced String-Manipulation Exercises

The preceding exercises are keyed to the text and designed to test your understanding of fundamental string-manipulation concepts. This section includes a collection of intermediate and advanced string-manipulation exercises. You should find these problems challenging, yet entertaining. The problems vary considerably in difficulty. Some require an hour or two of application writing and implementation. Others are useful for lab assignments that might require two or three weeks of study and implementation. Some are challenging term projects.

14.18 *(Text Analysis)* The availability of computers with string-manipulation capabilities has resulted in some rather interesting approaches to analyzing the writings of great authors. Much attention has been focused on whether William Shakespeare ever lived. Some scholars believe there's substantial evidence indicating that Christopher Marlowe actually penned the masterpieces attributed to Shakespeare. Researchers have used computers to find similarities in the writings of these two authors. This exercise examines three methods for analyzing texts with a computer.

   a) Write an application that reads a line of text from the keyboard and prints a table indicating the number of occurrences of each letter of the alphabet in the text. For example, the phrase

```
To be, or not to be: that is the question:
```

   contains one "a," two "b's," no "c's," and so on.

   b) Write an application that reads a line of text and prints a table indicating the number of one-letter words, two-letter words, three-letter words, and so on, appearing in the text. For example, Fig. 14.25 shows the counts for the phrase

```
Whether 'tis nobler in the mind to suffer
```

   c) Write an application that reads a line of text and prints a table indicating the number of occurrences of each different word in the text. The application should include the words in the table in the same order in which they appear in the text. For example, the lines

```
To be, or not to be: that is the question:
Whether 'tis nobler in the mind to suffer
```

   contain the word "to" three times, the word "be" two times, the word "or" once, etc.

Word length	Occurrences
1	0
2	2
3	1
4	2 (including 'tis)
5	0
6	2
7	1

Fig. 14.25 | Word-length counts for the string
"Whether 'tis nobler in the mind to suffer".

14.19 *(Printing Dates in Various Formats)* Dates are printed in several common formats. Two of the more common formats are

```
04/25/1955 and April 25, 1955
```

Write an application that reads a date in the first format and prints it in the second format.

14.20 *(Check Protection)* Computers are frequently employed in check-writing systems, such as payroll and accounts payable applications. There are many strange stories about weekly paychecks being printed (by mistake) for amounts in excess of $1 million. Incorrect amounts are printed by computerized check-writing systems because of human error or machine failure. Systems designers build controls into their systems to prevent such erroneous checks from being issued.

Another serious problem is the intentional alteration of a check amount by someone who plans to cash a check fraudulently. To prevent a dollar amount from being altered, some computerized check-writing systems employ a technique called check protection. Checks designed for imprinting by computer contain a fixed number of spaces in which the computer may print an amount. Suppose a paycheck contains eight blank spaces in which the computer is supposed to print the amount of a weekly paycheck. If the amount is large, then all eight of the spaces will be filled. For example,

```
1,230.60 (check amount)
--------
12345678 (position numbers)
```

On the other hand, if the amount is less than $1000, then several of the spaces would ordinarily be left blank. For example,

```
   99.87
--------
12345678
```

contains three blank spaces. If a check is printed with blank spaces, it's easier for someone to alter the amount. To prevent alteration, many check-writing systems insert *leading asterisks* to protect the amount as follows:

```
***99.87
--------
12345678
```

Write an application that inputs a dollar amount to be printed on a check, then prints the amount in check-protected format with leading asterisks if necessary. Assume that nine spaces are available for printing the amount.

14.21 *(Writing the Word Equivalent of a Check Amount)* Continuing the discussion in Exercise 14.20, we reiterate the importance of designing check-writing systems to prevent alteration of check amounts. One common security method requires that the amount be written in numbers and spelled out in words as well. Even if someone is able to alter the numerical amount of the check, it's extremely difficult to change the amount in words. Write an application that inputs a numeric check amount that's less than $1000 and writes the word equivalent of the amount. For example, the amount 112.43 should be written as

```
ONE hundred TWELVE and 43/100
```

14.22 *(Morse Code)* Perhaps the most famous of all coding schemes is the Morse code, developed by Samuel Morse in 1832 for use with the telegraph system. The Morse code assigns a series of dots and dashes to each letter of the alphabet, each digit, and a few special characters (e.g., period, comma, colon, semicolon). In sound-oriented systems, the dot represents a short sound and the dash a long sound. Other representations of dots and dashes are used with light-oriented systems and signal-flag systems. Separation between words is indicated by a space or, simply, the absence of a dot or dash. In a sound-oriented system, a space is indicated by a short time during which no sound is transmitted. The international version of the Morse code appears in Fig. 14.26.

Write an application that reads an English-language phrase and encodes it into Morse code. Also write an application that reads a phrase in Morse code and converts it into the English-language equivalent. Use one blank between each Morse-coded letter and three blanks between each Morse-coded word.

Character	Code	Character	Code	Character	Code
A	.-	N	-.	*Digits*	
B	-...	O	---	1	.----
C	-.-.	P	.--.	2	..---
D	-..	Q	--.-	3	...--
E	.	R	.-.	4	....-
F	..-.	S	...	5	.....
G	--.	T	-	6	-....
H	....	U	..-	7	--...
I	..	V	...-	8	---..
J	.---	W	.--	9	----.
K	-.-	X	-..-	0	-----
L	.-..	Y	-.--		
M	--	Z	--..		

Fig. 14.26 | Letters and digits as expressed in international Morse code.

14.23 *(Metric Conversions)* Write an application that will assist the user with metric conversions. Your application should allow the user to specify the names of the units as strings (i.e., centimeters, liters, grams, and so on, for the metric system and inches, quarts, pounds, and so on, for the English system) and should respond to simple questions, such as

```
"How many inches are in 2 meters?"
"How many liters are in 10 quarts?"
```

Your application should recognize invalid conversions. For example, the question

```
"How many feet are in 5 kilograms?"
```

is not meaningful because "feet" is a unit of length, whereas "kilograms" is a unit of mass.

Special Section: Challenging String-Manipulation Projects

14.24 *(Project: A Spelling Checker)* Many popular word-processing software packages have built-in spell checkers. In this project, you're asked to develop your own spell-checker utility. We make suggestions to help get you started. You should then consider adding more capabilities. Use a computerized dictionary (if you have access to one) as a source of words.

Why do we type so many words with incorrect spellings? In some cases, it's because we simply do not know the correct spelling, so we make a best guess. In some cases, it's because we transpose two letters (e.g., "defualt" instead of "default"). Sometimes we double-type a letter accidentally (e.g., "hanndy" instead of "handy"). Sometimes we type a nearby key instead of the one we intended (e.g., "biryhday" instead of "birthday"), and so on.

Design and implement a spell-checker application in Java. Your application should maintain an array wordList of strings. Enable the user to enter these strings. [*Note:* In Chapter 15, we introduce file processing. With this capability, you can obtain the words for the spell checker from a computerized dictionary stored in a file.]

Your application should ask a user to enter a word. The application should then look up that word in the wordList array. If the word is in the array, your application should print "Word is spelled correctly." If the word is not in the array, your application should print "Word is not spelled correctly." Then your application should try to locate other words in wordList that might be the word the user intended to type. For example, you can try all possible single transpositions of adjacent letters to discover that the word "default" is a direct match to a word in wordList. Of course, this implies that your application will check all other single transpositions, such as "edfault," "dfeault," "deafult," "defalut" and "defaultl." When you find a new word that matches one in wordList, print it in a message, such as

```
Did you mean "default"?
```

Implement other tests, such as replacing each double letter with a single letter, and any other tests you can develop to improve the value of your spell checker.

14.25 *(Project: A Crossword Puzzle Generator)* Most people have worked a crossword puzzle, but few have ever attempted to generate one. Generating a crossword puzzle is suggested here as a string-manipulation project requiring substantial sophistication and effort.

There are many issues the programmer must resolve to get even the simplest crossword-puzzle-generator application working. For example, how do you represent the grid of a crossword puzzle inside the computer? Should you use a series of strings or two-dimensional arrays?

The programmer needs a source of words (i.e., a computerized dictionary) that can be directly referenced by the application. In what form should these words be stored to facilitate the complex manipulations required by the application?

If you're really ambitious, you'll want to generate the clues portion of the puzzle, in which the brief hints for each across word and each down word are printed. Merely printing a version of the blank puzzle itself is not a simple problem.

Making a Difference

14.26 *(Cooking with Healthier Ingredients)* Obesity in America is increasing at an alarming rate. Check the map from the Centers for Disease Control and Prevention (CDC) at www.cdc.gov/nccdphp/dnpa/Obesity/trend/maps/index.htm, which shows obesity trends in the United States over the last 20 years. As obesity increases, so do occurrences of related problems (e.g., heart disease, high blood pressure, high cholesterol, type 2 diabetes). Write a program that helps users choose healthier ingredients when cooking, and helps those allergic to certain foods (e.g., nuts, gluten) find substitutes. The program should read a recipe from a JTextArea and suggest healthier replacements for some of the ingredients. For simplicity, your program should assume the recipe has no abbreviations for measures such as teaspoons, cups, and tablespoons, and uses numerical digits for quantities (e.g., 1 egg, 2 cups) rather than spelling them out (one egg, two cups). Some common substitutions are shown in Fig. 14.27. Your program should display a warning such as, "Always consult your physician before making significant changes to your diet."

Your program should take into consideration that replacements are not always one-for-one. For example, if a cake recipe calls for three eggs, it might reasonably use six egg whites instead. Conversion data for measurements and substitutes can be obtained at websites such as:

```
chinesefood.about.com/od/recipeconversionfaqs/f/usmetricrecipes.htm
www.pioneerthinking.com/eggsub.html
www.gourmetsleuth.com/conversions.htm
```

Your program should consider the user's health concerns, such as high cholesterol, high blood pressure, weight loss, gluten allergy, and so on. For high cholesterol, the program should suggest substitutes for eggs and dairy products; if the user wishes to lose weight, low-calorie substitutes for ingredients such as sugar should be suggested.

Ingredient	Substitution
1 cup sour cream	1 cup yogurt
1 cup milk	1/2 cup evaporated milk and 1/2 cup water
1 teaspoon lemon juice	1/2 teaspoon vinegar
1 cup sugar	1/2 cup honey, 1 cup molasses or 1/4 cup agave nectar
1 cup butter	1 cup margarine or yogurt
1 cup flour	1 cup rye or rice flour
1 cup mayonnaise	1 cup cottage cheese or 1/8 cup mayonnaise and 7/8 cup yogurt
1 egg	2 tablespoons cornstarch, arrowroot flour or potato starch or 2 egg whites or 1/2 of a large banana (mashed)
1 cup milk	1 cup soy milk
1/4 cup oil	1/4 cup applesauce
white bread	whole-grain bread

Fig. 14.27 | Common food substitutions.

14.27 *(Spam Scanner)* Spam (or junk e-mail) costs U.S. organizations billions of dollars a year in spam-prevention software, equipment, network resources, bandwidth, and lost productivity. Research online some of the most common spam e-mail messages and words, and check your own junk e-mail folder. Create a list of 30 words and phrases commonly found in spam messages. Write an application in which the user enters an e-mail message in a JTextArea. Then, scan the message for each of the 30 keywords or phrases. For each occurrence of one of these within the message, add a point to the message's "spam score." Next, rate the likelihood that the message is spam, based on the number of points it received.

14.28 *(SMS Language)* Short Message Service (SMS) is a communications service that allows sending text messages of 160 or fewer characters between mobile phones. With the proliferation of mobile phone use worldwide, SMS is being used in many developing nations for political purposes (e.g., voicing opinions and opposition), reporting news about natural disasters, and so on. For example, check out `comunica.org/radio2.0/archives/87`. Since the length of SMS messages is limited, SMS Language—abbreviations of common words and phrases in mobile text messages, e-mails, instant messages, etc.—is often used. For example, "in my opinion" is "imo" in SMS Language. Research SMS Language online. Write a GUI application in which the user can enter a message using SMS Language, then click a button to translate it into English (or your own language). Also provide a mechanism to translate text written in English (or your own language) into SMS Language. One potential problem is that one SMS abbreviation could expand into a variety of phrases. For example, IMO (as used above) could also stand for "International Maritime Organization," "in memory of," etc.

15

Files, Streams and Object Serialization

Consciousness ... does not appear to itself chopped up in bits. ... A "river" or a "stream" are the metaphors by which it is most naturally described.
—William James

Objectives

In this chapter you'll:

- Create, read, write and update files.

- Retrieve information about files and directories using features of the NIO.2 APIs.

- Learn the differences between text files and binary files.

- Use class **Formatter** to output text to a file.

- Use class **Scanner** to input text from a file.

- Write objects to and read objects from a file using object serialization, interface **Serializable** and classes **ObjectOutputStream** and **ObjectInputStream**.

- Use a **JFileChooser** dialog to allow users to select files or directories on disk.

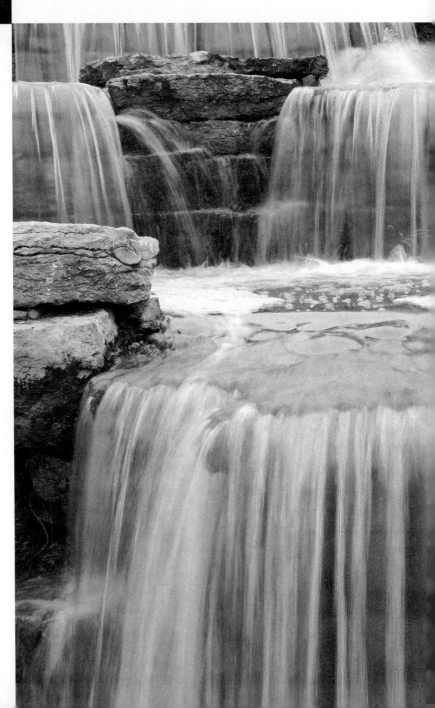

15.1 Introduction

Data stored in variables and arrays is *temporary*—it's lost when a local variable goes out of scope or when the program terminates. For long-term retention of data, even after the programs that create the data terminate, computers use **files**. You use files every day for tasks such as writing a document or creating a spreadsheet. Computers store files on **secondary storage devices**, including hard disks, flash drives, DVDs and more. Data maintained in files is **persistent data**—it exists beyond the duration of program execution. In this chapter, we explain how Java programs create, update and process files.

We begin with a discussion of Java's architecture for handling files programmatically. Next we explain that data can be stored in *text files* and *binary files*—and we cover the differences between them. We demonstrate retrieving information about files and directories using classes `Paths` and `Files` and interfaces `Path` and `DirectoryStream` (all from package `java.nio.file`), then consider the mechanisms for writing data to and reading data from files. We show how to create and manipulate sequential-access text files. Working with text files allows you to quickly and easily start manipulating files. As you'll learn, however, it's difficult to read data from text files back into object form. Fortunately, many object-oriented languages (including Java) provide ways to write objects to and read objects from files (known as *object serialization* and *deserialization*). To demonstrate this, we recreate some of our sequential-access programs that used text files, this time by storing objects in and retrieving objects from binary files.

15.2 Files and Streams

Java views each file as a sequential **stream of bytes** (Fig. 15.1).[1] Every operating system provides a mechanism to determine the end of a file, such as an **end-of-file marker** or a count of the total bytes in the file that's recorded in a system-maintained administrative data structure. A Java program processing a stream of bytes simply receives an indication from the operating system when it reaches the end of the stream—the program does *not* need to know how the underlying platform represents files or streams. In some cases, the

---

1. Java's NIO APIs also include classes and interfaces that implement so-called channel-based architecture for high-performance I/O. These topics are beyond the scope of this book.

end-of-file indication occurs as an exception. In others, the indication is a return value from a method invoked on a stream-processing object.

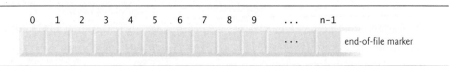

Fig. 15.1 | Java's view of a file of *n* bytes.

Byte-Based and Character-Based Streams
File streams can be used to input and output data as bytes or characters.

- **Byte-based streams** output and input data in its *binary* format—a char is two bytes, an int is four bytes, a double is eight bytes, etc.

- **Character-based streams** output and input data as a *sequence of characters* in which every character is two bytes—the number of bytes for a given value depends on the number of characters in that value. For example, the value 2000000000 requires 20 bytes (10 characters at two bytes per character) but the value 7 requires only two bytes (1 character at two bytes per character).

Files created using byte-based streams are referred to as **binary files**, while files created using character-based streams are referred to as **text files**. Text files can be read by text editors, while binary files are read by programs that understand the file's specific content and its ordering. A numeric value in a binary file can be used in calculations, whereas the character 5 is simply a character that can be used in a string of text, as in "Sarah Miller is 15 years old".

Standard Input, Standard Output and Standard Error Streams
A Java program **opens** a file by creating an object and associating a stream of bytes or characters with it. The object's constructor interacts with the operating system to *open* the file. Java can also associate streams with different devices. When a Java program begins executing, it creates three stream objects that are associated with devices—System.in, System.out and System.err. The System.in (standard input stream) object normally enables a program to input bytes from the keyboard. Object System.out (the standard output stream object) normally enables a program to output character data to the screen. Object System.err (the standard error stream object) normally enables a program to output character-based error messages to the screen. Each stream can be **redirected**. For System.in, this capability enables the program to read bytes from a different source. For System.out and System.err, it enables the output to be sent to a different location, such as a file on disk. Class System provides methods **setIn**, **setOut** and **setErr** to redirected the standard input, output and error streams, respectively.

The `java.io` and `java.nio` Packages
Java programs perform stream-based processing with classes and interfaces from package **java.io** and the subpackages of **java.nio**—Java's New I/O APIs that were first introduced in Java SE 6 and that have been enhanced since. There are also other packages throughout the Java APIs containing classes and interfaces based on those in the java.io and java.nio packages.

Character-based input and output can be performed with classes `Scanner` and **Formatter**, as you'll see in Section 15.4. You've used class `Scanner` extensively to input data from the keyboard. `Scanner` also can read data from a file. Class `Formatter` enables formatted data to be output to any text-based stream in a manner similar to method `System.out.printf`. Appendix I presents the details of formatted output with `printf`. All these features can be used to format text files as well. In Chapter 28, we use stream classes to implement networking applications.

Java SE 8 Adds Another Type of Stream
Chapter 17, Java SE 8 Lambdas and Streams, introduces a new type of stream that's used to process collections of elements (like arrays and `ArrayList`s), rather than the streams of bytes we discuss in this chapter's file-processing examples.

15.3 Using NIO Classes and Interfaces to Get File and Directory Information

Interfaces `Path` and `DirectoryStream` and classes `Paths` and `Files` (all from package java.nio.file) are useful for retrieving information about files and directories on disk:

- **Path** interface—Objects of classes that implement this interface represent the location of a file or directory. `Path` objects do not open files or provide any file-processing capabilities.

- **Paths** class—Provides `static` methods used to get a `Path` object representing a file or directory location.

- **Files** class—Provides `static` methods for common file and directory manipulations, such as copying files; creating and deleting files and directories; getting information about files and directories; reading the contents of files; getting objects that allow you to manipulate the contents of files and directories; and more

- **DirectoryStream** interface—Objects of classes that implement this interface enable a program to iterate through the contents of a directory.

Creating **Path** Objects
You'll use class `static` method **get** of class `Paths` to convert a `String` representing a file's or directory's location into a `Path` object. You can then use the methods of interface `Path` and class `Files` to determine information about the specified file or directory. We discuss several such methods momentarily. For complete lists of their methods, visit:

```
http://docs.oracle.com/javase/7/docs/api/java/nio/file/Path.html
http://docs.oracle.com/javase/7/docs/api/java/nio/file/Files.html
```

Absolute vs. Relative Paths
A file or directory's path specifies its location on disk. The path includes some or all of the directories leading to the file or directory. An **absolute path** contains *all* directories, starting with the **root directory**, that lead to a specific file or directory. Every file or directory on a particular disk drive has the *same* root directory in its path. A **relative path** is "relative" to another directory—for example, a path relative to the directory in which the application began executing.

*Getting **Path** Objects from URIs*
An overloaded version of Files static method get uses a URI object to locate the file or directory. A **Uniform Resource Identifier (URI)** is a more general form of the **Uniform Resource Locators (URLs)** that are used to locate websites. For example, the URL http:/ /www.deitel.com/ is the URL for the Deitel & Associates website. URIs for locating files vary across operating systems. On Windows platforms, the URI

```
file://C:/data.txt
```

identifies the file data.txt stored in the root directory of the C: drive. On UNIX/Linux platforms, the URI

```
file:/home/student/data.txt
```

identifies the file data.txt stored in the home directory of the user student.

Example: Getting File and Directory Information
Figure 15.2 prompts the user to enter a file or directory name, then uses classes Paths, Path, Files and DirectoryStream to output information about that file or directory.The program begins by prompting the user for a file or directory (line 16). Line 19 inputs the filename or directory name and passes it to Paths static method get, which converts the String to a Path. Line 21 invokes Files static method **exists**, which receives a Path and determines whether it exists (either as a file or as a directory) on disk. If the name does not exist, control proceeds to line 49, which displays a message containing the Path's String representation followed by "does not exist." Otherwise, lines 24–45 execute:

- Path method **getFileName** (line 24) gets the String name of the file or directory without any location information.

- Files static method **isDirectory** (line 26) receives a Path and returns a boolean indicating whether that Path represents a directory on disk.

- Path method **isAbsolute** (line 28) returns a boolean indicating whether that Path represents an absolute path to a file or directory.

- Files static method **getLastModifiedTime** (line 30) receives a Path and returns a FileTime (package java.nio.file.attribute) indicating when the file was last modified. The program outputs the FileTime's default String representation.

- Files static method **size** (line 31) receives a Path and returns a long representing the number of bytes in the file or directory. For directories, the value returned is platform specific.

- Path method **toString** (called implicitly at line 32) returns a String representing the Path.

- Path method **toAbsolutePath** (line 33) converts the Path on which it's called to an absolute path.

If the Path represents a directory (line 35), lines 40–41 use Files static method **newDirectoryStream** (lines 40–41) to get a DirectoryStream<Path> containing Path objects for the directory's contents. Lines 43–44 display the String representation of each Path in the DirectoryStream<Path>. Note that DirectoryStream is a generic type like ArrayList (Section 6.13).

The first output of this program demonstrates a Path for the folder containing this chapter's examples. The second output demonstrates a Path for this example's source code file. In both cases, we specified an absolute path.

```java
1  // Fig. 15.2: FileAndDirectoryInfo.java
2  // File class used to obtain file and directory information.
3  import java.io.IOException;
4  import java.nio.file.DirectoryStream;
5  import java.nio.file.Files;
6  import java.nio.file.Path;
7  import java.nio.file.Paths;
8  import java.util.Scanner;
9
10 public class FileAndDirectoryInfo
11 {
12    public static void main(String[] args) throws IOException
13    {
14       Scanner input = new Scanner(System.in);
15
16       System.out.println("Enter file or directory name:");
17
18       // create Path object based on user input
19       Path path = Paths.get(input.nextLine());
20
21       if (Files.exists(path)) // if path exists, output info about it
22       {
23          // display file (or directory) information
24          System.out.printf("%n%s exists%n", path.getFileName());
25          System.out.printf("%s a directory%n",
26             Files.isDirectory(path) ? "Is" : "Is not");
27          System.out.printf("%s an absolute path%n",
28             path.isAbsolute() ? "Is" : "Is not");
29          System.out.printf("Last modified: %s%n",
30             Files.getLastModifiedTime(path));
31          System.out.printf("Size: %s%n", Files.size(path));
32          System.out.printf("Path: %s%n", path);
33          System.out.printf("Absolute path: %s%n", path.toAbsolutePath());
34
35          if (Files.isDirectory(path)) // output directory listing
36          {
37             System.out.printf("%nDirectory contents:%n");
38
39             // object for iterating through a directory's contents
40             DirectoryStream<Path> directoryStream =
41                Files.newDirectoryStream(path);
42
43             for (Path p : directoryStream)
44                System.out.println(p);
45          }
46       }
47       else // not file or directory, output error message
48       {
```

Fig. 15.2 | File class used to obtain file and directory information. (Part 1 of 2.)

```
49          System.out.printf("%s does not exist%n", path);
50       }
51    } // end main
52 } // end class FileAndDirectoryInfo
```

```
Enter file or directory name:
c:\examples\ch15

ch15 exists
Is a directory
Is an absolute path
Last modified: 2013-11-08T19:50:00.838256Z
Size: 4096
Path: c:\examples\ch15
Absolute path: c:\examples\ch15

Directory contents:
C:\examples\ch15\fig15_02
C:\examples\ch15\fig15_12_13
C:\examples\ch15\SerializationApps
C:\examples\ch15\TextFileApps
```

```
Enter file or directory name:
C:\examples\ch15\fig15_02\FileAndDirectoryInfo.java

FileAndDirectoryInfo.java exists
Is not a directory
Is an absolute path
Last modified: 2013-11-08T19:59:01.848255Z
Size: 2952
Path: C:\examples\ch15\fig15_02\FileAndDirectoryInfo.java
Absolute path: C:\examples\ch15\fig15_02\FileAndDirectoryInfo.java
```

Fig. 15.2 | `File` class used to obtain file and directory information. (Part 2 of 2.)

 Error-Prevention Tip 15.1

Once you've confirmed that a `Path` exists, it's still possible that the methods demonstrated in Fig. 15.2 will throw `IOExceptions`. For example, the file or directory represented by the `Path` could be deleted from the system after the call to `Files` method `exists` and before the other statements in lines 24–45 execute. Industrial strength file- and directory-processing programs require extensive exception handling to recover from such possibilities.

Separator Characters

A **separator character** is used to separate directories and files in a path. On a Windows computer, the *separator character* is a backslash (\). On a Linux or Mac OS X system, it's a forward slash (/). Java processes both characters identically in a path name. For example, if we were to use the path

```
c:\Program Files\Java\jdk1.6.0_11\demo/jfc
```

which employs each separator character, Java would still process the path properly.

Good Programming Practice 15.1

When building Strings *that represent path information, use* File.separator *to obtain the local computer's proper separator character rather than explicitly using* / *or* \. *This constant is a* String *consisting of one character—the proper separator for the system.*

Common Programming Error 15.1

Using \ *as a directory separator rather than* \\ *in a string literal is a logic error. A single* \ *indicates that the* \ *followed by the next character represents an escape sequence. Use* \\ *to insert a* \ *in a string literal.*

15.4 Sequential-Access Text Files

Next, we create and manipulate *sequential-access files* in which records are stored in order by the record-key field. We begin with *text files*, enabling the reader to quickly create and edit human-readable files. We discuss creating, writing data to, reading data from and updating sequential-access text files. We also include a credit-inquiry program that retrieves data from a file. The programs in Sections 15.4.1—15.4.3 are all in the chapter's TextFileApps directory so that they can manipulate the same text file, which is also stored in that directory.

15.4.1 Creating a Sequential-Access Text File

Java imposes no structure on a file—notions such as records do not exist as part of the Java language. Therefore, you must structure files to meet the requirements of your applications. In the following example, we see how to impose a *keyed* record structure on a file.

The program in this section creates a simple sequential-access file that might be used in an accounts receivable system to keep track of the amounts owed to a company by its credit clients. For each client, the program obtains from the user an account number and the client's name and balance (i.e., the amount the client owes the company for goods and services received). Each client's data constitutes a "record" for that client. This application uses the account number as the *record key*—the file's records will be created and maintained in account-number order. The program assumes that the user enters the records in account-number order. In a comprehensive accounts receivable system (based on sequential-access files), a *sorting* capability would be provided so that the user could enter the records in *any* order. The records would then be sorted and written to the file.

Class CreateTextFile

Class CreateTextFile (Fig. 15.3) uses a Formatter to output formatted Strings, using the same formatting capabilities as method System.out.printf. A Formatter object can output to various locations, such as to a command window or to a file, as we do in this example. The Formatter object is instantiated in line 26 in method openFile (lines 22–38). The constructor used in line 26 takes one argument—a String containing the name of the file, including its path. If a path is not specified, as is the case here, the JVM assumes that the file is in the directory from which the program was executed. For text files, we use the .txt file extension. If the file does *not* exist, it will be *created*. If an *existing* file is opened, its contents are **truncated**—all the data in the file is *discarded*. If no exception occurs, the file is open for writing and the resulting Formatter object can be used to write data to the file.

```
 1   // Fig. 15.3: CreateTextFile.java
 2   // Writing data to a sequential text file with class Formatter.
 3   import java.io.FileNotFoundException;
 4   import java.lang.SecurityException;
 5   import java.util.Formatter;
 6   import java.util.FormatterClosedException;
 7   import java.util.NoSuchElementException;
 8   import java.util.Scanner;
 9
10   public class CreateTextFile
11   {
12      private static Formatter output; // outputs text to a file
13
14      public static void main(String[] args)
15      {
16         openFile();
17         addRecords();
18         closeFile();
19      }
20
21      // open file clients.txt
22      public static void openFile()
23      {
24         try
25         {
26            output = new Formatter("clients.txt"); // open the file
27         }
28         catch (SecurityException securityException)
29         {
30            System.err.println("Write permission denied. Terminating.");
31            System.exit(1); // terminate the program
32         }
33         catch (FileNotFoundException fileNotFoundException)
34         {
35            System.err.println("Error opening file. Terminating.");
36            System.exit(1); // terminate the program
37         }
38      }
39
40      // add records to file
41      public static void addRecords()
42      {
43         Scanner input = new Scanner(System.in);
44         System.out.printf("%s%n%s%n? ",
45            "Enter account number, first name, last name and balance.",
46            "Enter end-of-file indicator to end input.");
47
48         while (input.hasNext()) // loop until end-of-file indicator
49         {
50            try
51            {
```

Fig. 15.3 | Writing data to a sequential text file with class Formatter. (Part 1 of 2.)

```
52              // output new record to file; assumes valid input
53              output.format("%d %s %s %.2f%n", input.nextInt(),
54                 input.next(), input.next(), input.nextDouble());
55           }
56           catch (FormatterClosedException formatterClosedException)
57           {
58              System.err.println("Error writing to file. Terminating.");
59              break;
60           }
61           catch (NoSuchElementException elementException)
62           {
63              System.err.println("Invalid input. Please try again.");
64              input.nextLine(); // discard input so user can try again
65           }
66
67           System.out.print("? ");
68        } // end while
69     } // end method addRecords
70
71     // close file
72     public static void closeFile()
73     {
74        if (output != null)
75           output.close();
76     }
77  } // end class CreateTextFile
```

```
Enter account number, first name, last name and balance.
Enter end-of-file indicator to end input.
? 100 Bob Blue 24.98
? 200 Steve Green -345.67
? 300 Pam White 0.00
? 400 Sam Red -42.16
? 500 Sue Yellow 224.62
? ^Z
```

Fig. 15.3 | Writing data to a sequential text file with class `Formatter`. (Part 2 of 2.)

Lines 28–32 handle the **SecurityException**, which occurs if the user does not have permission to write data to the file. Lines 33–37 handle the **FileNotFoundException**, which occurs if the file does not exist and a new file cannot be created. This exception may also occur if there's an error *opening* the file. In both exception handlers we call static method **System.exit** and pass the value 1. This method terminates the application. An argument of 0 to method exit indicates *successful* program termination. A nonzero value, such as 1 in this example, normally indicates that an error has occurred. This value is passed to the command window that executed the program. The argument is useful if the program is executed from a **batch file** on Windows systems or a **shell script** on UNIX/Linux/Mac OS X systems. Batch files and shell scripts offer a convenient way of executing several programs in sequence. When the first program ends, the next program begins execution. It's possible to use the argument to method exit in a batch file or shell script to determine whether other programs should execute. For more information on batch files or shell scripts, see your operating system's documentation.

Method addRecords (lines 41–69) prompts the user to enter the various fields for each record or the end-of-file key sequence when data entry is complete. Figure 15.4 lists the key combinations for entering end-of-file for various computer systems.

Operating system	Key combination
UNIX/Linux/Mac OS X	*<Enter> <Ctrl> d*
Windows	*<Ctrl> z*

Fig. 15.4 | End-of-file key combinations.

Lines 44–46 prompt the user for input. Line 48 uses Scanner method hasNext to determine whether the end-of-file key combination has been entered. The loop executes until hasNext encounters end-of-file.

Lines 53–54 use a Scanner to read data from the user, then output the data as a record using the Formatter. Each Scanner input method throws a **NoSuchElementException** (handled in lines 61–65) if the data is in the wrong format (e.g., a String when an int is expected) or if there's no more data to input. The record's information is output using method **format**, which can perform identical formatting to the System.out.printf method used extensively in earlier chapters. Method format outputs a formatted String to the output destination of the Formatter object—the file clients.txt. The format string "%d %s %s %.2f%n" indicates that the current record will be stored as an integer (the account number) followed by a String (the first name), another String (the last name) and a floating-point value (the balance). Each piece of information is separated from the next by a space, and the double value (the balance) is output with two digits to the right of the decimal point (as indicated by the .2 in %.2f). The data in the text file can be viewed with a text editor or retrieved later by a program designed to read the file (Section 15.4.2).

When lines 66–68 execute, if the Formatter object is closed, a **FormatterClosedException** will be thrown. This exception is handled in lines 76–80. [*Note:* You can also output data to a text file using class **java.io.PrintWriter**, which provides format and printf methods for outputting formatted data.]

Lines 93–97 declare method closeFile, which closes the Formatter and the underlying output file. Line 96 closes the object by simply calling method **close**. If method close is not called explicitly, the operating system normally will close the file when program execution terminates—this is an example of operating-system "housekeeping." However, you should always explicitly close a file when it's no longer needed.

Sample Output
The sample data for this application is shown in Fig. 15.5. In the sample output, the user enters information for five accounts, then enters end-of-file to signal that data entry is complete. The sample output does not show how the data records actually appear in the file. In the next section, to verify that the file was created successfully, we present a program that reads the file and prints its contents. Because this is a text file, you can also verify the information simply by opening the file in a text editor.

Sample data			
100	Bob	Blue	24.98
200	Steve	Green	-345.67
300	Pam	White	0.00
400	Sam	Red	-42.16
500	Sue	Yellow	224.62

Fig. 15.5 | Sample data for the program in Fig. 15.3.

15.4.2 Reading Data from a Sequential-Access Text File

Data is stored in files so that it may be retrieved for processing when needed. Section 15.4.1 demonstrated how to create a file for sequential access. This section shows how to read data sequentially from a text file. We demonstrate how class Scanner can be used to input data from a file rather than the keyboard. The application (Fig. 15.6) reads records from the file "clients.txt" created by the application of Section 15.4.1 and displays the record contents. Line 13 declares a Scanner that will be used to retrieve input from the file.

```java
1   // Fig. 15.6: ReadTextFile.java
2   // This program reads a text file and displays each record.
3   import java.io.IOException;
4   import java.lang.IllegalStateException;
5   import java.nio.file.Files;
6   import java.nio.file.Path;
7   import java.nio.file.Paths;
8   import java.util.NoSuchElementException;
9   import java.util.Scanner;
10
11  public class ReadTextFile
12  {
13     private static Scanner input;
14
15     public static void main(String[] args)
16     {
17        openFile();
18        readRecords();
19        closeFile();
20     }
21
22     // open file clients.txt
23     public static void openFile()
24     {
25        try
26        {
27           input = new Scanner(Paths.get("clients.txt"));
28        }
```

Fig. 15.6 | Sequential file reading using a Scanner. (Part 1 of 2.)

```
29        catch (IOException ioException)
30        {
31            System.err.println("Error opening file. Terminating.");
32            System.exit(1);
33        }
34    }
35
36    // read record from file
37    public static void readRecords()
38    {
39        System.out.printf("%-10s%-12s%-12s%10s%n", "Account",
40            "First Name", "Last Name", "Balance");
41
42        try
43        {
44            while (input.hasNext()) // while there is more to read
45            {
46                // display record contents
47                System.out.printf("%-10d%-12s%-12s%10.2f%n", input.nextInt(),
48                    input.next(), input.next(), input.nextDouble());
49            }
50        }
51        catch (NoSuchElementException elementException)
52        {
53            System.err.println("File improperly formed. Terminating.");
54        }
55        catch (IllegalStateException stateException)
56        {
57            System.err.println("Error reading from file. Terminating.");
58        }
59    } // end method readRecords
60
61    // close file and terminate application
62    public static void closeFile()
63    {
64        if (input != null)
65            input.close();
66    }
67 } // end class ReadTextFile
```

```
Account    First Name  Last Name      Balance
100        Bob         Blue             24.98
200        Steve       Green          -345.67
300        Pam         White            0.00
400        Sam         Red            -42.16
500        Sue         Yellow         224.62
```

Fig. 15.6 | Sequential file reading using a Scanner. (Part 2 of 2.)

Method openFile (lines 23–34) opens the file for reading by instantiating a Scanner object in line 27. We pass a Path object to the constructor, which specifies that the Scanner object will read from the file "clients.txt" located in the directory from which the application executes. If the file cannot be found, an IOException occurs. The exception is handled in lines 29–33.

Method readRecords (lines 37–59) reads and displays records from the file. Lines 39–40 display headers for the columns in the application's output. Lines 44–49 read and display data from the file until the *end-of-file marker* is reached (in which case, method hasNext will return false at line 44). Lines 47–48 use Scanner methods nextInt, next and nextDouble to input an int (the account number), two Strings (the first and last names) and a double value (the balance). Each record is one line of data in the file. If the information in the file is not properly formed (e.g., there's a last name where there should be a balance), a NoSuchElementException occurs when the record is input. This exception is handled in lines 51–54. If the Scanner was closed before the data was input, an **IllegalStateException** occurs (handled in lines 55–58). Note in the format string in line 47 that the account number, first name and last name are left justified, while the balance is right justified and output with two digits of precision. Each iteration of the loop inputs one line of text from the text file, which represents one record. Lines 62–66 define method closeFile, which closes the Scanner.

15.4.3 Case Study: A Credit-Inquiry Program

To retrieve data sequentially from a file, programs start from the beginning of the file and read *all* the data consecutively until the desired information is found. It might be necessary to process the file sequentially several times (from the beginning of the file) during the execution of a program. Class Scanner does *not* allow repositioning to the beginning of the file. If it's necessary to read the file again, the program must *close* the file and *reopen* it.

The program in Figs. 15.7–15.8 allows a credit manager to obtain lists of customers with *zero balances* (i.e., customers who do not owe any money), customers with *credit balances* (i.e., customers to whom the company owes money) and customers with *debit balances* (i.e., customers who owe the company money for goods and services received). A credit balance is a *negative* amount, a debit balance a *positive* amount.

MenuOption enum

We begin by creating an enum type (Fig. 15.7) to define the different menu options the credit manager will have—this is required if you need to provide specific values for the enum constants. The options and their values are listed in lines 7–10.

```
1   // Fig. 15.7: MenuOption.java
2   // enum type for the credit-inquiry program's options.
3
4   public enum MenuOption
5   {
6      // declare contents of enum type
7      ZERO_BALANCE(1),
8      CREDIT_BALANCE(2),
9      DEBIT_BALANCE(3),
10     END(4);
11
12     private final int value; // current menu option
13
```

Fig. 15.7 | enum type for the credit-inquiry program's menu options. (Part 1 of 2.)

```
14       // constructor
15       private MenuOption(int value)
16       {
17          this.value = value;
18       }
19    } // end enum MenuOption
```

Fig. 15.7 | enum type for the credit-inquiry program's menu options. (Part 2 of 2.)

CreditInquiry Class

Figure 15.8 contains the functionality for the credit-inquiry program. The program displays a text menu and allows the credit manager to enter one of three options to obtain credit information:

- Option 1 (ZERO_BALANCE) displays accounts with zero balances.

- Option 2 (CREDIT_BALANCE) displays accounts with credit balances.

- Option 3 (DEBIT_BALANCE) displays accounts with debit balances.

- Option 4 (END) terminates program execution.

```
 1   // Fig. 15.8: CreditInquiry.java
 2   // This program reads a file sequentially and displays the
 3   // contents based on the type of account the user requests
 4   // (credit balance, debit balance or zero balance).
 5   import java.io.IOException;
 6   import java.lang.IllegalStateException;
 7   import java.nio.file.Paths;
 8   import java.util.NoSuchElementException;
 9   import java.util.Scanner;
10
11   public class CreditInquiry
12   {
13      private final static MenuOption[] choices = MenuOption.values();
14
15      public static void main(String[] args)
16      {
17         // get user's request (e.g., zero, credit or debit balance)
18         MenuOption accountType = getRequest();
19
20         while (accountType != MenuOption.END)
21         {
22            switch (accountType)
23            {
24               case ZERO_BALANCE:
25                  System.out.printf("%nAccounts with zero balances:%n");
26                  break;
27               case CREDIT_BALANCE:
28                  System.out.printf("%nAccounts with credit balances:%n");
29                  break;
```

Fig. 15.8 | Credit-inquiry program. (Part 1 of 4.)

```
30                  case DEBIT_BALANCE:
31                      System.out.printf("%nAccounts with debit balances:%n");
32                      break;
33              }
34
35              readRecords(accountType);
36              accountType = getRequest(); // get user's request
37          }
38      }
39
40      // obtain request from user
41      private static MenuOption getRequest()
42      {
43          int request = 4;
44
45          // display request options
46          System.out.printf("%nEnter request%n%s%n%s%n%s%n%s%n",
47              " 1 - List accounts with zero balances",
48              " 2 - List accounts with credit balances",
49              " 3 - List accounts with debit balances",
50              " 4 - Terminate program");
51
52          try
53          {
54              Scanner input = new Scanner(System.in);
55
56              do // input user request
57              {
58                  System.out.printf("%n? ");
59                  request = input.nextInt();
60              } while ((request < 1) || (request > 4));
61          }
62          catch (NoSuchElementException noSuchElementException)
63          {
64              System.err.println("Invalid input. Terminating.");
65          }
66
67          return choices[request - 1]; // return enum value for option
68      }
69
70      // read records from file and display only records of appropriate type
71      private static void readRecords(MenuOption accountType)
72      {
73          // open file and process contents
74          try (Scanner input = new Scanner(Paths.get("clients.txt")))
75          {
76              while (input.hasNext()) // more data to read
77              {
78                  int accountNumber = input.nextInt();
79                  String firstName = input.next();
80                  String lastName = input.next();
81                  double balance = input.nextDouble();
82
```

Fig. 15.8 | Credit-inquiry program. (Part 2 of 4.)

```
83                   // if proper acount type, display record
84                   if (shouldDisplay(accountType, balance))
85                      System.out.printf("%-10d%-12s%-12s%10.2f%n", accountNumber,
86                         firstName, lastName, balance);
87                   else
88                      input.nextLine(); // discard the rest of the current record
89               }
90            }
91            catch (NoSuchElementException |
92               IllegalStateException | IOException e)
93            {
94               System.err.println("Error processing file. Terminating.");
95               System.exit(1);
96            }
97      } // end method readRecords
98
99      // use record type to determine if record should be displayed
100     private static boolean shouldDisplay(
101        MenuOption accountType, double balance)
102     {
103        if ((accountType == MenuOption.CREDIT_BALANCE) && (balance < 0))
104           return true;
105        else if ((accountType == MenuOption.DEBIT_BALANCE) && (balance > 0))
106           return true;
107        else if ((accountType == MenuOption.ZERO_BALANCE) && (balance == 0))
108           return true;
109
110        return false;
111     }
112  } // end class CreditInquiry
```

```
Enter request
 1 - List accounts with zero balances
 2 - List accounts with credit balances
 3 - List accounts with debit balances
 4 - Terminate program

? 1


Accounts with zero balances:
300         Pam         White               0.00

Enter request
 1 - List accounts with zero balances
 2 - List accounts with credit balances
 3 - List accounts with debit balances
 4 - Terminate program

? 2


Accounts with credit balances:
200         Steve       Green           -345.67
400         Sam         Red              -42.16
```

Fig. 15.8 | Credit-inquiry program. (Part 3 of 4.)

```
Enter request
 1 - List accounts with zero balances
 2 - List accounts with credit balances
 3 - List accounts with debit balances
 4 - Terminate program

? 3

Accounts with debit balances:
100       Bob         Blue            24.98
500       Sue         Yellow         224.62

Enter request
 1 - List accounts with zero balances
 2 - List accounts with credit balances
 3 - List accounts with debit balances
 4 - Terminate program

? 4
```

Fig. 15.8 | Credit-inquiry program. (Part 4 of 4.)

The record information is collected by reading through the file and determining if each record satisfies the criteria for the selected account type. Line 18 in main calls method getRequest (lines 41–68) to display the menu options, translates the number typed by the user into a MenuOption and stores the result in MenuOption variable accountType. Lines 20–37 loop until the user specifies that the program should terminate. Lines 22–33 display a header for the current set of records to be output to the screen. Line 35 calls method readRecords (lines 71–97), which loops through the file and reads every record.

Method readRecords uses a try-with-resources statement (introduced in Section 11.12) to create a Scanner that opens the file for reading (line 74)—recall that try-with-resources will close its resource(s) when the try block terminates successfully or due to an exception. The file will be opened for reading with a new Scanner object each time readRecords is called, so that we can again read from the beginning of the file. Lines 78–81 read a record. Line 84 calls method shouldDisplay (lines 100–111) to determine whether the current record satisfies the account type requested. If shouldDisplay returns true, the program displays the account information. When the *end-of-file marker* is reached, the loop terminates and the try-with-resources statement closes the Scanner and the file. Once all the records have been read, control returns to main and getRequest is again called (line 36) to retrieve the user's next menu option.

15.4.4 Updating Sequential-Access Files

The data in many sequential files cannot be modified without the risk of destroying other data in the file. For example, if the name "White" needs to be changed to "Worthington," the old name cannot simply be overwritten, because the new name requires more space. The record for White was written to the file as

```
300 Pam White 0.00
```

If the record is rewritten beginning at the same location in the file using the new name, the record will be

```
300 Pam Worthington 0.00
```

The new record is larger (has more characters) than the original record. "Worthington" would overwrite the "0.00" in the current record and the characters beyond the second "o" in "Worthington" will overwrite the beginning of the next sequential record in the file. The problem here is that fields in a text file—and hence records—can vary in size. For example, 7, 14, −117, 2074 and 27383 are all ints stored in the same number of bytes (4) internally, but they're different-sized fields when written to a file as text. Therefore, records in a sequential-access file are not usually updated in place—instead, the entire file is rewritten. To make the preceding name change, the records before 300 Pam White 0.00 would be copied to a new file, the new record (which can be of a different size than the one it replaces) would be written and the records after 300 Pam White 0.00 would be copied to the new file. Rewriting the entire file is uneconomical to update just one record, but reasonable if a substantial number of records need to be updated.

15.5 Object Serialization

In Section 15.4, we demonstrated how to write the individual fields of a record into a file as text, and how to read those fields from a file. When the data was output to disk, certain information was lost, such as the type of each value. For instance, if the value "3" is read from a file, there's no way to tell whether it came from an int, a String or a double. We have only data, not type information, on a disk.

Sometimes we want to read an object from or write an object to a file or over a network connection. Java provides **object serialization** for this purposes. A **serialized object** is an object represented as a sequence of bytes that includes the object's data as well as information about the object's type and the types of data stored in the object. After a serialized object has been written into a file, it can be read from the file and **deserialized**—that is, the type information and bytes that represent the object and its data can be used to recreate the object in memory.

Classes *ObjectInputStream* and *ObjectOutputStream*

Classes **ObjectInputStream** and **ObjectOutputStream** (package java.io), which respectively implement the **ObjectInput** and **ObjectOutput** interfaces, enable entire objects to be read from or written to a stream (possibly a file). To use serialization with files, we initialize ObjectInputStream and ObjectOutputStream objects with stream objects that read from and write to files. Initializing stream objects with other stream objects in this manner is sometimes called **wrapping**—the new stream object being created wraps the stream object specified as a constructor argument.

Classes ObjectInputStream and ObjectOutputStream simply read and write the byte-based representation of objects—they don't know where to read the bytes from or write them to. The stream object that you pass to the ObjectInputStream constructor supplies the bytes that the ObjectInputStream converts into objects. Similarly, the stream object that you pass to the ObjectOutputStream constructor takes the byte-based representation of the object that the ObjectOutputStream produces and writes the bytes to the specified destination (e.g., a file, a network connection, etc.).

Interfaces ObjectOutput *and* ObjectInput

The ObjectOutput interface contains method **writeObject**, which takes an Object as an argument and writes its information to an OutputStream. A class that implements interface ObjectOutput (such as ObjectOutputStream) declares this method and ensures that the object being output implements interface Serializable (discussed shortly). Similarly, the ObjectInput interface contains method **readObject**, which reads and returns a reference to an Object from an InputStream. After an object has been read, its reference can be cast to the object's actual type. As you'll see in Chapter 28, applications that communicate via a network, such as the Internet, can also transmit objects across the network.

15.5.1 Creating a Sequential-Access File Using Object Serialization

This section and Section 15.5.2 create and manipulate sequential-access files using object serialization. The object serialization we show here is performed with byte-based streams, so the sequential files created and manipulated will be *binary files*. Recall that binary files typically cannot be viewed in standard text editors. For this reason, we write a separate application that knows how to read and display serialized objects. We begin by creating and writing serialized objects to a sequential-access file. The example is similar to the one in Section 15.4, so we focus only on the new features.

Defining Class Account

We begin by defining class Account (Fig. 15.9), which encapsulates the client record information used by the serialization examples. These examples and class Account are all located in the SerializationApps directory with the chapter's examples. This allows class Account to be used by both examples, because their files are defined in the same default package. Class Account contains private instance variables account, firstName, lastName and balance (lines 7–10) and *set* and *get* methods for accessing these instance variables. Though the *set* methods do not validate the data in this example, they should do so in an "industrial-strength" system. Class Account implements interface **Serializable** (line 5), which allows objects of this class to be *serialized* and *deserialized* with ObjectOutputStreams and ObjectInputStreams, respectively. Interface Serializable is a **tagging interface**. Such an interface does *not* contain methods. A class that implements Serializable is *tagged* as being a Serializable object. This is important, because an ObjectOutputStream will *not* output an object unless it *is a* Serializable object, which is the case for any object of a class that implements Serializable.

```
 1   // Fig. 15.9: Account.java
 2   // Serializable Account class for storing records as objects.
 3   import java.io.Serializable;
 4
 5   public class Account implements Serializable
 6   {
 7      private int account;
 8      private String firstName;
 9      private String lastName;
10      private double balance;
11
```

Fig. 15.9 | Account class for serializable objects. (Part 1 of 3.)

```
12        // initializes an Account with default values
13        public Account()
14        {
15            this(0, "", "", 0.0); // call other constructor
16        }
17
18        // initializes an Account with provided values
19        public Account(int account, String firstName,
20            String lastName, double balance)
21        {
22            this.account = account;
23            this.firstName = firstName;
24            this.lastName = lastName;
25            this.balance = balance;
26        }
27
28        // set account number
29        public void setAccount(int acct)
30        {
31            this.account = account;
32        }
33
34        // get account number
35        public int getAccount()
36        {
37            return account;
38        }
39
40        // set first name
41        public void setFirstName(String firstName)
42        {
43            this.firstName = firstName;
44        }
45
46        // get first name
47        public String getFirstName()
48        {
49            return firstName;
50        }
51
52        // set last name
53        public void setLastName(String lastName)
54        {
55            this.lastName = lastName;
56        }
57
58        // get last name
59        public String getLastName()
60        {
61            return lastName;
62        }
63
```

Fig. 15.9 | Account class for serializable objects. (Part 2 of 3.)

```
64    // set balance
65    public void setBalance(double balance)
66    {
67       this.balance = balance;
68    }
69
70    // get balance
71    public double getBalance()
72    {
73       return balance;
74    }
75 } // end class Account
```

Fig. 15.9 | Account class for serializable objects. (Part 3 of 3.)

In a Serializable class, every instance variable must be Serializable. Non-Serializable instance variables must be declared **transient** to indicate that they should be ignored during the serialization process. *By default, all primitive-type variables are serializable.* For reference-type variables, you must check the class's documentation (and possibly its superclasses) to ensure that the type is Serializable. For example, Strings are Serializable. By default, arrays *are* serializable; however, in a reference-type array, the referenced objects might *not* be. Class Account contains private data members account, firstName, lastName and balance—all of which are Serializable. This class also provides public *get* and *set* methods for accessing the private fields.

Writing Serialized Objects to a Sequential-Access File
Now let's discuss the code that creates the sequential-access file (Fig. 15.10). We concentrate only on new concepts here. To open the file, line 27 calls Files static method **newOutputStream**, which receives a Path specifying the file to open and, if the file exists, returns an OutputStream that can be used to write to the file. Existing files that are opened for output in this manner are *truncated*. There is no standard filename extension for files that store serialized objects, so we chose the .ser.

```
1  // Fig. 15.10: CreateSequentialFile.java
2  // Writing objects sequentially to a file with class ObjectOutputStream.
3  import java.io.IOException;
4  import java.io.ObjectOutputStream;
5  import java.nio.file.Files;
6  import java.nio.file.Paths;
7  import java.util.NoSuchElementException;
8  import java.util.Scanner;
9
10 public class CreateSequentialFile
11 {
12    private static ObjectOutputStream output; // outputs data to file
13
```

Fig. 15.10 | Sequential file created using ObjectOutputStream. (Part 1 of 3.)

```
14      public static void main(String[] args)
15      {
16         openFile();
17         addRecords();
18         closeFile();
19      }
20
21      // open file clients.ser
22      public static void openFile()
23      {
24         try
25         {
26            output = new ObjectOutputStream(
27               Files.newOutputStream(Paths.get("clients.ser")));
28         }
29         catch (IOException ioException)
30         {
31            System.err.println("Error opening file. Terminating.");
32            System.exit(1); // terminate the program
33         }
34      }
35
36      // add records to file
37      public static void addRecords()
38      {
39         Scanner input = new Scanner(System.in);
40
41         System.out.printf("%s%n%s%n? ",
42            "Enter account number, first name, last name and balance.",
43            "Enter end-of-file indicator to end input.");
44
45         while (input.hasNext()) // loop until end-of-file indicator
46         {
47            try
48            {
49               // create new record; this example assumes valid input
50               Account record = new Account(input.nextInt(),
51                  input.next(), input.next(), input.nextDouble());
52
53               // serialize record object into file
54               output.writeObject(record);
55            }
56            catch (NoSuchElementException elementException)
57            {
58               System.err.println("Invalid input. Please try again.");
59               input.nextLine(); // discard input so user can try again
60            }
61            catch (IOException ioException)
62            {
63               System.err.println("Error writing to file. Terminating.");
64               break;
65            }
```

Fig. 15.10 | Sequential file created using `ObjectOutputStream`. (Part 2 of 3.)

```
66
67                  System.out.print("? ");
68           }
69       }
70
71       // close file and terminate application
72       public static void closeFile()
73       {
74          try
75          {
76             if (output != null)
77                output.close();
78          }
79          catch (IOException ioException)
80          {
81             System.err.println("Error closing file. Terminating.");
82          }
83       }
84    } // end class CreateSequentialFile
```

```
Enter account number, first name, last name and balance.
Enter end-of-file indicator to end input.
? 100 Bob Blue 24.98
? 200 Steve Green -345.67
? 300 Pam White 0.00
? 400 Sam Red -42.16
? 500 Sue Yellow 224.62
? ^Z
```

Fig. 15.10 | Sequential file created using `ObjectOutputStream`. (Part 3 of 3.)

Class `OutputStream` provides methods for outputting byte arrays and individual bytes, but we wish to write *objects* to a file. For this reason, lines 26–27 pass the Input-Stream to class `ObjectInputStream`'s constructor, which *wrap* the OutputStream in an `ObjectOutputStream`. The ObjectOutputStream object uses the OutputStream to write into the file the bytes that represent entire objects. Lines 26–27 might throw an **IOException** if a problem occurs while opening the file (e.g., when a file is opened for writing on a drive with insufficient space or when a read-only file is opened for writing). If so, the program displays an error message (lines 29–33). If no exception occurs, the file is open, and variable output can be used to write objects to it.

This program assumes that data is input correctly and in the proper record-number order. Method addRecords (lines 37–69) performs the write operation. Lines 50–51 create an Account object from the data entered by the user. Line 54 calls ObjectOutput-Stream method writeObject to write the record object to the output file. Only one statement is required to write the *entire* object.

Method closeFile (lines 72–83) calls ObjectOutputStream method **close** on output to close both the ObjectOutputStream *and* its underlying OutputStream. The call to method close is contained in a try block, because close throws an IOException if the file cannot be closed properly. When using *wrapped* streams, closing the outermost stream *also* closes the wrapped stream as well.

In the sample execution for the program in Fig. 15.10, we entered information for five accounts—the same information shown in Fig. 15.5. The program does not show how the data records actually appear in the file. Remember that now we're using *binary files*, which are not humanly readable. To verify that the file has been created successfully, the next section presents a program to read the file's contents.

15.5.2 Reading and Deserializing Data from a Sequential-Access File

The preceding section showed how to create a file for sequential access using object serialization. In this section, we discuss how to *read serialized data* sequentially from a file.

The program in Fig. 15.11 reads records from a file created by the program in Section 15.5.1 and displays the contents. The program opens the file for input by calling Files static method **newInputStream**, which receives a Path specifying the file to open and, if the file exists, returns an InputStream that can be used to read from the file. In Fig. 15.10, we wrote objects to the file, using an ObjectOutputStream object. Data must be read from the file in the same format in which it was written. Therefore, we use an ObjectInputStream *wrapped* around an InputStream (lines 26–27). If no exceptions occur when opening the file, variable input can be used to read objects from the file.

```
1   // Fig. 15.11: ReadSequentialFile.java
2   // Reading a file of objects sequentially with ObjectInputStream
3   // and displaying each record.
4   import java.io.EOFException;
5   import java.io.IOException;
6   import java.io.ObjectInputStream;
7   import java.nio.file.Files;
8   import java.nio.file.Paths;
9
10  public class ReadSequentialFile
11  {
12     private static ObjectInputStream input;
13
14     public static void main(String[] args)
15     {
16        openFile();
17        readRecords();
18        closeFile();
19     }
20
21     // enable user to select file to open
22     public static void openFile()
23     {
24        try // open file
25        {
26           input = new ObjectInputStream(
27              Files.newInputStream(Paths.get("clients.ser")));
28        }
29        catch (IOException ioException)
30        {
```

Fig. 15.11 | Reading a file of objects sequentially with ObjectInputStream and displaying each record. (Part 1 of 3.)

```
31              System.err.println("Error opening file.");
32              System.exit(1);
33          }
34      }
35
36      // read record from file
37      public static void readRecords()
38      {
39          System.out.printf("%-10s%-12s%-12s%10s%n", "Account",
40              "First Name", "Last Name", "Balance");
41
42          try
43          {
44              while (true) // loop until there is an EOFException
45              {
46                  Account record = (Account) input.readObject();
47
48                  // display record contents
49                  System.out.printf("%-10d%-12s%-12s%10.2f%n",
50                      record.getAccount(), record.getFirstName(),
51                      record.getLastName(), record.getBalance());
52              }
53          }
54          catch (EOFException endOfFileException)
55          {
56              System.out.printf("%No more records%n");
57          }
58          catch (ClassNotFoundException classNotFoundException)
59          {
60              System.err.println("Invalid object type. Terminating.");
61          }
62          catch (IOException ioException)
63          {
64              System.err.println("Error reading from file. Terminating.");
65          }
66      } // end method readRecords
67
68      // close file and terminate application
69      public static void closeFile()
70      {
71          try
72          {
73              if (input != null)
74                  input.close();
75          }
76          catch (IOException ioException)
77          {
78              System.err.println("Error closing file. Terminating.");
79              System.exit(1);
80          }
81      }
82  } // end class ReadSequentialFile
```

Fig. 15.11 | Reading a file of objects sequentially with `ObjectInputStream` and displaying each record. (Part 2 of 3.)

```
Account     First Name  Last Name    Balance
100         Bob         Blue           24.98
200         Steve       Green        -345.67
300         Pam         White           0.00
400         Sam         Red           -42.16
500         Sue         Yellow        224.62

No more records
```

Fig. 15.11 | Reading a file of objects sequentially with `ObjectInputStream` and displaying each record. (Part 3 of 3.)

The program reads records from the file in method `readRecords` (lines 37–66). Line 46 calls `ObjectInputStream` method `readObject` to read an `Object` from the file. To use `Account`-specific methods, we *downcast* the returned `Object` to type `Account`. Method `readObject` throws an **EOFException** (processed at lines 54–57) if an attempt is made to read beyond the end of the file. Method `readObject` throws a `ClassNotFoundException` if the class for the object being read cannot be located. This may occur if the file is accessed on a computer that does not have the class.

> **Software Engineering Observation 15.1**
>
> *This section introduced object serialization and demonstrated basic serialization techniques. Serialization is a deep subject with many traps and pitfalls. Before implementing object serialization in industrial-strength applications, carefully read the online Java documentation for object serialization.*

15.6 Opening Files with `JFileChooser`

Class **JFileChooser** displays a dialog that enables the user to easily select files or directories. To demonstrate `JFileChooser`, we enhance the example in Section 15.3, as shown in Figs. 15.12–15.13. The example now contains a graphical user interface, but still displays the same data as before. The constructor calls method `analyzePath` in line 24. This method then calls method `getFileOrDirectoryPath` in line 31 to retrieve a `Path` object representing the selected file or directory.

Method `getFileOrDirectoryPath` (lines 71–85 of Fig. 15.12) creates a `JFileChooser` (line 74). Lines 75–76 call method **setFileSelectionMode** to specify what the user can select from the `fileChooser`. For this program, we use `JFileChooser` static constant **FILES_AND_DIRECTORIES** to indicate that files and directories can be selected. Other static constants include **FILES_ONLY** (the default) and **DIRECTORIES_ONLY**.

Line 77 calls method **showOpenDialog** to display the `JFileChooser` dialog titled **Open**. Argument `this` specifies the `JFileChooser` dialog's parent window, which determines the position of the dialog on the screen. If `null` is passed, the dialog is displayed in the center of the screen—otherwise, the dialog is centered over the application window (specified by the argument `this`). A `JFileChooser` dialog is a *modal dialog* that does not allow the user to interact with any other window in the program until the dialog is closed. The user selects the drive, directory or filename, then clicks **Open**. Method `showOpenDialog` returns an integer specifying which button (**Open** or **Cancel**) the user clicked to close the dialog. Line

48 tests whether the user clicked **Cancel** by comparing the result with `static` constant `CANCEL_OPTION`. If they're equal, the program terminates. Line 84 calls `JFileChooser` method **getSelectedFile** to retrieve a `File` object (package `java.io`) representing the file or directory that the user selected, then calls `File` method **toPath** to return a `Path` object. The program then displays information about the selected file or directory.

```java
1   // Fig. 15.12: JFileChooserDemo.java
2   // Demonstrating JFileChooser.
3   import java.io.IOException;
4   import java.nio.file.DirectoryStream;
5   import java.nio.file.Files;
6   import java.nio.file.Path;
7   import java.nio.file.Paths;
8   import javax.swing.JFileChooser;
9   import javax.swing.JFrame;
10  import javax.swing.JOptionPane;
11  import javax.swing.JScrollPane;
12  import javax.swing.JTextArea;
13
14  public class JFileChooserDemo extends JFrame
15  {
16     private final JTextArea outputArea; // displays file contents
17
18     // set up GUI
19     public JFileChooserDemo() throws IOException
20     {
21        super("JFileChooser Demo");
22        outputArea = new JTextArea();
23        add(new JScrollPane(outputArea)); // outputArea is scrollable
24        analyzePath(); // get Path from user and display info
25     }
26
27     // display information about file or directory user specifies
28     public void analyzePath() throws IOException
29     {
30        // get Path to user-selected file or directory
31        Path path = getFileOrDirectoryPath();
32
33        if (path != null && Files.exists(path)) // if exists, display info
34        {
35           // gather file (or directory) information
36           StringBuilder builder = new StringBuilder();
37           builder.append(String.format("%s:%n", path.getFileName()));
38           builder.append(String.format("%s a directory%n",
39              Files.isDirectory(path) ? "Is" : "Is not"));
40           builder.append(String.format("%s an absolute path%n",
41              path.isAbsolute() ? "Is" : "Is not"));
42           builder.append(String.format("Last modified: %s%n",
43              Files.getLastModifiedTime(path)));
44           builder.append(String.format("Size: %s%n", Files.size(path)));
45           builder.append(String.format("Path: %s%n", path));
```

Fig. 15.12 | Demonstrating `JFileChooser`. (Part 1 of 2.)

```
46          builder.append(String.format("Absolute path: %s%n",
47              path.toAbsolutePath()));
48
49          if (Files.isDirectory(path)) // output directory listing
50          {
51              builder.append(String.format("%nDirectory contents:%n"));
52
53              // object for iterating through a directory's contents
54              DirectoryStream<Path> directoryStream =
55                  Files.newDirectoryStream(path);
56
57              for (Path p : directoryStream)
58                  builder.append(String.format("%s%n", p));
59          }
60
61          outputArea.setText(builder.toString()); // display String content
62      }
63      else // Path does not exist
64      {
65          JOptionPane.showMessageDialog(this, path.getFileName() +
66              " does not exist.", "ERROR", JOptionPane.ERROR_MESSAGE);
67      }
68   } // end method analyzePath
69
70   // allow user to specify file or directory name
71   private Path getFileOrDirectoryPath()
72   {
73      // configure dialog allowing selection of a file or directory
74      JFileChooser fileChooser = new JFileChooser();
75      fileChooser.setFileSelectionMode(
76          JFileChooser.FILES_AND_DIRECTORIES);
77      int result = fileChooser.showOpenDialog(this);
78
79      // if user clicked Cancel button on dialog, return
80      if (result == JFileChooser.CANCEL_OPTION)
81          System.exit(1);
82
83      // return Path representing the selected file
84      return fileChooser.getSelectedFile().toPath();
85   }
86 } // end class JFileChooserDemo
```

Fig. 15.12 | Demonstrating `JFileChooser`. (Part 2 of 2.)

```
1  // Fig. 15.13: JFileChooserTest.java
2  // Tests class JFileChooserDemo.
3  import java.io.IOException;
4  import javax.swing.JFrame;
5
6  public class JFileChooserTest
7  {
```

Fig. 15.13 | Testing class `FileDemonstration`. (Part 1 of 2.)

```
 8       public static void main(String[] args) throws IOException
 9       {
10           JFileChooserDemo application = new JFileChooserDemo();
11           application.setSize(400, 400);
12           application.setDefaultCloseOperation(JFrame.EXIT_ON_CLOSE);
13           application.setVisible(true);
14       }
15   } // end class JFileChooserTest
```

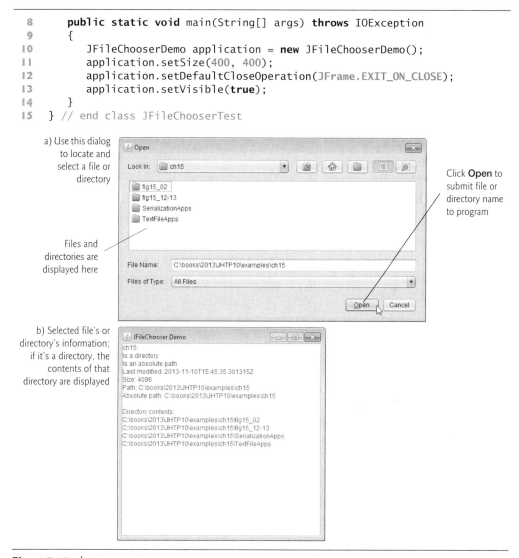

Fig. 15.13 | Testing class FileDemonstration. (Part 2 of 2.)

15.7 (Optional) Additional java.io Classes

This section overviews additional interfaces and classes (from package java.io).

15.7.1 Interfaces and Classes for Byte-Based Input and Output

InputStream and OutputStream are abstract classes that declare methods for performing byte-based input and output, respectively.

Pipe Streams

Pipes are synchronized communication channels between threads. We discuss threads in Chapter 23. Java provides **PipedOutputStream** (a subclass of OutputStream) and **Piped-**

InputStream (a subclass of InputStream) to establish pipes between two threads in a program. One thread sends data to another by writing to a PipedOutputStream. The target thread reads information from the pipe via a PipedInputStream.

Filter Streams
A **FilterInputStream** filters an InputStream, and a FilterOutputStream filters an OutputStream. **Filtering** means simply that the filter stream provides additional functionality, such as aggregating bytes into meaningful primitive-type units. FilterInputStream and FilterOutputStream are typically used as superclasses, so some of their filtering capabilities are provided by their subclasses.

A **PrintStream** (a subclass of FilterOutputStream) performs text output to the specified stream. Actually, we've been using PrintStream output throughout the text to this point—System.out and System.err are PrintStream objects.

Data Streams
Reading data as raw bytes is fast, but crude. Usually, programs read data as aggregates of bytes that form ints, floats, doubles and so on. Java programs can use several classes to input and output data in aggregate form.

Interface DataInput describes methods for reading primitive types from an input stream. Classes **DataInputStream** and RandomAccessFile each implement this interface to read sets of bytes and view them as primitive-type values. Interface DataInput includes methods such as readBoolean, readByte, readChar, readDouble, readFloat, readFully (for byte arrays), readInt, readLong, readShort, readUnsignedByte, readUnsignedShort, readUTF (for reading Unicode characters encoded by Java—we discuss UTF encoding in Appendix H) and skipBytes.

Interface DataOutput describes a set of methods for writing primitive types to an output stream. Classes **DataOutputStream** (a subclass of FilterOutputStream) and RandomAccessFile each implement this interface to write primitive-type values as bytes. Interface DataOutput includes overloaded versions of method write (for a byte or for a byte array) and methods writeBoolean, writeByte, writeBytes, writeChar, writeChars (for Unicode Strings), writeDouble, writeFloat, writeInt, writeLong, writeShort and writeUTF (to output text modified for Unicode).

Buffered Streams
Buffering is an I/O-performance-enhancement technique. With a **BufferedOutputStream** (a subclass of class FilterOutputStream), each output statement does *not* necessarily result in an actual physical transfer of data to the output device (which is a slow operation compared to processor and main memory speeds). Rather, each output operation is directed to a region in memory called a **buffer** that's large enough to hold the data of many output operations. Then, actual transfer to the output device is performed in one large **physical output operation** each time the buffer fills. The output operations directed to the output buffer in memory are often called **logical output operations**. With a BufferedOutputStream, a partially filled buffer can be forced out to the device at any time by invoking the stream object's **flush** method.

Using buffering can greatly increase the performance of an application. Typical I/O operations are extremely slow compared with the speed of accessing data in computer memory. Buffering reduces the number of I/O operations by first combining smaller outputs together in memory. The number of actual physical I/O operations is small compared with the number of I/O requests issued by the program. Thus, the program that's using buffering is more efficient.

Performance Tip 15.1

Buffered I/O can yield significant performance improvements over unbuffered I/O.

With a **BufferedInputStream** (a subclass of class `FilterInputStream`), many "logical" chunks of data from a file are read as one large **physical input operation** into a memory buffer. As a program requests each new chunk of data, it's taken from the buffer. (This procedure is sometimes referred to as a **logical input operation**.) When the buffer is empty, the next actual physical input operation from the input device is performed to read in the next group of "logical" chunks of data. Thus, the number of actual physical input operations is small compared with the number of read requests issued by the program.

Memory-Based **byte** Array Steams

Java stream I/O includes capabilities for inputting from byte arrays in memory and outputting to byte arrays in memory. A ByteArrayInputStream (a subclass of InputStream) reads from a byte array in memory. A ByteArrayOutputStream (a subclass of Output-Stream) outputs to a byte array in memory. One use of byte-array I/O is *data validation*. A program can input an entire line at a time from the input stream into a byte array. Then a validation routine can scrutinize the contents of the byte array and correct the data if necessary. Finally, the program can proceed to input from the byte array, "knowing" that the input data is in the proper format. Outputting to a byte array is a nice way to take advantage of the powerful output-formatting capabilities of Java streams. For example, data can be stored in a byte array, using the same formatting that will be displayed at a later time, and the byte array can then be output to a file to preserve the formatting.

Sequencing Input from Multiple Streams

A SequenceInputStream (a subclass of InputStream) logically concatenates several Input-Streams—the program sees the group as one continuous InputStream. When the program reaches the end of one input stream, that stream closes, and the next stream in the sequence opens.

15.7.2 Interfaces and Classes for Character-Based Input and Output

In addition to the byte-based streams, Java provides the **Reader** and **Writer** abstract classes, which are character-based streams like those you used for text-file processing in Section 15.4. Most of the byte-based streams have corresponding character-based concrete Reader or Writer classes.

Character-Based Buffering **Readers** and **Writers**

Classes **BufferedReader** (a subclass of abstract class Reader) and **BufferedWriter** (a subclass of abstract class Writer) enable buffering for character-based streams. Remember that character-based streams use Unicode characters—such streams can process data in any language that the Unicode character set represents.

Memory-Based **char** *Array* **Readers** *and* **Writers**

Classes **CharArrayReader** and **CharArrayWriter** read and write, respectively, a stream of characters to a char array. A **LineNumberReader** (a subclass of BufferedReader) is a buffered character stream that keeps track of the number of lines read—newlines, returns and carriage-return–line-feed combinations increment the line count. Keeping track of line numbers can be useful if the program needs to inform the reader of an error on a specific line.

Character-Based File, Pipe and String **Readers** *and* **Writers**

An InputStream can be converted to a Reader via class **InputStreamReader**. Similarly, an OutputStream can be converted to a Writer via class **OutputStreamWriter**. Class File-Reader (a subclass of InputStreamReader) and class FileWriter (a subclass of Output-StreamWriter) read characters from and write characters to a file, respectively. Class **PipedReader** and class **PipedWriter** implement piped-character streams for transferring data between threads. Class **StringReader** and **StringWriter** read characters from and write characters to Strings, respectively. A PrintWriter writes characters to a stream.

15.8 Wrap-Up

In this chapter, you learned how to manipulate persistent data. We compared byte-based and character-based streams, and introduced several classes from packages java.io and java.nio.file. You used classes Files and Paths and interfaces Path and DirectoryStream to retrieve information about files and directories. You used sequential-access file processing to manipulate records that are stored in order by the record-key field. You learned the differences between text-file processing and object serialization, and used serialization to store and retrieve entire objects. The chapter concluded with a small example of using a JFileChooser dialog to allow users to easily select files from a GUI. The next chapter discusses Java's classes for manipulating collections of data—such as class Array-List, which we introduced in Section 6.13.

Summary

Section 15.1 Introduction
• Computers use files for long-term retention of large amounts of persistent data (p. 637), even after the programs that created the data terminate.
• Computers store files on secondary storage devices (p. 637) such as hard disks.

Section 15.2 Files and Streams
• Java views each file as a sequential stream of bytes (p. 637).
• Every operating system provides a mechanism to determine the end of a file, such as an end-of-file marker (p. 637) or a count of the total bytes in the file.
• Byte-based streams (p. 638) represent data in binary format.
• Character-based streams (p. 638) represent data as sequences of characters.
• Files created using byte-based streams are binary files (p. 638). Files created using character-based streams are text files (p. 638). Text files can be read by text editors, whereas binary files are read by a program that converts the data to a human-readable format.

- Java also can associate streams with different devices. Three stream objects are associated with devices when a Java program begins executing—System.in, System.out and System.err.

Section 15.3 Using NIO Classes and Interfaces to Get File and Directory Information
- A Path (p. 639) represents the location of a file or directory. Path objects do not open files or provide any file-processing capabilities.
- Class Paths (p. 639) is used to get a Path object representing a file or directory location.
- Class Files (p. 639) provides static methods for common file and directory manipulations, including methods for copying files; creating and deleting files and directories; getting information about files and directories; reading the contents of files; getting objects that allow you to manipulate the contents of files and directories; and more.
- A DirectoryStream (p. 639) enables a program to iterate through the contents of a directory.
- The static method get (p. 639) of class Paths converts a String representing a file's or directory's location into a Path object.
- Character-based input and output can be performed with classes Scanner and Formatter.
- Class Formatter (p. 639) enables formatted data to be output to the screen or to a file in a manner similar to System.out.printf.
- An absolute path (p. 639) contains all the directories, starting with the root directory (p. 639), that lead to a specific file or directory. Every file or directory on a disk drive has the same root directory in its path.
- A relative path (p. 639) starts from the directory in which the application began executing.
- Files static method exists (p. 640) receives a Path and determines whether it exists (either as a file or as a directory) on disk.
- Path method getFileName (p. 640) gets the String name of a file or directory without any location information.
- Files static method isDirectory (p. 640) receives a Path and returns a boolean indicating whether that Path represents a directory on disk.
- Path method isAbsolute (p. 640) returns a boolean indicating whether a Path represents an absolute path to a file or directory.
- Files static method getLastModifiedTime (p. 640) receives a Path and returns a FileTime (package java.nio.file.attribute) indicating when the file was last modified.
- Files static method size (p. 640) receives a Path and returns a long representing the number of bytes in the file or directory. For directories, the value returned is platform specific.
- Path method toString (p. 640) returns a String representation of the Path.
- Path method toAbsolutePath (p. 640) converts the Path on which it's called to an absolute path.
- Files static method newDirectoryStream (p. 640) returns a DirectoryStream<Path> containing Path objects for a directory's contents.
- A separator character (p. 642) is used to separate directories and files in the path.

Section 15.4 Sequential-Access Text Files
- Java imposes no structure on a file. You must structure files to meet your application's needs.
- To retrieve data sequentially from a file, programs normally start from the beginning of the file and read all the data consecutively until the desired information is found.
- Data in many sequential files cannot be modified without the risk of destroying other data in the file. Records in a sequential-access file are usually updated by rewriting the entire file.

Section 15.5 Object Serialization

- Java provides a mechanism called object serialization (p. 654) that enables entire objects to be written to or read from a stream.

- A serialized object (p. 654) is represented as a sequence of bytes that includes the object's data as well as information about the object's type and the types of data it stores.

- After a serialized object has been written into a file, it can be read from the file and deserialized (p. 654) to recreate the object in memory.

- Classes ObjectInputStream (p. 654) and ObjectOutputStream (p. 654) enable entire objects to be read from or written to a stream (possibly a file).

- Only classes that implement interface Serializable (p. 655) can be serialized and deserialized.

- The ObjectOutput interface (p. 654) contains method writeObject (p. 655), which takes an Object as an argument and writes its information to an OutputStream. A class that implements this interface, such as ObjectOutputStream, would ensure that the Object is Serializable.

- The ObjectInput interface (p. 654) contains method readObject (p. 655), which reads and returns a reference to an Object from an InputStream. After an object has been read, its reference can be cast to the object's actual type.

Section 15.6 Opening Files with `JFileChooser`

- Class JFileChooser (p. 662) is used to display a dialog that enables users of a program to easily select files or directories from a GUI.

Section 15.7 (Optional) Additional `java.io` *Classes*

- InputStream and OutputStream are abstract classes for performing byte-based I/O.

- Pipes (p. 665) are synchronized communication channels between threads. One thread sends data via a PipedOutputStream (p. 665). The target thread reads information from the pipe via a PipedInputStream (p. 665).

- A filter stream (p. 666) provides additional functionality, such as aggregating data bytes into meaningful primitive-type units. FilterInputStream (p. 666) and FilterOutputStream are typically extended, so some of their filtering capabilities are provided by their concrete subclasses.

- A PrintStream (p. 666) performs text output. System.out and System.err are PrintStreams.

- Interface DataInput describes methods for reading primitive types from an input stream. Classes DataInputStream (p. 666) and RandomAccessFile each implement this interface.

- Interface DataOutput describes methods for writing primitive types to an output stream. Classes DataOutputStream (p. 666) and RandomAccessFile each implement this interface.

- Buffering is an I/O-performance-enhancement technique. Buffering reduces the number of I/O operations by combining smaller outputs together in memory. The number of physical I/O operations is much smaller than the number of I/O requests issued by the program.

- With a BufferedOutputStream (p. 666) each output operation is directed to a buffer (p. 666) large enough to hold the data of many output operations. Transfer to the output device is performed in one large physical output operation (p. 666) when the buffer fills. A partially filled buffer can be forced out to the device at any time by invoking the stream object's flush method (p. 666).

- With a BufferedInputStream (p. 667), many "logical" chunks of data from a file are read as one large physical input operation (p. 667) into a memory buffer. As a program requests data, it's taken from the buffer. When the buffer is empty, the next actual physical input operation is performed.

- A ByteArrayInputStream reads from a byte array in memory. A ByteArrayOutputStream outputs to a byte array in memory.

- A SequenceInputStream concatenates several InputStreams. When the program reaches the end of an input stream, that stream closes, and the next stream in the sequence opens.
- The Reader (p. 667) and Writer (p. 667) abstract classes are Unicode character-based streams. Most byte-based streams have corresponding character-based concrete Reader or Writer classes.
- Classes BufferedReader (p. 667) and BufferedWriter (p. 667) buffer character-based streams.
- Classes CharArrayReader (p. 668) and CharArrayWriter (p. 668) manipulate char arrays.
- A LineNumberReader (p. 668) is a buffered character stream that tracks the number of lines read.
- Classes FileReader (p. 668) and FileWriter (p. 668) perform character-based file I/O.
- Class PipedReader (p. 668) and class PipedWriter (p. 668) implement piped-character streams for transferring data between threads.
- Class StringReader (p. 668) and StringWriter (p. 668) read characters from and write characters to Strings, respectively. A PrintWriter (p. 646) writes characters to a stream.

Self-Review Exercises

15.1 Determine whether each of the following statements is *true* or *false*. If *false*, explain why.
a) You must explicitly create the stream objects System.in, System.out and System.err.
b) When reading data from a file using class Scanner, if you wish to read data in the file multiple times, the file must be closed and reopened to read from the beginning of the file.
c) Files static method exists receives a Path and determines whether it exists (either as a file or as a directory) on disk
d) Binary files are human readable in a text editor.
e) An absolute path contains all the directories, starting with the root directory, that lead to a specific file or directory.
f) Class Formatter contains method printf, which enables formatted data to be output to the screen or to a file.

15.2 Complete the following tasks, assuming that each applies to the same program:
a) Write a statement that opens file "oldmast.txt" for input—use Scanner variable inOldMaster.
b) Write a statement that opens file "trans.txt" for input—use Scanner variable inTransaction.
c) Write a statement that opens file "newmast.txt" for output (and creation)—use formatter variable outNewMaster.
d) Write the statements needed to read a record from the file "oldmast.txt". Use the data to create an object of class Account—use Scanner variable inOldMaster. Assume that class Account is the same as the Account class in Fig. 15.9.
e) Write the statements needed to read a record from the file "trans.txt". The record is an object of class TransactionRecord—use Scanner variable inTransaction. Assume that class TransactionRecord contains method setAccount (which takes an int) to set the account number and method setAmount (which takes a double) to set the amount of the transaction.
f) Write a statement that outputs a record to the file "newmast.txt". The record is an object of type Account—use Formatter variable outNewMaster.

15.3 Complete the following tasks, assuming that each applies to the same program:
a) Write a statement that opens file "oldmast.ser" for input—use ObjectInputStream variable inOldMaster to wrap an InputStream object.
b) Write a statement that opens file "trans.ser" for input—use ObjectInputStream variable inTransaction to wrap an InputStream object.

    c) Write a statement that opens file "newmast.ser" for output (and creation)—use ObjectOutputStream variable outNewMaster to wrap an OutputStream.

    d) Write a statement that reads a record from the file "oldmast.ser". The record is an object of class Account—use ObjectInputStream variable inOldMaster. Assume class Account is the same as the Account class in Fig. 15.9

    e) Write a statement that reads a record from the file "trans.ser". The record is an object of class TransactionRecord—use ObjectInputStream variable inTransaction.

    f) Write a statement that outputs a record of type Account to the file "newmast.ser"—use ObjectOutputStream variable outNewMaster.

Answers to Self-Review Exercises

15.1   a) False. These three streams are created for you when a Java application begins executing. b) True. c) True. d) False. Text files are human readable in a text editor. Binary files might be human readable, but only if the bytes in the file represent ASCII characters. e) True. f) False. Class Formatter contains method format, which enables formatted data to be output to the screen or to a file.

15.2
   a) `Scanner inOldMaster = new Scanner(Paths.get("oldmast.txt"));`
   b) `Scanner inTransaction = new Scanner(Paths.get("trans.txt"));`
   c) `Formatter outNewMaster = new Formatter("newmast.txt");`
   d) `Account account = new Account();`
      `account.setAccount(inOldMaster.nextInt());`
      `account.setFirstName(inOldMaster.next());`
      `account.setLastName(inOldMaster.next());`
      `account.setBalance(inOldMaster.nextDouble());`
   e) `TransactionRecord transaction = new Transaction();`
      `transaction.setAccount(inTransaction.nextInt());`
      `transaction.setAmount(inTransaction.nextDouble());`
   f) `outNewMaster.format("%d %s %s %.2f%n",`
        `account.getAccount(), account.getFirstName(),`
        `account.getLastName(), account.getBalance());`

15.3
   a) `ObjectInputStream inOldMaster = new ObjectInputStream(`
        `Files.newInputStream(Paths.get("oldmast.ser")));`
   b) `ObjectInputStream inTransaction = new ObjectInputStream(`
        `Files.newOutputStream(Paths.get("trans.ser")));`
   c) `ObjectOutputStream outNewMaster = new ObjectOutputStream(`
        `Files.newOutputStream(Paths.get("newmast.ser")));`
   d) `Account = (Account) inOldMaster.readObject();`
   e) `transactionRecord = (TransactionRecord) inTransaction.readObject();`
   f) `outNewMaster.writeObject(newAccount);`

Exercises

15.4   *(File Matching)* Self-Review Exercise 15.2 asked you to write a series of single statements. Actually, these statements form the core of an important type of file-processing program—namely, a file-matching program. In commercial data processing, it's common to have several files in each application system. In an accounts receivable system, for example, there's generally a master file containing detailed information about each customer, such as the customer's name, address, telephone number, outstanding balance, credit limit, discount terms, contract arrangements and possibly a condensed history of recent purchases and cash payments.

As transactions occur (i.e., sales are made and payments arrive in the mail), information about them is entered into a file. At the end of each business period (a month for some companies, a week for others, and a day in some cases), the file of transactions (called "trans.txt") is applied to the master file (called "oldmast.txt") to update each account's purchase and payment record. During an update, the master file is rewritten as the file "newmast.txt", which is then used at the end of the next business period to begin the updating process again.

File-matching programs must deal with certain problems that do not arise in single-file programs. For example, a match does not always occur. If a customer on the master file has not made any purchases or cash payments in the current business period, no record for this customer will appear on the transaction file. Similarly, a customer who did make some purchases or cash payments could have just moved to this community, and if so, the company may not have had a chance to create a master record for this customer.

Write a complete file-matching accounts receivable program. Use the account number on each file as the record key for matching purposes. Assume that each file is a sequential text file with records stored in increasing account-number order.

a) Define class TransactionRecord. Objects of this class contain an account number and amount for the transaction. Provide methods to modify and retrieve these values.

b) Modify class Account in Fig. 15.9 to include method combine, which takes a TransactionRecord object and combines the balance of the Account object and the amount value of the TransactionRecord object.

c) Write a program to create data for testing the program. Use the sample account data in Figs. 15.14 and 15.15. Run the program to create the files trans.txt and oldmast.txt to be used by your file-matching program.

Master file account number	Name	Balance
100	Alan Jones	348.17
300	Mary Smith	27.19
500	Sam Sharp	0.00
700	Suzy Green	-14.22

Fig. 15.14 | Sample data for master file.

Transaction file account number	Transaction amount
100	27.14
300	62.11
400	100.56
900	82.17

Fig. 15.15 | Sample data for transaction file.

d) Create class FileMatch to perform the file-matching functionality. The class should contain methods that read oldmast.txt and trans.txt. When a match occurs (i.e., records with the same account number appear in both the master file and the transaction file), add the dollar amount in the transaction record to the current balance in the master record, and write the "newmast.txt" record. (Assume that purchases are indicated by positive amounts in the transaction file and payments by negative amounts.) When there's a master record for a particular account, but no corresponding transaction record, merely write the master record to "newmast.txt". When there's a transaction record, but no corresponding master record, print to a log file the message "Unmatched transaction record for account number..." (fill in the account number from the transaction record). The log file should be a text file named "log.txt".

15.5   *(File Matching with Multiple Transactions)* It's possible (and actually common) to have several transaction records with the same record key. This situation occurs, for example, when a customer makes several purchases and cash payments during a business period. Rewrite your accounts receivable file-matching program from Exercise 15.4 to provide for the possibility of handling several transaction records with the same record key. Modify the test data of CreateData.java to include the additional transaction records in Fig. 15.16.

Account number	Dollar amount
300	83.89
700	80.78
700	1.53

Fig. 15.16 | Additional transaction records.

15.6   *(File Matching with Object Serialization)* Recreate your solution for Exercise 15.5 using object serialization. Use the statements from Exercise 15.3 as your basis for this program. You may want to create applications to read the data stored in the .ser files—the code in Section 15.5.2 can be modified for this purpose.

15.7   *(Telephone-Number Word Generator)* Standard telephone keypads contain the digits zero through nine. The numbers two through nine each have three letters associated with them (Fig. 15.17). Many people find it difficult to memorize phone numbers, so they use the correspondence between digits and letters to develop seven-letter words that correspond to their phone numbers. For example, a person whose telephone number is 686-2377 might use the correspondence indicated in Fig. 15.17 to develop the seven-letter word "NUMBERS." Every seven-letter word corresponds to exactly one seven-digit telephone number. A restaurant wishing to increase its takeout business could surely do so with the number 825-3688 (i.e., "TAKEOUT").

Digit	Letters	Digit	Letters	Digit	Letters
2	A B C	5	J K L	8	T U V
3	D E F	6	M N O	9	W X Y
4	G H I	7	P R S		

Fig. 15.17 | Telephone keypad digits and letters.

Every seven-letter phone number corresponds to many different seven-letter words, but most of these words represent unrecognizable juxtapositions of letters. It's possible, however, that the owner of a barbershop would be pleased to know that the shop's telephone number, 424-7288, corresponds to "HAIRCUT." A veterinarian with the phone number 738-2273 would be pleased to know that the number corresponds to the letters "PETCARE." An automotive dealership would be pleased to know that the dealership number, 639-2277, corresponds to "NEWCARS."

Write a program that, given a seven-digit number, uses a `PrintStream` object to write to a file every possible seven-letter word combination corresponding to that number. There are 2,187 (3^7) such combinations. Avoid phone numbers with the digits 0 and 1.

15.8   *(Student Poll)* Figure 6.8 contains an array of survey responses that's hard coded into the program. Suppose we wish to process survey results that are stored in a file. This exercise requires two separate programs. First, create an application that prompts the user for survey responses and outputs each response to a file. Use a `Formatter` to create a file called `numbers.txt`. Each integer should be written using method `format`. Then modify the program in Fig. 6.8 to read the survey responses from `numbers.txt`. The responses should be read from the file by using a `Scanner`. Use method `nextInt` to input one integer at a time from the file. The program should continue to read responses until it reaches the end of the file. The results should be output to the text file "output.txt".

15.9   *(Adding Object Serialization to the `MyShape` Drawing Application)* Modify Exercise 12.17 to allow the user to save a drawing into a file or load a prior drawing from a file using object serialization. Add buttons **Load** (to read objects from a file) and **Save** (to write objects to a file). Use an `ObjectOutputStream` to write to the file and an `ObjectInputStream` to read from the file. Write the array of `MyShape` objects using method `writeObject` (class `ObjectOutputStream`), and read the array using method `readObject` (`ObjectInputStream`). The object-serialization mechanism can read or write entire arrays—it's not necessary to manipulate each element of the array of `MyShape` objects individually. It's simply required that all the shapes be `Serializable`. For both the **Load** and **Save** buttons, use a `JFileChooser` to allow the user to select the file in which the shapes will be stored or from which they'll be read. When the user first runs the program, no shapes should be displayed on the screen. The user can display shapes by opening a previously saved file or by drawing new shapes. Once there are shapes on the screen, users can save them to a file using the **Save** button.

Making a Difference

15.10   *(Phishing Scanner)* Phishing is a form of identity theft in which, in an e-mail, a sender posing as a trustworthy source attempts to acquire private information, such as your user names, passwords, credit-card numbers and social security number. Phishing e-mails claiming to be from popular banks, credit-card companies, auction sites, social networks and online payment services may look quite legitimate. These fraudulent messages often provide links to spoofed (fake) websites where you're asked to enter sensitive information.

Search online for phishing scams. Also check out the Anti-Phishing Working Group (`www.antiphishing.org`), and the FBI's Cyber Investigations website (`www.fbi.gov/about-us/investigate/cyber/cyber`), where you'll find information about the latest scams and how to protect yourself.

Create a list of 30 words, phrases and company names commonly found in phishing messages. Assign a point value to each based on your estimate of its likeliness to be in a phishing message (e.g., one point if it's somewhat likely, two points if moderately likely, or three points if highly likely). Write an application that scans a file of text for these terms and phrases. For each occurrence of a keyword or phrase within the text file, add the assigned point value to the total points for that word or phrase. For each keyword or phrase found, output one line with the word or phrase, the number of occurrences and the point total. Then show the point total for the entire message. Does your program assign a high point total to some actual phishing e-mails you've received? Does it assign a high point total to some legitimate e-mails you've received?

16

Generic Collections

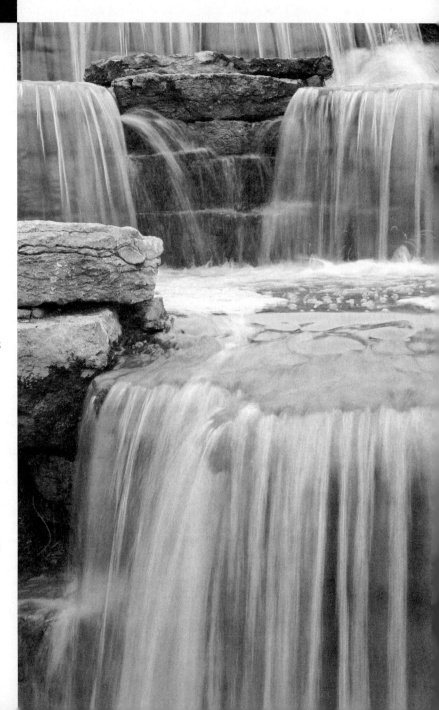

I think this is the most extraordinary collection of talent, of human knowledge, that has ever been gathered together at the White House— with the possible exception of when Thomas Jefferson dined alone.
—John F. Kennedy

Objectives

In this chapter you'll:

- Learn what collections are.

- Use class **Arrays** for array manipulations.

- Learn the type-wrapper classes that enable programs to process primitive data values as objects.

- Use prebuilt generic data structures from the collections framework.

- Use iterators to "walk through" a collection.

- Use persistent hash tables manipulated with objects of class **Properties**.

- Learn about synchronization and modifiability wrappers.

Outline

16.1 Introduction

In Section 6.13, we introduced the generic `ArrayList` collection—a dynamically resizable array-like data structure that stores references to objects of a type that you specify when you create the `ArrayList`. In this chapter, we continue our discussion of the Java **collections framework**, which contains many other *prebuilt* generic data-structures.

Some examples of collections are your favorite songs stored on your smartphone or media player, your contacts list, the cards you hold in a card game, the members of your favorite sports team and the courses you take at once in school.

We discuss the collections-framework interfaces that declare the capabilities of each collection type, various classes that implement these interfaces, methods that process collection objects, and **iterators** that "walk through" collections.

Java SE 8
After reading Chapter 17, Java SE 8 Lambdas and Streams, you'll be able to reimplement many of Chapter 16's examples in a more concise and elegant manner, and in a way that makes them easier to parallelize to improve performance on today's multi-core systems. In Chapter 23, Concurrency, you'll learn how to improve performance on multi-core systems using Java's *concurrent collections* and *parallel stream* operations.

16.2 Collections Overview

A **collection** is a data structure—actually, an object—that can hold references to other objects. Usually, collections contain references to objects of any type that has the *is-a* relationship with the type stored in the collection. The collections-framework interfaces declare the operations to be performed generically on various types of collections. Figure 16.1 lists some of the collections framework interfaces. Several implementations of these interfaces are provided within the framework. You may also provide your own implementations.

Interface	Description
Collection	The root interface in the collections hierarchy from which interfaces Set, Queue and List are derived.
Set	A collection that does *not* contain duplicates.
List	An ordered collection that *can* contain duplicate elements.
Map	A collection that associates keys to values and *cannot* contain duplicate keys. Map does not derive from Collection.
Queue	Typically a *first-in, first-out* collection that models a *waiting line*; other orders can be specified.

Fig. 16.1 | Some collections-framework interfaces.

Object-Based Collections

The collections framework classes and interfaces are members of package java.util. In early Java versions, the collections framework classes stored and manipulated *only* Object references, enabling you to store *any* object in a collection, because all classes directly or indirectly derive from class Object. Programs normally need to process *specific* types of objects. As a result, the Object references obtained from a collection need to be *downcast* to an appropriate type to allow the program to process the objects correctly. As we discussed in Chapter 10, downcasting generally should be avoided.

Generic Collections

To elminate this problem, the collections framework was enhanced with the *generics* capabilities that we introduced with generic ArrayLists in Chapter 6 and that we discuss in more detail in Chapter 20, Generic Classes and Methods. Generics enable you to specify the *exact type* that will be stored in a collection and give you the benefits of *compile-time type checking*—the compiler issues error messages if you use inappropriate types in your collections. Once you specify the type stored in a generic collection, any reference you retrieve from the collection will have that type. This eliminates the need for explicit type casts that can throw ClassCastExceptions if the referenced object is *not* of the appropriate type. In addition, the generic collections are *backward compatible* with Java code that was written before generics were introduced.

Good Programming Practice 16.1

Avoid reinventing the wheel—rather than building your own data structures, use the interfaces and collections from the Java collections framework, which have been carefully tested and tuned to meet most application requirements.

Choosing a Collection

The documentation for each collection discusses its memory requirements and its methods' performance characteristics for operations such as adding and removing elements, searching for elements, sorting elements and more. Before choosing a collection, review the online documentation for the collection category you're considering (Set, List, Map, Queue, etc.), then choose the implementation that best meets your application's needs. Chapter 19, Searching, Sorting and Big O, discusses a means for describing how hard an algorithm works to perform its task—based on the number of data items to be processed. After reading Chapter 19, you'll better understand each collection's performance characteristics as described in the online documentation.

16.3 Type-Wrapper Classes

Each primitive type (listed in Appendix D) has a corresponding **type-wrapper class** (in package `java.lang`). These classes are called `Boolean`, `Byte`, `Character`, `Double`, `Float`, `Integer`, `Long` and `Short`. These enable you to manipulate primitive-type values as objects. This is important because the data structures that we reuse or develop in Chapters 16–21 manipulate and share *objects*—they cannot manipulate variables of primitive types. However, they can manipulate objects of the type-wrapper classes, because every class ultimately derives from `Object`.

Each of the numeric type-wrapper classes—Byte, Short, Integer, Long, Float and Double—extends class `Number`. Also, the type-wrapper classes are `final` classes, so you cannot extend them. Primitive types do not have methods, so the methods related to a primitive type are located in the corresponding type-wrapper class (e.g., method `parseInt`, which converts a `String` to an `int` value, is located in class `Integer`).

16.4 Autoboxing and Auto-Unboxing

Java provides boxing and unboxing conversions that automatically convert between primitive-type values and type-wrapper objects. A **boxing conversion** converts a value of a primitive type to an object of the corresponding type-wrapper class. An **unboxing conversion** converts an object of a type-wrapper class to a value of the corresponding primitive type. These conversions are performed automatically—called **autoboxing** and **auto-unboxing**. Consider the following statements:

```
Integer[] integerArray = new Integer[5]; // create integerArray
integerArray[0] = 10; // assign Integer 10 to integerArray[0]
int value = integerArray[0]; // get int value of Integer
```

In this case, autoboxing occurs when assigning an int value (10) to `integerArray[0]`, because `integerArray` stores references to `Integer` objects, not int values. Auto-unboxing occurs when assigning `integerArray[0]` to int variable `value`, because variable `value` stores an int value, not a reference to an `Integer` object. Boxing conversions also occur in conditions, which can evaluate to primitive `boolean` values or `Boolean` objects. Many of the examples in Chapters 16–21 use these conversions to store primitive values in and retrieve them from data structures.

16.5 Interface `Collection` and Class `Collections`

Interface `Collection` contains **bulk operations** (i.e., operations performed on an *entire* collection) for operations such as *adding*, *clearing* and *comparing* objects (or elements) in a collection. A `Collection` can also be converted to an array. In addition, interface `Collection` provides a method that returns an **Iterator** object, which allows a program to walk through the collection and remove elements from it during the iteration. We discuss class `Iterator` in Section 16.6.1. Other methods of interface `Collection` enable a program to determine a collection's *size* and whether a collection is *empty*.

Software Engineering Observation 16.1

Collection is used commonly as a parameter type in methods to allow polymorphic processing of all objects that implement interface Collection.

Software Engineering Observation 16.2

Most collection implementations provide a constructor that takes a Collection argument, thereby allowing a new collection to be constructed containing the elements of the specified collection.

Class **Collections** provides static methods that *search*, *sort* and perform other operations on collections. Section 16.7 discusses more about Collections methods. We also cover Collections' **wrapper methods** that enable you to treat a collection as a *synchronized collection* (Section 16.13) or an *unmodifiable collection* (Section 16.14). Synchronized collections are for use with multithreading (discussed in Chapter 23), which enables programs to perform operations *in parallel*. When two or more threads of a program *share* a collection, problems might occur. As an analogy, consider a traffic intersection. If all cars were allowed to access the intersection at the same time, collisions might occur. For this reason, traffic lights are provided to control access to the intersection. Similarly, we can *synchronize* access to a collection to ensure that only *one* thread manipulates the collection at a time. The synchronization wrapper methods of class Collections return synchronized versions of collections that can be shared among threads in a program. Unmodifiable collections are useful when clients of a class need to *view* a collection's elements, but they should *not* be allowed to *modify* the collection by adding and removing elements.

16.6 Lists

A List (sometimes called a **sequence**) is an *ordered* Collection that can contain duplicate elements. Like array indices, List indices are zero based (i.e., the first element's index is zero). In addition to the methods inherited from Collection, List provides methods for manipulating elements via their indices, manipulating a specified range of elements, searching for elements and obtaining a **ListIterator** to access the elements.

Interface List is implemented by several classes, including **ArrayList**, **LinkedList** and **Vector**. Autoboxing occurs when you add primitive-type values to objects of these classes, because they store only references to objects. Classes ArrayList and Vector are resizable-array implementations of List. Inserting an element between existing elements of an ArrayList or Vector is an *inefficient* operation—all elements after the new one must be moved out of the way, which could be an expensive operation in a collection with a large number of elements. A LinkedList enables *efficient* insertion (or removal) of elements in the middle of a collection, but is much less efficient than an ArrayList for jumping to a specific element in the collection. We discuss the architecture of linked lists in Chapter 21.

ArrayList and Vector have nearly identical behaviors. Operations on Vectors are *synchronized* by default, whereas those on ArrayLists are not. Also, class Vector is from Java 1.0, before the collections framework was added to Java. As such, Vector has some methods that are not part of interface List and are not implemented in class ArrayList. For example, Vector methods addElement and add both append an element to a Vector, but only method add is specified in interface List and implemented by ArrayList. *Unsynchro-*

nized collections provide better performance than synchronized ones. For this reason, Array-List is typically preferred over Vector in programs that do not share a collection among threads. Separately, the Java collections API provides *synchronization wrappers* (Section 16.13) that can be used to add synchronization to the unsynchronized collections, and several powerful synchronized collections are available in the Java concurrency APIs.

Performance Tip 16.1

ArrayLists behave like Vectors without synchronization and therefore execute faster than Vectors, because ArrayLists do not have the overhead of thread synchronization.

Software Engineering Observation 16.3

LinkedLists can be used to create stacks, queues and deques (double-ended queues, pronounced "decks"). The collections framework provides implementations of some of these data structures.

The following three subsections demonstrate the List and Collection capabilities. Section 16.6.1 removes elements from an ArrayList with an Iterator. Section 16.6.2 uses ListIterator and several List- and LinkedList-specific methods.

16.6.1 ArrayList and Iterator

Figure 16.2 uses an ArrayList (introduced in Section 6.13) to demonstrate several capabilities of interface Collection. The program places two Color arrays in ArrayLists and uses an Iterator to remove elements in the second ArrayList collection from the first.

```
 1   // Fig. 16.2: CollectionTest.java
 2   // Collection interface demonstrated via an ArrayList object.
 3   import java.util.List;
 4   import java.util.ArrayList;
 5   import java.util.Collection;
 6   import java.util.Iterator;
 7
 8   public class CollectionTest
 9   {
10      public static void main(String[] args)
11      {
12         // add elements in colors array to list
13         String[] colors = {"MAGENTA", "RED", "WHITE", "BLUE", "CYAN"};
14         List<String> list = new ArrayList<String>();
15
16         for (String color : colors)
17            list.add(color); // adds color to end of list
18
19         // add elements in removeColors array to removeList
20         String[] removeColors = {"RED", "WHITE", "BLUE"};
21         List<String> removeList = new ArrayList<String>();
22
23         for (String color : removeColors)
24            removeList.add(color);
25
```

Fig. 16.2 | Collection interface demonstrated via an ArrayList object. (Part 1 of 2.)

```
26          // output list contents
27          System.out.println("ArrayList: ");
28
29          for (int count = 0; count < list.size(); count++)
30             System.out.printf("%s ", list.get(count));
31
32          // remove from list the colors contained in removeList
33          removeColors(list, removeList);
34
35          // output list contents
36          System.out.printf("%n%nArrayList after calling removeColors:%n");
37
38          for (String color : list)
39             System.out.printf("%s ", color);
40       }
41
42    // remove colors specified in collection2 from collection1
43    private static void removeColors(Collection<String> collection1,
44       Collection<String> collection2)
45    {
46       // get iterator
47       Iterator<String> iterator = collection1.iterator();
48
49       // loop while collection has items
50       while (iterator.hasNext())
51       {
52          if (collection2.contains(iterator.next()))
53             iterator.remove(); // remove current element
54       }
55    }
56 } // end class CollectionTest
```

```
ArrayList:
MAGENTA RED WHITE BLUE CYAN

ArrayList after calling removeColors:
MAGENTA CYAN
```

Fig. 16.2 | Collection interface demonstrated via an ArrayList object. (Part 2 of 2.)

Lines 13 and 20 declare and initialize String arrays colors and removeColors. Lines 14 and 21 create ArrayList<String> objects and assign their references to List<String> variables list and removeList, respectively. Recall that ArrayList is a *generic* class, so we can specify a *type argument* (String in this case) to indicate the type of the elements in each list. Because you specify the type to store in a collection at compile time, generic collections provide compile-time *type safety* that allows the compiler to catch attempts to use invalid types. For example, you cannot store Employees in a collection of Strings.

Lines 16–17 populate list with Strings stored in array colors, and lines 23–24 populate removeList with Strings stored in array removeColors using **List method add**. Lines 29–30 output each element of list. Line 29 calls **List method size** to get the number of elements in the ArrayList. Line 30 uses **List method get** to retrieve individual element values. Lines 29–30 also could have used the enhanced for statement (which we'll demonstrate with collections in other examples).

Line 33 calls method removeColors (lines 43–55), passing list and removeList as arguments. Method removeColors deletes the Strings in removeList from the Strings in list. Lines 38–39 print list's elements after removeColors completes its task.

Method removeColors declares two Collection<String> parameters (lines 43–44)—any two Collections containing Strings can be passed as arguments. The method accesses the elements of the first Collection (collection1) via an Iterator. Line 47 calls **Collection method iterator** to get an Iterator for the Collection. Interfaces Collection and Iterator are generic types. The loop-continuation condition (line 50) calls **Iterator method hasNext** to determine whether there are more elements to iterate through. Method hasNext returns true if another element exists and false otherwise.

The if condition in line 52 calls **Iterator method next** to obtain a reference to the next element, then uses method **contains** of the second Collection (collection2) to determine whether collection2 contains the element returned by next. If so, line 53 calls **Iterator method remove** to remove the element from the Collection collection1.

Common Programming Error 16.1

If a collection is modified by one of its methods after an iterator is created for that collection, the iterator immediately becomes invalid—any operation performed with the iterator fails immediate and throws a ConcurrentModificationException. For this reason, iterators are said to be "fail fast." Fail-fast iterators help ensure that a modifiable collection is not manipulated by two or more threads at the same time, which could corrupt the collection. In Chapter 23, Concurrency, you'll learn about concurrent collections (package java.util.concurrent) that can be safely manipulated by multiple concurrent threads.

Software Engineering Observation 16.4

We refer to the ArrayLists in this example via List variables. This makes our code more flexible and easier to modify—if we later determine that LinkedLists would be more appropriate, only the lines where we created the ArrayList objects (lines 14 and 21) need to be modified. In general, when you create a collection object, refer to that object with a variable of the corresponding collection interface type.

Type Inference with the <> Notation

Lines 14 and 21 specify the type stored in the ArrayList (that is, String) on the left and right sides of the initialization statements. Java SE 7 introduced *type inferencing* with the <> notation—known as the **diamond notation**—in statements that declare and create generic type variables and objects. For example, line 14 can be written as:

```
List<String> list = new ArrayList<>();
```

In this case, Java uses the type in angle brackets on the left of the declaration (that is, String) as the type stored in the ArrayList created on the right side of the declaration. We'll use this syntax for the remaining examples in this chapter.

16.6.2 LinkedList

Figure 16.3 demonstrates various operations on LinkedLists. The program creates two LinkedLists of Strings. The elements of one List are added to the other. Then all the Strings are converted to uppercase, and a range of elements is deleted.

```
 1   // Fig. 16.3: ListTest.java
 2   // Lists, LinkedLists and ListIterators.
 3   import java.util.List;
 4   import java.util.LinkedList;
 5   import java.util.ListIterator;
 6
 7   public class ListTest
 8   {
 9      public static void main(String[] args)
10      {
11         // add colors elements to list1
12         String[] colors =
13            {"black", "yellow", "green", "blue", "violet", "silver"};
14         List<String> list1 = new LinkedList<>();
15
16         for (String color : colors)
17            list1.add(color);
18
19         // add colors2 elements to list2
20         String[] colors2 =
21            {"gold", "white", "brown", "blue", "gray", "silver"};
22         List<String> list2 = new LinkedList<>();
23
24         for (String color : colors2)
25            list2.add(color);
26
27         list1.addAll(list2); // concatenate lists
28         list2 = null; // release resources
29         printList(list1); // print list1 elements
30
31         convertToUppercaseStrings(list1); // convert to uppercase string
32         printList(list1); // print list1 elements
33
34         System.out.printf("%nDeleting elements 4 to 6...");
35         removeItems(list1, 4, 7); // remove items 4-6 from list
36         printList(list1); // print list1 elements
37         printReversedList(list1); // print list in reverse order
38      }
39
40      // output List contents
41      private static void printList(List<String> list)
42      {
43         System.out.printf("%nlist:%n");
44
45         for (String color : list)
46            System.out.printf("%s ", color);
47
48         System.out.println();
49      }
50
51      // locate String objects and convert to uppercase
52      private static void convertToUppercaseStrings(List<String> list)
53      {
```

Fig. 16.3 | Lists, LinkedLists and ListIterators. (Part 1 of 2.)

```
54              ListIterator<String> iterator = list.listIterator();
55
56          while (iterator.hasNext())
57          {
58              String color = iterator.next(); // get item
59              iterator.set(color.toUpperCase()); // convert to upper case
60          }
61      }
62
63      // obtain sublist and use clear method to delete sublist items
64      private static void removeItems(List<String> list,
65          int start, int end)
66      {
67          list.subList(start, end).clear(); // remove items
68      }
69
70      // print reversed list
71      private static void printReversedList(List<String> list)
72      {
73          ListIterator<String> iterator = list.listIterator(list.size());
74
75          System.out.printf("%nReversed List:%n");
76
77          // print list in reverse order
78          while (iterator.hasPrevious())
79              System.out.printf("%s ", iterator.previous());
80      }
81  } // end class ListTest
```

```
list:
black yellow green blue violet silver gold white brown blue gray silver

list:
BLACK YELLOW GREEN BLUE VIOLET SILVER GOLD WHITE BROWN BLUE GRAY SILVER

Deleting elements 4 to 6...
list:
BLACK YELLOW GREEN BLUE WHITE BROWN BLUE GRAY SILVER

Reversed List:
SILVER GRAY BLUE BROWN WHITE BLUE GREEN YELLOW BLACK
```

Fig. 16.3 | Lists, LinkedLists and ListIterators. (Part 2 of 2.)

Lines 14 and 22 create LinkedLists list1 and list2 of type String. LinkedList is a generic class that has one type parameter for which we specify the type argument String in this example. Lines 16–17 and 24–25 call List method add to *append* elements from arrays colors and colors2 to the *ends* of list1 and list2, respectively.

Line 27 calls **List method addAll** to *append all elements* of list2 to the end of list1. Line 28 sets list2 to null, because list2 is no longer needed. Line 29 calls method printList (lines 41–49) to output list1's contents. Line 31 calls method convertToUppercaseStrings (lines 52–61) to convert each String element to uppercase, then line 32 calls printList again to display the modified Strings. Line 35 calls method removeItems (lines 64–68) to remove the range of elements starting at index 4 up to, but not including, index 7 of the list. Line 37 calls method printReversedList (lines 71–80) to print the list in reverse order.

Method *convertToUppercaseStrings*

Method convertToUppercaseStrings (lines 52–61) changes lowercase String elements in its List argument to uppercase Strings. Line 54 calls **List method listIterator** to get the List's **bidirectional iterator** (i.e., one that can traverse a List *backward* or *forward*). ListIterator is also a generic class. In this example, the ListIterator references String objects, because method listIterator is called on a List of Strings. Line 56 calls method hasNext to determine whether the List *contains another element*. Line 58 gets the next String in the List. Line 59 calls **String method toUpperCase** to get an uppercase version of the String and calls **ListIterator method set** to replace the current String to which iterator refers with the String returned by method toUpperCase. Like method toUpperCase, **String method toLowerCase** returns a lowercase version of the String.

Method *removeItems*

Method removeItems (lines 64–68) *removes a range of items* from the list. Line 67 calls **List method subList** to obtain a portion of the List (called a **sublist**). This is called a **range-view method,** which enables the program to view a portion of the list. The sublist is simply a view into the List on which subList is called. Method subList takes as arguments the beginning and ending index for the sublist. The ending index is *not* part of the range of the sublist. In this example, line 35 passes 4 for the beginning index and 7 for the ending index to subList. The sublist returned is the set of elements with indices 4 through 6. Next, the program calls **List method clear** on the sublist to remove the elements of the sublist from the List. Any changes made to a sublist are also made to the original List.

Method *printReversedList*

Method printReversedList (lines 71–80) prints the list backward. Line 73 calls List method listIterator with the starting position as an argument (in our case, the last element in the list) to get a *bidirectional iterator* for the list. **List method size** returns the number of items in the List. The while condition (line 78) calls **ListIterator's hasPrevious method** to determine whether there are more elements while traversing the list *backward*. Line 79 calls **ListIterator's previous method** to get the previous element from the list and outputs it to the standard output stream.

Views into Collections and *Arrays* Method *asList*

Class Arrays provides static method **asList** to *view* an array (sometimes called the **backing array**) as a **List** collection. A List view allows you to manipulate the array as if it were a list. This is useful for adding the elements in an array to a collection and for sorting array elements. The next example demonstrates how to create a LinkedList with a List view of an array, because we cannot pass the array to a LinkedList constructor. Sorting array elements with a List view is demonstrated in Fig. 16.7. Any modifications made through the List view change the array, and any modifications made to the array change the List view. The only operation permitted on the view returned by asList is *set*, which changes the value of the view and the backing array. Any other attempts to change the view (such as adding or removing elements) result in an **UnsupportedOperationException**.

Viewing Arrays as *Lists* and Converting *Lists* to Arrays

Figure 16.4 uses Arrays method asList to view an array as a List and uses **List method toArray** to get an array from a LinkedList collection. The program calls method asList to create a List view of an array, which is used to initialize a LinkedList object, then adds a series of Strings to the LinkedList and calls method toArray to obtain an array containing references to the Strings.

```
1   // Fig. 16.4: UsingToArray.java
2   // Viewing arrays as Lists and converting Lists to arrays.
3   import java.util.LinkedList;
4   import java.util.Arrays;
5
6   public class UsingToArray
7   {
8      // creates a LinkedList, adds elements and converts to array
9      public static void main(String[] args)
10     {
11         String[] colors = {"black", "blue", "yellow"};
12         LinkedList<String> links = new LinkedList<>(Arrays.asList(colors));
13
14         links.addLast("red"); // add as last item
15         links.add("pink"); // add to the end
16         links.add(3, "green"); // add at 3rd index
17         links.addFirst("cyan"); // add as first item
18
19         // get LinkedList elements as an array
20         colors = links.toArray(new String[links.size()]);
21
22         System.out.println("colors: ");
23
24         for (String color : colors)
25            System.out.println(color);
26     }
27  } // end class UsingToArray
```

```
colors:
cyan
black
blue
yellow
green
red
pink
```

Fig. 16.4 | Viewing arrays as Lists and converting Lists to arrays.

Line 12 constructs a LinkedList of Strings containing the elements of array colors. Arrays method asList returns a List view of the array, then uses that to initialize the LinkedList with its constructor that receives a Collection as an argument (a List *is a* Collection). Line 14 calls **LinkedList method addLast** to add "red" to the end of links. Lines 15–16 call **LinkedList method add** to add "pink" as the last element and "green" as the element at index 3 (i.e., the fourth element). Method addLast (line 14) functions identically to method add (line 15). Line 17 calls **LinkedList method addFirst** to add "cyan" as the new first item in the LinkedList. The add operations are permitted because they operate on the LinkedList object, not the view returned by asList. [*Note:* When "cyan" is added as the first element, "green" becomes the fifth element in the LinkedList.]

Line 20 calls the List interface's toArray method to get a String array from links. The array is a copy of the list's elements—modifying the array's contents does *not* modify the list. The array passed to method toArray is of the same type that you'd like method toArray to return. If the number of elements in that array is greater than or equal to the number of elements in the LinkedList, toArray copies the list's elements into its array argument and returns that array. If the LinkedList has more elements than the number of elements in the array passed to toArray, toArray *allocates a new array* of the same type it receives as an argument, *copies* the list's elements into the new array and returns the new array.

Common Programming Error 16.2

Passing an array that contains data to toArray *can cause logic errors. If the number of elements in the array is smaller than the number of elements in the list on which* toArray *is called, a new array is allocated to store the list's elements—without preserving the array argument's elements. If the number of elements in the array is greater than the number of elements in the list, the elements of the array (starting at index zero) are overwritten with the list's elements. Array elements that are not overwritten retain their values.*

16.7 Collections Methods

Class Collections provides several high-performance algorithms for manipulating collection elements. The algorithms (Fig. 16.5) are implemented as static methods. The methods sort, binarySearch, reverse, shuffle, fill and copy operate on Lists. Methods min, max, addAll, frequency and disjoint operate on Collections.

Method	Description
sort	Sorts the elements of a List.
binarySearch	Locates an object in a List, using the high-performance binary search algorithm which we introduced in Section 6.12 and discuss in detail in Section 19.4.
reverse	Reverses the elements of a List.
shuffle	Randomly orders a List's elements.
fill	Sets every List element to refer to a specified object.
copy	Copies references from one List into another.
min	Returns the smallest element in a Collection.
max	Returns the largest element in a Collection.
addAll	Appends all elements in an array to a Collection.
frequency	Calculates how many collection elements are equal to the specified element.
disjoint	Determines whether two collections have no elements in common.

Fig. 16.5 | Collections methods.

Software Engineering Observation 16.5

The collections framework methods are polymorphic. That is, each can operate on objects that implement specific interfaces, regardless of the underlying implementations.

16.7.1 Method sort

Method **sort** sorts the elements of a List, which must implement the **Comparable inter-face**. The order is determined by the natural order of the elements' type as implemented by a compareTo method. For example, the natural order for numeric values is ascending order, and the natural order for Strings is based on their lexicographical ordering (Section 14.3). Method compareTo is declared in interface Comparable and is sometimes called the **natural comparison method**. The sort call may specify as a second argument a **Comparator** object that determines an alternative ordering of the elements.

Sorting in Ascending Order
Figure 16.6 uses Collections method sort to order the elements of a List in *ascending* order (line 17). Method sort performs an iterative merge sort (we demonstrated a recursive merge sort in Section 19.8). Line 14 creates list as a List of Strings. Lines 15 and 18 each use an *implicit* call to the list's toString method to output the list contents in the format shown in the output.

```
1   // Fig. 16.6: Sort1.java
2   // Collections method sort.
3   import java.util.List;
4   import java.util.Arrays;
5   import java.util.Collections;
6
7   public class Sort1
8   {
9      public static void main(String[] args)
10     {
11        String[] suits = {"Hearts", "Diamonds", "Clubs", "Spades"};
12
13        // Create and display a list containing the suits array elements
14        List<String> list = Arrays.asList(suits);
15        System.out.printf("Unsorted array elements: %s%n", list);
16
17        Collections.sort(list); // sort ArrayList
18        System.out.printf("Sorted array elements: %s%n", list);
19     }
20  } // end class Sort1
```

```
Unsorted array elements: [Hearts, Diamonds, Clubs, Spades]
Sorted array elements: [Clubs, Diamonds, Hearts, Spades]
```

Fig. 16.6 | Collections method sort.

Sorting in Descending Order
Figure 16.7 sorts the same list of strings used in Fig. 16.6 in *descending* order. The example introduces the Comparator interface, which is used for sorting a Collection's elements in

a different order. Line 18 calls Collections's method sort to order the List in descending order. The static **Collections method reverseOrder** returns a Comparator object that orders the collection's elements in reverse order.

```
 1   // Fig. 16.7: Sort2.java
 2   // Using a Comparator object with method sort.
 3   import java.util.List;
 4   import java.util.Arrays;
 5   import java.util.Collections;
 6
 7   public class Sort2
 8   {
 9      public static void main(String[] args)
10      {
11         String[] suits = {"Hearts", "Diamonds", "Clubs", "Spades"};
12
13         // Create and display a list containing the suits array elements
14         List<String> list = Arrays.asList(suits); // create List
15         System.out.printf("Unsorted array elements: %s%n", list);
16
17         // sort in descending order using a comparator
18         Collections.sort(list, Collections.reverseOrder());
19         System.out.printf("Sorted list elements: %s%n", list);
20      }
21   } // end class Sort2
```

```
Unsorted array elements: [Hearts, Diamonds, Clubs, Spades]
Sorted list elements: [Spades, Hearts, Diamonds, Clubs]
```

Fig. 16.7 | Collections method sort with a Comparator object.

Sorting with a Comparator
Figure 16.8 creates a custom Comparator class, named TimeComparator, that implements interface Comparator to compare two Time2 objects. Class Time2, declared in Fig. 8.5, represents times with hours, minutes and seconds.

```
 1   // Fig. 16.8: TimeComparator.java
 2   // Custom Comparator class that compares two Time2 objects.
 3   import java.util.Comparator;
 4
 5   public class TimeComparator implements Comparator<Time2>
 6   {
 7      @Override
 8      public int compare(Time2 time1, Time2 time2)
 9      {
10         int hourDifference = time1.getHour() - time2.getHour();
11
12         if (hourDifference != 0) // test the hour first
13            return hourCompare;
```

Fig. 16.8 | Custom Comparator class that compares two Time2 objects. (Part 1 of 2.)

```
14
15          int minuteDifference = time1.getMinute() - time2.getMinute();
16
17          if (minuteDifference != 0) // then test the minute
18             return minuteDifference;
19
20          int secondDifference = time1.getSecond() - time2.getSecond();
21          return secondDifference;
22       }
23    } // end class TimeComparator
```

Fig. 16.8 │ Custom `Comparator` class that compares two `Time2` objects. (Part 2 of 2.)

Class `TimeComparator` implements interface `Comparator`, a generic type that takes one type argument (in this case `Time2`). A class that implements `Comparator` must declare a `compare` method that receives two arguments and returns a *negative* integer if the first argument is *less than* the second, 0 if the arguments are *equal* or a *positive* integer if the first argument is *greater than* the second. Method `compare` (lines 7–22) performs comparisons between `Time2` objects. Line 10 calculates the difference between the hours of the two `Time2` objects. If the hours are different (line 12), then we return this value. If this value is *positive*, then the first hour is greater than the second and the first time is greater than the second. If this value is *negative*, then the first hour is less than the second and the first time is less than the second. If this value is zero, the hours are the same and we must test the minutes (and maybe the seconds) to determine which time is greater.

Figure 16.9 sorts a list using the custom `Comparator` class `TimeComparator`. Line 11 creates an `ArrayList` of `Time2` objects. Recall that both `ArrayList` and `List` are generic types and accept a type argument that specifies the element type of the collection. Lines 13–17 create five `Time2` objects and add them to this list. Line 23 calls method `sort`, passing it an object of our `TimeComparator` class (Fig. 16.8).

```
1    // Fig. 16.9: Sort3.java
2    // Collections method sort with a custom Comparator object.
3    import java.util.List;
4    import java.util.ArrayList;
5    import java.util.Collections;
6
7    public class Sort3
8    {
9       public static void main(String[] args)
10      {
11         List<Time2> list = new ArrayList<>(); // create List
12
13         list.add(new Time2(6, 24, 34));
14         list.add(new Time2(18, 14, 58));
15         list.add(new Time2(6, 05, 34));
16         list.add(new Time2(12, 14, 58));
17         list.add(new Time2(6, 24, 22));
18
```

Fig. 16.9 │ `Collections` method `sort` with a custom `Comparator` object. (Part 1 of 2.)

```
19        // output List elements
20        System.out.printf("Unsorted array elements:%n%s%n", list);
21
22        // sort in order using a comparator
23        Collections.sort(list, new TimeComparator());
24
25        // output List elements
26        System.out.printf("Sorted list elements:%n%s%n", list);
27    }
28 } // end class Sort3
```

```
Unsorted array elements:
[6:24:34 AM, 6:14:58 PM, 6:05:34 AM, 12:14:58 PM, 6:24:22 AM]
Sorted list elements:
[6:05:34 AM, 6:24:22 AM, 6:24:34 AM, 12:14:58 PM, 6:14:58 PM]
```

Fig. 16.9 | Collections method sort with a custom Comparator object. (Part 2 of 2.)

16.7.2 Method shuffle

Method **shuffle** randomly orders a List's elements. Chapter 6 presented a card shuffling and dealing simulation that shuffled a deck of cards with a loop. Figure 16.10 uses method shuffle to shuffle a deck of Card objects that might be used in a card-game simulator.

```java
1   // Fig. 16.10: DeckOfCards.java
2   // Card shuffling and dealing with Collections method shuffle.
3   import java.util.List;
4   import java.util.Arrays;
5   import java.util.Collections;
6
7   // class to represent a Card in a deck of cards
8   class Card
9   {
10      public static enum Face {Ace, Deuce, Three, Four, Five, Six,
11         Seven, Eight, Nine, Ten, Jack, Queen, King };
12      public static enum Suit {Clubs, Diamonds, Hearts, Spades};
13
14      private final Face face;
15      private final Suit suit;
16
17      // constructor
18      public Card(Face face, Suit suit)
19      {
20         this.face = face;
21         this.suit = suit;
22      }
23
24      // return face of the card
25      public Face getFace()
26      {
```

Fig. 16.10 | Card shuffling and dealing with Collections method shuffle. (Part 1 of 3.)

```
27              return face;
28          }
29
30          // return suit of Card
31          public Suit getSuit()
32          {
33              return suit;
34          }
35
36          // return String representation of Card
37          public String toString()
38          {
39              return String.format("%s of %s", face, suit);
40          }
41      } // end class Card
42
43      // class DeckOfCards declaration
44      public class DeckOfCards
45      {
46          private List<Card> list; // declare List that will store Cards
47
48          // set up deck of Cards and shuffle
49          public DeckOfCards()
50          {
51              Card[] deck = new Card[52];
52              int count = 0; // number of cards
53
54              // populate deck with Card objects
55              for (Card.Suit suit: Card.Suit.values())
56              {
57                  for (Card.Face face: Card.Face.values())
58                  {
59                      deck[count] = new Card(face, suit);
60                      ++count;
61                  }
62              }
63
64              list = Arrays.asList(deck); // get List
65              Collections.shuffle(list);  // shuffle deck
66          } // end DeckOfCards constructor
67
68          // output deck
69          public void printCards()
70          {
71              // display 52 cards in two columns
72              for (int i = 0; i < list.size(); i++)
73                  System.out.printf("%-19s%s", list.get(i),
74                      ((i + 1) % 4 == 0) ? "%n" : "");
75          }
76
77          public static void main(String[] args)
78          {
```

Fig. 16.10 | Card shuffling and dealing with Collections method shuffle. (Part 2 of 3.)

```
79            DeckOfCards cards = new DeckOfCards();
80            cards.printCards();
81        }
82    } // end class DeckOfCards
```

Deuce of Clubs	Six of Spades	Nine of Diamonds	Ten of Hearts
Three of Diamonds	Five of Clubs	Deuce of Diamonds	Seven of Clubs
Three of Spades	Six of Diamonds	King of Clubs	Jack of Hearts
Ten of Spades	King of Diamonds	Eight of Spades	Six of Hearts
Nine of Clubs	Ten of Diamonds	Eight of Diamonds	Eight of Hearts
Ten of Clubs	Five of Hearts	Ace of Clubs	Deuce of Hearts
Queen of Diamonds	Ace of Diamonds	Four of Clubs	Nine of Hearts
Ace of Spades	Deuce of Spades	Ace of Hearts	Jack of Diamonds
Seven of Diamonds	Three of Hearts	Four of Spades	Four of Diamonds
Seven of Spades	King of Hearts	Seven of Hearts	Five of Diamonds
Eight of Clubs	Three of Clubs	Queen of Clubs	Queen of Spades
Six of Clubs	Nine of Spades	Four of Hearts	Jack of Clubs
Five of Spades	King of Spades	Jack of Spades	Queen of Hearts

Fig. 16.10 | Card shuffling and dealing with Collections method shuffle. (Part 3 of 3.)

Class Card (lines 8–41) represents a card in a deck of cards. Each Card has a face and a suit. Lines 10–12 declare two enum types—Face and Suit—which represent the face and the suit of the card, respectively. Method toString (lines 37–40) returns a String containing the face and suit of the Card separated by the string " of ". When an enum constant is converted to a String, the constant's identifier is used as the String representation. Normally we would use all uppercase letters for enum constants. In this example, we chose to use capital letters for only the first letter of each enum constant because we want the card to be displayed with initial capital letters for the face and the suit (e.g., "Ace of Spades").

Lines 55–62 populate the deck array with cards that have unique face and suit combinations. Both Face and Suit are public static enum types of class Card. To use these enum types outside of class Card, you must qualify each enum's type name with the name of the class in which it resides (i.e., Card) and a dot (.) separator. Hence, lines 55 and 57 use Card.Suit and Card.Face to declare the control variables of the for statements. Recall that method values of an enum type returns an array that contains all the constants of the enum type. Lines 55–62 use enhanced for statements to construct 52 new Cards.

The shuffling occurs in line 65, which calls static method shuffle of class Collections to shuffle the elements of the array. Method shuffle requires a List argument, so we must obtain a List view of the array before we can shuffle it. Line 64 invokes static method asList of class Arrays to get a List view of the deck array.

Method printCards (lines 69–75) displays the deck of cards in four columns. In each iteration of the loop, lines 73–74 output a card left justified in a 19-character field followed by either a newline or an empty string based on the number of cards output so far. If the number of cards is divisible by 4, a newline is output; otherwise, the empty string is output.

16.7.3 Methods reverse, fill, copy, max and min

Class Collections provides methods for *reversing, filling* and *copying* Lists. **Collections method reverse** reverses the order of the elements in a List, and **method fill** *overwrites* elements in a List with a specified value. The fill operation is useful for reinitializing a List. **Method copy** takes two arguments—a destination List and a source List. Each source List element is copied to the destination List. The destination List must be at least as long as the source List; otherwise, an IndexOutOfBoundsException occurs. If the destination List is longer, the elements not overwritten are unchanged.

Each method we've seen so far operates on Lists. Methods **min** and **max** each operate on any Collection. Method min returns the smallest element in a Collection, and method max returns the largest element in a Collection. Both of these methods can be called with a Comparator object as a second argument to perform *custom comparisons* of objects, such as the TimeComparator in Fig. 16.9. Figure 16.11 demonstrates methods reverse, fill, copy, max and min.

```java
1   // Fig. 16.11: Algorithms1.java
2   // Collections methods reverse, fill, copy, max and min.
3   import java.util.List;
4   import java.util.Arrays;
5   import java.util.Collections;
6
7   public class Algorithms1
8   {
9      public static void main(String[] args)
10     {
11        // create and display a List<Character>
12        Character[] letters = {'P', 'C', 'M'};
13        List<Character> list = Arrays.asList(letters); // get List
14        System.out.println("list contains: ");
15        output(list);
16
17        // reverse and display the List<Character>
18        Collections.reverse(list); // reverse order the elements
19        System.out.printf("%nAfter calling reverse, list contains:%n");
20        output(list);
21
22        // create copyList from an array of 3 Characters
23        Character[] lettersCopy = new Character[3];
24        List<Character> copyList = Arrays.asList(lettersCopy);
25
26        // copy the contents of list into copyList
27        Collections.copy(copyList, list);
28        System.out.printf("%nAfter copying, copyList contains:%n");
29        output(copyList);
30
31        // fill list with Rs
32        Collections.fill(list, 'R');
33        System.out.printf("%nAfter calling fill, list contains:%n");
34        output(list);
35     }
36
37     // output List information
38     private static void output(List<Character> listRef)
39     {
```

Fig. 16.11 | Collections methods reverse, fill, copy, max and min. (Part 1 of 2.)

```
40          System.out.print("The list is: ");
41
42          for (Character element : listRef)
43             System.out.printf("%s ", element);
44
45          System.out.printf("%nMax: %s", Collections.max(listRef));
46          System.out.printf(" Min: %s%n", Collections.min(listRef));
47       }
48    } // end class Algorithms1
```

```
list contains:
The list is: P C M
Max: P  Min: C

After calling reverse, list contains:
The list is: M C P
Max: P  Min: C

After copying, copyList contains:
The list is: M C P
Max: P  Min: C

After calling fill, list contains:
The list is: R R R
Max: R  Min: R
```

Fig. 16.11 | Collections methods reverse, fill, copy, max and min. (Part 2 of 2.)

Line 13 creates List<Character> variable list and initializes it with a List view of the Character array letters. Lines 14–15 output the current contents of the List. Line 18 calls Collections method reverse to reverse the order of list. Method reverse takes one List argument. Since list is a List view of array letters, the array's elements are now in reverse order. The reversed contents are output in lines 19–20. Line 27 uses Collections method copy to copy list's elements into copyList. Changes to copyList do not change letters, because copyList is a separate List that's not a List view of the array letters. Method copy requires two List arguments—the destination List and the source List. Line 32 calls Collections method fill to place the character 'R' in each list element. Because list is a List view of the array letters, this operation changes each element in letters to 'R'. Method fill requires a List for the first argument and an Object for the second argument—in this case, the Object is the *boxed* version of the character 'R'. Lines 45–46 call Collections methods max and min to find the largest and the smallest element of a Collection, respectively. Recall that interface List extends interface Collection, so a List *is a* Collection.

16.7.4 Method binarySearch

The high-speed binary search algorithm—which we discuss in detail in Section 19.4—is built into the Java collections framework as a static **Collections method binarySearch**. This method locates an object in a List (e.g., a LinkedList or an ArrayList). If the object is found, its index is returned. If the object is not found, binarySearch returns a negative value. Method `binarySearch` determines this negative value by first calculating the insertion point and making its sign negative. Then, `binarySearch` subtracts 1 from the insertion point to obtain the return value, which guarantees that method `binarySearch` returns positive numbers (>= 0) if and only if the object is found. If multiple elements in the list match the search key, there's no guarantee which one will be located first. Figure 16.12 uses method `binarySearch` to search for a series of strings in an `ArrayList`.

```java
 1   // Fig. 16.12: BinarySearchTest.java
 2   // Collections method binarySearch.
 3   import java.util.List;
 4   import java.util.Arrays;
 5   import java.util.Collections;
 6   import java.util.ArrayList;
 7
 8   public class BinarySearchTest
 9   {
10      public static void main(String[] args)
11      {
12         // create an ArrayList<String> from the contents of colors array
13         String[] colors = {"red", "white", "blue", "black", "yellow",
14            "purple", "tan", "pink"};
15         List<String> list =
16            new ArrayList<>(Arrays.asList(colors));
17
18         Collections.sort(list); // sort the ArrayList
19         System.out.printf("Sorted ArrayList: %s%n", list);
20
21         // search list for various values
22         printSearchResults(list, "black"); // first item
23         printSearchResults(list, "red"); // middle item
24         printSearchResults(list, "pink"); // last item
25         printSearchResults(list, "aqua"); // below lowest
26         printSearchResults(list, "gray"); // does not exist
27         printSearchResults(list, "teal"); // does not exist
28      }
29
30      // perform search and display result
31      private static void printSearchResults(
32         List<String> list, String key)
33      {
34         int result = 0;
35
36         System.out.printf("%nSearching for: %s%n", key);
37         result = Collections.binarySearch(list, key);
38
39         if (result >= 0)
40            System.out.printf("Found at index %d%n", result);
41         else
42            System.out.printf("Not Found (%d)%n",result);
43      }
44   } // end class BinarySearchTest
```

Fig. 16.12 | Collections method binarySearch. (Part 1 of 2.)

```
Sorted ArrayList: [black, blue, pink, purple, red, tan, white, yellow]

Searching for: black
Found at index 0

Searching for: red
Found at index 4

Searching for: pink
Found at index 2

Searching for: aqua
Not Found (-1)

Searching for: gray
Not Found (-3)

Searching for: teal
Not Found (-7)
```

Fig. 16.12 | Collections method binarySearch. (Part 2 of 2.)

Lines 15–16 initialize list with an ArrayList containing a copy of the elements in array colors. Collections method binarySearch expects its List argument's elements to be sorted in *ascending* order, so line 18 uses Collections method sort to sort the list. If the List argument's elements are *not* sorted, the result of using binarySearch is *undefined*. Line 19 outputs the sorted list. Lines 22–27 call method printSearchResults (lines 31–43) to perform searches and output the results. Line 37 calls Collections method binarySearch to search list for the specified key. Method binarySearch takes a List as the first argument and an Object as the second argument. Lines 39–42 output the results of the search. An overloaded version of binarySearch takes a Comparator object as its third argument, which specifies how binarySearch should compare the search key to the List's elements.

16.7.5 Methods addAll, frequency and disjoint

Class Collections also provides the methods addAll, frequency and disjoint. **Collections method addAll** takes two arguments—a Collection into which to *insert* the new element(s) and an array that provides elements to be inserted. **Collections method frequency** takes two arguments—a Collection to be searched and an Object to be searched for in the collection. Method frequency returns the number of times that the second argument appears in the collection. **Collections method disjoint** takes two Collections and returns true if they have *no elements in common*. Figure 16.13 demonstrates the use of methods addAll, frequency and disjoint.

```
1  // Fig. Fig. 16.13: Algorithms2.java
2  // Collections methods addAll, frequency and disjoint.
3  import java.util.ArrayList;
4  import java.util.List;
5  import java.util.Arrays;
6  import java.util.Collections;
```

Fig. 16.13 | Collections methods addAll, frequency and disjoint. (Part 1 of 2.)

```
7
8   public class Algorithms2
9   {
10      public static void main(String[] args)
11      {
12         // initialize list1 and list2
13         String[] colors = {"red", "white", "yellow", "blue"};
14         List<String> list1 = Arrays.asList(colors);
15         ArrayList<String> list2 = new ArrayList<>();
16
17         list2.add("black"); // add "black" to the end of list2
18         list2.add("red"); // add "red" to the end of list2
19         list2.add("green"); // add "green" to the end of list2
20
21         System.out.print("Before addAll, list2 contains: ");
22
23         // display elements in list2
24         for (String s : list2)
25            System.out.printf("%s ", s);
26
27         Collections.addAll(list2, colors); // add colors Strings to list2
28
29         System.out.printf("%nAfter addAll, list2 contains: ");
30
31         // display elements in list2
32         for (String s : list2)
33            System.out.printf("%s ", s);
34
35         // get frequency of "red"
36         int frequency = Collections.frequency(list2, "red");
37         System.out.printf(
38            "%nFrequency of red in list2: %d%n", frequency);
39
40         // check whether list1 and list2 have elements in common
41         boolean disjoint = Collections.disjoint(list1, list2);
42
43         System.out.printf("list1 and list2 %s elements in common%n",
44            (disjoint ? "do not have" : "have"));
45      }
46   } // end class Algorithms2
```

```
Before addAll, list2 contains: black red green
After addAll, list2 contains: black red green red white yellow blue
Frequency of red in list2: 2
list1 and list2 have elements in common
```

Fig. 16.13 | Collections methods addAll, frequency and disjoint. (Part 2 of 2.)

Line 14 initializes list1 with elements in array colors, and lines 17–19 add Strings "black", "red" and "green" to list2. Line 27 invokes method addAll to add elements in array colors to list2. Line 36 gets the frequency of String "red" in list2 using method frequency. Line 41 invokes method disjoint to test whether Collections list1 and list2 have elements in common, which they do in this example.

16.8 Stack Class of Package `java.util`

We introduced the concept of a *stack* in Section 5.6 when we discussed the method-call stack. In Chapter 21, Custom Generic Data Structures, we'll learn how to build data structures, including *linked lists*, *stacks*, *queues* and *trees*. In a world of software reuse, rather than building data structures as we need them, we can often take advantage of existing data structures. In this section, we investigate class **Stack** in the Java utilities package (`java.util`).

Class Stack extends class Vector to implement a stack data structure. Figure 16.14 demonstrates several Stack methods. For the details of class Stack, visit http://docs.oracle.com/javase/7/docs/api/java/util/Stack.html.

```java
1   // Fig. 16.14: StackTest.java
2   // Stack class of package java.util.
3   import java.util.Stack;
4   import java.util.EmptyStackException;
5
6   public class StackTest
7   {
8      public static void main(String[] args)
9      {
10        Stack<Number> stack = new Stack<>(); // create a Stack
11
12        // use push method
13        stack.push(12L); // push long value 12L
14        System.out.println("Pushed 12L");
15        printStack(stack);
16        stack.push(34567); // push int value 34567
17        System.out.println("Pushed 34567");
18        printStack(stack);
19        stack.push(1.0F); // push float value 1.0F
20        System.out.println("Pushed 1.0F");
21        printStack(stack);
22        stack.push(1234.5678); // push double value 1234.5678
23        System.out.println("Pushed 1234.5678 ");
24        printStack(stack);
25
26        // remove items from stack
27        try
28        {
29           Number removedObject = null;
30
31           // pop elements from stack
32           while (true)
33           {
34              removedObject = stack.pop(); // use pop method
35              System.out.printf("Popped %s%n", removedObject);
36              printStack(stack);
37           }
38        }
39        catch (EmptyStackException emptyStackException)
40        {
```

Fig. 16.14 | Stack class of package `java.util`. (Part 1 of 2.)

```
41              emptyStackException.printStackTrace();
42          }
43      }
44
45      // display Stack contents
46      private static void printStack(Stack<Number> stack)
47      {
48          if (stack.isEmpty())
49              System.out.printf("stack is empty%n%n"); // the stack is empty
50          else // stack is not empty
51              System.out.printf("stack contains: %s (top)%n", stack);
52      }
53  } // end class StackTest
```

```
Pushed 12L
stack contains: [12] (top)
Pushed 34567
stack contains: [12, 34567] (top)
Pushed 1.0F
stack contains: [12, 34567, 1.0] (top)
Pushed 1234.5678
stack contains: [12, 34567, 1.0, 1234.5678] (top)
Popped 1234.5678
stack contains: [12, 34567, 1.0] (top)
Popped 1.0
stack contains: [12, 34567] (top)
Popped 34567
stack contains: [12] (top)
Popped 12
stack is empty

java.util.EmptyStackException
        at java.util.Stack.peek(Unknown Source)
        at java.util.Stack.pop(Unknown Source)
        at StackTest.main(StackTest.java:34)
```

Fig. 16.14 | Stack class of package java.util. (Part 2 of 2.)

Error-Prevention Tip 16.1

Because Stack extends Vector, all public Vector methods can be called on Stack objects, even if the methods do not represent conventional stack operations. For example, Vector method add can be used to insert an element anywhere in a stack—an operation that could "corrupt" the stack. When manipulating a Stack, only methods push and pop should be used to add elements to and remove elements from the Stack, respectively. In Section 21.5, we create a Stack class using composition so that the Stack provides in its public interface only the capabilities that should be allowed by a Stack.

Line 10 creates an empty Stack of Numbers. Class Number (in package java.lang) is the superclass of the type-wrapper classes for the primitive numeric types (e.g., Integer, Double). By creating a Stack of Numbers, objects of any class that extends Number can be pushed onto the Stack. Lines 13, 16, 19 and 22 each call Stack method **push** to add a Number object to the *top* of the stack. Note the literals 12L (line 13) and 1.0F (line 19). Any integer literal that has the **suffix L** is a long value. An integer literal without a suffix is an int value. Similarly, any floating-point literal that has the **suffix F** is a float value. A floating-point literal without a suffix is a double value. You can learn more about numeric literals in the *Java Language Specification* at http://docs.oracle.com/javase/ specs/jls/se7/html/jls-15.html#jls-15.8.1.

An infinite loop (lines 32–37) calls **Stack method pop** to remove the *top* element of the stack. The method returns a Number reference to the removed element. If there are no elements in the Stack, method pop throws an **EmptyStackException**, which terminates the loop. Class Stack also declares **method peek**. This method returns the *top* element of the stack *without* popping the element off the stack.

Method printStack (lines 46–52) displays the stack's contents. The current *top* of the stack (the last value pushed onto the stack) is the *first* value printed. Line 48 calls **Stack method isEmpty** (inherited by Stack from class Vector) to determine whether the stack is empty. If it's empty, the method returns true; otherwise, false.

16.9 Class PriorityQueue and Interface Queue

Recall that a queue is a collection that represents a waiting line—typically, *insertions* are made at the back of a queue and *deletions* are made from the front. In Section 21.6, we'll discuss and implement a queue data structure. In this section, we investigate Java's **Queue** interface and **PriorityQueue** class from package java.util. Interface Queue extends interface Collection and provides additional operations for *inserting, removing* and *inspecting* elements in a queue. PriorityQueue, which implements the Queue interface, orders elements by their natural ordering as specified by Comparable elements' compareTo method or by a Comparator object that's supplied to the constructor.

Class PriorityQueue provides functionality that enables *insertions in sorted order* into the underlying data structure and *deletions* from the *front* of the underlying data structure. When adding elements to a PriorityQueue, the elements are inserted in priority order such that the *highest-priority element* (i.e., the largest value) will be the first element removed from the PriorityQueue.

The common PriorityQueue operations are **offer** to *insert* an element at the appropriate location based on priority order, **poll** to *remove* the highest-priority element of the priority queue (i.e., the head of the queue), **peek** to get a reference to the highest-priority element of the priority queue (without removing that element), **clear** to *remove all elements* in the priority queue and **size** to get the number of elements in the priority queue.

Figure 16.15 demonstrates the PriorityQueue class. Line 10 creates a PriorityQueue that stores Doubles with an *initial capacity* of 11 elements and orders the elements according to the object's natural ordering (the defaults for a PriorityQueue). PriorityQueue is a generic class. Line 10 instantiates a PriorityQueue with a type argument Double. Class PriorityQueue provides five additional constructors. One of these takes an int and a Comparator object to create a PriorityQueue with the *initial capacity* specified by the int and the *ordering* by the Comparator. Lines 13–15 use method offer to add elements to the priority queue. Method offer throws a NullPointerException if the program attempts to add a null object to the queue. The loop in lines 20–24 uses method size to determine whether the priority queue is *empty* (line 20). While there are more elements, line 22 uses PriorityQueue method peek to retrieve the *highest-priority element* in the queue for output (*without* actually removing it from the queue). Line 23 removes the highest-priority element in the queue with method poll, which returns the removed element.

```
 1   // Fig. 16.15: PriorityQueueTest.java
 2   // PriorityQueue test program.
 3   import java.util.PriorityQueue;
 4
 5   public class PriorityQueueTest
 6   {
 7      public static void main(String[] args)
 8      {
 9         // queue of capacity 11
10         PriorityQueue<Double> queue = new PriorityQueue<>();
11
12         // insert elements to queue
13         queue.offer(3.2);
14         queue.offer(9.8);
15         queue.offer(5.4);
16
17         System.out.print("Polling from queue: ");
18
19         // display elements in queue
20         while (queue.size() > 0)
21         {
22            System.out.printf("%.1f ", queue.peek()); // view top element
23            queue.poll(); // remove top element
24         }
25      }
26   } // end class PriorityQueueTest
```

```
Polling from queue: 3.2 5.4 9.8
```

Fig. 16.15 | PriorityQueue test program.

16.10 Sets

A **Set** is an *unordered* Collection of unique elements (i.e., *no duplicates*). The collections framework contains several Set implementations, including **HashSet** and **TreeSet**. HashSet stores its elements in a *hash table*, and TreeSet stores its elements in a *tree*. Hash tables are presented in Section 16.11. Trees are discussed in Section 21.7.

Figure 16.16 uses a HashSet to *remove duplicate strings* from a List. Recall that both List and Collection are generic types, so line 16 creates a List that contains String objects, and line 20 passes a Collection of Strings to method printNonDuplicates. Method printNonDuplicates (lines 24–35) takes a Collection argument. Line 27 constructs a HashSet<String> from the Collection<String> argument. By definition, Sets do *not* contain duplicates, so when the HashSet is constructed, it *removes any duplicates* in the Collection. Lines 31–32 output elements in the Set.

```
 1   // Fig. 16.16: SetTest.java
 2   // HashSet used to remove duplicate values from array of strings.
 3   import java.util.List;
 4   import java.util.Arrays;
```

Fig. 16.16 | HashSet used to remove duplicate values from an array of strings. (Part 1 of 2.)

```
5   import java.util.HashSet;
6   import java.util.Set;
7   import java.util.Collection;
8
9   public class SetTest
10  {
11     public static void main(String[] args)
12     {
13        // create and display a List<String>
14        String[] colors = {"red", "white", "blue", "green", "gray",
15           "orange", "tan", "white", "cyan", "peach", "gray", "orange"};
16        List<String> list = Arrays.asList(colors);
17        System.out.printf("List: %s%n", list);
18
19        // eliminate duplicates then print the unique values
20        printNonDuplicates(list);
21     }
22
23     // create a Set from a Collection to eliminate duplicates
24     private static void printNonDuplicates(Collection<String> values)
25     {
26        // create a HashSet
27        Set<String> set = new HashSet<>(values);
28
29        System.out.printf("%nNonduplicates are: ");
30
31        for (String value : set)
32           System.out.printf("%s ", value);
33
34        System.out.println();
35     }
36  } // end class SetTest
```

```
List: [red, white, blue, green, gray, orange, tan, white, cyan, peach, gray,
orange]

Nonduplicates are: orange green white peach gray cyan red blue tan
```

Fig. 16.16 | HashSet used to remove duplicate values from an array of strings. (Part 2 of 2.)

Sorted Sets

The collections framework also includes the **SortedSet interface** (which extends Set) for sets that maintain their elements in *sorted* order—either the *elements' natural order* (e.g., numbers are in *ascending* order) or an order specified by a Comparator. Class TreeSet implements SortedSet. The program in Fig. 16.17 places Strings into a TreeSet. The Strings are sorted as they're added to the TreeSet. This example also demonstrates *range-view* methods, which enable a program to view a portion of a collection.

Line 14 creates a TreeSet<String> that contains the elements of array colors, then assigns the new TreeSet<String> to SortedSet<String> variable tree. Line 17 outputs the initial set of strings using method printSet (lines 33–39), which we discuss momentarily. Line 31 calls **TreeSet method headSet** to get a subset of the TreeSet in which every element is less than "orange". The view returned from headSet is then output with printSet. If any changes are made to the subset, they'll *also* be made to the original TreeSet, because the subset returned by headSet is a view of the TreeSet.

Line 25 calls **TreeSet method tailSet** to get a subset in which each element is greater than or equal to "orange", then outputs the result. Any changes made through the tailSet view are made to the original TreeSet. Lines 28–29 call **SortedSet methods first** and **last** to get the smallest and largest elements of the set, respectively.

Method printSet (lines 33–39) accepts a SortedSet as an argument and prints it. Lines 35–36 print each element of the SortedSet using the enhanced for statement.

```
1   // Fig. 16.17: SortedSetTest.java
2   // Using SortedSets and TreeSets.
3   import java.util.Arrays;
4   import java.util.SortedSet;
5   import java.util.TreeSet;
6
7   public class SortedSetTest
8   {
9      public static void main(String[] args)
10     {
11        // create TreeSet from array colors
12        String[] colors = {"yellow", "green", "black", "tan", "grey",
13           "white", "orange", "red", "green"};
14        SortedSet<String> tree = new TreeSet<>(Arrays.asList(colors));
15
16        System.out.print("sorted set: ");
17        printSet(tree);
18
19        // get headSet based on "orange"
20        System.out.print("headSet (\"orange\"):  ");
21        printSet(tree.headSet("orange")  );
22
23        // get tailSet based upon "orange"
24        System.out.print("tailSet (\"orange\"):  ");
25        printSet(tree.tailSet("orange")  );
26
27        // get first and last elements
28        System.out.printf("first: %s%n", tree.first());
29        System.out.printf("last : %s%n", tree.last());
30     }
31
32     // output SortedSet using enhanced for statement
33     private static void printSet(SortedSet<String> set)
34     {
35        for (String s : set)
36           System.out.printf("%s ", s);
37
38        System.out.println();
39     }
40  } // end class SortedSetTest
```

Fig. 16.17 | Using SortedSets and TreeSets. (Part 1 of 2.)

```
sorted set: black green grey orange red tan white yellow
headSet ("orange"):  black green grey
tailSet ("orange"):  orange red tan white yellow
first: black
last : yellow
```

Fig. 16.17 | Using SortedSets and TreeSets. (Part 2 of 2.)

16.11 Maps

Maps associate *keys* to *values*. The keys in a Map must be *unique*, but the associated values need not be. If a Map contains both unique keys and unique values, it's said to implement a **one-to-one mapping**. If only the keys are unique, the Map is said to implement a **many-to-one mapping**—many keys can map to one value.

Maps differ from Sets in that Maps contain keys and values, whereas Sets contain only values. Three of the several classes that implement interface Map are **Hashtable**, **HashMap** and **TreeMap**. Hashtables and HashMaps store elements in hash tables, and TreeMaps store elements in trees. This section discusses hash tables and provides an example that uses a HashMap to store key–value pairs. **Interface SortedMap** extends Map and maintains its keys in *sorted* order—either the elements' *natural* order or an order specified by a Comparator. Class TreeMap implements SortedMap.

Map Implementation with Hash Tables

When a program creates objects, it may need to store and retrieve them efficiently. Storing and retrieving information with arrays is efficient if some aspect of your data directly matches a numerical key value and if the *keys are unique* and tightly packed. If you have 100 employees with nine-digit social security numbers and you want to store and retrieve employee data by using the social security number as a key, the task will require an array with over 800 million elements, because nine-digit Social Security numbers must begin with 001–899 (excluding 666) as per the Social Security Administration's website

```
http://www.socialsecurity.gov/employer/randomization.html
```

This is impractical for virtually all applications that use social security numbers as keys. A program having an array that large could achieve high performance for both storing and retrieving employee records by simply using the social security number as the array index.

Numerous applications have this problem—namely, that either the keys are of the wrong type (e.g., not positive integers that correspond to array subscripts) or they're of the right type, but *sparsely* spread over a *huge range*. What is needed is a high-speed scheme for converting keys such as social security numbers, inventory part numbers and the like into unique array indices. Then, when an application needs to store something, the scheme could convert the application's key rapidly into an index, and the record could be stored at that slot in the array. Retrieval is accomplished the same way: Once the application has a key for which it wants to retrieve a data record, the application simply applies the conversion to the key—this produces the array index where the data is stored and retrieved.

The scheme we describe here is the basis of a technique called **hashing**. Why the name? When we convert a key into an array index, we literally scramble the bits, forming a kind of "mishmashed," or hashed, number. The number actually has no real significance beyond its usefulness in storing and retrieving a particular data record.

A glitch in the scheme is called a **collision**—this occurs when two different keys "hash into" the same cell (or element) in the array. We cannot store two values in the same space, so we need to find an alternative home for all values beyond the first that hash to a particular array index. There are many schemes for doing this. One is to "hash again" (i.e., to apply another hashing transformation to the key to provide a next candidate cell in the array). The hashing process is designed to *distribute* the values throughout the table, so the assumption is that an available cell will be found with just a few hashes.

Another scheme uses one hash to locate the first candidate cell. If that cell is occupied, successive cells are searched in order until an available cell is found. Retrieval works the same way: The key is hashed once to determine the initial location and check whether it contains the desired data. If it does, the search is finished. If it does not, successive cells are searched linearly until the desired data is found.

The most popular solution to hash-table collisions is to have each cell of the table be a hash "bucket," typically a linked list of all the key–value pairs that hash to that cell. This is the solution that Java's Hashtable and HashMap classes (from package java.util) implement. Both Hashtable and HashMap implement the Map interface. The primary differences between them are that HashMap is *unsynchronized* (multiple threads should not modify a HashMap concurrently) and allows null keys and null values.

A hash table's **load factor** affects the performance of hashing schemes. The load factor is the ratio of the number of occupied cells in the hash table to the total number of cells in the hash table. The closer this ratio gets to 1.0, the greater the chance of collisions.

Performance Tip 16.2

The load factor in a hash table is a classic example of a memory-space/execution-time trade-off: By increasing the load factor, we get better memory utilization, but the program runs slower, due to increased hashing collisions. By decreasing the load factor, we get better program speed, because of reduced hashing collisions, but we get poorer memory utilization, because a larger portion of the hash table remains empty.

Computer science students study hashing schemes in courses called "Data Structures" and "Algorithms." Classes Hashtable and HashMap enable you to use hashing without having to implement hash-table mechanisms—a classic example of reuse. This concept is profoundly important in our study of object-oriented programming. As discussed in earlier chapters, classes encapsulate and hide complexity (i.e., implementation details) and offer user-friendly interfaces. Properly crafting classes to exhibit such behavior is one of the most valued skills in the field of object-oriented programming. Figure 16.18 uses a HashMap to count the number of occurrences of each word in a string.

```
1   // Fig. 16.18: WordTypeCount.java
2   // Program counts the number of occurrences of each word in a String.
3   import java.util.Map;
4   import java.util.HashMap;
5   import java.util.Set;
6   import java.util.TreeSet;
```

Fig. 16.18 | Program counts the number of occurrences of each word in a String. (Part 1 of 3.)

```
7    import java.util.Scanner;
8
9    public class WordTypeCount
10   {
11      public static void main(String[] args)
12      {
13         // create HashMap to store String keys and Integer values
14         Map<String, Integer> myMap = new HashMap<>();
15
16         createMap(myMap); // create map based on user input
17         displayMap(myMap); // display map content
18      }
19
20      // create map from user input
21      private static void createMap(Map<String, Integer> map)
22      {
23         Scanner scanner = new Scanner(System.in); // create scanner
24         System.out.println("Enter a string:"); // prompt for user input
25         String input = scanner.nextLine();
26
27         // tokenize the input
28         String[] tokens = input.split(" ");
29
30         // processing input text
31         for (String token : tokens)
32         {
33            String word = token.toLowerCase(); // get lowercase word
34
35            // if the map contains the word
36            if (map.containsKey(word)) // is word in map
37            {
38               int count = map.get(word); // get current count
39               map.put(word, count + 1); // increment count
40            }
41            else
42               map.put(word, 1); // add new word with a count of 1 to map
43         }
44      }
45
46      // display map content
47      private static void displayMap(Map<String, Integer> map)
48      {
49         Set<String> keys = map.keySet(); // get keys
50
51         // sort keys
52         TreeSet<String> sortedKeys = new TreeSet<>(keys);
53
54         System.out.printf("%nMap contains:%nKey\t\tValue%n");
55
56         // generate output for each key in map
57         for (String key : sortedKeys)
58            System.out.printf("%-10s%10s%n", key, map.get(key));
59
```

Fig. 16.18 | Program counts the number of occurrences of each word in a String. (Part 2 of 3.)

```
60          System.out.printf(
61              "%nsize: %d%nisEmpty: %b%n", map.size(), map.isEmpty());
62      }
63  } // end class WordTypeCount
```

```
Enter a string:
this is a sample sentence with several words this is another sample
sentence with several different words

Map contains:
Key            Value
a                1
another          1
different        1
is               2
sample           2
sentence         2
several          2
this             2
with             2
words            2

size: 10
isEmpty: false
```

Fig. 16.18 | Program counts the number of occurrences of each word in a `String`. (Part 3 of 3.)

Line 14 creates an empty `HashMap` with a *default initial capacity* (16 elements) and a default load factor (0.75)—these defaults are built into the implementation of `HashMap`. When the number of occupied slots in the `HashMap` becomes greater than the capacity times the load factor, the capacity is doubled automatically. `HashMap` is a generic class that takes two type arguments—the type of key (i.e., `String`) and the type of value (i.e., `Integer`). Recall that the type arguments passed to a generic class must be reference types, hence the second type argument is `Integer`, not `int`.

Line 16 calls method `createMap` (lines 21–44), which uses a `Map` to store the number of occurrences of each word in the sentence. Line 25 obtains the user input, and line 28 tokenizes it. Lines 31–43 convert the next token to lowercase letters (line 33), then call **Map method `containsKey`** (line 36) to determine whether the word is in the map (and thus has occurred previously in the string). If the `Map` does *not* contain the word, line 42 uses **Map method `put`** to create a new entry, with the word as the key and an `Integer` object containing 1 as the value. Autoboxing occurs when the program passes integer 1 to method `put`, because the map stores the number of occurrences as an `Integer`. If the word does exist in the map, line 38 uses **Map method `get`** to obtain the key's associated value (the count) in the map. Line 39 increments that value and uses `put` to replace the key's associated value. Method `put` returns the key's prior associated value, or `null` if the key was not in the map.

Error-Prevention Tip 16.2

Always use immutable keys with a `Map`. The key determines where the corresponding value is placed. If the key has changed since the insert operation, when you subsequently attempt to retrieve that value, it might not be found. In this chapter's examples, we use `String`s as keys and `String`s are immutable.

Method `displayMap` (lines 47–62) displays all the entries in the map. It uses **HashMap method keySet** (line 49) to get a set of the keys. The keys have type `String` in the map, so method keySet returns a generic type `Set` with type parameter specified to be `String`. Line 52 creates a `TreeSet` of the keys, in which the keys are sorted. The loop in lines 57–58 accesses each key and its value in the map. Line 58 displays each key and its value using format specifier %-10s to *left align* each key and format specifier %10s to *right align* each value. The keys are displayed in *ascending* order. Line 61 calls **Map method size** to get the number of key–value pairs in the Map. Line 61 also calls **Map method isEmpty**, which returns a `boolean` indicating whether the Map is empty.

16.12 Properties Class

A **Properties** object is a *persistent* `Hashtable` that stores *key–value pairs* of `Strings`—assuming that you use methods **setProperty** and **getProperty** to manipulate the table rather than inherited `Hashtable` methods put and get. By "persistent," we mean that the `Properties` object can be written to an output stream (possibly a file) and read back in through an input stream. A common use of `Properties` objects in prior versions of Java was to maintain application-configuration data or user preferences for applications. [*Note:* The **Preferences API** (package **java.util.prefs**) is meant to replace this particular use of class `Properties` but is beyond the scope of this book. To learn more, visit http://bit.ly/JavaPreferences.] Class `Properties` extends class `Hashtable<Object, Object>`. Figure 16.19 demonstrates several methods of class `Properties`.

Line 13 creates an empty `Properties` table with no default properties. Class `Properties` also provides an overloaded constructor that receives a reference to a `Properties` object containing default property values. Lines 16 and 17 each call `Properties` method setProperty to store a value for the specified key. If the key does not exist in the `table`, setProperty returns `null`; otherwise, it returns the previous value for that key.

```
1    // Fig. 16.19: PropertiesTest.java
2    // Demonstrates class Properties of the java.util package.
3    import java.io.FileOutputStream;
4    import java.io.FileInputStream;
5    import java.io.IOException;
6    import java.util.Properties;
7    import java.util.Set;
8
9    public class PropertiesTest
10   {
11      public static void main(String[] args)
12      {
13         Properties table = new Properties();
14
15         // set properties
16         table.setProperty("color", "blue");
17         table.setProperty("width", "200");
18
19         System.out.println("After setting properties");
20         listProperties(table);
```

Fig. 16.19 | Properties class of package `java.util`. (Part 1 of 3.)

```
21
22        // replace property value
23        table.setProperty("color", "red");
24
25        System.out.println("After replacing properties");
26        listProperties(table);
27
28        saveProperties(table);
29
30        table.clear(); // empty table
31
32        System.out.println("After clearing properties");
33        listProperties(table);
34
35        loadProperties(table);
36
37        // get value of property color
38        Object value = table.getProperty("color");
39
40        // check if value is in table
41        if (value != null)
42            System.out.printf("Property color's value is %s%n", value);
43        else
44            System.out.println("Property color is not in table");
45     }
46
47    // save properties to a file
48    private static void saveProperties(Properties props)
49    {
50        // save contents of table
51        try
52        {
53            FileOutputStream output = new FileOutputStream("props.dat");
54            props.store(output, "Sample Properties"); // save properties
55            output.close();
56            System.out.println("After saving properties");
57            listProperties(props);
58        }
59        catch (IOException ioException)
60        {
61            ioException.printStackTrace();
62        }
63     }
64
65    // load properties from a file
66    private static void loadProperties(Properties props)
67    {
68        // load contents of table
69        try
70        {
71            FileInputStream input = new FileInputStream("props.dat");
72            props.load(input); // load properties
73            input.close();
```

Fig. 16.19 | Properties class of package `java.util`. (Part 2 of 3.)

```
74                System.out.println("After loading properties");
75                listProperties(props);
76          }
77          catch (IOException ioException)
78          {
79                ioException.printStackTrace();
80          }
81    }
82
83    // output property values
84    private static void listProperties(Properties props)
85    {
86        Set<Object> keys = props.keySet(); // get property names
87
88        // output name/value pairs
89        for (Object key : keys)
90            System.out.printf(
91                "%s\t%s%n", key, props.getProperty((String) key));
92
93        System.out.println();
94    }
95 } // end class PropertiesTest
```

```
After setting properties
color    blue
width    200

After replacing properties
color    red
width    200

After saving properties
color    red
width    200

After clearing properties

After loading properties
color    red
width    200

Property color's value is red
```

Fig. 16.19 | Properties class of package java.util. (Part 3 of 3.)

Line 38 calls Properties method getProperty to locate the value associated with the specified key. If the key is *not* found in this Properties object, getProperty returns null. An overloaded version of this method receives a second argument that specifies the default value to return if getProperty cannot locate the key.

Line 54 calls **Properties method store** to save the Properties object's contents to the OutputStream specified as the first argument (in this case, a FileOutputStream). The second argument, a String, is a description written into the file. **Properties method list**, which takes a PrintStream argument, is useful for displaying the list of properties.

Line 72 calls **Properties method load** to restore the contents of the Properties object from the InputStream specified as the first argument (in this case, a FileInput-Stream). Line 86 calls Properties method keySet to obtain a Set of the property names. Because class Properties stores its contents as Objects, a Set of Object references is returned. Line 91 obtains the value of a property by passing a key to method getProperty.

16.13 Synchronized Collections

In Chapter 23, we discuss *multithreading*. Except for Vector and Hashtable, the collections in the collections framework are *unsynchronized* by default, so they can operate efficiently when multithreading is not required. Because they're unsynchronized, however, concurrent access to a Collection by multiple threads could cause indeterminate results or fatal errors—as we demonstrate in Chapter 23. To prevent potential threading problems, **synchronization wrappers** are used for collections that might be accessed by multiple threads. A **wrapper** object receives method calls, adds thread synchronization (to prevent concurrent access to the collection) and *delegates* the calls to the wrapped collection object. The Collections API provides a set of static methods for wrapping collections as synchronized versions. Method headers for the synchronization wrappers are listed in Fig. 16.20. Details about these methods are available at `http://docs.oracle.com/javase/7/docs/api/java/util/Collections.html`. All these methods take a generic type and return a *synchronized view* of the generic type. For example, the following code creates a synchronized List (list2) that stores String objects:

```
List<String> list1 = new ArrayList<>();
List<String> list2 = Collections.synchronizedList(list1);
```

```
public static method headers

<T> Collection<T> synchronizedCollection(Collection<T> c)
<T> List<T> synchronizedList(List<T> aList)
<T> Set<T> synchronizedSet(Set<T> s)
<T> SortedSet<T> synchronizedSortedSet(SortedSet<T> s)
<K, V> Map<K, V> synchronizedMap(Map<K, V> m)
<K, V> SortedMap<K, V> synchronizedSortedMap(SortedMap<K, V> m)
```

Fig. 16.20 | Synchronization wrapper methods.

16.14 Unmodifiable Collections

The Collections class provides a set of static methods that create **unmodifiable wrappers** for collections. Unmodifiable wrappers throw UnsupportedOperationExceptions if attempts are made to modify the collection. In an unmodifiable collection, the references stored in the collection are not modifiable, but the objects they refer *are modifiable* unless they belong to an immutable class like String. Headers for these methods are listed in Fig. 16.21. Details about these methods are available at `http://docs.oracle.com/javase/7/docs/api/java/util/Collections.html`. All these methods take a generic type and return an unmodifiable view of the generic type. For example, the following code creates an unmodifiable List (list2) that stores String objects:

```
List<String> list1 = new ArrayList<>();
List<String> list2 = Collections.unmodifiableList(list1);
```

Software Engineering Observation 16.6

You can use an unmodifiable wrapper to create a collection that offers read-only access to others, while allowing read–write access to yourself. You do this simply by giving others a reference to the unmodifiable wrapper while retaining for yourself a reference to the original collection.

```
public static method headers

<T> Collection<T> unmodifiableCollection(Collection<T> c)
<T> List<T> unmodifiableList(List<T> aList)
<T> Set<T> unmodifiableSet(Set<T> s)
<T> SortedSet<T> unmodifiableSortedSet(SortedSet<T> s)
<K, V> Map<K, V> unmodifiableMap(Map<K, V> m)
<K, V> SortedMap<K, V> unmodifiableSortedMap(SortedMap<K, V> m)
```

Fig. 16.21 | Unmodifiable wrapper methods.

16.15 Abstract Implementations

The collections framework provides various abstract implementations of Collection interfaces from which you can quickly "flesh out" complete customized implementations. These abstract implementations include a thin Collection implementation called an **AbstractCollection**, a List implementation that allows *array-like access* to its elements called an **AbstractList**, a Map implementation called an **AbstractMap**, a List implementation that allows *sequential access* (from beginning to end) to its elements called an **AbstractSequentialList**, a Set implementation called an **AbstractSet** and a Queue implementation called **AbstractQueue**. You can learn more about these classes at http://docs.oracle.com/javase/7/docs/api/java/util/package-summary.html. To write a *custom* implementation, you can extend the abstract implementation that best meets your needs, implement each of the class's abstract methods and override the class's concrete methods as necessary.

16.16 Wrap-Up

This chapter introduced the Java collections framework. You learned the collection hierarchy and how to use the collections-framework interfaces to program with collections polymorphically. You used classes ArrayList and LinkedList, which both implement the List interface. We presented Java's built-in interfaces and classes for manipulating stacks and queues. You used several predefined methods for manipulating collections. You learned how to use the Set interface and class HashSet to manipulate an unordered collection of unique values. We continued our presentation of sets with the SortedSet interface and class TreeSet for manipulating a sorted collection of unique values. You then learned about Java's interfaces and classes for manipulating key–value pairs—Map, SortedMap, Hashtable, HashMap and TreeMap. We discussed the specialized Properties class for manipulating key–value pairs of Strings that can be stored to a file and retrieved from a file. Finally, we discussed the Collections class's static methods for obtaining unmodifiable and synchronized views of collections. For additional information on the collections framework, visit http://docs.oracle.com/javase/7/docs/technotes/guides/collections. In Chapter 17, Java SE 8 Lambdas and Streams, you'll use Java SE 8's new functional programming capabilities to simplify collection operations. In Chapter 23, Concurrency, you'll learn how to improve performance on multi-core systems using Java's concurrent collections and parallel stream operations.

Summary

Section 16.1 Introduction
- The Java collections framework provides prebuilt data structures and methods to manipulate them.

Section 16.2 Collections Overview
- A collection is an object that can hold references to other objects.
- The classes and interfaces of the collections framework are in package java.util.

Section 16.3 Type-Wrapper Classes
- Type-wrapper classes (e.g., Integer, Double, Boolean) enable programmers to manipulate primitive-type values as objects (p. 679). Objects of these classes can be used in collections.

Section 16.4 Autoboxing and Auto-Unboxing
- Boxing (p. 679) converts a primitive value to an object of the corresponding type-wrapper class. Unboxing (p. 679) converts a type-wrapper object to the corresponding primitive value.
- Java performs boxing conversions and unboxing conversions automatically.

Section 16.5 Interface Collection and Class Collections
- Interfaces Set and List extend Collection (p. 678), which contains operations for adding, clearing, comparing and retaining objects in a collection, and method iterator (p. 683) to obtain a collection's Iterator (p. 679).
- Class Collections (p. 680) provides static methods for manipulating collections.

Section 16.6 Lists
- A List (p. 686) is an ordered Collection that can contain duplicate elements.
- Interface List is implemented by classes ArrayList, LinkedList and Vector. ArrayList (p. 680) is a resizable-array implementation. LinkedList (p. 680) is a linkedlist implementation of a List.
- Java SE 7 supports type inferencing with the <> notation in statements that declare and create generic type variables and objects.
- Iterator method hasNext (p. 683) determines whether a Collection contains another element. Method next returns a reference to the next object in the Collection and advances the Iterator.
- Method subList (p. 686) returns a view into a List. Changes made to this view are also made to the List.

- Method clear (p. 686) removes elements from a List.
- Method toArray (p. 687) returns the contents of a collection as an array.

Section 16.7 Collections Methods

- Algorithms sort (p. 689), binarySearch, reverse (p. 694), shuffle (p. 692), fill (p. 694), copy, addAll (p. 685), frequency and disjoint operate on Lists. Algorithms min and max (p. 695) operate on Collections.
- Algorithm addAll appends all the elements in an array to a collection (p. 698), frequency (p. 698) calculates how many elements in the collection are equal to the specified element, and disjoint (p. 698) determines whether two collections have elements in common.
- Algorithms min and max find the smallest and largest items in a collection.
- The Comparator interface (p. 689) provides a means of sorting a Collection's elements in an order other than their natural order.
- Collections method reverseOrder (p. 690) returns a Comparator object that can be used with sort to sort a collection's elements in reverse order.
- Algorithm shuffle (p. 692) randomly orders the elements of a List.
- Algorithm binarySearch (p. 696) locates an Object in a sorted List.

Section 16.8 **Stack** Class of Package **java.util**

- Class Stack (p. 700) extends Vector. Stack method push (p. 701) adds its argument to the top of the stack. Method pop (p. 702) removes the top element of the stack. Method peek returns a reference to the top element without removing it. Stack method isEmpty (p. 702) determines whether the stack is empty.

Section 16.9 Class **PriorityQueue** and Interface **Queue**

- Interface Queue (p. 702) extends interface Collection and provides additional operations for inserting, removing and inspecting elements in a queue.
- PriorityQueue (p. 702) implements interface Queue and orders elements by their natural ordering or by a Comparator object that's supplied to the constructor.
- PriorityQueue method offer (p. 702) inserts an element at the appropriate location based on priority order. Method poll (p. 702) removes the highest-priority element of the priority queue. Method peek (peek) gets a reference to the highest-priority element of the priority queue. Method clear (p. 702) removes all elements in the priority queue. Method size (p. 702) gets the number of elements in the priority queue.

Section 16.10 Sets

- A Set (p. 703) is an unordered Collection that contains no duplicate elements. HashSet (p. 703) stores its elements in a hash table. TreeSet (p. 703) stores its elements in a tree.
- Interface SortedSet (p. 704) extends Set and represents a set that maintains its elements in sorted order. Class TreeSet implements SortedSet.
- TreeSet method headSet (p. 704) gets a TreeSet view containing elements that are less than a specified element. Method tailSet (p. 705) gets a TreeSet view containing elements that are greater than or equal to a specified element. Any changes made to these views are made to the original TreeSet.

Section 16.11 Maps

- Maps (p. 706) store key–value pairs and cannot contain duplicate keys. HashMaps (p. 706) and Hashtables (p. 706) store elements in a hash table, and TreeMaps (p. 706) store elements in a tree.

- HashMap takes two type arguments—the type of key and the type of value.
- HashMap method put (p. 709) adds a key–value pair to a HashMap. Method get (p. 709) locates the value associated with the specified key. Method isEmpty (p. 710) determines if the map is empty.
- HashMap method keySet (p. 710) returns a set of the keys. Map method size (p. 710) returns the number of key–value pairs in the Map.
- Interface SortedMap (p. 706) extends Map and represents a map that maintains its keys in sorted order. Class TreeMap implements SortedMap.

Section 16.12 Properties Class
- A Properties object (p. 710) is a persistent subclass of Hashtable.
- The Properties no-argument constructor creates an empty Properties table. An overloaded constructor receives a Properties object containing default property values.
- Properties method setProperty (p. 710) specifies the value associated with its key argument. Method getProperty (p. 710) locates the value of the key specified as an argument. Method store (p. 712) saves the contents of a Properties object to specified OutputStream. Method load (p. 713) restores the contents of a Properties object from the specified InputStream.

Section 16.13 Synchronized Collections
- Collections from the collections framework are unsynchronized. Synchronization wrappers (p. 713) are provided for collections that can be accessed by multiple threads simultaneously.

Section 16.14 Unmodifiable Collections
- Unmodifiable collection wrappers (p. 713) throw UnsupportedOperationExceptions (p. 686) if attempts are made to modify the collection.

Section 16.15 Abstract Implementations
- The collections framework provides various abstract implementations of collection interfaces from which you can quickly flesh out complete customized implementations.

Self-Review Exercises

16.1 Fill in the blanks in each of the following statements:
a) A(n) _____ is used to iterate through a collection and can remove elements from the collection during the iteration.
b) An element in a List can be accessed by using the element's _____.
c) Assuming that myArray contains references to Double objects, _____ occurs when the statement "myArray[0] = 1.25;" executes.
d) Java classes _____ and _____ provide the capabilities of arraylike data structures that can resize themselves dynamically.
e) If you do not specify a capacity increment, the system will _____ the size of the Vector each time additional capacity is needed.
f) You can use a(n) _____ to create a collection that offers only read-only access to others while allowing read–write access to yourself.
g) Assuming that myArray contains references to Double objects, _____ occurs when the statement "double number = myArray[0];" executes.
h) Collections algorithm _____ determines if two collections have elements in common.

16.2 Determine whether each statement is *true* or *false*. If *false*, explain why.
a) Values of primitive types may be stored directly in a collection.
b) A Set can contain duplicate values.

c) A Map can contain duplicate keys.
d) A LinkedList can contain duplicate values.
e) Collections is an interface.
f) Iterators can remove elements.
g) With hashing, as the load factor increases, the chance of collisions decreases.
h) A PriorityQueue permits null elements.

Answers to Self-Review Exercises

16.1 a) Iterator. b) index. c) autoboxing. d) ArrayList, Vector. e) double. f) unmodifiable wrapper. g) auto-unboxing. h) disjoint.

16.2 a) False. Autoboxing occurs when adding a primitive type to a collection, which means the primitive type is converted to its corresponding type-wrapper class.
b) False. A Set cannot contain duplicate values.
c) False. A Map cannot contain duplicate keys.
d) True.
e) False. Collections is a class; Collection is an interface.
f) True.
g) False. As the load factor increases, fewer slots are available relative to the total number of slots, so the chance of a collision increases.
h) False. Attempting to insert a null element causes a NullPointerException.

Execises

16.3 Define each of the following terms:
a) Collection
b) Collections
c) Comparator
d) List
e) load factor
f) collision
g) space/time trade-off in hashing
h) HashMap

16.4 Explain briefly the operation of each of the following methods of class Vector:
a) add
b) set
c) remove
d) removeAllElements
e) removeElementAt
f) firstElement
g) lastElement
h) contains
i) indexOf
j) size
k) capacity

16.5 Explain why inserting additional elements into a Vector object whose current size is less than its capacity is a relatively fast operation and why inserting additional elements into a Vector object whose current size is at capacity is a relatively slow operation.

16.6 By extending class Vector, Java's designers were able to create class Stack quickly. What are the negative aspects of this use of inheritance, particularly for class Stack?

16.7   Briefly answer the following questions:
a) What is the primary difference between a `Set` and a `Map`?
b) What happens when you add a primitive type (e.g., `double`) value to a collection?
c) Can you print all the elements in a collection without using an `Iterator`? If yes, how?

16.8   Explain briefly the operation of each of the following `Iterator`-related methods:
a) `iterator`
b) `hasNext`
c) `next`

16.9   Explain briefly the operation of each of the following methods of class `HashMap`:
a) `put`
b) `get`
c) `isEmpty`
d) `containsKey`
e) `keySet`

16.10   Determine whether each of the following statements is *true* or *false*. If *false*, explain why.
a) Elements in a `Collection` must be sorted in ascending order before a `binarySearch` may be performed.
b) Method `first` gets the first element in a `TreeSet`.
c) A `List` created with `Arrays` method `asList` is resizable.

16.11   Explain the operation of each of the following methods of the `Properties` class:
a) `load`
b) `store`
c) `getProperty`
d) `list`

16.12   Rewrite lines 16–25 in Fig. 16.3 to be more concise by using the `asList` method and the `LinkedList` constructor that takes a `Collection` argument.

16.13   *(Duplicate Elimination)* Write a program that reads in a series of first names and eliminates duplicates by storing them in a `Set`. Allow the user to search for a first name.

16.14   *(Counting Letters)* Modify the program of Fig. 16.18 to count the number of occurrences of each letter rather than of each word. For example, the string `"HELLO THERE"` contains two `H`s, three `E`s, two `L`s, one `O`, one `T` and one `R`. Display the results.

16.15   *(Color Chooser)* Use a `HashMap` to create a reusable class for choosing one of the 13 predefined colors in class `Color`. The names of the colors should be used as keys, and the predefined `Color` objects should be used as values. Place this class in a package that can be imported into any Java program. Use your new class in an application that allows the user to select a color and draw a shape in that color.

16.16   *(Counting Duplicate Words)* Write a program that determines and prints the number of duplicate words in a sentence. Treat uppercase and lowercase letters the same. Ignore punctuation.

16.17   *(Inserting Elements in a `LinkedList` in Sorted Order)* Write a program that inserts 25 random integers from 0 to 100 in order into a `LinkedList` object. The program should sort the elements, then calculate the sum of the elements and the floating-point average of the elements.

16.18   *(Copying and Reversing `LinkedList`s)* Write a program that creates a `LinkedList` object of 10 characters, then creates a second `LinkedList` object containing a copy of the first list, but in reverse order.

16.19   *(Prime Numbers and Prime Factors)* Write a program that takes a whole number input from a user and determines whether it's prime. If the number is not prime, display its unique prime factors. Remember that a prime number's factors are only 1 and the prime number itself. Every number that's not prime has a unique prime factorization. For example, consider the number 54. The prime factors of 54 are 2, 3, 3 and 3. When the values are multiplied together, the result is 54. For the number 54, the prime factors output should be 2 and 3. Use Sets as part of your solution.

16.20 *(Sorting Words with a TreeSet)* Write a program that uses a String method split to tokenize a line of text input by the user and places each token in a TreeSet. Print the elements of the TreeSet. [*Note:* This should cause the elements to be printed in ascending sorted order.]

16.21 *(Changing a PriorityQueue's Sort Order)* The output of Fig. 16.15 shows that Priority-Queue orders Double elements in ascending order. Rewrite Fig. 16.15 so that it orders Double elements in descending order (i.e., 9.8 should be the highest-priority element rather than 3.2).

Java SE 8 Lambdas and Streams

Oh, could I flow like thee,
and make thy stream
My great example,
as it is my theme!
—Sir John Denham

Objectives

In this chapter you'll:

■ Learn what functional programming is and how it complements object-oriented programming.

■ Use functional programming to simplify programming tasks you've performed with other techniques.

■ Write lambda expressions that implement functional interfaces.

■ Learn what streams are and how stream pipelines are formed from stream sources, intermediate operations and terminal operations.

■ Perform operations on IntStreams, including forEach, count, min, max, sum, average, reduce, filter and sorted.

■ Perform operations on Streams, including filter, map, sorted, collect, forEach, findFirst, distinct, mapToDouble and reduce.

■ Create streams representing ranges of int values and random int values.

17.1 Introduction

The way you think about Java programming is about to change profoundly. Prior to Java SE 8, Java supported three programming paradigms—*procedural programming*, *object-oriented programming* and *generic programming*. Java SE 8 adds *functional programming*. The new language and library capabilities that support this paradigm were added to Java as part of *Project Lambda:*

```
http://openjdk.java.net/projects/lambda
```

In this chapter, we'll define functional programming and show how to use it to write programs faster, more concisely and with fewer bugs than programs written with previous techniques. In Chapter 23, Concurrency, you'll see that functional programs are easier to *parallelize* (i.e., perform multiple operations simultaneously) so that your programs can take advantage of multi-core architectures to enhance performance. Before reading this chapter, you should review Section 10.10, which introduced Java SE 8's new interface features (the ability to include `default` and `static` methods) and discussed the concept of functional interfaces.

This chapter presents many examples of functional programming, often showing simpler ways to implement tasks that you programmed in earlier chapters (Fig. 17.1)

Pre-Java-SE-8 topics	Corresponding Java SE 8 discussions and examples
Chapter 6, Arrays and ArrayLists	Sections 17.3—17.4 introduce basic lambda and streams capabilities that process one-dimensional arrays.
Chapter 10, Object-Oriented Programming: Polymorphism and Interfaces	Section 10.10 introduced the new Java SE 8 interface features (`default` methods, `static` methods and the concept of functional interfaces) that support functional programming.
Chapter 12, GUI Components: Part 1	Section 17.9 shows how to use a lambda to implement a Swing event-listener functional interface.
Chapter 14, Strings, Characters and Regular Expressions	Section 17.5 shows how to use lambdas and streams to process collections of `String` objects.
Chapter 15, Files, Streams and Object Serialization	Section 17.7 shows how to use lambdas and streams to process lines of text from a file.
Chapter 22, GUI Components: Part 2	Discusses using lambdas to implement Swing event-listener functional interfaces.
Chapter 23, Concurrency	Shows that functional programs are easier to parallelize so that they can take advantage of multi-core architectures to enhance performance. Demonstrates parallel stream processing. Shows that `Arrays` method `parallelSort` improves performance on multi-core architectures when sorting large arrays.
Chapter 25, JavaFX GUI: Part 1	Discusses using lambdas to implement JavaFX event-listener functional interfaces.

Fig. 17.1 | Java SE 8 lambdas and streams discussions and examples.

17.2 Functional Programming Technologies Overview

In the preceding chapters, you learned various procedural, object-oriented and generic programming techniques. Though you often used Java library classes and interfaces to perform various tasks, you typically determine *what* you want to accomplish in a task then specify precisely *how* to accomplish it. For example, let's assume that *what* you'd like to accomplish is to sum the elements of an array named `values` (the *data source*). You might use the following code:

```
int sum = 0;

for (int counter = 0; counter < values.length; counter++)
    sum += values[counter];
```

This loop specifies *how* we'd like to add each array element's value to the `sum`—with a `for` repetition statement that processes each element one at a time, adding each element's value to the sum. This iteration technique is known as **external iteration** (because you specify how to iterate, not the library) and requires you to access the elements sequentially from beginning to end in a single thread of execution. To perform the preceding task, you also create two variables (sum and counter) that are *mutated* repeatedly—that is, their values change—while the task is performed. You performed many similar array and collection tasks, such as displaying the elements of an array, summarizing the faces of a die that was rolled 6,000,000 times, calculating the average of an array's elements and more.

External Iteration Is Error Prone
Most Java programmers are comfortable with external iteration. However, there are several opportunities for error. For example, you could initialize variable sum incorrectly, initialize control variable counter incorrectly, use the wrong loop-continuation condition, increment control variable counter incorrectly or incorrectly add each value in the array to the sum.

Internal Iteration
In **functional programming**, you specify *what* you want to accomplish in a task, but *not how* to accomplish it. As you'll see in this chapter, to sum a numeric data source's elements (such as those in an array or collection), you can use new Java SE 8 library capabilities that allow you to say, "Here's a data source, give me the sum of its elements." You do *not* need to specify *how* to iterate through the elements or declare and use *any* mutable variables. This is known as **internal iteration**, because the *library* determines how to access all the elements to perform the task. With internal iteration, you can easily tell the library that you want to perform this task with *parallel processing* to take advantage of your computer's multi-core architecture—this can significantly improve the task's performance. As you'll learn in Chapter 23, it's hard to create parallel tasks that operate correctly if those tasks modify a program's state information (that is, its variable values). So the functional programming capabilities that you'll learn here focus on **immutability**—not modifying the data source being processed or any other program state.

17.2.1 Functional Interfaces

Section 10.10 introduced Java SE 8's new interface features—default methods and static methods—and discussed the concept of a *functional interface*—an interface that contains exactly one abstract method (and may also contain default and static methods). Such interfaces are also known as *single abstract method* (SAM) interfaces. Functional interfaces are used extensively in functional programming, because they act as an object-oriented model for a function.

Functional Interfaces in Package `java.util.function`
Package java.util.function contains several functional interfaces. Figure 17.2 shows the six basic generic functional interfaces. Throughout the table, T and R are generic type names that represent the type of the object on which the functional interface operates and the return type of a method, respectively. There are many other functional interfaces in package java.util.function that are specialized versions of those in Fig. 17.2. Most are for use with int, long and double primitive values, but there are also generic customizations of Consumer, Function and Predicate for binary operations—that is, methods that take two arguments.

Interface	Description
`BinaryOperator<T>`	Contains method `apply` that takes two T arguments, performs an operation on them (such as a calculation) and returns a value of type T. You'll see several examples of `BinaryOperators` starting in Section 17.3.
`Consumer<T>`	Contains method `accept` that takes a T argument and returns `void`. Performs a task with it's T argument, such as outputting the object, invoking a method of the object, etc. You'll see several examples of `Consumers` starting in Section 17.3.
`Function<T,R>`	Contains method `apply` that takes a T argument and returns a value of type R. Calls a method on the T argument and returns that method's result. You'll see several examples of `Functions` starting in Section 17.5.
`Predicate<T>`	Contains method `test` that takes a T argument and returns a `boolean`. Tests whether the T argument satisfies a condition. You'll see several examples of `Predicates` starting in Section 17.3.
`Supplier<T>`	Contains method `get` that takes no arguments and produces a value of type T. Often used to create a collection object in which a stream operation's results are placed. You'll see several examples of `Suppliers` starting in Section 17.7.
`UnaryOperator<T>`	Contains method `get` that takes no arguments and returns a value of type T. You'll see several examples of `UnaryOperators` starting in Section 17.3.

Fig. 17.2 | The six basic generic functional interfaces in package `java.util.function`.

17.2.2 Lambda Expressions

Functional programming is accomplished with lambda expressions. A **lambda expression** represents an *anonymous method*—a shorthand notation for implementing a functional interface, similar to an anonymous inner class (Section 12.11). The type of a lambda expression is the type of the functional interface that the lambda expression implements. Lambda expressions can be used anywhere functional interfaces are expected. From this point forward, we'll refer to lambda expressions simply as lambdas. We show basic lambda syntax in this section and discuss additional lambda features as we use them throughout this and later chapters.

Lambda Syntax
A lambda consists of a *parameter list* followed by the **arrow token** (->) and a body, as in:

```
(parameterList) -> {statements}
```

The following lambda receives two `int`s and returns their sum:

```
(int x, int y) -> {return x + y;}
```

In this case, the body is a *statement block* that may contain *one or more* statements enclosed in curly braces. There are several variations of this syntax. For example, the parameter types usually may be omitted, as in:

```
(x, y) -> {return x + y;}
```

in which case, the compiler determines the parameter and return types by the lambda's context—we'll say more about this later.

When the body contains only one expression, the return keyword and curly braces may be omitted, as in:

```
(x, y) -> x + y
```

in this case, the expression's value is *implicitly* returned. When the parameter list contains only one parameter, the parentheses may be omitted, as in:

```
value -> System.out.printf("%d ", value)
```

To define a lambda with an empty parameter list, specify the parameter list as empty parentheses to the left of the arrow token (->), as in:

```
() -> System.out.println("Welcome to lambdas!")
```

In addition, to the preceding lambda syntax, there are specialized shorthand forms of lambdas that are known as *method references*, which we introduce in Section 17.5.1.

17.2.3 Streams

Java SE 8 introduces the concept of **streams**, which are similar to the iterators you learned in Chapter 16. Streams are objects of classes that implement interface **Stream** (from the package java.util.stream) or one of the specialized stream interfacess for processing collections of int, long or double values (which we introduce in Section 17.3). Together with lambdas, streams enable you to perform tasks on collections of elements—often from an array or collection object.

Stream Pipelines

Streams move elements through a sequence of processing steps—known as a **stream pipeline**—that begins with a *data source* (such as an array or collection), performs various *intermediate operations* on the data source's elements and ends with a *terminal operation*. A stream pipeline is formed by *chaining* method calls. Unlike collections, streams do *not* have their own storage—once a stream is processed, it cannot be reused, because it does not maintain a copy of the original data source.

Intermediate and Terminal Operations

An **intermediate operation** specifies tasks to perform on the stream's elements and always results in a new stream. Intermediate operations are **lazy**—they aren't performed until a terminal operation is invoked. This allows library developers to optimize stream-processing performance. For example, if you have a collection of 1,000,000 Person objects and you're looking for the *first* one with the last name "Jones", stream processing can terminate as soon as the first such Person object is found.

A **terminal operation** initiates processing of a stream pipeline's intermediate operations and produces a result. Terminal operations are **eager**—they perform the requested operation when they are called. We say more about lazy and eager operations as we encounter them throughout the chapter and you'll see how lazy operations can improve performance. Figure 17.3 shows some common intermediate operations. Figure 17.4 shows some common terminal operations.

Intermediate Stream operations	
filter	Results in a stream containing only the elements that satisfy a condition.
distinct	Results in a stream containing only the unique elements.
limit	Results in a stream with the specified number of elements from the beginning of the original stream.
map	Results in a stream in which each element of the original stream is mapped to a new value (possibly of a different type)—e.g., mapping numeric values to the squares of the numeric values. The new stream has the same number of elements as the original stream.
sorted	Results in a stream in which the elements are in sorted order. The new stream has the same number of elements as the original stream.

Fig. 17.3 | Common intermediate Stream operations.

Terminal Stream operations	
forEach	Performs processing on every element in a stream (e.g., display each element).
Reduction operations—Take all values in the stream and return a single value	
average	Calculates the *average* of the elements in a numeric stream.
count	Returns the *number of elements* in the stream.
max	Locates the *largest* value in a numeric stream.
min	Locates the *smallest* value in a numeric stream.
reduce	Reduces the elements of a collection to a *single value* using an associative accumulation function (e.g., a lambda that adds two elements).
Mutable reduction operations—Create a container (such as a collection or StringBuilder)	
collect	Creates a *new collection* of elements containing the results of the stream's prior operations.
toArray	Creates an *array* containing the results of the stream's prior operations.
Search operations	
findFirst	Finds the *first* stream element based on the prior intermediate operations; immediately terminates processing of the stream pipeline once such an element is found.
findAny	Finds *any* stream element based on the prior intermediate operations; immediately terminates processing of the stream pipeline once such an element is found.
anyMatch	Determines whether *any* stream elements match a specified condition; immediately terminates processing of the stream pipeline if an element matches.
allMatch	Determines whether *all* of the elements in the stream match a specified condition.

Fig. 17.4 | Common terminal Stream operations.

Stream in File Processing vs. Stream in Functional Programming

Throughout this chapter, we use the term *stream* in the context of functional programming—this is not the same concept as the I/O streams we discussed in Chapter 15, Files,

Streams and Object Serialization, in which a program reads a stream of bytes from a file or outputs a stream of bytes to a file. As you'll see in Section 17.7, you also can use functional programming to manipulate the contents of a file.

17.3 IntStream Operations

[This section demonstrates how lambdas and streams can be used to simplify programming tasks that you learned in Chapter 6, Arrays and ArrayLists.]

Figure 17.5 demonstrates operations on an **IntStream** (package **java.util.stream**)—a specialized stream for manipulating int values. The techniques shown in this example also apply to **LongStreams** and **DoubleStreams** for long and double values, respectively.

```
1   // Fig. 17.5: IntStreamOperations.java
2   // Demonstrating IntStream operations.
3   import java.util.Arrays;
4   import java.util.stream.IntStream;
5
6   public class IntStreamOperations
7   {
8      public static void main(String[] args)
9      {
10        int[] values = {3, 10, 6, 1, 4, 8, 2, 5, 9, 7};
11
12        // display original values
13        System.out.print("Original values: ");
14        IntStream.of(values)
15              .forEach(value -> System.out.printf("%d ", value));
16        System.out.println();
17
18        // count, min, max, sum and average of the values
19        System.out.printf("%nCount: %d%n", IntStream.of(values).count());
20        System.out.printf("Min: %d%n",
21           IntStream.of(values).min().getAsInt());
22        System.out.printf("Max: %d%n",
23           IntStream.of(values).max().getAsInt());
24        System.out.printf("Sum: %d%n", IntStream.of(values).sum());
25        System.out.printf("Average: %.2f%n",
26           IntStream.of(values).average().getAsDouble());
27
28        // sum of values with reduce method
29        System.out.printf("%nSum via reduce method: %d%n",
30           IntStream.of(values)
31                 .reduce(0, (x, y) -> x + y));
32
33        // sum of squares of values with reduce method
34        System.out.printf("Sum of squares via reduce method: %d%n",
35           IntStream.of(values)
36                 .reduce(0, (x, y) -> x + y * y));
```

Fig. 17.5 | Demonstrating IntStream operations. (Part 1 of 2.)

```
37
38              // product of values with reduce method
39              System.out.printf("Product via reduce method: %d%n",
40                 IntStream.of(values)
41                        .reduce(1, (x, y) -> x * y));
42
43              // even values displayed in sorted order
44              System.out.printf("%nEven values displayed in sorted order: ");
45              IntStream.of(values)
46                     .filter(value -> value % 2 == 0)
47                     .sorted()
48                     .forEach(value -> System.out.printf("%d ", value));
49              System.out.println();
50
51              // odd values multiplied by 10 and displayed in sorted order
52              System.out.printf(
53                 "Odd values multiplied by 10 displayed in sorted order: ");
54              IntStream.of(values)
55                     .filter(value -> value % 2 != 0)
56                     .map(value -> value * 10)
57                     .sorted()
58                     .forEach(value -> System.out.printf("%d ", value));
59              System.out.println();
60
61              // sum range of integers from 1 to 10, exlusive
62              System.out.printf("%nSum of integers from 1 to 9: %d%n",
63                 IntStream.range(1, 10).sum());
64
65              // sum range of integers from 1 to 10, inclusive
66              System.out.printf("Sum of integers from 1 to 10: %d%n",
67                 IntStream.rangeClosed(1, 10).sum());
68        }
69  } // end class IntStreamOperations
```

```
Original values: 3 10 6 1 4 8 2 5 9 7

Count: 10
Min: 1
Max: 10
Sum: 55
Average: 5.50

Sum via reduce method: 55
Sum of squares via reduce method: 385
Product via reduce method: 3628800

Even values displayed in sorted order: 2 4 6 8 10
Odd values multiplied by 10 displayed in sorted order: 10 30 50 70 90

Sum of integers from 1 to 9: 45
Sum of integers from 1 to 10: 55
```

Fig. 17.5 | Demonstrating IntStream operations. (Part 2 of 2.)

17.3.1 Creating an `IntStream` and Displaying Its Values with the `forEach` Terminal Operation

`IntStream` static method **of** (line 14) receives an `int` array as an argument and returns an `IntStream` for processing the array's values. Once you create a stream, you can *chain* together multiple method calls to create a *stream pipeline*. The statement in lines 14–15 creates an `IntStream` for the `values` array, then uses `IntStream` method **forEach** (a terminal operation) to perform a task on each stream element. Method `forEach` receives as its argument an object that implements the **IntConsumer** functional interface (package **java.util.function**)—this is an `int`-specific version of the generic `Consumer` functional interface. This interface's **accept** method receives one `int` value and performs a task with it—in this case, displaying the value and a space. Prior to Java SE 8, you'd typically implement interface `IntConsumer` using an anonymous inner class like:

```
new IntConsumer()
{
   public void accept(int value)
   {
      System.out.printf("%d ", value);
   }
}
```

but in Java SE 8, you simply write the lambda

```
value -> System.out.printf("%d ", value)
```

The `accept` method's parameter name (`value`) becomes the lambda's parameter, and the `accept` method's body statement becomes the lambda expression's body. As you can see, the lambda syntax is clearer and more concise than the anonymous inner class.

Type Inference and a Lambda's Target Type

The Java compiler can usually *infer* the types of a lambda's parameters and the type returned by a lambda from the context in which the lambda is used. This is determined by the lambda's **target type**—the functional interface type that is expected where the lambda appears in the code. In line 15, the target type is `IntConsumer`. In this case, the lambda parameter's type is *inferred* to be `int`, because interface `IntConsumer`'s accept method expects to receive an `int`. You can *explicitly* declare the parameter's type, as in:

```
(int value) -> System.out.printf("%d ", value)
```

When doing so, the lambda's parameter list *must* be enclosed in parentheses. We generally let the compiler *infer* the lambda parameter's type in our examples.

`final` *Local Variables, Effectively* `final` *Local Variables and Capturing Lambdas*

Prior to Java SE 8, when implementing an anonymous inner class, you could use local variables from the enclosing method (known as the *lexical scope*), but you were required to declare those local variables `final`. Lambdas may also use `final` local variables. In Java SE 8, anonymous inner classes and lambdas can also use **effectively** `final` **local variables**—that is, local variables that are *not* modified after they're initially declared and initialized. A lambda that refers to a local variable in the enclosing lexical scope is known as a **capturing lambda**. The compiler captures the local variable's value and ensures that the value can be used when the lambda *eventually* executes, which may be *after* its lexical scope *no longer exists*.

*Using **this** in a Lambda That Appears in an Instance Method*
As in an anonymous inner class, a lambda can use the outer class's this reference. In an an anonymous inner class, you must use the syntax *OuterClassName*.this—otherwise, the this reference would refer to *the object of the anonymous inner class*. In a lambda, you refer to the object of the outer class, simply as this.

Parameter and Variable Names in a Lambda
The parameter names and variable names that you use in lambdas cannot be the same as as any other local variables in the lambda's lexical scope; otherwise, a compilation error occurs.

17.3.2 Terminal Operations count, min, max, sum and average

Class IntStream provides various terminal operations for common stream reductions on streams of int values. Terminal operations are *eager*—they immediately process the items in the stream. Common reduction operations for IntStreams include:

- **count** (line 19) returns the number of elements in the stream.
- **min** (line 21) returns the smallest int in the stream.
- **max** (line 23) returns the largest int in the stream.
- **sum** (line 24) returns the sum of all the ints in the stream.
- **average** (line 26) returns an **OptionalDouble** (package java.util) containing the average of the ints in the stream as a value of type double. For any stream, it's possible that there are *no elements* in the stream. Returning OptionalDouble enables method average to return the average if the stream contains *at least one element*. In this example, we know the stream has 10 elements, so we call class OptionalDouble's **getAsDouble** method to obtain the average. If there were no *elements*, the OptionalDouble would not contain the average and getAsDouble would throw a NoSuchElementException. To prevent this exception, you can instead call method **orElse**, which returns the OptionalDouble's value if there is one, or the value you pass to orElse, otherwise.

Class IntStream also provides method summaryStatistics that performs the count, min, max, sum and average operations *in one pass* of an IntStream's elements and returns the results as an IntSummaryStatistics object (package java.util). This provides a significant performance boost over reprocessing an IntStream repeatedly for each individual operation. This object has methods for obtaining each result and a toString method that summarizes all the results. For example, the statement:

```
System.out.println(IntStream.of(values).summaryStatistics());
```

produces:

```
IntSummaryStatistics{count=10, sum=55, min=1, average=5.500000,
max=10}
```

for the array values in Fig. 17.5.

17.3.3 Terminal Operation reduce

You can define your own reductions for an IntStream by calling its **reduce** method as shown in lines 29–31 of Fig. 17.5. Each of the terminal operations in Section 17.3.2 is a specialized implementation of reduce. For example, line 31 shows how to sum an Int-Steam's values using reduce, rather than sum. The first argument (0) is a value that helps you begin the reduction operation and the second argument is an object that implements the **IntBinaryOperator** functional interface (package java.util.function). The lambda:

```
(x, y) -> x + y
```

implements the interface's **applyAsInt** method, which receives two int values (representing the left and right operands of a binary operator) and performs a calculation with the values—in this case, adding the values. A lambda with two or more parameters *must* enclose them in parentheses. Evaluation of the reduction proceeds as follows:

- On the first call to reduce, lambda parameter x's value is the identity value (0) and lambda parameter y's value is the *first* int in the stream (3), producing the sum 3 (0 + 3).

- On the next call to reduce, lambda parameter x's value is the result of the first calculation (3) and lambda parameter y's value is the *second* int in the stream (10), producing the sum 13 (3 + 10).

- On the next call to reduce, lambda parameter x's value is the result of the previous calculation (13) and lambda parameter y's value is the *third* int in the stream (6), producing the sum 19 (13 + 6).

This process continues producing a running total of the IntSteam's values until they've all been used, at which point the final sum is returned.

Method reduce's Identity Value Argument

Method reduce's first argument is formally called an **identity value**—a value that, when combined with any stream element using the IntBinaryOperator produces that element's original value. For example, when summing the elements, the identity value is 0 (any int value added to 0 results in the original value) and when getting the product of the elements the identity value is 1 (any int value multiplied by 1 results in the original value).

Summing the Squares of the Values with Method reduce

Lines 34–36 of Fig. 17.5 use method reduce to calculate the sums of the squares of the IntSteam's values. The lambda in this case, adds the *square* of the current value to the running total. Evaluation of the reduction proceeds as follows:

- On the first call to reduce, lambda parameter x's value is the identity value (0) and lambda parameter y's value is the *first* int in the stream (3), producing the value 9 (0 + 3^2).

- On the next call to reduce, lambda parameter x's value is the result of the first calculation (9) and lambda parameter y's value is the *second* int in the stream (10), producing the sum 109 (9 + 10^2).

- On the next call to reduce, lambda parameter x's value is the result of the previous calculation (109) and lambda parameter y's value is the *third* int in the stream (6), producing the sum 145 (109 + 6^2).

This process continues producing a running total of the squares of the IntSteam's values until they've all been used, at which point the final sum is returned.

*Calculating the Product of the Values with Method **reduce***

Lines 39–41 of Fig. 17.5 use method `reduce` to calculate the product of the `IntSteam`'s values. In this case, the lambda multiplies its two arguments. Because we're producing a product, we begin with the identity value 1 in this case. Evaluation of the reduction proceeds as follows:

- On the first call to `reduce`, lambda parameter x's value is the identity value (1) and lambda parameter y's value is the *first* `int` in the stream (3), producing the value 3 (1 * 3).

- On the next call to `reduce`, lambda parameter x's value is the result of the first calculation (3) and lambda parameter y's value is the *second* `int` in the stream (10), producing the sum 30 (3 * 10).

- On the next call to `reduce`, lambda parameter x's value is the result of the previous calculation (30) and lambda parameter y's value is the *third* `int` in the stream (6), producing the sum 180 (30 * 6).

This process continues producing a running product of the `IntSteam`'s values until they've all been used, at which point the final product is returned.

17.3.4 Intermediate Operations: Filtering and Sorting `IntStream` Values

Lines 45–48 of Fig. 17.5 create a stream pipeline that *locates* the even integers in an `Int-Stream`, *sorts* them in ascending order and *displays* each value followed by a space.

*Intermediate Operation **filter***

You *filter* elements to produce a stream of intermediate results that match a condition—known as a *predicate*. `IntStream` method **filter** (line 46) receives an object that implements the **IntPredicate** functional interface (package `java.util.function`). The lambda in line 46:

```
value -> value % 2 == 0
```

implements the interface's **test** method, which receives an `int` and returns a `boolean` indicating whether the `int` satisfies the predicate—in this case, the `IntPredicate` returns `true` if the value it receives is divisible by 2. Calls to `filter` and other intermediate streams are *lazy*—they aren't evaluated until a *terminal operation* (which is *eager*) is performed—and produce new streams of elements. In lines 45–48, this occurs when `forEach` is called (line 48).

*Intermediate Operation **sorted***

`IntStream` method **sorted** orders the elements of the stream into *ascending* order. Like `filter`, `sorted` is a *lazy* operation; however, when the sorting is eventually performed, all prior intermediate operations in the stream pipeline must be complete so that method `sorted` knows which elements to sort.

Processing the Stream Pipeline and Stateless vs. Stateful Intermediate Operations

When `forEach` is called, the stream pipeline is processed. Line 46 produces an intermediate `IntStream` containing only the even integers, then line 47 sorts them and line 48 displays each element.

Method `filter` is a **stateless intermediate operation**—it does not require any information about other elements in the stream in order to test whether the current element satisfies the predicate. Similarly method `map` (discussed shortly) is a stateless intermediate operation. Method `sorted` is a **stateful intermediate operation** that requires information about *all* of the other elements in the stream in order to sort them. Similarly method `distinct` is a stateful intermediate operation. The online documentation for each intermediate stream operation specifies whether it is a stateless or stateful operation.

*Other Methods of the **IntPredicate** Functional Interface*
Interface `IntPredicate` also contains three `default` methods:

- **and**—performs a *logical AND* with *short-circuit evaluation* (Section 4.8) between the `IntPredicate` on which it's called and the `IntPredicate` it receives as an argument.

- **negate**—*reverses* the `boolean` value of the `IntPredicate` on which it's called.

- **or**—performs a *logical OR* with *short-circuit evaluation* between the `IntPredicate` on which it's called and the `IntPredicate` it receives as an argument.

Composing Lambda Expressions
You can use these methods and `IntPredicate` objects to compose more complex conditions. For example, consider the following two `IntPredicate`s:

```
IntPredicate even = value -> value % 2 == 0;
IntPredicate greaterThan5 = value -> value > 5;
```

To locate all the even integers greater than 5, you could replace the lambda in line 46 with the `IntPredicate`

```
even.and(greaterThan5)
```

17.3.5 Intermediate Operation: Mapping

Lines 54–58 of Fig. 17.5 create a stream pipeline that *locates* the odd integers in an `Int-Stream`, *multiplies* each odd integer by 10, *sorts* the values in ascending order and *displays* each value followed by a space.

*Intermediate Operation **map***
The new feature here is the *mapping* operation that takes each value and multiplies it by 10. Mapping is an *intermediate operation* that transforms a stream's elements to new values and produces a stream containing the resulting elements. Sometimes these are of different types from the original stream's elements.

`IntStream` method **map** (line 56) receives an object that implements the **IntUnary-Operator** functional interface (package `java.util.function`). The lambda in line 55:

```
value -> value * 10
```

implements the interface's **applyAsInt** method, which receives an `int` and maps it to a new `int` value. Calls to map are *lazy*. Method map is a *stateless* stream operation.

Processing the Stream Pipeline

When forEach is called (line 58), the stream pipeline is processed. First, line 55 produces an intermediate IntStream containing only the odd values. Next, line 56 multiplies each odd integer by 10. Then, line 57 sorts the values and line 58 displays each element.

17.3.6 Creating Streams of ints with IntStream Methods range and rangeClosed

If you need an *ordered sequence* of int values, you can create an IntStream containing such values with IntStream methods range (line 63 of Fig. 17.5) and rangeClosed (line 67). Both methods take two int arguments representing the range of values. Method **range** produces a sequence of values from its first argument up to, but *not* including its second argument. Method **rangeClosed** produces a sequence of values including *both* of its arguments. Lines 63 and 67 demonstrate these methods for producing sequences of int values from 1–9 and 1–10, respectively. For the complete list of IntStream methods, visit:

> http://download.java.net/jdk8/docs/api/java/util/stream/
>   IntStream.html

17.4 Stream<Integer> Manipulations

[This section demonstrates how lambdas and streams can be used to simplify programming tasks that you learned in Chapter 6, Arrays and ArrayLists.]

Just as class IntStream's method of can create an IntStream from an array of ints, class Array's **stream** method can be used to create a Stream from an array of objects. Figure 17.6 performs *filtering* and *sorting* on a Stream<Integer>, using the same techniques you learned in Section 17.3. The program also shows how to *collect* the results of a stream pipeline's operations into a new collection that you can process in subsequent statements. Throughout this example, we use the Integer array values (line 12) that's initialized with int values—the compiler *boxes* each int into an Integer object. Line 15 displays the contents of values before we perform any stream processing.

```
 1   // Fig. 17.6: ArraysAndStreams.java
 2   // Demonstrating lambdas and streams with an array of Integers.
 3   import java.util.Arrays;
 4   import java.util.Comparator;
 5   import java.util.List;
 6   import java.util.stream.Collectors;
 7
 8   public class ArraysAndStreams
 9   {
10      public static void main(String[] args)
11      {
12         Integer[] values = {2, 9, 5, 0, 3, 7, 1, 4, 8, 6};
13
14         // display original values
15         System.out.printf("Original values: %s%n", Arrays.asList(values));
```

Fig. 17.6 | Demonstrating lambdas and streams with an array of Integers. (Part 1 of 2.)

```
16
17        // sort values in ascending order with streams
18        System.out.printf("Sorted values: %s%n",
19            Arrays.stream(values)
20                .sorted()
21                .collect(Collectors.toList()));
22
23        // values greater than 4
24        List<Integer> greaterThan4 =
25            Arrays.stream(values)
26                  .filter(value -> value > 4)
27                  .collect(Collectors.toList());
28        System.out.printf("Values greater than 4: %s%n", greaterThan4);
29
30        // filter values greater than 4 then sort the results
31        System.out.printf("Sorted values greater than 4: %s%n",
32            Arrays.stream(values)
33                  .filter(value -> value > 4)
34                  .sorted()
35                  .collect(Collectors.toList()));
36
37        // greaterThan4 List sorted with streams
38        System.out.printf(
39            "Values greater than 4 (ascending with streams): %s%n",
40            greaterThan4.stream()
41                  .sorted()
42                  .collect(Collectors.toList()));
43    }
44 } // end class ArraysAndStreams
```

```
Original values: [2, 9, 5, 0, 3, 7, 1, 4, 8, 6]
Sorted values: [0, 1, 2, 3, 4, 5, 6, 7, 8, 9]
Values greater than 4: [9, 5, 7, 8, 6]
Sorted values greater than 4: [5, 6, 7, 8, 9]
Values greater than 4 (ascending with streams): [5, 6, 7, 8, 9]
```

Fig. 17.6 | Demonstrating lambdas and streams with an array of Integers. (Part 2 of 2.)

17.4.1 Creating a Stream<Integer>

When you pass an array of objects to class Arrays's static method stream, the method returns a Stream of the appropriate type—e.g., line 19 produces a Stream<Integer> from an Integer array. Interface **Stream** (package java.util.stream) is a generic interface for performing stream operations on any *non-primitive* type. The types of objects that are processed are determined by the Stream's source.

Class Arrays also provides overloaded versions of method stream for creating Int-Streams, LongStreams and DoubleStreams from entire int, long and double arrays or from ranges of elements in the arrays. The specialized IntStream, LongStream and Dou-bleStream classes provide various methods for common operations on numerical streams, as you learned in Section 17.3.

17.4.2 Sorting a Stream and Collecting the Results

In Section 6.12, you learned how to sort arrays with the sort and parallelSort static methods of class Arrays. You'll often sort the results of stream operations, so in lines 18–21 we'll sort the values array using stream techniques and display the sorted values. First, line 19 creates a Stream<Integer> from values. Next, line 20 calls Stream method sorted which sort the elements—this results in an intermediate Stream<Integers> with the values in *ascending* order.

To display the sorted results, we could output each value using Stream terminal operation forEach (as in line 15 of Fig. 17.5). However, when processing streams, you often create *new* collections containing the results so that you can perform additional operations on them. To create a collection, you can use Stream method **collect** (Fig. 17.6, line 21), which is a *terminal operation*. As the stream pipeline is processed, method collect performs a **mutable reduction** operation that places the results into an object which subsequently *can be modified*—often a collection, such as a List, Map or Set. The version of method collect in line 21 receives as it's argument an object that implements interface **Collector** (package java.util.stream), which specifies how to perform the mutable reduction. Class **Collectors** (package java.util.stream) provides static methods that return predefined Collector implementations. For example, Collectors method **toList** (line 21) transforms the Stream<Integer> into a List<Integer> collection. In lines 18–21, the resulting List<Integer> is then displayed with an *implicit* call to its toString method.

We demonstrate another version of method collect in Section 17.6. For more details on class Collectors, visit:

```
http://download.java.net/jdk8/docs/api/java/util/stream/
    Collectors.html
```

17.4.3 Filtering a Stream and Storing the Results for Later Use

Lines 24–27 of Fig. 17.6 create a Stream<Integer>, call Stream method filter (which receives a Predicate) to locate all the values greater than 4 and collect the results into a List<Integer>. Like IntPredicate (Section 17.3.4), functional interface Predicate has a test method that returns a boolean indicating whether the argument satisfies a condition, as well as methods **and**, **negate** and **or**.

We assign the stream pipeline's resulting List<Integer> to variable greaterThan4, which is used in line 28 to display the values greater than 4 and used again in lines 40–42 to perform additional operations on only the values greater than 4.

17.4.4 Filtering and Sorting a Stream and Collecting the Results

Lines 31–35 display the values greater than 4 in sorted order. First, line 32 creates a Stream<Integer>. Then line 33 filters the elements to locate all the values greater than 4. Next, line 34 indicates that we'd like the results sorted. Finally, line 35 collects the results into a List<Integer>, which is then displayed as a String.

17.4.5 Sorting Previously Collected Results

Lines 40–42 use the greaterThan4 collection that was created in lines 24–27 to show additional processing on a collection containing the results of a prior stream pipeline. In this case, we use streams to sort the values in greaterThan4, collect the results into a new List<Integers> and display the sorted values.

17.5 Stream<String> Manipulations

[This section demonstrates how lambdas and streams can be used to simplify programming tasks that you learned in Chapter 14, Strings, Characters and Regular Expressions.]
Figure 17.7 performs some of the same stream operations you learned in Sections 17.3—17.4 but on a Stream<String>. In addition, we demonstrate *case-insensitive sorting* and sorting in *descending* order. Throughout this example, we use the String array strings (lines 11–12) that's initialized with color names—some with an initial uppercase letter. Line 15 displays the contents of strings *before* we perform any stream processing.

```java
1   // Fig. 17.7: ArraysAndStreams2.java
2   // Demonstrating lambdas and streams with an array of Strings.
3   import java.util.Arrays;
4   import java.util.Comparator;
5   import java.util.stream.Collectors;
6
7   public class ArraysAndStreams2
8   {
9      public static void main(String[] args)
10     {
11        String[] strings =
12           {"Red", "orange", "Yellow", "green", "Blue", "indigo", "Violet"};
13
14        // display original strings
15        System.out.printf("Original strings: %s%n", Arrays.asList(strings));
16
17        // strings in uppercase
18        System.out.printf("strings in uppercase: %s%n",
19           Arrays.stream(strings)
20              .map(String::toUpperCase)
21              .collect(Collectors.toList()));
22
23        // strings less than "n" (case insensitive) sorted ascending
24        System.out.printf("strings greater than m sorted ascending: %s%n",
25           Arrays.stream(strings)
26              .filter(s -> s.compareToIgnoreCase("n") < 0)
27              .sorted(String.CASE_INSENSITIVE_ORDER)
28              .collect(Collectors.toList()));
29
30        // strings less than "n" (case insensitive) sorted descending
31        System.out.printf("strings greater than m sorted descending: %s%n",
32           Arrays.stream(strings)
33              .filter(s -> s.compareToIgnoreCase("n") < 0)
34              .sorted(String.CASE_INSENSITIVE_ORDER.reversed())
35              .collect(Collectors.toList()));
36     }
37  } // end class ArraysAndStreams2
```

Fig. 17.7 | Demonstrating lambdas and streams with an array of Strings. (Part 1 of 2.)

```
Original strings: [Red, orange, Yellow, green, Blue, indigo, Violet]
strings in uppercase: [RED, ORANGE, YELLOW, GREEN, BLUE, INDIGO, VIOLET]
strings greater than m sorted ascending: [orange, Red, Violet, Yellow]
strings greater than m sorted descending: [Yellow, Violet, Red, orange]
```

Fig. 17.7 | Demonstrating lambdas and streams with an array of Strings. (Part 2 of 2.)

17.5.1 Mapping Strings to Uppercase Using a Method Reference

Lines 18–21 display the Strings in uppercase letters. To do so, line 19 creates a Stream<String> from the array strings, then line 20 calls Stream method map to map each String to its uppercase version by calling String instance method toUpperCase. String::toUpperCase is known as a **method reference** and is a shorthand notation for a lambda expression—in this case, for a lambda expression like:

```
    (String s) -> {return s.toUpperCase();}
```

or

```
    s -> s.toUpperCase()
```

String::toUpperCase is a method reference for String instance method toUpperCase. Figure 17.8 shows the four method reference types.

Lambda	Description
String::toUpperCase	Method reference for an instance method of a class. Creates a one-parameter lambda that invokes the instance method on the lambda's argument and returns the method's result. Used in Fig. 17.7.
System.out::println	Method reference for an instance method that should be called on a specific object. Creates a one-parameter lambda that invokes the instance method on the specified object—passing the lambda's argument to the instance method—and returns the method's result. Used in Fig. 17.10.
Math::sqrt	Method reference for a static method of a class. Creates a one-parameter lambda in which the lambda's argument is passed to the specified a static method and the lambda returns the method's result.
TreeMap::new	Constructor reference. Creates a lambda that invokes the no-argument constructor of the specified class to create and initialize a new object of that class. Used in Fig. 17.17.

Fig. 17.8 | Types of method references.

Stream method map receives as an argument an object that implements the functional interface Function—the instance method reference String::toUpperCase is treated as a lambda that implements interface Function. This interface's **apply** method receives one parameter and returns a result—in this case, method apply receives a String and returns the uppercase version of the String. Line 21 *collects* the results into a List<String> that we output as a String.

17.5.2 Filtering Strings Then Sorting Them in Case-Insensitive Ascending Order

Lines 24–28 filter and sort the Strings. Line 25 creates a Stream<String> from the array strings, then line 26 calls Stream method filter to locate all the Strings that are greater than "m", using a *case-insensitive* comparison in the Predicate lambda. Line 27 sorts the results and line 28 collects them into a List<String> that we output as a String. In this case, line 27 invokes the version of Stream method sorted that receives a Comparator as an argument. As you learned in Section 16.7.1, a Comparator defines a compare method that returns a negative value if the first value being compared is less than the second, 0 if they're equal and a positive value if the first value is greater than the second. By default, method sorted uses the *natural order* for the type—for Strings, the natural order is case sensitive, which means that "Z" is less than "a". Passing the predefined Comparator String.CASE_INSENSITIVE_ORDER performs a *case-insensitive* sort.

17.5.3 Filtering Strings Then Sorting Them in Case-Insensitive Descending Order

Lines 31–35 perform the same tasks as lines 24–28, but sort the Strings in *descending* order. Functional interface Comparator contains default method **reversed**, which reverses an existing Comparator's ordering. When applied to String.CASE_INSENSITIVE_ORDER, the Strings are sorted in *descending* order.

17.6 Stream<Employee> Manipulations

The example in Figs. 17.9–17.16 demonstrates various lambda and stream capabilities using a Stream<Employee>. Class Employee (Fig. 17.9) represents an employee with a first name, last name, salary and department and provides methods for manipulating these values. In addition, the class provides a getName method (lines 69–72) that returns the combined first and last name as a String, and a toString method (lines 75–80) that returns a formatted String containing the employee's first name, last name, salary and department.

```
 1  // Fig. 17.9: Employee.java
 2  // Employee class.
 3  public class Employee
 4  {
 5     private String firstName;
 6     private String lastName;
 7     private double salary;
 8     private String department;
 9
10     // constructor
11     public Employee(String firstName, String lastName,
12        double salary, String department)
13     {
14        this.firstName = firstName;
15        this.lastName = lastName;
```

Fig. 17.9 | Employee class for use in Figs. 17.10–17.16. (Part 1 of 3.)

```
16          this.salary = salary;
17          this.department = department;
18       }
19
20       // set firstName
21       public void setFirstName(String firstName)
22       {
23          this.firstName = firstName;
24       }
25
26       // get firstName
27       public String getFirstName()
28       {
29          return firstName;
30       }
31
32       // set lastName
33       public void setLastName(String lastName)
34       {
35          this.lastName = lastName;
36       }
37
38       // get lastName
39       public String getLastName()
40       {
41          return lastName;
42       }
43
44       // set salary
45       public void setSalary(double salary)
46       {
47          this.salary = salary;
48       }
49
50       // get salary
51       public double getSalary()
52       {
53          return salary;
54       }
55
56       // set department
57       public void setDepartment(String department)
58       {
59          this.department = department;
60       }
61
62       // get department
63       public String getDepartment()
64       {
65          return department;
66       }
67
```

Fig. 17.9 | Employee class for use in Figs. 17.10–17.16. (Part 2 of 3.)

```
68        // return Employee's first and last name combined
69        public String getName()
70        {
71            return String.format("%s %s", getFirstName(), getLastName());
72        }
73
74        // return a String containing the Employee's information
75        @Override
76        public String toString()
77        {
78            return String.format("%-8s %-8s %8.2f   %s",
79                getFirstName(), getLastName(), getSalary(), getDepartment());
80        } // end method toString
81    } // end class Employee
```

Fig. 17.9 | Employee class for use in Figs. 17.10–17.16. (Part 3 of 3.)

17.6.1 Creating and Displaying a List<Employee>

Class ProcessingEmployees (Figs. 17.10–17.16) is split into several figures so we can show you the lambda and streams operations with their corresponding outputs. Figure 17.10 creates an array of Employees (lines 17–24) and gets its List view (line 27).

```
 1    // Fig. 17.10: ProcessingEmployees.java
 2    // Processing streams of Employee objects.
 3    import java.util.Arrays;
 4    import java.util.Comparator;
 5    import java.util.List;
 6    import java.util.Map;
 7    import java.util.TreeMap;
 8    import java.util.function.Function;
 9    import java.util.function.Predicate;
10    import java.util.stream.Collectors;
11
12    public class ProcessingEmployees
13    {
14        public static void main(String[] args)
15        {
16            // initialize array of Employees
17            Employee[] employees = {
18                new Employee("Jason", "Red", 5000, "IT"),
19                new Employee("Ashley", "Green", 7600, "IT"),
20                new Employee("Matthew", "Indigo", 3587.5, "Sales"),
21                new Employee("James", "Indigo", 4700.77, "Marketing"),
22                new Employee("Luke", "Indigo", 6200, "IT"),
23                new Employee("Jason", "Blue", 3200, "Sales"),
24                new Employee("Wendy", "Brown", 4236.4, "Marketing")};
25
26            // get List view of the Employees
27            List<Employee> list = Arrays.asList(employees);
```

Fig. 17.10 | Creating an array of Employees, converting it to a List and displaying the List. (Part 1 of 2.)

```
28
29          // display all Employees
30          System.out.println("Complete Employee list:");
31          list.stream().forEach(System.out::println);
32
```

```
Complete Employee list:
Jason    Red      5000.00    IT
Ashley   Green    7600.00    IT
Matthew  Indigo   3587.50    Sales
James    Indigo   4700.77    Marketing
Luke     Indigo   6200.00    IT
Jason    Blue     3200.00    Sales
Wendy    Brown    4236.40    Marketing
```

Fig. 17.10 | Creating an array of Employees, converting it to a List and displaying the List. (Part 2 of 2.)

Line 31 creates a Stream<Employee>, then uses Stream method forEach to display each Employee's String representation. The instance method reference System.out::println is converted by the compiler into an object that implements the Consumer functional interface. This interface's **accept** method receives one argument and returns void. In this example, the accept method passes each Employee to the System.out object's println instance method, which implicitly calls class Employee's toString method to get the String representation. The output at the end of Fig. 17.10 shows the results of displaying all the Employees.

17.6.2 Filtering Employees with Salaries in a Specified Range

Figure 17.11 demonstrates filtering Employees with an object that implements the functional interface Predicate<Employee>, which is defined with a lambda in lines 34–35. Defining lambdas in this manner enables you to reuse them multiple times, as we do in lines 42 and 49. Lines 41–44 output the Employees with salaries in the range 4000–6000 sorted by salary as follows:

- Line 41 creates a Stream<Employee> from the List<Employee>.

- Line 42 filters the stream using the Predicate named fourToSixThousand.

- Line 43 sorts by salary the Employees that remain in the stream. To specify a Comparator for salaries, we use the Comparator interface's static method comparing. The method reference Employee::getSalary that's passed as an argument is converted by the compiler into an object that implements the Function interface. This Function is used to extract a value from an object in the stream for use in comparisons. Method comparing returns a Comparator object that calls getSalary on each of two Employee objects, then returns a negative value if the first Employee's salary is less than the second, 0 if they're equal and a positive value if the first Employee's salary is greater than the second.

- Finally, line 44 performs the terminal forEach operation that processes the stream pipeline and outputs the Employees sorted by salary.

```
33        // Predicate that returns true for salaries in the range $4000-$6000
34        Predicate<Employee> fourToSixThousand =
35           e -> (e.getSalary() >= 4000 && e.getSalary() <= 6000);
36
37        // Display Employees with salaries in the range $4000-$6000
38        // sorted into ascending order by salary
39        System.out.printf(
40           "%nEmployees earning $4000-$6000 per month sorted by salary:%n");
41        list.stream()
42           .filter(fourToSixThousand)
43           .sorted(Comparator.comparing(Employee::getSalary))
44           .forEach(System.out::println);
45
46        // Display first Employee with salary in the range $4000-$6000
47        System.out.printf("%nFirst employee who earns $4000-$6000:%n%s%n",
48           list.stream()
49              .filter(fourToSixThousand)
50              .findFirst()
51              .get());
52
```

```
Employees earning $4000-$6000 per month sorted by salary:
Wendy    Brown     4236.40    Marketing
James    Indigo    4700.77    Marketing
Jason    Red       5000.00    IT

First employee who earns $4000-$6000:
Jason    Red       5000.00    IT
```

Fig. 17.11 | Filtering Employees with salaries in the range $4000–$6000.

Short-Circuit Stream Pipeline Processing

In Section 4.8, you studied short-circuit evaluation with the logical AND (&&) and logical OR (||) operators. One of the nice performance features of lazy evaluation is the ability to perform *short circuit evaluation*—that is, to stop processing the stream pipeline as soon as the desired result is available. Line 50 demonstrates Stream method **findFirst**—a *short-circuiting terminal operation* that processes the stream pipeline and terminates processing as soon as the *first* object from the stream pipeline is found. Based on the original list of Employees, the processing of the stream in lines 48–51—which filters Employees with salaries in the range $4000–$6000—proceeds as follows: The Predicate fourToSixThousand is applied to the first Employee (Jason Red). His salary ($5000.00) is in the range $4000–$6000, so the Predicate returns true and processing of the stream terminates *immediately*, having processed only one of the eight objects in the stream. Method findFirst then returns an Optional (in this case, an Optional<Employee>) containing the object that was found, if any. The call to Optional method get (line 51) returns the matching Employee object in this example. Even if the stream contained millions of Employee objects, the filter operation would be performed only until a match is found.

17.6.3 Sorting Employees By Multiple Fields

Figure 17.12 shows how to use streams to sort objects by *multiple* fields. In this example, we sort Employees by last name, then, for Employees with the same last name, we also sort them by first name. To do so, we begin by creating two Functions that each receive an Employee and return a String:

- byFirstName (line 54) is assigned a method reference for Employee instance method getFirstName

- byLastName (line 55) is assigned a method reference for Employee instance method getLastName

Next, we use these Functions to create a Comparator (lastThenFirst; lines 58–59) that first compares two Employees by last name, then compares them by first name. We use Comparator method comparing to create a Comparator that calls Function byLastName on an Employee to get its last name. On the resulting Comparator, we call Comparator method **thenComparing** to create a Comparator that first compares Employees by last name and, *if the last names are equal*, then compares them by first name. Lines 64–65 use this new lastThenFirst Comparator to sort the Employees in *ascending* order, then display the results. We reuse the Comparator in lines 71–73, but call its reversed method to indicate that the Employees should be sorted in *descending* order by last name, then first name.

```
53        // Functions for getting first and last names from an Employee
54        Function<Employee, String> byFirstName = Employee::getFirstName;
55        Function<Employee, String> byLastName = Employee::getLastName;
56
57        // Comparator for comparing Employees by first name then last name
58        Comparator<Employee> lastThenFirst =
59            Comparator.comparing(byLastName).thenComparing(byFirstName);
60
61        // sort employees by last name, then first name
62        System.out.printf(
63            "%nEmployees in ascending order by last name then first:%n");
64        list.stream()
65            .sorted(lastThenFirst)
66            .forEach(System.out::println);
67
68        // sort employees in descending order by last name, then first name
69        System.out.printf(
70            "%nEmployees in descending order by last name then first:%n");
71        list.stream()
72            .sorted(lastThenFirst.reversed())
73            .forEach(System.out::println);
74
```

```
Employees in ascending order by last name then first:
Jason     Blue      3200.00    Sales
Wendy     Brown     4236.40    Marketing
Ashley    Green     7600.00    IT
James     Indigo    4700.77    Marketing
Luke      Indigo    6200.00    IT
Matthew   Indigo    3587.50    Sales
Jason     Red       5000.00    IT
```

Fig. 17.12 | Sorting Employees by last name then first name. (Part 1 of 2.)

```
Employees in descending order by last name then first:
Jason     Red       5000.00    IT
Matthew   Indigo    3587.50    Sales
Luke      Indigo    6200.00    IT
James     Indigo    4700.77    Marketing
Ashley    Green     7600.00    IT
Wendy     Brown     4236.40    Marketing
Jason     Blue      3200.00    Sales
```

Fig. 17.12 | Sorting `Employees` by last name then first name. (Part 2 of 2.)

17.6.4 Mapping Employees to Unique Last Name Strings

You previously used `map` operations to perform calculations on `int` values and to convert `Strings` to uppercase letters. In both cases, the resulting streams contained values of the same types as the original streams. Figure 17.13 shows how to map objects of one type (`Employee`) to objects of a different type (`String`). Lines 77–81 perform the following tasks:

- Line 77 creates a `Stream<Employee>`.

- Line 78 maps the `Employees` to their last names using the instance method reference `Employee::getName` as method `map`'s `Function` argument. The result is a `Stream<String>`.

- Line 79 calls `Stream` method **distinct** on the `Stream<String>` to eliminate any duplicate `String` objects in a `Stream<String>`.

- Line 80 sorts the unique last names.

- Finally, line 81 performs a terminal `forEach` operation that processes the stream pipeline and outputs the unique last names in sorted order.

Lines 86–89 sort the `Employees` by last name then first name, then `map` the `Employees` to `Strings` with `Employee` instance method `getName` (line 88) and display the sorted names in a terminal `forEach` operation.

```
75       // display unique employee last names sorted
76       System.out.printf("%nUnique employee last names:%n");
77       list.stream()
78          .map(Employee::getLastName)
79          .distinct()
80          .sorted()
81          .forEach(System.out::println);
82
83       // display only first and last names
84       System.out.printf(
85          "%nEmployee names in order by last name then first name:%n");
86       list.stream()
87          .sorted(lastThenFirst)
88          .map(Employee::getName)
89          .forEach(System.out::println);
90
```

Fig. 17.13 | Mapping `Employee` objects to last names and whole names. (Part 1 of 2.)

```
Unique employee last names:
Blue
Brown
Green
Indigo
Red

Employee names in order by last name then first name:
Jason Blue
Wendy Brown
Ashley Green
James Indigo
Luke Indigo
Matthew Indigo
Jason Red
```

Fig. 17.13 | Mapping `Employee` objects to last names and whole names. (Part 2 of 2.)

17.6.5 Grouping Employees By Department

Figure 17.14 uses `Stream` method `collect` (line 95) to group `Employee`s by department. Method `collect`'s argument is a `Collector` that specifies how to summarize the data into a useful form. In this case, we use the `Collector` returned by `Collectors` static method **groupingBy**, which receives a `Function` that classifies the objects in the stream—the values returned by this function are used as the keys in a `Map`. The corresponding values, by default, are `List`s containing the stream elements in a given category. When method `collect` is used with this `Collector`, the result is a `Map<String, List<Employee>>` in which each `String` key is a department and each `List<Employee>` contains the `Employee`s in that department. We assign this `Map` to variable `groupedByDepartment`, which is used in lines 96–103 to display the `Employee`s grouped by department. `Map` method **forEach** performs an operation on each of the `Map`'s key–value pairs. The argument to the method is an object that implements functional interface **BiConsumer**. This interface's `accept` method has two parameters. For `Map`s, the first parameter represents the key and the second represents the corresponding value.

```
91      // group Employees by department
92      System.out.printf("%nEmployees by department:%n");
93      Map<String, List<Employee>> groupedByDepartment =
94         list.stream()
95            .collect(Collectors.groupingBy(Employee::getDepartment));
96      groupedByDepartment.forEach(
97         (department, employeesInDepartment) ->
98         {
99            System.out.println(department);
100           employeesInDepartment.forEach(
101              employee -> System.out.printf("   %s%n", employee));
102        }
103     );
104
```

Fig. 17.14 | Grouping `Employee`s by department. (Part 1 of 2.)

```
Employees by department:
Sales
    Matthew  Indigo   3587.50   Sales
    Jason    Blue     3200.00   Sales
IT
    Jason    Red      5000.00   IT
    Ashley   Green    7600.00   IT
    Luke     Indigo   6200.00   IT
Marketing
    James    Indigo   4700.77   Marketing
    Wendy    Brown    4236.40   Marketing
```

Fig. 17.14 | Grouping Employees by department. (Part 2 of 2.)

17.6.6 Counting the Number of Employees in Each Department

Figure 17.15 once again demonstrates Stream method collect and Collectors static method groupingBy, but in this case we count the number of Employees in each department. Lines 107–110 produce a Map<String, Long> in which each String key is a department name and the corresponding Long value is the number of Employees in that department. In this case, we use a version of Collectors static method groupingBy that receives two arguments—the first is a Function that classifies the objects in the stream and the second is another Collector (known as the **downstream Collector**). In this case, we use a call to Collectors static method counting as the second argument. This method returns a Collector that counts the number of objects in a given classification, rather than collecting them into a List. Lines 111–113 then output the key–value pairs from the resulting Map<String, Long>.

```
105        // count number of Employees in each department
106        System.out.printf("%nCount of Employees by department:%n");
107        Map<String, Long> employeeCountByDepartment =
108           list.stream()
109              .collect(Collectors.groupingBy(Employee::getDepartment,
110                 Collectors.counting()));
111        employeeCountByDepartment.forEach(
112           (department, count) -> System.out.printf(
113              "%s has %d employee(s)%n", department, count));
114
```

```
Count of Employees by department:
IT has 3 employee(s)
Marketing has 2 employee(s)
Sales has 2 employee(s)
```

Fig. 17.15 | Counting the number of Employees in each department.

17.6.7 Summing and Averaging Employee Salaries

Figure 17.16 demonstrates Stream method **mapToDouble** (lines 119, 126 and 132), which maps objects to double values and returns a DoubleStream. In this case, we map Employee objects to their salaries so that we can calculate the *sum* and *average*. Method mapToDouble receives an object that implements the functional interface **ToDoubleFunction** (package java.util.function). This interface's **applyAsDouble** method invokes an instance method on an object and returns a double value. Lines 119, 126 and 132 each pass to mapToDouble the Employee instance method reference Employee::getSalary, which returns the current Employee's salary as a double. The compiler converts this method reference into an object that implements the functional interface ToDoubleFunction.

```
115        // sum of Employee salaries with DoubleStream sum method
116        System.out.printf(
117           "%nSum of Employees' salaries (via sum method): %.2f%n",
118           list.stream()
119              .mapToDouble(Employee::getSalary)
120              .sum());
121
122        // calculate sum of Employee salaries with Stream reduce method
123        System.out.printf(
124           "Sum of Employees' salaries (via reduce method): %.2f%n",
125           list.stream()
126              .mapToDouble(Employee::getSalary)
127              .reduce(0, (value1, value2) -> value1 + value2));
128
129        // average of Employee salaries with DoubleStream average method
130        System.out.printf("Average of Employees' salaries: %.2f%n",
131           list.stream()
132              .mapToDouble(Employee::getSalary)
133              .average()
134              .getAsDouble());
135     } // end main
136 } // end class ProcessingEmployees
```

```
Sum of Employees' salaries (via sum method): 34524.67
Sum of Employees' salaries (via reduce method): 34525.67
Average of Employees' salaries: 4932.10
```

Fig. 17.16 | Summing and averaging Employee salaries.

Lines 118–120 create a Stream<Employee>, map it to a DoubleStream, then invoke DoubleStream method sum to calculate the sum of the Employees' salaries. Lines 125–127 also sum the Employees' salaries, but do so using DoubleStream method reduce rather than sum—we introduced method reduce in Section 17.3 with IntStreams. Finally, lines 131–134 calculate the average of the Employees' salaries using DoubleStream method average, which returns an OptionalDouble in case the DoubleStream does not contain any elements. In this case, we know the stream has elements, so we simply call method OptionalDouble method getAsDouble to get the result. Recall that you can also use method orElse to specify a value that should be used if the average method was called on an empty DoubleStream, and thus could not calculate the average.

17.7 Creating a Stream<String> from a File

Figure 17.17 uses lambdas and streams to summarize the number of occurrences of each word in a file then display a summary of the words in alphabetical order grouped by starting letter. This is commonly called a concordance (http://en.wikipedia.org/wiki/Concordance_(publishing)). Concordances are often used to analyze published works. For example, concordances of William Shakespeare's and Christopher Marlowe's works have been used to question whether they are the same person. Figure 17.18 shows the program's output. Line 16 of Fig. 17.17creates a regular expression Pattern that we'll use to split lines of text into their individual words. This Pattern represents one or more consecutive white-space characters. (We introduced regular expressions in Section 14.7.)

```java
 1   // Fig. 17.17: StreamOfLines.java
 2   // Counting word occurrences in a text file.
 3   import java.io.IOException;
 4   import java.nio.file.Files;
 5   import java.nio.file.Paths;
 6   import java.util.Map;
 7   import java.util.TreeMap;
 8   import java.util.regex.Pattern;
 9   import java.util.stream.Collectors;
10
11   public class StreamOfLines
12   {
13      public static void main(String[] args) throws IOException
14      {
15         // Regex that matches one or more consecutive whitespace characters
16         Pattern pattern = Pattern.compile("\\s+");
17
18         // count occurrences of each word in a Stream<String> sorted by word
19         Map<String, Long> wordCounts =
20            Files.lines(Paths.get("Chapter2Paragraph.txt"))
21               .map(line -> line.replaceAll("(?!')\\p{P}", ""))
22               .flatMap(line -> pattern.splitAsStream(line))
23               .collect(Collectors.groupingBy(String::toLowerCase,
24                  TreeMap::new, Collectors.counting()));
25
26         // display the words grouped by starting letter
27         wordCounts.entrySet()
28            .stream()
29            .collect(
30               Collectors.groupingBy(entry -> entry.getKey().charAt(0),
31                  TreeMap::new, Collectors.toList()))
32            .forEach((letter, wordList) ->
33               {
34                  System.out.printf("%n%C%n", letter);
35                  wordList.stream().forEach(word -> System.out.printf(
36                     "%13s: %d%n", word.getKey(), word.getValue()));
37               });
38      }
39   } // end class StreamOfLines
```

Fig. 17.17 | Counting word occurrences in a text file.

```
A                        I                        R
          a: 2                   inputs: 1                result: 1
        and: 3                 instruct: 1               results: 2
 application: 2               introduces: 1                  run: 1
  arithmetic: 1
                         J                        S
B                                 java: 1                   save: 1
      begin: 1                     jdk: 1                 screen: 1
                                                            show: 1
C                        L                                   sum: 1
 calculates: 1                    last: 1
calculations: 1                  later: 1           T
    chapter: 1                   learn: 1
   chapters: 1                                              that: 3
commandline: 1           M                                   the: 7
   compares: 1                                             their: 2
 comparison: 1                    make: 1                   then: 2
    compile: 1                messages: 2                   this: 2
   computer: 1           N                                    to: 4
D                                                           tools: 1
  decisions: 1                 numbers: 2                    two: 2
demonstrates: 1          O                        U
    display: 1
   displays: 2                  obtains: 1                   use: 2
                                    of: 1                   user: 1
E                                   on: 1
    example: 1                  output: 1         W
   examples: 1           P
                                                              we: 2
F                              perform: 1                   with: 1
        for: 1                 present: 1         Y
       from: 1                 program: 1
                           programming: 1                you'll: 2
H                             programs: 2
        how: 2
```

Fig. 17.18 | Output for the program of Fig. 17.17 arranged in three columns.

Summarizing the Occurrences of Each Word in the File

Lines 19–24 summarize contents of the text file "Chapter2Paragraph.txt" (which is located in the folder with the example) into a Map<String, Long> in which each String key is a word in the file and the corresponding Long value is the number of occurrences of that word. The statement performs the following tasks:

- Line 20 uses Files method **lines** to create a Stream<String> for reading the lines of text from a file. Class Files (package java.nio.file) is one of many classes throughout the Java APIs that have been enhanced to support Streams.

- Line 21 uses Stream method map to remove all the punctuation, except apostrophes, in the lines of text. The lambda argument represents a Function that invokes String method replaceAll on its String argument. This method receives two arguments—the first is a regular expression String to match and the second is a String with which every match is replaced. In the regular expression,

"(?!')" indicates that the rest of the regular expression should ignore apostrophes (such as in a contraction, like "you'll") and "\\p{P}" matches any punctuation character. For any match, the call to replaceAll removes the punctuation by replacing it with an empty String. The result of line 21 is an intermediate Stream<String> containing the lines without punctuation.

- Line 22 uses Stream method **flatMap** to break each line of text into its separate words. Method flatMap receives a Function that maps an object into a stream of elements. In this case, the object is a String containing words and the result is another intermediate Stream<String> for the individual words. The lambda in line 22 passes the String representing a line of text to Pattern method **splitAsStream** (new in Java SE 8), which uses the regular expression specified in the Pattern (line 16) to tokenize the String into its individual words.

- Lines 23–24 use Stream method collect to count the frequency of each word and place the words and their counts into the TreeMap<String, Long>. Here, we use a version of Collectors method groupingBy that receives three arguments— a classifier, a Map factory and a downstream Collector. The classifier is a Function that returns objects for use as keys in the resulting Map—the method reference String::toLowerCase converts each word in the Stream<String> to lowercase. The Map factory is an object that implements interface Supplier and returns a new Map collection—the *constructor reference* TreeMap::new returns a TreeMap that maintains its keys in sorted order. Collectors.counting() is the downstream Collector that determines the number of occurrences of each key in the stream.

Displaying the Summary Grouped by Starting Letter

Next, lines 27–37 group the key–value pairs in the Map wordCounts by the keys' first letter. This produces a new Map in which each key is a Character and the corresponding value is a List of the key–value pairs in wordCounts in which the key starts with the Character. The statement performs the following tasks:

- First we need to get a Stream for processing the key–value pairs in wordCounts. Interface Map does not contain any methods that return Streams. So, line 27 calls Map method entrySet on wordCounts to get a Set of **Map.Entry** objects that each contain one key–value pair from wordCounts. This produces an object of type Set<Map.Entry<String, Long>>.

- Line 28 calls Set method stream to get a Stream<Map.Entry<String, Long>>.

- Lines 29–31 call Stream method collect with three arguments—a classifier, a Map factory and a downstream Collector. The classifier Function in this case gets the key from the Map.Entry then uses String method charAt to get the key's first character—this becomes a Character key in the resulting Map. Once again, we use the constructor reference TreeMap::new as the Map factory to create a TreeMap that maintains its keys in sorted order. The downstream Collector (Collectors.toList()) places the Map.Entry objects into a List collection. The result of collect is a Map<Character, List<Map.Entry<String, Long>>>.

- Finally, to display the summary of the words and their counts by letter (i.e., the concordance), lines 32–37 pass a lambda to Map method forEach. The lambda (a BiConsumer) receives two parameters—letter and wordList represent the Character key and the List value, respectively, for each key–value pair in the Map produced by the preceding collect operation. The body of this lambda has two statements, so it *must* be enclosed in curly braces. The statement in line 34 displays the Character key on its own line. The statement in lines 35–36 gets a Stream<Map.Entry<String, Long>> from the wordList, then calls Stream method forEach to display the key and value from each Map.Entry object.

17.8 Generating Streams of Random Values

In Fig. 5.7, we demonstrated rolling a six-sided die 6,000,000 times and summarizing the frequencies of each face using *external iteration* (a for loop) and a switch statement that determined which counter to increment. We then displayed the results using separate statements that performed external iteration. In Fig. 6.7, we reimplemented Fig. 5.7, replacing the entire switch statement with a single statement that incremented counters in an array—that version of rolling the die still used external iteration to produce and summarize 6,000,000 random rolls and to display the final results. Both prior versions of this example, used mutable variables to control the external iteration and to summarize the results. Figure 17.19 reimplements those programs with a *single statement* that does it all, using lambdas, streams, internal iteration and no mutable variables to roll the die 6,000,000 times, calculate the frequencies and display the results.

```java
1   // Fig. 17.19: RandomIntStream.java
2   // Rolling a die 6,000,000 times with streams
3   import java.security.SecureRandom;
4   import java.util.Map;
5   import java.util.function.Function;
6   import java.util.stream.IntStream;
7   import java.util.stream.Collectors;
8
9   public class RandomIntStream
10  {
11     public static void main(String[] args)
12     {
13        SecureRandom random = new SecureRandom();
14
15        // roll a die 6,000,000 times and summarize the results
16        System.out.printf("%-6s%s%n", "Face", "Frequency");
17        random.ints(6_000_000, 1, 7)
18            .boxed()
19            .collect(Collectors.groupingBy(Function.identity(),
20                Collectors.counting()))
21            .forEach((face, frequency) ->
22                System.out.printf("%-6d%d%n", face, frequency));
23     }
24  } // end class RandomIntStream
```

Fig. 17.19 | Rolling a die 6,000,000 times with streams. (Part 1 of 2.)

```
Face   Frequency
1      999339
2      999937
3      1000302
4      999323
5      1000183
6      1000916
```

Fig. 17.19 | Rolling a die 6,000,000 times with streams. (Part 2 of 2.)

Creating an *IntStream* of Random Values

In Java SE 8, class SecureRandom has overloaded methods **ints**, **longs** and **doubles**, which it inherits from class Random (package java.util). These methods return IntStream, Long-Stream and DoubleStream, respectively, that represent streams of random numbers. Each method has four overloads. We describe the ints overloads here—methods longs and doubles perform the same tasks for streams of long and double values, respectively:

- ints()—creates an IntStream for an *infinite stream* of random ints. An **infinite stream** has an *unknown* number of elements—you use a short-circuiting terminal operation to complete processing on an infinite stream. We'll use an infinite stream in Chapter 23 to find prime numbers with the Sieve of Eratosthenes.

- ints(long)—creates an IntStream with the specified number of random ints.

- ints(int, int)—creates an IntStream for an *infinite stream* of random int values in the range starting with the first argument and up to, but not including, the second argument.

- ints(long, int, int)—creates an IntStream with the specified number of random int values in the range starting with the first argument and up to, but not including, the second argument.

Line 17 uses the last overloaded version of ints to create an IntStream of 6,000,000 random integer values in the range 1–6.

Converting an *IntStream* to a *Stream<Integer>*

We summarize the roll frequencies in this example by collecting them into a Map<Integer, Long> in which each Integer key is a side of the die and each Long value is the frequency of that side. Unfortunately, Java does not allow primitive values in collections, so to summarize the results in a Map, we must first convert the IntStream to a Stream<Integer>. We do this by calling IntStream method **boxed**.

Summarizing the Die Frequencies

Lines 19–20 call Stream method collect to summarize the results into a Map<Integer, Long>. The first argument to Collectors method groupingBy (line 19) calls static method **identity** from interface Function, which creates a Function that simply returns its argument. This allows the actual random values to be used as the Map's keys. The second argument to method groupingBy counts the number of occurrences of each key.

Displaying the Results

Lines 21–22 call the resulting Map's forEach method to display the summary of the results. This method receives an object that implements the BiConsumer functional interface as an argument. Recall that for Maps, the first parameter represents the key and the second represents the corresponding value. The lambda in lines 21–22 uses parameter face as the key and frequency as the value, and displays the face and frequency.

17.9 Lambda Event Handlers

In Section 12.11, you learned how to implement an event handler using an anonymous inner class. Some event-listener interfaces—such as ActionListener and ItemListener—are functional interfaces. For such interfaces, you can implement event handlers with lambdas. For example, the following statement from Fig. 12.21:

```
imagesJComboBox.addItemListener(
    new ItemListener() // anonymous inner class
    {
        // handle JComboBox event
        @Override
        public void itemStateChanged(ItemEvent event)
        {
            // determine whether item selected
            if (event.getStateChange() == ItemEvent.SELECTED)
                label.setIcon(icons[
                    imagesJComboBox.getSelectedIndex()]);
        }
    } // end anonymous inner class
); // end call to addItemListener
```

which registers an event handler for a JComboBox can be implemented more concisely as

```
imagesJComboBox.addItemListener(event -> {
    if (event.getStateChange() == ItemEvent.SELECTED)
        label.setIcon(icons[imagesJComboBox.getSelectedIndex()]);
});
```

For a simple event handler like this one, a lambda significantly reduces the amount of code you need to write.

17.10 Additional Notes on Java SE 8 Interfaces

Java SE 8 Interfaces Allow Inheritance of Method Implementations
Functional interfaces *must* contain only one abstract method, but may also contain default methods and static methods that are fully implemented in the interface declarations. For example, the Function interface—which is used extensively in functional programming—has methods apply (abstract), compose (default), andThen (default) and identity (static).

When a class implements an interface with default methods and does *not* override them, the class inherits the default methods' implementations. An interface's designer can now evolve an interface by adding new default and static methods without breaking existing code that implements the interface. For example, interface Comparator (Section 16.7.1) now contains many default and static methods, but older classes that implement this interface will still compile and operate properly in Java SE 8.

If one class inherits the same default method from two unrelated interfaces, the class *must* override that method; otherwise, the compiler will not know which method to use, so it will generate a compilation error.

Java SE 8: @FunctionalInterface Annotation

You can create your own functional interfaces by ensuring that each contains only one abstract method and zero or more default or static methods. Though not required, you can declare that an interface is a functional interface by preceding it with the **@FunctionalInterface annotation**. The compiler will then ensure that the interface contains only one abstract method; otherwise, it'll generate a compilation error.

17.11 Java SE 8 and Functional Programming Resources

Check out the book's web page at

```
http://www.deitel.com/books/jhtp10LOV
```

for links to the online Deitel Resource Centers that we built as we were writing *Java How to Program, 10/e, Late Objects Version.*

17.12 Wrap-Up

In this chapter, you learned about Java SE 8's new functional programming capabilities. We presented many examples, often showing simpler ways to implement tasks that you programmed in earlier chapters.

We overviewed the key functional programming technologies—functional interfaces, lambdas and streams. You learned how to process elements in an IntStream—a stream of int values. You created an IntStream from an array of ints, then used intermediate and terminal stream operations to create and process a stream pipeline that produced a result. You used lambdas to create anonymous methods that implemented functional interfaces.

We showed how to use a forEach terminal operation to perform an operation on each stream element. We used reduction operations to count the number of stream elements, determine the minimum and maximum values, and sum and average the values. You also learned how to use method reduce to create your own reduction operations.

You used intermediate operations to filter elements that matched a predicate and map elements to new values—in each case, these operations produced intermediate streams on which you could perform additional processing. You also learned how to sort elements in ascending and descending order and how to sort objects by multiple fields.

We demonstrated how to store the results of a stream pipeline into a collection for later use. To do so, you took advantage of various predefined Collector implementations provided by class Collectors. You also learned how to use a Collector to group elements into categories.

You learned that various Java SE 8 classes have been enhanced to support functional programming. You then used Files method lines to get a Stream<String> that read lines of text from a file and used SecureRandom method ints to get an IntStream of random values. You also learned how to convert an IntStream into a Stream<Integer> (via method boxed) so that you could use Stream method collect to summarize the frequencies of the Integer values and store the results in a Map.

Next, you learned how to implement an event-handling functional interface using a lambda. Finally, we presented some additional information about Java SE 8 interfaces and streams. In the next chapter, we discuss recursive programming in which methods call themselves either directly or indirectly.

Summary

Section 17.1 Introduction
- Prior to Java SE 8, Java supported three programming paradigms—procedural programming, object-oriented programming and generic programming. Java SE 8 adds functional programming.
- The new language and library capabilities that support functional programming were added to Java as part of Project Lambda.

Section 17.2 Functional Programming Technologies Overview
- Prior to functional programming, you typically determined what you wanted to accomplish, then specified the precise steps to accomplish that task.
- Using a loop to iterate over a collection of elements is known as external iteration (p. 723) and requires accessing the elements sequentially. Such iteration also requires mutable variables.
- In functional programming (p. 724), you specify what you want to accomplish in a task, but not how to accomplish it.
- Letting the library determine how to iterate over a collection of elements is known as internal iteration (p. 724). Internal iteration is easier to parallelize.
- Functional programming focuses on immutability (p. 724)—not modifying the data source being processed or any other program state.

Section 17.2.1 Functional Interfaces
- Functional interfaces are also known as single abstract method (SAM) interfaces.
- Package `java.util.function` contains six basic functional interfaces `BinaryOperator`, `Consumer`, `Function`, `Predicate`, `Supplier` and `UnaryOperator`.
- There are many specialized versions of the six basic functional interfaces for use with `int`, `long` and `double` primitive values. There are also generic customizations of `Consumer`, `Function` and `Predicate` for binary operations—that is, methods that take two arguments.

Section 17.2.2 Lambda Expressions
- A lambda expression (p. 725) represents an anonymous method—a shorthand notation for implementing a functional interface.
- The type of a lambda is the type of the functional interface that the lambda implements.
- Lambda expressions can be used anywhere functional interfaces are expected.
- A lambda consists of a parameter list followed by the arrow token (->, p. 725) and a body, as in:

      (*parameterList*) -> {*statements*}

  For example, the following lambda receives two `int`s and returns their sum:

      (**int** x, **int** y) -> {**return** x + y;}

  This lambda's body is a statement block that may contain one or more statements enclosed in curly braces.
- A lambda's parameter types may be omitted, as in:

      (x, y) -> {**return** x + y;}

  in which case, the parameter and return types are determined by the lambda's context.
- A lambda with a one-expression body can be written as:

      (x, y) -> x + y

  In this case, the expression's value is implicitly returned.

- When the parameter list contains only one parameter, the parentheses may be omitted, as in:
    ```
    value -> System.out.printf("%d ", value)
    ```
- A lambda with an empty parameter list is defined with () to the left of the arrow token (->), as in:
    ```
    () -> System.out.println("Welcome to lambdas!")
    ```
- There are also specialized shorthand forms of lambdas that are known as method references.

Section 17.2.3 Streams
- Streams (p. 726) are objects that implement interface Stream (from the package java.util.stream) and enable you to perform functional programming tasks. There are also specialized stream interfaces for processing int, long or double values.
- Streams move elements through a sequence of processing steps—known as a stream pipeline—that begins with a data source, performs various intermediate operations on the data source's elements and ends with a terminal operation. A stream pipeline is formed by chaining method calls.
- Unlike collections, streams do not have their own storage—once a stream is processed, it cannot be reused, because it does not maintain a copy of the original data source.
- An intermediate operation (p. 726) specifies tasks to perform on the stream's elements and always results in a new stream.
- Intermediate operations are lazy (p. 726)—they aren't performed until a terminal operation is invoked. This allows library developers to optimize stream-processing performance.
- A terminal operation (p. 726) initiates processing of a stream pipeline's intermediate operations and produces a result. Terminal operations are eager (p. 726)—they perform the requested operation when they are called.

Section 17.3 **IntStream** Operations
- An IntStream (package java.util.stream) is a specialized stream for manipulating int values.

Section 17.3.1 Creating an **IntStream** and Displaying Its Values with the **forEach** Terminal Operation
- IntStream static method of (p. 730) receives an int array as an argument and returns an IntStream for processing the array's values.
- IntStream method forEach (a terminal operation; p. 730) receives as its argument an object that implements the IntConsumer functional interface (package java.util.function). This interface's accept method receives one int value and performs a task with it.
- The Java compiler can infer the types of a lambda's parameters and the type returned by a lambda from the context in which the lambda is used. This is determined by the lambda's target type (p. 730)—the functional interface type that is expected where the lambda appears in the code.
- Lambdas may use final local variables or effectively final (p. 730) local variables.
- A lambda that refers to a local variable in the enclosing lexical scope is known as a capturing lambda.
- A lambda can use the outer class's this reference without qualifying it with the outer class's name.
- The parameter names and variable names that you use in lambdas cannot be the same as any other local variables in the lambda's lexical scope; otherwise, a compilation error occurs.

Section 17.3.2 Terminal Operations **count, min, max, sum** and **average**
- Class IntStream provides terminal operations for common stream reductions—count (p. 731) returns the number of elements, min returns the smallest int, max returns the largest int, sum returns the sum of all the ints and average returns an OptionalDouble (package java.util) containing the average of the ints as a value of type double.

- Class `OptionalDouble`'s `getAsDouble` method returns the `double` in the object or throws a `NoSuchElementException`. To prevent this exception, you can call method `orElse`, which returns the `OptionalDouble`'s value if there is one, or the value you pass to `orElse`, otherwise.

- `IntStream` method `summaryStatistics` performs the count, min, max, sum and average operations in one pass of an `IntStream`'s elements and returns the results as an `IntSummaryStatistics` object (package `java.util`).

Section 17.3.3 Terminal Operation *reduce*

- You can define your own reductions for an `IntStream` by calling its `reduce` method. The first argument is a value that helps you begin the reduction operation and the second argument is an object that implements the `IntBinaryOperator` (p. 732) functional interface.

- Method `reduce`'s first argument is formally called an identity value (p. 732)—a value that, when combined with any stream element using the `IntBinaryOperator` produces that element's original value.

Section 17.3.4 Intermediate Operations: Filtering and Sorting *IntStream Values*

- You filter elements to produce a stream of intermediate results that match a predicate. `IntStream` method `filter` (p. 733) receives an object that implements the `IntPredicate` functional interface (package `java.util.function`).

- `IntStream` method `sorted` (a lazy operation) orders the elements of the stream into ascending order (by default). All prior intermediate operations in the stream pipeline must be complete so that method `sorted` knows which elements to sort.

- Method `filter` a stateless intermediate operation—it does not require any information about other elements in the stream in order to test whether the current element satisfies the predicate.

- Method `sorted` is a stateful intermediate operation that requires information about all of the other elements in the stream in order to sort them.

- Interface `IntPredicate`'s `default` method and (p. 733) performs a logical AND operation with short-circuit evaluation between the `IntPredicate` on which it's called and its `IntPredicate` argument.

- Interface `IntPredicate`'s `default` method `negate` (p. 733) reverses the `boolean` value of the `IntPredicate` on which it's called.

- Interface `IntPredicate` `default` method or (p. 733) performs a logical OR operation with short-circuit evaluation between the `IntPredicate` on which it's called and its `IntPredicate` argument.

- You can use the interface `IntPredicate` `default` methods to compose more complex conditions.

Section 17.3.5 Intermediate Operation: Mapping

- Mapping is an intermediate operation that transforms a stream's elements to new values and produces a stream containing the resulting (possibly different type) elements.

- `IntStream` method `map` (a stateless intermediate operation; p. 734) receives an object that implements the `IntUnaryOperator` functional interface (package `java.util.function`).

Section 17.3.6 Creating Streams of *ints* with *IntStream Methods* range *and* rangeClosed

- `IntStream` methods range (p. 735) and `rangeClosed` each produce an ordered sequence of int values. Both methods take two int arguments representing the range of values. Method range produces a sequence of values from its first argument up to, but not including, its second argument. Method `rangeClosed` produces a sequence of values including both of its arguments.

Section 17.4 *Stream<Integer> Manipulations*

- Class `Array`'s `stream` method is used to create a `Stream` from an array of objects.

Section 17.4.1 Creating a **Stream<Integer>**

- Interface Stream (package java.util.stream; p. 736) is a generic interface for performing stream operations on objects. The types of objects that are processed are determined by the Stream's source.

- Class Arrays provides overloaded stream methods for creating IntStreams, LongStreams and DoubleStreams from int, long and double arrays or from ranges of elements in the arrays.

Section 17.4.2 Sorting a **Stream** and Collecting the Results

- Stream method sorted (p. 737) sorts a stream's elements into ascending order by default.

- To create a collection containing a stream pipeline's results, you can use Stream method collect (a terminal operation). As the stream pipeline is processed, method collect performs a mutable reduction operation that places the results into an object, such as a List, Map or Set.

- Method collect with one argument receives an object that implements interface Collector (package java.util.stream), which specifies how to perform the mutable reduction.

- Class Collectors (package java.util.stream) provides static methods that return predefined Collector implementations.

- Collectors method toList transforms a Stream<T> into a List<T> collection.

Section 17.4.3 Filtering a **Stream** and Storing the Results for Later Use

- Stream method filter (p. 737) receives a Predicate and results in a stream of objects that match the Predicate. Predicate method test returns a boolean indicating whether the argument satisfies a condition. Interface Predicate also has methods and, negate and or.

Section 17.4.5 Sorting Previously Collected Results

- Once you place the results of a stream pipeline into a collection, you can create a new stream from the collection for performing additional stream operations on the prior results.

Section 17.5.1 Mapping **Strings** to Uppercase Using a Method Reference

- Stream method map (p. 739) maps each element to a new value and produces a new stream with the same number of elements as the original stream.

- A method reference (p. 739) is a shorthand notation for a lambda expression.

- *ClassName*::*instanceMethodName* represents a method reference for an instance method of a class. Creates a one-parameter lambda that invokes the instance method on the lambda's argument and returns the method's result.

- *objectName*::*instanceMethodName* represents a method reference for an instance method that should be called on a specific object. Creates a one-parameter lambda that invokes the instance method on the specified object—passing the lambda's argument to the instance method—and returns the method's result.

- *ClassName*::*staticMethodName* represents a method reference for a static method of a class. Creates a one-parameter lambda in which the lambda's argument is passed to the specified static method and the lambda returns the method's result.

- *ClassName*::new represents a constructor reference. Creates a lambda that invokes the no-argument constructor of the specified class to create and initialize a new object of that class.

Section 17.5.2 Filtering **Strings** Then Sorting Them in Case-Insensitive Ascending Order

- Stream method sorted (p. 740) can receive a Comparator as an argument to specify how to compare stream elements for sorting.

- By default, method sorted uses the natural order for the stream's element type.

- For Strings, the natural order is case sensitive, which means that "Z" is less than "a". Passing the predefined Comparator String.CASE_INSENSITIVE_ORDER performs a case-insensitive sort.

Section 17.5.3 Filtering **String**s Then Sorting Them in Case-Insensitive Descending Order
- Functional interface Comparator's default method reversed (p. 740) reverses an existing Comparator's ordering.

Section 17.6.1 Creating and Displaying a **List<Employee>**
- When the instance method reference System.out::println is passed to Stream method forEach, it's converted by the compiler into an object that implements the Consumer functional interface. This interface's accept method receives one argument and returns void. In this case, the accept method passes the argument to the System.out object's println instance method.

Section 17.6.2 Filtering **Employee**s with Salaries in a Specified Range
- To reuse a lambda, you can assign it to a variable of the appropriate functional interface type.
- The Comparator interface's static method comparing (p. 745) receives a Function that's used to extract a value from an object in the stream for use in comparisons and returns a Comparator object.
- A nice performance feature of lazy evaluation is the ability to perform short circuit evaluation— that is, to stop processing the stream pipeline as soon as the desired result is available.
- Stream method findFirst is a short-circuiting terminal operation that processes the stream pipeline and terminates processing as soon as the first object from the stream pipeline is found. The method returns an Optional containing the object that was found, if any.

Section 17.6.3 Sorting **Employee**s By Multiple Fields
- To sort objects by two fields, you create a Comparator that uses two Functions. First you call Comparator method comparing to create a Comparator with the first Function. On the resulting Comparator, you call method thenComparing with the second Function. The resulting Comparator compares objects using the first Function then, for objects that are equal, compares them by the second Function.

Section 17.6.4 Mapping **Employee**s to Unique Last Name **String**s
- You can map objects in a stream to different types to produce another stream with the same number of elements as the original stream.
- Stream method distinct (p. 746) eliminates duplicate objects in a stream.

Section 17.6.5 Grouping **Employee**s By Department
- Collectors static method groupingBy (p. 747) with one argument receives a Function that classifies objects in the stream—the values returned by this function are used as the keys in a Map. The corresponding values, by default, are Lists containing the stream elements in a given category.
- Map method forEach performs an operation on each key–value pair. The method receives an object that implements functional interface BiConsumer. This interface's accept method has two parameters. For Maps, the first represents the key and the second the corresponding value.

Section 17.6.6 Counting the Number of **Employee**s in Each Department
- Collectors static method groupingBy with two arguments receives a Function that classifies the objects in the stream and another Collector (known as the downstream Collector; p. 748).
- Collectors static method counting returns a Collector that counts the number of objects in a given classification, rather than collecting them into a List.

*Section 17.6.7 Summing and Averaging **Employee** Salaries*

- Stream method mapToDouble (p. 748) maps objects to double values and returns a DoubleStream. The method receives an object that implements the functional interface ToDoubleFunction (package java.util.function). This interface's applyAsDouble method invokes an instance method on an object and returns a double value.

*Section 17.7 Creating a **Stream<String>** from a File*

- Files method lines creates a Stream<String> for reading the lines of text from a file.
- Stream method flatMap (p. 752) receives a Function that maps an object into a stream—e.g., a line of text into words.
- Pattern method splitAsStream (p. 752) uses a regular expression to tokenize a String.
- Collectors method groupingBy with three arguments receives a classifier, a Map factory and a downstream Collector. The classifier is a Function that returns objects which are used as keys in the resulting Map. The Map factory is an object that implements interface Supplier and returns a new Map collection. The downstream Collector determines how to collect each group's elements.
- Map method entrySet returns a Set of Map.Entry objects containing the Map's key–value pairs.
- Set method stream returns a stream for processing the Set's elements.

Section 17.8 Generating Streams of Random Values

- Class SecureRandom's methods ints (p. 754), longs and doubles (inherited from class Random) return IntStream, LongStream and DoubleStream, respectively, for streams of random numbers.
- Method ints with no arguments creates an IntStream for an infinite stream (p. 754) of random int values. An infinite stream is a stream with an unknown number of elements—you use a short-circuiting terminal operation to complete processing on an infinite stream.
- Method ints with a long argument creates an IntStream with the specified number of random int values.
- Method ints with two int arguments creates an IntStream for an infinite stream of random int values in the range starting with the first argument and up to, but not including, the second.
- Method ints with a long and two int arguments creates an IntStream with the specified number of random int values in the range starting with the first argument and up to, but not including, the second.
- To convert an IntStream to a Stream<Integer> call IntStream method boxed.
- Function static method identity creates a Function that simply returns its argument.

Section 17.9 Lambda Event Handlers

- Some event-listener interfaces are functional interfaces (p. 755). For such interfaces, you can implement event handlers with lambdas. For a simple event handler, a lambda significantly reduces the amount of code you need to write.

Section 17.10 Additional Notes on Java SE 8 Interfaces

- Functional interfaces must contain only one abstract method, but may also contain default methods and static methods that are fully implemented in the interface declarations.
- When a class implements an interface with default methods and does not override them, the class inherits the default methods' implementations. An interface's designer can now evolve an interface by adding new default and static methods without breaking existing code that implements the interface.

- If one class inherits the same `default` method from two interfaces, the class must override that method; otherwise, the compiler will generate a compilation error.
- You can create your own functional interfaces by ensuring that each contains only one `abstract` method and zero or more `default` or `static` methods.
- You can declare that an interface is a functional interface by preceding it with the `@Functional-Interface` annotation. The compiler will then ensure that the interface contains only one `abstract` method; otherwise, it'll generate a compilation error.

Self-Review Exercises

17.1 Fill in the blanks in each of the following statements:
a) Lambda expressions implement _____.
b) Functional programs are easier to _____ (i.e., perform multiple operations simultaneously) so that your programs can take advantage of multi-core architectures to enhance performance.
c) With _____ iteration the library determines how to access all the elements in a collection to perform a task.
d) The functional interface _____ contains method `apply` that takes two `T` arguments, performs an operation on them (such as a calculation) and returns a value of type `T`.
e) The functional interface _____ contains method `test` that takes a `T` argument and returns a `boolean`, and tests whether the `T` argument satisfies a condition.
f) A(n) _____ represents an anonymous method—a shorthand notation for implementing a functional interface.
g) Intermediate stream operations are _____—they aren't performed until a terminal operation is invoked.
h) The terminal stream operation _____ performs processing on every element in a stream.
i) _____ lambdas use local variables from the enclosing lexical scope.
j) A performance feature of lazy evaluation is the ability to perform _____ evaluation—that is, to stop processing the stream pipeline as soon as the desired result is available.
k) For Maps, a `BiConsumer`'s first parameter represents the _____ and its second represents the corresponding _____.

17.2 State whether each of the following is *true* or *false*. If *false*, explain why.
a) Lambda expressions can be used anywhere functional interfaces are expected.
b) Terminal operations are lazy—they perform the requested operation when they are called.
c) Method `reduce`'s first argument is formally called an identity value—a value that, when combined with a stream element using the `IntBinaryOperator` produces the stream element's original value. For example, when summing the elements, the identity value is 1 and when getting the product of the elements the identity value is 0.
d) `Stream` method `findFirst` is a short-circuiting terminal operation that processes the stream pipeline but terminates processing as soon as an object is found.
e) `Stream` method `flatMap` receives a `Function` that maps a stream into an object. For example, the object could be a `String` containing words and the result could be another intermediate `Stream<String>` for the individual words.
f) When a class implements an interface with `default` methods and overrides them, the class inherits the `default` methods' implementations. An interface's designer can now evolve an interface by adding new `default` and `static` methods without breaking existing code that implements the interface.

17.3 Write a lambda or method reference for each of the following tasks:

a) Write a lambda that can be used in place of the following anonymous inner class:

```
new IntConsumer()
{
    public void accept(int value)
    {
        System.out.printf("%d ", value);
    }
}
```

b) Write a method reference that can be used in place of the following lambda:

```
(String s) -> {return s.toUpperCase();}
```

c) Write a no-argument lambda that implicitly returns the String "Welcome to lambdas!".

d) Write a method reference for Math method sqrt.

e) Create a one-parameter lambda that returns the cube of its argument.

Answers to Self-Review Exercises

17.1 a) functional interfaces. b) parallelize. c) internal. d) BinaryOperator<T>. e) Predicate<T>. f) lambda expression. g) lazy. h) forEach. i) Capturing. j) short circuit. k) key, value.

17.2 a) True. b) False. Terminal operations are *eager*—they perform the requested operation when they are called. c) False. When summing the elements, the identity value is 0 and when getting the product of the elements the identity value is 1. d) True. e) False. Stream method flatMap receives a Function that maps an object into a stream. f) False. Should say: "…does not override them, …" instead of "overrides them."

17.3
```
a) value -> System.out.printf("%d ", value)
b) String::toUpperCase
c) () -> "Welcome to lambdas!"
d) Math::sqrt
e) value -> value * value * value
```

Exercises

17.4 Fill in the blanks in each of the following statements:

a) Stream _____ are formed from stream sources, intermediate operations and terminal operations.

b) The following code uses the technique of _____ iteration:

```
int sum = 0;

for (int counter = 0; counter < values.length; counter++)
    sum += values[counter];
```

c) Functional programming capabilities focus on _____—not modifying the data source being processed or any other program state.

d) The functional interface _____ contains method accept that takes a T argument and returns void; accept performs a task with its T argument, such as outputting the object, invoking a method of the object, etc.

e) The functional interface _____ contains method get that takes no arguments and produces a value of type T—this is often used to create a collection object in which a stream operation's results are placed.

f) Streams are objects that implement interface `Stream` and enable you to perform functional programming tasks on _____ of elements.

g) The intermediate stream operation _____ results in a stream containing only the elements that satisfy a condition.

h) _____ place the results of processing a stream pipeline into a collection such as a `List`, `Set` or `Map`.

i) Calls to `filter` and other intermediate streams are lazy—they aren't evaluated until an eager _____ operation is performed.

j) `Pattern` method _____ (new in Java SE 8) uses a regular expression to tokenize a `String`.

k) Functional interfaces *must* contain only one _____ method, but may also contain _____ methods and `static` methods that are fully implemented in the interface declarations.

17.5 State whether each of the following is *true* or *false*. If *false*, explain why.

a) An intermediate operation specifies tasks to perform on the stream's elements; this is efficient because it avoids creating a new stream.

b) Reduction operations take all values in the stream and turn them into a new stream.

c) If you need an ordered sequence of `int` values, you can create an `IntStream` containing such values with `IntStream` methods range and `rangeClosed`. Both methods take two `int` arguments representing the range of values. Method `rangeClosed` produces a sequence of values from its first argument up to, but not including, its second argument. Method range produces a sequence of values including both of its arguments.

d) Class `Files` (package `java.nio.file`) is one of many classes throughout the Java APIs that have been enhanced to support `Streams`.

e) Interface `Map` does not contain any methods that return `Streams`.

f) The `Function` functional interface—which is used extensively in functional programming—has methods `apply` (abstract), `compose` (abstract), `andThen` (default) and `identity` (static).

g) If one class inherits the same `default` method from two interfaces, the class *must* override that method; otherwise, the compiler does not know which method to use, so it generates a compilation error.

17.6 Write a lambda or method reference for each of the following tasks:

a) Write a lambda expression that receives two `double` parameters a and b and returns their product. Use the lambda form that explicitly lists the type of each parameter.

b) Rewrite the lambda expression in Part (a) using the lambda form that does not list the type of each parameter.

c) Rewrite the lambda expression in Part (b) using the lambda form that implicitly returns the value of the lambda's body expression.

d) Write a no-argument lambda that implicitly returns the string `"Welcome to lambdas!"`.

e) Write a constructor reference for class `ArrayList`.

f) Reimplement the following statement using a lambda as the event handler:

```
button.addActionListener(
    new ActionListener()
    {
        public void actionPerformed(ActionEvent event)
        {
            JOptionPane.showMessageDialog(ParentFrame.this,
                "JButton event handler");
        }
    }
);
```

17.7 Assuming that list is a List<Integer>, explain in detail the stream pipeline:

```
list.stream()
    .filter(value -> value % 2 != 0)
    .sum()
```

17.8 Assuming that random is a SecureRandom object, explain in detail the stream pipeline:

```
random.ints(1000000, 1, 3)
    .boxed()
    .collect(Collectors.groupingBy(Function.identity(),
        Collectors.counting()))
    .forEach((side, frequency) ->
        System.out.printf("%-6d%d%n", side, frequency));
```

17.9 *(Summarizing the Characters in a File)* Modify the program of Fig. 17.17 to summarize the number of occurrences of every character in the file.

17.10 *(Summarizing the File Types in a Directory)* Section 15.3 demonstrated how to get information about files and directories on disk. In addition, you used a DirectoryStream to display the contents of a directory. Interface DirectoryStream now contains default method entries, which returns a Stream. Use the techniques from Section 15.3, DirectoryStream method entries, lambdas and streams to summarize the types of files in a specified directory.

17.11 *(Manipulating a Stream<Invoice>)* Use the class Invoice provided in the exercises folder with this chapter's examples to create an array of Invoice objects. Use the sample data shown in Fig. 17.20. Class Invoice includes four properties—a PartNumber (type int), a PartDescription (type String), a Quantity of the item being purchased (type int) and a Price (type double). Perform the following queries on the array of Invoice objects and display the results:

a) Use lambdas and streams to sort the Invoice objects by PartDescription, then display the results.

b) Use lambdas and streams to sort the Invoice objects by Price, then display the results.

c) Use lambdas and streams to map each Invoice to its PartDescription and Quantity, sort the results by Quantity, then display the results.

d) Use lambdas and streams to map each Invoice to its PartDescription and the value of the Invoice (i.e., Quantity * Price). Order the results by Invoice value.

e) Modify Part (d) to select the Invoice values in the range $200 to $500.

Part number	Part description	Quantity	Price
83	Electric sander	7	57.98
24	Power saw	18	99.99
7	Sledge hammer	11	21.50
77	Hammer	76	11.99
39	Lawn mower	3	79.50
68	Screwdriver	106	6.99
56	Jig saw	21	11.00
3	Wrench	34	7.50

Fig. 17.20 | Sample data for Exercise 17.11.

17.12 *(Duplicate Word Removal)* Write a program that inputs a sentence from the user (assume no punctuation), then determines and displays the unique words in alphabetical order. Treat uppercase and lowercase letters the same.

17.13 *(Sorting Letters and Removing Duplicates)* Write a program that inserts 30 random letters into a List<Character>. Perform the following operations and display your results:

   a) Sort the List in ascending order.
   b) Sort the List in descending order.
   c) Display the List in ascending order with duplicates removed.

17.14 *(Mapping Then Reducing An **IntStream** for Parallelization)* The lambda you pass to a stream's reduce method should be *associative*—that is, regardless of the order in which its subexpressions are evaluated, the result should be the same. The lambda expression in lines 34–36 of Fig. 17.5 is *not* associative. If you were to use parallel streams (Chapter 23, Concurrency) with that lambda, you might get incorrect results for the sum of the squares, depending on the order in which the subexpressions are evaluated. The proper way to implement lines 34–36 would be *first* to map each int value to the square of that value, *then* to reduce the stream to the sum of the squares. Modify Fig. 17.5 to implement lines 34–36 in this manner.

18

Recursion

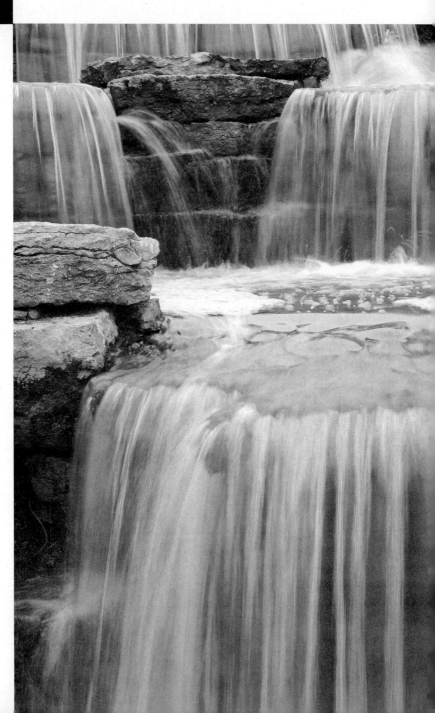

*O! thou hast damnable
iteration, and art indeed able to
corrupt a saint.*
—William Shakespeare

*It's a poor sort of memory that
only works backwards.*
—Lewis Carroll

*Life can only be understood
backwards; but it must be lived
forwards.*
—Soren Kierkegaard

Objectives

In this chapter you'll:

- Learn the concept of recursion.

- Write and use recursive methods.

- Determine the base case and recursion step in a recursive algorithm.

- Learn how recursive method calls are handled by the system.

- Learn the differences between recursion and iteration, and when to use each.

- Learn what fractals are and how to draw them using recursion.

- Learn what recursive backtracking is and why it's an effective problem-solving technique.

18.1 Introduction

The programs we've discussed so far are generally structured as methods that call one another in a hierarchical manner. For some problems, it's useful to have a method *call itself*. A method that does so is known as a **recursive method**. A recursive method can call itself either *directly* or *indirectly through another method*. Recursion is an important topic discussed at length in upper-level computer science courses. In this chapter, we consider recursion conceptually, then present several programs containing recursive methods. Figure 18.1 summarizes the recursion examples and exercises in this book.

Chapter	Recursion examples and exercises in this book
18	Factorial Method (Figs. 18.3 and 18.4) Fibonacci Method (Fig. 18.5) Towers of Hanoi (Fig. 18.11) Fractals (Figs. 18.18 and 18.19) What Does This Code Do? (Exercise 18.7, Exercise 18.12 and Exercise 18.13) Find the Error in the Following Code (Exercise 18.8) Raising an Integer to an Integer Power (Exercise 18.9) Visualizing Recursion (Exercise 18.10) Greatest Common Divisor (Exercise 18.11) Determine Whether a String Is a Palindrome (Exercise 18.14) Eight Queens (Exercise 18.15) Print an Array (Exercise 18.16) Print an Array Backward (Exercise 18.17) Minimum Value in an Array (Exercise 18.18) Star Fractal (Exercise 18.19) Maze Traversal Using Recursive Backtracking (Exercise 18.20) Generating Mazes Randomly (Exercise 18.21) Mazes of Any Size (Exercise 18.22) Time to Calculate a Fibonacci Number (Exercise 18.23)

Fig. 18.1 | Summary of the recursion examples and exercises in this text. (Part 1 of 2.)

Chapter	Recursion examples and exercises in this book
19	Merge Sort (Fig. 19.6)
	Linear Search (Exercise 19.8)
	Binary Search (Exercise 19.9)
	Quicksort (Exercise 19.10)
21	Binary-Tree Insert (Fig. 21.17)
	Preorder Traversal of a Binary Tree (Fig. 21.17)
	Inorder Traversal of a Binary Tree (Fig. 21.17)
	Postorder Traversal of a Binary Tree (Fig. 21.17)
	Print a Linked List Backward (Exercise 21.20)
	Search a Linked List (Exercise 21.21)

Fig. 18.1 | Summary of the recursion examples and exercises in this text. (Part 2 of 2.)

18.2 Recursion Concepts

Recursive problem-solving approaches have a number of elements in common. When a recursive method is called to solve a problem, it actually is capable of solving only the *simplest case(s)*, or **base case(s)**. If the method is called with a *base case*, it returns a result. If the method is called with a more complex problem, it divides the problem into two conceptual pieces—a piece that the method knows how to do and a piece that it does not know how to do. To make recursion feasible, the latter piece must resemble the original problem, but be a slightly simpler or smaller version of it. Because this new problem resembles the original problem, the method calls a fresh *copy* of itself to work on the smaller problem—this is referred to as a **recursive call** and is also called the **recursion step**. The recursion step normally includes a `return` statement, because its result will be combined with the portion of the problem the method knew how to solve to form a result that will be passed back to the original caller. This concept of separating the problem into two smaller portions is a form of the *divide-and-conquer* approach introduced in Chapter 5.

The recursion step executes while the original method call is still active (i.e., it has not finished executing). It can result in many more recursive calls as the method divides each new subproblem into two conceptual pieces. For the recursion to eventually terminate, each time the method calls itself with a simpler version of the original problem, the sequence of smaller and smaller problems must *converge on a base case*. When the method recognizes the base case, it returns a result to the previous copy of the method. A sequence of returns ensues until the original method call returns the final result to the caller. We'll illustrate this process with a concrete example in Section 18.3.

A recursive method may call another method, which may in turn make a call back to the recursive method. This is known as an **indirect recursive call** or **indirect recursion**. For example, method A calls method B, which makes a call back to method A. This is still recursion, because the second call to method A is made while the first call to method A is active—that is, the first call to method A has not yet finished executing (because it's waiting on method B to return a result to it) and has not returned to method A's original caller.

To better understand the concept of recursion, let's look at an example that's quite familiar to computer users—the recursive definition of a file system directory on a computer. A computer normally stores related files in a directory. A directory can be empty, can contain files and/or can contain other directories (usually referred to as subdirectories). Each of these subdirectories, in turn, may also contain both files and directories. If we want to list each file in a directory (including all the files in the directory's subdirectories), we need to create a method that first lists the initial directory's files, then makes recursive calls to list the files in each of that directory's subdirectories. The base case occurs when a directory is reached that does not contain any subdirectories. At this point, all the files in the original directory have been listed and no further recursion is necessary.

18.3 Example Using Recursion: Factorials

Let's write a recursive program to perform a popular mathematical calculation. Consider the *factorial* of a positive integer n, written $n!$ (pronounced "n factorial"), which is the product

$$n \cdot (n-1) \cdot (n-2) \cdot \ldots \cdot 1$$

with 1! equal to 1 and 0! defined to be 1. For example, 5! is the product $5 \cdot 4 \cdot 3 \cdot 2 \cdot 1$, which is equal to 120.

The factorial of integer number (where number ≥ 0) can be calculated *iteratively* (non-recursively) using a for statement as follows:

```
factorial = 1;
for (int counter = number; counter >= 1; counter--)
    factorial *= counter;
```

A recursive declaration of the factorial calculation for integers greater than 1 is arrived at by observing the following relationship:

$$n! = n \cdot (n-1)!$$

For example, 5! is clearly equal to $5 \cdot 4!$, as shown by the following equations:

$$5! = 5 \cdot 4 \cdot 3 \cdot 2 \cdot 1$$
$$5! = 5 \cdot (4 \cdot 3 \cdot 2 \cdot 1)$$
$$5! = 5 \cdot (4!)$$

The evaluation of 5! would proceed as shown in Fig. 18.2. Figure 18.2(a) shows how the succession of recursive calls proceeds until 1! (the base case) is evaluated to be 1, which terminates the recursion. Figure 18.2(b) shows the values returned from each recursive call to its caller until the final value is calculated and returned.

Figure 18.3 uses recursion to calculate and print the factorials of the integers 0 through 21. The recursive method factorial (lines 7–13) first tests to determine whether a *terminating condition* (line 9) is true. If number is less than or equal to 1 (the base case), factorial returns 1, no further recursion is necessary and the method returns. (A precondition of calling method factorial in this example is that its argument must be non-negative.) If number is greater than 1, line 12 expresses the problem as the product of number and a recursive call to factorial evaluating the factorial of number - 1, which is a slightly smaller problem than the original calculation, factorial(number).

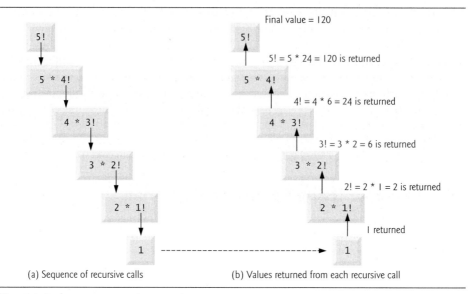

Fig. 18.2 | Recursive evaluation of 5!.

```
1    // Fig. 18.3: FactorialCalculator.java
2    // Recursive factorial method.
3
4    public class FactorialCalculator
5    {
6       // recursive method factorial (assumes its parameter is >= 0)
7       public static long factorial(long number)
8       {
9          if (number <= 1) // test for base case
10            return 1; // base cases: 0! = 1 and 1! = 1
11         else // recursion step
12            return number * factorial(number - 1);
13      }
14
15      // output factorials for values 0-21
16      public static void main(String[] args)
17      {
18         // calculate the factorials of 0 through 21
19         for (int counter = 0; counter <= 21; counter++)
20            System.out.printf("%d! = %d%n", counter, factorial(counter));
21      }
22   } // end class FactorialCalculator
```

```
0! = 1
1! = 1
2! = 2
3! = 6
4! = 24
5! = 120
```

Fig. 18.3 | Recursive factorial method. (Part 1 of 2.)

```
...
12! = 479001600 ——— 12! causes overflow for int variables
...
20! = 2432902008176640000
21! = -4249290049419214848 ——— 21! causes overflow for long variables
```

Fig. 18.3 | Recursive factorial method. (Part 2 of 2.)

Common Programming Error 18.1

*Either omitting the base case or writing the recursion step incorrectly so that it does not converge on the base case can cause a logic error known as **infinite recursion**, where recursive calls are continuously made until memory is exhausted or the method-call stack overflows. This error is analogous to the problem of an infinite loop in an iterative (non-recursive) solution.*

Method main (lines 16–21) displays the factorials of 0–21. The call to the factorial method occurs in line 20. Method factorial receives a parameter of type long and returns a result of type long. The program's output shows that factorial values become large quickly. We use type long (which can represent relatively large integers) so the program can calculate factorials greater than 12!. Unfortunately, the factorial method produces large values so quickly that we exceed the largest long value when we attempt to calculate 21!, as you can see in the last line of the program's output.

Due to the limitations of integral types, float or double variables may ultimately be needed to calculate factorials of larger numbers. This points to a weakness in some programming languages—namely, that they aren't easily *extended with new types* to handle unique application requirements. As we saw in Chapter 9, Java is an *extensible* language that allows us to create arbitrarily large integers if we wish. In fact, package java.math provides classes **BigInteger** and BigDecimal explicitly for arbitrary precision calculations that cannot be performed with primitive types. You can learn more about these classes at

```
docs.oracle.com/javase/7/docs/api/java/math/BigInteger.html
docs.oracle.com/javase/7/docs/api/java/math/BigDecimal.html
```

18.4 Reimplementing Class FactorialCalculator Using Class BigInteger

Figure 18.4 reimplements class FactorialCalculator using BigInteger variables. To demonstrate larger values than what long variables can store, we calculate the factorials of the numbers 0–50. Line 3 imports class BigInteger from package java.math. The new factorial method (lines 8–15) receives a BigInteger as an argument and returns a BigInteger.

```java
1  // Fig. 18.4: FactorialCalculator.java
2  // Recursive factorial method.
3  import java.math.BigInteger;
4
```

Fig. 18.4 | Factorial calculations with a recursive method. (Part 1 of 2.)

```
5    public class FactorialCalculator
6    {
7       // recursive method factorial (assumes its parameter is >= 0)
8       public static BigInteger factorial(BigInteger number)
9       {
10         if (number.compareTo(BigInteger.ONE) <= 0) // test base case
11            return BigInteger.ONE; // base cases: 0! = 1 and 1! = 1
12         else // recursion step
13            return number.multiply(
14               factorial(number.subtract(BigInteger.ONE)));
15      }
16
17      // output factorials for values 0-50
18      public static void main(String[] args)
19      {
20         // calculate the factorials of 0 through 50
21         for (int counter = 0; counter <= 50; counter++)
22            System.out.printf("%d! = %d%n", counter,
23               factorial(BigInteger.valueOf(counter)));
24      }
25   } // end class FactorialCalculator
```

```
0! = 1
1! = 1
2! = 2
3! = 6
...
21! = 51090942171709440000 ── 21! and larger values no longer cause overflow
22! = 1124000727777607680000
...
47! = 258623241511168180642964355153611979969197632389120000000000
48! = 12413915592536072670862289047373375038521486354677760000000000
49! = 608281864034267560872252163321295376887552831379210240000000000
50! = 30414093201713378043612608166064768844377641568960512000000000000
```

Fig. 18.4 | Factorial calculations with a recursive method. (Part 2 of 2.)

Since BigInteger is *not* a primitive type, we can't use the arithmetic, relational and equality operators with BigIntegers; instead, we must use BigInteger methods to perform these tasks. Line 10 tests for the base case using BigInteger method **compareTo**. This method compares the BigInteger number that calls the method to the method's BigInteger argument. The method returns -1 if the BigInteger that calls the method is less than the argument, 0 if they're equal or 1 if the BigInteger that calls the method is greater than the argument. Line 10 compares the BigInteger number with the BigInteger constant **ONE**, which represents the integer value 1. If compareTo returns -1 or 0, then number is less than or equal to 1 (the base case) and the method returns the constant BigInteger.ONE. Otherwise, lines 13–14 perform the recursion step using BigInteger methods **multiply** and **subtract** to implement the calculations required to multiply number by the factorial of number - 1. The program's output shows that BigInteger handles the large values produced by the factorial calculation.

18.5 Example Using Recursion: Fibonacci Series

The **Fibonacci series,**

> 0, 1, 1, 2, 3, 5, 8, 13, 21, ...

begins with 0 and 1 and has the property that each subsequent Fibonacci number is the sum of the previous two. This series occurs in nature and describes a form of spiral. The ratio of successive Fibonacci numbers converges on a constant value of 1.618..., a number that has been called the **golden ratio** or the **golden mean.** Humans tend to find the golden mean aesthetically pleasing. Architects often design windows, rooms and buildings whose length and width are in the ratio of the golden mean. Postcards are often designed with a golden-mean length-to-width ratio.

The Fibonacci series may be defined recursively as follows:

> fibonacci(0) = 0
> fibonacci(1) = 1
> fibonacci(n) = fibonacci(n – 1) + fibonacci(n – 2)

There are *two base cases* for the Fibonacci calculation: fibonacci(0) is defined to be 0, and fibonacci(1) to be 1. The program in Fig. 18.5 calculates the ith Fibonacci number recursively, using method fibonacci (lines 10–18). Method main (lines 21–26) tests fibonacci, displaying the Fibonacci values of 0–40. The variable counter created in the for header (line 23) indicates which Fibonacci number to calculate for each iteration of the loop. Fibonacci numbers tend to become large quickly (though not as quickly as factorials). Therefore, we use type BigInteger as the parameter type and the return type of method fibonacci.

```
 1   // Fig. 18.5: FibonacciCalculator.java
 2   // Recursive fibonacci method.
 3   import java.math.BigInteger;
 4
 5   public class FibonacciCalculator
 6   {
 7      private static BigInteger TWO = BigInteger.valueOf(2);
 8
 9      // recursive declaration of method fibonacci
10      public static BigInteger fibonacci(BigInteger number)
11      {
12         if (number.equals(BigInteger.ZERO) ||
13             number.equals(BigInteger.ONE)) // base cases
14            return number;
15         else // recursion step
16            return fibonacci(number.subtract(BigInteger.ONE)).add(
17               fibonacci(number.subtract(TWO)));
18      }
19
20      // displays the fibonacci values from 0-40
21      public static void main(String[] args)
22      {
```

Fig. 18.5 | Recursive fibonacci method. (Part 1 of 2.)

```
23            for (int counter = 0; counter <= 40; counter++)
24                System.out.printf("Fibonacci of %d is: %d%n", counter,
25                    fibonacci(BigInteger.valueOf(counter)));
26        }
27    } // end class FibonacciCalculator
```

```
Fibonacci of 0 is: 0
Fibonacci of 1 is: 1
Fibonacci of 2 is: 1
Fibonacci of 3 is: 2
Fibonacci of 4 is: 3
Fibonacci of 5 is: 5
Fibonacci of 6 is: 8
Fibonacci of 7 is: 13
Fibonacci of 8 is: 21
Fibonacci of 9 is: 34
Fibonacci of 10 is: 55
...
Fibonacci of 37 is: 24157817
Fibonacci of 38 is: 39088169
Fibonacci of 39 is: 63245986
Fibonacci of 40 is: 102334155
```

Fig. 18.5 | Recursive fibonacci method. (Part 2 of 2.)

The call to method fibonacci (line 25) from main is *not* a recursive call, but all subsequent calls to fibonacci performed from lines 16–17 of Fig. 18.5 are recursive, because at that point the calls are initiated by method fibonacci itself. Each time fibonacci is called, it immediately tests for the *base cases*—number equal to 0 or number equal to 1 (lines 12–13). We use BigInteger constants **ZERO** and ONE to represent the values 0 and 1, respectively. If the condition in lines 12–13 is true, fibonacci simply returns number, because fibonacci(0) is 0 and fibonacci(1) is 1. Interestingly, if number is greater than 1, the recursion step generates *two* recursive calls (lines 16–17), each for a slightly smaller problem than the original call to fibonacci. Lines 16–17 use BigInteger methods **add** and subtract to help implement the recursive step. We also use a constant of type BigInteger named TWO that we defined at line 7.

Analyzing the Calls to Method *Fibonacci*
Figure 18.6 shows how method fibonacci evaluates fibonacci(3). At the bottom of the figure we're left with the values 1, 0 and 1—the results of evaluating the *base cases*. The first two return values (from left to right), 1 and 0, are returned as the values for the calls fibonacci(1) and fibonacci(0). The sum 1 plus 0 is returned as the value of fibonacci(2). This is added to the result (1) of the call to fibonacci(1), producing the value 2. This final value is then returned as the value of fibonacci(3).

Figure 18.6 raises some interesting issues about *the order in which Java compilers evaluate the operands of operators*. This order is different from that in which operators are applied to their operands—namely, the order dictated by the rules of operator precedence. From Figure 18.6, it appears that while fibonacci(3) is being evaluated, two recursive calls will be made—fibonacci(2) and fibonacci(1). But in what order will they be

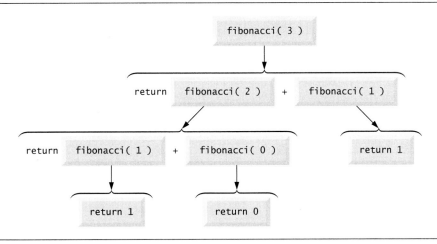

Fig. 18.6 | Set of recursive calls for `fibonacci`(3).

made? *The Java language specifies that the order of evaluation of the operands is from left to right.* Thus, the call `fibonacci(2)` is made first and the call `fibonacci(1)` second.

A word of caution is in order about recursive programs like the one we use here to generate Fibonacci numbers. Each invocation of the `fibonacci` method that does not match one of the *base cases* (0 or 1) results in *two more recursive calls* to the `fibonacci` method. Hence, this set of recursive calls rapidly gets out of hand. Calculating the Fibonacci value of 20 with the program in Fig. 18.5 requires 21,891 calls to the `fibonacci` method; calculating the Fibonacci value of 30 requires 2,692,537 calls! As you try to calculate larger Fibonacci values, you'll notice that each consecutive Fibonacci number you use the application to calculate results in a substantial increase in calculation time and in the number of calls to the `fibonacci` method. For example, the Fibonacci value of 31 requires 4,356,617 calls, and the Fibonacci value of 32 requires 7,049,155 calls! As you can see, the number of calls to `fibonacci` increases quickly—1,664,080 additional calls between Fibonacci values of 30 and 31 and 2,692,538 additional calls between Fibonacci values of 31 and 32! The difference in the number of calls made between Fibonacci values of 31 and 32 is more than 1.5 times the difference in the number of calls for Fibonacci values between 30 and 31. Problems of this nature can humble even the world's most powerful computers. [*Note:* In the field of complexity theory, computer scientists study how hard algorithms work to complete their tasks. Complexity issues are discussed in detail in the upper-level computer science curriculum course generally called "Algorithms." We introduce various complexity issues in Chapter 19, Searching, Sorting and Big O.] In this chapter's exercises, you'll be asked to enhance the Fibonacci program of Fig. 18.5 so that it calculates the approximate amount of time required to perform the calculation. For this purpose, you'll call `static System` method `currentTimeMillis`, which takes no arguments and returns the computer's current time in milliseconds.

Performance Tip 18.1
Avoid Fibonacci-style recursive programs, because they result in an exponential "explosion" of method calls.

18.6 Recursion and the Method-Call Stack

In Chapter 5, the *stack* data structure was introduced in the context of understanding how Java performs method calls. We discussed both the *method-call stack* and *stack frames*. In this section, we'll use these concepts to demonstrate how the program-execution stack handles *recursive* method calls.

Let's begin by returning to the Fibonacci example—specifically, calling method fibonacci with the value 3, as in Fig. 18.6. To show the *order* in which the method calls' stack frames are placed on the stack, we've lettered the method calls in Fig. 18.7.

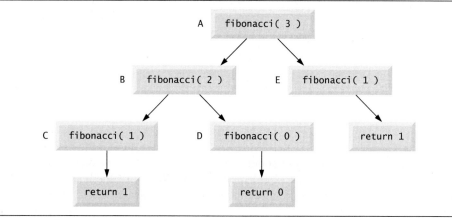

Fig. 18.7 | Method calls made within the call fibonacci(3).

When the first method call (A) is made, a *stack frame* containing the value of the local variable number (3, in this case) is *pushed* onto the *program-execution stack*. This stack, including the stack frame for method call A, is illustrated in part (a) of Fig. 18.8. [*Note:* We use a simplified stack here. An actual program-execution stack and its stack frames would be more complex than in Fig. 18.8, containing such information as where the method call is to *return* to when it has completed execution.]

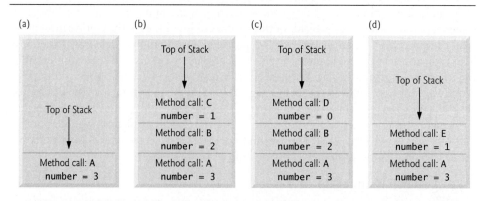

Fig. 18.8 | Method calls on the program-execution stack.

Within method call A, method calls B and E are made. The original method call has not yet completed, so its stack frame remains on the stack. The first method call to be made from within A is method call B, so the stack frame for method call B is pushed onto the stack on top of the one for method call A. Method call B must execute and complete before method call E is made. Within method call B, method calls C and D will be made. Method call C is made first, and its stack frame is pushed onto the stack [part (b) of Fig. 18.8]. Method call B has not yet finished, and its stack frame is still on the method-call stack. When method call C executes, it makes no further method calls, but simply returns the value 1. When this method returns, its stack frame is popped off the top of the stack. The method call at the top of the stack is now B, which continues to execute by performing method call D. The stack frame for method call D is pushed onto the stack [part (c) of Fig. 18.8]. Method call D completes without making any more method calls and returns the value 0. The stack frame for this method call is then popped off the stack. Now, both method calls made from within method call B have returned. Method call B continues to execute, returning the value 1. Method call B completes, and its stack frame is popped off the stack. At this point, the stack frame for method call A is at the top of the stack and the method continues its execution. This method makes method call E, whose stack frame is now pushed onto the stack [part (d) of Fig. 18.8]. Method call E completes and returns the value 1. The stack frame for this method call is popped off the stack, and once again method call A continues to execute. At this point, method call A will not be making any other method calls and can finish its execution, returning the value 2 to A's caller (`fibonacci(3) = 2`). A's stack frame is popped off the stack. The executing method is always the one whose stack frame is at the top of the stack, and the stack frame for that method contains the values of its local variables.

18.7 Recursion vs. Iteration

We've studied methods `factorial` and `fibonacci`, which can easily be implemented either recursively or iteratively. In this section, we compare the two approaches and discuss why you might choose one approach over the other in a particular situation.

Both iteration and recursion are *based on a control statement*: Iteration uses a repetition statement (e.g., `for`, `while` or `do...while`), whereas recursion uses a selection statement (e.g., `if`, `if...else` or `switch`). Both iteration and recursion involve *repetition*: Iteration explicitly uses a repetition statement, whereas recursion achieves repetition through repeated method calls. Iteration and recursion each involve a *termination test*: Iteration terminates when the loop-continuation condition fails, whereas recursion terminates when a base case is reached. Iteration with counter-controlled repetition and recursion both *gradually approach termination*: Iteration keeps modifying a counter until the counter assumes a value that makes the loop-continuation condition fail, whereas recursion keeps producing smaller versions of the original problem until the base case is reached. Both iteration and recursion *can occur infinitely*: An infinite loop occurs with iteration if the loop-continuation test never becomes false, whereas infinite recursion occurs if the recursion step does not reduce the problem each time in a manner that converges on the base case, or if the base case is not tested.

To illustrate the differences between iteration and recursion, let's examine an iterative solution to the factorial problem (Fig. 18.9). A repetition statement is used (lines 12–13) rather than the selection statement of the recursive solution (lines 9–12 of Fig. 18.3). Both solutions use a termination test. In the recursive solution (Fig. 18.3), line 9 tests for the *base case*. In the iterative solution, line 12 of Fig. 18.9 tests the loop-continuation condition—if the test fails, the loop terminates. Finally, instead of producing smaller versions of the original problem, the iterative solution uses a counter that is modified until the loop-continuation condition becomes false.

```java
1   // Fig. 18.9: FactorialCalculator.java
2   // Iterative factorial method.
3
4   public class FactorialCalculator
5   {
6      // recursive declaration of method factorial
7      public long factorial(long number)
8      {
9         long result = 1;
10
11         // iterative declaration of method factorial
12         for (long i = number; i >= 1; i--)
13            result *= i;
14
15         return result;
16      }
17
18      // output factorials for values 0-10
19      public static void main(String[] args)
20      {
21         // calculate the factorials of 0 through 10
22         for (int counter = 0; counter <= 10; counter++)
23            System.out.printf("%d! = %d%n", counter, factorial(counter));
24      }
25   } // end class FactorialCalculator
```

```
0! = 1
1! = 1
2! = 2
3! = 6
4! = 24
5! = 120
6! = 720
7! = 5040
8! = 40320
9! = 362880
10! = 3628800
```

Fig. 18.9 | Iterative factorial method.

Recursion has many *negatives*. It repeatedly invokes the mechanism, and consequently the *overhead, of method calls.* This repetition can be *expensive* in terms of both processor time and memory space. Each recursive call causes another *copy* of the method (actually, only the method's variables, stored in the stack frame) to be created—this set of copies *can consume considerable memory space.* Since iteration occurs within a method, repeated method calls and extra memory assignment are avoided.

Software Engineering Observation 18.1
Any problem that can be solved recursively can also be solved iteratively. A recursive approach is normally preferred over an iterative approach when the recursive approach more naturally mirrors the problem and results in a program that is easier to understand and debug. A recursive approach can often be implemented with fewer lines of code. Another reason to choose a recursive approach is that an iterative one might not be apparent.

Performance Tip 18.2
Avoid using recursion in situations requiring high performance. Recursive calls take time and consume additional memory.

Common Programming Error 18.2
Accidentally having a nonrecursive method call itself either directly or indirectly through another method can cause infinite recursion.

18.8 Towers of Hanoi

Earlier in this chapter we studied methods that can be easily implemented both recursively and iteratively. Now, we present a problem whose recursive solution demonstrates the elegance of recursion, and whose iterative solution may not be as apparent.

The **Towers of Hanoi** is one of the classic problems every budding computer scientist must grapple with. Legend has it that in a temple in the Far East, priests are attempting to move a stack of golden disks from one diamond peg to another (Fig. 18.10). The initial stack has 64 disks threaded onto one peg and arranged from bottom to top by decreasing size. The priests are attempting to move the stack from one peg to another under the constraints that exactly one disk is moved at a time and at no time may a larger disk be placed above a smaller disk. Three pegs are provided, one being used for temporarily holding disks. Supposedly, the world will end when the priests complete their task, so there's little incentive for us to facilitate their efforts.

Let's assume that the priests are attempting to move the disks from peg 1 to peg 3. We wish to develop an algorithm that prints the precise sequence of peg-to-peg disk transfers.

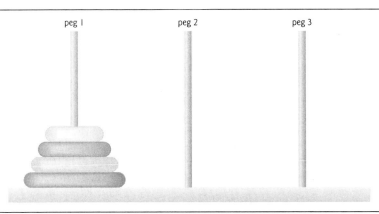

Fig. 18.10 | Towers of Hanoi for the case with four disks.

If we try to find an iterative solution, we'll likely find ourselves hopelessly "knotted up" in managing the disks. Instead, attacking this problem recursively quickly yields a solution. Moving n disks can be viewed in terms of moving only $n - 1$ disks (hence the recursion) as follows:

1. Move $n - 1$ disks from peg 1 to peg 2, using peg 3 as a temporary holding area.

2. Move the last disk (the largest) from peg 1 to peg 3.

3. Move $n - 1$ disks from peg 2 to peg 3, using peg 1 as a temporary holding area.

The process ends when the last task involves moving $n = 1$ disk (i.e., the base case). This task is accomplished by moving the disk, without using a temporary holding area.

In Fig. 18.11, method solveTowers (lines 6–25) solves the Towers of Hanoi, given the total number of disks (in this case 3), the starting peg, the ending peg, and the temporary holding peg as parameters. The base case (lines 10–14) occurs when only one disk needs to be moved from the starting peg to the ending peg. In the recursion step (lines 18–24), line 18 moves disks - 1 disks from the first peg (sourcePeg) to the temporary holding peg (tempPeg). When all but one of the disks have been moved to the temporary peg, line 21 moves the largest disk from the start peg to the destination peg. Line 24 finishes the rest of the moves by calling the method solveTowers to recursively move disks - 1 disks from the temporary peg (tempPeg) to the destination peg (destinationPeg), this time using the first peg (sourcePeg) as the temporary peg. Line 35 in main calls the recursive solveTowers method, which outputs the steps to the command prompt.

```java
 1   // Fig. 18.11: TowersOfHanoi.java
 2   // Towers of Hanoi solution with a recursive method.
 3   public class TowersOfHanoi
 4   {
 5      // recursively move disks between towers
 6      public static void solveTowers(int disks, int sourcePeg,
 7         int destinationPeg, int tempPeg)
 8      {
 9         // base case -- only one disk to move
10         if (disks == 1)
11         {
12            System.out.printf("%n%d --> %d", sourcePeg, destinationPeg);
13            return;
14         }
15
16         // recursion step -- move (disk - 1) disks from sourcePeg
17         // to tempPeg using destinationPeg
18         solveTowers(disks - 1, sourcePeg, tempPeg, destinationPeg);
19
20         // move last disk from sourcePeg to destinationPeg
21         System.out.printf("%n%d --> %d", sourcePeg, destinationPeg);
22
23         // move (disks - 1) disks from tempPeg to destinationPeg
24         solveTowers(disks - 1, tempPeg, destinationPeg, sourcePeg);
25      }
26
```

Fig. 18.11 | Towers of Hanoi solution with a recursive method. (Part 1 of 2.)

```
27      public static void main(String[] args)
28      {
29          int startPeg = 1; // value 1 used to indicate startPeg in output
30          int endPeg = 3; // value 3 used to indicate endPeg in output
31          int tempPeg = 2; // value 2 used to indicate tempPeg in output
32          int totalDisks = 3; // number of disks
33
34          // initial nonrecursive call: move all disks.
35          solveTowers(totalDisks, startPeg, endPeg, tempPeg);
36      }
37  } // end class TowersOfHanoi
```

```
1 --> 3
1 --> 2
3 --> 2
1 --> 3
2 --> 1
2 --> 3
1 --> 3
```

Fig. 18.11 | Towers of Hanoi solution with a recursive method. (Part 2 of 2.)

18.9 Fractals

A **fractal** is a geometric figure that can be generated from a pattern repeated recursively (Fig. 18.12). The figure is modified by recursively applying the pattern to each segment of the original figure. Although such figures had been studied before the 20th century, it was the mathematician Benoit Mandelbrot who in the 1970s introduced the term "fractal," along with the specifics of how a fractal is created and the practical applications of fractals. Mandelbrot's fractal geometry provides mathematical models for many complex forms found in nature, such as mountains, clouds and coastlines. Fractals have many uses in mathematics and science. They can be used to better understand systems or patterns that appear in nature (e.g., ecosystems), in the human body (e.g., in the folds of the brain), or in the universe (e.g., galaxy clusters). Not all fractals resemble objects in nature. Drawing fractals has become a popular art form. Fractals have a **self-similar property**—when subdivided into parts, each resembles a reduced-size copy of the whole. Many fractals yield an exact copy of the original when a portion of the fractal is magnified—such a fractal is said to be **strictly self-similar**.

18.9.1 Koch Curve Fractal

As an example, let's look at the strictly self-similar **Koch Curve** fractal (Fig. 18.12). It's formed by removing the middle third of each line in the drawing and replacing it with two lines that form a point, such that if the middle third of the original line remained, an equilateral triangle would be formed. Formulas for creating fractals often involve removing all or part of the previous fractal image. This pattern has already been determined for this fractal—we focus here on how to use those formulas in a recursive solution.

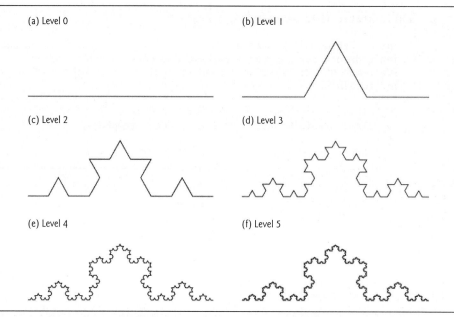

(a) Level 0   (b) Level 1

(c) Level 2   (d) Level 3

(e) Level 4   (f) Level 5

Fig. 18.12 | Koch Curve fractal.

We start with a straight line (Fig. 18.12(a)) and apply the pattern, creating a triangle from the middle third (Fig. 18.12(b)). We then apply the pattern again to each straight line, resulting in Fig. 18.12(c). Each time the pattern is applied, we say that the fractal is at a new **level**, or **depth** (sometimes the term **order** is also used). Fractals can be displayed at many levels—for instance, a fractal at level 3 has had three iterations of the pattern applied (Fig. 18.12(d)). After only a few iterations, this fractal begins to look like a portion of a snowflake (Fig. 18.12(e and f)). Since this is a strictly self-similar fractal, each portion of it contains an exact copy of the fractal. In Fig. 18.12(f), for example, we've highlighted a portion of the fractal with a dashed box. If the image in this box were increased in size, it would look exactly like the entire fractal of part (f).

A similar fractal, the **Koch Snowflake**, is similar to the Koch Curve but begins with a triangle rather than a line. The same pattern is applied to each side of the triangle, resulting in an image that looks like an enclosed snowflake. For simplicity, we've chosen to focus on the Koch Curve.

18.9.2 (Optional) Case Study: Lo Feather Fractal

We now demonstrate the use of recursion to draw fractals by writing a program to create a strictly self-similar fractal. We call this the "Lo feather fractal," named for Sin Han Lo, a Deitel & Associates colleague who created it. The fractal will eventually resemble one-half of a feather (see the outputs in Fig. 18.19). The base case, or fractal level of 0, begins as a line between two points, A and B (Fig. 18.13). To create the next higher level, we find the midpoint (C) of the line. To calculate the location of point C, use the following formula:

```
xC = (xA + xB) / 2;
yC = (yA + yB) / 2;
```

[*Note:* The x and y to the left of each letter refer to the *x*-coordinate and *y*-coordinate of that point, respectively. For instance, xA refers to the *x*-coordinate of point A, while yC refers to the *y*-coordinate of point C. In our diagrams we denote the point by its letter, followed by two numbers representing the *x*- and *y*-coordinates.]

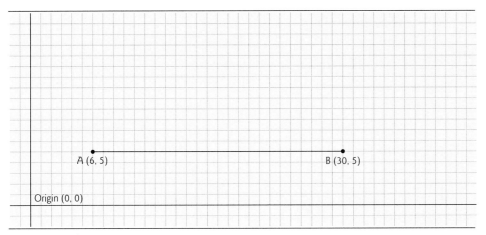

Fig. 18.13 | "Lo feather fractal" at level 0.

To create this fractal, we also must find a point D that lies left of segment AC and creates an isosceles right triangle ADC. To calculate point D's location, use the following formulas:

```
xD = xA + (xC - xA) / 2 - (yC - yA) / 2;
yD = yA + (yC - yA) / 2 + (xC - xA) / 2;
```

We now move from level 0 to level 1 as follows: First, add points C and D (as in Fig. 18.14). Then, remove the original line and add segments DA, DC and DB. The remaining lines will curve at an angle, causing our fractal to look like a feather. For the next level of the fractal, this algorithm is repeated on each of the three lines in level 1. For each line, the formulas above are applied, where the former point D is now considered to be point A, while the other end of each line is considered to be point B. Figure 18.15 contains the line from level 0 (now a dashed line) and the three added lines from level 1. We've changed point D to be point A, and the original points A, C and B to B1, B2 and B3, respectively. The preceding formulas have been used to find the new points C and D on each line. These points are also numbered 1–3 to keep track of which point is associated with each line. The points C1 and D1, for instance, represent points C and D associated with the line formed from points A to B1. To achieve level 2, the three lines in Fig. 18.15 are removed and replaced with new lines from the C and D points just added. Figure 18.16 shows the new lines (the lines from level 2 are shown as dashed lines for your convenience). Figure 18.17 shows level 2 without the dashed lines from level 1. Once this process has been repeated several times, the fractal created will begin to look like one-half of a feather, as shown in the output of Fig. 18.19. We'll present the code for this application shortly.

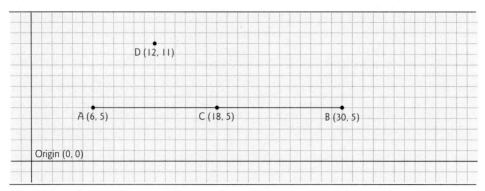

Fig. 18.14 | Determining points C and D for level 1 of the "Lo feather fractal."

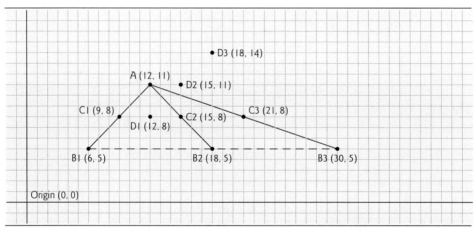

Fig. 18.15 | "Lo feather fractal" at level 1, with C and D points determined for level 2. [*Note:* The fractal at level 0 is included as a dashed line as a reminder of where the line was located in relation to the current fractal.]

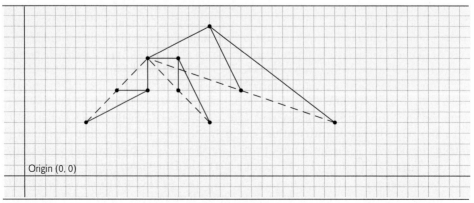

Fig. 18.16 | "Lo feather fractal" at level 2, with dashed lines from level 1 provided.

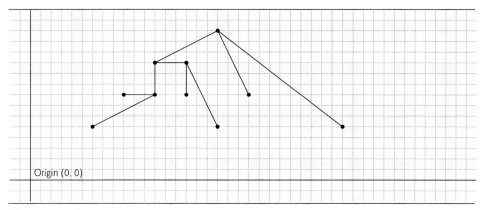

Fig. 18.17 | "Lo feather fractal" at level 2.

The application in Fig. 18.18 defines the user interface for drawing this fractal (shown at the end of Fig. 18.19). The interface consists of three buttons—one for the user to change the color of the fractal, one to increase the level of recursion and one to decrease the level of recursion. A JLabel keeps track of the current level of recursion, which is modified by calling method setLevel, to be discussed shortly. Lines 15–16 specify constants WIDTH and HEIGHT to be 400 and 480, respectively, for the size of the JFrame. The user triggers an ActionEvent by clicking the **Color** button. The event handler for this button is registered in lines 37–54. The method actionPerformed displays a JColorChooser. This dialog returns the selected Color object or blue (if the user presses **Cancel** or closes the dialog without pressing **OK**). Line 51 calls the setColor method in class FractalJPanel to update the color.

```
 1   // Fig. 18.18: Fractal.java
 2   // Fractal user interface.
 3   import java.awt.Color;
 4   import java.awt.FlowLayout;
 5   import java.awt.event.ActionEvent;
 6   import java.awt.event.ActionListener;
 7   import javax.swing.JFrame;
 8   import javax.swing.JButton;
 9   import javax.swing.JLabel;
10   import javax.swing.JPanel;
11   import javax.swing.JColorChooser;
12
13   public class Fractal extends JFrame
14   {
15      private static final int WIDTH = 400;   // define width of GUI
16      private static final int HEIGHT = 480; // define height of GUI
17      private static final int MIN_LEVEL = 0;
18      private static final int MAX_LEVEL = 15;
19
20      // set up GUI
21      public Fractal()
22      {
```

Fig. 18.18 | Fractal user interface. (Part 1 of 3.)

```
23              super("Fractal");
24
25              // set up levelJLabel to add to controlJPanel
26              final JLabel levelJLabel = new JLabel("Level: 0");
27
28              final FractalJPanel drawSpace = new FractalJPanel(0);
29
30              // set up control panel
31              final JPanel controlJPanel = new JPanel();
32              controlJPanel.setLayout(new FlowLayout());
33
34              // set up color button and register listener
35              final JButton changeColorJButton = new JButton("Color");
36              controlJPanel.add(changeColorJButton);
37              changeColorJButton.addActionListener(
38                  new ActionListener() // anonymous inner class
39                  {
40                      // process changeColorJButton event
41                      @Override
42                      public void actionPerformed(ActionEvent event)
43                      {
44                          Color color = JColorChooser.showDialog(
45                              Fractal.this, "Choose a color", Color.BLUE);
46
47                          // set default color, if no color is returned
48                          if (color == null)
49                              color = Color.BLUE;
50
51                          drawSpace.setColor(color);
52                      }
53                  } // end anonymous inner class
54              ); // end addActionListener
55
56              // set up decrease level button to add to control panel and
57              // register listener
58              final JButton decreaseLevelJButton = new JButton("Decrease Level");
59              controlJPanel.add(decreaseLevelJButton);
60              decreaseLevelJButton.addActionListener(
61                  new ActionListener() // anonymous inner class
62                  {
63                      // process decreaseLevelJButton event
64                      @Override
65                      public void actionPerformed(ActionEvent event)
66                      {
67                          int level = drawSpace.getLevel();
68                          --level;
69
70                          // modify level if possible
71                          if ((level >= MIN_LEVEL)) &&
72                              (level <= MAX_LEVEL))
73                          {
74                              levelJLabel.setText("Level: " + level);
```

Fig. 18.18 | Fractal user interface. (Part 2 of 3.)

```
75                            drawSpace.setLevel(level);
76                            repaint();
77                        }
78                    }
79                } // end anonymous inner class
80            ); // end addActionListener
81
82            // set up increase level button to add to control panel
83            // and register listener
84            final JButton increaseLevelJButton = new JButton("Increase Level");
85            controlJPanel.add(increaseLevelJButton);
86            increaseLevelJButton.addActionListener(
87                new ActionListener() // anonymous inner class
88                {
89                    // process increaseLevelJButton event
90                    @Override
91                    public void actionPerformed(ActionEvent event)
92                    {
93                        int level = drawSpace.getLevel();
94                        ++level;
95
96                        // modify level if possible
97                        if ((level >= MIN_LEVEL)) &&
98                            (level <= MAX_LEVEL))
99                        {
100                            levelJLabel.setText("Level: " + level);
101                            drawSpace.setLevel(level);
102                            repaint();
103                        }
104                    }
105                } // end anonymous inner class
106            ); // end addActionListener
107
108            controlJPanel.add(levelJLabel);
109
110            // create mainJPanel to contain controlJPanel and drawSpace
111            final JPanel mainJPanel = new JPanel();
112            mainJPanel.add(controlJPanel);
113            mainJPanel.add(drawSpace);
114
115            add(mainJPanel); // add JPanel to JFrame
116
117            setSize(WIDTH, HEIGHT); // set size of JFrame
118            setVisible(true); // display JFrame
119        } // end Fractal constructor
120
121        public static void main(String[] args)
122        {
123            Fractal demo = new Fractal();
124            demo.setDefaultCloseOperation(JFrame.EXIT_ON_CLOSE);
125        }
126    } // end class Fractal
```

Fig. 18.18 | Fractal user interface. (Part 3 of 3.)

The **Decrease Level** button's event handler is registered in lines 60–80. Method `actionPerformed` retrieves the current level of recursion and decrements it by 1 (lines 67–68). Lines 71–72 ensure that the level is greater than or equal to `MIN_LEVEL` and less than or equal to `MAX_LEVEL`—the fractal is not defined for recursion levels less than `MIN_LEVEL` and you can't see the additional detail above `MAX_LEVEL`. You can go up to any desired level, but around level 10 and higher, the fractal rendering becomes *slow* due to the details to be drawn. Lines 74–76 reset the level label to reflect the change—the new level is set and the `repaint` method is called to update the image to show the fractal at the new level.

The **Increase Level** `JButton` works like the **Decrease Level** `JButton`, but the level is incremented rather than decremented to show more details of the fractal (lines 93–94). When the application is first executed, the level will be set to 0, which will display a blue line between two points that were specified in the `FractalJPanel` class.

Class `FractalJPanel` (Fig. 18.19) specifies the drawing `JPanel`'s dimensions as 400 by 400 (lines 13–14). The `FractalJPanel` constructor (lines 18–24) takes the current level as a parameter and assigns it to its instance variable `level`. Instance variable `color` is set to blue by default. Lines 22–23 change the `JPanel`'s background color to white (so the fractal is easy to see), and set the drawing `FractalJPanel`'s dimensions.

```java
// Fig. 18.19: FractalJPanel.java
// Drawing the "Lo feather fractal" using recursion.
import java.awt.Graphics;
import java.awt.Color;
import java.awt.Dimension;
import javax.swing.JPanel;

public class FractalJPanel extends JPanel
{
   private Color color; // stores color used to draw fractal
   private int level;   // stores current level of fractal

   private static final int WIDTH = 400;  // defines width of JPanel
   private static final int HEIGHT = 400; // defines height of JPanel

   // set the initial fractal level to the value specified
   // and set up JPanel specifications
   public FractalJPanel(int currentLevel)
   {
      color = Color.BLUE;  // initialize drawing color to blue
      level = currentLevel; // set initial fractal level
      setBackground(Color.WHITE);
      setPreferredSize(new Dimension(WIDTH, HEIGHT));
   }

   // draw fractal recursively
   public void drawFractal(int level, int xA, int yA, int xB,
      int yB, Graphics g)
   {
```

Fig. 18.19 | Drawing the "Lo feather fractal" using recursion. (Part 1 of 4.)

```
30          // base case: draw a line connecting two given points
31          if (level == 0)
32             g.drawLine(xA, yA, xB, yB);
33          else // recursion step: determine new points, draw next level
34          {
35             // calculate midpoint between (xA, yA) and (xB, yB)
36             int xC = (xA + xB) / 2;
37             int yC = (yA + yB) / 2;
38
39             // calculate the fourth point (xD, yD) which forms an
40             // isosceles right triangle between (xA, yA) and (xC, yC)
41             // where the right angle is at (xD, yD)
42             int xD = xA + (xC - xA) / 2 - (yC - yA) / 2;
43             int yD = yA + (yC - yA) / 2 + (xC - xA) / 2;
44
45             // recursively draw the Fractal
46             drawFractal(level - 1, xD, yD, xA, yA, g);
47             drawFractal(level - 1, xD, yD, xC, yC, g);
48             drawFractal(level - 1, xD, yD, xB, yB, g);
49          }
50       }
51
52       // start drawing the fractal
53       @Override
54       public void paintComponent(Graphics g)
55       {
56          super.paintComponent(g);
57
58          // draw fractal pattern
59          g.setColor(color);
60          drawFractal(level, 100, 90, 290, 200, g);
61       }
62
63       // set the drawing color to c
64       public void setColor(Color c)
65       {
66          color = c;
67       }
68
69       // set the new level of recursion
70       public void setLevel(int currentLevel)
71       {
72          level = currentLevel;
73       }
74
75       // returns level of recursion
76       public int getLevel()
77       {
78          return level;
79       }
80    } // end class FractalJPanel
```

Fig. 18.19 | Drawing the "Lo feather fractal" using recursion. (Part 2 of 4.)

Fig. 18.19 | Drawing the "Lo feather fractal" using recursion. (Part 3 of 4.)

Fig. 18.19 | Drawing the "Lo feather fractal" using recursion. (Part 4 of 4.)

Lines 27–50 define the recursive method that creates the fractal. This method takes six parameters: the level, four integers that specify the x- and y-coordinates of two points, and the Graphics object g. The base case for this method (line 31) occurs when level equals 0, at which time a line will be drawn between the two points given as parameters. Lines 36–43 calculate (xC, yC), the midpoint between (xA, yA) and (xB, yB), and (xD, yD), the point that creates a right isosceles triangle with (xA, yA) and (xC, yC). Lines 46–48 make three recursive calls on three different sets of points.

In method paintComponent, line 60 makes the first call to method drawFractal to start the drawing. This method call is not recursive, but all subsequent calls to draw-Fractal performed from the body of drawFractal are. Since the lines will not be drawn until the base case is reached, the distance between two points decreases on each recursive call. As the level of recursion increases, the fractal becomes smoother and more detailed. The shape of this fractal stabilizes as the level approaches 11. Fractals will stabilize at different levels based on their shape and size.

The output of Fig. 18.19 shows the development of the fractal from levels 0 to 6. The last image shows the defining shape of the fractal at level 11. If we focus on one of the arms of this fractal, it will be identical to the whole image. This property defines the fractal to be strictly self-similar.

18.10 Recursive Backtracking

Our recursive methods all have a similar architecture—if the base case is reached, return a result; if not, make one or more recursive calls. This section explores a more complex recursive technique that finds a path through a maze, returning true if there's a possible solution. The solution involves moving through the maze one step at a time, where moves can be made by going down, right, up or left (diagonal moves are not permitted). From the current location in the maze (starting with the entry point), the following steps are taken: For each possible direction, the move is made in that direction and a recursive call is made to solve the remainder of the maze from the new location. When a dead end is reached (i.e., we cannot take any more steps forward without hitting a wall), we back up to the previous location and try to go in a different direction. If no other direction can be taken, we back up again. This process continues until we find a point in the maze where a move *can* be made in another direction. Once such a location is found, we move in the new direction and continue with another recursive call to solve the rest of the maze.

To back up to the previous location in the maze, our recursive method simply returns false, moving up the method-call chain to the previous recursive call (which references the previous location in the maze). Using recursion to return to an earlier decision point is known as **recursive backtracking**. If one set of recursive calls does not result in a solution to the problem, the program *backs up* to the previous decision point and makes a different decision, often resulting in another set of recursive calls. In this example, the previous decision point is the previous location in the maze, and the decision to be made is the direction that the next move should take. One direction has led to a *dead end*, so the search continues with a *different* direction. The recursive backtracking solution to the maze problem uses recursion to return only *partway* up the method-call chain, then try a different direction. If the backtracking reaches the entry location of the maze and the paths in all directions have been attempted, the maze does not have a solution.

The exercises ask you to implement recursive backtracking solutions to the maze problem (Exercises 18.20–18.22) and the Eight Queens problem (Exercise 18.15), which attempts to find a way to place eight queens on an empty chessboard so that no queen is "attacking" any other (i.e., no two queens are in the same row, in the same column or along the same diagonal).

18.11 Wrap-Up

In this chapter, you learned how to create recursive methods—i.e., methods that call themselves. You learned that recursive methods typically divide a problem into two conceptual pieces—a piece that the method knows how to do (the base case) and a piece that the method does not know how to do (the recursion step). The recursion step is a slightly smaller version of the original problem and is performed by a recursive method call. You saw some popular recursion examples, including calculating factorials and producing values in the Fibonacci series. You then learned how recursion works "under the hood," including the order in which recursive method calls are pushed on or popped off the program-execution stack. Next, you compared recursive and iterative approaches. You learned how to use recursion to solve more complex problems—the Towers of Hanoi and displaying fractals. The chapter concluded with an introduction to recursive backtracking, a technique for solving problems that involves backing up through recursive calls to try different possible solutions. In the next chapter, you'll learn numerous techniques for sorting lists of data and searching for an item in a list of data, and you'll explore the circumstances under which each searching and sorting technique should be used.

Summary

Section 18.1 Introduction

• A recursive method (p. 769) calls itself directly or indirectly through another method.

Section 18.2 Recursion Concepts

- When a recursive method is called (p. 770) to solve a problem, it can solve only the simplest case(s), or base case(s). If called with a base case (p. 770), the method returns a result.

- If a recursive method is called with a more complex problem than a base case, it typically divides the problem into two conceptual pieces—a piece that the method knows how to do and a piece that it does not know how to do.

- To make recursion feasible, the piece that the method does not know how to do must resemble the original problem, but be a slightly simpler or smaller version of it. Because this new problem resembles the original problem, the method calls a fresh copy of itself to work on the smaller problem—this is called the recursion step (p. 770).

- For recursion to eventually terminate, each time a method calls itself with a simpler version of the original problem, the sequence of smaller and smaller problems must converge on a base case. When, the method recognizes the base case, it returns a result to the previous copy of the method.

- A recursive call may be a call to another method, which in turn makes a call back to the original method. Such a process still results in a recursive call to the original method. This is known as an indirect recursive call or indirect recursion (p. 770).

Section 18.3 Example Using Recursion: Factorials

- Either omitting the base case or writing the recursion step incorrectly so that it does not converge on the base case can cause infinite recursion (p. 773), eventually exhausting memory. This error is analogous to the problem of an infinite loop in an iterative (nonrecursive) solution.

Section 18.5 Example Using Recursion: Fibonacci Series

- The Fibonacci series (p. 775) begins with 0 and 1 and has the property that each subsequent Fibonacci number is the sum of the preceding two.

- The ratio of successive Fibonacci numbers converges on a constant value of 1.618..., a number that has been called the golden ratio or the golden mean (p. 775).

- Some recursive solutions, such as Fibonacci, result in an "explosion" of method calls.

Section 18.6 Recursion and the Method-Call Stack

- The executing method is always the one whose stack frame is at the top of the stack, and the stack frame for that method contains the values of its local variables.

Section 18.7 Recursion vs. Iteration

- Both iteration and recursion are based on a control statement: Iteration uses a repetition statement, recursion a selection statement.

- Both iteration and recursion involve repetition: Iteration explicitly uses a repetition statement, whereas recursion achieves repetition through repeated method calls.

- Iteration and recursion each involve a termination test: Iteration terminates when the loop-continuation condition fails, recursion when a base case is recognized.

- Iteration with counter-controlled repetition and recursion each gradually approach termination: Iteration keeps modifying a counter until the counter assumes a value that makes the loop-continuation condition fail, whereas recursion keeps producing simpler versions of the original problem until the base case is reached.

- Both iteration and recursion can occur infinitely: An infinite loop occurs with iteration if the loop-continuation test never becomes false, whereas infinite recursion occurs if the recursion step does not reduce the problem each time in a manner that converges on the base case.

- Recursion repeatedly invokes the mechanism, and consequently the overhead, of method calls.
- Any problem that can be solved recursively can also be solved iteratively.
- A recursive approach is normally preferred over an iterative approach when it more naturally mirrors the problem and results in a program that is easier to understand and debug.
- A recursive approach can often be implemented with few lines of code, but a corresponding iterative approach might take a large amount of code. Another reason to choose a recursive solution is that an iterative solution might not be apparent.

Section 18.9 Fractals
- A fractal (p. 783) is a geometric figure that is generated from a pattern repeated recursively an infinite number of times.
- Fractals have a self-similar property (p. 783)—subparts are reduced-size copies of the whole.

Section 18.10 Recursive Backtracking
- In recursive backtracking (p. 794), if one set of recursive calls does not result in a solution to the problem, the program backs up to the previous decision point and makes a different decision, often resulting in another set of recursive calls.

Self-Review Exercises

18.1 State whether each of the following is *true* or *false*. If *false*, explain why.
  a) A method that calls itself indirectly is not an example of recursion.
  b) Recursion can be efficient in computation because of reduced memory-space usage.
  c) When a recursive method is called to solve a problem, it actually is capable of solving only the simplest case(s), or base case(s).
  d) To make recursion feasible, the recursion step in a recursive solution must resemble the original problem, but be a slightly larger version of it.

18.2 A _____ is needed to terminate recursion.
  a) recursion step
  b) break statement
  c) void return type
  d) base case

18.3 The first call to invoke a recursive method is _____.
  a) not recursive
  b) recursive
  c) the recursion step
  d) none of the above

18.4 Each time a fractal's pattern is applied, the fractal is said to be at a new _____.
  a) width
  b) height
  c) level
  d) volume

18.5 Iteration and recursion each involve a _____.
  a) repetition statement
  b) termination test
  c) counter variable
  d) none of the above

18.6 Fill in the blanks in each of the following statements:

a) The ratio of successive Fibonacci numbers converges on a constant value of 1.618..., a number that has been called the _____ or the _____.

b) Iteration normally uses a repetition statement, whereas recursion normally uses a(n) _____ statement.

c) Fractals have a(n) _____ property—when subdivided into parts, each is a reduced-size copy of the whole.

Answers to Self-Review Exercises

18.1 a) False. A method that calls itself in this manner is an example of indirect recursion. b) False. Recursion can be inefficient in computation because of multiple method calls and memory-space usage. c) True. d) False. To make recursion feasible, the recursion step in a recursive solution must resemble the original problem, but be a slightly *smaller* version of it.

18.2 d

18.3 a

18.4 c

18.5 b

18.6 a) golden ratio, golden mean. b) selection. c) self-similar.

Exercises

18.7 What does the following code do?

```
public int mystery(int a, int b)
{
    if (b == 1)
        return a;
    else
        return a + mystery(a, b - 1);
}
```

18.8 Find the error(s) in the following recursive method, and explain how to correct it (them). This method should find the sum of the values from 0 to n.

```
public int sum(int n)
{
    if (n == 0)
        return 0;
    else
        return n + sum(n);
}
```

18.9 *(Recursive power Method)* Write a recursive method power(base, exponent) that, when called, returns

$$base^{\ exponent}$$

For example, power(3,4) = 3 * 3 * 3 * 3. Assume that exponent is an integer greater than or equal to 1. *Hint:* The recursion step should use the relationship

$$base \ ^{exponent} = base \ \cdot \ base \ ^{exponent - 1}$$

and the terminating condition occurs when exponent is equal to 1, because

$$base^1 = base$$

Incorporate this method into a program that enables the user to enter the base and exponent.

18.10 *(Visualizing Recursion)* It's interesting to watch recursion "in action." Modify the factorial method in Fig. 18.3 to print its local variable and recursive-call parameter. For each recursive call, display the outputs on a separate line and add a level of indentation. Do your utmost to make the outputs clear, interesting and meaningful. Your goal here is to design and implement an output format that makes it easier to understand recursion. You may want to add such display capabilities to other recursion examples and exercises throughout the text.

18.11 *(Greatest Common Divisor)* The greatest common divisor of integers x and y is the largest integer that evenly divides into both x and y. Write a recursive method gcd that returns the greatest common divisor of x and y. The gcd of x and y is defined recursively as follows: If y is equal to 0, then gcd(x, y) is x; otherwise, gcd(x, y) is gcd(y, x % y), where % is the remainder operator. Use this method to replace the one you wrote in the application of Exercise 5.27.

18.12 What does the following program do?

```java
 1  // Exercise 18.12 Solution: MysteryClass.java
 2  public class MysteryClass
 3  {
 4     public static int mystery(int[] array2, int size)
 5     {
 6        if (size == 1)
 7           return array2[0];
 8        else
 9           return array2[size - 1] + mystery(array2, size - 1);
10     }
11
12     public static void main(String[] args)
13     {
14        int[] array = {1, 2, 3, 4, 5, 6, 7, 8, 9, 10};
15
16        int result = mystery(array, array.length);
17        System.out.printf("Result is: %d%n", result);
18     } // end method main
19  } // end class MysteryClass
```

18.13 What does the following program do?

```java
 1  // Exercise 18.13 Solution: SomeClass.java
 2  public class SomeClass
 3  {
 4     public static String someMethod(int[] array2, int x)
 5     {
 6        if (x < array2.length)
 7           return String.format(
 8              "%s%d ", someMethod(array2, x + 1), array2[x]);
 9        else
10           return "";
11     }
12
```

```
13        public static void main(String[] args)
14        {
15            int[] array = {1, 2, 3, 4, 5, 6, 7, 8, 9, 10};
16            String results = someMethod(array, 0);
17            System.out.println(results);
18        }
19    } // end class SomeClass
```

18.14 *(Palindromes)* A palindrome is a string that is spelled the same way forward and backward. Some examples of palindromes are "radar," "able was i ere i saw elba" and (if spaces are ignored) "a man a plan a canal panama." Write a recursive method `testPalindrome` that returns `boolean` value `true` if the string stored in the array is a palindrome and `false` otherwise. The method should ignore spaces and punctuation in the string.

18.15 *(Eight Queens)* A puzzler for chess buffs is the Eight Queens problem, which asks: Is it possible to place eight queens on an empty chessboard so that no queen is "attacking" any other (i.e., no two queens are in the same row, in the same column or along the same diagonal)? For instance, if a queen is placed in the upper-left corner of the board, no other queens could be placed in any of the marked squares shown in Fig. 18.20. Solve the problem recursively. [*Hint:* Your solution should begin with the first column and look for a location in that column where a queen can be placed—initially, place the queen in the first row. The solution should then recursively search the remaining columns. In the first few columns, there will be several locations where a queen may be placed. Take the first available location. If a column is reached with no possible location for a queen, the program should return to the previous column, and move the queen in that column to a new row. This continuous backing up and trying new alternatives is an example of recursive backtracking.]

18.16 *(Print an Array)* Write a recursive method `printArray` that displays all the elements in an array of integers, separated by spaces.

Fig. 18.20 | Squares eliminated by placing a queen in the upper-left corner of a chessboard.

18.17 *(Print an Array Backward)* Write a recursive method `stringReverse` that takes a character array containing a string as an argument and prints the string backward. [*Hint:* Use `String` method `toCharArray`, which takes no arguments, to get a `char` array containing the characters in the `String`.]

18.18 *(Find the Minimum Value in an Array)* Write a recursive method `recursiveMinimum` that determines the smallest element in an array of integers. The method should return when it receives an array of one element.

18.19 *(Fractals)* Repeat the fractal pattern in Section 18.9 to form a star. Begin with five lines (see Fig. 18.21) instead of one, where each line is a different arm of the star. Apply the "Lo feather fractal" pattern to each arm of the star.

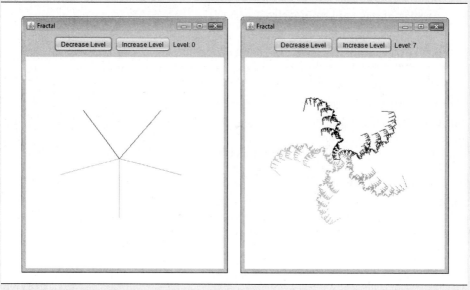

Fig. 18.21 | Sample outputs for Exercise 18.19.

18.20 *(Maze Traversal Using Recursive Backtracking)* The grid of #s and dots (.) in Fig. 18.22 is a two-dimensional array representation of a maze. The #s represent the walls of the maze, and the dots represent locations in the possible paths through the maze. A move can be made only to a location in the array that contains a dot.

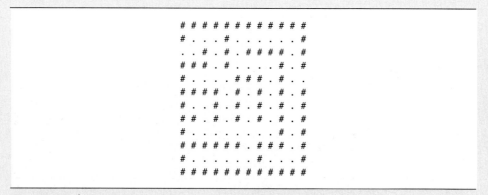

Fig. 18.22 | Two-dimensional array representation of a maze.

Write a recursive method (mazeTraversal) to walk through mazes like the one in Fig. 18.22. The method should receive as arguments a 12-by-12 character array representing the maze and the current location in the maze (the first time this method is called, the current location should be the entry point of the maze). As mazeTraversal attempts to locate the exit, it should place the character x in each square in the path. There's a simple algorithm for walking through a maze that guarantees finding the exit (assuming there's an exit). If there's no exit, you'll arrive at the starting location again. The algorithm is as follows: From the current location in the maze, try to move one space in any of the possible directions (down, right, up or left). If it's possible to move in at least one direction, call mazeTraversal recursively, passing the new spot on the maze as the current spot.

If it's not possible to go in any direction, "back up" to a previous location in the maze and try a new direction for that location (this is an example of recursive backtracking). Program the method to display the maze after each move so the user can watch as the maze is solved. The final output of the maze should display only the path needed to solve the maze—if going in a particular direction results in a dead end, the x's going in that direction should not be displayed. [*Hint:* To display only the final path, it may be helpful to mark off spots that result in a dead end with another character (such as '0').]

18.21   *(Generating Mazes Randomly)* Write a method mazeGenerator that takes as an argument a two-dimensional 12-by-12 character array and randomly produces a maze. The method should also provide the starting and ending locations of the maze. Test your method mazeTraversal from Exercise 18.20, using several randomly generated mazes.

18.22   *(Mazes of Any Size)* Generalize methods mazeTraversal and mazeGenerator of Exercise 18.20 and Exercise 18.21 to process mazes of any width and height.

18.23   *(Time to Calculate Fibonacci Numbers)* Enhance the Fibonacci program of Fig. 18.5 so that it calculates the approximate amount of time required to perform the calculation and the number of calls made to the recursive method. For this purpose, call static System method currentTimeMillis, which takes no arguments and returns the computer's current time in milliseconds. Call this method twice—once before and once after the call to fibonacci. Save each value and calculate the difference in the times to determine how many milliseconds were required to perform the calculation. Then, add a variable to the FibonacciCalculator class, and use this variable to determine the number of calls made to method fibonacci. Display your results.

19

Searching, Sorting and Big O

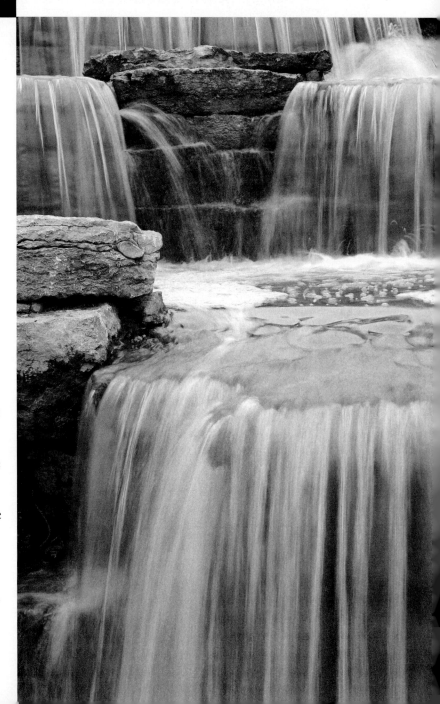

With sobs and tears
he sorted out
Those of the largest size ...
—Lewis Carroll

Attempt the end, and never
stand to doubt;
Nothing's so hard, but search
will find it out.
—Robert Herrick

'Tis in my memory lock'd,
And you yourself shall keep the
key of it.
—William Shakespeare

It is an immutable law in
business that words are words,
explanations are explanations,
promises are promises — but
only performance is reality.
—Harold S. Green

Objectives

In this chapter you'll:

- Search for a given value in an array using linear search and binary search.

- Sort arrays using the iterative selection and insertion sort algorithms.

- Sort arrays using the recursive merge sort algorithm.

- Determine the efficiency of searching and sorting algorithms.

- Introduce Big O notation for comparing the efficiency of algorithms.

19.1 Introduction

Searching data involves determining whether a value (referred to as the **search key**) is present in the data and, if so, finding its location. Two popular search algorithms are the simple linear search and the faster but more complex binary search. **Sorting** places data in ascending or descending order, based on one or more **sort keys**. A list of names could be sorted alphabetically, bank accounts could be sorted by account number, employee payroll records could be sorted by social security number, and so on. This chapter introduces two simple sorting algorithms, the selection sort and the insertion sort, along with the more efficient but more complex merge sort. Figure 19.1 summarizes the searching and sorting algorithms discussed in the examples and exercises of this book.

Software Engineering Observation 19.1

In apps that require searching and sorting, use the pre-defined capabilities of the Java Collections API (Chapter 16). The techniques presented in this chapter are provided to introduce students to the concepts behind searching and sorting algorithms—upper-level computer science courses typically discuss such algorithms in detail.

Chapter	Algorithm	Location
Searching Algorithms:		
16	binarySearch method of class Collections	Fig. 16.12
19	Linear search	Section 19.2
	Binary search	Section 19.4
	Recursive linear search	Exercise 19.8
	Recursive binary search	Exercise 19.9

Fig. 19.1 | Searching and sorting algorithms covered in this text. (Part 1 of 2.)

Chapter	Algorithm	Location
21	Linear search of a List	Exercise 21.21
	Binary tree search	Exercise 21.23
Sorting Algorithms:		
16	sort method of class Collections	Figs. 16.6–16.9
	SortedSet collection	Fig. 16.17
19	Selection sort	Section 19.6
	Insertion sort	Section 19.7
	Recursive merge sort	Section 19.8
	Bubble sort	Exercises 19.5 and 19.6
	Bucket sort	Exercise 19.7
	Recursive quicksort	Exercise 19.10
21	Binary tree sort	Section 21.7

Fig. 19.1 | Searching and sorting algorithms covered in this text. (Part 2 of 2.)

19.2 Linear Search

Looking up a phone number, finding a website via a search engine and checking the definition of a word in a dictionary all involve searching large amounts of data. This section and Section 19.4 discuss two common search algorithms—one that's easy to program yet relatively inefficient (linear search) and one that's relatively efficient but more complex to program (binary search).

Linear Search Algorithm

The **linear search algorithm** searches each element in an array sequentially. If the search key does not match an element in the array, the algorithm tests each element, and when the end of the array is reached, informs the user that the search key is not present. If the search key is in the array, the algorithm tests each element until it finds one that matches the search key and returns the index of that element.

As an example, consider an array containing the following values

34	56	2	10	77	51	93	30	5	52

and a program that's searching for 51. Using the linear search algorithm, the program first checks whether 34 matches the search key. It does not, so the algorithm checks whether 56 matches the search key. The program continues moving through the array sequentially, testing 2, then 10, then 77. When the program tests 51, which matches the search key, the program returns the index 5, which is the location of 51 in the array. If, after checking every array element, the program determines that the search key does not match any element in the array, it returns a sentinel value (e.g., -1).

Linear Search Implementation

Class LinearSearchTest (Fig. 19.2) contains static method linearSearch for performing searches of an int array and main for testing linearSearch.

```
 1  // Fig. 19.2: LinearSearchTest.java
 2  // Sequentially searching an array for an item.
 3  import java.security.SecureRandom;
 4  import java.util.Arrays;
 5  import java.util.Scanner;
 6
 7  public class LinearSearchTest
 8  {
 9     // perform a linear search on the data
10     public static int linearSearch(int data[], int searchKey)
11     {
12        // loop through array sequentially
13        for (int index = 0; index < data.length; index++)
14           if (data[index] == searchKey)
15              return index; // return index of integer
16
17        return -1; // integer was not found
18     } // end method linearSearch
19
20     public static void main(String[] args)
21     {
22        Scanner input = new Scanner(System.in);
23        SecureRandom generator = new SecureRandom();
24
25        int[] data = new int[10]; // create array
26
27        for (int i = 0; i < data.length; i++) // populate array
28           data[i] = 10 + generator.nextInt(90);
29
30        System.out.printf("%s%n%n", Arrays.toString(data)); // display array
31
32        // get input from user
33        System.out.print("Please enter an integer value (-1 to quit): ");
34        int searchInt = input.nextInt();
35
36        // repeatedly input an integer; -1 terminates the program
37        while (searchInt != -1)
38        {
39           int position = linearSearch(data, searchInt); // perform search
40
41           if (position == -1) // not found
42              System.out.printf("%d was not found%n%n", searchInt);
43           else // found
44              System.out.printf("%d was found in position %d%n%n",
45                 searchInt, position);
46
47           // get input from user
48           System.out.print("Please enter an integer value (-1 to quit): ");
49           searchInt = input.nextInt();
50        }
51     } // end main
52  } // end class LinearSearchTest
```

Fig. 19.2 | Sequentially searching an array for an item. (Part 1 of 2.)

```
[59, 97, 34, 90, 79, 56, 24, 51, 30, 69]
Please enter an integer value (-1 to quit): 79
79 was found in position 4

Please enter an integer value (-1 to quit): 61
61 was not found

Please enter an integer value (-1 to quit): 51
51 was found in position 7

Please enter an integer value (-1 to quit): -1
```

Fig. 19.2 | Sequentially searching an array for an item. (Part 2 of 2.)

Method *linearSearch*

Method linearSearch (lines 10–18) performs the linear search. The method receives as parameters the array to search (data) and the searchKey. Lines 13–15 loop through the elements in the array data. Line 14 compares each with searchKey. If the values are equal, line 15 returns the *index* of the element. If there are *duplicate* values in the array, linear search returns the index of the *first* element in the array that matches the search key. If the loop ends without finding the value, line 17 returns -1.

Method *main*

Method main (line 20–51) allows the user to search an array. Lines 25–28 create an array of 10 ints and populate it with random ints from 10–99. Then, line 30 displays the array's contents using Arrays static method toString, which returns a String representation of the array with the elements in square brackets ([and]) and separated by commas.

Lines 33–34 prompt the user for and store the search key. Line 39 calls method linearSearch to determine whether searchInt is in the array data. If it's not, linearSearch returns -1 and the program notifies the user (lines 41–42). If searchInt is in the array, linearSearch returns the position of the element, which the program outputs in lines 44–45. Lines 48–49 get the next search key from the user.

19.3 Big O Notation

Searching algorithms all accomplish the *same* goal—finding an element (or elements) that matches a given search key, if such an element does, in fact, exist. There are, however, a number of things that differentiate search algorithms from one another. *The major difference is the amount of effort they require to complete the search.* One way to describe this effort is with **Big O notation**, which indicates how hard an algorithm may have to work to solve a problem. For searching and sorting algorithms, this depends particularly on how many data elements there are. In this chapter, we use Big O to describe the worst-case run times for various searching and sorting algorithms.

19.3.1 O(1) Algorithms

Suppose an algorithm is designed to test whether the first element of an array is equal to the second. If the array has 10 elements, this algorithm requires one comparison. If the array has 1000 elements, it still requires one comparison. In fact, the algorithm is completely independent of the number of elements in the array. This algorithm is said to have a **constant run time**, which is represented in Big O notation as $O(1)$ and pronounced as "order one." An algorithm that's $O(1)$ does not necessarily require only one comparison. $O(1)$ just means that the number of comparisons is *constant*—it does not grow as the size of the array increases. An algorithm that tests whether the first element of an array is equal to any of the next three elements is still $O(1)$ even though it requires three comparisons.

19.3.2 O(n) Algorithms

An algorithm that tests whether the first array element is equal to *any* of the other array elements will require at most $n - 1$ comparisons, where n is the number of array elements. If the array has 10 elements, this algorithm requires up to nine comparisons. If the array has 1000 elements, it requires up to 999 comparisons. As n grows larger, the n part of the expression "dominates," and subtracting one becomes inconsequential. Big O is designed to highlight these dominant terms and ignore terms that become unimportant as n grows. For this reason, an algorithm that requires a total of $n - 1$ comparisons (such as the one we described earlier) is said to be $O(n)$. An $O(n)$ algorithm is referred to as having a **linear run time**. $O(n)$ is often pronounced "on the order of n" or simply "order n."

19.3.3 O(n²) Algorithms

Now suppose you have an algorithm that tests whether *any* element of an array is duplicated elsewhere in the array. The first element must be compared with every other element in the array. The second element must be compared with every other element except the first (it was already compared to the first). The third element must be compared with every other element except the first two. In the end, this algorithm will end up making $(n - 1) + (n - 2) + \ldots + 2 + 1$ or $n^2/2 - n/2$ comparisons. As n increases, the n^2 term dominates and the n term becomes inconsequential. Again, Big O notation highlights the n^2 term, leaving $n/2$. But, as we'll soon see, constant factors are omitted in Big O notation.

Big O is concerned with how an algorithm's run time grows in relation to the number of items processed. Suppose an algorithm requires n^2 comparisons. With four elements, the algorithm requires 16 comparisons; with eight elements, 64 comparisons. With this algorithm, *doubling* the number of elements *quadruples* the number of comparisons. Consider a similar algorithm requiring $n^2/2$ comparisons. With four elements, the algorithm requires eight comparisons; with eight elements, 32 comparisons. Again, *doubling* the number of elements *quadruples* the number of comparisons. Both of these algorithms grow as the square of n, so Big O ignores the constant and both algorithms are considered to be $O(n^2)$, which is referred to as **quadratic run time** and pronounced "on the order of n-squared" or more simply "order n-squared."

When n is small, $O(n^2)$ algorithms (running on today's computers) will not noticeably affect performance. But as n grows, you'll start to notice the performance degradation. An $O(n^2)$ algorithm running on a million-element array would require a trillion "operations" (where each could actually require several machine instructions to execute). This could take several hours. A billion-element array would require a quintillion operations, a number so large that the algorithm could take decades! $O(n^2)$ algorithms, unfortunately, are easy to write, as you'll see in this chapter. You'll also see algorithms with more favorable Big O measures. These efficient algorithms often take a bit more cleverness and work to create, but their superior performance can be well worth the extra effort, especially as n gets large and as algorithms are combined into larger programs.

19.3.4 Big O of the Linear Search

The linear search algorithm runs in $O(n)$ time. The worst case in this algorithm is that every element must be checked to determine whether the search item exists in the array. If the size of the array is *doubled*, the number of comparisons that the algorithm must perform is also *doubled*. Linear search can provide outstanding performance if the element matching the search key happens to be at or near the front of the array. But we seek algorithms that perform well, on average, across *all* searches, including those where the element matching the search key is near the end of the array.

Linear search is easy to program, but it can be slow compared to other search algorithms. If a program needs to perform many searches on large arrays, it's better to implement a more efficient algorithm, such as the binary search, which we present next.

Performance Tip 19.1

Sometimes the simplest algorithms perform poorly. Their virtue is that they're easy to program, test and debug. Sometimes more complex algorithms are required to realize maximum performance.

19.4 Binary Search

The **binary search algorithm** is more efficient than linear search, but it requires that the array be sorted. The first iteration of this algorithm tests the *middle* element in the array. If this matches the search key, the algorithm ends. Assuming the array is sorted in *ascending* order, then if the search key is *less than* the middle element, it cannot match any element in the second half of the array and the algorithm continues with only the first half of the array (i.e., the first element up to, but not including, the middle element). If the search key is *greater than* the middle element, it cannot match any element in the first half of the array and the algorithm continues with only the second half (i.e., the element *after* the middle element through the last element). Each iteration tests the middle value of the remaining portion of the array. If the search key does not match the element, the algorithm eliminates half of the remaining elements. The algorithm ends by either finding an element that matches the search key or reducing the subarray to zero size.

Example

As an example consider the sorted 15-element array

2	3	5	10	27	30	34	51	56	65	77	81	82	93	99

and a search key of 65. A program implementing the binary search algorithm would first check whether 51 is the search key (because 51 is the *middle* element of the array). The search key (65) is larger than 51, so 51 is ignored along with the first half of the array (all elements smaller than 51), leaving

56	65	77	81	82	93	99

Next, the algorithm checks whether 81 (the middle element of the remainder of the array) matches the search key. The search key (65) is smaller than 81, so 81 is discarded along with the elements larger than 81. After just two tests, the algorithm has narrowed the number of values to check to only three (56, 65 and 77). It then checks 65 (which indeed matches the search key) and returns the index of the array element containing 65.

This algorithm required just three comparisons to determine whether the search key matched an element of the array. Using a linear search algorithm would have required 10 comparisons. [*Note:* In this example, we've chosen to use an array with 15 elements so that there will always be an obvious middle element in the array. With an even number of elements, the middle of the array lies between two elements. We implement the algorithm to choose the higher of those two elements.]

19.4.1 Binary Search Implementation

Class `BinarySearchTest` (Fig. 19.3) contains:

- `static` method `binarySearch` to search an `int` array for a specified key
- `static` method `remainingElements` to display the remaining elements in the array being searched, and
- `main` to test method `binarySearch`.

The `main` method (lines 57–90) is nearly identical to `main` in Fig. 19.2. In this program, we create a 15-element array (line 62) and line 67 calls the `Arrays` class's `static` method **sort** to sort the array `data`'s elements in an array in ascending order (by default). Recall that the binary search algorithm will work only on a sorted array. The first line of output from this program shows the sorted array of `int`s. When the user instructs the program to search for 18, the program first tests the middle element, which is 57 (as indicated by *). The search key is less than 57, so the program eliminates the second half of the array and tests the middle element from the first half. The search key is smaller than 36, so the program eliminates the second half of the array, leaving only three elements. Finally, the program checks 18 (which matches the search key) and returns the index 1.

```
1    // Fig. 19.3: BinarySearchTest.java
2    // Use binary search to locate an item in an array.
3    import java.security.SecureRandom;
4    import java.util.Arrays;
5    import java.util.Scanner;
6
7    public class BinarySearchTest
8    {
9       // perform a binary search on the data
10      public static int binarySearch(int[] data, int key)
11      {
12         int low = 0; // low end of the search area
13         int high = data.length - 1; // high end of the search area
14         int middle = (low + high + 1) / 2; // middle element
15         int location = -1; // return value; -1 if not found
16
17         do // loop to search for element
18         {
19            // print remaining elements of array
20            System.out.print(remainingElements(data, low, high));
21
```

Fig. 19.3 | Use binary search to locate an item in an array (the * in the output marks the middle element). (Part 1 of 3.)

```
22          // output spaces for alignment
23          for (int i = 0; i < middle; i++)
24             System.out.print("   ");
25          System.out.println(" * "); // indicate current middle
26
27          // if the element is found at the middle
28          if (key == data[middle])
29             location = middle; // location is the current middle
30          else if (key < data[middle]) // middle element is too high
31             high = middle - 1; // eliminate the higher half
32          else  // middle element is too low
33             low = middle + 1; // eliminate the lower half
34
35          middle = (low + high + 1) / 2; // recalculate the middle
36       } while ((low <= high) && (location == -1));
37
38       return location; // return location of search key
39    } // end method binarySearch
40
41    // method to output certain values in array
42    private static String remainingElements(int[] data, int low, int high)
43    {
44       StringBuilder temporary = new StringBuilder();
45
46       // append spaces for alignment
47       for (int i = 0; i < low; i++)
48          temporary.append("   ");
49
50       // append elements left in array
51       for (int i = low; i <= high; i++)
52          temporary.append(data[i] + " ");
53
54       return String.format("%s%n", temporary);
55    } // end method remainingElements
56
57    public static void main(String[] args)
58    {
59       Scanner input = new Scanner(System.in);
60       SecureRandom generator = new SecureRandom();
61
62       int[] data = new int[15]; // create array
63
64       for (int i = 0; i < data.length; i++) // populate array
65          data[i] = 10 + generator.nextInt(90);
66
67       Arrays.sort(data); // binarySearch requires sorted array
68       System.out.printf("%s%n%n", Arrays.toString(data)); // display array
69
70       // get input from user
71       System.out.print("Please enter an integer value (-1 to quit): ");
72       int searchInt = input.nextInt();
73
```

Fig. 19.3 | Use binary search to locate an item in an array (the * in the output marks the middle element). (Part 2 of 3.)

```
74              // repeatedly input an integer; -1 terminates the program
75              while (searchInt != -1)
76              {
77                  // perform search
78                  int location = binarySearch(data, searchInt);
79
80                  if (location == -1) // not found
81                      System.out.printf("%d was not found%n%n", searchInt);
82                  else // found
83                      System.out.printf("%d was found in position %d%n%n",
84                          searchInt, location);
85
86                  // get input from user
87                  System.out.print("Please enter an integer value (-1 to quit): ");
88                  searchInt = input.nextInt();
89              }
90      } // end main
91  } // end class BinarySearchTest
```

```
[13, 18, 29, 36, 42, 47, 56, 57, 63, 68, 80, 81, 82, 88, 88]

Please enter an integer value (-1 to quit): 18
13 18 29 36 42 47 56 57 63 68 80 81 82 88 88
               *
13 18 29 36 42 47 56
         *
13 18 29
   *
18 was found in position 1

Please enter an integer value (-1 to quit): 82
13 18 29 36 42 47 56 57 63 68 80 81 82 88 88
               *
                        63 68 80 81 82 88 88
                                 *
                                 82 88 88
                                      *
                                 82
                                  *
82 was found in position 12

Please enter an integer value (-1 to quit): 69
13 18 29 36 42 47 56 57 63 68 80 81 82 88 88
               *
                        63 68 80 81 82 88 88
                                 *
                        63 68 80
                            *
                                 80
                                  *
69 was not found

Please enter an integer value (-1 to quit): -1
```

Fig. 19.3 | Use binary search to locate an item in an array (the * in the output marks the middle element). (Part 3 of 3.)

Lines 10–39 declare method `binarySearch`, which receives as parameters the array to search (`data`) and the search key (`key`). Lines 12–14 calculate the `low` end index, `high` end index and `middle` index of the portion of the array that the program is currently searching. At the beginning of the method, the `low` end is 0, the `high` end is the length of the array minus 1 and the `middle` is the average of these two values. Line 15 initializes the `location` of the element to -1—the value that will be returned if the `key` is not found. Lines 17–36 loop until `low` is greater than `high` (this occurs when the `key` is not found) or `location` does not equal -1 (indicating that the `key` was found). Line 28 tests whether the value in the `middle` element is equal to the `key`. If so, line 29 assigns `middle` to `location`, the loop terminates and `location` is returned to the caller. Each iteration of the loop tests a single value (line 28) and *eliminates half of the remaining values in the array* (line 31 or 33) if the value is not the `key`.

19.4.2 Efficiency of the Binary Search

In the worst-case scenario, searching a *sorted* array of 1023 elements takes *only 10 comparisons* when using a binary search. Repeatedly dividing 1023 by 2 (because after each comparison we can eliminate half the array) and rounding down (because we also remove the middle element) yields the values 511, 255, 127, 63, 31, 15, 7, 3, 1 and 0. The number 1023 (2^{10} – 1) is divided by 2 only 10 times to get the value 0, which indicates that there are no more elements to test. Dividing by 2 is equivalent to one comparison in the binary search algorithm. Thus, an array of 1,048,575 (2^{20} – 1) elements takes a *maximum of 20 comparisons* to find the key, and an array of over one billion elements takes a *maximum of 30 comparisons* to find the key. This is a tremendous improvement in performance over the linear search. For a one-billion-element array, this is a difference between an average of 500 million comparisons for the linear search and a maximum of only 30 comparisons for the binary search! The maximum number of comparisons needed for the binary search of any sorted array is the exponent of the first power of 2 greater than the number of elements in the array, which is represented as $\log_2 n$. All logarithms grow at roughly the same rate, so in big O notation the base can be omitted. This results in a big O of *O*(**log n**) for a binary search, which is also known as **logarithmic run time** and pronounced as "order log n."

19.5 Sorting Algorithms

Sorting data (i.e., placing the data into some particular order, such as ascending or descending) is one of the most important computing applications. A bank sorts all checks by account number so that it can prepare individual bank statements at the end of each month. Telephone companies sort their lists of accounts by last name and, further, by first name to make it easy to find phone numbers. Virtually every organization must sort some data, and often massive amounts of it. Sorting data is an intriguing, computer-intensive problem that has attracted intense research efforts.

An important item to understand about sorting is that the end result—the sorted array—will be the *same* no matter which algorithm you use to sort the array. The choice of algorithm affects only the run time and memory use of the program. The rest of this chapter introduces three common sorting algorithms. The first two—*selection sort* and *insertion sort*—are easy to program but *inefficient*. The last algorithm—*merge sort*—is much *faster* than selection sort and insertion sort but *harder to program*. We focus on sorting arrays of primitive-type data, namely ints. It's possible to sort arrays of class objects as well, as we demonstrated in Section 16.7.1 by using the built-in sorting capabilities of the Collections API.

19.6 Selection Sort

Selection sort is a simple, but inefficient, sorting algorithm. If you're sorting in increasing order, its first iteration selects the *smallest* element in the array and swaps it with the first element. The second iteration selects the *second-smallest* item (which is the smallest item of the remaining elements) and swaps it with the second element. The algorithm continues until the last iteration selects the *second-largest* element and swaps it with the second-to-last index, leaving the largest element in the last index. After the *i*th iteration, the smallest *i* items of the array will be sorted into increasing order in the first *i* elements of the array.

As an example, consider the array

| 34 | 56 | 4 | 10 | 77 | 51 | 93 | 30 | 5 | 52 |

A program that implements selection sort first determines the smallest element (4) of this array, which is contained in index 2. The program swaps 4 with 34, resulting in

| 4 | 56 | 34 | 10 | 77 | 51 | 93 | 30 | 5 | 52 |

The program then determines the smallest value of the remaining elements (all elements except 4), which is 5, contained in index 8. The program swaps 5 with 56, resulting in

| 4 | 5 | 34 | 10 | 77 | 51 | 93 | 30 | 56 | 52 |

On the third iteration, the program determines the next smallest value (10) and swaps it with 34.

| 4 | 5 | 10 | 34 | 77 | 51 | 93 | 30 | 56 | 52 |

The process continues until the array is fully sorted.

| 4 | 5 | 10 | 30 | 34 | 51 | 52 | 56 | 77 | 93 |

After the first iteration, the smallest element is in the first position. After the second iteration, the two smallest elements are in order in the first two positions. After the third iteration, the three smallest elements are in order in the first three positions.

19.6.1 Selection Sort Implementation

Class SelectionSortTest (Fig. 19.4) contains:

- static method selectionSort to sort an int array using the selection sort algorithm
- static method swap to swap the values of two array elements
- static method printPass to display the array contents after each pass, and
- main to test method selectionSort.

As in the searching examples, main (lines 57–72) creates an array of ints named data and populates it with random ints in the range 10–99. Line 68 tests method selectionSort.

```java
 1   // Fig. 19.4: SelectionSortTest.java
 2   // Sorting an array with selection sort.
 3   import java.security.SecureRandom;
 4   import java.util.Arrays;
 5
 6   public class SelectionSortTest
 7   {
 8      // sort array using selection sort
 9      public static void selectionSort(int[] data)
10      {
11         // loop over data.length - 1 elements
12         for (int i = 0; i < data.length - 1; i++)
13         {
14            int smallest = i; // first index of remaining array
15
16            // loop to find index of smallest element
17            for (int index = i + 1; index < data.length; index++)
18               if (data[index] < data[smallest])
19                  smallest = index;
20
21            swap(data, i, smallest); // swap smallest element into position
22            printPass(i + 1, smallest); // output pass of algorithm
23         }
24      } // end method selectionSort
25
26      // helper method to swap values in two elements
27      private static void swap(int[] data, int first, int second)
28      {
29         int temporary = data[first]; // store first in temporary
30         data[first] = data[second]; // replace first with second
31         data[second] = temporary; // put temporary in second
32      }
33
34      // print a pass of the algorithm
35      private static void printPass(int[] data, int pass, int index)
36      {
37         System.out.printf("after pass %2d: ", pass);
38
39         // output elements till selected item
40         for (int i = 0; i < index; i++)
41            System.out.printf("%d  ", data[i]);
42
43         System.out.printf("%d* ", data[index]); // indicate swap
44
45         // finish outputting array
46         for (int i = index + 1; i < data.length; i++)
47            System.out.printf("%d  ", data[i]);
48
49         System.out.printf("%n                   "); // for alignment
50
51         // indicate amount of array that's sorted
52         for (int j = 0; j < pass; j++)
53            System.out.print("-- ");
```

Fig. 19.4 | Sorting an array with selection sort. (Part 1 of 2.)

```
54              System.out.println();
55          }
56
57      public static void main(String[] args)
58      {
59          SecureRandom generator = new SecureRandom();
60
61          int[] data = new int[10]; // create array
62
63          for (int i = 0; i < data.length; i++) // populate array
64              data[i] = 10 + generator.nextInt(90);
65
66          System.out.printf("Unsorted array:%n%s%n%n",
67              Arrays.toString(data)); // display array
68          selectionSort(data); // sort array
69
70          System.out.printf("Sorted array:%n%s%n%n",
71              Arrays.toString(data)); // display array
72      }
73  } // end class SelectionSortTest
```

```
Unsorted array:
[40, 60, 59, 46, 98, 82, 23, 51, 31, 36]

after pass  1: 23  60  59  46  98  82  40* 51  31  36
               --
after pass  2: 23  31  59  46  98  82  40  51  60* 36
               --  --
after pass  3: 23  31  36  46  98  82  40  51  60  59*
               --  --  --
after pass  4: 23  31  36  40  98  82  46* 51  60  59
               --  --  --  --
after pass  5: 23  31  36  40  46  82  98* 51  60  59
               --  --  --  --  --
after pass  6: 23  31  36  40  46  51  98  82* 60  59
               --  --  --  --  --  --
after pass  7: 23  31  36  40  46  51  59  82  60  98*
               --  --  --  --  --  --  --
after pass  8: 23  31  36  40  46  51  59  60  82* 98
               --  --  --  --  --  --  --  --
after pass  9: 23  31  36  40  46  51  59  60  82* 98
               --  --  --  --  --  --  --  --  --
Sorted array:
[23, 31, 36, 40, 46, 51, 59, 60, 82, 98]
```

Fig. 19.4 | Sorting an array with selection sort. (Part 2 of 2.)

Methods selectionSort and swap

Lines 9–24 declare the selectionSort method. Lines 12–23 loop data.length - 1 times. Line 14 declares and initializes (to the current index i) the variable smallest, which stores the index of the smallest element in the remaining array. Lines 17–19 loop over the remaining elements in the array. For each of these elements, line 18 compares its value to the value of the smallest element. If the current element is smaller than the smallest element, line 19 assigns the current element's index to smallest. When this loop finishes, smallest will contain the index of the smallest element in the remaining array. Line 21 calls method swap (lines 27–32) to place the smallest remaining element in the next ordered spot in the array.

Methods printPass

The output of method printPass uses dashes (lines 52–53) to indicate the portion of the array that's sorted after each pass. An asterisk is placed next to the position of the element that was swapped with the smallest element on that pass. On each pass, the element next to the asterisk (specified at line 43) and the element above the rightmost set of dashes were swapped.

19.6.2 Efficiency of the Selection Sort

The selection sort algorithm runs in $O(n^2)$ time. Method selectionSort (lines 9–24) contains two for loops. The outer one (lines 12–23) iterates over the first $n - 1$ elements in the array, swapping the smallest remaining item into its sorted position. The inner loop (lines 17–19) iterates over each item in the remaining array, searching for the smallest element. This loop executes $n - 1$ times during the first iteration of the outer loop, $n - 2$ times during the second iteration, then $n - 3$, …, 3, 2, 1. This inner loop will iterate a total of $n(n - 1)/2$ or $(n^2 - n)/2$. In Big O notation, smaller terms drop out and constants are ignored, leaving a Big O of $O(n^2)$.

19.7 Insertion Sort

Insertion sort is another *simple, but inefficient,* sorting algorithm. The first iteration of this algorithm takes the *second element* in the array and, if it's *less than* the *first element, swaps it with the first element.* The second iteration looks at the third element and inserts it into the correct position with respect to the first two, so all three elements are in order. At the *i*th iteration of this algorithm, the first *i* elements in the original array will be sorted.

Consider as an example the following array, which is identical to the one used in the discussions of selection sort and merge sort.

| 34 | 56 | 4 | 10 | 77 | 51 | 93 | 30 | 5 | 52 |

A program that implements the insertion sort algorithm will first look at the first two elements of the array, 34 and 56. These are already in order, so the program continues. (If they were out of order, the program would swap them.)

In the next iteration, the program looks at the third value, 4. This value is less than 56, so the program stores 4 in a temporary variable and moves 56 one element to the right. The program then checks and determines that 4 is less than 34, so it moves 34 one element to the right. The program has now reached the beginning of the array, so it places 4 in the zeroth element. The array now is

| 4 | 34 | 56 | 10 | 77 | 51 | 93 | 30 | 5 | 52 |

In the next iteration, the program stores 10 in a temporary variable. Then it compares 10 to 56 and moves 56 one element to the right because it's larger than 10. The program then compares 10 to 34, moving 34 right one element. When the program compares 10 to 4, it observes that 10 is larger than 4 and places 10 in element 1. The array now is

| 4 | 10 | 34 | 56 | 77 | 51 | 93 | 30 | 5 | 52 |

Using this algorithm, at the *i*th iteration, the first *i* elements of the original array are sorted, but they may not be in their final locations—smaller values may be located later in the array.

19.7.1 Insertion Sort Implementation

Class InsertionSortTest (Fig. 19.5) contains:

- static method insertionSort to sort ints using the insertion sort algorithm
- static method printPass to display the array contents after each pass, and
- main to test method insertionSort.

Method main (lines 53–68) is identical to main in Fig. 19.4 except that line 64 calls method insertionSort.

```java
1   // Fig. 19.5: InsertionSortTest.java
2   // Sorting an array with insertion sort.
3   import java.security.SecureRandom;
4   import java.util.Arrays;
5
6   public class InsertionSortTest
7   {
8      // sort array using insertion sort
9      public static void insertionSort(int[] data)
10     {
11        // loop over data.length - 1 elements
12        for (int next = 1; next < data.length; next++)
13        {
14           int insert = data[next]; // value to insert
15           int moveItem = next; // location to place element
16
17           // search for place to put current element
18           while (moveItem > 0 && data[moveItem - 1] > insert)
19           {
20              // shift element right one slot
21              data[moveItem] = data[moveItem - 1];
22              moveItem--;
23           }
24
25           data[moveItem] = insert; // place inserted element
26           printPass(data, next, moveItem); // output pass of algorithm
27        }
28     }
29
30     // print a pass of the algorithm
31     public static void printPass(int[] data, int pass, int index)
32     {
33        System.out.printf("after pass %2d: ", pass);
34
35        // output elements till swapped item
36        for (int i = 0; i < index; i++)
37           System.out.printf("%d  ", data[i]);
```

Fig. 19.5 | Sorting an array with insertion sort. (Part 1 of 3.)

```
38
39          System.out.printf("%d* ", data[index]); // indicate swap
40
41          // finish outputting array
42          for (int i = index + 1; i < data.length; i++)
43             System.out.printf("%d  ", data[i]);
44
45          System.out.printf("%n                     "); // for alignment
46
47          // indicate amount of array that's sorted
48          for(int i = 0; i <= pass; i++)
49             System.out.print("--  ");
50          System.out.println();
51       }
52
53       public static void main(String[] args)
54       {
55          SecureRandom generator = new SecureRandom();
56
57          int[] data = new int[10]; // create array
58
59          for (int i = 0; i < data.length; i++) // populate array
60             data[i] = 10 + generator.nextInt(90);
61
62          System.out.printf("Unsorted array:%n%s%n%n",
63             Arrays.toString(data)); // display array
64          insertionSort(data); // sort array
65
66          System.out.printf("Sorted array:%n%s%n%n",
67             Arrays.toString(data)); // display array
68       }
69    } // end class InsertionSortTest
```

```
Unsorted array:
[34, 96, 12, 87, 40, 80, 16, 50, 30, 45]

after pass 1: 34  96* 12  87  40  80  16  50  30  45
              --  --
after pass 2: 12* 34  96  87  40  80  16  50  30  45
              --  --  --
after pass 3: 12  34  87* 96  40  80  16  50  30  45
              --  --  --  --
after pass 4: 12  34  40* 87  96  80  16  50  30  45
              --  --  --  --  --
after pass 5: 12  34  40  80* 87  96  16  50  30  45
              --  --  --  --  --  --
after pass 6: 12  16* 34  40  80  87  96  50  30  45
              --  --  --  --  --  --  --
after pass 7: 12  16  34  40  50* 80  87  96  30  45
              --  --  --  --  --  --  --  --
after pass 8: 12  16  30* 34  40  50  80  87  96  45
              --  --  --  --  --  --  --  --  --
```

Fig. 19.5 | Sorting an array with insertion sort. (Part 2 of 3.)

```
after pass  9: 12  16  30  34  40  45* 50  80  87  96
               --  --  --  --  --  --  --  --  --  --
Sorted array:
[12, 16, 30, 34, 40, 45, 50, 80, 87, 96]
```

Fig. 19.5 | Sorting an array with insertion sort. (Part 3 of 3.)

Method `insertionSort`

Lines 9–28 declare the `insertionSort` method. Lines 12–27 loop over `data.length - 1` items in the array. In each iteration, line 14 declares and initializes variable `insert`, which holds the value of the element that will be inserted into the sorted portion of the array. Line 15 declares and initializes the variable `moveItem`, which keeps track of where to insert the element. Lines 18–23 loop to locate the correct position where the element should be inserted. The loop will terminate either when the program reaches the front of the array or when it reaches an element that's less than the value to be inserted. Line 21 moves an element to the right in the array, and line 22 decrements the position at which to insert the next element. After the loop ends, line 25 inserts the element into place.

Method `printPass`

The output of method `printPass` (lines 31–51) uses dashes to indicate the portion of the array that's sorted after each pass. An asterisk is placed next to the element that was inserted into place on that pass.

19.7.2 Efficiency of the Insertion Sort

The insertion sort algorithm also runs in $O(n^2)$ time. Like selection sort, the implementation of insertion sort (lines 9–28) contains two loops. The `for` loop (lines 12–27) iterates `data.length - 1` times, inserting an element into the appropriate position in the elements sorted so far. For the purposes of this application, `data.length - 1` is equivalent to $n - 1$ (as `data.length` is the size of the array). The `while` loop (lines 18–23) iterates over the preceding elements in the array. In the worst case, this `while` loop will require $n - 1$ comparisons. Each individual loop runs in $O(n)$ time. In Big O notation, nested loops mean that you must *multiply* the number of comparisons. For each iteration of an outer loop, there will be a certain number of iterations of the inner loop. In this algorithm, for each $O(n)$ iterations of the outer loop, there will be $O(n)$ iterations of the inner loop. Multiplying these values results in a Big O of $O(n^2)$.

19.8 Merge Sort

Merge sort is an *efficient* sorting algorithm but is conceptually *more complex* than selection sort and insertion sort. The merge sort algorithm sorts an array by *splitting* it into two equal-sized subarrays, *sorting* each subarray, then *merging* them into one larger array. With an odd number of elements, the algorithm creates the two subarrays such that one has one more element than the other.

The implementation of merge sort in this example is recursive. The base case is an array with one element, which is, of course, sorted, so the merge sort immediately returns in this case. The recursion step splits the array into two approximately equal pieces, recursively sorts them, then merges the two sorted arrays into one larger, sorted array.

Suppose the algorithm has already merged smaller arrays to create sorted arrays A:

4	10	34	56	77

and B:

5	30	51	52	93

Merge sort combines these two arrays into one larger, sorted array. The smallest element in A is 4 (located in the zeroth index of A). The smallest element in B is 5 (located in the zeroth index of B). In order to determine the smallest element in the larger array, the algorithm compares 4 and 5. The value from A is smaller, so 4 becomes the first element in the merged array. The algorithm continues by comparing 10 (the second element in A) to 5 (the first element in B). The value from B is smaller, so 5 becomes the second element in the larger array. The algorithm continues by comparing 10 to 30, with 10 becoming the third element in the array, and so on.

19.8.1 Merge Sort Implementation

Figure 19.6 declares the MergeSortTest class, which contains:

- static method mergeSort to initiate the sorting of an int array using the merge sort algorithm
- static method sortArray to perform the recursive merge sort algorithm—this is called by method mergeSort
- static method merge to merge two sorted subarrays into a single sorted subarray
- static method subarrayString to get a subarray's String representation for output purposes, and
- main to test method mergeSort.

Method main (lines 101–116) is identical to main in Figs. 19.4–19.5 except that line 112 calls method mergeSort. The output from this program displays the splits and merges performed by merge sort, showing the progress of the sort at each step of the algorithm. It's well worth your time to step through these outputs to fully understand this elegant sorting algorithm.

```java
1   // Fig. 19.6: MergeSortTest.java
2   // Sorting an array with merge sort.
3   import java.security.SecureRandom;
4   import java.util.Arrays;
5
6   public class MergeSortTest
7   {
8      // calls recursive split method to begin merge sorting
9      public static void mergeSort(int[] data)
10     {
11        sortArray(data, 0, data.length - 1); // sort entire array
12     } // end method sort
13
```

Fig. 19.6 | Sorting an array with merge sort. (Part 1 of 5.)

```
14      // splits array, sorts subarrays and merges subarrays into sorted array
15      private static void sortArray(int[] data, int low, int high)
16      {
17         // test base case; size of array equals 1
18         if ((high - low) >= 1) // if not base case
19         {
20            int middle1 = (low + high) / 2; // calculate middle of array
21            int middle2 = middle1 + 1; // calculate next element over
22
23            // output split step
24            System.out.printf("split:   %s%n",
25               subarrayString(data, low, high));
26            System.out.printf("         %s%n",
27               subarrayString(data, low, middle1));
28            System.out.printf("         %s%n%n",
29               subarrayString(data, middle2, high));
30
31            // split array in half; sort each half (recursive calls)
32            sortArray(data, low, middle1); // first half of array
33            sortArray(data, middle2, high); // second half of array
34
35            // merge two sorted arrays after split calls return
36            merge (data, low, middle1, middle2, high);
37         } // end if
38      } // end method sortArray
39
40      // merge two sorted subarrays into one sorted subarray
41      private static void merge(int[] data, int left, int middle1,
42         int middle2, int right)
43      {
44         int leftIndex = left; // index into left subarray
45         int rightIndex = middle2; // index into right subarray
46         int combinedIndex = left; // index into temporary working array
47         int[] combined = new int[data.length]; // working array
48
49         // output two subarrays before merging
50         System.out.printf("merge:   %s%n",
51            subarrayString(data, left, middle1));
52         System.out.printf("         %s%n",
53            subarrayString(data, middle2, right));
54
55         // merge arrays until reaching end of either
56         while (leftIndex <= middle1 && rightIndex <= right)
57         {
58            // place smaller of two current elements into result
59            // and move to next space in arrays
60            if (data[leftIndex] <= data[rightIndex])
61               combined[combinedIndex++] = data[leftIndex++];
62            else
63               combined[combinedIndex++] = data[rightIndex++];
64         }
65
```

Fig. 19.6 | Sorting an array with merge sort. (Part 2 of 5.)

```
66          // if left array is empty
67          if (leftIndex == middle2)
68              // copy in rest of right array
69              while (rightIndex <= right)
70                  combined[combinedIndex++] = data[rightIndex++];
71          else // right array is empty
72              // copy in rest of left array
73              while (leftIndex <= middle1)
74                  combined[combinedIndex++] = data[leftIndex++];
75
76          // copy values back into original array
77          for (int i = left; i <= right; i++)
78              data[i] = combined[i];
79
80          // output merged array
81          System.out.printf("          %s%n%n",
82              subarrayString(data, left, right));
83      } // end method merge
84
85      // method to output certain values in array
86      private static String subarrayString(int[] data, int low, int high)
87      {
88          StringBuilder temporary = new StringBuilder();
89
90          // output spaces for alignment
91          for (int i = 0; i < low; i++)
92              temporary.append("   ");
93
94          // output elements left in array
95          for (int i = low; i <= high; i++)
96              temporary.append(" " + data[i]);
97
98          return temporary.toString();
99      }
100
101     public static void main(String[] args)
102     {
103         SecureRandom generator = new SecureRandom();
104
105         int[] data = new int[10]; // create array
106
107         for (int i = 0; i < data.length; i++) // populate array
108             data[i] = 10 + generator.nextInt(90);
109
110         System.out.printf("Unsorted array:%n%s%n%n",
111             Arrays.toString(data)); // display array
112         mergeSort(data); // sort array
113
114         System.out.printf("Sorted array:%n%s%n%n",
115             Arrays.toString(data)); // display array
116     }
117 } // end class MergeSortTest
```

Fig. 19.6 | Sorting an array with merge sort. (Part 3 of 5.)

```
Unsorted array:
[75, 56, 85, 90, 49, 26, 12, 48, 40, 47]
split:      75 56 85 90 49 26 12 48 40 47
            75 56 85 90 49
                           26 12 48 40 47
split:      75 56 85 90 49
            75 56 85
                    90 49
split:      75 56 85
            75 56
                  85
split:      75 56
            75
               56
merge:      75
               56
            56 75
merge:      56 75
                  85
            56 75 85
split:              90 49
                    90
                       49
merge:              90
                       49
                    49 90
merge:      56 75 85
                       49 90
            49 56 75 85 90
split:                 26 12 48 40 47
                       26 12 48
                                40 47
split:                 26 12 48
                       26 12
                             48
split:                 26 12
                       26
                          12
merge:                 26
                          12
                       12 26
merge:                 12 26
                             48
                       12 26 48
split:                       40 47
                             40
                                47
```

Fig. 19.6 │ Sorting an array with merge sort. (Part 4 of 5.)

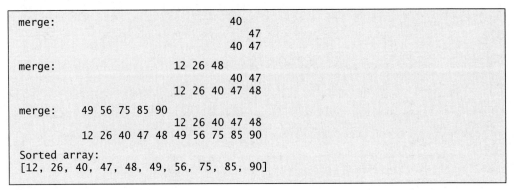

```
merge:                              40
                                       47
                                    40 47
merge:                  12 26 48
                                    40 47
                        12 26 40 47 48
merge:      49 56 75 85 90
                                    12 26 40 47 48
            12 26 40 47 48 49 56 75 85 90
Sorted array:
[12, 26, 40, 47, 48, 49, 56, 75, 85, 90]
```

Fig. 19.6 | Sorting an array with merge sort. (Part 5 of 5.)

Method mergeSort

Lines 9–12 of Fig. 19.6 declare the mergeSort method. Line 11 calls method sortArray with 0 and data.length - 1 as the arguments—corresponding to the beginning and ending indices, respectively, of the array to be sorted. These values tell method sortArray to operate on the entire array.

Method sortArray

Recursive method sortArray (lines 15–38) performs the recursive merge sort algorithm. Line 18 tests the base case. If the size of the array is 1, the array is already sorted, so the method returns immediately. If the size of the array is greater than 1, the method splits the array in two, recursively calls method sortArray to sort the two subarrays, then merges them. Line 32 recursively calls method sortArray on the first half of the array, and line 33 recursively calls method sortArray on the second half. When these two method calls return, each half of the array has been sorted. Line 36 calls method merge (lines 41–83) on the two halves of the array to combine the two sorted arrays into one larger sorted array.

Method merge

Lines 41–83 declare method merge. Lines 56–64 in merge loop until the end of either subarray is reached. Line 60 tests which element at the beginning of the arrays is smaller. If the element in the left array is smaller, line 61 places it in position in the combined array. If the element in the right array is smaller, line 63 places it in position in the combined array. When the while loop completes, one entire subarray has been placed in the combined array, but the other subarray still contains data. Line 67 tests whether the left array has reached the end. If so, lines 69–70 fill the combined array with the elements of the right array. If the left array has not reached the end, then the right array must have reached the end, and lines 73–74 fill the combined array with the elements of the left array. Finally, lines 77–78 copy the combined array into the original array.

19.8.2 Efficiency of the Merge Sort

Merge sort is *far more efficient* than insertion or selection sort. Consider the first (non-recursive) call to sortArray. This results in two recursive calls to sortArray with subarrays each approximately half the original array's size, and a single call to merge, which requires, at worst, $n - 1$ comparisons to fill the original array, which is $O(n)$. (Recall that each array element can be chosen by comparing one element from each subarray.) The two calls to sort-

Array result in four more recursive sortArray calls, each with a subarray approximately a quarter of the original array's size, along with two calls to merge that each require, at worst, $n/2 - 1$ comparisons, for a total number of comparisons of $O(n)$. This process continues, each sortArray call generating two additional sortArray calls and a merge call, until the algorithm has *split* the array into one-element subarrays. At each level, $O(n)$ comparisons are required to *merge* the subarrays. Each level splits the the arrays in half, so doubling the array size requires one more level. Quadrupling the array size requires two more levels. This pattern is logarithmic and results in $\log_2 n$ levels. This results in a total efficiency of **$O(n \log n)$**.

19.9 Big O Summary for This Chapter's Searching and Sorting Algorithms

Figure 19.7 summarizes the searching and sorting algorithms covered in this chapter with the Big O for each. Figure 19.8 lists the Big O values we've covered in this chapter along with a number of values for n to highlight the differences in the growth rates.

Algorithm	Location	Big O
Searching Algorithms:		
Linear search	Section 19.2	$O(n)$
Binary search	Section 19.4	$O(\log n)$
Recursive linear search	Exercise 19.8	$O(n)$
Recursive binary search	Exercise 19.9	$O(\log n)$
Sorting Algorithms:		
Selection sort	Section 19.6	$O(n^2)$
Insertion sort	Section 19.7	$O(n^2)$
Merge sort	Section 19.8	$O(n \log n)$
Bubble sort	Exercises 19.5 and 19.6	$O(n^2)$

Fig. 19.7 | Searching and sorting algorithms with Big O values.

$n =$	$O(\log n)$	$O(n)$	$O(n \log n)$	$O(n^2)$
1	0	1	0	1
2	1	2	2	4
3	1	3	3	9
4	1	4	4	16
5	1	5	5	25
10	1	10	10	100
100	2	100	200	10,000
1000	3	1000	3000	10^6
1,000,000	6	1,000,000	6,000,000	10^{12}
1,000,000,000	9	1,000,000,000	9,000,000,000	10^{18}

Fig. 19.8 | Number of comparisons for common Big O notations.

19.10 Wrap-Up

This chapter introduced searching and sorting. We discussed two searching algorithms—linear search and binary search—and three sorting algorithms—selection sort, insertion sort and merge sort. We introduced Big O notation, which helps you analyze the efficiency of an algorithm. The next two chapters continue our discussion of dynamic data structures that can grow or shrink at execution time. Chapter 20 demonstrates how to use Java's generics capabilities to implement generic methods and classes. Chapter 21 discusses the details of implementing generic data structures. Each of the algorithms in this chapter is "single threaded"—in Chapter 23, Concurrency, we'll discuss multithreading and how it can help you program for better performance on today's multi-core systems.

Summary

Section 19.1 Introduction
- Searching (p. 803) involves determining if a search key is in the data and, if so, finding its location.
- Sorting (p. 803) involves arranging data into order.

Section 19.2 Linear Search
- The linear search algorithm (p. 804) searches each element in the array sequentially until it finds the correct element, or until it reaches the end of the array without finding the element.

Section 19.3 Big O Notation
- A major difference among searching algorithms is the amount of effort they require.
- Big O notation (p. 806) describes an algorithm's efficiency in terms of the work required to solve a problem. For searching and sorting algorithms typically it depends on the number of elements in the data.
- An algorithm that's $O(1)$ does not necessarily require only one comparison (p. 807). It just means that the number of comparisons does not grow as the size of the array increases.
- An $O(n)$ algorithm is referred to as having a linear run time (p. 807).
- Big O highlights dominant factors and ignores terms that become unimportant with high n values.
- Big O notation is concerned with the growth rate of algorithm run times, so constants are ignored.
- The linear search algorithm runs in $O(n)$ time.
- The worst case in linear search is that every element must be checked to determine whether the search key (p. 808) exists, which occurs if the search key is the last array element or is not present.

Section 19.4 Binary Search
- Binary search (p. 808) is more efficient than linear search, but it requires that the array be sorted.
- The first iteration of binary search tests the middle element in the array. If this is the search key, the algorithm returns its location. If the search key is less than the middle element, the search continues with the first half of the array. If the search key is greater than the middle element, the search continues with the second half of the array. Each iteration tests the middle value of the remaining array and, if the element is not found, eliminates half of the remaining elements.
- Binary search is a more efficient searching algorithm than linear search because each comparison eliminates from consideration half of the elements in the array.

- Binary search runs in $O(\log n)$ time because each step removes half of the remaining elements; this is also known as logarithmic run time (p. 812).

- If the array size is doubled, binary search requires only one extra comparison.

Section 19.6 Selection Sort
- Selection sort (p. 813) is a simple, but inefficient, sorting algorithm.

- The sort begins by selecting the smallest item and swaps it with the first element. The second iteration selects the second-smallest item (which is the smallest remaining item) and swaps it with the second element. The sort continues until the last iteration selects the second-largest element and swaps it with the second-to-last element, leaving the largest element in the last index. At the ith iteration of selection sort, the smallest i items of the whole array are sorted into the first i indices.

- The selection sort algorithm runs in $O(n^2)$ time (p. 816).

Section 19.7 Insertion Sort
- The first iteration of insertion sort (p. 816) takes the second element in the array and, if it's less than the first element, swaps it with the first element. The second iteration looks at the third element and inserts it in the correct position with respect to the first two elements. After the ith iteration of insertion sort, the first i elements in the original array are sorted.

- The insertion sort algorithm runs in $O(n^2)$ time (p. 819).

Section 19.8 Merge Sort
- Merge sort (p. 819) is a sorting algorithm that's faster, but more complex to implement, than selection sort and insertion sort. The merge sort algorithm sorts an array by splitting it into two equal-sized subarrays, sorting each subarray recursively and merging the subarrays into one larger array.

- Merge sort's base case is an array with one element. A one-element array is already sorted, so merge sort immediately returns when it's called with a one-element array. The merge part of merge sort takes two sorted arrays and combines them into one larger sorted array.

- Merge sort performs the merge by looking at the first element in each array, which is also the smallest element in the array. Merge sort takes the smallest of these and places it in the first element of the larger array. If there are still elements in the subarray, merge sort looks at the second of these (which is now the smallest element remaining) and compares it to the first element in the other subarray. Merge sort continues this process until the larger array is filled.

- In the worst case, the first call to merge sort has to make $O(n)$ comparisons to fill the n slots in the final array.

- The merging portion of the merge sort algorithm is performed on two subarrays, each of approximately size $n/2$. Creating each of these subarrays requires $n/2 - 1$ comparisons for each subarray, or $O(n)$ comparisons total. This pattern continues as each level works on twice as many arrays, but each is half the size of the previous array.

- Similar to binary search, this halving results in $\log n$ levels for a total efficiency of $O(n \log n)$ (p. 825).

Self-Review Exercises

19.1   Fill in the blanks in each of the following statements:

  a) A selection sort application would take approximately _____ times as long to run on a 128-element array as on a 32-element array.

  b) The efficiency of merge sort is _____.

19.2   What key aspect of both the binary search and the merge sort accounts for the logarithmic portion of their respective Big Os?

19.3 In what sense is the insertion sort superior to the merge sort? In what sense is the merge sort superior to the insertion sort?

19.4 In the text, we say that after the merge sort splits the array into two subarrays, it then sorts these two subarrays and merges them. Why might someone be puzzled by our statement that "it then sorts these two subarrays"?

Answers to Self-Review Exercises

19.1 a) 16, because an $O(n^2)$ algorithm takes 16 times as long to sort four times as much information. b) $O(n \log n)$.

19.2 Both of these algorithms incorporate "halving"—somehow reducing something by half. The binary search eliminates from consideration one-half of the array after each comparison. The merge sort splits the array in half each time it's called.

19.3 The insertion sort is easier to understand and to program than the merge sort. The merge sort is far more efficient [$O(n \log n)$] than the insertion sort [$O(n^2)$].

19.4 In a sense, it does not really sort these two subarrays. It simply keeps splitting the original array in half until it provides a one-element subarray, which is, of course, sorted. It then builds up the original two subarrays by merging these one-element arrays to form larger subarrays, which are then merged, and so on.

Exercises

19.5 *(Bubble Sort)* Implement bubble sort—another simple yet inefficient sorting technique. It's called bubble sort or sinking sort because smaller values gradually "bubble" their way to the top of the array (i.e., toward the first element) like air bubbles rising in water, while the larger values sink to the bottom (end) of the array. The technique uses nested loops to make several passes through the array. Each pass compares successive pairs of elements. If a pair is in increasing order (or the values are equal), the bubble sort leaves the values as they are. If a pair is in decreasing order, the bubble sort swaps their values in the array. The first pass compares the first two elements of the array and swaps their values if necessary. It then compares the second and third elements in the array. The end of this pass compares the last two elements in the array and swaps them if necessary. After one pass, the largest element will be in the last index. After two passes, the largest two elements will be in the last two indices. Explain why bubble sort is an $O(n^2)$ algorithm.

19.6 *(Enhanced Bubble Sort)* Make the following simple modifications to improve the performance of the bubble sort you developed in Exercise 19.5:
    a) After the first pass, the largest number is guaranteed to be in the highest-numbered array element; after the second pass, the two highest numbers are "in place"; and so on. Instead of making nine comparisons on every pass for a ten-element array, modify the bubble sort to make eight comparisons on the second pass, seven on the third pass, and so on.
    b) The data in the array may already be in proper or near-proper order, so why make nine passes if fewer will suffice? Modify the sort to check at the end of each pass whether any swaps have been made. If there were none, the data must already be sorted, so the program should terminate. If swaps have been made, at least one more pass is needed.

19.7 *(Bucket Sort)* A bucket sort begins with a one-dimensional array of positive integers to be sorted and a two-dimensional array of integers with rows indexed from 0 to 9 and columns indexed from 0 to $n-1$, where n is the number of values to be sorted. Each row of the two-dimensional array is referred to as a *bucket*. Write a class named `BucketSort` containing a method called `sort` that operates as follows:

    a) Place each value of the one-dimensional array into a row of the bucket array, based on the value's "ones" (rightmost) digit. For example, 97 is placed in row 7, 3 is placed in row 3 and 100 is placed in row 0. This procedure is called a *distribution pass*.

    b) Loop through the bucket array row by row, and copy the values back to the original array. This procedure is called a *gathering pass*. The new order of the preceding values in the one-dimensional array is 100, 3 and 97.

    c) Repeat this process for each subsequent digit position (tens, hundreds, thousands, etc.). On the second (tens digit) pass, 100 is placed in row 0, 3 is placed in row 0 (because 3 has no tens digit) and 97 is placed in row 9. After the gathering pass, the order of the values in the one-dimensional array is 100, 3 and 97. On the third (hundreds digit) pass, 100 is placed in row 1, 3 is placed in row 0 and 97 is placed in row 0 (after the 3). After this last gathering pass, the original array is in sorted order.

        The two-dimensional array of buckets is 10 times the length of the integer array being sorted. This sorting technique provides better performance than a bubble sort, but requires much more memory—the bubble sort requires space for only one additional element of data. This comparison is an example of the space/time trade-off: The bucket sort uses more memory than the bubble sort, but performs better. This version of the bucket sort requires copying all the data back to the original array on each pass. Another possibility is to create a second two-dimensional bucket array and repeatedly swap the data between the two bucket arrays.

19.8   *(Recursive Linear Search)* Modify Fig. 19.2 to use recursive method `recursiveLinearSearch` to perform a linear search of the array. The method should receive the search key and starting index as arguments. If the search key is found, return its index in the array; otherwise, return –1. Each call to the recursive method should check one index in the array.

19.9   *(Recursive Binary Search)* Modify Fig. 19.3 to use recursive method `recursiveBinarySearch` to perform a binary search of the array. The method should receive the search key, starting index and ending index as arguments. If the search key is found, return its index in the array. If the search key is not found, return –1.

19.10   *(Quicksort)* The recursive sorting technique called quicksort uses the following basic algorithm for a one-dimensional array of values:

    a) *Partitioning Step*: Take the first element of the unsorted array and determine its final location in the sorted array (i.e., all values to the left of the element in the array are less than the element, and all values to the right of the element in the array are greater than the element—we show how to do this below). We now have one element in its proper location and two unsorted subarrays.

    b) *Recursive Step*: Perform *Step 1* on each unsorted subarray. Each time *Step 1* is performed on a subarray, another element is placed in its final location of the sorted array, and two unsorted subarrays are created. When a subarray consists of one element, that element is in its final location (because a one-element array is already sorted).

        The basic algorithm seems simple enough, but how do we determine the final position of the first element of each subarray? As an example, consider the following set of values (the element in bold is the partitioning element—it will be placed in its final location in the sorted array):

        37 2 6 4 89 8 10 12 68 45

Starting from the rightmost element of the array, compare each element with 37 until an element less than 37 is found; then swap 37 and that element. The first element less than 37 is 12, so 37 and 12 are swapped. The new array is

> *12* 2 6 4 89 8 10 37 68 45

Element 12 is in italics to indicate that it was just swapped with 37.

Starting from the left of the array, but beginning with the element after 12, compare each element with 37 until an element greater than 37 is found—then swap 37 and that element. The first element greater than 37 is 89, so 37 and 89 are swapped. The new array is

> 12 2 6 4 *37* 8 10 *89* 68 45

Starting from the right, but beginning with the element before 89, compare each element with 37 until an element less than 37 is found—then swap 37 and that element. The first element less than 37 is 10, so 37 and 10 are swapped. The new array is

> 12 2 6 4 *10* 8 *37* 89 68 45

Starting from the left, but beginning with the element after 10, compare each element with 37 until an element greater than 37 is found—then swap 37 and that element. There are no more elements greater than 37, so when we compare 37 with itself, we know that 37 has been placed in its final location in the sorted array. Every value to the left of 37 is smaller than it, and every value to the right of 37 is larger than it.

Once the partition has been applied on the previous array, there are two unsorted subarrays. The subarray with values less than 37 contains 12, 2, 6, 4, 10 and 8. The subarray with values greater than 37 contains 89, 68 and 45. The sort continues recursively, with both subarrays being partitioned in the same manner as the original array.

Based on the preceding discussion, write recursive method `quickSortHelper` to sort a one-dimensional integer array. The method should receive as arguments a starting index and an ending index on the original array being sorted.

Generic Classes and Methods

20

Objectives

In this chapter you'll:

- Create generic methods that perform identical tasks on arguments of different types.

- Create a generic **Stack** class that can be used to store objects of any class or interface type.

- Undestand compile-time translation of generic methods and classes.

- Understand how to overload generic methods with nongeneric methods or other generic methods.

- Understand raw types.

- Use wildcards when precise type information about a parameter is not required in the method body.

20.1 Introduction

You've used existing generic methods and classes in Chapters 6 and 16. In this chapter, you'll learn how to write your own.

It would be nice if we could write a single sort method to sort the elements in an Integer array, a String array or an array of any type that supports ordering (i.e., its elements can be compared). It would also be nice if we could write a single Stack class that could be used as a Stack of integers, a Stack of floating-point numbers, a Stack of Strings or a Stack of any other type. It would be even nicer if we could detect type mismatches at *compile time*—known as **compile-time type safety**. For example, if a Stack should store only integers, an attempt to push a String onto that Stack should issue a *compilation* error. This chapter discusses **generics**—specifically **generic methods** and **generic classes**—which provide the means to create the type-safe general models mentioned above.

20.2 Motivation for Generic Methods

Overloaded methods are often used to perform *similar* operations on *different* types of data. To motivate generic methods, let's begin with an example (Fig. 20.1) containing overloaded printArray methods (lines 22–29, 32–39 and 42–49) that print the String representations of the elements of an Integer array, a Double array and a Character array, respectively. We could have used arrays of primitive types int, double and char. We're using arrays of the type-wrapper classes to set up our generic method example, because *only reference types can be used to specify generic types in generic methods and classes*.

```
1   // Fig. 20.1: OverloadedMethods.java
2   // Printing array elements using overloaded methods.
3
4   public class OverloadedMethods
5   {
6       public static void main(String[] args)
7       {
8           // create arrays of Integer, Double and Character
9           Integer[] integerArray = {1, 2, 3, 4, 5, 6};
10          Double[] doubleArray = {1.1, 2.2, 3.3, 4.4, 5.5, 6.6, 7.7};
11          Character[] characterArray = {'H', 'E', 'L', 'L', 'O'};
```

Fig. 20.1 | Printing array elements using overloaded methods. (Part I of 2.)

```
12
13          System.out.printf("Array integerArray contains:%n");
14          printArray(integerArray); // pass an Integer array
15          System.out.printf("%nArray doubleArray contains:%n");
16          printArray(doubleArray); // pass a Double array
17          System.out.printg("%nArray characterArray contains:%n");
18          printArray(characterArray); // pass a Character array
19       }
20
21       // method printArray to print Integer array
22       public static void printArray(Integer[] inputArray)
23       {
24          // display array elements
25          for (Integer element : inputArray)
26             System.out.printf("%s ", element);
27
28          System.out.println();
29       }
30
31       // method printArray to print Double array
32       public static void printArray(Double[] inputArray)
33       {
34          // display array elements
35          for (Double element : inputArray)
36             System.out.printf("%s ", element);
37
38          System.out.println();
39       }
40
41       // method printArray to print Character array
42       public static void printArray(Character[] inputArray)
43       {
44          // display array elements
45          for (Character element : inputArray)
46             System.out.printf("%s ", element);
47
48          System.out.println();
49       }
50    } // end class OverloadedMethods
```

```
Array integerArray contains:
1 2 3 4 5 6

Array doubleArray contains:
1.1 2.2 3.3 4.4 5.5 6.6 7.7

Array characterArray contains:
H E L L O
```

Fig. 20.1 | Printing array elements using overloaded methods. (Part 2 of 2.)

The program begins by declaring and initializing three arrays—six-element Integer array integerArray (line 9), seven-element Double array doubleArray (line 10) and five-element Character array characterArray (line 11). Then lines 13–18 display the contents of each array.

When the compiler encounters a method call, it attempts to locate a method declaration with the same name and with parameters that match the argument types in the call. In this example, each printArray call matches one of the printArray method declarations. For example, line 14 calls printArray with integerArray as its argument. The compiler determines the argument's type (i.e., Integer[]) and attempts to locate a print-Array method that specifies an Integer[] parameter (lines 22–29), then sets up a call to that method. Similarly, when the compiler encounters the call at line 16, it determines the argument's type (i.e., Double[]), then attempts to locate a printArray method that specifies a Double[] parameter (lines 32–39), then sets up a call to that method. Finally, when the compiler encounters the call at line 18, it determines the argument's type (i.e., Character[]), then attempts to locate a printArray method that specifies a Character[] parameter (lines 42–49), then sets up a call to that method.

*Common Features in the Overloaded **printArray** Methods*
Study each printArray method. The array element type appears in each method's header (lines 22, 32 and 42) and for-statement header (lines 25, 35 and 45). If we were to replace the element types in each method with a generic name—T by convention—then all three methods would look like the one in Fig. 20.2. It appears that if we can replace the array element type in each of the three methods with a *single generic type*, then we should be able to declare *one* printArray method that can display the String representations of the elements of *any* array that contains objects. The method in Fig. 20.2 is similar to the generic printArray method declaration you'll see in Section 20.3. The one shown here *will not compile*—we use this simply to show that the three printArray methods of Fig. 20.1 are identical except for the types they process.

```
1   public static void printArray(T[] inputArray)
2   {
3      // display array elements
4      for (T element : inputArray)
5         System.out.printf("%s ", element);
6
7      System.out.println();
8   }
```

Fig. 20.2 | printArray method in which actual type names are replaced with a generic type name (in this case T).

20.3 Generic Methods: Implementation and Compile-Time Translation

If the operations performed by several overloaded methods are *identical* for each argument type, the overloaded methods can be more conveniently coded using a generic method. You can write a single generic method declaration that can be called with arguments of different types. Based on the types of the arguments passed to the generic method, the compiler handles each method call appropriately. At *compilation time*, the compiler ensures the *type safety* of your code, preventing many runtime errors.

Figure 20.3 reimplements Fig. 20.1 using a generic printArray method (lines 22–29 of Fig. 20.3). The printArray calls in lines 14, 16 and 18 are identical to those of

Fig. 20.1 (lines 14, 16 and 18) and the outputs of the two applications are identical. This demonstrates the expressive power of generics.

```
 1   // Fig. 20.3: GenericMethodTest.java
 2   // Printing array elements using generic method printArray.
 3
 4   public class GenericMethodTest
 5   {
 6      public static void main(String[] args)
 7      {
 8         // create arrays of Integer, Double and Character
 9         Integer[] intArray = {1, 2, 3, 4, 5};
10         Double[] doubleArray = {1.1, 2.2, 3.3, 4.4, 5.5, 6.6, 7.7};
11         Character[] charArray = {'H', 'E', 'L', 'L', 'O'};
12
13         System.out.printf("Array integerArray contains:%n");
14         printArray(integerArray); // pass an Integer array
15         System.out.printf("%nArray doubleArray contains:%n");
16         printArray(doubleArray); // pass a Double array
17         System.out.printf("%nArray characterArray contains:%n");
18         printArray(characterArray); // pass a Character array
19      }
20
21      // generic method printArray
22      public static <T> void printArray(T[] inputArray)
23      {
24         // display array elements
25         for (T element : inputArray)
26            System.out.printf("%s ", element);
27
28         System.out.println();
29      }
30   } // end class GenericMethodTest
```

```
Array integerArray contains:
1 2 3 4 5 6

Array doubleArray contains:
1.1 2.2 3.3 4.4 5.5 6.6 7.7

Array characterArray contains:
H E L L O
```

Fig. 20.3 | Printing array elements using generic method `printArray`.

Type Parameter Section of a Generic Method

Line 22 begins method `printArray`'s declaration. All generic method declarations have a **type-parameter section** (`<T>` in this example) delimited by **angle brackets** that precedes the method's return type. Each type-parameter section contains one or more **type parameters**, separated by commas. A type parameter, also known as a **type variable**, is an identifier that specifies a generic type name. The type parameters can be used to declare the return type, parameter types and local variable types in a generic method declaration, and they act as placeholders for the types of the arguments passed to the generic method, which are known as **actual type arguments**. A generic method's body is declared like that of any other method. *Type parameters can represent only reference types*—not primitive types (like int, double and char). Note, too, that the type-parameter names throughout the method declaration must match those declared in the type-parameter section. For example, line 25 declares element as type T, which matches the type parameter (T) declared in line 22. Also, a type parameter can be declared only once in the type-parameter section but can appear more than once in the method's parameter list. For example, the type-parameter name T appears twice in the following method's parameter list:

```
public static <T> T maximum(T value1, T value2)
```

Type-parameter names need not be unique among different generic methods. In method printArray, T appears in the same two locations where the overloaded printArray methods of Fig. 20.1 specified Integer, Double or Character as the array element type. The remainder of printArray is identical to the versions presented in Fig. 20.1.

Good Programming Practice 20.1

The letters T (for "type"), E (for "element"), K (for "key") and V (for "value") are commonly used as type parameters. For other common ones, see http://docs.oracle.com/javase/tutorial/java/generics/types.html.

Testing the Generic **printArray** *Method*

As in Fig. 20.1, the program in Fig. 20.3 begins by declaring and initializing six-element Integer array integerArray (line 9), seven-element Double array doubleArray (line 10) and five-element Character array characterArray (line 11). Then each array is output by calling printArray (lines 14, 16 and 18)—once with argument integerArray, once with argument doubleArray and once with argument characterArray.

When the compiler encounters line 14, it first determines argument integerArray's type (i.e., Integer[]) and attempts to locate a method named printArray that specifies a single Integer[] parameter. There's no such method in this example. Next, the compiler determines whether there's a generic method named printArray that specifies a single array parameter and uses a type parameter to represent the array element type. The compiler determines that printArray (lines 22–29) is a match and sets up a call to the method. The same process is repeated for the calls to method printArray at lines 16 and 18.

Common Programming Error 20.1

If the compiler cannot match a method call to a nongeneric or a generic method declaration, a compilation error occurs.

Common Programming Error 20.2

If the compiler doesn't find a method declaration that matches a method call exactly, but does find two or more methods that can satisfy the method call, a compilation error occurs. For the complete details of resolving calls to overloaded and generic methods, see http://docs.oracle.com/javase/specs/jls/se7/html/jls-15.html#jls-15.12.

In addition to setting up the method calls, the compiler also determines whether the operations in the method body can be applied to elements of the type stored in the array argument. The only operation performed on the array elements in this example is to output their String representation. Line 26 performs an *implicit toString call* on every element. *To work with generics, every element of the array must be an object of a class or interface type.* Since all objects have a toString method, the compiler is satisfied that line 26 performs a *valid* operation for any object in printArray's array argument. The toString methods of classes Integer, Double and Character return the String representation of the underlying int, double or char value, respectively.

Erasure at Compilation Time

When the compiler translates generic method printArray into Java bytecodes, it removes the type-parameter section and *replaces the type parameters with actual types.* This process is known as **erasure**. By default all generic types are replaced with type Object. So the compiled version of method printArray appears as shown in Fig. 20.4—there's only *one* copy of this code, which is used for all printArray calls in the example. This is quite different from similar mechanisms in other programming languages, such as C++'s templates, in which a *separate copy of the source code* is generated and compiled for *every* type passed as an argument to the method. As you'll see in Section 20.4, the translation and compilation of generics is a bit more involved than what we've discussed in this section.

By declaring printArray as a generic method in Fig. 20.3, we eliminated the need for the overloaded methods of Fig. 20.1 and created a reusable method that can output the String representations of the elements in any array that contains objects. However, this particular example could have simply declared the printArray method as shown in Fig. 20.4, using an Object array as the parameter. This would have yielded the same results, because any Object can be output as a String. In a generic method, the benefits become more apparent when you place restrictions on the type parameters, as we demonstrate in the next section.

```
1   public static void printArray(Object[] inputArray)
2   {
3      // display array elements
4      for (Object element : inputArray)
5         System.out.printf("%s ", element);
6
7      System.out.println();
8   }
```

Fig. 20.4 | Generic method printArray after the compiler performs erasure.

20.4 Additional Compile-Time Translation Issues: Methods That Use a Type Parameter as the Return Type

Let's consider a generic method in which type parameters are used in the return type and in the parameter list (Fig. 20.5). The application uses a generic method maximum to determine and return the largest of its three arguments of the same type. Unfortunately, *the relational operator > cannot be used with reference types.* However, it's possible to compare two objects of the same class if that class implements the generic **interface Comparable<T>** (from package java.lang). All the type-wrapper classes for primitive types implement this interface.

Generic interfaces enable you to specify, with a single interface declaration, a set of related types. Comparable<T> objects have a **compareTo method**. For example, if we have two Integer objects, integer1 and integer2, they can be compared with the expression:

```
integer1.compareTo(integer2)
```

When you declare a class that implements Comparable<T>, you must implement method compareTo such that it compares the contents of two objects of that class and returns the comparison results. As specified in interface Comparable<T>'s documentation, compareTo *must* return 0 if the objects are equal, a negative integer if object1 is less than object2 or a positive integer if object1 is greater than object2. For example, class Integer's compareTo method compares the int values stored in two Integer objects. A benefit of implementing interface Comparable<T> is that Comparable<T> objects can be used with the sorting and searching methods of class Collections (package java.util). We discussed those methods in Chapter 16. In this example, we'll use method compareTo in method maximum to help determine the largest value.

```java
 1   // Fig. 20.5: MaximumTest.java
 2   // Generic method maximum returns the largest of three objects.
 3
 4   public class MaximumTest
 5   {
 6      public static void main(String[] args)
 7      {
 8         System.out.printf("Maximum of %d, %d and %d is %d%n%n", 3, 4, 5,
 9            maximum(3, 4, 5));
10         System.out.printf("Maximum of %.1f, %.1f and %.1f is %.1f%n%n",
11            6.6, 8.8, 7.7, maximum(6.6, 8.8, 7.7));
12         System.out.printf("Maximum of %s, %s and %s is %s%n", "pear",
13            "apple", "orange", maximum("pear", "apple", "orange"));
14      }
15
16      // determines the largest of three Comparable objects
17      public static <T extends Comparable<T>> T maximum(T x, T y, T z)
18      {
19         T max = x; // assume x is initially the largest
20
21         if (y.compareTo(max) > 0)
22            max = y; // y is the largest so far
23
24         if (z.compareTo(max) > 0)
25            max = z; // z is the largest
26
27         return max; // returns the largest object
28      }
29   } // end class MaximumTest
```

```
Maximum of 3, 4 and 5 is 5

Maximum of 6.6, 8.8 and 7.7 is 8.8

Maximum of pear, apple and orange is pear
```

Fig. 20.5 | Generic method maximum with an upper bound on its type parameter.

Generic Method `maximum` *and Specifying a Type Parameter's Upper Bound*

Generic method `maximum` (lines 17–28) uses type parameter `T` as the return type of the method (line 17), as the type of method parameters `x`, `y` and `z` (line 17), and as the type of local variable `max` (line 19). The type-parameter section specifies that `T extends Comparable<T>`—only objects of classes that implement interface `Comparable<T>` can be used with this method. `Comparable<T>` is known as the type parameter's **upper bound**. By default, `Object` is the upper bound, meaning that an object of any type can be used. Type-parameter declarations that bound the parameter always use keyword `extends` regardless of whether the type parameter extends a class or implements an interface. The upper bound may be a comma-separated list that contains zero or one class and zero or more interfaces.

Method `maximum`'s type parameter is more restrictive than the one specified for `print-Array` in Fig. 20.3, which was able to output arrays containing any type of object. The `Comparable<T>` restriction is important, because not all objects can be compared. However, `Comparable<T>` objects are guaranteed to have a `compareTo` method.

Method `maximum` uses the same algorithm that we used in Section 5.4 to determine the largest of its three arguments. The method assumes that its first argument (`x`) is the largest and assigns it to local variable `max` (line 19). Next, the `if` statement at lines 21–22 determines whether `y` is greater than `max`. The condition invokes `y`'s `compareTo` method with the expression `y.compareTo(max)`, which returns a negative integer, 0 or a positive integer, to determine `y`'s relationship to `max`. If the return value of the `compareTo` is greater than 0, then `y` is greater and is assigned to variable `max`. Similarly, the `if` statement at lines 24–25 determines whether `z` is greater than `max`. If so, line 25 assigns `z` to `max`. Then line 27 returns `max` to the caller.

Calling Method `maximum`

In `main` (lines 6–14), line 9 calls `maximum` with the integers 3, 4 and 5. When the compiler encounters this call, it first looks for a `maximum` method that takes three arguments of type `int`. There's no such method, so the compiler looks for a generic method that can be used and finds generic method `maximum`. However, recall that the arguments to a generic method must be of a *reference type*. So the compiler autoboxes the three `int` values as `Integer` objects and specifies that the three `Integer` objects will be passed to `maximum`. Class `Integer` (package `java.lang`) implements the `Comparable<Integer>` interface such that method `compareTo` compares the `int` values in two `Integer` objects. Therefore, `Integer`s are valid arguments to method `maximum`. When the `Integer` representing the maximum is returned, we attempt to output it with the `%d` format specifier, which outputs an `int` primitive-type value. So `maximum`'s return value is output as an `int` value.

A similar process occurs for the three `double` arguments passed to `maximum` in line 11. Each `double` is autoboxed as a `Double` object and passed to `maximum`. Again, this is allowed because class `Double` (package `java.lang`) implements the `Comparable<Double>` interface. The `Double` returned by `maximum` is output with the format specifier `%.1f`, which outputs a `double` primitive-type value. So `maximum`'s return value is auto-unboxed and output as a `double`. The call to `maximum` in line 13 receives three `String`s, which are also `Comparable<String>` objects. We intentionally placed the largest value in a different position in each method call (lines 9, 11 and 13) to show that the generic method always finds the maximum value, regardless of its position in the argument list.

Erasure and the Upper Bound of a Type Parameter
When the compiler translates method `maximum` into bytecodes, it uses erasure to replace the type parameters with actual types. In Fig. 20.3, all generic types were replaced with type `Object`. Actually, all type parameters are replaced with the *upper bound* of the type parameter, which is specified in the type-parameter section. Figure 20.6 simulates the erasure of method `maximum`'s types by showing the method's source code after the type-parameter section is removed and type parameter `T` is replaced with the upper bound, `Comparable`, throughout the method declaration. The erasure of `Comparable<T>` is simply `Comparable`.

```
 1   public static Comparable maximum(Comparable x, Comparable y, Comparable z)
 2   {
 3      Comparable max = x; // assume x is initially the largest
 4
 5      if (y.compareTo(max) > 0)
 6         max = y; // y is the largest so far
 7
 8      if (z.compareTo(max) > 0)
 9         max = z; // z is the largest
10
11      return max; // returns the largest object
12   }
```

Fig. 20.6 | Generic method `maximum` after erasure is performed by the compiler.

After erasure, method `maximum` specifies that it returns type `Comparable`. However, the calling method does not expect to receive a `Comparable`. It expects to receive an object of the same type that was passed to `maximum` as an argument—`Integer`, `Double` or `String` in this example. When the compiler replaces the type-parameter information with the upper-bound type in the method declaration, it also inserts *explicit cast operations* in front of each method call to ensure that the returned value is of the type expected by the caller. Thus, the call to `maximum` in line 9 (Fig. 20.5) is preceded by an `Integer` cast, as in

```
(Integer) maximum(3, 4, 5)
```

the call to `maximum` in line 11 is preceded by a `Double` cast, as in

```
(Double) maximum(6.6, 8.8, 7.7)
```

and the call to `maximum` in line 13 is preceded by a `String` cast, as in

```
(String) maximum("pear", "apple", "orange")
```

In each case, the type of the cast for the return value is *inferred* from the types of the method arguments in the particular method call, because, according to the method declaration, the return type and the argument types match. Without generics, you'd be responsible for implementing the cast operation.

20.5 Overloading Generic Methods

A generic method may be overloaded like any other method. A class can provide two or more generic methods that specify the same method name but different method parameters. For example, generic method `printArray` of Fig. 20.3 could be overloaded with another printArray generic method with the additional parameters `lowSubscript` and `highSub``script` to specify the portion of the array to output (see Exercise 20.5).

A generic method can also be overloaded by nongeneric methods. When the compiler encounters a method call, it searches for the method declaration that best matches the method name and the argument types specified in the call—an error occurs if two or more overloaded methods both could be considered best matches. For example, generic method `printArray` of Fig. 20.3 could be overloaded with a version that's specific to `Strings`, which outputs the `Strings` in neat, tabular format (see Exercise 20.6).

20.6 Generic Classes

The concept of a data structure, such as a stack, can be understood *independently* of the element type it manipulates. Generic classes provide a means for describing the concept of a stack (or any other class) in a *type-independent* manner. We can then instantiate *type-specific* objects of the generic class. Generics provide a nice opportunity for software reusability.

Once you have a generic class, you can use a simple, concise notation to indicate the type(s) that should be used in place of the class's type parameter(s). At compilation time, the compiler ensures the *type safety* of your code and uses the *erasure* techniques described in Sections 20.3—20.4 to enable your client code to interact with the generic class.

One generic `Stack` class, for example, could be the basis for creating many logical `Stack` classes (e.g., "Stack of `Double`," "Stack of `Integer`," "Stack of `Character`," "Stack of `Employee`"). These classes are known as **parameterized classes** or **parameterized types** because they accept one or more type parameters. Recall that type parameters represent only *reference types*, which means the `Stack` generic class cannot be instantiated with primitive types. However, we can instantiate a `Stack` that stores objects of Java's type-wrapper classes and allow Java to use *autoboxing* to convert the primitive values into objects. Recall that autoboxing occurs when a value of a primitive type (e.g., `int`) is pushed onto a `Stack` that contains wrapper-class objects (e.g., `Integer`). *Auto-unboxing* occurs when an object of the wrapper class is popped off the `Stack` and assigned to a primitive-type variable.

Implementing a Generic Stack Class
Figure 20.7 declares a generic `Stack` class for demonstration purposes—the `java.util` package already contains a generic `Stack` class. A generic class declaration looks like a nongeneric one, but the class name is followed by *a type-parameter section* (line 5). In this case, type parameter `T` represents the element type the `Stack` will manipulate. As with generic methods, the type-parameter section of a generic class can have one or more type parameters separated by commas. (You'll create a generic class with two type parameters in Exercise 20.8.) Type parameter `T` is used throughout the `Stack` class declaration to represent the element type. This example implements a `Stack` as an `ArrayList`.

Class `Stack` declares variable `elements` as an `ArrayList<T>` (line 7). This `ArrayList` will store the `Stack`'s elements. As you know, an `ArrayList` can grow dynamically, so objects of our `Stack` class can also grow dynamically. The `Stack` class's no-argument constructor (lines 10–13) invokes the one-argument constructor (lines 16–20) to create a `Stack` in which the underlying `ArrayList` has a capacity of 10 elements. The one-argument constructor can also be called directly to create a `Stack` with a specified initial capacity. Line 18 validates the constructor's argument. Line 19 creates the `ArrayList` of the specified capacity (or 10 if the capacity was invalid).

```
1   // Fig. 20.7: Stack.java
2   // Stack generic class declaration.
3   import java.util.ArrayList;
4
5   public class Stack<T>
6   {
7      private final ArrayList<T> elements; // ArrayList stores stack elements
8
9      // no-argument constructor creates a stack of the default size
10     public Stack()
11     {
12        this(10); // default stack size
13     }
14
15     // constructor creates a stack of the specified number of elements
16     public Stack(int capacity)
17     {
18        int initCapacity = capacity > 0 ? capacity : 10; // validate
19        elements = new ArrayList<T>(initCapacity); // create ArrayList
20     }
21
22     // push element onto stack
23     public void push(T pushValue)
24     {
25        elements.add(pushValue); // place pushValue on Stack
26     }
27
28     // return the top element if not empty; else throw EmptyStackException
29     public T pop()
30     {
31        if (elements.isEmpty()) // if stack is empty
32           throw new EmptyStackException("Stack is empty, cannot pop");
33
34        // remove and return top element of Stack
35        return elements.remove(elements.size() - 1);
36     }
37   } // end class Stack<T>
```

Fig. 20.7 | Stack generic class declaration.

Method push (lines 23–26) uses ArrayList method add to append the pushed item to the end of the ArrayList elements. The last element in the ArrayList represents the *top* of the stack.

Method pop (lines 29–36) first determines whether an attempt is being made to pop an element from an empty Stack. If so, line 32 throws an EmptyStackException (declared in Fig. 20.8). Otherwise, line 35 in Fig. 20.7 returns the top element of the Stack by removing the last element in the underlying ArrayList.

Class EmptyStackException (Fig. 20.8) provides a no-argument constructor and a one-argument constructor. The no-argument constructor sets the default error message, and the one-argument constructor sets a custom error message.

As with generic methods, when a generic class is compiled, the compiler performs *erasure* on the class's type parameters and replaces them with their upper bounds. For class

Stack (Fig. 20.7), no upper bound is specified, so the default upper bound, Object, is used. The scope of a generic class's type parameter is the entire class. However, type parameters *cannot* be used in a class's static variable declarations.

```
1   // Fig. 20.8: EmptyStackException.java
2   // EmptyStackException class declaration.
3   public class EmptyStackException extends RuntimeException
4   {
5      // no-argument constructor
6      public EmptyStackException()
7      {
8         this("Stack is empty");
9      }
10
11     // one-argument constructor
12     public EmptyStackException(String message)
13     {
14        super(message);
15     }
16  } // end class EmptyStackException
```

Fig. 20.8 | EmptyStackException class declaration.

Testing the Generic Stack Class of Fig. 20.7

Now, let's consider the application (Fig. 20.9) that uses the Stack generic class (Fig. 20.7). Lines 12–13 in Fig. 20.9 create and initialize variables of type Stack<Double> (pronounced "Stack of Double") and Stack<Integer> (pronounced "Stack of Integer"). The types Double and Integer are known as the Stack's **type arguments**. The compiler uses them to replace the type parameters so that it can perform type checking and insert cast operations as necessary. We'll discuss the cast operations in more detail shortly. Lines 12–13 instantiate doubleStack with a capacity of 5 and integerStack with a capacity of 10 (the default). Lines 16–17 and 20–21 call methods testPushDouble (lines 25–36), testPopDouble (lines 39–59), testPushInteger (lines 62–73) and testPopInteger (lines 76–96), respectively, to demonstrate the two Stacks in this example.

```
1   // Fig. 20.9: StackTest.java
2   // Stack generic class test program.
3
4   public class StackTest
5   {
6      public static void main(String[] args)
7      {
8         double[] doubleElements = {1.1, 2.2, 3.3, 4.4, 5.5};
9         int[] integerElements = {1, 2, 3, 4, 5, 6, 7, 8, 9, 10};
10
11        // Create a Stack<Double> and a Stack<Integer>
12        Stack<Double> doubleStack = new Stack<>(5);
13        Stack<Integer> integerStack = new Stack<>();
14
```

Fig. 20.9 | Stack generic class test program. (Part 1 of 3.)

```
15          // push elements of doubleElements onto doubleStack
16          testPushDouble(doubleStack, doubleElements);
17          testPopDouble(doubleStack); // pop from doubleStack
18
19          // push elements of integerElements onto integerStack
20          testPushInteger(integerStack, integerElements);
21          testPopInteger(integerStack); // pop from integerStack
22       }
23
24       // test push method with double stack
25       private static void testPushDouble(
26          Stack<Double> stack, double[] values)
27       {
28          System.out.printf("%nPushing elements onto doubleStack%n");
29
30          // push elements to Stack
31          for (double value : values)
32          {
33             System.out.printf("%.1f ", value);
34             stack.push(value); // push onto doubleStack
35          }
36       }
37
38       // test pop method with double stack
39       private static void testPopDouble(Stack<Double> stack)
40       {
41          // pop elements from stack
42          try
43          {
44             System.out.printf("%nPopping elements from doubleStack%n");
45             double popValue; // store element removed from stack
46
47             // remove all elements from Stack
48             while (true)
49             {
50                popValue = stack.pop(); // pop from doubleStack
51                System.out.printf("%.1f ", popValue);
52             }
53          }
54          catch(EmptyStackException emptyStackException)
55          {
56             System.err.println();
57             emptyStackException.printStackTrace();
58          }
59       }
60
61       // test push method with integer stack
62       private static void testPushInteger(
63          Stack<Integer> stack, int[] values)
64       {
65          System.out.printf("%nPushing elements onto integerStack%n");
66
```

Fig. 20.9 | Stack generic class test program. (Part 2 of 3.)

```
67              // push elements to Stack
68              for (int value : values)
69              {
70                  System.out.printf("%d ", value);
71                  stack.push(value); // push onto integerStack
72              }
73          }
74
75          // test pop method with integer stack
76          private static void testPopInteger(Stack<Integer> stack)
77          {
78              // pop elements from stack
79              try
80              {
81                  System.out.printf("%nPopping elements from integerStack%n");
82                  int popValue; // store element removed from stack
83
84                  // remove all elements from Stack
85                  while (true)
86                  {
87                      popValue = stack.pop(); // pop from intStack
88                      System.out.printf("%d ", popValue);
89                  }
90              }
91              catch(EmptyStackException emptyStackException)
92              {
93                  System.err.println();
94                  emptyStackException.printStackTrace();
95              }
96          }
97      } // end class StackTest
```

```
Pushing elements onto doubleStack
1.1 2.2 3.3 4.4 5.5
Popping elements from doubleStack
5.5 4.4 3.3 2.2 1.1
EmptyStackException: Stack is empty, cannot pop
        at Stack.pop(Stack.java:32)
        at StackTest.testPopDouble(StackTest.java:50)
        at StackTest.main(StackTest.java:17)

Pushing elements onto integerStack
1 2 3 4 5 6 7 8 9 10
Popping elements from integerStack
10 9 8 7 6 5 4 3 2 1
EmptyStackException: Stack is empty, cannot pop
        at Stack.pop(Stack.java:32)
        at StackTest.testPopInteger(StackTest.java:87)
        at StackTest.main(StackTest.java:21)
```

Fig. 20.9 | Stack generic class test program. (Part 3 of 3.)

Methods testPushDouble *and* testPopDouble

Method testPushDouble (lines 25–36) invokes method push (line 34) to place the double values 1.1, 2.2, 3.3, 4.4 and 5.5 from array doubleElements onto doubleStack. *Autobox-*

ing occurs in line 34 when the program tries to push a primitive double value onto the doubleStack, which stores only references to Double objects.

Method testPopDouble (lines 39–59) invokes Stack method pop (line 50) in an infinite loop (lines 48–52) to remove all the values from the stack. The output shows that the values indeed pop off in last-in, first-out order (the defining characteristic of stacks). When the loop attempts to pop a sixth value, the doubleStack is empty, so pop throws an EmptyStackException, which causes the program to proceed to the catch block (lines 54–58). The stack trace indicates the exception that occurred and shows that method pop generated the exception at line 32 of the file Stack.java (Fig. 20.7). The trace also shows that pop was called by StackTest method testPopDouble at line 50 (Fig. 20.9) of Stack-Test.java and that method testPopDouble was called from method main at line 17 of StackTest.java. This information enables you to determine the methods that were on the method-call stack at the time that the exception occurred. Because the program catches the exception, the exception is considered to have been handled and the program can continue executing.

Auto-unboxing occurs in line 50 when the program assigns the Double object popped from the stack to a double primitive variable. Recall from Section 20.4 that the compiler inserts casts to ensure that the proper types are returned from generic methods. After erasure, Stack method pop returns type Object, but the client code in testPopDouble expects to receive a double when method pop returns. So the compiler inserts a Double cast, as in

```
popValue = (Double) stack.pop();
```

The value assigned to popValue will be *unboxed* from the Double object returned by pop.

Methods *testPushInteger* and *testPopInteger*

Method testPushInteger (lines 62–73) invokes Stack method push to place values onto integerStack until it's full. Method testPopInteger (lines 76–96) invokes Stack method pop to remove values from integerStack. Once again, the values are popped in last-in, first-out order. During *erasure*, the compiler recognizes that the client code in method testPopInteger expects to receive an int when method pop returns. So the compiler inserts an Integer cast, as in

```
popValue = (Integer) stack.pop();
```

The value assigned to popValue will be unboxed from the Integer object returned by pop.

Creating Generic Methods to Test Class *Stack<T>*

The code in methods testPushDouble and testPushInteger is *almost identical* for pushing values onto a Stack<Double> or a Stack<Integer>, respectively, and the code in methods testPopDouble and testPopInteger is almost identical for popping values from a Stack<Double> or a Stack<Integer>, respectively. This presents another opportunity to use generic methods. Figure 20.10 declares generic method testPush (lines 24–35) to perform the same tasks as testPushDouble and testPushInteger in Fig. 20.9—that is, push values onto a Stack<T>. Similarly, generic method testPop (Fig. 20.10, lines 38–58) performs the same tasks as testPopDouble and testPopInteger in Fig. 20.9—that is, pop values off a Stack<T>. The output of Fig. 20.10 precisely matches that of Fig. 20.9.

```
 1   // Fig. 20.10: StackTest2.java
 2   // Passing generic Stack objects to generic methods.
 3   public class StackTest2
 4   {
 5      public static void main(String[] args)
 6      {
 7         Double[] doubleElements = {1.1, 2.2, 3.3, 4.4, 5.5};
 8         Integer[] integerElements = {1, 2, 3, 4, 5, 6, 7, 8, 9, 10};
 9
10         // Create a Stack<Double> and a Stack<Integer>
11         Stack<Double> doubleStack = new Stack<>(5);
12         Stack<Integer> integerStack = new Stack<>();
13
14         // push elements of doubleElements onto doubleStack
15         testPush("doubleStack", doubleStack, doubleElements);
16         testPop("doubleStack", doubleStack); // pop from doubleStack
17
18         // push elements of integerElements onto integerStack
19         testPush("integerStack", integerStack, integerElements);
20         testPop("integerStack", integerStack); // pop from integerStack
21      }
22
23      // generic method testPush pushes elements onto a Stack
24      public static <T> void testPush(String name , Stack<T> stack,
25         T[] elements)
26      {
27         System.out.printf("%nPushing elements onto %s%n", name);
28
29         // push elements onto Stack
30         for (T element : elements)
31         {
32            System.out.printf("%s ", element);
33            stack.push(element); // push element onto stack
34         }
35      }
36
37      // generic method testPop pops elements from a Stack
38      public static <T> void testPop(String name, Stack<T> stack)
39      {
40         // pop elements from stack
41         try
42         {
43            System.out.printf("%nPopping elements from %s%n", name);
44            T popValue; // store element removed from stack
45
46            // remove all elements from Stack
47            while (true)
48            {
49               popValue = stack.pop();
50               System.out.printf("%s ", popValue);
51            }
52         }
```

Fig. 20.10 | Passing generic Stack objects to generic methods. (Part 1 of 2.)

```
53          catch(EmptyStackException emptyStackException)
54          {
55             System.out.println();
56             emptyStackException.printStackTrace();
57          }
58       }
59    } // end class StackTest2
```

```
Pushing elements onto doubleStack
1.1 2.2 3.3 4.4 5.5
Popping elements from doubleStack
5.5 4.4 3.3 2.2 1.1
EmptyStackException: Stack is empty, cannot pop
        at Stack.pop(Stack.java:32)
        at StackTest2.testPop(StackTest2.java:50)
        at StackTest2.main(StackTest2.java:17)

Pushing elements onto integerStack
1 2 3 4 5 6 7 8 9 10
Popping elements from integerStack
10 9 8 7 6 5 4 3 2 1
EmptyStackException: Stack is empty, cannot pop
        at Stack.pop(Stack.java:32)
        at StackTest2.testPop(StackTest2.java:50)
        at StackTest2.main(StackTest2.java:21
```

Fig. 20.10 | Passing generic Stack objects to generic methods. (Part 2 of 2.)

Lines 11–12 create the Stack<Double> and Stack<Integer> objects, respectively. Lines 15–16 and 19–20 invoke generic methods testPush and testPop to test the Stack objects. Because type parameters can represent only reference types, to be able to pass arrays doubleElements and integerElements to generic method testPush, the arrays declared in lines 7–8 must be declared with the wrapper types Double and Integer. When these arrays are initialized with primitive values, the compiler *autoboxes* each primitive value.

Generic method testPush (lines 24–35) uses type parameter T (specified at line 24) to represent the data type stored in the Stack<T>. The generic method takes three arguments—a String that represents the name of the Stack<T> object for output purposes, a reference to an object of type Stack<T> and an array of type T—the type of elements that will be pushed onto Stack<T>. The compiler enforces *consistency* between the type of the Stack and the elements that will be pushed onto the Stack when push is invoked, which is the real value of the generic method call. Generic method testPop (lines 38–58) takes two arguments—a String that represents the name of the Stack<T> object for output purposes and a reference to an object of type Stack<T>.

20.7 Raw Types

The test programs for generic class Stack in Section 20.6 instantiate Stacks with type arguments Double and Integer. It's also possible to instantiate generic class Stack without specifying a type argument, as follows:

```
Stack objectStack = new Stack(5); // no type argument specified
```

In this case, the objectStack has a **raw type**—the compiler implicitly uses type Object throughout the generic class for each type argument. Thus the preceding statement creates a Stack that can store objects of *any* type. This is important for *backward compatibility* with prior Java versions. For example, the data structures of the Java Collections Framework (Chapter 16) all stored references to Objects, but are now implemented as generic types.

A raw-type Stack variable can be assigned a Stack that specifies a type argument, such as a Stack<Double> object, as follows:

```
Stack rawTypeStack2 = new Stack<Double>(5);
```

because type Double is a subclass of Object. This assignment is allowed because the elements in a Stack<Double> (i.e., Double objects) are certainly objects—class Double is an indirect subclass of Object.

Similarly, a Stack variable that specifies a type argument in its declaration can be assigned a raw-type Stack object, as in:

```
Stack<Integer> integerStack = new Stack(10);
```

Although this assignment is permitted, it's *unsafe*, because a Stack of raw type might store types other than Integer. In this case, the compiler issues a warning message which indicates the unsafe assignment.

Using Raw Types with Generic Class Stack
The test program of Fig. 20.11 uses the notion of raw type. Line 11 instantiates generic class Stack with raw type, which indicates that rawTypeStack1 can hold objects of any type. Line 14 assigns a Stack<Double> to variable rawTypeStack2, which is declared as a Stack of raw type. Line 17 assigns a Stack of raw type to Stack<Integer> variable, which is legal but causes the compiler to issue a warning message (Fig. 20.12) indicating a *potentially unsafe assignment*—again, this occurs because a Stack of raw type might store types other than Integer. Also, the calls to generic methods testPush and testPop in lines 19–22 result in compiler warning messages (Fig. 20.12). These occur because rawTypeStack1 and rawTypeStack2 are declared as Stacks of raw type, but methods testPush and testPop each expect a second argument that is a Stack with a specific type argument. The warnings indicate that the compiler cannot guarantee the types manipulated by the stacks to be the correct types, since we did not supply a variable declared with a type argument. Methods testPush (Fig. 20.11, lines 28–39) and testPop (lines 42–62) are the same as in Fig. 20.10.

```
 1   // Fig. 20.11: RawTypeTest.java
 2   // Raw type test program.
 3   public class RawTypeTest
 4   {
 5      public static void main(String[] args)
 6      {
 7         Double[] doubleElements = {1.1, 2.2, 3.3, 4.4, 5.5};
 8         Integer[] integerElements = {1, 2, 3, 4, 5, 6, 7, 8, 9, 10};
 9
10         // Stack of raw types assigned to Stack of raw types variable
11         Stack rawTypeStack1 = new Stack(5);
```

Fig. 20.11 | Raw-type test program. (Part 1 of 3.)

```
12
13        // Stack<Double> assigned to Stack of raw types variable
14        Stack rawTypeStack2 = new Stack<Double>(5);
15
16        // Stack of raw types assigned to Stack<Integer> variable
17        Stack<Integer> integerStack = new Stack(10);
18
19        testPush("rawTypeStack1", rawTypeStack1, doubleElements);
20        testPop("rawTypeStack1", rawTypeStack1);
21        testPush("rawTypeStack2", rawTypeStack2, doubleElements);
22        testPop("rawTypeStack2", rawTypeStack2);
23        testPush("integerStack", integerStack, integerElements);
24        testPop("integerStack", integerStack);
25    }
26
27    // generic method pushes elements onto stack
28    public static <T> void testPush(String name, Stack<T> stack,
29        T[] elements)
30    {
31        System.out.printf("%nPushing elements onto %s%n", name);
32
33        // push elements onto Stack
34        for (T element : elements)
35        {
36            System.out.printf("%s ", element);
37            stack.push(element); // push element onto stack
38        }
39    }
40
41    // generic method testPop pops elements from stack
42    public static <T> void testPop(String name, Stack<T> stack)
43    {
44        // pop elements from stack
45        try
46        {
47            System.out.printf("%nPopping elements from %s%n", name);
48            T popValue; // store element removed from stack
49
50            // remove elements from Stack
51            while (true)
52            {
53                popValue = stack.pop(); // pop from stack
54                System.out.printf("%s ", popValue);
55            }
56        } // end try
57        catch(EmptyStackException emptyStackException)
58        {
59            System.out.println();
60            emptyStackException.printStackTrace();
61        }
62    }
63 } // end class RawTypeTest
```

Fig. 20.11 | Raw-type test program. (Part 2 of 3.)

```
Pushing elements onto rawTypeStack1
1.1 2.2 3.3 4.4 5.5
Popping elements from rawTypeStack1
5.5 4.4 3.3 2.2 1.1
EmptyStackException: Stack is empty, cannot pop
        at Stack.pop(Stack.java:32)
        at RawTypeTest.testPop(RawTypeTest.java:53)
        at RawTypeTest.main(RawTypeTest.java:20)

Pushing elements onto rawTypeStack2
1.1 2.2 3.3 4.4 5.5
Popping elements from rawTypeStack2
5.5 4.4 3.3 2.2 1.1
EmptyStackException: Stack is empty, cannot pop
        at Stack.pop(Stack.java:32)
        at RawTypeTest.testPop(RawTypeTest.java:53)
        at RawTypeTest.main(RawTypeTest.java:22)

Pushing elements onto integerStack
1 2 3 4 5 6 7 8 9 10
Popping elements from integerStack
10 9 8 7 6 5 4 3 2 1
EmptyStackException: Stack is empty, cannot pop
        at Stack.pop(Stack.java:32)
        at RawTypeTest.testPop(RawTypeTest.java:53)
        at RawTypeTest.main(RawTypeTest.java:24)
```

Fig. 20.11 | Raw-type test program. (Part 3 of 3.)

Compiler Warnings

Figure 20.12 shows the warning messages generated by the compiler when the file Raw-TypeTest.java (Fig. 20.11) is compiled with the -Xlint:unchecked option, which provides more information about potentially unsafe operations in code that uses generics. The first warning in Fig. 20.11 is generated for line 17, which assigned a raw-type Stack to a Stack<Integer> variable—the compiler cannot ensure that all objects in the Stack will be Integer objects. The next warning occurs at line 19. The compiler determines method testPush's type argument from the Double array passed as the third argument, because the second method argument is a raw-type Stack variable. In this case, Double is the type argument, so the compiler expects a Stack<Double> as the second argument. The warning occurs because the compiler cannot ensure that a raw-type Stack contains only Doubles. The warning at line 21 occurs for the same reason, even though the actual Stack that rawTypeStack2 references is a Stack<Double>. The compiler cannot guarantee that the variable will always refer to the same Stack object, so it must use the variable's declared type to perform all type checking. Lines 20 and 22 each generate warnings because method testPop expects as an argument a Stack for which a type argument has been specified. However, in each call to testPop, we pass a raw-type Stack variable. Thus, the compiler indicates a warning because it cannot check the types used in the body of the method. In general, you should avoid using raw types.

```
RawTypeTest.java:17: warning: [unchecked] unchecked conversion
found   : Stack
required: Stack<java.lang.Integer>
      Stack<Integer> integerStack = new Stack(10);
                                    ^
RawTypeTest.java:19: warning: [unchecked] unchecked conversion
found   : Stack
required: Stack<java.lang.Double>
      testPush("rawTypeStack1", rawTypeStack1, doubleElements);
                               ^
RawTypeTest.java:19: warning: [unchecked] unchecked method invocation:
<T>testPush(java.lang.String,Stack<T>,T[]) in RawTypeTest is applied to
(java.lang.String,Stack,java.lang.Double[])
      testPush("rawTypeStack1", rawTypeStack1, doubleElements);
              ^
RawTypeTest.java:20: warning: [unchecked] unchecked conversion
found   : Stack
required: Stack<T>
      testPop("rawTypeStack1", rawTypeStack1);
                              ^
RawTypeTest.java:20: warning: [unchecked] unchecked method invocation:
<T>testPop(java.lang.String,Stack<T>) in RawTypeTest is applied to
(java.lang.String,Stack)
      testPop("rawTypeStack1", rawTypeStack1);
             ^
RawTypeTest.java:21: warning: [unchecked] unchecked conversion
found   : Stack
required: Stack<java.lang.Double>
      testPush("rawTypeStack2", rawTypeStack2, doubleElements);
                               ^
RawTypeTest.java:21: warning: [unchecked] unchecked method invocation:
<T>testPush(java.lang.String,Stack<T>,T[]) in RawTypeTest is applied to
(java.lang.String,Stack,java.lang.Double[])
      testPush("rawTypeStack2", rawTypeStack2, doubleElements);
              ^
RawTypeTest.java:22: warning: [unchecked] unchecked conversion
found   : Stack
required: Stack<T>
      testPop("rawTypeStack2", rawTypeStack2);
                              ^
RawTypeTest.java:22: warning: [unchecked] unchecked method invocation:
<T>testPop(java.lang.String,Stack<T>) in RawTypeTest is applied to
(java.lang.String,Stack)
      testPop("rawTypeStack2", rawTypeStack2);
             ^
9 warnings
```

Fig. 20.12 | Warning messages from the compiler.

20.8 Wildcards in Methods That Accept Type Parameters

In this section, we introduce a powerful generics concept known as **wildcards**. Let's consider an example that motivates wildcards. Suppose that you'd like to implement a generic method sum that totals the numbers in a collection, such as an ArrayList. You'd begin by inserting the numbers in the collection. Because generic classes can be used only with class or interface types, the numbers would be *autoboxed* as objects of the type-wrapper classes. For example, any int value would be *autoboxed* as an Integer object, and any double value would be *autoboxed* as a Double object. We'd like to be able to total all the numbers in the ArrayList regardless of their type. For this reason, we'll declare the ArrayList with the type argument Number, which is the superclass of both Integer and Double. In addition, method sum will receive a parameter of type ArrayList<Number> and total its elements. Figure 20.13 demonstrates totaling the elements of an ArrayList of Numbers.

```java
1   // Fig. 20.13: TotalNumbers.java
2   // Totaling the numbers in an ArrayList<Number>.
3   import java.util.ArrayList;
4
5   public class TotalNumbers
6   {
7      public static void main(String[] args)
8      {
9         // create, initialize and output ArrayList of Numbers containing
10        // both Integers and Doubles, then display total of the elements
11        Number[] numbers = {1, 2.4, 3, 4.1}; // Integers and Doubles
12        ArrayList<Number> numberList = new ArrayList<>();
13
14        for (Number element : numbers)
15           numberList.add(element); // place each number in numberList
16
17        System.out.printf("numberList contains: %s%n", numberList);
18        System.out.printf("Total of the elements in numberList: %.1f%n",
19           sum(numberList));
20     }
21
22     // calculate total of ArrayList elements
23     public static double sum(ArrayList<Number> list)
24     {
25        double total = 0; // initialize total
26
27        // calculate sum
28        for (Number element : list)
29           total += element.doubleValue();
30
31        return total;
32     }
33  } // end class TotalNumbers
```

```
numberList contains: [1, 2.4, 3, 4.1]
Total of the elements in numberList: 10.5
```

Fig. 20.13 | Totaling the numbers in an ArrayList<Number>.

Line 11 declares and initializes an array of Numbers. Because the initializers are primitive values, Java *autoboxes* each primitive value as an object of its corresponding wrapper type. The int values 1 and 3 are *autoboxed* as Integer objects, and the double values 2.4

and 4.1 are *autoboxed* as Double objects. Line 12 declares and creates an ArrayList object that stores Numbers and assigns it to variable numberList.

Lines 14–15 traverse array numbers and place each element in numberList. Line 17 outputs the contents of the ArrayList as a String. This statement implicitly invokes the ArrayList's toString method, which returns a String of the form "[*elements*]" in which *elements* is a comma-separated list of the elements' String representations. Lines 18–19 display the sum of the elements that is returned by the call to method sum.

Method sum (lines 23–32) receives an ArrayList of Numbers and calculates the total of the Numbers in the collection. The method uses double values to perform the calculations and returns the result as a double. Lines 28–29 use the enhanced for statement, which is designed to work with both arrays and the collections of the Collections Framework, to total the elements of the ArrayList. The for statement assigns each Number in the ArrayList to variable element, then uses **Number method doubleValue** to obtain the Number's underlying primitive value as a double value. The result is added to total. When the loop terminates, the method returns the total.

Implementing Method **sum** With a Wildcard Type Argument in Its Parameter

Recall that the purpose of method sum in Fig. 20.13 was to total any type of Numbers stored in an ArrayList. We created an ArrayList of Numbers that contained both Integer and Double objects. The output of Fig. 20.13 demonstrates that method sum worked properly. Given that method sum can total the elements of an ArrayList of Numbers, you might expect that the method would also work for ArrayLists that contain elements of only one numeric type, such as ArrayList<Integer>. So we modified class TotalNumbers to create an ArrayList of Integers and pass it to method sum. When we compile the program, the compiler issues the following error message:

```
sum(java.util.ArrayList<java.lang.Number>) in TotalNumbersErrors
cannot be applied to (java.util.ArrayList<java.lang.Integer>)
```

Although Number is the superclass of Integer, the compiler doesn't consider the type ArrayList<Number> to be a superclass of ArrayList<Integer>. If it were, then every operation we could perform on ArrayList<Number> would also work on an ArrayList<Integer>. Consider the fact that you can add a Double object to an ArrayList<Number> because a Double *is a* Number, but you cannot add a Double object to an ArrayList<Integer> because a Double *is not an* Integer. Thus, the subtype relationship does not hold.

How do we create a more flexible version of the sum method that can total the elements of any ArrayList containing elements of any subclass of Number? This is where **wildcard type arguments** are important. Wildcards enable you to specify method parameters, return values, variables or fields, and so on, that act as supertypes or subtypes of parameterized types. In Fig. 20.14, method sum's parameter is declared in line 50 with the type:

```
ArrayList<? extends Number>
```

A wildcard type argument is denoted by a question mark (**?**), which by itself represents an "unknown type." In this case, the wildcard extends class Number, which means that the wildcard has an upper bound of Number. Thus, the unknown-type argument must be either Number or a subclass of Number. With the parameter type shown here, method sum can receive an ArrayList argument that contains any type of Number, such as ArrayList<Integer> (line 20), ArrayList<Double> (line 33) or ArrayList<Number> (line 46).

```
 1    // Fig. 20.14: WildcardTest.java
 2    // Wildcard test program.
 3    import java.util.ArrayList;
 4
 5    public class WildcardTest
 6    {
 7       public static void main(String[] args)
 8       {
 9          // create, initialize and output ArrayList of Integers, then
10          // display total of the elements
11          Integer[] integers = {1, 2, 3, 4, 5};
12          ArrayList<Integer> integerList = new ArrayList<>();
13
14          // insert elements in integerList
15          for (Integer element : integers)
16             integerList.add(element);
17
18          System.out.printf("integerList contains: %s%n", integerList);
19          System.out.printf("Total of the elements in integerList: %.0f%n%n",
20             sum(integerList));
21
22          // create, initialize and output ArrayList of Doubles, then
23          // display total of the elements
24          Double[] doubles = {1.1, 3.3, 5.5};
25          ArrayList<Double> doubleList = new ArrayList<>();
26
27          // insert elements in doubleList
28          for (Double element : doubles)
29             doubleList.add(element);
30
31          System.out.printf("doubleList contains: %s%n", doubleList);
32          System.out.printf("Total of the elements in doubleList: %.1f%n%n",
33             sum(doubleList));
34
35          // create, initialize and output ArrayList of Numbers containing
36          // both Integers and Doubles, then display total of the elements
37          Number[] numbers = {1, 2.4, 3, 4.1}; // Integers and Doubles
38          ArrayList<Number> numberList = new ArrayList<>();
39
40          // insert elements in numberList
41          for (Number element : numbers)
42             numberList.add(element);
43
44          System.out.printf("numberList contains: %s%n", numberList);
45          System.out.printf("Total of the elements in numberList: %.1f%n",
46             sum(numberList));
47       } // end main
48
49       // total the elements; using a wildcard in the ArrayList parameter
50       public static double sum(ArrayList<? extends Number> list)
51       {
52          double total = 0; // initialize total
53
```

Fig. 20.14 | Wildcard test program. (Part I of 2.)

```
54          // calculate sum
55          for (Number element : list)
56              total += element.doubleValue();
57
58          return total;
59      }
60  } // end class WildcardTest
```

```
integerList contains: [1, 2, 3, 4, 5]
Total of the elements in integerList: 15

doubleList contains: [1.1, 3.3, 5.5]
Total of the elements in doubleList: 9.9

numberList contains: [1, 2.4, 3, 4.1]
Total of the elements in numberList: 10.5
```

Fig. 20.14 | Wildcard test program. (Part 2 of 2.)

Lines 11–20 create and initialize an ArrayList<Integer>, output its elements and total them by calling method sum (line 20). Lines 24–33 perform the same operations for an ArrayList<Double>. Lines 37–46 perform the same operations for an Array-List<Number> that contains Integers and Doubles.

In method sum (lines 50–59), although the ArrayList argument's element types are not directly known by the method, they're known to be at least of type Number, because the wildcard was specified with the upper bound Number. For this reason line 56 is allowed, because all Number objects have a doubleValue method.

Although wildcards provide flexibility when passing parameterized types to a method, they also have some disadvantages. Because the wildcard (?) in the method's header (line 50) does not specify a type-parameter name, you cannot use it as a type name throughout the method's body (i.e., you cannot replace Number with ? in line 55). You could, however, declare method sum as follows:

public static <T extends Number> double sum(ArrayList<T> list)

which allows the method to receive an ArrayList that contains elements of any Number subclass. You could then use the type parameter T throughout the method body.

If the wildcard is specified without an upper bound, then only the methods of type Object can be invoked on values of the wildcard type. Also, methods that use wildcards in their parameter's type arguments cannot be used to add elements to a collection referenced by the parameter.

Common Programming Error 20.3

Using a wildcard in a method's type-parameter section or using a wildcard as an explicit type of a variable in the method body is a syntax error.

20.9 Wrap-Up

This chapter introduced generics. You learned how to declare generic methods and classes with type parameters specified in type-parameter sections. You also learned how to specify the upper bound for a type parameter and how the Java compiler uses erasure and casts to support multiple types with generic methods and classes. We discussed how backward compatibility is achieved via raw types. You also learned how to use wildcards in a generic method or a generic class.

In Chapter 21, you'll learn how to implement your own custom dynamic data structures that can grow or shrink at execution time. In particular, you'll implement these data structures using the generics capabilities you learned in this chapter.

Summary

Section 20.1 Introduction
- Generic methods enable you to specify, with one method declaration, a set of related methods.
- Generic classes and interfaces enable you to specify sets of related types.

Section 20.2 Motivation for Generic Methods
- Overloaded methods are often used to perform similar operations on different types of data.
- When the compiler encounters a method call, it attempts to locate a method declaration with a name and parameters that are compatible with the argument types in the method call.

Section 20.3 Generic Methods: Implementation and Compile-Time Translation
- If the operations performed by several overloaded methods are identical for each argument type, they can be more compactly and conveniently coded using a generic method. A single generic method declaration can be called with arguments of different data types. Based on the types of the arguments passed to a generic method, the compiler handles each method call appropriately.
- All generic method declarations have a type-parameter section (p. 835) delimited by angle brackets (< and >) that precedes the method's return type (p. 835).
- A type-parameter section contains one or more type parameters separated by commas.
- A type parameter (p. 835) is an identifier that specifies a generic type name. Type parameters can be used as the return type, parameter types and local variable types in a generic method declaration, and they act as placeholders for the types of the arguments passed to the generic method, which are known as actual type arguments (p. 836). Type parameters can represent only reference types.
- Type-parameter names used throughout a method declaration must match those declared in the type-parameter section. A type-parameter name can be declared only once in the type-parameter section but can appear more than once in the method's parameter list.
- When the compiler encounters a method call, it determines the argument types and attempts to locate a method with the same name and parameters that match the argument types. If there's no such method, the compiler searches for methods with the same name and compatible parameters and for matching generic methods.
- Objects of a class that implements generic interface Comparable (Comparable) can be compared with method compareTo (p. 838), which returns 0 if the objects are equal, a negative integer if the first object is less than the second or a positive integer if the first object is greater than the second.
- All the type-wrapper classes for primitive types implement Comparable.
- Comparable objects can be used with the sorting and searching methods of class Collections.

Section 20.4 Additional Compile-Time Translation Issues: Methods That Use a Type Parameter as the Return Type

- When a generic method is compiled, the compiler performs erasure (p. 848) to remove the type-parameter section and replace the type parameters with actual types. By default each type parameter is replaced with its upper bound (p. 848), which is `Object` unless specified otherwise.

- When erasure is performed on a method that returns a type variable (p. 848), explicit casts are inserted in front of each method call to ensure that the returned value has the type expected by the caller.

Section 20.5 Overloading Generic Methods

- A generic method may be overloaded with other generic methods or with nongeneric methods.

Section 20.6 Generic Classes

- Generic classes provide a means for describing a class in a type-independent manner. We can then instantiate type-specific objects of the generic class.

- A generic class declaration looks like a nongeneric class declaration, except that the class name is followed by a type-parameter section. The type-parameter section of a generic class can have one or more type parameters separated by commas.

- When a generic class is compiled, the compiler performs erasure on the class's type parameters and replaces them with their upper bounds.

- Type parameters cannot be used in a class's `static` declarations.

- When instantiating an object of a generic class, the types specified in angle brackets after the class name are known as type arguments (p. 843). The compiler uses them to replace the type parameters so that it can perform type checking and insert cast operations as necessary.

Section 20.7 Raw Types

- It's possible to instantiate a generic class without specifying a type argument. In this case, the new object of the class is said to have a raw type (p. 849)—the compiler implicitly uses type `Object` (or the type parameter's upper bound) throughout the generic class for each type argument.

Section 20.8 Wildcards in Methods That Accept Type Parameters

- Class `Number` is the superclass of both `Integer` and `Double`.

- `Number` method `doubleValue` (p. 854) obtains the `Number`'s underlying primitive value as a `double` value.

- Wildcard type arguments enable you to specify method parameters, return values, variables, and so on, that act as supertypes of parameterized types. A wildcard-type argument is denoted by `?` (p. 854), which represents an "unknown type." A wildcard can also have an upper bound.

- Because a wildcard (`?`) is not a type-parameter name, you cannot use it as a type name throughout a method's body.

- If a wildcard is specified without an upper bound, then only the methods of type `Object` can be invoked on values of the wildcard type.

- Methods that use wildcards as type arguments (p. 854) cannot be used to add elements to a collection referenced by the parameter.

Self-Review Exercises

20.1   State whether each of the following is *true* or *false*. If *false*, explain why.

a)   A generic method cannot have the same method name as a nongeneric method.

b) All generic method declarations have a type-parameter section that immediately precedes the method name.

c) A generic method can be overloaded by another generic method with the same method name but different method parameters.

d) A type parameter can be declared only once in the type-parameter section but can appear more than once in the method's parameter list.

e) Type-parameter names among different generic methods must be unique.

f) The scope of a generic class's type parameter is the entire class except its `static` members.

20.2 Fill in the blanks in each of the following:

a) _____ and _____ enable you to specify, with a single method declaration, a set of related methods, or with a single class declaration, a set of related types, respectively.

b) A type-parameter section is delimited by _____.

c) A generic method's _____ can be used to specify the method's argument types, to specify the method's return type and to declare variables within the method.

d) The statement `"Stack objectStack = new Stack();"` indicates that `objectStack` stores _____.

e) In a generic class declaration, the class name is followed by a(n) _____.

f) The syntax _____ specifies that the upper bound of a wildcard is type `T`.

Answers to Self-Review Exercises

20.1 a) False. Generic and nongeneric methods can have the same method name. A generic method can overload another generic method with the same method name but different method parameters. A generic method also can be overloaded by providing nongeneric methods with the same method name and number of arguments. b) False. All generic method declarations have a type-parameter section that immediately precedes the method's return type. c) True. d) True. e) False. Type-parameter names among different generic methods need not be unique. f) True.

20.2 a) Generic methods, generic classes. b) angle brackets (< and >). c) type parameters. d) a raw type. e) type-parameter section. f) `? extends T`.

Exercises

20.3 *(Explain Notation)* Explain the use of the following notation in a Java program:

```
public class Array<T> { }
```

20.4 *(Generic Method `selectionSort`)* Write a generic method `selectionSort` based on the sort program of Fig. 19.4. Write a test program that inputs, sorts and outputs an `Integer` array and a `Float` array. [*Hint:* Use `<T extends Comparable<T>>` in the type-parameter section for method `selectionSort`, so that you can use method `compareTo` to compare the objects of the type that `T` represents.]

20.5 *(Overloaded Generic Method `printArray`)* Overload generic method `printArray` of Fig. 20.3 so that it takes two additional integer arguments, `lowSubscript` and `highSubscript`. A call to this method prints only the designated portion of the array. Validate `lowSubscript` and `highSubscript`. If either is out of range, the overloaded `printArray` method should throw an `InvalidSubscriptException`; otherwise, `printArray` should return the number of elements printed. Then modify `main` to exercise both versions of `printArray` on arrays `integerArray`, `doubleArray` and `characterArray`. Test all capabilities of both versions of `printArray`.

20.6 *(Overloading a Generic Method with a Nongeneric Method))* Overload generic method printArray of Fig. 20.3 with a nongeneric version that specifically prints an array of Strings in neat, tabular format, as shown in the sample output that follows:

```
Array stringArray contains:
one      two      three    four
five     six      seven    eight
```

20.7 *(Generic isEqualTo Method)* Write a simple generic version of method isEqualTo that compares its two arguments with the equals method and returns true if they're equal and false otherwise. Use this generic method in a program that calls isEqualTo with a variety of built-in types, such as Object or Integer. What result do you get when you attempt to run this program?

20.8 *(Generic Class Pair)* Write a generic class Pair which has two type parameters—F and S— each representing the type of the first and second element of the pair, respectively. Add *get* and *set* methods for the first and second elements of the pair. [*Hint:* The class header should be public class Pair<F, S>.]

20.9 *(Overloading Generic Methods)* How can generic methods be overloaded?

20.10 *(Overload Resolution)* The compiler performs a matching process to determine which method to call when a method is invoked. Under what circumstances does an attempt to make a match result in a compile-time error?

20.11 *(What Does this Statement Do?)* Explain why a Java program might use the statement

```
ArrayList<Employee> workerList = new ArrayList<>();
```

Custom Generic Data Structures

21

Much that I bound,
I could not free;
Much that I freed
returned to me.
—Lee Wilson Dodd

There is always room at the top.
—Daniel Webster

I think that I shall never see
A poem lovely as a tree.
—Joyce Kilmer

Objectives

In this chapter you'll learn:

■ To form linked data structures using references, self-referential classes, recursion and generics.

■ To create and manipulate dynamic data structures, such as linked lists, queues, stacks and binary trees.

■ Various important applications of linked data structures.

■ How to create reusable data structures with classes, inheritance and composition.

■ To organize classes in packages to promote reuse.

21.1 Introduction

This chapter shows how to build **dynamic data structures** that grow and shrink at execution time. **Linked lists** are collections of data items "linked up in a chain"—insertions and deletions can be made *anywhere* in a linked list. **Stacks** are important in compilers and operating systems; insertions and deletions are made only at one end of a stack—its **top**. **Queues** represent waiting lines; insertions are made at the back (also referred to as the **tail**) of a queue and deletions are made from the front (also referred to as the **head**). **Binary trees** facilitate high-speed searching and sorting of data, eliminating duplicate data items efficiently, representing file-system directories, compiling expressions into machine language and many other interesting applications.

We discuss each of these major data-structure types and implement programs that create and manipulate them. We use classes, inheritance and composition to create them for reusability and maintainability. We also explain how to organize classes into your own packages to promote reuse. We include this chapter for computer-science and computer-engineering students who need to know how to build linked data structures.

Software Engineering Observation 21.1

The vast majority of software developers should use the predefined generic collection classes that we discussed in Chapter 16, rather than developing customized linked data structures.

Optional Online "Building Your Own Compiler" Project

If you feel ambitious, you might want to attempt the major project described in the special section entitled Building Your Own Compiler, which we've posted online at `http://www.deitel.com/books/jhtp10LOV`. You've been using a Java compiler to translate your Java programs to bytecodes so that you could execute these programs. In this project, you'll actually build your own compiler. It will read statements written in a simple, yet powerful high-level language similar to early versions of the popular language BASIC and translate these statements into Simpletron Machine Language (SML) instructions—SML is the language you learned in the Chapter 6 special section, Building Your Own Computer. Your Simpletron Simulator program will then execute the SML program produced by your compiler! Implementing this project by using an object-oriented approach will give you an opportunity to exercise most of what you've learned in this book. The special section carefully walks you through the specifications of the high-level language and describes the algorithms you'll need to convert each high-level language statement into machine-language instructions. If you enjoy being challenged, you might attempt the enhancements to both the compiler and the Simpletron Simulator suggested in the exercises.

21.2 Self-Referential Classes

A **self-referential class** contains an instance variable that refers to another object of the same class type. For example, the generic Node class declaration

```
class Node<T>
{
    private T data;
    private Node<T> nextNode; // reference to next linked node

    public Node(T data) { /* constructor body */ }
    public void setData(T data) { /* method body */ }
    public T getData() { /* method body */ }
    public void setNext(Node<T> next) { /* method body */ }
    public Node<T> getNext() { /* method body */ }
}
```

has two private instance variables—data (of the generic type T) and Node<T> variable nextNode. Variable nextNode references a Node<T> object, an object of the same class being declared here—hence the term "self-referential class." Field nextNode is a **link**—it "links" an object of type Node<T> to another object of the same type. Type Node<T> also has five methods: a constructor that receives a value to initialize data, a setData method to set the value of data, a getData method to return the value of data, a setNext method to set the value of nextNode and a getNext method to return a reference to the next node.

Programs can link self-referential objects together to form such useful data structures as lists, queues, stacks and trees. Figure 21.1 illustrates two self-referential objects linked together to form a list. A backslash—representing a null reference—is placed in the link member of the second self-referential object to indicate that the link does *not* refer to another object. The backslash is illustrative; it does not correspond to the backslash character in Java. By convention, in code we use the null reference to indicate the end of a data structure.

Fig. 21.1 | Self-referential-class objects linked together.

21.3 Dynamic Memory Allocation

Creating and maintaining dynamic data structures requires **dynamic memory allocation**—allowing a program to obtain more memory space at execution time to hold new nodes and to release space no longer needed. Remember that Java does not require you to explicitly release dynamically allocated memory. Rather, Java performs automatic *garbage collection* of objects that are no longer referenced in a program.

The limit for dynamic memory allocation can be as large as the amount of available physical memory in the computer or the amount of available disk space in a virtual-memory system. Often the limits are much smaller, because the computer's available memory must be shared among many applications.

The declaration and class-instance-creation expression

```
// 10 is nodeToAdd's data
Node<Integer> nodeToAdd = new Node<Integer>(10);
```

allocates a Node<Integer> object and returns a reference to it, which is assigned to node-ToAdd. If *insufficient memory* is available, the preceding expression throws an OutOfMemory-Error. The sections that follow discuss lists, stacks, queues and trees—all of which use dynamic memory allocation and self-referential classes to create dynamic data structures.

21.4 Linked Lists

A linked list is a linear collection (i.e., a sequence) of self-referential-class objects, called **nodes**, connected by reference *links*—hence, the term "linked" list. Typically, a program accesses a linked list via a reference to its first node. The program accesses each subsequent node via the link reference stored in the previous node. By convention, the link reference in the last node of the list is set to null to indicate "end of list." Data is stored in and removed from linked lists dynamically—the program creates and deletes nodes as necessary. Stacks and queues are also linear data structures and, as we'll see, are constrained versions of linked lists. Trees are *nonlinear* data structures.

Lists of data can be stored in conventional Java arrays, but linked lists provide several advantages. A linked list is appropriate when the number of data elements to be represented in the data structure is *unpredictable*. Linked lists are dynamic, so the length of a list can increase or decrease as necessary, whereas the size of a conventional Java array cannot be altered—it's fixed when the program creates the array. [Of course, ArrayLists *can* grow and shrink.] Conventional arrays can become full. Linked lists become full only when the system has *insufficient memory* to satisfy dynamic storage allocation requests. Package java.util contains class LinkedList (discussed in Chapter 16) for implementing and manipulating linked lists that grow and shrink during program execution.

Performance Tip 21.1

Insertion into a linked list is fast—only two references have to be modified (after locating the insertion point). All existing node objects remain at their current locations in memory.

Linked lists can be maintained in sorted order simply by inserting each new element at the proper point in the list. (It does, of course, take time to *locate* the proper insertion point.) *Existing list elements do not need to be moved.*

Performance Tip 21.2

Insertion and deletion in a sorted array can be time consuming—all the elements following the inserted or deleted element must be shifted appropriately.

21.4.1 Singly Linked Lists

Linked list nodes normally are *not stored contiguously* in memory. Rather, they're logically contiguous. Figure 21.2 illustrates a linked list with several nodes. This diagram presents a **singly linked list**—each node contains one reference to the next node in the list. Often, linked lists are implemented as *doubly linked lists*—each node contains a reference to the next node in the list *and* a reference to the preceding one.

Performance Tip 21.3

The elements of an array are contiguous in memory. This allows immediate access to any array element, because its address can be calculated directly as its offset from the beginning of the array. Linked lists do not afford such immediate access—an element can be accessed only by traversing the list from the front (or the back in a doubly linked list).

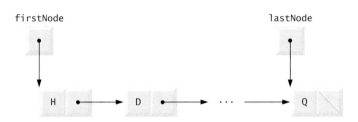

Fig. 21.2 | Linked-list graphical representation.

21.4.2 Implementing a Generic List Class

The program of Figs. 21.3–21.5 uses an object of our generic List class to manipulate a list of miscellaneous objects. The program consists of four classes—ListNode (Fig. 21.3, lines 6–37), List (Fig. 21.3, lines 40–147), EmptyListException (Fig. 21.4) and List-Test (Fig. 21.5). Encapsulated in each List object is a linked list of ListNode objects.

[*Note:* The List, ListNode and EmptyListException classes are placed in the package com.deitel.datastructures, so that they can be reused throughout this chapter. In Section 21.4.10, we discuss the package statement (line 3 of Figs. 21.3 and 21.4), and show how to compile and run programs that use classes in your own packages.]

```
1   // Fig. 21.3: List.java
2   // ListNode and List class declarations.
3   package com.deitel.datastructures;
4
5   // class to represent one node in a list
6   class ListNode<T>
7   {
8      // package access members; List can access these directly
9      T data; // data for this node
10     ListNode<T> nextNode; // reference to the next node in the list
11
12     // constructor creates a ListNode that refers to object
13     ListNode(T object)
14     {
15        this(object, null);
16     }
17
```

Fig. 21.3 | ListNode and List class declarations. (Part 1 of 4.)

```
18      // constructor creates ListNode that refers to the specified
19      // object and to the next ListNode
20      ListNode(T object, ListNode<T> node)
21      {
22         data = object;
23         nextNode = node;
24      }
25
26      // return reference to data in node
27      T getData()
28      {
29         return data;
30      }
31
32      // return reference to next node in list
33      ListNode<T> getNext()
34      {
35         return nextNode;
36      }
37   } // end class ListNode<T>
38
39   // class List definition
40   public class List<T>
41   {
42      private ListNode<T> firstNode;
43      private ListNode<T> lastNode;
44      private String name; // string like "list" used in printing
45
46      // constructor creates empty List with "list" as the name
47      public List()
48      {
49         this("list");
50      }
51
52      // constructor creates an empty List with a name
53      public List(String listName)
54      {
55         name = listName;
56         firstNode = lastNode = null;
57      }
58
59      // insert item at front of List
60      public void insertAtFront(T insertItem)
61      {
62         if (isEmpty()) // firstNode and lastNode refer to same object
63            firstNode = lastNode = new ListNode<T>(insertItem);
64         else // firstNode refers to new node
65            firstNode = new ListNode<T>(insertItem, firstNode);
66      }
67
68      // insert item at end of List
69      public void insertAtBack(T insertItem)
70      {
```

Fig. 21.3 | ListNode and List class declarations. (Part 2 of 4.)

```
71          if (isEmpty()) // firstNode and lastNode refer to same object
72              firstNode = lastNode = new ListNode<T>(insertItem);
73          else // lastNode's nextNode refers to new node
74              lastNode = lastNode.nextNode = new ListNode<T>(insertItem);
75      }
76
77      // remove first node from List
78      public T removeFromFront() throws EmptyListException
79      {
80          if (isEmpty()) // throw exception if List is empty
81              throw new EmptyListException(name);
82
83          T removedItem = firstNode.data; // retrieve data being removed
84
85          // update references firstNode and lastNode
86          if (firstNode == lastNode)
87              firstNode = lastNode = null;
88          else
89              firstNode = firstNode.nextNode;
90
91          return removedItem; // return removed node data
92      }
93
94      // remove last node from List
95      public T removeFromBack() throws EmptyListException
96      {
97          if (isEmpty()) // throw exception if List is empty
98              throw new EmptyListException(name);
99
100         T removedItem = lastNode.data; // retrieve data being removed
101
102         // update references firstNode and lastNode
103         if (firstNode == lastNode)
104             firstNode = lastNode = null;
105         else // locate new last node
106         {
107             ListNode<T> current = firstNode;
108
109             // loop while current node does not refer to lastNode
110             while (current.nextNode != lastNode)
111                 current = current.nextNode;
112
113             lastNode = current; // current is new lastNode
114             current.nextNode = null;
115         }
116
117         return removedItem; // return removed node data
118     }
119
```

Fig. 21.3 | ListNode and List class declarations. (Part 3 of 4.)

```
120    // determine whether list is empty
121    public boolean isEmpty()
122    {
123        return firstNode == null; // return true if list is empty
124    }
125
126    // output list contents
127    public void print()
128    {
129        if (isEmpty())
130        {
131            System.out.printf("Empty %s%n", name);
132            return;
133        }
134
135        System.out.printf("The %s is: ", name);
136        ListNode<T> current = firstNode;
137
138        // while not at end of list, output current node's data
139        while (current != null)
140        {
141            System.out.printf("%s ", current.data);
142            current = current.nextNode;
143        }
144
145        System.out.println();
146    }
147 } // end class List<T>
```

Fig. 21.3 | ListNode and List class declarations. (Part 4 of 4.)

```
1    // Fig. 21.4: EmptyListException.java
2    // Class EmptyListException declaration.
3    package com.deitel.datastructures;
4
5    public class EmptyListException extends RuntimeException
6    {
7        // constructor
8        public EmptyListException()
9        {
10            this("List"); // call other EmptyListException constructor
11        }
12
13        // constructor
14        public EmptyListException(String name)
15        {
16            super(name + " is empty"); // call superclass constructor
17        }
18    } // end class EmptyListException
```

Fig. 21.4 | Class EmptyListException declaration.

```
 1  // Fig. 21.5: ListTest.java
 2  // ListTest class to demonstrate List capabilities.
 3  import com.deitel.datastructures.List;
 4  import com.deitel.datastructures.EmptyListException;
 5
 6  public class ListTest
 7  {
 8     public static void main(String[] args)
 9     {
10        List<Integer> list = new List<>();
11
12        // insert integers in list
13        list.insertAtFront(-1);
14        list.print();
15        list.insertAtFront(0);
16        list.print();
17        list.insertAtBack(1);
18        list.print();
19        list.insertAtBack(5);
20        list.print();
21
22        // remove objects from list; print after each removal
23        try
24        {
25           int removedItem = list.removeFromFront();
26           System.out.printf("%n%d removed%n", removedItem);
27           list.print();
28
29           removedItem = list.removeFromFront();
30           System.out.printf("%n%d removed%n", removedItem);
31           list.print();
32
33           removedItem = list.removeFromBack();
34           System.out.printf("%n%d removed%n", removedItem);
35           list.print();
36
37           removedItem = list.removeFromBack();
38           System.out.printf("%n%d removed%n", removedItem);
39           list.print();
40        }
41        catch (EmptyListException emptyListException)
42        {
43           emptyListException.printStackTrace();
44        }
45     }
46  } // end class ListTest
```

```
The list is: -1
The list is: 0 -1
The list is: 0 -1 1
The list is: 0 -1 1 5
```

Fig. 21.5 | ListTest class to demonstrate List capabilities. (Part 1 of 2.)

```
0 removed
The list is: -1 1 5

-1 removed
The list is: 1 5

5 removed
The list is: 1

1 removed
Empty list
```

Fig. 21.5 | ListTest class to demonstrate List capabilities. (Part 2 of 2.)

21.4.3 Generic Classes ListNode and List

Generic class ListNode (Fig. 21.3, lines 6–37) declares package-access fields data and nextNode. The data field is a reference of type T, so its type will be determined when the client code creates the corresponding List object. Variable nextNode stores a reference to the next ListNode object in the linked list (or null if the node is the last one in the list).

Lines 42–43 of class List (Fig. 21.3, lines 40–47) declare references to the first and last ListNodes in a List (firstNode and lastNode, respectively). The constructors (lines 47–50 and 53–57) initialize both references to null. The most important methods of class List are insertAtFront (lines 60–66), insertAtBack (lines 69–75), removeFromFront (lines 78–92) and removeFromBack (lines 95–118). Method isEmpty (lines 121–124) is a *predicate method* that determines whether the list is empty (i.e., the reference to the first node of the list is null). Predicate methods typically test a condition and do not modify the object on which they're called. If the list is empty, method isEmpty returns true; otherwise, it returns false. Method print (lines 127–146) displays the list's contents. We discuss class List's methods in more detail after we discuss class ListTest.

21.4.4 Class ListTest

Method main of class ListTest (Fig. 21.5) creates a List<Integer> object (line 10), then inserts objects at the beginning of the list using method insertAtFront, inserts objects at the end of the list using method insertAtBack, deletes objects from the front of the list using method removeFromFront and deletes objects from the end of the list using method removeFromBack. After each insert and remove operation, ListTest calls List method print to display the current list contents. If an attempt is made to remove an item from an empty list, an EmptyListException (Fig. 21.4) is thrown, so the method calls to removeFromFront and removeFromBack are placed in a try block that's followed by an appropriate exception handler. Notice in lines 13, 15, 17 and 19 (Fig. 21.5) that the application passes literal primitive int values to methods insertAtFront and insertAtBack. Each of these methods was declared with a parameter of the generic type T (Fig. 21.3, lines 60 and 69). Since this example manipulates a List<Integer>, the type T represents the type-wrapper class Integer. In this case, the JVM *autoboxes* each literal value in an Integer object, and that object is actually inserted into the list.

21.4.5 List Method insertAtFront

Now we discuss each method of class List (Fig. 21.3) in detail and provide diagrams showing the reference manipulations performed by methods insertAtFront, insertAt-

Back, removeFromFront and removeFromBack. Method insertAtFront (lines 60–66 of Fig. 21.3) places a new node at the front of the list. The steps are:

1. Call isEmpty to determine whether the list is empty (line 62).

2. If the list is empty, assign to firstNode and lastNode the new ListNode that was initialized with insertItem (line 63). (Recall that assignment operators evaluate right to left.) The ListNode constructor at lines 13–16 calls the ListNode constructor at lines 20–24 to set instance variable data to refer to the insertItem passed as an argument and to set reference nextNode to null, because this is the first and last node in the list.

3. If the list is not empty, the new node is "linked" into the list by setting firstNode to a new ListNode object and initializing that object with insertItem and firstNode (line 65). When the ListNode constructor (lines 20–24) executes, it sets instance variable data to refer to the insertItem passed as an argument and performs the insertion by setting the nextNode reference of the new node to the ListNode passed as an argument, which previously was the first node.

In Fig. 21.6, part (a) shows a list and a new node during the insertAtFront operation and before the program links the new node into the list. The dotted arrows in part (b) illustrate *Step 3* of the insertAtFront operation that enables the node containing 12 to become the new first node in the list.

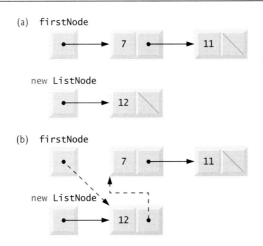

Fig. 21.6 | Graphical representation of operation insertAtFront.

21.4.6 List Method insertAtBack

Method insertAtBack (lines 69–75 of Fig. 21.3) places a new node at the back of the list. The steps are:

1. Call isEmpty to determine whether the list is empty (line 71).

2. If the list is empty, assign to firstNode and lastNode the new ListNode that was initialized with insertItem (line 72). The ListNode constructor at lines 13–16

calls the constructor at lines 20–24 to set instance variable `data` to refer to the `insertItem` passed as an argument and to set reference `nextNode` to `null`.

3. If the list is not empty, line 74 links the new node into the list by assigning to `lastNode` and `lastNode.nextNode` the reference to the new `ListNode` that was initialized with `insertItem`. `ListNode`'s constructor (lines 13–16) sets instance variable `data` to refer to the `insertItem` passed as an argument and sets reference `nextNode` to `null`, because this is the last node in the list.

In Fig. 21.7, part (a) shows a list and a new node during the `insertAtBack` operation and before linking the new node into the list. The dotted arrows in part (b) illustrate *Step 3* of method `insertAtBack`, which adds the new node to the end of a list that's not empty.

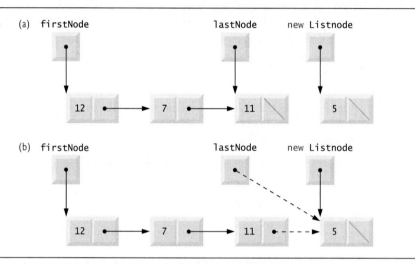

Fig. 21.7 | Graphical representation of operation `insertAtBack`.

21.4.7 List Method removeFromFront

Method `removeFromFront` (lines 78–92 of Fig. 21.3) removes the first node of the list and returns a reference to the removed data. If the list is empty when the program calls this method, the method throws an `EmptyListException` (lines 80–81). Otherwise, the method returns a reference to the removed data. The steps are:

1. Assign `firstNode.data` (the data being removed) to `removedItem` (line 83).

2. If `firstNode` and `lastNode` refer to the same object (line 86), the list has only one element at this time. So, the method sets `firstNode` and `lastNode` to `null` (line 87) to remove the node from the list (leaving the list empty).

3. If the list has more than one node, then the method leaves reference `lastNode` as is and assigns the value of `firstNode.nextNode` to `firstNode` (line 89). Thus, `firstNode` references the node that was previously the second node in the list.

4. Return the `removedItem` reference (line 91).

In Fig. 21.8, part (a) illustrates the list before the removal operation. The dashed lines and arrows in part (b) show the reference manipulations.

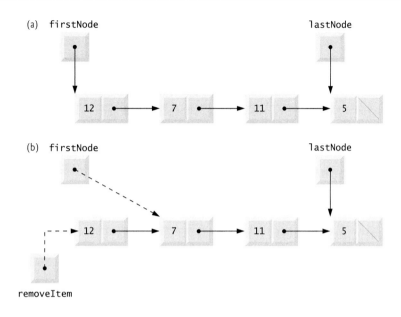

Fig. 21.8 | Graphical representation of operation removeFromFront.

21.4.8 List Method removeFromBack

Method removeFromBack (lines 95–118 of Fig. 21.3) removes the last node of a list and returns a reference to the removed data. The method throws an EmptyListException (lines 97–98) if the list is empty when the program calls this method. The steps are:

1. Assign lastNode.data (the data being removed) to removedItem (line 100).

2. If the firstNode and lastNode refer to the same object (line 103), the list has only one element at this time. So, line 104 sets firstNode and lastNode to null to remove that node from the list (leaving the list empty).

3. If the list has more than one node, create the ListNode reference current and assign it firstNode (line 107).

4. Now "walk the list" with current until it references the node before the last node. The while loop (lines 110–111) assigns current.nextNode to current as long as current.nextNode (the next node in the list) is not lastNode.

5. After locating the second-to-last node, assign current to lastNode (line 113) to update which node is last in the list.

6. Set the current.nextNode to null (line 114) to remove the last node from the list and terminate the list at the current node.

7. Return the removedItem reference (line 117).

In Fig. 21.9, part (a) illustrates the list before the removal operation. The dashed lines and arrows in part (b) show the reference manipulations. [We limited the List insertion

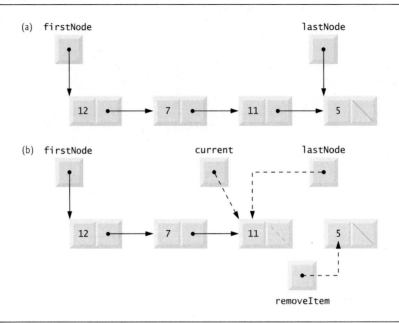

Fig. 21.9 | Graphical representation of operation `removeFromBack`.

and removal operations to the front and the back of the list. In Exercise 21.26, you'll enhance the `List` class to enable insertions and deletions *anywhere* in the `List`.]

21.4.9 List Method print

Method `print` (lines 127–146 of Fig. 21.3) first determines whether the list is empty (lines 129–133). If so, `print` displays a message indicating that the list is empty and returns control to the calling method. Otherwise, `print` outputs the list's data. Line 136 creates `ListNode` `current` and initializes it with `firstNode`. While `current` is not `null`, there are more items in the list. Therefore, line 141 outputs a string representation of `current.data`. Line 142 moves to the next node in the list by assigning the value of reference `current.nextNode` to `current`. This printing algorithm is identical for linked lists, stacks and queues.

21.4.10 Creating Your Own Packages

As you know, the Java API types (classes, interfaces and enums) are organized in *packages* that group related types. Packages facilitate software reuse by enabling programs to `import` existing classes, rather than *copying* them into the folders of each program that uses them. Programmers use packages to organize program components, especially in large programs. For example, you might have one package containing the types that make up your program's graphical user interface, another for the types that manage your application's data and another for the types that communicate with servers over a network. In addition, packages help you specify unique names for every type you declare, which (as we'll discuss) helps prevent class-name conflicts. This section introduces how to create and use your own packages. Much of what we discuss here is handled for you by IDEs such as NetBeans, Eclipse and IntelliJ IDEA. We focus on creating and using packages with the JDK's command-line tools.

Steps for Declaring a Reusable Class

Before a class can be imported into multiple programs, it must be placed in a package to make it reusable. The steps for creating a reusable class are:

1. Declare one or more `public` types (classes, interfaces and enums). Only `public` types can be reused outside the package in which they're declared.

2. Choose a unique package name and add a **package declaration** to the source-code file for each reusable type that should be part of the package.

3. Compile the types so that they're placed in the appropriate package directory.

4. Import the reusable types into a program and use them.

We'll now discuss each of these steps in more detail.

Step 1: Creating `public` Types for Reuse

For *Step 1*, you declare the types that will be placed in the package, including both the reusable types and any supporting types. In Fig. 21.3, class `List` is `public`, so it's reusable outside its package. Class `ListNode`, however, is not `public`, so it can be used *only* by class `List` and any other types declared in the *same* package. In Fig. 21.4, class `EmptyListException` is `public`, so it, too, is reusable. If a source-code file contains more than one type, all types in the file are placed in the same package when the file is compiled.

Step 2: Adding the `package` Statements

For *Step 2*, you provide a `package` declaration containing the package's name. All source-code files containing types that should be part of the same package must contain the *same* package declaration. Figures 21.3 and 21.4 each contain:

```
package com.deitel.datastructures;
```

indicating that all the types declared in those files—`ListNode` and `List` in Fig. 21.3 and `EmptyListException` in Fig. 21.4—are part of the `com.deitel.datastructures` package.

Each Java source-code file may contain only *one* package declaration, and it must *precede* all other declarations and statements. If no `package` statement is provided in a Java source-code file, the types declared in that file are placed in the so-called *default package* and are accessible only to other classes in the default package that are located in the *same directory*. All prior programs in this book have used this default package.

Package Naming Conventions

A package name's parts are separated by dots (`.`), and there typically are two or more parts. To ensure *unique* package names, you typically begin the name with your institution's or company's Internet domain name in reverse order—e.g., our domain name is `deitel.com`, so we begin our package names with `com.deitel`. For the domain name *yourcollege*.edu, you'd begin the package name with edu.*yourcollege*.

After the reversed domain name, you can specify additional parts in a package name. If you're part of a university with many schools or company with many divisions, you might use the school or division name as the next part of the package name. Similarly, if the types are for a specific project, you might include the project name as part of the package name. We chose `datastructures` as the next part in our package name to indicate that classes `ListNode`, `List` and `EmptyListException` are from this data structures chapter.

Fully Qualified Names

The package name is part of the **fully qualified type name**, so the name of class List is actually com.deitel.datastructures.List. You can use this fully qualified name in your programs, or you can import the class and use its **simple name** (the class name by itself— List) in the program. If another package also contains a List class, the fully qualified class names can be used to distinguish between the classes in the program and prevent a **name conflict** (also called a **name collision**).

Step 3: Compiling Packaged Types

Step 3 is to compile the class so that it's stored in the appropriate package. When a Java file containing a package declaration is compiled, the resulting class file is placed in a directory specified by the declaration. Classes in the package com.deitel.datastructures are placed in the directory

```
com
    deitel
        datastructures
```

The names in the package declaration specify the exact location of the package's classes.

The javac command-line option **-d** causes the compiler to create the directories based on the package declaration. The option also specifies where the top-level directory in the package name should be placed on your system—you may specify a relative or complete path to this location. For example, the command

```
javac -d . List.java EmptyListException.java
```

specifies that the first directory in our package name (com) should be placed in the current directory. The period (.) after -d in the preceding command represents the *current directory* on the Windows, UNIX, Linux and Mac OS X operating systems (and several others as well). Similarly, the command

```
javac -d .. List.java EmptyListException.java
```

specifies that the first directory in our package name (com) should be placed in the *parent* directory—we did this for all the reusable classes in this chapter. Once you compile with the -d option, the package's datastructures directory contains the files ListNode.class, List.class and EmptyListException.class.

Step 4: Importing Types from Your Package

Once types are compiled into a package, they can be imported (*Step 4*). Class ListTest (Fig. 21.5) is in the *default package* because its .java file does not contain a package declaration. Because class ListTest is in a *different* package from List and EmptyListException, you must either import these classes so that class ListTest can use them (lines 3–4 of Fig. 21.5) or you must *fully qualify* the names List and EmptyListException everywhere they're used throughout class ListTest. For example, line 10 of Fig. 21.5 could have been written as:

```
com.deitel.datastructures.List<Integer> list =
    new com.deitel.datastructures.List<>();
```

Single-Type-Import vs. Type-Import-On-Demand Declarations

Lines 3–4 of Fig. 21.5 are **single-type-import declarations**—they each specify *one* class to import. When a source-code file uses *multiple* classes from a package, you can import those classes with a a **type-import-on-demand declaration** of the form

```
import packagename.*;
```

which uses an asterisk (*) at its end to inform the compiler that *all* `public` classes from the *packagename* package can be used in the file containing the `import`. Only those classes that are *used* are loaded at execution time. The preceding `import` allows you to use the simple name of any type from the *packagename* package. Throughout this book, we provide single-type-import declarations as a form of documentation to show you specifically which types are used in each program.

Common Programming Error 21.1

Using the `import` *declaration* `import java.*;` *causes a compilation error. You must specify the full package name from which you want to import classes.*

Error-Prevention Tip 21.1

Using single-type-import declarations helps avoid naming conflicts by importing only the types you actually use in your code.

Specifying the Classpath When Compiling a Program

When compiling `ListTest`, javac must locate the `.class` files for classes `List` and `EmptyListException` to ensure that class `ListTest` uses them correctly. The compiler uses a special object called a **class loader** to locate the classes it needs. The class loader begins by searching the standard Java classes that are bundled with the JDK. Then it searches for **optional packages**. Java provides an **extension mechanism** that enables new (optional) packages to be added to Java for development and execution purposes. If the class is not found in the standard Java classes or in the extension classes, the class loader searches the **classpath**—a list of directories or **archive files** containing reusable types. Each directory or archive file is separated from the next by a **directory separator**—a semicolon (;) on Windows or a colon (:) on UNIX/Linux/Mac OS X. Archive files are individual files that contain directories of other files, typically in a compressed format. For example, the standard classes used by your programs are contained in the archive file `rt.jar`, which is installed with the JDK. Archive files normally end with the `.jar` or `.zip` file-name extensions.

By default, the classpath consists only of the current directory. However, the classpath can be modified by

1. providing the **-classpath** *listOfDirectories* option to the javac compiler or

2. setting the **CLASSPATH environment variable** (a special variable that you define and the operating system maintains so that programs can search for classes in the specified locations).

If you compile `ListTest.java` without specifying the -classpath option, as in

```
javac ListTest.java
```

the class loader assumes that the additional package(s) used by the `ListTest` program are in the *current directory*. As we mentioned, we placed our package in the *parent* directory so that it could be used by other programs in this chapter. To compile `ListTest.java`, use the command

```
javac -classpath .;.. ListTest.java
```

on Windows or the command

```
javac -classpath .:.. ListTest.java
```

on UNIX/Linux/Mac OS X. The `.` in the classpath enables the class loader to locate `List-Test` in the current directry. The `..` enables the class loader to locate the contents of package `com.deitel.datastructures` in the parent directory.

Common Programming Error 21.2

Specifying an explicit classpath eliminates the current directory from the classpath. This prevents classes in the current directory (including packages in the current directory) from loading properly. If classes must be loaded from the current directory, include a dot (.) in the classpath to specify the current directory.

Software Engineering Observation 21.2

In general, it's a better practice to use the -classpath option of the compiler, rather than the CLASSPATH environment variable, to specify the classpath for a program. This enables each program to have its own classpath.

Error-Prevention Tip 21.2

Specifying the classpath with the CLASSPATH environment variable can cause subtle and difficult-to-locate errors in programs that use different versions of the same package.

Specifying the Classpath When Executing a Program
When you execute a program, the JVM must be able to locate the `.class` files for the program's classes. Like the compiler, the `java` command uses a *class loader* that searches the standard classes and extension classes first, then searches the classpath (the current directory by default). The classpath can be specified explicitly by using the same techniques discussed for the compiler. As with the compiler, it's better to specify an individual program's classpath via command-line JVM options. You can specify the classpath in the `java` command via the **-classpath** or **-cp** command-line options, followed by a list of directories or archive files. Again, if classes must be loaded from the current directory, be sure to include a dot (.) in the classpath to specify the current directory. To execute the `ListTest` program, use the following command:

```
java -classpath .:.. ListTest
```

You'll need to use similar `javac` and `java` commands for each of this chapter's remaining examples. For more information on the classpath, visit `docs.oracle.com/javase/7/docs/technotes/tools/index.html#general`.

21.5 Stacks

A stack is a constrained version of a list—*new nodes can be added to and removed from a stack only at the top*. For this reason, a stack is referred to as a **last-in, first-out** (**LIFO**) data structure. The link member in the bottom node is set to `null` to indicate the bottom of the stack. A stack is not required to be implemented as a linked list—it can also be implemented using an array.

The primary methods for manipulating a stack are **push** and **pop**, which add a new node to the top of the stack and remove a node from the top of the stack, respectively. Method pop also returns the data from the popped node.

Stacks have many interesting applications. For example, when a program calls a method, the called method must know how to return to its caller, so the return address of the calling method is pushed onto the program-execution stack (discussed in Section 5.6). If a series of method calls occurs, the successive return addresses are pushed onto the stack in last-in, first-out order so that each method can return to its caller. Stacks support recursive method calls in the *same* manner as they do conventional nonrecursive method calls.

The program-execution stack also contains the memory for local variables on each invocation of a method during a program's execution. When the method returns to its caller, the memory for that method's local variables is popped off the stack, and those variables are no longer known to the program. If the local variable is a reference and the object to which it referred has no other variables referring to it, the object can be garbage collected.

Compilers use stacks to evaluate arithmetic expressions and generate machine-language code to process them. The exercises in this chapter explore several applications of stacks, including using them to develop a complete working compiler. Also, package `java.util` contains class `Stack` (see Chapter 16) for implementing and manipulating stacks that can grow and shrink during program execution.

In this section, we take advantage of the close relationship between lists and stacks to implement a stack class by reusing the `List<T>` class of Fig. 21.3. We demonstrate two different forms of reusability. First, we implement the stack class by extending class `List`. Then we implement an identically performing stack class through *composition* by including a reference to a `List` object as a `private` instance variable. The list, stack and queue data structures in this chapter are implemented to store references to objects of any type to encourage further reusability.

Stack Class That Inherits from *List<T>*

Figures 21.10 and 21.11 create and manipulate a stack class that extends the `List<T>` class of Fig. 21.3. We want the stack to have methods `push`, `pop`, `isEmpty` and `print`. Essentially, these are the `List<T>` methods `insertAtFront`, `removeFromFront`, `isEmpty` and `print`. Of course, class `List<T>` contains other methods (such as `insertAtBack` and `removeFromBack`) that we would rather not make accessible through the `public` interface to the stack class. It's important to remember that all methods in `List<T>`'s `public` interface class also are `public` methods of the subclass `StackInheritance<T>` (Fig. 21.10). Each method of `StackInheritance<T>` calls the appropriate `List<T>` method—for example, method `push` calls `insertAtFront` and method `pop` calls `removeFromFront`. `StackInheritance<T>` clients can call methods `isEmpty` and `print` because they're inherited from `List<T>`. Class `StackInheritance<T>` is declared in package `com.deitel.datastructures` (line 3) for reuse. `StackInheritance<T>` does not import `List<T>`—the classes are in the same package.

Class `StackInheritanceTest`'s method `main` (Fig. 21.11) creates an object of class `StackInheritance<T>` called `stack` (line 10). The program pushes integers onto the stack (lines 13, 15, 17 and 19). *Autoboxing* is used here to insert `Integer` objects into the data

```
 1   // Fig. 21.10: StackInheritance.java
 2   // StackInheritance extends class List.
 3   package com.deitel.datastructures;
 4
 5   public class StackInheritance<T> extends List<T>
 6   {
 7      // constructor
 8      public StackInheritance()
 9      {
10         super("stack");
11      }
12
13      // add object to stack
14      public void push(T object)
15      {
16         insertAtFront(object);
17      }
18
19      // remove object from stack
20      public T pop() throws EmptyListException
21      {
22         return removeFromFront();
23      }
24   } // end class StackInheritance
```

Fig. 21.10 | StackInheritance extends class List.

structure. Lines 27–32 pop the objects from the stack in an infinite while loop. If method pop is invoked on an empty stack, the method throws an EmptyListException. In this case, the program displays the exception's stack trace, which shows the methods on the program-execution stack at the time the exception occurred. The program uses method print (inherited from List) to output the contents of the stack.

```
 1   // Fig. 21.11: StackInheritanceTest.java
 2   // Stack manipulation program.
 3   import com.deitel.datastructures.StackInheritance;
 4   import com.deitel.datastructures.EmptyListException;
 5
 6   public class StackInheritanceTest
 7   {
 8      public static void main(String[] args)
 9      {
10         StackInheritance<Integer> stack = new StackInheritance<>();
11
12         // use push method
13         stack.push(-1);
14         stack.print();
15         stack.push(0);
16         stack.print();
17         stack.push(1);
```

Fig. 21.11 | Stack manipulation program. (Part 1 of 2.)

```
18              stack.print();
19              stack.push(5);
20              stack.print();
21
22              // remove items from stack
23              try
24              {
25                  int removedItem;
26
27                  while (true)
28                  {
29                      removedItem = stack.pop(); // use pop method
30                      System.out.printf("%n%d popped%n", removedItem);
31                      stack.print();
32                  }
33              }
34              catch (EmptyListException emptyListException)
35              {
36                  emptyListException.printStackTrace();
37              }
38          }
39      } // end class StackInheritanceTest
```

```
The stack is: -1
The stack is: 0 -1

The stack is: 1  0 -1
The stack is: 5  1  0 -1

5 popped
The stack is: 1 0 -1

1 popped
The stack is: 0 -1

0 popped
The stack is: -1

-1 popped
Empty stack
com.deitel.datastructures.EmptyListException: stack is empty
        at com.deitel.datastructures.List.removeFromFront(List.java:81)
        at com.deitel.datastructures.StackInheritance.pop(
            StackInheritance.java:22)
        at StackInheritanceTest.main(StackInheritanceTest.java:29)
```

Fig. 21.11 | Stack manipulation program. (Part 2 of 2.)

Forming a Stack Class Via Composition Rather Than Inheritance

A better way to implement a stack class is by reusing a list class through *composition*. Figure 21.12 uses a private List<T> (line 7) in class StackComposition<T>'s declaration. Composition enables us to hide the List<T> methods that should not be in our stack's public interface. We provide public interface methods that use only the required List<T> methods. Implementing each stack method as a call to a List<T> method is called

delegation—the stack method invoked delegates the call to the appropriate List<T> method. In particular, StackComposition<T> delegates calls to List<T> methods insert-AtFront, removeFromFront, isEmpty and print. In this example, we do not show class StackCompositionTest, because the only difference is that we change the type of the stack from StackInheritance to StackComposition (lines 3 and 10 of Fig. 21.11).

```java
1   // Fig. 21.12: StackComposition.java
2   // StackComposition uses a composed List object.
3   package com.deitel.datastructures;
4
5   public class StackComposition<T>
6   {
7      private List<T> stackList;
8
9      // constructor
10     public StackComposition()
11     {
12        stackList = new List<T>("stack");
13     }
14
15     // add object to stack
16     public void push(T object)
17     {
18        stackList.insertAtFront(object);
19     }
20
21     // remove object from stack
22     public T pop() throws EmptyListException
23     {
24        return stackList.removeFromFront();
25     }
26
27     // determine if stack is empty
28     public boolean isEmpty()
29     {
30        return stackList.isEmpty();
31     }
32
33     // output stack contents
34     public void print()
35     {
36        stackList.print();
37     }
38  } // end class StackComposition
```

Fig. 21.12 | StackComposition uses a composed List object.

21.6 Queues

Another commonly used data structure is the queue. A queue is similar to a checkout line in a supermarket—the cashier services the person at the *beginning* of the line *first*. Other customers enter the line only at the end and wait for service. *Queue nodes are removed only from the head (or front) of the queue and are inserted only at the tail (or end).* For this reason, a queue is a **first-in, first-out** (FIFO) data structure. The insert and remove operations are known as **enqueue** and **dequeue**.

Queues have many uses in computer systems. Each CPU in a computer can service only one application at a time. Each application requiring processor time is placed in a queue. The application at the front of the queue is the next to receive service. Each application gradually advances to the front as the applications before it receive service.

Queues are also used to support **print spooling**. For example, a single printer might be shared by all users of a network. Many users can send print jobs to the printer, even when the printer is already busy. These print jobs are placed in a queue until the printer becomes available. A program called a **spooler** manages the queue to ensure that, as each print job completes, the next one is sent to the printer.

Information packets also *wait* in queues in computer networks. Each time a packet arrives at a network node, it must be routed to the next node along the path to the packet's final destination. The routing node routes one packet at a time, so additional packets are enqueued until the router can route them.

A file server in a computer network handles file-access requests from many clients throughout the network. Servers have a limited capacity to service requests from clients. When that capacity is exceeded, client requests *wait* in queues.

Figure 21.13 creates a Queue<T> class that contains a List<T> (Fig. 21.3) object and provides methods enqueue, dequeue, isEmpty and print. Class List<T> contains some methods (e.g., insertAtFront and removeFromBack) that we'd rather not make accessible through Queue<T>'s public interface. Using composition enables us to hide class List<T>'s other public methods from clients of class Queue<T>. Each Queue<T> method calls an appropriate List<T> method—method enqueue calls List<T> method insertAt-Back, method dequeue calls List<T> method removeFromFront, method isEmpty calls List<T> method isEmpty and method print calls List<T> method print. For reuse, class Queue<T> is declared in package com.deitel.datastructures.

```
 1   // Fig. 21.13: Queue.java
 2   // Queue uses class List.
 3   package com.deitel.datastructures;
 4
 5   public class Queue
 6   {
 7      private List<T> queueList;
 8
 9      // constructor
10      public Queue()
11      {
12         queueList = new List<T>("queue");
13      }
14
15      // add object to queue
16      public void enqueue(T object)
17      {
18         queueList.insertAtBack(object);
19      }
```

Fig. 21.13 | Queue uses class List. (Part 1 of 2.)

```
20
21          // remove object from queue
22          public T dequeue() throws EmptyListException
23          {
24              return queueList.removeFromFront();
25          }
26
27          // determine if queue is empty
28          public boolean isEmpty()
29          {
30              return queueList.isEmpty();
31          }
32
33          // output queue contents
34          public void print()
35          {
36              queueList.print();
37          }
38      } // end class Queue
```

Fig. 21.13 | Queue uses class List. (Part 2 of 2.)

Class QueueTest's (Fig. 21.14) main method creates and initializes Queue<T> variable queue (line 10). Lines 13, 15, 17 and 19 enqueue four integers, taking advantage of *auto-boxing* to insert Integer objects into the queue. Lines 27–32 use an infinite loop to dequeue the objects in first-in, first-out order. When the queue is empty, method dequeue throws an EmptyListException, and the program displays the exception's stack trace.

```
1       // Fig. 21.14: QueueTest.java
2       // Class QueueTest.
3       import com.deitel.datastructures.Queue;
4       import com.deitel.datastructures.EmptyListException;
5
6       public class QueueTest
7       {
8           public static void main(String[] args)
9           {
10              Queue<Integer> queue = new Queue<>();
11
12              // use enqueue method
13              queue.enqueue(-1);
14              queue.print();
15              queue.enqueue(0);
16              queue.print();
17              queue.enqueue(1);
18              queue.print();
19              queue.enqueue(5);
20              queue.print();
21
```

Fig. 21.14 | Queue processing program. (Part 1 of 2.)

```
22          // remove objects from queue
23          try
24          {
25              int removedItem;
26
27              while (true)
28              {
29                  removedItem = queue.dequeue(); // use dequeue method
30                  System.out.printf("%n%d dequeued%n", removedItem);
31                  queue.print();
32              }
33          }
34          catch (EmptyListException emptyListException)
35          {
36              emptyListException.printStackTrace();
37          }
38      }
39  } // end class QueueTest
```

```
The queue is: -1
The queue is: -1 0
The queue is: -1 0 1
The queue is: -1 0 1 5

-1 dequeued
The queue is: 0 1 5

0 dequeued
The queue is: 1 5

1 dequeued
The queue is: 5

5 dequeued
Empty queue
com.deitel.datastructures.EmptyListException: queue is empty
        at com.deitel.datastructures.List.removeFromFront(List.java:81)
        at com.deitel.datastructures.Queue.dequeue(Queue.java:24)
        at QueueTest.main(QueueTest.java:29)
```

Fig. 21.14 | Queue processing program. (Part 2 of 2.)

21.7 Trees

Lists, stacks and queues are **linear data structures** (i.e., **sequences**). A tree is a nonlinear, two-dimensional data structure with special properties. Tree nodes contain two or more links. This section discusses binary trees (Fig. 21.15)—trees whose nodes each contain two links (one or both of which may be null). The **root node** is the first node in a tree. Each link in the root node refers to a **child**. The **left child** is the first node in the **left subtree** (also known as the root node of the left subtree), and the **right child** is the first node in the **right subtree** (also known as the root node of the right subtree). The children of a specific node are called **siblings**. A node with no children is called a **leaf node**. Computer scientists normally draw trees from the root node down—the opposite of the way most trees grow in nature.

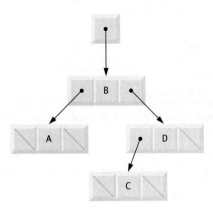

Fig. 21.15 | Binary tree graphical representation.

In our example, we create a special binary tree called a **binary search tree**. A binary search tree (with no duplicate node values) has the characteristic that the values in any left subtree are less than the value in that subtree's parent node, and the values in any right subtree are greater than the value in that subtree's parent node. Figure 21.16 illustrates a binary search tree with 12 integer values. The shape of the binary search tree that corresponds to a set of data can vary, depending on the order in which the values are inserted into the tree.

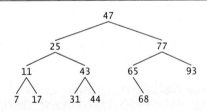

Fig. 21.16 | Binary search tree containing 12 values.

Figures 21.17 and 21.18 create a generic binary search tree class and use it to manipulate a tree of integers. The application in Fig. 21.18 *traverses* the tree (i.e., walks through all its nodes) three ways—using recursive **inorder, preorder** and **postorder** traversals (trees are almost always processed recursively). The program generates 10 random numbers and inserts each into the tree. Class Tree<T> is declared in package com.deitel.datastructures for reuse.

```
1   // Fig. 21.17: Tree.java
2   // TreeNode and Tree class declarations for a binary search tree.
3   package com.deitel.datastructures;
4
```

Fig. 21.17 | TreeNode and Tree class declarations for a binary search tree. (Part 1 of 4.)

```
 5    // class TreeNode definition
 6    class TreeNode<T extends Comparable<T>>
 7    {
 8       // package access members
 9       TreeNode<T> leftNode;
10       T data; // node value
11       TreeNode<T> rightNode;
12
13       // constructor initializes data and makes this a leaf node
14       public TreeNode(T nodeData)
15       {
16          data = nodeData;
17          leftNode = rightNode = null; // node has no children
18       }
19
20       // locate insertion point and insert new node; ignore duplicate values
21       public void insert(T insertValue)
22       {
23          // insert in left subtree
24          if (insertValue.compareTo(data) < 0)
25          {
26             // insert new TreeNode
27             if (leftNode == null)
28                leftNode = new TreeNode<T>(insertValue);
29             else // continue traversing left subtree recursively
30                leftNode.insert(insertValue);
31          }
32          // insert in right subtree
33          else if (insertValue.compareTo(data) > 0)
34          {
35             // insert new TreeNode
36             if (rightNode == null)
37                rightNode = new TreeNode<T>(insertValue);
38             else // continue traversing right subtree recursively
39                rightNode.insert(insertValue);
40          }
41       }
42    } // end class TreeNode
43
44    // class Tree definition
45    public class Tree<T extends Comparable<T>>
46    {
47       private TreeNode<T> root;
48
49       // constructor initializes an empty Tree of integers
50       public Tree()
51       {
52          root = null;
53       }
54
55       // insert a new node in the binary search tree
56       public void insertNode(T insertValue)
57       {
```

Fig. 21.17 | TreeNode and Tree class declarations for a binary search tree. (Part 2 of 4.)

```
58          if (root == null)
59             root = new TreeNode<T>(insertValue); // create root node
60          else
61             root.insert(insertValue); // call the insert method
62       }
63
64       // begin preorder traversal
65       public void preorderTraversal()
66       {
67          preorderHelper(root);
68       }
69
70       // recursive method to perform preorder traversal
71       private void preorderHelper(TreeNode<T> node)
72       {
73          if (node == null)
74             return;
75
76          System.out.printf("%s ", node.data); // output node data
77          preorderHelper(node.leftNode); // traverse left subtree
78          preorderHelper(node.rightNode); // traverse right subtree
79       }
80
81       // begin inorder traversal
82       public void inorderTraversal()
83       {
84          inorderHelper(root);
85       }
86
87       // recursive method to perform inorder traversal
88       private void inorderHelper(TreeNode<T> node)
89       {
90          if (node == null)
91             return;
92
93          inorderHelper(node.leftNode); // traverse left subtree
94          System.out.printf("%s ", node.data); // output node data
95          inorderHelper(node.rightNode); // traverse right subtree
96       }
97
98       // begin postorder traversal
99       public void postorderTraversal()
100      {
101         postorderHelper(root);
102      }
103
104      // recursive method to perform postorder traversal
105      private void postorderHelper(TreeNode<T> node)
106      {
107         if (node == null)
108            return;
109
```

Fig. 21.17 | TreeNode and Tree class declarations for a binary search tree. (Part 3 of 4.)

```
110          postorderHelper(node.leftNode); // traverse left subtree
111          postorderHelper(node.rightNode); // traverse right subtree
112          System.out.printf("%s ", node.data); // output node data
113       }
114    } // end class Tree
```

Fig. 21.17 | TreeNode and Tree class declarations for a binary search tree. (Part 4 of 4.)

```
1    // Fig. 21.18: TreeTest.java
2    // Binary tree test program.
3    import java.security.SecureRandom;
4    import com.deitel.datastructures.Tree;
5
6    public class TreeTest
7    {
8       public static void main(String[] args)
9       {
10         Tree<Integer> tree = new Tree<Integer>();
11         SecureRandom randomNumber = new SecureRandom();
12
13         System.out.println("Inserting the following values: ");
14
15         // insert 10 random integers from 0-99 in tree
16         for (int i = 1; i <= 10; i++)
17         {
18            int value = randomNumber.nextInt(100);
19            System.out.printf("%d ", value);
20            tree.insertNode(value);
21         }
22
23         System.out.printf("%n%nPreorder traversal%n");
24         tree.preorderTraversal();
25
26         System.out.printf("%n%nInorder traversal%n");
27         tree.inorderTraversal();
28
29         System.out.printf("%n%nPostorder traversal%n");
30         tree.postorderTraversal();
31         System.out.println();
32      }
33   } // end class TreeTest
```

```
Inserting the following values:
49 64 14 34 85 64 46 14 37 55

Preorder traversal
49 14 34 46 37 64 55 85

Inorder traversal
14 34 37 46 49 55 64 85

Postorder traversal
37 46 34 14 55 85 64 49
```

Fig. 21.18 | Binary tree test program.

Let's walk through the binary tree program. Method `main` of class `TreeTest` (Fig. 21.18) begins by instantiating an empty `Tree<T>` object and assigning its reference to variable `tree` (line 10). Lines 16–21 randomly generate 10 integers, each of which is inserted into the binary tree by calling method `insertNode` (line 20). The program then performs preorder, inorder and postorder traversals (these will be explained shortly) of `tree` (lines 24, 27 and 30, respectively).

Overview of Class **Tree**
Class `Tree` (Fig. 21.17, lines 45–114) requires its type argument to implement interface `Comparable`, so that each value inserted in the tree can be *compared* with the existing values to find the insertion point. The class has `private` field `root` (line 47)—a `TreeNode` reference to the root node of the tree. `Tree`'s constructor (lines 50–53) initializes `root` to `null` to indicate that the tree is *empty*. The class contains method `insertNode` (lines 56–62) to insert a new node in the tree and methods `preorderTraversal` (lines 65–68), `inorder-Traversal` (lines 82–85) and `postorderTraversal` (lines 99–102) to begin traversals of the tree. Each of these methods calls a recursive utility method to perform the traversal operations on the internal representation of the tree.

Tree Method **insertNode**
Class `Tree`'s method `insertNode` (lines 56–62) first determines whether the tree is empty. If so, line 59 allocates a new `TreeNode`, initializes the node with the value being inserted in the tree and assigns the new node to reference `root`. If the tree is not empty, line 61 calls `TreeNode` method `insert` (lines 21–41). This method uses recursion to determine the location for the new node in the tree and inserts the node at that location. A node can be inserted only as a leaf node in a binary search tree.

TreeNode Method **insert**
`TreeNode` method `insert` compares the value to insert with the `data` value in the root node. If the insert value is less than the root node data (line 24), the program determines whether the left subtree is empty (line 27). If so, line 28 allocates a new `TreeNode`, initializes it with the value being inserted and assigns the new node to reference `leftNode`. Otherwise, line 30 recursively calls `insert` for the left subtree to insert the value into the left subtree. If the insert value is greater than the root node data (line 33), the program determines whether the right subtree is empty (line 36). If so, line 37 allocates a new `TreeNode`, initializes it with the value being inserted and assigns the new node to reference `right-Node`. Otherwise, line 39 recursively calls `insert` for the right subtree to insert the value in the right subtree. If the `insertValue` is already in the tree, it's simply ignored.

Tree Methods **inorderTraversal**, **preorderTraversal** *and* **postorderTraversal**
Methods `inorderTraversal`, `preorderTraversal` and `postorderTraversal` call `Tree` helper methods `inorderHelper` (lines 88–96), `preorderHelper` (lines 71–79) and `post-orderHelper` (lines 105–113), respectively, to traverse the tree and print the node values. The helper methods in class `Tree` enable you to start a traversal without having to pass the root node to the method. Reference `root` is an *implementation detail* that a programmer should not be able to access. Methods `inorderTraversal`, `preorderTraversal` and `postorderTraversal` simply take the private `root` reference and pass it to the appropriate helper method to initiate a traversal of the tree. The base case for each helper method determines whether the reference it receives is `null` and, if so, returns immediately.

Method `inorderHelper` (lines 88–96) defines the steps for an inorder traversal:

1. Traverse the left subtree with a call to `inorderHelper` (line 93).

2. Process the value in the node (line 94).

3. Traverse the right subtree with a call to `inorderHelper` (line 95).

The inorder traversal does not process the value in a node until the values in that node's left subtree are processed. The inorder traversal of the tree in Fig. 21.19 is

6 13 17 27 33 42 48

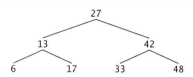

Fig. 21.19 | Binary search tree with seven values.

The inorder traversal of a binary search tree prints the node values in *ascending order*. The process of creating a binary search tree actually sorts the data; thus, it's called the **binary tree sort**.

Method `preorderHelper` (lines 71–79) defines the steps for a preorder traversal:

1. Process the value in the node (line 76).

2. Traverse the left subtree with a call to `preorderHelper` (line 77).

3. Traverse the right subtree with a call to `preorderHelper` (line 78).

The preorder traversal processes the value in each node as the node is visited. After processing the value in a particular node, it processes the values in the left subtree, then processes the values in the right subtree. The preorder traversal of the tree in Fig. 21.19 is

27 13 6 17 42 33 48

Method `postorderHelper` (lines 105–113) defines the steps for a postorder traversal:

1. Traverse the left subtree with a call to `postorderHelper` (line 110).

2. Traverse the right subtree with a call to `postorderHelper` (line 111).

3. Process the value in the node (line 112).

The postorder traversal processes the value in each node after the values of all that node's children are processed. The `postorderTraversal` of the tree in Fig. 21.19 is

6 17 13 33 48 42 27

The binary search tree facilitates **duplicate elimination**. While building a tree, the insertion operation recognizes attempts to insert a duplicate value, because a duplicate follows the same "go left" or "go right" decisions on each comparison as the original value did. Thus, the insertion operation eventually compares the duplicate with a node containing the same value. At this point, the insertion operation can decide to *discard* the duplicate value (as we do in this example).

Searching a binary tree for a value that matches a key value is fast, especially for **tightly packed** (or **balanced**) **trees**. In a tightly packed tree, each level contains about twice as many elements as the previous level. Figure 21.19 is a tightly packed binary tree. A tightly packed binary search tree with n elements has $\log_2 n$ levels. Thus, at most $\log_2 n$ comparisons are required either to find a match or to determine that no match exists. Searching a (tightly packed) 1000-element binary search tree requires at most 10 comparisons, because $2^{10} > 1000$. Searching a (tightly packed) 1,000,000-element binary search tree requires at most 20 comparisons, because $2^{20} > 1,000,000$.

The chapter exercises present algorithms for several other binary tree operations, such as deleting an item from a binary tree, printing a binary tree in a two-dimensional tree format and performing a **level-order traversal of a binary tree**. The level-order traversal visits the nodes of the tree row by row, starting at the root node level. On each level of the tree, a level-order traversal visits the nodes from left to right. Other binary tree exercises include allowing a binary search tree to contain duplicate values, inserting string values in a binary tree and determining how many levels are contained in a binary tree.

21.8 Wrap-Up

This chapter completes our presentation of data structures. We began in Chapter 16 with an introduction to the built-in collections of the Java Collections Framework and continued in Chapter 20 by showing you how to implement generic methods and collections. In this chapter, you learned to build generic dynamic data structures that grow and shrink at execution time. You learned that linked lists are collections of data items that are "linked up in a chain." You also saw that an application can perform insertions and deletions at the beginning and end of a linked list. You learned that the stack and queue data structures are constrained versions of lists. For stacks, you saw that insertions and deletions are made only at the top. For queues that represent waiting lines, you saw that insertions are made at the tail and deletions are made from the head. You also learned the binary tree data structure. You saw a binary search tree that facilitated high-speed searching and sorting of data and eliminating duplicate data items efficiently. Throughout the chapter, you learned how to create and package these data structures for reusability and maintainability.

In the next chapter, you'll continue your study of Swing GUI concepts, building on the techniques you learned in Chapter 12. In Chapter 25, we'll introduce JavaFX GUI and include in-depth treatments of JavaFX GUI, graphics and multimedia in the online chapters.

Summary

Section 21.1 Introduction
- Dynamic data structures (p. 862) can grow and shrink at execution time.
- Linked lists (p. 862) are collections of data items "linked up in a chain"—insertions and deletions can be made anywhere in a linked list.
- Stacks (p. 862) are important in compilers and operating systems—insertions and deletions are made only at the top (p. 862) of a stack.
- In a queue, insertions are made at the tail (p. 862) and deletions are made from the head (p. 862).
- Binary trees (p. 862) facilitate high-speed searching and sorting, eliminating duplicate data items efficiently, representing file-system directories and compiling expressions into machine language.

Section 21.2 Self-Referential Classes

- A self-referential class (p. 863) contains a reference that refers to another object of the same class type. Self-referential objects can be linked together to form dynamic data structures.

Section 21.3 Dynamic Memory Allocation

- The limit for dynamic memory allocation (p. 863) can be as large as the available physical memory in the computer or the available disk space in a virtual-memory system. Often the limits are much smaller, because the computer's available memory must be shared among many users.

- If no memory is available, an OutOfMemoryError is thrown.

Section 21.4 Linked Lists

- A linked list is accessed via a reference to the first node of the list. Each subsequent node is accessed via the link-reference member stored in the previous node.

- By convention, the link reference in the last node of a list is set to null to mark the end of the list.

- A node can contain data of any type, including objects of other classes.

- A linked list is appropriate when the number of data elements to be stored is unpredictable. Linked lists are dynamic, so the length of a list can increase or decrease as necessary.

- The size of a "conventional" Java array cannot be altered—it's fixed at creation time.

- List nodes normally are not stored in contiguous memory. Rather, they're logically contiguous.

- Packages help manage program components and facilitate software reuse.

- Packages provide a convention for unique type names that helps prevent naming conflicts (p. 876).

- Before a type can be imported into multiple programs, it must be placed in a package. There can be only one package declaration (p. 875) in each Java source-code file, and it must precede all other declarations and statements in the file.

- Every package name should start with your Internet domain name in reverse order. After the domain name is reversed, you can choose any other names you want for your package.

- When compiling types in a package, the javac command-line option -d (p. 876) specifies where to store the package and causes the compiler to create the package's directories if they do not exist.

- The package name is part of the fully qualified type name (p. 876).

- A single-type-import declaration (p. 877) specifies one class to import. A type-import-on-demand declaration (p. 877) imports only the classes that the program uses from a particular package.

- The compiler uses a class loader (p. 877) to locate the classes it needs in the classpath. The classpath consists of a list of directories or archive files, each separated by a directory separator (p. 877).

- The classpath for the compiler and JVM can be specified by providing the -classpath option (p. 878) to the javac or java command, or by setting the CLASSPATH environment variable. If classes must be loaded from the current directory, include a dot (.) in the classpath.

Section 21.5 Stacks

- A stack is a last-in, first-out (LIFO) data structure (p. 878). The primary methods used to manipulate a stack are push (p. 879) and pop (p. 879), which add a new node to the stack's top and remove a node from the top, respectively. Method pop returns the removed node's data.

- When a method call is made, the called method must know how to return to its caller, so the return address is pushed onto the program-execution stack. If a series of method calls occurs, the successive return values are pushed onto the stack in last-in, first-out order.

- The program-execution stack contains the space created for local variables on each invocation of a method. When the method returns to its caller, the space for that method's local variables is popped off the stack, and those variables are no longer available to the program.

- Stacks are used by compilers to evaluate arithmetic expressions and generate machine-language code to process the expressions.

- The technique of implementing each stack method as a call to a List method is called delegation—the stack method invoked delegates (p. 882) the call to the appropriate List method.

Section 21.6 Queues

- A queue (p. 890) is similar to a checkout line in a supermarket—the first person in line is serviced first, and other customers enter the line only at the end and wait to be serviced.

- Queue nodes are removed only from the head (p. 890) of the queue and are inserted only at the tail. For this reason, a queue is referred to as a first-in, first-out FIFOaaaa data structure.

- The insert and remove operations for a queue are known as enqueue (p. 883) and dequeue (p. 883).

- Queues have many uses in computer systems. Most computers have only a single processor, so only one application at a time can be serviced. Entries for the other applications are placed in a queue. The entry at the front of the queue is the next to receive service. Each entry gradually advances to the front of the queue as applications receive service.

Section 21.7 Trees

- A tree is a nonlinear, two-dimensional data structure. Tree nodes contain two or more links.

- A binary tree (p. 885) is a tree whose nodes all contain two links. The root node (p. 885) is the first node in a tree.

- Each link in the root node refers to a child (p. 885). The left child (p. 885) is the first node in the left subtree (p. 885), and the right child (p. 885) is the first node in the right subtree (p. 885).

- The children of a node are called siblings (p. 885). A node with no children is a leaf node (p. 885).

- In a binary search tree (p. 886) with no duplicate values, the values in any left subtree are less than the value in the subtree's parent node, and the values in any right subtree are greater than the value in the subtree's parent node. A node can be inserted only as a leaf node in a binary search tree.

- An inorder traversal (p. 886) of a binary search tree processes the node values in ascending order.

- In a preorder traversal (p. 886), the value in each node is processed as the node is visited. Then the values in the left subtree are processed, then the values in the right subtree.

- In a postorder traversal (p. 886), the value in each node is processed after the values of its children.

- The binary search tree facilitates duplicate elimination (p. 891). As the tree is created, attempts to insert a duplicate value are recognized, because a duplicate follows the same "go left" or "go right" decisions on each comparison as the original value did. Thus, the duplicate eventually is compared with a node containing the same value. The duplicate value can be discarded at this point.

- In a tightly packed tree (p. 892), each level contains about twice as many elements as the previous one. So a tightly packed binary search tree with n elements has $\log_2 n$ levels, and thus at most $\log_2 n$ comparisons would have to be made either to find a match or to determine that no match exists. Searching a (tightly packed) 1000-element binary search tree requires at most 10 comparisons, because $2^{10} > 1000$. Searching a (tightly packed) 1,000,000-element binary search tree requires at most 20 comparisons, because $2^{20} > 1,000,000$.

Self-Review Exercises

21.1 Fill in the blanks in each of the following statements:

    a) A self-_____ class is used to form dynamic data structures that can grow and shrink at execution time.

b) A(n) _____ is a constrained version of a linked list in which nodes can be inserted and deleted only from the start of the list.

c) A method that does not alter a linked list, but simply looks at it to determine whether it's empty, is referred to as a(n) _____ method.

d) A queue is referred to as a(n) _____ data structure because the first nodes inserted are the first ones removed.

e) The reference to the next node in a linked list is referred to as a(n) _____.

f) Automatically reclaiming dynamically allocated memory in Java is called _____.

g) A(n) _____ is a constrained version of a linked list in which nodes can be inserted only at the end of the list and deleted only from the start of the list.

h) A(n) _____ is a nonlinear, two-dimensional data structure that contains nodes with two or more links.

i) A stack is referred to as a(n) _____ data structure because the last node inserted is the first node removed.

j) The nodes of a(n) _____ tree contain two link members.

k) The first node of a tree is the _____ node.

l) Each link in a tree node refers to a(n) _____ or _____ of that node.

m) A tree node that has no children is called a(n) _____ node.

n) The three traversal algorithms we mentioned in the text for binary search trees are _____, _____ and _____.

o) When compiling types in a package, the javac command-line option _____ specifies where to store the package and causes the compiler to create the package's directories if they do not exist.

p) The compiler uses a(n) _____ to locate the classes it needs in the classpath.

q) The classpath for the compiler and JVM can be specified with the _____ option to the javac or java command, or by setting the _____ environment variable.

r) There can be only one _____ in a Java source-code file, and it must precede all other declarations and statements in the file.

21.2 What are the differences between a linked list and a stack?

21.3 What are the differences between a stack and a queue?

21.4 Comment on how each of the following entities or concepts contributes to the reusability of data structures:
a) classes
b) inheritance
c) composition

21.5 Provide the inorder, preorder and postorder traversals of the binary search tree of Fig. 21.20.

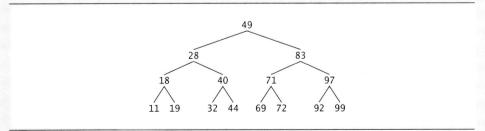

Fig. 21.20 | Binary search tree with 15 nodes.

Answers to Self-Review Exercises

21.1 a) referential. b) stack. c) predicate. d) first-in, first-out (FIFO). e) link. f) garbage collection. g) queue. h) tree i) last-in, first-out (LIFO). j) binary. k) root. l) child or subtree. m) leaf. n) inorder, preorder, postorder. o) -d. p) class loader. q) -classpath, CLASSPATH. r) package declaration.

21.2 It's possible to insert a node anywhere in a linked list and remove a node from anywhere in a linked list. Nodes in a stack may be inserted only at the top of the stack and removed only from the top.

21.3 A queue is a FIFO data structure that has references to both its head and its tail, so that nodes may be inserted at the tail and deleted from the head. A stack is a LIFO data structure that has a single reference to the stack's top, where both insertion and deletion of nodes are performed.

21.4 a) Classes allow us to create as many data structure objects as we wish.
   b) Inheritance enables a subclass to reuse the functionality from a superclass. Public and protected superclass methods can be accessed through a subclass to eliminate duplicate logic.
   c) Composition enables a class to reuse code by storing a reference to an instance of another class in a field. Public methods of the instance can be called by methods in the class that contains the reference.

21.5 The inorder traversal is

    11 18 19 28 32 40 44 49 69 71 72 83 92 97 99

The preorder traversal is

    49 28 18 11 19 40 32 44 83 71 69 72 97 92 99

The postorder traversal is

    11 19 18 32 44 40 28 69 72 71 92 99 97 83 49

Exercises

21.6 *(Concatenating Lists)* Write a program that concatenates two linked list objects of characters. Class ListConcatenate should include a static method concatenate that takes references to both list objects as arguments and concatenates the second list to the first list.

21.7 *(Inserting into an Ordered List)* Write a program that inserts 25 random integers from 0 to 100 in order into a linked-list object. For this exercise, you'll need to modify the List<T> class (Fig. 21.3) to maintain an ordered list. Name the new version of the class SortedList.

21.8 *(Merging Ordered Lists)* Modify the SortedList class from Exercise 21.7 to include a merge method that can merge the SortedList it receives as an argument with the SortedList that calls the method. Write an application to test method merge.

21.9 *(Copying a List Backward)* Write a static method reverseCopy that receives a List<T> as an argument and returns a copy of that List<T> with its elements reversed. Test this method in an application.

21.10 *(Printing a Sentence in Reverse Using a Stack)* Write a program that inputs a line of text and uses a stack to display the words of the line in reverse order.

21.11 *(Palindrome Tester)* Write a program that uses a stack to determine whether a string is a palindrome (i.e., the string is spelled identically backward and forward). The program should ignore spaces and punctuation.

21.12 *(Infix-to-Postfix Converter)* Stacks are used by compilers to help in the process of evaluating expressions and generating machine-language code. In this and the next exercise, we investigate how compilers evaluate arithmetic expressions consisting only of constants, operators and parentheses.

Humans generally write expressions like 3 + 4 and 7 / 9 in which the operator (+ or / here) is written between its operands—this is called *infix notation*. Computers "prefer" *postfix notation*, in which the operator is written to the right of its two operands. The preceding infix expressions would appear in postfix notation as 3 4 + and 7 9 /, respectively.

To evaluate a complex infix expression, a compiler would first convert the expression to postfix notation and evaluate the postfix version. Each of these algorithms requires only a single left-to-right pass of the expression. Each algorithm uses a stack object in support of its operation, but each uses the stack for a different purpose.

In this exercise, you'll write a Java version of the infix-to-postfix conversion algorithm. In the next exercise, you'll write a Java version of the postfix expression evaluation algorithm. In a later exercise, you'll discover that code you write in this exercise can help you implement a complete working compiler.

Write class `InfixToPostfixConverter` to convert an ordinary infix arithmetic expression (assume a valid expression is entered) with single-digit integers such as

```
(6 + 2) * 5 - 8 / 4
```

to a postfix expression. The postfix version (no parentheses are needed) of the this infix expression is

```
6 2 + 5 * 8 4 / -
```

The program should read the expression into `StringBuffer infix` and use one of the stack classes implemented in this chapter to help create the postfix expression in `StringBuffer postfix`. The algorithm for creating a postfix expression is as follows:

a) Push a left parenthesis `'('` onto the stack.
b) Append a right parenthesis `')'` to the end of `infix`.
c) While the stack is not empty, read `infix` from left to right and do the following:
  If the current character in `infix` is a digit, append it to `postfix`.
  If the current character in `infix` is a left parenthesis, push it onto the stack.
  If the current character in `infix` is an operator:
      Pop operators (if there are any) at the top of the stack while they have equal
          or higher precedence than the current operator, and append the popped
          operators to `postfix`.
      Push the current character in `infix` onto the stack.
  If the current character in `infix` is a right parenthesis:
      Pop operators from the top of the stack and append them to `postfix` until
          a left parenthesis is at the top of the stack.
      Pop (and discard) the left parenthesis from the stack.

The following arithmetic operations are allowed in an expression:

+ addition
- subtraction
* multiplication
/ division
^ exponentiation
% remainder

The stack should be maintained with stack nodes that each contain an instance variable and a reference to the next stack node. Some methods you may want to provide are as follows:

a) Method `convertToPostfix`, which converts the infix expression to postfix notation.
b) Method `isOperator`, which determines whether c is an operator.

c) Method `precedence`, which determines whether the precedence of `operator1` (from the infix expression) is less than, equal to or greater than that of `operator2` (from the stack). The method returns `true` if `operator1` has lower precedence than `operator2`. Otherwise, `false` is returned.

d) Method `peek` (this should be added to the stack class), which returns the top value of the stack without popping the stack.

21.13 *(Postfix Evaluator)* Write class `PostfixEvaluator` that evaluates a postfix expression such as

```
6 2 + 5 * 8 4 / -
```

The program should read a postfix expression consisting of digits and operators into a `StringBuffer`. Using modified versions of the stack methods implemented earlier in this chapter, the program should scan the expression and evaluate it (assume it's valid). The algorithm is as follows:

a) Append a right parenthesis `')'` to the end of the postfix expression. When the right-parenthesis character is encountered, no further processing is necessary.

b) Until the right parenthesis is encountered, read the expression from left to right.
   If the current character is a digit, do the following:
       Push its integer value onto the stack (the integer value of a digit character is its value in the Unicode character set minus the value of `'0'` in Unicode).
   Otherwise, if the current character is an *operator*:
       Pop the two top elements of the stack into variables `x` and `y`.
       Calculate `y` *operator* `x`.
       Push the result of the calculation onto the stack.

c) When the right parenthesis is encountered in the expression, pop the top value of the stack. This is the result of the postfix expression.

[*Note:* In b) above (based on the sample expression at the beginning of this exercise), if the operator is `'/'`, the top of the stack is 4 and the next element in the stack is 40, then pop 4 into x, pop 40 into y, evaluate 40 / 4 and push the result, 10, back on the stack. This note also applies to operator `'-'`.] The arithmetic operations allowed in an expression are: + (addition), - (subtraction), * (multiplication), / (division), ∧ (exponentiation) and % (remainder).

The stack should be maintained with one of the stack classes introduced in this chapter. You may want to provide the following methods:

a) Method `evaluatePostfixExpression`, which evaluates the postfix expression.

b) Method `calculate`, which evaluates the expression op1 operator op2.

21.14 *(Postfix Evaluator Modification)* Modify the postfix evaluator program of Exercise 21.13 so that it can process integer operands larger than 9.

21.15 *(Supermarket Simulation)* Write a program that simulates a checkout line at a supermarket. The line is a queue object. Customers (i.e., customer objects) arrive in random integer intervals of from 1 to 4 minutes. Also, each customer is serviced in random integer intervals of from 1 to 4 minutes. Obviously, the rates need to be balanced. If the average arrival rate is larger than the average service rate, the queue will grow infinitely. Even with "balanced" rates, randomness can still cause long lines. Run the supermarket simulation for a 12-hour day (720 minutes), using the following algorithm:

a) Choose a random integer between 1 and 4 to determine the minute at which the first customer arrives.

b) At the first customer's arrival time, do the following:
   Determine customer's service time (random integer from 1 to 4).
   Begin servicing the customer.
   Schedule arrival time of next customer (random integer 1 to 4 added to the current time).

    c) For each simulated minute of the day, consider the following:

        If the next customer arrives, proceed as follows:

            Say so.

            Enqueue the customer.

            Schedule the arrival time of the next customer.

        If service was completed for the last customer, do the following:

            Say so.

            Dequeue next customer to be serviced.

            Determine customer's service completion time (random integer from 1 to 4 added to the current time).

Now run your simulation for 720 minutes and answer each of the following:

    a) What is the maximum number of customers in the queue at any time?

    b) What is the longest wait any one customer experiences?

    c) What happens if the arrival interval is changed from 1 to 4 minutes to 1 to 3 minutes?

21.16 *(Allowing Duplicates in a Binary Tree)* Modify Figs. 21.17 and 21.18 to allow the binary tree to contain duplicates.

21.17 *(Processing a Binary Search Tree of Strings)* Write a program based on the program of Figs. 21.17 and 21.18 that inputs a line of text, tokenizes it into separate words, inserts the words in a binary search tree and prints the inorder, preorder and postorder traversals of the tree.

21.18 *(Duplicate Elimination)* In this chapter, we saw that duplicate elimination is straightforward when creating a binary search tree. Describe how you'd perform duplicate elimination when using only a one-dimensional array. Compare the performance of array-based duplicate elimination with the performance of binary-search-tree-based duplicate elimination.

21.19 *(Depth of a Binary Tree)* Modify Figs. 21.17 and 21.18 so the Tree class provides a method getDepth that determines how many levels are in the tree. Test the method in an application that inserts 20 random integers in a Tree.

21.20 *(Recursively Print a List Backward)* Modify the List<T> class of Fig. 21.3 to include method printListBackward that recursively outputs the items in a linked-list object in reverse order. Write a test program that creates a list of integers and prints the list in reverse order.

21.21 *(Recursively Search a List)* Modify the List<T> class of Fig. 21.3 to include method search that recursively searches a linked-list object for a specified value. The method should return a reference to the value if it's found; otherwise, it should return null. Use your method in a test program that creates a list of integers. The program should prompt the user for a value to locate in the list.

21.22 *(Binary Tree Delete)* In this exercise, we discuss deleting items from binary search trees. The deletion algorithm is not as straightforward as the insertion algorithm. Three cases are encountered when deleting an item—the item is contained in a leaf node (i.e., it has no children), or in a node that has one child or in a node that has two children.

    If the item to be deleted is contained in a leaf node, the node is deleted and the reference in the parent node is set to null.

    If the item to be deleted is contained in a node with one child, the reference in the parent node is set to reference the child node and the node containing the data item is deleted. This causes the child node to take the place of the deleted node in the tree.

    The last case is the most difficult. When a node with two children is deleted, another node in the tree must take its place. However, the reference in the parent node cannot simply be assigned to reference one of the children of the node to be deleted. In most cases, the resulting binary search tree would not embody the following characteristic of binary search trees (with no duplicate values): *The values in any left subtree are less than the value in the parent node, and the values in any right subtree are greater than the value in the parent node.*

Which node is used as a *replacement node* to maintain this characteristic? It's either the node containing the largest value in the tree less than the value in the node being deleted, or the node containing the smallest value in the tree greater than the value in the node being deleted. Let's consider the node with the smaller value. In a binary search tree, the largest value less than a parent's value is located in the left subtree of the parent node and is guaranteed to be contained in the rightmost node of the subtree. This node is located by walking down the left subtree to the right until the reference to the right child of the current node is null. We're now referencing the replacement node, which is either a leaf node or a node with one child to its left. If the replacement node is a leaf node, the steps to perform the deletion are as follows:

a) Store the reference to the node to be deleted in a temporary reference variable.

b) Set the reference in the parent of the node being deleted to reference the replacement node.

c) Set the reference in the parent of the replacement node to null.

d) Set the reference to the right subtree in the replacement node to reference the right subtree of the node to be deleted.

e) Set the reference to the left subtree in the replacement node to reference the left subtree of the node to be deleted.

The deletion steps for a replacement node with a left child are similar to those for a replacement node with no children, but the algorithm also must move the child into the replacement node's position in the tree. If the replacement node is a node with a left child, the steps to perform the deletion are as follows:

a) Store the reference to the node to be deleted in a temporary reference variable.

b) Set the reference in the parent of the node being deleted to refer to the replacement node.

c) Set the reference in the parent of the replacement node to reference the left child of the replacement node.

d) Set the reference to the right subtree in the replacement node to reference the right subtree of the node to be deleted.

e) Set the reference to the left subtree in the replacement node to reference the left subtree of the node to be deleted.

Write method `deleteNode`, which takes as its argument the value to delete. Method `deleteNode` should locate in the tree the node containing the value to delete and use the algorithms discussed here to delete the node. If the value is not found in the tree, the method should display a message saying so. Modify the program of Figs. 21.17 and 21.18 to use this method. After deleting an item, call the methods `inorderTraversal`, `preorderTraversal` and `postorderTraversal` to confirm that the delete operation was performed correctly.

21.23 *(Binary Tree Search)* Modify class `Tree` of Fig. 21.17 to include method `contains`, which attempts to locate a specified value in a binary-search-tree object. The method should take as an argument a search key to locate. If the node containing the search key is found, the method should return a reference to that node's data; otherwise, it should return `null`.

21.24 *(Level-Order Binary Tree Traversal)* The program of Figs. 21.17 and 21.18 illustrated three recursive methods of traversing a binary tree—inorder, preorder and postorder traversals. This exercise presents the *level-order traversal* of a binary tree, in which the node values are printed level by level, starting at the root node level. The nodes on each level are printed from left to right. The level-order traversal is not a recursive algorithm. It uses a queue object to control the output of the nodes. The algorithm is as follows:

a) Insert the root node in the queue.

b) While there are nodes left in the queue, do the following:
Get the next node in the queue.
Print the node's value.
If the reference to the left child of the node is not null:
    Insert the left child node in the queue.
If the reference to the right child of the node is not null:
    Insert the right child node in the queue.

Write method `levelOrder` to perform a level-order traversal of a binary tree object. Modify the program of Figs. 21.17 and 21.18 to use this method. [*Note:* You'll also need to use the queue-processing methods of Fig. 21.13 in this program.]

21.25 *(Printing Trees)* Modify class `Tree` of Fig. 21.17 to include a recursive `outputTree` method to display a binary tree object. The method should output the tree row by row, with the top of the tree at the left of the screen and the bottom of the tree toward the right. Each row is output vertically. For example, the binary tree illustrated in Fig. 21.20 is output as shown in Fig. 21.21.

The rightmost leaf node appears at the top of the output in the rightmost column and the root node appears at the left of the output. Each column starts five spaces to the right of the preceding column. Method `outputTree` should receive an argument `totalSpaces` representing the number of spaces preceding the value to be output. (This variable should start at zero so that the root node is output at the left of the screen.) The method uses a modified inorder traversal to output the tree—it starts at the rightmost node in the tree and works back to the left. The algorithm is as follows:

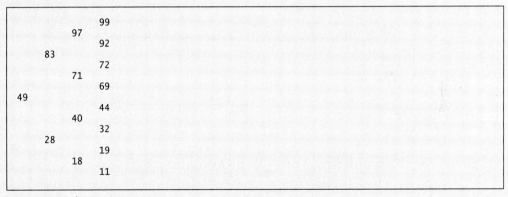

Fig. 21.21 | Sample output of recursive method `outputTree`.

While the reference to the current node is not null, perform the following:
    Recursively call `outputTree` with the right subtree of the current node and
        `totalSpaces + 5`.
    Use a `for` statement to count from 1 to `totalSpaces` and output spaces.
    Output the value in the current node.
    Set the reference to the current node to refer to the left subtree of the current node.
    Increment `totalSpaces` by 5.

21.26 *(Insert/Delete Anywhere in a Linked List)* Our linked-list class allowed insertions and deletions at only the front and the back of the linked list. These capabilities were convenient for us when we used inheritance or composition to produce a stack class and a queue class with minimal code simply by reusing the list class. Linked lists are normally more general than those we provided. Modify the linked-list class we developed in this chapter to handle insertions and deletions *anywhere* in the list. Create diagrams comparable to Figs. 21.6 (`insertAtFront`), 21.7 (`insertAtBack`), 21.8

(removeFromFront) and 21.9 (removeFromBack) that show how to insert a new node in the middle of a linked list and how to remove an existing node from the middle of a linked list.

21.27 *(Lists and Queues without Tail References)* Our linked-list implementation (Fig. 21.3) used both a firstNode and a lastNode. The lastNode was useful for the insertAtBack and removeFrom-Back methods of the List class. The insertAtBack method corresponds to the enqueue method of the Queue class. Rewrite the List class so that it does not use a lastNode. Thus, any operations on the tail of a list must begin searching the list from the front. Does this affect our implementation of the Queue class (Fig. 21.13)?

21.28 *(Performance of Binary Tree Sorting and Searching)* One problem with the binary tree sort is that the order in which the data is inserted affects the shape of the tree—for the same collection of data, different orderings can yield binary trees of dramatically different shapes. The performance of the binary tree sorting and searching algorithms is sensitive to the shape of the binary tree. What shape would a binary tree have if its data were inserted in increasing order? in decreasing order? What shape should the tree have to achieve maximal searching performance?

21.29 *(Indexed Lists)* As presented in the text, linked lists must be searched sequentially. For large lists, this can result in poor performance. A common technique for improving list-searching performance is to create and maintain an index to the list. An index is a set of references to key places in the list. For example, an application that searches a large list of names could improve performance by creating an index with 26 entries—one for each letter of the alphabet. A search operation for a last name beginning with 'Y' would then first search the index to determine where the 'Y' entries began, then "jump into" the list at that point and search linearly until the desired name was found. This would be much faster than searching the linked list from the beginning. Use the List class of Fig. 21.3 as the basis of an IndexedList class. Write a program that demonstrates the operation of indexed lists. Be sure to include methods insertInIndexedList, searchIndexedList and delete-FromIndexedList.

21.30 *(Queue Class that Inherits from a List Class)* In Section 21.5, we created a stack class from class List with inheritance (Fig. 21.10) and with composition (Fig. 21.12). In Section 21.6 we created a queue class from class List with composition (Fig. 21.13). Create a queue class by inheriting from class List. What are the differences between this class and the one we created with composition?

Special Section: Building Your Own Compiler

In Exercises 6.30–6.32, we introduced Simpletron Machine Language (SML), and you implemented a Simpletron computer simulator to execute SML programs. In Exercises 21.31–21.35, we build a compiler that converts programs written in a high-level programming language to SML. This section "ties" together the entire programming process. You'll write programs in this new high-level language, compile them on the compiler you build and run them on the simulator you built in Exercise 6.31. You should make every effort to implement your compiler in an object-oriented manner. [*Note:* Due to the size of the descriptions for Exercises 21.31–21.35, we've posted them in a PDF document located at www.deitel.com/books/jhtp10LOV.]

GUI Components: Part 2

...the force of events wakes slumberous talents.
—Edward Hoagland

You and I would see more interesting photography if they would stop worrying, and instead, apply horse-sense to the problem of recording the look and feel of their own era.
—Jessie Tarbox Beals

Objectives

In this chapter you'll:

■ Create and manipulate sliders, menus, pop-up menus and windows.

■ Programatically change the look-and-feel of a GUI, using Swing's pluggable look-and-feel.

■ Create a multiple-document interface with `JDesktopPane` and `JInternalFrame`.

■ Use additional layout managers `BoxLayout` and `GridBagLayout`.

22.1 Introduction

In this chapter, we continue our study of Swing GUIs. We discuss additional components and layout managers and lay the groundwork for building more complex GUIs. We begin with sliders for selecting from a range of integer values, then discuss additional details of windows. Next, you'll use menus to organize an application's commands.

The look-and-feel of a Swing GUI can be uniform across all platforms on which a Java program executes, or the GUI can be customized by using Swing's **pluggable look-and-feel** (**PLAF**). We provide an example that illustrates how to change between Swing's default metal look-and-feel (which looks and behaves the same across platforms), the Nimbus look-and-feel (introduced in Chapter 12), a look-and-feel that simulates **Motif** (a UNIX look-and-feel) and one that simulates the Microsoft Windows look-and-feel.

Many of today's applications use a multiple-document interface (MDI)—a main window (often called the *parent window*) containing other windows (often called *child windows*) to manage several open documents in parallel. For example, many e-mail programs allow you to have several e-mail windows open at the same time so that you can compose or read multiple e-mail messages. We demonstrate Swing's classes for creating multiple-document interfaces. Finally, you'll learn about additional layout managers for organizing graphical user interfaces. We use several more Swing GUI components in later chapters as they're needed.

Swing is now considered a legacy technology. For GUIs, graphics and multimedia in new Java apps, you should use the features presented in this book's JavaFX chapters.

Java SE 8: Implementing Event Listeners with Lambdas
Throughout this chapter, we use anonymous inner classes and nested classes to implement event handlers so that the examples can compile and execute with both Java SE 7 and Java SE 8. In many of the examples, you could implement the functional event-listener interfaces with Java SE 8 lambdas (as demonstrated in Section 17.9).

22.2 JSlider

JSliders enable a user to select from a range of integer values. Class JSlider inherits from JComponent. Figure 22.1 shows a horizontal JSlider with **tick marks** and the **thumb** that allows a user to select a value. JSliders can be customized to display *major tick marks*, *minor tick marks* and labels for the tick marks. They also support **snap-to ticks**, which cause the *thumb*, when positioned between two tick marks, to snap to the closest one.

Thumb ——————— Tick mark

Fig. 22.1 | JSlider component with horizontal orientation.

Most Swing GUI components support mouse and keyboard interactions—e.g., if a JSlider has the focus (i.e., it's the currently selected GUI component in the user interface), pressing the left arrow key or right arrow key causes the JSlider's thumb to decrease or increase by 1, respectively. The down arrow key and up arrow key also cause the thumb to decrease or increase by 1 tick, respectively. The *PgDn* (page down) *key* and *PgUp* (page up) *key* cause the thumb to decrease or increase by **block increments** of one-tenth of the range of values, respectively. The *Home key* moves the thumb to the minimum value of the JSlider, and the *End key* moves the thumb to the maximum value of the JSlider.

JSliders have either a horizontal or a vertical orientation. For a horizontal JSlider, the minimum value is at the left end and the maximum is at the right end. For a vertical JSlider, the minimum value is at the bottom and the maximum is at the top. The minimum and maximum value positions on a JSlider can be reversed by invoking JSlider method **setInverted** with boolean argument true. The relative position of the thumb indicates the current value of the JSlider.

The program in Figs. 22.2–22.4 allows the user to size a circle drawn on a subclass of JPanel called OvalPanel (Fig. 22.2). The user specifies the circle's diameter with a horizontal JSlider. Class OvalPanel knows how to draw a circle on itself, using its own instance variable diameter to determine the diameter of the circle—the diameter is used as the width and height of the bounding box in which the circle is displayed. The diameter value is set when the user interacts with the JSlider. The event handler calls method set-Diameter in class OvalPanel to set the diameter and calls repaint to draw the new circle. The repaint call results in a call to OvalPanel's paintComponent method.

```
 1   // Fig. 22.2: OvalPanel.java
 2   // A customized JPanel class.
 3   import java.awt.Graphics;
 4   import java.awt.Dimension;
 5   import javax.swing.JPanel;
 6
 7   public class OvalPanel extends JPanel
 8   {
 9      private int diameter = 10; // default diameter
10
11      // draw an oval of the specified diameter
12      @Override
13      public void paintComponent(Graphics g)
14      {
15         super.paintComponent(g);
16         g.fillOval(10, 10, diameter, diameter);
17      }
18
```

Fig. 22.2 | JPanel subclass for drawing circles of a specified diameter. (Part 1 of 2.)

```
19      // validate and set diameter, then repaint
20      public void setDiameter(int newDiameter)
21      {
22         // if diameter invalid, default to 10
23         diameter = (newDiameter >= 0 ? newDiameter : 10);
24         repaint(); // repaint panel
25      }
26
27      // used by layout manager to determine preferred size
28      public Dimension getPreferredSize()
29      {
30         return new Dimension(200, 200);
31      }
32
33      // used by layout manager to determine minimum size
34      public Dimension getMinimumSize()
35      {
36         return getPreferredSize();
37      }
38   } // end class OvalPanel
```

Fig. 22.2 | JPanel subclass for drawing circles of a specified diameter. (Part 2 of 2.)

```
1    // Fig. 22.3: SliderFrame.java
2    // Using JSliders to size an oval.
3    import java.awt.BorderLayout;
4    import java.awt.Color;
5    import javax.swing.JFrame;
6    import javax.swing.JSlider;
7    import javax.swing.SwingConstants;
8    import javax.swing.event.ChangeListener;
9    import javax.swing.event.ChangeEvent;
10
11   public class SliderFrame extends JFrame
12   {
13      private final JSlider diameterJSlider; // slider to select diameter
14      private final OvalPanel myPanel; // panel to draw circle
15
16      // no-argument constructor
17      public SliderFrame()
18      {
19         super("Slider Demo");
20
21         myPanel = new OvalPanel(); // create panel to draw circle
22         myPanel.setBackground(Color.YELLOW);
23
24         // set up JSlider to control diameter value
25         diameterJSlider =
26            new JSlider(SwingConstants.HORIZONTAL, 0, 200, 10);
27         diameterJSlider.setMajorTickSpacing(10); // create tick every 10
28         diameterJSlider.setPaintTicks(true); // paint ticks on slider
29
```

Fig. 22.3 | JSlider value used to determine the diameter of a circle. (Part 1 of 2.)

```
30          // register JSlider event listener
31          diameterJSlider.addChangeListener(
32             new ChangeListener() // anonymous inner class
33             {
34                // handle change in slider value
35                @Override
36                public void stateChanged(ChangeEvent e)
37                {
38                   myPanel.setDiameter(diameterJSlider.getValue());
39                }
40             }
41          );
42
43          add(diameterJSlider, BorderLayout.SOUTH);
44          add(myPanel, BorderLayout.CENTER);
45       }
46    } // end class SliderFrame
```

Fig. 22.3 | JSlider value used to determine the diameter of a circle. (Part 2 of 2.)

```
1    // Fig. 22.4: SliderDemo.java
2    // Testing SliderFrame.
3    import javax.swing.JFrame;
4
5    public class SliderDemo
6    {
7       public static void main(String[] args)
8       {
9          SliderFrame sliderFrame = new SliderFrame();
10         sliderFrame.setDefaultCloseOperation(JFrame.EXIT_ON_CLOSE);
11         sliderFrame.setSize(220, 270);
12         sliderFrame.setVisible(true);
13      }
14   } // end class SliderDemo
```

a) Initial GUI with default circle

b) GUI after the user moves the JSlider's thumb to the right

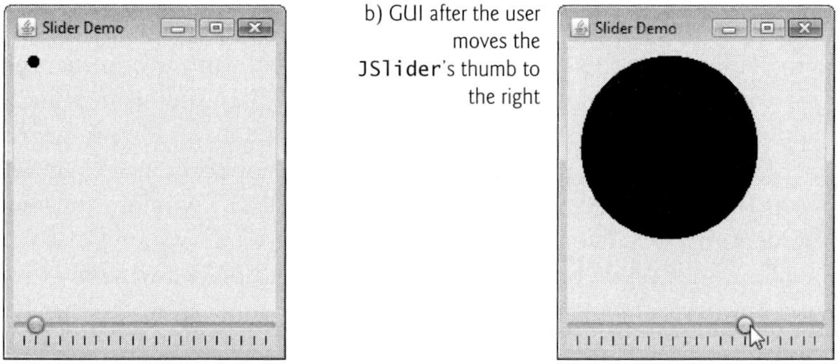

Fig. 22.4 | Test class for SliderFrame.

Class OvalPanel (Fig. 22.2) contains a paintComponent method (lines 12–17) that draws a filled oval (a circle in this example), a setDiameter method (lines 20–25) that changes the circle's diameter and repaints the OvalPanel, a getPreferredSize method (lines 28–31) that returns the preferred width and height of an OvalPanel and a getMinimumSize method (lines 34–37) that returns an OvalPanel's minimum width and height. Methods getPreferredSize and getMinimumSize are used by some layout managers to determine the size of a component.

Class SliderFrame (Fig. 22.3) creates the JSlider that controls the diameter of the circle. Class SliderFrame's constructor (lines 17–45) creates OvalPanel object myPanel (line 21) and sets its background color (line 22). Lines 25–26 create JSlider object diameterJSlider to control the diameter of the circle drawn on the OvalPanel. The JSlider constructor takes four arguments. The first specifies the orientation of diameterJSlider, which is HORIZONTAL (a constant in interface SwingConstants). The second and third arguments indicate the minimum and maximum integer values in the range of values for this JSlider. The last argument indicates that the initial value of the JSlider (i.e., where the thumb is displayed) should be 10.

Lines 27–28 customize the appearance of the JSlider. Method **setMajorTickSpacing** indicates that each major tick mark represents 10 values in the range of values supported by the JSlider. Method **setPaintTicks** with a true argument indicates that the tick marks should be displayed (they aren't displayed by default). For other methods that are used to customize a JSlider's appearance, see the JSlider online documentation (docs.oracle.com/javase/7/docs/api/javax/swing/JSlider.html).

JSliders generate **ChangeEvents** (package javax.swing.event) in response to user interactions. An object of a class that implements interface **ChangeListener** (package javax.swing.event) and declares method **stateChanged** can respond to ChangeEvents. Lines 31–41 register a ChangeListener to handle diameterJSlider's events. When method stateChanged (lines 35–39) is called in response to a user interaction, line 38 calls myPanel's setDiameter method and passes the current value of the JSlider as an argument. JSlider method **getValue** returns the current thumb position.

22.3 Understanding Windows in Java

A JFrame is a **window** with a **title bar** and a **border**. Class JFrame is a subclass of Frame (package java.awt), which is a subclass of Window (package java.awt). As such, JFrame is one of the *heavyweight* Swing GUI components. When you display a window from a Java program, the window is provided by the local platform's windowing toolkit, and therefore the window will look like every other window displayed on that platform. When a Java application executes on a Macintosh and displays a window, the window's title bar and borders will look like those of other Macintosh applications. When a Java application executes on a Microsoft Windows system and displays a window, the window's title bar and borders will look like those of other Microsoft Windows applications. And when a Java application executes on a UNIX platform and displays a window, the window's title bar and borders will look like those of other UNIX applications on that platform.

Returning Window Resources to the System
By default, when the user closes a JFrame window, it's hidden (i.e., removed from the screen), but you can control this with JFrame method **setDefaultCloseOperation**. Interface **WindowConstants** (package javax.swing), which class JFrame implements, declares three constants—DISPOSE_ON_CLOSE, DO_NOTHING_ON_CLOSE and HIDE_ON_CLOSE (the default)—for use with this method. Some platforms allow only a limited number of windows

to be displayed on the screen. Thus, a window is a valuable resource that should be given back to the system when it's no longer needed. Class `Window` (an indirect superclass of `JFrame`) declares method **dispose** for this purpose. When a `Window` is no longer needed in an application, you should explicitly dispose of it. This can be done by calling the `Window`'s `dispose` method or by calling method `setDefaultCloseOperation` with the argument `WindowConstants.DISPOSE_ON_CLOSE`. Terminating an application also returns window resources to the system. Using `DO_NOTHING_ON_CLOSE` indicates that the program will determine what to do when the user attempts to close the window. For example, the program might want to ask whether to save a file's changes before closing a window.

Displaying and Positioning Windows
By default, a window is not displayed on the screen until the program invokes the window's `setVisible` method (inherited from class `java.awt.Component`) with a `true` argument. A window's size should be set with a call to method `setSize` (inherited from class `java.awt.Component`). The position of a window when it appears on the screen is specified with method **setLocation** (inherited from class `java.awt.Component`).

Window Events
When the user manipulates the window, this action generates **window events**. Event listeners are registered for window events with `Window` method **addWindowListener**. The **WindowListener** interface provides seven window-event-handling methods—**windowActivated** (called when the user makes a window the active window), **windowClosed** (called after the window is closed), **windowClosing** (called when the user initiates closing of the window), **windowDeactivated** (called when the user makes another window the active window), **windowDeiconified** (called when the user restores a minimized window), **windowIconified** (called when the user minimizes a window) and **windowOpened** (called when a program first displays a window on the screen).

22.4 Using Menus with Frames

Menus are an integral part of GUIs. They allow the user to perform actions without unnecessarily cluttering a GUI with extra components. In Swing GUIs, menus can be attached only to objects of the classes that provide method **setJMenuBar**. Two such classes are `JFrame` and `JApplet`. The classes used to declare menus are `JMenuBar`, `JMenu`, `JMenuItem`, `JCheckBoxMenuItem` and class `JRadioButtonMenuItem`.

Look-and-Feel Observation 22.1
Menus simplify GUIs because components can be hidden within them. These components will be visible only when the user looks for them by selecting the menu.

Overview of Several Menu-Related Components
Class **JMenuBar** (a subclass of `JComponent`) contains the methods necessary to manage a **menu bar**, which is a container for menus. Class **JMenu** (a subclass of `javax.swing.JMenuItem`) contains the methods necessary for managing menus. Menus contain menu items and are added to menu bars or to other menus as submenus. When a menu is clicked, it expands to show its list of menu items.

Class **JMenuItem** (a subclass of `javax.swing.AbstractButton`) contains the methods necessary to manage **menu items**. A menu item is a GUI component inside a menu that, when selected, causes an action event. A menu item can be used to initiate an action, or it can be a **submenu** that provides more menu items from which the user can select. Submenus are useful for grouping related menu items in a menu.

Class **JCheckBoxMenuItem** (a subclass of `javax.swing.JMenuItem`) contains the methods necessary to manage menu items that can be toggled on or off. When a JCheckBoxMenuItem is selected, a check appears to the left of the menu item. When the JCheckBoxMenuItem is selected again, the check is removed.

Class **JRadioButtonMenuItem** (a subclass of `javax.swing.JMenuItem`) contains the methods necessary to manage menu items that can be toggled on or off like JCheckBoxMenuItems. When multiple JRadioButtonMenuItems are maintained as part of a ButtonGroup, only one item in the group can be selected at a given time. When a JRadioButtonMenuItem is selected, a filled circle appears to the left of the menu item. When another JRadioButtonMenuItem is selected, the filled circle of the previously selected menu item is removed.

Using Menus in an Application

Figures 22.5–22.6 demonstrate various menu items and how to specify special characters called **mnemonics** that can provide quick access to a menu or menu item from the keyboard. Mnemonics can be used with all subclasses of `javax.swing.AbstractButton`. Class MenuFrame (Fig. 22.5) creates the GUI and handles the menu-item events. Most of the code in this application appears in the class's constructor (lines 34–151).

```java
1   // Fig. 22.5: MenuFrame.java
2   // Demonstrating menus.
3   import java.awt.Color;
4   import java.awt.Font;
5   import java.awt.BorderLayout;
6   import java.awt.event.ActionListener;
7   import java.awt.event.ActionEvent;
8   import java.awt.event.ItemListener;
9   import java.awt.event.ItemEvent;
10  import javax.swing.JFrame;
11  import javax.swing.JRadioButtonMenuItem;
12  import javax.swing.JCheckBoxMenuItem;
13  import javax.swing.JOptionPane;
14  import javax.swing.JLabel;
15  import javax.swing.SwingConstants;
16  import javax.swing.ButtonGroup;
17  import javax.swing.JMenu;
18  import javax.swing.JMenuItem;
19  import javax.swing.JMenuBar;
20
21  public class MenuFrame extends JFrame
22  {
23     private final Color[] colorValues =
24        {Color.BLACK, Color.BLUE, Color.RED, Color.GREEN};
```

Fig. 22.5 | JMenus and mnemonics. (Part 1 of 5.)

```java
25        private final JRadioButtonMenuItem[] colorItems; // color menu items
26        private final JRadioButtonMenuItem[] fonts; // font menu items
27        private final JCheckBoxMenuItem[] styleItems; // font style menu items
28        private final JLabel displayJLabel; // displays sample text
29        private final ButtonGroup fontButtonGroup; // manages font menu items
30        private final ButtonGroup colorButtonGroup; // manages color menu items
31        private int style; // used to create style for font
32
33        // no-argument constructor set up GUI
34        public MenuFrame()
35        {
36           super("Using JMenus");
37
38           JMenu fileMenu = new JMenu("File"); // create file menu
39           fileMenu.setMnemonic('F'); // set mnemonic to F
40
41           // create About... menu item
42           JMenuItem aboutItem = new JMenuItem("About...");
43           aboutItem.setMnemonic('A'); // set mnemonic to A
44           fileMenu.add(aboutItem); // add about item to file menu
45           aboutItem.addActionListener(
46              new ActionListener() // anonymous inner class
47              {
48                 // display message dialog when user selects About...
49                 @Override
50                 public void actionPerformed(ActionEvent event)
51                 {
52                    JOptionPane.showMessageDialog(MenuFrame.this,
53                       "This is an example\nof using menus",
54                       "About", JOptionPane.PLAIN_MESSAGE);
55                 }
56              }
57           );
58
59           JMenuItem exitItem = new JMenuItem("Exit"); // create exit item
60           exitItem.setMnemonic('x'); // set mnemonic to x
61           fileMenu.add(exitItem); // add exit item to file menu
62           exitItem.addActionListener(
63              new ActionListener() // anonymous inner class
64              {
65                 // terminate application when user clicks exitItem
66                 @Override
67                 public void actionPerformed(ActionEvent event)
68                 {
69                    System.exit(0); // exit application
70                 }
71              }
72           );
73
74           JMenuBar bar = new JMenuBar(); // create menu bar
75           setJMenuBar(bar); // add menu bar to application
76           bar.add(fileMenu); // add file menu to menu bar
77
```

Fig. 22.5 | JMenus and mnemonics. (Part 2 of 5.)

```
78      JMenu formatMenu = new JMenu("Format"); // create format menu
79      formatMenu.setMnemonic('r'); // set mnemonic to r
80
81      // array listing string colors
82      String[] colors = { "Black", "Blue", "Red", "Green" };
83
84      JMenu colorMenu = new JMenu("Color"); // create color menu
85      colorMenu.setMnemonic('C'); // set mnemonic to C
86
87      // create radio button menu items for colors
88      colorItems = new JRadioButtonMenuItem[colors.length];
89      colorButtonGroup = new ButtonGroup(); // manages colors
90      ItemHandler itemHandler = new ItemHandler(); // handler for colors
91
92      // create color radio button menu items
93      for (int count = 0; count < colors.length; count++)
94      {
95         colorItems[count] =
96            new JRadioButtonMenuItem(colors[count]); // create item
97         colorMenu.add(colorItems[count]); // add item to color menu
98         colorButtonGroup.add(colorItems[count]); // add to group
99         colorItems[count].addActionListener(itemHandler);
100     }
101
102     colorItems[0].setSelected(true); // select first Color item
103
104     formatMenu.add(colorMenu); // add color menu to format menu
105     formatMenu.addSeparator(); // add separator in menu
106
107     // array listing font names
108     String[] fontNames = { "Serif", "Monospaced", "SansSerif" };
109     JMenu fontMenu = new JMenu("Font"); // create font menu
110     fontMenu.setMnemonic('n'); // set mnemonic to n
111
112     // create radio button menu items for font names
113     fonts = new JRadioButtonMenuItem[fontNames.length];
114     fontButtonGroup = new ButtonGroup(); // manages font names
115
116     // create Font radio button menu items
117     for (int count = 0; count < fonts.length; count++)
118     {
119        fonts[count] = new JRadioButtonMenuItem(fontNames[count]);
120        fontMenu.add(fonts[count]); // add font to font menu
121        fontButtonGroup.add(fonts[count]); // add to button group
122        fonts[count].addActionListener(itemHandler); // add handler
123     }
124
125     fonts[0].setSelected(true); // select first Font menu item
126     fontMenu.addSeparator(); // add separator bar to font menu
127
128     String[] styleNames = { "Bold", "Italic" }; // names of styles
129     styleItems = new JCheckBoxMenuItem[styleNames.length];
130     StyleHandler styleHandler = new StyleHandler(); // style handler
```

Fig. 22.5 | JMenus and mnemonics. (Part 3 of 5.)

```
131
132        // create style checkbox menu items
133        for (int count = 0; count < styleNames.length; count++)
134        {
135            styleItems[count] =
136                new JCheckBoxMenuItem(styleNames[count]); // for style
137            fontMenu.add(styleItems[count]); // add to font menu
138            styleItems[count].addItemListener(styleHandler); // handler
139        }
140
141        formatMenu.add(fontMenu); // add Font menu to Format menu
142        bar.add(formatMenu); // add Format menu to menu bar
143
144        // set up label to display text
145        displayJLabel = new JLabel("Sample Text", SwingConstants.CENTER);
146        displayJLabel.setForeground(colorValues[0]);
147        displayJLabel.setFont(new Font("Serif", Font.PLAIN, 72));
148
149        getContentPane().setBackground(Color.CYAN); // set background
150        add(displayJLabel, BorderLayout.CENTER); // add displayJLabel
151    } // end MenuFrame constructor
152
153    // inner class to handle action events from menu items
154    private class ItemHandler implements ActionListener
155    {
156        // process color and font selections
157        @Override
158        public void actionPerformed(ActionEvent event)
159        {
160            // process color selection
161            for (int count = 0; count < colorItems.length; count++)
162            {
163                if (colorItems[count].isSelected())
164                {
165                    displayJLabel.setForeground(colorValues[count]);
166                    break;
167                }
168            }
169
170            // process font selection
171            for (int count = 0; count < fonts.length; count++)
172            {
173                if (event.getSource() == fonts[count])
174                {
175                    displayJLabel.setFont(
176                        new Font(fonts[count].getText(), style, 72));
177                }
178            }
179
180            repaint(); // redraw application
181        }
182    } // end class ItemHandler
183
```

Fig. 22.5 | JMenus and mnemonics. (Part 4 of 5.)

```
184    // inner class to handle item events from checkbox menu items
185    private class StyleHandler implements ItemListener
186    {
187       // process font style selections
188       @Override
189       public void itemStateChanged(ItemEvent e)
190       {
191          String name = displayJLabel.getFont().getName(); // current Font
192          Font font; // new font based on user selections
193
194          // determine which items are checked and create Font
195          if (styleItems[0].isSelected() &&
196                styleItems[1].isSelected())
197             font = new Font(name, Font.BOLD + Font.ITALIC, 72);
198          else if (styleItems[0].isSelected())
199             font = new Font(name, Font.BOLD, 72);
200          else if (styleItems[1].isSelected())
201             font = new Font(name, Font.ITALIC, 72);
202          else
203             font = new Font(name, Font.PLAIN, 72);
204
205          displayJLabel.setFont(font);
206          repaint(); // redraw application
207       }
208    }
209 } // end class MenuFrame
```

Fig. 22.5 | JMenus and mnemonics. (Part 5 of 5.)

```
1  // Fig. 22.6: MenuTest.java
2  // Testing MenuFrame.
3  import javax.swing.JFrame;
4
5  public class MenuTest
6  {
7     public static void main(String[] args)
8     {
9        MenuFrame menuFrame = new MenuFrame();
10       menuFrame.setDefaultCloseOperation(JFrame.EXIT_ON_CLOSE);
11       menuFrame.setSize(500, 200);
12       menuFrame.setVisible(true);
13    }
14 } // end class MenuTest
```

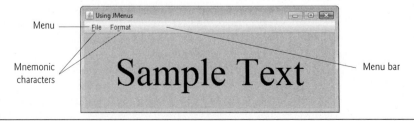

Fig. 22.6 | Test class for MenuFrame. (Part 1 of 2.)

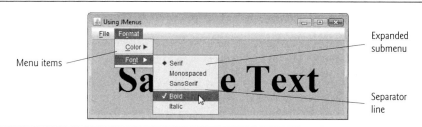

Fig. 22.6 | Test class for `MenuFrame`. (Part 2 of 2.)

Setting Up the File Menu

Lines 38–76 set up the **File** menu and attach it to the menu bar. The **File** menu contains an **About...** menu item that displays a message dialog when the menu item is selected and an **Exit** menu item that can be selected to terminate the application. Line 38 creates a `JMenu` and passes to the constructor the string `"File"` as the name of the menu. Line 39 uses `JMenu` method **`setMnemonic`** (inherited from class `AbstractButton`) to indicate that F is the mnemonic for this menu. Pressing the *Alt* key and the letter *F* opens the menu, just as clicking the menu name with the mouse would. In the GUI, the mnemonic character in the menu's name is displayed with an underline. (See the screen captures in Fig. 22.6.)

Look-and-Feel Observation 22.2

Mnemonics provide quick access to menu commands and button commands through the keyboard.

Look-and-Feel Observation 22.3

*Different mnemonics should be used for each button or menu item. Normally, the first letter in the label on the menu item or button is used as the mnemonic. If several buttons or menu items start with the same letter, choose the next most prominent letter in the name (e.g., **x** is commonly chosen for an **Exit** button or menu item). Mnemonics are case insensitive.*

Lines 42–43 create `JMenuItem aboutItem` with the text "About..." and set its mnemonic to the letter A. This menu item is added to `fileMenu` at line 44 with `JMenu` method **add**. To access the **About...** menu item through the keyboard, press the *Alt* key and letter *F* to open the **File** menu, then press *A* to select the **About...** menu item. Lines 46–56 create an `ActionListener` to process `aboutItem`'s action event. Lines 52–54 display a message dialog box. In most prior uses of `showMessageDialog`, the first argument was `null`. The purpose of the first argument is to specify the **parent window** that helps determine where the dialog box will be displayed. If the parent window is specified as `null`, the dialog box appears in the center of the screen. Otherwise, it appears centered over the specified parent window. In this example, the program specifies the parent window with `Menu-Frame.this`—the `this` reference of the `MenuFrame` object. When using the `this` reference in an inner class, specifying `this` by itself refers to the inner-class object. To reference the outer-class object's `this` reference, qualify `this` with the outer-class name and a dot (`.`).

Recall that dialog boxes are typically modal. A modal dialog box does not allow any other window in the application to be accessed until the dialog box is dismissed. The dialogs displayed with class `JOptionPane` are modal dialogs. Class **`JDialog`** can be used to create your own modal or nonmodal dialogs.

Lines 59–72 create menu item exitItem, set its mnemonic to x, add it to fileMenu and register an ActionListener that terminates the program when the user selects exit-Item. Lines 74–76 create the JMenuBar, attach it to the window with JFrame method set-JMenuBar and use JMenuBar method **add** to attach the fileMenu to the JMenuBar.

Look-and-Feel Observation 22.4

Menus appear left to right in the order they're added to a JMenuBar.

Setting Up the *Format Menu*

Lines 78–79 create the formatMenu and set its mnemonic to r. F is not used because that's the **File** menu's mnemonic. Lines 84–85 create colorMenu (this will be a submenu in **Format**) and set its mnemonic to C. Line 88 creates JRadioButtonMenuItem array colorItems, which refers to the menu items in colorMenu. Line 89 creates ButtonGroup colorButtonGroup, which ensures that only one of the **Color** submenu items is selected at a time. Line 90 creates an instance of inner class ItemHandler (declared at lines 154–181) that responds to selections from the **Color** and **Font** submenus (discussed shortly). The loop at lines 93–100 creates each JRadioButtonMenuItem in array colorItems, adds each menu item to colorMenu and to colorButtonGroup and registers the ActionListener for each menu item.

Line 102 invokes AbstractButton method **setSelected** to select the first element in array colorItems. Line 104 adds colorMenu as a submenu of formatMenu. Line 105 invokes JMenu method **addSeparator** to add a horizontal **separator** line to the menu.

Look-and-Feel Observation 22.5

A submenu is created by adding a menu as a menu item in another menu.

Look-and-Feel Observation 22.6

Separators can be added to a menu to group menu items logically.

Look-and-Feel Observation 22.7

Any JComponent can be added to a JMenu or to a JMenuBar.

Lines 108–126 create the **Font** submenu and several JRadioButtonMenuItems and select the first element of JRadioButtonMenuItem array fonts. Line 129 creates a JCheckBoxMenu-Item array to represent the menu items for specifying bold and italic styles for the fonts. Line 130 creates an instance of inner class StyleHandler (declared at lines 185–208) to respond to the JCheckBoxMenuItem events. The for statement at lines 133–139 creates each JCheck-BoxMenuItem, adds it to fontMenu and registers its ItemListener. Line 141 adds fontMenu as a submenu of formatMenu. Line 142 adds the formatMenu to bar (the menu bar).

Creating the Rest of the GUI and Defining the Event Handlers

Lines 145–147 create a JLabel for which the **Format** menu items control the font, font color and font style. The initial foreground color is set to the first element of array color-Values (Color.BLACK) by invoking JComponent method **setForeground**. The initial font is set to Serif with PLAIN style and 72-point size. Line 149 sets the background color of the window's content pane to cyan, and line 150 attaches the JLabel to the CENTER of the content pane's BorderLayout.

ItemHandler method actionPerformed (lines 157–181) uses two for statements to determine which font or color menu item generated the event and sets the font or color of the JLabel displayLabel, respectively. The if condition at line 163 uses Abstract-Button method **isSelected** to determine the selected JRadioButtonMenuItem. The if condition at line 173 invokes the event object's getSource method to get a reference to the JRadioButtonMenuItem that generated the event. Line 176 invokes AbstractButton method getText to obtain the name of the font from the menu item.

StyleHandler method itemStateChanged (lines 188–207) is called if the user selects a JCheckBoxMenuItem in the fontMenu. Lines 195–203 determine which JCheckBoxMenu-Items are selected and use their combined state to determine the new font style.

22.5 JPopupMenu

Applications often provide **context-sensitive pop-up menus** for several reasons—they can be convenient, there might not be a menu bar and the options they display can be specific to individual on-screen components. In Swing, such menus are created with class **JPopup-Menu** (a subclass of JComponent). These menus provide options that are specific to the component for which the **popup trigger event** occurred—on most systems, when the user presses and releases the right mouse button.

Look-and-Feel Observation 22.8

The pop-up trigger event is platform specific. On most platforms that use a mouse with multiple buttons, the pop-up trigger event occurs when the user clicks the right mouse button on a component that supports a pop-up menu.

The application in Figs. 22.7–22.8 creates a JPopupMenu that allows the user to select one of three colors and change the background color of the window. When the user clicks the right mouse button on the PopupFrame window's background, a JPopupMenu containing colors appears. If the user clicks a JRadioButtonMenuItem for a color, ItemHandler method actionPerformed changes the background color of the window's content pane.

Line 25 of the PopupFrame constructor (Fig. 22.7, lines 21–70) creates an instance of class ItemHandler (declared in lines 73–89) that will process the item events from the menu items in the pop-up menu. Line 29 creates the JPopupMenu. The for statement (lines 33–39) creates a JRadioButtonMenuItem object (line 35), adds it to popupMenu (line 36), adds it to ButtonGroup colorGroup (line 37) to maintain one selected JRadioButton-MenuItem at a time and registers its ActionListener (line 38). Line 41 sets the initial background to white by invoking method setBackground.

```
1   // Fig. 22.7: PopupFrame.java
2   // Demonstrating JPopupMenus.
3   import java.awt.Color;
4   import java.awt.event.MouseAdapter;
5   import java.awt.event.MouseEvent;
6   import java.awt.event.ActionListener;
```

Fig. 22.7 | JPopupMenu for selecting colors. (Part 1 of 3.)

```java
7   import java.awt.event.ActionEvent;
8   import javax.swing.JFrame;
9   import javax.swing.JRadioButtonMenuItem;
10  import javax.swing.JPopupMenu;
11  import javax.swing.ButtonGroup;
12
13  public class PopupFrame extends JFrame
14  {
15     private final JRadioButtonMenuItem[] items; // holds items for colors
16     private final Color[] colorValues =
17        { Color.BLUE, Color.YELLOW, Color.RED }; // colors to be used
18     private final JPopupMenu popupMenu; // allows user to select color
19
20     // no-argument constructor sets up GUI
21     public PopupFrame()
22     {
23        super("Using JPopupMenus");
24
25        ItemHandler handler = new ItemHandler(); // handler for menu items
26        String[] colors = { "Blue", "Yellow", "Red" };
27
28        ButtonGroup colorGroup = new ButtonGroup(); // manages color items
29        popupMenu = new JPopupMenu(); // create pop-up menu
30        items = new JRadioButtonMenuItem[colors.length];
31
32        // construct menu item, add to pop-up menu, enable event handling
33        for (int count = 0; count < items.length; count++)
34        {
35           items[count] = new JRadioButtonMenuItem(colors[count]);
36           popupMenu.add(items[count]); // add item to pop-up menu
37           colorGroup.add(items[count]); // add item to button group
38           items[count].addActionListener(handler); // add handler
39        }
40
41        setBackground(Color.WHITE);
42
43        // declare a MouseListener for the window to display pop-up menu
44        addMouseListener(
45           new MouseAdapter() // anonymous inner class
46           {
47              // handle mouse press event
48              @Override
49              public void mousePressed(MouseEvent event)
50              {
51                 checkForTriggerEvent(event);
52              }
53
54              // handle mouse release event
55              @Override
56              public void mouseReleased(MouseEvent event)
57              {
58                 checkForTriggerEvent(event);
59              }
```

Fig. 22.7 | JPopupMenu for selecting colors. (Part 2 of 3.)

```
60
61                    // determine whether event should trigger pop-up menu
62                    private void checkForTriggerEvent(MouseEvent event)
63                    {
64                       if (event.isPopupTrigger())
65                          popupMenu.show(
66                             event.getComponent(), event.getX(), event.getY());
67                    }
68                 }
69            );
70       } // end PopupFrame constructor
71
72       // private inner class to handle menu item events
73       private class ItemHandler implements ActionListener
74       {
75          // process menu item selections
76          @Override
77          public void actionPerformed(ActionEvent event)
78          {
79             // determine which menu item was selected
80             for (int i = 0; i < items.length; i++)
81             {
82                if (event.getSource() == items[i])
83                {
84                   getContentPane().setBackground(colorValues[i]);
85                   return;
86                }
87             }
88          }
89       } // end private inner class ItemHandler
90    } // end class PopupFrame
```

Fig. 22.7 | JPopupMenu for selecting colors. (Part 3 of 3.)

```
1    // Fig. 22.8: PopupTest.java
2    // Testing PopupFrame.
3    import javax.swing.JFrame;
4
5    public class PopupTest
6    {
7       public static void main(String[] args)
8       {
9          PopupFrame popupFrame = new PopupFrame();
10         popupFrame.setDefaultCloseOperation(JFrame.EXIT_ON_CLOSE);
11         popupFrame.setSize(300, 200);
12         popupFrame.setVisible(true);
13      }
14   } // end class PopupTest
```

Fig. 22.8 | Test class for PopupFrame. (Part 1 of 2.)

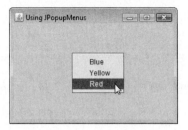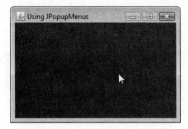

Fig. 22.8 | Test class for `PopupFrame`. (Part 2 of 2.)

Lines 44–69 register a `MouseListener` to handle the mouse events of the application window. Methods `mousePressed` (lines 48–52) and `mouseReleased` (lines 55–59) check for the pop-up trigger event. Each method calls private utility method `checkForTrigger-Event` (lines 62–67) to determine whether the pop-up trigger event occurred. If it did, `MouseEvent` method **`isPopupTrigger`** returns `true`, and `JPopupMenu` method **`show`** displays the `JPopupMenu`. The first argument to method `show` specifies the **origin component**, whose position helps determine where the `JPopupMenu` will appear on the screen. The last two arguments are the *x-y* coordinates (measured from the origin component's upper-left corner) at which the `JPopupMenu` is to appear.

Look-and-Feel Observation 22.9
Displaying a `JPopupMenu` for the pop-up trigger event of multiple GUI components requires registering mouse-event handlers for each of those GUI components.

When the user selects a menu item from the pop-up menu, class `ItemHandler`'s method `actionPerformed` (lines 76–88) determines which `JRadioButtonMenuItem` the user selected and sets the background color of the window's content pane.

22.6 Pluggable Look-and-Feel

A program that uses Java's AWT GUI components (package `java.awt`) takes on the look-and-feel of the platform on which the program executes. A Java application running on a Mac OS X looks like other Mac OS X applications, one running on Microsoft Windows looks like other Windows applications, and one running on a Linux platform looks like other applications on that Linux platform. This is sometimes desirable, because it allows users of the application on each platform to use GUI components with which they're already familiar. However, it also introduces interesting portability issues.

Portability Tip 22.1
GUI components often look different on different platforms (fonts, font sizes, component borders, etc.) and might require different amounts of space to display. This could change their layout and alignments.

Portability Tip 22.2
GUI components on different platforms have might different default functionality—e.g., not all platforms allow a button with the focus to be "pressed" with the space bar.

Swing's lightweight GUI components eliminate many of these issues by providing uniform functionality across platforms and by defining a uniform cross-platform look-and-feel. Section 12.2 introduced the *Nimbus* look-and-feel. Earlier versions of Java used the **metal look-and-feel**, which is still the default. Swing also provides the flexibility to customize the look-and-feel to appear as a Microsoft Windows-style look-and-feel (only on Windows systems), a Motif-style (UNIX) look-and-feel (across all platforms) or a Macintosh look-and-feel (only on Mac systems).

Figures 22.9–22.10 demonstrate a way to change the look-and-feel of a Swing GUI. It creates several GUI components, so you can see the change in their look-and-feel at the same time. The output windows show the Metal, Nimbus, CDE/Motif, Windows and Windows Classic look-and-feels that are available on Windows systems. The installed look-and-feels will vary by platform.

We've covered the GUI components and event-handling concepts in this example previously, so we focus here on the mechanism for changing the look-and-feel. Class **UIManager** (package javax.swing) contains nested class **LookAndFeelInfo** (a public static class) that maintains information about a look-and-feel. Line 20 (Fig. 22.9) declares an array of type UIManager.LookAndFeelInfo (note the syntax used to identify the static inner class LookAndFeelInfo). Line 34 uses UIManager static method **getInstalledLookAndFeels** to get the array of UIManager.LookAndFeelInfo objects that describe each look-and-feel available on your system.

Performance Tip 22.1

Each look-and-feel is represented by a Java class. UIManager method getInstalled-LookAndFeels does not load each class. Rather, it provides the names of the available look-and-feel classes so that a choice can be made (presumably once at program start-up). This reduces the overhead of having to load all the look-and-feel classes even if the program will not use some of them.

```java
1  // Fig. 22.9: LookAndFeelFrame.java
2  // Changing the look-and-feel.
3  import java.awt.GridLayout;
4  import java.awt.BorderLayout;
5  import java.awt.event.ItemListener;
6  import java.awt.event.ItemEvent;
7  import javax.swing.JFrame;
8  import javax.swing.UIManager;
9  import javax.swing.JRadioButton;
10 import javax.swing.ButtonGroup;
11 import javax.swing.JButton;
12 import javax.swing.JLabel;
13 import javax.swing.JComboBox;
14 import javax.swing.JPanel;
15 import javax.swing.SwingConstants;
16 import javax.swing.SwingUtilities;
17
18 public class LookAndFeelFrame extends JFrame
19 {
```

Fig. 22.9 | Look-and-feel of a Swing-based GUI. (Part 1 of 3.)

```
20      private final UIManager.LookAndFeelInfo[] looks;
21      private final String[] lookNames; // look-and-feel names
22      private final JRadioButton[] radio; // for selecting look-and-feel
23      private final ButtonGroup group; // group for radio buttons
24      private final JButton button; // displays look of button
25      private final JLabel label; // displays look of label
26      private final JComboBox<String> comboBox; // displays look of combo box
27
28      // set up GUI
29      public LookAndFeelFrame()
30      {
31         super("Look and Feel Demo");
32
33         // get installed look-and-feel information
34         looks = UIManager.getInstalledLookAndFeels();
35         lookNames = new String[looks.length];
36
37         // get names of installed look-and-feels
38         for (int i = 0; i < looks.length; i++)
39            lookNames[i] = looks[i].getName();
40
41         JPanel northPanel = new JPanel();
42         northPanel.setLayout(new GridLayout(3, 1, 0, 5));
43
44         label = new JLabel("This is a " + lookNames[0] + " look-and-feel",
45            SwingConstants.CENTER);
46         northPanel.add(label);
47
48         button = new JButton("JButton");
49         northPanel.add(button);
50
51         comboBox = new JComboBox<String>(lookNames);
52         northPanel.add(comboBox);
53
54         // create array for radio buttons
55         radio = new JRadioButton[looks.length];
56
57         JPanel southPanel = new JPanel();
58
59         // use a GridLayout with 3 buttons in each row
60         int rows = (int) Math.ceil(radio.length / 3.0);
61         southPanel.setLayout(new GridLayout(rows, 3));
62
63         group = new ButtonGroup(); // button group for look-and-feels
64         ItemHandler handler = new ItemHandler(); // look-and-feel handler
65
66         for (int count = 0; count < radio.length; count++)
67         {
68            radio[count] = new JRadioButton(lookNames[count]);
69            radio[count].addItemListener(handler); // add handler
70            group.add(radio[count]); // add radio button to group
71            southPanel.add(radio[count]); // add radio button to panel
72         }
```

Fig. 22.9 | Look-and-feel of a Swing-based GUI. (Part 2 of 3.)

```
73
74        add(northPanel, BorderLayout.NORTH); // add north panel
75        add(southPanel, BorderLayout.SOUTH); // add south panel
76
77        radio[0].setSelected(true); // set default selection
78     } // end LookAndFeelFrame constructor
79
80     // use UIManager to change look-and-feel of GUI
81     private void changeTheLookAndFeel(int value)
82     {
83        try // change look-and-feel
84        {
85           // set look-and-feel for this application
86           UIManager.setLookAndFeel(looks[value].getClassName());
87
88           // update components in this application
89           SwingUtilities.updateComponentTreeUI(this);
90        }
91        catch (Exception exception)
92        {
93           exception.printStackTrace();
94        }
95     }
96
97     // private inner class to handle radio button events
98     private class ItemHandler implements ItemListener
99     {
100        // process user's look-and-feel selection
101        @Override
102        public void itemStateChanged(ItemEvent event)
103        {
104           for (int count = 0; count < radio.length; count++)
105           {
106              if (radio[count].isSelected())
107              {
108                 label.setText(String.format(
109                    "This is a %s look-and-feel", lookNames[count]));
110                 comboBox.setSelectedIndex(count); // set combobox index
111                 changeTheLookAndFeel(count); // change look-and-feel
112              }
113           }
114        }
115     } // end private inner class ItemHandler
116  } // end class LookAndFeelFrame
```

Fig. 22.9 | Look-and-feel of a Swing-based GUI. (Part 3 of 3.)

```
1   // Fig. 22.10: LookAndFeelDemo.java
2   // Changing the look-and-feel.
3   import javax.swing.JFrame;
4
```

Fig. 22.10 | Test class for LookAndFeelFrame. (Part 1 of 2.)

```
 5   public class LookAndFeelDemo
 6   {
 7      public static void main(String[] args)
 8      {
 9         LookAndFeelFrame lookAndFeelFrame = new LookAndFeelFrame();
10         lookAndFeelFrame.setDefaultCloseOperation(JFrame.EXIT_ON_CLOSE);
11         lookAndFeelFrame.setSize(400, 220);
12         lookAndFeelFrame.setVisible(true);
13      }
14   } // end class LookAndFeelDemo
```

Fig. 22.10 | Test class for LookAndFeelFrame. (Part 2 of 2.)

Our utility method changeTheLookAndFeel (lines 81–95) is called by the event handler for the JRadioButtons at the bottom of the user interface. The event handler (declared in private inner class ItemHandler at lines 98–115) passes an integer representing the element in array looks that should be used to change the look-and-feel. Line 86 invokes static method **setLookAndFeel** of UIManager to change the look-and-feel. The **getClassName** method of class UIManager.LookAndFeelInfo determines the name of the look-and-feel class that corresponds to the UIManager.LookAndFeelInfo object. If the look-and-feel is not already loaded, it will be loaded as part of the call to setLookAndFeel. Line 89 invokes the static method **updateComponentTreeUI** of class **SwingUtilities** (package javax.swing) to change the look-and-feel of every GUI component attached to its argument (this instance of our application class LookAndFeelFrame) to the new look-and-feel.

22.7 **JDesktopPane and JInternalFrame**

A **multiple-document interface** (MDI) is a main window (called the **parent window**) containing other windows (called **child windows**) and is often used to manage several open documents. For example, many e-mail programs allow you to have several windows open at the same time, so you can compose or read multiple e-mail messages simultaneously. Similarly, many word processors allow the user to open multiple documents in separate windows within in a main window, making it possible to switch between them without having to close one to open another. The application in Figs. 22.11–22.12 demonstrates Swing's **JDesktopPane** and **JInternalFrame** classes for implementing multiple-document interfaces.

```
 1   // Fig. 22.11: DesktopFrame.java
 2   // Demonstrating JDesktopPane.
 3   import java.awt.BorderLayout;
 4   import java.awt.Dimension;
 5   import java.awt.Graphics;
 6   import java.awt.event.ActionListener;
 7   import java.awt.event.ActionEvent;
 8   import java.util.Random;
 9   import javax.swing.JFrame;
10   import javax.swing.JDesktopPane;
11   import javax.swing.JMenuBar;
12   import javax.swing.JMenu;
13   import javax.swing.JMenuItem;
14   import javax.swing.JInternalFrame;
15   import javax.swing.JPanel;
16   import javax.swing.ImageIcon;
17
18   public class DesktopFrame extends JFrame
19   {
20      private final JDesktopPane theDesktop;
21
22      // set up GUI
23      public DesktopFrame()
24      {
25         super("Using a JDesktopPane");
26
27         JMenuBar bar = new JMenuBar();
28         JMenu addMenu = new JMenu("Add");
29         JMenuItem newFrame = new JMenuItem("Internal Frame");
30
31         addMenu.add(newFrame); // add new frame item to Add menu
32         bar.add(addMenu); // add Add menu to menu bar
33         setJMenuBar(bar); // set menu bar for this application
34
35         theDesktop = new JDesktopPane();
36         add(theDesktop); // add desktop pane to frame
37
38         // set up listener for newFrame menu item
39         newFrame.addActionListener(
```

Fig. 22.11 | Multiple-document interface. (Part 1 of 2.)

```
40              new ActionListener() // anonymous inner class
41              {
42                  // display new internal window
43                  @Override
44                  public void actionPerformed(ActionEvent event)
45                  {
46                      // create internal frame
47                      JInternalFrame frame = new JInternalFrame(
48                          "Internal Frame", true, true, true, true);
49
50                      MyJPanel panel = new MyJPanel();
51                      frame.add(panel, BorderLayout.CENTER);
52                      frame.pack(); // set internal frame to size of contents
53
54                      theDesktop.add(frame); // attach internal frame
55                      frame.setVisible(true); // show internal frame
56                  }
57              }
58          );
59      } // end DesktopFrame constructor
60  } // end class DesktopFrame
61
62  // class to display an ImageIcon on a panel
63  class MyJPanel extends JPanel
64  {
65      private static final SecureRandom generator = new SecureRandom();
66      private final ImageIcon picture; // image to be displayed
67      private final static String[] images = { "yellowflowers.png",
68          "purpleflowers.png", "redflowers.png", "redflowers2.png",
69          "lavenderflowers.png" };
70
71      // load image
72      public MyJPanel()
73      {
74          int randomNumber = generator.nextInt(images.length);
75          picture = new ImageIcon(images[randomNumber]); // set icon
76      }
77
78      // display imageIcon on panel
79      @Override
80      public void paintComponent(Graphics g)
81      {
82          super.paintComponent(g);
83          picture.paintIcon(this, g, 0, 0); // display icon
84      }
85
86      // return image dimensions
87      public Dimension getPreferredSize()
88      {
89          return new Dimension(picture.getIconWidth(),
90              picture.getIconHeight());
91      }
92  } // end class MyJPanel
```

Fig. 22.11 | Multiple-document interface. (Part 2 of 2.)

Lines 27–33 create a JMenuBar, a JMenu and a JMenuItem, add the JMenuItem to the JMenu, add the JMenu to the JMenuBar and set the JMenuBar for the application window. When the user selects the JMenuItem newFrame, the application creates and displays a new JInternalFrame object containing an image.

Line 35 assigns JDesktopPane (package javax.swing) variable theDesktop a new JDesktopPane object that will be used to manage the JInternalFrame child windows. Line 36 adds the JDesktopPane to the JFrame. By default, the JDesktopPane is added to the center of the content pane's BorderLayout, so the JDesktopPane expands to fill the entire application window.

```
 1   // Fig. 22.12: DesktopTest.java
 2   // Demonstrating JDesktopPane.
 3   import javax.swing.JFrame;
 4
 5   public class DesktopTest
 6   {
 7      public static void main(String[] args)
 8      {
 9         DesktopFrame desktopFrame = new DesktopFrame();
10         desktopFrame.setDefaultCloseOperation(JFrame.EXIT_ON_CLOSE);
11         desktopFrame.setSize(600, 480);
12         desktopFrame.setVisible(true);
13      }
14   } // end class DesktopTest
```

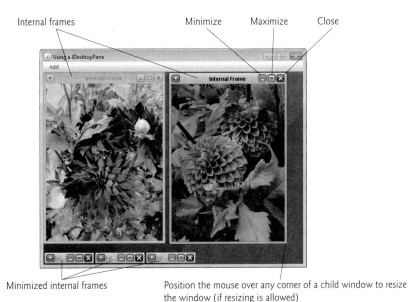

Internal frames   Minimize   Maximize   Close

Minimized internal frames   Position the mouse over any corner of a child window to resize the window (if resizing is allowed)

Fig. 22.12 | Test class for DeskTopFrame. (Part 1 of 2.)

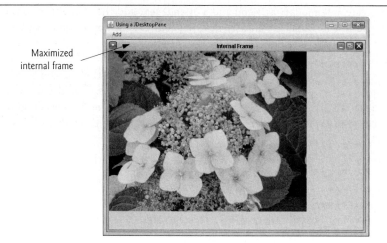

Maximized internal frame

Fig. 22.12 | Test class for `DeskTopFrame`. (Part 2 of 2.)

Lines 39–58 register an `ActionListener` to handle the event when the user selects the `newFrame` menu item. When the event occurs, method `actionPerformed` (lines 43–56) creates a `JInternalFrame` object in lines 47–48. The `JInternalFrame` constructor used here takes five arguments—a `String` for the title bar of the internal window, a `boolean` indicating whether the internal frame can be resized by the user, a `boolean` indicating whether the internal frame can be closed by the user, a `boolean` indicating whether the internal frame can be maximized by the user and a `boolean` indicating whether the internal frame can be minimized by the user. For each of the `boolean` arguments, a `true` value indicates that the operation should be allowed (as is the case here).

As with `JFrame`s and `JApplet`s, a `JInternalFrame` has a content pane to which GUI components can be attached. Line 50 creates an instance of our class `MyJPanel` (declared at lines 63–91) that is added to the `JInternalFrame` at line 51.

Line 52 uses `JInternalFrame` method **pack** to set the size of the child window. Method `pack` uses the preferred sizes of the components to determine the window's size. Class `MyJPanel` declares method `getPreferredSize` (lines 87–91) to specify the panel's preferred size for use by the pack method. Line 54 adds the `JInternalFrame` to the `JDesktopPane`, and line 55 displays the `JInternalFrame`.

Classes `JInternalFrame` and `JDesktopPane` provide many methods for managing child windows. See the `JInternalFrame` and `JDesktopPane` online API documentation for complete lists of these methods:

```
docs.oracle.com/javase/7/docs/api/javax/swing/JInternalFrame.html
docs.oracle.com/javase/7/docs/api/javax/swing/JDesktopPane.html
```

22.8 JTabbedPane

A **JTabbedPane** arranges GUI components into layers, of which only one is visible at a time. Users access each layer via a tab—similar to folders in a file cabinet. When the user clicks a tab, the appropriate layer is displayed. The tabs appear at the top by default but also can be positioned at the left, right or bottom of the `JTabbedPane`. Any component can be placed on a tab. If the component is a container, such as a panel, it can use any layout manager to lay out several components on the tab. Class JTabbedPane is a subclass of JComponent. The application in Figs. 22.13–22.14 creates one tabbed pane with three tabs. Each tab displays one of the JPanels—panel1, panel2 or panel3.

```java
 1   // Fig. 22.13: JTabbedPaneFrame.java
 2   // Demonstrating JTabbedPane.
 3   import java.awt.BorderLayout;
 4   import java.awt.Color;
 5   import javax.swing.JFrame;
 6   import javax.swing.JTabbedPane;
 7   import javax.swing.JLabel;
 8   import javax.swing.JPanel;
 9   import javax.swing.JButton;
10   import javax.swing.SwingConstants;
11
12   public class JTabbedPaneFrame extends JFrame
13   {
14      // set up GUI
15      public JTabbedPaneFrame()
16      {
17         super("JTabbedPane Demo ");
18
19         JTabbedPane tabbedPane = new JTabbedPane(); // create JTabbedPane
20
21         // set up panel1 and add it to JTabbedPane
22         JLabel label1 = new JLabel("panel one", SwingConstants.CENTER);
23         JPanel panel1 = new JPanel();
24         panel1.add(label1);
25         tabbedPane.addTab("Tab One", null, panel1, "First Panel");
26
27         // set up panel2 and add it to JTabbedPane
28         JLabel label2 = new JLabel("panel two", SwingConstants.CENTER);
29         JPanel panel2 = new JPanel();
30         panel2.setBackground(Color.YELLOW);
31         panel2.add(label2);
32         tabbedPane.addTab("Tab Two", null, panel2, "Second Panel");
33
34         // set up panel3 and add it to JTabbedPane
35         JLabel label3 = new JLabel("panel three");
36         JPanel panel3 = new JPanel();
37         panel3.setLayout(new BorderLayout());
38         panel3.add(new JButton("North"), BorderLayout.NORTH);
39         panel3.add(new JButton("West"), BorderLayout.WEST);
40         panel3.add(new JButton("East"), BorderLayout.EAST);
41         panel3.add(new JButton("South"), BorderLayout.SOUTH);
42         panel3.add(label3, BorderLayout.CENTER);
43         tabbedPane.addTab("Tab Three", null, panel3, "Third Panel");
44
45         add(tabbedPane); // add JTabbedPane to frame
46      }
47   } // end class JTabbedPaneFrame
```

Fig. 22.13 | JTabbedPane used to organize GUI components.

```
 1   // Fig. 22.14: JTabbedPaneDemo.java
 2   // Demonstrating JTabbedPane.
 3   import javax.swing.JFrame;
 4
 5   public class JTabbedPaneDemo
 6   {
 7      public static void main(String[] args)
 8      {
 9         JTabbedPaneFrame tabbedPaneFrame = new JTabbedPaneFrame();
10         tabbedPaneFrame.setDefaultCloseOperation(JFrame.EXIT_ON_CLOSE);
11         tabbedPaneFrame.setSize(250, 200);
12         tabbedPaneFrame.setVisible(true);
13      }
14   } // end class JTabbedPaneDemo
```

Fig. 22.14 | Test class for `JTabbedPaneFrame`.

The constructor (lines 15–46) builds the GUI. Line 19 creates an empty JTabbedPane with default settings—that is, tabs across the top. If the tabs do not fit on one line, they'll wrap to form additional lines of tabs. Next the constructor creates the JPanels panel1, panel2 and panel3 and their GUI components. As we set up each panel, we add it to tabbedPane, using JTabbedPane method **addTab** with four arguments. The first argument is a String that specifies the title of the tab. The second argument is an Icon reference that specifies an icon to display on the tab. If the Icon is a null reference, no image is displayed. The third argument is a Component reference that represents the GUI component to display when the user clicks the tab. The last argument is a String that specifies the tool tip for the tab. For example, line 25 adds JPanel panel1 to tabbedPane with title "Tab One" and the tool tip "First Panel". JPanels panel2 and panel3 are added to tabbedPane at lines 32 and 43. To view a tab, click it with the mouse or use the arrow keys to cycle through the tabs.

22.9 BoxLayout Layout Manager

In Chapter 12, we introduced three layout managers—FlowLayout, BorderLayout and GridLayout. This section and Section 22.10 present two additional layout managers (summarized in Fig. 22.15). We discuss them in the examples that follow.

Layout manager	Description
BoxLayout	Allows GUI components to be arranged left-to-right or top-to-bottom in a container. Class Box declares a container that uses BoxLayout and provides static methods to create a Box with a horizontal or vertical BoxLayout.
GridBagLayout	Similar to GridLayout, but the components can vary in size and can be added in any order.

Fig. 22.15 | Additional layout managers.

The BoxLayout layout manager (in package java.swing) arranges GUI components horizontally along a container's x-axis or vertically along its y-axis. The application in Figs. 22.16–22.17 demonstrate BoxLayout and the container class Box that uses Box-Layout as its default layout manager.

```java
1   // Fig. 22.16: BoxLayoutFrame.java
2   // Demonstrating BoxLayout.
3   import java.awt.Dimension;
4   import javax.swing.JFrame;
5   import javax.swing.Box;
6   import javax.swing.JButton;
7   import javax.swing.BoxLayout;
8   import javax.swing.JPanel;
9   import javax.swing.JTabbedPane;
10
11  public class BoxLayoutFrame extends JFrame
12  {
13     // set up GUI
14     public BoxLayoutFrame()
15     {
16        super("Demonstrating BoxLayout");
17
18        // create Box containers with BoxLayout
19        Box horizontal1 = Box.createHorizontalBox();
20        Box vertical1 = Box.createVerticalBox();
21        Box horizontal2 = Box.createHorizontalBox();
22        Box vertical2 = Box.createVerticalBox();
23
24        final int SIZE = 3; // number of buttons on each Box
25
26        // add buttons to Box horizontal1
27        for (int count = 0; count < SIZE; count++)
28           horizontal1.add(new JButton("Button " + count));
29
30        // create strut and add buttons to Box vertical1
31        for (int count = 0; count < SIZE; count++)
32        {
33           vertical1.add(Box.createVerticalStrut(25));
34           vertical1.add(new JButton("Button " + count));
35        }
```

Fig. 22.16 | BoxLayout layout manager. (Part 1 of 2.)

```
36
37        // create horizontal glue and add buttons to Box horizontal2
38        for (int count = 0; count < SIZE; count++)
39        {
40            horizontal2.add(Box.createHorizontalGlue());
41            horizontal2.add(new JButton("Button " + count));
42        }
43
44        // create rigid area and add buttons to Box vertical2
45        for (int count = 0; count < SIZE; count++)
46        {
47            vertical2.add(Box.createRigidArea(new Dimension(12, 8)));
48            vertical2.add(new JButton("Button " + count));
49        }
50
51        // create vertical glue and add buttons to panel
52        JPanel panel = new JPanel();
53        panel.setLayoutnew BoxLayout(panel, BoxLayout.Y_AXIS) ();
54
55        for (int count = 0; count < SIZE; count++)
56        {
57            panel.add(Box.createGlue());
58            panel.add(new JButton("Button " + count));
59        }
60
61        // create a JTabbedPane
62        JTabbedPane tabs = new JTabbedPane(
63            JTabbedPane.TOP, JTabbedPane.SCROLL_TAB_LAYOUT);
64
65        // place each container on tabbed pane
66        tabs.addTab("Horizontal Box", horizontal1);
67        tabs.addTab("Vertical Box with Struts", vertical1);
68        tabs.addTab("Horizontal Box with Glue", horizontal2);
69        tabs.addTab("Vertical Box with Rigid Areas", vertical2);
70        tabs.addTab("Vertical Box with Glue", panel);
71
72        add(tabs); // place tabbed pane on frame
73    } // end BoxLayoutFrame constructor
74 } // end class BoxLayoutFrame
```

Fig. 22.16 | BoxLayout layout manager. (Part 2 of 2.)

```
1   // Fig. 22.17: BoxLayoutDemo.java
2   // Demonstrating BoxLayout.
3   import javax.swing.JFrame;
4
5   public class BoxLayoutDemo
6   {
7       public static void main(String[] args)
8       {
9           BoxLayoutFrame boxLayoutFrame = new BoxLayoutFrame();
```

Fig. 22.17 | Test class for BoxLayoutFrame. (Part 1 of 2.)

```
10          boxLayoutFrame.setDefaultCloseOperation(JFrame.EXIT_ON_CLOSE);
11          boxLayoutFrame.setSize(400, 220);
12          boxLayoutFrame.setVisible(true);
13      }
14  } // end class BoxLayoutDemo
```

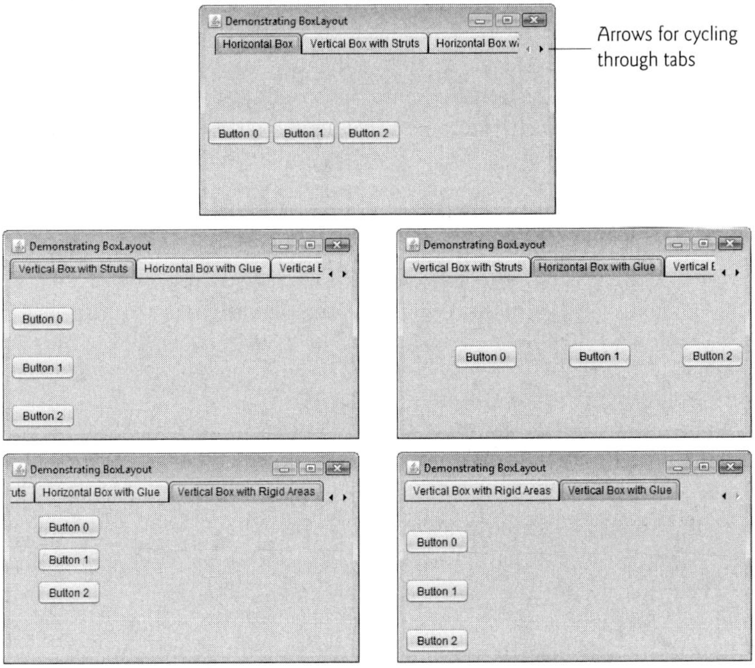

Fig. 22.17 | Test class for BoxLayoutFrame. (Part 2 of 2.)

Creating *Box* Containers

Lines 19–22 create Box containers. References horizontal1 and horizontal2 are initialized with static Box method createHorizontalBox, which returns a Box container with a horizontal BoxLayout in which GUI components are arranged left-to-right. Variables vertical1 and vertical2 are initialized with static Box method **createVerticalBox**, which returns references to Box containers with a vertical BoxLayout in which GUI components are arranged top-to-bottom.

Struts

The loop at lines 27–28 adds three JButtons to horizontal1. The for statement at lines 31–35 adds three JButtons to vertical1. Before adding each button, line 33 adds a **vertical strut** to the container with static Box method **createVerticalStrut**. A vertical strut is an invisible GUI component that has a fixed pixel height and is used to guarantee a fixed amount of space between GUI components. The int argument to method create-VerticalStrut determines the height of the strut in pixels. When the container is resized, the distance between GUI components separated by struts does not change. Class Box also declares method **createHorizontalStrut** for horizontal BoxLayouts.

Glue

The for statement at lines 38–42 adds three JButtons to horizontal2. Before adding each button, line 40 adds **horizontal glue** to the container with static Box method **create-HorizontalGlue**. Horizontal glue is an invisible GUI component that can be used between fixed-size GUI components to occupy additional space. Normally, extra space appears to the right of the last horizontal GUI component or below the last vertical one in a BoxLayout. Glue allows the extra space to be placed between GUI components. When the container is resized, components separated by glue components remain the same size, but the glue stretches or contracts to occupy the space between them. Class Box also declares method **createVerticalGlue** for vertical BoxLayouts.

Rigid Areas

The for statement at lines 45–49 adds three JButtons to vertical2. Before each button is added, line 47 adds a **rigid area** to the container with static Box method **create-RigidArea**. A rigid area is an invisible GUI component that always has a fixed pixel width and height. The argument to method createRigidArea is a Dimension object that specifies the area's width and height.

*Setting a **BoxLayout** for a **Container***

Lines 52–53 create a JPanel object and set its layout to a BoxLayout in the conventional manner, using Container method setLayout. The BoxLayout constructor receives a reference to the container for which it controls the layout and a constant indicating whether the layout is horizontal (**BoxLayout.X_AXIS**) or vertical (**BoxLayout.Y_AXIS**).

*Adding **Glue** and **JButtons***

The for statement at lines 55–59 adds three JButtons to panel. Before adding each button, line 57 adds a glue component to the container with static Box method **create-Glue**. This component expands or contracts based on the size of the Box.

*Creating the **JTabbedPane***

Lines 62–63 create a JTabbedPane to display the five containers in this program. The argument **JTabbedPane.TOP** sent to the constructor indicates that the tabs should appear at the top of the JTabbedPane. The argument **JTabbedPane.SCROLL_TAB_LAYOUT** specifies that the tabs should wrap to a new line if there are too many to fit on one line.

*Attaching the **Box** Containers and **JPanel** to the **JTabbedPane***

The Box containers and the JPanel are attached to the JTabbedPane at lines 66–70. Try executing the application. When the window appears, resize the window to see how the glue components, strut components and rigid area affect the layout on each tab.

22.10 GridBagLayout Layout Manager

One of the most powerful predefined layout managers is **GridBagLayout** (in package java.awt). This layout is similar to GridLayout in that it arranges components in a grid, but it's more flexible. The components can vary in size (i.e., they can occupy multiple rows and columns) and can be added in any order.

The first step in using GridBagLayout is determining the appearance of the GUI. For this step you need only a piece of paper. Draw the GUI, then draw a grid over it, dividing the components into rows and columns. The initial row and column numbers should be 0, so that the GridBagLayout layout manager can use the row and column numbers to properly place the components in the grid. Figure 22.18 demonstrates drawing the lines for the rows and columns over a GUI.

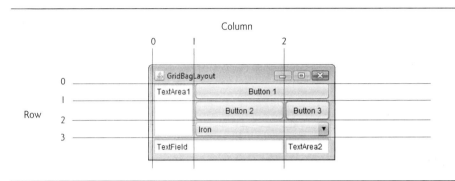

Fig. 22.18 | Designing a GUI that will use GridBagLayout.

GridBagConstraints

A **GridBagConstraints** object describes how a component is placed in a GridBagLayout. Several GridBagConstraints fields are summarized in Fig. 22.19.

Field	Description
anchor	Specifies the relative position (NORTH, NORTHEAST, EAST, SOUTHEAST, SOUTH, SOUTHWEST, WEST, NORTHWEST, CENTER) of the component in an area that it does not fill.
fill	Resizes the component in the specified direction (NONE, HORIZONTAL, VERTICAL, BOTH) when the display area is larger than the component.
gridx	The column in which the component will be placed.
gridy	The row in which the component will be placed.
gridwidth	The number of columns the component occupies.
gridheight	The number of rows the component occupies.
weightx	The amount of extra space to allocate horizontally. The grid slot can become wider when extra space is available.
weighty	The amount of extra space to allocate vertically. The grid slot can become taller when extra space is available.

Fig. 22.19 | GridBagConstraints fields.

GridBagConstraints *Field* anchor

GridBagConstraints field **anchor** specifies the relative position of the component in an area that it does not fill. The variable anchor is assigned one of the following GridBagConstraints constants: **NORTH, NORTHEAST, EAST, SOUTHEAST, SOUTH, SOUTHWEST, WEST, NORTHWEST** or **CENTER**. The default value is CENTER.

GridBagConstraints *Field* fill
GridBagConstraints field fill defines how the component grows if the area in which it can be displayed is larger than the component. The variable fill is assigned one of the following GridBagConstraints constants: **NONE**, **VERTICAL**, **HORIZONTAL** or **BOTH**. The default value is NONE, which indicates that the component will not grow in either direction. VERTICAL indicates that it will grow vertically. HORIZONTAL indicates that it will grow horizontally. BOTH indicates that it will grow in both directions.

GridBagConstraints *Fields* gridx *and* gridy
Variables **gridx** and **gridy** specify where the upper-left corner of the component is placed in the grid. Variable gridx corresponds to the column, and variable gridy corresponds to the row. In Fig. 22.18, the JComboBox (displaying "Iron") has a gridx value of 1 and a gridy value of 2.

GridBagConstraints *Field* gridwidth
Variable **gridwidth** specifies the number of columns a component occupies. The JCombo-Box occupies two columns. Variable **gridheight** specifies the number of rows a component occupies. The JTextArea on the left side of Fig. 22.18 occupies three rows.

GridBagConstraints *Field* weightx
Variable **weightx** specifies how to distribute extra horizontal space to grid slots in a Grid-BagLayout when the container is resized. A zero value indicates that the grid slot does not grow horizontally on its own. However, if the component spans a column containing a component with nonzero weightx value, the component with zero weightx value will grow horizontally in the same proportion as the other component(s) in that column. This is because each component must be maintained in the same row and column in which it was originally placed.

GridBagConstraints *Field* weighty
Variable **weighty** specifies how to distribute extra vertical space to grid slots in a Grid-BagLayout when the container is resized. A zero value indicates that the grid slot does not grow vertically on its own. However, if the component spans a row containing a component with nonzero weighty value, the component with zero weighty value grows vertically in the same proportion as the other component(s) in the same row.

Effects of weightx *and* weighty
In Fig. 22.18, the effects of weighty and weightx cannot easily be seen until the container is resized and additional space becomes available. Components with larger weight values occupy more of the additional space than those with smaller weight values.

Components should be given nonzero positive weight values—otherwise they'll "huddle" together in the middle of the container. Figure 22.20 shows the GUI of Fig. 22.18 with all weights set to zero.

Demonstrating GridBagLayout
The application in Figs. 22.21–22.22 uses the GridBagLayout layout manager to arrange the components of the GUI in Fig. 22.18. The application does nothing except demonstrate how to use GridBagLayout.

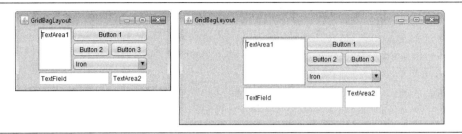

Fig. 22.20 | GridBagLayout with the weights set to zero.

```
 1   // Fig. 22.21: GridBagFrame.java
 2   // Demonstrating GridBagLayout.
 3   import java.awt.GridBagLayout;
 4   import java.awt.GridBagConstraints;
 5   import java.awt.Component;
 6   import javax.swing.JFrame;
 7   import javax.swing.JTextArea;
 8   import javax.swing.JTextField;
 9   import javax.swing.JButton;
10   import javax.swing.JComboBox;
11
12   public class GridBagFrame extends JFrame
13   {
14      private final GridBagLayout layout; // layout of this frame
15      private final GridBagConstraints constraints; // layout's constraints
16
17      // set up GUI
18      public GridBagFrame()
19      {
20         super("GridBagLayout");
21         layout = new GridBagLayout();
22         setLayout(layout); // set frame layout
23         constraints = new GridBagConstraints(); // instantiate constraints
24
25         // create GUI components
26         JTextArea textArea1 = new JTextArea("TextArea1", 5, 10);
27         JTextArea textArea2 = new JTextArea("TextArea2", 2, 2);
28
29         String[] names = { "Iron", "Steel", "Brass" };
30         JComboBox<String> comboBox = new JComboBox<String>(names);
31
32         JTextField textField = new JTextField("TextField");
33         JButton button1 = new JButton("Button 1");
34         JButton button2 = new JButton("Button 2");
35         JButton button3 = new JButton("Button 3");
36
37         // weightx and weighty for textArea1 are both 0: the default
38         // anchor for all components is CENTER: the default
39         constraints.fill = GridBagConstraints.BOTH;
40         addComponent(textArea1, 0, 0, 1, 3);
```

Fig. 22.21 | GridBagLayout layout manager. (Part 1 of 2.)

```
41
42        // weightx and weighty for button1 are both 0: the default
43        constraints.fill = GridBagConstraints.HORIZONTAL;
44        addComponent(button1, 0, 1, 2, 1);
45
46        // weightx and weighty for comboBox are both 0: the default
47        // fill is HORIZONTAL
48        addComponent(comboBox, 2, 1, 2, 1);
49
50        // button2
51        constraints.weightx = 1000;  // can grow wider
52        constraints.weighty = 1;        // can grow taller
53        constraints.fill = GridBagConstraints.BOTH;
54        addComponent(button2, 1, 1, 1, 1);
55
56        // fill is BOTH for button3
57        constraints.weightx = 0;
58        constraints.weighty = 0;
59        addComponent(button3, 1, 2, 1, 1);
60
61        // weightx and weighty for textField are both 0, fill is BOTH
62        addComponent(textField, 3, 0, 2, 1);
63
64        // weightx and weighty for textArea2 are both 0, fill is BOTH
65        addComponent(textArea2, 3, 2, 1, 1);
66     } // end GridBagFrame constructor
67
68     // method to set constraints on
69     private void addComponent(Component component,
70        int row, int column, int width, int height)
71     {
72        constraints.gridx = column;
73        constraints.gridy = row;
74        constraints.gridwidth = width;
75        constraints.gridheight = height;
76        layout.setConstraints(component, constraints); // set constraints
77        add(component); // add component
78     }
79  } // end class GridBagFrame
```

Fig. 22.21 | GridBagLayout layout manager. (Part 2 of 2.)

```
1   // Fig. 22.22: GridBagDemo.java
2   // Demonstrating GridBagLayout.
3   import javax.swing.JFrame;
4
5   public class GridBagDemo
6   {
7      public static void main(String[] args)
8      {
9         GridBagFrame gridBagFrame = new GridBagFrame();
```

Fig. 22.22 | Test class for GridBagFrame. (Part 1 of 2.)

```
10          gridBagFrame.setDefaultCloseOperation(JFrame.EXIT_ON_CLOSE);
11          gridBagFrame.setSize(300, 150);
12          gridBagFrame.setVisible(true);
13      }
14  } // end class GridBagDemo
```

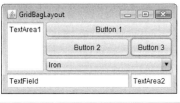

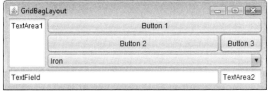

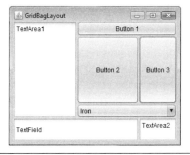

Fig. 22.22 | Test class for `GridBagFrame`. (Part 2 of 2.)

GUI Overview

The GUI contains three `JButton`s, two `JTextArea`s, a `JComboBox` and a `JTextField`. The layout manager is `GridBagLayout`. Lines 21–22 create the `GridBagLayout` object and set the layout manager for the `JFrame` to `layout`. Line 23 creates the `GridBagConstraints` object used to determine the location and size of each component in the grid. Lines 26–35 create each GUI component that will be added to the content pane.

JTextArea textArea1

Lines 39–40 configure `JTextArea` `textArea1` and add it to the content pane. The values for `weightx` and `weighty` values are not specified in `constraints`, so each has the value zero by default. Thus, the `JTextArea` will not resize itself even if space is available. However, it spans multiple rows, so the vertical size is subject to the `weighty` values of `JButton`s `button2` and `button3`. When either button is resized vertically based on its `weighty` value, the `JTextArea` is also resized.

Line 39 sets variable `fill` in `constraints` to `GridBagConstraints.BOTH`, causing the `JTextArea` to always fill its entire allocated area in the grid. An anchor value is not specified in `constraints`, so the default `CENTER` is used. We do not use variable anchor in this application, so all the components will use the default. Line 40 calls our utility method addComponent (declared at lines 69–78). The JTextArea object, the row, the column, the number of columns to span and the number of rows to span are passed as arguments.

JButton button1
JButton button1 is the next component added (lines 43–44). By default, the weightx and weighty values are still zero. The fill variable is set to HORIZONTAL—the component will always fill its area in the horizontal direction. The vertical direction is not filled. The weighty value is zero, so the button will become taller only if another component in the same row has a nonzero weighty value. JButton button1 is located at row 0, column 1. One row and two columns are occupied.

JComboBox comboBox
JComboBox comboBox is the next component added (line 48). By default, the weightx and weighty values are zero, and the fill variable is set to HORIZONTAL. The JComboBox button will grow only in the horizontal direction. The weightx, weighty and fill variables retain the values set in constraints until they're changed. The JComboBox button is placed at row 2, column 1. One row and two columns are occupied.

JButton button2
JButton button2 is the next component added (lines 51–54). It's given a weightx value of 1000 and a weighty value of 1. The area occupied by the button is capable of growing in the vertical and horizontal directions. The fill variable is set to BOTH, which specifies that the button will always fill the entire area. When the window is resized, button2 will grow. The button is placed at row 1, column 1. One row and one column are occupied.

JButton button3
JButton button3 is added next (lines 57–59). Both the weightx value and weighty value are set to zero, and the value of fill is BOTH. JButton button3 will grow if the window is resized—it's affected by the weight values of button2. The weightx value for button2 is much larger than that for button3. When resizing occurs, button2 will occupy a larger percentage of the new space. The button is placed at row 1, column 2. One row and one column are occupied.

JTextField textField *and* JTextArea textArea2
Both the JTextField textField (line 62) and JTextArea textArea2 (line 65) have a weightx value of 0 and a weighty value of 0. The value of fill is BOTH. The JTextField is placed at row 3, column 0, and the JTextArea at row 3, column 2. The JTextField occupies one row and two columns, the JTextArea one row and one column.

Method addComponent
Method addComponent's parameters are a Component reference component and integers row, column, width and height. Lines 72–73 set the GridBagConstraints variables gridx and gridy. The gridx variable is assigned the column in which the Component will be placed, and the gridy value is assigned the row in which the Component will be placed. Lines 74–75 set the GridBagConstraints variables gridwidth and gridheight. The gridwidth variable specifies the number of columns the Component will span in the grid,

and the gridheight variable specifies the number of rows the Component will span in the grid. Line 76 sets the GridBagConstraints for a component in the GridBagLayout. Method **setConstraints** of class GridBagLayout takes a Component argument and a GridBag-Constraints argument. Line 77 adds the component to the JFrame.

When you execute this application, try resizing the window to see how the constraints for each GUI component affect its position and size in the window.

GridBagConstraints Constants **RELATIVE** *and* **REMAINDER**

Instead of gridx and gridy, a variation of GridBagLayout uses GridBagConstraints constants **RELATIVE** and **REMAINDER**. RELATIVE specifies that the next-to-last component in a particular row should be placed to the right of the previous component in the row. REMAINDER specifies that a component is the last component in a row. Any component that is not the second-to-last or last component on a row must specify values for GridbagCon-straints variables gridwidth and gridheight. The application in Figs. 22.23–22.24 arranges components in GridBagLayout, using these constants.

```java
1   // Fig. 22.23: GridBagFrame2.java
2   // Demonstrating GridBagLayout constants.
3   import java.awt.GridBagLayout;
4   import java.awt.GridBagConstraints;
5   import java.awt.Component;
6   import javax.swing.JFrame;
7   import javax.swing.JComboBox;
8   import javax.swing.JTextField;
9   import javax.swing.JList;
10  import javax.swing.JButton;
11
12  public class GridBagFrame2 extends JFrame
13  {
14     private final GridBagLayout layout; // layout of this frame
15     private final GridBagConstraints constraints; // layout's constraints
16
17     // set up GUI
18     public GridBagFrame2()
19     {
20        super("GridBagLayout");
21        layout = new GridBagLayout();
22        setLayout(layout); // set frame layout
23        constraints = new GridBagConstraints(); // instantiate constraints
24
25        // create GUI components
26        String[] metals = { "Copper", "Aluminum", "Silver" };
27        JComboBox comboBox = new JComboBox(metals);
28
29        JTextField textField = new JTextField("TextField");
30
31        String[] fonts = { "Serif", "Monospaced" };
32        JList list = new JList(fonts);
33
```

Fig. 22.23 | GridBagConstraints constants RELATIVE and REMAINDER. (Part 1 of 2.)

```
34          String[] names = { "zero", "one", "two", "three", "four" };
35          JButton[] buttons = new JButton[names.length];
36
37          for (int count = 0; count < buttons.length; count++)
38             buttons[count] = new JButton(names[count]);
39
40          // define GUI component constraints for textField
41          constraints.weightx = 1;
42          constraints.weighty = 1;
43          constraints.fill = GridBagConstraints.BOTH;
44          constraints.gridwidth = GridBagConstraints.REMAINDER;
45          addComponent(textField);
46
47          // buttons[0] -- weightx and weighty are 1: fill is BOTH
48          constraints.gridwidth = 1;
49          addComponent(buttons[0]);
50
51          // buttons[1] -- weightx and weighty are 1: fill is BOTH
52          constraints.gridwidth = GridBagConstraints.RELATIVE;
53          addComponent(buttons[1]);
54
55          // buttons[2] -- weightx and weighty are 1: fill is BOTH
56          constraints.gridwidth = GridBagConstraints.REMAINDER;
57          addComponent(buttons[2]);
58
59          // comboBox -- weightx is 1: fill is BOTH
60          constraints.weighty = 0;
61          constraints.gridwidth = GridBagConstraints.REMAINDER;
62          addComponent(comboBox);
63
64          // buttons[3] -- weightx is 1: fill is BOTH
65          constraints.weighty = 1;
66          constraints.gridwidth = GridBagConstraints.REMAINDER;
67          addComponent(buttons[3]);
68
69          // buttons[4] -- weightx and weighty are 1: fill is BOTH
70          constraints.gridwidth = GridBagConstraints.RELATIVE;
71          addComponent(buttons[4]);
72
73          // list -- weightx and weighty are 1: fill is BOTH
74          constraints.gridwidth = GridBagConstraints.REMAINDER;
75          addComponent(list);
76       } // end GridBagFrame2 constructor
77
78       // add a component to the container
79       private void addComponent(Component component)
80       {
81          layout.setConstraints(component, constraints);
82          add(component); // add component
83       }
84    } // end class GridBagFrame2
```

Fig. 22.23 | GridBagConstraints constants RELATIVE and REMAINDER. (Part 2 of 2.)

```
 1   // Fig. 22.24: GridBagDemo2.java
 2   // Demonstrating GridBagLayout constants.
 3   import javax.swing.JFrame;
 4
 5   public class GridBagDemo2
 6   {
 7      public static void main(String[] args)
 8      {
 9         GridBagFrame2 gridBagFrame = new GridBagFrame2();
10         gridBagFrame.setDefaultCloseOperation(JFrame.EXIT_ON_CLOSE);
11         gridBagFrame.setSize(300, 200);
12         gridBagFrame.setVisible(true);
13      }
14   } // end class GridBagDemo2
```

 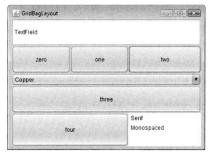

Fig. 22.24 | Test class for GridBagDemo2.

*Setting the **JFrame**'s Layout to a **GridBagLayout***

Lines 21–22 create a GridBagLayout and use it to set the JFrame's layout manager. The components that are placed in GridBagLayout are created in lines 27–38—they are a JComboBox, a JTextField, a JList and five JButtons.

*Configuring the **JTextField***

The JTextField is added first (lines 41–45). The weightx and weighty values are set to 1. The fill variable is set to BOTH. Line 44 specifies that the JTextField is the last component on the line. The JTextField is added to the content pane with a call to our utility method addComponent (declared at lines 79–83). Method addComponent takes a Component argument and uses GridBagLayout method setConstraints to set the constraints for the Component. Method add attaches the component to the content pane.

*Configuring **JButton buttons[0]***

JButton buttons[0] (lines 48–49) has weightx and weighty values of 1. The fill variable is BOTH. Because buttons[0] is not one of the last two components on the row, it's given a gridwidth of 1 and so will occupy one column. The JButton is added to the content pane with a call to utility method addComponent.

Configuring JButton buttons[1]
JButton buttons[1] (lines 52–53) has weightx and weighty values of 1. The fill variable is BOTH. Line 52 specifies that the JButton is to be placed relative to the previous component. The Button is added to the JFrame with a call to addComponent.

Configuring JButton buttons[2]
JButton buttons[2] (lines 56–57) has weightx and weighty values of 1. The fill variable is BOTH. This JButton is the last component on the line, so REMAINDER is used. The JButton is added to the content pane with a call to addComponent.

Configuring JComboBox
The JComboBox (lines 60–62) has a weightx of 1 and a weighty of 0. The JComboBox will not grow vertically. The JComboBox is the only component on the line, so REMAINDER is used. The JComboBox is added to the content pane with a call to addComponent.

Configuring JButton buttons[3]
JButton buttons[3] (lines 65–67) has weightx and weighty values of 1. The fill variable is BOTH. This JButton is the only component on the line, so REMAINDER is used. The JButton is added to the content pane with a call to addComponent.

Configuring JButton buttons[4]
JButton buttons[4] (lines 70–71) has weightx and weighty values of 1. The fill variable is BOTH. This JButton is the next-to-last component on the line, so RELATIVE is used. The JButton is added to the content pane with a call to addComponent.

Configuring JList
The JList (lines 74–75) has weightx and weighty values of 1. The fill variable is BOTH. The JList is added to the content pane with a call to addComponent.

22.11 Wrap-Up

This chapter completes our introduction to GUIs. In this chapter, we discussed additional GUI topics, such as menus, sliders, pop-up menus, multiple-document interfaces, tabbed panes and Java's pluggable look-and-feel. All these components can be added to existing applications to make them easier to use and understand. We also presented additional layout managers for organizing and sizing GUI components. In the next chapter, you'll learn about multithreading, which allows you to specify that an application should perform multiple tasks at once.

Summary

Section 22.2 JSlider
• JSliders (p. 904) enable you to select from a range of integer values. They can display major and minor tick marks, and labels for the tick marks (p. 904). They also support snap-to ticks (p. 904)—positioning the thumb (p. 904) between two tick marks snaps it to the closest tick mark.

- JSliders have either horizontal or vertical orientation. For a horizontal JSlider, the minimum value is at the extreme left and the maximum value at the extreme right. For a vertical JSlider, the minimum value is at the extreme bottom and the maximum value at the extreme top. The position of the thumb indicates the current value of the JSlider. Method getValue (p. 908) of class JSlider returns the current thumb position.

- JSlider method setMajorTickSpacing () sets the spacing for tick marks on a JSlider. Method setPaintTicks (p. 908) with a true argument indicates that the tick marks should be displayed.

- JSliders generate ChangeEvents when the user interacts with a JSlider. A ChangeListener (p. 908) declares method stateChanged (p. 908) that can respond to ChangeEvents.

Section 22.3 Understanding Windows in Java
- A window's (p. 908) events can be handled by a WindowListener (p. 909), which provides seven window-event-handling methods—windowActivated, windowClosed, windowClosing, window-Deactivated, windowDeiconified, windowIconified and windowOpened.

Section 22.4 Using Menus with Frames
- Menus neatly organize commands in a GUI. In Swing GUIs, menus can be attached only to objects of classes with method setJMenuBar (p. 909).

- A JMenuBar (p. 909) is a container for menus. A JMenuItem appears in a menu. A JMenu (p. 909) contains menu items and can be added to a JMenuBar or to other JMenus as submenus.

- When a menu is clicked, it expands to show its list of menu items.

- When a JCheckBoxMenuItem (p. 910) is selected, a check appears to the left of the menu item. When the JCheckBoxMenuItem is selected again, the check is removed.

- In a ButtonGroup, only one JRadioButtonMenuItem (p. 910) can be selected at a time.

- AbstractButton method setMnemonic (p. 915) specifies the mnemonic (p. 910) for a button. Mnemonic characters are normally displayed with an underline.

- A modal dialog box (p. 915) does not allow access to any other window in the application until the dialog is dismissed. The dialogs displayed with class JOptionPane are modal dialogs. Class JDialog (p. 915) can be used to create your own modal or nonmodal dialogs.

Section 22.5 JPopupMenu
- Context-sensitive pop-up menus (p. 917) are created with class JPopupMenu. The pop-up trigger event occurs normally when the user presses and releases the right mouse button. MouseEvent method isPopupTrigger (p. 920) returns true if the pop-up trigger event occurred.

- JPopupMenu method show (p. 920) displays a JPopupMenu. The first argument specifies the origin component, which helps determine where the JPopupMenu will appear. The last two arguments are the coordinates from the origin component's upper-left corner, at which the JPopupMenu appears.

Section 22.6 Pluggable Look-and-Feel
- Class UIManager.LookAndFeelInfo (p. 921) maintains information about a look-and-feel.

- UIManager (p. 921) static method getInstalledLookAndFeels (p. 921) returns an array of UIManager.LookAndFeelInfo objects that describe the available look-and-feels.

- UIManager static method setLookAndFeel (p. 924) changes the look-and-feel. SwingUtilities (p. 924) static method updateComponentTreeUI (p. 924) changes the look-and-feel of every component attached to its Component argument to the new look-and-feel.

Section 22.7 *JDesktopPane and JInternalFrame*
- Many of today's applications use a multiple-document interface (MDI; p. 925) to manage several open documents that are being processed in parallel. Swing's JDesktopPane (p. 925) and JInternalFrame (p. 925) classes provide support for creating multiple-document interfaces.

Section 22.8 *JTabbedPane*
- A JTabbedPane (p. 928) arranges GUI components into layers, of which only one is visible at a time. Users access each layer by clicking its tab.

Section 22.9 *BoxLayout Layout Manager*
- BoxLayout)p. 939) arranges GUI components left-to-right or top-to-bottom in a container.
- Class Box represents a container with BoxLayout as its default layout manager and provides static methods to create a Box with a horizontal or vertical BoxLayout.

Section 22.10 *GridBagLayout Layout Manager*
- GridBagLayout (p. 934) is similar to GridLayout, but each component size can vary.
- A GridBagConstraints object (p. 935) specifies how a component is placed in a GridBagLayout.

Self-Review Exercises

22.1 Fill in the blanks in each of the following statements:
- a) The _____ class is used to create a menu object.
- b) The _____ method of class JMenu places a separator bar in a menu.
- c) JSlider events are handled by the _____ method of interface _____.
- d) The GridBagConstraints instance variable _____ is set to CENTER by default.

22.2 State whether each of the following is *true* or *false*. If *false*, explain why.
- a) When the programmer creates a JFrame, a minimum of one menu must be created and added to the JFrame.
- b) The variable fill belongs to the GridBagLayout class.
- c) Drawing on a GUI component is performed with respect to the (0, 0) upper-left corner coordinate of the component.
- d) The default layout for a Box is BoxLayout.

22.3 Find the error(s) in each of the following and explain how to correct the error(s).
- a) JMenubar b;
- b) mySlider = JSlider(1000, 222, 100, 450);
- c) gbc.fill = GridBagConstraints.NORTHWEST;   // set fill
- d) // override to paint on a customized Swing component
```
public void paintcomponent(Graphics g)
{
    g.drawString("HELLO", 50, 50);
}
```
- e) // create a JFrame and display it
```
JFrame f = new JFrame("A Window");
f.setVisible(true);
```

Answers to Self-Review Exercises

22.1 a) JMenu. b) addSeparator. c) stateChanged, ChangeListener. d) anchor.

22.2 a) False. A JFrame does not require any menus.

b) False. The variable `fill` belongs to the `GridBagConstraints` class.

c) True.

d) True.

22.3 a) `JMenubar` should be `JMenuBar`.

b) The first argument to the constructor should be `SwingConstants.HORIZONTAL` or `Swing-Constants.VERTICAL`, and the keyword new must be used after the = operator. Also, the minimum value should be less than the maximum and the initial value should be in range.

c) The constant should be either `BOTH`, `HORIZONTAL`, `VERTICAL` or `NONE`.

d) `paintcomponent` should be `paintComponent`, and the method should call `super.paint-Component(g)` as its first statement.

e) The `JFrame`'s `setSize` method must also be called to establish the size of the window.

Exercises

22.4 *(Fill-in-the-Blanks)* Fill in the blanks in each of the following statements:

a) A `JMenuItem` that is a `JMenu` is called a(n) _____.

b) Method _____ attaches a `JMenuBar` to a `JFrame`.

c) Container class _____ has a default `BoxLayout`.

d) A(n) _____ manages a set of child windows declared with class `JInternalFrame`.

22.5 *(True or False)* State whether each of the following is *true* or *false*. If *false*, explain why.

a) Menus require a `JMenuBar` object so they can be attached to a `JFrame`.

b) `BoxLayout` is the default layout manager for a `JFrame`.

c) `JApplet`s can contain menus.

22.6 *(Find the Code Errors)* Find the error(s) in each of the following. Explain how to correct the error(s).

a) `x.add(new JMenuItem("Submenu Color")); // create submenu`

b) `container.setLayout(new GridbagLayout());`

22.7 *(Display a Circle and Its Attributes)* Write a program that displays a circle of random size and calculates and displays the area, radius, diameter and circumference. Use the following equations: *diameter* = 2 × *radius*, *area* = π × *radius*², *circumference* = 2 × π × *radius*. Use the constant `Math.PI` for pi (π). All drawing should be done on a subclass of `JPanel`, and the results of the calculations should be displayed in a read-only `JTextArea`.

22.8 *(Using a JSlider)* Enhance the program in Exercise 22.7 by allowing the user to alter the radius with a `JSlider`. The program should work for all radii in the range from 100 to 200. As the radius changes, the diameter, area and circumference should be updated and displayed. The initial radius should be 150. Use the equations from Exercise 22.7. All drawing should be done on a subclass of `JPanel`, and the results of the calculations should be displayed in a read-only `JTextArea`.

22.9 *(Varying `weightx` and `weighty`)* Explore the effects of varying the `weightx` and `weighty` values of the program in Fig. 22.21. What happens when a slot has a nonzero weight but is not allowed to fill the whole area (i.e., the `fill` value is not `BOTH`)?

22.10 *(Synchronizing a JSlider and a JTextField)* Write a program that uses the `paintComponent` method to draw the current value of a `JSlider` on a subclass of `JPanel`. In addition, provide a `JTextField` where a specific value can be entered. The `JTextField` should display the current value of the `JSlider` at all times. Changing the value in the `JTextField` should also update the `JSlider`. A `JLabel` should be used to identify the `JTextField`. The `JSlider` methods `setValue` and `getValue` should be used. [*Note:* The `setValue` method is a `public` method that does not return a value and takes one integer argument, the `JSlider` value, which determines the position of the thumb.]

22.11 *(Creating a Color Chooser)* Declare a subclass of JPanel called MyColorChooser that provides three JSlider objects and three JTextField objects. Each JSlider represents the values from 0 to 255 for the red, green and blue parts of a color. Use these values as the arguments to the Color constructor to create a new Color object. Display the current value of each JSlider in the corresponding JTextField. When the user changes the value of the JSlider, the JTextField should be changed accordingly. Use your new GUI component as part of an application that displays the current Color value by drawing a filled rectangle.

22.12 *(Creating a Color Chooser: Modification)* Modify the MyColorChooser class of Exercise 22.11 to allow the user to enter an integer value into a JTextField to set the red, green or blue value. When the user presses *Enter* in the JTextField, the corresponding JSlider should be set to the appropriate value.

22.13 *(Creating a Color Chooser: Modification)* Modify the application in Exercise 22.12 to draw the current color as a rectangle on an instance of a subclass of JPanel which provides its own paintComponent method to draw the rectangle and provides *set* methods to set the red, green and blue values for the current color. When any *set* method is invoked, the drawing panel should automatically repaint itself.

22.14 *(Drawing Application)* Modify the application in Exercise 22.13 to allow the user to drag the mouse across the drawing panel (a subclass of JPanel) to draw a shape in the current color. Enable the user to choose what shape to draw.

22.15 *(Drawing Application Modification)* Modify the application in Exercise 22.14 to allow the user to terminate the application by clicking the close box on the window that is displayed and by selecting Exit from a File menu. Use the techniques shown in Fig. 22.5.

22.16 *(Complete Drawing Application)* Using the techniques developed in this chapter and Chapter 12, create a complete drawing application. The program should use the GUI components from Chapter 12 and this chapter to enable the user to select the shape, color and fill characteristics. Each shape should be stored in an array of MyShape objects, where MyShape is the superclass in your hierarchy of shape classes. Use a JDesktopPane and JInternalFrames to allow the user to create multiple separate drawings in separate child windows. Create the user interface as a separate child window containing all the GUI components that allow the user to determine the characteristics of the shape to be drawn. The user can then click in any JInternalFrame to draw the shape.

Concurrency

23

The most general definition of beauty…Multeity in Unity.
—Samuel Taylor Coleridge

Do not block the way of inquiry.
—Charles Sanders Peirce

Learn to labor and to wait.
—Henry Wadsworth Longfellow

Objectives

In this chapter you'll:

- Understand concurrency, parallelism and multithreading.

- Learn the thread life cycle.

- Use `ExecutorService` to launch concurrent threads that execute `Runnable`s.

- Use `synchronized` methods to coordinate access to shared mutable data.

- Understand producer/ consumer relationships.

- Use `SwingWorker` to update Swing GUIs in a thread-safe manner.

- Compare the performance of `Arrays` methods `sort` and `parallelSort` on a multi-core system.

- Use parallel streams for better performance on multi-core systems.

- Use `CompletableFuture`s to execute long calculations asynchronously and get the results in the future.

23.1 Introduction

[Note: Sections marked "Advanced" are intended for readers who wish a deeper treatment of concurrency and may be skipped by readers preferring only basic coverage.] It would be nice if we could focus our attention on performing only one task at a time and doing it well. That's usually difficult to do in a complex world in which there's so much going on at once. This chapter presents Java's capabilities for developing programs that create and manage multiple tasks. As we'll demonstrate, this can greatly improve program performance.

When we say that two tasks are operating **concurrently**, we mean that they're both *making progress* at once. Until recently, most computers had only a single processor. Operating systems on such computers execute tasks concurrently by rapidly switching between them, doing a small portion of each before moving on to the next, so that all tasks keep progressing. For example, it's common for personal computers to compile a program, send a file to a printer, receive electronic mail messages over a network and more, concurrently. Since its inception, Java has supported concurrency.

When we say that two tasks are operating **in parallel**, we mean that they're executing *simultaneously*. In this sense, parallelism is a subset of concurrency. The human body performs a great variety of operations in parallel. Respiration, blood circulation, digestion, thinking and walking, for example, can occur in parallel, as can all the senses—sight, hearing, touch, smell and taste. It's believed that this parallelism is possible because the human brain is thought to contain billions of "processors." Today's multi-core computers have multiple processors that can perform tasks in parallel.

Java Concurrency

Java makes concurrency available to you through the language and APIs. Java programs can have multiple **threads of execution**, where each thread has its own method-call stack and program counter, allowing it to execute concurrently with other threads while sharing with them application-wide resources such as memory and file handles. This capability is called **multithreading**.

Performance Tip 23.1

A problem with single-threaded applications that can lead to poor responsiveness is that lengthy activities must complete before others can begin. In a multithreaded application, threads can be distributed across multiple cores (if available) so that multiple tasks execute in parallel and the application can operate more efficiently. Multithreading can also increase performance on single-processor systems—when one thread cannot proceed (because, for example, it's waiting for the result of an I/O operation), another can use the processor.

Concurrent Programming Uses

We'll discuss many applications of **concurrent programming**. For example, when streaming an audio or video over the Internet, the user may not want to wait until the entire audio or video downloads before starting the playback. To solve this problem, multiple threads can be used—one to download the audio or video (later in the chapter we'll refer to this as a *producer*), and another to play it (later in the chapter we'll refer to this as a *consumer*). These activities proceed concurrently. To avoid choppy playback, the threads are **synchronized** (that is, their actions are coordinated) so that the player thread doesn't begin until there's a sufficient amount of the audio or video in memory to keep the player thread busy. Producer and consumer threads *share memory*—we'll show how to coordinate these threads to ensure correct execution. The Java Virtual Machine (JVM) creates threads to run programs and threads to perform housekeeping tasks such as garbage collection.

Concurrent Programming Is Difficult

Writing multithreaded programs can be tricky. Although the human mind can perform functions concurrently, people find it difficult to jump between parallel trains of thought. To see why multithreaded programs can be difficult to write and understand, try the following experiment: Open three books to page 1, and try reading the books concurrently. Read a few words from the first book, then a few from the second, then a few from the third, then loop back and read the next few words from the first book, and so on. After this experiment, you'll appreciate many of the challenges of multithreading—switching between the books, reading briefly, remembering your place in each book, moving the book you're reading closer so that you can see it and pushing the books you're not reading aside—and, amid all this chaos, trying to comprehend the content of the books!

Use the Prebuilt Classes of the Concurrency APIs Whenever Possible

Programming concurrent applications is difficult and error prone. If you must use synchronization in a program, follow these guidelines:

1. *The vast majority of programmers should use existing collection classes and interfaces from the concurrency APIs that manage synchronization for you—such as the* Array-

BlockingQueue class (an implementation of interface BlockingQueue) we discuss in Section 23.6. Two other concurrency API classes that you'll use frequently are `LinkedBlockingQueue` and `ConcurrentHashMap` (each summarized in Fig. 23.22). The concurrency API classes are written by experts, have been thoroughly tested and debugged, operate efficiently and help you avoid common traps and pitfalls. Section 23.10 overviews Java's pre-built concurrent collections.

2. For advanced programmers who want to control synchronization, use the `synchronized` keyword and `Object` methods `wait`, `notify` and `notifyAll`, which we discuss in the optional Section 23.7.

3. Only the most advanced programmers should use `Locks` and `Conditions`, which we introduce in the optional Section 23.9, and classes like `LinkedTransferQueue`—an implementation of interface `TransferQueue`—which we summarize in Fig. 23.22.

You might want to read our discussions of the more advanced features in items 2 and 3 above, even though you most likely will not use them. We explain these because:

• They provide a solid basis for understanding how concurrent applications synchronize access to shared memory.

• By showing you the complexity involved in using these low-level features, we hope to impress upon you the message: *Use the simpler prebuilt concurrency capabilities whenever possible.*

23.2 Thread States and Life Cycle

At any time, a thread is said to be in one of several **thread states**—illustrated in the UML state diagram in Fig. 23.1. Several of the terms in the diagram are defined in later sections. We include this discussion to help you understand what's going on "under the hood" in a Java multithreaded environment. Java hides most of this detail from you, greatly simplifying the task of developing multithreaded applications.

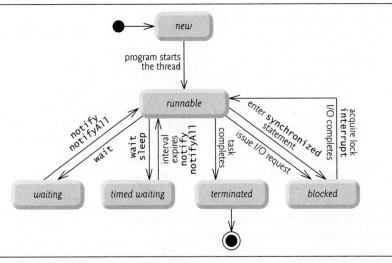

Fig. 23.1 | Thread life-cycle UML state diagram.

23.2.1 *New* and *Runnable* States

A new thread begins its life cycle in the *new* state. It remains in this state until the program starts the thread, which places it in the *runnable* state. A thread in the *runnable* state is considered to be executing its task.

23.2.2 *Waiting* State

Sometimes a *runnable* thread transitions to the *waiting* state while it waits for another thread to perform a task. A *waiting* thread transitions back to the *runnable* state only when another thread notifies it to continue executing.

23.2.3 *Timed Waiting* State

A *runnable* thread can enter the *timed waiting* state for a specified interval of time. It transitions back to the *runnable* state when that time interval expires or when the event it's waiting for occurs. *Timed waiting* threads and *waiting* threads cannot use a processor, even if one is available. A *runnable* thread can transition to the *timed waiting* state if it provides an optional wait interval when it's waiting for another thread to perform a task. Such a thread returns to the *runnable* state when it's notified by another thread or when the timed interval expires—whichever comes first. Another way to place a thread in the *timed waiting* state is to put a *runnable* thread to sleep—a **sleeping thread** remains in the *timed waiting* state for a designated period of time (called a **sleep interval**), after which it returns to the *runnable* state. Threads sleep when they momentarily do not have work to perform. For example, a word processor may contain a thread that periodically backs up (i.e., writes a copy of) the current document to disk for recovery purposes. If the thread did not sleep between successive backups, it would require a loop in which it continually tested whether it should write a copy of the document to disk. This loop would consume processor time without performing productive work, thus reducing system performance. In this case, it's more efficient for the thread to specify a sleep interval (equal to the period between successive backups) and enter the *timed waiting* state. This thread is returned to the *runnable* state when its sleep interval expires, at which point it writes a copy of the document to disk and reenters the *timed waiting* state.

23.2.4 *Blocked* State

A *runnable* thread transitions to the *blocked* state when it attempts to perform a task that cannot be completed immediately and it must temporarily wait until that task completes. For example, when a thread issues an input/output request, the operating system blocks the thread from executing until that I/O request completes—at that point, the *blocked* thread transitions to the *runnable* state, so it can resume execution. A *blocked* thread cannot use a processor, even if one is available.

23.2.5 *Terminated* State

A *runnable* thread enters the *terminated* state (sometimes called the *dead* state) when it successfully completes its task or otherwise terminates (perhaps due to an error). In the UML state diagram of Fig. 23.1, the *terminated* state is followed by the UML final state (the bull's-eye symbol) to indicate the end of the state transitions.

23.2.6 Operating-System View of the *Runnable* State

At the operating system level, Java's *runnable* state typically encompasses *two separate* states (Fig. 23.2). The operating system hides these states from the Java Virtual Machine (JVM), which sees only the *runnable* state. When a thread first transitions to the *runnable* state from the *new* state, it's in the *ready* state. A *ready* thread enters the **running** state (i.e., begins executing) when the operating system assigns it to a processor—also known as **dispatching the thread**. In most operating systems, each thread is given a small amount of processor time—called a **quantum** or **timeslice**—with which to perform its task. Deciding how large the quantum should be is a key topic in operating systems courses. When its quantum expires, the thread returns to the *ready* state, and the operating system assigns another thread to the processor. Transitions between the *ready* and *running* states are handled solely by the operating system. The JVM does not "see" the transitions—it simply views the thread as being *runnable* and leaves it up to the operating system to transition the thread between *ready* and *running*. The process that an operating system uses to determine which thread to dispatch is called **thread scheduling** and is dependent on thread priorities.

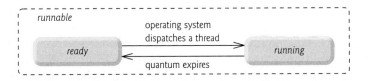

Fig. 23.2 | Operating system's internal view of Java's *runnable* state.

23.2.7 Thread Priorities and Thread Scheduling

Every Java thread has a **thread priority** that helps determine the order in which threads are scheduled. Each new thread inherits the priority of the thread that created it. Informally, higher-priority threads are more important to a program and should be allocated processor time before lower-priority threads. *Nevertheless, thread priorities cannot guarantee the order in which threads execute.*

It's recommended that you do not explicitly create and use `Thread` objects to implement concurrency, but rather use the `Executor` interface (which is described in Section 23.3). The `Thread` class does contain some useful `static` methods, which you *will* use later in the chapter.

Most operating systems support timeslicing, which enables threads of equal priority to share a processor. Without timeslicing, each thread in a set of equal-priority threads runs to completion (unless it leaves the *runnable* state and enters the *waiting* or *timed waiting* state, or gets interrupted by a higher-priority thread) before other threads of equal priority get a chance to execute. With timeslicing, even if a thread has *not* finished executing when its quantum expires, the processor is taken away from the thread and given to the next thread of equal priority, if one is available.

An *operating system's* **thread scheduler** determines which thread runs next. One simple thread-scheduler implementation keeps the highest-priority thread *running* at all times and, if there's more than one highest-priority thread, ensures that all such threads execute for a quantum each in **round-robin** fashion. This process continues until all threads run to completion.

Software Engineering Observation 23.1
Java provides higher-level concurrency utilities to hide much of this complexity and make multithreaded programming less error prone. Thread priorities are used behind the scenes to interact with the operating system, but most programmers who use Java multithreading will not be concerned with setting and adjusting thread priorities.

Portability Tip 23.1
Thread scheduling is platform dependent—the behavior of a multithreaded program could vary across different Java implementations.

23.2.8 Indefinite Postponement and Deadlock

When a higher-priority thread enters the *ready* state, the operating system generally preempts the currently *running* thread (an operation known as **preemptive scheduling**). Depending on the operating system, a steady influx of higher-priority threads could postpone—possibly indefinitely—the execution of lower-priority threads. Such **indefinite postponement** is sometimes referred to more colorfully as **starvation**. Operating systems employ a technique called *aging* to prevent starvation—as a thread waits in the *ready* state, the operating system gradually increases the thread's priority to ensure that the thread will eventually run.

Another problem related to indefinite postponement is called **deadlock**. This occurs when a waiting thread (let's call this thread1) cannot proceed because it's waiting (either directly or indirectly) for another thread (let's call this thread2) to proceed, while simultaneously thread2 cannot proceed because it's waiting (either directly or indirectly) for thread1 to proceed. The two threads are waiting for each other, so the actions that would enable each thread to continue execution can never occur.

23.3 Creating and Executing Threads with the Executor Framework

This section demonstrates how to perform concurrent tasks in an application by using Executors and Runnable objects.

Creating Concurrent Tasks with the **Runnable** Interface
You implement the **Runnable** interface (of package java.lang) to specify a task that can execute concurrently with other tasks. The Runnable interface declares the single method **run**, which contains the code that defines the task that a Runnable object should perform.

Executing **Runnable** Objects with an **Executor**
To allow a Runnable to perform its task, you must execute it. An **Executor** object executes Runnables. It does this by creating and managing a group of threads called a **thread pool**. When an Executor begins executing a Runnable, the Executor calls the Runnable object's run method, which executes in the new thread.

The Executor interface declares a single method named **execute** which accepts a Runnable as an argument. The Executor assigns every Runnable passed to its execute method to one of the available threads in the thread pool. If there are no available threads, the Executor creates a new thread or waits for a thread to become available and assigns that thread the Runnable that was passed to method execute.

Using an Executor has many advantages over creating threads yourself. Executors can *reuse existing threads* to eliminate the overhead of creating a new thread for each task and can improve performance by *optimizing the number of threads* to ensure that the processor stays busy, without creating so many threads that the application runs out of resources.

Software Engineering Observation 23.2

Though it's possible to create threads explicitly, it's recommended that you use the Executor interface to manage the execution of Runnable objects.

Using Class *Executors* to Obtain an *ExecutorService*

The **ExecutorService** interface (of package java.util.concurrent) *extends* Executor and declares various methods for managing the life cycle of an Executor. You obtain an ExecutorService object by calling one of the **static** methods declared in class **Executors** (of package java.util.concurrent). We use interface ExecutorService and a method of class Executors in our example, which executes three tasks.

Implementing the *Runnable* Interface

Class PrintTask (Fig. 23.3) implements Runnable (line 5), *so that multiple PrintTasks can execute concurrently.* Variable sleepTime (line 8) stores a random integer value from 0 to 5 seconds created in the PrintTask constructor (line 17). Each thread running a Print-Task sleeps for the amount of time specified by sleepTime, then outputs its task's name and a message indicating that it's done sleeping.

```
 1   // Fig. 23.3: PrintTask.java
 2   // PrintTask class sleeps for a random time from 0 to 5 seconds
 3   import java.security.SecureRandom;
 4
 5   public class PrintTask implements Runnable
 6   {
 7      private static final SecureRandom generator = new SecureRandom();
 8      private final int sleepTime; // random sleep time for thread
 9      private final String taskName;
10
11      // constructor
12      public PrintTask(String taskName)
13      {
14         this.taskName = taskName;
15
16         // pick random sleep time between 0 and 5 seconds
17         sleepTime = generator.nextInt(5000); // milliseconds
18      }
19
20      // method run contains the code that a thread will execute
21      public void run()
22      {
23         try // put thread to sleep for sleepTime amount of time
24         {
25            System.out.printf("%s going to sleep for %d milliseconds.%n",
26               taskName, sleepTime);
```

Fig. 23.3 | PrintTask class sleeps for a random time from 0 to 5 seconds. (Part 1 of 2.)

```
27                Thread.sleep(sleepTime); // put thread to sleep
28            }
29            catch (InterruptedException exception)
30            {
31                exception.printStackTrace();
32                Thread.currentThread().interrupt(); // re-interrupt the thread
33            }
34
35            // print task name
36            System.out.printf("%s done sleeping%n", taskName);
37        }
38  } // end class PrintTask
```

Fig. 23.3 | PrintTask class sleeps for a random time from 0 to 5 seconds. (Part 2 of 2.)

A PrintTask executes when a thread calls the PrintTask's run method. Lines 25–26 display a message indicating the name of the currently executing task and that the task is going to sleep for sleepTime milliseconds. Line 27 invokes static method **sleep** of class Thread to place the thread in the *timed waiting* state for the specified amount of time. At this point, the thread loses the processor, and the system allows another thread to execute. When the thread awakens, it reenters the *runnable* state. When the PrintTask is assigned to a processor again, line 36 outputs a message indicating that the task is done sleeping, then method run terminates. The catch at lines 29–33 is required because method sleep might throw a *checked* exception of type **InterruptedException** if a sleeping thread's **interrupt** method is called.

Let the Thread Handle *InterruptedExceptions*

It's considered good practice to let the executing thread handle InterruptedExceptions. Normally, you'd do this by declaring that method run throws the exception, rather than catching the exception. However, recall from Chapter 11 that when you override a method, the throws may contain only the same exception types or a subset of the exception types declared in the original method's throws clause. Runnable method run does not have a throws clause in its original declaration, so we cannot provide one in line 21. To ensure that the executing thread receives the InterruptedException, line 32 first obtains a reference to the currently executing Thread by calling static method **currentThread**, then uses that Thread's interrupt method to deliver the InterruptedException to the current thread.[1]

Using the *ExecutorService* to Manage Threads that Execute *PrintTasks*

Figure 23.4 uses an ExecutorService object to manage threads that execute PrintTasks (as defined in Fig. 23.3). Lines 11–13 create and name three PrintTasks to execute. Line 18 uses Executors method **newCachedThreadPool** to obtain an ExecutorService that's capable of creating new threads as they're needed by the application. These threads are used by ExecutorService to execute the Runnables.

---

1. For detailed information on handling thread interruptions, see Chapter 7 of *Java Concurrency in Practice* by Brian Goetz, et al., Addison-Wesley Professional, 2006.

```
 1   // Fig. 23.4: TaskExecutor.java
 2   // Using an ExecutorService to execute Runnables.
 3   import java.util.concurrent.Executors;
 4   import java.util.concurrent.ExecutorService;
 5
 6   public class TaskExecutor
 7   {
 8      public static void main(String[] args)
 9      {
10         // create and name each runnable
11         PrintTask task1 = new PrintTask("task1");
12         PrintTask task2 = new PrintTask("task2");
13         PrintTask task3 = new PrintTask("task3");
14
15         System.out.println("Starting Executor");
16
17         // create ExecutorService to manage threads
18         ExecutorService executorService = Executors.newCachedThreadPool();
19
20         // start the three PrintTasks
21         executorService.execute(task1); // start task1
22         executorService.execute(task2); // start task2
23         executorService.execute(task3); // start task3
24
25         // shut down ExecutorService--it decides when to shut down threads
26         executorService.shutdown();
27
28         System.out.printf("Tasks started, main ends.%n%n");
29      }
30   } // end class TaskExecutor
```

```
Starting Executor
Tasks started, main ends

task1 going to sleep for 4806 milliseconds
task2 going to sleep for 2513 milliseconds
task3 going to sleep for 1132 milliseconds
task3 done sleeping
task2 done sleeping
task1 done sleeping
```

```
Starting Executor
task1 going to sleep for 3161 milliseconds.
task3 going to sleep for 532 milliseconds.
task2 going to sleep for 3440 milliseconds.
Tasks started, main ends.

task3 done sleeping
task1 done sleeping
task2 done sleeping
```

Fig. 23.4 | Using an ExecutorService to execute Runnables.

Lines 21–23 each invoke the ExecutorService's execute method, which executes its Runnable argument (in this case a PrintTask) some time in the future. The specified task may execute in one of the threads in the ExecutorService's thread pool, in a new thread created to execute it, or in the thread that called the execute method—the ExecutorService manages these details. Method execute returns immediately from each invocation—the program does *not* wait for each PrintTask to finish. Line 26 calls ExecutorService method **shutdown**, which notifies the ExecutorService to *stop accepting new tasks, but continues executing tasks that have already been submitted*. Once all of the previously submitted Runnables have completed, the ExecutorService terminates. Line 28 outputs a message indicating that the tasks were started and the main thread is finishing its execution.

Main Thread

The code in main executes in the **main thread**, which is created by the JVM. The code in the run method of PrintTask (lines 21–37 of Fig. 23.3) executes whenever the Executor starts each PrintTask—again, this is sometime after they're passed to the ExecutorService's execute method (Fig. 23.4, lines 21–23). When main terminates, the program itself continues running because there are still tasks that must finish executing. The program will not terminate until these tasks complete.

Sample Outputs

The sample outputs show each task's name and sleep time as the thread goes to sleep. The thread with the shortest sleep time *in most cases* awakens first, indicates that it's done sleeping and terminates. In Section 23.8, we discuss multithreading issues that could prevent the thread with the shortest sleep time from awakening first. In the first output, the main thread terminates *before* any of the PrintTasks output their names and sleep times. This shows that the main thread runs to completion before any of the PrintTasks gets a chance to run. In the second output, all of the PrintTasks output their names and sleep times *before* the main thread terminates. This shows that the PrintTasks started executing before the main thread terminated. Also, notice in the second example output, task3 goes to sleep before task2 last, even though we passed task2 to the ExecutorService's execute method before task3. This illustrates the fact that *we cannot predict the order in which the tasks will start executing, even if we know the order in which they were created and started*.

Waiting for Previously Scheduled Tasks to Terminate

After scheduling tasks to execute, you'll typically want to *wait for the tasks to complete*—for example, so that you can use the tasks' results. After calling method shutdown, you can call ExecutorService method awaitTermination to wait for scheduled tasks to complete. We demonstrate this in Fig. 23.7. We purposely did not call awaitTermination in Fig. 23.4 to demonstrate that a program can continue executing after the main thread terminates.

23.4 Thread Synchronization

When multiple threads share an object and it's *modified* by one or more of them, indeterminate results may occur (as we'll see in the examples) unless access to the shared object is managed properly. If one thread is in the process of updating a shared object and another thread also tries to update it, it's uncertain which thread's update takes effect. Similarly, if one thread is in the process of updating a shared object and another thread tries to read it, it's uncertain whether the reading thread will see the old value or the new one. In such cases, the program's behavior cannot be trusted—sometimes the program will produce the correct results, and sometimes it won't, and there won't be any indication that the shared object was manipulated incorrectly.

The problem can be solved by giving only one thread at a time *exclusive access* to code that accesses the shared object. During that time, other threads desiring to access the object are kept waiting. When the thread with exclusive access finishes accessing the object, one of the waiting threads is allowed to proceed. This process, called **thread synchronization**, coordinates access to shared data by multiple concurrent threads. By synchronizing threads in this manner, you can ensure that each thread accessing a shared object *excludes* all other threads from doing so simultaneously—this is called **mutual exclusion**.

23.4.1 Immutable Data

Actually, thread synchronization is necessary *only* for shared **mutable data**, i.e., data that may *change* during its lifetime. With shared **immutable data** that will *not* change, it's not possible for a thread to see old or incorrect values as a result of another thread's manipulation of that data.

When you share *immutable data* across threads, declare the corresponding data fields `final` to indicate that the values of the variables will *not* change after they're initialized. This prevents accidental modification of the shared data, which could compromise thread safety. *Labeling object references as `final` indicates that the reference will not change, but it does not guarantee that the referenced object is immutable—this depends entirely on the object's properties.* However, it's still good practice to mark references that will not change as `final`.

> **Software Engineering Observation 23.3**
>
> *Always declare data fields that you do not expect to change as `final`. Primitive variables that are declared as `final` can safely be shared across threads. An object reference that's declared as `final` ensures that the object it refers to will be fully constructed and initialized before it's used by the program, and prevents the reference from pointing to another object.*

23.4.2 Monitors

A common way to perform synchronization is to use Java's built-in **monitors**. Every object has a monitor and a **monitor lock** (or **intrinsic lock**). The monitor ensures that its object's monitor lock is held by a maximum of only one thread at any time. Monitors and monitor locks can thus be used to enforce mutual exclusion. If an operation requires the executing thread to *hold a lock* while the operation is performed, a thread must *acquire the lock* before proceeding with the operation. Other threads attempting to perform an operation that requires the same lock will be *blocked* until the first thread *releases the lock*, at which point the *blocked* threads may attempt to acquire the lock and proceed with the operation.

To specify that a thread must hold a monitor lock to execute a block of code, the code should be placed in a **synchronized statement**. Such code is said to be **guarded** by the monitor lock; a thread must **acquire the lock** to execute the guarded statements. The monitor allows only one thread at a time to execute statements within `synchronized` statements that lock on the same object, as only one thread at a time can hold the monitor lock. The `synchronized` statements are declared using the **synchronized** keyword:

```
synchronized (object)
{
    statements
}
```

where *object* is the object whose monitor lock will be acquired; *object* is normally this if it's the object in which the synchronized statement appears. If several synchronized statements in different threads are trying to execute on an object at the same time, only one of them may be active on the object—all the other threads attempting to enter a synchronized statement on the same object are placed in the *blocked* state.

When a synchronized statement finishes executing, the object's monitor lock is released and one of the *blocked* threads attempting to enter a synchronized statement can be allowed to acquire the lock to proceed. Java also allows **synchronized methods**. Before executing, a synchronized instance method must acquire the lock on the object that's used to call the method. Similarly, a static synchronized method must acquire the lock on the class that's used to call the method.

Software Engineering Observation 23.4
Using a synchronized block to enforce mutual exclusion is an example of the design pattern known as the Java Monitor Pattern (see section 4.2.1 of Java Concurrency in Practice *by Brian Goetz, et al., Addison-Wesley Professional, 2006).*

23.4.3 Unsynchronized Mutable Data Sharing

First, we illustrate the dangers of sharing an object across threads *without* proper synchronization. In this example (Figs. 23.5–23.7), two Runnables maintain references to a single integer array. Each Runnable writes three values to the array, then terminates. This may seem harmless, but we'll see that it can result in errors if the array is manipulated without synchronization.

Class *SimpleArray*
A SimpleArray object (Fig. 23.5) will be *shared* across multiple threads. SimpleArray will enable those threads to place int values into array (declared at line 9). Line 10 initializes variable writeIndex, which will be used to determine the array element that should be written to next. The constructor (lines 13–16) creates an integer array of the desired size.

```
 1   // Fig. 23.5: SimpleArray.java
 2   // Class that manages an integer array to be shared by multiple threads.
 3   import java.security.SecureRandom;
 4   import java.util.Arrays;
 5
 6   public class SimpleArray // CAUTION: NOT THREAD SAFE!
 7   {
 8       private static final SecureRandom generator = new SecureRandom();
 9       private final int[] array; // the shared integer array
10       private int writeIndex = 0; // shared index of next element to write
11
```

Fig. 23.5 | Class that manages an integer array to be shared by multiple threads. (*Caution:* The example of Figs. 23.5–23.7 is *not* thread safe.) (Part 1 of 2.)

```
12      // construct a SimpleArray of a given size
13      public SimpleArray(int size)
14      {
15          array = new int[size];
16      }
17
18      // add a value to the shared array
19      public void add(int value)
20      {
21          int position = writeIndex; // store the write index
22
23          try
24          {
25              // put thread to sleep for 0-499 milliseconds
26              Thread.sleep(generator.nextInt(500));
27          }
28          catch (InterruptedException ex)
29          {
30              Thread.currentThread().interrupt(); // re-interrupt the thread
31          }
32
33          // put value in the appropriate element
34          array[position] = value;
35          System.out.printf("%s wrote %2d to element %d.%n",
36              Thread.currentThread().getName(), value, position);
37
38          ++writeIndex; // increment index of element to be written next
39          System.out.printf("Next write index: %d%n", writeIndex);
40      }
41
42      // used for outputting the contents of the shared integer array
43      public String toString()
44      {
45          return Arrays.toString(array);
46      }
47  } // end class SimpleArray
```

Fig. 23.5 | Class that manages an integer array to be shared by multiple threads. (*Caution:* The example of Figs. 23.5–23.7 is *not* thread safe.) (Part 2 of 2.)

Method add (lines 19–40) allows new values to be inserted at the end of the array. Line 21 stores the current writeIndex value. Line 26 puts the thread that invokes add to sleep for a random interval from 0 to 499 milliseconds. This is done to make the problems associated with *unsynchronized access to shared mutable data* more obvious. After the thread is done sleeping, line 34 inserts the value passed to add into the array at the element specified by position. Lines 35–36 output a message indicating the executing thread's name, the value that was inserted in the array and where it was inserted. The expression Thread.currentThread().getName() (line 36) first obtains a reference to the currently executing Thread, then uses that Thread's getName method to obtain its name. Line 38 increments writeIndex so that the next call to add will insert a value in the array's next element. Lines 43–46 override method toString to create a String representation of the array's contents.

Class *ArrayWriter*

Class ArrayWriter (Fig. 23.6) implements the interface Runnable to define a task for inserting values in a SimpleArray object. The constructor (lines 10–14) takes two arguments—an integer value, which is the first value this task will insert in the SimpleArray object, and a reference to the SimpleArray object. Line 20 invokes method add on the SimpleArray object. The task completes after three consecutive integers beginning with startValue are inserted in the SimpleArray object.

```
1   // Fig. 23.6: ArrayWriter.java
2   // Adds integers to an array shared with other Runnables
3   import java.lang.Runnable;
4
5   public class ArrayWriter implements Runnable
6   {
7      private final SimpleArray sharedSimpleArray;
8      private final int startValue;
9
10     public ArrayWriter(int value, SimpleArray array)
11     {
12        startValue = value;
13        sharedSimpleArray = array;
14     }
15
16     public void run()
17     {
18        for (int i = startValue; i < startValue + 3; i++)
19        {
20           sharedSimpleArray.add(i); // add an element to the shared array
21        }
22     }
23  } // end class ArrayWriter
```

Fig. 23.6 | Adds integers to an array shared with other Runnables. (*Caution:* The example of Figs. 23.5–23.7 is *not* thread safe.)

Class *SharedArrayTest*

Class SharedArrayTest (Fig. 23.7) executes two ArrayWriter tasks that add values to a single SimpleArray object. Line 12 constructs a six-element SimpleArray object. Lines 15–16 create two new ArrayWriter tasks, one that places the values 1–3 in the Simple-Array object, and one that places the values 11–13. Lines 19–21 create an ExecutorSer-vice and execute the two ArrayWriters. Line 23 invokes the ExecutorService's shutDown method to *prevent additional tasks from starting* and to enable the application to terminate when the currently executing tasks complete execution.

```
1   // Fig. 23.7: SharedArrayTest.java
2   // Executing two Runnables to add elements to a shared SimpleArray.
3   import java.util.concurrent.Executors;
```

Fig. 23.7 | Executing two Runnables to add elements to a shared array. (*Caution:* The example of Figs. 23.5–23.7 is *not* thread safe.) (Part 1 of 3.)

```
4   import java.util.concurrent.ExecutorService;
5   import java.util.concurrent.TimeUnit;
6
7   public class SharedArrayTest
8   {
9      public static void main(String[] arg)
10     {
11        // construct the shared object
12        SimpleArray sharedSimpleArray = new SimpleArray(6);
13
14        // create two tasks to write to the shared SimpleArray
15        ArrayWriter writer1 = new ArrayWriter(1, sharedSimpleArray);
16        ArrayWriter writer2 = new ArrayWriter(11, sharedSimpleArray);
17
18        // execute the tasks with an ExecutorService
19        ExecutorService executorService = Executors.newCachedThreadPool();
20        executorService.execute(writer1);
21        executorService.execute(writer2);
22
23        executorService.shutdown();
24
25        try
26        {
27           // wait 1 minute for both writers to finish executing
28           boolean tasksEnded =
29              executorService.awaitTermination(1, TimeUnit.MINUTES);
30
31           if (tasksEnded)
32           {
33              System.out.printf("%nContents of SimpleArray:%n");
34              System.out.println(sharedSimpleArray); // print contents
35           }
36           else
37              System.out.println(
38                 "Timed out while waiting for tasks to finish.");
39        }
40        catch (InterruptedException ex)
41        {
42           ex.printStackTrace();
43        }
44     } // end main
45  } // end class SharedArrayTest
```

```
pool-1-thread-1 wrote  1 to element 0.
Next write index: 1
pool-1-thread-1 wrote  2 to element 1.
Next write index: 2
pool-1-thread-1 wrote  3 to element 2.
Next write index: 3
pool-1-thread-2 wrote 11 to element 0.
Next write index: 4
```

First **pool-1-thread-1** wrote the value 1 to element 0. Later **pool-1-thread-2** wrote the value 11 to element 0, thus *overwriting* the previously stored value.

Fig. 23.7 | Executing two **Runnables** to add elements to a shared array. (*Caution:* The example of Figs. 23.5–23.7 is *not* thread safe.) (Part 2 of 3.)

```
pool-1-thread-2 wrote 12 to element 4.
Next write index: 5
pool-1-thread-2 wrote 13 to element 5.
Next write index: 6

Contents of SimpleArray:
[11, 2, 3, 0, 12, 13]
```

Fig. 23.7 | Executing two Runnables to add elements to a shared array. (*Caution:* The example of Figs. 23.5–23.7 is *not* thread safe.) (Part 3 of 3.)

ExecutorService *Method* awaitTermination
Recall that ExecutorService method shutdown returns immediately. Thus any code that appears *after* the call to ExecutorService method shutdown in line 23 *will continue executing as long as the* main *thread is still assigned to a processor.* We'd like to output the SimpleArray object to show you the results *after* the threads complete their tasks. So, we need the program to wait for the threads to complete before main outputs the SimpleArray object's contents. Interface ExecutorService provides the **awaitTermination** method for this purpose. This method returns control to its caller either when all tasks executing in the ExecutorService complete or when the specified timeout elapses. If all tasks are completed before awaitTermination times out, this method returns true; otherwise it returns false. The two arguments to awaitTermination represent a timeout value and a unit of measure specified with a constant from class TimeUnit (in this case, TimeUnit.MINUTES).

Method awaitTermination throws an InterruptedException if the calling thread is interrupted while waiting for other threads to terminate. Because we catch this exception in the application's main method, there's no need to re-interrupt the main thread as this program will terminate as soon as main terminates.

In this example, if *both* tasks complete before awaitTermination times out, line 34 displays the SimpleArray object's contents. Otherwise, lines 37–38 display a message indicating that the tasks did not finish executing before awaitTermination timed out.

Sample Program Output
Figure 23.7's output shows the problems (highlighted in the output) that can be caused by *failure to synchronize access to shared mutable data.* The value 1 was written to element 0, then *overwritten* later by the value 11. Also, when writeIndex was incremented to 3, *nothing was written to that element*, as indicated by the 0 in that element of the printed array.

Recall that we added calls to Thread method sleep between operations on the shared mutable data to emphasize the *unpredictability of thread scheduling* and increase the likelihood of producing erroneous output. Even if these operations were allowed to proceed at their normal pace, you could still see errors in the program's output. However, modern processors can handle the simple operations of the SimpleArray method add so quickly that you might not see the errors caused by the two threads executing this method concurrently, even if you tested the program dozens of times. *One of the challenges of multithreaded programming is spotting the errors—they may occur so infrequently and unpredictably that a broken program does not produce incorrect results during testing, creating the illusion that the program is correct.* This is all the more reason to use predefined collections that handle the synchronization for you.

23.4.4 Synchronized Mutable Data Sharing—Making Operations Atomic

The output errors of Fig. 23.7 can be attributed to the fact that the shared object, Simple-Array, is not **thread safe**—SimpleArray is susceptible to errors if it's *accessed concurrently by multiple threads.* The problem lies in method add, which stores the value of writeIndex, places a new value in that element, then increments writeIndex. Such a method would present no problem in a single-threaded program. However, if one thread obtains the value of writeIndex, there's no guarantee that another thread cannot come along and increment writeIndex *before* the first thread has had a chance to place a value in the array. If this happens, the first thread will be writing to the array based on a **stale value** of writeIndex—a value that's no longer valid. Another possibility is that one thread might obtain the value of writeIndex *after* another thread adds an element to the array but *before* writeIndex is incremented. In this case, too, the first thread would write to the array based on an invalid value for writeIndex.

SimpleArray is *not thread safe because it allows any number of threads to read and modify shared mutable data concurrently*, which can cause errors. To make SimpleArray thread safe, we must ensure that no two threads can access its shared mutable data at the same time. While one thread is in the process of storing writeIndex, adding a value to the array, and incrementing writeIndex, *no other thread* may read or change the value of writeIndex or modify the contents of the array at any point during these three operations. In other words, we want these three operations—storing writeIndex, writing to the array, incrementing writeIndex—to be an **atomic operation**, which cannot be divided into smaller suboperations. (As you'll see in later examples, read operations on shared mutable data should also be atomic.) We can simulate atomicity by ensuring that only one thread carries out the three operations at a time. Any other threads that need to perform the operation must *wait* until the first thread has finished the add operation in its entirety.

Atomicity can be achieved using the synchronized keyword. By placing our three suboperations in a synchronized statement or synchronized method, we allow only one thread at a time to acquire the lock and perform the operations. When that thread has completed all of the operations in the synchronized block and releases the lock, another thread may acquire the lock and begin executing the operations. This ensures that a thread executing the operations will see the actual values of the shared mutable data and that *these values will not change unexpectedly in the middle of the operations as a result of another thread's modifying them.*

 Software Engineering Observation 23.5

Place all accesses to mutable data that may be shared by multiple threads inside synchronized statements or synchronized methods that synchronize on the same lock. When performing multiple operations on shared mutable data, hold the lock for the entirety of the operation to ensure that the operation is effectively atomic.

Class *SimpleArray* with Synchronization

Figure 23.8 displays class SimpleArray with the proper synchronization. Notice that it's identical to the SimpleArray class of Fig. 23.5, except that add is now a synchronized method (line 20). So, only one thread at a time can execute this method. We reuse classes ArrayWriter (Fig. 23.6) and SharedArrayTest (Fig. 23.7) from the previous example.

```java
 1   // Fig. 23.8: SimpleArray.java
 2   // Class that manages an integer array to be shared by multiple
 3   // threads with synchronization.
 4   import java.security.SecureRandom;
 5   import java.util.Arrays;
 6
 7   public class SimpleArray
 8   {
 9      private static final SecureRandom generator = new SecureRandom();
10      private final int[] array; // the shared integer array
11      private int writeIndex = 0; // index of next element to be written
12
13      // construct a SimpleArray of a given size
14      public SimpleArray(int size)
15      {
16         array = new int[size];
17      }
18
19      // add a value to the shared array
20      public synchronized void add(int value)
21      {
22         int position = writeIndex; // store the write index
23
24         try
25         {
26            // in real applications, you shouldn't sleep while holding a lock
27            Thread.sleep(generator.nextInt(500)); // for demo only
28         }
29         catch (InterruptedException ex)
30         {
31            Thread.currentThread().interrupt();
32         }
33
34         // put value in the appropriate element
35         array[position] = value;
36         System.out.printf("%s wrote %2d to element %d.%n",
37            Thread.currentThread().getName(), value, position);
38
39         ++writeIndex; // increment index of element to be written next
40         System.out.printf("Next write index: %d%n", writeIndex);
41      }
42
43      // used for outputting the contents of the shared integer array
44      public synchronized String toString()
45      {
46         return Arrays.toString(array);
47      }
48   } // end class SimpleArray
```

Fig. 23.8 | Class that manages an integer array to be shared by multiple threads with synchronization. (Part 1 of 2.)

```
pool-1-thread-1 wrote  1 to element 0.
Next write index: 1
pool-1-thread-2 wrote 11 to element 1.
Next write index: 2
pool-1-thread-2 wrote 12 to element 2.
Next write index: 3
pool-1-thread-2 wrote 13 to element 3.
Next write index: 4
pool-1-thread-1 wrote  2 to element 4.
Next write index: 5
pool-1-thread-1 wrote  3 to element 5.
Next write index: 6

Contents of SimpleArray:
[1, 11, 12, 13, 2, 3]
```

Fig. 23.8 | Class that manages an integer array to be shared by multiple threads with synchronization. (Part 2 of 2.)

Line 20 declares method `add` as `synchronized`, making all of the operations in this method behave as a single, atomic operation. Line 22 performs the first suboperation—storing the value of `writeIndex`. Line 35 defines the second suboperation, writing an element to the element at the index `position`. Line 39 increments `writeIndex`. When the method finishes executing at line 41, the executing thread implicitly *releases* the Simple-Array lock, making it possible for another thread to begin executing the `add` method.

In the `synchronized` add method, we print messages to the console indicating the progress of threads as they execute this method, in addition to performing the actual operations required to insert a value in the array. We do this so that the messages will be printed in the correct order, allowing us to see whether the method is properly synchronized by comparing these outputs with those of the previous, unsynchronized example. We continue to output messages from `synchronized` blocks in later examples for demonstration purposes only; typically, however, I/O *should not* be performed in `synchronized` blocks, because it's important to minimize the amount of time that an object is "locked." [***Note:*** Line 27 in this example calls **Thread** method **sleep** (for demo purposes only) to emphasize the unpredictability of thread scheduling. You should never call **sleep** while holding a lock in a real application.]

Performance Tip 23.2

Keep the duration of synchronized statements as short as possible while maintaining the needed synchronization. This minimizes the wait time for blocked threads. Avoid performing I/O, lengthy calculations and operations that do not require synchronization while holding a lock.

23.5 Producer/Consumer Relationship without Synchronization

In a **producer/consumer relationship**, the **producer** portion of an application generates data and *stores it in a shared object*, and the **consumer** portion of the application *reads data* *from the shared object.* The producer/consumer relationship separates the task of identifying work to be done from the tasks involved in actually carrying out the work.

Examples of Producer/Consumer Relationship

One example of a common producer/consumer relationship is **print spooling**. Although a printer might not be available when you want to print from an application (i.e., the producer), you can still "complete" the print task, as the data is temporarily placed on disk until the printer becomes available. Similarly, when the printer (i.e., a consumer) is available, it doesn't have to wait until a current user wants to print. The spooled print jobs can be printed as soon as the printer becomes available. Another example of the producer/consumer relationship is an application that copies data onto DVDs by placing data in a fixed-size buffer, which is emptied as the DVD drive "burns" the data onto the DVD.

Synchronization and State Dependence

In a multithreaded producer/consumer relationship, a **producer thread** generates data and places it in a shared object called a **buffer**. A **consumer thread** reads data from the buffer. This relationship requires *synchronization* to ensure that values are produced and consumed properly. All operations on *mutable* data that's shared by multiple threads (e.g., the data in the buffer) must be guarded with a lock to prevent corruption, as discussed in Section 23.4. Operations on the buffer data shared by a producer and consumer thread are also **state dependent**—the operations should proceed only if the buffer is in the correct state. If the buffer is in a *not-full state*, the producer may produce; if the buffer is in a *not-empty state*, the consumer may consume. All operations that access the buffer must use synchronization to ensure that data is written to the buffer or read from the buffer only if the buffer is in the proper state. If the producer attempting to put the next data into the buffer determines that it's full, the producer thread must *wait* until there's space to write a new value. If a consumer thread finds the buffer empty or finds that the previous data has already been read, the consumer must also *wait* for new data to become available. Other examples of state dependence are that you can't drive your car if its gas tank is empty and you can't put more gas into the tank if it's already full.

Logic Errors from Lack of Synchronization

Consider how logic errors can arise if we do not synchronize access among multiple threads manipulating shared mutable data. Our next example (Figs. 23.9–23.13) implements a producer/consumer relationship *without the proper synchronization*. A producer thread writes the numbers 1 through 10 into a shared buffer—a single memory location shared between two threads (a single `int` variable called `buffer` in line 6 of Fig. 23.12 in this example). The consumer thread reads this data from the shared buffer and displays the data. The program's output shows the values that the producer writes (produces) into the shared buffer and the values that the consumer reads (consumes) from the shared buffer.

Each value the producer thread writes to the shared buffer must be consumed *exactly once* by the consumer thread. However, the threads in this example are not synchronized. Therefore, *data can be lost or garbled if the producer places new data into the shared buffer before the consumer reads the previous data.* Also, data can be incorrectly *duplicated* if the consumer consumes data again before the producer produces the next value. To show these possibilities, the consumer thread in the following example keeps a total of all the values it reads. The producer thread produces values from 1 through 10. If the consumer reads each value produced once and only once, the total will be 55. However, if you execute this program several times, you'll see that the total is not always 55 (as shown in the outputs in Fig. 23.13). To emphasize the point, the producer and consumer threads in the example each sleep for random intervals of up to three seconds between performing their tasks. Thus, we do not know when the producer thread will attempt to write a new value, or when the consumer thread will attempt to read a value.

Interface *Buffer*

The program consists of interface Buffer (Fig. 23.9) and classes Producer (Fig. 23.10), Consumer (Fig. 23.11), UnsynchronizedBuffer (Fig. 23.12) and SharedBufferTest (Fig. 23.13). Interface Buffer (Fig. 23.9) declares methods blockingPut (line 6) and blockingGet (line 9) that a Buffer (such as UnsynchronizedBuffer) must implement to enable the Producer thread to place a value in the Buffer and the Consumer thread to retrieve a value from the Buffer, respectively. In subsequent examples, methods blockingPut and blockingGet will call methods that throw InterruptedExceptions—typically this indicates that a method temporarily could be blocked from performing a task. We declare each method with a throws clause here so that we don't have to modify this interface for the later examples.

```
1   // Fig. 23.9: Buffer.java
2   // Buffer interface specifies methods called by Producer and Consumer.
3   public interface Buffer
4   {
5      // place int value into Buffer
6      public void blockingPut(int value) throws InterruptedException;
7
8      // return int value from Buffer
9      public int blockingGet() throws InterruptedException;
10  } // end interface Buffer
```

Fig. 23.9 | Buffer interface specifies methods called by Producer and Consumer. (*Caution:* The example of Figs. 23.9–23.13 is *not* thread safe.)

Class *Producer*

Class Producer (Fig. 23.10) implements the Runnable interface, allowing it to be executed as a task in a separate thread. The constructor (lines 11–14) initializes the Buffer reference sharedLocation with an object created in main (line 15 of Fig. 23.13) and passed to the constructor. As we'll see, this is an UnsynchronizedBuffer object that implements interface Buffer *without synchronizing access to the shared object*. The Producer thread in this program executes the tasks specified in the method run (Fig. 23.10, lines 17–39). Each iteration of the loop (lines 21–35) invokes Thread method sleep (line 25) to place the Producer thread into the *timed waiting* state for a random time interval between 0 and 3 seconds. When the thread awakens, line 26 passes the value of control variable count to the Buffer object's blockingPut method to set the shared buffer's value. Lines 27–28 keep a total of all the values produced so far and output that value. When the loop completes, lines 36–37 display a message indicating that the Producer has finished producing data and is terminating. Next, method run terminates, which indicates that the Producer completed its task. Any method called from a Runnable's run method (e.g., Buffer method blockingPut) executes as part of that task's thread of execution. This fact becomes important in Sections 23.6—23.8 when we add synchronization to the producer/consumer relationship.

```java
 1   // Fig. 23.10: Producer.java
 2   // Producer with a run method that inserts the values 1 to 10 in buffer.
 3   import java.security.SecureRandom;
 4
 5   public class Producer implements Runnable
 6   {
 7      private static final SecureRandom generator = new SecureRandom();
 8      private final Buffer sharedLocation; // reference to shared object
 9
10      // constructor
11      public Producer(Buffer sharedLocation)
12      {
13         this.sharedLocation = sharedLocation;
14      }
15
16      // store values from 1 to 10 in sharedLocation
17      public void run()
18      {
19         int sum = 0;
20
21         for (int count = 1; count <= 10; count++)
22         {
23            try // sleep 0 to 3 seconds, then place value in Buffer
24            {
25               Thread.sleep(generator.nextInt(3000)); // random sleep
26               sharedLocation.blockingPut(count); // set value in buffer
27               sum += count; // increment sum of values
28               System.out.printf("\t%2d%n", sum);
29            }
30            catch (InterruptedException exception)
31            {
32               Thread.currentThread().interrupt();
33            }
34         }
35
36         System.out.printf(
37            "Producer done producing%nTerminating Producer%n");
38      }
39   } // end class Producer
```

Fig. 23.10 | Producer with a run method that inserts the values 1 to 10 in buffer. (*Caution:* The example of Figs. 23.9–23.13 is *not* thread safe.)

Class *Consumer*
Class Consumer (Fig. 23.11) also implements interface Runnable, allowing the Consumer to execute concurrently with the Producer. Lines 11–14 initialize Buffer reference sharedLocation with an object that implements the Buffer interface (created in main, Fig. 23.13) and passed to the constructor as the parameter shared. As we'll see, this is the same UnsynchronizedBuffer object that's used to initialize the Producer object—thus,

the two threads share the same object. The Consumer thread in this program performs the tasks specified in method run (lines 17–39). Lines 21–34 iterate 10 times. Each iteration invokes Thread method sleep (line 26) to put the Consumer thread into the *timed waiting* state for up to 3 seconds. Next, line 27 uses the Buffer's blockingGet method to retrieve the value in the shared buffer, then adds the value to variable sum. Line 28 displays the total of all the values consumed so far. When the loop completes, lines 36–37 display a line indicating the sum of the consumed values. Then method run terminates, which indicates that the Consumer completed its task. Once both threads enter the *terminated* state, the program ends.

```java
1  // Fig. 23.11: Consumer.java
2  // Consumer with a run method that loops, reading 10 values from buffer.
3  import java.security.SecureRandom;
4
5  public class Consumer implements Runnable
6  {
7     private static final SecureRandom generator = new SecureRandom();
8     private final Buffer sharedLocation; // reference to shared object
9
10    // constructor
11    public Consumer(Buffer sharedLocation)
12    {
13       this.sharedLocation = sharedLocation;
14    }
15
16    // read sharedLocation's value 10 times and sum the values
17    public void run()
18    {
19       int sum = 0;
20
21       for (int count = 1; count <= 10; count++)
22       {
23          // sleep 0 to 3 seconds, read value from buffer and add to sum
24          try
25          {
26             Thread.sleep(generator.nextInt(3000));
27             sum += sharedLocation.blockingGet();
28             System.out.printf("\t\t\t%2d%n", sum);
29          }
30          catch (InterruptedException exception)
31          {
32             Thread.currentThread().interrupt();
33          }
34       }
35
36       System.out.printf("%n%s %d%n%s%n",
37          "Consumer read values totaling", sum, "Terminating Consumer");
38    }
39 } // end class Consumer
```

Fig. 23.11 | Consumer with a run method that loops, reading 10 values from buffer. (*Caution:* The example of Figs. 23.9–23.13 is *not* thread safe.)

We Call Thread Method *sleep* Only for Demonstration Purposes

We call method `sleep` in method `run` of the `Producer` and `Consumer` classes to emphasize the fact that, *in multithreaded applications, it's unpredictable when each thread will perform its task and for how long it will perform the task when it has a processor.* Normally, these thread scheduling issues are beyond the control of the Java developer. In this program, our thread's tasks are quite simple—the `Producer` writes the values 1 to 10 to the buffer, and the `Consumer` reads 10 values from the buffer and adds each value to variable `sum`. Without the `sleep` method call, and if the `Producer` executes first, given today's phenomenally fast processors, the `Producer` would likely complete its task before the `Consumer` got a chance to execute. If the `Consumer` executed first, it would likely consume garbage data ten times, then terminate before the `Producer` could produce the first real value.

Class *UnsynchronizedBuffer* Does Not Synchronize Access to the Buffer

Class `UnsynchronizedBuffer` (Fig. 23.12) implements interface `Buffer` (line 4), but does *not* synchronize access to the buffer's state—we purposely do this to demonstrate the problems that occur when multiple threads access *shared mutable data* in *without* synchronization. Line 6 declares instance variable `buffer` and initializes it to –1. This value is used to demonstrate the case in which the `Consumer` attempts to consume a value *before* the Producer ever places a value in `buffer`. Again, methods `blockingPut` (lines 9–13) and `blockingGet` (lines 16–20) do *not* synchronize access to the `buffer` instance variable. Method `blockingPut` simply assigns its argument to `buffer` (line 12), and method `blockingGet` simply returns the value of `buffer` (line 19). As you'll see in Fig. 23.13, `Unsynchronized-Buffer` object is shared between the `Producer` and the `Consumer`.

```java
1   // Fig. 23.12: UnsynchronizedBuffer.java
2   // UnsynchronizedBuffer maintains the shared integer that is accessed by
3   // a producer thread and a consumer thread.
4   public class UnsynchronizedBuffer implements Buffer
5   {
6      private int buffer = -1; // shared by producer and consumer threads
7
8      // place value into buffer
9      public void blockingPut(int value) throws InterruptedException
10     {
11        System.out.printf("Producer writes\t%2d", value);
12        buffer = value;
13     }
14
15     // return value from buffer
16     public int blockingGet() throws InterruptedException
17     {
18        System.out.printf("Consumer reads\t%2d", buffer);
19        return buffer;
20     }
21  } // end class UnsynchronizedBuffer
```

Fig. 23.12 | UnsynchronizedBuffer maintains the shared integer that is accessed by a producer thread and a consumer thread. (*Caution:* The example of Fig. 23.9–Fig. 23.13 is *not* thread safe.)

*Class **SharedBufferTest***

In class SharedBufferTest (Fig. 23.13), line 12 creates an ExecutorService to execute the Producer and Consumer Runnables. Line 15 creates an UnsynchronizedBuffer and assigns it to Buffer variable sharedLocation. This object stores the data that the Producer and Consumer threads will share. Lines 24–25 create and execute the Producer and Consumer. The Producer and Consumer constructors are each passed the same Buffer object (sharedLocation), so each object refers to the same Buffer. These lines also implicitly launch the threads and call each Runnable's run method. Finally, line 27 calls method shutdown so that the application can terminate when the threads executing the Producer and Consumer complete their tasks and line 28 waits for the scheduled tasks to complete. When main terminates (line 29), the main thread of execution enters the *terminated* state.

```java
1   // Fig. 23.13: SharedBufferTest.java
2   // Application with two threads manipulating an unsynchronized buffer.
3   import java.util.concurrent.ExecutorService;
4   import java.util.concurrent.Executors;
5   import java.util.concurrent.TimeUnit;
6
7   public class SharedBufferTest
8   {
9      public static void main(String[] args) throws InterruptedException
10     {
11        // create new thread pool with two threads
12        ExecutorService executorService = Executors.newCachedThreadPool();
13
14        // create UnsynchronizedBuffer to store ints
15        Buffer sharedLocation = new UnsynchronizedBuffer();
16
17        System.out.println(
18           "Action\t\tValue\tSum of Produced\tSum of Consumed");
19        System.out.printf(
20           "------\t\t-----\t---------------\t---------------%n%n");
21
22        // execute the Producer and Consumer, giving each
23        // access to the sharedLocation
24        executorService.execute(new Producer(sharedLocation));
25        executorService.execute(new Consumer(sharedLocation));
26
27        executorService.shutdown(); // terminate app when tasks complete
28        executorService.awaitTermination(1, TimeUnit.MINUTES);
29     }
30  } // end class SharedBufferTest
```

Action	Value	Sum of Produced	Sum of Consumed
Producer writes	1	1	
Producer writes	2	3	—— 1 is lost
Producer writes	3	6	—— 2 is lost

Fig. 23.13 | Application with two threads manipulating an unsynchronized buffer. (*Caution:* The example of Figs. 23.9–23.13 is *not* thread safe.) (Part 1 of 2.)

```
Consumer reads   3                      3
Producer writes  4      10
Consumer reads   4                      7
Producer writes  5      15
Producer writes  6      21         —— 5 is lost
Producer writes  7      28         —— 6 is lost
Consumer reads   7              14
Consumer reads   7              21  —— 7 read again
Producer writes  8      36
Consumer reads   8              29
Consumer reads   8              37  —— 8 read again
Producer writes  9      45
Producer writes 10      55         —— 9 is lost

Producer done producing
Terminating Producer
Consumer reads  10              47
Consumer reads  10              57  —— 10 read again
Consumer reads  10              67  —— 10 read again
Consumer reads  10              77  —— 10 read again

Consumer read values totaling 77
Terminating Consumer
```

```
Action          Value   Sum of Produced Sum of Consumed
------          -----   --------------- ---------------

Consumer reads  -1                      -1  —— reads -1 bad data
Producer writes  1       1
Consumer reads   1                       0
Consumer reads   1                       1  —— 1 read again
Consumer reads   1                       2  —— 1 read again
Consumer reads   1                       3  —— 1 read again
Consumer reads   1                       4  —— 1 read again
Producer writes  2       3
Consumer reads   2                       6
Producer writes  3       6
Consumer reads   3                       9
Producer writes  4      10
Consumer reads   4                      13
Producer writes  5      15
Producer writes  6      21         —— 5 is lost
Consumer reads   6                      19

Consumer read values totaling 19
Terminating Consumer
Producer writes  7      28         —— 7 never read
Producer writes  8      36         —— 8 never read
Producer writes  9      45         —— 9 never read
Producer writes 10      55         —— 10 never read

Producer done producing
Terminating Producer
```

Fig. 23.13 | Application with two threads manipulating an unsynchronized buffer. (*Caution:* The example of Figs. 23.9–23.13 is *not* thread safe.) (Part 2 of 2.)

Recall from this example's overview that the Producer should execute first and every value produced by the Producer should be consumed exactly once by the Consumer. However, when you study the first output of Fig. 23.13, notice that the Producer writes the values 1, 2 and 3 before the Consumer reads its first value (3). Therefore, the values 1 and 2 are *lost*. Later, the values 5, 6 and 9 are *lost*, while 7 and 8 are *read twice* and 10 is read four times. So the first output produces an incorrect total of 77, instead of the correct total of 55. In the second output, the Consumer reads the value -1 *before* the Producer ever writes a value. The Consumer reads the value 1 *five times* before the Producer writes the value 2. Meanwhile, the values 5, 7, 8, 9 and 10 are all *lost*—the last four because the Consumer terminates *before* the Producer. An incorrect consumer total of 19 is displayed. (Lines in the output where the Producer or Consumer has acted out of order are highlighted.)

Error-Prevention Tip 23.1

Access to a shared object by concurrent threads must be controlled carefully or a program may produce incorrect results.

To solve the problems of *lost* and *duplicated* data, Section 23.6 presents an example in which we use an ArrayBlockingQueue (from package java.util.concurrent) to synchronize access to the shared object, guaranteeing that each and every value will be processed once and only once.

23.6 Producer/Consumer Relationship: ArrayBlockingQueue

The best way to synchronize producer and consumer threads is to use classes from Java's java.util.concurrent package that *encapsulate the synchronization for you*. Java includes the class **ArrayBlockingQueue**—a fully implemented, *thread-safe buffer class* that implements interface **BlockingQueue**. This interface extends the Queue interface discussed in Chapter 16 and declares methods **put** and **take**, the blocking equivalents of Queue methods offer and poll, respectively. Method put places an element at the end of the BlockingQueue, waiting if the queue is full. Method take removes an element from the head of the BlockingQueue, waiting if the queue is empty. These methods make class ArrayBlockingQueue a good choice for implementing a shared buffer. Because method put blocks until there's room in the buffer to write data, and method take blocks until there's new data to read, the producer must produce a value first, the consumer correctly consumes only after the producer writes a value and the producer correctly produces the next value (after the first) only after the consumer reads the previous (or first) value. ArrayBlockingQueue stores the shared mutable data in an array, the size of which is specified as an ArrayBlockingQueue constructor argument. Once created, an ArrayBlockingQueue is fixed in size and will not expand to accommodate extra elements.

Class *BlockingBuffer*
Figures 23.14–23.15 demonstrate a Producer and a Consumer accessing an ArrayBlockingQueue. Class BlockingBuffer (Fig. 23.14) uses an ArrayBlockingQueue object that stores an Integer (line 7). Line 11 creates the ArrayBlockingQueue and passes 1 to the constructor so that the object holds a single value to mimic the UnsynchronizedBuffer example in Fig. 23.12. Lines 7 and 11 (Fig. 23.14) use generics, which we discussed in

Chapters 16–20. We discuss *multiple-element buffers* in Section 23.8. Because our Block-ingBuffer class uses the *thread-safe* ArrayBlockingQueue class to manage all of its shared state (the shared buffer in this case), BlockingBuffer is itself *thread safe*, even though we have not implemented the synchronization ourselves.

```java
 1   // Fig. 23.14: BlockingBuffer.java
 2   // Creating a synchronized buffer using an ArrayBlockingQueue.
 3   import java.util.concurrent.ArrayBlockingQueue;
 4
 5   public class BlockingBuffer implements Buffer
 6   {
 7      private final ArrayBlockingQueue<Integer> buffer; // shared buffer
 8
 9      public BlockingBuffer()
10      {
11         buffer = new ArrayBlockingQueue<Integer>(1);
12      }
13
14      // place value into buffer
15      public void blockingPut(int value) throws InterruptedException
16      {
17         buffer.put(value); // place value in buffer
18         System.out.printf("%s%2d\t%s%d%n", "Producer writes ", value,
19            "Buffer cells occupied: ", buffer.size());
20      }
21
22      // return value from buffer
23      public int blockingGet() throws InterruptedException
24      {
25         int readValue = buffer.take(); // remove value from buffer
26         System.out.printf("%s %2d\t%s%d%n", "Consumer reads ",
27            readValue, "Buffer cells occupied: ", buffer.size());
28
29         return readValue;
30      }
31   } // end class BlockingBuffer
```

Fig. 23.14 | Creating a synchronized buffer using an `ArrayBlockingQueue`.

BlockingBuffer implements interface Buffer (Fig. 23.9) and uses classes Producer (Fig. 23.10 modified to remove line 28) and Consumer (Fig. 23.11 modified to remove line 28) from the example in Section 23.5. This approach demonstrates encapsulated syn-chronization—*the threads accessing the shared object are unaware that their buffer accesses are now synchronized*. The synchronization is handled entirely in the blockingPut and block-ingGet methods of BlockingBuffer by calling the synchronized ArrayBlockingQueue methods put and take, respectively. Thus, the Producer and Consumer Runnables are properly synchronized simply by calling the shared object's blockingPut and block-ingGet methods.

Line 17 in method blockingPut (Fig. 23.14, lines 15–20) calls the ArrayBlocking-Queue object's put method. This method call blocks if necessary until there's room in the buffer to place the value. Method blockingGet (lines 23–30) calls the ArrayBlocking-

Queue object's take method (line 25). This method call *blocks* if necessary until there's an element in the buffer to remove. Lines 18–19 and 26–27 use the ArrayBlockingQueue object's **size** method to display the total number of elements currently in the Array-BlockingQueue.

Class BlockingBufferTest
Class BlockingBufferTest (Fig. 23.15) contains the main method that launches the application. Line 13 creates an ExecutorService, and line 16 creates a BlockingBuffer object and assigns its reference to the Buffer variable sharedLocation. Lines 18–19 execute the Producer and Consumer Runnables. Line 21 calls method shutdown to end the application when the threads finish executing the Producer and Consumer tasks and line 22 waits for the scheduled tasks to complete.

```
1   // Fig. 23.15: BlockingBufferTest.java
2   // Two threads manipulating a blocking buffer that properly
3   // implements the producer/consumer relationship.
4   import java.util.concurrent.ExecutorService;
5   import java.util.concurrent.Executors;
6   import java.util.concurrent.TimeUnit;
7
8   public class BlockingBufferTest
9   {
10     public static void main(String[] args) throws InterruptedException
11     {
12        // create new thread pool with two threads
13        ExecutorService executorService = Executors.newCachedThreadPool();
14
15        // create BlockingBuffer to store ints
16        Buffer sharedLocation = new BlockingBuffer();
17
18        executorService.execute(new Producer(sharedLocation));
19        executorService.execute(new Consumer(sharedLocation));
20
21        executorService.shutdown();
22        executorService.awaitTermination(1, TimeUnit.MINUTES);
23     }
24  } // end class BlockingBufferTest
```

```
Producer writes  1     Buffer cells occupied: 1
Consumer reads   1     Buffer cells occupied: 0
Producer writes  2     Buffer cells occupied: 1
Consumer reads   2     Buffer cells occupied: 0
Producer writes  3     Buffer cells occupied: 1
Consumer reads   3     Buffer cells occupied: 0
Producer writes  4     Buffer cells occupied: 1
Consumer reads   4     Buffer cells occupied: 0
Producer writes  5     Buffer cells occupied: 1
Consumer reads   5     Buffer cells occupied: 0
Producer writes  6     Buffer cells occupied: 1
```

Fig. 23.15 | Two threads manipulating a blocking buffer that properly implements the producer/consumer relationship. (Part 1 of 2.)

```
Consumer reads   6      Buffer cells occupied: 0
Producer writes  7      Buffer cells occupied: 1
Consumer reads   7      Buffer cells occupied: 0
Producer writes  8      Buffer cells occupied: 1
Consumer reads   8      Buffer cells occupied: 0
Producer writes  9      Buffer cells occupied: 1
Consumer reads   9      Buffer cells occupied: 0
Producer writes 10      Buffer cells occupied: 1

Producer done producing
Terminating Producer
Consumer reads  10      Buffer cells occupied: 0

Consumer read values totaling 55
Terminating Consumer
```

Fig. 23.15 | Two threads manipulating a blocking buffer that properly implements the producer/consumer relationship. (Part 2 of 2.)

While methods `put` and `take` of `ArrayBlockingQueue` are properly synchronized, `BlockingBuffer` methods `blockingPut` and `blockingGet` (Fig. 23.14) are not declared to be synchronized. Thus, the statements performed in method `blockingPut`—the `put` operation (line 17) and the output (lines 18–19)—are *not atomic*; nor are the statements in method `blockingGet`—the `take` operation (line 25) and the output (lines 26–27). So there's no guarantee that each output will occur immediately after the corresponding `put` or `take` operation, and the outputs may appear out of order. Even if they do, the `Array-BlockingQueue` object is properly synchronizing access to the data, as evidenced by the fact that the sum of values read by the consumer is always correct.

23.7 (Advanced) Producer/Consumer Relationship with synchronized, wait, notify and notifyAll

[*Note:* This section is intended for *advanced* programmers who want to control synchronization.[2]] The previous example showed how multiple threads can share a single-element buffer in a thread-safe manner by using the `ArrayBlockingQueue` class that encapsulates the synchronization necessary to protect the shared mutable data. For educational purposes, we now explain how you can implement a shared buffer yourself using the synchronized keyword and methods of class `Object`. *Using an ArrayBlockingQueue generally results in more-maintainable, better-performing code.*

After identifying the shared mutable data and the *synchronization policy* (i.e., associating the data with a lock that guards it), the next step in synchronizing access to the buffer is to implement methods `blockingGet` and `blockingPut` as synchronized methods. This requires that a thread obtain the *monitor lock* on the `Buffer` object before attempting to access the buffer data, but it does not automatically ensure that threads proceed with an operation only if the buffer is in the proper state. We need a way to allow our threads to *wait*, depending on whether certain conditions are true. In the case of placing a new item in the buffer, the condition that allows the operation to proceed is that the *buffer is not full*.

---

2. For detailed information on `wait`, `notify` and `notifyAll`, see Chapter 14 of *Java Concurrency in Practice* by Brian Goetz, et al., Addison-Wesley Professional, 2006.

In the case of fetching an item from the buffer, the condition that allows the operation to proceed is that the *buffer is not empty*. If the condition in question is true, the operation may proceed; if it's false, the thread must *wait* until it becomes true. When a thread is waiting on a condition, it's removed from contention for the processor and placed into the *waiting* state and the lock it holds is released.

Methods `wait`, `notify` and `notifyAll`

`Object` methods `wait`, `notify` and `notifyAll` can be used with conditions to make threads *wait* when they cannot perform their tasks. If a thread obtains the *monitor lock* on an object, then determines that it cannot continue with its task on that object until some condition is satisfied, the thread can call `Object` method **wait** on the synchronized object; this *releases the monitor lock* on the object, and the thread waits in the *waiting* state while the other threads try to enter the object's synchronized statement(s) or method(s). When a thread executing a synchronized statement (or method) completes or satisfies the condition on which another thread may be waiting, it can call `Object` method **notify** on the synchronized object to allow a waiting thread to transition to the *runnable* state again. At this point, the thread that was transitioned from the *waiting* state to the *runnable* state can attempt to *reacquire the monitor lock* on the object. Even if the thread is able to reacquire the monitor lock, it still might not be able to perform its task at this time—in which case the thread will reenter the *waiting* state and implicitly *release the monitor lock*. If a thread calls **notifyAll** on the synchronized object, then *all* the threads waiting for the monitor lock become eligible to *reacquire the lock* (that is, they all transition to the *runnable* state).

Remember that only *one* thread at a time can obtain the monitor lock on the object—other threads that attempt to acquire the same monitor lock will be *blocked* until the monitor lock becomes available again (i.e., until no other thread is executing in a synchronized statement on that object).

> **Common Programming Error 23.1**
> *It's an error if a thread issues a wait, a notify or a notifyAll on an object without having acquired a lock for it. This causes an* `IllegalMonitorStateException`.

> **Error-Prevention Tip 23.2**
> *It's a good practice to use* `notifyAll` *to notify waiting threads to become runnable. Doing so avoids the possibility that your program would forget about waiting threads, which would otherwise starve.*

Figures 23.16 and 23.17 demonstrate a `Producer` and a `Consumer` accessing a shared buffer with synchronization. In this case, the `Producer` always produces a value *first*, the `Consumer` correctly consumes only *after* the `Producer` produces a value and the `Producer` correctly produces the next value only after the `Consumer` consumes the previous (or first) value. We reuse interface `Buffer` and classes `Producer` and `Consumer` from the example in Section 23.5, except that line 28 is removed from class `Producer` and class `Consumer`.

Class *SynchronizedBuffer*

The synchronization is handled in class `SynchronizedBuffer`'s `blockingPut` and `blockingGet` methods (Fig. 23.16), which implements interface `Buffer` (line 4). Thus, the `Producer`'s and `Consumer`'s run methods simply call the shared object's synchronized `blockingPut` and blockingGet methods. Again, we output messages from this class's synchronized methods for demonstration purposes only—I/O *should not* be performed in synchronized blocks, because it's important to minimize the amount of time that an object is "locked."

```
 1   // Fig. 23.16: SynchronizedBuffer.java
 2   // Synchronizing access to shared mutable data using Object
 3   // methods wait and notifyAll.
 4   public class SynchronizedBuffer implements Buffer
 5   {
 6      private int buffer = -1; // shared by producer and consumer threads
 7      private boolean occupied = false;
 8
 9      // place value into buffer
10      public synchronized void blockingPut(int value)
11         throws InterruptedException
12      {
13         // while there are no empty locations, place thread in waiting state
14         while (occupied)
15         {
16            // output thread information and buffer information, then wait
17            System.out.println("Producer tries to write."); // for demo only
18            displayState("Buffer full. Producer waits."); // for demo only
19            wait();
20         }
21
22         buffer = value; // set new buffer value
23
24         // indicate producer cannot store another value
25         // until consumer retrieves current buffer value
26         occupied = true;
27
28         displayState("Producer writes " + buffer); // for demo only
29
30         notifyAll(); // tell waiting thread(s) to enter runnable state
31      } // end method blockingPut; releases lock on SynchronizedBuffer
32
33      // return value from buffer
34      public synchronized int blockingGet() throws InterruptedException
35      {
36         // while no data to read, place thread in waiting state
37         while (!occupied)
38         {
39            // output thread information and buffer information, then wait
40            System.out.println("Consumer tries to read."); // for demo only
41            displayState("Buffer empty. Consumer waits."); // for demo only
42            wait();
43         }
44
45         // indicate that producer can store another value
46         // because consumer just retrieved buffer value
47         occupied = false;
```

Fig. 23.16 | Synchronizing access to shared mutable data using Object methods wait and notifyAll. (Part 1 of 2.)

```
48
49          displayState("Consumer reads " + buffer); // for demo only
50
51          notifyAll(); // tell waiting thread(s) to enter runnable state
52
53          return buffer;
54      } // end method blockingGet; releases lock on SynchronizedBuffer
55
56      // display current operation and buffer state; for demo only
57      private synchronized void displayState(String operation)
58      {
59          System.out.printf("%-40s%d\t\t%b%n%n", operation, buffer,
60              occupied);
61      }
62  } // end class SynchronizedBuffer
```

Fig. 23.16 | Synchronizing access to shared mutable data using `Object` methods `wait` and `notifyAll`. (Part 2 of 2.)

Fields and Methods of Class *SynchronizedBuffer*

Class SynchronizedBuffer contains fields buffer (line 6) and occupied (line 7)—you must synchronize access to *both* fields to ensure that class SynchronizedBuffer is thread safe. Methods blockingPut (lines 10–31) and blockingGet (lines 34–54) are declared as synchronized—only *one* thread can call either of these methods at a time on a particular SynchronizedBuffer object. Field occupied is used to determine whether it's the Producer's or the Consumer's turn to perform a task. This field is used in conditional expressions in both the blockingPut and blockingGet methods. If occupied is false, then buffer is empty, so the Consumer cannot read the value of buffer, but the Producer can place a value into buffer. If occupied is true, the Consumer can read a value from buffer, but the Producer cannot place a value into buffer.

Method *blockingPut* and the *Producer Thread*

When the Producer thread's run method invokes synchronized method blockingPut, the thread implicitly attempts to acquire the SynchronizedBuffer object's monitor lock. If the monitor lock is available, the Producer thread *implicitly* acquires the lock. Then the loop at lines 14–20 first determines whether occupied is true. If so, buffer is *full* and we want to wait until the buffer is empty, so line 17 outputs a message indicating that the Producer thread is trying to write a value, and line 18 invokes method displayState (lines 57–61) to output another message indicating that buffer is *full* and that the Producer thread is *waiting* until there's space. Line 19 invokes method wait (inherited from Object by SynchronizedBuffer) to place the thread that called method blockingPut (i.e., the Producer thread) in the *waiting* state for the SynchronizedBuffer object. The call to wait causes the calling thread to *implicitly* release the lock on the SynchronizedBuffer object. This is important because the thread cannot currently perform its task and because other threads (in this case, the Consumer) should be allowed to access the object to allow the condition (occupied) to change. Now another thread can attempt to acquire the SynchronizedBuffer object's lock and invoke the object's blockingPut or blockingGet method.

The Producer thread remains in the *waiting* state until another thread *notifies* the Producer that it may proceed—at which point the Producer returns to the *runnable* state and attempts to implicitly reacquire the lock on the SynchronizedBuffer object. If the lock is available, the Producer thread reacquires it, and method blockingPut continues executing with the next statement after the wait call. Because wait is called in a loop, the loop-continuation condition is tested again to determine whether the thread can proceed. If not, then wait is invoked again—otherwise, method blockingPut continues with the next statement after the loop.

Line 22 in method blockingPut assigns the value to the buffer. Line 26 sets occupied to true to indicate that the buffer now contains a value (i.e., a consumer can read the value, but a Producer cannot yet put another value there). Line 28 invokes method displayState to output a message indicating that the Producer is writing a new value into the buffer. Line 30 invokes method notifyAll (inherited from Object). If any threads are *waiting* on the SynchronizedBuffer object's monitor lock, those threads enter the *runnable* state and can now attempt to *reacquire the lock*. Method notifyAll returns immediately, and method blockingPut then returns to the caller (i.e., the Producer's run method). When method blockingPut returns, it *implicitly releases the monitor lock* on the SynchronizedBuffer object.

Method *blockingGet* and the *Consumer Thread*

Methods blockingGet and blockingPut are implemented similarly. When the Consumer thread's run method invokes synchronized method blockingGet, the thread attempts to *acquire the monitor lock* on the SynchronizedBuffer object. If the lock is available, the Consumer thread acquires it. Then the while loop at lines 37–43 determines whether occupied is false. If so, the buffer is empty, so line 40 outputs a message indicating that the Consumer thread is trying to read a value, and line 41 invokes method displayState to output a message indicating that the buffer is *empty* and that the Consumer thread is *waiting*. Line 42 invokes method wait to place the thread that called method blockingGet (i.e., the Consumer) in the *waiting* state for the SynchronizedBuffer object. Again, the call to wait causes the calling thread to *implicitly release the lock* on the SynchronizedBuffer object, so another thread can attempt to acquire the SynchronizedBuffer object's lock and invoke the object's blockingPut or blockingGet method. If the lock on the SynchronizedBuffer is not available (e.g., if the Producer has not yet returned from method blockingPut), the Consumer is *blocked* until the lock becomes available.

The Consumer thread remains in the *waiting* state until it's *notified* by another thread that it may proceed—at which point the Consumer thread returns to the *runnable* state and attempts to *implicitly reacquire the lock* on the SynchronizedBuffer object. If the lock is available, the Consumer reacquires it, and method blockingGet continues executing with the next statement after wait. Because wait is called in a loop, the loop-continuation condition is tested again to determine whether the thread can proceed with its execution. If not, wait is invoked again—otherwise, method blockingGet continues with the next statement after the loop. Line 47 sets occupied to false to indicate that buffer is now empty (i.e., a Consumer cannot read the value, but a Producer can place another value in buffer), line 49 calls method displayState to indicate that the consumer is reading and line 51 invokes method notifyAll. If any threads are in the *waiting* state for the lock on this SynchronizedBuffer object, they enter the *runnable* state and can now attempt to *reacquire the lock*. Method notifyAll returns immediately, then method blockingGet returns the value of buffer to its caller. When method blockingGet returns, the lock on the SynchronizedBuffer object is *implicitly released*.

Error-Prevention Tip 23.3

Always invoke method wait *in a loop that tests the condition the task is waiting on. It's possible that a thread will reenter the* runnable *state (via a timed wait or another thread calling* notifyAll*) before the condition is satisfied. Testing the condition again ensures that the thread will not erroneously execute if it was notified early.*

Method displayState Is Also synchronized

Notice that method displayState is a synchronized method. This is important because it, too, reads the SynchronizedBuffer's shared mutable data. Though only one thread at a time may acquire a given object's lock, one thread may acquire the same object's lock *multiple* times—this is known as a **reentrant lock** and enables one synchronized method to invoke another on the same object.

Testing Class SynchronizedBuffer

Class SharedBufferTest2 (Fig. 23.17) is similar to class SharedBufferTest (Fig. 23.13). SharedBufferTest2 contains method main (Fig. 23.17, lines 9–26), which launches the application. Line 12 creates an ExecutorService to run the Producer and Consumer tasks. Line 15 creates a SynchronizedBuffer object and assigns its reference to Buffer variable sharedLocation. This object stores the data that will be shared between the Producer and Consumer. Lines 17–18 display the column heads for the output. Lines 21–22 execute a Producer and a Consumer. Finally, line 24 calls method shutdown to end the application when the Producer and Consumer complete their tasks and line 25 waits for the scheduled tasks to complete. When method main ends (line 26), the main thread of execution terminates.

```
1   // Fig. 23.17: SharedBufferTest2.java
2   // Two threads correctly manipulating a synchronized buffer.
3   import java.util.concurrent.ExecutorService;
4   import java.util.concurrent.Executors;
5   import java.util.concurrent.TimeUnit;
6
7   public class SharedBufferTest2
8   {
9      public static void main(String[] args) throws InterruptedException
10     {
11        // create a newCachedThreadPool
12        ExecutorService executorService = Executors.newCachedThreadPool();
13
14        // create SynchronizedBuffer to store ints
15        Buffer sharedLocation = new SynchronizedBuffer();
16
17        System.out.printf("%-40s%s\t\t%s%n%-40s%s%n%n", "Operation",
18           "Buffer", "Occupied", "---------", "------\t\t--------");
19
```

Fig. 23.17 | Two threads correctly manipulating a synchronized buffer. (Part 1 of 3.)

```
20          // execute the Producer and Consumer tasks
21          executorService.execute(new Producer(sharedLocation));
22          executorService.execute(new Consumer(sharedLocation));
23
24          executorService.shutdown();
25          executorService.awaitTermination(1, TimeUnit.MINUTES);
26      }
27   } // end class SharedBufferTest2
```

Operation	Buffer	Occupied
---------	------	--------
Consumer tries to read. Buffer empty. Consumer waits.	-1	false
Producer writes 1	1	true
Consumer reads 1	1	false
Consumer tries to read. Buffer empty. Consumer waits.	1	false
Producer writes 2	2	true
Consumer reads 2	2	false
Producer writes 3	3	true
Consumer reads 3	3	false
Producer writes 4	4	true
Producer tries to write. Buffer full. Producer waits.	4	true
Consumer reads 4	4	false
Producer writes 5	5	true
Consumer reads 5	5	false
Producer writes 6	6	true
Producer tries to write. Buffer full. Producer waits.	6	true
Consumer reads 6	6	false
Producer writes 7	7	true
Producer tries to write. Buffer full. Producer waits.	7	true
Consumer reads 7	7	false
Producer writes 8	8	true
Consumer reads 8	8	false
Consumer tries to read. Buffer empty. Consumer waits.	8	false

Fig. 23.17 | Two threads correctly manipulating a synchronized buffer. (Part 2 of 3.)

Producer writes 9	9	true
Consumer reads 9	9	false
Consumer tries to read. Buffer empty. Consumer waits.	9	false
Producer writes 10	10	true
Consumer reads 10	10	false
Producer done producing Terminating Producer		
Consumer read values totaling 55 Terminating Consumer		

Fig. 23.17 | Two threads correctly manipulating a synchronized buffer. (Part 3 of 3.)

Study the outputs in Fig. 23.17. Observe that *every integer produced is consumed exactly once—no values are lost, and no values are consumed more than once*. The synchronization ensures that the Producer produces a value only when the buffer is *empty* and the Consumer consumes only when the buffer is *full*. The Producer always goes first, the Consumer *waits* if the Producer has not produced since the Consumer last consumed, and the Producer waits if the Consumer has not yet consumed the value that the Producer most recently produced. Execute this program several times to confirm that every integer produced is consumed exactly *once*. In the sample output, note the highlighted lines indicating when the Producer and Consumer must *wait* to perform their respective tasks.

23.8 (Advanced) Producer/Consumer Relationship: Bounded Buffers

The program in Section 23.7 uses thread synchronization to guarantee that two threads manipulate data in a shared buffer correctly. However, the application may not perform optimally. If the two threads operate at different speeds, one of them will spend more (or most) of its time waiting. For example, in the program in Section 23.7 we shared a single integer variable between the two threads. If the Producer thread produces values *faster* than the Consumer can consume them, then the Producer thread *waits* for the Consumer, because there are no other locations in the buffer in which to place the next value. Similarly, if the Consumer consumes values *faster* than the Producer produces them, the Consumer *waits* until the Producer places the next value in the shared buffer. Even when we have threads that operate at the *same* relative speeds, those threads may occasionally become "out of sync" over a period of time, causing one of them to *wait* for the other.

Performance Tip 23.3

We cannot make assumptions about the relative speeds of concurrent threads— *interactions that occur with the operating system, the network, the user and other components can cause the threads to operate at different and ever-changing speeds. When this happens, threads wait. When threads wait excessively, programs become less efficient, interactive programs become less responsive and applications suffer longer delays.*

Bounded Buffers

To minimize the amount of waiting time for threads that share resources and operate at the same average speeds, we can implement a **bounded buffer** that provides a fixed number of buffer cells into which the Producer can place values, and from which the Consumer can retrieve those values. (In fact, we've already done this with the ArrayBlockingQueue class in Section 23.6.) If the Producer temporarily produces values faster than the Consumer can consume them, the Producer can write additional values into the extra buffer cells, if any are available. This capability enables the Producer to perform its task even though the Consumer is not ready to retrieve the current value being produced. Similarly, if the Consumer consumes faster than the Producer produces new values, the Consumer can read additional values (if there are any) from the buffer. This enables the Consumer to keep busy even though the Producer is not ready to produce additional values. An example of the producer/consumer relationship that uses a bounded buffer is video streaming, which we discussed in Section 23.1.

Even a *bounded buffer* is inappropriate if the Producer and the Consumer operate consistently at different speeds. If the Consumer always executes faster than the Producer, then a buffer containing one location is enough. If the Producer always executes faster, only a buffer with an "infinite" number of locations would be able to absorb the extra production. However, if the Producer and Consumer execute at about the same average speed, a bounded buffer helps to smooth the effects of any occasional speeding up or slowing down in either thread's execution.

The key to using a *bounded buffer* with a Producer and Consumer that operate at about the same speed is to provide the buffer with enough locations to handle the anticipated "extra" production. If, over a period of time, we determine that the Producer often produces as many as three more values than the Consumer can consume, we can provide a buffer of at least three cells to handle the extra production. Making the buffer too small would cause threads to wait longer.

[*Note:* As we mention in Fig. 23.22, ArrayBlockingQueue can work with multiple producers and multiple consumers. For example, a factory that produces its product very fast will need to have many more delivery trucks (i.e., consumers) to remove those products quickly from the warehousing area (i.e., the bounded buffer) so that the factory can continue to produce products at full capacity.]

Performance Tip 23.4

Even when using a bounded buffer, it's possible that a producer thread could fill the buffer, which would force the producer to wait until a consumer consumed a value to free an element in the buffer. Similarly, if the buffer is empty at any given time, a consumer thread must wait until the producer produces another value. The key to using a bounded buffer is to optimize the buffer size to minimize the amount of thread wait time, while not wasting space.

Bounded Buffers Using *ArrayBlockingQueue*

The simplest way to implement a bounded buffer is to use an ArrayBlockingQueue for the buffer so that *all of the synchronization details are handled for you*. This can be done by modifying the example from Section 23.6 to pass the desired size for the bounded buffer into the ArrayBlockingQueue constructor. Rather than repeat our previous ArrayBlockingQueue example with a different size, we instead present an example that illustrates how you can build a bounded buffer yourself. Again, using an `ArrayBlockingQueue` will result in more-maintainable and better-performing code. In Exercise 23.13, we ask you to reimplement this section's example, using the Java Concurrency API techniques presented in Section 23.9.

Implementing Your Own Bounded Buffer as a Circular Buffer

The program in Figs. 23.18 and 23.19 demonstrates a `Producer` and a `Consumer` accessing a *bounded buffer with synchronization*. Again, we reuse interface `Buffer` and classes `Producer` and `Consumer` from the example in Section 23.5, except that line 28 is removed from class `Producer` and class `Consumer`. We implement the bounded buffer in class `CircularBuffer` (Fig. 23.18) as a **circular buffer** that uses a shared array of three elements. A circular buffer writes into and reads from the array elements in order, beginning at the first cell and moving toward the last. When a `Producer` or `Consumer` reaches the last element, it returns to the first and begins writing or reading, respectively, from there. In this version of the producer/consumer relationship, the `Consumer` consumes a value only when the array is not empty and the `Producer` produces a value only when the array is not full. Once again, the output statements used in this class's `synchronized` methods are for *demonstration purposes only*.

```
 1   // Fig. 23.18: CircularBuffer.java
 2   // Synchronizing access to a shared three-element bounded buffer.
 3   public class CircularBuffer implements Buffer
 4   {
 5      private final int[] buffer = {-1, -1, -1}; // shared buffer
 6
 7      private int occupiedCells = 0; // count number of buffers used
 8      private int writeIndex = 0; // index of next element to write to
 9      private int readIndex = 0; // index of next element to read
10
11      // place value into buffer
12      public synchronized void blockingPut(int value)
13         throws InterruptedException
14      {
15         // wait until buffer has space available, then write value;
16         // while no empty locations, place thread in blocked state
17         while (occupiedCells == buffer.length)
18         {
19            System.out.printf("Buffer is full. Producer waits.%n");
20            wait(); // wait until a buffer cell is free
21         } // end while
22
23         buffer[writeIndex] = value; // set new buffer value
24
25         // update circular write index
26         writeIndex = (writeIndex + 1) % buffer.length;
27
28         ++occupiedCells; // one more buffer cell is full
29         displayState("Producer writes " + value);
30         notifyAll(); // notify threads waiting to read from buffer
31      }
```

Fig. 23.18 | Synchronizing access to a shared three-element bounded buffer. (Part 1 of 3.)

```
32
33      // return value from buffer
34      public synchronized int blockingGet() throws InterruptedException
35      {
36         // wait until buffer has data, then read value;
37         // while no data to read, place thread in waiting state
38         while (occupiedCells == 0)
39         {
40            System.out.printf("Buffer is empty. Consumer waits.%n");
41            wait(); // wait until a buffer cell is filled
42         } // end while
43
44         int readValue = buffer[readIndex]; // read value from buffer
45
46         // update circular read index
47         readIndex = (readIndex + 1) % buffer.length;
48
49         --occupiedCells; // one fewer buffer cells are occupied
50         displayState("Consumer reads " + readValue);
51         notifyAll(); // notify threads waiting to write to buffer
52
53         return readValue;
54      }
55
56      // display current operation and buffer state
57      public synchronized void displayState(String operation)
58      {
59         // output operation and number of occupied buffer cells
60         System.out.printf("%s%s%d)%n%s", operation,
61            " (buffer cells occupied: ", occupiedCells, "buffer cells:  ");
62
63         for (int value : buffer)
64            System.out.printf(" %2d  ", value); // output values in buffer
65
66         System.out.printf("%n                ");
67
68         for (int i = 0; i < buffer.length; i++)
69            System.out.print("---- ");
70
71         System.out.printf("%n                ");
72
73         for (int i = 0; i < buffer.length; i++)
74         {
75            if (i == writeIndex && i == readIndex)
76               System.out.print(" WR"); // both write and read index
77            else if (i == writeIndex)
78               System.out.print(" W  "); // just write index
79            else if (i == readIndex)
80               System.out.print("  R "); // just read index
81            else
82               System.out.print("    "); // neither index
83      }
84
```

Fig. 23.18 | Synchronizing access to a shared three-element bounded buffer. (Part 2 of 3.)

```
85          System.out.printf("%n%n");
86      }
87  } // end class CircularBuffer
```

Fig. 23.18 | Synchronizing access to a shared three-element bounded buffer. (Part 3 of 3.)

Line 5 initializes array `buffer` as a three-element `int` array that represents the circular buffer. Variable `occupiedCells` (line 7) counts the number of elements in `buffer` that contain data to be read. When `occupiedBuffers` is 0, the circular buffer is *empty* and the `Consumer` must *wait*—when `occupiedCells` is 3 (the size of the circular buffer), the circular buffer is *full* and the `Producer` must *wait*. Variable `writeIndex` (line 8) indicates the next location in which a value can be placed by a `Producer`. Variable `readIndex` (line 9) indicates the position from which the next value can be read by a `Consumer`. `CircularBuffer`'s instance variables are *all* part of the class's shared mutable data, thus access to all of these variables must be synchronized to ensure that a `CircularBuffer` is thread safe.

CircularBuffer Method blockingPut

`CircularBuffer` method `blockingPut` (lines 12–31) performs the same tasks as in Fig. 23.16, with a few modifications. The loop at lines 17–21 determines whether the `Producer` must *wait* (i.e., all buffer cells are *full*). If so, line 19 indicates that the `Producer` is *waiting* to perform its task. Then line 20 invokes method `wait`, causing the `Producer` thread to *release* the `CircularBuffer`'s *lock* and *wait* until there's space for a new value to be written into the buffer. When execution continues at line 23 after the `while` loop, the value written by the `Producer` is placed in the circular buffer at location `writeIndex`. Then line 26 updates `writeIndex` for the next call to `CircularBuffer` method `blockingPut`. This line is the key to the buffer's *circularity*. When `writeIndex` is incremented *past the end of the buffer*, the line sets it to 0. Line 28 increments `occupiedCells`, because there's now one more value in the buffer that the `Consumer` can read. Next, line 29 invokes method `displayState` (lines 57–86) to update the output with the value produced, the number of occupied buffer cells, the contents of the buffer cells and the current `writeIndex` and `readIndex`. Line 30 invokes method `notifyAll` to transition *waiting* threads to the *runnable* state, so that a waiting `Consumer` thread (if there is one) can now try again to read a value from the buffer.

CircularBuffer Method blockingGet

`CircularBuffer` method `blockingGet` (lines 34–54) also performs the same tasks as it did in Fig. 23.16, with a few minor modifications. The loop at lines 38–42 (Fig. 23.18) determines whether the `Consumer` must wait (i.e., all buffer cells are *empty*). If the `Consumer` must *wait*, line 40 updates the output to indicate that the `Consumer` is *waiting* to perform its task. Then line 41 invokes method `wait`, causing the current thread to *release the lock* on the `CircularBuffer` and *wait* until data is available to read. When execution eventually continues at line 44 after a `notifyAll` call from the `Producer`, `readValue` is assigned the value at location `readIndex` in the circular buffer. Then line 47 updates `readIndex` for the next call to `CircularBuffer` method `blockingGet`. This line and line 26 implement the *circularity* of the buffer. Line 49 decrements `occupiedCells`, because there's now one more position in the buffer in which the `Producer` thread can place a value. Line 50 invokes method `displayState` to update the output with the consumed value, the number of occupied buffer cells, the contents of the buffer cells and the current writeIndex and readIndex. Line 51 invokes method notifyAll to allow any Producer threads *waiting to write* into the CircularBuffer object to attempt to write again. Then line 53 returns the consumed value to the caller.

CircularBuffer *Method* displayState
Method displayState (lines 57–86) outputs the application's state. Lines 63–64 output the values of the buffer cells. Line 64 uses method printf with a "%2d" format specifier to print the contents of each buffer with a leading space if it's a single digit. Lines 71–83 output the current writeIndex and readIndex with the letters W and R, respectively. Once again, displayState is a synchronized method because it accesses class CircularBuffer's shared mutable data.

Testing Class CircularBuffer
Class CircularBufferTest (Fig. 23.19) contains the main method that launches the application. Line 12 creates the ExecutorService, and line 15 creates a CircularBuffer object and assigns its reference to CircularBuffer variable sharedLocation. Line 18 invokes the CircularBuffer's displayState method to show the initial state of the buffer. Lines 21–22 execute the Producer and Consumer tasks. Line 24 calls method shutdown to end the application when the threads complete the Producer and Consumer tasks and line 25 waits for the tasks to complete.

```java
1   // Fig. 23.19: CircularBufferTest.java
2   // Producer and Consumer threads correctly manipulating a circular buffer.
3   import java.util.concurrent.ExecutorService;
4   import java.util.concurrent.Executors;
5   import java.util.concurrent.TimeUnit;
6
7   public class CircularBufferTest
8   {
9      public static void main(String[] args) throws InterruptedException
10     {
11        // create new thread pool with two threads
12        ExecutorService executorService = Executors.newCachedThreadPool();
13
14        // create CircularBuffer to store ints
15        CircularBuffer sharedLocation = new CircularBuffer();
16
17        // display the initial state of the CircularBuffer
18        sharedLocation.displayState("Initial State");
19
20        // execute the Producer and Consumer tasks
21        executorService.execute(new Producer(sharedLocation));
22        executorService.execute(new Consumer(sharedLocation));
23
24        executorService.shutdown();
25        executorService.awaitTermination(1, TimeUnit.MINUTES);
26     }
27  } // end class CircularBufferTest
```

Fig. 23.19 | Producer and Consumer threads correctly manipulating a circular buffer. (Part 1 of 3.)

```
Initial State (buffer cells occupied: 0)
buffer cells:   -1   -1   -1
                ---- ---- ----
                 WR

Producer writes 1 (buffer cells occupied: 1)
buffer cells:    1   -1   -1
                ---- ---- ----
                 R    W

Consumer reads 1 (buffer cells occupied: 0)
buffer cells:    1   -1   -1
                ---- ---- ----
                      WR

Buffer is empty. Consumer waits.
Producer writes 2 (buffer cells occupied: 1)
buffer cells:    1    2   -1
                ---- ---- ----
                      R    W

Consumer reads 2 (buffer cells occupied: 0)
buffer cells:    1    2   -1
                ---- ---- ----
                           WR

Producer writes 3 (buffer cells occupied: 1)
buffer cells:    1    2    3
                ---- ---- ----
                 W         R

Consumer reads 3 (buffer cells occupied: 0)
buffer cells:    1    2    3
                ---- ---- ----
                 WR

Producer writes 4 (buffer cells occupied: 1)
buffer cells:    4    2    3
                ---- ---- ----
                 R    W

Producer writes 5 (buffer cells occupied: 2)
buffer cells:    4    5    3
                ---- ---- ----
                 R         W

Consumer reads 4 (buffer cells occupied: 1)
buffer cells:    4    5    3
                ---- ---- ----
                      R    W

Producer writes 6 (buffer cells occupied: 2)
buffer cells:    4    5    6
                ---- ---- ----
                 W    R
```

Fig. 23.19 | Producer and Consumer threads correctly manipulating a circular buffer. (Part 2 of 3.)

```
Producer writes 7 (buffer cells occupied: 3)
buffer cells:    7    5    6
                ---- ---- ----
                      WR

Consumer reads 5 (buffer cells occupied: 2)
buffer cells:    7    5    6
                ---- ---- ----
                 W         R

Producer writes 8 (buffer cells occupied: 3)
buffer cells:    7    8    6
                ---- ---- ----
                           WR

Consumer reads 6 (buffer cells occupied: 2)
buffer cells:    7    8    6
                ---- ---- ----
                 R         W

Consumer reads 7 (buffer cells occupied: 1)
buffer cells:    7    8    6
                ---- ---- ----
                 R    W

Producer writes 9 (buffer cells occupied: 2)
buffer cells:    7    8    9
                ---- ---- ----
                 W    R

Consumer reads 8 (buffer cells occupied: 1)
buffer cells:    7    8    9
                ---- ---- ----
                 W         R

Consumer reads 9 (buffer cells occupied: 0)
buffer cells:    7    8    9
                ---- ---- ----
                 WR

Producer writes 10 (buffer cells occupied: 1)
buffer cells:   10    8    9
                ---- ---- ----
                 R    W


Producer done producing
Terminating Producer
Consumer reads 10 (buffer cells occupied: 0)
buffer cells:   10    8    9
                ---- ---- ----
                      WR


Consumer read values totaling: 55
Terminating Consumer
```

Fig. 23.19 | Producer and Consumer threads correctly manipulating a circular buffer. (Part 3 of 3.)

Each time the Producer writes a value or the Consumer reads a value, the program outputs a message indicating the action performed (a read or a write), the contents of buffer, and the location of writeIndex and readIndex. In the output of Fig. 23.19, the Producer first writes the value 1. The buffer then contains the value 1 in the first cell and the value –1 (the default value that we use for output purposes) in the other two cells. The write index is updated to the second cell, while the read index stays at the first cell. Next, the Consumer reads 1. The buffer contains the same values, but the read index has been updated to the second cell. The Consumer then tries to read again, but the buffer is empty and the Consumer is forced to wait. Only once in this execution of the program was it necessary for either thread to wait.

23.9 (Advanced) Producer/Consumer Relationship: The Lock and Condition Interfaces

Though the synchronized keyword provides for most basic thread-synchronization needs, Java provides other tools to assist in developing concurrent programs. In this section, we discuss the Lock and Condition interfaces. These interfaces give you more precise control over thread synchronization, but are more complicated to use. *Only the most advanced programmers should use these interfaces.*

Interface *Lock* and Class *ReentrantLock*

Any object can contain a reference to an object that implements the **Lock** interface (of package java.util.concurrent.locks). A thread calls the Lock's **lock** method (analogous to entering a synchronized block) to acquire the lock. Once a Lock has been obtained by one thread, the Lock object will not allow another thread to obtain the Lock until the first thread releases the Lock (by calling the Lock's **unlock** method—analogous to exiting a synchronized block). If several threads are trying to call method lock on the same Lock object at the same time, only one of these threads can obtain the lock—all the others are placed in the *waiting* state for that lock. When a thread calls method unlock, the lock on the object is released and a waiting thread attempting to lock the object proceeds.

Error-Prevention Tip 23.4

Place calls to Lock method unlock in a finally block. If an exception is thrown, unlock must still be called or deadlock could occur.

Class **ReentrantLock** (of package java.util.concurrent.locks) is a basic implementation of the Lock interface. The constructor for a ReentrantLock takes a boolean argument that specifies whether the lock has a **fairness policy**. If the argument is true, the ReentrantLock's fairness policy is "the longest-waiting thread will acquire the lock when it's available." Such a fairness policy guarantees that *indefinite postponement* (also called *starvation*) cannot occur. If the fairness policy argument is set to false, there's no guarantee as to which waiting thread will acquire the lock when it's available.

Software Engineering Observation 23.6

Using a ReentrantLock with a fairness policy avoids indefinite postponement.

> ### Performance Tip 23.5
> *In most cases, a non-fair lock is preferable, because using a fair lock can decrease program performance.*

Condition Objects and Interface Condition

If a thread that owns a `Lock` determines that it cannot continue with its task until some condition is satisfied, the thread can wait on a **condition object**. Using `Lock` objects allows you to explicitly declare the condition objects on which a thread may need to wait. For example, in the producer/consumer relationship, producers can wait on *one* object and consumers can wait on *another*. This is not possible when using the `synchronized` keywords and an object's built-in monitor lock. Condition objects are associated with a specific `Lock` and are created by calling a `Lock`'s **`newCondition`** method, which returns an object that implements the **`Condition`** interface (of package `java.util.concurrent.locks`). To wait on a condition object, the thread can call the `Condition`'s **`await`** method (analogous to `Object` method `wait`). This immediately releases the associated `Lock` and places the thread in the *waiting* state for that `Condition`. Other threads can then try to obtain the `Lock`. When a *runnable* thread completes a task and determines that the *waiting* thread can now continue, the *runnable* thread can call `Condition` method **`signal`** (analogous to `Object` method `notify`) to allow a thread in that `Condition`'s *waiting* state to return to the *runnable* state. At this point, the thread that transitioned from the *waiting* state to the *runnable* state can attempt to reacquire the `Lock`. Even if it's able to *reacquire* the `Lock`, the thread still might not be able to perform its task at this time—in which case the thread can call the `Condition`'s `await` method to *release* the `Lock` and reenter the *waiting* state. If multiple threads are in a `Condition`'s *waiting* state when `signal` is called, the default implementation of `Condition` signals the longest-waiting thread to transition to the *runnable* state. If a thread calls `Condition` method **`signalAll`** (analogous to `Object` method `notifyAll`), then all the threads waiting for that condition transition to the *runnable* state and become eligible to reacquire the `Lock`. Only one of those threads can obtain the `Lock` on the object—the others will wait until the `Lock` becomes available again. If the `Lock` has a *fairness policy*, the longest-waiting thread acquires the `Lock`. When a thread is finished with a shared object, it must call method `unlock` to release the `Lock`.

> ### Error-Prevention Tip 23.5
> *When multiple threads manipulate a shared object using locks, ensure that if one thread calls method `await` to enter the* waiting *state for a condition object, a separate thread eventually will call `Condition` method `signal` to transition the thread waiting on the condition object back to the* runnable *state. If multiple threads may be waiting on the condition object, a separate thread can call `Condition` method `signalAll` as a safeguard to ensure that all the waiting threads have another opportunity to perform their tasks. If this is not done, starvation might occur.*

> ### Common Programming Error 23.2
> *An `IllegalMonitorStateException` occurs if a thread issues an `await`, a `signal`, or a `signalAll` on a `Condition` object that was created from a `ReentrantLock` without having acquired the lock for that `Condition` object.*

Lock *and* Condition *vs. the* synchronized *Keyword*

In some applications, using Lock and Condition objects may be preferable to using the synchronized keyword. Locks allow you to *interrupt* waiting threads or to specify a *timeout* for waiting to acquire a lock, which is not possible using the synchronized keyword. Also, a Lock is *not* constrained to be acquired and released in the *same* block of code, which is the case with the synchronized keyword. Condition objects allow you to specify multiple conditions on which threads may *wait*. Thus, it's possible to indicate to waiting threads that a specific condition object is now true by calling signal or signalAll on that Condition object. With synchronized, there's no way to explicitly state the condition on which threads are waiting, and thus there's no way to notify threads waiting on one condition that they may proceed without also signaling threads waiting on any other conditions. There are other possible advantages to using Lock and Condition objects, but generally it's best to use the synchronized keyword unless your application requires advanced synchronization capabilities.

Software Engineering Observation 23.7

Think of Lock and Condition as an advanced version of synchronized. Lock and Condition support timed waits, interruptible waits and multiple Condition queues per Lock—if you do not need one of these features, you do not need Lock and Condition.

Error-Prevention Tip 23.6

Using interfaces Lock and Condition is error prone—unlock is not guaranteed to be called, whereas the monitor in a synchronized statement will always be released when the statement completes execution. Of course, you can guarantee that unlock will be called if it's placed in a finally block, as we do in Fig. 23.20.

Using Locks *and* Conditions *to Implement Synchronization*

We now implement the producer/consumer relationship using Lock and Condition objects to coordinate access to a shared single-element buffer (Figs. 23.20 and 23.21). In this case, each produced value is correctly consumed exactly once. Again, we reuse interface Buffer and classes Producer and Consumer from the example in Section 23.5, except that line 28 is removed from class Producer and class Consumer.

Class *SynchronizedBuffer*

Class SynchronizedBuffer (Fig. 23.20) contains five fields. Line 11 creates a new object of type ReentrantLock and assigns its reference to Lock variable accessLock. The ReentrantLock is created without the *fairness policy* because at any time only a single Producer or Consumer will be waiting to acquire the Lock in this example. Lines 14–15 create two Conditions using Lock method newCondition. Condition canWrite contains a queue for a Producer thread waiting while the buffer is *full* (i.e., there's data in the buffer that the Consumer has not read yet). If the buffer is *full*, the Producer calls method await on this Condition. When the Consumer reads data from a *full* buffer, it calls method signal on this Condition. Condition canRead contains a queue for a Consumer thread waiting while the buffer is *empty* (i.e., there's no data in the buffer for the Consumer to read). If the buffer is *empty*, the Consumer calls method await on this Condition. When the Producer writes to the *empty* buffer, it calls method signal on this Condition. The int variable buffer (line 17) holds the shared mutable data. The boolean variable occupied (line 18) keeps track of whether the buffer currently holds data (that the Consumer should read).

```
I    // Fig. 23.20: SynchronizedBuffer.java
2    // Synchronizing access to a shared integer using the Lock and Condition
3    // interfaces
4    import java.util.concurrent.locks.Lock;
5    import java.util.concurrent.locks.ReentrantLock;
6    import java.util.concurrent.locks.Condition;
7
8    public class SynchronizedBuffer implements Buffer
9    {
10      // Lock to control synchronization with this buffer
11      private final Lock accessLock = new ReentrantLock();
12
13      // conditions to control reading and writing
14      private final Condition canWrite = accessLock.newCondition();
15      private final Condition canRead = accessLock.newCondition();
16
17      private int buffer = -1; // shared by producer and consumer threads
18      private boolean occupied = false; // whether buffer is occupied
19
20      // place int value into buffer
21      public void blockingPut(int value) throws InterruptedException
22      {
23         accessLock.lock(); // lock this object
24
25         // output thread information and buffer information, then wait
26         try
27         {
28            // while buffer is not empty, place thread in waiting state
29            while (occupied)
30            {
31               System.out.println("Producer tries to write.");
32               displayState("Buffer full. Producer waits.");
33               canWrite.await(); // wait until buffer is empty
34            }
35
36            buffer = value; // set new buffer value
37
38            // indicate producer cannot store another value
39            // until consumer retrieves current buffer value
40            occupied = true;
41
42            displayState("Producer writes " + buffer);
43
44            // signal any threads waiting to read from buffer
45            canRead.signalAll();
46         }
47         finally
48         {
49            accessLock.unlock(); // unlock this object
50         }
51      }
```

Fig. 23.20 | Synchronizing access to a shared integer using the Lock and Condition interfaces. (Part I of 2.)

```
52
53      // return value from buffer
54      public int blockingGet() throws InterruptedException
55      {
56         int readValue = 0; // initialize value read from buffer
57         accessLock.lock(); // lock this object
58
59         // output thread information and buffer information, then wait
60         try
61         {
62            // if there is no data to read, place thread in waiting state
63            while (!occupied)
64            {
65               System.out.println("Consumer tries to read.");
66               displayState("Buffer empty. Consumer waits.");
67               canRead.await(); // wait until buffer is full
68            }
69
70            // indicate that producer can store another value
71            // because consumer just retrieved buffer value
72            occupied = false;
73
74            readValue = buffer; // retrieve value from buffer
75            displayState("Consumer reads " + readValue);
76
77            // signal any threads waiting for buffer to be empty
78            canWrite.signalAll();
79         }
80         finally
81         {
82            accessLock.unlock(); // unlock this object
83         }
84
85         return readValue;
86      }
87
88      // display current operation and buffer state
89      private void displayState(String operation)
90      {
91         try
92         {
93            accessLock.lock(); // lock this object
94            System.out.printf("%-40s%d\t\t%b%n%n", operation, buffer,
95               occupied);
96         }
97         finally
98         {
99            accessLock.unlock(); // unlock this objects
100        }
101     }
102  } // end class SynchronizedBuffer
```

Fig. 23.20 | Synchronizing access to a shared integer using the Lock and Condition interfaces. (Part 2 of 2.)

Line 23 in method `blockingPut` calls method `lock` on the `SynchronizedBuffer`'s `accessLock`. If the lock is *available* (i.e., no other thread has acquired it), this thread now owns the lock and the thread continues. If the lock is *unavailable* (i.e., it's held by another thread), method `lock` waits until the lock is released. After the lock is acquired, lines 26–46 execute. Line 29 tests `occupied` to determine whether `buffer` is full. If it is, lines 31–32 display a message indicating that the thread will *wait*. Line 33 calls `Condition` method `await` on the `canWrite` condition object, which temporarily releases the `Synchronized-Buffer`'s `Lock` and *waits* for a signal from the `Consumer` that `buffer` is available for writing. When `buffer` is available, the method proceeds, writing to `buffer` (line 36), setting `occupied` to `true` (line 40) and displaying a message indicating that the producer wrote a value (line 42). Line 45 calls `Condition` method `signal` on condition object `canRead` to notify the waiting `Consumer` (if there is one) that the buffer has new data to be read. Line 49 calls method `unlock` from a `finally` block to *release* the lock and allow the `Consumer` to proceed.

Line 57 of method `blockingGet` (lines 54–86) calls method `lock` to *acquire* the `Lock`. This method *waits* until the `Lock` is *available*. Once the `Lock` is *acquired*, line 63 tests whether `occupied` is `false`, indicating that the buffer is *empty*. If so, line 67 calls method `await` on condition object `canRead`. Recall that method `signal` is called on variable `can-Read` in the `blockingPut` method (line 45). When the `Condition` object is *signaled*, the `blockingGet` method continues. Lines 72–74 set `occupied` to `false`, store the value of `buffer` in `readValue` and output the `readValue`. Then line 78 *signals* the condition object `canWrite`. This awakens the `Producer` if it's indeed *waiting* for the buffer to be *emptied*. Line 82 calls method `unlock` from a `finally` block to *release* the lock, and line 85 returns `readValue` to the caller.

Common Programming Error 23.3

Forgetting to `signal` *a waiting thread is a logic error. The thread will remain in the* wait-*ing state, which will prevent it from proceeding. Such waiting can lead to indefinite post-ponement or deadlock.*

*Class **SharedBufferTest2***
Class `SharedBufferTest2` (Fig. 23.21) is identical to that of Fig. 23.17. Study the outputs in Fig. 23.21. *Observe that every integer produced is consumed exactly once—no values are lost, and no values are consumed more than once.* The `Lock` and `Condition` objects ensure that the `Producer` and `Consumer` cannot perform their tasks unless it's their turn. The Pro-ducer *must* go first, the `Consumer` *must wait* if the `Producer` has not produced since the `Consumer` last consumed and the `Producer` *must wait* if the `Consumer` has not yet con-sumed the value that the `Producer` most recently produced. Execute this program several times to confirm that every integer produced is consumed exactly once. In the sample out-put, note the highlighted lines indicating when the `Producer` and `Consumer` must *wait* to perform their respective tasks.

```
1   // Fig. 23.21: SharedBufferTest2.java
2   // Two threads manipulating a synchronized buffer.
3   import java.util.concurrent.ExecutorService;
```

Fig. 23.21 | Two threads manipulating a synchronized buffer. (Part 1 of 3.)

```
 4    import java.util.concurrent.Executors;
 5    import java.util.concurrent.TimeUnit;
 6
 7    public class SharedBufferTest2
 8    {
 9       public static void main(String[] args) throws InterruptedException
10       {
11          // create new thread pool with two threads
12          ExecutorService executorService = Executors.newCachedThreadPool();
13
14          // create SynchronizedBuffer to store ints
15          Buffer sharedLocation = new SynchronizedBuffer();
16
17          System.out.printf("%-40s%s\t\t%s%n%-40s%s%n%n", "Operation",
18             "Buffer", "Occupied", "---------", "------\t\t--------");
19
20          // execute the Producer and Consumer tasks
21          executorService.execute(new Producer(sharedLocation));
22          executorService.execute(new Consumer(sharedLocation));
23
24          executorService.shutdown();
25          executorService.awaitTermination(1, TimeUnit.MINUTES);
26       }
27    } // end class SharedBufferTest2
```

Operation	Buffer	Occupied
Producer writes 1	1	true
Producer tries to write. Buffer full. Producer waits.	1	true
Consumer reads 1	1	false
Producer writes 2	2	true
Producer tries to write. Buffer full. Producer waits.	2	true
Consumer reads 2	2	false
Producer writes 3	3	true
Consumer reads 3	3	false
Producer writes 4	4	true
Consumer reads 4	4	false
Consumer tries to read. Buffer empty. Consumer waits.	4	false

Fig. 23.21 | Two threads manipulating a synchronized buffer. (Part 2 of 3.)

Producer writes 5	5	true
Consumer reads 5	5	false
Consumer tries to read. Buffer empty. Consumer waits.	5	false
Producer writes 6	6	true
Consumer reads 6	6	false
Producer writes 7	7	true
Consumer reads 7	7	false
Producer writes 8	8	true
Consumer reads 8	8	false
Producer writes 9	9	true
Consumer reads 9	9	false
Producer writes 10	10	true
Producer done producing Terminating Producer Consumer reads 10	10	false
Consumer read values totaling 55 Terminating Consumer		

Fig. 23.21 | Two threads manipulating a synchronized buffer. (Part 3 of 3.)

23.10 Concurrent Collections

In Chapter 16, we introduced various collections from the Java Collections API. We also mentioned that you can obtain *synchronized* versions of those collections to allow only one thread at a time to access a collection that might be shared among several threads. The collections from the java.util.concurrent package are specifically designed and optimized for sharing collections among multiple threads.

Figure 23.22 lists the many concurrent collections in package java.util.concurrent. The entries for ConcurrentHashMap and LinkedBlockingQueue are shown in bold because these are by far the most frequently used concurrent collections. Like the collections introduced in Chapter 16, the concurrent collections have been enhanced to support lambdas. However, rather than providing methods to support streams, the concurrent collections provide their own implementations of various stream-like operations—e.g., ConcurrentHashMap has methods forEach, reduce and search—that are designed and optimized for concurrent collections that are shared among threads. For more information on the concurrent collections, visit

Java SE 7:
```
http://docs.oracle.com/javase/7/docs/api/java/util/concurrent/
    package-summary.html
```
Java SE 8
```
http://download.java.net/jdk8/docs/api/java/util/concurrent/
    package-summary.html
```

Collection	Description
ArrayBlockingQueue	A fixed-size queue that supports the producer/consumer relationship—possibly with many producers and consumers.
ConcurrentHashMap	**A hash-based map (similar to the HashMap introduced in Chapter 16) that allows an arbitrary number of reader threads and a limited number of writer threads. This and the LinkedBlockingQueue are by far the most frequently used concurrent collections.**
ConcurrentLinkedDeque	A concurrent linked-list implementation of a double-ended queue.
ConcurrentLinkedQueue	A concurrent linked-list implementation of a queue that can grow dynamically.
ConcurrentSkipListMap	A concurrent map that is sorted by its keys.
ConcurrentSkipListSet	A sorted concurrent set.
CopyOnWriteArrayList	A thread-safe ArrayList. Each operation that modifies the collection first creates a new copy of the contents. Used when the collection is traversed much more frequently than the collection's contents are modified.
CopyOnWriteArraySet	A set that's implemented using CopyOnWriteArrayList.
DelayQueue	A variable-size queue containing Delayed objects. An object can be removed only after its delay has expired.
LinkedBlockingDeque	A double-ended blocking queue implemented as a linked list that can optionally be fixed in size.
LinkedBlockingQueue	**A blocking queue implemented as a linked list that can optionally be fixed in size. This and the ConcurrentHashMap are by far the most frequently used concurrent collections.**
LinkedTransferQueue	A linked-list implementation of interface TransferQueue. Each producer has the option of waiting for a consumer to take an element being inserted (via method transfer) or simply placing the element into the queue (via method put). Also provides overloaded method tryTransfer to immediately transfer an element to a waiting consumer or to do so within a specified timeout period. If the transfer cannot be completed, the element is not placed in the queue. Typically used in applications that pass messages between threads.
PriorityBlockingQueue	A variable-length priority-based blocking queue (like a PriorityQueue).
SynchronousQueue	[For experts.] A blocking queue implementation that does not have an internal capacity. Each insert operation by one thread must wait for a remove operation from another thread and vice versa.

Fig. 23.22 | Concurrent collections summary (package `java.util.concurrent`).

23.11 Multithreading with GUI: SwingWorker

Swing applications present a unique set of challenges for multithreaded programming. All Swing applications have a single thread, called the **event dispatch thread**, to handle interactions with the application's GUI components. Typical interactions include *updating GUI components* or *processing user actions* such as mouse clicks. All tasks that require interaction with an application's GUI are placed in an *event queue* and are executed sequentially by the event dispatch thread.

Swing GUI components are not thread safe—they cannot be manipulated by multiple threads without the risk of incorrect results that might corrupt the GUI. Unlike the other examples presented in this chapter, thread safety in GUI applications is achieved not by synchronizing thread actions, but by *ensuring that Swing components are accessed from only the event dispatch thread.* This technique is called **thread confinement.** Allowing just one thread to access non-thread-safe objects eliminates the possibility of corruption due to multiple threads accessing these objects concurrently.

It's acceptable to perform brief calculations on the event dispatch thread in sequence with GUI component manipulations. If an application must perform a lengthy computation in response to a user interaction, the event dispatch thread cannot attend to other tasks in the event queue while the thread is tied up in that computation. This causes the GUI components to become unresponsive. It's preferable to handle a long-running computation in a separate thread, freeing the event dispatch thread to continue managing other GUI interactions. Of course, you must update the GUI with the computation's results from the event dispatch thread, rather than from the worker thread that performed the computation.

Class SwingWorker

Class **SwingWorker** (in package `javax.swing`) enables you to perform an asynchronous task in a worker thread (such as a long-running computation) then update Swing components from the event dispatch thread based on the task's results. SwingWorker implements the Runnable interface, meaning that *a SwingWorker object can be scheduled to execute in a separate thread.* The SwingWorker class provides several methods to simplify performing a task in a worker thread and making its results available for display in a GUI. Some common SwingWorker methods are described in Fig. 23.23.

Method	Description
doInBackground	Defines a long computation and is called in a worker thread.
done	Executes on the event dispatch thread when doInBackground returns.
execute	Schedules the SwingWorker object to be executed in a worker thread.
get	Waits for the computation to complete, then returns the result of the computation (i.e., the return value of doInBackground).
publish	Sends intermediate results from the doInBackground method to the process method for processing on the event dispatch thread.

Fig. 23.23 | Commonly used SwingWorker methods. (Part 1 of 2.)

Method	Description
process	Receives intermediate results from the publish method and processes these results on the event dispatch thread.
setProgress	Sets the progress property to notify any property change listeners on the event dispatch thread of progress bar updates.

Fig. 23.23 | Commonly used SwingWorker methods. (Part 2 of 2.)

23.11.1 Performing Computations in a Worker Thread: Fibonacci Numbers

In the next example, the user enters a number n and the program gets the nth Fibonacci number, which we calculate using the recursive algorithm discussed in Section 18.5. Since the algorithm is time consuming for large values, we use a SwingWorker object to perform the calculation in a worker thread. The GUI also provides a separate set of components that get the next Fibonacci number in the sequence with each click of a button, beginning with fibonacci(1). This set of components performs its short computation directly in the event dispatch thread. This program is capable of producing up to the 92nd Fibonacci number—subsequent values are outside the range that can be represented by a long. Recall that you can use class BigInteger to represent arbitrarily large integer values.

Class BackgroundCalculator (Fig. 23.24) performs the recursive Fibonacci calculation in a *worker thread*. This class extends SwingWorker (line 8), overriding the methods doInBackground and done. Method doInBackground (lines 21–24) computes the nth Fibonacci number in a worker thread and returns the result. Method done (lines 27–43) displays the result in a JLabel.

```
1   // Fig. 23.24: BackgroundCalculator.java
2   // SwingWorker subclass for calculating Fibonacci numbers
3   // in a background thread.
4   import javax.swing.SwingWorker;
5   import javax.swing.JLabel;
6   import java.util.concurrent.ExecutionException;
7
8   public class BackgroundCalculator extends SwingWorker<Long, Object>
9   {
10      private final int n; // Fibonacci number to calculate
11      private final JLabel resultJLabel; // JLabel to display the result
12
13      // constructor
14      public BackgroundCalculator(int n, JLabel resultJLabel)
15      {
16         this.n = n;
17         this.resultJLabel = resultJLabel;
18      }
```

Fig. 23.24 | SwingWorker subclass for calculating Fibonacci numbers in a background thread. (Part 1 of 2.)

```
19
20      // long-running code to be run in a worker thread
21      public Long doInBackground()
22      {
23         return nthFib = fibonacci(n);
24      }
25
26      // code to run on the event dispatch thread when doInBackground returns
27      protected void done()
28      {
29         try
30         {
31            // get the result of doInBackground and display it
32            resultJLabel.setText(get().toString());
33         }
34         catch (InterruptedException ex)
35         {
36            resultJLabel.setText("Interrupted while waiting for results.");
37         }
38         catch (ExecutionException ex)
39         {
40            resultJLabel.setText(
41               "Error encountered while performing calculation.");
42         }
43      }
44
45      // recursive method fibonacci; calculates nth Fibonacci number
46      public long fibonacci(long number)
47      {
48         if (number == 0 || number == 1)
49            return number;
50         else
51            return fibonacci(number - 1) + fibonacci(number - 2);
52      }
53   } // end class BackgroundCalculator
```

Fig. 23.24 | SwingWorker subclass for calculating Fibonacci numbers in a background thread. (Part 2 of 2.)

SwingWorker is a *generic class*. In line 8, the first type parameter is Long and the second is Object. The first type parameter indicates the type returned by the doInBackground method; the second indicates the type that's passed between the publish and process methods to handle intermediate results. Since we do not use publish and process in this example, we simply use Object as the second type parameter. We discuss publish and process in Section 23.11.2.

A BackgroundCalculator object can be instantiated from a class that controls a GUI. A BackgroundCalculator maintains instance variables for an integer that represents the Fibonacci number to be calculated and a JLabel that displays the results of the calculation (lines 10–11). The BackgroundCalculator constructor (lines 14–18) initializes these instance variables with the arguments that are passed to the constructor.

Software Engineering Observation 23.8
*Any GUI components that will be manipulated by SwingWorker methods, such as
components that will be updated from methods process or done, should be passed to the
SwingWorker subclass's constructor and stored in the subclass object. This gives these
methods access to the GUI components they'll manipulate.*

When method execute is called on a BackgroundCalculator object, the object is
scheduled for execution in a worker thread. Method doInBackground is called from the
worker thread and invokes the fibonacci method (lines 46–52), passing instance variable
n as an argument (line 23). Method fibonacci uses recursion to compute the Fibonacci
of n. When fibonacci returns, method doInBackground returns the result.

After doInBackground returns, method done is called from the event dispatch thread.
This method attempts to set the result JLabel to the return value of doInBackground by
calling method get to retrieve this return value (line 32). Method get *waits* for the result to
be ready if necessary, but since we call it from method done, the computation will be complete *before* get is called. Lines 34–37 catch InterruptedException if the current thread is
interrupted while waiting for get to return. This exception will not occur in this example
since the calculation will have already completed by the time get is called. Lines 38–42 catch
ExecutionException, which is thrown if an exception occurs during the computation.

Class FibonacciNumbers

Class FibonacciNumbers (Fig. 23.25) displays a window containing two sets of GUI components—one set to compute a Fibonacci number in a worker thread and another to get
the next Fibonacci number in response to the user's clicking a JButton. The constructor
(lines 38–109) places these components in separate titled JPanels. Lines 46–47 and 78–
79 add two JLabels, a JTextField and a JButton to the workerJPanel to allow the user
to enter an integer whose Fibonacci number will be calculated by the BackgroundWorker.
Lines 84–85 and 103 add two JLabels and a JButton to the eventThreadJPanel to allow
the user to get the next Fibonacci number in the sequence. Instance variables n1 and n2
contain the previous two Fibonacci numbers in the sequence and are initialized to 0 and
1, respectively (lines 29–30). Instance variable count stores the most recently computed
sequence number and is initialized to 1 (line 31). The two JLabels display count and n2
initially, so that the user will see the text Fibonacci of 1: 1 in the eventThreadJPanel
when the GUI starts.

```
 1   // Fig. 23.25: FibonacciNumbers.java
 2   // Using SwingWorker to perform a long calculation with
 3   // results displayed in a GUI.
 4   import java.awt.GridLayout;
 5   import java.awt.event.ActionEvent;
 6   import java.awt.event.ActionListener;
 7   import javax.swing.JButton;
 8   import javax.swing.JFrame;
 9   import javax.swing.JPanel;
10   import javax.swing.JLabel;
```

Fig. 23.25 | Using SwingWorker to perform a long calculation with results displayed in a GUI.
(Part 1 of 4.)

```
11   import javax.swing.JTextField;
12   import javax.swing.border.TitledBorder;
13   import javax.swing.border.LineBorder;
14   import java.awt.Color;
15   import java.util.concurrent.ExecutionException;
16
17   public class FibonacciNumbers extends JFrame
18   {
19      // components for calculating the Fibonacci of a user-entered number
20      private final JPanel workerJPanel =
21         new JPanel(new GridLayout(2, 2, 5, 5));
22      private final JTextField numberJTextField = new JTextField();
23      private final JButton goJButton = new JButton("Go");
24      private final JLabel fibonacciJLabel = new JLabel();
25
26      // components and variables for getting the next Fibonacci number
27      private final JPanel eventThreadJPanel =
28         new JPanel(new GridLayout(2, 2, 5, 5));
29      private long n1 = 0; // initialize with first Fibonacci number
30      private long n2 = 1; // initialize with second Fibonacci number
31      private int count = 1; // current Fibonacci number to display
32      private final JLabel nJLabel = new JLabel("Fibonacci of 1: ");
33      private final JLabel nFibonacciJLabel =
34         new JLabel(String.valueOf(n2));
35      private final JButton nextNumberJButton = new JButton("Next Number");
36
37      // constructor
38      public FibonacciNumbers()
39      {
40         super("Fibonacci Numbers");
41         setLayout(new GridLayout(2, 1, 10, 10));
42
43         // add GUI components to the SwingWorker panel
44         workerJPanel.setBorder(new TitledBorder(
45            new LineBorder(Color.BLACK), "With SwingWorker"));
46         workerJPanel.add(new JLabel("Get Fibonacci of:"));
47         workerJPanel.add(numberJTextField);
48         goJButton.addActionListener(
49            new ActionListener()
50            {
51               public void actionPerformed(ActionEvent event)
52               {
53                  int n;
54
55                  try
56                  {
57                     // retrieve user's input as an integer
58                     n = Integer.parseInt(numberJTextField.getText());
59                  }
```

Fig. 23.25 | Using SwingWorker to perform a long calculation with results displayed in a GUI. (Part 2 of 4.)

```
60              catch(NumberFormatException ex)
61              {
62                  // display an error message if the user did not
63                  // enter an integer
64                  fibonacciJLabel.setText("Enter an integer.");
65                  return;
66              }
67
68              // indicate that the calculation has begun
69              fibonacciJLabel.setText("Calculating...");
70
71              // create a task to perform calculation in background
72              BackgroundCalculator task =
73                  new BackgroundCalculator(n, fibonacciJLabel);
74              task.execute(); // execute the task
75          }
76      } // end anonymous inner class
77      ); // end call to addActionListener
78      workerJPanel.add(goJButton);
79      workerJPanel.add(fibonacciJLabel);
80
81      // add GUI components to the event-dispatching thread panel
82      eventThreadJPanel.setBorder(new TitledBorder(
83          new LineBorder(Color.BLACK), "Without SwingWorker"));
84      eventThreadJPanel.add(nJLabel);
85      eventThreadJPanel.add(nFibonacciJLabel);
86      nextNumberJButton.addActionListener(
87          new ActionListener()
88          {
89              public void actionPerformed(ActionEvent event)
90              {
91                  // calculate the Fibonacci number after n2
92                  long temp = n1 + n2;
93                  n1 = n2;
94                  n2 = temp;
95                  ++count;
96
97                  // display the next Fibonacci number
98                  nJLabel.setText("Fibonacci of " + count + ": ");
99                  nFibonacciJLabel.setText(String.valueOf(n2));
100             }
101         } // end anonymous inner class
102     ); // end call to addActionListener
103     eventThreadJPanel.add(nextNumberJButton);
104
105     add(workerJPanel);
106     add(eventThreadJPanel);
107     setSize(275, 200);
108     setVisible(true);
109 } // end constructor
```

Fig. 23.25 | Using SwingWorker to perform a long calculation with results displayed in a GUI. (Part 3 of 4.)

```
110
111      // main method begins program execution
112      public static void main(String[] args)
113      {
114          FibonacciNumbers application = new FibonacciNumbers();
115          application.setDefaultCloseOperation(EXIT_ON_CLOSE);
116      }
117  } // end class FibonacciNumbers
```

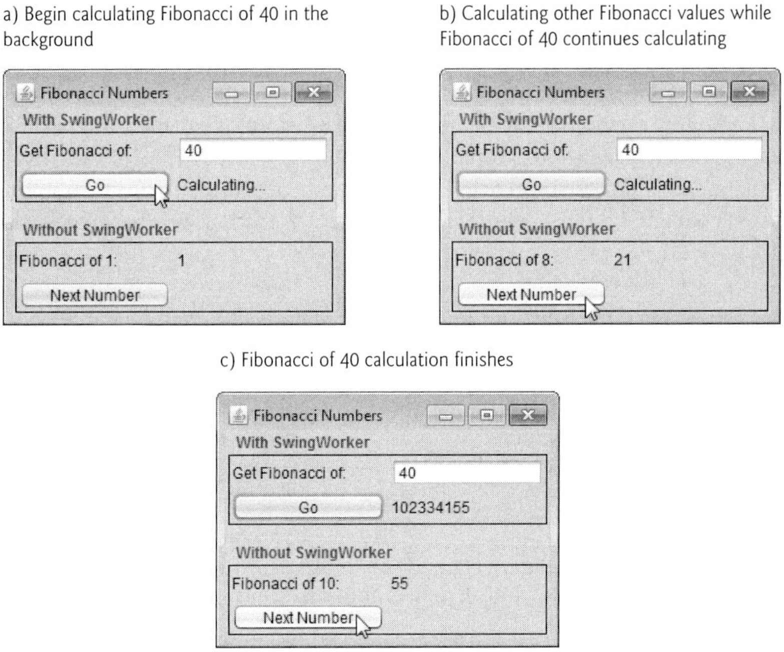

a) Begin calculating Fibonacci of 40 in the background

b) Calculating other Fibonacci values while Fibonacci of 40 continues calculating

c) Fibonacci of 40 calculation finishes

Fig. 23.25 | Using `SwingWorker` to perform a long calculation with results displayed in a GUI. (Part 4 of 4.)

Lines 48–77 register the event handler for the `goJButton`. If the user clicks this `JButton`, line 58 gets the value entered in the `numberJTextField` and attempts to parse it as an integer. Lines 72–73 create a new `BackgroundCalculator` object, passing in the user-entered value and the `fibonacciJLabel` that's used to display the calculation's results. Line 74 calls method `execute` on the `BackgroundCalculator`, scheduling it for execution in a separate worker thread. Method `execute` does not wait for the `BackgroundCalculator` to finish executing. It returns immediately, allowing the GUI to continue processing other events while the computation is performed.

If the user clicks the `nextNumberJButton` in the `eventThreadJPanel`, the event handler registered in lines 86–102 executes. Lines 92–95 add the previous two Fibonacci numbers stored in n1 and n2 to determine the next number in the sequence, update n1 and n2 to their new values and increment count. Then lines 98–99 update the GUI to display the next number. The code for these calculations is in method `actionPerformed`, so they're performed on the *event dispatch thread*. Handling such short computations in the event dispatch thread does not cause the GUI to become unresponsive, as with the recursive algorithm for calculating the Fibonacci of a large number. Because the longer Fibonacci computation is performed in a separate worker thread using the SwingWorker, it's possible to get the next Fibonacci number while the recursive computation is still in progress.

23.11.2 Processing Intermediate Results: Sieve of Eratosthenes

We've presented an example that uses the SwingWorker class to execute a long process in a *background thread* and update the GUI when the process is finished. We now present an example of updating the GUI with intermediate results before the long process completes. Figure 23.26 presents class PrimeCalculator, which extends SwingWorker to compute the first *n* prime numbers in a *worker thread*. In addition to the doInBackground and done methods used in the previous example, this class uses SwingWorker methods publish, process and setProgress. In this example, method publish sends prime numbers to method process as they're found, method process displays these primes in a GUI component and method setProgress updates the progress property. We later show how to use this property to update a JProgressBar.

```java
1   // Fig. 23.26: PrimeCalculator.java
2   // Calculates the first n primes, displaying them as they are found.
3   import javax.swing.JTextArea;
4   import javax.swing.JLabel;
5   import javax.swing.JButton;
6   import javax.swing.SwingWorker;
7   import java.security.SecureRandom;
8   import java.util.Arrays;
9   import java.util.List;
10  import java.util.concurrent.CancellationException;
11  import java.util.concurrent.ExecutionException;
12
13  public class PrimeCalculator extends SwingWorker<Integer, Integer>
14  {
15     private static final SecureRandom generator = new SecureRandom();
16     private final JTextArea intermediateJTextArea; // displays found primes
17     private final JButton getPrimesJButton;
18     private final JButton cancelJButton;
19     private final JLabel statusJLabel; // displays status of calculation
20     private final boolean[] primes; // boolean array for finding primes
21
22     // constructor
23     public PrimeCalculator(int max, JTextArea intermediateJTextArea,
24        JLabel statusJLabel, JButton getPrimesJButton,
25        JButton cancelJButton)
26     {
27        this.intermediateJTextArea = intermediateJTextArea;
28        this.statusJLabel = statusJLabel;
29        this.getPrimesJButton = getPrimesJButton;
30        this.cancelJButton = cancelJButton;
31        primes = new boolean[max];
32
```

Fig. 23.26 | Calculates the first *n* primes, displaying them as they are found. (Part 1 of 3.)

```
33              Arrays.fill(primes, true); // initialize all primes elements to true
34          }
35
36          // finds all primes up to max using the Sieve of Eratosthenes
37          public Integer doInBackground()
38          {
39              int count = 0; // the number of primes found
40
41              // starting at the third value, cycle through the array and put
42              // false as the value of any greater number that is a multiple
43              for (int i = 2; i < primes.length; i++)
44              {
45                  if (isCancelled()) // if calculation has been canceled
46                      return count;
47                  else
48                  {
49                      setProgress(100 * (i + 1) / primes.length);
50
51                      try
52                      {
53                          Thread.sleep(generator.nextInt(5));
54                      }
55                      catch (InterruptedException ex)
56                      {
57                          statusJLabel.setText("Worker thread interrupted");
58                          return count;
59                      }
60
61                      if (primes[i]) // i is prime
62                      {
63                          publish(i); // make i available for display in prime list
64                          ++count;
65
66                          for (int j = i + i; j < primes.length; j += i)
67                              primes[j] = false; // i is not prime
68                      }
69                  }
70              }
71
72              return count;
73          }
74
75          // displays published values in primes list
76          protected void process(List<Integer> publishedVals)
77          {
78              for (int i = 0; i < publishedVals.size(); i++)
79                  intermediateJTextArea.append(publishedVals.get(i) + "\n");
80          }
81
82          // code to execute when doInBackground completes
83          protected void done()
84          {
85              getPrimesJButton.setEnabled(true); // enable Get Primes button
```

Fig. 23.26 | Calculates the first *n* primes, displaying them as they are found. (Part 2 of 3.)

```
86            cancelJButton.setEnabled(false); // disable Cancel button
87
88         try
89         {
90            // retrieve and display doInBackground return value
91            statusJLabel.setText("Found " + get() + " primes.");
92         }
93         catch (InterruptedException | ExecutionException |
94            CancellationException ex)
95         {
96            statusJLabel.setText(ex.getMessage());
97         }
98      }
99   } // end class PrimeCalculator
```

Fig. 23.26 | Calculates the first *n* primes, displaying them as they are found. (Part 3 of 3.)

Class `PrimeCalculator` extends `SwingWorker` (line 13), with the first type parameter indicating the return type of method `doInBackground` and the second indicating the type of intermediate results passed between methods `publish` and `process`. In this case, both type parameters are `Integers`. The constructor (lines 23–34) takes as arguments an integer that indicates the upper limit of the prime numbers to locate, a `JTextArea` used to display primes in the GUI, one `JButton` for initiating a calculation and one for canceling it, and a `JLabel` used to display the status of the calculation.

Sieve of Eratosthenes
Line 33 initializes the elements of the `boolean` array `primes` to `true` with `Arrays` method `fill`. `PrimeCalculator` uses this array and the **Sieve of Eratosthenes** algorithm (described in Exercise 6.27) to find all primes less than `max`. The Sieve of Eratosthenes takes a list of integers and, beginning with the first prime number, filters out all multiples of that prime. It then moves to the next prime, which will be the next number that's not yet filtered out, and eliminates all of its multiples. It continues until the end of the list is reached and all nonprimes have been filtered out. Algorithmically, we begin with element 2 of the boolean array and set the cells corresponding to all values that are multiples of 2 to `false` to indicate that they're divisible by 2 and thus not prime. We then move to the next array element, check whether it's `true`, and if so set all of its multiples to `false` to indicate that they're divisible by the current index. When the whole array has been traversed in this way, all indices that contain `true` are prime, as they have no divisors.

Method *doInBackground*
In method `doInBackground` (lines 37–73), the control variable `i` for the loop (lines 43–70) controls the current index for implementing the Sieve of Eratosthenes. Line 45 calls the inherited `SwingWorker` method **isCancelled** to determine whether the user has clicked the **Cancel** button. If `isCancelled` returns `true`, method `doInBackground` returns the number of primes found so far (line 46) without finishing the computation.

If the calculation isn't canceled, line 49 calls `setProgress` to update the percentage of the array that's been traversed so far. Line 53 puts the currently executing thread to sleep for up to 4 milliseconds. We discuss the reason for this shortly. Line 61 tests whether the element of array `primes` at the current index is `true` (and thus prime). If so, line 63 passes the index to method `publish` so that it can be displayed as an *intermediate result* in the GUI and line 64 increments the number of primes found. Lines 66–67 set all multiples of the current index to `false` to indicate that they're not prime. When the entire array has been traversed, line 72 returns the number of primes found.

Method process

Lines 76–80 declare method `process`, which executes in the event dispatch thread and receives its argument `publishedVals` from method `publish`. The passing of values between `publish` in the worker thread and `process` in the event dispatch thread is asynchronous; `process` might not be invoked for every call to `publish`. All `Integer`s published since the last call to `process` are received as a `List` by method `process`. Lines 78–79 iterate through this list and display the published values in a `JTextArea`. Because the computation in method `doInBackground` progresses quickly, publishing values often, updates to the `JTextArea` can pile up on the event dispatch thread, causing the GUI to become sluggish. In fact, when searching for a large number of primes, the *event dispatch thread* may receive so many requests in quick succession to update the `JTextArea` that it *runs out of memory in its event queue*. This is why we put the worker thread to *sleep* for a few milliseconds between calls to `publish`. The calculation is slowed just enough to allow the event dispatch thread to keep up with requests to update the `JTextArea` with new primes, enabling the GUI to update smoothly and remain responsive.

Method done

Lines 83–98 define method `done`. When the calculation is finished or canceled, method done enables the **Get Primes** button and disables the **Cancel** button (lines 85–86). Line 91 gets and displays the return value—the number of primes found—from method `doInBackground`. Lines 93–97 catch the exceptions thrown by method `get` and display an appropriate message in the `statusJLabel`.

Class FindPrimes

Class `FindPrimes` (Fig. 23.27) displays a `JTextField` that allows the user to enter a number, a `JButton` to begin finding all primes less than that number and a `JTextArea` to display the primes. A `JButton` allows the user to cancel the calculation, and a `JProgressBar` shows the calculation's progress. The constructor (lines 32–125) sets up the GUI.

```
1   // Fig. 23.27: FindPrimes.java
2   // Using a SwingWorker to display prime numbers and update a JProgressBar
3   // while the prime numbers are being calculated.
4   import javax.swing.JFrame;
5   import javax.swing.JTextField;
6   import javax.swing.JTextArea;
7   import javax.swing.JButton;
8   import javax.swing.JProgressBar;
9   import javax.swing.JLabel;
10  import javax.swing.JPanel;
11  import javax.swing.JScrollPane;
12  import javax.swing.ScrollPaneConstants;
```

Fig. 23.27 | Using a `SwingWorker` to display prime numbers and update a `JProgressBar` while the prime numbers are being calculated. (Part 1 of 4.)

```
13   import java.awt.BorderLayout;
14   import java.awt.GridLayout;
15   import java.awt.event.ActionListener;
16   import java.awt.event.ActionEvent;
17   import java.util.concurrent.ExecutionException;
18   import java.beans.PropertyChangeListener;
19   import java.beans.PropertyChangeEvent;
20
21   public class FindPrimes extends JFrame
22   {
23      private final JTextField highestPrimeJTextField = new JTextField();
24      private final JButton getPrimesJButton = new JButton("Get Primes");
25      private final JTextArea displayPrimesJTextArea = new JTextArea();
26      private final JButton cancelJButton = new JButton("Cancel");
27      private final JProgressBar progressJProgressBar = new JProgressBar();
28      private final JLabel statusJLabel = new JLabel();
29      private PrimeCalculator calculator;
30
31      // constructor
32      public FindPrimes()
33      {
34         super("Finding Primes with SwingWorker");
35         setLayout(new BorderLayout());
36
37         // initialize panel to get a number from the user
38         JPanel northJPanel = new JPanel();
39         northJPanel.add(new JLabel("Find primes less than: "));
40         highestPrimeJTextField.setColumns(5);
41         northJPanel.add(highestPrimeJTextField);
42         getPrimesJButton.addActionListener(
43            new ActionListener()
44            {
45               public void actionPerformed(ActionEvent e)
46               {
47                  progressJProgressBar.setValue(0); // reset JProgressBar
48                  displayPrimesJTextArea.setText(""); // clear JTextArea
49                  statusJLabel.setText(""); // clear JLabel
50
51                  int number; // search for primes up through this value
52
53                  try
54                  {
55                     // get user input
56                     number = Integer.parseInt(
57                        highestPrimeJTextField.getText());
58                  }
59                  catch (NumberFormatException ex)
60                  {
61                     statusJLabel.setText("Enter an integer.");
62                     return;
63                  }
64
```

Fig. 23.27 | Using a SwingWorker to display prime numbers and update a JProgressBar while the prime numbers are being calculated. (Part 2 of 4.)

```
65              // construct a new PrimeCalculator object
66              calculator = new PrimeCalculator(number,
67                 displayPrimesJTextArea, statusJLabel, getPrimesJButton,
68                 cancelJButton);
69
70              // listen for progress bar property changes
71              calculator.addPropertyChangeListener(
72                 new PropertyChangeListener()
73                 {
74                    public void propertyChange(PropertyChangeEvent e)
75                    {
76                       // if the changed property is progress,
77                       // update the progress bar
78                       if (e.getPropertyName().equals("progress"))
79                       {
80                          int newValue = (Integer) e.getNewValue();
81                          progressJProgressBar.setValue(newValue);
82                       }
83                    }
84                 } // end anonymous inner class
85              ); // end call to addPropertyChangeListener
86
87              // disable Get Primes button and enable Cancel button
88              getPrimesJButton.setEnabled(false);
89              cancelJButton.setEnabled(true);
90
91              calculator.execute(); // execute the PrimeCalculator object
92           }
93        } // end anonymous inner class
94     ); // end call to addActionListener
95     northJPanel.add(getPrimesJButton);
96
97     // add a scrollable JList to display results of calculation
98     displayPrimesJTextArea.setEditable(false);
99     add(new JScrollPane(displayPrimesJTextArea,
100        ScrollPaneConstants.VERTICAL_SCROLLBAR_ALWAYS,
101        ScrollPaneConstants.HORIZONTAL_SCROLLBAR_NEVER));
102
103    // initialize a panel to display cancelJButton,
104    // progressJProgressBar, and statusJLabel
105    JPanel southJPanel = new JPanel(new GridLayout(1, 3, 10, 10));
106    cancelJButton.setEnabled(false);
107    cancelJButton.addActionListener(
108       new ActionListener()
109       {
110          public void actionPerformed(ActionEvent e)
111          {
112             calculator.cancel(true); // cancel the calculation
113          }
114       } // end anonymous inner class
115    ); // end call to addActionListener
```

Fig. 23.27 | Using a SwingWorker to display prime numbers and update a JProgressBar while the prime numbers are being calculated. (Part 3 of 4.)

```
116        southJPanel.add(cancelJButton);
117        progressJProgressBar.setStringPainted(true);
118        southJPanel.add(progressJProgressBar);
119        southJPanel.add(statusJLabel);
120
121        add(northJPanel, BorderLayout.NORTH);
122        add(southJPanel, BorderLayout.SOUTH);
123        setSize(350, 300);
124        setVisible(true);
125    } // end constructor
126
127    // main method begins program execution
128    public static void main(String[] args)
129    {
130        FindPrimes application = new FindPrimes();
131        application.setDefaultCloseOperation(EXIT_ON_CLOSE);
132    } // end main
133 } // end class FindPrimes
```

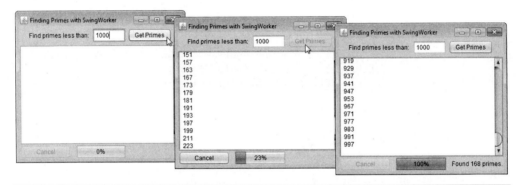

Fig. 23.27 | Using a SwingWorker to display prime numbers and update a JProgressBar while the prime numbers are being calculated. (Part 4 of 4.)

Lines 42–94 register the event handler for the getPrimesJButton. When the user clicks this JButton, lines 47–49 reset the JProgressBar and clear the displayPrimes-JTextArea and the statusJLabel. Lines 53–63 parse the value in the JTextField and display an error message if the value is not an integer. Lines 66–68 construct a new PrimeCalculator object, passing as arguments the integer the user entered, the display-PrimesJTextArea for displaying the primes, the statusJLabel and the two JButtons.

Lines 71–85 register a PropertyChangeListener for the PrimeCalculator object. **PropertyChangeListener** is an interface from package java.beans that defines a single method, propertyChange. Every time method setProgress is invoked on a PrimeCalculator, the PrimeCalculator generates a PropertyChangeEvent to indicate that the progress property has changed. Method propertyChange listens for these events. Line 78 tests whether a given PropertyChangeEvent indicates a change to the progress property. If so, line 80 gets the new value of the property and line 81 updates the JProgressBar with the new progress property value.

The **Get Primes** JButton is disabled (line 88) so only one calculation that updates the GUI can execute at a time, and the **Cancel** JButton is enabled (line 89) to allow the user to stop the computation before it completes. Line 91 executes the PrimeCalculator to begin finding primes. If the user clicks the cancelJButton, the event handler registered at lines 107–115 calls PrimeCalculator's method **cancel** (line 112), which is inherited from class SwingWorker, and the calculation returns early. The argument true to method cancel indicates that the thread performing the task should be interrupted in an attempt to cancel the task.

23.12 sort/parallelSort Timings with the Java SE 8 Date/Time API

In Section 6.12, we used class Arrays's static method sort to sort an array and we introduced static method parallelSort for sorting large arrays more efficiently on multi-core systems. Figure 23.28 uses both methods to sort 15,000,000 element arrays of random int values so that we can demonstrate parallelSort's performance improvement of over sort on a multi-core system (we ran this on a dual-core system).

```java
 1   // SortComparison.java
 2   // Comparing performance of Arrays methods sort and parallelSort.
 3   import java.time.Duration;
 4   import java.time.Instant;
 5   import java.text.NumberFormat;
 6   import java.util.Arrays;
 7   import java.security.SecureRandom;
 8
 9   public class SortComparison
10   {
11      public static void main(String[] args)
12      {
13         SecureRandom random = new SecureRandom();
14
15         // create array of random ints, then copy it
16         int[] array1 = random.ints(15_000_000).toArray();
17         int[] array2 = new int[array1.length];
18         System.arraycopy(array1, 0, array2, 0, array1.length);
19
20         // time the sorting of array1 with Arrays method sort
21         System.out.println("Starting sort");
22         Instant sortStart = Instant.now();
23         Arrays.sort(array1);
24         Instant sortEnd = Instant.now();
25
26         // display timing results
27         long sortTime = Duration.between(sortStart, sortEnd).toMillis();
28         System.out.printf("Total time in milliseconds: %d%n%n", sortTime);
29
30         // time the sorting of array2 with Arrays method parallelSort
31         System.out.println("Starting parallelSort");
32         Instant parallelSortStart = Instant.now();
```

Fig. 23.28 | Comparing performance of Arrays methods sort and parallelSort. (Part 1 of 2.)

```
33          Arrays.parallelSort(array2);
34          Instant parallelSortEnd = Instant.now();
35
36          // display timing results
37          long parallelSortTime =
38              Duration.between(parallelSortStart, parallelSortEnd).toMillis();
39          System.out.printf("Total time in milliseconds: %d%n%n",
40              parallelSortTime);
41
42          // display time difference as a percentage
43          String percentage = NumberFormat.getPercentInstance().format(
44              (double) sortTime / parallelSortTime);
45          System.out.printf("%nsort took %s more time than parallelSort%n",
46              percentage);
47      }
48  } // end class SortComparison
```

```
Starting sort
Total time in milliseconds: 1319

Starting parallelSort
Total time in milliseconds: 323

sort took 408% more time than parallelSort
```

Fig. 23.28 | Comparing performance of Arrays methods sort and parallelSort. (Part 2 of 2.)

Creating the Arrays
Line 16 uses SecureRandom method ints to create an IntStream of 15,000,000 random int values, then calls IntStream method toArray to place the values into an array. Lines 17 and 18 copy the array so that the calls to both sort and parallelSort work with the same set of values.

*Timing **Arrays** Method **sort** with Date/Time API Classes **Instant** and **Duration***
Lines 22 and 24 each call class Instant's static method **now** to get the current time before and after the call to sort. To determine the difference between two Instants, line 27 uses class Duration's static method **between**, which returns a Duration object containing the time difference. Next, we call Duration method **toMillis** to get the difference in milliseconds.

*Timing **Arrays** Method **parallelSort** with Date/Time API Classes **Instant** and **Duration***
Lines 32–34 time the call to Arrays method parallelSort. Then, lines 37–38 calculate the difference between the Instants.

Displaying the Percentage Difference Between the Sorting Times
Lines 43–44 use a NumberFormat (package java.text) to format the ratio of the sort times as a percentage. NumberFormat static method **getPercentInstance** returns a NumberFormat that's used to format a number as a percentage. NumberFormat method format performs the formatting. As you can see in the sample output, the sort method took over *400% more time* to sort the 15,000,000 random int values.

Other Parallel Array Operations

In addition to method parallelSort, class Arrays now contains methods parallelSetAll and parallelPrefix, which perform the following tasks:

- **parallelSetAll**—Fills an array with values produced by a generator function that receives an int and returns a value of type int, long or double. Depending on which overload of method parallelSetAll is used, the generator function is an object of a class that implements IntToDoubleFunction (for double arrays), IntUnaryOperator (for int arrays), IntToLongFunction (for long arrays) or IntFunction (for arrays of any non-primitive type).

- **parallelPrefix**—Applies a BinaryOperator to the current and previous array elements and stores the result in the current element. For example, consider:

```
int[] values = {1, 2, 3, 4, 5};
Arrays.parallelPrefix(values, (x, y) -> x + y);
```

This call to parallelPrefix uses a BinaryOperator that *adds* two values. After the call completes, the array contains 1, 3, 6, 10 and 15. Similarly, the following call to parallelPrefix, uses a BinaryOperator that *multiplies* two values. After the call completes, the array contains 1, 2, 6, 24 and 120:

```
int[] values = {1, 2, 3, 4, 5};
Arrays.parallelPrefix(values, (x, y) -> x * y);
```

23.13 Java SE 8: Sequential vs. Parallel Streams

In Chapter 17, you learned about Java SE 8 lambdas and streams. We mentioned that streams are easy to *parallelize*, enabling programs to benefit from enhanced performance on multi-core systems. Using the timing capabilities introduced in Section 23.12, Fig. 23.29 demonstrates both *sequential* and *parallel* stream operations on a 10,000,000-element array of random long values (created at line 17) to compare the performance.

```
1   // StreamStatisticsComparison.java
2   // Comparing performance of sequential and parallel stream operations.
3   import java.time.Duration;
4   import java.time.Instant;
5   import java.util.Arrays;
6   import java.util.LongSummaryStatistics;
7   import java.util.stream.LongStream;
8   import java.security.SecureRandom;
9
10  public class StreamStatisticsComparison
11  {
12     public static void main(String[] args)
13     {
14        SecureRandom random = new SecureRandom();
15
16        // create array of random long values
17        long[] values = random.longs(10_000_000, 1, 1001).toArray();
```

Fig. 23.29 | Comparing performance of sequential and parallel stream operations. (Part 1 of 3.)

```
18
19        // perform calculcations separately
20        Instant separateStart = Instant.now();
21        long count = Arrays.stream(values).count();
22        long sum = Arrays.stream(values).sum();
23        long min = Arrays.stream(values).min().getAsLong();
24        long max = Arrays.stream(values).max().getAsLong();
25        double average = Arrays.stream(values).average().getAsDouble();
26        Instant separateEnd = Instant.now();
27
28        // display results
29        System.out.println("Calculations performed separately");
30        System.out.printf("   count: %,d%n", count);
31        System.out.printf("     sum: %,d%n", sum);
32        System.out.printf("     min: %,d%n", min);
33        System.out.printf("     max: %,d%n", max);
34        System.out.printf("  average: %f%n", average);
35        System.out.printf("Total time in milliseconds: %d%n%n",
36           Duration.between(separateStart, separateEnd).toMillis());
37
38        // time sum operation with sequential stream
39        LongStream stream1 = Arrays.stream(values);
40        System.out.println("Calculating statistics on sequential stream");
41        Instant sequentialStart = Instant.now();
42        LongSummaryStatistics results1 = stream1.summaryStatistics();
43        Instant sequentialEnd = Instant.now();
44
45        // display results
46        displayStatistics(results1);
47        System.out.printf("Total time in milliseconds: %d%n%n",
48           Duration.between(sequentialStart, sequentialEnd).toMillis());
49
50        // time sum operation with parallel stream
51        LongStream stream2 = Arrays.stream(values).parallel();
52        System.out.println("Calculating statistics on parallel stream");
53        Instant parallelStart = Instant.now();
54        LongSummaryStatistics results2 = stream2.summaryStatistics();
55        Instant parallelEnd = Instant.now();
56
57        // display results
58        displayStatistics(results1);
59        System.out.printf("Total time in milliseconds: %d%n%n",
60           Duration.between(parallelStart, parallelEnd).toMillis());
61     }
62
63     // display's LongSummaryStatistics values
64     private static void displayStatistics(LongSummaryStatistics stats)
65     {
66        System.out.println("Statistics");
67        System.out.printf("   count: %,d%n", stats.getCount());
68        System.out.printf("     sum: %,d%n", stats.getSum());
69        System.out.printf("     min: %,d%n", stats.getMin());
70        System.out.printf("     max: %,d%n", stats.getMax());
```

Fig. 23.29 | Comparing performance of sequential and parallel stream operations. (Part 2 of 3.)

```
71          System.out.printf("   average: %f%n", stats.getAverage());
72      }
73  } // end class StreamStatisticsComparison
```

```
Calculations performed separately
    count: 10,000,000
      sum: 5,003,695,285
      min: 1
      max: 1,000
  average: 500.369529
Total time in milliseconds: 173

Calculating statistics on sequential stream
Statistics
    count: 10,000,000
      sum: 5,003,695,285
      min: 1
      max: 1,000
  average: 500.369529
Total time in milliseconds: 69

Calculating statistics on parallel stream
Statistics
    count: 10,000,000
      sum: 5,003,695,285
      min: 1
      max: 1,000
  average: 500.369529
Total time in milliseconds: 38
```

Fig. 23.29 | Comparing performance of sequential and parallel stream operations. (Part 3 of 3.)

Performing Stream Operations with Separate Passes of a Sequential Stream
Section 17.3 demonstrated various numerical operations on IntStreams. Lines 20–26 perform and time the count, sum, min, max and average stream operations each performed individually on a LongStream returned by Arrays method stream. Lines 29–36 then display the results and the total time required to perform all five operations.

Performing Stream Operations with a Single Pass of a Sequential Stream
Lines 39–48 demonstrate the performance improvement you get by using LongStream method summaryStatistics to determine the count, sum, minimum value, maximum value and average in one pass of a *sequential* LongStream—all streams are sequential by default. This operation took approximately 40% of the time required to perform the five operations separately.

Performing Stream Operations with a Single Pass of a Parallel Stream
Lines 51–60 demonstrate the performance improvement you get by using LongStream method summaryStatistics on a *parallel* LongStream. To obtain a parallel stream that can take advantage of multi-core processors, simply invoke method parallel on an existing stream. As you can see from the sample output, performing the operations on a parallel stream decreased the total time required even further—taking approximately 55% of the

calculation time for the sequential `LongStream` and just 22% of the time required to perform the five operations separately.

23.14 (Advanced) Interfaces `Callable` and `Future`

Interface `Runnable` provides only the most basic functionality for multithreaded programming. In fact, this interface has limitations. Suppose a `Runnable` is performing a long calculation and the application wants to retrieve the result of that calculation. The `run` method cannot return a value, so *shared mutable data* would be required to pass the value back to the calling thread. As you now know, this would require thread synchronization. The **Callable** interface (of package `java.util.concurrent`) fixes this limitation. The interface declares a single method named **call** which returns a value representing the result of the `Callable`'s task—such as the result of a long running calculation.

An application that creates a `Callable` likely wants to run it concurrently with other `Runnables` and `Callables`. `ExecutorService` method **submit** executes its `Callable` argument and returns an object of type **Future** (of package `java.util.concurrent`), which represents the `Callable`'s future result. The `Future` interface **get** method *blocks* the calling thread, and waits for the `Callable` to complete and return its result. The interface also provides methods that enable you to cancel a `Callable`'s execution, determine whether the `Callable` was cancelled and determine whether the `Callable` completed its task.

Executing Aysnchronous Tasks with *CompletableFuture*

Java SE 8 introduces class **CompletableFuture** (package `java.util.concurrent`), which implements the `Future` interface and enables you to *asynchronously* execute `Runnables` that perform tasks or `Suppliers` that return values. Interface **Supplier**, like interface `Callable`, is a functional interface with a single method (in this case, `get`) that receives no arguments and returns a result. Class `CompletableFuture` provides many additional capabilities that for advanced programmers, such as creating `CompletableFutures` without executing them immediately, composing one or more `CompletableFutures` so that you can wait for any or all of them to complete, executing code after a `CompletableFuture` completes and more.

Figure 23.30 performs two long-running calculations sequentially, then performs them again asynchronously using `CompletableFutures` to demonstrate the performance improvement from asynchronous execution on a multi-core system. For demonstration purposes, our long-running calculation is performed by a recursive `fibonacci` method (lines 73–79; similar to the one presented in Section 18.5). For larger Fibonacci values, the recursive implementation can require *significant* computation time—in practice, it's much faster to calculate Fibonacci values using a loop.

```
1  // FibonacciDemo.java
2  // Fibonacci calculations performed synchronously and asynchronously
3  import java.time.Duration;
4  import java.text.NumberFormat;
5  import java.time.Instant;
6  import java.util.concurrent.CompletableFuture;
7  import java.util.concurrent.ExecutionException;
8
```

Fig. 23.30 | Fibonacci calculations performed synchronously and asynchronously. (Part 1 of 4.)

```java
9    // class that stores two Instants in time
10   class TimeData
11   {
12      public Instant start;
13      public Instant end;
14
15      // return total time in seconds
16      public double timeInSeconds()
17      {
18         return Duration.between(start, end).toMillis() / 1000.0;
19      }
20   } // end class TimeData
21
22   public class FibonacciDemo
23   {
24      public static void main(String[] args)
25         throws InterruptedException, ExecutionException
26      {
27         // perform synchronous fibonacci(45) and fibonacci(44) calculations
28         System.out.println("Synchronous Long Running Calculations");
29         TimeData synchronousResult1 = startFibonacci(45);
30         TimeData synchronousResult2 = startFibonacci(44);
31         double synchronousTime =
32            calculateTime(synchronousResult1, synchronousResult2);
33         System.out.printf(
34            "   Total calculation time = %.3f seconds%n", synchronousTime);
35
36         // perform asynchronous fibonacci(45) and fibonacci(44) calculations
37         System.out.printf("%nAsynchronous Long Running Calculations%n");
38         CompletableFuture<TimeData> futureResult1 =
39            CompletableFuture.supplyAsync(() -> startFibonacci(45));
40         CompletableFuture<TimeData> futureResult2 =
41            CompletableFuture.supplyAsync(() -> startFibonacci(44));
42
43         // wait for results from the asynchronous operations
44         TimeData asynchronousResult1 = futureResult1.get();
45         TimeData asynchronousResult2 = futureResult2.get();
46         double asynchronousTime =
47            calculateTime(asynchronousResult1, asynchronousResult2);
48         System.out.printf(
49            "   Total calculation time = %.3f seconds%n", asynchronousTime);
50
51         // display time difference as a percentage
52         String percentage = NumberFormat.getPercentInstance().format(
53            synchronousTime / asynchronousTime);
54         System.out.printf("%nSynchronous calculations took %s" +
55            " more time than the asynchronous calculations%n", percentage);
56      }
57
58      // executes function fibonacci asynchronously
59      private static TimeData startFibonacci(int n)
60      {
```

Fig. 23.30 | Fibonacci calculations performed synchronously and asynchronously. (Part 2 of 4.)

```
61          // create a TimeData object to store times
62          TimeData timeData = new TimeData();
63
64          System.out.printf(" Calculating fibonacci(%d)%n", n);
65          timeData.start = Instant.now();
66          long fibonacciValue = fibonacci(n);
67          timeData.end = Instant.now();
68          displayResult(n, fibonacciValue, timeData);
69          return timeData;
70       }
71
72       // recursive method fibonacci; calculates nth Fibonacci number
73       private static long fibonacci(long n)
74       {
75          if (n == 0 || n == 1)
76             return n;
77          else
78             return fibonacci(n - 1) + fibonacci(n - 2);
79       }
80
81       // display fibonacci calculation result and total calculation time
82       private static void displayResult(int n, long value, TimeData timeData)
83       {
84          System.out.printf(" fibonacci(%d) = %d%n", n, value);
85          System.out.printf(
86             " Calculation time for fibonacci(%d) = %.3f seconds%n",
87             n, timeData.timeInSeconds());
88       }
89
90       // display fibonacci calculation result and total calculation time
91       private static double calculateTime(TimeData result1, TimeData result2)
92       {
93          TimeData bothThreads = new TimeData();
94
95          // determine earlier start time
96          bothThreads.start = result1.start.compareTo(result2.start) < 0 ?
97             result1.start : result2.start;
98
99          // determine later end time
100         bothThreads.end = result1.end.compareTo(result2.end) > 0 ?
101            result1.end : result2.end;
102
103         return bothThreads.timeInSeconds();
104      }
105 } // end class FibonacciDemo
```

```
Synchronous Long Running Calculations
   Calculating fibonacci(45)
   fibonacci(45) = 1134903170
   Calculation time for fibonacci(45) = 5.884 seconds
   Calculating fibonacci(44)
   fibonacci(44) = 701408733
```

Fig. 23.30 | Fibonacci calculations performed synchronously and asynchronously. (Part 3 of 4.)

```
    Calculation time for fibonacci(44) = 3.605 seconds
    Total calculation time = 9.506 seconds

Asynchronous Long Running Calculations
    Calculating fibonacci(45)
    Calculating fibonacci(44)
    fibonacci(44) = 701408733
    Calculation time for fibonacci(44) = 3.650 seconds
    fibonacci(45) = 1134903170
    Calculation time for fibonacci(45) = 5.911 seconds
    Total calculation time = 5.911 seconds

Synchronous calculations took 161% more time than the asynchronous ones
```

Fig. 23.30 | Fibonacci calculations performed synchronously and asynchronously. (Part 4 of 4.)

Class *TimeData*

Class TimeData (lines 10–20) stores two Instants representing the start and end time of a task, and provides method timeInSeconds to calculate the total time between them. We use TimeData objects throughout this example to calculate the time required to perform Fibonacci calculations.

Method *startFibonacci* for Performing and Timing Fibonacci Calculations

Method startFibonacci (lines 59–70) is called several times in main (lines 29, 30, 39 and 41) to initiate Fibonacci calculations and to calculate the time each calculation requires. The method receives the Fibonacci number to calculate and performs the following tasks:

- Line 62 creates a TimeData object to store the calculation's start and end times.

- Line 64 displays the Fibonacci number to be calculated.

- Line 65 stores the current time before method fibonacci is called.

- Line 66 calls method fibonacci to perform the calculation.

- Line 67 stores the current time after the call to fibonacci completes.

- Line 68 displays the result and the total time required for the calculation.

- Line 69 returns the TimeData object for use in method main.

Performing Fibonacci Calculations Synchronously

Method main (lines 24–56) first demonstrates synchronous Fibonacci calculations. Line 29 calls startFibonacci(45) to initiate the fibonacci(45) calculation and store the TimeData object containing the calculation's start and end times. When this call completes, line 30 calls startFibonacci(44) to initiate the fibonacci(44) calculation and store its TimeData. Next, lines 31–32 pass both TimeData objects to method calculate-Time (lines 91–104), which returns the total calculation time in seconds. Lines 33–34 display the total calculation time for the synchronous Fibonacci calculations.

Performing Fibonacci Calculations Asynchronously

Lines 38–41 in main launch the asynchronous Fibonacci calculations in separate threads. CompletableFuture static method **supplyAsync** executes an asynchronous task that returns a value. The method receives as its argument an object that implements interface Sup-

plier—in this case, we use a lambdas with empty parameter lists to invoke
`startFibonacci(45)` (line 39) and `startFibonacci(44)` (line 41). The compiler infers that
`supplyAsync` returns a `CompletableFuture<TimeData>` because method `startFibonacci`
returns type `TimeData`. Class `CompletableFuture` also provides `static` method **runAsync** to
execute an asynchronous task that does not return a result—this method receives a `Runnable`.

Getting the Asynchronous Calculations' Results
Class `CompletableFuture` implements interface `Future`, so we can obtain the asynchronous
tasks' results by calling `Future` method `get` (lines 44–45). These are *blocking* calls—they
cause the `main` thread to *wait* until the asynchronous tasks complete and return their results.
In our case, the results are `TimeData` objects. Once both tasks return, lines 46–47 pass both
`TimeData` objects to method `calculateTime` (lines 91–104) to get the total calculation
time in seconds. Then, lines 48–49 display the total calculation time for the asynchronous
Fibonacci calculations. Finally, lines 52–55 calculate and display the percentage difference
in execution time for the synchronous and asynchronous calculations.

Program Outputs
On our dual-core computer, the synchronous calculations took a total of 9.506 seconds.
Though the individual asynchronous calculations took approximately the same amount of
time as the corresponding synchronous calculations, the total time for the asynchronous
calculations was only 5.911 seconds, because the two calculations were actually performed
in parallel. As you can see in the output, the synchronous calculations took 161% more time
to complete, so asynchronous execution provided a significant performance improvement.

23.15 (Advanced) Fork/Join Framework

Java's concurrency APIs include the fork/join framework, which helps programmers parallelize algorithms. The framework is beyond the scope of this book. Experts tell us that
most Java programmers will nevertheless benefit by the fork/join framework's use "behind
the scenes" in the Java API and other third party libraries. For example, the parallel capabilities of Java SE 8 streams are implemented using this framework.

The fork/join framework is particularly well suited to divide-and-conquer-style algorithms, such as the merge sort that we implemented in Section 19.8. Recall that the recursive merge-sort algorithm sorts an array by *splitting* it into two equal-sized subarrays,
sorting each subarray, then *merging* them into one larger array. Each subarray is sorted by
performing the same algorithm on the subarray. For algorithms like merge sort, the fork/
join framework can be used to create concurrent tasks so that they can be distributed across
multiple processors and be truly performed in parallel—the details of assigning the tasks
to different processors are handled for you by the framework.

23.16 Wrap-Up

In this chapter, we presented Java's concurrency capabilities for enhancing application performance on multi-core systems. You learned the differences between concurrent and parallel execution. We discussed that Java makes concurrency available to you through
multithreading. You also learned that the JVM itself creates threads to run a program, and
that it also can create threads to perform housekeeping tasks such as garbage collection.

We discussed the life cycle of a thread and the states that a thread may occupy during its lifetime. Next, we presented the interface Runnable, which is used to specify a task that can execute concurrently with other tasks. This interface's run method is invoked by the thread executing the task. We showed how to execute a Runnable object by associating it with an object of class Thread. Then we showed how to use the Executor interface to manage the execution of Runnable objects via thread pools, which can reuse existing threads to eliminate the overhead of creating a new thread for each task and can improve performance by optimizing the number of threads to ensure that the processor stays busy.

You learned that when multiple threads share an object and one or more of them modify that object, indeterminate results may occur unless access to the shared object is managed properly. We showed you how to solve this problem via thread synchronization, which coordinates access to shared mutable data by multiple concurrent threads. You learned several techniques for performing synchronization—first with the built-in class ArrayBlockingQueue (which handles *all* the synchronization details for you), then with Java's built-in monitors and the synchronized keyword, and finally with interfaces Lock and Condition.

We discussed the fact that Swing GUIs are not thread safe, so all interactions with and modifications to the GUI must be performed in the event dispatch thread. We also discussed the problems associated with performing long-running calculations in the event dispatch thread. Then we showed how you can use the SwingWorker class to perform long-running calculations in worker threads. You learned how to display the results of a Swing-Worker in a GUI when the calculation completed and how to display intermediate results while the calculation was still in process.

We revisited the Arrays class's sort and parallelSort methods to demonstrate the benefit of using a parallel sorting algorithm on a multi-core processor. We used the Java SE 8 Date/Time API's Instant and Duration classes to time the sort operations.

You learned that Java SE 8 streams are easy to parallelize, enabling programs to benefit from enhanced performance on multi-core systems, and that to obtain a parallel stream, you simply invoke method parallel on an existing stream.

We discussed the Callable and Future interfaces, which enable you to execute tasks that return results and to obtain those results, respectively. We then presented an example of performing long-running tasks synchronously and asynchronously using Java SE 8's new CompletableFuture class. We use the multithreading techniques introduced in this chapter again in Chapter 28, Networking, to help build multithreaded servers that can interact with multiple clients concurrently. In the next chapter, we introduce database-application development with Java's JDBC API.

Summary

Section 23.1 Introduction
- Two tasks that are operating concurrently are both making progress at once.
- Two tasks that are operating in parallel are executing simultaneously. In this sense, parallelism is a subset of concurrency. Today's multi-core computers have multiple processors that can perform tasks in parallel.
- Java makes concurrency available to you through the language and APIs.

- Java programs can have multiple threads of execution, where each thread has its own method-call stack and program counter, allowing it to execute concurrently with other threads. This capability is called multithreading.

- In a multithreaded application, threads can be distributed across multiple processors (if available) so that multiple tasks execute in parallel and the application can operate more efficiently.

- The JVM creates threads to run a program and for housekeeping tasks such as garbage collection.

- Multithreading can also increase performance on single-processor systems—when one thread cannot proceed (because, for example, it's waiting for the result of an I/O operation), another can use the processor.

- The vast majority of programmers should use existing collection classes and interfaces from the concurrency APIs that manage synchronization for you.

Section 23.2 Thread States and Life Cycle

- A new thread begins its life cycle in the *new* state (p. 953). When the program starts the thread, it's placed in the *runnable* state. A thread in the *runnable* state is considered to be executing its task.

- A *runnable* thread transitions to the *waiting* state (p. 953) to wait for another thread to perform a task. A *waiting* thread transitions to *runnable* when another thread notifies it to continue executing.

- A *runnable* thread can enter the *timed waiting* state (p. 953) for a specified interval of time, transitioning back to *runnable* when that time interval expires or when the event it's waiting for occurs.

- A *runnable* thread can transition to the *timed waiting* state if it provides an optional wait interval when it's waiting for another thread to perform a task. Such a thread will return to the *runnable* state when it's notified by another thread or when the timed interval expires.

- A sleeping thread (p. 953) remains in the *timed waiting* state for a designated period of time, after which it returns to the *runnable* state.

- A *runnable* thread transitions to the *blocked* state (p. 953) when it attempts to perform a task that cannot be completed immediately and the thread must temporarily wait until that task completes. At that point, the *blocked* thread transitions to the *runnable* state, so it can resume execution.

- A *runnable* thread enters the *terminated* state (p. 953) when it successfully completes its task or otherwise terminates (perhaps due to an error).

- At the operating-system level, the *runnable* state (p. 954) encompasses two separate states. When a thread first transitions to the *runnable* state from the *new* state, it's in the *ready* state (p. 954). A *ready* thread enters the *running* state (p. 954) when the operating system dispatches it.

- Most operating systems allot a quantum (p. 954) in which a thread performs its task. When this expires, the thread returns to the *ready* state and another thread is assigned to the processor.

- Thread scheduling determines which thread to dispatch based on thread priorities.

- The job of an operating system's thread scheduler (p. 954) is to determine which thread runs next.

- When a higher-priority thread enters the *ready* state, the operating system generally preempts the currently *running* thread (an operation known as preemptive scheduling; p. 955).

- Depending on the operating system, higher-priority threads could postpone—possibly indefinitely (p. 955)—the execution of lower-priority threads.

Section 23.3 Creating and Executing Threads with the **Executor** Framework

- A Runnable (p. 955) object represents a task that can execute concurrently with other tasks.

- Interface Runnable declares method run (p. 955) in which you place the code that defines the task to perform. The thread executing a Runnable calls method run to perform the task.

- A program will not terminate until its last thread completes execution.

- You cannot predict the order in which threads will be scheduled, even if you know the order in which they were created and started.

- It's recommended that you use the Executor interface (p. 955) to manage the execution of Runnable objects. An Executor object typically creates and manages a group of threads—called a thread pool (p. 955).

- Executors (p. 956) can reuse existing threads and can improve performance by optimizing the number of threads to ensure that the processor stays busy.

- Executor method execute (p. 955) receives a Runnable and assigns it to an available thread in a thread pool. If there are none, the Executor creates a new thread or waits for one to become available.

- Interface ExecutorService (of package java.util.concurrent; p. 956) extends interface Executor and declares other methods for managing the life cycle of an Executor.

- An object that implements the ExecutorService interface can be created using static methods declared in class Executors (of package java.util.concurrent).

- Executors method newCachedThreadPool (p. 957) returns an ExecutorService that creates new threads as they're needed by the application.

- ExecutorService method execute executes its Runnable sometime in the future. The method returns immediately from each invocation—the program does not wait for each task to finish.

- ExecutorService method shutdown (p. 959) notifies the ExecutorService to stop accepting new tasks, but continues executing existing tasks and terminates when those tasks complete execution.

Section 23.4 Thread Synchronization

- Thread synchronization (p. 960) coordinates access to shared mutable data by multiple concurrent threads.

- By synchronizing threads, you can ensure that each thread accessing a shared object excludes all other threads from doing so simultaneously—this is called mutual exclusion (p. 960).

- A common way to perform synchronization is to use Java's built-in monitors. Every object has a monitor and a monitor lock (p. 960). The monitor ensures that its object's monitor lock is held by a maximum of only one thread at any time, and thus can be used to enforce mutual exclusion.

- If an operation requires the executing thread to hold a lock while the operation is performed, a thread must acquire the lock (p. 960) before it can proceed with the operation. Any other threads attempting to perform an operation that requires the same lock will be *blocked* until the first thread releases the lock, at which point the *blocked* threads may attempt to acquire the lock.

- To specify that a thread must hold a monitor lock to execute a block of code, the code should be placed in a synchronized statement (p. 960). Such code is said to be guarded by the monitor lock.

- The synchronized statements are declared using the synchronized keyword:

```
synchronized (object)
{
    statements
} // end synchronized statement
```

where *object* is the object whose monitor lock will be acquired; *object* is normally this if it's the object in which the synchronized statement appears.

- Java also allows synchronized methods (p. 961). Before executing, a synchronized instance method must acquire the lock on the object that's used to call the method. Similary, a static synchronized method must acquire the lock on the class that's used to call the method.

- ExecutorService method awaitTermination (p. 965) forces a program to wait for threads to terminate. It returns control to its caller either when all tasks executing in the ExecutorService complete or when the specified timeout elapses. If all tasks complete before the timeout elapses, the method returns true; otherwise, it returns false.

- You can simulate atomicity (p. 966) by ensuring that only one thread performs a set of operations at a time. Atomicity can be achieved with synchronized statements or synchronized methods.

- When you share immutable data across threads, you should declare the corresponding data fields final to indicate that variables' values will not change after they're initialized.

Section 23.5 Producer/Consumer Relationship without Synchronization

- In a multithreaded producer/consumer relationship (p. 968), a producer thread generates data and places it in a shared object called a buffer. A consumer thread reads data from the buffer.

- Operations on a buffer data shared by a producer and a consumer should proceed only if the buffer is in the correct state. If the buffer is not full, the producer may produce; if the buffer is not empty, the consumer may consume. If the buffer is full when the producer attempts to write into it, the producer must wait until there's space. If the buffer is empty or the previous value was already read, the consumer must wait for new data to become available.

Section 23.6 Producer/Consumer Relationship: `ArrayBlockingQueue`

- ArrayBlockingQueue (p. 976) is a fully implemented buffer class from package java.util.concurrent that implements the BlockingQueue interface.

- An ArrayBlockingQueue can implement a shared buffer in a producer/consumer relationship. Method put (p. 976) places an element at the end of the BlockingQueue, waiting if the queue is full. Method take (p. 976) removes an element from the head of the BlockingQueue, waiting if the queue is empty.

- ArrayBlockingQueue stores shared mutable data in an array that's sized with an argument passed to the constructor. Once created, an ArrayBlockingQueue is fixed in size.

Section 23.7 (Advanced) Producer/Consumer Relationship with `synchronized`, `wait`, `notify` and `notifyAll`

- You can implement a shared buffer yourself using the synchronized keyword and Object methods wait, notify and notifyAll (p. 980).

- A thread can call Object method wait to release an object's monitor lock, and wait in the *waiting* state while the other threads try to enter the object's synchronized statement(s) or method(s).

- When a thread executing a synchronized statement (or method) completes or satisfies the condition on which another thread may be waiting, it can call Object method notify (p. 980) to allow a waiting thread to transition to the *runnable* state. At this point, the thread that was transitioned can attempt to reacquire the monitor lock on the object.

- If a thread calls notifyAll (p. 980), then all the threads waiting for the monitor lock become eligible to reacquire the lock (that is, they all transition to the *runnable* state).

Section 23.8 (Advanced) Producer/Consumer Relationship: Bounded Buffers

- You cannot make assumptions about the relative speeds of concurrent threads.

- A bounded buffer (p. 987) can be used to minimize the amount of waiting time for threads that share resources and operate at the same average speeds. If the producer temporarily produces values faster than the consumer can consume them, the producer can write additional values into the extra buffer space (if any are available). If the consumer consumes faster than the producer produces new values, the consumer can read additional values (if there are any) from the buffer.

- The key to using a bounded buffer with a producer and consumer that operate at about the same speed is to provide the buffer with enough locations to handle the anticipated "extra" production.

- The simplest way to implement a bounded buffer is to use an `ArrayBlockingQueue` for the buffer so that all of the synchronization details are handled for you.

Section 23.9 (Advanced) Producer/Consumer Relationship: The `Lock` and `Condition` Interfaces

- The `Lock` and `Condition` interfaces (p. 994) give programmers more precise control over thread synchronization, but are more complicated to use.

- Any object can contain a reference to an object that implements the `Lock` interface (of package `java.util.concurrent.locks`). A thread calls a `Lock`'s `lock` method (p. 994) to acquire the lock. Once a `Lock` has been obtained by one thread, the `Lock` will not allow another thread to obtain it until the first thread releases it (by calling the `Lock`'s `unlock` method; p. 994).

- If several threads are trying to call method `lock` on the same `Lock` object at the same time, only one thread can obtain the lock—the others are placed in the *waiting* state. When a thread calls `unlock`, the object's lock is released and a waiting thread attempting to lock the object proceeds.

- Class `ReentrantLock` (p. 994) is a basic implementation of the `Lock` interface.

- The `ReentrantLock` constructor takes a `boolean` that specifies whether the lock has a fairness policy (p. 994). If `true`, the `ReentrantLock`'s fairness policy is "the longest-waiting thread will acquire the lock when it's available"—this prevents indefinite postponement. If the argument is set to `false`, there's no guarantee as to which waiting thread will acquire the lock when it's available.

- If a thread that owns a `Lock` determines that it cannot continue with its task until some condition is satisfied, the thread can wait on a condition object (p. 995). Using `Lock` objects allows you to explicitly declare the condition objects on which a thread may need to wait.

- `Condition` (p. 995) objects are associated with a specific `Lock` and are created by calling `Lock` method `newCondition`, which returns a `Condition` object. To wait on a `Condition`, the thread can call the `Condition`'s `await` method. This immediately releases the associated `Lock` and places the thread in the *waiting* state for that `Condition`. Other threads can then try to obtain the `Lock`.

- When a *runnable* thread completes a task and determines that a *waiting* thread can now continue, the *runnable* thread can call `Condition` method `signal` to allow a thread in that `Condition`'s *waiting* state to return to the *runnable* state. At this point, the thread that transitioned from the *waiting* state to the *runnable* state can attempt to reacquire the `Lock`.

- If multiple threads are in a `Condition`'s *waiting* state when `signal` is called, the default implementation of `Condition` signals the longest-waiting thread to transition to the *runnable* state.

- If a thread calls `Condition` method `signalAll`, then all the threads waiting for that condition transition to the *runnable* state and become eligible to reacquire the `Lock`.

- When a thread is finished with a shared object, it must call method `unlock` to release the `Lock`.

- `Lock`s allow you to interrupt waiting threads or to specify a timeout for waiting to acquire a lock—not possible with `synchronized`. Also, a `Lock` object is not constrained to be acquired and released in the same block of code, which is the case with the `synchronized` keyword.

- `Condition` objects allow you to specify multiple conditions on which threads may wait. Thus, it's possible to indicate to waiting threads that a specific condition object is now true by calling that `Condition` object's `signal` or `signallAll` methods (p. 995). With `synchronized`, there's no way to explicitly state the condition on which threads are waiting.

Section 23.11 Multithreading with GUI: `SwingWorker`

- The event dispatch thread (p. 1003) handles interactions with the application's GUI components. All tasks that interact with the GUI are placed in an event queue and executed sequentially by this thread.

- Swing GUI components are not thread safe. Thread safety is achieved by ensuring that Swing components are accessed from only the event dispatch thread.

- Performing a lengthy computation in response to a user interface interaction ties up the event dispatch thread, preventing it from attending to other tasks and causing the GUI components to become unresponsive. Long-running computations should be handled in separate threads.

- You can extend generic class SwingWorker (package javax.swing; p. 1003), which implements Runnable, to perform a task in a worker thread then update Swing components from the event dispatch thread based on the task's results. You override its doInBackground and done methods. Method doInBackground performs the computation and returns the result. Method done displays the results in the GUI.

- Class SwingWorker's first type parameter indicates the type returned by the doInBackground method; the second indicates the type that's passed between the publish and process methods to handle intermediate results.

- Method doInBackground is called from a worker thread. After doInBackground returns, method done is called from the event dispatch thread to display the results.

- An ExecutionException is thrown if an exception occurs during the computation.

- SwingWorker method publish repeatedly sends intermediate results to method process, which displays the results in a GUI component. Method setProgress updates the progress property.

- Method process executes in the event dispatch thread and receives data from method publish. The passing of values between publish in the worker thread and process in the event dispatch thread is asynchronous; process is not necessarily invoked for every call to publish.

- PropertyChangeListener (p. 1016) is an interface from package java.beans that defines a single method, propertyChange. Every time method setProgress is invoked, a PropertyChangeEvent is generated to indicate that the progress property has changed.

Section 23.12 Timing **sort** and **parallelSort** with the Java SE 8 Date/Time API

- Class Instant's static method now gets the current time.

- To determine the difference between two Instants, use class Duration's static method between, which returns a Duration object containing the time difference.

- Duration method toMillis returns the Duration as a long value milliseconds.

- NumberFormat static method getPercentInstance returns a NumberFormat that's used to format a number as a percentage.

- NumberFormat method format returns a String representation of its argument in the specified numeric format.

- Arrays static method parallelSetAll fills an array with values produced by a generator function that receives an int and returns a value of type int, long or double. Depending on which overload of method parallelSetAll is used the generator function is an object of a class that implements IntToDoubleFunction (for double arrays), IntUnaryOperator (for int arrays), IntToLongFunction (for long arrays) or IntFunction (for arrays of any non-primitive type).

- Arrays static method parallelPrefix applies a BinaryOperator to the current and previous array elements and stores the result in the current element.

Section 23.13 Java SE 8: Sequential vs. Parallel Streams

- Streams are easy to parallelize, enabling programs to benefit from enhanced performance on multi-core systems.

- To obtain a parallel stream, simply invoke method parallel on an existing stream.

Section 23.14 (Advanced) Interfaces **Callable** and **Future**

- The Callable (p. 1022) interface (of package java.util.concurrent) declares a single method named call that allows a task to return a value.

- ExecutorService method submit (p. 1022) executes a Callable passed in as its argument. Method submit returns an object of type Future (of package java.util.concurrent) that represents the future result of the executing Callable.

- Interface Future (p. 1022) declares method get to return the result of the Callable. The interface also provides methods that enable you to cancel a Callable's execution, determine whether the Callable was cancelled and determine whether the Callable completed its task.

- Java SE 8 introduces a new CompletableFuture class (package java.util.concurrent; p. 1022), which implements the Future interface and enables you to asynchronously execute Runnables that perform tasks or Suppliers that return values.

- Interface Supplier (p. 1022), like interface Callable, is a functional interface with a single method (in this case, get) that receives no arguments and returns a result.

- CompletableFuture static method supplyAsync (p. 1033) asynchronously executes a Supplier task that returns a value.

- CompletableFuture static method runAsync (p. 1034) asynchronously executes a Runnable task that does not return a result.

- CompletableFuture method get is a blocking method—it causes the calling thread to wait until the asynchronous task completes and returns its results.

Section 23.15 (Advanced) Fork/Join Framework

- Java's concurrency APIs include the fork/join framework, which helps programmers parallelize algorithms. The fork/join framework particularly well suited to divide-and-conquer-style algorithms, like the merge sort.

Self-Review Exercises

23.1 Fill in the blanks in each of the following statements:
- a) A thread enters the *terminated* state when _____.
- b) To pause for a designated number of milliseconds and resume execution, a thread should call method _____ of class _____.
- c) A *runnable* thread can enter the _____ state for a specified interval of time.
- d) At the operating-system level, the *runnable* state actually encompasses two separate states, _____ and _____.
- e) Runnables are executed using a class that implements the _____ interface.
- f) ExecutorService method _____ ends each thread in an ExecutorService as soon as it finishes executing its current Runnable, if any.
- g) In a(n) _____ relationship, the _____ generates data and stores it in a shared object, and the _____ reads data from the shared object.
- h) Keyword _____ indicates that only one thread at a time should execute on an object.

23.2 *(Advanced Optional Sections)* Fill in the blanks in each of the following statements:
- a) Method _____ of class Condition moves a single thread in an object's *waiting* state to the *runnable* state.
- b) Method _____ of class Condition moves every thread in an object's *waiting* state to the *runnable* state.

c) A thread can call method _____ on a `Condition` object to release the associated Lock and place that thread in the _____ state.

d) Class _____ implements the `BlockingQueue` interface using an array.

e) Class `Instant`'s static method _____ gets the current time.

f) `Duration` method _____ returns the `Duration` as a `long` value milliseconds.

g) `NumberFormat` static method _____ returns a `NumberFormat` that's used to format a number as a percentage.

h) `NumberFormat` method _____ returns a `String` representation of its argument in the specified numeric format.

i) `Arrays` static method _____ fills an array with values produced by a generator function.

j) `Arrays` static method _____ applies a `BinaryOperator` to the current and previous array elements and stores the result in the current element.

k) To obtain a parallel stream, simply invoke method _____ on an existing stream.

l) Among its many features a `CompletableFuture` enables you to asynchronously execute _____ that perform tasks or _____ that return values.

23.3 State whether each of the following is *true* or *false*. If *false*, explain why.

a) A thread is not *runnable* if it has terminated.

b) Some operating systems use timeslicing with threads. Therefore, they can enable threads to preempt threads of the same priority.

c) When the thread's quantum expires, the thread returns to the *running* state as the operating system assigns it to a processor.

d) On a single-processor system without timeslicing, each thread in a set of equal-priority threads (with no other threads present) runs to completion before other threads of equal priority get a chance to execute.

23.4 *(Advanced Optional Sections)* State whether each of the following is *true* or *false*. If *false*, explain why.

a) To determine the difference between two `Instant`s, use class `Duration`'s static method `difference`, which returns a `Duration` object containing the time difference.

b) Streams are easy to parallelize, enabling programs to benefit from enhanced performance on multi-core systems.

c) Interface `Supplier`, like interface `Callable`, is a functional interface with a single method that receives no arguments and returns a result.

d) `CompletableFuture` static method `runAsync` asynchronously executes a `Supplier` task that returns a value.

e) `CompletableFuture` static method `supplyAsync` asynchronously executes a `Runnable` task that does not return a result.

Answers to Self-Review Exercises

23.1 a) its run method ends. b) `sleep`, `Thread`. c) *timed waiting*. d) *ready*, *running*. e) `Executor`. f) `shutdown`. g) producer/consumer, producer, consumer. h) `synchronized`.

23.2 a) `signal`. b) `signalAll`. c) `await`, *waiting*. d) `ArrayBlockingQueue`. e) `now`. f) `toMillis`. g) `getPercentInstance`. h) `format`. i) `parallelSetAll`. j) `parallelPrefix`. k) `parallel`. l) `Runnables`, `Suppliers`.

23.3 a) True. b) False. Timeslicing allows a thread to execute until its timeslice (or quantum) expires. Then other threads of equal priority can execute. c) False. When a thread's quantum expires, the thread returns to the *ready* state and the operating system assigns to the processor another thread. d) True.

23.4   a) False. The `Duration` method for calculating the difference between two `Instants` is named `between`. b) True. c) True. d) False. The method that asynchronously executes a `Supplier` is `supplyAsync`. e) False. The method that asynchronously executes a `Runnable` is `runAsync`.

Exercises

23.5   *(True or False)* State whether each of the following is *true* or *false*. If *false*, explain why.
   a) Method `sleep` does not consume processor time while a thread sleeps.
   b) Swing components are thread safe.
   c) *(Advanced)* Declaring a method `synchronized` guarantees that deadlock cannot occur.
   d) *(Advanced)* Once a `ReentrantLock` has been obtained by a thread, the `ReentrantLock` object will not allow another thread to obtain the lock until the first thread releases it.

23.6   *(Multithreading Terms)* Define each of the following terms.
   a) thread
   b) multithreading
   c) *runnable* state
   d) *timed waiting* state
   e) preemptive scheduling
   f) `Runnable` interface
   g) producer/consumer relationship
   h) quantum

23.7   *(Advanced: Multithreading Terms)* Discuss each of the following terms in the context of Java's threading mechanisms:
   a) `synchronized`
   b) `wait`
   c) `notify`
   d) `notifyAll`
   e) `Lock`
   f) `Condition`

23.8   *(Blocked State)* List the reasons for entering the *blocked* state. For each of these, describe how the program will normally leave the *blocked* state and enter the *runnable* state.

23.9   *(Deadlock and Indefinite Postponement)* Two problems that can occur in systems that allow threads to wait are deadlock, in which one or more threads will wait forever for an event that cannot occur, and indefinite postponement, in which one or more threads will be delayed for some unpredictably long time. Give an example of how each of these problems can occur in multithreaded Java programs.

23.10   *(Bouncing Ball)* Write a program that bounces a blue ball inside a `JPanel`. The ball should begin moving with a `mousePressed` event. When the ball hits the edge of the `JPanel`, it should bounce off the edge and continue in the opposite direction. The ball should be updated using a `Runnable`.

23.11   *(Bouncing Balls)* Modify the program in Exercise 23.10 to add a new ball each time the user clicks the mouse. Provide for a minimum of 20 balls. Randomly choose the color for each new ball.

23.12   *(Bouncing Balls with Shadows)* Modify the program in Exercise 23.11 to add shadows. As a ball moves, draw a solid black oval at the bottom of the `JPanel`. You may consider adding a 3-D effect by increasing or decreasing the size of each ball when it hits the edge of the `JPanel`.

23.13 *(Advanced: Circular Buffer with Locks and Conditions)* Reimplement the example in Section 23.8 using the Lock and Condition concepts presented in Section 23.9.

23.14 *(Bounded Buffer: A Real-World Example)* Describe how a highway off-ramp onto a local road is a good example of a producer/consumer relationship with a bounded buffer. In particular, discuss how the designers might choose the size of the off-ramp.

Parallel Streams

For Exercises 23.15–23.17, you may need to create larger data sets to see a significant performance difference.

23.15 *(Summarizing the Words in a File)* Reimplement Fig. 17.17 using parallel streams. Use the Date/Time API timing techniques you learned in Section 23.12 to compare the time required for the sequential and parallel versions of the program.

23.16 *(Summarizing the Characters in a File)* Reimplement Exercise 17.9 using parallel streams. Use the Date/Time API timing techniques you learned in Section 23.12 to compare the time required for the sequential and parallel versions of the program.

23.17 *(Summarizing the File Types in a Directory)* Reimplement Exercise 17.10 using parallel streams. Use the Date/Time API timing techniques you learned in Section 23.12 to compare the time required for the sequential and parallel versions of the program.

Accessing Databases with JDBC

24

It is a capital mistake to theorize before one has data.
—Arthur Conan Doyle

Now go, write it before them in a table, and note it in a book, that it may be for the time to come for ever and ever.
—The Holy Bible, Isaiah 30:8

Get your facts first, and then you can distort them as much as you please.
—Mark Twain

I like two kinds of men: domestic and foreign.
—Mae West

Objectives

In this chapter you'll learn:

- Relational database concepts.
- To use Structured Query Language (SQL) to retrieve data from and manipulate data in a database.
- To use the JDBC™ API to access databases.
- To use the RowSet interface from package javax.sql to manipulate databases.
- To use JDBC 4's automatic JDBC driver discovery.
- To create precompiled SQL statements with parameters via PreparedStatements.
- How transaction processing makes database applications more robust.

24.1 Introduction

A **database** is an organized collection of data. There are many different strategies for organizing data to facilitate easy access and manipulation. A **database management system** (**DBMS**) provides mechanisms for storing, organizing, retrieving and modifying data for many users. Database management systems allow for the access and storage of data without concern for the internal representation of data.

Structured Query Language
Today's most popular database systems are *relational databases* (Section 24.2). A language called **SQL**—pronounced "sequel," or as its individual letters—is the international standard language used almost universally with relational databases to perform **queries** (i.e., to request information that satisfies given criteria) and to manipulate data. [*Note:* As you learn about SQL, you'll see some authors writing "a SQL statement" (which assumes the pronunciation "sequel") and others writing "an SQL statement" (which assumes that the individual letters are pronounced). In this book we pronounce SQL as "sequel."]

Popular Relational Database Management Systems
Some popular **relational database management systems** (**RDBMSs**) are Microsoft SQL Server®, Oracle®, Sybase®, IBM DB2®, Informix®, PostgreSQL and MySQL™. The JDK comes with a pure-Java RDBMS called Java DB—the Oracle-branded version of Apache Derby™.

JDBC
Java programs interact with databases using the **Java Database Connectivity** (**JDBC**™) **API**. A **JDBC driver** enables Java applications to connect to a database in a particular DBMS and allows you to manipulate that database using the JDBC API.

Software Engineering Observation 24.1
The JDBC API is portable—the same code can manipulate databases in various RDBMSs.

Most popular database management systems provide JDBC drivers. In this chapter, we introduce JDBC and use it to manipulate Java DB databases. The techniques we demonstrate here can be used to manipulate other databases that have JDBC drivers. If not, third-party vendors provide JDBC drivers for many DBMSs. This chapter's examples were tested with Java DB using both the Java SE 7 and Java SE 8 JDKs.

Java Persistence API (JPA)
In online Chapter 29, we introduce Java Persistence API (JPA). In that chapter, you'll learn how to autogenerate Java classes that represent the tables in a database and the relationships between them—known as object-relational mapping—then use objects of those classes to interact with a database. As you'll see, storing data in and retrieving data from a database will be handled for you—the techniques you learn in this chapter will typically be hidden from you by JPA.

24.2 Relational Databases

A **relational database** is a logical representation of data that allows the data to be accessed without consideration of its physical structure. A relational database stores data in **tables**. Figure 24.1 illustrates a sample table that might be used in a personnel system. The table name is Employee, and its primary purpose is to store the attributes of employees. Tables are composed of **rows**, each describing a single entity—in Fig. 24.1, an employee. Rows are composed of **columns** in which values are stored. This table consists of six rows. The Number column of each row is the table's **primary key**—a column (or group of columns) with a value that is *unique* for each row. This guarantees that each row can be identified by its primary key. Good examples of primary-key columns are a social security number, an employee ID number and a part number in an inventory system, as values in each of these columns are guaranteed to be unique. The rows in Fig. 24.1 are displayed in order by primary key. In this case, the rows are listed in ascending order by primary key, but they could be listed in descending order or in no particular order at all.

Number	Name	Department	Salary	Location
23603	Jones	413	1100	New Jersey
24568	Kerwin	413	2000	New Jersey
34589	Larson	642	1800	Los Angeles
35761	Myers	611	1400	Orlando
47132	Neumann	413	9000	New Jersey
78321	Stephens	611	8500	Orlando

Row { (34589, Larson, 642, 1800, Los Angeles)

Primary key   Column

Fig. 24.1 | Employee table sample data.

Each column represents a different data attribute. Rows are unique (by primary key) within a table, but particular column values may be duplicated between rows. For example, three different rows in the Employee table's Department column contain number 413.

Selecting Data Subsets
Different users of a database are often interested in different data and different relationships among the data. Most users require only subsets of the rows and columns. Queries specify which subsets of the data to select from a table. You use SQL to define queries. For example, you might select data from the Employee table to create a result that shows where each department is located, presenting the data sorted in increasing order by department number. This result is shown in Fig. 24.2. SQL is discussed in Section 24.4.

Department	Location
413	New Jersey
611	Orlando
642	Los Angeles

Fig. 24.2 | Distinct Department and Location data from the Employees table.

24.3 A books Database

We introduce relational databases in the context of this chapter's books database, which you'll use in several examples. Before we discuss SQL, we discuss the *tables* of the books database. We use this database to introduce various database concepts, including how to use SQL to obtain information from the database and to manipulate the data. We provide a script to create the database. You can find the script in the examples directory for this chapter. Section 24.5 explains how to use this script.

Authors Table
The database consists of three tables: Authors, AuthorISBN and Titles. The Authors table (described in Fig. 24.3) consists of three columns that maintain each author's unique ID number, first name and last name. Figure 24.4 contains sample data from the Authors table.

Column	Description
AuthorID	Author's ID number in the database. In the books database, this integer column is defined as **autoincremented**—for each row inserted in this table, the AuthorID value is increased by 1 automatically to ensure that each row has a unique AuthorID. This column represents the table's primary key. Autoincremented columns are so-called identity columns. The SQL script we provide for this database uses the SQL **IDENTITY** keyword to mark the AuthorID column as an identity column. For more information on using the IDENTITY keyword and creating databases, see the Java DB Developer's Guide at http://docs.oracle.com/javadb/10.10.1.1/devguide/derbydev.pdf.
FirstName	Author's first name (a string).
LastName	Author's last name (a string).

Fig. 24.3 | Authors table from the books database.

AuthorID	FirstName	LastName
1	Paul	Deitel
2	Harvey	Deitel
3	Abbey	Deitel
4	Dan	Quirk
5	Michael	Morgano

Fig. 24.4 | Sample data from the Authors table.

Titles Table

The Titles table described in Fig. 24.5 consists of four columns that maintain information about each book in the database, including its ISBN, title, edition number and copyright year. Figure 24.8 contains the data from the Titles table.

Column	Description
ISBN	ISBN of the book (a string). The table's primary key. ISBN is an abbreviation for "International Standard Book Number"—a numbering scheme that publishers use to give every book a unique identification number.
Title	Title of the book (a string).
EditionNumber	Edition number of the book (an integer).
Copyright	Copyright year of the book (a string).

Fig. 24.5 | Titles table from the books database.

ISBN	Title	EditionNumber	Copyright
0132151006	Internet & World Wide Web How to Program	5	2012
0133807800	Java How to Program	10	2015
0132575655	Java How to Program, Late Objects Version	10	2015
013299044X	C How to Program	7	2013
0132990601	Simply Visual Basic 2010	4	2013
0133406954	Visual Basic 2012 How to Program	6	2014
0133379337	Visual C# 2012 How to Program	5	2014
0136151574	Visual C++ 2008 How to Program	2	2008
0133378713	C++ How to Program	9	2014
0133570924	Android How to Program	2	2015
0133570924	Android for Programmers: An App-Driven Approach, Volume 1	2	2014
0132121360	Android for Programmers: An App-Driven Approach	1	2012

Fig. 24.6 | Sample data from the Titles table of the books database .

AuthorISBN Table

The AuthorISBN table (described in Fig. 24.7) consists of two columns that maintain ISBNs for each book and their corresponding authors' ID numbers. This table associates authors with their books. The AuthorID column is a **foreign key**—a column in this table that matches the primary-key column in another table (that is, AuthorID in the Authors table). The ISBN column is also a foreign key—it matches the primary-key column (that is, ISBN) in the Titles table. A database might consist of many tables. A goal when designing a database is to *minimize* the amount of *duplicated* data among the database's tables. Foreign keys, which are specified when a database table is created in the database, link the data in *multiple* tables. Together the AuthorID and ISBN columns in this table form a *composite primary key*. Every row in this table *uniquely* matches *one* author to *one* book's ISBN. Figure 24.8 contains the data from the AuthorISBN table of the books database.

Column	Description
AuthorID	The author's ID number, a foreign key to the Authors table.
ISBN	The ISBN for a book, a foreign key to the Titles table.

Fig. 24.7 | AuthorISBN table from the books database.

AuthorID	ISBN	AuthorID	ISBN
1	0132151006	2	0133379337
2	0132151006	1	0136151574
3	0132151006	2	0136151574
1	0133807800	4	0136151574
2	0133807800	1	0133378713
1	0132575655	2	0133378713
2	0132575655	1	0133764036
1	013299044X	2	0133764036
2	013299044X	3	0133764036
1	0132990601	1	0133570924
2	0132990601	2	0133570924
3	0132990601	3	0133570924
1	0133406954	1	0132121360
2	0133406954	2	0132121360
3	0133406954	3	0132121360
1	0133379337	5	0132121360

Fig. 24.8 | Sample data from the AuthorISBN table of books.

Every foreign-key value must appear as another table's primary-key value so the DBMS can ensure that the foreign key value is valid—this is known as the **Rule of Referential Integrity**. For example, the DBMS ensures that the AuthorID value for a particular row of the `AuthorISBN` table is valid by checking that there is a row in the `Authors` table with that `AuthorID` as the primary key.

Foreign keys also allow *related* data in *multiple* tables to be *selected* from those tables—this is known as **joining** the data. There is a **one-to-many relationship** between a primary key and a corresponding foreign key (for example, one author can write many books and one book can be written by many authors). This means that a foreign key can appear *many* times in its own table but only *once* (as the primary key) in another table. For example, the ISBN 0132151006 can appear in several rows of `AuthorISBN` (because this book has several authors) but only once in `Titles`, where ISBN is the primary key.

Entity-Relationship (ER) Diagram

There's a one-to-many relationship between a primary key and a corresponding foreign key (e.g., one author can write many books). A foreign key can appear many times in its own table, but only once (as the primary key) in another table. Figure 24.9 is an **entity-relationship (ER) diagram** for the books database. This diagram shows the *database tables* and the *relationships* among them. The first compartment in each box contains the table's name and the remaining compartments contain the table's columns. The names in italic are primary keys. *A table's primary key uniquely identifies each row in the table.* Every row must have a primary-key value, and that value must be unique in the table. This is known as the **Rule of Entity Integrity**. Again, for the `AuthorISBN` table, the primary key is the combination of both columns—this is known as a composite primary key.

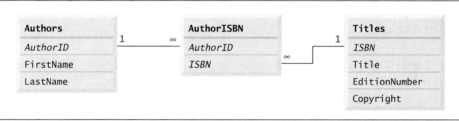

Fig. 24.9 | Table relationships in the books database.

The lines connecting the tables in Fig. 24.9 represent the *relationships* among the tables. Consider the line between the `Authors` and `AuthorISBN` tables. On the `Authors` end of the line, there's a 1, and on the `AuthorISBN` end, an infinity symbol (∞). This indicates a *one-to-many relationship*—for *each* author in the `Authors` table, there can be an *arbitrary number* of ISBNs for books written by that author in the `AuthorISBN` table (that is, an author can write *any* number of books). Note that the relationship line links the `AuthorID` column in the `Authors` table (where `AuthorID` is the primary key) to the `AuthorID` column in the `AuthorISBN` table (where `AuthorID` is a foreign key)—the line between the tables links the primary key to the matching foreign key.

The line between the `Titles` and `AuthorISBN` tables illustrates a *one-to-many relationship*—one book can be written by many authors. Note that the line between the tables links the primary key ISBN in table `Titles` to the corresponding foreign key in table `AuthorISBN`. The relationships in Fig. 24.9 illustrate that the sole purpose of the `AuthorISBN` table is to provide a **many-to-many relationship** between the `Authors` and `Titles` tables—an author can write *many* books, and a book can have *many* authors.

24.4 SQL

We now discuss SQL in the context of our books database. You'll be able to use the SQL discussed here in the examples later in the chapter. The next several subsections demonstrate SQL queries and statements using the SQL keywords in Fig. 24.10. Other SQL keywords are beyond this text's scope.

SQL keyword	Description
SELECT	Retrieves data from one or more tables.
FROM	Tables involved in the query. Required in every SELECT.
WHERE	Criteria for selection that determine the rows to be retrieved, deleted or updated. Optional in a SQL query or a SQL statement.
GROUP BY	Criteria for grouping rows. Optional in a SELECT query.
ORDER BY	Criteria for ordering rows. Optional in a SELECT query.
INNER JOIN	Merge rows from multiple tables.
INSERT	Insert rows into a specified table.
UPDATE	Update rows in a specified table.
DELETE	Delete rows from a specified table.

Fig. 24.10 | SQL query keywords.

24.4.1 Basic SELECT Query

Let's consider several SQL queries that extract information from database books. A SQL query "selects" rows and columns from one or more tables in a database. Such selections are performed by queries with the **SELECT** keyword. The basic form of a SELECT query is

SELECT * **FROM** *tableName*

in which the **asterisk (*)** *wildcard character* indicates that all columns from the *tableName* table should be retrieved. For example, to retrieve all the data in the Authors table, use

SELECT * **FROM** Authors

Most programs do not require all the data in a table. To retrieve only specific columns, replace the * with a comma-separated list of column names. For example, to retrieve only the columns AuthorID and LastName for all rows in the Authors table, use the query

SELECT AuthorID, LastName **FROM** Authors

This query returns the data listed in Fig. 24.11.

AuthorID	LastName	AuthorID	LastName
1	Deitel	4	Quirk
2	Deitel	5	Morgano
3	Deitel		

Fig. 24.11 | Sample AuthorID and LastName data from the Authors table.

Software Engineering Observation 24.2

In general, you process results by knowing in advance the order of the columns in the result—for example, selecting AuthorID *and* LastName *from table* Authors *ensures that the columns will appear in the result with* AuthorID *as the first column and* LastName *as the second column. Programs typically process result columns by specifying the column number in the result (starting from number 1 for the first column). Selecting columns by name avoids returning unneeded columns and protects against changes in the actual order of the columns in the table(s) by returning the columns in the exact order specified.*

Common Programming Error 24.1

If you assume that the columns are always returned in the same order from a query that uses the asterisk (*), the program may process the results incorrectly. If the column order in the table(s) changes or if additional columns are added at a later time, the order of the columns in the result will change accordingly.

24.4.2 WHERE Clause

In most cases, it's necessary to locate rows in a database that satisfy certain **selection criteria**. Only rows that satisfy the selection criteria (formally called **predicates**) are selected. SQL uses the optional **WHERE clause** in a query to specify the selection criteria for the query. The basic form of a query with selection criteria is

> **SELECT** *columnName1*, *columnName2*, ... **FROM** *tableName* **WHERE** *criteria*

For example, to select the Title, EditionNumber and Copyright columns from table Titles for which the Copyright date is greater than 2013, use the query

```
SELECT Title, EditionNumber, Copyright
    FROM Titles
    WHERE Copyright > '2013'
```

Strings in SQL are delimited by single (') rather than double (") quotes. Figure 24.12 shows the result of the preceding query.

Title	EditionNumber	Copyright
Java How to Program	10	2015
Java How to Program, Late Objects Version	10	2015
Visual Basic 2012 How to Program	6	2014
Visual C# 2012 How to Program	5	2014
C++ How to Program	9	2014
Android How to Program	2	2015
Android for Programmers: An App-Driven Approach, Volume 1	2	2014

Fig. 24.12 | Sampling of titles with copyrights after 2005 from table Titles.

Pattern Matching: Zero or More Characters
The WHERE clause criteria can contain the operators <, >, <=, >=, =, <> and LIKE. Operator **LIKE** is used for **pattern matching** with wildcard characters **percent (%)** and **underscore** (_). Pattern matching allows SQL to search for strings that match a given pattern.

A pattern that contains a percent character (%) searches for strings that have zero or more characters at the percent character's position in the pattern. For example, the next query locates the rows of all the authors whose last name starts with the letter D:

```
SELECT AuthorID, FirstName, LastName
    FROM Authors
    WHERE LastName LIKE 'D%'
```

This query selects the two rows shown in Fig. 24.13—three of the five authors have a last name starting with the letter D (followed by zero or more characters). The % symbol in the WHERE clause's LIKE pattern indicates that any number of characters can appear after the letter D in the LastName. The pattern string is surrounded by single-quote characters.

AuthorID	FirstName	LastName
1	Paul	Deitel
2	Harvey	Deitel
3	Abbey	Deitel

Fig. 24.13 | Authors whose last name starts with D from the Authors table.

Portability Tip 24.1

See the documentation for your database system to determine whether SQL is case sensitive on your system and to determine the syntax for SQL keywords.

Portability Tip 24.2

Read your database system's documentation carefully to determine whether it supports the LIKE operator as discussed here.

Pattern Matching: Any Character

An underscore (_) in the pattern string indicates a single wildcard character at that position in the pattern. For example, the following query locates the rows of all the authors whose last names start with any character (specified by _), followed by the letter o, followed by any number of additional characters (specified by %):

```
SELECT AuthorID, FirstName, LastName
    FROM Authors
    WHERE LastName LIKE '_o%'
```

The preceding query produces the row shown in Fig. 24.14, because only one author in our database has a last name that contains the letter o as its second letter.

AuthorID	FirstName	LastName
5	Michael	Morgano

Fig. 24.14 | The only author from the Authors table whose last name contains o as the second letter.

24.4.3 ORDER BY Clause

The rows in the result of a query can be sorted into ascending or descending order by using the optional **ORDER BY clause**. The basic form of a query with an ORDER BY clause is

SELECT *columnName1*, *columnName2*, ... **FROM** *tableName* **ORDER BY** *column* **ASC**
SELECT *columnName1*, *columnName2*, ... **FROM** *tableName* **ORDER BY** *column* **DESC**

where ASC specifies ascending order (lowest to highest), DESC specifies descending order (highest to lowest) and *column* specifies the column on which the sort is based. For example, to obtain the list of authors in ascending order by last name (Fig. 24.15), use the query

```
SELECT AuthorID, FirstName, LastName
    FROM Authors
    ORDER BY LastName ASC
```

AuthorID	FirstName	LastName
1	Paul	Deitel
2	Harvey	Deitel
3	Abbey	Deitel
5	Michael	Morgano
4	Dan	Quirk

Fig. 24.15 | Sample data from table Authors in ascending order by LastName.

Sorting in Descending Order
The default sorting order is ascending, so ASC is optional. To obtain the same list of authors in descending order by last name (Fig. 24.16), use the query

```
SELECT AuthorID, FirstName, LastName
    FROM Authors
    ORDER BY LastName DESC
```

AuthorID	FirstName	LastName
4	Dan	Quirk
5	Michael	Morgano
1	Paul	Deitel
2	Harvey	Deitel
3	Abbey	Deitel

Fig. 24.16 | Sample data from table Authors in descending order by LastName.

Sorting By Multiple Columns
Multiple columns can be used for sorting with an ORDER BY clause of the form

ORDER BY *column1 sortingOrder*, *column2 sortingOrder*, ...

where *sortingOrder* is either ASC or DESC. The *sortingOrder* does not have to be identical for each column. The query

```
SELECT AuthorID, FirstName, LastName
   FROM Authors
   ORDER BY LastName, FirstName
```

sorts all the rows in ascending order by last name, then by first name. If any rows have the same last-name value, they're returned sorted by first name (Fig. 24.17).

AuthorID	FirstName	LastName
3	Abbey	Deitel
2	Harvey	Deitel
1	Paul	Deitel
5	Michael	Morgano
4	Dan	Quirk

Fig. 24.17 | Sample data from `Authors` in ascending order by `LastName` and `FirstName`.

*Combining the **WHERE** and **ORDER BY** Clauses*
The WHERE and ORDER BY clauses can be combined in one query, as in

```
SELECT ISBN, Title, EditionNumber, Copyright
   FROM Titles
   WHERE Title LIKE '%How to Program'
   ORDER BY Title ASC
```

which returns the ISBN, Title, EditionNumber and Copyright of each book in the Titles table that has a Title ending with "How to Program" and sorts them in ascending order by Title. The query results are shown in Fig. 24.18.

ISBN	Title	EditionNumber	Copyright
0133764036	Android How to Program	2	2015
013299044X	C How to Program	7	2013
0133378713	C++ How to Program	9	2014
0132151006	Internet & World Wide Web How to Program	5	2012
0133807800	Java How to Program	10	2015
0133406954	Visual Basic 2012 How to Program	6	2014
0133379337	Visual C# 2012 How to Program	5	2014
0136151574	Visual C++ 2008 How to Program	2	2008

Fig. 24.18 | Sampling of books from table `Titles` whose titles end with `How to Program` in ascending order by `Title`.

24.4.4 Merging Data from Multiple Tables: INNER JOIN

Database designers often split related data into separate tables to ensure that a database does not store data redundantly. For example, in the books database, we use an AuthorISBN table to store the relationship data between authors and their corresponding titles. If we did not separate this information into individual tables, we'd need to include author information with each entry in the Titles table. This would result in the database's storing *duplicate* author information for authors who wrote multiple books. Often, it's necessary to merge data from multiple tables into a single result. Referred to as joining the tables, this is specified by an **INNER JOIN** operator, which merges rows from two tables by matching values in columns that are common to the tables. The basic form of an INNER JOIN is:

```
SELECT columnName1, columnName2, ...
FROM table1
INNER JOIN table2
    ON table1.columnName = table2.columnName
```

The **ON clause** of the INNER JOIN specifies the columns from each table that are compared to determine which rows are merged—these fields almost always correspond to the foreign-key fields in the tables being joined. For example, the following query produces a list of authors accompanied by the ISBNs for books written by each author:

```
SELECT FirstName, LastName, ISBN
FROM Authors
INNER JOIN AuthorISBN
    ON Authors.AuthorID = AuthorISBN.AuthorID
ORDER BY LastName, FirstName
```

The query merges the FirstName and LastName columns from table Authors with the ISBN column from table AuthorISBN, sorting the results in ascending order by LastName and FirstName. Note the use of the syntax *tableName.columnName* in the ON clause. This syntax, called a **qualified name**, specifies the columns from each table that should be compared to join the tables. The *"tableName."* syntax is required if the columns have the same name in both tables. The same syntax can be used in any SQL statement to distinguish columns in different tables that have the same name. In some systems, table names qualified with the database name can be used to perform cross-database queries. As always, the query can contain an ORDER BY clause. Figure 24.19 shows the results of the preceding query, ordered by LastName and FirstName. [*Note:* To save space, we split the result of the query into two columns, each containing the FirstName, LastName and ISBN columns.]

 Common Programming Error 24.2

Failure to qualify names for columns that have the same name in two or more tables is an error. In such cases, the statement must precede those column names with their table names and a dot (e.g., Authors.AuthorID).

FirstName	LastName	ISBN	FirstName	LastName	ISBN
Abbey	Deitel	0132121360	Harvey	Deitel	0133764036
Abbey	Deitel	0133570924	Harvey	Deitel	0133378713
Abbey	Deitel	0133764036	Harvey	Deitel	0136151574
Abbey	Deitel	0133406954	Harvey	Deitel	0133379337
Abbey	Deitel	0132990601	Harvey	Deitel	0133406954
Abbey	Deitel	0132151006	Harvey	Deitel	0132990601
Harvey	Deitel	0132121360	Harvey	Deitel	013299044X
Harvey	Deitel	0133570924	Harvey	Deitel	0132575655

Fig. 24.19 | Sampling of authors and ISBNs for the books they have written in ascending order by LastName and FirstName. (Part 1 of 2.)

FirstName	LastName	ISBN	FirstName	LastName	ISBN
Harvey	Deitel	0133807800	Paul	Deitel	0133406954
Harvey	Deitel	0132151006	Paul	Deitel	0132990601
Paul	Deitel	0132121360	Paul	Deitel	013299044X
Paul	Deitel	0133570924	Paul	Deitel	0132575655
Paul	Deitel	0133764036	Paul	Deitel	0133807800
Paul	Deitel	0133378713	Paul	Deitel	0132151006
Paul	Deitel	0136151574	Michael	Morgano	0132121360
Paul	Deitel	0133379337	Dan	Quirk	0136151574

Fig. 24.19 | Sampling of authors and ISBNs for the books they have written in ascending order by LastName and FirstName. (Part 2 of 2.)

24.4.5 INSERT Statement

The **INSERT** statement inserts a row into a table. The basic form of this statement is

```
INSERT INTO tableName (columnName1, columnName2, ..., columnNameN)
    VALUES (value1, value2, ..., valueN)
```

where *tableName* is the table in which to insert the row. The *tableName* is followed by a comma-separated list of column names in parentheses (this list is not required if the IN-SERT operation specifies a value for every column of the table in the correct order). The list of column names is followed by the SQL keyword **VALUES** and a comma-separated list of values in parentheses. The values specified here must match the columns specified after the table name in both order and type (e.g., if *columnName1* is supposed to be the FirstName column, then *value1* should be a string in single quotes representing the first name). Always explicitly list the columns when inserting rows. If the table's column order changes or a new column is added, using only VALUES may cause an error. The INSERT statement

```
INSERT INTO Authors (FirstName, LastName)
    VALUES ('Sue', 'Red')
```

inserts a row into the Authors table. The statement indicates that values are provided for the FirstName and LastName columns. The corresponding values are 'Sue' and 'Smith'. We do not specify an AuthorID in this example because AuthorID is an autoincremented column in the Authors table. For every row added to this table, the DBMS assigns a unique AuthorID value that is the next value in the autoincremented sequence (i.e., 1, 2, 3 and so on). In this case, Sue Red would be assigned AuthorID number 6. Figure 24.20 shows the Authors table after the INSERT operation. [*Note:* Not every database management system supports autoincremented columns. Check the documentation for your DBMS for alternatives to autoincremented columns.]

Common Programming Error 24.3

SQL delimits strings with single quotes ('). A string containing a single quote (e.g., O'Malley) must have two single quotes in the position where the single quote appears (e.g., 'O''Malley'). The first acts as an escape character for the second. Not escaping single-quote characters in a string that's part of a SQL statement is a SQL syntax error.

Common Programming Error 24.4

It's normally an error to specify a value for an autoincrement column.

AuthorID	FirstName	LastName
1	Paul	Deitel
2	Harvey	Deitel
3	Abbey	Deitel
4	Dan	Quirk
5	Michael	Morgano
6	Sue	Red

Fig. 24.20 | Sample data from table Authors after an INSERT operation.

24.4.6 UPDATE Statement

An **UPDATE** statement modifies data in a table. Its basic form is

```
UPDATE tableName
    SET columnName1 = value1, columnName2 = value2, ..., columnNameN = valueN
    WHERE criteria
```

where *tableName* is the table to update. The *tableName* is followed by keyword **SET** and a comma-separated list of *columnName* = *value* pairs. The optional WHERE clause provides criteria that determine which rows to update. Though not required, the WHERE clause is typically used, unless a change is to be made to every row. The UPDATE statement

```
UPDATE Authors
    SET LastName = 'Black'
    WHERE LastName = 'Red' AND FirstName = 'Sue'
```

updates a row in the Authors table. The statement indicates that LastName will be assigned the value Black for the row where LastName is Red and FirstName is Sue. [*Note:* If there are multiple matching rows, this statement will modify *all* such rows to have the last name "Black."] If we know the AuthorID in advance of the UPDATE operation (possibly because we searched for it previously), the WHERE clause can be simplified as follows:

```
WHERE AuthorID = 6
```

Figure 24.21 shows the Authors table after the UPDATE operation has taken place.

AuthorID	FirstName	LastName
1	Paul	Deitel
2	Harvey	Deitel
3	Abbey	Deitel
4	Dan	Quirk
5	Michael	Morgano
6	Sue	Black

Fig. 24.21 | Sample data from table Authors after an UPDATE operation.

24.4.7 DELETE Statement

A SQL **DELETE** statement removes rows from a table. Its basic form is

DELETE FROM *tableName* **WHERE** *criteria*

where *tableName* is the table from which to delete. The optional WHERE clause specifies the criteria used to determine which rows to delete. If this clause is omitted, all the table's rows are deleted. The DELETE statement

```
DELETE FROM Authors
    WHERE LastName = 'Black' AND FirstName = 'Sue'
```

deletes the row for Sue Black in the Authors table. If we know the AuthorID in advance of the DELETE operation, the WHERE clause can be simplified as follows:

```
WHERE AuthorID = 5
```

Figure 24.22 shows the Authors table after the DELETE operation has taken place.

AuthorID	FirstName	LastName
1	Paul	Deitel
2	Harvey	Deitel
3	Abbey	Deitel
4	Dan	Quirk
5	Michael	Morgano

Fig. 24.22 | Sample data from table Authors after a DELETE operation.

24.5 Setting up a Java DB Database

This chapter's examples use Oracle's pure Java database **Java DB**, which is installed with Oracle's JDK on Windows, Mac OS X and Linux. Before you can execute this chapter's applications, you must set up in Java DB the books database that's used in Sections 24.6––24.7 and the addressbook database that's used in Section 24.8.

For this chapter, you'll be using the embedded version of Java DB. This means that the database you manipulate in each example must be located in that example's folder. This chapter's examples are located in two subfolders of the ch24 examples folder—books_examples and addressbook_example. Java DB may also act as a server that can receive database requests over a network, but that is beyond this chapter's scope.

JDK Installation Folders
The Java DB software is located in the db subdirectory of your JDK's installation directory. The directories listed below are for Oracle's JDK 7 update 51:

- 32-bit JDK on Windows:
  ```
  C:\Program Files (x86)\Java\jdk1.7.0_51
  ```

- 64-bit JDK on Windows:
  ```
  C:\Program Files\Java\jdk1.7.0_51
  ```

- Mac OS X:
  `/Library/Java/JavaVirtualMachines/jdk1.7.0_51.jdk/Contents/Home`
- Ubuntu Linux:
  `/usr/lib/jvm/java-7-oracle`

For Linux, the install location depends on the installer you use and possibly the version of Linux that you use. We used Ubuntu Linux for testing purposes.

Depending on your platform, the JDK installation folder's name might differ if you're using a different update of JDK 7 or using JDK 8. In the following instructions, you should update the JDK installation folder's name based on the JDK version you're using.

Java DB Configuration

Java DB comes with several files that enable you to configure and run it. Before executing these files from a command window, you must set the environment variable `JAVA_HOME` to refer to the JDK's exact installation directory listed above (or the location where you installed the JDK if it differs from those listed above). See the Before You Begin section of this book for information on setting environment variables.

24.5.1 Creating the Chapter's Databases on Windows

After setting the `JAVA_HOME` environment variable, perform the following steps:

1. Run Notepad as an administrator. To do this on Windows 7, select **Start > All Programs > Accessories**, right click Notepad and select **Run as administrator**. On Windows 8, search for Notepad, right click it in the search results and select **Advanced** in the app bar, then select **Run as administrator**.

2. From Notepad, open the batch file `setEmbeddedCP.bat` that is located in the JDK installation folder's `db\bin` folder.

3. Locate the line

   ```
   @rem set DERBY_INSTALL=
   ```

   and change it to

   ```
   @set DERBY_INSTALL=%JAVA_HOME%\db
   ```

   Save your changes and close this file.

4. Open a Command Prompt window and change directories to the JDK installation folder's `db\bin` folder. Then, type `setEmbeddedCP.bat` and press *Enter* to set the environment variables required by Java DB.

5. Use the `cd` command to change to this chapter's `books_examples` directory. This directory contains a SQL script `books.sql` that builds the `books` database.

6. Execute the following command (with the quotation marks):

   ```
   "%JAVA_HOME%\db\bin\ij"
   ```

   to start the command-line tool for interacting with Java DB. The double quotes are necessary because the path that the environment variable `%JAVA_HOME%` represents contains a space. This will display the `ij>` prompt.

7. At the ij> prompt type

```
connect 'jdbc:derby:books;create=true;user=deitel;
    password=deitel';
```

and press *Enter* to create the books database in the current directory and to create the user deitel with the password deitel for accessing the database.

8. To create the database table and insert sample data in it, we've provided the file address.sql in this example's directory. To execute this SQL script, type

```
run 'books.sql';
```

Once you create the database, you can execute the SQL statements presented in Section 24.4 to confirm their execution. Each command you enter at the ij> prompt must be terminated with a semicolon (;).

9. To terminate the Java DB command-line tool, type

```
exit;
```

10. Change directories to the addressbook_example subfolder of the ch24 examples folder, which contains the SQL script addressbook.sql that builds the addressbook database. Repeat Steps 6–9. In each step, replace books with addressbook.

You're now ready to execute this chapter's examples.

24.5.2 Creating the Chapter's Databases on Mac OS X

After setting the JAVA_HOME environment variable, perform the following steps:

1. Open a Terminal, then type:

```
DERBY_HOME=/Library/Java/JavaVirtualMachines/jdk1.7.0_51.jdk/
    Contents/Home/db
```

and press *Enter*. Then type

```
export DERBY_HOME
```

and press *Enter*. This specifies where Java DB is located on your Mac.

2. In the Terminal window, change directories to the JDK installation folder's db/bin folder. Then, type ./setEmbeddedCP and press *Enter* to set the environment variables required by Java DB.

3. In the Terminal window, use the cd command to change to the books_examples directory. This directory contains a SQL script books.sql that builds the books database.

4. Execute the following command (with the quotation marks):

```
$JAVA_HOME/db/bin/ij
```

to start the command-line tool for interacting with Java DB. This will display the ij> prompt.

5. Perform Steps 7–9 of Section 24.5.1 to create the books database.

6. Use the cd command to change to the addressbook_example directory. This directory contains a SQL script addressbook.sql that builds the addressbook database.

7. Perform Steps 7–9 of Section 24.5.1 to create the `addressbook` database. In each step, replace `books` with `addressbook`.

You're now ready to execute this chapter's examples.

24.5.3 Creating the Chapter's Databases on Linux

After setting the `JAVA_HOME` environment variable, perform the following steps:

1. Open a shell window.

2. Perform the steps in Section 24.5.2, but in Step 1, set `DERBY_HOME` to

`DERBY_HOME=`*YourLinuxJDKInstallationFolder*`/db`

On our Ubuntu Linux system, this was:

`DERBY_HOME=/usr/lib/jvm/java-7-oracle/db`

You're now ready to execute this chapter's examples.

24.6 Manipulating Databases with JDBC

This section presents two examples. The first introduces how to connect to a database and query it. The second demonstrates how to display the result of the query in a `JTable`.

24.6.1 Connecting to and Querying a Database

The example of Fig. 24.23 performs a simple query on the `books` database that retrieves the entire `Authors` table and displays the data. The program illustrates connecting to the database, querying the database and processing the result. The discussion that follows presents the key JDBC aspects of the program.

Lines 3–8 import the JDBC interfaces and classes from package `java.sql` used in this program. Method `main` (lines 12–48) connects to the `books` database, queries the database, displays the query result and closes the database connection. Line 14 declares a `String` constant for the database URL. This identifies the name of the database to connect to, as well as information about the protocol used by the JDBC driver (discussed shortly). Lines 15–16 declare a `String` constant representing the SQL query that will select the `authorID`, `firstName` and `lastName` columns in the database's `authors` table.

```
1   // Fig. 24.23: DisplayAuthors.java
2   // Displaying the contents of the Authors table.
3   import java.sql.Connection;
4   import java.sql.Statement;
5   import java.sql.DriverManager;
6   import java.sql.ResultSet;
7   import java.sql.ResultSetMetaData;
8   import java.sql.SQLException;
9
10  public class DisplayAuthors
11  {
```

Fig. 24.23 | Displaying the contents of the `Authors` table. (Part 1 of 2.)

```
12        public static void main(String args[])
13        {
14            final String DATABASE_URL = "jdbc:derby:books";
15            final String SELECT_QUERY =
16                "SELECT authorID, firstName, lastName FROM authors";
17
18            // use try-with-resources to connect to and query the database
19            try (
20                Connection connection = DriverManager.getConnection(
21                    DATABASE_URL, "deitel", "deitel");
22                Statement statement = connection.createStatement();
23                ResultSet resultSet = statement.executeQuery(SELECT_QUERY))
24            {
25                // get ResultSet's meta data
26                ResultSetMetaData metaData = resultSet.getMetaData();
27                int numberOfColumns = metaData.getColumnCount();
28
29                System.out.printf("Authors Table of Books Database:%n%n");
30
31                // display the names of the columns in the ResultSet
32                for (int i = 1; i <= numberOfColumns; i++)
33                    System.out.printf("%-8s\t", metaData.getColumnName(i));
34                System.out.println();
35
36                // display query results
37                while (resultSet.next())
38                {
39                    for (int i = 1; i <= numberOfColumns; i++)
40                        System.out.printf("%-8s\t", resultSet.getObject(i));
41                    System.out.println();
42                }
43            } // AutoCloseable objects' close methods are called now
44            catch (SQLException sqlException)
45            {
46                sqlException.printStackTrace();
47            }
48        }
49    } // end class DisplayAuthors
```

```
Authors Table of Books Database:

AUTHORID        FIRSTNAME       LASTNAME
1               Paul            Deitel
2               Harvey          Deitel
3               Abbey           Deitel
4               Dan             Quirk
5               Michael         Morgano
```

Fig. 24.23 | Displaying the contents of the Authors table. (Part 2 of 2.)

JDBC supports **automatic driver discovery**—it loads the database driver into memory for you. To ensure that the program can locate the driver class, you must include the class's location in the program's classpath when you execute the program. You did this for Java DB in Section 24.5 when you executed the setEmbeddedCP.bat or setEmbeddedCP file on your system—that step configured a CLASSPATH environment variable in the command window for your platform. After doing so, you can run this application simply using the command

```
java DisplayAuthors
```

Connecting to the Database

The JDBC interfaces we use in this example each extend the AutoCloseable interface, so you can use objects that implement these interfaces with the try-with-resources statement (introduced in Section 11.12). Lines 19–23 create this example's AutoCloseable objects in the parentheses following keyword try—such objects are automatically closed when the try block terminates (line 43) or if an exception occurs during the try block's execution. Each object created in the parentheses following keyword try must be separated from the next by a semicolon (;).

Lines 20–21 create a **Connection** object (package java.sql) referenced by connection. An object that implements interface Connection manages the connection between the Java program and the database. Connection objects enable programs to create SQL statements that manipulate databases. The program initializes connection with the result of a call to static method **getConnection** of class **DriverManager** (package java.sql), which attempts to connect to the database specified by its URL.

Method getConnection takes three arguments

- a String that specifies the database URL,
- a String that specifies the username and
- a String that specifies the password.

The username and password for the books database were set in Section 24.5. If you used a different username and password there, you'll need to replace the username (second argument) and password (third argument) passed to method getConnection in line 21.

The URL locates the database (possibly on a network or in the local file system of the computer). The URL jdbc:derby:books specifies the protocol for communication (jdbc), the **subprotocol** for communication (derby) and the location of the database (books). The subprotocol derby indicates that the program uses a Java DB/Apache Derby-specific subprotocol to connect to the database—recall that Java DB is simply the Oracle branded version of Apache Derby. If the DriverManager cannot connect to the database, method getConnection throws a **SQLException** (package java.sql). Figure 24.24 lists the JDBC driver names and database URL formats of several popular RDBMSs.

RDBMS	Database URL format
MySQL	jdbc:mysql://*hostname*:*portNumber*/*databaseName*
ORACLE	jdbc:oracle:thin:@*hostname*:*portNumber*:*databaseName*
DB2	jdbc:db2:*hostname*:*portNumber*/*databaseName*
PostgreSQL	jdbc:postgresql://*hostname*:*portNumber*/*databaseName*
Java DB/Apache Derby	jdbc:derby:*dataBaseName* (embedded)
	jdbc:derby://*hostname*:*portNumber*/*databaseName* (network)

Fig. 24.24 | Popular JDBC database URL formats. (Part 1 of 2.)

RDBMS	Database URL format
Microsoft SQL Server	jdbc:sqlserver://*hostname*:*portNumber*;databaseName=*dataBaseName*
Sybase	jdbc:sybase:Tds:*hostname*:*portNumber*/*databaseName*

Fig. 24.24 | Popular JDBC database URL formats. (Part 2 of 2.)

Software Engineering Observation 24.3

Most database management systems require the user to log in before accessing the database contents. DriverManager *method* getConnection *is overloaded with versions that enable the program to supply the username and password to gain access.*

*Creating a **Statement** for Executing Queries*
Line 22 of Fig. 24.23 invokes Connection method **createStatement** to obtain an object that implements interface Statement (package java.sql). The program uses the **Statement** object to submit SQL statements to the database.

Executing a Query
Line 23 use the Statement object's **executeQuery** method to submit a query that selects all the author information from table Authors. This method returns an object that implements interface **ResultSet** and contains the query results. The ResultSet methods enable the program to manipulate the query result.

*Processing a Query's **ResultSet***
Lines 26–42 process the ResultSet. Line 26 obtains the ResultSet's **ResultSetMetaData** (package java.sql) object. The **metadata** describes the ResultSet's contents. Programs can use metadata programmatically to obtain information about the ResultSet's column names and types. Line 27 uses ResultSetMetaData method **getColumnCount** to retrieve the number of columns in the ResultSet. Lines 32–33 display the column names.

Software Engineering Observation 24.4

Metadata enables programs to process ResultSet *contents dynamically when detailed information about the* ResultSet *is not known in advance.*

Lines 37–42 display the data in each ResultSet row. First, the program positions the ResultSet cursor (which points to the row being processed) to the first row in the ResultSet with method **next** (line 37). Method next returns boolean value true if it's able to position to the next row; otherwise, the method returns false.

Common Programming Error 24.5

Initially, a ResultSet *cursor is positioned before the first row. A* SQLException *occurs if you attempt to access a* ResultSet's *contents before positioning the* ResultSet *cursor to the first row with method* next.

If there are rows in the ResultSet, lines 39–40 extract and display the contents of each column in the current row. When a ResultSet is processed, each column can be extracted as a specific Java type—ResultSetMetaData method **getColumnType** returns a constant integer from class **Types** (package java.sql) indicating the type of a specified column. Programs can use these values in a switch statement to invoke ResultSet methods that return the column values as appropriate Java types. For example, if the type of a column is Types.INTEGER, ResultSet method **getInt** can be used to get the column value as an int. For simplicity, this example treats each value as an Object. We retrieve each column value with ResultSet method **getObject** (line 40), then print the Object's String representation. ResultSet *get* methods typically receive as an argument either a column number (as an int) or a column name (as a String) indicating which column's value to obtain. Unlike array indices, ResultSet *column numbers start at 1.*

Performance Tip 24.1

If a query specifies the exact columns to select from the database, the ResultSet contains the columns in the specified order. In this case, using the column number to obtain the column's value is more efficient than using the column name. The column number provides direct access to the specified column. Using the column name requires a search of the column names to locate the appropriate column.

Error-Prevention Tip 24.1

Using column names to obtain values from a ResultSet produces code that is less error prone than obtaining values by column number—you don't need to remember the column order. Also, if the column order changes, your code does not have to change.

Common Programming Error 24.6

Specifying column index 0 when obtaining values from a ResultSet causes a SQL-Exception—the first column index in a ResultSet is always 1.

When the end of the try block is reached (line 43), the close method is called on the ResultSet, Statement and Connection that were obtained by the try-with-resources statement.

Common Programming Error 24.7

A SQLException occurs if you attempt to manipulate a ResultSet after closing the Statement that created it. The ResultSet is discarded when the Statement is closed.

Software Engineering Observation 24.5

Each Statement object can open only one ResultSet object at a time. When a Statement returns a new ResultSet, the Statement closes the prior ResultSet. To use multiple ResultSets in parallel, separate Statement objects must return the ResultSets.

24.6.2 Querying the books Database

The next example (Figs. 24.25 and 24.28) allows the user to enter any query into the program. The example displays the result of a query in a **JTable**, using a **TableModel** object to provide the ResultSet data to the JTable. A JTable is a swing GUI component that can be bound to a database to display the results of a query. Class ResultSetTableModel (Fig. 24.25) performs the connection to the database via a TableModel and maintains the ResultSet. Class DisplayQueryResults (Fig. 24.28) creates the GUI and specifies an instance of class ResultSetTableModel to provide data for the JTable.

ResultSetTableModel Class

Class ResultSetTableModel (Fig. 24.25) extends class **AbstractTableModel** (package javax.swing.table), which implements interface TableModel. ResultSetTableModel overrides TableModel methods **getColumnClass**, **getColumnCount**, **getColumnName**, **get-RowCount** and **getValueAt**. The default implementations of TableModel methods is-CellEditable and setValueAt (provided by AbstractTableModel) are not overridden, because this example does not support editing the JTable cells. The default implementations of TableModel methods **addTableModelListener** and **removeTableModelListener** (provided by AbstractTableModel) are not overridden, because the implementations of these methods in AbstractTableModel properly add and remove event listeners.

```java
1   // Fig. 24.25: ResultSetTableModel.java
2   // A TableModel that supplies ResultSet data to a JTable.
3   import java.sql.Connection;
4   import java.sql.Statement;
5   import java.sql.DriverManager;
6   import java.sql.ResultSet;
7   import java.sql.ResultSetMetaData;
8   import java.sql.SQLException;
9   import javax.swing.table.AbstractTableModel;
10
11  // ResultSet rows and columns are counted from 1 and JTable
12  // rows and columns are counted from 0. When processing
13  // ResultSet rows or columns for use in a JTable, it is
14  // necessary to add 1 to the row or column number to manipulate
15  // the appropriate ResultSet column (i.e., JTable column 0 is
16  // ResultSet column 1 and JTable row 0 is ResultSet row 1).
17  public class ResultSetTableModel extends AbstractTableModel
18  {
19     private final Connection connection;
20     private final Statement statement;
21     private ResultSet resultSet;
22     private ResultSetMetaData metaData;
23     private int numberOfRows;
24
25     // keep track of database connection status
26     private boolean connectedToDatabase = false;
27
28     // constructor initializes resultSet and obtains its metadata object;
29     // determines number of rows
30     public ResultSetTableModel(String url, String username,
31        String password, String query) throws SQLException
32     {
33        // connect to database
34        connection = DriverManager.getConnection(url, username, password);
35
36        // create Statement to query database
37        statement = connection.createStatement(
38           ResultSet.TYPE_SCROLL_INSENSITIVE,
39           ResultSet.CONCUR_READ_ONLY);
```

Fig. 24.25 | A TableModel that supplies ResultSet data to a JTable. (Part 1 of 4.)

```
40
41          // update database connection status
42          connectedToDatabase = true;
43
44          // set query and execute it
45          setQuery(query);
46       }
47
48       // get class that represents column type
49       public Class getColumnClass(int column) throws IllegalStateException
50       {
51          // ensure database connection is available
52          if (!connectedToDatabase)
53             throw new IllegalStateException("Not Connected to Database");
54
55          // determine Java class of column
56          try
57          {
58             String className = metaData.getColumnClassName(column + 1);
59
60             // return Class object that represents className
61             return Class.forName(className);
62          }
63          catch (Exception exception)
64          {
65             exception.printStackTrace();
66          }
67
68          return Object.class; // if problems occur above, assume type Object
69       }
70
71       // get number of columns in ResultSet
72       public int getColumnCount() throws IllegalStateException
73       {
74          // ensure database connection is available
75          if (!connectedToDatabase)
76             throw new IllegalStateException("Not Connected to Database");
77
78          // determine number of columns
79          try
80          {
81             return metaData.getColumnCount();
82          }
83          catch (SQLException sqlException)
84          {
85             sqlException.printStackTrace();
86          }
87
88          return 0; // if problems occur above, return 0 for number of columns
89       }
90
```

Fig. 24.25 | A TableModel that supplies ResultSet data to a JTable. (Part 2 of 4.)

```
91      // get name of a particular column in ResultSet
92      public String getColumnName(int column) throws IllegalStateException
93      {
94         // ensure database connection is available
95         if (!connectedToDatabase)
96            throw new IllegalStateException("Not Connected to Database");
97
98         // determine column name
99         try
100        {
101           return metaData.getColumnName(column + 1);
102        }
103        catch (SQLException sqlException)
104        {
105           sqlException.printStackTrace();
106        }
107
108        return ""; // if problems, return empty string for column name
109     }
110
111     // return number of rows in ResultSet
112     public int getRowCount() throws IllegalStateException
113     {
114        // ensure database connection is available
115        if (!connectedToDatabase)
116           throw new IllegalStateException("Not Connected to Database");
117
118        return numberOfRows;
119     }
120
121     // obtain value in particular row and column
122     public Object getValueAt(int row, int column)
123        throws IllegalStateException
124     {
125        // ensure database connection is available
126        if (!connectedToDatabase)
127           throw new IllegalStateException("Not Connected to Database");
128
129        // obtain a value at specified ResultSet row and column
130        try
131        {
132           resultSet.absolute(row + 1);
133           return resultSet.getObject(column + 1);
134        }
135        catch (SQLException sqlException)
136        {
137           sqlException.printStackTrace();
138        }
139
140        return ""; // if problems, return empty string object
141     }
```

Fig. 24.25 | A TableModel that supplies ResultSet data to a JTable. (Part 3 of 4.)

```
142
143      // set new database query string
144      public void setQuery(String query)
145         throws SQLException, IllegalStateException
146      {
147         // ensure database connection is available
148         if (!connectedToDatabase)
149            throw new IllegalStateException("Not Connected to Database");
150
151         // specify query and execute it
152         resultSet = statement.executeQuery(query);
153
154         // obtain metadata for ResultSet
155         metaData = resultSet.getMetaData();
156
157         // determine number of rows in ResultSet
158         resultSet.last(); // move to last row
159         numberOfRows = resultSet.getRow(); // get row number
160
161         // notify JTable that model has changed
162         fireTableStructureChanged();
163      }
164
165      // close Statement and Connection
166      public void disconnectFromDatabase()
167      {
168         if (connectedToDatabase)
169         {
170            // close Statement and Connection
171            try
172            {
173               resultSet.close();
174               statement.close();
175               connection.close();
176            }
177            catch (SQLException sqlException)
178            {
179               sqlException.printStackTrace();
180            }
181            finally  // update database connection status
182            {
183               connectedToDatabase = false;
184            }
185         }
186      }
187   } // end class ResultSetTableModel
```

Fig. 24.25 | A TableModel that supplies ResultSet data to a JTable. (Part 4 of 4.)

ResultSetTableModel Constructor

The ResultSetTableModel constructor (lines 30–46) accepts four String arguments—
the URL of the database, the username, the password and the default query to perform.
The constructor throws any exceptions that occur in its body back to the application that
created the ResultSetTableModel object, so that the application can determine how to

handle the exception (e.g., report an error and terminate the application). Line 34 establishes a connection to the database. Lines 37–39 invoke `Connection` method `createStatement` to create a `Statement` object. This example uses a version of method `createStatement` that takes two arguments—the result set type and the result set concurrency. The **result set type** (Fig. 24.26) specifies whether the `ResultSet`'s cursor is able to scroll in both directions or forward only and whether the `ResultSet` is sensitive to changes made to the underlying data.

ResultSet constant	Description
TYPE_FORWARD_ONLY	Specifies that a `ResultSet`'s cursor can move only in the forward direction (i.e., from the first to the last row in the `ResultSet`).
TYPE_SCROLL_INSENSITIVE	Specifies that a `ResultSet`'s cursor can scroll in either direction and that the changes made to the underlying data during `ResultSet` processing are not reflected in the `ResultSet` unless the program queries the database again.
TYPE_SCROLL_SENSITIVE	Specifies that a `ResultSet`'s cursor can scroll in either direction and that the changes made to the underlying data during `ResultSet` processing are reflected immediately in the `ResultSet`.

Fig. 24.26 | `ResultSet` constants for specifying `ResultSet` type.

Portability Tip 24.3

Some JDBC drivers do not support scrollable `ResultSet`s. In such cases, the driver typically returns a `ResultSet` in which the cursor can move only forward. For more information, see your database driver documentation.

Common Programming Error 24.8

Attempting to move the cursor backward through a `ResultSet` when the database driver does not support backward scrolling causes a `SQLFeatureNotSupportedException`.

`ResultSet`s that are sensitive to changes reflect those changes immediately after they're made with methods of interface `ResultSet`. If a `ResultSet` is insensitive to changes, the query that produced the `ResultSet` must be executed again to reflect any changes made. The **result set concurrency** (Fig. 24.27) specifies whether the `ResultSet` can be updated with `ResultSet`'s update methods.

ResultSet static concurrency constant	Description
CONCUR_READ_ONLY	Specifies that a `ResultSet` can't be updated—changes to the `ResultSet` contents cannot be reflected in the database with `ResultSet`'s update methods.
CONCUR_UPDATABLE	Specifies that a `ResultSet` can be updated (i.e., changes to its contents can be reflected in the database with `ResultSet`'s update methods).

Fig. 24.27 | `ResultSet` constants for specifying result properties.

Portability Tip 24.4

Some JDBC drivers do not support updatable ResultSets. *In such cases, the driver typi-cally returns a read-only* ResultSet. *For more information, see your database driver doc-umentation.*

Common Programming Error 24.9

Attempting to update a ResultSet *when the database driver does not support updatable* ResultSets *causes* SQLFeatureNotSupportedExceptions.

This example uses a ResultSet that is scrollable, insensitive to changes and read only. Line 45 (Fig. 24.25) invokes method setQuery (lines 144–163) to perform the default query.

ResultSetTableModel Method getColumnClass

Method getColumnClass (lines 49–69) returns a Class object that represents the superclass of all objects in a particular column. The JTable uses this information to configure the default cell renderer and cell editor for that column in the JTable. Line 58 uses ResultSet-MetaData method **getColumnClassName** to obtain the fully qualified class name for the specified column. Line 61 loads the class and returns the corresponding Class object. If an exception occurs, the catch in lines 63–66 prints a stack trace and line 68 returns Object.class—the Class instance that represents class Object—as the default type. [*Note:* Line 58 uses the argument column + 1. Like arrays, JTable row and column numbers are counted from 0. However, ResultSet row and column numbers are counted from 1. Thus, when processing ResultSet rows or columns for use in a JTable, it's necessary to add 1 to the row or column number to manipulate the appropriate ResultSet row or column.]

ResultSetTableModel Method getColumnCount

Method getColumnCount (lines 72–89) returns the number of columns in the model's underlying ResultSet. Line 81 uses ResultSetMetaData method **getColumnCount** to obtain the number of columns in the ResultSet. If an exception occurs, the catch in lines 83–86 prints a stack trace and line 88 returns 0 as the default number of columns.

ResultSetTableModel Method getColumnName

Method getColumnName (lines 92–109) returns the name of the column in the model's underlying ResultSet. Line 101 uses ResultSetMetaData method **getColumnName** to obtain the column name from the ResultSet. If an exception occurs, the catch in lines 103–106 prints a stack trace and line 108 returns the empty string as the default column name.

ResultSetTableModel Method getRowCount

Method getRowCount (lines 112–119) returns the number of rows in the model's underlying ResultSet. When method setQuery (lines 144–163) performs a query, it stores the number of rows in variable numberOfRows.

ResultSetTableModel Method getValueAt

Method getValueAt (lines 122–141) returns the Object in a particular row and column of the model's underlying ResultSet. Line 132 uses ResultSet method **absolute** to position the ResultSet cursor at a specific row. Line 133 uses ResultSet method getObject to obtain the Object in a specific column of the current row. If an exception occurs, the catch in lines 135–138 prints a stack trace and line 140 returns an empty string as the default value.

ResultSetTableModel Method *setQuery*

Method setQuery (lines 144–163) executes the query it receives as an argument to obtain a new ResultSet (line 152). Line 155 gets the ResultSetMetaData for the new Result-Set. Line 158 uses ResultSet method **last** to position the ResultSet cursor at the last row in the ResultSet. [*Note:* This can be slow if the table contains many rows.] Line 159 uses ResultSet method **getRow** to obtain the row number for the current row in the Re-sultSet. Line 162 invokes method **fireTableStructureChanged** (inherited from class AbstractTableModel) to notify any JTable using this ResultSetTableModel object as its model that the structure of the model has changed. This causes the JTable to repopulate its rows and columns with the new ResultSet data. Method setQuery throws any exceptions that occur in its body back to the application that invoked setQuery.

ResultSetTableModel Method *disconnectFromDatabase*

Method disconnectFromDatabase (lines 166–186) implements an appropriate termination method for class ResultSetTableModel. A class designer should provide a public method that clients of the class must invoke explicitly to free resources that an object has used. In this case, method disconnectFromDatabase closes the ResultSet, Statement and Connection (lines 173–175), which are considered limited resources. Clients of the ResultSetTableModel class should always invoke this method when the instance of this class is no longer needed. Before releasing resources, line 168 verifies whether the connection is already terminated. If not, the method proceeds. The other methods in class Re-sultSetTableModel each throw an IllegalStateException if connectedToDatabase is false. Method disconnectFromDatabase sets connectedToDatabase to false (line 183) to ensure that clients do not use an instance of ResultSetTableModel after that instance has already been terminated. IllegalStateException is an exception from the Java librar-ies that is appropriate for indicating this error condition.

DisplayQueryResults Class

Class DisplayQueryResults (Fig. 24.28) implements the application's GUI and interacts with the ResultSetTableModel via a JTable object. This application also demonstrates the JTable sorting and filtering capabilities.

```
1   // Fig. 24.28: DisplayQueryResults.java
2   // Display the contents of the Authors table in the books database.
3   import java.awt.BorderLayout;
4   import java.awt.event.ActionListener;
5   import java.awt.event.ActionEvent;
6   import java.awt.event.WindowAdapter;
7   import java.awt.event.WindowEvent;
8   import java.sql.SQLException;
9   import java.util.regex.PatternSyntaxException;
10  import javax.swing.JFrame;
11  import javax.swing.JTextArea;
12  import javax.swing.JScrollPane;
13  import javax.swing.ScrollPaneConstants;
14  import javax.swing.JTable;
15  import javax.swing.JOptionPane;
```

Fig. 24.28 | Display the contents of the Authors table in the books database. (Part 1 of 5.)

```
16  import javax.swing.JButton;
17  import javax.swing.Box;
18  import javax.swing.JLabel;
19  import javax.swing.JTextField;
20  import javax.swing.RowFilter;
21  import javax.swing.table.TableRowSorter;
22  import javax.swing.table.TableModel;
23
24  public class DisplayQueryResults extends JFrame
25  {
26     // database URL, username and password
27     private static final String DATABASE_URL = "jdbc:derby:books";
28     private static final String USERNAME = "deitel";
29     private static final String PASSWORD = "deitel";
30
31     // default query retrieves all data from Authors table
32     private static final String DEFAULT_QUERY = "SELECT * FROM Authors";
33
34     private static ResultSetTableModel tableModel;
35
36     public static void main(String args[])
37     {
38        // create ResultSetTableModel and display database table
39        try
40        {
41           // create TableModel for results of query SELECT * FROM Authors
42           tableModel = new ResultSetTableModel(DATABASE_URL,
43              USERNAME, PASSWORD, DEFAULT_QUERY);
44
45           // set up JTextArea in which user types queries
46           final JTextArea queryArea = new JTextArea(DEFAULT_QUERY, 3, 100);
47           queryArea.setWrapStyleWord(true);
48           queryArea.setLineWrap(true);
49
50           JScrollPane scrollPane = new JScrollPane(queryArea,
51              ScrollPaneConstants.VERTICAL_SCROLLBAR_AS_NEEDED,
52              ScrollPaneConstants.HORIZONTAL_SCROLLBAR_NEVER);
53
54           // set up JButton for submitting queries
55           JButton submitButton = new JButton("Submit Query");
56
57           // create Box to manage placement of queryArea and
58           // submitButton in GUI
59           Box boxNorth = Box.createHorizontalBox();
60           boxNorth.add(scrollPane);
61           boxNorth.add(submitButton);
62
63           // create JTable based on the tableModel
64           JTable resultTable = new JTable(tableModel);
65
66           JLabel filterLabel = new JLabel("Filter:");
67           final JTextField filterText = new JTextField();
68           JButton filterButton = new JButton("Apply Filter");
```

Fig. 24.28 | Display the contents of the Authors table in the books database. (Part 2 of 5.)

```
69              Box boxSouth = Box.createHorizontalBox();
70
71              boxSouth.add(filterLabel);
72              boxSouth.add(filterText);
73              boxSouth.add(filterButton);
74
75              // place GUI components on JFrame's content pane
76              JFrame window = new JFrame("Displaying Query Results");
77              add(boxNorth, BorderLayout.NORTH);
78              add(new JScrollPane(resultTable), BorderLayout.CENTER);
79              add(boxSouth, BorderLayout.SOUTH);
80
81              // create event listener for submitButton
82              submitButton.addActionListener(
83                 new ActionListener()
84                 {
85                    public void actionPerformed(ActionEvent event)
86                    {
87                       // perform a new query
88                       try
89                       {
90                          tableModel.setQuery(queryArea.getText());
91                       }
92                       catch (SQLException sqlException)
93                       {
94                          JOptionPane.showMessageDialog(null,
95                             sqlException.getMessage(), "Database error",
96                             JOptionPane.ERROR_MESSAGE);
97
98                          // try to recover from invalid user query
99                          // by executing default query
100                         try
101                         {
102                            tableModel.setQuery(DEFAULT_QUERY);
103                            queryArea.setText(DEFAULT_QUERY);
104                         }
105                         catch (SQLException sqlException2)
106                         {
107                            JOptionPane.showMessageDialog(null,
108                               sqlException2.getMessage(), "Database error",
109                               JOptionPane.ERROR_MESSAGE);
110
111                            // ensure database connection is closed
112                            tableModel.disconnectFromDatabase();
113
114                            System.exit(1); // terminate application
115                         }
116                      }
117                   }
118                }
119             );
120
```

Fig. 24.28 | Display the contents of the Authors table in the books database. (Part 3 of 5.)

```
121              final TableRowSorter<TableModel> sorter =
122                 new TableRowSorter<TableModel>(tableModel);
123              resultTable.setRowSorter(sorter);
124
125              // create listener for filterButton
126              filterButton.addActionListener(
127                 new ActionListener()
128                 {
129                    // pass filter text to listener
130                    public void actionPerformed(ActionEvent e)
131                    {
132                       String text = filterText.getText();
133
134                       if (text.length() == 0)
135                          sorter.setRowFilter(null);
136                       else
137                       {
138                          try
139                          {
140                             sorter.setRowFilter(
141                                RowFilter.regexFilter(text));
142                          }
143                          catch (PatternSyntaxException pse)
144                          {
145                             JOptionPane.showMessageDialog(null,
146                                "Bad regex pattern", "Bad regex pattern",
147                                JOptionPane.ERROR_MESSAGE);
148                          }
149                       }
150                    }
151                 }
152              );
153              // dispose of window when user quits application (this overrides
154              // the default of HIDE_ON_CLOSE)
155              window.setDefaultCloseOperation(DISPOSE_ON_CLOSE);
156              window.setSize(500, 250);
157              window.setVisible(true);
158
159              // ensure database is closed when user quits application
160              addWindowListener(
161                 new WindowAdapter()
162                 {
163                    // disconnect from database and exit when window has closed
164                    public void windowClosed(WindowEvent event)
165                    {
166                       tableModel.disconnectFromDatabase();
167                       System.exit(0);
168                    }
169                 }
170              );
171           }
172           catch (SQLException sqlException)
173           {
```

Fig. 24.28 | Display the contents of the Authors table in the books database. (Part 4 of 5.)

```
174              JOptionPane.showMessageDialog(null, sqlException.getMessage(),
175                 "Database error", JOptionPane.ERROR_MESSAGE);
176              tableModel.disconnectFromDatabase();
177              System.exit(1); // terminate application
178           }
179        }
180     } // end class DisplayQueryResults
```

a) Displaying all authors from the `Authors` table

🔷 Displaying Query Results	☐ ◻ ✕

```
SELECT * FROM authors
```
                                                    `Submit Query`

AUTHORID	FIRSTNAME	LASTNAME
1	Paul	Deitel
2	Harvey	Deitel
3	Abbey	Deitel
4	Dan	Quirk
5	Michael	Morgano

Filter: `_____`   `Apply Filter`

b) Displaying the the authors' first and last names joined with the titles and edition numbers of the books they've authored

🔷 Displaying Query Results	☐ ◻ ✕

```
SELECT firstName, lastName, title, editionNumber FROM authors
INNER JOIN authorISBN ON authors.authorID = authorISBN.authorID
INNER JOIN titles ON authorISBN.isbn=titles.isbn
```
                                                    `Submit Query`

FIRSTNAME	LASTNAME	TITLE	EDITIONNUMBER
Paul	Deitel	Internet & World W...	5
Harvey	Deitel	Internet & World W...	5
Abbey	Deitel	Internet & World W...	5
Paul	Deitel	Java How to Progr...	10
Harvey	Deitel	Java How to Progr...	10
Paul	Deitel	Java How to Progr...	10

Filter: `_____`   `Apply Filter`

c) Filtering the results of the previous query to show only the books with Java in the title

🔷 Displaying Query Results	☐ ◻ ✕

```
SELECT firstName, lastName, title, editionNumber FROM authors
INNER JOIN authorISBN ON authors.authorID = authorISBN.authorID
INNER JOIN titles ON authorISBN.isbn=titles.isbn
```
                                                    `Submit Query`

FIRSTNAME	LASTNAME	TITLE	EDITIONNUMBER
Paul	Deitel	Java How to Progr...	10
Harvey	Deitel	Java How to Progr...	10
Paul	Deitel	Java How to Progr...	10
Harvey	Deitel	Java How to Progr...	10

Filter: Java `_____`   `Apply Filter`

Fig. 24.28 | Display the contents of the `Authors` table in the `books` database. (Part 5 of 5.)

Lines 27–29 and 32 declare the URL, username, password and default query that are passed to the `ResultSetTableModel` constructor to make the initial connection to the database and perform the default query. The `main` method (lines 36–179) creates a

ResultSetTableModel object and the GUI for the application and displays the GUI in a JFrame. Line 64 creates the JTable object and passes a ResultSetTableModel object (created at lines 42–43) to the JTable constructor, which then registers the JTable as a listener for TableModelEvents generated by the ResultSetTableModel.

The local variables queryArea (line 46), filterText (line 67) and sorter (lines 121–122) are declared final because they're used from anonymous inner classes. Recall that any local variable that will be used in an anonymous inner class must be declared final; otherwise, a compilation error occurs. (In Java SE 8, this program would compile without declaring these variables final because these variables would be effectively final, as discussed in Chapter 17.)

Lines 82–119 register an event handler for the submitButton that the user clicks to submit a query to the database. When the user clicks the button, method actionPerformed (lines 85–117) invokes method setQuery from the class ResultSetTableModel to execute the new query (line 90). If the user's query fails (e.g., because of a syntax error in the user's input), lines 102–103 execute the default query. If the default query also fails, there could be a more serious error, so line 112 ensures that the database connection is closed and line 114 exits the program. The screen captures in Fig. 24.28 show the results of two queries. The first screen capture shows the default query that retrieves all the data from table Authors of database books. The second screen capture shows a query that selects each author's first name and last name from the Authors table and combines that information with the title and edition number from the Titles table. Try entering your own queries in the text area and clicking the **Submit Query** button to execute the query.

Lines 161–170 register a **WindowListener** for the **windowClosed** event, which occurs when the user closes the window. Since WindowListeners can handle several window events, we extend class **WindowAdapter** and override only the windowClosed event handler.

Sorting Rows in a JTable

JTables allow users to sort rows by the data in a specific column. Lines 121–122 use the **TableRowSorter** class (from package **javax.swing.table**) to create an object that uses our ResultSetTableModel to sort rows in the JTable that displays query results. When the user clicks the title of a particular JTable column, the TableRowSorter interacts with the underlying TableModel to reorder the rows based on the data in that column. Line 123 uses JTable method **setRowSorter** to specify the TableRowSorter for resultTable.

Filtering Rows in a JTable

JTables can now show subsets of the data from the underlying TableModel. This is known as filtering the data. Lines 126–152 register an event handler for the filterButton that the user clicks to filter the data. In method actionPerformed (lines 130–150), line 132 obtains the filter text. If the user did not specify filter text, line 135 uses JTable method **setRowFilter** to remove any prior filter by setting the filter to null. Otherwise, lines 140–141 use setRowFilter to specify a **RowFilter** (from package javax.swing) based on the user's input. Class RowFilter provides several methods for creating filters. The static method **regexFilter** receives a String containing a regular expression pattern as its argument and an optional set of indices that specify which columns to filter. If no indices are specified, then all the columns are searched. In this example, the regular expression pattern is the text the user typed. Once the filter is set, the data displayed in the JTable is updated based on the filtered TableModel.

24.7 RowSet Interface

In the preceding examples, you learned how to query a database by explicitly establishing a Connection to the database, preparing a Statement for querying the database and executing the query. In this section, we demonstrate the **RowSet interface**, which configures the database connection and prepares query statements automatically. The interface RowSet provides several *set* methods that allow you to specify the properties needed to establish a connection (such as the database URL, username and password of the database) and create a Statement (such as a query). RowSet also provides several *get* methods that return these properties.

Connected and Disconnected RowSets
There are two types of RowSet objects—connected and disconnected. A **connected RowSet** object connects to the database once and remains connected while the object is in use. A **disconnected RowSet** object connects to the database, executes a query to retrieve the data from the database and then closes the connection. A program may change the data in a disconnected RowSet while it's disconnected. Modified data can be updated in the database after a disconnected RowSet reestablishes the connection with the database.

Package **javax.sql.rowset** contains two subinterfaces of RowSet—JdbcRowSet and CachedRowSet. **JdbcRowSet**, a connected RowSet, acts as a wrapper around a ResultSet object and allows you to scroll through and update the rows in the ResultSet. Recall that by default, a ResultSet object is nonscrollable and read only—you must explicitly set the result-set type constant to TYPE_SCROLL_INSENSITIVE and set the result-set concurrency constant to CONCUR_UPDATABLE to make a ResultSet object scrollable and updatable. A JdbcRowSet object is scrollable and updatable by default. **CachedRowSet**, a disconnected RowSet, caches the data of a ResultSet in memory and disconnects from the database. Like JdbcRowSet, a CachedRowSet object is scrollable and updatable by default. A CachedRowSet object is also *serializable*, so it can be passed between Java applications through a network, such as the Internet. However, CachedRowSet has a limitation—the amount of data that can be stored in memory is limited. Package javax.sql.rowset contains three other subinterfaces of RowSet.

> **Portability Tip 24.5**
> *A RowSet can provide scrolling capability for drivers that do not support scrollable ResultSets.*

Using a RowSet
Figure 24.29 reimplements the example of Fig. 24.23 using a RowSet. Rather than establish the connection and create a Statement explicitly, Fig. 24.29 uses a JdbcRowSet object to create a Connection and a Statement automatically.

Class **RowSetProvider** (package javax.sql.rowset) provides static method **newFactory** which returns a an object that implements interface **RowSetFactory** (package javax.sql.rowset) that can be used to create various types of RowSets. Lines 18–19 in the try-with-resources statement use RowSetFactory method **createJdbcRowSet** to obtain a JdbcRowSet object.

Lines 22–24 set the RowSet properties that the DriverManager uses to establish a database connection. Line 22 invokes JdbcRowSet method **setUrl** to specify the database

```
 1    // Fig. 24.29: JdbcRowSetTest.java
 2    // Displaying the contents of the Authors table using JdbcRowSet.
 3    import java.sql.ResultSetMetaData;
 4    import java.sql.SQLException;
 5    import javax.sql.rowset.JdbcRowSet;
 6    import javax.sql.rowset.RowSetProvider;
 7
 8    public class JdbcRowSetTest
 9    {
10       // JDBC driver name and database URL
11       private static final String DATABASE_URL = "jdbc:derby:books";
12       private static final String USERNAME = "deitel";
13       private static final String PASSWORD = "deitel";
14
15       public static void main(String args[])
16       {
17          // connect to database books and query database
18          try (JdbcRowSet rowSet =
19             RowSetProvider.newFactory().createJdbcRowSet())
20          {
21             // specify JdbcRowSet properties
22             rowSet.setUrl(DATABASE_URL);
23             rowSet.setUsername(USERNAME);
24             rowSet.setPassword(PASSWORD);
25             rowSet.setCommand("SELECT * FROM Authors"); // set query
26             rowSet.execute(); // execute query
27
28             // process query results
29             ResultSetMetaData metaData = rowSet.getMetaData();
30             int numberOfColumns = metaData.getColumnCount();
31             System.out.printf("Authors Table of Books Database:%n%n");
32
33             // display rowset header
34             for (int i = 1; i <= numberOfColumns; i++)
35                System.out.printf("%-8s\t", metaData.getColumnName(i));
36             System.out.println();
37
38             // display each row
39             while (rowSet.next())
40             {
41                for (int i = 1; i <= numberOfColumns; i++)
42                   System.out.printf("%-8s\t", rowSet.getObject(i));
43                System.out.println();
44             }
45          }
46          catch (SQLException sqlException)
47          {
48             sqlException.printStackTrace();
49             System.exit(1);
50          }
51       }
52    } // end class JdbcRowSetTest
```

Fig. 24.29 | Displaying the contents of the Authors table using JdbcRowSet. (Part 1 of 2.)

```
Authors Table of Books Database:

AUTHORID        FIRSTNAME       LASTNAME
1               Paul            Deitel
2               Harvey          Deitel
3               Abbey           Deitel
4               Dan             Quirk
5               Michael         Morgano
```

Fig. 24.29 | Displaying the contents of the Authors table using JdbcRowSet. (Part 2 of 2.)

URL. Line 23 invokes JdbcRowSet method **setUsername** to specify the username. Line 24 invokes JdbcRowSet method **setPassword** to specify the password. Line 25 invokes Jdbc-RowSet method **setCommand** to specify the SQL query that will be used to populate the RowSet. Line 26 invokes JdbcRowSet method **execute** to execute the SQL query. Method execute performs four actions—it establishes a Connection to the database, prepares the query Statement, executes the query and stores the ResultSet returned by query. The Connection, Statement and ResultSet are encapsulated in the JdbcRowSet object.

The remaining code is almost identical to Fig. 24.23, except that line 29 (Fig. 24.29) obtains a ResultSetMetaData object from the JdbcRowSet, line 39 uses the JdbcRowSet's next method to get the next row of the result and line 42 uses the JdbcRowSet's getObject method to obtain a column's value. When the end of the try block is reached, the try-with-resources statement invokes JdbcRowSet method **close**, which closes the RowSet's encapsulated ResultSet, Statement and Connection. In a CachedRowSet, invoking close also releases the resources held by that RowSet. The output of this application is the same as that of Fig. 24.23.

24.8 PreparedStatements

A **PreparedStatement** enables you to create compiled SQL statements that execute more efficiently than Statements. PreparedStatements can also specify parameters, making them more flexible than Statements—you can execute the same query repeatedly with different parameter values. For example, in the books database, you might want to locate all book titles for an author with a specific last and first name, and you might want to execute that query for several authors. With a PreparedStatement, that query is defined as follows:

```
PreparedStatement authorBooks = connection.prepareStatement(
   "SELECT LastName, FirstName, Title " +
   "FROM Authors INNER JOIN AuthorISBN " +
      "ON Authors.AuthorID=AuthorISBN.AuthorID " +
   "INNER JOIN Titles " +
      "ON AuthorISBN.ISBN=Titles.ISBN " +
   "WHERE LastName = ? AND FirstName = ?");
```

The two question marks (?) in the the preceding SQL statement's last line are placeholders for values that will be passed as part of the query to the database. Before executing a PreparedStatement, the program must specify the parameter values by using the Prepared-Statement interface's *set* methods.

For the preceding query, both parameters are strings that can be set with Prepared-Statement method **setString** as follows:

```
      authorBooks.setString(1, "Deitel");
      authorBooks.setString(2, "Paul");
```

Method setString's first argument represents the parameter number being set, and the second argument is that parameter's value. Parameter numbers are *counted from 1*, starting with the first question mark (?). When the program executes the preceding Prepared-Statement with the parameter values set above, the SQL passed to the database is

```
      SELECT LastName, FirstName, Title
      FROM Authors INNER JOIN AuthorISBN
         ON Authors.AuthorID=AuthorISBN.AuthorID
      INNER JOIN Titles
         ON AuthorISBN.ISBN=Titles.ISBN
      WHERE LastName = 'Deitel' AND FirstName = 'Paul'
```

Method setString automatically escapes String parameter values as necessary. For example, if the last name is O'Brien, the statement

```
      authorBooks.setString(1, "O'Brien");
```

escapes the ' character in O'Brien by replacing it with two single-quote characters, so that the ' appears correctly in the database.

Performance Tip 24.2

PreparedStatements are more efficient than Statements when executing SQL statements multiple times and with different parameter values.

Error-Prevention Tip 24.2

Use PreparedStatements with parameters for queries that receive String values as arguments to ensure that the Strings are quoted properly in the SQL statement.

Error-Prevention Tip 24.3

PreparedStatements help prevent SQL injection attacks, which typically occur in SQL statements that include user input improperly. To avoid this security issue, use Prepared-Statements in which user input can be supplied only via parameters—indicated with ? when creating a PreparedStatement. Once you've created such a PreparedStatement, you can use its set methods to specify the user input as arguments for those parameters.

Interface PreparedStatement provides *set* methods for each supported SQL type. It's important to use the *set* method that is appropriate for the parameter's SQL type in the database—SQLExceptions occur when a program attempts to convert a parameter value to an incorrect type.

Address Book Application that Uses *PreparedStatements*

We now present an address book app that enables you to browse existing entries, add new entries and search for entries with a specific last name. Our AddressBook Java DB database contains an Addresses table with the columns addressID, FirstName, LastName, Email and PhoneNumber. The column addressID is an identity column in the Addresses table.

Class *Person*

Our address book application consists of three classes—Person (Fig. 24.30), PersonQueries (Fig. 24.31) and AddressBookDisplay (Fig. 24.32). Class Person is a simple class that represents one person in the address book. The class contains fields for the address ID, first name, last name, email address and phone number, as well as *set* and *get* methods for manipulating these fields.

```java
1    // Fig. 24.30: Person.java
2    // Person class that represents an entry in an address book.
3    public class Person
4    {
5       private int addressID;
6       private String firstName;
7       private String lastName;
8       private String email;
9       private String phoneNumber;
10
11      // constructor
12      public Person()
13      {
14      }
15
16      // constructor
17      public Person(int addressID, String firstName, String lastName,
18         String email, String phoneNumber)
19      {
20         setAddressID(addressID);
21         setFirstName(firstName);
22         setLastName(lastName);
23         setEmail(email);
24         setPhoneNumber(phoneNumber);
25      }
26
27      // sets the addressID
28      public void setAddressID(int addressID)
29      {
30         this.addressID = addressID;
31      }
32
33      // returns the addressID
34      public int getAddressID()
35      {
36         return addressID;
37      }
38
39      // sets the firstName
40      public void setFirstName(String firstName)
41      {
42         this.firstName = firstName;
43      }
44
45      // returns the first name
46      public String getFirstName()
47      {
```

Fig. 24.30 | Person class that represents an entry in an **AddressBook**. (Part 1 of 2.)

```
48        return firstName;
49     }
50
51     // sets the lastName
52     public void setLastName(String lastName)
53     {
54        this.lastName = lastName;
55     }
56
57     // returns the last name
58     public String getLastName()
59     {
60        return lastName;
61     }
62
63     // sets the email address
64     public void setEmail(String email)
65     {
66        this.email = email;
67     }
68
69     // returns the email address
70     public String getEmail()
71     {
72        return email;
73     }
74
75     // sets the phone number
76     public void setPhoneNumber(String phone)
77     {
78        this.phoneNumber = phone;
79     }
80
81     // returns the phone number
82     public String getPhoneNumber()
83     {
84        return phoneNumber;
85     }
86  } // end class Person
```

Fig. 24.30 | Person class that represents an entry in an AddressBook. (Part 2 of 2.)

Class *PersonQueries*

Class PersonQueries (Fig. 24.31) manages the address book application's database connection and creates the PreparedStatements that the application uses to interact with the database. Lines 18–20 declare three PreparedStatement variables. The constructor (lines 23–49) connects to the database at lines 27–28.

```
1   // Fig. 24.31: PersonQueries.java
2   // PreparedStatements used by the Address Book application.
3   import java.sql.Connection;
```

Fig. 24.31 | PreparedStatements used by the Address Book application. (Part 1 of 5.)

```
4   import java.sql.DriverManager;
5   import java.sql.PreparedStatement;
6   import java.sql.ResultSet;
7   import java.sql.SQLException;
8   import java.util.List;
9   import java.util.ArrayList;
10
11  public class PersonQueries
12  {
13     private static final String URL = "jdbc:derby:AddressBook";
14     private static final String USERNAME = "deitel";
15     private static final String PASSWORD = "deitel";
16
17     private Connection connection; // manages connection
18     private PreparedStatement selectAllPeople;
19     private PreparedStatement selectPeopleByLastName;
20     private PreparedStatement insertNewPerson;
21
22     // constructor
23     public PersonQueries()
24     {
25        try
26        {
27           connection =
28              DriverManager.getConnection(URL, USERNAME, PASSWORD);
29
30           // create query that selects all entries in the AddressBook
31           selectAllPeople =
32              connection.prepareStatement("SELECT * FROM Addresses");
33
34           // create query that selects entries with a specific last name
35           selectPeopleByLastName = connection.prepareStatement(
36              "SELECT * FROM Addresses WHERE LastName = ?");
37
38           // create insert that adds a new entry into the database
39           insertNewPerson = connection.prepareStatement(
40              "INSERT INTO Addresses " +
41              "(FirstName, LastName, Email, PhoneNumber) " +
42              "VALUES (?, ?, ?, ?)");
43        }
44        catch (SQLException sqlException)
45        {
46           sqlException.printStackTrace();
47           System.exit(1);
48        }
49     }
50
51     // select all of the addresses in the database
52     public List< Person > getAllPeople()
53     {
54        List< Person > results = null;
55        ResultSet resultSet = null;
56
```

Fig. 24.31 | PreparedStatements used by the Address Book application. (Part 2 of 5.)

```
57              try
58              {
59                  // executeQuery returns ResultSet containing matching entries
60                  resultSet = selectAllPeople.executeQuery();
61                  results = new ArrayList< Person >();
62
63                  while (resultSet.next())
64                  {
65                      results.add(new Person(
66                          resultSet.getInt("addressID"),
67                          resultSet.getString("FirstName"),
68                          resultSet.getString("LastName"),
69                          resultSet.getString("Email"),
70                          resultSet.getString("PhoneNumber")));
71                  }
72              }
73              catch (SQLException sqlException)
74              {
75                  sqlException.printStackTrace();
76              }
77              finally
78              {
79                  try
80                  {
81                      resultSet.close();
82                  }
83                  catch (SQLException sqlException)
84                  {
85                      sqlException.printStackTrace();
86                      close();
87                  }
88              }
89
90              return results;
91          }
92
93          // select person by last name
94          public List< Person > getPeopleByLastName(String name)
95          {
96              List< Person > results = null;
97              ResultSet resultSet = null;
98
99              try
100             {
101                 selectPeopleByLastName.setString(1, name); // specify last name
102
103                 // executeQuery returns ResultSet containing matching entries
104                 resultSet = selectPeopleByLastName.executeQuery();
105
106                 results = new ArrayList< Person >();
107
108                 while (resultSet.next())
109                 {
```

Fig. 24.31 | PreparedStatements used by the Address Book application. (Part 3 of 5.)

```
110                results.add(new Person(resultSet.getInt("addressID"),
111                    resultSet.getString("FirstName"),
112                    resultSet.getString("LastName"),
113                    resultSet.getString("Email"),
114                    resultSet.getString("PhoneNumber")));
115            }
116        }
117        catch (SQLException sqlException)
118        {
119            sqlException.printStackTrace();
120        }
121        finally
122        {
123            try
124            {
125                resultSet.close();
126            }
127            catch (SQLException sqlException)
128            {
129                sqlException.printStackTrace();
130                close();
131            }
132        }
133
134        return results;
135    }
136
137    // add an entry
138    public int addPerson(
139        String fname, String lname, String email, String num)
140    {
141        int result = 0;
142
143        // set parameters, then execute insertNewPerson
144        try
145        {
146            insertNewPerson.setString(1, fname);
147            insertNewPerson.setString(2, lname);
148            insertNewPerson.setString(3, email);
149            insertNewPerson.setString(4, num);
150
151            // insert the new entry; returns # of rows updated
152            result = insertNewPerson.executeUpdate();
153        }
154        catch (SQLException sqlException)
155        {
156            sqlException.printStackTrace();
157            close();
158        }
159
160        return result;
161    }
162
```

Fig. 24.31 | PreparedStatements used by the Address Book application. (Part 4 of 5.)

```
163     // close the database connection
164     public void close()
165     {
166        try
167        {
168           connection.close();
169        }
170        catch (SQLException sqlException)
171        {
172           sqlException.printStackTrace();
173        }
174     }
175  } // end class PersonQueries
```

Fig. 24.31 | PreparedStatements used by the Address Book application. (Part 5 of 5.)

Creating *PreparedStatements*

Lines 31–32 invoke Connection method **prepareStatement** to create the Prepared-Statement named selectAllPeople that selects all the rows in the Addresses table. Lines 35–36 create the PreparedStatement named selectPeopleByLastName with a parameter. This statement selects all the rows in the Addresses table that match a particular last name. Notice the ? character that's used to specify the last-name parameter. Lines 39–42 create the PreparedStatement named insertNewPerson with four parameters that represent the first name, last name, email address and phone number for a new entry. Again, notice the ? characters used to represent these parameters.

PersonQueries *Method* getAllPeople

Method getAllPeople (lines 52–91) executes PreparedStatement selectAllPeople (line 60) by calling method **executeQuery**, which returns a ResultSet containing the rows that match the query (in this case, all the rows in the Addresses table). Lines 61–71 place the query results in an ArrayList of Person objects, which is returned to the caller at line 90. Method getPeopleByLastName (lines 94–135) uses PreparedStatement method setString to set the parameter to selectPeopleByLastName (line 101). Then, line 104 executes the query and lines 106–115 place the query results in an ArrayList of Person objects. Line 134 returns the ArrayList to the caller.

PersonQueries *Methods* addPerson *and* Close

Method addPerson (lines 138–161) uses PreparedStatement method setString (lines 146–149) to set the parameters for the insertNewPerson PreparedStatement. Line 152 uses PreparedStatement method **executeUpdate** to insert the new record. This method returns an integer indicating the number of rows that were updated (or inserted) in the database. Method close (lines 164–174) simply closes the database connection.

Class *AddressBookDisplay*

The AddressBookDisplay (Fig. 24.32) application uses a PersonQueries object to interact with the database. Line 59 creates the PersonQueries object. When the user presses the **Browse All Entries** JButton, the browseButtonActionPerformed handler (lines 309–335) is called. Line 313 calls the method getAllPeople on the PersonQueries object to obtain all the entries in the database. The user can then scroll through the entries using the

Previous and **Next** JButtons. When the user presses the **Find** JButton, the queryButtonActionPerformed handler (lines 265–287) is called. Lines 267–268 call method getPeopleByLastName on the PersonQueries object to obtain the entries in the database that match the specified last name. If there are several such entries, the user can then scroll through them using the **Previous** and **Next** JButtons.

```java
 1   // Fig. 24.32: AddressBookDisplay.java
 2   // A simple address book
 3   import java.awt.event.ActionEvent;
 4   import java.awt.event.ActionListener;
 5   import java.awt.event.WindowAdapter;
 6   import java.awt.event.WindowEvent;
 7   import java.awt.FlowLayout;
 8   import java.awt.GridLayout;
 9   import java.util.List;
10   import javax.swing.JButton;
11   import javax.swing.Box;
12   import javax.swing.JFrame;
13   import javax.swing.JLabel;
14   import javax.swing.JPanel;
15   import javax.swing.JTextField;
16   import javax.swing.WindowConstants;
17   import javax.swing.BoxLayout;
18   import javax.swing.BorderFactory;
19   import javax.swing.JOptionPane;
20
21   public class AddressBookDisplay extends JFrame
22   {
23      private Person currentEntry;
24      private PersonQueries personQueries;
25      private List<Person> results;
26      private int numberOfEntries = 0;
27      private int currentEntryIndex;
28
29      private JButton browseButton;
30      private JLabel emailLabel;
31      private JTextField emailTextField;
32      private JLabel firstNameLabel;
33      private JTextField firstNameTextField;
34      private JLabel idLabel;
35      private JTextField idTextField;
36      private JTextField indexTextField;
37      private JLabel lastNameLabel;
38      private JTextField lastNameTextField;
39      private JTextField maxTextField;
40      private JButton nextButton;
41      private JLabel ofLabel;
42      private JLabel phoneLabel;
43      private JTextField phoneTextField;
44      private JButton previousButton;
45      private JButton queryButton;
46      private JLabel queryLabel;
```

Fig. 24.32 | A simple address book. (Part 1 of 8.)

```
47        private JPanel queryPanel;
48        private JPanel navigatePanel;
49        private JPanel displayPanel;
50        private JTextField queryTextField;
51        private JButton insertButton;
52
53        // constructor
54        public AddressBookDisplay()
55        {
56           super("Address Book");
57
58           // establish database connection and set up PreparedStatements
59           personQueries = new PersonQueries();
60
61           // create GUI
62           navigatePanel = new JPanel();
63           previousButton = new JButton();
64           indexTextField = new JTextField(2);
65           ofLabel = new JLabel();
66           maxTextField = new JTextField(2);
67           nextButton = new JButton();
68           displayPanel = new JPanel();
69           idLabel = new JLabel();
70           idTextField = new JTextField(10);
71           firstNameLabel = new JLabel();
72           firstNameTextField = new JTextField(10);
73           lastNameLabel = new JLabel();
74           lastNameTextField = new JTextField(10);
75           emailLabel = new JLabel();
76           emailTextField = new JTextField(10);
77           phoneLabel = new JLabel();
78           phoneTextField = new JTextField(10);
79           queryPanel = new JPanel();
80           queryLabel = new JLabel();
81           queryTextField = new JTextField(10);
82           queryButton = new JButton();
83           browseButton = new JButton();
84           insertButton = new JButton();
85
86           setLayout(new FlowLayout(FlowLayout.CENTER, 10, 10));
87           setSize(400, 300);
88           setResizable(false);
89
90           navigatePanel.setLayout(
91              new BoxLayout(navigatePanel, BoxLayout.X_AXIS));
92
93           previousButton.setText("Previous");
94           previousButton.setEnabled(false);
95           previousButton.addActionListener(
96              new ActionListener()
97              {
98                 public void actionPerformed(ActionEvent evt)
99                 {
```

Fig. 24.32 | A simple address book. (Part 2 of 8.)

```
100                        previousButtonActionPerformed(evt);
101                     }
102                  }
103              );
104
105              navigatePanel.add(previousButton);
106              navigatePanel.add(Box.createHorizontalStrut(10));
107
108              indexTextField.setHorizontalAlignment(
109                 JTextField.CENTER);
110              indexTextField.addActionListener(
111                 new ActionListener()
112                 {
113                    public void actionPerformed(ActionEvent evt)
114                    {
115                       indexTextFieldActionPerformed(evt);
116                    }
117                 }
118              );
119
120              navigatePanel.add(indexTextField);
121              navigatePanel.add(Box.createHorizontalStrut(10));
122
123              ofLabel.setText("of");
124              navigatePanel.add(ofLabel);
125              navigatePanel.add(Box.createHorizontalStrut(10));
126
127              maxTextField.setHorizontalAlignment(
128                 JTextField.CENTER);
129              maxTextField.setEditable(false);
130              navigatePanel.add(maxTextField);
131              navigatePanel.add(Box.createHorizontalStrut(10));
132
133              nextButton.setText("Next");
134              nextButton.setEnabled(false);
135              nextButton.addActionListener(
136                 new ActionListener()
137                 {
138                    public void actionPerformed(ActionEvent evt)
139                    {
140                       nextButtonActionPerformed(evt);
141                    }
142                 }
143              );
144
145              navigatePanel.add(nextButton);
146              add(navigatePanel);
147
148              displayPanel.setLayout(new GridLayout(5, 2, 4, 4));
149
150              idLabel.setText("Address ID:");
151              displayPanel.add(idLabel);
152
```

Fig. 24.32 | A simple address book. (Part 3 of 8.)

```
153            idTextField.setEditable(false);
154            displayPanel.add(idTextField);
155
156            firstNameLabel.setText("First Name:");
157            displayPanel.add(firstNameLabel);
158            displayPanel.add(firstNameTextField);
159
160            lastNameLabel.setText("Last Name:");
161            displayPanel.add(lastNameLabel);
162            displayPanel.add(lastNameTextField);
163
164            emailLabel.setText("Email:");
165            displayPanel.add(emailLabel);
166            displayPanel.add(emailTextField);
167
168            phoneLabel.setText("Phone Number:");
169            displayPanel.add(phoneLabel);
170            displayPanel.add(phoneTextField);
171            add(displayPanel);
172
173            queryPanel.setLayout(
174               new BoxLayout(queryPanel, BoxLayout.X_AXIS));
175
176            queryPanel.setBorder(BorderFactory.createTitledBorder(
177               "Find an entry by last name"));
178            queryLabel.setText("Last Name:");
179            queryPanel.add(Box.createHorizontalStrut(5));
180            queryPanel.add(queryLabel);
181            queryPanel.add(Box.createHorizontalStrut(10));
182            queryPanel.add(queryTextField);
183            queryPanel.add(Box.createHorizontalStrut(10));
184
185            queryButton.setText("Find");
186            queryButton.addActionListener(
187               new ActionListener()
188               {
189                  public void actionPerformed(ActionEvent evt)
190                  {
191                     queryButtonActionPerformed(evt);
192                  }
193               }
194            );
195
196            queryPanel.add(queryButton);
197            queryPanel.add(Box.createHorizontalStrut(5));
198            add(queryPanel);
199
200            browseButton.setText("Browse All Entries");
201            browseButton.addActionListener(
202               new ActionListener()
203               {
204                  public void actionPerformed(ActionEvent evt)
205                  {
```

Fig. 24.32 | A simple address book. (Part 4 of 8.)

```
206                          browseButtonActionPerformed(evt);
207                       }
208                    }
209                 );
210
211              add(browseButton);
212
213              insertButton.setText("Insert New Entry");
214              insertButton.addActionListener(
215                 new ActionListener()
216                 {
217                    public void actionPerformed(ActionEvent evt)
218                    {
219                       insertButtonActionPerformed(evt);
220                    }
221                 }
222              );
223
224              add(insertButton);
225
226              addWindowListener(
227                 new WindowAdapter()
228                 {
229                    public void windowClosing(WindowEvent evt)
230                    {
231                       personQueries.close(); // close database connection
232                       System.exit(0);
233                    }
234                 }
235              );
236
237              setVisible(true);
238           } // end constructor
239
240           // handles call when previousButton is clicked
241           private void previousButtonActionPerformed(ActionEvent evt)
242           {
243              currentEntryIndex--;
244
245              if (currentEntryIndex < 0)
246                 currentEntryIndex = numberOfEntries - 1;
247
248              indexTextField.setText("" + (currentEntryIndex + 1));
249              indexTextFieldActionPerformed(evt);
250           }
251
252           // handles call when nextButton is clicked
253           private void nextButtonActionPerformed(ActionEvent evt)
254           {
255              currentEntryIndex++;
256
257              if (currentEntryIndex >= numberOfEntries)
258                 currentEntryIndex = 0;
```

Fig. 24.32 | A simple address book. (Part 5 of 8.)

```
259
260          indexTextField.setText("" + (currentEntryIndex + 1));
261          indexTextFieldActionPerformed(evt);
262       }
263
264       // handles call when queryButton is clicked
265       private void queryButtonActionPerformed(ActionEvent evt)
266       {
267          results =
268             personQueries.getPeopleByLastName(queryTextField.getText());
269          numberOfEntries = results.size();
270
271          if (numberOfEntries != 0)
272          {
273             currentEntryIndex = 0;
274             currentEntry = results.get(currentEntryIndex);
275             idTextField.setText("" + currentEntry.getAddressID());
276             firstNameTextField.setText(currentEntry.getFirstName());
277             lastNameTextField.setText(currentEntry.getLastName());
278             emailTextField.setText(currentEntry.getEmail());
279             phoneTextField.setText(currentEntry.getPhoneNumber());
280             maxTextField.setText("" + numberOfEntries);
281             indexTextField.setText("" + (currentEntryIndex + 1));
282             nextButton.setEnabled(true);
283             previousButton.setEnabled(true);
284          }
285          else
286             browseButtonActionPerformed(evt);
287       }
288
289       // handles call when a new value is entered in indexTextField
290       private void indexTextFieldActionPerformed(ActionEvent evt)
291       {
292          currentEntryIndex =
293             (Integer.parseInt(indexTextField.getText()) - 1);
294
295          if (numberOfEntries != 0 && currentEntryIndex < numberOfEntries)
296          {
297             currentEntry = results.get(currentEntryIndex);
298             idTextField.setText("" + currentEntry.getAddressID());
299             firstNameTextField.setText(currentEntry.getFirstName());
300             lastNameTextField.setText(currentEntry.getLastName());
301             emailTextField.setText(currentEntry.getEmail());
302             phoneTextField.setText(currentEntry.getPhoneNumber());
303             maxTextField.setText("" + numberOfEntries);
304             indexTextField.setText("" + (currentEntryIndex + 1));
305          }
306        }
307
308       // handles call when browseButton is clicked
309       private void browseButtonActionPerformed(ActionEvent evt)
310       {
```

Fig. 24.32 | A simple address book. (Part 6 of 8.)

```
311         try
312         {
313             results = personQueries.getAllPeople();
314             numberOfEntries = results.size();
315
316             if (numberOfEntries != 0)
317             {
318                 currentEntryIndex = 0;
319                 currentEntry = results.get(currentEntryIndex);
320                 idTextField.setText("" + currentEntry.getAddressID());
321                 firstNameTextField.setText(currentEntry.getFirstName());
322                 lastNameTextField.setText(currentEntry.getLastName());
323                 emailTextField.setText(currentEntry.getEmail());
324                 phoneTextField.setText(currentEntry.getPhoneNumber());
325                 maxTextField.setText("" + numberOfEntries);
326                 indexTextField.setText("" + (currentEntryIndex + 1));
327                 nextButton.setEnabled(true);
328                 previousButton.setEnabled(true);
329             }
330         }
331         catch (Exception e)
332         {
333             e.printStackTrace();
334         }
335     }
336
337     // handles call when insertButton is clicked
338     private void insertButtonActionPerformed(ActionEvent evt)
339     {
340         int result = personQueries.addPerson(firstNameTextField.getText(),
341             lastNameTextField.getText(), emailTextField.getText(),
342             phoneTextField.getText());
343
344         if (result == 1)
345             JOptionPane.showMessageDialog(this, "Person added!",
346                 "Person added", JOptionPane.PLAIN_MESSAGE);
347         else
348             JOptionPane.showMessageDialog(this, "Person not added!",
349                 "Error", JOptionPane.PLAIN_MESSAGE);
350
351         browseButtonActionPerformed(evt);
352     }
353
354     // main method
355     public static void main(String args[])
356     {
357         new AddressBookDisplay();
358     }
359 } // end class AddressBookDisplay
```

Fig. 24.32 | A simple address book. (Part 7 of 8.)

a) Initial **Address Book** screen.

b) Results of clicking **Browse All Entries**.

c) Browsing to the next entry.

d) Finding entries with the last name **Green**.

e) After adding a new entry and browsing to it.

Fig. 24.32 | A simple address book. (Part 8 of 8.)

To add a new entry into the AddressBook database, the user can enter the first name, last name, email and phone number (the AddressID will *autoincrement*) in the JTextFields and press the **Insert New Entry** JButton. The insertButtonActionPerformed handler (lines 338–352) is called. Lines 340–342 call the method addPerson on the PersonQueries object to add a new entry to the database. Line 351 calls browseButtonActionPerformed to obtain the updated set of people in the address book and update the GUI accordingly.

The user can then view different entries by pressing the **Previous** JButton or **Next** JButton, which results in calls to methods previousButtonActionPerformed (lines 241–250) or nextButtonActionPerformed (lines 253–262), respectively. Alternatively, the user can enter a number in the indexTextField and press *Enter* to view a particular entry. This results in a call to method indexTextFieldActionPerformed (lines 290–306) to display the specified record.

24.9 Stored Procedures

Many database management systems can store individual or sets of SQL statements in a database, so that programs accessing that database can invoke them. Such named collections of SQL statements are called **stored procedures**. JDBC enables programs to invoke stored procedures using objects that implement the interface **CallableStatement**. CallableStatements can receive arguments specified with the methods inherited from interface PreparedStatement. In addition, CallableStatements can specify **output parameters** in which a stored procedure can place return values. Interface CallableStatement includes methods to specify which parameters in a stored procedure are output parameters. The interface also includes methods to obtain the values of output parameters returned from a stored procedure.

Portability Tip 24.6

Although the syntax for creating stored procedures differs across database management systems, the interface CallableStatement provides a uniform interface for specifying input and output parameters for stored procedures and for invoking stored procedures.

Portability Tip 24.7

According to the Java API documentation for interface CallableStatement, for maximum portability between database systems, programs should process the update counts (which indicate how many rows were updated) or ResultSets returned from a CallableStatement before obtaining the values of any output parameters.

24.10 Transaction Processing

Many database applications require guarantees that a series of database insertions, updates and deletions executes properly before the application continues processing the next database operation. For example, when you transfer money electronically between bank accounts, several factors determine if the transaction is successful. You begin by specifying the source account and the amount you wish to transfer from that account to a destination account. Next, you specify the destination account. The bank checks the source account to determine whether its funds are sufficient to complete the transfer. If so, the bank withdraws the specified amount and, if all goes well, deposits it into the destination account to complete the transfer. What happens if the transfer fails after the bank withdraws the money from the source account? In a proper banking system, the bank redeposits the money in the source account. How would you feel if the money was subtracted from your source account and the bank *did not* deposit the money in the destination account?

Transaction processing enables a program that interacts with a database to *treat a database operation (or set of operations) as a single operation*. Such an operation also is known as an **atomic operation** or a **transaction**. At the end of a transaction, a decision can be made either to **commit the transaction** or **roll back the transaction**. Committing the transaction finalizes the database operation(s); all insertions, updates and deletions performed as part of the transaction cannot be reversed without performing a new database operation. Rolling back the transaction leaves the database in its state prior to the database operation. This is useful when a portion of a transaction fails to complete properly. In our bank-account-transfer discussion, the transaction would be rolled back if the deposit could not be made into the destination account.

Java provides transaction processing via methods of interface `Connection`. Method `setAutoCommit` specifies whether each SQL statement commits after it completes (a `true` argument) or whether several SQL statements should be grouped as a transaction (a `false` argument). If the argument to `setAutoCommit` is `false`, the program must follow the last SQL statement in the transaction with a call to `Connection` method **commit** (to commit the changes to the database) or `Connection` method **rollback** (to return the database to its state prior to the transaction). Interface `Connection` also provides method **getAutoCommit** to determine the autocommit state for the `Connection`.

24.11 Wrap-Up

In this chapter, you learned basic database concepts, how to query and manipulate data in a database using SQL and how to use JDBC to allow Java applications to interact with Java DB databases. You learned about the SQL commands SELECT, INSERT, UPDATE and DELETE, as well as clauses such as WHERE, ORDER BY and INNER JOIN. You created and configured databases in Java DB by using predefined SQL scripts. You learned the steps for obtaining a `Connection` to the database, creating a `Statement` to interact with the database's data, executing the statement and processing the results. Then you used a `RowSet` to simplify the process of connecting to a database and creating statements. You used `PreparedStatements` to create precompiled SQL statements. We also provided overviews of `CallableStatements` and transaction processing. In the next chapter, you'll build graphical user interfaces using JavaFX—Java's GUI technology of the future.

Summary

Section 24.1 Introduction
- A database (p. 1038) is an integrated collection of data. A database management system (DBMS; p. 1038) provides mechanisms for storing, organizing, retrieving and modifying data.
- Today's most popular database management systems are relational database (p. 1038) systems.
- SQL (p. 1038) is the international standard language used to query (p. 1038) and manipulate relational data.
- Programs connect to, and interact with, relational databases via an interface—software that facilitates communications between a database management system and a program.
- A JDBC driver (p. 1038) enables Java applications to connect to a database in a particular DBMS and allows you to retrieve and manipulate database data.

Section 24.2 Relational Databases

- A relational database (p. 1039) stores data in tables (p. 1039). Tables are composed of rows (p. 1039), and rows are composed of columns in which values are stored.

- A table's primary key (p. 1039) has a unique in each row.

- Each column (p. 1039) of a table represents a different attribute.

- The primary key can be composed of more than one column.

- An identity column is the SQL standard way to represent an autoincremented (p. 1040) column. The SQL IDENTITY keyword (p. 1040) marks a column as an identity column.

- A foreign key is a column in a table that must match the primary-key column in another table. This is known as the Rule of Referential Integrity (p. 1042).

- A one-to-many relationship (p. 1043) between tables indicates that a row in one table can have many related rows in a separate table.

- Every column in a primary key must have a value, and the value of the primary key must be unique. This is known as the Rule of Entity Integrity (p. 1043).

- Foreign keys enable information from multiple tables to be joined together. There's a one-to-many relationship between a primary key and its corresponding foreign key.

Section 24.4.1 Basic **SELECT** Query

- The basic form of a query (p. 1044) is

      SELECT * FROM *tableName*

  where the asterisk (*; p. 1044) indicates that all columns from *tableName* should be selected, and *tableName* specifies the table in the database from which rows will be retrieved.

- To retrieve specific columns, replace the * with a comma-separated list of column names.

Section 24.4.2 **WHERE** Clause

- The optional WHERE clause (p. 1045) in a query specifies the selection criteria for the query. The basic form of a query with selection criteria (p. 1044) is

      SELECT *columnName1*, *columnName2*, ... FROM *tableName* WHERE *criteria*

- The WHERE clause can contain operators <, >, <=, >=, =, <> and LIKE. LIKE (p. 1045) is used for string pattern matching (p. 1045) with wildcard characters percent (%) and underscore (_).

- A percent character (%; p. 1045) in a pattern indicates that a string matching the pattern can have zero or more characters at the percent character's location in the pattern.

- An underscore (_ ; p. 1045) in the pattern string indicates a single character at that position in the pattern.

Section 24.4.3 **ORDER BY** Clause

- A query's result can be sorted with the ORDER BY clause (p. 1047). The simplest form of an ORDER BY clause is

      SELECT *columnName1*, *columnName2*, ... FROM *tableName* ORDER BY *column* ASC
      SELECT *columnName1*, *columnName2*, ... FROM *tableName* ORDER BY *column* DESC

  where ASC specifies ascending order, DESC specifies descending order and *column* specifies the column on which the sort is based. The default sorting order is ascending, so ASC is optional.

- Multiple columns can be used for ordering purposes with an ORDER BY clause of the form

      ORDER BY *column1 sortingOrder*, *column2 sortingOrder*, ...

- The WHERE and ORDER BY clauses can be combined in one query. If used, ORDER BY must be the last clause in the query.

Section 24.4.4 Merging Data from Multiple Tables: **INNER JOIN**
- An INNER JOIN (p. 1049) merges rows from two tables by matching values in columns that are common to the tables. The basic form for the INNER JOIN operator is:

      SELECT *columnName1, columnName2, ...*
      FROM *table1*
      INNER JOIN *table2*
          ON *table1.columnName* = *table2.columnName*

The ON clause (p. 1049) specifies the columns from each table that are compared to determine which rows are joined. If a SQL statement uses columns with the same name from multiple tables, the column names must be fully qualified (p. 1049) by prefixing them with their table names and a dot (.).

Section 24.4.5 **INSERT** *Statement*
- An INSERT statement (p. 1050) inserts a new row into a table. The basic form of this statement is

      INSERT INTO *tableName* (*columnName1, columnName2, ..., columnNameN*)
          VALUES (*value1, value2, ..., valueN*)

where *tableName* is the table in which to insert the row. The *tableName* is followed by a comma-separated list of column names in parentheses. The list of column names is followed by the SQL keyword VALUES (p. 1050) and a comma-separated list of values in parentheses.
- SQL uses single quotes (') to delimit strings. To specify a string containing a single quote in SQL, escape the single quote with another single quote (i.e., ' ').

Section 24.4.6 **UPDATE** *Statement*
- An UPDATE statement (p. 1051) modifies data in a table. The basic form of an UPDATE statement is

      UPDATE *tableName*
          SET *columnName1 = value1, columnName2 = value2, ..., columnNameN = valueN*
          WHERE *criteria*

where *tableName* is the table to update. Keyword SET (p. 1051) is followed by a comma-separated list of *columnName = value* pairs. The optional WHERE clause determines which rows to update.

Section 24.4.7 **DELETE** *Statement*
- A DELETE statement (p. 1052) removes rows from a table. The simplest form for a DELETE statement is

      DELETE FROM *tableName* WHERE *criteria*

where *tableName* is the table from which to delete a row (or rows). The optional WHERE *criteria* determines which rows to delete. If this clause is omitted, all the table's rows are deleted.

Section 24.5 Setting up a Java DB Database
- Oracle's pure Java database Java DB (p. 1052) is installed with the JDK on Windows, Mac OS X and Linux.
- Java DB has both an embedded version and a network version.
- The Java DB software is located in the db subdirectory of your JDK's installation directory.
- Java DB comes with several files that enable you to configure and run it. Before executing these files from a command window, you must set the environment variable JAVA_HOME to refer to the JDK's exact installation directory.

- You use the `setEmbeddedCP.bat` or `setEmbeddedCP` file (depending on your OS platform) to configure the CLASSPATH for working with Java DB embedded databases.

- The Java DB `ij` tool allows you to interact with Java DB from the command line. You can use it to create databases, run SQL scripts and perform SQL queries. Each command you enter at the `ij>` prompt must be terminated with a semicolon (`;`).

Section 24.6.1 Connecting to and Querying a Database

- Package `java.sql` contains classes and interfaces for accessing relational databases in Java.

- A `Connection` object (p. 1057) manages the connection between a Java program and a database. `Connection` objects enable programs to create SQL statements that access data.

- `DriverManager` (p. 1057) method `getConnection` (p. 1057) attempts to connect to a database at a URL that specifies the protocol for communication, the subprotocol (p. 1057) for communication and the database name.

- `Connection` method `createStatement` (p. 1058) creates a `Statement` object (p. 1058), which can be used to submit SQL statements to the database.

- `Statement` method `executeQuery` (p. 1058) executes a query and returns a `ResultSet` object (p. 1058). `ResultSet` methods enable a program to manipulate query results.

- A `ResultSetMetaData` object (p. 1058) describes a `ResultSet`'s contents. Programs can use metadata programmatically to obtain information about the `ResultSet` column names and types.

- `ResultSetMetaData` method `getColumnCount` (p. 1058) retrieves the number of `ResultSet` columns.

- `ResultSet` method `next` (p. 1058) positions the `ResultSet` cursor to the next row and returns true if the row exists; otherwise, it returns `false`. This method must be called to begin processing a `ResultSet` because the cursor is intially positioned before the first row.

- It's possible to extract each `ResultSet` column as a specific Java type. `ResultSetMetaData` method `getColumnType` (p. 1058) returns a `Types` (p. 1059) constant (package `java.sql`) indicating the column's type.

- `ResultSet` *get* methods typically receive as an argument either a column number (as an `int`) or a column name (as a `String`) indicating which column's value to obtain.

- `ResultSet` row and column numbers start at 1.

- Each `Statement` object can open only one `ResultSet` at a time. When a `Statement` returns a new `ResultSet`, the `Statement` closes the prior `ResultSet`.

Section 24.6.2 Querying the **books** Database

- `TableModel` (p. 1059) method `getColumnClass` (p. 1060) returns a `Class` object that represents the superclass of all objects in a particular column. A `JTable` (p. 1059) uses this information to set up the default cell renderer and cell editor for that column in a `JTable`.

- `Connection` method `createStatement` has an overloaded version that receives the result type and concurrency. The result type specifies whether the `ResultSet`'s cursor is able to scroll in both directions or forward only and whether the `ResultSet` is sensitive to changes. The result concurrency (p. 1064) specifies whether the `ResultSet` can be updated.

- Some JDBC drivers (p. 1064) do not support scrollable or updatable `ResultSets`.

- `ResultSetMetaData` method `getColumnClassName` (p. 1065) obtains a column's fully qualified class name.

- `TableModel` method `getColumnCount` (p. 1065) returns the number of columns in the `ResultSet`.

- `TableModel` method `getColumnName` (p. 1065) returns the column name in the `ResultSet`.

- `ResultSetMetaData` method `getColumnName` (p. 1065) obtains a `ResultSet` column's name.
- `TableModel` method `getRowCount` (p. 1065) returns the number of rows in the model's `ResultSet`.
- `TableModel` method `getValueAt` (p. 1065) returns the `Object` at a particular row and column of the model's underlying `ResultSet`.
- `ResultSet` method `absolute` (p. 1065) positions the `ResultSet` cursor at a specific row.
- `AbstractTableModel` method `fireTableStructureChanged` (p. 1066) notifies any `JTable` using a particular `TableModel` object as its model that the data in the model has changed.

Section 24.7 RowSet Interface
- Interface `RowSet` (p. 1072) configures a database connection and executes a query automatically.
- A connected `RowSet` (p. 1072) remains connected to the database while the object is in use. A disconnected `RowSet` (p. 1072) connects, executes a query, then closes the connection.
- `JdbcRowSet` (p. 1072) (a connected `RowSet`) wraps a `ResultSet` object and allows you to scroll and update its rows. Unlike a `ResultSet` object, a `JdbcRowSet` is scrollable and updatable by default.
- `CachedRowSet` (p. 1072), a disconnected `RowSet`, caches a `ResultSet`'s data in memory. A `CachedRowSet` is scrollable and updatable. A `CachedRowSet` is also serializable.
- Class `RowSetProvider` (package `javax.sql.rowset`; p. 1072) provides `static` method `newFactory` which returns an object that implements interface `RowSetFactory` (package `javax.sql.rowset`) that can be used to create various types of `RowSet`s.
- `RowSetFactory` (p. 1072) method `createJdbcRowSet` returns a `JdbcRowSet` object.
- `JdbcRowSet` method `setUrl` specifies the database URL.
- `JdbcRowSet` method `setUsername` specifies the username.
- `JdbcRowSet` method `setPassword` specifies the password.
- `JdbcRowSet` method `setCommand` specifies the SQL query that will be used to populate a `RowSet`.
- `JdbcRowSet` method `execute` executes the SQL query. Method `execute` performs establishes a `Connection` to the database, prepares the query `Statement`, executes the query and stores the `ResultSet` returned by query. The `Connection`, `Statement` and `ResultSet` are encapsulated in the `JdbcRowSet` object.

Section 24.8 PreparedStatements
- `PreparedStatement`s (p. 1074) are compiled, so they execute more efficiently than `Statement`s.
- `PreparedStatement`s can have parameters, so the same query can execute with different arguments.
- A parameter is specified with a question mark (?) in the SQL statement. Before executing a `PreparedStatement`, you must use `PreparedStatement`'s *set* methods to specify the arguments.
- `PreparedStatement` method `setString`'s (p. 1074) first argument represents the parameter number being set and the second argument is that parameter's value.
- Parameter numbers are counted from 1, starting with the first question mark (?).
- Method `setString` automatically escapes `String` parameter values as necessary.
- Interface `PreparedStatement` provides set methods for each supported SQL type.

Section 24.9 Stored Procedures
- JDBC enables programs to invoke stored procedures (p. 1090) using `CallableStatement` (p. 1090) objects.
- `CallableStatement` can specify input parameters. `CallableStatement` can specify output parameters (p. 1090) in which a stored procedure can place return values.

Section 24.10 Transaction Processing

- Transaction processing (p. 1090) enables a program that interacts with a database to treat a database operation (or set of operations) as a single operation—known as an atomic operation (p. 1091) or a transaction (p. 1091).

- At the end of a transaction, a decision can be made to either commit or roll back the transaction.

- Committing a transaction (p. 1091) finalizes the database operation(s)—inserts, updates and deletes cannot be reversed without performing a new database operation.

- Rolling back a transaction (p. 1091) leaves the database in its state prior to the database operation.

- Java provides transaction processing via methods of interface `Connection`.

- Method `setAutoCommit` (p. 1091) specifies whether each SQL statement commits after it completes (a `true` argument) or whether several SQL statements should be grouped as a transaction.

- When autocommit is disabled, the program must follow the last SQL statement in the transaction with a call to `Connection` method `commit` (to commit the changes to the database; p. 1091) or `Connection` method `rollback` (to return the database to its state prior to the transaction; p. 1091).

- Method `getAutoCommit` (p. 1091) determines the autocommit state for the `Connection`.

Self-Review Exercise

24.1   Fill in the blanks in each of the following statements:
   a) The international standard database language is _____.
   b) A table in a database consists of _____ and _____.
   c) Statement objects return SQL query results as _____ objects.
   d) The _____ uniquely identifies each row in a table.
   e) SQL keyword _____ is followed by the selection criteria that specify the rows to select in a query.
   f) SQL keywords _____ specify the order in which rows are sorted in a query.
   g) Merging rows from multiple database tables is called _____ the tables.
   h) A(n) _____ is an organized collection of data.
   i) A(n) _____ is a set of columns whose values match the primary-key values of another table.
   j) _____ method _____ is used to obtain a `Connection` to a database.
   k) Interface _____ helps manage the connection between a Java program and a database.
   l) A(n) _____ object is used to submit a query to a database.
   m) Unlike a `ResultSet` object, _____ and _____ objects are scrollable and updatable by default.
   n) _____, a disconnected `RowSet`, caches the data of a `ResultSet` in memory.

Answers to Self-Review Exercise

24.1   a) SQL. b) rows, columns. c) `ResultSet`. d) primary key. e) `WHERE`. f) `ORDER BY`. g) joining. h) database. i) foreign key. j) `DriverManager`, `getConnection`. k) `Connection`. l) `Statement`. m) `JdbcRowSet`, `CachedRowSet`. n) `CachedRowSet`.

Exercises

24.2   *(Query Application for the **books** Database)* Using the techniques shown in this chapter, define a complete query application for the books database. Provide the following predefined queries:

a) Select all authors from the Authors table.
b) Select a specific author and list all books for that author. Include each book's title, year and ISBN. Order the information alphabetically by the author's last name then by first name.
c) Select a specific title and list all authors for that title. Order the authors alphabetically by last name then by first name.
d) Provide any other queries you feel are appropriate.

Display a JComboBox with appropriate names for each predefined query. Also allow users to supply their own queries.

24.3 *(Data-Manipulation Application for the **books** Database)* Define a data-manipulation application for the books database. The user should be able to edit existing data and add new data to the database (obeying referential and entity integrity constraints). Allow the user to edit the database in the following ways:
a) Add a new author.
b) Edit the existing information for an author.
c) Add a new title for an author. (Remember that the book must have an entry in the AuthorISBN table.).
d) Add a new entry in the AuthorISBN table to link authors with titles.

24.4 *(Employee Database)* In Section 10.5, we introduced an employee-payroll hierarchy to calculate each employee's payroll. In this exercise, we provide a database of employees that corresponds to the employee-payroll hierarchy. (A SQL script to create the employees database is provided with the examples for this chapter.) Write an application that allows the user to:
a) Add employees to the employee table.
b) Add payroll information to the appropriate table for each new employee. For example, for a salaried employee add the payroll information to the salariedEmployees table.

Figure 24.33 is the entity-relationship diagram for the employees database.

24.5 *(Employee Database Query Application)* Modify Exercise 24.4 to provide a JComboBox and a JTextArea to allow the user to perform a query that is either selected from the JComboBox or defined in the JTextArea. Sample predefined queries are:
a) Select all employees working in Department SALES.
b) Select hourly employees working over 30 hours.
c) Select all commission employees in descending order of the commission rate.

24.6 *(Employee Database Data-Manipulation Application)* Modify Exercise 24.5 to perform the following tasks:
a) Increase base salary by 10% for all base-plus-commission employees.
b) If the employee's birthday is in the current month, add a $100 bonus.
c) For all commission employees with gross sales over $10,000, add a $100 bonus.

24.7 *(Address Book Modification: Update an Existing Entry)* Modify the program in Figs. 24.30–24.32 to provide a JButton that allows the user to call a method named updatePerson in PersonQueries class to update the current entry in the AddressBook database.

24.8 *(Address Book Modification: Delete an Existing Entry)* Modify the program of Exercise 24.7 to provide a JButton that allows the user to call a method named deletePerson in PersonQueries class to delete the current entry in the AddressBook database.

24.9 *(Optional Project: ATM Case Study with a Database)* Modify the optional ATM Case Study (online Chapters 33–34) to use an actual database to store the account information. We provide a SQL script to create BankDatabase, which has a single table consisting of four columns—AccountNumber (an int), PIN (an int), AvailableBalance (a double) and TotalBalance (a double).

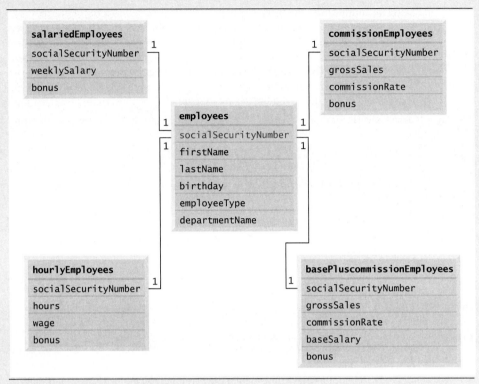

Fig. 24.33 | Table relationships in the `employees` database.

JavaFX GUI: Part 1

But, soft! what light through yonder window breaks? It is the east, and Juliet is the sun!
—William Shakespeare

Even a minor event in the life of a child is an event of that child's world and thus a world event.
—Gaston Bachelard

... the wisest prophets make sure of the event first.
—Horace Walpole

Do you think I can listen all day to such stuff?
—Lewis Carroll

Objectives

In this chapter you'll:

- Build JavaFX GUIs and handle events generated by user interactions with them.

- Understand the structure of a JavaFX app window.

- Use JavaFX Scene Builder to create FXML files that describe JavaFX scenes containing Labels, ImageViews, TextFields, Sliders and Buttons without writing any code.

- Arrange GUI components using the **VBox** and **GridPane** layout containers.

- Use a controller class to define event handlers for JavaFX FXML GUI.

- Build two JavaFX apps.

25.1 Introduction

[*Note:* The prerequisites for this chapter are Chapters 1–11. This chapter does not require that you've read Chapter 12, GUI Components: Part 1, which discusses Swing GUI.]

A **graphical user interface** (**GUI**) presents a user-friendly mechanism for interacting with an app. A GUI (pronounced "GOO-ee") gives an app a distinctive "look-and-feel." GUIs are built from **GUI components**. These are sometimes called *controls* or *widgets*—short for window gadgets. A GUI component is an object with which the user interacts via the mouse, the keyboard or another form of input, such as voice recognition.

Look-and-Feel Observation 25.1

Providing different apps with consistent, intuitive user-interface components gives users a sense of familiarity with a new app, so that they can learn it more quickly and use it more productively.

History of GUI in Java

Java's original GUI library was the Abstract Window Toolkit (AWT). Swing (Chapters 12 and 22) was added to the platform in Java SE 1.2. Since then, Swing has remained the primary Java GUI technology. Swing is now in maintenance mode—Oracle has stopped development and will provide only bug fixes going forward; however, it will remain part of Java and is still widely used.

Java's GUI, graphics and multimedia API of the future is **JavaFX**. Sun Microsystems (acquired by Oracle in 2010) announced JavaFX in 2007 as a competitor to Adobe Flash and Microsoft Silverlight. JavaFX 1.0 was released in 2008. Prior to version 2.0, developers used JavaFX Script—which was similar to JavaScript—to write JavaFX apps. The JavaFX Script source code compiled to Java bytecode, allowing JavaFX apps to run on the Java Virtual Machine. Starting with version 2.0 in 2011, JavaFX was reimplemented as a set of Java libraries that could be used directly in Java apps. Some of the benefits of JavaFX vs. Swing include:

- JavaFX is easier to use—it provides one API for GUI, graphics and multimedia (images, animation, audio and video), whereas Swing is only for GUIs, so you need to use other APIs for graphics and multimedia apps.

- With Swing, many IDEs provided GUI design tools for dragging and dropping components onto a layout; however, each IDE produced different code. JavaFX Scene Builder (Section 25.2) can be used standalone or integrated with many IDEs and it produces the same code regardless of the IDE.

- Though Swing components could be customized, JavaFX gives you complete control over a JavaFX GUI's look-and-feel (online Chapter 26) via Cascading Style Sheets (CSS).

- JavaFX was designed for improved thread safety, which is important for today's multi-core systems.

- JavaFX supports transformations for repositioning and reorienting JavaFX components, and animations for changing the properties of JavaFX components over time. These can be used to make apps more intuitive and easier to use.

JavaFX Version Used in This Chapter

In this chapter, we use JavaFX 2.2 (released in late 2012) with Java SE 7. We tested the chapter's apps on Windows, Mac OS X and Linux. At the time of this writing, Oracle was about to release JavaFX 8 and Java SE 8. Our online Chapters 26 and 27—located on the book's companion website (see the inside front cover of this book)—present additional JavaFX GUI features and introduce JavaFX graphics and multimedia features in the context of JavaFX 8 and Java SE 8.

25.2 JavaFX Scene Builder and the NetBeans IDE

Most Java textbooks that introduce GUI programming provide hand-coded GUIs—that is, the authors build the GUIs from scratch in Java code, rather than using a visual GUI design tool. This is due to the fractured Java IDE market—there are many Java IDEs, so authors can't depend on any one IDE being used.

JavaFX is organized differently. The **JavaFX Scene Builder** tool is a standalone JavaFX GUI visual layout tool that can also be used with various IDEs, including the most popular ones—NetBeans, Eclipse and IntelliJ IDEA. JavaFX Scene Builder is most tightly integrated with NetBeans,[1] which is why we use it in our JavaFX presentation.

JavaFX Scene Builder enables you to create GUIs by dragging and dropping GUI components from Scene Builder's library onto a design area, then modifying and styling the GUI—all without writing any code. JavaFX Scene Builder's live editing and preview features allow you to view your GUI as you create and modify it, without compiling and running the app. You can use **Cascading Style Sheets (CSS)** to change the entire look-and-feel of your GUI—a concept sometimes called **skinning**. In online Chapter 26, we'll demonstrate the basics of styling with CSS.

In this chapter, we use JavaFX Scene Builder version 1.1 and NetBeans 7.4 to create two complete introductory JavaFX apps. Online Chapters 26–27 use JavaFX Scene Builder 2.0, which was about to be released when this book went to publication.

---

1. `http://www.oracle.com/technetwork/java/javafx/tools/index.html`.

What is FXML?
As you create and modify a GUI, JavaFX Scene Builder generates **FXML (FX Markup Language)**—an XML vocabulary for defining and arranging JavaFX GUI controls without writing any Java code. You do not need to know FXML or XML to study this chapter. As you'll see in Section 25.4, JavaFX Scene Builder hides the FXML details from you, so you can focus on defining *what* the GUI should contain without specifying *how* to generate it—this is another example of declarative programming, which we used with Java SE lambdas in Chapter 17.

 Software Engineering Observation 25.1

The FXML code is separate from the program logic that's defined in Java source code—this separation of the interface (the GUI) from the implementation (the Java code) makes it easier to debug, modify and maintain JavaFX GUI apps.

25.3 JavaFX App Window Structure

A JavaFX app window consists of several parts (Fig. 25.1) that you'll use in Sections 25.4– –25.5:

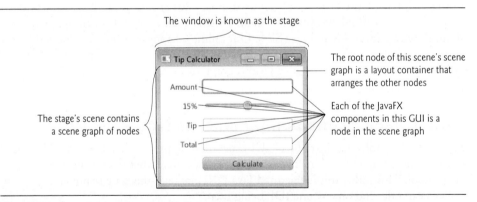

Fig. 25.1 | JavaFX app window parts.

- The window in which a JavaFX app's GUI is displayed is known as the **stage** and is an instance of class **Stage** (package `javafx.stage`).

- The stage contains one active **scene** that defines the GUI as a **scene graph**—a tree data structure of an app's visual elements, such as GUI controls, shapes, images, video, text and more. The scene is an instance of class **Scene** (package `javafx.scene`).

- Each visual element in the scene graph is a **node**—an instance of a subclass of **Node** (package `javafx.scene`), which defines common attributes and behaviors for all nodes in the scene graph. With the exception of the first node in the scene graph—known as the **root node**—each node has one parent. Nodes can have transforms (e.g., moving, rotating, scaling and skewing), opacity (which controls whether a node is transparent, partially transparent or opaque), effects (e.g., drop shadows, blurs, reflection and lighting) and more that we'll introduce in online Chapter 26.

- Nodes that have children are typically **layout containers** that arrange their child nodes in the scene. You'll use two layout containers (VBox and GridPane) in this chapter and learn several more in online Chapters 26–27.

- The nodes arranged in a layout container are a combination of controls and, in more complex GUIs, possibly other layout containers. **Controls** are GUI components, such as Labels that display text, TextFields that enable a program to receive text typed by the user, Buttons that initiate actions and more. When the user interacts with a control, such as clicking a Button, the control generates an event. Programs can respond to these events—known as event handling—to specify what should happen when each user interaction occurs.

- An event handler is a method that responds to a user interaction. An FXML GUI's event handlers are defined in a so-called **controller class** (as you'll see in Section 25.5.5).

25.4 Welcome App—Displaying Text and an Image

In this section, *without writing any code* you'll build a JavaFX **Welcome** app that displays text in a **Label** and an image in an **ImageView** (Fig. 25.2). First, you'll create a JavaFX app project in the *NetBeans IDE*. Then, you'll use visual-programming techniques and JavaFX Scene Builder to *drag-and-drop* JavaFX components onto the design area. Next, you'll use JavaFX Scene Builder's **Inspector** window to configure options, such as the Label's text and font size, and the ImageView's image. Finally, you'll execute the app from NetBeans. This section assumes that you've read the Before You Begin section, and installed NetBeans and Scene Builder. We used NetBeans 7.4, Scene Builder 1.1 and Java SE 7 for this chapter's examples.

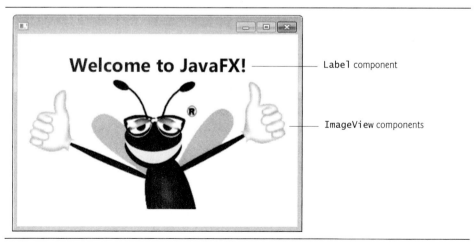

Fig. 25.2 | Final **Welcome** app running on Windows 7.

25.4.1 Creating the App's Project

You'll now use NetBeans to create a **JavaFX FXML App**. Open NetBeans on your system. Initially, the **Start Page** (Fig. 25.3) is displayed—this page gives you links to the NetBeans documentation and displays a list of your recent projects, if any.

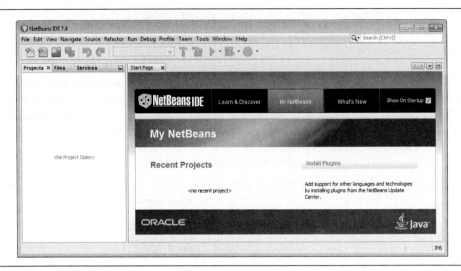

Fig. 25.3 | NetBeans IDE showing the **Start Page**.

Creating a New Project

To create an app, you must first create a **project**—a group of related files, such as code files and images that make up an app. Click the **New Project...** (☐) button on the toolbar or select **File > New Project...** to display the **New Project dialog** (Fig. 25.4). Under **Categories**, select **JavaFX** and under **Projects** select **JavaFX FXML Application**, then click **Next >**.

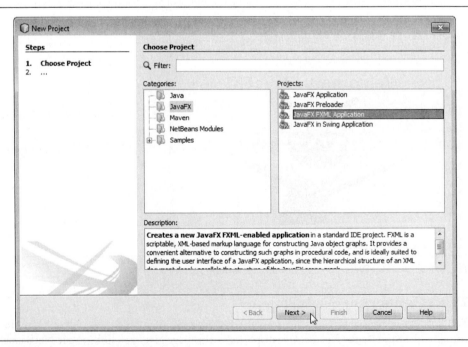

Fig. 25.4 | **New Project** dialog.

New JavaFX Application Dialog

In the **New JavaFX Application** dialog (Fig. 25.5), specify the following information:

1. **Project Name:** field—This is your app's name. Enter `Welcome` in this field.

2. **Project Location:** field—The project's location on your system. NetBeans places new projects in a subdirectory of `NetBeansProjects` within your user account's `Documents` folder. You can click the **Browse...** button to specify a different location. Your project's name is used as the subdirectory name.

3. **FXML name:** field—The name of the FXML filename that will contain the app's GUI. Enter `Welcome` here—the IDE creates the file `Welcome.fxml` in the project.

4. **Create Application Class:** checkbox—When this is checked, NetBeans creates a class with the specified name. This class contains the app's `main` method. Enter `Welcome` in this field. If you precede the class name with a package name, NetBeans creates the class in that package; otherwise, NetBeans will place the class in the default package.

Click **Finish** to create the project.

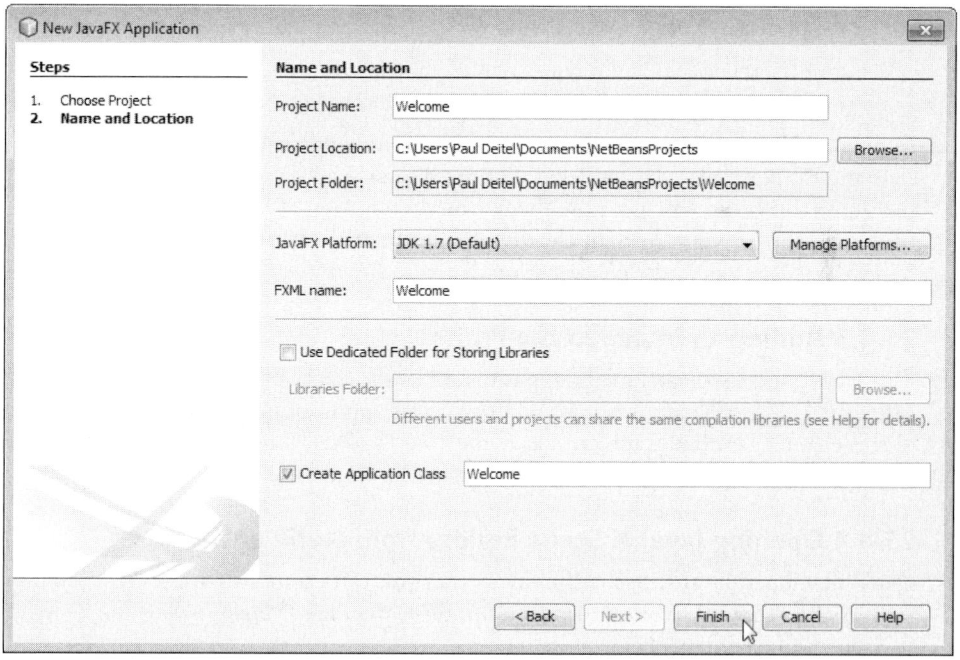

Fig. 25.5 | New JavaFX Application dialog.

25.4.2 NetBeans Projects Window—Viewing the Project Contents

The NetBeans **Projects** window provides access to all of your projects. The **Welcome** node represents this app's project. You can have many projects open at once—each will have its own top-level node. Within a project's node, the contents are organized into folders and files. You can view the `Welcome` project's contents by expanding the **Welcome > Source**

Packages > <default package> node (Fig. 25.6). If you specified a package name for the app class in Fig. 25.5, then that package's name will appear rather than **<default package>**.

Fig. 25.6 | NetBeans **Projects** window.

NetBeans creates and opens three files for a **JavaFX FXML Application** project:

- `Welcome.fxml`—This file contains the FXML markup for the GUI. By default, the IDE creates a GUI containing a `Button` and a `Label`.

- `Welcome.java`—This is the main class that creates the GUI from the FXML file and displays the GUI in a window.

- `WelcomeController.java`—This is the class in which you'd define the GUI's event handlers that allow the app to respond to user interactions with the GUI.

In Section 25.5, when we present an app with event handlers, we'll discuss the main app class and the controller class in detail. For the **Welcome** app, you will not edit any of these files in NetBeans, so you can close them. You do not need the `WelcomeController.java` file in this app, so you can right click the file in the **Projects** window and select **Delete** to remove it. Click **Yes** in the confirmation dialog to delete the file.

25.4.3 Adding an Image to the Project

One way to use an image in your app is to add its file to the project, then display it on an `ImageView`. The `bug.png` image you'll use for this app is located in the `images` subfolder of this chapter's examples folder. Locate the `images` folder on your file system, then drag `bug.png` onto the project's **<default package>** node to add the file to the project.

25.4.4 Opening JavaFX Scene Builder from NetBeans

You'll now open JavaFX Scene Builder so that you can create this app's GUI. To do so, right click `Welcome.fxml` in the **Projects** window, then select **Open** to view the FXML file in Scene Builder (Fig. 25.7).

Deleting the Default Controls
The FXML file provided by NetBeans contains a default GUI consisting of a `Button` control and a `Label` control. The **Welcome** app will not use these default controls, so you can delete them. To do so, click each in the content panel (or in the **Hierarchy** window at the bottom-left of Scene Builder's window), then press the *Backspace* or *Delete* key. In each case, Scene Builder displays the warning "**Some components have an fx:id. Do you really want to delete them?**". This means that there could be Java code in the project that refers

The **Library** contains JavaFX **Containers**, **Controls** and other items that can be dragged and dropped on the canvas

You use the content panel to design the GUI

You use the **Inspector** window to configure the currently selected item in the content panel

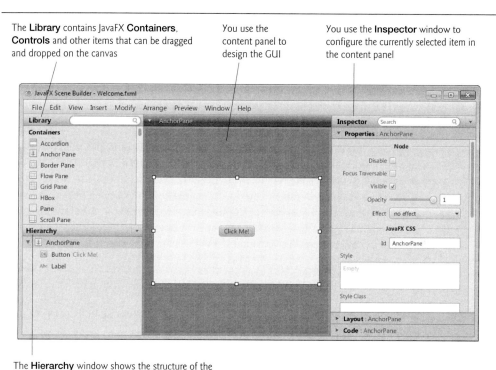

The **Hierarchy** window shows the structure of the GUI and allows you to select and reorganize controls

Fig. 25.7 | JavaFX Scene Builder displaying the default GUI in `Welcome.fxml`.

to these controls—for this app, there will not be any such code, so you can click **Delete** to remove these controls.

Deleting the Reference to the `WelcomeController` Class

As you'll learn in Section 25.5, in Scene Builder, you can specify the name of the controller class that contains methods for responding to the user's interactions with the GUI. The **Welcome** app does not need to respond to any user interactions, so you'll remove the reference in the FXML file to class `WelcomeController`. To do so, select the `AnchorPane` node in the **Hierarchy** window, then click the **Inspector** window's **Code** section to expand it and delete the value specified in the **Controller class** field. You're now ready to create the **Welcome** app's GUI.

25.4.5 Changing to a VBox Layout Container

For this app, you'll place a `Label` and an `ImageView` in a **VBox layout container** (package `javafx.scene.layout`), which will be the scene graph's root node. Layout containers help you arrange and size GUI components. A `VBox` arranges its nodes *vertically* from top to bottom. `VBox` is one of several JavaFX layout containers for arranging controls in a GUI. We discuss the `GridPane` layout container in Section 25.5 and several others in online Chapter 26. By default, NetBeans provides an `AnchorPane` as the root layout. To change from the default `AnchorPane` to a `VBox`:

1. *Adding a VBox to the Default Layout.* Drag a VBox from the **Library** window's **Containers** section onto the default AnchorPane in Scene Builder's content panel.

2. *Making the VBox the Root Layout.* Select **Edit > Trim Document to Selection** to make the VBox the root layout and remove the AnchorPane.

25.4.6 Configuring the VBox Layout Container

You'll now specify the VBox's alignment, initial size and padding:

1. *Specifying the VBox's Alignment.* A VBox's **alignment** determines the layout positioning of the VBox's children. In this app, we'd like each child node (the Label and the ImageView) to be centered horizontally in the scene, and we'd like both children to be centered vertically, so that there is an equal amount of space above the Label and below the ImageView. To accomplish this, select the VBox, then in the **Inspector**'s **Properties** section, set the **Alignment** property to CENTER. When you set the **Alignment**, notice the variety of potential alignment values you can use.

2. *Specifying the VBox's Preferred Size.* The **preferred size** (width and height) of the scene graph's root node is used by the scene to determine its window size when the app begins executing. To set the preferred size, select the VBox, then in the **Inspector**'s **Layout** section, set the **Pref Width** property to 450 and the **Pref Height** property to 300.

25.4.7 Adding and Configuring a Label

Next, you'll create the Label that displays "Welcome to JavaFX!":

1. *Adding a Label to the VBox.* Drag a Label from the **Library** window's **Controls** section onto the VBox. The Label is automatically centered in the VBox because you set the VBox's alignment to CENTER in Section 25.4.6.

2. *Changing the Label's text.* You can set a Label's text either by double clicking it and typing the text, or by selecting the Label and setting its **Text** property in the **Inspector**'s **Properties** section. Set the Label's text to "Welcome to JavaFX!".

3. *Changing the Label's font.* For this app, we set the Label to display in a large bold font. To do so, select the Label, then in the **Inspector**'s **Preferences** section, click the value to the right of the **Font** property. In the window that appears, set the **style** property to Bold and the **size** property to 30.

25.4.8 Adding and Configuring an ImageView

Finally, you'll add the ImageView that displays bug.png:

1. *Adding an ImageView to the VBox.* Drag an ImageView from the **Library** window's **Controls** section onto the VBox. The ImageView is automatically placed below the Label. Each new control you add to a VBox is placed below the VBox's other children, though you can change the order by dragging the children in Scene Builder's **Hierarchy** window. Like the Label, the ImageView is also automatically centered in the VBox.

2. *Setting the ImageViews's image.* To set the image to display, select the ImageView and click the ellipsis (...) button to the right of the **Image** property in the **Inspec-**

tor's **Properties** section. By default, Scene Builder opens a dialog showing the project's source-code folder, which is where you placed the image file bug.png in Section 25.4.3. Select the image file, then click **Open**. Scene Builder displays the image and resizes the ImageView to match the image's aspect ratio—the ratio of the image's width to its height—by setting the ImageView's **Fit Width** and **Fit Height** properties.

3. *Changing the ImageView's size.* We'd like to display the image in its original size. To do so, you must delete the default values for the ImageView's **Fit Width** and **Fit Height** properties, which are located in the **Inspector**'s **Layout** section. Once you delete these values, Scene Builder resizes the ImageView to the image's exact dimensions. Save the FXML file.

You've now completed the GUI. Scene Builder's content panel should now appear as shown in Fig. 25.8.

Fig. 25.8 | Completed design of the **Welcome** app's GUI in Scene Builder.

25.4.9 Running the Welcome App

You can run the app from NetBeans in one of three ways:

- Select the project's root node in the NetBeans **Projects** window, then click the **Run Project** (▷) button on the toolbar.
- Select the project's root node in the NetBeans **Projects** window, then press F6.
- Right click the project's root node in the NetBeans **Projects** window, then select **Run**.

In each case, the IDE will compile the app (if it isn't already compiled), then run the app. The **Welcome** app should now appear as shown in Fig. 25.2.

25.5 Tip Calculator App—Introduction to Event Handling

The **Tip Calculator** app (Fig. 25.9(a)) calculates and displays a restaurant bill tip and total. By default, the app calculates the total with a 15% tip. You can specify a tip percentage from 0% to 30% by moving the Slider *thumb*—this updates the tip percentage (Fig. 25.9(b) and (c)). In this section, you'll build a **Tip Calculator** app using several JavaFX components and learn how to respond to user interactions with the GUI.

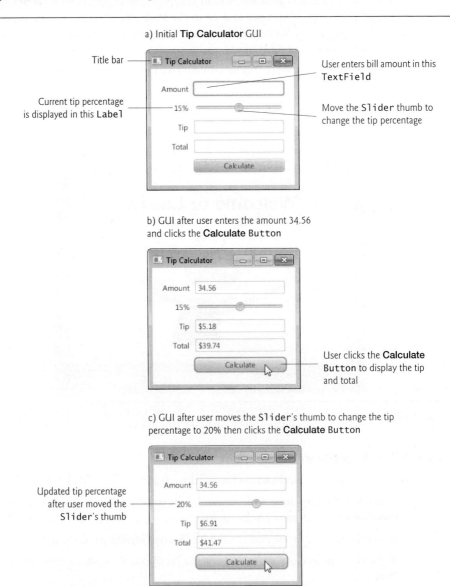

a) Initial **Tip Calculator** GUI

Title bar — User enters bill amount in this TextField

Current tip percentage is displayed in this Label — Move the Slider thumb to change the tip percentage

b) GUI after user enters the amount 34.56 and clicks the **Calculate** Button

User clicks the **Calculate** Button to display the tip and total

c) GUI after user moves the Slider's thumb to change the tip percentage to 20% then clicks the **Calculate** Button

Updated tip percentage after user moved the Slider's thumb

Fig. 25.9 | Entering the bill amount and calculating the tip.

You'll begin by test-driving the app, using it to calculate 15% and 10% tips. Then we'll overview the technologies you'll use to create the app. You'll build the app's GUI using the NetBeans and JavaFX SceneBuilder. Finally, we'll present the complete Java code for the app and do a detailed code walkthrough.

25.5.1 Test-Driving the Tip Calculator App

Opening and Running the App

Open the NetBeans IDE, then perform the following steps to open the **Tip Calculator** app's project and run it:

1. *Opening the Tip Calculator app's project.* Select **File > Open Project...** or click the **Open Project...** (🗂) button on the toolbar to display the **Open Project** dialog. Navigate to this chapter's examples folder, select TipCalculator and click the **Open Project** button. A TipCalculator node now appears in the **Projects** window.

2. *Running the Tip Calculator app.* Right click the TipCalculator project in the **Projects** window, then click the **Run Project** (▷) button on the toolbar.

Entering a Bill Total

Using your keyboard, enter 34.56, then press the **Calculate** Button. The **Tip** and **Total** TextFields show the tip amount and the total bill for a 15% tip (Fig. 25.9(b)).

Selecting a Custom Tip Percentage

Use the Slider to specify a *custom* tip percentage. Drag the Slider's *thumb* until the percentage reads **20%** (Fig. 25.9(c)), then press the **Calculate** Button to display the updated tip and total. As you drag the thumb, the tip percentage in the Label to the Slider's left updates continuously. By default, the Slider allows you to select values from 0.0 to 100.0, but in this app we'll restrict the Slider to selecting whole numbers from 0 to 30.

25.5.2 Technologies Overview

This section introduces the technologies you'll use to build the **Tip Calculator** app.

Class Application

The main class in a JavaFX app is a subclass of **Application** (package **javafx.application.Application**). The app's main method calls class Application's static **launch** method to begin executing a JavaFX app. This method, in turn, causes the JavaFX runtime to create an object of the Application subclass and call its **start** method, which creates the GUI, attaches it to a Scene and places it on the Stage that method start receives as an argument.

Arranging JavaFX Components with a GridPane

Recall that layout containers arrange JavaFX components in a Scene. A **GridPane** (package **javafx.scene.layout**) arranges JavaFX components into *columns* and *rows* in a rectangular grid.

This app uses a GridPane (Fig. 25.10) to arrange views into two columns and five rows. Each cell in a GridPane can be empty or can hold one or more JavaFX components, including layout containers that arrange other controls. Each component in a GridPane can span *multiple* columns or rows, though we did not use that capability in this GUI.

When you drag a GridPane onto Scene Builder's content panel, Scene Builder creates the GridPane with two columns and three rows by default. You can add and remove columns and rows as necessary. We'll discuss other GridPane features as we present the GUI-building steps. To learn more about class GridPane, visit:

```
http://docs.oracle.com/javafx/2/api/javafx/scene/layout/GridPane.html
```

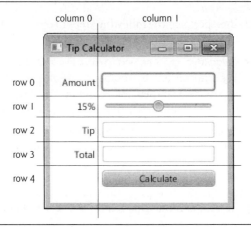

Fig. 25.10 | Tip Calculator GUI's GridPane labeled by its rows and columns.

Creating and Customizing the GUI with Scene Builder

You'll create Labels, TextFields, a Slider and a Button by dragging them onto the content panel in Scene Builder, then customize them using the **Inspector** window.

- A **TextField** (package javafx.scene.control) can accept text input from the user or display text. You'll use one editable TextField to input the bill amount from the user and two *uneditable* TextFields to display the tip and total amounts.

- A **Slider** (package javafx.scene.control) represents a value in the range 0.0–100.0 by default and allows the user to select a number in that range by moving the Slider's thumb. You'll customize the Slider so the user can choose a custom tip percentage *only* from the more limited range 0 to 30.

- A **Button** (package javafx.scene.control) allows the user to initiate an action—in this app, pressing the **Calculate** Button calculates and displays the tip and total amounts.

Formatting Numbers as Locale-Specific Currency and Percentage Strings

You'll use class **NumberFormat** (package **java.text**) to create *locale-specific* currency and percentage strings—an important part of *internationalization*.

Event Handling

Normally, a user interacts with an app's GUI to indicate the tasks that the app should perform. For example, when you write an e-mail in an e-mail app, clicking the **Send** button tells the app to send the e-mail to the specified e-mail addresses. GUIs are **event driven**. When the user interacts with a GUI component, the interaction—known as an **event**—

drives the program to perform a task. Some common user interactions that cause an app to perform a task include *clicking* a button, *typing* in a text field, *selecting* an item from a menu, *closing* a window and *moving* the mouse. The code that performs a task in response to an event is called an **event handler**, and the process of responding to events is known as **event handling**.

Before an app can respond to an event for a particular control, you must:

1. Create a class that represents the event handler and implements an appropriate interface—known as an **event-listener interface**.

2. Indicate that an object of that class should be notified when the event occurs—known as **registering the event handler**.

In this app, you'll respond to two events—when the user moves the Slider's thumb, the app will update the Label that displays the current tip percentage, and when the user clicks the **Calculate** Button, the app will calculate and display the tip and total bill amount.

You'll see that for certain events—such as when the user clicks a Button—you can link a control to its event-handling method by using the **Code** section of Scene Builder's **Inspector** window. In this case, the class that implements the event-listener interface will be created for you and will call the method you specify. For events that occur when the value of control's property changes—such as when the user moves a Slider's thumb to change the Slider's value—you'll see that you must create the event handler entirely in code.

Implementing Interface ChangeListener for Handling Slider Thumb Position Changes

You'll implement the **ChangeListener** interface (from package javafx.beans.value) to respond to the user moving the Slider's thumb. In particular, you'll use method changed to display the user-selected tip percentage as the user moves the Slider's thumb.

Model-View-Controller (MVC) Architecture

JavaFX applications in which the GUI is implemented as FXML adhere to the **Model-View-Controller (MVC) design pattern**, which separates an app's data (contained in the **model**) from the app's GUI (the **view**) and the app's processing logic (the **controller**).

The controller implements logic for processing user inputs. The model contains application data, and the view presents the data stored in the model. When a user provides some input, the controller modifies the model with the given input. In the **Tip Calculator**, the model is the bill amount, the tip and the total. When the model changes, the controller updates the view to present the changed data.

In a JavaFX FXML app, you define the app's event handlers in a **controller class**. The controller class defines instance variables for interacting with controls programmatically, as well as event-handling methods. The controller class may also declare additional instance variables, static variables and methods that support the app's operation. In a simple app like the **Tip Calculator**, the model and controller are often combined into a single class, as we'll do in this example.

FXMLLoader Class

When a JavaFX FXML app begins executing, class **FXMLLoader**'s static method **load** is used to load the FXML file that represents the app's GUI. This method:

- Creates the GUI's scene graph and returns a **Parent** (package javafx.scene) reference to the scene graph's root node.

- Initializes the controller's instance variables for the components that are manipulated programmatically.

- Creates and registers the event handlers for any events specified in the FXML.

We'll discuss these steps in more detail in Sections 25.5.4—25.5.5.

25.5.3 Building the App's GUI

In this section, we'll show the precise steps for using Scene Builder to create the **Tip Calculator**'s GUI. The GUI will not look like the one shown in Fig. 25.9 until you've completed the steps.

fx:id Property Values for This App's Controls

If a control or layout will be manipulated programmatically in the controller class (as we'll do with one of the Labels, all of the TextFields and the Slider in this app), you must provide a name for that control or layout. In Section 25.5.4, you'll learn how to declare variables in your source code for each such component in the FXML, and we'll discuss how those variables are initialized for you. Each object's name is specified via its **fx:id** property. You can set this property's value by selecting a component in your scene, then expanding the **Inspector** window's **Code** section—the **fx:id** property appears at the top of the **Code** section. Figure 25.11 shows the **fx:id** properties of the **Tip Calculator**'s programmatically manipulated controls. For clarity, our naming convention is to use the control's class name in the **fx:id** property.

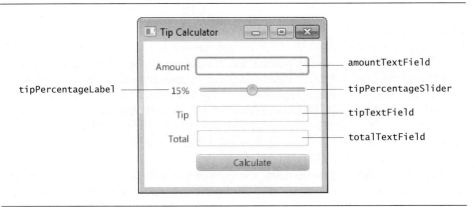

Fig. 25.11 | **Tip Calculator**'s programmatically manipulated controls labeled with their **fx:id**s.

Creating the TipCalculator Project

Click the **New Project...** ( ) button on the toolbar or select **File > New Project...**. In the **New Project** dialog. Under **Categories**, select **JavaFX** and under **Projects** select **JavaFX FXML Application**, then click **Next >** and specify TipCalculator in the **Project Name, FXML name** and **Create Application Class** fields. Click **Finish** to create the project.

*Step 1: Changing the Root Layout from an **AnchorPane** to a **GridPane***
Open TipCalculator.fxml in Scene Builder so that you can build the GUI and delete the default controls, then change from the default AnchorPane to a GridPane:

1. *Adding a **GridPane** to the Default Layout.* Drag a GridPane from the **Library** window's **Containers** section onto the default AnchorPane in Scene Builder's content panel.

2. *Making the **GridPane** the Root Layout.* Select **Edit > Trim Document to Selection** to make the GridPane the root layout and remove the AnchorPane.

*Step 2: Adding Rows to the **GridPane***
By default, the GridPane contains two columns and three rows. Recall that the GUI in Fig. 25.10 consists of five rows. You can add a row above or below an existing row by right clicking a row and selecting **Grid Pane > Add Row Above** or **Grid Pane > Add Row Below**. After adding two rows, the GridPane should appear as shown in Fig. 25.12. You can use similar steps to add columns. You can delete a row or column by right clicking the tab containing its row or column number and selecting **Delete**.

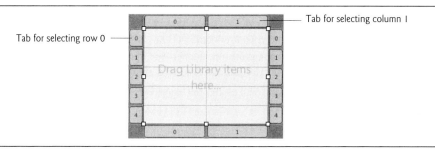

Fig. 25.12 | GridPane with five rows.

*Step 3: Adding the Controls to the **GridPane***
You'll now add the controls in Fig. 25.10 to the GridPane. For those that have **fx:ids** (see Fig. 25.11), while the control is selected, set its **fx:id** property in the **Inspector** window's **Code** section. Perform the following steps:

1. *Adding the **Labels.*** Drag Labels from the **Library** window's **Controls** section into the first four rows of the GridPane's left column (i.e., column 0). As you add each Label, set its text as shown Fig. 25.10.

2. *Adding the **TextFields.*** Drag TextFields from the **Library** window's **Controls** section into rows 0, 2 and 3 of the GridPane's right column (i.e., column 1).

3. *Adding a **Slider.*** Drag a horizontal Slider from the **Library** window's **Controls** section into row 1 of the GridPane's right column.

4. *Adding a **Button.*** Drag a Button from the **Library** window's **Controls** section into row 4 of the GridPane's right column. You can set the Button's text by double clicking it, or by selecting the Button, then setting its **Text** property in the **Inspector** window's **Properties** section.

The GridPane should appear as shown in Fig. 25.13.

Fig. 25.13 | GridPane filled with the **Tip Calculator**'s controls.

*Step 4: Right-Aligning **GridPane** Column 0's Contents*
A GridPane column's contents are left-aligned by default. To right-align the contents of column 0, select it by clicking the tab at the top or bottom of the column, then in the In-spector's **Layout** section, set the **Halignment** (horizontal alignment) property to RIGHT.

*Step 5: Sizing the **GridPane** Columns to Fit Their Contents*
By default, Scene Builder sets each GridPane column's width to 100 pixels and each row's height to 30 pixels to ensure that you can easily drag controls into the GridPane's cells. In this app, we sized each column to fit its contents. To do so, select the column 0 by clicking the tab at the top or bottom of the column, then in the **Inspector**'s **Layout** section, set the **Pref Width** property to USE_COMPUTED_SIZE to indicate that the column's width should be based on the widest child—the **Amount** Label in this case. Repeat this process for column 1. The GridPane should appear as shown in Fig. 25.14.

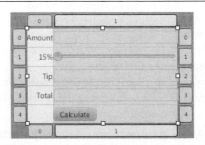

Fig. 25.14 | GridPane with columns sized to fit their contents.

*Step 6: Sizing the **TextFields***
Scene Builder sets each TextField's width to 200 pixels by default. You may size controls as appropriate for each GUI you create. In this app, we do not need the TextFields to be so wide, so we used the preferred width for each TextField, which is somewhat narrower. When setting a property to the same value for several controls, you can select all of them and specify the value once. To select all three TextFields, hold the *Ctrl* (or *Command*) key and click each TextField. Then in the **Inspector**'s **Layout** section, set the **Pref Width** property to USE_COMPUTED_SIZE. This indicates that each TextField should use its pre-ferred width (as defined by JavaFX). Notice that the GridPane's right column resizes to the TextFields' preferred widths.

*Step 7: Sizing the **Button***
By default, Scene Builder sets a Button's width based on its text. For this app, we chose to make the Button the same width as the other controls in the GridPane's right column. To do so, select the Button, then in the Inspector's **Layout** section, set the **Max Width** property to MAX_VALUE. This causes the Button's width to grow to fill the column's width.

Previewing the GUI
As you design your GUI, you can preview it by selecting **Preview > Show Preview in Window**. As you can see in Fig. 25.15, there's no space between the Labels in the left column and the controls in the right column. In addition, there's no space around the GridPane, because the Stage is sized to fit the Scene's content. Thus, many of the controls touch or come close to the window's borders. You'll fix these issues in the next step.

Fig. 25.15 | GridPane with the TextFields and Button resized.

*Step 8: Configuring the **GridPane**'s Padding and Horizontal Gap Between Its Columns*
The space between a node's contents and its top, right, bottom and left edges is known as the **padding**, which separates the contents from the node's edges. Since the GridPane's size determines the size of the Stage's window, the padding in this example also separates the GridPane's children from the window's edges. To set the padding, select the GridPane, then in the Inspector's **Layout** section, set the **Padding** property's four values (**TOP**, **RIGHT**, **BOTTOM** and **LEFT**) to 14—the JavaFX recommended distance between the edge of a control and the edge of a Scene.

You can specify the default amount of space between a GridPane's columns and rows with its **Hgap** (horizontal gap) and **Vgap** (vertical gap) properties, respectively. Because Scene Builder sets each GridPane row's height to 30 pixels—which is greater than the heights of this app's controls—there's already some vertical space between the components. To specify the horizontal gap between the columns, select the GridPane in the **Hierarchy** window, then in the Inspector's **Layout** section, set the **Hgap** property to 8. If you'd like to precisely control the vertical space between components, you can set each row's **Pref Height** property to USE_COMPUTED_SIZE (as we did for the columns' **Pref Width** property in Step 5), then set the GridPane's **Vgap** property.

*Step 9: Making the **tipTextField** and **totalTextField** Uneditable and Not Focusable*
The tipTextField and totalTextField are used in this app only to display results, not receive text input. For this reason, they should not be interactive. You can type in a Text-Field only if it's "in **focus**"—that is, it's the control that the user is interacting with. When

you click an interactive control, it receives the focus. Similarly, when you press the *Tab* key, the focus transfers from the current focusable control to the next one—this occurs in the order the controls were added to the GUI. Interactive controls—such as TextFields, Sliders and Buttons—are focusable by default. Non-interactive controls—like Labels— are not focusable.

In this app, the tipTextField and totalTextField are neither editable nor focusable. To make these changes, select both TextFields, then in the **Inspector**'s **Properties** section, uncheck the **Editable** and **Focus Traversable** properties.

Step 10: Setting the Slider's Properties

To complete the GUI, you'll now configure the **Tip Calculator**'s Slider. By default, a Slider's range is 0.0 to 100.0 and its initial value is 0.0. This app allows tip percentages from 0 to 30 with a default of 15. To make these changes, select the Slider, then in the **Inspector**'s **Properties** section, set the Slider's **Max** property to 30 and the **Value** property to 15. We also set the **Block Increment** property to 5—this is the amount by which the **Value** property increases or decreases when the user clicks between an end of the Slider and the Slider's thumb. Save the FXML file by selecting **File > Save**.

Previewing the Final Layout

Select **Preview > Show Preview in Window** to view the final GUI (Fig. 25.16). When we discuss the TipCalculatorController class in Section 25.5.5, we'll show how to specify the **Calculate** Button's event handler in the FXML file.

Fig. 25.16 | Final GUI design previewed in Scene Builder.

25.5.4 TipCalculator Class

When you created the **Tip Calculator** app's project, NetBeans created two Java source-code files for you:

- TipCalculator.java—This file contains the TipCalculator class, in which the main method (discussed in this section) loads the FXML file to create the GUI and attaches the GUI to a Scene that's displayed on the app's Stage.

- TipCalculatorController.java—This file contains the TipCalculatorController class (discussed in Section 25.5.5), which is where you'll specify the Slider and Button controls' event handlers.

Figure 25.17 presents class TipCalculator. We reformatted the code to meet our conventions. With the exception of line 18, all of the code in this class was generated by Net-

Beans. As we discussed in Section 25.5.2, the `Application` subclass is the starting point for a JavaFX app. The `main` method calls class `Application`'s `static launch` method (line 26) to begin executing the app. This method, in turn, causes the JavaFX runtime to create an object of the `TipCalculator` class and calls its `start` method.

```java
1  // Fig. 25.17: TipCalculator.java
2  // Main app class that loads and displays the Tip Calculator's GUI
3  import javafx.application.Application;
4  import javafx.fxml.FXMLLoader;
5  import javafx.scene.Parent;
6  import javafx.scene.Scene;
7  import javafx.stage.Stage;
8
9  public class TipCalculator extends Application
10 {
11    @Override
12    public void start(Stage stage) throws Exception
13    {
14       Parent root =
15          FXMLLoader.load(getClass().getResource("TipCalculator.fxml"));
16
17       Scene scene = new Scene(root); // attach scene graph to scene
18       stage.setTitle("Tip Calculator"); // displayed in window's title bar
19       stage.setScene(scene); // attach scene to stage
20       stage.show(); // display the stage
21    }
22
23    public static void main(String[] args)
24    {
25       // create a TipCalculator object and call its start method
26       launch(args);
27    }
28 }
```

Fig. 25.17 | Main app class that loads and displays the **Tip Calculator**'s GUI.

Overridden *Application* Method *start*

Method `start` (lines 11–21) creates the GUI, attaches it to a `Scene` and places it on the `Stage` that method `start` receives as an argument. Lines 14–15 use class `FXMLLoader`'s `static` method `load` to create the GUI's scene graph. This method:

- Returns a `Parent` (package `javafx.scene`) reference to the scene graph's root node (the `GridPane` in this example).

- Creates an object of the controller class.

- Initializes the controller's instance variables for the components that are manipulated programmatically.

- Registers the event handlers for any events specified in the FXML.

We discuss the initialization of the controller's instance variables and the registration of the event handlers in Section 25.5.5.

Creating the **Scene**

To display the GUI, you must attach it to a Scene, then attach the Scene to the Stage that's passed into method start. Line 17 creates a Scene, passing root (the scene graph's root node) as an argument to the constructor. By default, the Scene's size is determined by the size of the scene graph's root node. Overloaded versions of the Scene constructor allow you to specify the Scene's size and fill (a color, gradient or image), which appears in the Scene's background. Line 18 uses Scene method setTitle to specify the text that appears in the Stage window's title bar. Line 19 places Stage method setScene to place the Scene onto the Stage. Finally, line 20 calls Stage method show to display the Stage window.

25.5.5 TipCalculatorController Class

Figures 25.18–25.21 present the TipCalculatorController class that responds to user interactions with the app's Button and Slider. Replace the code that NetBeans generated in TipCalculatorController.java with the code in Figs. 25.18–25.21.

Class **TipCalculatorController**'s **import** *Statements*

Figure 25.18 shows class TipCalculatorController's import statements.

```
 1   // TipCalculatorController.jav
 2   // Controller that handles calculateButton and tipPercentageSlider events
 3   import java.math.BigDecimal;
 4   import java.math.RoundingMode;
 5   import java.text.NumberFormat;
 6   import javafx.beans.value.ChangeListener;
 7   import javafx.beans.value.ObservableValue;
 8   import javafx.event.ActionEvent;
 9   import javafx.fxml.FXML;
10   import javafx.scene.control.Label;
11   import javafx.scene.control.Slider;
12   import javafx.scene.control.TextField;
13
```

Fig. 25.18 | TipCalculatorController's import declarations.

Lines 3–12 import the classes and interfaces used by class TipCalculatorController:

- Class BigDecimal of package java.math (line 3) is used to perform precise monetary calculations. The RoundingMode enum of package java.math (line 4) is used to specify how BigDecimal values are rounded during calculations or when formatting floating-point numbers as Strings.

- Class NumberFormat of package java.text (line 5) provides numeric formatting capabilities, such as locale-specific currency and percentage formats. For example, in the U.S. locale, the monetary value 34.56 is formatted as $34.95 and the percentage 15 is formatted as 15%. Class NumberFormat determines the locale of the system on which your app runs, then formats currency amounts and percentages accordingly.

- You implement interface ChangeListener of package javafx.beans.value (line 6) to respond to the user moving the Slider's thumb. This interface's changed method receives an object that implements interface ObservableValue (line 7)—that is, a value that generates an event when it changes.

- A Button's event handler receives an ActionEvent (line 8; package javafx.event), which indicates that the Button was clicked. As you'll see in online Chapter 26, many JavaFX controls support ActionEvents.

- The annotation FXML (line 9; package javafx.fxml) is used in a JavaFX controller class's code to mark instance variables that should refer to JavaFX components in the GUI's FXML file and methods that can respond to the events of JavaFX components in the GUI's FXML file.

- Package javafx.scene.control (lines 10–12) contains many JavaFX control classes, including Label, Slider and TextField.

As you write code with various classes and interfaces, you can use the the NetBeans IDE's **Source > Organize Imports** command to let the IDE insert the import statements for you. If the same class or interface name appears in more than one package, the IDE will display a dialog in which you can select the appropriate import statement.

TipCalculatorController's static Variables and Instance Variables

Lines 17–38 of Fig. 25.19 present class TipCalculatorController's static and instance variables. The NumberFormat objects (lines 17–20) are used to format currency values and percentages, respectively. Method getCurrencyInstance returns a NumberFormat object that formats values as currency using the default locale for the system on which the app is running. Similarly, method getPercentInstance returns a NumberFormat object that formats values as percentages using the system's default locale. The BigDecimal object tipPercentage (line 22) stores the current tip percentage and is used in the tip calculation (Fig. 25.20) when the user clicks the app's **Calculate** Button.

```
14   public class TipCalculatorController
15   {
16      // formatters for currency and percentages
17      private static final NumberFormat currency =
18         NumberFormat.getCurrencyInstance();
19      private static final NumberFormat percent =
20         NumberFormat.getPercentInstance();
21
22      private BigDecimal tipPercentage = new BigDecimal(0.15); // 15% default
23
24      // GUI controls defined in FXML and used by the controller's code
25      @FXML
26      private TextField amountTextField;
27
28      @FXML
29      private Label tipPercentageLabel;
30
31      @FXML
32      private Slider tipPercentageSlider;
33
```

Fig. 25.19 | TipCalculatorController's static variables and instance variables. (Part 1 of 2.)

```
34        @FXML
35        private TextField tipTextField;
36
37        @FXML
38        private TextField totalTextField;
39
```

Fig. 25.19 | TipCalculatorController's static variables and instance variables. (Part 2 of 2.)

@FXML Annotation
Recall from Section 25.5.3 that each control that this app manipulates in its Java source code needs an **fx:id**. Lines 25–38 (Fig. 25.19) declare the controller class's corresponding instance variables. The **@FXML annotation** that precedes each declaration (lines 25, 28, 31, 34 and 37) indicates that the variable name can be used in the FXML file that describes the app's GUI. The variable names that you specify in the controller class must precisely match the **fx:id** values you specified when building the GUI. When the FXMLLoader loads TipCalculator.fxml to create the GUI, it also initializes each of the controller's instance variables that are declared with @FXML to ensure that they refer to the corresponding GUI components in the FXML file.

TipCalculatorController's calculateButtonPressed Event Handler
Figure 25.20 presents class TipCalculatorController's calculateButtonPressed method, which is called with the user clicks the **Calculate** Button. The @FXML annotation (line 41) preceding the method indicates that this method can be used to specify a control's event handler in the FXML file that describes the app's GUI. For a control that generates an ActionEvent (as is the case for many JavaFX controls), the event-handling method must return void and receive one ActionEvent parameter (line 42).

```
40        // calculates and displays the tip and total amounts
41        @FXML
42        private void calculateButtonPressed(ActionEvent event)
43        {
44           try
45           {
46              BigDecimal amount = new BigDecimal(amountTextField.getText());
47              BigDecimal tip = amount.multiply(tipPercentage);
48              BigDecimal total = amount.add(tip);
49
50              tipTextField.setText(currency.format(tip));
51              totalTextField.setText(currency.format(total));
52           }
53           catch (NumberFormatException ex)
54           {
55              amountTextField.setText("Enter amount");
56              amountTextField.selectAll();
57              amountTextField.requestFocus();
58           }
59        }
60
```

Fig. 25.20 | TipCalculatorController's calculateButtonPressed event handler.

Specifying the Calculate Button's Event Handler in Scene Builder

When you created the TipCalculator project with NetBeans, it preconfigured the class TipCalculatorController as the controller for the GUI in TipCalculator.fxml. You can see this in Scene Builder by selecting the scene's root node (i.e., the GridPane), then expanding the **Inspector** window's **Code** section. The controller class's name is specified in the **Controller class** field. If you declare the method calculateButtonPressed in the controller class before specifying the **Calculate** Button's event handler in the FXML, when you open Scene Builder it scans the controller class for methods prefixed with @FXML and allows you to select from those methods to configure event handlers.

To indicate that calculateButtonPressed should be called when the user clicks the **Calculate** Button, open TipCalculator.fxml in Scene Builder, then:

1. Select the **Calculate** Button.

2. In the **Inspector** window, expand the **Code** section.

3. Under **On Action**, select #calculateButtonPressed from the drop-down list and save the FXML file.

When the FXMLLoader loads TipCalculator.fxml to create the GUI, it creates and registers an event handler for the **Calculate** Button's ActionEvent. An ActionEvent's handler is an object of a class that implements the **EventHandler<ActionEvent>** interface, which contains a handle method that returns void and receives an ActionEvent parameter. This method, in turn, calls method calculateButtonPressed when the user clicks the **Calculate** Button. The FXMLLoader performs similar tasks for every event listener you specified via the **Inspector** window's **Code** section.

Calculating and Displaying the Tip and Total Amounts

Lines 46–51 calculate and display the tip and total amounts. Line 46 calls method getText to get from the amountTextField the bill amount typed by the user. This String is passed to the BigDecimal constructor, which throws a NumberFormatException if its argument is not a number. In that case, line 55 calls amountTextField's setText method to display the message "Enter amount" in the TextField. Line 56 then calls method selectAll to select the TextField's text and line 57 calls requestFocus, which gives the TextField the focus. This allows the user to immediately type a new value in the amountTextField without having to first select its text. Methods getText, setText and selectAll are inherited into class TextField from class TextInputControl (package javafx.scene.control), and method requestFocus is inherited into class TextField from class Node (package javafx.scene).

If line 46 does not throw an exception, line 47 calculates the tip by calling method multiply to multiply the amount by the tipPercentage, and line 48 calculates the total by calling method add to add the tip to the bill amount. Next lines 50 and 51 use the currency object's format method to create currency-formatted Strings representing the tip and total amounts—these are displayed in tipTextField and totalTextField, respectively.

TipCalculatorController's initalize Method

Figure 25.21 presents class TipCalculatorController's initialize method. When the FXMLLoader creates an object of class TipCalculatorController, it determines whether the class contains an initialize method with no parameters and, if so, calls that method to initialize the controller. This method can be used to configure the controller before the GUI is displayed. Line 65 calls the currency object's setRoundingMode method to specify how currency values should be rounded. The value RoundingMode.HALF_UP indicates that values greater than or equal to .5 should round up—for example, 34.567 would be formatted as 34.57 and 34.564 would be formatted as 34.56.

```
61    // called by FXMLLoader to initialize the controller
62    public void initialize()
63    {
64       // 0-4 rounds down, 5-9 rounds up
65       currency.setRoundingMode(RoundingMode.HALF_UP);
66
67       // listener for changes to tipPercentageSlider's value
68       tipPercentageSlider.valueProperty().addListener(
69          new ChangeListener<Number>()
70          {
71             @Override
72             public void changed(ObservableValue<? extends Number> ov,
73                Number oldValue, Number newValue)
74             {
75                tipPercentage =
76                   BigDecimal.valueOf(newValue.intValue() / 100.0);
77                tipPercentageLabel.setText(percent.format(tipPercentage));
78             }
79          }
80       );
81    }
82 }
```

Fig. 25.21 | TipCalculatorController's initalize method.

Using an Anonymous Inner Class for Event Handling
Each JavaFX control has various properties, some of which—such as a Slider's value—can notify an event listener when they change. For such properties, you must manually register as the event handler an object of a class that implements the ChangeListener interface from package javafx.beans.value. If such an event handler is not reused, you'd typically define it as an instance of an **anonymous inner class**—a class that's declared without a name and typically appears inside a method declaration. Lines 68–80 are one statement that declares the event listener's class, creates an object of that class and registers it as the listener for changes to the tipPercentageSlider's value.

The call to method valueProperty (line 68) returns an object of class DoubleProperty (package javax.beans.property) that represents the Slider's value. A DoubleProperty is an ObservableValue that can notify listeners when the value changes. Each class that implements interface ObservableValue provides method addListener (called on line 68) for registering a ChangeListener. In the case of a Slider's value, addListener's argument is an object that implements ChangeListener<Number>, because the Slider's value is a numeric value.

Since an anonymous inner class has no name, one object of the class must be created at the point where the class is declared (starting at line 69). Method addListener's argument is defined in lines 69–79 as a class-instance creation expression that declares an anonymous inner class and creates one object of that class. A reference to that object is then passed to addListener. After the new keyword, the syntax ChangeListener<Number>() (line 69) begins the declaration of an anonymous inner class that implements interface ChangeListener<Number>. This is similar to beginning a class declaration with

```
public class MyHandler implements ChangeListener<Number>
```

The opening left brace at 70 and the closing right brace at line 79 delimit the body of the anonymous inner class. Lines 71–78 declare the ChangeListener<Number>'s changed method, which receives a reference to the ObservableValue that changed, a Number containing the Slider's old value before the event occurred and a Number containing the Slider's new value. When the user moves the Slider's thumb, lines 75–76 store the new tip percentage and line 77 updates the tipPercentageLabel.

An anonymous inner class can access its top-level class's instance variables, static variables and methods—in this case, the anonymous inner class uses instance variables tipPercentage and tipPercentageLabel, and static variable percent. However, an anonymous inner class has limited access to the local variables of the method in which it's declared—it can access only the final local variables declared in the enclosing method's body. (As of Java SE 8, an anonymous inner class may also access a class's effectively final local variables—see Section 17.3.1 for more information.)

Java SE 8: Using a Lambda to Implement the ChangeListener

Recall from Section 10.10 that in Java SE 8 an interface containing one method is a functional interface and recall from Chapter 17 that such interfaces may be implemented with lambdas. Section 17.9 showed how to implement an event-handling functional interface using a lambda. The event handler in Fig. 25.21 can be implemented with a lambda as follows:

```
tipPercentageSlider.valueProperty().addListener(
    (ov, oldValue, newValue) ->
    {
        tipPercentage =
            BigDecimal.valueOf(newValue.intValue() / 100.0);
        tipPercentageLabel.setText(percent.format(tipPercentage));
    });
```

25.6 Features Covered in the Online JavaFX Chapters

JavaFX is a robust GUI, graphics and multimedia technology. In the online Chapters 26 and 27, you'll:

- Learn additional JavaFX layouts and controls.
- Handle other event types (such as MouseEvents).
- Apply transformations (such as moving, rotating, scaling and skewing) and effects (such as drop shadows, blurs, reflection and lighting) to a scene graph's nodes.
- Use CSS to specify the look-and-feel of controls.
- Use JavaFX properties and data binding to enable automatic updating of controls as corresponding data changes.
- Use JavaFX graphics capabilities.

• Perform JavaFX animations.
• Use JavaFX multimedia capabilities to play audio and video.

In addition, our JavaFX Resource Center

        http://www.deitel.com/JavaFX

contains links to online resources where you can learn more about JavaFX's capabilities.

25.7 Wrap-Up

In this chapter, we introduced JavaFX. We presented the structure of a JavaFX stage (the application window). You learned that the stage displays a scene's scene graph, that the scene graph is composed of nodes and that nodes consist of layouts and controls.

You designed GUIs using visual programming techniques in JavaFX Scene Builder, which enabled you to create GUIs without writing any Java code. You arranged `Label`, `ImageView`, `TextField`, `Slider` and `Button` controls using the `VBox` and `GridPane` layout containers. You learned how class `FXMLLoader` uses the FXML created in Scene Builder to create the GUI.

You implemented a controller class to respond to user interactions with `Button` and `Slider` controls. We showed that certain event handlers can be specified directly in FXML from Scene Builder, but event handlers for changes to a control's property values must be implemented directly in the controllers code. You also learned that the `FXMLLoader` creates and initializes an instance of an application's controller class, initializes the controller's instance variables that are declared with the `@FXML` annotation, and creates and registers event handlers for any events specified in the FXML.

In the next chapter, you'll use additional JavaFX controls and layouts and use CSS to style your GUI. You'll also learn more about JavaFX properties and how to use a technique called data binding to automatically update elements in a GUI with new data.

Summary

Section 25.1 Introduction
• A graphical user interface (GUI) presents a user-friendly mechanism for interacting with an app. A GUI (pronounced "GOO-ee") gives an app a distinctive "look-and-feel."
• GUIs are built from GUI components—sometimes called controls or widgets.
• Providing different apps with consistent, intuitive user-interface components gives users a sense of familiarity with a new app, so that they can learn it more quickly and use it more productively.
• Java's GUI, graphics and multimedia API of the future is JavaFX.

Section 25.2 JavaFX Scene Builder and the NetBeans IDE
• JavaFX Scene Builder is a standalone JavaFX GUI visual layout tool that can also be used with various IDEs.
• JavaFX Scene Builder enables you to create GUIs by dragging and dropping GUI components from Scene Builder's library onto a design area, then modifying and styling the GUI—all without writing any code.
• JavaFX Scene Builder generates FXML (FX Markup Language)—an XML vocabulary for defining and arranging JavaFX GUI controls without writing any Java code.

- The FXML code is separate from the program logic that's defined in Java source code—this separation of the interface (the GUI) from the implementation (the Java code) makes it easier to debug, modify and maintain JavaFX GUI apps.

Section 25.3 JavaFX App Window Structure

- The window in which a JavaFX app's GUI is displayed is known as the stage and is an instance of class Stage (package javafx.stage).
- The stage contains one scene that defines the GUI as a scene graph—a tree structure of an app's visual elements, such as GUI controls, shapes, images, video, text and more. The scene is an instance of class Scene (package javafx.scene).
- Each visual element in the scene graph is a node—an instance of a subclass of Node (package javafx.scene), which defines common attributes and behaviors for all nodes in the scene graph.
- The first node in the scene graph is known as the root node.
- Nodes that have children are typically layout containers that arrange their child nodes in the scene.
- The nodes arranged in a layout container are a combination of controls and possibly other layout containers.
- When the user interacts with a control, it generates an event. Programs can use event handling to specify what should happen when each user interaction occurs.
- An event handler is a method that responds to a user interaction. An FXML GUI's event handlers are defined in a controller class.

Section 25.4 Welcome App—Displaying Text and an Image

- To create an app in NetBeans, you must first create a project—a group of related files, such as code files and images that make up an app.
- The NetBeans **Projects** window provides access to all of your projects. Within a project's node, the contents are organized into folders and files.
- NetBeans creates three files for a JavaFX FXML Application project: an FXML markup file for the GUI, a file containing the app's main class and a file containing the app's controller class.
- To open a project's FXML file in JavaFX Scene Builder, right click the FXML file in the **Projects** window, then select **Open**.
- Layout containers help you arrange GUI components. A VBox arranges its nodes vertically from top to bottom.
- To make a layout container the root node in a scene graph, select the layout container, then select Scene Builder's **Edit > Trim Document to Selection** menu item.
- A VBox's alignment determines the layout positioning of its children.
- The preferred size (width and height) of the scene graph's root node is used by the scene to determine its window size when the app begins executing.
- You can set a Label's text either by double clicking it and typing the text, or by selecting the Label and setting its Text property in the **Inspector**'s **Properties** section.
- When adding controls to a VBox, each new control is placed below the preceding ones by default. You can change the order by dragging the children in **Scene Builder**'s **Hierarchy** window.
- To set the image to display, select the ImageView then set its **Image** property in the **Inspector**'s **Properties** section. An image's aspect ratio is the ratio of the image's width to its height.
- To specify an ImageView's size, set its **Fit Width** and **Fit Height** properties in the **Inspector**'s **Layout** section.

Section 25.5.2 Technologies Overview

- A JavaFX app's main class inherits from Application (package javafx.application.Application).

- The main class's main method calls class Application's static launch method to begin executing a JavaFX app. This method, in turn, causes the JavaFX runtime to create an object of the Application subclass and call its start method, which creates the GUI, attaches it to a Scene and places it on the Stage that method start recevies as an argument.

- A GridPane (package javafx.scene.layout) arranges JavaFX nodes into columns and rows in a rectangular grid.

- Each cell in a GridPane can be empty or can hold one or more JavaFX components, including layout containers that arrange other controls.

- Each component in a GridPane can span multiple columns or rows.

- A TextField (package javafx.scene.control) can accept text input or display text.

- A Slider (package javafx.scene.control) represents a value in the range 0.0–100.0 by default and allows the user to select a number in that range by moving the Slider's thumb.

- A Button (package javafx.scene.control) allows the user to initiate an action.

- Class NumberFormat (package java.text) can format locale-specific currency and percentage strings.

- GUIs are event driven. When the user interacts with a GUI component, the interaction—known as an event—drives the program to perform a task.

- The code that performs a task in response to an event is called an event handler.

- For certain events you can link a control to its event-handling method by using the **Code** section of Scene Builder's **Inspector** window. In this case, the class that implements the event-listener interface will be created for you and will call the method you specify.

- For events that occur when the value of a control's property changes, you must create the event handler entirely in code.

- You implement the ChangeListener interface (package javafx.beans.value) to respond to the user moving the Slider's thumb.

- JavaFX applications in which the GUI is implemented as FXML adhere to the Model-View-Controller (MVC) design pattern, which separates an app's data (contained in the model) from the app's GUI (the view) and the app's processing logic (the controller). The controller implements logic for processing user inputs. The view presents the data stored in the model. When a user provides input, the controller modifies the model with the given input. When the model changes, the controller updates the view to present the changed data. In a simple app, the model and controller are often combined into a single class.

- In a JavaFX FXML app, you define the app's event handlers in a controller class. The controller class defines instance variables for interacting with controls programmatically, as well as event-handling methods.

- Class FXMLLoader's static method load uses the FXML file that represents the app's GUI to creates the GUI's scene graph and returns a Parent (package javafx.scene) reference to the scene graph's root node. It also initializes the controller's instance variables, and creates and registers the event handlers for any events specified in the FXML.

Section 25.5.3 Building the App's GUI

- If a control or layout will be manipulated programmatically in the controller class, you must provide a name for that control or layout. Each object's name is specified via its **fx:id** property. You can set this property's value by selecting a component in your scene, then expanding the **Inspector** window's **Code** section—the **fx:id** property appears at the top.

- By default, the GridPane contains two columns and three rows. You can add a row above or below an existing row by right clicking a row and selecting **Grid Pane > Add Row Above** or **Grid Pane > Add Row Below**. You can delete a row or column by right clicking the tab containing its row or column number and selecting **Delete**.

- You can set a Button's text by double clicking it, or by selecting the Button, then setting its **Text** property in the **Inspector** window's **Properties** section.

- A GridPane column's contents are left-aligned by default. To change the alignment, select the column by clicking the tab at the top or bottom of the column, then in the **Inspector**'s **Layout** section, set the **Halignment** property.

- Setting a node's **Pref Width** property of a GridPane column to USE_COMPUTED_SIZE indicates that the width should be based on the widest child.

- To size a Button the same width as the other controls in a GridPane's column, select the Button, then in the **Inspector**'s **Layout** section, set the **Max Width** property to MAX_VALUE.

- As you design your GUI, you can preview it in Scene Builder by selecting **Preview > Show Preview in Window**.

- The space between a node's contents and its top, right, bottom and left edges is known as the padding, which separates the contents from the node's edges. To set the padding, select the node, then in the **Inspector**'s **Layout** section, set the **Padding** property's values.

- You can specify the default amount of space between a GridPane's columns and rows with its **Hgap** (horizontal gap) and **Vgap** (vertical gap) properties, respectively.

- You can type in a TextField only if it's "in focus"—that is, it's the control that the user is interacting with. When you click an interactive control, it receives the focus. Similarly, when you press the *Tab* key, the focus transfers from the current focusable control to the next one—this occurs in the order the controls were added to the GUI.

Section 25.5.4 TipCalculator Class

- To display a GUI, you must attach it to a Scene, then attach the Scene to the Stage that's passed into Application method start.

- By default, the Scene's size is determined by the size of the scene graph's root node. Overloaded versions of the Scene constructor allow you to specify the Scene's size and fill (a color, gradient or image), which appears in the c's background.

- Scene method setTitle specifies the text that appears in the Stage window's title bar.

- Stage method setScene places a Scene onto a Stage.

- Stage method show displays the Stage window.

Section 25.5.5 TipCalculatorController Class

- The RoundingMode enum of package java.math is used to specify how BigDecimal values are rounded during calculations or when formatting floating-point numbers as Strings.

- Class NumberFormat of package java.text provides numeric formatting capabilities, such as locale-specific currency and percentage formats.

- A Button's event handler receives an ActionEvent, which indicates that the Button was clicked. Many JavaFX controls support ActionEvents.

- Package javafx.scene.control contains many JavaFX control classes.

- The @FXML annotation preceding an instance variable indicates that the variable's name can be used in the FXML file that describes the app's GUI. The variable names that you specify in the controller class must precisely match the **fx:id** values you specified when building the GUI.

- When the FXMLLoader loads an FXML file to create a GUI, it also initializes each of the controller's instance variables that are declared with @FXML to ensure that they refer to the corresponding GUI components in the FXML file.
- The @FXML annotation preceding a method indicates that the method can be used to specify a control's event handler in the FXML file that describes the app's GUI.
- When the FXMLLoader creates an object of a controller class, it determines whether the class contains an initialize method with no parameters and, if so, calls that method to initialize the controller. This method can be used to configure the controller before the GUI is displayed.
- An anonymous inner class is a class that's declared without a name and typically appears inside a method declaration.
- Since an anonymous inner class has no name, one object of the class must be created at the point where the class is declared.
- An anonymous inner class can access its top-level class's instance variables, static variables and methods, but has limited access to the local variables of the method in which it's declared—it can access only the final local variables declared in the enclosing method's body. (As of Java SE 8, an anonymous inner class may also access a class's effectively final local variables.)

Self-Review Exercises

25.1 Fill in the blanks in each of the following statements:
a) A(n) _____ can display text and accept text input from the user.
b) Use a(n) _____ to arrange GUI components into cells in a rectangular grid.
c) JavaFX Scene Builder's _____ window shows the structure of the GUI and allows you to select and reorganize controls.
d) You implement interface _____ to respond to events when the user moves a Slider's thumb.
e) A(n) _____ represents the app's window.
f) The method _____ is called by the FXMLLoader before the GUI is displayed.
g) The contents of a scene are placed in its _____.
h) The elements in the scene graph are called _____.
i) _____ allows you to build JavaFX GUIs using drag-and-drop techniques.
j) A(n) _____ file contains the description of a JavaFX GUI.

25.2 State whether each of the following is *true* or *false*. If *false*, explain why.
a) You must create JavaFX GUIs by hand coding them in Java.
b) The layout VBox arranges components vertically in a scene.
c) To right align controls in a GridPane column, set its **Alignment** property to RIGHT.
d) The FXMLLoader initializes the controller's @FXML instance variables.
e) You override class Application's launch method to display a JavaFX app's stage.
f) The control that the user is interacting with "has the focus."
g) By default, a Slider allows you to select values from 0 to 255.
h) A node can span multiple columns in a GridPane.
i) Every Application subclass must override the start method.

Answers to Self-Review Exercises

25.1 a) TextField. b) GridPane. c) **Hierarchy**. d) ChangeListener<Number>. e) Stage. f) initialize. g) scene graph. h) nodes. i) JavaFX Scene Builder. j) FXML.

25.2 a) False. You can use JavaFX Scene Builder to create JavaFX GUIs without writing any code. b) True. c) False. The name of the property is **Halignment**. d) True. e) False. You override class

Application's start method to display a JavaFX app's stage. f) True. g) False. By default a Slider allows you to select values from 0.0 to 100.0. h) True. i) True.

Exercises

25.3   *(Scrapbooking App)* Find four images of famous landmarks using websites such as Flickr. Create an app similar to the **Welcome** app in which you arrange the images in a collage. Add text that identifies each landmark. You can use images that are part of your project or you can specify the URL of an image that's online.

25.4   *(Enhanced Tip Calculator App)* Modify the **Tip Calculator** app to allow the user to enter the number of people in the party. Calculate and display the amount owed by each person if the bill were to be split evenly among the party members.

25.5   *(Mortgage Calculator App)* Create a mortgage calculator app that allows the user to enter a purchase price, down-payment amount and an interest rate. Based on these values, the app should calculate the loan amount (purchase price minus down payment) and display the monthly payment for 10-, 20- and 30-year loans. Allow the user to select a custom loan duration (in years) by using a Slider and display the monthly payment for that custom loan duration.

25.6   *(College Loan Payoff Calculator App)* A bank offers college loans that can be repaid in 5, 10, 15, 20, 25 or 30 years. Write an app that allows the user to enter the amount of the loan and the annual interest rate. Based on these values, the app should display the loan lengths in years and their corresponding monthly payments.

25.7   *(Car Payment Calculator App)* Typically, banks offer car loans for periods ranging from two to five years (24 to 60 months). Borrowers repay the loans in monthly installments. The amount of each monthly payment is based on the length of the loan, the amount borrowed and the interest rate. Create an app that allows the customer to enter the price of a car, the down-payment amount and the loan's annual interest rate. The app should display the loan's duration in months and the monthly payments for two-, three-, four- and five-year loans. The variety of options allows the user to easily compare repayment plans and choose the most appropriate.

25.8   *(Miles-Per-Gallon Calculator App)* Drivers often want to know the miles per gallon their cars get so they can estimate gasoline costs. Develop an app that allows the user to input the number of miles driven and the number of gallons used and calculates and displays the corresponding miles per gallon.

Making a Difference

25.9   *(Body Mass Index Calculator App)* The formulas for calculating the BMI are

$$BMI = \frac{weightInPounds \times 703}{heightInInches \times heightInInches}$$

or

$$BMI = \frac{weightInKilograms}{heightInMeters \times heightInMeters}$$

Create a BMI calculator app that allows users to enter their weight and height and whether they are entering these values in English or metric units, then calculates and displays the user's body mass index. The app should also display the following information from the Department of Health and Human Services/National Institutes of Health so that users can evaluate their BMIs:

```
BMI VALUES
Underweight: less than 18.5
Normal:      between 18.5 and 24.9
Overweight:  between 25 and 29.9
Obese:       30 or greater
```

25.10 *(Target-Heart-Rate Calculator App)* While exercising, you can use a heart-rate monitor to see that your heart rate stays within a safe range suggested by your trainers and doctors. According to the American Heart Association (AHA), the formula for calculating your *maximum heart rate* in beats per minute is *220 minus your age in years* (`http://bit.ly/AHATargetHeartRates`). Your *target heart rate* is a range that is 50–85% of your maximum heart rate. [*Note:* These formulas are estimates provided by the AHA. Maximum and target heart rates may vary based on the health, fitness and gender of the individual. Always consult a physician or qualified health care professional before beginning or modifying an exercise program.] Write an app that inputs the person's age, then calculates and displays the person's maximum heart rate and target-heart-rate range.

Chapters on the Web

The following chapters are available at *Java How to Program, 10/e, Late Objects Version*'s Companion Website (www.pearsonhighered.com/deitel) as PDF documents:

- Chapter 26, JavaFX GUI: Part 2
- Chapter 27, JavaFX Graphics and Multimedia
- Chapter 28, Networking
- Chapter 29, Java Persistence API (JPA)
- Chapter 30, JavaServer™ Faces Web Apps: Part 1
- Chapter 31, JavaServer™ Faces Web Apps: Part 2
- Chapter 32, REST-Based Web Services
- Chapter 33, (Optional) ATM Case Study, Part 1: Object-Oriented Design with the UML
- Chapter 34, (Optional) ATM Case Study, Part 2: Implementing an Object-Oriented Design

These files can be viewed in Adobe® Reader® (get.adobe.com/reader).

Operator Precedence Chart

Operators are shown in decreasing order of precedence from top to bottom (Fig. A.1).

Operator	Description	Associativity
++ --	unary postfix increment unary postfix decrement	right to left
++ -- + - ! ~ (*type*)	unary prefix increment unary prefix decrement unary plus unary minus unary logical negation unary bitwise complement unary cast	right to left
* / %	multiplication division remainder	left to right
+ -	addition or string concatenation subtraction	left to right
<< >> >>>	left shift signed right shift unsigned right shift	left to right
< <= > >= instanceof	less than less than or equal to greater than greater than or equal to type comparison	left to right
== !=	is equal to is not equal to	left to right
&	bitwise AND boolean logical AND	left to right
^	bitwise exclusive OR boolean logical exclusive OR	left to right

Fig. A.1 | Operator precedence chart. (Part 1 of 2.)

Operator	Description	Associativity
|	bitwise inclusive OR boolean logical inclusive OR	left to right
&&	conditional AND	left to right
||	conditional OR	left to right
? :	conditional	right to left
= += -= *= /= %= &= ^= |= <<= >>= >>>=	assignment addition assignment subtraction assignment multiplication assignment division assignment remainder assignment bitwise AND assignment bitwise exclusive OR assignment bitwise inclusive OR assignment bitwise left-shift assignment bitwise signed-right-shift assignment bitwise unsigned-right-shift assignment	right to left

Fig. A.1 | Operator precedence chart. (Part 2 of 2.)

B

ASCII Character Set

	0	1	2	3	4	5	6	7	8	9
0	nul	soh	stx	etx	eot	enq	ack	bel	bs	ht
1	nl	vt	ff	cr	so	si	dle	dc1	dc2	dc3
2	dc4	nak	syn	etb	can	em	sub	esc	fs	gs
3	rs	us	sp	!	"	#	$	%	&	'
4	(	)	*	+	,	-	.	/	0	1
5	2	3	4	5	6	7	8	9	:	;
6	<	=	>	?	@	A	B	C	D	E
7	F	G	H	I	J	K	L	M	N	O
8	P	Q	R	S	T	U	V	W	X	Y
9	Z	[	\	]	^	_	'	a	b	c
10	d	e	f	g	h	i	j	k	l	m
11	n	o	p	q	r	s	t	u	v	w
12	x	y	z	{			}	~	del		

Fig. B.1 | ASCII character set.

The digits at the left of the table are the left digits of the decimal equivalents (0–127) of the character codes, and the digits at the top of the table are the right digits of the character codes. For example, the character code for "F" is 70, and the character code for "&" is 38.

Most users of this book are interested in the ASCII character set used to represent English characters on many computers. The ASCII character set is a subset of the Unicode character set used by Java to represent characters from most of the world's languages. For more information on the Unicode character set, see the web bonus Appendix H.

Keywords and Reserved Words

Java Keywords				
abstract	assert	boolean	break	byte
case	catch	char	class	continue
default	do	double	else	enum
extends	final	finally	float	for
if	implements	import	instanceof	int
interface	long	native	new	package
private	protected	public	return	short
static	strictfp	super	switch	synchronized
this	throw	throws	transient	try
void	volatile	while		
Keywords that are not currently used				
const	goto			

Fig. C.1 | Java keywords.

Java also contains the reserved words true and false, which are boolean literals, and null, which is the literal that represents a reference to nothing. Like keywords, these reserved words cannot be used as identifiers.

Primitive Types

Type	Size in bits	Values	Standard
boolean		true or false	
[*Note:* A boolean's representation is specific to the Java Virtual Machine on each platform.]			
char	16	'\u0000' to '\uFFFF' (0 to 65535)	(ISO Unicode character set)
byte	8	-128 to $+127$ (-2^7 to $2^7 - 1$)	
short	16	$-32,768$ to $+32,767$ (-2^{15} to $2^{15} - 1$)	
int	32	$-2,147,483,648$ to $+2,147,483,647$ (-2^{31} to $2^{31} - 1$)	
long	64	$-9,223,372,036,854,775,808$ to $+9,223,372,036,854,775,807$ (-2^{63} to $2^{63} - 1$)	
float	32	*Negative range:* $-3.4028234663852886E+38$ to $-1.40129846432481707e-45$ *Positive range:* $1.40129846432481707e-45$ to $3.4028234663852886E+38$	(IEEE 754 floating point)
double	64	*Negative range:* $-1.7976931348623157E+308$ to $-4.94065645841246544e-324$ *Positive range:* $4.94065645841246544e-324$ to $1.7976931348623157E+308$	(IEEE 754 floating point)

Fig. D.1 | Java primitive types.

You can use underscores to make numeric literal values more readable. For example, 1_000_000 is equivalent to 1000000.

For more information on IEEE 754 visit http://grouper.ieee.org/groups/754/. For more information on Unicode, see Appendix H.

E

Using the Debugger

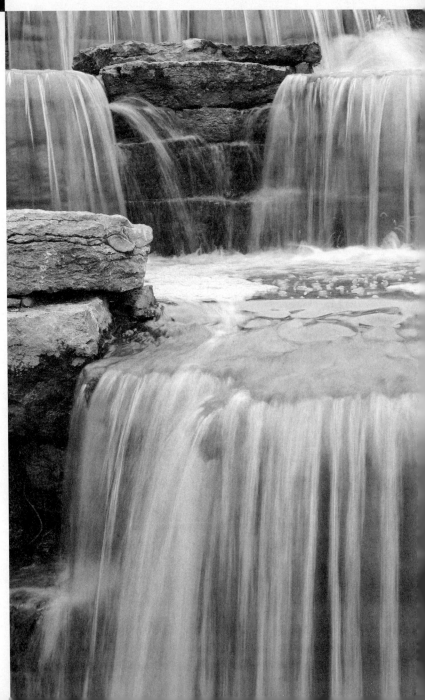

And so shall I catch the fly.
—William Shakespeare

*We are built to make mistakes,
coded for error.*
—Lewis Thomas

*What we anticipate seldom
occurs; what we least expect
generally happens.*
—Benjamin Disraeli

Objectives

In this appendix you'll learn:

- To set breakpoints to debug applications.

- To use the **run** command to run an application through the debugger.

- To use the **stop** command to set a breakpoint.

- To use the **cont** command to continue execution.

- To use the **print** command to evaluate expressions.

- To use the **set** command to change variable values during program execution.

- To use the **step**, **step up** and **next** commands to control execution.

- To use the **watch** command to see how a field is modified during program execution.

- To use the **clear** command to list breakpoints or remove a breakpoint.

E.1 Introduction

In Chapter 2, you learned that there are two types of errors—syntax errors and logic errors—and you learned how to eliminate syntax errors from your code. Logic errors do not prevent the application from compiling successfully, but they do cause an application to produce erroneous results when it runs. The JDK includes software called a **debugger** that allows you to monitor the execution of your applications so you can locate and remove logic errors. The debugger will be one of your most important application development tools. Many IDEs provide their own debuggers similar to the one included in the JDK or provide a graphical user interface to the JDK's debugger.

This appendix demonstrates key features of the JDK's debugger using command-line applications that receive no input from the user. The same debugger features discussed here can be used to debug applications that take user input, but debugging such applications requires a slightly more complex setup. To focus on the debugger features, we've opted to demonstrate the debugger with simple command-line applications involving no user input. For more information on the Java debugger visit http://docs.oracle.com/javase/7/docs/technotes/tools/windows/jdb.html.

E.2 Breakpoints and the run, stop, cont and print Commands

We begin our study of the debugger by investigating **breakpoints**, which are markers that can be set at any executable line of code. When application execution reaches a breakpoint, execution pauses, allowing you to examine the values of variables to help determine whether logic errors exist. For example, you can examine the value of a variable that stores the result of a calculation to determine whether the calculation was performed correctly. Setting a breakpoint at a line of code that is not executable (such as a comment) causes the debugger to display an error message.

To illustrate the features of the debugger, we use application AccountTest (Fig. E.1), which creates and manipulates an object of class Account (Fig. 7.8). Execution of AccountTest begins in main (lines 7–24). Line 9 creates an Account object with an initial balance of $50.00. Recall that Account's constructor accepts one argument, which specifies the Account's initial balance. Lines 12–13 output the initial account balance using Account method getBalance. Line 15 declares and initializes a local variable depositAmount. Lines 17–19 then print depositAmount and add it to the Account's balance using its credit method. Finally, lines 22–23 display the new balance. [*Note:* The Appendix E examples directory contains a copy of Account.java identical to the one in Fig. 7.8.]

```java
1   // Fig. E.1: AccountTest.java
2   // Create and manipulate an Account object.
3
4   public class AccountTest
5   {
6      // main method begins execution
7      public static void main(String[] args)
8      {
9         Account account = new Account("Jane Green", 50.00);
10
11         // display initial balance of Account object
12         System.out.printf("initial account balance: $%.2f%n",
13            account.getBalance());
14
15         double depositAmount = 25.0; // deposit amount
16
17         System.out.printf("%nadding %.2f to account balance%n%n",
18            depositAmount);
19         account.deposit(depositAmount); // add to account balance
20
21         // display new balance
22         System.out.printf("new account balance: $%.2f%n",
23            account.getBalance());
24      }
25   } // end class AccountTest
```

```
initial account balance: $50.00

adding 25.00 to account balance

new account balance: $75.00
```

Fig. E.1 | Create and manipulate an Account object.

In the following steps, you'll use breakpoints and various debugger commands to examine the value of the variable depositAmount declared in AccountTest (Fig. E.1).

1. *Opening the* Command Prompt *window and changing directories.* Open the Command Prompt window by selecting Start > Programs > Accessories > Command Prompt. Change to the directory containing the Appendix E examples by typing cd C:\examples\debugger [*Note:* If your examples are in a different directory, use that directory here.]

2. *Compiling the application for debugging.* The Java debugger works only with .class files that were compiled with the **-g** compiler option, which generates information that is used by the debugger to help you debug your applications. Compile the application with the -g command-line option by typing javac -g AccountTest.java Account.java. This command compiles both Account-

Test.java and Account.java. The command java -g *.java compiles all of the working directory's .java files for debugging.

3. **Starting the debugger.** In the **Command Prompt**, type **jdb** (Fig. E.2). This command will start the Java debugger and enable you to use its features. [*Note:* We modified the colors of our **Command Prompt** window for readability.]

```
C:\examples\debugger>javac -g AccountTest.java Account.java

C:\examples\debugger>jdb
Initializing jdb ...
>
```

Fig. E.2 | Starting the Java debugger.

4. **Running an application in the debugger.** Run the AccountTest application through the debugger by typing **run** AccountTest (Fig. E.3). If you do not set any breakpoints before running your application in the debugger, the application will run just as it would using the java command.

```
C:\examples\debugger>jdb
Initializing jdb ...
> run AccountTest
run  AccountTest
Set uncaught java.lang.Throwable
Set deferred uncaught java.lang.Throwable
>
VM Started: initial account balance: $50.00

adding 25.00 to account balance

new account balance: $75.00

The application exited
```

Fig. E.3 | Running the AccountTest application through the debugger.

5. **Restarting the debugger.** To make proper use of the debugger, you must set at least one breakpoint before running the application. Restart the debugger by typing jdb.

6. **Inserting breakpoints in Java.** You set a breakpoint at a specific line of code in your application. The line numbers used in these steps are from the source code in Fig. E.1. Set a breakpoint at line 12 in the source code by typing stop at AccountTest:12 (Fig. E.4). The **stop command** inserts a breakpoint at the line number specified after the command. You can set as many breakpoints as necessary. Set another breakpoint at line 19 by typing stop at AccountTest:19 (Fig. E.4). When the application runs, it suspends execution at any line that contains a break-

point. The application is said to be in **break mode** when the debugger pauses the application's execution. Breakpoints can be set even after the debugging process has begun. The debugger command `stop in`, followed by a class name, a period and a method name (e.g., `stop in Account.credit`) instructs the debugger to set a breakpoint at the first executable statement in the specified method. The debugger pauses execution when program control enters the method.

```
C:\examples\debugger>jdb
Initializing jdb ...
> stop at AccountTest:12
Deferring breakpoint AccountTest:12.
It will be set after the class is loaded.
> stop at AccountTest:19
Deferring breakpoint AccountTest:19.
It will be set after the class is loaded.
>
```

Fig. E.4 | Setting breakpoints at lines 12 and 19.

7. *Running the application and beginning the debugging process.* Type `run AccountTest` to execute the application and begin the debugging process (Fig. E.5). The debugger prints text indicating that breakpoints were set at lines 12 and 19. It calls each breakpoint a "deferred breakpoint" because each was set before the application began running in the debugger. The application pauses when execution reaches the breakpoint on line 12. At this point, the debugger notifies you that a breakpoint has been reached and it displays the source code at that line (12). That line of code is the next statement that will execute.

```
It will be set after the class is loaded.
>run AccountTest
run  AccountTest
Set uncaught java.lang.Throwable
Set deferred uncaught java.lang.Throwable
>
VM Started: Set deferred breakpoint AccountTest:19
Set deferred breakpoint AccountTest:12

Breakpoint hit: "thread=main", AccountTest.main(), line=12 bci=13
12            System.out.printf("initial account balance: $%.2f%n",

main[1]
```

Fig. E.5 | Restarting the AccountTest application.

8. *Using the cont command to resume execution.* Type `cont`. The **cont command** causes the application to continue running until the next breakpoint is reached (line 19), at which point the debugger notifies you (Fig. E.6). AccountTest's normal output appears between messages from the debugger.

```
main[1] cont
> initial account balance: $50.00

adding 25.00 to account balance

Breakpoint hit: "thread=main", AccountTest.main(), line=19 bci=60
19              account.deposit(depositAmount); // add to account balance

main[1]
```

Fig. E.6 | Execution reaches the second breakpoint.

9. *Examining a variable's value.* Type print depositAmount to display the current value stored in the depositAmount variable (Fig. E.7). The **print command** allows you to peek inside the computer at the value of one of your variables. This command will help you find and eliminate logic errors in your code. The value displayed is 25.0—the value assigned to depositAmount in line 15 of Fig. E.1.

```
main[1] print depositAmount
 depositAmount = 25.0
main[1]
```

Fig. E.7 | Examining the value of variable depositAmount.

10. *Continuing application execution.* Type cont to continue the application's execution. There are no more breakpoints, so the application is no longer in break mode. The application continues executing and eventually terminates (Fig. E.8). The debugger will stop when the application ends.

```
main[1] cont
> new account balance: $75.00

The application exited
```

Fig. E.8 | Continuing application execution and exiting the debugger.

E.3 The print and set Commands

In the preceding section, you learned how to use the debugger's print command to examine the value of a variable during program execution. In this section, you'll learn how to use the print command to examine the value of more complex expressions. You'll also learn the **set command**, which allows the programmer to assign new values to variables.

For this section, we assume that you've followed *Step 1* and *Step 2* in Section E.2 to open the **Command Prompt** window, change to the directory containing the Appendix E examples (e.g., C:\examples\debugger) and compile the AccountTest application (and class Account) for debugging.

1. *Starting debugging.* In the **Command Prompt**, type jdb to start the Java debugger.

2. *Inserting a breakpoint.* Set a breakpoint at line 19 in the source code by typing stop at AccountTest:19.

3. *Running the application and reaching a breakpoint.* Type run AccountTest to begin the debugging process (Fig. E.9). This will cause AccountTest's main to execute until the breakpoint at line 19 is reached. This suspends application execution and switches the application into break mode. At this point, the statements in lines 9–13 created an Account object and printed the initial balance of the Account obtained by calling its getBalance method. The statement in line 15 (Fig. E.1) declared and initialized local variable depositAmount to 25.0. The statement in line 19 is the next statement that will execute.

```
C:\examples\debugger>jdb
Initializing jdb ...
> stop at AccountTest:19
Deferring breakpoint AccountTest:19.
It will be set after the class is loaded.
> run AccountTest
run  AccountTest
Set uncaught java.lang.Throwable
Set deferred uncaught java.lang.Throwable
>
VM Started: Set deferred breakpoint AccountTest:19
initial account balance: $50.00

adding 25.00 to account balance

Breakpoint hit: "thread=main", AccountTest.main(), line=19 bci=60
19              account.deposit(depositAmount); // add to account balance

main[1]
```

Fig. E.9 | Application execution suspended when debugger reaches the breakpoint at line 19.

4. *Evaluating arithmetic and boolean expressions.* Recall from Section E.2 that once the application has entered break mode, you can explore the values of the application's variables using the debugger's print command. You can also use the print command to evaluate arithmetic and boolean expressions. In the **Command Prompt** window, type print depositAmount - 2.0. The print command returns the value 23.0 (Fig. E.10). However, this command does not actually change the value of depositAmount. In the **Command Prompt** window, type print depositAmount == 23.0. Expressions containing the == symbol are treated as boolean expressions. The value returned is false (Fig. E.10) because depositAmount does not currently contain the value 23.0—depositAmount is still 25.0.

```
main[1] print depositAmount - 2.0
 depositAmount - 2.0 = 23.0
main[1] print depositAmount == 23.0
 depositAmount == 23.0 = false
main[1]
```

Fig. E.10 | Examining the values of an arithmetic and boolean expression.

5. *Modifying values.* The debugger allows you to change the values of variables during the application's execution. This can be valuable for experimenting with different values and for locating logic errors in applications. You can use the debugger's set command to change the value of a variable. Type set deposit-Amount = 75.0. The debugger changes the value of depositAmount and displays its new value (Fig. E.11).

```
main[1] set depositAmount = 75.0
 depositAmount = 75.0 = 75.0
main[1]
```

Fig. E.11 | Modifying values.

6. *Viewing the application result.* Type cont to continue application execution. Line 19 of AccountTest (Fig. E.1) executes, passing depositAmount to Account method credit. Method main then displays the new balance. The result is $125.00 (Fig. E.12). This shows that the preceding step changed the value of depositAmount from its initial value (25.0) to 75.0.

```
main[1] cont
> new account balance: $125.00

The application exited

C:\examples\debugger>
```

Fig. E.12 | Output showing new account balance based on altered value of depositAmount.

E.4 Controlling Execution Using the step, step up and next Commands

Sometimes you'll need to execute an application line by line to find and fix errors. Walking through a portion of your application this way can help you verify that a method's code executes correctly. In this section, you'll learn how to use the debugger for this task. The commands you learn in this section allow you to execute a method line by line, execute all the statements of a method at once or execute only the remaining statements of a method (if you've already executed some statements within the method).

Once again, we assume you're working in the directory containing the Appendix E examples and have compiled for debugging with the -g compiler option.

1. *Starting the debugger.* Start the debugger by typing jdb.

2. *Setting a breakpoint.* Type stop at AccountTest:19 to set a breakpoint at line 19.

3. *Running the application.* Run the application by typing run AccountTest. After the application displays its two output messages, the debugger indicates that the breakpoint has been reached and displays the code at line 19. The debugger and application then pause and wait for the next command to be entered.

4. *Using the* **step** *command.* The **step** command executes the next statement in the application. If the next statement to execute is a method call, control transfers to the called method. The step command enables you to enter a method and study the individual statements of that method. For instance, you can use the print and set commands to view and modify the variables within the method. You'll now use the step command to enter the credit method of class Account (Fig. 7.8) by typing step (Fig. E.13). The debugger indicates that the step has been completed and displays the next executable statement—in this case, line 21 of class Account (Fig. 7.8).

```
main[1] step
>
Step completed: "thread=main", Account.deposit(), line=24 bci=0
24              if (depositAmount > 0.0) // if the depositAmount is valid

main[1]
```

Fig. E.13 | Stepping into the credit method.

5. *Using the* **step up** *command.* After you've stepped into the credit method, type **step up**. This command executes the remaining statements in the method and returns control to the place where the method was called. The credit method contains only one statement to add the method's parameter amount to instance variable balance. The step up command executes this statement, then pauses before line 22 in AccountTest. Thus, the next action to occur will be to print the new account balance (Fig. E.14). In lengthy methods, you may want to look at a few key lines of code, then continue debugging the caller's code. The step up command is useful for situations in which you do not want to continue stepping through the entire method line by line.

```
main[1] step up
>
Step completed: "thread=main", AccountTest.main(), line=22 bci=65
22              System.out.printf("new account balance: $%.2f%n",

main[1]
```

Fig. E.14 | Stepping out of a method.

6. *Using the cont command to continue execution.* Enter the cont command (Fig. E.15) to continue execution. The statement at lines 22–23 executes, displaying the new balance, then the application and the debugger terminate.

```
main[1] cont
> new account balance: $75.00

The application exited

C:\examples\debugger>
```

Fig. E.15 | Continuing execution of the AccountTest application.

7. *Restarting the debugger.* Restart the debugger by typing jdb.

8. *Setting a breakpoint.* Breakpoints persist only until the end of the debugging session in which they're set—once the debugger exits, all breakpoints are removed. (In Section E.6, you'll learn how to manually clear a breakpoint before the end of the debugging session.) Thus, the breakpoint set for line 19 in *Step 2* no longer exists upon restarting the debugger in *Step 7*. To reset the breakpoint at line 19, once again type stop at AccountTest:19.

9. *Running the application.* Type run AccountTest to run the application. As in *Step 3*, AccountTest runs until the breakpoint at line 19 is reached, then the debugger pauses and waits for the next command.

10. *Using the next command.* Type **next**. This command behaves like the step command, except when the next statement to execute contains a method call. In that case, the called method executes in its entirety and the application advances to the next executable line after the method call (Fig. E.16). Recall from *Step 4* that the step command would enter the called method. In this example, the next command causes Account method credit to execute, then the debugger pauses at line 22 in AccountTest.

```
main[1] next
>
Step completed: "thread=main", AccountTest.main(), line=22 bci=65
22          System.out.printf("new account balance: $%.2f%n",

main[1]
```

Fig. E.16 | Stepping over a method call.

11. *Using the exit command.* Use the **exit command** to end the debugging session (Fig. E.17). This command causes the AccountTest application to immediately terminate rather than execute the remaining statements in main. When debugging some types of applications (e.g., GUI applications), the application continues to execute even after the debugging session ends.

```
main[1] exit

C:\examples\debugger>
```

Fig. E.17 | Exiting the debugger.

E.5 The watch Command

In this section, we present the **watch command**, which tells the debugger to watch a field. When that field is about to change, the debugger will notify you. In this section, you'll learn how to use the watch command to see how the Account object's field balance is modified during the execution of the AccountTest application.

As in the preceding two sections, we assume that you've followed *Step 1* and *Step 2* in Section E.2 to open the **Command Prompt**, change to the correct examples directory and compile classes AccountTest and Account for debugging (i.e., with the -g compiler option).

1. *Starting the debugger.* Start the debugger by typing jdb.

2. *Watching a class's field.* Set a watch on Account's balance field by typing watch Account.balance (Fig. E.18). You can set a watch on any field during execution of the debugger. Whenever the value in a field is about to change, the debugger enters break mode and notifies you that the value will change. Watches can be placed only on fields, not on local variables.

```
C:\examples\debugger>jdb
Initializing jdb ...
> watch Account.balance
Deferring watch modification of Account.balance.
It will be set after the class is loaded.
>
```

Fig. E.18 | Setting a watch on Account's balance field.

3. *Running the application.* Run the application with the command run Account-Test. The debugger will now notify you that field balance's value will change (Fig. E.19). When the application begins, an instance of Account is created with an initial balance of $50.00 and a reference to the Account object is assigned to the local variable account (line 9, Fig. E.1). Recall from Fig. 7.8 that when the constructor for this object runs, if parameter initialBalance is greater than 0.0, instance variable balance is assigned the value of parameter initialBalance. The debugger notifies you that the value of balance will be set to 50.0.

4. *Adding money to the account.* Type cont to continue executing the application. The application executes normally before reaching the code on line 19 of Fig. E.1 that calls Account method credit to raise the Account object's balance by a specified amount. The debugger notifies you that instance variable balance will change (Fig. E.20). Although line 19 of class AccountTest calls method deposit, line 25 in Account's method deposit actually changes the value of balance.

```
> run AccountTest
run  AccountTest
Set uncaught java.lang.Throwable
Set deferred uncaught java.lang.Throwable
>
VM Started: Set deferred watch modification of Account.balance

Field (Account.balance) is 0.0, will be 50.0: "thread=main", Acount.<init>(),
line=18 bci=17
18               this.balance = balance; // assign to instance variable balance

main[1]
```

Fig. E.19 | AccountTest application stops when account is created and its balance field will be modified.

```
main[1] cont
> initial account balance: $50.00

adding 25.00 to account balance
Field (Account.balance) is 50.0, will be 75.0: "thread=main",
Account.deposit(), line=25 bci=13

25               balance = balance + depositAmount; // add it to the balance

main[1]
```

Fig. E.20 | Changing the value of balance by calling Account method credit.

5. *Continuing execution.* Type cont—the application will finish executing because the application does not attempt any additional changes to balance (Fig. E.21).

```
main[1] cont
> new account balance: $75.00

The application exited

C:\examples\debugger>
```

Fig. E.21 | Continuing execution of AccountTest.

6. *Restarting the debugger and resetting the watch on the variable.* Type jdb to restart the debugger. Once again, set a watch on the Account instance variable balance by typing the watch Account.balance, then type run AccountTest to run the application.

7. *Removing the watch on the field.* Suppose you want to watch a field for only part of a program's execution. You can remove the debugger's watch on variable balance by typing **unwatch** Account.balance (Fig. E.22). Type cont—the application will finish executing without reentering break mode.

```
main[1] unwatch Account.balance
Removed: watch modification of Account.balance
main[1] cont
> initial account balance: $50.00

adding 25.00 to account balance

new account balance: $75.00

The application exited

C:\examples\debugger>
```

Fig. E.22 | Removing the watch on variable `balance`.

E.6 The `clear` Command

In the preceding section, you learned to use the `unwatch` command to remove a watch on a field. The debugger also provides the `clear` command to remove a breakpoint from an application. You'll often need to debug applications containing repetitive actions, such as a loop. You may want to examine the values of variables during several, but possibly not all, of the loop's iterations. If you set a breakpoint in the body of a loop, the debugger will pause before each execution of the line containing a breakpoint. After determining that the loop is working properly, you may want to remove the breakpoint and allow the remaining iterations to proceed normally. In this section, we use the compound interest application in Fig. 4.6 to demonstrate how the debugger behaves when you set a breakpoint in the body of a `for` statement and how to remove a breakpoint in the middle of a debugging session.

1. *Opening the* Command Prompt *window, changing directories and compiling the application for debugging.* Open the Command Prompt window, then change to the directory containing the Appendix E examples. For your convenience, we've provided a copy of the `Interest.java` file in this directory. Compile the application for debugging by typing `javac -g Interest.java`.

2. *Starting the debugger and setting breakpoints.* Start the debugger by typing `jdb`. Set breakpoints at lines 13 and 22 of class `Interest` by typing `stop at Interest:13`, then `stop at Interest:22`.

3. *Running the application.* Run the application by typing `run Interest`. The application executes until reaching the breakpoint at line 13 (Fig. E.23).

4. *Continuing execution.* Type `cont` to continue—the application executes line 13, printing the column headings `"Year"` and `"Amount on deposit"`. Line 13 appears before the `for` statement at lines 16–23 in `Interest` (Fig. 4.6) and thus executes only once. Execution continues past line 13 until the breakpoint at line 22 is reached during the first iteration of the `for` statement (Fig. E.24).

5. *Examining variable values.* Type `print year` to examine the current value of variable `year` (i.e., the `for`'s control variable). Print the value of variable `amount` too (Fig. E.25).

```
It will be set after the class is loaded.
> run Interest
run  Interest
Set uncaught java.lang.Throwable
Set deferred uncaught java.lang.Throwable
>
VM Started: Set deferred breakpoint Interest:22
Set deferred breakpoint Interest:13

Breakpoint hit: "thread=main", Interest.main(), line=13 bci=9
13              System.out.printf("%s%20s%n", "Year", "Amount on deposit");

main[1]
```

Fig. E.23 | Reaching the breakpoint at line 13 in the Interest application.

```
main[1] cont
> Year    Amount on deposit
Breakpoint hit: "thread=main", Interest.main(), line=22 bci=55
22              System.out.printf("%4d%,20.2f%n", year, amount);

main[1]
```

Fig. E.24 | Reaching the breakpoint at line 22 in the Interest application.

```
main[1] print year
 year = 1
main[1] print amount
 amount = 1050.0
main[1]
```

Fig. E.25 | Printing year and amount during the first iteration of Interest's for.

6. *Continuing execution.* Type cont to continue execution. Line 22 executes and prints the current values of year and amount. After the for enters its second iteration, the debugger notifies you that the breakpoint at line 22 has been reached a second time. The debugger pauses each time a line where a breakpoint has been set is about to execute—when the breakpoint appears in a loop, the debugger pauses during each iteration. Print the values of variables year and amount again to see how the values have changed since the first iteration of the for (Fig. E.26).

```
main[1] cont
>    1              1,050.00
Breakpoint hit: "thread=main", Interest.main(), line=22 bci=55
22              System.out.printf("%4d%,20.2f%n", year, amount);

main[1] print amount
 amount = 1102.5
main[1] print year
 year = 2
main[1]
```

Fig. E.26 | Printing year and amount during the second iteration of Interest's for.

7. *Removing a breakpoint.* You can display a list of all of the breakpoints in the application by typing **clear** (Fig. E.27). Suppose you're satisfied that the Interest application's for statement is working properly, so you want to remove the breakpoint at line 22 and allow the remaining iterations of the loop to proceed normally. You can remove the breakpoint at line 22 by typing clear Interest:22. Now type clear to list the remaining breakpoints in the application. The debugger should indicate that only the breakpoint at line 13 remains (Fig. E.27). This breakpoint has already been reached and thus will no longer affect execution.

```
main[1] clear
Breakpoints set:
        breakpoint Interest:13
        breakpoint Interest:22
main[1] clear Interest:22
Removed: breakpoint Interest:22
main[1] clear
Breakpoints set:
        breakpoint Interest:13
main[1]
```

Fig. E.27 | Removing the breakpoint at line 22.

8. *Continuing execution after removing a breakpoint.* Type cont to continue execution. Recall that execution last paused before the printf statement in line 22. If the breakpoint at line 22 was removed successfully, continuing the application will produce the correct output for the current and remaining iterations of the for statement without the application halting (Fig. E.28).

```
main[1] cont
>     2              1,102.50
      3              1,157.63
      4              1,215.51
      5              1,276.28
      6              1,340.10
      7              1,407.10
      8              1,477.46
      9              1,551.33
     10              1,628.89

The application exited

C:\examples\debugger>
```

Fig. E.28 | Application executes without a breakpoint set at line 22.

E.7 Wrap-Up

In this appendix, you learned how to insert and remove breakpoints in the debugger. Breakpoints allow you to pause application execution so you can examine variable values with the debugger's `print` command. This capability will help you locate and fix logic errors in your applications. You saw how to use the `print` command to examine the value of an expression and how to use the `set` command to change the value of a variable. You also learned debugger commands (including the `step`, `step up` and `next` commands) that can be used to determine whether a method is executing correctly. You learned how to use the `watch` command to keep track of a field throughout the life of an application. Finally, you learned how to use the `clear` command to list all the breakpoints set for an application or remove individual breakpoints to continue execution without breakpoints.

Appendices on the Web

The following appendices are available at Java How to Program, 9/e's Companion Web-site (www.pearsonhighered.com/deitel) as PDF documents:

- Appendix F, Using the Java API Documentation
- Appendix G, Creating Documentation with javadoc
- Appendix H, Unicode®
- Appendix I, Formatted Output
- Appendix J, Number Systems
- Appendix K, Bit Manipulation
- Appendix L, Labeled break and continue Statements
- Appendix M, UML 2: Additional Diagram Types
- Appendix N, Design Patterns

These files can be viewed in Adobe® Reader® (get.adobe.com/reader).

Index

Additional Comments from Recent Editions Reviewers

"Fantastic textbook and reference. Provides great detail on the latest Java features including lambdas. The code examples make it easy to understand the concepts." —**Lance Andersen, Principal Member of the Technical Staff, Oracle Corporation**

"If you think a 10th edition is just going to be a repeat then you would not do this book justice. It has the breadth and depth to get a beginning Java programmer started, but at the same time it is a good companion for a more seasoned programmer who wants to get updated to the latest version of Java. Perfect introduction to strings. Good explanation of static vs. non-static methods and variables. Best introduction to Java 2D I've seen! The collections framework is well explained. Good introduction to the most essential data structures. A nice introduction to JavaFX."
—**Manfred Riem, Java Champion**

"Clearly describes the use cases for different parts of the Java APIs. The tips and observations are very useful. Clearly explains opportunities and pitfalls in Java. Rather than telling the reader what to do and not do, the rationale behind these opportunities and pitfalls is explained. The new features introduced in Java 8 are well mixed with older functionality." —**Johan Vos, LodgON and Java Champion**

"Really good, clear explanation of object-oriented programming fundamentals. Excellent polymorphism chapter. Covers all the essentials of strings. Good to see things like try-with-resources and DirectoryStream being used. Excellent generic collections chapter. Covering lambdas and streams in one chapter is a tough challenge; you've done pretty well. Concurrency chapter gives good coverage of numerous aspects. Good data structures chapter. Introduces JavaFX, the great new way to develop client applications in Java; I like the use of Scene Builder to create the GUI with drag-and-drop design rather than doing it by hand, which shows the way it should be done." —**Simon Ritter, Oracle Corporation**

"GUI examples are very good and the exercises are well thought out. Graphics examples are easy to follow; good and challenging exercises. Recursion is a well-written chapter; factorials, the Fibonacci series and the Tower of Hanoi are good examples. The JavaFX GUI chapter provides a solid introduction to using the JavaFX Scene Builder demonstrating how easy it is to create Java-based GUI applications."
—**Lance Andersen, Principal Member of the Technical Staff, Oracle Corporation**

"The Making a Difference exercises are well thought through. I like the DeckOfCards example [in the Introduction to Classes and Objects chapter]. The evolving inheritance example is a good approach to motivating inheritance. I like the employee [polymorphism] example. Very thorough and well explained GUI chapter; I liked the layout exercises. Thorough strings chapter; I like the clear definitions of regular expressions and the Pig Latin exercise. Good introduction to collections; Hashtable performance discussion was good. I like the summary of searching and sorting algorithms with Big O values. Solid treatment of threading." —**Dr. Danny Coward, Oracle Corporation**

"Nice breadth of coverage of traditional core Java and programming topics as well as newer areas such as lambda expressions and areas becoming more critical such as concurrent programming. A fine intro chapter. I like the [Intro to Classes] bank account example. [Arrays and ArrayLists] is a fine chapter. [Classes and Objects: A Deeper Look] provides a good examination of data type creation. Nice chapter on exception handling. Very nice coverage of files, streams and object serialization. Very nice chapter on generics. Nice overview of hand-managed node-based data structures."
—**Evan Golub, University of Maryland**

"I like the references to big data, Moore's Law and encapsulation. The inheritance chapter is excellent; examples are gender neutral which is perfect; the University Community Member inheritance hierarchy is a great example."
—**Khallai Taylor, Assistant Professor, Triton College and Adjunct Professor, Lonestar College—Kingwood**

"Good explanation of control statements, and translating from pseudocode to a Java program. Good approach to important concepts like static, accessors and private fields and their validation. [Classes and Objects: A Deeper Look] coverage is very interesting—I like how the book flows. Excellent explanation of Java SE 8 interfaces. Excellent explanation of exceptions." —**Jorge Vargas, Yumbling and a Java Champion**

"Very interesting and entertaining introduction. Good job explaining arrays before the more abstract collections. Guiding the reader to avoid dangerous patterns is equally important as explaining the correct syntax; great work! Excellent introduction to object-oriented concepts; rather than just a theoretical overview, it points the reader to how OO is implemented. Great polymorphism chapter—should help the reader distinguish between abstract classes and Java 8 interfaces with default methods. Good discussion of analyzing stack traces, since exceptions provide useful debugging information. Great job explaining Java2D. Shows how easily files and the file system are accessible using Java. Very good introduction to hashtables. Pushing all lambda-related content into a single chapter is hard, but the authors succeeded; I like the way they show how lambda expressions compare to existing code with inner classes; they show that it's the compiler that does the work. Recursion is well explained. Great introduction to BigInteger and BigDecimal. One of the best explanations of generics I've read. Clearly explains collections, and when and how they should be used; it's important that developers understand this, since choosing a wrong implementation can lead to massive performance penalties or hard-to-understand programs. The explanations of linked lists, stacks and queues are excellent." —**Johan Vos, LodgON and Java Champion**